LAWRENCE C. KOLB, M.D.

Distinguished Physician,
Veterans Administration Hospital;
Professor of Psychiatry,
Albany Medical College, Albany, New York;
Professor Emeritus of Psychiatry,
Columbia University College of Physicians and Surgeons;
Consultant to Presbyterian Hospital of New York City

H. KEITH H. BRODIE, M.D.

Professor and Chairman, Department of Psychiatry
Duke University School of Medicine, Durham, North Carolina

MODERN CLINICAL PSYCHIATRY

TENTH EDITION

1982

W. B. SAUNDERS COMPANY

Philadelphia, London, Toronto, Mexico City, Rio de Janeiro, Sydney, Tokyo

W. B. Saunders Company: West Washington Square
Philadelphia, PA   19105

1 St. Anne's Road
Eastbourne, East Sussex BN21 3UN, England

1 Goldthorne Avenue
Toronto, Ontario M8Z 5T9, Canada

Apartado 26370 – Cedro 512
Mexico 4, D.F., Mexico

Rua Coronel Cabrita, 8
Sao Cristovao Caixa Postal 21176
Rio de Janeiro, Brazil

9 Waltham Street
Artarmon, N.S.W. 2064, Australia

Ichibancho, Central Bldg., 22-1 Ichibancho
Chiyoda-Ku, Tokyo 102, Japan

Library of Congress Cataloging in Publication Data

Kolb, Lawrence Coleman, 1911–

Modern clinical psychiatry.

1. Psychiatry.   I. Title. [DNLM: 1. Mental disorders.
WM 100 K801m]

RC454.K59 1982   616.89   81–40564

ISBN 0–7216–5496–7   AACR2

Listed here are the latest translated editions of this
book together with the language of the translation
and the publisher.

Polish (*6th Edition*) – Panst, Zaklad Wydawn
Lekarskich, Warsaw, Poland

Spanish (*8th Edition*) – La Prensa Medica Mexicana
Mexico City, Mexico

Portuguese (*8th Edition*) – Editora Interamericana Ltda.,
Rio de Janeiro, Brazil

Japanese (*8th Edition*) – Hirokawa Publishing Co.
Tokyo, Japan

Italian (*8th Edition*) – Editrice Libraria V. Idelson
Naples, Italy

Modern Clinical Psychiatry   ISBN   0-7216-5496-7

Last digit is the print number: 9   8   7   6   5   4   3   2   1

PREFACE

With the publication of this tenth edition of *Modern Clinical Psychiatry*, the senior author welcomes with pleasure his new associate, H. Keith H. Brodie, M.D. Doctor Brodie is well known in psychiatry as an educator, investigator, and clinician. Since 1974, he has served as Professor and Chairman of the Department of Psychiatry, Duke University, Durham, North Carolina. His intensive and extensive experience, as witnessed by his many research publications in the scientific literature, in the biological substrates of the affective states and in the areas of alcohol and drug abuse, brings to the writing of this text a new depth and perspective. Dr. Brodie's career, however, is remarkable for his earlier study and interest in social and community psychiatry. His diverse studies and viewpoints are applied now as a generalist in psychiatric education. Recently, as chairman of an ad hoc committee of the Board of Trustees of the American Psychiatric Association, he devoted considerable effort, with the Task Force on Nomenclature and Statistics, to complete the final form of the Association's *Diagnostic and Statistical Manual of Mental Disorders*, Third Edition (DSM-III). His collaboration in the writing of *Modern Clinical Psychiatry* brings a fresh and thoroughly up-to-date viewpoint to its preparation.

During the interval between the publication of the ninth and tenth editions of this text, much discussion and debate has been heard over the many changes suggested in psychiatric nomenclature by those who developed DSM-III. That new edition, while accepted in the United States of America, has yet to achieve international recognition and is not thought to be fully satisfactory by all psychiatric groups within this country. Accordingly, Doctor Brodie and I present classifications and nomenclature from DSM-III as well as from the Ninth International Classification of Diseases. DSM-III diagnostic criteria for major psychotic disorders and for conditions for which the criteria may not be widely accepted are included as tables in appropriate chapters. We placed the order of chapters concerned with clinical syndromes essentially as in previous editions.

We have elected to maintain a chapter on neurosis but within that chapter have used the DSM-III classifications as section headings. New chapters are added to deal with the classification Psychotic Disorders Not Elsewhere Classified (Chapter 21, Other Psychotic Disorders) and with Psychosexual Disorders (Chapter 23). The chapter on affective disorders (Chapter 19) is largely rewritten. Where DSM-III classifications delete psychopathological entities recognized for years by experienced clinicians, we have continued sections pertaining to these; an example is the retention of the discussion of cyclothymic personality in Chapter 25, Personality Disorders.

The text is updated and expanded once again, with emphasis on the chemical basis of neurotransmission and the effects of psychoactive drugs upon this process. The potential role of endorphins in mental illness and its prevention, the biochemistry of sleep, and the relationship of circadian rhythms to the development of affective disease are included. Discussions have been added on attachment theory, the action of benzodiazapenes on the central nervous system, the modes of action of the tricyclic antidepressants, the utilization of plasma levels in monitoring the action of such drugs, and the concept of the therapeutic window.

Doctor Brodie and I wish to express our personal appreciation to David Lane of the Library of the New York State Psychiatric Institute, who assisted in providing reference material and development of the biographies; Cathy Smith, who helped in the search for illustrations; Kandie Jones and Lisa Vint, for secretarial and typing assistance; and Barbara Minton, for proofreading.

Lawrence C. Kolb, M.D.

Use of the words *man, he,* and *him* throughout this book, when not referring to a specific male, is at all times to convey the generic concept of a human being.

CONTENTS

1

THE BEGINNINGS OF PSYCHIATRY

"Times past and times present are both perhaps present in time future, and time future contained in time past."

T. S. Eliot

"Those who cannot remember the past are condemned to repeat it."

Santayana

THE RAKE'S PROGRESS: BEDLAM, by William Hogarth (Courtesy of the Metropolitan Museum of Art, New York.)

Modern psychiatry is that branch of medicine concerned with the manifestations and treatments of the disordered functioning of personality, which affects an individual's subjective life, his or her relations with others, or the capacity to adapt to life in society. Psychiatry is directed to the origins and the dynamic interactions of the personality as they contribute to the development of mental disease. "Origins" include the genetic determinants, whether of chromosomal derivation or resulting from prenatal factors, family and social transactions, and experiential deprivations, which often underlie the specific selection of forms of behavior. "Dynamic" refers to the motivations that

1

direct behavior, and the adaptive processes and mechanisms utilized for maintenance of personality functioning at
the biological, familial, and social levels
of life. The variations of disturbance
include disorders of overt behavior
as well as those influencing feeling,
thought, and the functioning of various
organ systems. Psychiatry's concern is
with both personality's maldevelopment, expressed in certain persisting
immaturities, and its disorganizations.

Since disordered behavior touches
upon many aspects of life in society, the
psychiatrist and psychiatry are interested in the knowledge obtained from
the biological sciences, which contribute information on personality growth
and pathology, and also in scientific and
humanitarian studies that contribute to
the understanding of individuals with
personality disturbances. These include
psychology, the social sciences, law,
philosophy, and theology.

In the biological sciences, modern
psychiatry seeks for explanations in the
individual's genetic inheritance. This includes predispositions, the influence of
anatomical, physiological, and biochemical processes, and the determining effect upon the maturing nervous system
of the recording of the individual's life
experiences. The recording begins in
the prenatal period and extends
through childhood within the family, to
the later environmental and cultural
pressures. To the psychiatrist, the interaction of these factors determines
the personality of the individual.

Personality has been defined in a multitude of ways; some are concerned only
with the outward expressions of behavior, while others consider man's
subjective experiences as well. For
psychiatrists, both aspects of individual
experience are covered by the term
"personality." Personality is perhaps
best recognized as each individual's
characteristically recurring patterns of
behavior. These patterns are evident
in response to both the sudden and the
persistent stresses of life.

THE BEGINNINGS: PRIMITIVE CONCEPTS

The origins of most of psychiatry's
scientific concepts are rooted in the past.
The study of the primitive tribes of this
day lends support to conjectures concerning the concepts of illness held by
prehistoric men which are reflected in
the myths and records of the early
pages of history. Comparative studies
also have provided valuable insights
into the ranges of man's behavior
under varying conditions. They have
made evident the modifying influence
of culture on the symptom expressions
of psychopathology and illuminated the
deficiencies in certain theoretical explanations of behavior that come from a
study of man in a particular culture
during a given time span.

The concepts of disease found
among primitive people differ from
those held by the scientific communities
of today, although remnants of such
primitive ideas of illness may be noted
from time to time in the general populations of even the most technologically
advanced societies. To primitive people, all illnesses are attributed to forces
acting outside the body. Such forces are
seen as supernatural; they are the evil
spirits, witches, demons, gods, or magi-
cians. These demonological explanations are particularly strong for illnesses affecting behavior. It is pertinent
to speculate that primitive people came
to such ideas from their own personal
experiences and contacts with the sick.
Their own dreams of return of the
dead and the remembrance of the dead
ones' threats, demands, and affections
perhaps fostered the belief in influence
from beyond life. Their observations of
the nonsensical, impertinent, meaningless, and destructive behavior of the
delirious and psychotic, their apprehensions in the face of a convulsive attack, and their efforts to explain the
phantom limb phenomenon must have
fostered the concept of demonological
possession as the causal means for the

peculiar or frightening changes of behavior which fell upon their close and familiar associates.

Primitive societies devised methods of treatment which are used even now almost exclusively in the framework of magical and religious practices. Within these methods (which often were followed by recovery of the afflicted) one may perceive the rudiments of psychotherapy.

Since like produces like to primitive man and since objects once in contact continue to have an influence even at a distance, the use of charms for their protective or healing force is frequent among such people. Charms may be viewed as homeopathic or imitative magic. Another way in which imitative magic is used constructively is in the rites of the healers who act out the experience of the person to aid him. Good examples are the healer among the Dyaks of Borneo who plays the role of the parturient woman or the medicine man who enters a state of trance before indicating the treatment. The effectiveness of such methods of treatment may have rested on the patient's identifying with the healer and entering into a state of death and rebirth. The therapeutic use of trance states is another widespread measure among primitive groups. In some tribes, trance states are induced by fixation on objects much as one may induce hypnotic states.

The quest of the medicine man is often to find the lost or afflicted soul, to drive out the demon, and then to return the soul to the body. Exorcism, the forcing of an evil spirit from the possessed, is brought about by many means in different groups and areas and may be easily recognized as a form of psychotherapy in which the ill person is encouraged to speak of those actions and misdeeds that have guilty connotations. The rites of self-punishment appear to have the same purpose. Other primitive ways include the use of spells and incantations with their repetitive offerings, the rituals of silence,

and also the applications internally and externally of herbs and other medicines. Throughout, one may recognize the primitive methods as beginning with simple cause-and-effect explanations and empirical observations, without recognition of the operation of internal forces of either a biological or a psychological nature. Nor does the medicine man direct his efforts to the individual but rather to a malignant invading force foreign to his primitive patient. The meanings and aims of primitive rites, while psychotherapeutic, hold no relationship to modern treatments which find the sources of illness within the biosocial organization and development of man.

GRECO-ROMAN ERA

References to mental disorders in the early writings of Egypt, India, China, Greece, and Rome disclose the beginnings of those major streams of thought and action which now pervade the growth of psychiatry as a science. The beginnings of the humanitarian attitude, reflected today in the area of social psychiatry, were seen as early as 860 B.C. when Greek priests supplemented incantations and exorcisms for the mentally disturbed with recommendations for kindness and suggestions for the use of physical and recreational activities.

A significant move occurred in the sixth century B.C. as the Greek healer's interest turned toward observation and experimentation; these were the first scientific steps in biological science. Alcmaeon dissected and noted the connections of the sense organs to the brain, from which he inferred that the seat of reason and the soul were located in this organ.

This early scientific movement is best observed in the writings of Hippocrates (460–375 B.C.). He initiated a classification of mental disorders into mania, melancholia, and phrenites. His descriptions of disease indicate the existence then of knowledge of epilepsy, hysteria, postpartum psychosis, and the acute brain syndromes (delirious states) that occur with infectious diseases and after hemorrhage. He flatly rejected the influence of the gods as causative of mental disease. Hippocrates influenced, as well, the social attitudes of his day. While Athenian courts recognized the rights of the mentally disturbed in civil affairs, they gave no consideration to their rights in a capital offense. Through his influence, if it could be proved that the individual on trial suffered from a condition which Hippocrates designated as paranoia, the court appointed a guardian for the accused.

Although others expanded the Hippocratic approach, undoubtedly the high point of scientific observation during the Greco-Roman period was reached in the time of the Roman physician Galen (A.D. 130–200). Using the scientific approach, he studied the anatomy and physiology of the nervous system and postulated that the existence of symptoms did not necessarily indicate that the organ or part of the body which served as their expression was the affected part. Galen developed a theory of the rational soul as divided into external and internal parts. The former, in his system, consisted of the five senses; the functions of the latter were such things as imagination, judgment, perception, and movement. Galen concluded, as Plato thought but Aristotle denied, that the brain and not the heart was the seat of the soul.

The problem of mental disorders occupied the attention of the Greek philosophers as well. Empedocles spoke of the importance of the emotions and pointed out that love and hate were fundamental in determining changes in human behavior. His concepts were incorporated by Plato in his consideration of Eros in the personal life of man. Plato propounded the idea that a psychologic biography might be written of the individual man, commencing with his earliest years through his relations with his family members and educators, to explain his adult behavior. So, too, he conceived of a tripartite soul composed of rational, libidinous, and "spirited" portions, the latter containing various animal qualities. This concept of the soul has been likened to Freud's structural concept of the personality. Thus, one of the mainstreams of modern psychiatry, the psychodynamic, had its recorded beginnings in the Greco-Roman period, largely disappeared in the Dark Ages, and occasionally reemerged in the philosophical writings of the Middle Ages. It is finally recaptured in the modern psychodynamic movement initiated by Sigmund Freud.

With the decline of the Roman Empire and throughout the Dark Ages of Western man, there occurred a revival of demonology, spiritual explanations, and tortuous exorcisms, with disagreement from only a few solitary individuals.

At times throughout the Middle Ages and even later, in Europe and in the Americas, large groups of individuals simultaneously seemed affected with psychic epidemics. The majority were poor peasants, artisans, and other impoverished members of the societies in which they lived. In the belief that they were infected by the devil, masses danced together in the streets, cried out the names of demons, publicly exposed and exorcised themselves, and told of their ecstatic visions. The study of these epidemics led to some of the earliest conceptions of social factors as causation of mental derangement—the beginning of social psychiatry.

The physician whom some describe as the first psychiatrist, Johann Weyer, worked openly against the then current beliefs of supernatural possession as the cause of mental phenomena, condemned those who accused women of witchcraft, gave explanations of the mass psychoses, and described many as arising from symptoms of melancholia proceeding from love. He suggested that reputable physicians be called in before adjudging women as witches, as in his opinion their behavior was due to illness. Weyer advised that one might find the pathogenesis of mental phenomena through developing detailed information about the sufferer. He successfully treated some accused of witchcraft by sitting alone and talking with them for long periods.

Beginning with Francis Bacon in the seventeenth century, the philosophers recognized that the functions of "mind" were of concern to the natural order of the universe. These views came to have a profound influence on medical thought. At this time the philosophic interest of Descartes and others in the "mind" and its function established a dualistic explanation of human behavior. It will be noted that in the definition of psychiatry there was no mention of the word *mind*. There need not be, however, any objection to the use of the word, provided it is employed as a collective designation for certain functional activities of the organism, particularly those of the organism as an individual personality. As a corollary to this definition of mind, the reactions of parts of the organism would be designated as physiological, while "mind" would be considered the integrated response of the organism to the complex physiological, psychological, and sociological forces that impinge upon it. The "mind," therefore, is merely one aspect — the psychological aspect — of biological functioning of the organism and not a metaphysical entity having an existence parallel to the body. The dichotomy implied by "mind and body" does not exist in the organism.

THE MODERN ERA

Social Psychological Change

At this historical time, there again took place a revival of interest in the humanitarian care of the mentally ill. Under the leadership of Chiaruggi in Italy (1759–1820), Philippe Pinel (1745–1826) in France, Daniel Tuke (1827–1895) in England, and Dorothea Dix (1802–1887) in the United States of America, the shackles of patients were removed and hospital surroundings were developed for their care. This humanitarian drive was aligned with the same political and social forces that led to the revolutionary movements in western European countries and America. As Pinel struck the chains from the limbs of the maniacal sick at the Bicêtre in Paris, he called for public support to apply to the insane the same humaneness demanded for all by the French National Assembly — the rights of liberty and equality. He laid the groundwork in the treatment of the mentally ill for acceptance of the humanitarian tenet that man's condition may be improved by man through his own efforts. The revolutionary climate also fostered the first demonstrations of hypnosis by Anton Mesmer.

As Dain has emphasized, the moral treatment emerging at that time used psychological forces to bring about behavioral change. It was psychotherapeutic; those advocating such moral treatment thought that the attitudes and behaviors of the caretakers were the important elements in bringing relief to the suffering and abnormal behavior of those considered ill. Respect for the patient's personality and kindness in meeting his needs were specified as the psychotherapeutic alleviating actions between those treating and those brought to treatment.

In the U.S.A., Benjamin Rush (1745–1813) was the first physician to undertake serious studies of mental illnesses. He perceived the significance of the physician-patient relationship in bringing about certain "cures" and encouraged physicians to recognize the importance of their commanding social position. It is striking that, in his era, he realized that antisocial acts had origins in emotional disturbances, recommended gentleness in contacts with the depressed, firmness with the manic, and attention-getting actions with the distracted. Rush observed that in some instances threats were necessary to induce fear for the modification of antisocial behaviors.

The interest in psychotherapy and the humanitarian attitudes toward mental illness have undergone major revivals during the past half-century. Various forms of psychotherapy now flourish worldwide. Differing from the simple application of attitudes of acceptance toward the mentally and emotionally distressed, the modern psychotherapies are based upon a series of hypothetical propositions and operational tenets lacking in the earlier "moral therapy."

The current humanitarian posture in western European and North American societies is typified by the "open hospital" movement in England and enactment of the British Mental Health Act early in the 1950's. In the U.S.A. the National Mental Health Act of 1946 initiated support for nationwide programs of community mental health services, and education of mental health specialists and researchers. This was followed in 1963 by the Community Mental Health Services Act. The goal of the community mental health movement is to strengthen development of therapeutic services in local communities. It is hoped this will eventually eliminate long-term institutional care of the mentally disturbed and retarded in facilities isolated from their families and communities. The social deterioration of individuals through continued isolation in the large facilities that had developed throughout the world is now recognized.

Biomedical Influence

More or less coincident with the humanitarian reforms in treatment occurred the growth of medical interest in mental illnesses. Following a long series of observations by the brilliant clinicians in Europe, the German Emil Kraepelin (1856–1926) gave to psychiatry the first comprehensive description of what he believed were entities of mental disease. Prior to his time, psychiatric attention had been directed to the symptom, which was regarded as the illness. Kraepelin assumed that mental disorders were definite disease entities analogous to the physical diseases and defined by etiology, symptomatology, course, and outcome. This led him to stress clinical observations and the search for physical origins for mental diseases. His system of classification was based on descriptions, symptoms, and outcome, since it was frequently impossible to make the diagnosis by laboratory examinations. Thus the classifications were not based on an understanding of etiologic factors, including those of psychodynamic processes. While his system brought clarity to a mélange of psychiatric observations and thereby aided scientific study, Kraepelin appears to have had a limited appreciation of the inner life of his patients. His work did little to promote understanding of mental disorders, particularly the psychodynamic forces operative in them. His name, nevertheless, must be considered among those of the psychiatric great, as he observed with discernment and systematized the results of his observations—a necessary stage through which every science must pass.

Coincident with the successes that followed the late nineteenth century discoveries of the pathology and etiology of disease, scientists turned to similar attempts to understand the etiology of mental disorders. Just as institutes for the study of general medical illnesses were established in western Europe, in 1896 the State of New York established the Pathological Institute (now known as the New York State Psychiatric Institute) to study the etiology of the mental disturbances then recognized and to develop therapeutic and preventive measures for them. This was the first research organization in which investigators from the biological, psychological and social sciences were associated. It brought together scientists from the fields of anatomy, histology, pathology, microbiology and cellular biology, psychology, and anthropology. Within short order, a worker attached to the Institute, in collaboration with another in the younger Rockefeller Institute, established the cause of paresis as the spirochete *Treponema pallidum.*

It is presumed that Ira Van Gieson, the pathologist who was the first director of this Institute, derived many of his ideas from the great German pathologist Rudolph Virchow. Virchow had a broad perspective of the study of mankind, which superseded his extraordinary studies of organ pathology. He encouraged early archeological studies and involved himself actively in the social policies and political life of his nation.

Research institutes devoted to the field of psychiatry have spread throughout the world and vigorous investigative units have sprung up in universities and in many independent teaching hospitals. From these research efforts has evolved the enormous expansion of the knowledge of personality functioning, psychopathology, and brain structure and function. New therapeutic and preventive approaches and hypotheses with powerful, heuristic potentials have emerged.

BIBLIOGRAPHY

Ackerknecht, E. H.: A Short History of Psychiatry. 2nd revised ed. New York, Hafner Publishing Company, 1968.

Alexander, F. G., and Selesnick, S. T.: The History of Psychiatry. New York, Harper & Row, 1966.

Braceland, F. J.: Kraepelin, his system and his influence. Am. J. Psychiatry, *113*:871–876, 1957.

Dain, N.: Concepts of Insantiy in the United States, 1789–1865. New Brunswick, N.J., Rutgers University Press, 1964.

Kiev, A. (ed.): Magic, Faith and Healing. New York, Free Press of Glencoe, 1964.

Kolb, L. C.: The institutes of psychiatry: growth, development and future. Psychol. Med., *1*:86–95, 1970.

Kriegman, G., Gardner, R. D., and Absey, D. W. (Eds.): American Psychiatry: Past, Present, and Future. Charlottesville, Va., University Press of Virginia, 1975.

Mora, G.: On the 400th Anniversary of Johann Weyer's "De Praestigiis Daemonum." Am. J. Psychiatry, *120*:417–428, 1963.

Rosen, G.: Madness in Society. Chicago, University of Chicago Press, 1966.

Schneck, J. M.: A History of Psychiatry. Springfield, Ill., Charles C Thomas, 1960.

Zilboorg, G., and Henry, G. W.: A History of Medical Psychology. New York, Norton & Company, 1941.

2

DEVELOPMENT OF MODERN PSYCHIATRY

"Now we, like all animals, carry with us vestigial traces of our past ancestry, not least in our mental processes. To develop psychologically we must understand ourselves, and it should help us to do so if we can find ways to investigate those hidden depths in our minds from which we draw our impulses."

Sir Walter Langdon-Brown

CHARCOT DEMONSTRATING HYPONOSIS
(From The Bettmann Archive, Inc.)

That body of knowledge which is directed to understanding the psychological influences and maturations that determine psychopathology is known as dynamic psychiatry. It rests essentially on an evolutionary basis. In its theory, behavior, no matter how abnormal, is the result of needs and drives, which are built into the personality through the biological inheritance. Behavior is complicated and modified by other needs, affects, and counter-strivings acquired in the long learning experience of family and cultural interactions that establish the foundations for man's social life. The basic maturational forces or drives are considered often to operate beyond the range of conscious awareness; that is, they are "unconscious." While dynamic psychiatry is oriented toward the understanding of motivations as determinants of behavior, it also recognizes the capacity to function as a central determinant in eventual adaptation. Capacity to function rests on the genetically determined anatomic-physiologic structure. Its development is influenced through experience and learning, and, in turn, by the biological and social motivations that determine aspiration and drive intensities. *Psychodynamics* is the term generally applied to the systematized knowledge and theory of human behavior and its motivations.

EVOLUTIONARY BASIS OF PSYCHODYNAMICS

It is now generally conceded that many of the symptomatic expressions of personality disorders are rooted in modes of behavior that have been manifested earlier in life; that is, they are ontogenetically determined. Through failure of maturation, which may be the consequence of either physical maldevelopment or deprivation of those experiences necessary to foster maturation of a function, evidences of immature and maladaptive behavior may persist into later life. Another type of failure in the maturational growth of the personality occurs through excessive stimulation or gratification during the sequential stages of personality development. Whether it be through deprivation or excessive gratification, the term *fixation* is applied to the process by which facets of the personality do not progress to maturity.

The recurrence of infantile and childish behavior is noted frequently in the clinic when the patient is unable to solve some emotional conflict. In the face of a physical illness or a severe emotional arousal in adult life, such *regressions* may occur and present as abnormal illness behavior or as characteristic psychopathological indicators.

The evolutionary orientation of modern psychodynamics stems directly from the genius of Charles Darwin, and later Herbert Spencer, who influenced the great English theoretical neurologist John Hughlings Jackson (1835–1911). Jackson set forth an evolutionary theory to explain the functions of the nervous system in health and disease. He drew from his careful clinical observations of epilepsy and other diseases of the brain. Jackson postulated that the functions of the nervous system were integrated at progressively more complex levels, with mentation, the highest level of function, being subserved by the vast cell aggregations of the human cerebral cortex. He viewed the symptoms accompanying disordered brain function as representative of both the loss of more recently acquired functions of the brain and the reappearance of more primitive functions which are submerged in evolutionary growth. According to him, when a brain injury produced a permanent deficit in the functioning of the nervous system, the re-emergence of more primitive actions could be recognized as symptoms in addition to the symptoms due to loss of function. A classic example is the Babinski reflex, a primitive toe sign, which disappears during infantile life with myelination of the corticospinal pathways to re-emerge as the result of disease to the pathways from the cortex. Jackson also indicated that the organism tends to adapt to the loss of function by a substitutive or compensatory behavior, which sometimes also is viewed as a symptom by the clinician.

The Jacksonian theories on evolution and dissolution of function within the nervous system inherently contain the postulate that the understanding of any behavioral disturbance is dependent upon knowledge of the progressive development of that behavior in a given organism. While Jackson's attention was directed principally to the functions and dysfunctions at the lower levels of integration of nervous activity, he wrote briefly on higher functions and commented that the study of dreams and jokes would provide an important means of furthering understanding of the origins of psychological pathology. Jackson's works and his concepts were known well and were incorporated into the later theories of Sigmund Freud, then a promising neurologist, who established the major premises of dynamic psychiatry, and also of Adolf Meyer, the proponent of the dynamic evolutionary school of psychobiology.

HISTORICAL BASIS OF PSYCHODYNAMICS

Anton Mesmer

When Anton Mesmer (1734–1815), a Viennese outcast, stirred a furor in Paris by curing many diseases, including hysteria, by his technique of "animal magnetism," the scientific world first noted the influence of purely psychological processes on symptoms of illness. Members of the committee of the French Academy of Science, which included Benjamin Franklin on its roster of distinguished members, were impressed by the results of Mesmer's touching of his patients but duly noted the lack of evidence of animal magnetic fluids. While Mesmer's success was short-lived, his technique was picked up and used in both England and the United States. The English surgeon James Braid (1795–1860) provided a descriptive formulation of mesmerism and introduced the term *hypnotism*. The Fench country physician A. Liebault (1823–1904) learned to use hypnotism widely in his practice and was responsible for teaching the technique to Jean Martin Charcot, the renowned French neurologist. Liebault's work represents perhaps the first direct use of psychological forces in the practice of medicine—its use in an equivalent sense with other conventional techniques for the relief of suffering of the ill.

Jean Martin Charcot

While Charcot (1825–1893) questioned the growing view that psychological forces could cause hysteria, his eminent position in French neurology brought the study of this disturbance and others directly into the stream of serious medical investigation. From his own studies, Charcot presented a report to the French Academy of Science that the phenomena of hypnotism were manifestations of abnormality and that the hypnotic state occurred only in those with hysteria. Charcot's fame and numerous publications brought him many students, including Sigmund Freud.

Hippolyte-Marie Bernheim

Bernheim (1840–1919), professor of clinical medicine at Nancy, vigorously disagreed with Charcot's views and maintained that the phenomena Charcot observed took place only when conditions of suggestion were set up by the hypnotist. He stripped the subject of hypnosis of much of its mystery, dispelled ideas of special hypnotic powers and magnetic influences, and demonstrated that patients are also susceptible to suggestion in the waking state. Bernheim advanced the theory that hysteria was of mental origin. He was probably the first to apply the term *psychoneurosis* to hysteria and similar states. Some consider Bernheim's work to be the first effort to evolve a general understanding of behavior. From his studies came new questions pertaining to the legal responsibilities of criminals and the etiology of criminal behavior. Bernheim challenged the thought that "will" was the agent of crime and evil by advancing the belief that the mechanism of suggestion underlies the endless variety of both normal and abnormal behavior.

Pierre Janet

Another of Charcot's students at the Sâlpetrière was Pierre Janet (1859–1947), who also fostered the growth of the psychodynamic viewpoint. Contrary to his teacher, he recognized that the hysteric's fixed ideas and inner conflict with reality were neurotic and insisted on treatment by psychological means. His therapy was essentially persuasion and the use of techniques for altering the environment of the patient.

Janet evolved the theory that the neuroses represent a lack of psychic tension on the part of the patient. By psychic tension, he meant an integrating force which, when abundant, held the stream of conscious activity intact. Through constitutional deficiency or as the consequence of fatigue or stress, the psychic energy became defective. Janet saw the disintegration of the stream of consciousness as the expression of psychoneuroses. Based on this concept, the idea of *dissociation* was formulated. As the result of dissociation, elements of consciousness were considered to take on an independent existence and express themselves clinically in the form of alternating personalities, fugues, anesthesias, and other hysterical expressions. The concept of dissociation has an established position in the field of abnormal psychology. Janet also introduced the idea of subconscious processes occurring independently on the mainstream of consciousness but later rejected Freud's explanation of "repression."

Sigmund Freud

Initiating his practice as a neurologist well acquainted with Jackson and the French school, Sigmund Freud (1856–1939) turned his attention to the psychoneuroses, following his studies in Paris with Charcot. On his return to Vienna, he became associated with Josef Breuer, who was perhaps the first to recognize that neurotic symptoms had "meaning" in relation to the patient's previous life. Breuer and Freud observed that under hypnosis their patients recalled old ideas, impulses, and experiences which they had found necessary otherwise to put aside or repress. As the patient disclosed and "talked out" his emotional upheavals, his symptoms subsided. Breuer gave up this treatment, presumably concerned over the deep attachment to the therapist evidenced by patients. Freud continued alone and soon found that it was unnecessary to hypnotize the patient. He persuaded his patients to speak freely and to bring up anything that came to their minds no matter how irrelevant it might initially seem. With the use of this "free associational" technique, Freud found that he had a means of widely exploring the earlier experiences upon which the patient's mental processes and current symptoms rested. He was able to analyze the meanings of dreams, slips of the tongue, mistakes and errors in everyday life, such as simple forgetting. From his careful clinical observations, he constructed a system of psychology to which he gave the name "psychoanalysis."

Freud's psychoanalytic psychology is fundamentally psychogenetic and evolutionary. It aims to discover the motivational conflicts that determine behavior, whether healthy or disordered. It provides as well a concept of personality structure and development not previously advanced by other schools. His clear penetration of the relationship existing between patient and physician — the overdetermined attitudes of affection or dislike, which he termed *transference* and in which he saw the recapitulations of earlier infantile and childish relations to a parental figure — represents a monumental insight. The analyses of the transference relationship and the patient's resistance were to Freud the essential elements in his psychoanalytic therapy.

Freud also insisted that much of mental life is unconscious, beyond the realm of awareness. The concept of the unconscious has been one of the great contributions to psychiatry. While some psychologists dislike the use of such a metaphorical word as "the unconscious" for those impulses, desires, and emotional responses which are inaccessible to our introspective observation, such a hypothesis is required for the explanation of many mental phenomena.

Freud's emphasis upon personality as a process developing step by step has given us a clearer understanding of personality manifestations. Many, however, do not accept Freud's concept of infantile sexuality, with its uncompleted differentiation, and the influence of its persistent hangovers on personality. Freud's demonstration of the importance of inner conflict with infantile sexuality's dynamically opposed impulses is the first theoretical system to provide meaning to the genesis of neurotic and psychotic reactions and other psychological phenomena. Although some have misinterpreted Freud as referring to the generalized systems of drives and to the structural elements of the personality (the id, the ego, and the superego) as though they were entities, the use of such terms for certain dynamic parts or functions of the personality has simplified thinking concerning personality functioning. Freud's emphasis upon a determinism of psychic processes has led to a greater clarity in our thinking. His psychological theory revolves around the problem of the development of infantile drives into adult personality. He contended that psychopathology resulted from failure of a smooth, scheduled progress through the successive stages of psychosexual development

Alfred Adler

This Viennese psychiatrist (1870–1937), an early student and associate of Freud, later came to dissent from Freud's emphasis on infantile sexuality. He believed that the child's resistance to domination and his drive to self-assertion, domination, and superiority were more important than the sexual drive in the development and structuring of the personality. Adler's psychological formula may be stated as follows: Because of a sense of inferiority—organic, intellectual, social, or the result of past experiences—a will to power is stimulated, resulting in compensatory reactions directed to goals of superiority. Adler included these various compensatory activities under the term *masculine protest*. He adopted this term on the assumption that the exaggerated "will to power," with its drive to prestige, superiority, and achievement, might be compared to what he believed was the reaction of women to their feminine status. He observed that in European culture, women were usually regarded as inferior, a status to which he considered they reacted by a so-called "masculine protest," that is, by trying to act like men. The will to power need not have its origin in a patent organic defect but in whatever feeling of inferiority leads to feelings of inadequacy, be it organic, sexual, economic, or social.

Adler gave his psychological movement the name *individual psychology*, to indicate that each individual has his or her own special goals and a unique manner of attempting to achieve them. These methods mark the individual off from others and largely determine the structure of his personality. The various psychological processes by which he seeks to deny his inferiority and maintain the fiction of achievement constitute the symptoms of the neurosis. Adler's emphasis on power and prestige motivations, on cultural determinants of neurosis, and on therapy as a re-education have been absorbed to a greater extent than is conceded by adherents to other schools of thought.

Carl G. Jung

A native of Switzerland, Jung (1875–1961) became closely associated with Freud during the early days of the latter's development of psychoanalytic theory. In 1911 he broke with Freud over the importance of infantile and childhood levels or stages of sexuality development and the effect upon personality of trauma sustained during these developmental phases.

Jung believed that the unconscious is made up of material derived from two sources. He called one of these sources the "personal unconscious" and the other the "collective or racial unconscious." He considered the personal unconscious to be superficial to the collective unconscious and therefore more accessible to consciousness. He contended that the personal unconscious contains the individual's personal urges and thoughts that developed in his individual history, forgotten impressions, and reactions to environmental experiences. The contents of the deeper racial or collective unconscious consist of instinctive impulses and primitive fears, feelings, trends, and thoughts connected with racial experience and belief. According to Jung, feelings and desires related to modes of thinking and acting that have undergone racial repression and belong to phases of past human cultural epochs belong in the collective unconscious. To this psychological movement Jung gave the name *analytic psychology.*

Jung contributed other concepts which have received wide acceptance. Among them was the word association test for investigating hidden regions of personality, which is discussed in a later chapter. Jung was among the first to emphasize the nature of the child's interpersonal relationships and to point out that neurotic difficulties of parents are decisive influences in the difficulties of children. Working with Bleuler, Jung applied psychoanalytic concepts to the psychoses and was the first psychiatrist to suggest a psychological approach to the study of dementia praecox (1907). He presented a penetrating analytic description of personality types, developed the extravert-introvert concept, and studied artistic creation's, mythological themes, and religion and their relation to dreams, fantasies, and neuroses. He stressed the importance of symbolism and religion. His critics comment upon the extent to which he combined psychological philosophical, mystical, and metaphysical elements.

Adolf Meyer

Slightly younger than Freud, with a similar interest in the basic sciences of neurology, neuroanatomy, and pathology, and having knowledge of the foremost works of the French and British schools, Adolf Meyer (1866–1950) played a prominent role in the development of dynamic psychiatry in the United States through his pluralistic and interactional concepts of human behavior. He insisted that multiple biological, psychological, and social forces contribute to the growth and determination of personality. This approach he designated as "psychobiological." Meyer, as well as Freud, stressed the importance of early parental influences in shaping the development of the child's personality and conceived of mental disturbances as progressive habit formations.

The techniques Meyer devised for the psychiatric examination form the basis for most of those now used in English-speaking countries. He taught that the understanding of maladaptive behavior requires a comprehensive study of the life history of the individual in which is traced the growth of personality through each unfolding stage to that of the individual's life situation. In his teaching, Meyer condemned the focus upon a single complaint or single aspect of the patient's problem or the examination of it from the standpoint of a particular system of psychiatry. He inveighed against the Kraepelinian nosology with its prognostic import and spoke of psychiatric illnesses as reaction patterns.

Meyer emphasized that each personality has its assets and liabilities. The existence of faulty habit patterns implies the potentiality for teaching healthy socialization. Psychobiology, then, is the biology of the whole personality — the whole person in the whole situation — which must be accounted for and understood in assessing the personality reactions.

The weakness of the psychobiological school lies in its failure to work through the study of intrapsychic processes and their origins in the dynamic interactions of the life of the individual. It remained for the psychoanalysts to clarify through their work these processes, which, however, were always clearly perceived as important in psychobiology. As the first to emphasize that psychiatry is a biological science and that its practitioners must study the actual and complete dynamic situation in which the patient lives, Meyer has left an indelible imprint on psychiatry.

Other Contributors

The concepts developed by these workers were perceived as incomplete by later psychoanalytic investigators. Anna Freud expanded psychoanalytic understanding through her elaboration of the defense mechanisms; Theodor Reik made a major contribution in his studies and interpretations of character analysis; Heinz Hartmann contributed by emphasizing the adaptive functions of ego; and Karen Horney made important contributions through her broadening understanding of neurotic development and the contributing social forces.

Meanwhile, the American Harry Stack Sullivan, strongly influenced by Adolf Meyer, the philosopher George Mead, and the linguist Edward Sapir, emphasized and studied in particular the analysis of the communicative processes between the growing infant and its parents as the means of specifying the dynamic evolution of human behavior, which to him evolved as a social phenomenon. He applied his hypotheses to the study of the patient-therapist relationship and thereby redefined the role of the therapist as a participant observer. Sullivan's orientation goes beyond the explanation of personality development occurring in an isolated organism, which typified the earlier psychodynamic framework of the psychoanalytic movement. He believed that observations of interactions occurring in the interpersonal field are the legimate area of psychiatry and that only those events expressed through the "public" communicative process are capable of observation and examination. Sullivan reported about the inner life of the individual — dreams and fantasies are transferred by the process of communication from the absolute private into something public. Personality to him was not a static entity. He defined personality as "the relative and enduring patterns of recurring interpersonal situations which characterize human life."

Currently, there is ongoing analysis and synthesis of the psychodynamic theories with the theories derived from the learning and behavioral investigations of Ivan Pavlov and John B. Watson, and later C. L. Hull, B. F. Skinner, and others.

THE STUDY OF BEHAVIOR

Kraepelin's effort to classify conglomerations of human behavior into identifiable syndromes represents one of the major beginnings of the study of the source of behavior. While his system of classification has been widely criticized, all subsequent attempts at improvement or modification are essentially based upon it.

The comparative studies of behavior in many species make it possible to identify a variety of patterns of activity that are directed to maintaining the life adaptation of each individual in each species. There are those forms of activity which are directed essentially to maintaining the biological needs of the individual for food, water, oxygen, elimination of waste products, warmth, and protection against attack. These may be classified as (1) ingestive, (2) eliminative, (3) shelter-seeking, and (4) agonistic patterns of behavior, the latter being any activity resulting in contact or contest, whether it results in fighting or flight. The other forms of behavior are concerned with the procreative and social existence of species, the identifiable activities of which are (5) sexual and mating, (6) care-giving and care-taking, (7) mimetic and communicative, and (8) exploratory or investigative.

Human behavior, in times of either health or illness, may be examined in one or all of the above contexts. People differ from other animals in several ways. First is the outstanding capacity for flexible and intricate manipulatory activity acquired through the freeing of the upper extremities from locomotion by the assumption of bipedal gait. The major adaptive power, however, rests upon the range and versatility of the communicative, social, and investigatory activities associated with the enormous growth of the human brain and its expanded capacities for storing and aggregating experiences. Humans are able to express through language those thought processes and affective states that accompany the arousal of their needs and the outcome of those drives motivated for their satisfaction. This, in turn, has led to the evolution of the complex symbolizations that people utilize for communication with each other and the capacity to perpetuate knowledge over time through their re-

cording and dissemination by cultural institutions. These progressive accretions of knowledge have enabled the solving of increasingly intricate problems.

The disorders of human behavior now recognized involve not only various groupings of defects in the behaviors directed to satisfying basic biological needs, but, more important, those affecting the essentially human elements of behavior: social relations, the ability to communicate, act, think, and feel appropriate to maturational state and situation.

General Systems Theory

Adolf Meyer's psychobiological theory rests upon the tenet that one must approach the study of mental illness or health by a comprehensive examination and analysis of all the numerous factors and stresses that act over time to influence the growth and emergence of the whole personality. The psychobiological perspective embodies and outlines in a very broad way the lines of study and analysis of personality in health and disease.

The generality of this theory, that is, its failure to define the role functioning of the various scientific disciplines and techniques as they might be employed in the study of personality, has left a void. That void may well be filled today by *general systems theory*, particularly as it applies to living systems. This theory, as the author perceives it, has an organizing capacity for placing the data at hand in the hierarchy of systems that comprise or bear upon man's personality functioning. So, too, that organizational frame should set the limits of these data and the definition of their relevance in terms of effecting man's own actions within his own system, as well as upon other levels of the social systems within which he lives. Furthermore, within the general systems framework of living system organizations, one can recognize the contributions of others who have offered hypotheses relating to various aspects of man's behavior.

All living systems function to maintain a steady state within by taking in inputs of matter energy so as to restore or maintain their own energy and support repair in their own structures. These systems are open—means are available for input of energy as well as its output. Their walling off in any aspect leads to a failure in functioning or death. They are complex in structure. Each contains genetic materials which provide the informational template for the development of its structures and processes from origin onward. They are composed of protoplasm, containing water, proteins, and other organic compounds. Each system contains an integrating organ (the brain: the critical subsystem which controls the entire system). The brain determines appropriate co-actions between all other subsystems. Each contains other critical subsystems or maintains symbiotic or parasitic relations with other living or nonliving systems. These subordinate subsystems are integrated to form self-regulatory, developing, reproducing systems with purposes or goals.

To put it another way, living systems, including man, contain three critical subsystems. They are (1) that concerned with processing information; (2) that concerned with matter energy processing; and (3) that concerned with processing matter, energy, and information—the reproduction subsystem.

The first, the brain, receives inputs from the internal and external environment. The internal environment includes the two previously mentioned subsystems concerned with matter energy.

As for the information-processing subsystem—transformations related to immediate and continued species survival—information input is received at various receptors and carried by channels or nets to central decoders. The various inputs are relayed to and associated with stored information (memory) gained from the past. The total input related through the associative and stored information subsystems is integrated. A decoder then directs incoding of various information to various output transducers in the subsystems, thus leading to actions appropriate to maintaining or reaffirming the steady states within the system.

In all living systems steady states are brought about by feedback mechanisms that operate on the input channels and nets to either increase or decrease the input, thus providing a method of maximizing or minimizing input or stress. Cybernetics is the study of methods of feedback control. The feedback net provides a channel from the decoder to the input receptors and channels which modulate their functioning.

Man as a living system functions through the integrated actions of various subcellular, cellular, and organ subsystems. As an individual system he relates to other single individuals and group, social, organization, societal, or national suprasystems.

As for the decision-making processes within living systems, they are conceived of as evolving from the processing of information. In the case of behavior each system develops a "preferential hierarchy of values" from its past experiences of success or failure in the goal-seeking actions required to hold the steady state. Preferential values are acquired through experience; they constrict the decision procedures as rules to facilitate rapid adaptation to the preferred steady state—its purpose. Since each system may simultaneously have multiple purposes, inputs may direct the total system toward several incompatible actions; thus conflict ensues. Effective living systems comply with conflicting inputs by responding to the commands with higher priority values.

Systems theory holds that more complex systems evolve characteristics beyond those of the sum of their subsystems. These characteristics are emergent; they appear through novel associations in the critical informational subsystems. Thus in examining function of a living system one may not extrapolate as identical the functions and actions of its subsystems or less complex living systems. One must identify the emergent functions of the more complex system.

Studies or theories about the complex system based on observations of its subsystems which fail to reflect upon the characteristic emergent functions of the former are incomplete and cannot be used as explanatory for functioning of the total system.

Earlier, comment was made on the emergent biological characteristics of man, which separate him from all other mammalian forms. These emergent characteristics have provided the source for the emergence of the species-characteristic functional behavioral process that serves as an adaptive interface between individual men and the necessary social suprasystems necessary for his survival — his personality.

The heuristic value of general systems theory for research related to personality functioning, its potential for cross systems hypotheses and experimentation, and the uncovering of new information on behavior remain to be realized. As Grinker commented, "General systems theories and other global theories such as transaction only encompass smaller theories, each one of which may contribute hypotheses that require well-designed operational research in order to increase our understanding." The psychiatrist may profitably perceive his efforts as those of a clinical scientist with background to draw upon the informational network as it relates to the operations of the organ subsystems of man, as well as being concerned with man's personality functioning in transaction with the social suprasystems necessary for his survival. From his analysis of these complex systems relations, the psychiatrist may formulate the genesis and driving forces that determine aspects of maladaptive and adaptive behavior.

Motivation: Forces and Systems

Behavior may be generally recognized as directed toward some goal, some aim that promises or provides satisfaction or a state of well-being. Behavior may be stated to be motivated, that is, activated and also selected as the appropriate means to accomplish a goal. Within the concept of motivation, questions may be asked as to the forces that lead to the activation or inhibition of a particular form of behavior and those forces that select one or another form as the appropriate one at a particular time.

BIOLOGICAL NEEDS. Each form of behavior has as its goal the satisfaction of a need. Thus, the lack of food, water, or warmth impels the individual to activity aimed at satisfying the bodily lack. Needs are determined by the unique biological organization of the species. It is assumed theoretically that a *drive* is induced by the establishment of a need, which provides the physiological substrata for the motivation to behavior. In all species, there exist certain biologically primitive or physiological needs necessary for the survival of the individual and the species. The needs for oxygen, water, food, maintenance of body temperature, and avoidance of tissue damage exist at birth and persist throughout life. The need to copulate and to procreate the species and care for the young, while innately given with vertebrate life, is activated only after full maturation of the genital apparatus of the organism, coupled with appropriate stimulation and later mating behavior with another member of the species.

In recent years it has been found that another fundamental driving force exists in both man and animals, that is, a drive to explore, or, as it has sometimes been described, innate curiosity. This exploratory drive seems, from experimental evidence, to exist without direct relevance to satisfaction of general bodily functions related to self-preservation or procreation. Even very young monkeys will press levers to open and reopen windows for prolonged periods with no other reward than to look out and observe what is on the other side. Yet the drive is capable of enhancement and may be seen as one of a chain of brain-directed activities which later are molded through experience to bring about highly skilled acts to achieve the satisfaction of a need. Thus, a monkey's activity in lever manipulation is enhanced if he is allowed as a reward to sight another monkey, enhanced beyond that produced by sight of a bowl of food or a moving toy. Furthermore, this exploratory drive to satisfy a perceptual need, in this instance mediated through the visual system, provides an additional reward. Monkeys that have attempted for days to solve a mechanical problem and finally are successful then repeat the satisfying manipulations many times, apparently because of the gratification gained through mastery.

Before such animal studies were made there were innumerable observations of the exploratory efforts of infants and young children, which brought forth various hypotheses about the function of exploration and play. It would seem that work satisfaction relieves tension states induced by subcellular metabolic events which are translated into the integrated exploratory drive expressed in perceptual motor activity.

Exploratory behavior, associated with the protective blanket of long-continued dependence upon older members of a species, offers an unexcelled opportunity of evolutionary adaptation to a diversity of environments. It extends the chance of survival of those who live beyond infancy by increasing their adaptive potential through learning. It is not surprising that prolonged periods of both family dependence and

exploratory behavior exist side by side in the widely ranging primate species, including man.

SOCIAL NEEDS. While all of the biologically primitive needs are observed early in phylogenetic growth, they are neither psychologically primitive nor simple in their mechanisms of operation. This is particularly true in man who, as a result of his long period of dependency and the influence of socially determined goals, has evolved through learning many other desires.

In the growing child, the satisfaction of the need for food passes through numerous stages of development beyond that of making the need known through crying and satisfying the need by sucking and the ingestion of milk. With this behavior, there is associated contact not only with the ingested liquids or foods with all their variegated tastes, consistencies, and other characteristics, but also with the mother, or food giver, who thus comes to signify a source of pleasure and security. Her care determines further associations and behavior, including all those ways in which people in various cultures eventually obtain food, prepare it, and finally eat to satisfy hunger or engage in social exchange. The many patterns of food acquisition and ingestion are learned acquisitions or derivatives of the original need for food.

While the physiological needs are innately determined, those acquired through association are learned and are the products of the unique interaction of one individual with others. The acquired needs of man then develop in particular family cultures and are determined by associations. Needs for social status, whether acquired through power or prestige and whether or not they are satisfied by the different means of birth, material wealth, creativity, conformity, or capacity to gain the confidence of others, are learned.

"INSTINCT." In the past, the term *instinct* was widely used to explain patterns of behavior innately given to the organism. It is clear that the existence of an unsatisfied need establishes in the organism a set or attitude which primes it for action in the face of an adequate excitant or stimulus in the external environment. This stimulus leads to arousal of the function and also guides or cues the response to satisfy the need—whether the response will be action or inhibition, fight or flight, leaping or stalking, speech or silence.

Many studies by animal psychologists have demonstrated the necessity for the proper maturation of the organism, its necessary exposure to the appropriate stimuli, and the influence of actual experience in determining the development of the effective adaptive behavior. Likewise, a deprivation experienced at a critical stage in the maturational process may result in a continuing deficiency in the evolution of particular behavior sequences.

The accumulated evidence indicates that it is misleading and incorrect to consider "instinctive" behavior as a separate form entirely unrelated to "learned" behavior. The two types blend into each other. What is desirable in the study of the behavior of man as well as animals is the eventual isolation and understanding of the various fragments of each behavioral act and also the contribution of the total bodily structure. That of the brain as the integrating organ will be found the most important.

The value of attempting to separate learned from innate responses in humans is most significant from the standpoint of treatment. Learned processes, deficient or disordered, may perhaps be modified by learning or relearning—in other words, by one of the varieties of psychotherapy. Those disorders dependent primarily on dysfunctions of primary organization, that is, "innate," are unlikely to be so modified and will require other interventions for their modification.

In psychiatry, the term *instinct* is used in a psychological sense and denotes the innate biological drives that determine motivations. They are the dynamic agents not only for the maintenance of the life of the individual, including his social adaptations, but also of the energy for creative purposes in all walks of life.

Emotion, Drives, and Affects

As mentioned in the discussion of general systems theory and as may be inferred from the foregoing in man as in all living systems, there exists a continuing drive to maintain a constant internal steady state. That state is characterized by the absence of the tension aroused by a need, a lack sensed in one or several subsystems. We have indicated that in man the tension of need may result from deficiencies sensed or existing in the systems concerned with maintaining his biological integrity. Tensions may also be aroused through the need to discharge, as for example, the mounting pressure in the maturing seminal vesicles for discharge of semen, or the pressures in the rectum or bladder which lead to defecation and urination. So, too, through the long process of social learning, continuous need states evolve with related tensions, which drive to many complex social behaviors.

Even in the resting or *homeostatic state*, as it was designated by Cannon, there exists a continuous dynamic interchange of energy and activity in all bodily systems, accompanied by a continuous barrage of information delivered from both the internal bodily and external sensory receptors. A constant quantum of such information derived from all sources establishes the steady state; variations of any sort signal the need and motivate to corrective action.

We may assume that much of the vast and continuous barrage of sensed information reaching the brain is nonmotivational and never achieves conscious attention. If it has psychological meaning, it is as a sense of general awareness of personal well-being. Also, many of the tensions of need are undoubtedly so minor, leading to immediate corrections through the reserve subsystems within the body, that they, too, are nonmotivating for behavior.

EMOTION. When a need state exceeds a critical level, there is aroused in human beings, and very probably in all mammalian species, subjective states of tension or excitement, which we denote in terms of threat, craving, or satiation. These states, drives, and affects, as we shall discriminate them here, set in process complex behavioral and physiological activities which generally are known as emotions.

During the earliest days of life, the crying of the baby signifies subjective distress. It indicates either distress due to tension of hunger, thirst, respiratory embarrassment, or threatened local or general change in bodily temperature or of the integrity of the skin or mucous membrane. Subjective evidences of infantile satisfaction — that is, the satiation of needs — abound plentifully in the baby's short periods of relaxed external interest, while positively pleasurable subjective states may be inferred when the excitement of play with the mother is begun.

These early evidences of distress or unpleasure, as well as satisfaction and pleasure, become differentiated as infants develop and their perceptual powers lead to progressive discrimination of both distress-producing and pleasure-rewarding sensations from both internal and external stimuli. Those the infant has learned as tending most often to follow transactions with caretakers — fear and rage, satisfaction and excitement — are states that Arieti has denoted as "protoemotions" but have been labeled as "drive states" by others.

DRIVE STATES. As motivating forces, the drive states required to maintain the physical integrity of the organism are primitive. In human beings, they have been observed to operate in anen-

cephalic infants. The tensions of the need and its later satisfaction are inferred to be distressing and satisfying, painful or pleasurable. But they are obviously experienced passively; the infant is incapable of directing actions to obtain (approach behavior) or to escape from (avoidance behavior) the circumstances arousing the need tensions. Nor has an infant the potential for use of actions and behaviors to decrease or increase discomfort or comfort. As Tomkins states it, the primary function of the *drive systems* is providing motivating information concerning what systems are to be activated and deactivated and when.

AFFECT SYSTEM. The states of fear, rage, hunger, thirst, or joy in which the growing infant's behavior indicates awareness to either move toward or move away from objects in order to allay tension, gain satisfaction, or maximize excitement require the development of considerable capacity for perception (recognition) as well as imaging of the environment. These prehensive states of pleasure or distress always are associated with ideas that may or may not be fully the center of consciousness in the experiences.

Affects, which may be defined as feeling-tones, are pain-pleasure accompaniments of an idea or mental representation. By stimulating or facilitating some innate drive, they exercise a strongly determinative influence in giving direction both to thought associations and to overt behavior reactions. The terms *affect* and *emotion* often are used loosely as if these two aspects of mental life were the same. This is because the term emotion is used with many, and therefore ambiguous, meanings. Its use probably should be confined to indicate either the complex biochemical-physiological processes or functions concerned with the somatic expression of feeling or else the patterns of behavior that express affect. The word "affect" is more applicable to subjectively experienced feeling phenomena. The primary function of the *affect system* may be regarded as solely *motivational.* Furthermore, it is the driving force of this system upon which the essential characteristics of human personality evolve: the cognitive, attitudinal, decision-making, and action powers.

Affects, then, may be recognized as painful or pleasurable, warning of a need or signaling satiation. Thus, fear and rage emerge when bodily integrity is threatened, as inferred from the cries and other neuromuscular activity concerned with escape from some unpleasant stimulus or injury. Rage, fear, and anxiety are primitive affects aroused as concomitants of the reactive processes of aggression, escape, and helplessness (fight, flight, or helplessness). Other unpleasant affects (loneliness) are aroused by frustration of the drive state for attachment. Satisfaction of the needs in turn is associated with a pleasurable subjective appreciation of satiation. With later growth, and particularly as the consequence of the transaction within the family, primitive pain-pleasure affects are elaborated so that in maturity one discriminates such positively motivating or attractive affects as interest, joy, affection, tenderness, love, and compassion as well as the aversive affects of fear, anxiety, guilt, shame, disgust, and hatred.

It is evident that the highly discriminative affective states, which influence man's personality development, arise only through the long process of family and cultural evolution. Of necessity their evolution has required the vast potential of the human brain for recording, analyzing, and synthesizing information.

Affects serve as the subjective signals warning of threat or lack of satisfaction; they also provide a feedback indicating the approach of satisfaction or satiation and the relaxation of tension. Affects may be rapidly aroused and as quickly dispelled, or they may be slow to evolve and be sustained for prolonged periods.

Affects are perceptions of the internal state of the environment and, as such, in psychoanalytic theory are designated as ego states. Affects direct the integrating and executive aspects of ego functioning; however, they also direct the development of many human behaviors which are defensive in nature and serve to disguise the existence of the underlying affect so as to lessen or deflect the associated drive state. Thus, while guilt signals a need to give up a socially prohibited act—to refrain from it if it is intended or to undertake expiatory rituals if the act has taken place—guilt may also evoke behaviors indicating its defiance, denial or repression. Behaviors associated with affective states may indeed be used to offset and deny the existence of tension induced by other emotions, as, for example, the use of laughter, crying, or rage to modify a variety of other anxieties.

It is widely thought that the recognition of the affective states, of the variability in their relative intensities, and of the evolution of their control through the developmental process is central to the explanation of individual personality functioning and its pathological expressions. These states are discussed further under Disturbances of Affect in Chapter 6, Psychopathology.

There now exist many analyses and theories of emotions wherein the term is defined largely as behavioral expression. Earlier theories are well reviewed by de Rivera, who proposes a structural theory of his own.

While defining the emotional state as a whole, he indicates the potential of characterizing it as (1) a special perception of the situation in which the experiencer finds himself or herself, (2) as a response to the perception that involves "movement" or "transformation" of the experiencer's relation persisting until either successful completion or a change in meaning of the situation, (3) through either an internal bodily transformation or the individual's relation to the environment (as an example of the latter, de

Rivera suggests the strengthening of the intention to assertion through arousal of anger), and (4) as an adaptation to the exigencies of the experiencer's total situation.

To him, any emotion is the result of choices made by the experiencer in his relationship to another.

Intelligence

In vertebrates, the modifiable and integrative aspects of behavior are greatly increased. In them appears the cerebral cortex, developed for the purpose of providing a mechanism capable of elaborating, integrating, and controlling impulses and functions more perfectly than is possible with a more elementary nervous system. In fact, evolutionary stages in development are traceable in the cerebral cortex itself, associated with a corresponding hierarchy of functions. The older part of the cortex, the archipallium or limbic system, as MacLean designates it, is concerned with self-preservative and self-procreative functions and the basic emotional response and visceral functions, in contrast to the more recently developed neopallium, the portion essential for progressively complex discriminations and integrations characteristic of the highest psychic functions. The biological advantage of its development was that the organism obtained a more flexible capacity for adaptation.

Biological processes have evolved from conditions of simplicity and diffusiveness to complexity, differentiation, and definiteness. Similarly, an imperceptible transition has evolved from innate drive states to cognitive ability of that adaptive attribute called intelligence. Since, from a practical standpoint, the intelligence of an organism is fundamentally its psychological capacity for adapting to and making use of its environment, it is quite arbitrary to say where in the phyletic series intelligence was acquired. In fact, intelligence probably was not superimposed on earlier instinctive processes at some definite stage of evolution but was an outgrowth of them. Whether we speak of species or of individual human beings, those that possess the greatest capacity in these respects are the most intelligent.

Attention

Intelligence requires that the organism explore vast bits of information and retain them within its nervous system. Also, the information-processing organ must select from among the incoming barrage of sensory registrations recurrent ensembles of sensory inputs and recode them as recognizable percepts. It must decide which percepts have priority in terms of immediate and later adaptation, and must attend or focus on the most significant. Finally, the decision-making process requires that actions be taken or be delayed.

We may deduce that over time the most intelligent of the species have recorded a vast sum of sensory impressions. They have retained what constitutes a memory bank. They have evolved a process of rapid and clear perceptivity through the progressive differentiation of the incoming sensory inputs—their perceptivity is both acute and extensive. Also, they have evolved a number of processes which we identify as attention. *Vigilance* is one aspect of the attention processes. It may be defined as the means of scanning sensory inputs obtained from the internal and the external world to select those prepotent for survival. *Concentration* is another aspect of attention; the narrowing down of interest onto one part of the perceptual input, focusing, is another. Again, the attentive process may be varied to allow the alert and continuing scanning of a stream of inputs to discover similarities or discontinuities—the *associative process*. The latter is used effectively by diagnosticians, whether they be physicians or psychoanalysts scanning freely the auditory and visual signals provided by their patients, or engineers attempting to discover the source of malfunctioning of a machine.

Over a time all individuals tend to evolve certain preferences in their scanning activities, decision-making, and action-taking processes. They do so through the learning motivated by affect. Those sets, attitudes, and decisions that have been reinforced by reward-pleasure or through the relief or avoidance of distress and pain, become the preferred modes of functioning.

In the analysis of behavior we must then attend carefully to these aspects of intelligence: attention, whether it be vigilance, concentration, or association; memory as recording and recall; perception and cognition; and the acquired attitudes toward attending, decision-making, and action designated in earlier psychologies as conation.

Attitudes, Sets, and Conations

For the evolution of man's personality, the functioning unit between his inner world and the social environment in which he largely lives, the major determining force rests in his capacity to learn to control and modulate his affects. Each family and each society rewards or constrains individual members through the affection it bestows, withholds, and withdraws or the punishment it renders. Excitement, joy, and contentment are the rewarding affects. Guilt and shame, anxiety and fear, and rage are the aversive affects. The learning processes by which affect display is modulated so that others are less distressed by its emergence in behavior are the molding process for personality evolution. For man in all modern societies, affect control is more significant than the motivations of the primitive drive states concerned with simple biological survival. Thus, to be accepted in the human world, even activation of the craving for food in

hunger demands that one receive, prepare, and consume food by customs that elaborately obscure the craving. Only under extreme conditions of prolonged starvation do the human customs derived from learned control of affect break down to reveal the immediacy of the drive states in their primitive egocentric expression.

Man's affective states, too, differentiate from the primitive pain-pleasure paradigm we ascribe to the helpless infant lying in the crib. That differentiation comes about through the long process of human socialization. From attraction, to interest, to joy in company and attentive care, we identify in adults the state of love—a conative set.

What is often overlooked in consideration of personality is that through the long experiences and learning over time, in the social system there is established within each individual positive and negative sets for action, which regularly put in motion recurring patterns of behavioral response directed toward avoidance of unpleasure or distress or assistance toward an affective reward. The idea of the perceptual motor set is an old one in general psychology as related to action tendencies. While it continues to be studied in that field by those interested in cognition, the sets and assets, as such, are the determining factors in the establishment of the individual character traits that establish social acceptability and competence or their obverse.

In the love of mature people, a series of differentiated states has evolved related to parental care: tenderness, compassion, and pity. From loss of love, people suffer sadness, but they also have learned its variants as depression, as well as hatefulness, vengefulness, enviousness, and jealousy. From early distress and fear they have elaborated anxiety, apprehension, shame, and guilt. From the pleasure in consummation people have defined the character sets pride and vanity. And from each of these affects and derived attitudes, human creative intelligence and capacity for leisure have provided the myriad behaviors that identify characteristic responses in the face of stress, in the anticipation of success and failure or their aftermath, in relaxed satiation, or in distressing despondency.

The senior author has proposed recently that a series of assertive sets or character traits evolve on the basis of pleasurable learning experiences in infancy and childhood. Thus they balance and contrast with the functions of the defensive traits that evolve to protect the ego from anxiety and other unpleasant affects. These assertive sets of characteristics have been of critical importance in the evolution of human civilization: trust, empathy, likability, and humor as well as commitment, responsibility, perseverance, curiosity, courage, and flexibility.

These attitudes determine successful social adaptations. They determine adaptations in many who are crippled by the appalling limitations of the maladaptive expressions of psychopathology to be described later in this book. There is underway now in psychologic research a movement to re-examine personality dynamics in the light of the development and role function of such attitudes in establishing a healthy balance within the individual personality. Much of the diagnostic and prognostic weakness that exists in modern psychiatric practice and psychosocial research has its origins in preoccupation with the maladaptive to the exclusion of the important ongoing and highly adaptive attitudinal sets to action.

Consciousness

A prerequisite for that degree of adapting to and making use of the environment to which we apply the term *intelligence* is that function we know as "consciousness." By this term is meant a sense of awareness of self and of the environment. Its major biological advantage is that it permits the organism to adapt itself to novel circumstances.

ORIGIN. How consciousness develops is unknown, but it seems reasonable to assume that, in common with higher functions in general, it is a specialized development of lower ones. Such an assumption is in agreement with the general evolutionary propositions. Although no conclusions as to the origin or nature of consciousness can be secured by objective observation, one may speculate that it originates in the properties of irritability of protoplasm. When protoplasm—let us assume it to be in the form of an extremely simple organism such as a protozoon—is stimulated, a response occurs. A response, however simple, implies a change, a difference. As evolution progresses and the organism becomes more complex, and as the types of stimuli and responses multiply, one can imagine that the organism becomes gradually but dimly aware that modifications are induced, that changes occur in itself. Thus, a sense of comparison arises until, finally, sensations are produced, an awareness of which constitutes the dawning of consciousness.

DEVELOPMENT. These beginnings of perceptive processes undergo evolutionary expansion from the simple to the more complex until, finally, a conceptual consciousness with ideative and affective components is reached. It seems safe to assume that its development was through an expanding process, a successive integration, which has progressed simultaneously with zoological evolution. At the psychological level is to be found the highest phase in integration in the continuity of nature. A consideration of the evolutionary process suggests that there is no sharp distinction between the conscious and the unconscious and that conscious thinking represents the most highly developed and most fully integrated process of organizing and dealing with experience.

DEGREE OF CONSCIOUSNESS. Many psychobiological activities occur beyond conscious awareness. It was formerly assumed that consciousness or sense of awareness was a prerequisite for all those expressions of the organism we refer to as "mental." While many of these functions are manifested only under conditions of clear awareness, observation of mental processes under varying states of consciousness, such as those induced by drugs, hyponosis, or occurring in states of pathology, reveals that highly significant psychic processes operate under widely varying degrees of awareness, and even in the absence of awareness.

Responsiveness alone is not indicative of conscious awareness. Reflex activities may be observed in deep states of coma, and complex behavior, including pertinent verbal communication and interpersonal exchange, may take place following a head injury or in other psychopathologic conditions without the individual's later recalling these actions. Dreaming sleep also represents a state of consciousness which differs from full awareness in which there is a capacity to relate inner perceptions when attention is directed to the immediate external environment.

Full awareness or full consciousness in man demands, then, the capacity for immediate memory and the reproduction of his actions on request with, as well, the ability to perceive the surrounding environment and relate to it in terms of immediate drives and interests. Since at times these responses are held in abeyance, consciousness must be seen as a state in which thought processes, the mediating activities of the brain, intervene between the perceptions and the motivating activities of the organism.

Most students of man's mental life agree that one is greatly influenced by unrecognized psychological forces and that much behavior originates from motives of which one is not aware in the normal waking state. Psychological motivations are undoubtedly a result usually of combinations of causes, of which those least acceptable socially and morally possess the greatest driving force and are farthest removed from consciousness, whereas those which the individual considers the most acceptable are in the forefront of consciousness and are manifest.

The Unconscious

In order to explain many mental phenomena, the features of which are not manifest, it is necessary to hypothesize the existence of a stratum of the personality referred to as the *unconscious*. It includes material that under ordinary circumstances does not enter the conscious part of the personality. For the most part, those drive states determining behavior to satisfy the physiological needs of man operate unconsciously. The diabetic favors foods containing sugar, drinks excessively, and urinates frequently because of a defect in sugar metabolism and its ultimate influence on the body's fluid balance. All this behavior is determined beyond the level of conscious awareness. The individual only knows consciously what he does or must do to remain comfortable.

Various psychological drives exist beyond conscious awareness and are manifested in such forms as dreams, amnesias, purposeful forgetting, mistakes, and split personality. There is abundant evidence that unconscious drives exercise a fundamental influence upon behavior, feelings, decisions, and interpersonal relationships. In psychopathological states, it is particularly apparent that unconscious psychic forces are powerfully active in influencing personality. Emotional forces of which the individual is unaware may be in conflict and act in such a way as to determine his behavior, even though he knows nothing about them consciously.

As will be discussed later, conscious

and unconscious forces or motivations may cause the individual to pursue opposing goals. Much behavior, in fact, is a complex of conscious and unconscious motivations. It is only through active repression or through dissociation that any sharp division is produced between the conscious and the unconscious. Some psychiatrists, instead of speaking of the unconscious, emphasize "unconscious mental processes."

The Preconscious

Preconscious is a term applied to mental processes that are not conscious but possess the attribute of easy recall to consciousness. Unconscious mental processes differ in that they do not have access to consciousness except under special conditions, such as psychoanalytic therapy or the psychoses.

BIBLIOGRAPHY

Alexander, F. G., and Selesnick, S. T.: The History of Psychiatry. New York, Harper & Row, 1966.
Arieti, S.: The Intrapsychic Self. New York, Basic Books, 1967.
Bailey, P.: Janet and Freud. Arch. Neurol. Psychiatry, *76*:76–89, 1956.
Brenner, C.: On the nature and development of affects. Psychoanal. Q., *43*:532–556, 1974.
Bruch, H.: Interpersonal Theory: Harry Stack Sullivan. *In* Burton, A. (ed.): Operational Theories of Personality. New York, Brunner-Mazel, 1974.
Cannon, W. B.: Bodily Changes in Pain, Hunger, Fear and Rage. 2nd ed. New York, D. Appleton Co., 1929.
De Rivera, J.: A Structural Theory of the Emotions. Psychol. Issues, *10*:4, Monograph 40. New York, International Universities Press, 1977.
Grinker, R. R., Sr.: Preface. *In* Gray, W., Duhl, F. J., and Rizzo, N. D. (eds.): General Systems Theory and Psychiatry. Boston, Little, Brown and Company, 1974.
Hendrick, I.: Work and the pleasure principle. Psychoanal. Q., *12*:34–329, 1943.
Hendrick, I.: The discussion of the "instinct to master." Psychoanal. Q., *12*:561–565, 1943.
Jones, E.: The Life and Work of Sigmund Freud. Vols. I–III. New York, Basic Books, 1953–1957.
Kolb, L. C.: The adaptive functions of the ego: a reconceptualization. The assertive sets or sublimated character traits. (In press.)
Lief, A. (ed.): The Commonsense Psychiatry of Adolf Meyer. New York, McGraw-Hill Book Co., Inc., 1948.
MacLean, P. D.: Contrasting functions of limbic and neocortical systems of the brain and their relevance to psychophysiological aspects of medicine. Am. J. Med., *25*:611–626, 1958.
Miller, J. C.: Living Systems. New York, McGraw-Hill Book Co., 1978.
Pribram, K. H.: Looking to see. Some experiments on the brain mechanism of attention in perception and its distortions. Assoc. Res. Nerv. Ment. Dis., *48*:150–162, 1968.
Sullivan, H. S.: The Interpersonal Theory of Psychiatry. (Eds., H. S. Perry and M. L. Gawel.) New York, Norton & Co., 1953.
Taylor, J. (ed.): Selected Writings of John Hughlings Jackson. Vols. I, II. New York, Basic Books, Inc., 1958.
Tomkins, S. S.: Affect Imagery Consciousness. 2 Vols. New York, Springer Publishing Company, Inc., 1962.
Winters, E. (ed.): The Collected Papers of Adolf Meyer. Vols. I–IV. Baltimore, Johns Hopkins Press, 1950–1952.

3

THE BRAIN AND BEHAVIOR

"Now the general causes of the emotions are indubitably physiology."

William James, 1890

IVAN P. PAVLOV
(From the National Library of Medicine,
Bethesda, Maryland.)

Most of the earlier neurophysiologic studies have been directed on the one hand to examination of control of various systems or organs by the central nervous system and its spinal and peripheral extensions or systems, and on the other hand to examination of cognitive, perceptual, and volitional performances. Increasingly over the past two decades researchers have concentrated upon the structural-functional subsystems of the brain as they relate to behavior.

Inferences drawn from the study of clinical phenomena, commencing at the turn of the twentieth century, provided the impetus for the growth of physiology of behaviors and emotions which now has direct pertinence to functions significant in the daily living of the individual members of all species. Careful analysis of sequences or patterns of activity by ethologists and students of animal psychology, and their correlation with the activity of various portions of the nervous system as demonstrated during electrical or pharmacological stimulation or after ablations, have laid the groundwork for an expanding understanding of the dynamic structural-functional relationships within the nervous system which lead to arousal and execution of integrated goal-directed behaviors. Also, the empiric clinical discoveries of the powerful actions of the phenothiazines and, later, of the various antidepressant pharmaceuticals have stimulated much study. This study has in turn added to our capacity to formulate powerful new hypotheses of concern in understanding the process of synaptic transmission, particularly as related to the subsystems of the brain concerned with drives and affects.

By far the largest proportion of the observations on behavior and its relation to brain function reported in this chapter are derived from studies in animal species. Likewise, most of the hypotheses presented in this chapter are based on observations made by those whose principal concern is the study of nonhuman species. The extent to which one may extrapolate from the physiology of nonhuman species to that of man remains an open question. Yet those basic biological functions upon which the interest of neurophysiologists has focused are common to all species, including man. Furthermore, the majority of social drives recognized as essentially human are considered their derivatives. In the past there has been notable success in applying to human organ functioning the knowledge gained by physiologists from experimentation in animals.

The ethologist Konrad Lorenz argues convincingly that analogies in behavior between differing species indicate a parallel adaptation developed for survival value in the course of evolution. Studies in the new discipline of sociobiology, including the examination in animal species of behaviors labeled altruism, faithfulness to one's mate, parental sacrifices, friendship, enmity, or jealousy, indeed may be highly significant in relationship to understanding human growth and personality development. These actions in animal species are to be regarded as more than simple anthropomorphism. They have the potential, when carefully analyzed, of providing information about the shaping processes that influence the evolution of these and other behaviors. Many observations now exist that demonstrate how differing social environments have profound physiological effects. This evidence has recently been reviewed by Kiritz and Moos.

At best the information available today on brain function as it relates to behavior provides a structure for speculation upon the relationship between that function and its abnormal expressions in psychiatric disorder. At the least it has heuristic value.

The human brain differs from that of other mammalian species in the extent to which the cerebral cortex has expanded. Upon this growth rest the extensive cognitive functions of man: his capacities for language, elaborate communications systems, retention of information in memory, exquisitely discriminative and variable affective and conative sets, and the ability to solve problems and inquire. Man retains, however, the primitive brain structures found in subhuman species. Thus, the midbrain hypothalamic systems common to all vertebrates appear to control the regulating functions concerned with those primary activities needed to sustain life: feeding, drinking, breathing, sexual activity, and thermal control.

MacLean has hypothesized that the human cortex is "triune." His researches and those of others show that the striatal cortex is concerned not only with movement but with the storing of ancestrally learned behaviors. The limbic system (Fig. 3–1), a paleocortical development, is conceived today to have

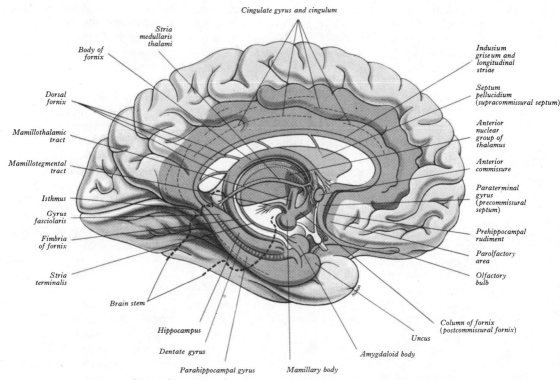

Figure 3–1 The limbic system. A diagram of a dissection of the medial aspect of a cerebral hemisphere to demonstrate the majority of the structures included under the term limbic system. The anterior nuclear group of the dorsal thalamus is included with the limbic system. The approximate position of the brainstem that was removed in the course of dissection is outlined in a heavy interrupted line. (From Warwick, R., and Williams, P. L., (eds.): Gray's Anatomy. 35th Br. ed. © Longman Group, Ltd., 1973.)

emerged in the evolutionary process to function in connection with emotionally determined behaviors that are related principally to preservation of the self or the species. Cognitive functioning, including the processing of information, recognition and recall, decision-making and action-taking or action-inhibiting, relates to the extent and development of the neocortex.

Thus, the human brain may be thought of as a hierarchical structure which, in effective functioning, demands the integration of each of the successively more complex systems extending from the hindbrain through the forebrain. Dysfunction at any level in the successively more complex structures and their interconnecting links, whether in the midbrain, the hypothalamus, the limbic system, or the various

regions of the cortex, distorts behavior and in man may lead to symptoms impairing personality function.

In the previous chapter emotion was defined as those bodily processes and activities that are generated through threats to existence or frustration and delay in gratification of a drive state. These processes include the activation of organ systems by the involuntary nervous system as well as the brain subsystem concerned with affect.

Direct attack induces the emotional states of rage or fear. Pain, hunger, and thirst, with their attendant drives and associated affects, may be regarded as primitive emotional states. Satiation of these needs—or expectation of satiation—leads to varying degrees of satisfaction or pleasure, another variety of affect with attendant emotional behavior. With the procreative drives, both stressing and satisfying drive and affective states are aroused in the seeking period, in copulatory and protective activities, and in the complexly organized rearing of the young characteristic of the mammalian species.

In an attempt to summarize findings derived from neurophysiology, Magda Arnold has suggested that emotion derives from an appraisal of inputs from the sensory system mediated by the limbic system and related to an affective recall discharged through cingulum, hippocampus, postcommissural fornix, and interthalamic nuclei of the limbic subsystem of the brain. She suggests that the affective tone of the perceptive memory established in this brain subsystem establishes the next step of the move to action, which is mediated by circuits connected with the frontal lobe.

For the psychiatrist the most significant behaviors are those connected with the arousal of emotion, and particularly affect, and its variable modulation and control through a wide range of socially learned behavioral sequences. The mentally ill suffer as a consequence of their defective control of socially prohibited emotional expression, or their inept learning of defenses or socially adaptive and self-esteeming behaviors against it.

Abnormalities in social functioning are seen in the senseless rages, the grotesque posturings, and the bizarre delusional and hallucinatory experiences of the psychotic, the seemingly irrational repetitions of the compulsive, or the sensorimotor inhibitions of the hysteric. In contrast to such behaviors there is the flexible and constructive expression of emotion displayed by those more fortunate in their growth and development.

Owing to development of a verbal communicative system, man alone of all the species is capable of reporting upon the variety of subjectively perceived affective states that attend the arousal of emotional behaviors. Tenderness and love, jealousy, anxiety, sadness and lonesomeness, guilt and shame, envy and hatred—all are shadings of the primitive affects of love, fear, and rage that may be defined only through the verbal reporting of the affective state in man: emotional states at best capable of inference in other mammalian forms.

Emotional behavior, then, is a complex organismal response to a perception of threat or of satiety. Such behavior represents a response to signals or cues sensed from either the internal or the external environment. Its expression may be examined in terms of the arousing percept, the goal-directed activity, or those associated subjective states capable of study only through man's verbal communications, his fantasy, and his thought. Thus, in man, one may examine the repetitive situations in which aggressive behavior occurs; the pattern of overt expression of aggressive behavior or its covert expressions in passivity and withdrawal, or, finally, the subjective accounts of perceived rage, jealousy, envy, fear, or anxiety that represent the many manifestations of human affect when the aggressive drive is stimulated.

Each emotional response varies quantitatively. The rage response may be intense or may be shown only through minor behavioral expression. The percept that calls out one emotion may be interrupted by another more prepotent for the organism's survival. Emotional behavior results from an infinity of triggering mechanisms: unfamiliar percepts, an inner awareness of lack of strength, a perceived threat. The same cause may produce differing reactions in the same subject at differing times. Each emotional state may be capable of expression in a number of behaviors. In the same subject these expressions change as the individual becomes habituated to the stimulating condition and learns different adaptations to the arousing stimulus situation.

ANALYSIS OF BEHAVIOR

For the understanding and evaluation of behavior one must comprehend not only the range and variety of pathological patterns but also the adaptive processes which maintain performance in the homeostatic state.

For the most part the physiological analyses of central nervous system function have been concerned with behaviors considered "instinctive." As defined by Tinbergen and other ethologists, instinctive behavior exists as innate hierarchically organized nervous mechanisms susceptible to certain priming, releasing, and directing impulses coming from both *within* and *without* the organism. In turn these mechanisms evince response by coordinated actions that contribute to the maintenance of the individual and the species. Such innate behavioral mechanisms are capable of discrimination in simpler vertebrate forms, as the stickleback fish or the herring gull. In mammalian forms, however, much of behavior is thought by animal psychologists to be derived from the innate drive states and learned. While the instinctive drives certainly exist in man, it is unknown whether innate stereotypes of behavior still exist. Because of the overriding importance of the learning capacity and opportunity inherent in the vast growth of the cerebral hemispheres and projected through the existing social systems, the analysis which might identify simple instinctive activity in man has as yet escaped accomplishment.

Study of submammalian species by ethologists has shown that in any sequence, whether it be to feed and relieve hunger, to find water and quench thirst, to obtain a mate and satisfy the sexual drive, or to progress through the successive states concerned with nurturing and preparing the young for independent growth, one may find "priming" and "releasing" mechanisms. The former consist of facilitating processes which build up the potential to act. Internally, the accumulation of appropriate hormonal agents sets the attention of the neuromuscular systems. The releasing mechanism initiates or triggers the sequence of acts which make up a coordinated series of behaviors leading to the achievement of the necessary goal. Such releasing mechanisms may come about by either the development of a certain intensity of tissue need or the perception of some stimuli in the environment facilitating the potential of the innate releasing mechanism.

In the sequence of behaviors considered instinctive the initial actions are "appetitive" or "exploratory"; they occur through the development of internal tensions. Following the preparatory appetitive and exploratory behaviors there follow the "consummatory" actions.

During the appetitive stage of a behavioral sequence, which may be very short or of prolonged duration, extending over days, the animal appears restless and agitated. Superficially, his actions sometimes appear aimless. He seems to have reserves of energy and strength, exposed in such aggressive actions as fighting to obtain food or gain a mate. Alertness to environmental stimuli is acute, and perceptual attentiveness is magnified toward those cues subserving the prepotent organismal goal, while sensitivity to other stimuli outside that urge is diminished. Organs concerned with the need demanding eventual gratification are placed in a state of readiness for functioning.

With the realization of the external goal—food, water, a sexual mate—there takes place the consummatory act, usually a stereotyped pattern of behavior. Satisfactory consummation is followed by a state of satiation accompanied by resting behavior, lessened alertness to and interest in the environment, and, as we know from man, a subjective state of satisfaction.

As the animal grows and records experience within his nervous system, his susceptibility to response through exposure to the releasing mechanisms is enhanced. Furthermore, the external releasing perceptions for particular behavior may assume a wider range of configurations or become more differentiated through learning processes. Without consummation for prolonged periods, actions directed toward certain goals may discharge spontaneously even though presentation of the external releasing stimulus has not taken place. Thus, it is apparent that innate behaviors constitute in themselves a sequence of complexly organized actions dependent upon the internal state of each organism and each species. Furthermore, such behaviors become subject to increasingly greater modifications through experience and learning according to the extent and the peculiar organization of the nervous system of the species. The components of a behavioral sequence may vary then in their capacity for arousal, in the intensity and complexity of response of the various perceptual motor components in appetitive, consummatory, and satiated states.

It seems from the analysis of behavioral sequences that the brain, as the integrative organ of each organism, must be so organized in all animal species as to assure sensitivity to environmental and internal stimuli, to effect arousal, with increased alertness and attentiveness, as well as rest and satiation. It must contain subsystems that establish the innate drives and in some species the stereotyped behaviors which take place without previous experience and learning. In the more highly differentiated mammalian species, including man, there exist the cortical systems upon which the multivariate discrimination of sensory experiences develops as well as the encoding denoted as "memories" and upon which are based those highly discriminated learned patterns of perception, mediation, and action. From these derive the many flexi-

ble behavioral approaches available to man to serve his appetitive and consummatory drives.

INFORMATION PROCESSING

From the analytic descriptions of goal-seeking behavior as provided by ethologists, one must conceive of brain function in terms other than those offered earlier and derived from learning theory and simple stimulus—response physiology. As an integrating organ, the brain must continuously process information registered upon the body from its exterior and interior surfaces, from the internal organ systems, and from its own structure. In this integrative process the brain utilizes systems that have laid down a record over time of past sensory experience and the recorded consequences of actions taken which succeeded or failed in goal-seeking or protective behavior. It must relate the incoming registrations to each other, collate them, and compare them with previous registrations.

The brain must attend to those registrations that signal threat to the function of the organism as a whole or to any of its subsystems, and must determine the general or local response most likely to protect and preserve function. In carrying out the integrative and executive functions of the organism, brain subsystems sustain a constant watch to sense opportunity or threat and to attend to the stimulus. In so doing conscious percepts in man emerge from memories of the past.

So, too, in relation to the needs of the other major bodily systems concerned with energy processing and reproduction, man and other species, depending upon the selective needs deriving from the systems, variously attend to differing stimuli. When hungry, vigilance is intensified to cues indicating food. In man, only when the reproductive system has evolved to maturity is the brain alerted to attend to and enhance further behavior directed toward consummation with the sexual object.

AROUSAL AND SATIATION

Largely through the work of Magoun and his collaborators, it is now recognized that within the central gray matter of the brain stem exist cells rich in afferent and efferent connections with the spinal cord, hypothalamus, limbic system, and various areas of the cerebral cortex. Their activation is known to facilitate or inhibit the postural tonus of muscles throughout the body, to influence endocrine and visceral functions, and to be concerned as well with states of wakefulness, orienting, and attention. Thus stimulation of the corticoparietal projections of the central reticular formations sets up the low-voltage frequencies in the electroencephalogram associated with states of attention and wakefulness. Similar behavior, with associated EEG patterns of arousal, follows stimulation in the sub and dorsal hypothalamus and the nonspecific thalamic nuclei, as well as activation of the well-known specific afferent pathways in the brain stem. It appears from stimulation experiments in animals that arousal of the cortex may follow impulses reaching it from the midbrain by either of two routes: an extrathalamic route, passing through the internal capsule from the subthalamic areas, or via the cortical projections of the nonspecific thalamic nuclei. Destruction of the central tegmental areas in animals leads to comatose behavior (high-voltage slow EEG patterns are seen in such states) even though the specific sensory pathways to the brain are intact, nor is it possible to bring about arousal even by the most intense stimulation thereafter.

That the reticular activating system is concerned with the modulations of consciousness and attention seems evident Its activity now is known to be sup-pressed by general anesthetics, the barbiturates, the phenothiazines, reserpine, and other pharmacological agents. As we shall note in discussing innate alimentary, sexual, and aggressive behaviors, the electrical activity within the activating system is modified likewise by other metabolic and endocrine imbalances.

ATTENTION AND VIGILANCE

The modifications of consciousness and attention to stimulations are not only dependent upon the afferent inflow to the midbrain activating system from the spinal and central sensory neurons but are also subject to "feedback" control from the cerebral cortex. Thus, electrical stimulation of diverse points in the cingulate, orbital, and lateral frontal areas, central and paraoccipital areas, superior gyrus, and tip of the temporal lobe of the cortex leads to both augmentation and reduction of activity within the brain stem reticular system. It seems likely, then, that as facilitation of performance is brought about through cortical arousal by activity in the activating system, there occurs an inverse inhibitory corticoreticular discharge or feedback which obviates overexcitation and also dampens or inhibits sensory stimulation irrelevant to the prepotent behavioral sequence.

Little is known of the means by which the brain maintains its ability to attend selectively to one set of sensory registrations and not another. Acts of attention seem enormously different. On the one hand one may be struck by the precise visual attentiveness that must be exerted for an otherwise preoccupied man to suddenly catch a ball thrown past him by a playing child. Against this, one may conceive the narrowed attention of a microscopist as he focuses upon the tissue viewed through his scope. Then again there is the consciously determined scanning attention to a large stream of incoming registrations, such as might be given by a music critic while preparing to write his appraisal of the playing of a symphony orchestra, or that of the psychoanalyst attempting to discover a meaningful thread in scanning the sequence of the often apparently unrelated free association of his patient.

Arguing from a series of experiments, Pribram has suggested that attention derives from other than associations established by means of transcortical or cortico-cortical associations and that the brain's intrinsic processing system is other than a passive receptacle of information. He is of the belief that mnemic functions (memory) occur as active recoding and that the processing cortex regulates ongoing processes under the sensory system.

Thus from his work upon the association areas of the cerebral cortex concerned with recognition, we find it divisible into the *posterior part,* concerned with *recognition,* and the *frontal part,* concerned with *recall.* As for the latter, it is divided according to sense modality. Clinical studies and experiments over time indicate that the inferior temporal cortex functions in relation to visual recognition, the middle temporal to auditory recognition, the anterior temporal to gustation, and the posterior parietal to somesthesias. Pribram was struck with the anatomical fact that the aforementioned associative processing areas are separated by a considerable span from their related primary cortical sensory receptive and the mnestic or associational cortex without loss of visual recognition of patterns in monkeys. What does take place is impairment in behaviors in which animals are required to process a number of visual cues to complete a task. Such animals fail, even though they "track" easily. Pribram states that behavioral learning (that is, identification) is based on a progressive differentiation and not on associative abstraction. He suggests the attention required in simple visual motor tracking as used in catching a fly

depends only on the functioning of the primary sensory receptive cortex. Probably corticofugal impulses from that area to subthalamic system areas direct alerting. Scanning, requiring searching, relating, and selection of a series of cues, comes about through actions of the intrinsic (associative) processing cortex. Here the scanning attention might be directed by corticofugal pathways to the subthalamic alerting spheres. Vigilance, the monitoring of external and internal registrations to determine their prepotency, seems most likely the function of the limbic system. Cognitive factors, perhaps, are the consequence of diffuse corticocortical associational actions.

Physiologists have found that the reticular activating system facilitates sensory inputs from the spinal cord and brain stem. Additional feedback control is exerted centrally by an inverse inhibitory corticoreticular discharge which dampens sensory stimulation and overexcitation as well as at peripheral sensory receptors outside the central nervous system, in the cochlea and retina. It is of interest that Freud predicted the existence of a *stimulus barrier* (Reizschutz) to protect the organism from destructive and overwhelming stimulation. The discovery of the physiological arrangements within the nervous system preventing overactivation of sensory neurons and the *excessive overload* of the brain itself provides experimental support for his hypotheses.

The exigencies of life and adaptation to it have required the establishment of flexible gates excluding, reducing, or facilitating the inflow of sensory impressions from one or several sources, depending upon the immediate adaptive function demanded of the individual organism. That this protective barrier may fail to function, through maldevelopment or overload, and lead to disease is a distinct possibility. Such occurrences perhaps are exemplified in the sensory hypersensitivities noted in childhood schizophrenia, in such toxic states as delirium tremens, and in the stress reaction observed in man following prolonged battle exposure or after other catastrophes. The application of this knowledge to the clinic has suggested modulating the input of auditory stimulation to mask the pain incurred during dental procedures. The concepts of the gating theory may contribute to our understanding of the potent analgesic effects produced by acupuncture.

Still another characteristic of the activating system is its deactivation of the cortex on the presentation of repetitive, unvarying stimulation which may be interpreted as monotonous. Here the system functions by progressive reduction of electrocortical arousal even though the sensory input reaches the cortex. The system then is concerned with the process of *habituation*. Prolonged deprivation of cortical arousal now is known also to have deleterious effects, as described in Chapter 7.

While the activating systems in the brain stem and thalamus are concerned principally with alerting the organism and directing its attention to external or internal cues, there exist brain systems that reinforce sequences of behavior. These systems are concerned with emotional arousal and related affect. As noted in the previous chapter, the anlages of the finely differentiated affective states of human beings rest upon primitive feeling states of pleasure and distress — states experienced first in the helpless dependency of infancy.

NEUROTRANSMISSION

As with other brain systems, cellular interconnections are now understood to be made through electrochemical events taking place at the synaptic junctions between cells. The most popular of the current hypotheses relating to affect variability centers on presumed functional levels of concentration of the biogenic amines at the synaptic junction, the cleft, and the postsynaptic receptor site. Thus the passage of a nerve impulse from activated neurons across the synaptic junction to other nerve cells is considered to take place by discharge of the biogenic amine (see Figure 3–2) into the synaptic cleft where it is bound momentarily to the postsynaptic receptor.

Numerous compounds serve as neurotransmitters in the human brain. The catecholamines (dopamine, norepinephrine, and epinephrine), the indolamines (serotonin), gamma-aminobutyric acid, and acetylcholine represent only a few. Concentrations of these substances vary throughout the various major nuclear constructs of the sections of the brain.

The catecholamines in the neurons are synthesized from the amino acid tyrosine, derived either from dietary protein or through liver synthesis from phenylalanine. Catecholamine biosynthesis comes about through the hydroxylation of tyrosine to form dihydroxyphenylalanine (L-dopa). The next step in catecholamine synthesis involves the decarboxylation of dopa to form dopamine. Dopamine under the action of dopamine β-oxidase is hydroxylated to form L-norepinephrine. As a final step, neurons that contain the enzyme phenylethanolamine-n-methyltransferase (PNMT) transfer the methyl group from s-adenosylmethionine to the primary amine of the norepinephrine molecule to form epinephrine.

Catecholamine molecules are released into synapses and are either taken up again or are metabolized prior to their excretion into the urine. Their end products, most generally examined quantitatively in current research, are homovanillic acid from dopamine or methoxy-4-hydroxyphenyl glycol (MHPG) from norepinephrine.

The metabolites of noradrenalin are present in cerebral spinal fluid. It is possible to tell how much noradrenalin is metabolized within the brain by

Figure 3–2   *See legend on opposite page*

measuring the cerebrospinal fluid after ingestion of probenecid, which blocks the dispersion of acid metabolites from spinal fluid.

In contrast to the catecholamines, serotonin (5-hydroxytryptamine) is synthesized from dietary tryptophan. This agent is related to several congeners, including N,N,dimethyltryptamine and its 5-hydroxy derivative, bufotenin, which has been known to produce mental changes. Serotonin too is related biochemically to other hallucinogenic substances, including psilocybin and lysergic acid diethylamide (LSD). The 5-hydroxytryptamine–containing neurons are concentrated in a raphe nuclei of the lower brain stem but innervate numerous, widely dispersed regions of the central nervous system, including the cortex and spinal cord.

Gamma-aminobutyric acid (GABA), according to Roberts, may be a pretransmitter mediating presynaptic inhibition in the vertebrate central nervous system. Its absence or relative lack in the balance of neurotransmitters operative at the synaptic junctions possibly leads to variations in the rate of functioning of certain neuronal circuits and thereby disturbs steady discharges or produces dystonia. It is of interest that, recently, diminution in GABA levels has been found in the substantia nigra, globus pallidus, and caudate nucleus of patients with Huntington's chorea.

Throughout the brain the neurons synthesizing, storing, and releasing acetylcholine (ACh) are believed to have a much wider distribution than those containing the catecholamines. The histochemical staining of cholinesterase defines the cholinergic pathways in the intersegmental projections of the limbic and reticular systems, as well as other locally restricted interneurons.

Of the biogenic amines, norepinephrine is found in highest concentration in the hypothalamus but is also present elsewhere, including in the limbic system. The biogenic amine serotonin has a similar distribution. Dopamine, on the other hand, is most highly concentrated in the basal ganglia. It has been suggested, but not yet proved, that all three of these biogenic amines may act as chemical transmitters. Some believe that one or more of these amines may act as modulators of synaptic transmissions that depend on other substances.

Synthesized from tyrosine, norepinephrine is stored in intraneuronal granules at the presynaptic endings. When discharged into the synaptic cleft it is inactivated by conversion by the enzyme catechol-O-methyltransferase or is taken up again by the cell. Released within the cell, it is inactivated by mitochondrial monoamine oxidase, forming metabolites. The latter enzyme may then regulate the levels of norepinephrine within the cell. Epinephrine exists only in low concentrations in the brain. Peripherally, it exists in the adrenal medulla. Serotonin is synthesized by the hydroxylation of tryptophan, its amino acid dietary precursor, to form 5-hydroxytryptophan. This compound is decarboxylated to form serotonin. It, too, is metabolized by monoamine oxidase to form 5-hydroxyindolacetic acid.

Earlier inference from clinical investigations related states of anger to the state of physiological arousal produced by injections of norepinephrine,

Figure 3–2 Chemical transmission across the synapse, the narrow gap between two neurons in the brain, involves an elaborate sequence of molecular events. Here the process of transmission at a norepinephrine synapse is diagrammed. First, norepinephrine is manufactured from the amino acid tyrosine in three steps, each of which is catalyzed by an enzyme. The transmitter is then stored within membrane-bound vesicles in association with storage proteins (indicated by light gray pathways). The arrival in the axon terminal of a nerve impulse triggers an influx of calcium ions, which induces the release of norepinephrine from the vesicles into the synaptic space (dark gray pathways). The liberated transmitter molecules bind to specific receptor proteins embedded in the postsynaptic membrane, triggering a series of reactions that culminate in short-term (electrical) and long-term effects on the receiving neuron (light brown pathways). The action of norepinephrine is then terminated by a variety of means, including rapid re-uptake of the transmitter into the axon terminal and degradation by enzymes (dark brown pathways). The release of some norepinephrine into the synaptic space activates presynaptic receptors on the axon terminal, initiating production of cyclic AMP, which activates protein kinase, thus stimulating more norepinephrine production (black pathways).

(From Iverson, L.: The chemistry of the brain. © Scientific American, September 1979. All rights reserved.)

whereas fear was thought to resemble those related to states induced by both norepinephrine and epinephrine injections. In monkeys in which blood levels of these amines may be measured, release of norepinephrine takes place with presentation of familiar and threatening stimuli. On the other hand, when the threatening situation is unknown or uncertain, increased epinephrine levels occur in the peripheral blood. Improved performance of work under stress is associated with increased norepinephrine excretion. Exposure of human beings to emotionally arousing feelings leads to increased excretion of both norephinephrine and epinephrine; exposure to bland film is followed by diminution in the steady-state release of these compounds.

It appears that the nature of differential perception of the external cues determines differentially the relative levels of excretion of these amines within the body. In animals, decrements in brain norepinephrine take place with fear and immobilization, and even after intracerebral stimulation productive of heightened emotional arousal. Also, in animals adrenocorticosteroids enhance the activity of the enzymes that convert norepinephrine to epinephrine in the adrenal.

As will be discussed in the chapter on pharmacological therapy, those agents that are considered to increase norepinephrine concentrations in the synaptic cleft are associated with relief of depressive affect with its components of impounded rage and fear.

Experienced psychiatrists are impressed with the powerful effects of the new pharmaceuticals in modulating and changing pathologic affect and drive. The current biological interpretations of modifications of synaptic transmission by these drugs must be recognized as oversimplified. Since synaptic transmission is involved in integration of all brain and peripheral neuronal interaction, one must realize that specificity as it relates to subsystem

function must involve other variables. These may arise in either qualitative or quantitative production or degradation of transmitter substances. We remain far from a chemical control of man's affective state.

There is physiological evidence for a central affective system within the brain. Olds and Milner found that animals with permanently implanted electrodes through which the animals might deliver stimuli to a portion of their own basal forebrains learned shortly to re-excite this brain area repeatedly and autonomously. When the electrodes were placed properly, rats stimulated themselves as often as 8000 times per hour.

Heath and his coworkers have reported pleasurable affects in some men with similar electrode placement carried out as a treatment of schizophrenia. When the electrode was placed in sites in the posterior hypothalamus or mid-brain, self-stimulation was much less frequent. Chlorpromazine and reserpine obliterate or inhibit self-stimulation in the latter sites but not in the more potently rewarding cephalic structures. The drive for autonomous self-stimulation can be modified by increasing the intensity of needs. In rats the drive for self-stimulation is much greater when they are exposed to the shock pain of crossing an electric grid than when they are deprived of food for a day.

This system, with its capacity to reinforce behaviors, should be contrasted with the long-known sensory system concerned with pain—an emotional state that regularly leads to withdrawal behavior. Repetitive induction of this unpleasant emotion establishes behaviors of avoidance or aversion.

Recently, it has been discovered that the human brain contains receptors for opium derivatives. Further, a new class of compounds, endorphins, has been shown to activate these receptors and to be synthesized in human brain. The endorphins are polypeptide fragments, principally derived from β-lipoprotein, a large polypeptide molecule. The discovery of endorphins, together with receptors for these compounds, may make possible better analgesic drugs and may also allow an increase in endorphin release, thus producing a highly potent form of analgesia. The relationship of endorphins to a state of well-being indicates that these compounds may play a role in the etiology or in the treatment of mental illness.

CYCLIC REINFORCEMENT AND INHIBITION

Many of the drive states, which serve to maintain the health of man and other species and assure their procreative activities, take place on time-fixed cycles of activity. Undoubtedly the most autonomous and least conscious cyclical activity is the spontaneously recurring movement of the chest cage and diaphragm concerned with the maintenance of respiration. In man this unconsciously maintained cyclical behavior is sometimes distorted in the form of respiratory tics, grunts, bouts of hyperventilation, and breath holding, or even in the disturbances of vocalization that take place in stuttering.

Equally important to the maintenance of health — and its disruption is symptomatic of psychiatric disorder — is the sleep-wakefulness cycle. Also, in procreative life the estrous cycle represents a time-recurrent event characteristic of women and the females of other mammalian species. Disruptions of this cycle are among the most telling symptoms of stress.

Time-bound behavior sequences are less evident in human life than in our mammalian relatives. The flexibility with which we are endowed through this capacity for learning has detached us from the rigid behavioral cycles so characteristic of many simpler species. Yet evidence exists that we remain bound to behaviors determined by the function of "biological clocks." Disruption of these rhythmic functions by conflicting learned activities has been associated with serious psychopathology.

Richter's studies of cyclical behaviors in man and animals have led him to hypothesize the presence of three types of "clocks": homeostatic, central, and peripheral. The estrous cycle represents a homeostatic "clock" wherein hormonal feedback mechanisms exist between distant target organs (in this case the ovary and uterus), an endocrine gland (the pituitary), and the hypothalamus. The timing systems of the central and peripheral clocks do not appear to be homeostatic and are capable of imposing recurrent behaviors through learning. Thus, one may learn to awaken at precise times; certain pathologic behaviors recurring in patients in regular time cycles appear to be learned. The *anniversary reactions,* to be described in Chapter 7 in connection with bereavements, are an example. While Richter states that the homeostatic systems are somewhat irregular, the central timing systems function with high constancy over long periods. The cellular timing devices exist outside the nervous system; they cycle certain phenomena of primary physical disease, such as the regularly recurring fever of Hodgkin's disease. Such rhythms are thought to be ingrained into cellular and organ systems by the day-night and seasonal cycles, which modify metabolic potentials and are modified in the evolutionary process.

With the capacity for man to move rapidly by means of air travel from one time zone to another across the world, there has been a recognition that interruption of the *chronobiological functions* significantly impairs personality functioning. The significance of sustaining the usual chronobiological rhythms has necessitated consideration of the conventionally accepted hypothesis about homeostasis, as Kiritz has emphasized.

For some time it has been thought that a reciprocally innervated biphasic catabolic-anabolic sequence has existed in response to psychological disturbances. The first phase of the response consists of secretion of hormones with catabolic effects (cortisol, epinephrine, norepinephrine, and thyroid and growth hormones). At such time the anabolic hormones (insulin, estrogen and androgen) are thought to be suppressed.

In the second phase, the opposite trend of hormonal activation tends to occur. Thus, it has been found that urinary norepinephrine, epinephrine and corticoid steroid excretions are low during late evening and early morning and tend to rise sharply as sleeping hours end — preceding awakening by some three hours. Such a shift suggests an anticipated adaptation to the stresses of daytime activities. (See Fig. 3–3.)

Figure 3–3 Phase map of daily cycle of endocrine measures and urine in man in relation to habitual sleep and feeding schedule. (From Curitis, G. C.: Psychosom. Med., *34*:245, 1972.)

It has been shown that there exists in infants as young as 2 or 3 months a well developed rhythm of adrenal excretion, which becomes synchronized to social routines at this time. Longer chronobiological rhythms appear to exist in adrenal function, with peaks occurring in the late fall and winter. There appears also to be a cyclic rhythm in thyroid secretion and possibly in insulin secretion. The levels of the sexual hormones vary on a diurnal basis. Plasma testosterone values tend to be at the maximum level during the mornings, as do estrogen values. On the other hand, plasma aldosterone and renin are at maximum values in late afternoon.

It is now known that the rhythms of corticoid steroid and catecholamine secretion and urine volume do not immediately change their phase or period when environmental and living schedules are modified. After such sudden shifts in the phases of environmental living schedules as experienced today in east-west air travel, it takes several days to bring about change in the circadian rhythms. Experimental work in animals suggests the possibility that severe psychological stress also may bring about changes in the circadian rhythms, which we assume have been established adaptively to foster patterns of behavior dedicated to survival. Recent studies by Wehr suggest the possibility that certain of the affective disorders may be associated with abnormalities in the sleep-wake cycle and that drugs used in the treatment of these disorders may alter this cycle in humans. In terms of prevention of behavioral disorganization, based as it is upon appropriate physiological functioning, much more needs to be discovered about the processes establishing the circadian rhythms and their related neuroendocrinological changes.

Sleep-Wakefulness Behavior

For centuries the preservation of the regularly recurring sleep cycle has been recognized as imperative for the maintenance of health. Typical disruptions of the sleep cycle occur in depressive reactions and in various neurotic conditions and are represented as well by the somnambulistic trances seen most frequently in children. Less frequently met are those symptomatic eruptions of sleep which intrude upon the waking state: narcoleptic and hypersomniac attacks. The physiology of sleep has direct bearing upon the understanding of this clinical phenomenology.

Both the sleeping and the waking states are associated with characteristic electrocencephalographic patterns. The sleeping period is associated with at least two quite distinct types of brain activity. During 80 per cent of sleeping time there occurs an electroencephalographic pattern of large-amplitude slow waves and spindle bursts. This segment of sleep time is thought to represent inhibition of activity of the cerebral cortex. The other segment of sleep is characterized by an electroencephalographic pattern of low-voltage fast activity; this is thought to be a period in which subcortical function is predominantly impaired. It is now designated as "fast," "paradoxical," or "dreaming" sleep (Fig. 3–4).

In the human adult, periods of dreaming sleep recur each night at intervals of approximately 90 minutes. Associated with the electroencephalographic pattern of dreaming sleep are bursts of rapid conjugate eye movements (REM). At times of such electroencephalographic and ocular activity, the awakened sleeper almost regularly reports dreaming, in contrast to his behavior when awakened during other periods of the sleep cycle. Other significant physiological changes also take place during REM sleep. Thus, respiration is irregular, heart rate and blood pressure are elevated, skin resistance is lowered, spontaneous middle ear activity takes place, penile erection occurs, and there is a rapid and distinctive diminution in muscle tone as shown by the electroencephalograph.

Figure 3–4   NREM AND REM sleep—30 second recordings. *Left* and *Right Eyes*, electrooculographs of the lateral canthi referred to the opposite mastoid; *EMG*, chin to cheek surface electromyograph; *C3-EEG*, left central to right mastoid electroencephalograph.

In NREM sleep, stages 1, 2, 3 and 4 are shown on successive lines of the EEG. All are consistent with the eye and EMG tracings shown for NREM, but the stage 2 EEG is the actual EEG that was recorded with the eyes and EMG. Note the characteristic low voltage, relatively fast EEG and vertex spikes of stage 1 NREM; the 14 Hz spindles and K complexes (also seen in the eye leads) of stage 2 NREM; the high voltage, 1 to 2 Hz delta waves that comprise 20 to 50 per cent of the EEG of stage 3 NREM and more than 50 per cent (almost continuous) of the stage 4 NREM EEG.

A spontaneous awakening interrupts REM sleep, contributing 10 to 11 Hz alpha activity to the EEG. In REM sleep, note the out-of-phase deflections in the eye channels, indicating rapid consensual eye deflections; the low muscle tone in the EMG; and the low voltage, relatively fast EEG with "sawtooth" waves accompanying the phasic eye movements.

(Courtesy of Howard Roffwarg, M.D., Professor of Psychiatry, University of Texas, Southwestern Medical School.)

Dreaming sleep occupies as much as 50 per cent of the sleep cycle in infants, decreasing in amount with aging (Fig. 3–5). Similar cycles of REM sleep have been identified in many mammalian species other than man. One may infer from the periodic sleep activity of animals that they dream in association with this distinctive physiological phase of the sleep cycle.

Whether REM sleep is of greater or less depth or whether it represents a more primitive form of the dominant sleep periods remains a matter of discussion. While it has been assumed that dreaming sleep is light, at times the arousal threshold is higher during the REM period and at other times it is barely in excess of the waking threshold.

The recent clinical experiment by Greenberg, Pillard, and Pearlman seems to substantiate Freud's suggestion that dreaming serves an important function in reducing or working through anxiety. These researchers discovered that individuals who were made anxious by viewing a certain film and were then subjected to dream deprivation adapted less well to a second viewing of the same film in contrast to a control group who were not subjected to deprivation of REM sleep.

Hartmann has speculated that deep sleep is linked with the general restorative anabolic processes, while dreaming

REM SLEEP/NREM SLEEP RELATIONSHIP THROUGHOUT HUMAN LIFE

Figure 3–5 Graph showing changes (with age) in total amounts of daily sleep, daily REM sleep, and in percentage of REM sleep. Note sharp diminution of REM sleep in the early years. REM sleep falls from eight hours at birth to less than one hour in old age. The amount of NREM sleep throughout life remains more constant, falling from eight hours to five hours. In contrast to the steep decline of REM sleep, the quantity of NREM sleep is undiminished for many years. Although total daily REM sleep falls steadily during life, the percentage rises slightly in adolescence and early adulthood. This rise does not reflect an increase in amount; it is due to the fact that REM sleep does not diminish as quickly as total sleep.

(Courtesy of Howard Roffwarg, M.D., Professor of Psychiatry, University of Texas, Southwestern Medical School.)

sleep occurs in relation to brain synthetic processes. He suggests that the brain protein molecules are synthesized in the brain during deep sleep or used during the REM periods in reconnecting and restoring cerebral functioning. It is of interest to note that distance runners have more slow-wave sleep than others who engage in regular exercise of a less strenuous nature. Starvation, too, in man significantly increases deep sleep and leads to a fall in REM sleeping time.

Physiological studies have established the fact that the occurrence of the rapid low-voltage electrical activity depends upon the functioning of nuclear aggregations in the pontine reticular formations. REM records persist in mammals, including man, following decortication; they have been absent in several electroencephalographic recordings of patients with evidence of pontine damage. Even in decorticate animals, deprivation of "fast sleep" by repeated awakening leads to a pattern of sleep in which REM outbursts occur at increasingly frequent intervals. Cerebral tracts other than the ascending reticular formation are involved in the cortical driving mechanism in animals. "Fast sleep" disappears only with interruption of tracts in the ventral mesencephalon. It is of interest that there has been reported in man a syndrome of "peduncular hallucinosis" characterized by isolated visual hallucinations which occur at onset of sleep in those with lesions in the area of the ventral mesencephalon.

In the past five years much research has been done upon the effects of drugs in expressions of REM and nonREM sleep. Atropine reduces or abolishes REM sleep, whereas cholinergic agents such as eserine prolong its expression. Atropine administered to cats just prior to the time of the expected circadian rise of 17-hydroxy steroids blocks that biological rhythmic activity. The barbiturates pentobarbital (Nembutal) and secobarbital (Seconal),

glutethimide (Doriden), methyprylon (Noludar), and diphenhydramine (Benadryl) all reduce the amount of time spent in REM sleep. Of these drugs the barbiturates have the most effect. Dextroamphetamine, combined with pentobarbital, eliminates dreaming sleep. Following the withdrawal of the aforementioned drugs there occurs an increase in REM sleep in subsequent nights—a "rebound."

Particularly after the withdrawal of barbiturates and alcohol administered over prolonged periods, the increased REM periods are punctuated by frightening nightmares. This is in contrast to deprivation of REM sleep by awakening; although increased REM sleep occurs on subsequent nights following interruption of REM by awakening, frightening dreaming is not usually reported.

The phenothiazines tend to change the electroencephalographic patterns of sleep toward that consistent with the state of coma. Antidepressants such as amitriptyline and imipramine decrease REM sleep activity, but over a few days of administration they expand the nonREM periods and lengthen the usual 90 minute cycles of REM expression up to 120 minutes. Their withdrawal is not followed by REM rebound. The monoamine oxidase inhibitors completely obliterate REM sleep.

On the other hand reserpine and lysergic acid diethylamide (LSD) enhance REM sleep, as does L-tryptophan and the tyrosine hydroxylase inhibitor alpha-methyl-para-tyrosine, which blocks the synthesis of catecholamines.

The relative amounts of REM and non-REM sleep may depend on the balance in neurotransmitter activities in the cholinergic, catecholaminergic, and serotonergic systems in the brain.

"Napping" sleep apparently varies greatly with the time of day. Afternoon napping is associated with an earlier appearance and greater proportion of REM sleep than is evening napping.

This observation suggests a greater potential for REM sleep expression during the daytime.

COGNITIVE SYSTEM

The capacity to respond with increasingly effective goal-directed behavior to variable but previously unspecified circumstances defines adaptation. That capacity, in living systems, requires that incoming information be registered and encoded, that a memory of the experience be established. On the basis of the earlier memories presentation of information resembling that registered at any early time is recognized as familiar — is perceived. So, too, the responses to past experience are recorded, including those internal events that determine emotion and affect. With each succeeding experience of goal seeking or avoidance of threat, the organism learns of the comparative effectiveness of present and previous behaviors by comparative analysis. It thus progressively discriminates the most significant cues in percepts, evolves more skillful and economical behavioral responses, and in the more complex mammalian species progressively analyzes and solves problems concerned with increasingly variable and complex environmental situations. Memory, perception, and cognition depend upon evolution of the brain.

Memory

It is now assumed that a series of electrochemical processes takes place to fix in the neuronal network of the brain those records of past sensory experiences that form the basis for perception and the development of motor and cognitive behaviors necessary for adaptation and defensive purposes. Much of what is written pertaining to these processes is highly speculative. Yet the mounting information and available hypotheses have heuristic value.

Memory processing is considered to be determined through two distinct but overlapping stages. The recall of immediately experienced events is recognized as different than the recall of past events. Electroshock will eradicate recall of recent events.

Clinical studies make it evident that extensive brain damage early in life impairs the storage of information and the potential for learning. With brain damage later in life specific deficits are noted in ability to retain recent percepts, while the memories encoded from the past are retained. Such impairment of storage or retention of experiences is a prominent symptom in certain of the alcoholic psychoses and characterizes the psychosis associated with the senium. Similarly, during the induction of anesthesia and after electroshock therapy, memory processing is impaired. While immediate memory of short spans is possible, the recall of long-span percepts, which involves storage, is defective.

Within the past decade it has been observed that patients treated neurosurgically for epilepsy by bilateral temporal lobe resections lose their ability to process current experience into memory. Thus, retention of any cognitive material is severely impaired and there may occur as well impairment of recall extending backward for several years (retrograde amnesia). Retention of earlier memories is unaffected. The anterior mesial surfaces of the temporal lobe are significantly concerned with the processing of perceptions to become permanent memories, but such encoding of perceptions involves as well widespread processes throughout the cerebral cortex. DeJong has placed on record one human case in which precise bilateral localized necrosis of the hippocampi led to impairment of memory recording. Animal experiments have shown that bilateral hippocampal ablation is the significant lesion responsible for impairing acquistion of avoidance learning.

It has been suggested that in the processing of sensory experiences into the electrochemical mechanisms that establish permanent coding within the brain, both specific and nonspecific sensory pathways are activated, the latter discharging into the hippocampus via the fornix. In studies in animals of the electrical activity of the hippocampus, regularly recurring high-voltage theta rhythms are generally evoked in this structure. Such rhythms become localized when a learned behavioral response takes place as the result of conditioning. Early in the conditioned learning process the electrical activity in the hippocampus precedes that in the adjacent cerebral cortex. When conditioned learning is established, the electrical activity in the cortex appears to precede that in the hippocampus. It has been suggested that these shifting electrical wave changes between hippocampus and cortex, which occur in the course of learning, bring about enduring biochemical changes in the cytoplasm of fast synaptic neurons and related neuroglia upon which permanent registrations depend.

Since it is now known that the processes of the astrocytic glia are intimately applied to the neurons and seem to serve as metabolic bridges between them and the circulating blood, they may be implicated in any biochemical process that determines structural change related to acquisition of memory.

The permanent recording of sensory experiences—long-term memory—would seem to require the transformation of electrical energy generated in the neurons into some permanent changes in their structure or their relationship within the net. The analogy of the genetic code information-processing through the template of RNA (ribonucleic acid) has been offered as a possible explanation for the structural change in the neurons which establishes the codes for a permanent memory. Yet in order to establish with certainty the evidence that one or another neurochemical process takes place to assure permanent encoding of an electroneural impulse and thus to demonstrate that a given molecule or set of molecules, or structure or set of structures, is specifically concerned in effecting a memory trace, a number of convincing demonstrations pertaining to that molecule or structure must be assured. Thus the molecule or structure must be shown to undergo a change of state in response to the experience to be remembered. That altered state must be shown to persist as long as the memory. The disappearance of the alteration must coincide with the loss of the memory.

Today convincing evidence meeting the general criteria above does not exist to establish any protein, lipid, or other brain constituent as the substance involved in structural alteration related to memory storage.

The metabolism of RNA may relate to memory storage, as its major function is participation in the synthesis of proteins. Many are convinced that the structural changes related to storage do concern brain proteins, but point out that cellular metabolism is dynamic and not fixed, and that there are many regulatory mechanisms within the neuron and between the neuron, its processes, and its numerous synaptic functions. It has been suggested that coding then is not related to a permanently enduring state of change in the human. It occurs only when brain protein synthesis takes place above a certain critical rate. Experiments have shown that in small mammals (mice) interference with the rate of protein sythesis in the brain by such an inhibitor as the antibiotic puromycin prevents learning of new behavioral expressions and disrupts old learning as well. Flexner has suggested that the establishment of enduring memory traces depends upon the existence within the brain of a self-sustaining system for synthesis of necessary proteins. He suggests that in the evolution of the process of long-term memory the initial learning experience triggers the synthesis of one or more species of messenger ribonucleic acid (mRNA). This mRNA alters the synthetic rate of one or more proteins essential for structural change in various neurons. In turn, these proteins modify the characteristics of the synaptic network so as to variously effect the transmission of nerve impulses. Finally, the proteins or their products induce the related mRNA production to sustain a critical level of their synthesis. When the level of synthesis falls, there takes place a temporary memory failure. It is unlikely that this hypothesis alone is sufficient to explain either short-term or long-term memory.

More recent studies have shown that such sodium pump inhibitors as lithium and ouabain in increasing doses cause rapid loss of memory in young chicks. This occurs independently of the actions of the protein synthesis inhibitors in impairing memory fixation. The sodium pump inhibitors have been found to block the formation of long-term memory only if present at the time of learning, while protein synthesis inhibitors will prevent long-term memory formation even when administered after learning. In animal experiments, when one combines an inhibitor of protein synthesis, such as cycloheximide, with electroconvulsive shock, complete amnesia of single trial learning may be produced.

Earlier theorists postulated memory as based upon the establishment of synaptic resistances or efficiency of reverberating electrical circuits. Probably in the future the electrochemical hypothesis will be related to the current, fashionable molecular theories of memory. The integrity of the hippocampal structures bilaterally seems necessary for the fixing of a trace event for immediate or long-term recall. Perhaps, as was discussed earlier under the subject of vigilance, this structure is concerned with the monitoring of meaningful internal and external information to determine its priority in terms of survival of the organism. High-priority information is likely to be recorded. For a thorough examination of the past and present hypotheses and data relative to mnestic function, the reader is referred to John.

LEARNING

From both clinical and laboratory evidence there is reason to believe that the cerebral processes associated with learning in early life are fundamentally different from those that take place after maturation of the nervous system. For many years it has been known that children born blind because of corneal opacities do not develop good vision unless that defect is repaired by corneal transplant very early in life. Likewise the dreams of children born blind or deaf never contain visual or auditory images, presumably because the patterns of cerebral organization fail to evolve without early perceptual experience. The same holds true for the organization of the body percepts: children born without a limb do not experience a limb phantom as do adults who suffer amputation.

Hebb has suggested that early sensing is necessary for the establishment of perceptual functioning. Furthermore, all later learning depends upon the appropriate early experiencing, which apparently stimulates the basic organization and integration of cerebral systems concerned with perception and cognition.

A long series of animal experiments now makes it clear that the organization of various sensory systems and behaviors depends upon experiencing at critical periods in the early life of each species. In the absence of the appropriate experiencing at the "critical time," the organism may be left with an enduring deficit in perception or behavior—an ego deficit, in psychoanalytic terms—a defect of personality functioning. The degree to which such deficits may be repaired by later experience is unknown.

"Imprinting," the specific emotional attachment of the young of some species to their parents, is a case in point. Discovered first in various birds, "imprinting" takes place when the young bird perceives a moving object during certain critical days following hatching. The attachment may be made to any moving object at this point in maturational development. Thus, when contact with man or some mobile inanimate object is substituted for contact with the parent, birds exposed to the substitute will thereafter follow that substitute when it is presented. From his observations on imprinting Hess distinguishes between *imprinting*, the early type of learning, and later *associational learning*. The former is dependent upon an experience that takes place at a critical period in early life. It is depressed by the prior administration of such pharmacologic agents as meprobamate or carisoprodol, and it is enhanced when painful stimuli occur with the visual percept. In contrast, later associational learning does not depend upon experience at critical periods in life, is not depressed by meprobamate, and leads to avoidance behaviors when associated with pain. In imprinting, the first percept is the most significant in the formation of the bond that leads to following behavior; in later associational learning the more recent learning has greater influence on behavior. Since this form of early learning, so important in establishing a social bond between young and their parents, may be adversely influenced by drugs which disturb electrochemical events in the brain,* we may generalize and assume that the electrochemical events of learning differ in the nervous system of the immature as compared to the mature member of the species.

_____

*Whereas associational learning is not affected by such drugs.

In the adult brain the evidence for the occurrence of electrochemical change comes from several sources. By using the Pavlovian technique of conditioning, the classic method of associational learning, it is possible to establish a blocking of the alpha rhythm of the electroencephalogram on presentation of a click as a conditional stimulus associated with eye opening that regularly acts in such a way as the unconditioned stimulus. In the initial stages of learning to respond to the clinic, the blocking of the alpha rhythm is generalized over the cortex; later it is localized to the occipital cortex, the projection site of the visual unconditioned stimulus. Other experiments in animals have shown that painful and pleasurable stimuli both augment the amplitude of cerebral electrical discharges and increase the distribution of afferent signals over the brain. As effective reinforcement is continued and learning occurs, the electrical discharges that were generally distributed initially are restricted to the site of projection of the unconditioned stimuli.

Learning theorists tend to distinguish between classical Pavlovian conditioning, associational learning, and instrumental conditioning. In the former an unconditioned stimulus, such as food that would lead a dog to salivate, when paired repeatedly with another signal such as a light or noise, would over a span of time bring an animal to salivate on presentation of the hitherto biologically unimportant but paired light or sound. Pavlov spoke of the latter as the conditioned stimulus and the salivation following its presentation as the conditioned response. So, too, he found it possible to pair signals with painful stimuli to produce conditioned evasive responses. Pavlov pointed out the necessity to assess the state of need or satiety of the animals he had under study. He came to know of the influence of the human experimenter upon the responsivity of his subjects and recognized that symbols could replace physical stimuli as signals for conditioned learning. To him sensations, perceptions, and direct impressions formed the primary signals of reality for man. Words constituted the secondary signals, as abstractions of reality, that permitted generalizations. In this psychology the reflex concept is primary, but reflex here represents a behavior response with afferent, mediating central, and efferent portions. Pavlov conceived of processes of cortical excitation and inhibition, sleep and hypnosis as representing inhibitory cortical states.

Instrumental learning differs from conditioned learning in the sense that the animal is rewarded when he performs a desired task. Thus an animal comes to learn that if he carries out such an action as striking a lever he will receive a food reward. So, too, he may learn to depress a lever in order to avoid a painful shock. In the course of instrumental learning, each time the correct response is given for either need reduction or escape, the animal is rewarded. When he fails to carry out the desired behavior the positive reward is denied or the aversive stimulus is given. Such instrumental or operant conditioning is associated with the work of a long line of American psychologists, of whom Skinner is the best known current spokesman.

Doubt was expressed in the past that visceral responses could be "learned" through trial-and-error rewarding methods of instrumental conditioning. As DiCara reports, a long series of experiments by Neal Miller and his associates has demonstrated otherwise. Increase and decrease in heart rate, blood pressure, constriction and relaxation of the vascular bed, intestinal contraction, and rate of urinary secretions may all be influenced by such learning procedures. So, too, the learning is relieved by periodic reinforcement and extinguishes or disappears if the reinforcement is not provided. It is of interest that the same reward may be used to obtain learned visceral responses of opposing character. It seems from this ex-

perimental work that conditioning through the sympathetic nervous system may occur with a much greater degree of specificity than thought possible earlier. The work on visceral conditioning is of paramount significance in considering the operational forces concerned in the psychophysiological (psychosomatic) disorders.

While imprinting, conditioned, or instrumental learning paradigms are of importance in comprehending the evolution of adaptive and maladaptive (psychopathological) behavior in man, they have yet to explain many phenomena evident in his learning or creative conceptualizations. Thus many behaviors follow single exposures to stimulating events. Brilliant conceptualizations often appear to arise from sudden coalescence of internal associations.

It appears now that learning may be affected by the level of the pituitary hormones within the individual. In rats, removal of the pituitary glands decreases the ability of the animals to acquire conditioned avoidance behavior while administration of adrenocorticotropic hormone (ACTH), melanocyte-stimulating hormone (MSH), or vasopressin to hypophysectomized rats corrects this deficiency. There is a difference in the effects of the various hormones in the sense that injection of ACTH or MSH appears to delay the loss of avoidance responses by intact rats for a few hours whereas similar injections of vasopressin delay it several days or longer. It has been suggested that ACTH and MSH effect motivational processes while vasopressin effects long-term memory.

In comparative psychopathology, the paradigm of a conditioned emotional response (CER) in animals represents most closely the acute stress reactions or traumatic neuroses suffered by people immediately after threatening catastrophes—as in battle experiences in war time, or the multitude of sudden catastrophes of modern civil life. It is of interest, too, that the strength of acquired CER in animals varies in relation to the circadian rhythm. Thus if an animal is trained by an unavoidable shock at 8 A.M. daily, it will show the strongest response thereafter at the time of training and the weakest 12 hours later. So, too, this response is inhibited by adrenalectomy, or by suppression of adrenal function with phenothiazines.

Understanding the learning process is of paramount importance in human beings, since our large brain gives us a learning capacity far beyond that of other species. This capacity for learning new behaviors has made possible both the increased complexity of our intellectual creativeness and the extraordinary range of our socially maladjustive behavior and psychological defenses, described in later chapters. The gap remains great between the known physiology of behavior and the explanations it offers now of psychopathology.

While much of the investigation of these symptoms has been concerned with the discernment of their anatomical location and interpreted in electrophysiologic terms or in terms of neurohumoral transmission, it must be appreciated that the expanding knowledge of the ultrastructure of the cell and its intricate biochemical interchanges later may add an even more significant basis for understanding the regulatory systems of the brain and the influence of pharmacologic agents on behavior.

SPECIAL COGNITIVE FUNCTIONS

Within recent years there has been a revival of clinical and research interest in the special functioning of the brain hemispheres. From studies of language function following acute hemiplegia in infancy, the study of those who have undergone hemispherectomy, and also study of the cognitive abilities in both man and animals following sectioning of the corpus callosum, it seems clear now that the two cerebral hemispheres develop a differing yet complementary specialization. Clinical observation has established that left hemispheric function is predominantly concerned with language function and arithmetical ability in right-handed people. The right hemisphere is particularly specialized for musical ability and discernment of spatial relations.

Brown and Jaffe have hypothesized that cerebral dominance for these specialized functions is a continuous process evolving throughout life. Before the age of 5, either hemisphere may assume the language function. Later, when lateralized specialization has taken place, this is no longer the case. Furthermore, the kinds of language impairment that develop as a result of brain damage vary, depending on the age the cerebral defects occur. Young children who develop an aphasia show mutism or agrammatism, whether that lesion occurs in frontal, temporal, or parietal lobes. After the age of 10, lesions in the left hemisphere may produce mutism or agrammatism but anomia and parphasia also appear.

The differing and complementary functions of the hemispheres have been stated in other ways. The left hemisphere is thought of now as being dominantly specialized for verbal, analytical and temporal functions while the right is dominant for visual, configurational and spatial functions. We find then that melody, although depending on auditory and temporal sensation, is better perceived in the right hemisphere, as are the other nonverbal sounds. The same is true for tactual perception of pattern, number, direction, and shape. Perception of visual, auditory, and tactual configurations appears to be a right hemisphere–dependent function.

There are indications that during development divergences in structural functional relations may result. Undoubtedly, the superior evolution of one or the other hemispheres relates to the extraordinary talents shown by some persons in language, arithmetical ability, musical ability, and so on. On the other hand, discontinuities or impairments of ability may derive from variable temporal development of the hemispheres and their interconnections. On such subtle discontinuities of brain structural evolution may rest the framework for certain of the scholastic deficiencies in some youngsters who are labeled today as suffering from minimal brain damage. Their limited abilities may relate to uneven development of hemispheric functions, which effect either delay or conflict in adaptive cognitive abilities, rather than to brain damage.

MATTER-ENERGY PROCESSING

RESPIRATORY, ALIMENTARY, AND EXCRETORY BEHAVIOR. All those functions directly concerned with the intake of substances and elimination of wastes occur in organs which embryologically are outgrowths of the alimentary tract. Accordingly, in this section are considered those physiologic processes concerned with respiration, feeding, and drinking, as well as the elimination of carbon dioxide, fecal matter, and urine.

Psychopathological disturbances of respiration were described earlier. Perverted eating and drinking behaviors are common symptomatic expressions of psychiatric disorders: prolonged anorexia, specific food aversions and obsessions, compulsive eating and drinking, constipation, and various diarrheas.

While the majority of the symptomatic disturbances of alimentation are learned to gratify symbolically some psychosocial need, they are mediated through and distort the functioning of related neuronal and organic systems. Others, however, are directly expressive of disturbances in the brain subsystem concerned with alimentary self-preservation. It is well known that through learning techniques one may induce in an animal erotic-like behavior

which may impair eating. For example, it is possible to train rats by offering them the self-satisfaction of bar pressing which evokes lateral hypothalamic brain stimulation, and couple this experience with food deprivation. In this experimental condition the rat may demonstrate continued preference for brain self-stimulation when both that opportunity and food are simultaneously available. Under such a training program, there evolves the maladaptive behavior of self-starvation which is like that recognized in the clinic as anorexia nervosa.

The arousal of the need for oxygen, food, or fluids, recognized affectively as suffocation, hunger, or thirst, is mediated through the reticular activating system. In asphyxia, either a diminution in the oxygen in the blood or an increase in the carbon dioxide (the two components of asphyxia) powerfully stimulates the bulbar respiratory center as well as the mesencephalic reticular formation. During starvation, when the blood sugar level falls, there is an increase in circulating epinephrine, which effects a compensatory release of glucose from glycogen. But as this latter process runs out, with depletion of glycogen stores, epinephrine may directly activate the ascending and descending reticular system, thereby facilitating cortical arousal and motor activity. Probably similar physiological processes lead to arousal in the face of emerging thirst, although there does not now exist experimental evidence for this assumption.

The innate processes that direct feeding behavior have been located in the hypothalamus and the limbic system (visceral brain) (Fig. 3–6). Thus, electrical stimulation of the lateral hypothalamus elicits feeding behavior in the satiated animal; its destruction causes aphagia and adipsia. A dual control of eating seems probable, as stimulation of the hypothalamic ventromedial nucleus inhibits feeding and lesions in this area lead to hyperphagia and eventual obe-

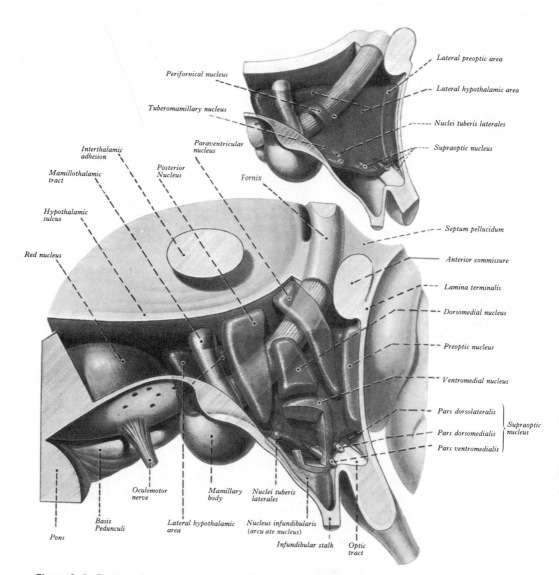

Figure 3–6 The hypothalamus. Schemata of the hypothalamic region of the left cerebral hemisphere from the medial aspect to display the major hypothalamic nuclei. In the upper diagram the medially placed nuclear groups have been removed, while in the lower diagram both lateral and medial groups are included. Lateral to the fornix and the mamillothalamic tract is the lateral hypothalamic region, in which the tuberomamillary nucleus is situated. Situated rostrally in this area is the lateral preoptic nucleus. Surrounding the fornix is the perifornical nucleus, which joins the lateral hypothalamic area with the posterior hypothalamic nucleus. The medially situated nuclei fill in much of the region between the mamillothalamic tract and the lamina terminalis, but also project caudal to the tract. The nuclei tuberis laterales are situated ventrally, largely in the lateral hypothalamic area. The supraoptic nucleus consists of three parts. (From Homans, J.: A Textbook of Surgery. 6th ed. 1945. Courtesy of Charles C Thomas, Publisher, Springfield, Illinois.)

sity. Similarly, stimulation in the closely situated paraventricular nuclei elicits polydipsia, while electrical discharges related to fluid satiation have been observed in the supraoptic neurons following injection into animals of hypertonic solutions of saline and glucose.

Although it would seem that the hypothalamus is concerned solely with specifying the direction of the drive for food or fluid, shaping of the feeding behavior in mammals has been thought to depend upon the functioning of the limbic system, consisting of the olfactory bulb, septum pellucidum, cingulum, fornix, and amygdala. Electrophysiological studies by Rolls show that neurons in the region of the lateral amygdala and piriform cortex in animals are directly excited when eating, drinking, or reward is elicited by electrical stimulation of the lateral hypothalamus. These neurons are also transynaptically excited during self-stimulation of the nucleus accumbens.

Activation of the hypothalamic center is related to catecholamine transmission which has differing effects, apparently, in relation to the circadian rhythms. For instance, during the dark, direct application of l-norepinephrine to the hypothalamus of rats suppresses feeding behavior while in light the same dosage facilitates such behavior.

The extent to which drinking behavior is related to cholinergic drive is unknown. Thus, carbachol will elicit drinking when applied to various segments of the limbic system but eserine is effective only when applied to the nuclei. Central atropine blocks the cholinergic induction of drinking at some sites. It should be noted, however, that Levitt has questioned whether the cholinergically induced drinking is related to the usual homeostatic water balance mechanisms.

For many years clinicians have recognized that some epileptic seizures are initiated with one or several of the subjective experiences of hunger, thirst, choking, retching, or the wish to urinate or defecate, or by chewing or other oral activity, including automatisms of eating and drinking. In addition there may occur in such attacks manifestations of rage or fright expressed in screaming, running, or attack. It is known now that such convulsive seizures are due to focal lesions in the temporal lobe involving the structures of the limbic system. This system in turn projects to the hypothalamus and central gray matter of the mesencephalon through the median forebrain bundle. MacLean has found particularly that excitation in the amygdalar projections and ventral hypothalamus leads to oral activities; others have demonstrated that stimulation of the cingulate cortex in animals may inhibit feeding behaviors and related organ functions concerned with alimentation, including secretion of gastric juices.

REPRODUCTIVE PROCESSING

Arousal of the sexual drive, the finding of a mate, and the consummatory acts of copulation represent only the initial sequence of sexual behavior. Parturition in man, as well as other mammals, is followed by a long series of interdependent actions between the parents and the young designed to nurture the growth and development of the young. It is now recognized that the wide variety of behaviors evolved in reproduction of different species depend increasingly, as one ascends the evolutionary series, upon learned behaviors, particularly those concerned with socialization.

It appears from experimental work in animals that the quantities of circulating hormone testosterone exercise an organizing action upon the midbrain structures in order to bring about masculinization. From his work, Phoenix has hypothesized that the genetic male, deprived of testosterone during a critical period in development, will not develop the normal patterns of male sexual behavior as an adult. His work and that of others seem to support this contention even for the sexual behavior of primates. On the other hand, the contention that the presence of abnormally high prenatal estrogen levels or the exposure to exogenous synthetic progestins which masculinize the fetus might lead to enhanced postnatal intellectual development has not been borne out in recent studies by Baker and Erhard published by Money and Ehrhardt. The association of high intelligence levels with the possible early exposure to high levels of prenatal androgens came from the observation that many sufferers of the adrenal genital syndrome had superior intelligence quotients (IQs). Nevertheless, in the laboratory even a single injection of testosterone propionate given prenatally or postnatally firmly alters an animal's metabolism of testosterone, androstenedione, and cortisone. Altered steroid metabolism persists for the entire lifetime of an animal following such intervention. The data suggest then that effects of sex steroids are attributable to differential central nervous system development.

Other aspects of reproductive behavior are also under hormonal control. Thus, maternal behavior would appear to be inhibited by hormonal secretions in both sexes.

The midbrain activating system is known to become progressively more sensitive to electrical stimulation as estrous behavior evolves. In the period following coitus in female rabbits, when the animal relaxes, is inactive, or may sleep, its electroencephalographic recordings have shown spindle bursting, followed by REM sleep and hypersynchrony in limbic patterns.

Electrical stimulation of the tubular structures in animals induces ovulation. Lesions or implantations of estrogen in this area inhibit ovulation following coitus and later tend to cause atrophy of the ovary and reproductive tract. Similarly, testosterone implanted in this area in male dogs causes aspermia and testicular and prostatic atrophy. This system then responds to both neural influx and direct endocrine action as circulating gonadal hormones check pituitary gonadotropin secretion.

As for other components of the consummatory act, MacLean has found that in male monkeys penile erection and its modifications, pelvic movements, and ejaculation follow stimulation of the hippocampal projections, parts of the anterior and midline thalamic nuclei, and the hypothalamus, with the septopreoptic and medial dorsal nuclei being the most sensitive areas.

Even more impressive is the enormous significance to sexual behavior in man of early experience in learning patterns of socialization that lead to successful mating, copulation, and eventual child rearing. The thesis is now corroborated by a long line of experimental observations culminating in the reports of Harlow, who found that young monkeys isolated from a mother and contacted only through an experimental wire frame for nutrition, or else isolated from their peers, were defective in sexual approach, in the consummatory act, and in mothering behavior in adulthood. Here again the recording of experience over time is dependent upon the functioning of the cerebral cortex and allows the eventual patterning of the complex series of behaviors that determine the various phases of both procreation and child rearing. In man, particularly, each of the phases may be enhanced, distorted, or arrested through his extensive capacity for symbolizing during learning.

AGONISTIC SYSTEM

Expressions of and reactions to aggression—rage and fight, immobilization, flight, and fear—are the agonistic responses designed to protect each species from attack and also to facilitate alimentary and sexual activities.

Aggression, defined in the narrow sense of initiating attack, is a universal form of behavior in all classes of vertebrates and arthropods but rarely in lower invertebrates. In the animal kingdom fighting is common, useful, and apparently adaptive. The young of many mammalian species exhibit the beginnings of fighting behavior in their play. Both external and internal environments influence the emergence of aggressivity and impulsivity. Hunger, territorial restriction, and increase in male sexual hormone increase fighting activity in various vertebrates.

Man alone resorts to violent aggressiveness with widespread maiming and killing of members of his own species. He alone has evolved exquisite means of cruelty and torture as well as equally subtle controls through social methods of inducing guilty and shameful affects and inhibiting ritualistic and expiatory behaviors. It has been said that the crowning achievement of man's evolution was the emergence of conscience — to control aggressivity. Man's aggressivity and the psychological control devices evolved for its control depend upon the vast growth of his cerebral cortex.

Perhaps because the socially feared and inappropriate aggressiveness of the psychotic has been most difficult to control, both clinical and laboratory studies of the physiological processes related to the expression of rage preceded those of other forms of behavior. As early as 1892 Goltz reported upon the astounding behavior of his decorticated dog, which had displayed strong actions of growling, barking, and biting on slight stimulation, actions expressive of the emotion of rage. Walter Cannon coined the term "sham rage" after he observed lashing of the tail, arching of the back, display of claws, biting, and panting respirations, behaviors which showed the components of rage and attack, in acutely decorticated cats. A long series of experiments by Bard and others demonstrated that "savage" behavior in cats followed precise lesions in the ventromedial nucleus of the hypothalamus.

It is now known that both ablation and stimulation of the ventromedial nucleus may produce what was termed by Montcastle and Bard as "savage" behavior. Probably it is more appropriate to state that animals with bilateral lesions in these nuclei live in a unique state of hyperirritability wherein light stimulation elicits aggressive behavior as the animals never launch unprovoked attacks. Furthermore, the condition only comes on after some weeks following the surgical procedures. The neurotransmitter norepinephrine and its related pathways are believed to be the concerned brain subsystem. Yet there is considerable pharmacological evidence that central cholinergic mechanisms participate as well, particularly in the regulation of predatory killing.

It is known that removal of the neocortex alone, leaving the old brain rhinencephalic structures intact, leads to the behavioral expression of placidity — the obverse of rage. Rage reactions emerge spontaneously when both new and old cortices are removed or when the amygdala and piriform cortex are resected, but not after damage to the hippocampus. The neocortex then appears to have both a facilitatory and an inhibitory influence on aggressive behaviors characterized by rage, and in addition influences the direction and timing of such behaviors. The inhibitory influence is dependent upon the cingulate gyrus and transmitted through the amygdala to influence the ventromedial hypothalamic nuclei.

It was the introduction of prefrontal lobotomy that established the relationship of function of brain to control of emotional behaviors. As the result of the many studies of psychiatrically ill persons treated by prefrontal lobotomy, the clinical indications for the procedure have been narrowed to the presence of certain symptoms which represent the expression of rage or related aggressive states. These are assaultive and destructive behavior, including self-destructive behaviors such as self-mutilation and suicidal attempts, chronic irascibility, agitation, undue anxiety, impulsiveness, and overactivity. Other behavioral symptoms often modified by lobotomy are depression, hypochondriasis, chronic pain, and refusal to eat—symptoms that often are recognized as symbolic of inhibition of rage or hostility. Lobotomy was found to offer little in terms of the social adaptation of the psychotic patient who showed apathy and indifference. It was found as well that prefrontal cortical resections made in a posterior plane, which presumably damaged the amygdala, induced apathy or placidity that militated against the social recovery of the patient.

Thus agonistic responses are affected by lobotomy, a psychosurgical therapy described in Chapter 33.

BIBLIOGRAPHY

Brain and Behavior: General

Arnold, M. D.: Brain function in emotion: A phenomenological analysis. In Black, P., (ed.): Physiological Correlates of Emotion. New York, Academic Press, 1970.

Cannon, W. B.: Wisdom of the Body. New York, Norton, 1939.

Kiritz, S., and Moos, R. H.: Physiological effects of social environments. Psychosom. Med., 36:96–114, 1974.

Kolata, G. B.: Sociobiology (1): Models of social behavior. Science, 187:50–51, 1975.

Lorenz, K. Z.: Analogy as a source of knowledge. Science, 185:229–234, 1974.

MacLean, P. D.: A triune concept of the brain and behavior. In Boag, T. J. and Campbell, D. (eds.): The Clarence M. Hincks Memorial Lecture. Toronto, University of Toronto Press, 1973.

MacLean, P. D.: Cerebral evolution and emotional processes: New findings on the striatal complex. Ann. N.Y. Acad. Sci., 193:137–149, 1973.

Tinbergen, N.: The Study of Instinct. Oxford, Clarendon Press, 1951.

Information Processing

Andry, D. K., and Luttges, M. W.: Memory traces: Experimental separation by cycloheximide and electroconvulsive shock. Science, 178:518–520, 1972.

Curtis, G. C.: Psychosomatics and chronobiology: Possible implications of neuroendocrine rhythms. A review. Psychosom. Med., 34:235–256, 1972.

Greenberg, R., Pillard, R., and Pearlman, C.: The effect of dream (stage REM) deprivation on adaptation to stress. Psychosom. Med., 34:257–262, 1972.

Hartmann, E. L.: The Functions of Sleep. New Haven, Conn., Yale University Press, 1973.

Heath, R. G., Cox, A. W., and Lustick, L. S.: Brain activity during emotional states. Am. J. Psychiatry, 131:858–862, 1974.

Kales, H. (ed.): Sleep. Physiology and Pathology. Philadelphia, J. B. Lippincott Company, 1968.

Kopin, E. J. (ed.): Neurotransmitters. Vol. 50, Association for Research in Nervous and Mental Disease. Baltimore, Williams & Wilkins, 1972.

MacFadyen, U. M., Oswald, I., and Lewis, S. A.: Starvation and human slow-wave sleep. J. Appl. Physiol., 35:391–394, 1973.

Magoun, H. W.: The Waking Brain. 2nd ed. Springfield, Ill., Charles C Thomas, 1963.

Marx, J. L.: Learning and behavior: Effects of pituitary hormones. Science, 190:367–370, 1975.

Olds, J., and Milner, P.: Positive reinforcement produced by electrical stimulation of septal area and other regions of the rat brain. J. Comp. Physiol. Psychol., 47:419–429, 1954.

Pessah, M. A., and Roffwarg, H. P.: Spontaneous middle ear muscle activity in man: A rapid eye movement sleep phenomenon. Science, 178:773–776, 1972.

Pribram, K. H.: Looking to see: Some experiments on the brain mechanisms of attention in perception. Res. Publ. Assoc. Res. Nerv. Ment. Dis., 48:150–162, 1970.

Richter, C. P.: Biological Clocks in Medicine and Psychiatry. Springfield, Ill., Charles C Thomas, 1965.

Roberts, E.: Y-aminobutyric acid and nervous system function—a perspective. Biochem. Pharmacol., 23:2637–2649, 1974.

Usdin, E., Bunney, W. E., and Kline, N. S.: Endorphins in Mental Health Research. New York, Oxford University Press, 1979.

Vogel, L. W.: A review of REM sleep deprivation. Arch. Gen. Psychiatry, 32:749–761, 1975.

Wehr, T. A., and Goodwin, F. K.: Biological Rhythms and Psychiatry. Vol. 7, American Handbook of Psychiatry, 2nd ed. New York, Basic Books, 1981.

Wurtman, R. J., and Moskowitz, M. H.: Brain catecholamines and neurological disease. Trans. Am. Neurol. Assoc., *99*:148–159, 1974.

Zloty, R. B., Burdick, J. A., and Adamson, J. D.: Sleep of distance runners. Act. Nerv. Super. (Praha), *15*:217–221, 1973.

Cognitive System

Brown, J. W., and Jaffe, J.: Hypothesis on cerebral dominance. Neuropsychologia, *13*:107–110, 1975.

DiCara, L. V.: Learning in the autonomic nervous system. Sci. Am., *222*:31–39, 1970.

DeJong, R. N., Itabashi, H. H., and Olson, J. R.: "Pure" memory loss with hippocampal lesions. Trans. Am. Neurol. Assoc., *93*:31–34, 1968.

Galin, D.: Implications for psychiatry of left and right cerebral specialization. Arch. Gen. Psychiatry, *31*:572–583, 1974.

Harlow, H. F., and Harlow, M. K.: Social deprivation in monkeys. Sci. Am., *207*:136–146, 1962.

Hebb, D. O.: The Organization of Behavior. New York, John Wiley & Sons, Inc., 1949.

Hess, E. H.: Imprinting in birds. Science, *146*:1128–1130, 1964.

John, E. R.: Mechanisms of Memory. New York, Academic Press, 1967.

Mark, R. F., and Watts, M. D.: Drug inhibition of memory formation in chickens. Proc. R. Soc. Lond., *178*:439–464, 1971.

Pavlov, I. P.: Experimental Psychology and Other Essays. New York, Philosophical Library, 1959.

Scott, J. P.: Critical periods in behavioral development. Science, *138*:949–958, 1962.

Matter-Energy Processing

Levitt, R. A.: Cholinergic substrate for drinking in the rat. Psychol. Rep., *29*:431–448, 1971.

Margules, D. L., Lewis, M. J., Dragovich, J. A., and Margules, A. S.: Hypothalamic norepinephrine: Circadian rhythms and the control of feeding behavior. Science, *178*:640–643, 1972.

Rolls, E. T.: Activation of amygdaloid neurones in reward, eating and drinking elicited by electrical stimulation of the brain. Brain Res., *45*:365–381, 1972.

Santos, R. M., and Routtenberg, A.: Attenuation of brain stimulation self-starvation: Adaptation effects. Physiol. Behav., *9*:831–837, 1972.

Reproductive Processing

Friedman, R. C., Richart, R. M., and Vande Wiele, R. L.: Sex Differences in Behavior. New York, John Wiley & Sons, 1974.

Leon, M., Numan, M., and Maltz, H.: Maternal behavior in the rat: Facilitation through gonadectomy. Science, *179*:1018–1019, 1973.

Money, J. and Ehrhardt, A. A.: Man and Woman, Boy and Girl: The Differentiation and Dimorphism of Gender Identity from Conception to Maturity. Baltimore, Johns Hopkins Press, 1973.

Phoenix, C. H., Gay, R. W., and Blizzard, R. M.: Sexual behavior: General aspects. *In* Martini, L., and Ganong, W. F. (eds.): Neuroendocrinology. Vol. II. New York, Academic Press, 1967.

Agonistic System

Frazier, S. H. (ed.): Aggression. Vol. 52, Association for Research in Nervous and Mental Disease. Baltimore, Williams & Wilkins Co., 1974.

4 PERSONALITY DEVELOPMENT

"We must watch the infant in his mother's arms; we must see the first images which the external world casts upon the dark mirror of his mind; the first occurrence which he witnesses; we must hear the first words which awaken the sleeping powers of thought and stand by his earliest efforts if we would understand the prejudices, the habits and the passions which rule his life."

Alexis de Tocqueville, 1855

SIGMUND FREUD
(From The Bettmann Archive, Inc.)

Each organism undergoes a process of development of biological structure from the time of the fusion of the male and female germ cells until maturity has been reached. At any time during this maturational process, noxious factors may impair the growth of the organism, produce malformations, or limit the functioning of an organ or of the entire living being. Lack of appropriate foodstuffs and nutrients, including the necessary vitamins and minerals, also limits bodily growth. It is well established now that growth may be restricted also by lack of appropriate stimulation: an experiential deficit at critical periods in maturation prevents the full unfolding of the functions of a system or organ. Thus environments in which the diet or social stimulation is restricted or impoverished will tend to limit brain growth and personality development in the growing child. Also, lack of early experiencing may lay down a continuing vulnerability to various stresses throughout the remainder of life.

Each person, then, has an anatomical structure conforming in general to the species pattern yet unique in certain details. It is this structure and its physiological functioning, that in part determines and limits personality development. The growth of the central nervous system establishes the limits of *temperament* and *intelligence*. Temperamental variations, those capacities for range of active responsiveness to the environment, are considered both to influence the experiential effect of an environmental change and perhaps in turn to be modified by that change. That distinguishing property of the nervous system—the capacity to register, store, and integrate the experiences of the organism so as to bring about the most effective behavioral responses for adaptation—makes it possible for human personality to evolve. Thus, over time, through a prolonged series of social experiencing, more or less enduring and consistent attitudes, beliefs, desires, values, and patterns of adaptation develop which make each individual unique. The distinctive whole formed by these relatively permanent behavioral patterns and tendencies of a given individual is spoken of as *personality*.

To a limited extent, certain patterns are already laid down at birth, but for the most part only the potentials for the development of personality components exist at that time. Whether the successive stages of the unfolding of personality proceed in a wholesome manner and in a harmonious sequence of biopsychological and biosocial maturation through infancy, childhood, maturity, and old age, with realization of personal potentials, subjective satisfactions, and social adaptations, or whether there is an arrest or uneven growth of various personality compo-

nents, depends upon complex interactions between various genetic, environmental, social, and emotional factors.

There is normally a *maturational sequence* in personality development, each stage developing as a logical sequel to the previous one—an emergent growth through distinctively different stages, each having its particular needs and problems. If residues of an earlier stage are carried over to later ones, they may produce malformations of the personality and become a source of psychopathology. Early experiences also continue to exert their influence on the developing personality, even though they are not available to conscious recall.

Genes cannot transmit acquired characteristics. Although the biological development of the fetus may be influenced by the intrauterine environment, there is no reason to believe that personality, as just defined, is largely influenced by prenatal life or even that it exists in the newborn infant. This statement does not deny a genetic anlage or congenital aspects of biochemistry and reactivity which create biological predispositions to the temperamental components of personality in later life. However, while extreme abnormalities in vegetative, central nervous, and endocrine systems may have a demonstrable relation to personality characteristics, there seems to be little relation between them and persistent features of the normal personality.

The observations of Money and Ehrhardt and Stoller make evident for human beings the overriding importance of human transactions of early life in determination of even such an important aspect of personality as sexual gender identity. The former researchers, who followed the development of infants known to have genetic and hormonal deviance, concluded that the rearing of these children during the first two years of life is the major force establishing gender identity. As an example, a group of infants, who suffered complete absence of gonadal hormones in the prenatal period and at birth were genetically determined to be male children though born with female-appearing genitalia, developed along feminine lines if their parents related to them as girls in the first 18 months of life.

It is convenient to think of personality as having parts or divisions that perform specific functions—in other words, as having structure. Such a concept facilitates the idea of dynamics in the functioning of the personality. However, these parts must not be considered as concrete realities or self-acting entities but as groups of forces and functions. The concept of personality structure now generally followed is that proposed by Freud, who postulated three psychic segments in the structure of the personality. While these structural divisions are hypothetical, they offer a useful classification of the system of drives. Many of the terms used in describing their dynamic interrelationships are highly figurative.

The Id

The *id* is a collective name for the primitive biological impulses. It represents the innate portion of the personality. The physiologically determined drives for air, food, water, and other nutrient substances, maintenance of bodily temperature and physical integrity, and procreation are thought of as id functions. Thus dependent longings, aggressive and flight tendencies, and sexuality are thought of as id drives and affects. Associated with these primitive drives are the protective aversive states of pain, distress, and rage and the cravings to satisfy hunger, thirst, and avoid suffocation. The major affective states of man only unfold with development of perception and cognition; they more properly must be recognized as components of the ego. When ego functions are maldeveloped or impaired, id derivatives appear in conscious fantasies or may erupt as overt behavior expressions.

The Ego

The *ego*, or reality-testing self, is that part or function of the personality that establishes a relationship with the world in which we live. The ego, of course, is a group of functions for which a metaphor is employed for ease of conceptualization. The ego deals with the environment through conscious perception, thought, feeling, and action. It contains the evaluating, judging, compromising, solution-forming, and defense-creating aspects of the personality. The ego organization, concerned as it is with such important functions as perception, memory, evaluating and testing reality, synthesizing experience, and acting as intermediary between the inner and outer worlds, may be regarded as the integrative and executive agency. Its functions are to deal rationally with the requirements of reality, to adapt behavior to the environment, and to maintain harmony between the urges of the id and the demands and aspirations of the superego.

For normal development of the personality, the ego must be able to modify both the id drives and the superego's demands for acceptable conduct without extreme sacrifice of either emotional and instinctive satisfactions or of ethical ideals. In this way the ego serves as mediator and directs behavior into acceptable compromises between the blind drives of the id and the inhibitions of the superego. In contrast to the id drives, which press for immediate satisfaction and are thus stated to operate by the *pleasure principle*, ego functions are guided by the *reality principle*. Thus, the ego directs instinctual energy into channels that will, in the long run, bring maximum pleasure and satisfaction. Its processes take place largely, but not entirely, at the conscious level. It constructively integrates impulses and thus secures mastery over them. If, through conscious control, it deals effectively with inner and outer stresses, and through reason and circumspection it deals rationally with the requirements of reality and of society, the ego is said to be strong and healthy.

The individual with a well developed and mature ego shows flexibility in handling the various stresses of life without resorting to the inflexible and repetitive defenses that distinguish neurotic or psychotic symptoms or to character defects. If the ego structure is underdeveloped or dominated by unconscious factors, it may undergo disintegrative processes and may be unable to withstand the strain of continued repression, with the result that mental symptoms or character defects appear.

Ego development takes place through the series of transactions between the growing infant and child and his or her parents and others who influence growth. While the adaptive and defensive functions of the ego, to be described in detail in Chapter 5, are born through resolution of conflict between the id and the evolving superego, other ego functions develop from conflict-free activities and have intrinsic generating and satisfying properties of their own. Thus, Hartmann notes the development of perception, intention, object comprehension, thinking, language, and memory as autonomous functions of the ego which take place in conflict-free experiencing. One might conclude from the study of exploratory behavior in monkeys, described by Burton, that there is a primary drive state serving to satisfy a perceptual need. Perceptual privations, in turn, may lead to serious impairment of ego functions.

Ego functions are directed, then, to bring about psychosocial adaptation. But such adaptation requires as well the evolution of a series of interpersonal attitudes which establish for the individual a certain consistency in his relations with others—the means by which he customarily perceives them and functions in relation to them. In addition, others have expectations of his social responses—his ego identity. Erikson has described the development of ego attitudes from the growing child's progressive identification with aspects of parents and others immediately affecting him. Erikson postulated specific psychosocial crises at each stage of interaction, whose solution establishes an attitudinal position upon which the growing child proceeds to work through the succeeding stages in his psychosocial evolution, either relatively free of conflict or laden with conflict. Infancy, with varying degrees of mutually satisfying and dissatisfying exchanges, lays the basis for varying degrees of *trust* or *mistrust* of others. The psychosocial crises of early childhood lay the basis for degrees of *personal autonomy* as against degrees of personal *shame and doubt*; later childhood brings the forerunner of *initiative* versus acceptance of *guilt*; school age, that of *industriousness* versus a *sense of inferiority*; adolescence, the crises of *identity formation* or *diffusion*.

The phases of adult life, too, bring their special crises. The young adult must work through the issue of intimacy against that of isolation, the later adult that of procreation versus self-absorption, and the mature adult that of integrity versus despair.

The primary requisite of the transactional process required for personality development is the learning of satisfying and acceptable attitudes and actions designed to control and modulate man's affects. Man's complex affective states are themselves the consequence of the long ongoing process of socialization which allows their progressive unfolding and differentiation. We recognize the syntonic affects of interest and excitement, as well as joy. In addition there are the dystonic and aversive motivating states of distress, fear, shame and guilt, disgust, anger, contempt, love, tenderness and compassion, or sadness.

These motivating and sometimes conflicting affects over time become established within the personality as prevailing mood characteristics, too: curiosity, cheerfulness, apprehensiveness, contemptuousness, or hatefulness. Again affective reaction formations may establish transient or enduring attitudes of envy, jealousy, pride, and courage.

Aside from the work of S. S. Tomkins, little attention has been paid to the dynamics of affective differentiation and its relation to ego development and personality.

Beyond the ego attitudes and affective sets described, psychopathologists are now striving to define and search for forces that establish conative sets, found in the mood action complexes which exist in the ego organization of those who successfully adapt to life or cope with its many enduring or sudden stresses. We mentioned in a previous chapter the balancing force of such ego assets as commitment, responsibility, perseverance, empathy, likability, humor and playfulness, flexibility, curiosity, and courage—the complex traits found in creative and constructive persons even though they may often be burdened with severe pathological ego defenses.

The Superego

The third hypothetical segment of the personality structure is the *superego*, that segment conceptualized as observer and evaluator of ego functioning, comparing it with an ideal standard—an ideal derived from standards of behavior perceived over time in parents, teachers, and others significant to the growing child. The *ego ideal*, the internalized picture or image of what one desires to become and toward which the ego strives, provides the aspirational direction and demand for achievement within each personality.

The concept of the superego had its origin in Freud's analysis of psychotic delusions of being watched. He conceived then of an "observing" portion of the personality.

Around the ages of 4 to 6 children evolve a sense of constraint in their actions as they give in to the superior strength of the parents. They accept the parental dictates as absolute, demanding unquestioned obedience. They are unable then to judge their acts or those of another in terms of their social meanings, but only as right or wrong. Only after children have shared their perspectives with other children and adults in play, action, and thought do they evolve the differential perspectives that allow a less bound and more open and cooperative moral realism. Young children respond only with the narrow and rigid moralism of their homes, and particularly so when insecure. As they discover new images of morality in their play with peers or adults other than their parents, the earlier moral absolutes of the parental figures give way to a wider, more realistic appraisal of morality in general social values and goals.

The superego is derived particularly from identification with parents and their substitutes—figures of authority capable of punishing or rewarding. The prohibitions and obligations noted in these identifications are internalized and incorporated into the unconscious psychological structure of the child. Later, the injunctions and prohibitions of other authorities and of cultural influences are absorbed into the superego, the whole acting as censor. It acts as the supervisor of the ego and of inner, unconscious tendencies and, therefore, as the repressing part of the personality.

If early training has been severely punitive and shaming and unrelieved by later broadening experiences in role playing with others, the superego will contain irrational elements. Retroflexly, within the individual personality, it may threaten and punish and thereby seek to maintain its authority when the ego tends to accept impulses from the repressed part of the id. It does this by creating anxiety and by producing guilt, shame, and remorse. If the superego is severe and inflexible, the resulting fear of it will lead to a rigid, inhibited, unhappy, anxious, and often neurotic personality. Alternatively, the superego facilitates pleasurable satisfactions when ego functioning is evaluated as striving toward or achieving the ideals and goals. Thus, gratification comes from increased self-respect, personal integrity, pride in effort or accomplishment, or self-righteousness.

The Self Concept

As mentioned earlier, perception is one of the functions of the ego. The ego or "I" of the personality learns to and does perceive the world about, including the "me" of the personality. It takes itself, the body in which the person resides, its various parts, and all facets of its functioning as an object; it assesses, evaluates, and aspires for that self. These envolving and changing percepts establish the *self concept*—defined by Rosenberg as "the totality of the individual's thoughts and feelings having reference to himself as an object"—"the picture of the self." The self concept defines the social identity of the individual: sex, age, race, nationality, religion, family and legal status, name, and, later, the various social roles in which one acts and one's personal evaluation of each of the foregoing. It includes the extensions of the ego—personal relations, social background, properties, and works. It contains the attitudes toward one's self and thereby defines levels of self-esteem and self-confidence related to functioning as measured against self-ideals.

The self concept is built up over time through the quality of the early parent-child relationships and the later continual discriminations of the ego as it perceives its "me" functioning in comparison with others and with the emergent ideals and aspirations as personality unfolds. With growing maturity, a committed self concept comes into being, a self concept realistically separated from but related to earlier desired and fantasied concepts of self.

Self-assessment stirs affect and emotion. Various affective states influence and color that assessment. In recent years there has been an increasing recognition of the importance of the status of the self concept as a means of comprehending both healthy and pathological personality functioning.

Balance of Segments

In the well adjusted person, behavior simultaneously and successfully meets the demands of the id, the ego, and the superego. On the other hand, the behavior of the neurotic, the psychotic, and the pathological personality with serious and repetitive social maladjustment may be considered to result from a disturbance in the dynamic checks and balances of these segments of the personality.

DEVELOPMENTAL PROCESS

Neonatal Period

At birth, the healthy infant already has well established psychophysiological processes available to assure adaptation to extrauterine life. Yet birth brings with it a major shift in the physiological functioning of the infant. Thus, there take place the establishment of respiration and the closure of the umbilical blood flow and the cardiac bypasses, upon opening of the pulmonary circulation. As Leboyer has so touchingly demonstrated, the stress of separation of the infant at birth from the mother may be done without violence. The termination of transplacental nourishment means commencement of alimentary feeding, which demands the establishment of a *symbiotic* relationship of the infant with the mother or a mother substitute. The body surface and its active sensory receptors are exposed now to a wide variety of variable stimuli, and the homeostatic mechanisms of the central nervous system must establish means of protecting the growing infant from overwhelming excitation and must also assure water balance, nourishment, oxygenation, and temperature regulation. The period of physiological shift and adaptation to the extrauterine environment is one of inconstant and irregular physiological regulation. It extends for two to eight weeks after birth.

At first the neonate's respirations are shallow, irregular, and noisy, but later they become steady and deep. Sucking is uncertain, and, while the infant may ingest well, regurgitation is frequent. Initially, there is a loss of weight. Urination and defecation occur spontaneously, but sweat glands will not function for the first month after birth.

Much time is spent in variable stages of sleep, with periods of quiet or regular sleep and irregular active sleep. In quiet sleep the infant appears fully relaxed and his limb resistance is low. There is limited neuromuscular activity—occasional mouthings or muscular jerks. Eyelids are closed and spontaneous eye movements are rare. The infant's facial expression is relaxed without grimacing or chewing and respirations, at a frequency of approximately 36 per minute, are regular and constant. In contrast, during irregular sleep the eyelids may appear either pinched or closed and intermittent rapid eye movements (REM) occur. Grimacing is frequent and the infant chews, chomps, and mouths. Muscular activity is common in limbs and body and respiration is irregular and at greater rate. Of the sleep time, 50 per cent is spent in the later stage associated with the electroencephalographic patterns of REM. And half of the infant's day is spent in sleep.

When awake the neonate appears alert and active, crying, or inactive. Total daytime sleep decreases from one half at birth to about one quarter at 3 months of age.

Awake and crying, the infant gives vent to the signals that establish and sustain the needed relationship with the mother. Not only nourishment through nursing is received but also those bodily contacts that stimulate particularly the kinesthetic and tactile systems. There exists, then, between infant and mother a new extrauterine biological relationship. Even within the short period of two weeks, there is evidence of smiling and ability to initiate facial and manual gestures by human neonates.

While awake and alert the infant also at times initiates contact with the external environment other than his mother through the early functioning of his distance receptors—his eyes and ears. The infant responds to most sudden and intense stimuli such as noise, pressure, or jars with a *startle reaction* under all conditions except when vigorously crying. The response to less intense stimuli depends on the infant's initial state; activity is increased when the infant is inactive and is reduced when he is active (except during periods of vigorous nursing or crying). Similarly, the heart rate accelerates if it is slow initially and decelerates if it is rapid initially (law of initial values). The infant's capacity to respond to auditory and other stimulation varies depending upon the development of his nervous system. Schulyan has reported that heart rate responds in that premature infants at high risk for developmental defect had accelerated heart rate whereas the full term infant did not.

The responsiveness of individual infants is highly variable, however, indicating temperamental predispositions even in the neonatal state. These predispositions, in turn, influence the pattern of mutual interaction with the mother. In some infants the startle response is vigorous, while in others it is slight. Infants are dissimilar even in their response to soothing contact.

Bridger and Birns have found that there is a discrepancy between many neonates' behavior and the responsiveness of the autonomic nervous system to various stresses. From his observations he has postulated that those infants who show little behavioral response to stressing stimuli but respond strongly in terms of such indicators of autonomic activity as increased heart rate may later show autonomic hyperactivity and predisposition to psychosomatic disease. The evidence suggests that in the early developmental stage the autonomic nervous system has a lower threshold for reaction than the musculoskeletal system. Thus, with intense soothing stimulation neither system responds to stress, but if that stimulation is lessened, autonomic responses appear without musculoskeletal reactions.

While the physiological needs of the human infant are innately determined, their satisfaction both in the prenatal period and for a prolonged period after birth is dependent entirely upon maternal care-giving. The ongoing dependent relationship of the infant establishes from the very beginning of extrauterine life the association with others from which derive the forces that mold personality and eventual capacities for social adaptation.

Oral Interaction

Because of its pleasure-giving potentiality during the nursing stage of development, the mouth is spoken of as an erogenous zone. Satisfactions secured from such pleasure-giving zones are called *autoerotic*. Too little or inconsistent "psychological mothering" is apt to promote autoerotism in the form of prolonged or excessive thumb-sucking, constipation, or early and excessive masturbation. On the other hand, consistent and healthy emotional satisfactions in the child's relationships to his or her parents shorten the autoerotic period of development and promote a natural sublimation of the instinctive drives — a wholesome progress in the successive stages of these aspects of personality development and differentiation.

Individuals who continue to be mouth-centered far beyond the age when the mouth should have ceased to be a focus of satisfaction are said to be of an oral type of personality. Their characteristics are dependency, egocentricity, demanding and taking but not giving, and preoccupation with mouthing as well as ingestive and alimentary fantasies and satisfaction.

Eliminative Interaction

With the stage of increasing motor skills, the interaction between the child and mother focuses on the effort to have the child learn to control his eliminative activities; it is bladder and bowel centered.

The manner in which the mother attempts to instruct her child in these first efforts at personal autonomy determines the development of later personality traits. If, for example, urinary or bowel control is attempted before physiological maturation with myelination of the necessary pathways in the spinal cord has made the child capable of recognizing, announcing, or controlling his need to eliminate, or before the child can walk to the toilet or manipulate his clothing, and if the child is punished for his failures, rage or fear will be directed toward the controlling parent. The child then centers his attention on the power struggle between himself and parent. He may respond with fear of the parent and gradually evolve a pattern of cleanliness, orderliness, submissiveness, and punctuality sometimes referred to as the *anal character*. Or again, his subjective response may be one of rage with the evolving defiant reactions of dirtiness, obstinacy, and unreliability. Most frequently the response to the usual mothering process is vacillating.

From the experiences in this period of interaction, the beginnings of the capacities for self-control, personal independence, and a sense of autonomy and pride may be envisaged. With them arise the learned affects of shame and disgust which are incorporated in response to the parents' attitudes toward the child's excretory functions and are communicated to him through various means. Shame must be recognized as an important infantile emotion, learned by early training—a feeling of being exposed. Too much shaming may lead to defiant shamelessness as a character trait.

As mentioned in the foregoing discussion, the initial manifestations of *aggression* may be thought of as taking place during the oral stage of psychosexual development. Even at a very tender age, the nursling is not a passive recipient of his mother's milk. On the contrary, the milk is secured by a surprisingly vigorous activity. According to this point of view, aggression makes its first appearance in infantile personality traits characterized by energy, application, and determination and is of a constructive nature. Others suggest that the arousal of aggression arises relatively later in personality development and only as a reaction to frustration, particularly to the frustrations which the child inevitably feels that he suffers at the hands of parents during the process of being brought up. Undoubtedly, there are many occasions in the child's life for developing resentments and aggressive impulses against a frustrating parent.

MOTILITY

As the child develops, the focus of maternal attention gradually shifts from the giving of food to assisting the child to develop his maturing capacity for motility, the manipulation of objects with his hands, and later walking and speaking. The general motility of the child appears to arise from an autonomous drive. The patterning of motor activity and its successive and more intricate mastery in various actions, play, and games is in itself satisfying and induces pleasurable affects. Likewise, restriction of motor activity induces conflict with the arousal of rage. Commencing at about the age of 10 months, the infant engages in two different types of motor activity. There are those that seem to serve no other purpose than the experience of movement, such as crawling, running, jumping, and whirling; many of these activities are rhythmic and circular. The second type are those motor activities undertaken to manipulate objects; these activities are often autonomous and appear driven. It is through his motor activities that the child expresses his impulsive urge to action, an urge which must later be controlled for effective social participation. Activity is used in the service of aggression and sexuality and as a means of communication through imitation, gesture, and posture. It is associated with a range of affective stages including joy, rage, anxiety, and depression.

Motility, too, is the means by which the ego gains competence and security in its executive and synthetic functions. The carrying out and trying of intentions in action—the accomplishment of a successful series of operant behaviors that are processed as such by the rewarded ego—assist in establishment of sound concepts of reality about self-functioning, as well as the outer world. Also, they support the establishment of the ego sets of autonomy, initiative, and competence.

It is not surprising that patterns of disturbed motility frequently present as symptoms of personality disturbance in adults. Thus, one finds tics and other compulsive activities, the motor inhibitions of the hysteric, the grimacing and posturing of the schizophrenic, and the waxy flexibility of the catatonic.

ATTACHMENT BEHAVIOR

Beyond the symbiotic relationship between infant and mother that assures the baby's biological sustenance, students of both human and mammalian development now recognize the existence of complementary transactions between the two. The activities of the infant and growing child in these transactions, considered to establish protection and a sense of security, are now designated by Bowlby and others as *attachment behavior*. Attachment theory and the related behaviors are most significant to the comprehension of healthy and psychopathological evolution and their various manifestations. Also, they underly the capacity for later social attachments to others, including physicians and health caretakers; the vagaries of these relationships often stem from failures and discontinuities in the early mother-child contacts.

These first acts of mothering center on satisfying the infant's needs for food, warmth, and contact. The mother must provide constant attention to maintain the child's comfort through avoiding the irritations caused by wet and dirty clothing or exposure to other damaging forces. Maternal care is directed to much more than satisfying the "oral" needs of the infant, who senses in the early days not only through the oral mucosa and perioral musculature but also by means of the general tactile-kinesthetic sensory systems that are known to be myelinated at the time of birth. The infant is stimulated by the play of the mother, by the fondling received, and also by the mother's attempts to gain responses by facial gestures and vocal signs. As early as three or four months infants respond differently to people; they are in contact with those upon whom their lives depend.

In the first several weeks of life, the infant demands, through crying, immediate help in relief of tensions, whether they are induced through external discomfort or from internal unrest. In this stage as well, the earliest indications of a smile have been noticed — a slight upward inflection of the mouth taking place usually just after feeding and during periods of alert inactivity, drowsiness, or irregular sleep. The infant's smiling is innately programmed and does not derive directly in response to maternal approach or smiling, for children born blind or deaf display this and other basic facial expressions. Soon the response of the facial musculature can be elicited by high-pitched sounds, particularly by the mother or nurse. A fuller smile is evident by the third week; this, in turn, generates in the mothering one efforts to reproduce it through rocking, cuddling, or cooing at the baby. Thus, the smiling response is reinforced in the infant and further intensifies the mutually gratifying, stimulating, and nourishing mother-child relationship. This crying and smiling are the infant's earliest indication of the affects of distress and joy or pleasure.

The infant may be described as directed by the "pleasure principle," unable to delay gratification of his demands. Until he is several years old, he will be unable to stand the urgency of his needs or to accept delay of response for some future gain or greater satisfaction of desires in terms of the perceived problems and goals and the problems of others — that is, to be guided by the "reality principle." The persistence into later life of emotional states characterized by dependency and the immediacy and urgency of demands, with absence of responsibility for or consideration of others and associated with stages of rage when the need is not met, may be identified then as *infantile*.

The early mothering process, if warm and consistent, lays the groundwork for a continuing sense of security and trust in others. Its absence, as Erikson suggests, may establish the early roots of mistrust and insecurity. These are the origins of ego attitudes significant for carrying the infant through later stages of growth.

It may be surmised as well that the intermittent contacts with the mother, alternating with states of discomfort and comfort, establish those varying sensory experiences that set down the infant's slowly growing discriminations of *self* from another, the beginnings of a separate identity, the basis for a sense of space, and also the rhythms that establish time as a modality.

An impressive body of evidence from studies of both child development and animal psychology demonstrates the major significance of the healthy development of the early mother-child relationship. Thus, infants deprived of the stimulation of mothering, even though good care of bodily functions is assured, appear weak and listless, cry much more than others, and become apathetic. Odd grimaces and gestures appear. These phenomena disappear if the mother rejoins the infant within the first three months of life but are more obvious and severe when maternal deprivation takes place during the second half of the first year. Rutter's critical article, which reassesses the work on the consequences of maternal deprivation, emphasizes the necessity for critical analysis of this presumed factor in leading to psychopathology. In many instances the pathology is due to other than simple privation of the bonding transaction between mother and child, as shall be discussed in later chapters.

Attachment behavior provides the means by which the growing infant and child progressively learns to explore the world about yet to maintain the security of the symbiotic bond to the mothering one. Attachment behavior is generated when the child is exposed to strange or unfamiliar situations—either through separation from the mother or the perception of the unfamiliar. In such circumstances, exploratory behaviors generally terminate, the child gives evidence of distress or behaves in a fearful or wary manner, and demands or retreats to the mother. Exploratory behavior brings the infant toward new stimuli in the surroundings and thus away from the attachment person. When alarmed, the infant seeks proximity to his or her attachment figure; his "secure haven," as Ainsworth puts it.

Through the progressive development of the growing child's memory and cognitive systems as he or she repeatedly explores the environment and personal bodily parts and functions, he comes to perceive himself and others as separate individuals with distinctive features. Activation of attachment behavior diminishes progressively as infants recognize their mothers and later develop a permanent mental representation of the mother that sustains their sense of security during her disappearance and absence.

This developmental process has been studied by Mahler and others, who speak of it as *separation-individuation*. This ends when the child moves from perceiving another person as an immediately available object satisfying a need to perception of *object constancy*, in which need satisfaction is always available through the capacity to call up a mental representation of the satisfier, with expectation of soon-to-be-achieved satisfaction.

While there is some discrepancy about the timing in the opinions of child psychiatrists who have studied the process of separation-individuation and the establishment of object constancy, Mahler believes that it is between the ages of 25 and 36 months that the child tolerates brief separations from the mother without distress. By then it is thought that children have established in their memories imagery or mental representations of both mother and self. When the process is completed favorably, early development of a sense of personal permanence as well as a stable basis for self conceptualization is possible.

Inconstant mothering and inability of the child to maintain security through retreat to the attachment figure, as well as mothers' failures to allow exploratory behavior, set the stage both for excessive dependency demands later in life and for inhibition of curiosity, courage, and other flexible sets within the growing child—with resultant self-doubt as well as over- or under-idealization of self and others. Inconstant mothering, too, may lay the groundwork for "splitting" perceptions of others into "all good" or "all bad" projections that arise in the perceptive-affective life during the separation-individuation transactions.

Mahler describes the separation-individuation process as proceeding through four phases. By the fifth month, the infant clearly has established the attachment to the mother, both in perception and emotion. He or she recognizes her by smiling and greets her vocally, follows her visually, and quiets when picked up by her. There exists then a "recognition memory" at this time. From five to seven months (the differentiation subphase), the memory is active in the presence of the mother, but the beginnings of mother memory at times of need, expressed by signs of distress, seem to emerge. These memory traces are too fleeting to sustain the infant away from mother's presence. Mahler's practicing subphase, from 10 to 16 months, is evident in the infant's anticipatory behavior at the potential departure of the mother, which is protested by efforts to follow her or by calling to her. In the later stages of this developmental subphase, the child shows by play the beginnings of both initiative and symbolic activity. Dolls may be mothered, or the child may precede the mother to the door and say such things as "by-bye" or "Mama." McDevitt interprets from these behaviors that the child now is able to effect mental representations of behavior patterns separate from actions.

Later children initiate activities in which they move away from the mother, and actively separate and explore but, as described, use her as a secure base when alarmed. From 16 to 18 months (Mahler's reapproachment subphase), concern with the mother's absence and her approval and disapproval is evident and there are indications of depressive moods, in contrast to the apparent less concern and overall good mood when children are briefly separated from the mother. In this phase the child's representation of the mother or her surrogate becomes attached affectively to "good" or "bad" feelings; thus the beginning of ambivalence in relations, or the imaging characteristics of "splitting" — with perceptions of mothers or others as "all good" or "all bad."

Equally important is the discovery of critical experiential periods needed for the formation of the primary social bonds that are basic for later social relations and for learning. *Critical periods* for establishing the early social bond in mammals and birds are timed in development by the appearance of behavioral mechanisms that maintain or prevent contact and thus perhaps are related to internal processes associated with emotional arousal. From animal studies it has been inferred that the establishment of the important dependent relationship comes about through the presence of the mother, whether her behavior may be judged as gratifying or thwarting, rewarding or punishing. The essential feature is her presence to the infant as an object arousing emotion. The process of socialization is accelerated by the arousal of any strong emotion related to contact, whether it be hunger, fear, pain, or loneliness.

The primary bond between mother and child takes place irrespective of learning through contact gained in the feeding process. Thus, "imprinting" in birds is immediately related to the muscular effort made to follow an object during a critical period and can be reduced in intensity if ducklings are given the muscle relaxants meprobamate or carisoprodol. Harlow has shown that young monkeys isolated at birth and supplied with dummy mothers prefer a dummy with a cloth-covered surface without a feeding nipple to a wire-framed dummy with a feeding nipple. Monkeys raised on such dummy monkeys become, as adults, uniformly poor mothers in turn, neglecting and punishing their young.

BODY IMAGE

Body Percepts

By the third or fourth month, the maturing infant shows by his responses to others that he perceives the world about him. He perceives smiles and returns them; he is beginning to learn to express emotion through gestures. By the sixth month, the child is capable of binocular vision and appreciates vision at a distance. Also, coordinated activity is possible between several parts of the body; earlier, the eyes turned toward sound, and now so does the body. At the same time, hand and arm movements are well coordinated; and the hand brings objects to the mouth easily. This is the beginning of the infant's exploration of his own body, first with the mouth and then with the hand (Table 4–1). These perceptions, largely tactile and kinesthetic sensations in the early months, establish for him the integrated percept of his physical wholeness. They function at a level below conscious awareness to position the body in space, to manipulate objects it may control, and to provide knowledge of the body surface. That percepts of body parts exist is strikingly demonstrated after the loss of a limb in an adult, when the hallucinated "phantom" of the lost arm or leg causes a continuing sensation of its presence.

Early Sensory Experiences

Early perception by the infant of the body members is necessary for the evolution of these body percepts. If the infant or growing child fails in this experience, either because of congenital absence of a body part or because the limb is lost before the child is five years old, the sensory projection of a limb as a phantom never occurs.

The importance of early infantile sensory experiences in effecting the funtioning growth of various integrative systems in the brain is established by other clinical and experimental observations. The most convincing illustration has to do with the permanent defects in vision which occur in children with congenital cataracts but intact retinas and visual apparatus who fail to have the corneal defect repaired by implanting of a healthy transparent cornea before five years of age. Such children are unable to develop adequate vision, while others with earlier transplants go through long periods of learning before they can perceive accurately and recognize formed images. Artificial blinding of infant chimpanzees with later uncovering of the eyes has duplicated these findings.

Such clinical observations indicate once more the importance of critical

TABLE 4–1　Onset of Hand-to-body Exploration in 100 Normal Infants

PART EXPLORED	NO. OF INFANTS	FIRST EXPLORATION RANGE (WEEKS)	MEDIAN AGE (WEEKS)
Hand	100	4.5–15.5	12
Body	97	8–18	14
Knee	92	9.5–22	16
Foot	100	11.5–27	19.5
Penis	28	15–39	23.5
Buttock	14	24–38	—
Vagina	12	28–50	—

(Modified from Harvey Kravitz, M.D., Children's Memorial Hospital; Clinical Assistant Professor of Pediatrics, University of Illinois, Chicago, Illinois.)

periods in infancy for experiencing certain sensations and establishing the neural patterns required for later functional maturation of various sensory systems. Much more knowledge is needed of the critical periods of growth in various systems, of the nature of deficits caused by infantile sensory deprivations, and of the capacity and means for correcting the functional impairments. Undoubtedly, this information will influence our appreciation of the etiology of many personality problems as well as the treatment of such defects.

Body Concept

It must be recalled that the child not only develops bodily perceptions over time which are modified gradually and extended in the course of growth so as to conform with the current body structure, but also takes unto himself the attitudes of others toward his body and its parts. He may develop a satisfying body concept, or he may come to view his body and its parts as unpleasant, dirty, shameful, or disgusting, by which he reflects the interaction between himself, the parental figures, and, later, other significant persons. The clinician will find it useful to distinguish *body percepts* from *body concepts*. Theoretically both are included within the well-known term *body image*. Body image is that perception of the body by the ego. The body ego contains percepts, concepts, and affects related to the body. Children's concepts of their bodies form a nuclear structure of their later self-concepts and will, in large part, determine their capacities to adapt successfully to the stresses of illness, trauma, and physical changes.

PERIOD OF CHILDHOOD

For purposes of descriptive analysis and study it is useful to distinguish between various periods of growth. Yet these distinctions are arbitrary, and it must be kept in mind that stages of maturation gradually melt into one another; there are no real distinctions. Childhood is here conceived as beginning with the capacity to speak — some time during the second year of life. Of course, it runs coincidently with those processes of maturation concerned with increasing motility of the child, his growing capacity for elimination and control of excrements. It also marks a major shift in his interpersonal relations as he now grows beyond signaling by means of cries or those early gestures learned in later infancy.

Since the earliest experiences of the child occur in the family setting, his perceptions and interpretations of these experiences will determine his attitudes toward and evaluations of later, even adult, experiences that contain some apparent similarities. Such a *transference* of an attitude derived from some personal relationship in the family to others in the larger world will exert either favorable or unfavorable influences on his relations with others and thus upon his ability to reach his ultimate social goals. Persistent attitudes of resentment or hostility that are built into the personality structure through the early experiences may form the repetitive responses of the neurotic in later life and may become the focus upon which paralyzing reaction-formations are built.

For example, if a young child sees a comforting and protecting mother repeatedly hurt or made to cry by a cruel father, he may acquire a lasting hatred for the father and later transfer this attitude to all men who resemble him in some way. Again, if the mother is vacillating in her care, sometimes comforting and at other times cruel, the child will be unable to make the clear discrimination from which unambivalent attitudes of love or hatred would emerge.

A major determinant in personality development is the unconscious modeling of the growing child upon the parents, spoken of as *identification*. The child identifies with the perceived aspects of the behavior of the parent; included are those which arouse tension or pleasure, the overrated body parts, and actions and capacities which, in the child's growing fantasies, probably give the parent the strength and power he wishes for himself. If the parents are emotionally mature persons, the adaptive process of identification promotes healthy growth.

The widening ability of the child to care for himself now brings him deeper relationships with the father, and other siblings in the family; his social development extends beyond that of the primary relationship with the mother. With this period of expanding social contact there evolves the necessity to share. In these experiences with others, the associated emotions of jealousy, rage, envy, and guilt develop. His greater activity provides him the opportunity to exercise his exploratory tendencies, his curiosity, and his initiative at solving simple problems. Differences are discerned between the sexes, and the foundations for eventual sexual identification are laid down. The striving for the first place in affection and acquisition, from the mother against the father and in a struggle with brothers and sisters, establishes competitive rivalries that stimulate those wish-fulfilling dreams and fantasies of overwhelming strength and reward or, later, the fear of retaliation, of harm and attack from others.

With the striving initiative of the child and the arousal of the emotions of jealous rage and anger, there also emerges the superego, the *conscience*. In the face of his struggles the child is curbed by one or both parents, and in turn develops both feelings of hatefulness and those adaptations of escape from retaliatory attack that may be retained in some form to adulthood — sulking, withdrawal, and finally the internalization of the prohibitions against his expressions of anger.

For psychoanalysis, this period represents the *phallic stage*. Attention has already been called to the theory that at about one year of age the source of pleasure shifts from the oral to the anal region. Similarly, at about three years of age there appears another stage in the development of pleasurable interest with a shift of source from the anal to the genital region. This phase continues until about the seventh year. With the advent of this phase, there is a concern with the difference between sexes and the size, presence, or absence of the phallic organs. There is a predominance of genital sensations, and masturbation may become a source of psychosexual pleasure. The interest is not a sexual one in the adult sense of the term. The boy merely comes to realize that his penis is important and devotes narcissistic attention to it. The girl may become aware that she has no penis and may believe she had one but lost it, with the result that she might develop feelings of inferiority and jealousy. The oral, anal, and phallic stages of libido development are often spoken of as the pregenital stages.

Continuous throughout the phallic stage up to the fifth or sixth year there exists a period of attraction to the parent of the opposite sex accompanied by jealousy and rivalrous hostility toward the parent of the same sex. To this situation between father, mother, and child, Freud gave the term *Oedipus complex*. Various anthropologists reject the universality of the Oedipus complex. That it is, however, a basically correct psychological feature of our own culture is generally accepted. Some suggest that the Oedipus reaction is determined by the behavior of the parents, not of the child. It is certainly frequently true that fathers are more severe with their sons and more indulgent with their daughters. That mothers frequently reverse this relationship is constantly observed by psychiatrists. In either case, the rivalry and hostility associated with the Oedipus reaction would follow quite naturally. Others regard the oedipal period as a convenient and expressive metaphorical term for designating the phase of personality development in which the child feels and expresses hostility against one of the parents because of the frustrations experienced.

Normally, this potentially pathogenic relation is resolved by the mechanisms of identification in which the boy identifies with his father and incorporates his father's goals and standards into his own pattern of behavior. Likewise the girl identifies with her mother, advances toward a healthy emotional maturation, and finds gratification and security in a feminine role.

From clinical observation, it is frequently recognized that when the Oedipus complex is inadequately resolved, the individual may introject some of the qualities of the parent of the opposite sex, with the result that the development of "normal" relationships with persons of the opposite sex is precluded. Familiar examples are the adult son who lives with a widowed mother and is oblivious to the charm of women of his own age, or the young man who falls in love with a much older woman who in some way resembles his mother. Psychoanalytically it is said that such fixation occurs at the homosexual stage of personality development.

Socialization Period

Later childhood, that period from 6 or 7 to 12 years of age, is one in which the child's socialization is relegated to others outside the family in our Western culture. The influence of teachers as authority figures outside the home, of older and younger playmates, and of other relatives and friends provides important opportunities for new identifications and discriminations which allay, modify, or intensify the patterns of behavioral reactions established in the family and also offer opportunities for the acquisition of new skills and roles. The child is eager to do things; he has the opportunity to learn habits of industry. Yet, if he fails to gain the patterns and otherwise measure up to his peers in school and on the playground, a sense of inferiority is instilled. His play activities provide him the opportunity for gaining pleasure in mastering tasks and, for some, that of prestige in accomplishment. Through socialized play he has the opportunity to learn mastery of his glee in triumph and his frustration and rage in failure. Group play activities allow the gradual growth and pleasure in the companionsip of others, in sharing their problems. The era carries with it as well the learning of other patterns of group behavior, those of teasing, disparagement, and ostracism. If the juvenile suffers as a consequence of group actions, his responses may seem to deepen the already existing personality reactions to frustrations at home.

At this time in the child's life, his sexual curiosity is limited; this is the latency period of psychoanalytic psychosexual development. While sex interests and activities do not disappear, there are no such marked and significant psychosexual changes as are seen in both the preceding and the following periods. The child does, however, identify more strongly than before with the parent of the same sex and begins more differentiation along masculine or feminine lines. Therefore at this time it is important that there be close association with a parent or some other satisfactory person of the same sex with whom the child may identify in establishing masculinity or femininity. This period is notably one of training in the customs and attitudes of society. There is a progressive development of the ego as a result of growth on the one hand and of education and experience on the other. It is a period during which ideals are formed. The child is exposed to more complex and social pressures; also environmental opportunities play an important part in directing individual interests and capacities. In the latter part of the latency period, a quest for status becomes a strong motivating force. It is, too, the period when inner control of aggressive-destructive impulses should be attained.

PERIOD OF ADOLESCENCE

With increasing group relations, the juvenile often develops an intense interest in one other child, usually of the same sex. This interest extends to consideration of the feelings and sensitivities of the friend. It represents the first efforts at those intimate contacts that occur in adulthood. This interest in the friend extends to satisfying his or her wishes as well as being moved by and interested in his or her successes and failures. Groups of juveniles get together and the roles of leader and supporter are learned. These social interactions provide satisfaction and security for the growing youngster.

Adolescence proper sets in with puberty, with its rapid physiological development of the sex organs. The maturation of sexual and reproductive capacities stimulates genital and heterosexual interests and activities in the genital stage of psychosexual development. Sexuality is no longer diffused throughout the body as in the pregenital phases of personality development but becomes focalized on the genital organs. The sexual area, however, is only one aspect of the personality in which there is an inherent drive toward maturation.

The growing adolescent is now preoccupied with how he appears to others and how he perceives himself. He is in search of a *personal identity,* a sense of self. Since the adolescent stands midway between personal independence and continued dependence on the parents, many acts of emancipatory behavior occur. For example, the effort to establish a sexual identification leads the boy to seek reinforcement with men or other older boys who are idealized, while the girl finds similar sources for her growing femininity. Overaggressive and competitive attitudes, exhibitionist poses, or cynical and antisocial actions may represent these struggles for a masculine independence from authority at home. Usually there is a searching out of members of the other sex, with courting as a preparation for eventual intimacy and mating. These adolescent interests break up the more juvenile friendships and call upon the adolescent to relive the separation experiences of early life and also the emotions of sadness and jealous hatefulness engendered in the oedipal conflict. Concomitant with his sexual drive, the adolescent develops a fantasy life filled with fulfillment of his desires, yet finds himself in conflict between the latter and the prohibitions of his family and society.

The adolescent must commit himself eventually to a choice of intimacy with another and must make, as well, an occupational decision, and he must couple this with a persistent and energetic competitive drive. Without much commitment the adolescent is exposed to a sense of personal isolation, or else he becomes preoccupied with a multiplicity of sexual relations of varying kinds or becomes involved in self-effacing attachments to others. He may attempt to maintain the illusion of youth, refusing to believe that the passage of time will affect his choices or his ability to find opportunities in industry and to acquire skills. Fear of and oversensitivity to competitive activity may develop. Some adolescents choose a *negative identity* founded in the presumed strengths and fascinations of the most undesirable and dangerous figures offered for identification.

Since the crises to which the adolescent is exposed are so varied and so critical, it is not surprising that personality disturbances are common in this period.

ADULTHOOD AND MATURITY

While chronological age may be recognized legally as an indication of responsible maturity, it is no guarantee of the emotional growth of the individual. The mature adult is one who has developed a clear personal identity, demonstrated by the ability to form an intimate, satisfying, and loving relationship with a mature member of the opposite sex and to take on the responsibilities of rearing children. He is able both to assume personal responsibilities when necessary and to accept the decisions of those with competent authority for the general good. He independently pursues his own goals, with recognition of his limitations and with willingness to seek advice from others when indicated, and is able to maintain and enjoy his personal relations with others, making due allowances for their deficits with an understanding tolerance. The healthy adult is one who is absorbed and satisfied in achievement relative to his family, vocation, and avocations rather than in personal self-assertions. He functions well at home and at work in terms of developing gratifying relations with others as well as in being generally free of symptoms of illness.

Problems of Maturity

In all periods of adult life, the conflicts that occur recapitulate those of earlier life. For the young adult, these struggles center largely over the necessity for decisions relative to the selection of a mate and a vocation. In each instance the young adult may find himself in conflict between his personal drives and estimates of capacity and opportunity and those expressed by his parents or their representatives. Anxieties that develop in arriving at these decisions may adversely affect both marital and vocational life. Undue dependence upon the parents, if marriage occurs, will deprive the marital partner of the tenderness and attentiveness required to establish a satisfying and growth-promoting home. Attitudes of unusual defiance or submissiveness, originating in the relations to parents and teachers, are likely to be transferred to those in authority in the vocational world. In turn, these may lead either to derogatory attitudes toward the defiant young adult or to failure of associates to recognize potentialities of the submissive person that might lead to advancement. The birth of children often revives the sibling rivalries of earlier years in one or both parents, with reappearance of inappropriate hostilities or resurgence of infantile demands.

In middle adulthood, with advancement to senior positions, the rearousal of sibling rivalries may lead to paralyzing anxieties over envy and hostility suspected in peers, or to overbearing attitudes of revenge for their assumed earlier punitiveness. Failure to be advanced also can bring forth hostilities and resentments that produce sulky withdrawal, depression, or accusations of favoritism or influence. With menopause, women experience the conflicts centered on waning sexuality and inability to bear children. Later life poses again the problems of increasing dependence, with surrender of personal responsibility owing to increasing physical weakness or relinquishment of positions of power and prestige, with consequent recurrence of drives of rivalry. The older person must also face the anxieties consequent upon impending death.

Separation and Death

One of the major emotional problems of the elderly, but one to which people are exposed throughout all periods of life, is separation from those whom one loves and upon whom one is dependent. Mourning, the period of grief that follows loss through death or an important separation, or even the loss of a body part as from amputation, must be regarded as a process of anxiety with restitution and re-establishment of the personality in the face of the loss. During mourning the intensity of grief leads to both physiological and psychological disturbances which are evidenced in withdrawal from others and preoccupation with the loss. The process of mourning is the psychological effort to maintain the lost object by fantasy reviewing of the experiences, meanings, and emotional significance of the relationship and the eventual taking in of certain qualities derived from the association.

Older people frequently suffer this process and may defend themselves against it by adopting attitudes of personal omnipotence and pride in self-sufficiency, or they may be recurrently overcome by overt anxiety and other defenses against it.

For the infant and child, death of a person upon whom they are dependent leads to profound emotional disturbances, as many have demonstrated.

The growing child's appreciation of death is not that of the adult, however. Until the age of 5 or thereabouts, death is perceived by the child as a departure, a further existence under other conditions, without finality, to which the separated child responds by asking for the lost person. The child at this time interprets the loss frequently as a malignant, premeditated act to which he responds with the emotions of both sadness and rage. He is taught to repress these emotions. Later, between ages 5 and 10, children tend to personify death as someone who carries others off, a fearful person. It is only after this age that death is recognized as a universal process with final dissolution of life.

Deaths in the family through suicide or illness, or threats of suicide, may be perceived by the young child as hateful or manipulative acts and may in turn lead to retaliatory fantasies, which form the basis for later suicidal thoughts and acts that have revenge as their motive.

Thus mourning and separation anxiety must be recognized as regular emotional responses to a loss, with a recognizable course of development and resolutions. Mourning for adults runs a course of 6 to 12 months; it is to be differentiated from depression.

SPECIAL FACTORS INFLUENCING DEVELOPMENT

Family Constellation

While the *only child* may develop well and has often been reported to be superior to others in terms of health, physique, intelligence, and facility at school, his emotional position in the family exposes him to the full intensity of any emotional disturbances that may exist in the parents. As an only child, he may represent the parents' single effort to appear as sexually mature adults and thus he represents a denial of interested and wanted parenthood. The parents' exploitative drives are channeled into the only child, and their oversolicitude leads to an excessive protection, which further isolates him from his peers. He is deprived of the learning experiences of living and sharing with siblings; frequently he has fantasies of brothers and sisters and may blame himself for having no siblings. With others of his own age he may be shy, awkward, or intensely competitive, thus becoming the victim of teasing and rejection; this induces either further withdrawal or overcompensatory efforts to gain attention and prestige. Such efforts may be expressed in exhibitionistic activities, boastfulness, or bribery of others if the means exist. His isolation often leads to the persistence of childish dependency on others, which impairs his capacity for adult relations.

Yet, the attention given to the only child may serve as a driving force in his personality growth and enhance the unfolding of many social assets and talents.

The *adopted child,* particularly when adopted outside the parental family, also is exposed to developmental difficulties that lead to a high incidence of personality disorder in later life. Thus, the adopted child may perpetuate intrapsychically a split in his parenteral object relations, since in reality he has two sets of parents and maintains one as "bad" and the other as "good." Also, one or both of the adoptive parents may be disturbed by unconscious guilt, which is then projected onto the heredity or conception of the adopted child. Adopted children frequently have wish-fulfilling fantasies that their real mothers will reclaim them. Their ambivalence toward their adoptive parents often is difficult to resolve, as they tend to perceive these parents as inadequate and support their conflict with fantasied satisfactions in the relationship with the lost parents. Such fantasies maintain and generate their frequent desires to come to find and know their real parents. Furthermore, the adoptive status is often used by the new parents as a means of shaming the child and controlling his behavior, thus magnifying a sense of being unwanted and unloved. Adopted children exposed to such family transactions more often appear to be aggressive and to indulge in sexual "acting out" in adolescence and later life.

The *institutionalized child* is often exposed as well to an environment unfavorable to emotional maturation. Deprived of a close, continuing, and warm emotional contact with an interested mother substitute and later a paternal figure, the child reared in an institution lacks the personal stimulation and the opportunity for the growth of affection and trust that permits development later of the capacity for successful relations and identifications with others. Thus impairment occurs in the maturation of both ego and superego functions. It has been found that such children show a greater frequency of problem behavior characterized by lack of control, anxiety, aggression, cognitive limitations, and an affective impoverishment. Specifically, they are more restless, overactive, and limited in concentration, may have temper tantrums and may be impudent, cruel, and destructive. More frequently, they show impairment of speech and mental activities which resemble retardation and lead to difficulty in school.

Twins, both identical and nonidentical, as well as those born in other multiple sibships, have special problems in personality growth. The maternal attitude toward twins is sometimes one of shame and rejection followed later by efforts to explore and differentiate the siblings as a means for the mother to direct appropriately her responses to one or other of the children. The care of twins demands much of the mother; each receives less attention than the single child. Yet this drives the pair together and establishes the matrix which makes it difficult for them to establish independent self-identities. Their constant closeness interferes with their independent learning of social functions. Twins develop more intense rivalry problems to which they may adapt by attaching themselves to one or the other parent or, more commonly, by assuming similar desires and thereby repressing their individual drives. The strong jealousy for the parents generated in the relationship intensifies hostile drives toward the other twin which, in turn, require compensatory efforts at repressions that again bring the twins together. While these pressures are not inevitable, they occur frequently in twin development and make the individual both insecure in his own identity and extremely vulnerable to the loss of his sibling on whom he is usually excessively dependent.

ORDINAL POSITION AND FAMILY SIZE. Both the quantity and quality of interaction between the growing infant or child and his parents will be influenced by the maternal drive and affective satisfaction of the parents and by the time available to them from their other goal strivings. Thus large families will tend to decrease the amount of parental contact for those most recently born. On the other hand peer transactions tend to increase and may therefore make up for the relative degree of deprivation of maternal and paternal interactions. First-born children usually arouse and obtain the greatest degree of maternal and paternal interest and joy. They obtain the most attention because there is less competition for parental time. As the new and shared object expressive of parental aspirations, the first-born's hold on both parents exceeds that of the later siblings. As one might predict, studies of those who have achieved most in terms of creative effort demonstrate a preponderance in first-born status. Yet a child in this position is highly vulnerable, too. When his physique or his early or later development disappoint or deviate from parental expectations, he often suffers severe rejection and may become overloaded with distress, anguish, guilt, or shame, which in turn stimulates the development of pathological defenses.

So, too, the youngest child may generate a greater maternal interest and attention as a way of recapturing or retaining the satisfactions of the mother's earlier years. Spoiling or overprotection is more likely here than for the oldest; maternal attitudes are conducive to maintenance of oral dependent characteristics.

Infinite variations exist for highly variable personality development in the many differing transactions stimulated between parents and children of moderate and large-sized families. At the same time, extended kinships or friendships offer many alternative modes for identification for the growing child. In the attempt to understand the individual personality, the diagnostician must seek to identify all the significant relations and the nature and result of their transactions with the child or adult who has become his concern.

BIBLIOGRAPHY

Adler, A.: Individual Psychology. London, Routledge, 1946.

Ainsworth, M. D. S., Blehar, M. C., Waters, E., and Wall, S.: Patterns of Attachment. New York, John Wiley & Sons, 1978.

Arlow, J. A.: The only child. Psychoanal. Q., 41:507–536, 1972.

Bowlby, J.: Attachment and Loss. Vol. 1. New York, Basic Books, 1969.

Bowlby, J.: Attachment and Loss. Vol. 2. Separation, Anxiety and Anger. New York, Basic Books, 1973.

Burlingham, D.: Twins: A Study of Three Pairs of Identical Twins. New York, International Universities Press, 1952.

Chassell, J. C.: Old wine in new bottles. Superego as a structuring of roles. In Gibson, R. W. (ed.): Cross Currents in Psychiatry and Psychoanalysis. Philadelphia, J. B. Lippincott, 1967.

Dubos, R., Lee, C. J., and Costello, R.: Lasting biological effects of early environmental influences. J. Exp. Med., 130:963–977, 1969.

Dyrud, J. E., and Donnelly, C.: Executive functions of the ego. Arch. Gen. Psychiatry, 20:257–261, 1961.

Erikson, E. H.: Childhood and Society. 2nd ed. New York, W. W. Norton, 1963.

Frank, L. K.: Play in personality development. Am. J. Orthopsychiatry, 25:576–590, 1955.

Freud, S.: Collected Papers. London, Hogarth Press, 1924.

Freud, S.: The Ego and the Id. Translated by J. Riviere. London, Hogarth Press, 1927.

Galenson, E., and Roiphe, H.: Some suggested revisions concerning early female development. In Blum, H. P. (ed.): Female Psychology. New York, International Universities Press, 1977.

Harlow, H. F., and Harlow, M. K.: Social deprivation in monkeys. Sci. Am., 207:136–146, 1962.

Hartmann, H.: Ego Psychology and the Problem of Adaptation. New York, International University Press, 1958.

Hinde, R. A.: Maternal deprivation in rhesus monkeys. J. Psychosom. Res., 16:227–228, 1972.

Kastenbaum, R., and Aisenberg, R.: The Psychology of Death. New York, Springer Publishing Company, 1972.

Kohut, H.: The Analysis of the Self. New York, International Universities Press, 1971.

Kolb, L. C.: Disturbances of the body image. In Arieti, S. (ed.): American Handbook of Psychiatry. 2nd ed. Vol. IV. New York, Basic Books, 1975, pp. 810–837.

Leboyer, F.: Birth Without Violence. New York, Alfred Knopf, 1975.

Mahler, M. S.: The Psychological Birth of the Human Infant. Symbiosis and Individuation. New York, Basic Books, 1975.

McDevitt, J. B.: The role of internalization in the development of object relations during the separation-individuation phase. J. Am. Psychoanal. Assoc. 27:327–343, 1979.

Nurnberger, J. I. (ed.): Biological and Environmental Determinants of Early Development. Vol. 51, Association for Research in Nervous and Mental Disease. Baltimore, Williams & Wilkins Company, 1973.

Rosenberg, M.: Conceiving the Self. New York, Basic Books, 1979.

Rutter, M.: Maternal deprivation reconsidered. J. Psychosom. Res., 16:241–250, 1972.

Rynearson, E. K.: Humans and pets and attachment. Br. J. Psychol. 133:550–555, 1978.

Sandler, J.: On the concept of superego. Psychoanal. Study Child, 15:128–162, 1966.

Schechter, M. D., Carlson, P. V., Simmons, J. A., and Work, H. H.: Emotional problems of the adoptee. Arch. Gen. Psychiat., 10:109–118, 1964.

Schoenberg, B. C., Carr, A. C., Peretz, D., and Kutscher, A. H. (eds.): Loss and Grief: Psychological Management in Medical Practice. New York, Columbia University Press, 1970.·

Scott, J. P.: Critical periods in behavioral development. Science, 138:949–958, 1962.

Stone, A. A.: Consciousness: Altered levels in blind children. Psychosom. Med., 26:14–19, 1964.

Tomkins, S. S.: Affect, Imagery and Consciousness. 2 Vols. New York, Springer Publishing Company, 1963.

5

ADAPTIVE PROCESSES
AND MENTAL MECHANISMS

"During man's growth, mere individuality becomes personality: and the developed individual personality is not only the most complex type of organization known, and one which exhibits a far greater range of diversity among its members than any other single type of organization, but the highest product of evolution of which we have any knowledge."

Julian Huxley

ANNA FREUD
(Courtesy of Edmund Engelman.)

NEED FOR ADAPTIVE MECHANISMS

In the course of evolution, all species have developed various means and mechanisms to adapt to the life conditions which confront them. Some butterflies, for example, develop a protective coloring simulating the surface on which they rest to escape detection by their enemies, and members of the same species adapt their coloring when the environment to which they are exposed differs from that of their original habitat. Since adaptation is the very essence of life, it is not strange that man, the most highly developed species, has evolved not only anatomical adjustments, which protect him structurally or physiologically in respect to his environment, but also psychological devices, which assist him in dealing with emotional needs and stresses. These devices help meet the needs for affection, personal security, personal significance, and defense against perturbing affects. By acting without conscious recognition on man's part, such devices effect adaptation to inner situations and experiences that would otherwise be intolerable. The self-conscious personality, with its intense need for a sense of security and self-esteem, evolves mechanisms of a protective nature as instinctively as self-preservation prompts the avoidance of approaching physical danger. Just as the body through its physical and biochemical processes strives to maintain a physiological equilibrium or homeostasis, so the personality through automatic and unconscious psychological processes seeks to maintain a psychological stability.

The evolution of a healthy personality requires especially the development of those behavioral processes necessary for adapting to life in human society. Therefore the development of the communicative and explorative or problem-solving behaviors, especially language and the thought processes, must be considered of paramount importance as human adaptive processes. These processes are acquired through learning, as are the various mental mechanisms by which the personality attempts to enhance and defend itself, to mediate between its conflicting drives, and to allay tensions. In terms of psychopathology, the definitions of disturbance will be found particularly in failures of the integrative function of the personality—its ego functions. Thus disturbances of language, perception, thought, and memory and of the capacity to delay gratifications of needs, discharge tensions, and learn the ordinary social behaviors, or the acquisition of inflexible character defenses against such tensions, provide the recognizable symptomatic expressions of the personality disorders.

LANGUAGE AND COMMUNICATION

There is strong reason to believe that man's neocortex alone evolved the structural and functional organization necessary for human speech. Judging from experimental brain stimulation, vocalization in nonhuman primates appears to be functionally organized, outside the neocortex in the areas of emotional behavior. According to Lenneberg's work, language development follows a regular maturational process even in children in whom the process is impeded owing to retardation, such as in Down's syndrome (Mongolism; see Chapter 29). The acquisition of language in children is not prevented by physical impairments such as blindness or deafness, or by deprivation of rearing by deaf parents, if appropriate stimulation is provided early in life. It has been suggested that the "critical period" for language acquisition extends from the age of two until puberty. Fluent second language acquisition is easy between these ages and difficult afterward.

Chomsky and other linguists propose that the human brain is organized to act upon a "generative grammar" and that the varieties of grammar required to cover all languages are small. Thus, all of language is not learned. The neocortical organization of man is programmed to accept language. Observations that language comprehension always develops before language expression and that language comprehension evolves in children incapable of any form of verbal expression seem to support these opinions.

While the acquisition of language as a communicative device distinguishes man from all other living species, it is often overlooked that man retains and uses other forms of communication as well. Among methods of influencing others and eliciting responses from them are the various motoric forms of nonverbal communication. These must be considered for understanding conflictual and abnormal behaviors.

To return again to the developmental history of man, the infant's original communications consist essentially of vocalizations that signal his distress and need for help. These vocalizations essentially signal emotional states. The responses from the mother set up the pattern for the growth of the later and more complex communicative systems, the smiles, pointings, and other gesturings between the two, which again signal emotional reactions—signs that later may be adapted, as in the language of the deaf-mutes, for an elaborate nonverbal symbolic communicative system. The early gestures are the rudiments of the kinesthetic system wherein bodily movements and postures provide information and convey messages to others. Thus the tightstepped gluteal-pressed walk and stiff posture of a young woman signifies her overconcern with the taboos of sexual behavior, while the condescendingly haughty walk of a young man—erect, head thrown back, stiffarmed—tells of his effort to cover up his unspoken feeling of social inadequacy with disdainful poise.

Many recent observations have been made of the early interactions between infant and mother, which initiate the communication process. By the third or fourth month of life, the healthy infant has a functional visual motor system, permitting voluntary control of the eyes. About the same time he enters the babbling stage of prelinguistic verbalization, which gives him a considerable measure of control over his perceptual input. Even at this early period of life a number of major lines of social and behavioral activities (gazing, smiling, vocalizing) are brought together in the transactions of play activity with the mother. The infant seeks stimulation actively but appears to be innately disposed to orient toward and remain attentive to a certain range of stimulus quantities and qualities. An effectively lively caregiver will provide stimulation that corresponds to the range of stimulus events most suitable for the innate capacities of the individual infant. Thus, both mother and infant in their early communication move toward a mutual maintenance of arousal wherein the infant responds affectively with rewarding social behavior, such as smiles and coos. It has been observed that if the level of stimulation is too low, the infant fails to attend or loses interest quickly in the caregiver; if stimulation is excessive he avoids it by turning away. Various observations make it clear that infants can discriminate pitch, loudness, and rhythm in the voice of the mother or caregiver and they may discriminate brightness, form and pattern contrasts on complex levels, and movement. Mothers demonstrate a remarkable range of visual, auditory, and facial expressions as well as tactile movements in their play with infants.

From the clinical standpoint and in relation to the infant's later affective development and his gestures, speech, and language, the variety and attunement of the mother's playfulness clearly are most significant. So too, impairment of an infant's participation, as in retardation, or visual or auditory defect, may impinge upon the mothering process and limit the mother's capacity to effectively stimulate the child's beginning social transactions.

It must be held in mind that the gestural characteristics of human communication vary not only from individual to individual but also from culture to culture. Gestures have now come under study by anthropologists, who indicate that each culture has a limited range of these communicative acts; in the U.S.A. there are said to exist approximately 30 which may be regularly recognized.

Verbal communication, language, begins between the first and second year, when the necessary neuromuscular structures are fully developed. First the child uses interjections to inform of his emotional states. Later he denotes those about him by naming, and still later designates objects with nouns. Next comes the use of verbs, and by the end of the second year simple sentences are formed. The child indicates his ability to separate himself from others clearly by using pronouns and enriches his informational activity by learning the use of adjectives and adverbs.

If the child has failed to speak by the end of three and one-half years, some defect almost invariably exists in the neuroanatomical structures concerned with speech. The possibilities are failures in the auditory apparatus per se leading to deafness, in the auditory nerves, or in those brain pathways and interconnections mediating the reception, cognition, and activations of speech—or failure in the teaching and learning of speech, in the intercommunication processes that structure language through interplay between parent and child. Language does not evolve in nonspeaking environments, as various observations have shown.

A distinction worthy of note is the difference between *speech* as a system of verbal signals and signs and *language* as a transactional process serving social functions. The former is a trainable function capable of imitation and exists in a small way in infants around the end of the first year. But language as a complex adaptive device used to influence the social behavior of others appears several years later.

But even with the development of verbal communication, language continues to reflect the emotional states and attitudes of the speaker in the hidden meanings of accompanying tone, inflection, volume, and gesture. Wit and humor especially, as well as various creative efforts, reflect and reveal the hidden and conflicting motivations through their nonverbal meanings.

The psychiatrist must observe the discrepancies between the content of language, verbal communication, and the meanings conveyed in the nonverbal accompaniments of language, including the postures and gestures which establish the speaker's character. In these discrepancies the psychiatrist may detect evidence of conflict, the subtle expression of hidden affect, and the modes of defending against its expression. It is of utmost significance to bear in mind that there is not only verbal language but also a nonverbal organ and action language.

Communication involves relations between peoples. As has been described in Chapter 4, growth is associated with establishing successively the capacity to communicate well with one other (the mother), then with the family members, and finally with increasingly varied and complex groups of persons, in the process of which the individual assumes at one time one social role and at another time another social role.

PERCEPTION AND THOUGHT

Even more distinctive of man than language has been his unparalleled evolution of a system for problem solving which has demanded an organization of neural functions of much greater complexity than that of a simple receptor-effector relationship with the environment. In contrast to the simple organizations of a reflex-stimulus-reflex system, the interposition of the highly elaborate cellular structure of the brain establishes delay in response, storing, and retention of previous experiences and the capacity for increasingly effective discriminations in exploring the environment.

It has been said that man never contacts reality directly; he first reacts with himself and his preconceived emotions, hopes, fears, and aspirations. It is the interposition of this mediating system, the human brain, that has made possible the potential for the use of symbols. Through the progressive storing of accumulated knowledge and its transmission from one generation to another by the various cultural institutions, modern civilizations have arisen.

Beyond its communicative function, language with its purposive drives made possible for man the designation and categorization of objects and thus the ability to regroup words to form different meanings or to use the same word in different combinations to specify still further meanings. Thus in the development of language the ranges of discrimination and thought were extended far beyond that found in animal species, which use only a nonverbal communicative system.

Yet, if thought is considered the means for problem solving, verbal language is not a necessary precursor. Experimental psychology has acquired a wealth of data to show that animals may solve problems and also use symbols as signs. Nor is problem solving dependent upon learning, as new insights and solutions depend upon recombinations of previous experience. The parts of the old experience used in the new solutions or conceptions nevertheless must have been explored or learned. Thus, animals reared in isolation and denied the experiences of those reared in groups prove inferior in problem-solving tests. Man's great capacity for thought as a purposive problem-solving device rests upon his greater capacity for recording past experiences, for remembering, for questioning—and therefore for making progressively precise discriminations and complex combinations. Fixation of the past through memory allows those comparisons with current percepts or images that establish the capacity to formulate questions, the other component of man's thought processes, which distinguish him from other species.

Perception and learning are necessary concomitants of the thinking process. Perception is not sensation; it implies the recognition of an object, an image, or a thought. Perceptions then often represent integrations of many sensations recorded in the brain as the central integrating organ. Thus perception of an orange implies the sensing of both color and form visually. The latter requires the kinesthetic sensing of the ocular muscles as they circumscribe the shape, as well as the olfactory and gustatory memories of previous contacts with the orange. Perception, then, is the act of knowing objects, images, and thoughts, by sensory experiences or by recollective thought. *Imagery* takes place when some central brain process is set in action which is similar to the process aroused on earlier occasions on sensing the object. *Concepts,* in contradistinction to percepts, are mental images of something formed by generalizations from the particulars.

The acquisition of percepts takes place only through a long process of repetitive experiencing of the object, a learning process that involves the mental processes of discrimination and generalization. The child who perceives the orange discriminates it from other round objects and is now able to transfer this percept to other images of an orange, such as pictures or models. He generalizes the percept. Yet now he again recognizes the orange image and discriminates it from the real object.

In the previous chapter, reference was made to the serious defects that occur if the growing child is prevented before the age of five from experiencing visual sensation, which lays down the patterns of arousal in the central nervous system that lead to recall and the potentiality for effective visual perception. Mention was also made of the acquisition of perception of one's body, through experiencing it in the sensing and explorations of the early growth process, as well as perception of other objects external to the body.

Early Perceptual Processes

To return once more to development, the beginnings of perceptual and conceptual processes are hypothesized to occur in the experiences associated with the early mothering of the infant. Through the repeated experiences of sensing diffuse internal and external bodily cravings, discomforts, and relaxations, as well as their relationship to the nursing, caring, and playful contacts with the mother, the infant comes to associate satisfaction or discomfort with the presence or absence of contact with the mother. These early percepts are diffuse, and represent the physiological responses later associated with emotion in the sense that the internal state of the infant is recorded. It is unlikely that the infant distinguishes himself from the mother—the "me" or "not me." What is perceived, then, is hunger or satiation, satisfaction, cold or warmth, and pain, but without conscious meaning.

The continuing contact with the mother leads to a discrimination of nipple and breast as distinct from the infant's self and later to the percept of the mother's face, with eventual recognition of its varying expression of affect in smiling, laughing, frowning, or indifference. It is assumed that at this time the infant's brain has made the perceptual distinction between the body of the infant as separate from that of the mother and has established the fundamental basis for a personal identity.

As time proceeds, it is assumed that in periods of frustration unrelieved by the immediacy of mothering the infant develops an image, or hallucinates the presence, of the breast or the mother as a wish-fulfilling substitute for gratification. Electroencephalographic studies now indicate a capacity for dream life in earliest infancy which supports the contention of the emergence of early, if diffuse, imagery, a form of substitutive mental representation, the infantile prototype of ideation. The unsatisfied need also may be thought of as leading to a heightened awareness and attention which establish the set that determines what eventually appears in consciousness.

In infancy attentiveness is short-lived, yet the infant, with his limited capacity to sense, has difficulty shifting from one percept to another. He may be said to be "stimulus bound." When he is exposed to a number of objects, his incapacity to attend the multiplicity of impressions is evinced in crying or other behavior indicating tension.

With recognition through repeated experience, the infantile percepts take on meaning as the external objects, human or inanimate, repeatedly induce feeling states within him. About the fourth month of life, when he commences to grasp, external percepts are given another meaning in terms of what the infant may do to them. The early percepts are largely tactile—kinesthetic senses. At about six months of age visual perception enlarges and becomes dominant.

Conceptual Development

Piaget's direct study of the growing child provides the best source of information on the development of the early perceptual and underlying cognitive processes. Within the first 18 months of life, before any evidence of language expression, the child's sensorimotor behavior demonstrates the existence of a practical intelligence centered on a logic of action. Once he has pulled toward him a blanket on which a toy has been placed, he will then pull the blanket to reach any other object placed upon it. Further, he will generalize that action to pull a string to which an object is attached. Piaget argues that the growing child's sensorimotor experiences with objects lead him to assimilate into himself that which is repeatable and capable of generalization as a logic or scheme. These sensorimotor actions organize reality outside the child by constructing action categories which define objects, space, time, and causes. By so manipulating objects beyond himself the child comes to separate himself from the outer world. At five to seven months objects are not permanent; their withdrawal sets off indifference or screaming. By nine months the child will look for an object he has seen if it is placed behind a screen—yet then he does not search elsewhere. A few months later he will use inferences to look for it elsewhere. The object has become permanently fixed in his mind; he organizes space and time as he searches and finds objects. So, too, as in the blanket experience described earlier, he has commenced to recognize that his own actions offer a cause.

By the beginning of the second year the child has an understanding of space—that a movement in one direction may be cancelled by a movement in another or that a point in space may be reached by several routes.

From a year and a half to seven or eight the sensorimotor knowledge seems to be internalized and shaped as representations or symbols, of which language is the best one. Gestures and imitations are highly important. The evidence for the young child's use of internalized representational thought is seen in the imitative acts performed when alone and separated from the model. Now the child in transit to the use of representational intelligence may be observed to solve problems by sudden insights (interiorized combinations) rather than by trial and error as in the past. The child needs to explore and experiment with objects many times before he assimilates their various properties and relations. Such development takes place in deaf and dumb as well as blind children; the latter, however, are delayed in their symbol development as they are impaired in their ability to explore space.

To Piaget, percepts and concepts of objects are derived from early sensorimotor experiencing. They may evolve simultaneously. The percepts may precede conceptualization by a long period; or, in the case of perspective,

there occurs a divergent evolution of percept and concept. Thus not until after age seven will the child commence to recognize changes in size and shape and to represent perspective in drawing—a development progressive to age ten.

To Piaget, the symbolic or semiotic function takes place through *operations:* the child begins by imitating in the presence of a model. Later he will carry out the imitations alone. A child may imitate the stamping or crying of an angry playmate, but later will repeat the same actions when alone—a deferred imitation. So, too, through the play of pretending, the child establishes a gestural symbol of some act such as sleeping. Not until after two and a half years is the child capable of a graphic image—a way station between the symbolic play and a mental image or concept.

Imitation is the prefiguration of representation. Symbolic play and drawing form the next way station before the establishment of mental images. Symbolic play for the child assimilates reality to the self, the play representing both affective states and cognitive interests. The child may play as an object, holding himself stiff "like a skyscraper." His symbolic play may deal as well with the unconscious conflicts of the child—aggressive, sexual, and so on.

Before age seven, the images are static; motion or change is difficult to reproduce. In this period of life his thinking is absolute and unidirectional. Although he may identify his left hand from his right, this will be difficult when he is asked to make the distinction before a mirror. To Piaget this suggests that imaginal reproductions require anticipation and depend on operations which make it possible for the child to understand these processes.

From seven onward to approximately twelve, the healthy child turns to concrete operations, classifying objects according to similarities and ordering them in series. His thought processes are reversible, and the child now increases his capacity to think of points of view of others. Yet he is incapable of abstract thought. His command of language symbols expands his knowledge over vast ranges of time and space. It is the communicative process in gesture, language, and play that broadens the child's perceptivity of this world — decenters it from himself to others. This conceptual decentering occurs simultaneously with the decentering of affective and social (moral) thinking. Thus while children before age seven will state that the quantity of liquid being poured from one glass to a narrower or wider one is increased or decreased, after this age they note that the water poured is the same and may be returned to the original container, and they will argue that the quantity is unchanged. States are subordinated to transformations and are reversible. They relate directly to concrete objects and not yet to verbal abstracts. With the thinking abilities mentioned, the child is able to play games with other children, to learn the social rules. These are first received as absolute dictates from elders, are applied without allowances, and only later are softened as group decisions between contemporaries.

It is only in the preadolescent period that the beginnings are made in accepting and thinking in terms of abstractions — not in relation to observations or representations regarded as true. The reader is referred to the extensive observational data reported by Piaget. The important point for psychiatry is the recognition that many clinical phenomena related to communication and thought are recognizable as partial regressions to or fixations at earlier levels of conceptual development.

Social Perception and Cognition

While the descriptions of the development of perceptual cognitive behavior from infancy onward provide a useful background for establishing norms for these adaptive processes, it is evident from the studies of psychopathology that they are insufficient to explain the discrepancies easily discovered between social behavior and intellectual functioning. Such discrepancies are particularly typical of major psychoses — especially schizophrenia — but they occur as well in other psychotic states and impinge upon those with neurotic behavioral processes. The essential issue relates to the development of percepts and cognitions pertaining to the social fields in which each individual functions — the way in which he conceives of his relationships to the network of significant persons with whom he is in contact throughout life.

The earliest process that determines social perception — separation-individuation, described in the previous chapter — is significant. In this process the child evolves a sense of identity and a recognition that others exist beyond himself. As he proceeds through the transactions with the mother, his behavior suggests that he evolves images of self and mother associated with variable affects, both pleasant and distressing, which in turn translate in imagery to "good" or "bad" images of self and mother. Such images arise as the child is treated affectionately or related to critically. Such disparate polar attitudes to self and others coalesce and fuse when mothering is constant but may remain and emerge later in ambivalent social attitudes when the caring transactions are intense and contradictory. Only when the developmental transactions are conducted over time and in such a way that the intensity of affective interchange between child and mother is within tolerable limits is the growing child capable of fusing the disparate, affectively charged, part images of self and mother into a coherent, integrated representation that accepts the reality of ambivalent and multifaceted affective relations.

These percepts and concepts evolve in

the context of family life where valida-
tion occurs through the interpretations
of social reality provided by parents,
siblings and, distantly or closely, other
members of the kinship, and family
helpers who relate to the growing child
and adolescent.

Reiss has suggested that the consensual experience within the family may
explain the way in which individuals
employ their cognitive and perceptual
resources in intimate relationships with
others. Furthermore, such experiences
account for the means by which these
intimate relationships mold the cognitive and perceptual processes so as to
provide a generally shared sense of
social reality or to distort it psychopathologically. Each family tends to evolve
and share a distinctive view of its social
environment as well as the patterns that
are perceived or understood to govern
that environment. To Reiss, the perceptual and cognitive abilities of each
family member play a significant role in
forming and continuing the family constructs. On the other hand, the same
constructs determine how the family
members interact with each other in
response to outside influences. Reiss
suggests the existence of at least three
types of family. In the *environment-sensi-
tive* variety, family members together
perceive a problem as external or "out
there" without personal relevance for
the family. In this type of family logical
principles govern a solution. The family
attempts to observe as much as possible
from beyond its circle; individual family members recognize that others' percepts and thoughts are responses to the
external problem, to be included in the
understanding sought. Their acceptance will be based on objective accuracy. There is full sharing of observations
and ideas so that the family agrees on
the final solution to the problem The
sharing requires that each family
member delays closure on definition
until he has examined as much information as possible.

In a second type of family, described
as the *interpersonal distance-sensitive* vari-

ety, each member tends to demonstrate
to the others his independence from
the family and to emphasize his own
sense of mastery. Individual family
members find acceptance of others' observations or suggestions a sign of personal weakness and tend to see the externally arising problem as unique to
their own perceptions or cognitions. As
a result, neither the behaviors nor the
results of behavior of a family member
may be evaluated or useful to others in
the family. Members of such families
are conceptualized as reaching decisions precipitously with little information or as accumulating massive
amounts of information without coming to any closure.

Finally, in the *consensual-sensitive* variety of family, the tendency is for all
members to perceive the goal of analysis and solution of any problem as a
means of maintaining family agreement at all times. In this situation, dissent between family members is intolerable so each member quickly gives up
his percepts or concepts to others without accepting views from the outside.
Consensus is quickly voiced; if information continues to be given, the family
members ignore or oversimplify it.

The suggestion is made that the latter type of family is very similar to families of schizophrenics. The interpersonal distance-sensitive variety tends to
produce the impulsive or delinquent
person whereas the environment-sensi-
tive family essentially adapts well to the
general social scene. Admixtures of
these various forms of family consensual
experience are foreseen by Reiss as producing the varieties of different behaviors that one indeed finds in the
universe of individuals who come to the
attention of the psychopathologist.

Within the family framework, Reiss'
formulation may have general merit in
explaining the tendency of successive
members of families to conform in the
development of their social perceptual
cognitive fields. As will be described
later in this chapter, however, the potential exists for reaction formations

between family members that lead to the obverse in the processes of thinking even in the consensual-sensitive type of family.

Registration and Stimulus Barrier

Consciousness includes not only percepts and images of current happenings and those of the past, but also the images of the possible future. There is now mounting evidence that conscious percepts and images are influenced not only by consciously available past percepts, but also those that have been *repressed*. More recently there have accumulated some data to indicate, in addition, the registration of external stimuli that go unrecognized, since they are so subliminal that no immediate conscious recording ever occurs, yet such registrations appear to influence other perceptions. Thus experiments have demonstrated that subliminal exposures of emotionally toned words such as "angry" and "happy" given simultaneously by subliminal tachistoscopic projection will modify the percept of a clearly exposed photograph of a man's face to include the subject's report of the associated subliminal affect word.

It appears, then, that of the many stimuli impinging on the human receptor system, many more register and achieve some subjective representation than may be surmised from simple examination of the thoughts or overt behaviors of the subject. Man, then, is much more receptive of his world and its impingements upon him; his senses range actively and restlessly over wide areas that fall outside the range of perception and immediate consciousness. For such "incidental registrations" to reach consciousness, it seems likely that they must be recruited to reality-attuned schemata.

Registration and perception are considered now by many researchers as distinct processes, the former highly efficient but less selective. The barriers to perception of registered stimuli depend upon their endowment with qualities significant to consciousness at a particular time. Accordingly, it may be said that the state of consciousness at a particular time determines the structure of perceptions and registrations. The mind's "set" or "attitude" selects from the vast barrage of incoming sensory registrations, both internal and external, those to which the individual attends; this establishes an effective barrier to perception so as to make adaptations to those most significant to the state of the organism at the moment. Recent neurophysiological work has shown as well that stimuli may be blocked from registration centrally by "feedback" which reduces registrations at the peripheral sensory organs, again providing the organism a *stimulus barrier*. The foregoing discussion is consistent with clinical observations. As an example, many soldiers fail to recall perception of pain at the time of impact when wounded in battle, when other threats and activities preclude attending to the pain-inducing wound.

The concept of the stimulus barrier, now supported by physiological studies, bears directly upon such issues as the sensitivity of individuals to varying degrees and kinds of sensory experiences as well as preferences in the selection of perceptual experiences. Thus, many childhood schizophrenics are hypersensitive to auditory stimuli and prefer to use the contact receptors of touch, taste, and smell rather than the distance receptors of vision and audition.

Overwhelming of the stimulus barrier is conceived as the etiologic factor in the catastrophic or post-traumatic stress disorders of adults or as underlying many childhood neurotic states when there has been exposure to psychically traumatic percepts that induce massive stimulation and border on the unbearable.

Early Fantasies

The psychoanalytic theories of the early beginnings of hallucinated wishes in the infant have been mentioned. Later, waking images or fantasies, thoughts, and dreams also are considered to fulfill the function of damping the tensions of unmet needs. It has been further suggested that these fantasies evolve in relation to the growth of the child. Thus with the period of toilet training and the exposure of the child to efforts to control him, the thought processes are repetitive, oscillating between the wish to excrete and the defiance of withholding. Here one may conceive of establishing the polar thinking of "is it right" or "is it wrong," or "I am good," "I am bad," or "I shall do it" or "I shall not do it"; modes of thought that are fixed characteristically in the obsessive-compulsive mind. Later on, with the child's exposure to the emotional interplay between himself and both parents and siblings, there arise those fantasies dealing with the consequences of relations with others. "If I love father, mother will punish me," or pseudo-masochistic, "If I die, you will be sorry." Finally, the child evolves a variety of thought in which he projects himself into the future and attempts to organize his world for satisfactions to be attained at a later time. By using his past, he attempts to organize his future through thought to both avoid dangers and attain pleasures.

A distinction is made between the type of prelogical emotional thinking or fantasy of the young child, which emerges as well in states of fatigue, intoxication, or psychoses, and the dreams of adults. Designated by psychoanalysts as *primary process thinking,* it is highly charged affectively. Its images are relatively unorganized, usually visual, and/or subject to the ego defensive operations of condensation, displacement, and symbolization. In contradistinction to primary process thinking, *secondary process thinking* is highly organized and logical and is related to ordered word representation or abstractions concerned with the realities of the external world.

The Uses of Fantasy

The child's capacity to separate himself from the early fantasy world and to achieve freedom for organizational thought depends not only on his innate intellectual endowment, but also upon the preservation of his curiosity and a limitation of early fears and anxieties. The parental relationship again, through its capacities for guiding the child's exploratory behavior, protecting him from too great arousal of emotions, allows the potentiality for gaining a period of autonomous thought, free from the intrusive and disturbing fantasies of early infancy and childhood just described. Thereby his capacity for the progressive differentiations, generalizations, transfers, and recombinations that constitute new conceptualizations and underlie creative thought and productive human activity is fostered by contact with adults who desire to impart their knowledge and protect the child through their own mature behavior from behavioral sequences that lead to emotional fixations and repetitive intrusion of immature fantasies.

In the next chapter the deleterious effects on mentation due to isolation from others will be described as an etiologic factor in the disruption of personality functioning. However, it must be mentioned that the healthy individual often finds periods of limited isolation highly significant in terms of creative thinking. In such instances it may be surmised that numerous perceptions and registrations from the past are brought to preconscious and conscious states that allow their associations and recombinations for purposes of gaining new insights and solutions of formerly insoluble problems. There are on record numerous instances of sudden insights leading to highly important scientific discoveries which took place under such circumstances. Kekulé's conceptualization of the benzene ring is one of the best known.

Such emergent and creative thought

is considered by some to take place through associative linkage between repressed primary and secondary thought processes. If such is the case, the suggestion of Noy that primary processes be considered not as an infantile side of thinking but rather as one of two ongoing and continuously developing processes of thought must receive serious consideration. To him, primary processes of thinking are used for all functions aimed at preserving self-continuity and identity, and for assimilation (as used by Piaget) of new experiences and lines of action into the life scheme. Secondary process thinking is used for encountering reality, for integration and mastery in relation to reality. The latter is subject to continuous feedback from the environment; only portions of the former are so directed. Both methods of thinking continue throughout life, and both mature through experience during the life span. For most of daily living the secondary, reality-centered thought fills consciousness. Secondary process is concerned with processing more and more information, of representing complex events by quick and effective symbols and signs—the bits of conceptual thinking. This is in contrast to the more subjectively oriented primary process concerned with assimilating feelings, ideas, memories, and values and integrating them into the self system.

The sudden emergence of a new creative act perhaps occurs at moments of reflection or withdrawal from ongoing external feedback, allowing the emergence of new insight. Much of the recent Western fascination with experiencing altered states of consciousness by drug usage and transcendental meditation has been caused by the possibility of release of creative insights during withdrawal from secondary process thought and the limiting of external stimulation and ordinary perception.

An encounter with reality may be processed first by the logical thought activities and later dealt with in dream and fantasy. The coalescence of these several processes achieves mastery sometimes in the sudden insight. Or the emergence of a personal motivation may emerge in fantasy or dream, to be worked through by secondary process thought. These suggestions do not dismiss the continued existence of early life primary process condensations which may arise, in consciousness, in psychotic or neurotic imagery of thought, or in dream or fantasy.

Other Adaptive Processes

In the last chapter we mentioned the existence of certain ego assets as important in defining the total personality. The relative strength of such ongoing attitudes or conative sets as trust, autonomy, initiative, as well as others, is not well understood. The sets of personal responsibility, perseverance, humor, commitment, courage, curiosity, flexibility, and empathy must be recognized as powerful forces in ongoing attempts at coping with both acute and enduring stresses to the individual personality.

DEFENSIVE PROCESSES

Through the long period of development, the personality acquires various psychological techniques by which it attempts to defend itself, establish compromises between conflicting impulses, and allay inner tensions. These functions of the ego are internal mechanisms of control, operative below the level of conscious awareness. The personality develops defenses designed to manage anxiety, aggressive impulses, hostilities, resentments, and frustrations. All of us make continual use of defense mechanisms. In themselves they are not necessarily pathological. Life would be unbearable without resort to rationalization and similar psychic protections. Neither it is always the goal of therapy to eliminate them. Since at times they may promote the individual's ability to live in peace with himself or herself, it may, in fact, be a therapeutic objective to strengthen them. The type of motivating device unconsciously selected to meet emotional needs and stresses and to provide a defense against anxiety, the extent of its employment, and the degree to which it distorts the personality, dominates the behavior, and disturbs the adjustment with others determine the measure of mental health. Processes similar in kind take place, therefore, in both the "normal" and the "abnormal."

Conflict

Unfortunately, the conscious desires of the individual, the recognition he craves, and the gratification of biological impulses with which he was endowed are frequently not compatible with the conventionally sanctioned habits, attitudes, demands, and values of the larger social group of which he is a member, nor with the prohibiting and censoring forces of his personality. Conscious and unconscious forces pursue incompatible goals. A struggle exists between two powerful incompatible response-tendencies—between the attitudes, habits, and values absorbed from the family, school, church, and various other carriers of ethical and moral standards and traditions on the one hand, and unconscious needs and strivings on the other.

The dilemma in which the individual is impelled by mutually incompatible mental forces and irreconcilable, competing impulses and personality needs is known as a *psychic conflict*. The conflict may be thought of as a clashing—an internal struggle—between different parts of the personality. According to psychoanalytical theory, many conflicts have their origin in the early struggles of infancy and childhood but through repression become inaccessible to conscious introspection. In this dynamic clashing of impulses, the individual is torn between his conflictful drives, his wishes and aversions, his loves and hostilities, his fears and longings, his urges and resistances. His satisfactions, stability, and peace of mind may be seriously disturbed because of conflict between his drives and wishes on the one hand, and the codes, traditions, beliefs, and loyalties which he has adopted from his social group on the other.

There is, as it were, a civil war within the personality. The individual is driven simultaneously toward behaviors of opposite types. The personality becomes divided against itself, and a sense of tension or inner restlessness exists. It is the task of personality, often a difficult and painful one, to establish a compromise satisfactory to its conflictful strivings. Frequently it is not successful, and as a result the individual experiences anxiety, a condition of diffuse apprehension and of heightened and persistent inner tension.

Anxiety

Conflict induces the affect of *anxiety*, considered central to the understanding of the psychodynamic processes. Anxiety is generally considered now as a state of tension signaling the potentiality of an impending disaster, a warning of danger from the pressure of unacceptable internal attitudes erupting into either consciousness or action, with the consequent responses of the individual personality or society to this eruption. To put it in another way, in the face of emerging aggressive or sexual drives, the tension of loneliness or sadness or the revelation of love or tenderness, which might expose the individual to suffering of affects of guilt or shame, anxiety is first felt in the context of the conflict situation.

While anxiety and *fear* have much in common, in that both represent signals of danger, there are certain fundamental differences. Fear is the affective response to an actual, current danger. It subsides with the elimination of the threatening situation through conquest or escape. The danger most frequently is to the physical integrity of the individual, whether from the threat of illness or from an external physical attack. Anxiety, on the other hand, may be thought of as the signal of an impending threat to the personality in the context of the social environment. Sullivan has provided a useful operational definition of anxiety in this context. He describes anxiety as a state of tension existing when one apprehends an unfavorable estimate by a significant person. The sufferer of anxiety is at best dimly aware of the conflict, aware only of the state of dread.

During development of personality, various mental mechanisms evolve to protect the individual from anxiety and other affects and their physiological accompaniments. These are described and illustrated in the following paragraphs. Overt anxiety and its associated physiological expressions are observed only when the defensive mental mechanisms break down as the consequence of overwhelming inner or outer threat to the personality.

Serious personality disorder exists when personality functioning is limited through repetitive and inflexible use of a limited number of "narcissistic" and "immature" ego defense mechanisms. Such defensive limitation may occur either through arousal of intense and ongoing anxiety as the consequence of persistent conflict within the personality, or through failures to evolve a full and unlimited range of potential psychological devices useful in warding off and protecting from impairing intensities of affective arousal.

Psychotic behavior is characterized by the use of such defenses as delusional projection, denial, fantasy, regression, symbolization, and acting out. The neurotic will more frequently utilize repression, isolation (intellectualization), reaction formation, displacement, or dissociation. For both there will be a limitation or lack of effective balance in the personality's ego adaptive attitudes. (See Table 5–1.) This chapter contains descriptions of those ego defensive processes related particularly to the explanation of psychopathology.

Repression

One of the commonest of mental mechanisms developed for the purpose of dealing with conflict, i.e., with irreconcilable desires, competing strivings, tendencies toward acts that constitute a threat to the image we have of ourselves, is that of *repression*. By this mechanism, desires, impulses, thoughts, and strivings incompatible with, or disturbing to, the individual's conscious self-requirements and motivations are excluded from the field of conscious awareness, being pushed into the unconscious. Here, through a psychological inhibition of recall, they remain inaccessible so that they may not be recognized and give rise to unbearable anxiety. Repression acts as a defense against drives and memories that cannot be controlled by the ego. It is not produced by a deliberate and conscious effort or rejection on the part of the person in whom it operates. Rather, it is an involuntary repudiation or denial, a nonconscious process acting automatically. Experiences involving guilt, shame, or the lowering of self-esteem are particularly apt to be repressed. In repression there is an elimination from consciousness of unrecognized motives and of all ideas or memories that might tend to arouse a painful anxiety.

Impulses that the ego cannot handle except by repression nevertheless retain their dynamic drive and tension. They continue to lead a subterranean life beneath a conventional surface, yet they are liable to manifest their influence in traits of personality, in special interests, in some system of beliefs or code of values, or in more marked form as neurotic, psychosomatic, or psychotic symptoms. Frequently, repressed material may be dealt with rationally if it can become conscious. It is therefore often desirable to make such

TABLE 5-1   Ego Defense Mechanisms*

EGO MECHANISM	SYMONDS	BIBRING ET AL.	A. FREUD	FENICHEL
Delusional projection	—	*Level I—"Narcissistic"*	—	—
Denial (psychotic) (1894)	—	Denial	Denial	—
Distortion (1896)	—	? Depersonalization	Distortion	Denial
Projection (1895)	Projection	*Level II—"Immature"* Projection	Projection	Projection
Schizoid fantasy (1908)	Fantasy	Denial through fantasy	Denial through fantasy	—
Hypochondriasis (1896)	—	Falling ill	Introjection	Introjection
Passive-aggressive behavior (1915)	Compromise formation	Compliance	Turning against the self	—
Acting out	—	Acting out	—	—
Intellectualization (1894)	Intellectualization, undoing, isolation	*Level III—"Neurotic"* Intellectualization, undoing, isolation	Intellectualization, undoing, isolation	Isolation, undoing
Repression (1894)	Repression	Repression	Repression	Repression
Displacement (1894)	Displacement	Displacement	Displacement	Displacement
Reaction formation (1905)	Reaction formation	Reaction formation	Reaction formation	Reaction formation
Dissociation (1893)	? Regression	Affectualization, counterphobia	Reversal	—
Altruism (1916–1917)	Regression	*Level IV—"Mature"* Altruistic surrender	Altruism	Sublimation
Humor (1905)	—	Avoidance, withdrawal	—	—
Suppression (1894)	—	Control through thinking	—	—
Anticipation	—		—	—
Sublimation (1905)	Sublimation	Sublimation	Sublimation	Sublimation

*Years in parentheses indicate the dates Freud considered these problems.
Modified from Vaillant, G. E.: Arch. Gen. Psychiatry, 24:107–118, 1971.

recall possible. As will be pointed out later, this may be done by the technique known as free association.

Repression, then, is a primary defense against anxiety which is likely to arise when unbearable ideas and impulses threaten to enter conscious awareness. From a different point of view, one may think of repression as having been induced by anxiety rather than the reverse. In either case, the present tendency is to think of repression as the cornerstone of dynamic psychiatry. If repression is unable to prevent anxiety, then other mechanisms, such as projection or symbolization, may be called on to assist in its failing efforts. If repression breaks down, the capacity for evaluating reality may be impaired and infantile defenses disregardful of reality may be called into action. These may, for example, permit patients to disown an unacceptable impulse or threatening feeling of hostility by having it attributed to a source, perhaps a voice, outside themselves. As we come to consider symptoms, we shall find that the patterns of defense against anxiety may be of various and even of changing forms.

By forbidding the undisguised expression of instinctive strivings and socially forbidden tendencies, repression operates to maintain ethical and social conventions, thus assisting the individual in adjusting to the mores and social institutions. Unfortunately, repression is not without disadvantages. Deep-seated drives and urges are not destroyed by repression; on the contrary, although automatically restrained, they remain unchanged in quality and intensity. These drives and urges are, in fact, unmodified in any respect save that the individual is not consciously aware of the disowned strivings. Though frustrated, they constantly seek satisfaction. To make sure, however, that the undesired awareness and expression of these strivings and wishes may not be permitted, the personality functions automatically and without conscious de-

liberation to crush the strivings, wishes, and thoughts and to reverse their effect by the cultivation and promotion of characteristics sharply opposed in nature. These contrasting aims and efforts, designed to reinforce repression, lead to the formation of prejudices and of pronounced character defenses known as *reaction-formations*. These will be discussed later in the chapter. The more repressions a person has, the more prejudices and biases he develops in order to prevent the arousal of his repressed desires. Similarly, intolerance of the wrongdoings of others is often indicative of the effort required to repress similar unrecognized tendencies on his own part.

Repression is not always pathological and its results undesirable. If it operates smoothly and without undue effort, this mechanism may result in a well-adjusted life. In some instances, repression and other mechanisms designed to deal with conflicts and unacceptable impulses may result in the formation of qualities of character that are estimable and yet, because of the sources from which those qualities have arisen, the psychological purposes and needs they fulfill, and the uncompromising tenacity with which they are pursued, they must be looked upon as psychopathological products. We need not be unduly concerned about the genetic source and psychodynamic function that these commendable personality traits are serving. Such desirable character traits might be characterized as representing the conversion of liabilities into assets. Many personality traits serve the same psychological purpose as do neurotic symptoms. Intolerance, submissiveness, meticulousness, extreme shyness, and other traits may, like neurotic symptoms, be developed as protection against an awareness of early fear, hate, or resentment long buried in the unconsciousness.

Repression should not be confused with *suppression,* in which a conscious effort is made to dismiss repudiated strivings and undesired memories from awareness.

Conscious Control

From what has been said, it is plain that repression is a mechanism that, when employed, operates without conscious recognition. The most successful adjustment to life conditions is not possible if there are tendencies or feelings of which one is not aware so that they are therefore beyond the reach of control. The motives directing our behavior cannot be guided into desirable constructive channels unless their hidden sources are exposed to the light of full consciousness, permitting us to face all the facts and direct our promptings by the mechanism of conscious control. It enables us to replace automatic adaptations and repressions by conscious and flexible adjustments. Likewise, if we can learn to recognize and understand our mechanisms of escape and defense, we may exercise a greater measure of conscious control. Conscious control requires a realistic and efficient capacity for perceiving, deciding, and regulating—that is, a strong ego.

Identification

Identification is the most important of the psychological mechanisms for determining the growth of the ego. As mentioned in the discussion of personality development, the child takes over the attitudes and behavior patterns of his parents and others significant to him. The motivation for identification is wish-fulfillment, in that the child admires or aspires to the strength and qualities of his elders and their associates and attempts to gain for himself their patterns of success by acquiring their modes of behavior. Identification contributes also to the growth of the superego functions. Thus a son may identify with his father and mold his personality on that of his parent, following his patterns of behavior and in-

terest and sharing his ways. This mechanism is not one of conscious deliberation nor of simple imitation.

The process of identification takes place in the family setting and is related to the child's drive to mastery, and excitement in novelty. It occurs in the repeated transactions of separation from the supporting parents, first from the mother, as the child gains mobility to move away from her and to explore little by little. Later he seeks strength for other tasks in his imitative play—attempts to assimilate the actions of parents, teachers, playmates, and others. Significant identification demands continued reinforcement through constancy of the presence of persons to whom the child relates, and through the child's gaining a sense of competence and rising self-esteem from the use of the identified actions.

Successive identifications over time gradually evolve into *adult individuation*—a firm personal identity separate from the pathological identifications characteristic of psychopathology.

Early and traumatic separations from parents sometimes stimulate drives toward "parenting identities"—such as over-anxious concerns for children, pets, or others.

Although identification provides a means for constructive influence on personality growth, this depends upon the personality of those to whom the child is exposed. A child may take on, as well, the socially undesirable characteristics of a parent if these appear to him to provide some special strength or merit. This occurrence is sometimes referred to as *hostile identification*. The brutality of young Germans preceding and during World War II may be interpreted as hostile identification with the actions of the Nazi storm troopers of that time. Identification is seldom complete, since the personality of the admired person is never perceived in its totality by either child or adult. Certain traits alone may be picked up and assumed.

A young male school teacher was observed by his friends to change in the sense that he developed an erect posture and spoke to them looking over his glasses with a precise and clipped speech. He had moved from one city to another to assist in teaching under an outstanding superintendent of schools. His friends were surprised, on meeting the superintendent, to note that his posture and speech were those assumed by their friend.

Identification may be wish-fulfilling in its psychological purpose. This function may, for example, be observed in the self-gratifying sense of superiority felt by the servant of a distinguished personage with whom he identifies himself, or again it may explain the self-satisfaction of the psychotic patient who believes he is Christ and who, to complete the role, wears his hair and beard in the manner in which Christ is ordinarily represented.

Through this mechanism, certain circumstances, including relationships with certain people, may be selected because they fit into specific personality needs. The exaggerated sympathy at times shown by one person for another (even though the second person may be charged with some serious legal offense) results from identification —from a certain unconscious sensing of a common quality of impulse shared with the second individual. Through this mechanism, some desire may be vicariously satisfied, any fulfillment or even a conscious recognition of which would not be knowingly permitted. The false confessions of crime of which one occasionally reads in the newspapers are the results of identification which is based on a desire to commit the confessed offense.

The mechanism sometimes is utilized repetitively by those who have failed to establish a well-organized personality identity. As mentioned before, stable identifications require the presence over time of constant and reliable models, who provide emotional support and encouragement.

Pathological identifications are those wherein the ego attempts to achieve a sense of power through magical efforts of symbiosis with an ideal. Thus pseudo-identifications occur that are often transient, stilted, or caricatured, and that fail to relate convincingly to others. Now referred to in psychoanalytic writings as *"as if"* characters, such persons strive for security by successively attaching themselves to one person after another in whom they perceive some desired strengths. Many attempt to take on their wished-for traits. Since such identifications represent an infantile wish-fulfillment, these are usually transient and cast off when the seeker for a magical security loses or feels rejected by his current supportive image.

TRANSFERENCE. As thus far described, identification is an individual's unconscious molding of himself after the fashion of another or his feeling of a sort of effective oneness with a second person. It is more than the conscious modeling of a child after the pattern of a loved and admired parent.

In a second type of identification, more properly recognized as *transference*, the image of one person is unconsciously identified with that of another. The more recent acquaintance becomes the surrogate of the person previously known and is invested with the same attitudes and emotions with which the individual has come to surround the image of the original party. Here identification is transferred and projected on to the other. This explains some of our apparently causeless likes and dislikes of persons whom we have unwittingly identified with other persons who had once aroused similar emotions. A person representing authority may come to be identified with a tyrannical father, and the surrogate may be regarded with the same emotions as was the original image. This is doubtless the dynamic determinant of the activity shown by some persons who constantly struggle against the regulations and institutions of society. Hostile and other negative feelings having their original source in attitudes created in early childhood may be displaced or transferred to others in later life and thereby seriously distort human relationships.

EMPATHY. *Empathy* is a healthy form of identification that is limited and temporary, but enables one person to feel for and with another and to understand the other's experiences and feelings. Empathetic individuals possess a warm capacity for projecting themselves into the situations and feelings of others. They also reflectively stand outside of the other and maintain their own sense of personal identity. This quality will be found only in those with a flexible, mature, and well-established personality.

INTROJECTION. *Introjection* is best understood as a development in an earlier phase of personality than that during which identification occurs. The child introjects or perceives pleasure-pain experiences from which there are derived "good" or "bad" images of the self. In these early experiences the child hardly discriminates between his need and the gratifying or denying source. Thus, satisfaction or frustration of the need is unrelated to its human source and taken in as part of the childish personality. Identification, on the other hand, occurs after the child has been able to differentiate himself clearly from others; it originates in well-defined perceptions of others rather than in the primitive perceptions of inner bodily sensations. Introjection is the obverse of *projection*, to be discussed later.

INCORPORATION. *Incorporation*, another psychoanalytic term, refers to a defense in which a lost or abandoned source of identification is introduced into the ego structure without transformation of the ego. It takes place with an open expression of unneutralized aggression toward the incorporated object. With incorporation, representation of the self becomes like representation of the hated object.

A young married woman was referred for treatment by her husband because of her recent crying spells, self-denunciation and deprecation, and inability to care for her home and infant. She quickly stated that her mother was frequently in tears, held her on her lap only then, and constantly denounced the injustices done her. The patient stated she was afraid she was like her mother and she disliked herself for these traits.

Reaction-Formation

Another important device for the establishment of character is that known as *reaction-formation*. This is a character trait that is usually the exact opposite of what would follow naturally from the expression of unfettered tendencies, a trait developed to maintain the repression of these impulses and to deny and disguise personality trends that have existed under cover. Perfectionistic and uncompromising character traits are often reaction-formations against forbidden tendencies, desires, or impulses. Often such traits unwittingly reveal troublesome aspects of the personality. The defensive character of conspicuous traits and attitudes is betrayed by the very quality of their exaggeration and at times by their inappropriateness. Such overemphasized character and personality traits may be described as constituting the first line of psychological defense. They can scarcely be called pathological unless they disturb adjustment. Feelings of rejection and hostility may be disguised by scrupulous politeness or effusive expressions of gratitude. So far as conscious intention is concerned, a reaction-formation is always honest and sincere. The overtly aggressive person, constantly demanding his rights and ready to fight at any provocation, may be defending himself against a deeply seated sense of insecurity. On the other hand, submissiveness may be a reaction-formation that serves to cover up unrecognized aggressive tendencies. A façade of excessive amiability may conceal intense hostility.

Great concern for a certain person may be a disguise for unrecognized feelings of hostility, jealousy, or even wishes for the person's death. Beneath devotion may lurk a concealed wish for death—e.g., of a widowed mother for whom a spinster daughter has sacrificed herself and refused an offer of marriage. Such devotion serves to appease a sense of guilt. If employed within rational limits, reaction-formation may be a desirable choice of defense against anxiety.

The unmarried sibling of an identical twin pair presented himself for treatment due to mounting anxiety over his flagrant promiscuous homosexual activity. His brother was happily married. He described his adolescent hatred of his mother for her betrayal of the family in a sordid extramarital affair and his conviction that he could obtain a trusting relationship only with another man—like his brother—indicating that no woman could be trusted. Later he revealed his close and tender relationship with his mother during early boyhood and his expressed wish for a similar feminine companion. The homosexual orientation represented a spiteful reaction-formation against the, to him, fearful wish for a woman.

Compensation

Physiological and physical compensations are phenomena that the internist and the surgeon observe daily. If a valve of the heart is incompetent, the heart muscle hypertrophies in order to compensate for the impairment in circulation that would otherwise result from the valvular defect. If a spinal scoliosis develops from disease or faulty habits of posture, a secondary curve, opposite in direction to the primary one, is produced above or below the former in order that the center of gravity may not be displaced. Such compensations represent attempts of organs to adjust to physiological defects and inadequacies. Similarly, the organism as a whole, in distinction from its component organs, by compensating for its inadequacies and imperfections attempts to secure the recognition it craves.

Such compensations may easily become exaggerated and are often unwittingly betrayed by behavior. The person of small stature but with aggressive and dominating traits is an example of overcompensation familiar to all. His pompous and pretentious manner may have been adopted to indicate the strength and authority which a diminutive size fails to suggest. His deportment may make the undersized person feel more comfortable and secure and help him forget his physical inadequacies.

Prestige seems to be one of the fundamental needs of the personality. Methods of enhancing our self-esteem and of covering up deficiencies are widespread and vary from the simple showing off seen daily on the playground or the pretentious displays of unusual dress or symbols of material success to the formations of delusions of grandeur. It should not be forgotten, moreover, that socially acceptable degrees of compensation and even admirable personality traits may be an expression of neurotic needs. Their neurotic origin is often betrayed by the striking degree to which they are developed.

Handicaps and limitations, as factors in the production of compensatory products, may be of a widely diversified nature, being in some instances physical, in others mental. The inferiority, too, which lies at the basis of compensatory mechanisms may be either real or fancied. In persons whose reactions in relation to reality in general and to social stimuli in particular are well integrated, the existence of a physical inferiority may provoke constructive activities, which result in qualities of outstanding social usefulness. Handicaps may spur one on to greater efforts, as in the case of Wordsworth's happy warrior who "turned his necessity to glorious gain." On the other hand, diseases or deformities that thwart normal instincts or ambitions or cause the individual to stand out unpleasantly from the group may fail to promote desirable qualities of the personality but may lead to wishful thinking, unpleasant traits, or even at times to a psychotic sacrifice of reality. In whatever form manifested, the products represent the results of the personality's efforts to attain a satisfying self-esteem and sense of security. All too often, unfortunately, the mechanism leads to overcompensations which, although satisfying to the individual, are fictitious so far as social values are concerned.

A boy who was so tall, angular, and ungainly that he had always been extremely self-conscious enlisted in the Army. (It is quite probable that, without consciously realizing it, he had been prompted to enlist because the military uniform and a certain glamor connected with the military life seemed to offer hope of relief from the unpleasant sense of being different.) Here he soon became an object of raillery because of his clumsiness in attempting to execute the various drills. After having struggled in vain for adeptness, the boy was placed in the "awkward squad," where he naturally felt even more self-conscious and more painfully aware of his deficiencies. The indignity suffered by his self-esteem was too great; the need of his personality for a more satisfying recognition and for a sense of security exceeded its limited resources and he therefore constructed a fictitious substitute by developing the belief that he was a major general. He was no longer the awkward soldier, unable to compete with his associates, but their commander, directing affairs of great military importance. The compensatory delusion satisfied the recruit's emotional needs but destroyed his usefulness for the realities of military life and required his hospitalization.

Rationalization

Probably none of us realizes the extent to which the mental mechanisms operative in our everyday lives are defensive in nature. One of the commonest of these devices designed to maintain self-respect and prevent feelings of guilt is that of rationalization, a term introduced into psychiatric literature by Ernest Jones.

We prefer to believe that our behavior is the result of thoughtful deliberation, unbiased judgment, and full awareness of all the motives prompting it. As a matter of fact, only to a minor extent is behavior the result of such conscious intellectual considerations. After we have acted in response to these unrecognized motives, we formulate presentable reasons that we believe determined our conduct, although they are really but *ex post facto* justifications. This mechanism provides rational intellectual explanations of behavior that has really been prompted by unrecognized motives. We think we can fully explain our conduct but are deceived by pseudorational explanations. Our real desires and attitudes remain concealed and disguised.

At times certain of our rationalizations contain a minor element of truth which, however, is so unduly emphasized that it serves to conceal the essential prompting motive. Those motives that are acceptable are selected and considered to be the only ones. Our thinking defends our feeling. Since we believe that our behavior ought to be determined by certain motives, rationalization through its self-deception leads us to believe that it is. In fact, several motives usually combine and are operative in originating our behavior, some of them having a distinctly ethical value. Other components are of a more selfish, emotional, or instinctive nature.

When behavior is determined by such a coalescence of motives, it will be found that the individual selects the most acceptable from the complex group to explain his behavior. The more self-centered and instinctive ones are the more dynamic, and these exercise greater influence in determining behavior, yet they are not those recognized in consciousness as determinative of it. The motives that are the highest from an ethical standpoint are those that dominate consciousness and are therefore offered as the real motives, although they are of less influence in determining behavior than are the unrecognized components.

The student may ask whether or not

the individual is aware that the reasons he offers for his behavior are not the actual ones so that he is guilty of a falsehood. In a lie, one consciously knows that the reason is fictitious. Rationalization is so thoroughly a nonconscious mechanism, one does not recognize that motives cannot always be taken at face value. To employ rationalization in discussing his behavior does not mean that he is not honest and sincere. The self-deceptions of rationalization are usually defended with great emotional intensity, since their creation was designed to conceal a truth that would be painful to the ego.

Rationalization is a mechanism that serves a useful purpose insofar as it is conducive to psychic self-protection and comfort. It leads, however, to self-deception and its conclusions are untrustworthy guides for further conduct. Its products, which are often employed deductively as premises, are so fallacious that they may readily contribute to the formation of delusions.

A not uncommon reaction closely allied to rationalization, which helps to maintain self-esteem in the face of inadequacy, is the depreciation often spoken of as "sour grapes." In this defensive devaluation reaction, the individual disparages some particular goal which, inwardly at least, he would greatly like to attain but which, because of some obstacle, often personal inadequacy, he cannot reach. Depreciating that for which one is unqualified is frequent. It is, of course, one form of response to anxiety. Somewhat allied as a defensive mechanism is a blasé indifference in the face of circumstances that would naturally offend self-esteem.

Substitution

Substitution is a mechanism which may be employed to reduce tension resulting from frustration. Through it are secured alternative or substitutive gratifications comparable to those that would have been enjoyed had frustration not occurred. To yield satisfaction and reduce tension, the substitutive action must have certain similarities to the frustrated one. Many psychiatric symptoms represent substitutive and symbolic satisfactions.

In the effort to solve a conflict, the organism has available to itself the options of (1) continuing to strive toward the desired goal; (2) overcoming the obstacles to achievement of the goal by some aggressive drive; or (3) avoiding or fleeing from the obstacle. Among the adjustments possible in personality functioning when it is not possible to utilize aggression or avoidance is the acceptance of a substitute goal or insight. Such a potential exists when the commitment to the goal or the use of a particular adaptive technique prevents the individual from relinquishing that goal. If he is so committed, frustration and the inevitable affective response must follow, although defense against the latter may be achieved with some other mental mechanism.

Displacement

Another anxiety-reducing device which also operates by a process of substitution is displacement. By this defense mechanism, an emotional feeling is transferred from its actual object to a substitute. The feeling originally directed toward a certain person, object, or situation is transferred and attached to another person, object, or situation, which becomes invested with the emotional significance originally associated with the former. In a phobia, for example, there is an unconscious transfer of fear and threat from its original hidden and internal unconscious source to another one, which is external and apparently unrelated insofar as the patient is consciously aware. In the frequent handwashing observed in certain compulsive neuroses, affect is displaced from an earlier experience in which a feeling of moral uncleanness was associated with the idea of dirt.

Dirt then evokes the feeling value originally attached to the consciously repudiated experience.

A 30-year-old housewife entered the hospital for treatment of a phobic condition which prevented her from leaving her home. Her condition started after the birth of her third child, when she developed feelings of panic associated with the idea of being sexually attacked. In treatment she proved to have been very dependent since early childhood and to be seductive. She eventually revealed that in her desire to have men care for her she feared loss of sexual control to the point of becoming a prostitute. This anxiety was displaced by fear of street walking.

Feelings and attitudes, such as love and hate, are particularly apt to be displaced from one person to someone else, who comes to be a surrogate for the first person. A feeling of hostility toward a parent may, for example, be so intense that it cannot be consciously entertained. By shifting the hatred to someone who has a resemblance to the parent, the person may be protected against conscious recognition of his attitude toward the parent.

In many instances, symbolism is a kind of displacement. An object becomes a symbol of the person or thing that originally stimulated the feeling or impulse. Displacement enables the individual to maintain repression of dangerous or unacceptable impulses, wishes, or thoughts. The displacement of anxiety from the significant to the less significant is common. Allied to displacement is the mechanism described by Freud whereby the conscious may defend itself from material in the unconscious by treating it as a joke.

Restitution

The mechanism of relieving the mind of a load of guilt by restitutive acts (a making up for, or reparation) is common. Restitution arising from feelings of guilt may become the main motive in life, as exemplified by the indefatigably, almost wearisomely, benevolent person. Operating to a less extreme degree and in a less obvious manner, the restitutive reaction to unconscious guilt may play a large part in a drive toward creativeness.

Projection

This mechanism is, in many respects, a form of displacement, a means of defense which, to a limited degree, one may observe daily among his associates and which is seen to a psychotic degree in paranoia and in other paranoid psychoses. Acting as a defense against anxiety, projection is directed outward; it attributes to other persons those objectionable character traits, attitudes, motives, and desires one wishes to disclaim. The mechanism enables one to remain blind to important drives in the personality, while their influence distorts one's picture of the outside world.

One constantly meets people who severely criticize in other persons the very faults that are the weak points of their own character, utterly failing to recognize that they themselves possess the despised traits and motives. The material projected might be said to be an echo of the projector's own unconscious. By projection, one's own aggressive designs and id impulses are attributed to others. Through it, repudiated tendencies find outlet.

Feelings of guilt which give rise to anxiety may be alleviated if one is able to cast the blame for shameful tendencies or wishes onto the outer world, leaving one's self guiltless or even victimized. One may feel less guilty, too, if someone else can be made to feel guilty. As a further defense against anxiety, one may respond with hostility and aggressive behavior toward the external object that is the focus of projection. Some treat others with projections of certain of their own unconscious trends — hate, fear, and similar feelings. Often they hold others responsible for their difficulties.

It will be noted that projection is closely associated with the mechanism of denial. This is well illustrated by the formula stated by Freud: A, unable to tolerate the anxiety aroused by his hatred of B, unconsciously changes his attitude, "I hate B," to "B hates me." Repression and projection protect the ego from being overwhelmed or disorganized by the effects of aggression, hate, or guilt.

Sometimes a striving for supremacy and security by persons who, compared with others, are actually or in imagination at a disadvantage in life may lead to projection as a defensive means. If the ego fails or becomes disorganized, other phenomena — hallucinations, ideas of reference, and delusions — often become associated with projection.

DELUSIONS AND PROJECTIONS. Material may be projected in the form either of ideas or of perceptions. In the former case, projection may lead to the formation of delusions, particularly ones of persecution.

During the World War an American soldier, in order to escape from a highly dangerous situation, shot himself in the foot. He was first treated in an Army hospital and later transferred to the United States, where the self-inflicted wound healed slowly. The retrospective discomfort or sense of guilt created by his cowardice and dereliction was alleviated psychologically by projection. He believed that the delay in the healing of the wound was a result of neglect on the part of the physician. The soldier felt no self-reproach since it was not he but the physician who was culpable. He was, of course, quite unaware that the attempt he later made on the life of the physician was an effort to destroy *qualities of which he was the actual possessor.*

Such a projection stimulated by a sense of guilt is at times one of the important mechanisms in the production of paranoia. By this mechanism, a patient may persuade himself that his persecutor is so unspeakably evil that he deserves death, and to kill him, far from being a criminal act, is a laudable one.

HALLUCINATIONS AND PROJECTION. Frequently in the psychotic, the disowned aspects of the personality are projected, not in terms of ideation but in terms of perception. In such a case, the repressed mental material or unacceptable tendencies, striving, or qualities may be externalized in the form of hallucinated voices accusing the patient of practices that represent the rejected aspects.

The soldier just mentioned, in his effort to kill the physician, naturally did not destroy the sense of guilt produced by the violations of his code of mental honor, nor did his attempt to kill his physician destroy the despised defects of character. Finally, their projection led to a still greater distortion of reality in the form of hallucinations. One day, as he was walking along a city street, he heard accusing remarks that seemed to refer to him. Glancing about, he saw that the person in the direction from which the accusing voices apparently came was the driver of a passing automobile. Without warning, the former soldier shot and killed the man. Thus he killed a person who, by projection, had become the representative and incarnation of his own hated but unrecognized qualities.

IDEAS OF REFERENCE. The symptom known as *ideas of reference* arises through the operation of the mechanism of projection. The individual who utilizes this type of projective mechanism egocentrically believes that he is the object of special and ill-disposed attention by those about him. Casual remarks by others, for example, are understood as relating to him and interpreted as accusatory or vilifying.

Symbolization

At first people communicated with each other through the use of concrete objects, but with the development of language they used words in place of objects. Gradually words were employed to represent ideas as well as objects. Similarly, objects became the symbols or substitutes for ideas, feelings, and tendencies. *Symbolization* with its meaning-carrying signs is therefore a mechanism whereby one idea or object is employed to represent some other idea or object. It is characteristic that words or objects used are significantly charged with meaning. This arises from the fact that the displacement of emotional values from the object to the symbol is the essence of symbolization. Symbolization is a mechanism extensively employed in psychopathology.

We have seen that conflicting drives and· ideas, or groups of associated ideas, with which painful emotions are associated may be repressed because they are distressing to the conscious personality. Since they are denied direct, conscious, and frank expression, the repressed impulses and other psychic content break through and obtain expression at the conscious level in a disguised symbolic form. The wish or drive, therefore, that cannot be acknowledged consciously may be dealt with or satisfied in a symbolic manner.

The resemblance between the symbol and the object symbolized is generally so slight or superficial that the conscious mind will overlook it. The individual is, therefore, quite unaware of the meaning of the symbol he has employed; indeed, he is often unaware that he has used one. at all. To his conscious mind, the symbol is not a symbol; it is reality in and of itself. He therefore treats symbols as if they were real and directs his behavior in accordance with the affective value with which the symbols are invested.

In both the normal and the psychotic individual, repressed material may be expressed through symbolism. The symbolism could be manifested in forms of esthetic value by an artist, but most often is disguised and difficult to read. It is frequently said that symbolism is the language of the unconscious. Symbolism characteristic of neurotic and psychotic processes is related to primary process thinking. It differs, then, from words or other symbols used for purposes of rational thought and communication. In symbolism, the defense of repression is inaction. Appearing in the content of dreams, hallucinations, and obscure or apparently meaningless ideas, symbols express particularly those contents of the individual's inner life with which much feeling is connected.

The disguises under which such material may be manifested are numerous. Various affectations of dress, gait, speech, or manner as observed among persons who are never regarded as suffering from mental disorder are often' symbolic disguises expressing products of repression.

A recently married woman was admitted to a hospital for treatment because of her unusual behavior. She stood on her head, was mute, and would communicate by using ball point pens which wrote in red ink. Later she explained her behavior as a means of expressing her anger at her husband for taking her money. She was in love with him so could not speak of her rage, yet the red ink symbolized it. Standing on her head represented both a defiant gesture and a wish for help by being found ill.

Dreams, which are products of thinking that lack the awareness and direction supplied by consciousness, involve various processes, one of the most frequent of which is symbolization. Although not all dreams contain symbolic material and not all psychiatrists agree as to the interpretation to be placed upon dream imagery, many of the images and experiences of dreams represent such products of repression as unacknowledged motives and desires.

Fixation

We know that from infancy to maturity there should be a progressive development, differentiation, and maturation in the instinctive, emotional, and other aspects of the personality. Unfortunately, the development of some aspect of the personality may be halted at an incomplete stage of its evolution with a resulting persistence of certain incompletely matured elements. Such a personality shows a lack of harmonious integration. Its emotional organization, particularly, remains at an immature level, and there is a lag between biological status and emotional independence.

This cessation of the process of development of the personality at a stage short of complete and uniform mature independence is known as *fixation.*

Certain phases of development are not successfully passed through and left behind. Just as the child may continue baby talk and dependence on mother beyond the period when these characteristics should have been outgrown, so phases of personality development may be arrested at various stages. The arrest is not in the intellectual but in the emotional, dispositional aspect of personality maturation.

According to one theory, fixation is the result of experiencing such excessive satisfactions at a given level that this level can be renounced only with reluctance. According to another theory, a similar effect may be produced by excessive frustration at a given level.

Regression

Attention has just been called to the fact that certain aspects of the personality may be arrested in their maturing process, with the result that a full and harmonious development never occurs. By another anxiety-evading mechanism known as *regression*, the personality may suffer loss of some of the development already attained and revert to a lower level of integration, adaptation, and expression. The retreat to a lower level of personality development is characterized by immature patterns of thought, emotion, or behavior.

A child who is toilet trained again wets his bed following the birth of a sibling who now takes the maternal attention from him. He seeks by his regression to regain the gratifications of an earlier period of life.

An infantile or juvenile approach to the world, which may have been latent for many years, may be awakened by some frustrating experience or situation later in life. Regression to the dependence of infancy or childhood allays the fears and insecurities arising from the necessity for adult existence to meet life situations and responsibilities in an independent fashion. While adjustive in its purpose, regres-

sion is disruptive and does not promote a desirable adaptation.

The stronger the fixations may have been established during the course of development, the more readily will frustrating and conflictive situations be evaded by regression to those fixations. Extreme forms and degrees of regression result in a serious disorganization of personality and often constitute an important element in schizophrenia. In the process of regression, the total personality does not regress from one developmental stage to the next lower in clearly defined stages or as a total unit. Certain aspects of the patient's feelings, thinking, and behavior may be perceived as operating at various 'levels within various stages concurrently. The patient may, for example, think, feel, and behave partially as an adult but at the same time may manifest infantile needs.

Following a trip abroad with some friends, an 18-year-old adopted child became withdrawn and preoccupied herself with religious matters and fantasies about her own parents. Some few days before her hospital admission she commenced to repeat whatever was said to her (echolalia). This behavior persisted for some weeks after her admission. Later she said she had suffered early in life from other children mocking her through echoing her words but learned that she could satisfy her own angry feelings to her teasers by adopting the same method.

Dissociation

Another mechanism to which the organism may resort to secure a measure of satisfaction when the various components of the personality are not well integrated is that of dissociation. A portion of the personality that is a source of emotional distress may be eliminated by this mechanism. In dissociation, certain aspects of activities of the personality escape from the control of the individual, become separated from normal consciousness, and, thus segregated, function as a unitary whole.

DUAL OR MULTIPLE PERSONALITIES. We are accustomed to looking upon our perceptions, ideas, emotions, memories, and wishes as all belonging to a consciousness, a personality, that cannot be divided. Ordinarily a given topic occupies one's consciousness one moment and some other topic the next moment, but it is felt that there is some connection between the two topics, that both are part of awareness, that consciousness has been continuous, and that one's mental life has not been divided. Occasionally, however, in a person in whom there is an active incompatibility between repressed elements in his mental life and the rest of his personality, the repressed components may escape from the forces that are repressing them, become separated from the usual consciousness, organize a personality of their own, as it were, and thus dictate behavior. This new or secondary personality has its own consciousness which has no recollection of the usual or primary personality and carries out acts independent of it. The consciousness possessed by this independently functioning experience was designated by Morton Prince as the coconsciousness.

The disposition and character possessed by the secondary personality may be quite different from that shown by the primary personality. This contrast should naturally be expected, since the secondary personality is made up of material that has been repressed, that is, has been rejected by the primary personality because it was not of a nature to be consciously entertained or satisfied.

Occasionally more than one body of associated repressions and affective experiences may become sufficiently organized to acquire independent activity, in which case there will be more than one secondary personality, each possessing a character and disposition different from the others and from the primary personality. To these independently acting personalities is given the term *multiple personalities*.

A 28-year-old married woman was admitted to a hospital, depressed and retarded, after a suicidal attempt. Several days later she became angry and assaultive, claimed that it was "her" fault that she was depressed. She then stated that "Mary" was the depressed person; she was Cynthia. As Cynthia she reported frequently leaving home, picking up sailors and lesbians, and acting in a loose and lascivious manner. As Mary she acted as a dutiful, quiet, submissive housewife and mother, angry and depressed over her husband's poor relationship to her. Periodically she abruptly assumed the character of Cynthia and became loud, boisterous, and uninhibited. In the depressed state she accepted the dictates of her superego, repressed the rage toward her husband, and dutifully attempted to assume her responsibilities as a housewife, as Mary. When overwhelmed by rage, she expressed her rage through defiance and acted her aggressive and sexual urges as Cynthia. Only the latter dissociation recognized the former

SOMNAMBULISM. One of the simplest forms of dissociation is that of somnambulism, in which, while the usual personality is asleep, a fragment or some aspect of the personality assumes direction, with the result that, without the awareness of his usual personality, the sleeper arises and executes some complicated act. Other examples of automatisms, or dissociations of personality in which unconscious factors temporarily gain control, act independently and dictate behavior, are *automatic writing* and *fugues*. In all these dissociated states, the organization of the repressed tendencies and desires into systems has usually been aided by daydreams. Recently it has been demonstrated that somnambulism occurs only in association with the electroencephalographic concomitants of nondreaming sleep.

AUTOMATIC WRITING. In automatic writing, the usual consciousness may or may not be aware that an automatism is being executed, but in all other forms of dissociation the usual or primary personality is not aware.

FUGUE. Sometimes the organized material that has broken away from usual consciousness to form the secondary personality may initiate activities that lead the patient far from the scenes and efforts of his ordinary life. Such a flight or *fugue* state consists of "transitory abnormal behavior characterized by aimless wandering and more or less alteration of consciousness, usually, but not necessarily, followed by amnesia." A desire for. escape from some intolerable situation is usually the immediately precipitating factor in the production of the fugue. Frequently the prompting desire is escape either from justice or from domestic stress. An accompanying depressive mood is common. In fugues of short duration, the patient wanders aimlessly, is highly emotional, and when found is agitated and confused. In long fugues he travels far, appears self-possessed, and lives in every way like a normal person except that he is not where he should be. The patient may be his normal self when he emerges from his fugue, aware of his identity with full memory of his past life except for the fugue period, or he may be unaware of his identity and of his past life. Clinically most cases fall into a poorly defined psychopathic-neurotic group. Many have shown a previous tendency to lying or to hysterical features.

Resistance

This defensive mechanism produces a deep-seated opposition to the bringing of repressed (unconscious) data into awareness. Through its operation, the individual seeks to avoid memories and insights which would arouse anxiety and be painful for him to face consciously. It is also observed in psychoanalytical therapy when the psychiatrist encourages the patient to bring repressed material into awareness through free associations. It was through the difficulties and obstructions encountered in free association—the blocking, embarrassment, silences, and anxieties shown by the patient to which he gave the name

resistance—that Freud built up his concept of repression. Resistances afford a clue to the existence of repressed material.

Denial

Denial is an intrapsychic defense mechanism by means of which consciously intolerable perceptions are ignored or insufficiently appreciated. It is accompanied by a splitting of ego function since the individual maintains simultaneously but unconsciously the significance and affective connotation of the denied percept. What is consciously intolerable is unconsciously rejected by a protective mechanism of nonawareness. By this means, reality is transformed so that it is no longer unpleasant or painful. The term denial used in a psychiatric sense does not include a consciously attempted endeavor to repudiate or disown as in malingering or lying.

A distinguished neurologist in his mid-40's developed headaches, over subsequent weeks incurring weakness of his left hand. He suddenly became comatose and was admitted to the hospital, where a craniotomy revealed the presence of a rapidly growing glioma in the left cerebral hemisphere. Following decompression and recovery of consciousness, he repeatedly assured his family and friends that he had had a minor cerebrovascular accident.

Denial as a defense evolves early in a child's development. Winnicott suggests that the infant's *transitional object*—a cloth, doll, or some other soft object to which he or she seems inordinately attached—represents a denial of separation from the mother. The object aids transition from merger with the mother to being outside the mother but yet related.

Splitting

This term is widely used today to explain the coexistence within the ego of contradictory affective states, representative of self and others, as well as attitudes to self and others. Other individuals or the self are perceived as "all good" or "all bad." It has received most application by those who have studied the borderline personalities (unstable personalities, DSM-III). Splitting earlier was conceptualized as a result of denial, which arose when patients became anxious as they were unable to tolerate ambivalent ("good" or "bad") feelings about a wanted person. By denial that the other had been the cause of their anger, they relieved their anxiety and were able to maintain a fantasized relationship with an idealized image of the wanted person. If denial alone is insufficient to relieve anxiety, patients may call up other defensive operations to assist, such as displacement, identification with the bad aspects, and the turning of danger toward themselves or projection of the good or bad representation onto others.

Some psychiatrists limit the term splitting to disavowal of whole percepts, while others use it to designate a mental mechanism that exists before the child has evolved constant representations of others. It refers, then, to a clinical phenomenon in which it is presumed that the growing child separates the longed-for image of the love object from the hated image of it and may do the same with self-representation.

Sublimation

We have seen that repression is a mental mechanism designed to deal with conflicting drives and desires. If it is successful in its purpose and there are no accompanying feelings of anxiety, it facilitates a well-adjusted life. Since, however, repression is, in effect, the overcoming of one force by another, the energy in the repressed impulse is not available for constructive, consciously directed activity. It would be highly desirable, therefore, if the energy inherent in primitive or unacceptable impulses could somehow be transformed and flow with relative freedom into the conscious mind and there direct the individual's interests and activities. The mechanism by which this energy is transformed and directed to socially useful goals is known as *sublimation.* Instinctive needs and unacceptable impulses find an acceptable outlet and mode of expression when anxiety arising from the threat of these needs and impulses is channeled into patterns of social acceptability. Instead of utilizing primitive tendencies and impulses for selfish or forbidden purposes, sublimation transforms and directs them into vocational channels or into art, literature, religion, science, or other activities that promote cultural development and a richer life for both the individual and the social group. Aggressive impulses, for example, may be sublimated through sports and games or other socially accepted channels.

Rarely does the individual recognize that his activity which serves the material, mental, and cultural welfare of himself and his fellows derives its energy from impulses originally developed for biological and selfish ends. The scientist engaged in research on problems of importance to the health or welfare of the entire race does not consciously recognize that his researches are but the disguised and refined expression of a pronounced, innate drive of curiosity.

DEFENSIVE COMPLEXES

We may designate as defensive complexes of the ego, rather than as specific mental processes, those more complexly organized ideomotor, perceptual, and cognitive ego functions in which one may discern the utilization of a variety of the previously described mental mechanisms. Among such processes are certain character formations, conversions, some fantasies, and dreams.

Thus the frequently encountered excessive behavioral reaction or sudden emotional outburst in response to an apparently slight stimulus, as well as certain mannerisms, slips of speech, or forgetfulness, are seen to occur as the result of complex internal responses to an outwardly insignificant or seemingly trivial external stimulus. These reactions are linked to deeply repressed experiences that are highly charged emotionally, against which the individual has erected a complex of defenses. Repression plays the major role in the evolution of such processes. Not only may taboo instinctive desires, strivings, and tendencies be repressed, but also ideas, particularly those with painful affect loading. A group of associated ideas invested with common affective accompaniments becomes associated as a complex. The affect imparts the dynamic element, as a result of which it comes to constitute a sphere of emotionally charged thought and thus exercises a strong unconscious influence on behavior.

Character Defenses

A variety of persisting attitudes, modes of approaching or responding to others, mannerisms, and affectations which give each individual his particular character are means by which anxiety and other long-continuing affects are walled off or discharged. By such character defenses conflict between id impulses and the requirements of reality are maintained in an equilibrium which often is compatible with a more or less satisfactory, if inflexible and narrow, social adaptation. Such character formations represent the means by which the personality habitually copes with enduring states of anxiety. Often these character formations offer the symbolic means of fulfilling some perceived demand from the outside world and simultaneously provide a form of gratification for the hidden and repressed drive. Character defenses are to be contrasted with psychopathological symptoms, which erupt to contain anxiety that occurs despite character defenses. The symptom is an exaggerated expression of one or several of the ego-defensive mental mechanisms; it conspicuously impairs the social adaptation of the individual and appears as a regression in reaction to some acute stress.

Certain character traits represent sublimations of drives, whereas others are reactive. Thus unremitting striving for power or prestige may represent a reaction to the anxiety evoked by deeply repressed perceptions of inferiority, while excessive kindliness may be a defense against hidden aggressive and sadistic drives. Particular aggregations of traits are referred to as establishing the oral, anal, and urethral characters. These character formations are seen as the reactions to vicissitudes of early development and the consequence of excessive tension at that particular stage of growth, or as the consequence of relative denial of satisfaction at a later period leading to a regressive fixation.

Perfectionism represents a common character defense wherein one demands of oneself and others a higher quality of performance than situations require. Thus the insecure child who seeks affection from his parents by complying with their demands for high performance characteristically must excel to allay his anxiety in later life. Perfectionism as a character defense offers a means of sustaining a satisfying self-image as well as a way of life that avoids self-disparagement. Again it appears to offer the means of continually satisfying the need for affectionate appreciation by others. The symptom of compulsiveness, on the other hand, fends off unacceptable feelings and impulses. It must be kept in mind that character formations occur with symptomatic expressions that may or may not have common psychodynamic roots.

Conversion

Conversion is a psychological process in which one finds utilized the mechanisms of repression, identification, displacement, denial, and symbolization. Thus a conflict inducing a painful affect is converted to an inhibition of some motor or sensory functions and in so doing neutralizes the affect discharge. With the paralysis or sensory disturbance the conflict is denied, the affect repressed, and yet the inhibition of function symbolizes the repressed wish and the need for its inhibition. It appears as well that those utilizing conversion often select the symptoms on the basis of identification.

Fantasy

Earlier, fantasy was discussed as an ego-adaptive process, one important for mental health and creative thinking. Fantasy may also be defensive. If, however, the gratifications of reality are insufficient, thinking may not be controlled by the demands of reality but may serve as a regressive or substitute satisfaction. Such musing is known as fantasy. Fantasy provides the illusion of a fulfillment of wishes that cannot be satisfied, either because of the frustrations of reality or because the individual's standards of behavior forbid actual gratification of strivings and wishes. Often these strivings and wishes are of such a character that direct reflection on them would scarcely be permitted. Fantasy is a defensive or tension-relieving mechanism offering either solace and an illusionary release from unsatisfying reality or an imaginary satisfaction of wishes, any actual gratification of which has been forbidden by repression.

In Freud's words: "The pleasure-principle triumphs over the reality-principle." By the former, he meant the unconscious processes that strive toward the immediate gaining of affective pleasure. By the latter, he meant the conscious tendency of the individual in his attempt to satisfy his pleasure to consider such practical necessities as the outer world imposes and, if necessary, to postpone the satisfaction of these pleasures. Because so seductive and so satisfying in itself, fantasy may replace necessary reality thinking or effective action and serve as a substitute for effort directed at adjustment to the actualities of life. Fantasy has much in common with dreams, differing chiefly in being more coherent and in occurring during waking hours.

Fantasy is not an isolated function but an integrated synthesis of idea, conation, feeling, interpretation, and memory in which instinctive and affective elements predominate and largely direct it. By disregarding reality and providing a substitute satisfaction, it aids in resolving conflicts and in preventing the development of anxiety. In extreme cases it tends to enlist the aid of delusions and hallucinations; wishes, particularly those that remain unsatisfied and beyond full conscious awareness, are projected and come back realized. In many cases, at least, fantasy may be regarded as a defense against anxiety. The psychotic patient may live simultaneously in two unrelated worlds—one of fantasy and one of reality.

One patient in his fantasy world owned the United States Treasury and its contents; he built and controlled the hospital in which he lived but had just lost the key to it. Almost daily he would hand his physician an order for a billion dollars, at the same time begging for some tobacco and that he be given parole of the grounds.

One form of fantasy is that of mysticism, in which the urge for peace and love represents the obverse of one's own aggressive drives. Such mystical fantasy may take on delusional characteristics in which the conflicted sufferer assumes and even acts out a saintlike character.

This coexistence of the consciousness of fantasy and the consciousness of reality is made possible by the mechanism of rationalization and its production of what is known as a "logic-tight compartment." Related ideas exist in each compartment, undisturbed by those in the other, each group pursuing its course segregated from those which are incompatible by a barrier through which no reasoning or argument can force a passage. "Logic-tight" and "affective-tight" compartments produced by rationalization are not confined to the psychotic but may be seen among those who are considered of sound mental health. In such cases, the compartments assure an affective segregation of incompatible strivings and emotional material.

Dreams

Dreams, like fantasy and conversion formation, combine and expose many of the defense mechanisms, as Freud so beautifully showed in the study of dreams. In dreams one may find condensations, displacements, symbolizations, regressions, and other ego mechanisms. The mental representations of dreams are a form of sleeping fantasy or imagery, commonly considered to represent a means by which the ego attempts to resolve problems, protect against unpleasant affects, and offer wish-fulfilling gratifications. The analysis of the psychic content of dreams is an established technique in psychoanalytic therapy and is described in Chapter 30.

The recently discovered fact that dreaming sleep represents a distinctive aspect of the sleep cycle characterized by a number of associated physiological concomitants has provoked many new explanations for sleep and dreaming sleep, regarding their physiology, their function, and their relation to healthy and disturbed psychological processes. The physiology of sleep is discussed in detail in Chapter 3.

BIBLIOGRAPHY

Birdwhistell, R. L.: Kinesis and Context. Essay on Body Motion Communication. Philadelphia, University of Pennsylvania Press, 1970.

Blum, H. D.: Symbolic processes and symbol formation. Int. J. Psychoanal., 59:455–471, 1978.

Brody, M. W.: Introjection, identification and incorporation. Int. J. Psychoanal., 45:57–63, 1964.

Dorpat, T. L.: Is splitting a defense? Int. Rev. Psychoanal., 6:105–113, 1979.

Fenichel, B.: The Psychoanalytic Theory of the Neuroses. New York, W. W. Norton & Company, 1946.

Freud, A.: The Ego and the Mechanisms of Defense. (Translated by C. M. Baines.) London, Hogarth Press, 1927.

Freud, S.: A General Introduction to Psychoanalysis. New York, Garden City Publishing Company, 1938.

Hollender, M. H.: Perfectionism, Compr. Psychiatry, 6:94–103, 1965.

Klein, G.: Perceptions, Motives and Personality. New York, Alfred A. Knopf, 1970.

Lenneberg, E. H.: Biological Foundations of Language. New York, John Wiley & Sons, 1967.

Lezine, I.: The transition from sensorimotor to earliest symbolic function in early development. In Nurnberger, J. I. (ed.): Biological and Environmental Determinants of Early Development. Res. Publ. Assoc. Res. Nerv. Ment. Dis. 51:221–232, 1973.

Miller, G. A. (ed.): Communication, Language and Meaning. New York, Basic Books, 1973.

Noy, P.: A revision of the psychoanalytic theory of the primary process. Int. J. Psychoanal., 50:155–178, 1969.

Piaget, J., and Garcia, M.: Understanding Causality. (Translated by D. and M. Miles.) New York, W. W. Norton & Company, 1974.

Rapaport, D.: The Organization and Pathology of Thought. New York, Columbia University Press, 1951.

Reiss, D.: Varieties of consensual experience. 1. A theory for relating family interaction to individual thinking. Family Process., 10:1–28, 1971.

Rioch, D. M., and Weinstein, E. H. (eds.): Disorders of Communication. Baltimore, Williams & Wilkins Company, 1964.

Ross, N.: The "as if" concept. J. Am. Psychoanal. Assoc., 15:59–82, 1967.

Ruesch, W.: Disturbed Communication. New York, W. W. Norton & Company, 1957.

Schechter, D. E.: Identification and individuation. J. Am. Psychoanal. Assoc., 16:48–80, 1968.

Stern, D.: The First Relationship. Infant and Mother. Cambridge, Mass., Harvard University Press, 1977.

Trunnill, E. E., and Holt, W. E.: The concept of denial or disavowal. J. Am. Psychoanal. Assoc., 22:768–784, 1974.

Vaillant, G. E.: Theoretical hierarchy of adaptive ego mechanisms. Arch. Gen. Psychiatry, 24:107–118, 1971.

Winnicott, D. W.: Playing and Reality. New York, Basic Books, 1971.

6

PSYCHOPATHOLOGY

"... They see not us, nor any Sunday caller
among the geraniums and wicker chairs,
for they are Jacks who climb the beanstalk country ..."

Tennessee Williams

EMIL KRAEPELIN
(From Roback, A. A., and Kiernan, T.: Pictorial History of
Psychology and Psychiatry. New York, Philosophical Library,
1969, p. 219.)

Psychopathology, the definition of abnormal personality functioning, has evolved from the recognition of easily discernible and gross disturbances of human behavior in terms of action, thought, and consciousness to an expanding awareness of the variations in the individual's total reaction pattern—his personality. The gross symptomatic expressions of disturbed behav-ior were known centuries ago; their occurrence in more or less persistent and recognizable groupings led to the Kraepelinian elaboration of the various categories of psychotic behavior which still constitute the matrix for the syndromes now recognized in modern clinical diagnostic nomenclature. Further studies of abnormal behavior have established the various forms of the psychoneuroses, the expressions of mental retardation, and personality disorders of both adult and early life.

Just as mechanical objects subjected to stress beyond the limits of their elasticity suffer distortion, so the personality subjected to anxiety-producing stresses beyond the limits of its capacity for adaptation may suffer disorganization in both overt and symbolic behavior. Doubtless everyone, however healthy his adaptation appears to be, has particular psychological spheres vulnerable to stress. If his experiences touch these areas and the degree of their anxiety-producing nature exceeds his ability to deal with their stresses by healthy adaptive methods, he will be compelled to deal with them by neurotic or psychotic ones. Through repeated or cumulative stress, the individual's adaptive sets and "normal" defenses no longer suffice and his adaptive capacity is exhausted. Stress alone, however, should not be considered the precipitating factor in mental disorder. It must be a particular stress for a particular person and, perhaps, at a particular time.

Criteria of Mental Illness

Definitions of mental health or absence of illness, though more general, are useful in assessing the presence and extent of illness. In addition they have made more precise a series of personality assets which define capacities for readaptation in the face of stress or recovery from illness. The World Health Organization speaks of health in broad terms as "the presence of physical and emotional well being." To the psychiatrist, the healthy adult shows behavior that confirms an awareness of self or personal identity, coupled with a life purpose, a sense of personal autonomy, and willingness to perceive reality and cope with its vicissitudes. The healthy adult has a capacity to invest in others, to understand their needs, to achieve a mutually satisfying heterosexual relationship, to be active and productive with evidence of persistence and endurance in pursuing tasks to their accomplishment, to respond flexibly in the face of stress, to receive pleasure from a variety of sources, and to accept his limitations realistically.

In the field of mental health, as elsewhere, there are no fixed boundaries. The presence of character fixations, with their limitations of self-actualization, the appearance of symptoms, the loss or impairment of pre-existing functions, the recurrence of regressive behavior, and the distortion or impoverishment of affects provide the clinical evidence of illness.

Like more narrowly biological phenomena, such as fever, inflammation, and other morbid processes, mental disorders are defensive, protective, and reparative in purpose, but as they deal largely with the affective and psychosocial aspects of the organism, the adaptive ends they serve are those of personal situations. The symptomatology of the personality disorder represents either the individual's attempt to effect an adjustment to the interplay of psychological, social, and physiological forces impinging upon him or his failure in that effort. Again, the symptoms may represent an attempt to hide the truth from one's self, to retreat from difficult situations, to deal with anxiety, or to shut out the stresses of life. The result then is that one employs substitutive methods of adjustment that lead away from reality, which is sacrificed to attain emotional comfort, maintain self-respect, or provide satisfaction in the easiest way. The comforts and compensations, however, are highly egotistic and limit full expression of the individual's capacities or are objectionable to the social group.

Personality Disorder

Although each person has his own particular characteristics which distinguish him from all others, certain general types of personality have been defined as disordered. For the most part the groupings are descriptive; a better understanding of the dynamics of personality development in each instance represents one of the areas in which study is greatly needed.

The task of the physician and psychiatrist in clinical practice is to define the psychopathology of the patient and then attempt to understand the genesis of the abnormality. As has been pointed out, the personality of the patient determines largely the manner in which he will respond to stress and thereby the specific definitions of the symptomatic expressions of his illness. In the study of the patient, the type of personality organization that the patient has acquired must be defined as well as the symptomatic psychopathology he brings with him. The varieties of personality disorders, per se, are described in Chapter 25.

SYMPTOMS AS PSYCHOBIOLOGICAL REACTIONS

Origin and Function of Symptoms

· Symptoms are the results of many forces, some of them from without but more of them from within the patient. Symptoms, therefore, even though they may be bizarre and therefore baffling to our understanding, have a cause and meaning.

Some symptoms, such as impairment of memory in senile dementia, or confusion in a toxic state, are the results of physiological disturbances of neuron activity involved in the process of thinking. As such they represent a loss of function.

Neurotic symptoms, however, in contrast to those due to impairment or loss of physiological or biochemical function, are manifestations of psychological processes of which the patient is little aware. These symptoms represent defenses or substitutions to cope with

some impairment of psychosocial functioning.

To discover the meaning of those unusual personality manifestations that are called symptoms and the functions they perform in the life history of the patient, one must ascertain the needs and meaningful factors or situations that led to their production. It should be remembered that *the pathological psychiatric formations termed symptoms represent the patient's attempt, in the face of great difficulties, to maintain his existence in the best possible way.* Symptoms, too, may be not only an expression of a mental illness but also an attempt by the patient to fight the illness. Regression, for example, with its withdrawal to an earlier developmental level, may be not only a symptom of mental illness but also an attempt to deal on that level with tasks consonant with his reduced ability.

The method of approach to an understanding of mental disorder is to correlate the symptoms with the current physical and emotional status of the patient, with his life history, and with forces that have played a part in molding his personality. The psychiatrist attempts to interpret symptoms not only in their relationship to past experiences but also in terms of the known dynamics of behavior.

DISORDERS OF MOTOR ASPECTS OF BEHAVIOR

The disturbances to be considered here lie in the field the psychologists designate as *conation*, action tendency, or impulse toward action. This includes an implication of affect and desire. Conversely, all affects have conative elements and impulses. Conation is the intention-set or striving aspect of the personality. It represents the purposive activity of the personality but lacks the degree of consciousness that has usually been associated with the idea of will or volition.

Attitude

Certain other terms dealing with the action sphere of the personality may be briefly mentioned. By attitude is meant a continuing set or predisposition to react in a characteristic feeling or manner. Attitudes are determined largely by one's feeling state and may be consciously or unconsciously acquired. They may become ingrained in the character structure of the personality and influence personality functioning. A bitter feeling, for example, may affect memory, judgment, and reasoning.

Disposition

By disposition is meant the sum of one's tendencies or inclinations as determined by the affective and conative components of the personality.

Assertion

Assertion may be defined as a deep-seated drive or pattern of the personality to react in a definitely forceful way. The term assertion carries a certain implication of will to overt action, in contrast to aggression, with its implication of hostility.

DISTURBANCE OF ACTIVITY

Increased Activity

Disturbances of activity may conveniently be classified as overactivity (typically seen in mania), underactivity (depression), and dysactivity (schizoid and paranoic).

An increase in *psychomotor* activity may be purposeful but no objective is attained, as the goal of the activity is constantly changing. The patient is very busy but his activities are not productive. A new activity is undertaken before there has been opportunity to complete the task already begun. This celerity is often shared by all conative aspects of the individual so that the stream of thought is characterized by a flight of ideas.

Decreased Activity

A distinct slowing up of expression occurs in decreased psychomotor activity or *psychomotor retardation.* Typically, there is a prolonged delay before initiating the intended activity and, once begun, it is executed slowly and as if with painful effort. In extreme cases, the patient is mute and motionless and does not spontaneously undertake any activity. As in increased psychomotor activity, the other conative aspects of behavior may participate in the disturbance, with the result that a retardation of the stream of thought is often associated.

Repetitious Activities

In certain mental diseases, especially in the compulsive reactions and schizophrenia, it may be found that, when an activity has been initiated, there is a tendency to repeat it in the same manner for an indefinite period. This persistent and constant repetition of certain activities is known as *stereotypy* and may be of position, movement of body, or speech. A constantly maintained immobility of position is known as *catalepsy.* A cataleptic form of immobility frequently seen in schizophrenia and probably to be regarded as the expression of a high degree of suggestibility is *cerea flexibilitas,* or *waxy flexibility.* This is so called from the fact that the joints of the patient's extremities may be flexed or extended with a wax-like rigidity, continuing to retain the position imposed as do the jointed limbs of a doll. The extremities may thus be placed and maintained in an uncomfortable position for a much longer period than would be permitted by a normal person. Stereotyped movements, known as *mannerisms,* are common as well in schizophrenia. These may be in the form of grimaces, repeated gestures, peculiarities of gait, or numerous other types. Sometimes a complicated series of movements may be repeated and constitute a fairly definite ritual. The same rather meaningless word, phase, or sentence may be repeated. Such a reiteration in which no coherent thought is expressed is known as *verbigeration*. Stereotypies have a definite psychological meaning, the symbolic significance in each case being peculiar to the individual and determined by his complexes or other affective experiences. After a time, their repetition may become a matter of habit, in which case the original affective value is largely lost.

Automatic Behavior

A phenomenological but not psychological counterpart of negativism is observed in *command automatism,* in which suggestions or requests from without are compulsively or automatically followed. Automatic obedience may also assume the form of repeating words or phrases uttered in the presence of the patient *(echolalia),* or it may be exhibited by the imitation of movements noted in others *(echopraxia).* Echolalia and echopraxia sometimes represent regressions to childish forms of "mocking" behavior or mimicry in which hostility and resentment are expressed under the guise of compliance. Mimicry is seen as one of the evolving sensorimotor activities, in childhood, moving from simple imitation to take on significant meanings in terms of interpersonal relations.

Negativism

Negativism is a psychological defense reaction characterized by opposition and resistance to what is suggested. It may be manifested by behavior opposite to what would ordinarily be called for in a given situation. It is frequently expressed in such forms as mutism, re-

fusal of food, noncompliance with requests, and resistance to efforts to care for the patient. Psychodynamically, the negativistic act provides gratification by the acting out of hostile, revengeful feelings toward significant persons—acts which the sufferer has learned are specifically anxiety provoking to the other and lead through the latter's evident concern to an expression of interest in the negativistic person.

Compulsions

A morbid and often an irresistible urge to perform an apparently unreasonable act repetitiously is known as a *compulsion.* The obligatory act may be of a simple nature, such as touching an object twice, or walking on cracks in the sidewalk, or it may be complex and constitute more or less of a ritual. A compulsion may be regarded as the result of an obsession—an obsession in action. Such acts are so closely linked with obsession that the combination is often referred to as the compulsive-obsessive syndrome. The acts are not meaningless, but, through the operation of the mechanisms of displacement, substitution, and symbolism, serve as defenses against anxiety. A common form of compulsion is handwashing. Frequently the basic force behind this is guilt over masturbation, the repetitious act serving through the mechanisms of displacement and symbolism as an anxiety-relieving measure. Many people whom no one thinks of as suffering from mental disease have various obsessive-compulsive habits, which serve as defense reactions for keeping anxiety, feelings of guilt, and unacceptable instinctual drives at a minimum. Among such personality traits are tendencies to exaggerate the importance of carefulness and details and to stress cleanliness and orderliness. Various perfectionistic strivings and a rigid adherence to routine are obvious.

Violence

As discussed in previous chapters, aggressive behavior must be recognized in vertebrates as facilitative to species survival through its functions in protection from attack and in support of the ingestive and procreative drives. Violence as practiced by man—in war, assassination, murder, assault, rape, cruelty in mutilating others and the self, and suicide—is an expression of aggressivity unique to his species.

Such expressions of violence may be regarded as pathological when they are expressive of a deficit in development or an impairment of function of the superego. In some, deficiency in brain growth leading to mental retardation may determine inability to absorb the family and cultural values which lead to internalization of control of rage. In others, severe emotional deprivation in early life owing to parental loss, neglect, or hatred may impair the process of identification and internalization of values necessary to constitute superego control and ego ideals. In still others, parental discipline or that provided in schools or other institutions may be so brutal and hateful as to establish identification with the aggressor, thus allowing acting out of similar violence to others later in life. In the instance of some emotionally deprived children thirsting for support, frustration leads to reaction formations with denial of internalized social values. Such children—and adolescents and adults—reared to produce these formations may evolve a repertoire of shrewd and devious expressions of cruelty and destructiveness as a means of revenge and testing of others. Still others, raised in seemingly healthy and socially conscious and law-abiding families, express violent or destructive behavior in a narrowly defined form owing to *superego lacunae* derived from some subtle expression of condoning behavior of parents or other persons in authority.

Socially sanctioned violent or destructive acts ordered and allowed by public authority in wartime may not be considered as psychopathological. Nor should violent acts aroused in protection of self in the political interactions of various groups be so construed. Regarding both these categories of violent actions, certain individuals predisposed to violence through impairment of superego formations often indulge their individual psychopathology in overdetermined ways during wartime or in revolutionary periods.

Persistent and continued expressions of cruel, destructive, or other violent behavior on the part of an individual require a social accomplice. Sadomasochistic matches between individuals are common.

Among adults impairment of superego control with impulsive acting out of violence in murder or assault is commonly associated with impairment of brain function by poisons or other damage. Thus murder and assault are more frequently committed by the alcoholic than by others. The hallucinogens also act to impair brain function and related superego control. Brain damage from any cause may predispose to lack of impulse control when the individual is aroused to rage. Psychiatrists have found that perpetrators of unmotivated murders (those without preconceived planning) are more likely to show electroencephalographic evidence of brain damage than are the perpetrators of premeditated murders. In the instance of mass murders, a paranoid personality development usually exists, in which increasing frustration leads suddenly to revengeful acting out against a humanity conceived of as unsympathetic. The act is demonstrative, too, of the megalomaniac wish fulfillment of the murderer.

Studies in the past of patients hospitalized for psychiatric illness have shown that those discharged are less likely to be detained for criminal action, including violence, than the population at large. There is need today for

TABLE 6–1   Psychiatric Diagnoses of 30
               Violent Patients

Chronic alcoholism*	12
Schizophrenia	10
Affective disorder	6
Mental retardation	3
Organic brain syndrome	2
Antisocial personality	2
Anxiety neurosis	1

*Six patients have another primary diagnosis.
(From Tuason, V. B.: Dis. Nerv. Syst., 32:764–
768, 1971.)

investigation of the association of mental illness with violence in general society, particularly as management of mental hospital patients has moved rapidly in most Western countries from legal confinement in institutions to community care.

Psychiatric conditions in which violence is most likely to be directed toward others are tabulated from a small group of patients in Table 6–1. Violent assault or murder of another frequently precedes suicide. Among patients who threaten homicide, the risk of that act is greater if the individual has never threatened suicide. When a suicidal threat precedes a homicidal one, patients are more likely to attempt to kill themselves than to act against another. About 40 per cent of psychiatric patients who make suicidal attempts give histories of previous assaultive behaviors.

Until recent years, violence against children received little attention. One study showed that in England and Wales a quarter of all victims of homicide were under 16 years of age. Four fifths of these children had been killed by their parents—the majority by their mothers. Children under one year of age are especially vulnerable to both abuse and homicide. D'Orban discriminates six types of maternal filicide in the following order of frequency: battering mothers who impulsively killed in reaction to aggression from the victim, mentally ill mothers, mothers who attempted to kill their children within a day of birth (neonaticides), retaliating mothers whose aggression is directed against the spouse, mothers who killed unwanted children by either passive neglect or direct aggression, and mothers who killed to relieve suffering in the victim.

Suicide

In Western societies, most persons who suicide or have suicidal impulses consult their physicians beforehand. In the vast majority of instances, appropriate intervention through immediate treatment or referral to a psychiatrist for therapy would prevent either the attempt, with its significant loss of self-esteem, or the actual act leading to death. *In the United States, less than one third of those who commit suicide had been seen by a psychiatrist but about one half consulted a physician beforehand.*

Suicide, suicidal attempts, and suicidal ideation are generally considered evidence of psychopathology, although this is not necessarily so. Transient thoughts of death and dying are universal, and thoughts of self-destruction are frequent. Obsessive preoccupation with suicidal ruminations, however, is pathological.

Although suicide has many precipitating events and motivating forces, all persons with suicidal ideation have an intense underlying sense of deprivation of affection, love, and power, leading to a deep sense of personal rejection or lack of control of their social environment. The suicidal attempt is motivated by the wish for revenge, by hopelessness, or by wish-fulfilling fantasies of reunion, or, as in the case of the *countersymbiotic* suicide, represents a displacement onto the self of an aggressive wish toward the mother. Perhaps the most commonly recognized motive is the wish to instill guilt in the significant person who is perceived as abandoning; in this case, suicide is a means of control and revenge. Similar motives exist in those groups of patients who indulge in repeated acts of wrist cutting or *self-mutilation* — often carried out with a seeming delicacy. Overwhelmed by an acute sense of despairing loneliness following an actual or fantasied abandonment, the patients impulsively act out their revenge, often in a fuguelike condition, upon their bodies as an object entirely owned. Those who make unsuccessful suicidal attempts and those who threaten suicide manage to give warning of their distress in such a way as to prevent success and also to influence favorably their important interpersonal relation.

Fantasies precede suicidal acts. Fantasies of identification and reunion in death with a loved person are frequently the motive for the "anniversary" suicide — an attempt that takes place on the anniversary of death of the wished-for person. Sometimes there is a regressive wish for reunion with the mother, a wish to live once more in an ideal state of passivity and infantile gratification. Another fantasy is of rebirth, of recommencing life in a more satisfying manner. This fantasy is said to be usual in periods of recovery following depressions or acute schizophrenic episodes. With splitting of the self-image into "good" or "bad" parts, the wish to destroy the maligned part of the self may, in periods of great tension, lead to an impulsive attempt at its elimination. This fantasy often precedes self-mutilative acts as well, particularly in the schizophrenic, who sometimes makes horrifying efforts to remove an organ or body part conceived of as the source of evil. Finally there are the fantasies of escape into death from the hopelessness arising in the course of psychotic or other illness or even from the stringencies of living. Such fantasies apparently may be stimulated by the reading of much-publicized suicide stories. Motor vehicle fatalities increase following these stories. There remain some presumed suicidal attempts, particularly in patients with

delirium, that represent a desperate effort to escape fearfully imminent illusory or hallucinatory threats.

Suicidal threats are pervasive in society as a means of interpersonal domination and control. They are used to induce both heterosexual and homosexual love relationships, including marriage, to prevent dissolution of such relations, to force parental acquiescence to the desires of children or vice versa, to obtain favored treatment, and to avoid certain varieties of required service (such as military service) to friends and country.

Unsuccessful suicidal attempts are estimated to occur from five to fifty times as frequently as successful suicides. The suicide rate varies among countries and cultures and is inversely proportionate to the homicide rate.

Suicide is significantly more frequent in discharged mental hospital patients in the *six* months immediately following their release. In Japan and Austria the annual rate of successful suicides equals approximately 23 per 100,000. The United States rate of around 10 per 100,000 ranks in the middle of the listing of countries; suicide is the tenth leading cause of death in this country.

The suicide rate has remained relatively stable over the past decade but apparently a marked increase in suicide attempts has taken place. In a review of studies in English between 1960 and 1971, Weissman documents the increase in the magnitude and characteristics of suicide attempts. Although there are many weaknesses in collecting data on suicide attempts, it can be deduced that the rapidly changing personal and social economic status of worldwide populations, particularly in the hitherto less deprived Western countries, may play a significant role.

It is striking that in Western countries there is a preponderance of attempted suicides of women over men, amounting to ratios of 3 to 1, while in countries such as Poland the ratio is greater for males. Possibly in the studies done there was a failure to note the high rates of suicide attempts in jails, where the male population is higher than the female.

More suicidal attempts are made among urban than rural populations. In urban suicides, the majority suffer affective psychosis or are alcoholic. Immigrants or visitors from other countries are at higher risk than native-borns for the attempt. For suicide, there is a striking difference in the rate between blacks and whites across the world, although a recent study suggests that the urban black suicide rate has tended to rise. In the black population, the homicide rate greatly exceeds that of whites, suggesting the inverse relationship posited by sociologists many years ago. High suicide rates occur among American Indians.

For physicians, it is important to note that the major method of death by suicide or for attempts at suicide is self-medication. The barbiturates have headed the list for years as the most frequently used medication. However, with the increasing availability of psychotropic drugs since the 1960s, there has been greater usage of minor tranquilizers and antidepressives.

While a survey of hospital populations would suggest that wrist slashing occurred largely among intelligent, unmarried, young women, recent studies have shown that the wrist cutters are frequently young, single men.

The rate of completion of suicide among those who are hospitalized following attempts is estimated to be about 1 per cent per year. Among wrist slashers, the later suicide rate has been found to be about 16 per cent. The risk of successful suicide is higher in the first two years after the attempt and in the first three months particularly. It is significant that those who eventually are successful usually have made a serious attempt and seldom have maintained a continuing therapeutic contact with a psychiatric or other facility.

In assessment of those at risk for suicide attempt repetition, 80 per cent of repeaters may be identified by organic brain disease, previous attempts, marital status (widowed, separated, or divorced), or aspiration to membership in a higher social class.

A recent clinical study by Barraclough, Bunch, Nelson, and Sainsbury provides an analysis of suicide in relation to the nature of the personality disorder or lack of one in 100 cases. Table 6–2 summarizes that information.

Suicide is rare in the very young; it occurs with increasing frequency as adolescence advances. Among adolescents in the United States it constitutes the second largest cause of death. It is more frequent among the aged, in men, and among the single, isolated, divorced, and widowed. At least a third of those who have attempted suicide unsuccessfully are without psychopathology, but the vast majority of this group give evidence of recent serious socio-economic distress.

For the psychiatrist, the significant judgment has to do with the recognition that there is a high risk of suicide attempts in those patients who admit to suicidal ruminations. A history of successful suicide in other family members has been found to be statistically related to successful suicide. Clinical experience indicates that suicidal attempts are more common in patients who have been brought up in families in which they were coerced by suicidal threats or made to feel guilty by their parents by being told they were responsible for impending death. It may be surmised that such family transactions lead to impairment of superego development which allows the acting out of suicidal impulses. In psychotherapy such patients may be expected to threaten the psychiatrist. On the other hand, it has been found that the risk of successful suicide is low in those who have made a previous attempt.

TABLE 6–2   Psychiatric Diagnoses of Cases of Successful Suicide

PRINCIPAL DIAGNOSIS	OTHER DIAGNOSIS	N	
Depression	None	64	
	Malignant terminal illness	2	
	Nonmalignant terminal illness	2	
	Barbiturate dependence	1	
	Dementia and barbiturate dependence	1	
			70
Alcoholism	None	4	
	Depression	9	
	Depression and nonmalignant terminal illness	1	
	Nonmalignant terminal illness	1	
			15
Schizophrenia		3	
			3
Phobic anxiety state	None	2	
	Barbiturate dependence	1	
			3
Barbiturate dependence		1	
			1
Acute (schizo-affective) psychosis		1	
			1
Total mentally ill		93	
Total not mentally ill		7	
			100

(From Barraclough, B., Bunch, J., Nelson, B., and Sainsbury, P.: Br. J. Psychiatry, *125*:355–373, 1974.)

Most of those who commit suicide suffer as well from self-derogatory attitudes, profound feelings of hopelessness and helplessness, and a sense of rejection prior to the act. Suicide and suicidal attempts are unrelated to particular forms of psychopathology, although they are most frequent among those with depressive reactions.

Prevention of suicide depends upon the recognition of risk. While risk scales for suicide have been developed, their general clinical usage remains impractical. In a number of countries, suicide prevention centers or crises centers have been established to respond to telephone calls for assistance from the acutely distressed. No evidence now exists that the incidence of suicide has fallen because of the operations of such centers, even though suicide rates have dropped dramatically in some countries (England and Wales) in recent years.

DISORDERS OF PERCEPTION

Illusions

It will be remembered that the various end-organs or receptors are constructed to analyze the environmental energy and select certain kinds which are transformed in the receptor and give rise to a nervous impulse. On arrival in the appropriate area in the brain, this impulse produces a visual, auditory, or other sensory image, the interpretation and meaning of which will depend upon one's previous experiences and interpretations.

One of the ways in which the mental life of the individual may express emotional or striving elements that touch it with particular significance is through a perceptual misinterpretation of such sensory images. The elements that are particularly likely to lead to misinterpretations of these images are intense affective states, ardent wishes, or urgent drives and impulses. Repressed elements are especially apt to be highly dynamic and produce misinterpretations that reflect some affect or express some wish or drive. A patient with a deep feeling of guilt, for example, may interpret the rustling of leaves as reproaching voices. Such a perceptual misinterpretation is known as an *illusion*.

The illusion has the same psychological function as a hallucination, but less reality distortion is involved. The nature of illusions is especially likely to be determined by the prevailing trend of the patient's emotional state and needs. Strained expectation or fear predisposes to illusional interpretations. In mental health, but particularly in mental disorder, the emotional life imbues and tends to influence perceptual experience according to the needs of the personality. In confused toxic states, caused either by ingested poisons or by infection, perceptions may be misinterpreted because the sensory stimuli and impressions are not properly transmitted and integrated in the brain. Such illusions usually possess less psychological significance than do those occurring in fully clear consciousness.

Hallucinations

In an illusion, an image symbol of a real object is formed, but for psychological reasons it is misinterpreted. Hallucinations are generally regarded arbitrarily as perceptions which occur when there is no impulse created by the stimulation of a receptor. Whether the absence of sensory receptor activity actually occurs remains undetermined, since the casual observer has no means of verifying this assumption. The word *hallucination* was introduced by Esquirol (1772–1840), a pupil of Philippe Pinel (1745–1826). He defined it in accordance with its present meaning as a perception without object and clearly differentiated it from illusion.

Although lacking a basis of reality in the sense that the percept is not aroused by a current stimulus in the periphery, hallucinations constitute an actual part of mental life. They should be looked upon as mental products that, arising from within and therefore not related to any external stimulus, possess an idiosyncratic certainty, which, however, may not attain the vividness usually associated with impressions derived from the external world.

The content of the hallucinations usually suggests their dynamic significance. They represent a breakthrough of preconscious or unconscious material into consciousness in the form of sensory images. These hallucinated images, which the patient accepts as reality, represent the projection onto the outer world of such psychological needs and situations as wish-fulfillment, enhancement of self-esteem, criticism, censure, a sense of guilt, self-punishment, the satisfaction of repressed and rejected impulses, or the desire for a more satisfying reality. The dreams of normal persons are prototypes of the mental patient's hallucinations. Sometimes in cases of internal conflict there is hallucinatory expression of the internal debate; some of the hallucinations express approbation or commendation, while others express insults and antagonism.

The way in which escape from a harsh and unsatisfying reality may be secured through hallucinatory perceptual experiences is illustrated in the actions of a woman whose natural biological tendencies had been frustrated and who, because of personality inadequacies, had found economic and social adjustments too great a burden. One day as she was sitting on the bank of the Potomac River, preoccupied with her problems and dreaming of some means of satisfactory escape from them, she heard the voice of a former lover who had ceased his attentions as her personality limitations had become more apparent. In this thwarted and distressing state of affairs, she received from the old admirer a message pointing the way to an enchanting fulfillment of her fondest hopes. Although she could not see him, the patient heard the lover direct her to jump into the water, from which he promised to rescue her and row her to Norfolk, whence they would sail to Egypt, there to occupy a beautiful castle.

So convinced by the vividness of the message that reality was ignored, the woman threw herself into the water, where she would have perished except for some chance passers. A correct appreciation of her experience would have been too painful and disillusioning, and so she continued to believe in the reality of these autogenous perceptions.

The hallucinated object may be perceived at an extreme distance, as closely related to the experiences, or indeed as introjected into the body. Leston Havens' study on placement of hallucinations in space pointed out that the distancing of the object, particularly if human, is related to differing affective states. In those schizophrenics who hallucinate persons at a distance, the hallucinated person is perceived as threatening or abusive and the subject feels angry or flat toward the hallucinated individual. When the person is hallucinated as a companion close by, the affective state is more likely to be one of friendliness. In the case of the hallucinated person felt inside the patient's body, the pathologically hallucinated individual is berated, hated or accused, although sometimes expressions of admiration and friendliness are expressed. In all instances, the hallucinated person is recognized as not a part of one's self—"not me." Havens speaks, too, of certain hypochondriacal body parts as potential hallucinated percepts. He has suggested that in shifts of distancing over time toward the hallucinated objects in schizophrenics, movement takes place in connection with clinical improvement in the course of treatment.

In the mentally healthy person the majority of perceptions produced by casual stimuli from the environment are ignored. The content of perceptions in hallucinations is so intimately subjective that in their acute phases, at least, they cannot be ignored and therefore not only absorb the attention but require that reality be made to harmonize with them. As a result, the functional capacity of the ego for testing any reality that does not harmonize with the hallucinations is usually suspended.

In so-called *anticipatory illusions* and *hallucinations*, a person in a tense emotional state, say of fear, intently expects to see or hear the object that has excited the emotion. The result is that the perception momentarily expected in vivid clearness appears, but in a projected, hallucinatory, or illusional form.

Sometimes various gradations between normal representation and hallucinations may occur, with the result that the patient is uncertain whether his mental experience has been of a perceptual (unreal) nature or whether it has been merely a thought.

Hallucinations are to be differentiated from images which the individual locates within and as part of the inner self-experience. Images are usually less clearly defined and inconstant than the hallucinatory experience. *Pseudohallucinations* are those perceptions recognized by the subject as not real. Most frequently, the latter are experienced as images of deceased relatives or others who may call to or speak with the experiencing person.

Defining the existence of a hallucinatory experience is particularly difficult in children. One must be peculiarly sensitive to the diagnosis of hallucinatory experience among the young. It is insufficient to conclude that a child is suffering pathological auditory hallucinations merely on the basis of observing his behavior in distractively looking about, gazing at some object, or seeming to be listening to voices. The child should be led to describe the nature of the experience in detail before the determination is made whether a hallucination has actually occurred. Among children there are several recurring phenomena which cannot be regarded as pathological hallucinations. Some children describe clear images, in external objective space, of imaginary companions, either human or animal-like, and may play with or treat the image as real. Close questioning will reveal that he or she recognizes the nonexistence of the image or succumbs easily to the conviction that it does not exist. More often than not, the child's use of the imaginary companion is a representation of loneliness.

Nor should the *eidetic image* be confused with hallucinatory experience. Eidetic imagery is the ability to produce vivid and almost perfect images of visually presented material. Such imagery is not confused with reality. It is a frequent perceptual capacity of the young and developing child, which tends to decrease in incidence with age. It has been reported that 60 per cent of 4-year-olds have this perceptual capacity whereas it will be found in only 7 per cent of adults.

Pseudohallucinations in children are transient, shadowy, and often considered visions, which the child at a later age is capable of verbalizing and identifying as imagination. Such pseudohallucinations may be associated with anxiety or fright in the youngsters, and are more often discovered in those who show some indications of maladaptation or have been raised in distressing family situations. Another form of experience that is sometimes confused with pseudohallucination is the "night terror," in which the child, while seemingly not asleep, is unaware of his surroundings or the efforts of others to reassure him. He is, in fact, in a dreaming sleep. In this situation he may stare in an evident affective state of great fear. Such night terror attacks last from a few minutes up to half an hour and are followed by amnesia.

Hallucinations may occur in any diseases in which cerebral functioning is impaired. Although in these cases there is perhaps an irritation of the association centers connected with the special sense hallucinated, the nature of the material hallucinated is doubtless influenced by the psychological experiences of the patient.

Psychological material may be projected in the image symbols of any of the senses, although the images are characteristically of that sense best fitted to symbolize the particular material seeking expression. Feelings of guilt, for example, may best be expressed in spoken language, and so the patient hears accusing voices. Such accusing voices represent the projection of the critical voice of the superego. Fear of some aspect of the personality may well be symbolized by the sight of terrifying objects, and so the patient sees frightful animals. One patient with an experience he looked upon as one of moral contamination complained of a constant odor of carbolic acid. To him this chemical had always represented a purifying agent, and its hallucination was well adapted to symbolize his desire for a feeling of moral purification.

Hallucinations are more marked during the early and acute stages of psychotic reactions. This is to be expected, since it is the period when repression is failing and the solution of the conflict is proving unsuccessful. Hallucinations with clearness of consciousness are of much more serious prognostic import than those occurring with clouding of consciousness. Hallucinations occur less frequently when the patient is occupied with reality than when attention slackens or he begins to daydream. They are often associated with delusions, to which they add support or corroboration. At times, they seem to be the concrete symbolic expression of delusional ideas.

Hypnagogic hallucinations take place in healthy persons in that period between sleeping and waking.

Hypnopompic hallucinations occur when the subject is awakening; such hallucinations are observed in both those with psychiatric disability and the healthy. In a recent study Carrick McDonald found that hypnopompic hallucinations persist for shorter periods of time when they are related to a mental illness rather than a mental illness in association with brain disease. His study suggests, therefore, that the frequently stated clinical opinion of the nonpathological nature of the hypnopompic hallucination should be revised. McDonald noted as well that many of those with such hallucinations also had diurnal hallucinations. The patients with hypnagogic hallucinations most frequently suffered visual hallucinatory experiences, whereas those with both diurnal and hypnagogic hallucinations frequently had auditory impressions. Table 6–3 provides a summary of the illnesses occurring with those found to suffer hypnagogic hallucinations.

The occurrence of hallucinatory experience is not synonymous with mental disorder. Hallucinations and illusions may occur in healthy people in periods of prolonged isolation or under the influence of certain pharmacologic agents such as mescaline or d-lysergic acid diethylamide-25. Hallucinations induced by such agents are seldom formed, are usually lacking in ideational content, and are experienced as outside or beyond the self of the subject. In these respects they differ from the usual hallucinations of the psychotic person, who fails to distinguish the experience from reality and as beyond himself or herself. Otherwise these experiences are *ego*

dystonic. Again, they occasionally occur as transient phenomena and in a benign sense in familiar situations in which the perceiver is experiencing a special need for foods, fluids, or some other unrequited physiological need.

As a psychophysiological explanation for hallucinatory phenomena, West has proposed a "perceptual release theory." As he sees it, the brain constantly receives sensory impulses of all sorts, selectively excluding from consciousness the majority that are irrelevant to attentiveness and not needed to adapt to external reality. Concentration to maintain a clear focus is then a process both of scanning and screening incoming information from the external and internal worlds. When sensory input is diminished or impaired either by excessive affect or by disturbed synaptic transmission in toxic states of other processes affecting neural transmission, diminution of the stimulating effect of the sensory inputs occurs, but also increased cortical arousal. In such instances, perceptual "traces" otherwise occluded in the healthy scanning and selection process are released and re-experienced in consciousness, either familiarly or in new and bizarre combinations as hallucinations. For such release, the level of

TABLE 6–3   Illnesses Associated with Hypnagogic Hallucinations

	HYPNAGOGIC	HYPNAGOGIC + DIURNAL	ALL CASES
Functional group			
Psychoneurosis	1	1	2
Personality disorder	2	1	3
Paranoid state	1	0	1
Schizophrenia	7	12	19
Depression	2	2	4
Organic group			
Alcoholism	4	3	7
Epilepsy	2	2	4
Post encephalitic	1	1	2
Puerperal psychosis	0	3	3
Acute brain syndrome	0	1	1
Drug addiction	0	1	1
Tuberculosis (pulmonary)	0	1	1

(From McDonald, C.: Br. J. Psychiatry, *118*:543–547, 1971.)

arousal must be sufficient for conscious awareness to exist, and the particular perception-bearing circuits are in reverberation so as to command that awareness.

HALLUCINATIONS OF HEARING. As already indicated, hallucinations of hearing are the most frequent form of perceptual disturbance. Sometimes the hallucinations are in the form of various noises, but most often they consist of words arranged in more or less complete sentences. Usually these sentences are remarks concerning the patient or addressed to him. The patient may converse or quarrel with the "voices." He may locate them as coming from any part of his body or from a distance. Sometimes the remarks are of a pleasant nature but usually they are unpleasant, derogatory, obscene, or accusatory. These unpleasant remarks represent the projection of disowned personality aspects or desires which may not be allowed into the consciousness in undisguised form. Hallucinations conveying a command are often convincing and compelling. They may therefore lead to direct and dangerous action. Considerations of reality are of little weight in comparison to their influence.

Auditory hallucinatory experiences often are associated with movement of the laryngeal musculature, suggesting that the patient is uttering subvocally the words he perceives in his hallucination, just as a child does as he learns to read silently.

Miles H. Miller and his colleagues have found that auditory hallucinations are reported less commonly in patients with higher cognitive abilities and that the delusional schizophrenic who reports such hallucinations often shows an impoverishment in descriptive language skills. These findings suggest that in the patient's attempt to describe unfamiliar or stressful internal experiences, the degree of deviancy and vividness of the language of the psychotic not only reflects the intensity of the affective experiences to which he is exposed but his linguistic limitations as well.

HALLUCINATIONS OF SIGHT. These are not rare but are much less frequent than auditory hallucinations. They occur most typically in the deliria of acute infectious diseases or of toxic psychoses. In each of these states the visual hallucinations are apt to be accompanied by some clouding of consciousness. In general, visual hallucinations are confined to acute, reversible organic brain disorders. Visual hallucinations more frequently excite fear in the patient than do auditory ones, since they produce a greater distortion of reality. One of the most frequent mental disorders accompanied by visual images is delirium tremens, in which the images tend to be terrifying.

Most commonly, unformed visual hallucinations occur with disease of the occipital cortex, while formed hallucinations, sometimes consisting of complex scenes, result from disease of the temporoparietal cortex. Recently it has been suggested that formed visual hallucinations are more often associated with excitation or lesions of the dominant hemisphere. There are exceptions to these general observations; for example, various drugs may produce either type. Visual hallucinatory experiences have been induced not only by such agents as mescaline but also by amphetamine, atropine, and similar agents used in the treatment of parkinsonism.

HALLUCINATIONS OF OLFACTION. Hallucinations of smell are not uncommon in schizophrenic states and with lesions of the temporal lobe. Olfactory hallucinations are usually of an unpleasant or even of a strongly objectionable character. Their repulsive nature is not surprising, since they are particularly apt to represent feelings of disgust or guilt.

HALLUCINATIONS OF TASTE. True gustatory hallucinations are uncommon but at times are associated with hallucinations of smell. Illusions of taste are much more frequent.

TACTILE HALLUCINATIONS. Hallucinations of touch occur principally in toxic states, such as delirium tremens, and in cocaine addiction. Hallucinated sexual sensations are observed in schizophrenia and are often associated with grotesque delusions concerning bodily organs.

KINESTHETIC HALLUCINATIONS. The *phantom phenomenon*, that is, the hallucinatory perception of an amputated limb or of a limb denervated peripherally or through spinal cord transection, represents the most common form of kinesthetic hallucinatory experience. Such phantoms may change shape or size, or they may move. Distortions of the body image most frequently noted in schizophrenia or toxic states, particularly those induced by such drugs as mescaline, psilocybin, or *d*-LSD-25, also largely fall into this category of hallucinatory experience.

DISORDERS OF THINKING

The joining of ideas one to another by imagining, conceiving, inferring, and other processes, and the formation of new ideas by these processes, constitute a function we know as thinking. This may be looked upon as a form of internal or implicit behavior. Thought is the most highly organized of psychobiological integrations. In considering this function from the standpoint of psychiatry, attention should be directed to the production of thought, the progression of thought, and the content of thought. It should be remembered, too, that thought takes place on several levels, ranging from the fully conscious, dealing perhaps with highly abstract topics, to that on a primitive, emotional level.

DISORDERS IN FORM OF THOUGHT

As just indicated, thinking is a form of behavior which implies the existence of stimulus and response, the latter serving some psychologic purpose. In mental health, the stimuli for thought come from various sources, including unconscious and affective ones, but thinking is corrected by reason and logic. Such thought is known as rational or realistic. It appears to be directed by, and to take place in, conscious awareness. In daydreaming, thinking is guided not only by realistic considerations but to a considerable extent by egocentric wishes and instinctual needs. In mental disorder, and particularly in schizophrenia, thinking may be directed even more by unconscious factors and become of the type first designated by Bleuler as *autistic* and later as *dereistic*. In dereistic thinking (in contrast to realistic thinking), complexes, drives, and other affective and conative motivations are given free rein and operate without conscious regard for reality. As a result, associations of ideas are no longer logical.

DISORDERS IN PROGRESSION OF THOUGHT

The rate and manner of associative activity cannot, of course, be learned except through the patient's stream of talk. It is a familiar observation that, as one's thoughts are expressed in language, there is a pertinent association or linkage of each idea with the one that has preceded—that one's thinking moves in a logical progression toward a more or less definite end. This progression of thought is often known as the "stream of thought" or "stream of talk." Normally, there is a logical and coherent sequence of related ideas passing uninterruptedly and without digression from an initial idea to a goal idea.

Flight of Ideas

In certain mental disorders, there occurs a disturbance in the progression of thought characterized by an increased associative activity, a rapid digression from one idea to another. Ideas follow in quick succession but do not progress toward the goal idea, which is therefore never reached. This disturbance of the stream of thought in which the thinking processes appear to run too quickly and in which no idea is completed is known as *flight of ideas*. Flight of ideas is associated with an accelerated inner drive and distractability, as a result of which the patient is unable to sustain his attention and direct it toward a goal idea. Observation will usually disclose an associated relation between the thought· and a prompting stimulus springing from either an external or an internal source. Frequently a word similar in sound, but not at all so in significance, calls up the new thought. This is known as *clang association* and may lead to a senseless rhyme.

One patient with a rapid flow of thought, when asked if he were sad, replied, "Yes, you have to be quiet to be sad. Everything having to do with 's' is quiet—on the q.t.—sit, sob, sigh, sin, sorrow, surcease, sought, sand, sweet mother's love, and salvation. This is my first case—I am kind of a bum lawyer or liar—too damned honest to be a lawyer, so had to be a liar."

Retardation

As noted, the flow of thought in flight of ideas is abnormally rapid. In retardation, on the other hand, the initiation and movement of thought are slow. Often the patient will state that his thoughts come slowly or that he has difficulty in thinking. It will be noted that he speaks slowly and usually in a low tone. Retardation is most frequently observed in the depressive phases of the affective psychoses but may be noted in schizophrenia.

Perseveration

By perseveration is meant an abnormally persistent repetition or continuance in expression of an idea. This clinging to a thought may be observed at times in aphasia, catatonia, and in those with senile dementia.

Circumstantiality

Another disturbance in the flow of thought is that known as circumstantiality. In this disturbance, the patient finally reaches his ideational objective, but only after many unnecessary and trivial details have led him into tiresome digressions. Circumstantiality occurs largely among persons who do not form sharply defined concepts or are unable to distinguish essentials from nonessentials. In mental disorder, therefore, it is frequently observed among the feeble-minded, epileptics, and cases of moderately advanced senile mental disorder.

Incoherence

Sometimes the progression of thinking is so disorderly that one idea runs into another without logical consecution, and speech is not bound by any law. The result is a disorganization of syntactical structure with a lapse into disjointed phrases or even into parts of sentences and it is known as incoherence.

One schizophrenic patient, when asked how long she had been in the hospital, answered, "Oh, three weeks—since different statements are made—because it is hot—Mr. Smith is a cheap guy—French—how goes about it?"

In incoherence there is a tendency for ideas to arise from a confusion of complexes, viz., repressed material highly charged affectively. As might be expected, incoherence occurs particularly in schizophrenia, a disease in which the thinking is characteristically dominated by complexes. Much of the thinking of the schizophrenic is described as scattered, which simply means that the thinking is a little less disorderly than in incoherence.

Blocking

Another disturbance in the flow of thought is that known as blocking. In this disorder, sometimes known as thought deprivation or thought obstruction, both expression and progression of thought suddenly cease. To a degree it may be considered as having a prototype in the sudden inhibition of the train of thought sometimes occurring when one is overcome by some strong affect, such as anger or terror. After a time, the apparent obstruction seems to be removed, and the flow of thought is resumed. This interruption of the progression of thought is probably caused by the activity of a dominant complex with its associated unpleasant affect. At first the blocking may be caused by some definite thought, or rather by the disagreeable affect attached to it, but it quickly becomes general so that nothing more is initiated. Blocking to a severe degree seems to be confined to schizophrenia.

DISORDERS OF CONTENT OF THOUGHT

Trends and Overdetermined Ideas

There is a tendency for the associative evolution of ideas, and therefore for thought content, to be determined more by affective factors than by logical reasoning. Ideas having the strongest feeling tones tend to dominate. It is because of this fact that thought content may exhibit a trend, viz., a propensity to center around a special topic. When an idea comes to have an extreme feeling-tone connected with it, it is spoken of as an *overdetermined* or *overvalued idea.*

The importance or value and the meaning attached to an idea are directly proportional to the inner need for such a belief. When an overvalued idea exists, it blinds the individual to all else so that only those observations and memories are selected which suit its purpose or confirm it. Anything that conflicts with it is denied admission into consciousness.

The whole personality, including its thinking and feeling aspects, is absorbed by the idea and placed at its disposal, so to speak, with the result that the overvalued idea becomes one of the most important determinants of behavior. Trends and overdetermined ideas, like delusions, serve to satisfy some pressing inner need of the personality, such as a sense of security, defense, or self-esteem.

Delusions

Everyone is prone to develop comforting and other psychologically useful fictions to afford support and security to the personality. Apparently, mankind has always developed or adopted elaborate beliefs in an effort to satisfy inner needs. The construction of reassuring delusive beliefs as protection against anxiety and insecurity has been universally characteristic. This has been the unrecognized purpose in our fairy tales, in the folk stories about powerful persons, and in our father-image myths, beliefs, and creeds.

Sometimes the demand for the satisfaction of special inner needs of the personality may be so insistent that the claims of reality are disregarded and delusional ideas appear. Actuality is transformed to make it compatible with the emotional needs of the personality. The delusion is usually defined as a false belief. As we consider delusions and their meaning, value, and purpose, we shall see, however, that such a definition is fallaciously inadequate. It is often said that to be considered delusional, a false belief must be one that a person of similar education and experience would consider improbable or impossible and is not corrected in response to reason or logic. Even this definition is inadequate, since it ignores any consideration of the important principle that the incorrect understanding and use of facts and evidence are in response to definite purposes and needs of the personality and that the prevailing factors which control delusional thinking are affective rather than ideative or cognitive.

How inner needs may produce misinterpretations, denial, and misuse of facts in a way to be considered delusional is illustrated in the following case report:

During a recent foreign war, a woman was notified by the War Department that her husband had been killed on a certain date and buried where he died. Several months later, she visited the Department and expressed the conviction that her husband was alive and that the body of her supposed husband was actually that of no person known to her. The military authorities presented evidence that no error had been made, but the widow remained unconvinced and demanded that the body of her alleged husband be returned to America and examined. This was done and the identification number and the location of wounds were found to correspond to the records of the War Department. Still the woman remained unconvinced. Finally the reason for the delusion appeared. Among the officer's papers collected after his death and forwarded to the widow were affectionate letters from another woman. The patient had protected herself from the painful realization that she was not first in the affections of her husband by developing the belief that the man who had been killed and whose papers had been forwarded to her was someone other than her husband.

We thus see that situations containing highly affective factors are accompanied by a lowering of the critical faculty and of the threshold of beliefs. Attempts through factual disproof to convince the patient that his beliefs are delusional are therefore rarely successful. The patient's experiences are assimilated and the picture of the external world supplied by his thinking is falsified according to his nonadjusted affective and instinctive demands. He acts as if his delusional system constituted reality—as to him it does.

As indicated, the thinking we characterize as delusional is quite similar in kind, although different in degree, to that in which we all indulge. Our beliefs tend to be subjectively colored, and doubtless all of us resort to certain fictions of security. Employment of wishful thinking by "normal" persons in their struggle for a realization of their hopes, and of rationalization or projection for defensive purposes, serves the same psychological ends as do the delusions of the psychotic and imperceptibly merges into them. Prejudices, likewise, often arise from intrapsychic conflict and serve as defensive measures.

From what has been said, it will be seen that delusions are attempts to deal with the special problems and stresses of one's particular life situation in which fantasy is called upon to supply what real life has denied. They differ from the beliefs of the healthy, however, in their irrational fixity, even in the face of what would be considered incontrovertible evidence to the contrary.

Delusions, therefore, require an individual approach. Their trend is determined by the personality problems and needs of the patient before he became psychotic; the content will be found to reveal significant aspects of the patient's personal problems. The sources of these problems may often be found in thwarted trends and drives, frustrated hopes, feelings of inferiority, biological inadequacies, rejected qualities, teasing desires, gnawing feelings of guilt, and other situations that require a defense against anxiety. A deep-seated need for consolation, for example, may be met by self-flattering delusions.

Often the problem-solving value of the delusion and its relation to the situation by which it was produced are psychologically plain. Many times, however, the function of the delusion is far from obvious and its interpretation must remain a matter of speculation. This does not mean that the delusion is without significance or purpose. It possesses a definite adjustment value, but its source and purpose are concealed by its symbolically disguised content. When this central theme is extensively developed and conclusions are so logically deduced from the premises assumed that a coherent and connected organization of ideas is established, the patient's delusions are said to be *systematized*.

Since the psychological purposes and needs by which delusions are created fall into certain general classifications, and since well-defined mental mechanisms are employed in their creation, delusions may be classified according to certain types.

DELUSIONS OF GRANDEUR. Expansive delusions or delusions of grandeur arise from feelings of inadequacy, insecurity, or inferiority, any conscious recognition of which is prevented by the exaggerated ideative and affective components of the delusion. The content of grandiose delusions frequently suggests the nature of previous frustrations or insecurities. The patient who insists that he is God has, by the aid of his delusion, escaped from the troubles of reality which are too great a threat to his emotional security. If his distress was one of guilt, he has achieved perfection; if it was one of intolerable inferiority, he has achieved distinction; if it was one of fear, he has gained security and safety. The symbolic meaning of grandiose delusions is not greatly complicated and is fairly easily analyzed. Such delusions misidentify the self with another more powerful person.

DELUSIONS OF SELF-ACCUSATION. Delusions of self-accusation are believed to arise because the repression of unacceptable trends and desires weakens and the superego becomes increasingly critical. In such a case, repression is not destroyed, but the threat, as it were, that consciously forbidden tendencies might be permitted expression creates in the patient a vague feeling of guilt. This sense of guilt is then rationalized in consciousness into ideas of remorse and self-accusation. Feelings of guilt may be appeased through self-punishment.

DELUSIONS OF PERSECUTION. Ideas of persecution are among the most frequent forms of delusions, occurring especially in chronic psychotic disorders. The threat of unworthy desires and of troublesome and disowned aspects of the personality is projected as hostility from the environment. Sensitive dissatisfactions with self, arising from unadjusted elements in the personality, may be projected as a dissatisfaction, and therefore as hostility, felt toward one by others.

The formation of delusions of persecution is facilitated by the mechanism of projection which easily leads to misjudgments of reality. The hostile and aggressive motives that the patient attributes to others reflect his own inclinations. High aspirations without qualities necessary for satisfying success accompanied by an inability to accept defeat may lead to brooding, distrust, suspicion, misinterpretations, resentment, and ideas of persecution, coupled perhaps with aggressiveness. Delusions of persecution permit a shifting of responsibility and otherwise serve to relieve anxiety arising from guilt.

As a further measure for averting blows to self-esteem, the patient with ideas of persecution may develop compensatory reactions in the form of an exaggerated self-assurance. It will often be found that persons who develop delusions of persecution have, since childhood, been critical, resentful, suspicious, and unhappy. Not a few of them have been lonely, brooding, and insecure, and have lacked friends with whom they could share confidences. Ready to criticize others, they have been unable to tolerate criticism themselves.

It is not uncommon to find delusions of grandeur and of persecution associated. This is not surprising, since they serve much the same purpose, one tending to supplement the other. By his delusions of grandeur, the patient psychopathologically enhances his self-esteem and magnifies his ego. In the delusions of persecution, he repudiates and rejects those aspects and tendencies which self-respect would disavow by attaching them to others.

IDEAS OF REFERENCE. Through ideas of reference, remarks or actions on the part of other persons, although in no way referring to the patient, are interpreted by him as being significantly related to himself and often as expressing accusation or depreciation. In paranoid states, ideas of reference represent a projection of the patient's own self-criticism onto the external world. In depression, feelings of guilt may stimulate ideas of reference, and these, in turn, contribute to loosely organized paranoid delusions.

DELUSIONS OF SIN, GUILT, IMPOVERISHMENT, AND ILLNESS. In depression, delusions frequently represent the ideational expression of rationalization of an affective depression. If repression weakens, material, such as wishes, memories, or ideas, which is of such a nature that it would cause emotional pain if admitted to consciousness is apt to give rise to depression. Depressive delusions often represent the rationalization of a sense of depression that has had its source in unconscious hostile tendencies felt toward persons against whom such feelings and tendencies should not be directed.

Depressive delusions are most frequently expressed in ideas concerning guilt, disease, or poverty. Ideas of guilt and of loss of self-esteem may arise when the repression of unconsciously desired, but consciously repudiated, tendencies is weakened. The patient, in his attempt to rationalize the vague feelings of wickedness rising into consciousness, formulates ideas of self-accusation based on criticisms by the superego. Unconscious hostile tendencies may be projected outward, giving rise to fear of punishment. Any psychological factor which makes the patient feel that he stands out in an undesirable or unacceptable way from the rest of his social group may lead to *delusions of guilt* and therefore of depression.

Ideas of disease have similar meanings. The illness represents punishment for unacceptable and hostile drives to another; they may originate in identifications with the hated person.

Ideas of poverty are often the ideational representation of subjective sense of loss of social value. Such ideas of poverty may accompany delusions of guilt, the idea of unworthiness being displaced to the most generally recognized symbol of value—money. Appearing at times with depressive delusions are *nihilistic ideas* expressing the patient's belief that he has no brain, that he has no feeling, that he is dead, or that other sections of reality no longer exist. Such nihilistic ideas probably have their origin in vague feelings of emotional change and in a subjective feeling of unreality and of changed personality. This subjective sense of absence and of change is rationalized into ideas of annihilation.

In *passivity feelings* or *ideas of control*, the patient may express the delusional belief that he is controlled or that people read his mind. Such feelings probably represent the denial of an impulse to yield to threatening internal needs or demands which, however, are disowned through the mechanism of projection.

DELUSIONAL LOVING. In this delusional state, the sufferer believes that he or she is loved by another when in fact little or no relationship exists. Several delusional loving syndromes have been described: the phantom lover syndrome, erotomania, and De Clérambault s syndrome. In the phantom lover syndrome, the deluded person is convinced of having the love of a nonexistent person. Other less obvious variants are convictions of being loved by a person who is dead or one who has moved away, in denial of the death or absence. Others so deluded have spoken of being loved by a stranger or by someone they have never met or spoken to. Erotomania is the conviction that someone is intensely in love with the patient;

in De Clérambault's syndrome, a deluded woman believes a distinguished man is pursuing her erotically and is deeply in love with her.

In a recent study, Seeman describes two varieties of delusional lovers: those with fixed delusions and those with recurrent delusional lovers. The former are more seriously ill and are generally schizophrenic; the latter are schizoaffective or affectively disturbed.

DELUSIONAL REJECTION. In the Capgras syndrome, the sufferer has the fixed idea that a person is not real but is impersonating or taking the role of someone else.

Hypochondria

Although containing important affective elements of a depressive nature, hypochondria, with its exaggerated concern over physical health, may perhaps best be considered as a disturbance of ideational content. In hypochondria, the patient's attention is abnormally concentrated on his own body; he is depressed, and his thoughts are obsessively preoccupied with some organ which he is convinced is incurably diseased, although no pathological process can be demonstrated. A changed feeling of self may be present. Anxiety is displaced from unconscious mental sources to organs which thereby become the center of affective distress and preoccupation. The organ that is the focus of bodily complaint is usually one particularly subject to physiological expressions of anxiety or to the muscular tension of the anxious state. Hypochondria is more frequently manifested by persons who have learned through childhood transactions to solicit affection or to evade the responsibilities of life through illness.

In its milder forms, hypochondria may have its origin in a sense of insecurity which is rationalized as a threat to physical health. During the involutional period, the changing psychological outlook on life, as well as the regressive physiological processes and the failing psychobiological security, may cause hypochondria. If hypochondriasis is consistent with the mood, it tends to disappear as the pathological mood does. If it is symbolic or inconsistent with the mood, as in schizophrenia, it indicates a serious disorder.

Obsessions

Thoughts that persistently thrust themselves into consciousness against the conscious desire of the patient are known as obsessions. Obsessions persist in the conscious mind so tenaciously that they cannot be dispelled by conscious processes and are uninfluenced by logic or reasoning. The obsessive thought is strongly charged with the emotions of guilt or depression, is unwanted, and usually plagues the individual almost constantly. The sufferer cannot understand why he is obsessed with the thought.

Obsessive ruminations are of various content. Often the constant preoccupation concerns some metaphysical question. The patient, for example, may be compelled to keep asking himself why he was born. The explanation of obsessive thought is to be found in the activity of the unconscious and of repression. As a defensive device, a guilty anxiety is displaced to an innocuous idea and the anxiety thereby decreased. The obsessive thought that is consciously distasteful may be related to what is unconsciously desired. Obsessive thoughts are closely related to compulsive acts, in which, after a distressing resistance to its performance, the patient feels impelled to perform some act that, because of its elaborate and repetitive nature, often seems almost ritualistic.

Phobias

Allied to obsessive thoughts are phobias, or fears, doubts, and indecisions.

Like the obsessive idea, a phobia thrusts itself persistently into consciousness. Morbid anxiety always accompanies a phobia, in contrast to the guilt or depression of the obsessed. Among common phobias are fears of dirt, bacteria, cancer, or crowds. In general, one may say that the patient's anxiety becomes detached from a specific idea, object, or situation in his daily life and is displaced to some situation in the form of a specific neurotic fear. The fear that he feels in the presence of a certain object or experience is really the displaced fear of some anxiety-producing component within his own personality. The situation about which he is phobic symbolizes or represents the incidents arousing affects of rage or shame, affects that must be prevented from coming to the surface, usually out of anxiety of rupturing an important relationship. The patient is not, of course, aware of the psychological source or significance of his fear, and while he may acknowledge that his fear is irrational, he is quite unable to regulate his life except as dictated by the phobia. He is constantly attempting to control his anxiety by avoiding the object or situation to which the anxiety has been displaced.

Dysmorphophobia, the fear of some physical defect thought to be noticeable to others although the patient appears normal, probably represents a bodily delusion. It generally is regarded as having serious prognostic implications.

DISTURBANCES OF AFFECT

Affectivity penetrates and colors the whole psychic life, determining the general attitude, whether of rejection or of acceptance, in relation to any experience, promoting any tendency in harmony with it, and inhibiting any impulse not in agreement. As pointed out in an earlier chapter, the affective states provide the dynamic motivating drives. By *mood* is meant a sustained affective state of considerable duration.

Thus, affects serve as a signal or warning function for the ego and, at the same time, are the driving force that establishes the psychological defenses that lead to their repression. As an example, guilty affect serves as a warning to refrain or desist from a forbidden act or to make restitutive actions if the act has been committed. If, however, guilty affect is too intense, ego functioning may bring about its repression and denial or evolve methods of control through defiance or masochistic reaction formation. Shame, too, warns against failure to perform to standards acceptable to the ego ideal or is suffered in restitution for performance of an unworthy act. As an anticipatory defense against shame, pride may evolve. The motor components of certain affects such as laughter and crying also serve as a means of reducing tension.

Affective factors may interfere with associative tendencies and prevent one from becoming aware of certain strivings or other consciously unacceptable aspects of his mental life. There seems to be reason to believe that profound disturbances of affectivity may even produce disturbances of consciousness, as in the perplexed, bewildered states of deep depression. In fact, as patients are observed while they are suffering from mental disorders and their feelings are largely determined by unconscious factors, it becomes evident that affective factors influence not only all other psychic functions but other physiological ones as well.

The role of affects for psychopathology is well summarized by Bleuler: "Just as those abnormalities which we call psychopathies are practically nothing but thymopathies (disturbances of affects) so affective influences play such a dominant role in psychopathology in general that practically everything else is merely incidental. Only the feeblemindednesses, the confusions and most delirious states are predominantly disturbances of intellect. But even these are colored by affective mechanisms, and often in both their practical and theoretical significance are determined by affective factors."*

Psychiatric literature strongly stresses the importance of psychogenic factors in mental disorder. Although not clearly so denoted, such dynamic etiological factors are really affective in nature. It is not ideas themselves that are the important factors in determining the patient's mental content or his forms of behavior but the affects attached to his ideas. One thinks, therefore, according to the nature and intensity of his moods.

In the full evaluation of the significance of affect or feeling-tone in mental disorders, consideration must not be confined to that of pathological variations, since, directly and indirectly, affect exercises profound influence upon the thought and behavior of every individual. Not only is the thought content composed largely of affectively valued ideas, but judgment is constantly distorted and rendered unreliable by those ideas that are overvalued for emotional reasons. Associations are to a large degree directed by affective factors which facilitate those associations that tend to magnify the ego or aid in attaining some objective, while affects inhibit those associations that are unpleasant or opposed to some psychological need. If the tension of his emotional need or conflict exceeds the individual's capacity for evaluating reality, for appreciating its significance and remaining in contact with it, his experiences may be interpreted in accordance with affective needs and become hallucinatory or delusional.

By the mechanism of identification, an affect may be projected from the subject to which it was originally attached to one associated with or suggested by it. If, for example, a child came to hate a person who chanced to have some particular striking physical characteristic, then the child might always thereafter dislike persons who have a similar physical characteristic. In psychopathological states there is this constant tendency for the transfer of affects from material beyond conscious recognition to conscious thought content. In the psychoses, affective states of great intensity are often determined by unrecognized but highly dynamic factors.

Pleasurable Affects

A moderately pleasurable affect is known as *euphoria*. The euphoric patient is of an optimistic mental "set," is imbued with a subjectively pleasant feeling of well-being, and is confident and assured in attitude. Euphoria is most frequently noted in hypomanic states and in certain organic disorders such as general paresis, multiple sclerosis, and some cases of frontal lobe tumor. In *elation* an air of enjoyment and of self-confidence radiates from the patient, and his motor activity and drive are exaggerated. His circumstances may be such that unhappiness should be produced, yet everything that would normally produce that feeling is lightly brushed aside. It imparts a false sense of reality. Elation is often labile and readily shifts to irritability.

In *exaltation* there is an intense elation accompanied by an attitude of grandeur. A less frequent affective disorder is *ecstasy*. In this the mood is one of a peculiar, entrancing, peaceful rapture and tranquil sense of power. A religious feeling is an essential part of the state. The patient identifies himself with an immense cosmic power. He feels detached from outside things and on a new plane of existence, accompanied often by a feeling of having been reborn. He feels that he has attained a state beyond which there is nothing better. After having emerged from the experience, the patient retains a vivid recollection of it. Dynamically, ecstasy probably represents the achievement of the maximum of wish-fulfillment. Sometimes ecstasy occurs in persons

---

*Naturgeschichte der Seele, Zweite Auflage, S. 185. Julius Springer, 1932.

who have had a strong sense of guilt. It has been observed in dissociative, epileptic, schizophrenic, and affective reactions.

Depression

Depression, an affective feeling-tone of sadness, is probably the commonest type of complaint in psychiatric patients. Depression may vary from a mild downheartedness or feeling of indifference to a despair beyond hope. In the milder depressive syndrome, the patient is quiet, restrained, inhibited, unhappy, pessimistic, and self-depreciative and has a feeling of lassitude, inadequacy, discouragement, and hopelessness. He is unable to make decisions and experiences difficulty with customarily easy mental activities. He is overconcerned with personal problems. Some depressed persons are petulant, querulous, and distrustful. In somewhat deeper depression, there is a constant unpleasant tension; every experience is accompanied by mental pain; the patient is impenetrably absorbed with a few topics of a melancholy nature. Conversation may be painfully difficult. He is dejected and hopeless in attitude and manner. The patient's dispirited affective attitude is projected toward his environment, which reflects his dolesome outlook. He feels rejected and unloved. He may be so preoccupied with depressive ruminations that attention, concentration, and memory are impaired.

Depression has its roots in unconscious guilt arising from interpersonal issues, perhaps from unconscious ambivalence and hostility with resentful and aggressive impulses directed toward persons who are the objects of an undesired obligation (a mother whose dependency prevents her daughter's desired marriage) or toward persons on whom one is dependent for security. The hostile impulses originally directed against other persons become directed against one's own self.

It should be recognized that the affect of depression may include varying degrees of sadness, guilt, and shame simultaneously—sadness because of a loss, guilt over a repressed hostile drive, and shame due to failure to live up to some personal standard. Helplessness, too, may be associated. The further study of depressions and the analysis of the prepotent affect underlying the various forms of this state will go far toward providing knowledge of those types most amenable to alleviation. It is said that states of shame are much less accessible to change than those in which guilt predominates.

Grief is to be differentiated from depression as an affect of sadness suffered from a loss of a close personal relation and unassociated with the affects of guilt or shame due to some repressed hostility toward the lost person. Grief, while leading to a withdrawal and preoccupation with the lost person, is self-limiting and seldom leads to serious impairment of usual activities, personal derogation, suicidal thoughts, or serious domestic disturbance.

Anxiety

Anxiety is a persistent feeling of dread, apprehension, and impending disaster. It is a response to threats from repressed dangerous impulses deep within the personality or to repressed feelings striving for consciousness, a warning of danger from the pressure of unacceptable internal attitudes. It differs from fear in not being referable to specific objects or events. The patient is ignorant of its source.

Most psychiatrists, in using the word "anxiety" without a qualifying adjective, mean neurotic anxiety arising from self-inaccessible sources as just described. Some speak of "normal" anxiety, meaning thereby that there is an actual danger which is realistically appraised and that the degree of anxiety is not out of proportion to the threat. Such an anxiety does not have to be managed by forcing it out of awareness by such mechanisms as repression or dissociation or by using neurotic defenses.

Anxiety is often displaced from its original, but unrecognized, source to some other situation which appears to the patient to afford reasonable grounds for apprehension, to be the excitant of his diffuse, unformulated uneasiness and painful apprehension. Sometimes the anxiety is not attached to any ideational content but is felt as a morbid fear without apparent source. Anxiety felt directly and expressed in this manner is known as *free-floating* anxiety. Again anxiety may be covert. In this hidden form, there are no obvious tension and painful apprehension with their physical manifestations. The various personality traits of the individual, together with the mental mechanisms he has developed to conceal or displace his anxiety, may serve sufficiently well as defenses to prevent its overt expression. It may still, however, be the fundamental basis for the development of serious personality deviations or disorders. Anxiety is the presenting symptom in the so-called anxiety neuroses and may often be openly manifest in other neuroses. Anxiety, therefore, together with the various defensive mechanisms, such as repression, regression, conversion, and displacement, constitutes an important factor in the psychopathology of abnormal personalities, psychoneuroses, psychoses, and psychosomatic disease.

Anxiety occupies a position of great importance in psychoanalytical theory, according to which it results from the threat either of uncontrollable id forces or of self-destructive superego forces. According to this theory, anxiety is of significance in two roles: It serves not only as a signal or indicator of conflict but also as a reinforcing agent for repression, reaction-formation, and projection. In fact, the various mental mechanisms and devices which serve a defensive purpose exercise that function through their ability to reduce the strength of anxiety.

Through its effect upon the autonomic system, anxiety is particularly apt to lead to disturbances of physiological functions and to find expression in psychophysiological symptoms. In acute forms, it may, through stimulation of the autonomic system, produce generalized visceral tension and therefore hyperventilation, spasm of the cardiac and pyloric portions of the stomach, intestinal irritability, hyperchlorhydria, diarrhea or constipation, palpitation, tachycardia, extrasystoles, vasomotor flushing, and respiratory distress. It may be accompanied by fainting, weakness, nausea, and tremor. Hands and face may perspire; the patient may assume a tense posture and show excessive vigilance and fidgety movements of the hands or feet; the voice may be uneven or strained and the pupils widely dilated. When anxiety is severe and overflows in this way into the muscular system, producing gross motor restlessness, the reaction of the patient is spoken of as *agitation*.

Tension is sometimes confused with the affect of anxiety. In tension, the patient has a continuing feeling of tautness, both emotionally and in his muscles. He senses a restlessness, dissatisfaction, dread, and discomforting expectancy. He presents a strained, tense expression of the facies, his fingers are tremulous, and he manifests an abrupt haste in movement. The patient may experience difficulty in concentration and complains of tightness or other unpleasant sensations in the head. Tension may arise when a person is torn between contradictory desires and strivings, by a struggle for security, and by various other situations. Its origin may be from either conscious or unconscious sources. It is a component of anxiety, expressive of a continuing inner perception of this affect accompanied by neuromuscular setting.

Panic is a pronounced state of anxiety which produces disorganization of ego functions. One of the best descriptions is that of Diethelm: "Panic is not merely a high degree of fear, but a fear based on prolonged tension, with a sudden climax which is characterized by fear, extreme insecurity, suspiciousness and a tendency to projection and disorganization." Misinterpretations are followed by projections that may assume the form of hallucinations having a threatening and accusatory content, and also may have the form of delusions of persecution. The situations giving rise to panic are ones in which some long-standing insecurity of the personality has created tension and become particularly threatening. Homosexual and, occasionally, disowned heterosexual tendencies are the most frequent factors. Because of the underlying sense of insecurity, the patient may react with self-assertion and aggressiveness and may rush about; in other cases, he may exhibit dilated pupils and the other usual sympathicotonic manifestations of great anxiety, yet remain immobile because he does not dare move. He often has difficulty in thinking and at times has a sense and appearance of bewilderment. Suicide is not uncommon in panic states. This state of panic differs from the panic disorder described in the new American nomenclature (DSM-III).

Inadequate Affect

Emotional dulling or detachment in the form of indifference or *apathy* is a frequent form of affective disturbance and is characterized by an inadequate sensitiveness to those experiences that normally give rise to pleasure or pain. The facies shows an emptiness of expression. Patients suffering from this affective impoverishment show a lack of drive and interest in matters that have previously appealed to them. There is an indifference to esthetic and other finer sentiments. Such qualities as gratitude, sympathy, hope, anticipation, grief, regret, pride, or shame no longer appear to form part of the patient's subjective experience. This absence of emotional responsiveness may cause the patient to seem out of touch with reality. Apathy may be regarded as a protective, defensive reaction, perhaps against painful perceptions.

Inappropriateness of Affect

Disharmony of affect is a common emotional disturbance, particularly noted in schizophrenia. The patient smiles when the social situation suggests a serious mien as appropriate. He laughs or cries out of context to the interpersonal milieu and apparently in relation to his inner percepts and associations, to which the affect may be quite appropriate.

Ambivalence

Recognizing that each feature of the personality has a double aspect, each having a counterpart closely connected with it, Bleuler introduced into psychiatric thought the concept of ambivalence. In affective ambivalence, contradictory feeling attitudes may exist toward the same object. Both of these conflicting attitudes are faces on the same coin; while only one may be visible, the other is nevertheless present. One of the two components of ambivalence remains repressed but may give rise to anxiety and feelings of guilt. A common form of ambivalent polarity is a subtle combination of love and hate. A person caring for an invalid member of his family may, for example, have mixed feelings. One feeling may be that of love, of wanting to be helpful, but another, of which he is not conscious, may be that of annoyance and hostility. Affection is linked with a sentiment of rejection. In the confusion of hostile and affectionate impulses, there may be an intensification of conscious love in order to repress the fundamental hatred. An expression of hostility toward one to whom a person should be indebted, a parent, for example, is not consciously tolerable. The hostility, therefore, necessarily remains unconscious lest it give rise to anxiety. The ambivalent attitudes of hostility and love are accordingly developed. Often when ambivalence of feelings exists, the repressed component of the dual affective attitude will be projected; for example, repressed hatred may be experienced as hatred directed toward one's self by the other party.

Depersonalization

Depersonalization, a pervasive and distressing feeling of estrangement, known sometimes as the depersonalization syndrome, may be defined as an affective disorder in which feelings of unreality and a loss of conviction of one's own identity and of a sense of identification with and control over one's own body are the principal symptoms. The term was introduced by Dugas in 1898. The unreality symptoms are of two kinds: a feeling of changed personality and a feeling that the outside world is unreal. The patient feels that he is no longer himself, but he does not feel that he has become someone else. The condition is, therefore, not one of so-called transformation of personality. Experience loses emotional meaning and may be colored by a frightening sense of strangeness and unreality. The onset may be acute, following a severe emotional shock, or it may be of gradual onset following prolonged physical or emotional stress. It is more frequent in personalities of an intelligent, sensitive, affectionate, introverted, and imaginative type. The patient may say his feelings are "frozen," that his thoughts are strange; his thoughts and acts seem to be carried on mechanically, as if he were a machine or an automaton. People and objects appear unreal, far away, and lacking in normal color and vividness. The patient may say he feels as if he were going about in a trance or dream. He appears perplexed and bewildered because of the strangeness of unreality feelings. He has difficulty in concentrat-

ing and may complain that his brain is "dead" or has "stopped working."

Depersonalization is probably not a specific disorder but occurs in various neurotic and psychotic states such as depressions, hypochondria, obsessional states, and hysteria, and in some early schizophrenias. Apparently it may occur in some normal persons after exhaustion or shock. It is more common at puberty and in women. The reaction may be regarded psychopathologically as a form of withdrawal from reality or as a means of escape from an intolerable situation. Frances and associates regard it as an affect denoting the sufferer s sense of disruption of self-constancy.

DISTURBANCES OF CONSCIOUSNESS

Perhaps from a descriptive standpoint the words "clearmindedness" and "awareness" best indicate what we designate as consciousness. The sensorium is clear, i.e., the functioning of the special senses is intact, and the apprehension of external stimuli presented to them is unimpaired. The individual is able to apprehend his environment as to place, time, person, and general setting, to understand questions, and to reflect upon them.

Full consciousness demands attentiveness as well as that complex function known as *apperception,* by which through active, attentive thoughts one analyzes, integrates, evaluates, and absorbs experience. It is through apperception that new ideas are formulated and related to ones already familiar, with the result that one is able to understand or grasp new situations, events, and experiences. In *disturbances of apperception,* the patient has difficulty in understanding questions, unaccustomed situations, and experiences. Disorders of apperception occur in psychogenic diseases involving intense preoccupation and in other disturbances of attention, as well as in toxic and organic states. Faulty capacity for apperception exists, of course, in mental deficiency. The projective psychological tests (Rorschach and thematic apperception) are examinations of this function.

Among the disturbances of consciousness are those imposed by *disordered attention.* The conscious, selective reaction by which the organism examines the external world for useful data is known as attention. Successful examination requires a certain degree of vigilance and a certain tenacity. Attention is greatly influenced by conation, affect, and associations. Feelings and attitudes influence attention, not only directly but indirectly, through their effect upon associations. Fatigue, toxic states, and organic lesions strongly modify both vigilance and tenacity and so influence attention. Toxic and organic factors, by interfering also with associations, tend to lower attention. Similarly, a poverty of associations is largely responsible for defects of attention in the mentally deficient. Even a normal person who has few associations connected with an object submitted for examination will, in the absence of strongly affective factors, exhibit but little attention. The inability to hold the attention a sufficient length of time to render adequate examination possible is known as *distractibility.* In this disorder, every fleeting stimulus or an abnormal lability of affect redirects the attention, which is lacking in normal tenacity. Profound depression, on the other hand, may cause too great tenacity of attention. No stimulus or experience can divert the attention to an idea or object not related to the patient's depressive mental content or not in harmony with it. Emotional disorganization as seen in the apathetic schizophrenic may greatly diminish the degree of attention.

As indicated in an earlier chapter, consciousness may be considered to exist at varying levels of awareness of one's environment. Thus it is to be suspected that the clinical disturbances of this function roughly describe pro-gressively serious levels of impairment. The clinician defines as successive steps in defects, from the least to the greatest impairments, states of confusion, clouding of consciousness, delirium, dream, and fugue states, to complete stupor.

Confusion

Confusion is a disturbance of consciousness characterized by bewilderment, perplexity, disorientation, disturbance of associative functions, and poverty of ideas. The face of the confused patient presents a distressed, puzzled, and, at times, surprised expression. Confusion is confined largely to conditions in which there is a diffuse impairment of brain tissue function, especially associated with toxic, infectious, or traumatic agents, although it occurs also in dissociative reactions and epileptic dream states. Most psychiatrists believe that the term confusion should not be loosely applied to those subjects, such as retarded, depressive, or perplexed schizophrenic patients, whose replies are neither prompt nor pertinent. Many consider that true confusion is found only in toxic-organic reactions. Certainly clouding of consciousness is the basic feature in the toxic-organic states.

Clouding of Consciousness

Clouding of consciousness is a disturbance in which clear-mindedness is not complete, usually because there are physical or chemical disturbances producing functional impairment of the associative apparatus of the cerebrum. The threshold of consciousness is high, and perceptions are not produced by those sensory stimuli which ordinarily result in clear perceptions. The capacity to think clearly and with customary rapidity, to perceive, respond to, and remember current stimuli is impaired. To make the patient understand a question, it may be necessary to shake him, to shout the question, and perhaps to repeat this procedure several times before he apprehends sufficiently to reply. Attention wanders, and the patient's apprehension of his environment is incomplete and inaccurate. The symptom is often seen in general hospitals in patients suffering from infectious diseases and other conditions affecting cerebral oxygenation and metabolism. Clouding of consciousness may also occur in psychogenic disturbances, such as dissociative reactions. In this case, the clouding and the subsequent amnesia for events of the clouded period may serve the purpose of excluding from awareness material which deep-seated wishes would shut out. Clouding of consciousness may be of various degrees, ranging from hebetude to somnolence, stupor, or coma.

Delirium*

Although involving much more than a disturbance of consciousness, mention should be made of the symptom-complex known as *delirium*, also designated as the *acute brain syndrome*. This syndrome, ordinarily acute in both development and course, consists of clouding of consciousness, bewilderment, restlessness, confusion, disorientation, incoherent or dreamlike thinking, illusions and hallucinations, and apprehension or fear. Its occurrence is usually associated with infections accompanied by fever, toxic states, metabolic disturbances (uremia, pellagra, pernicious anemia), cardiac decompensation, or head trauma, which impair cerebral functioning and cause cerebral insufficiency. Some persons develop delirium more readily than do others. Perhaps in some cases this tendency is caused either by an inherently greater vulnerability of the brain to toxins or by a less resistant blood-cerebrospinal

---

*The clinical picture of delirium is well depicted in Shakespeare's description of Falstaff's death: "For after I saw him fumble with the sheets, and play with flowers, and smile upon his finger's ends, I knew there was but one way; for his nose was sharp as a pen, and 'a babbled of green fields." Henry V, Act II, Scene iii.

fluid barrier. On the other hand, the susceptibility may depend upon the integration and stability of the personality. Electroencephalographic changes are usually found in delirium. Generally, the greater the reduction in the level of awareness, the greater the shift toward slower-frequency ranges. The electroencephalographic changes are reversible to the extent to which the clinical delirium is reversible.

Delirium is usually more marked at night, when the ordinary background of sensory input is reduced; at times it may be limited to nighttime, the patient seeming normal during the day. The most frequent prodromal symptoms are drowsiness, restless sleep, difficulty in grasp, and impaired attention. In very mild cases, the patient may merely appear mentally dull and sluggish and not keenly aware of just what is happening to him. He may show a little "wandering" but become clear when addressed. Attention is impaired, and there is a reduction in capacity for abstract thinking. The patient usually has difficulty in performing tests requiring concentration and sustained attention, e.g., the serial subtraction of 7s from 100. As the delirium becomes more marked, the patient seems dazed, baffled, and bewildered and fails to recognize members of his family.

Important symptoms are fluctuations in grasp or perception of reality, orientation, and consciousness. Shifting degrees of awareness and of orientation should always suggest the possibility of delirium. Moments of rationality often alternate with moments of irrationality. If the clouding of consciousness has been marked, the patient, after recovery, has no recollection of what occurred during the delirium. Frequently the memory is patchy, varying with the fluctuations of consciousness that occurred during the delirious episode. Other variations in the clinical picture often coexist and are also suggestive. Comparative calmness, for example, may exist for a period, to be followed suddenly by restlessness or impulsive activity. The patient's mood may shift rapidly or be characterized by doubt, perplexity, irritability, apprehension, fear, and even panic. Frightening dreams and fantasies may arise, and both illusions and hallucinations occur, the former being more frequent. Visual hallucinations are more frequent than auditory ones and at first are often in the form of ill-defined or shadowy figures. The content of thought and of hallucinations is more dependent upon the patient's personality problems and tendencies and his previous life experiences than upon the nature of the underlying physical process responsible for the delirium. Frequently the patient shows motor disturbance, manifested in mild cases by tremulousness in writing, but in more severe cases by picking, grasping, and groping. Activity may vary from mild restlessness to intense and uncontrollable overactivity.

Delirium rarely continues for more than a month and in infectious diseases may be of only fleeting duration. Later delirious episodes tend to resemble any previous ones, in both content and course. Following his recovery, the patient often describes his hallucinations and other delirious experiences as having been dreamlike in nature. Although the delirious syndrome occurs frequently in infectious diseases and in their febrile period, it is by no means confined to such association. Toxic-delirious reactions occur in old age in a wide variety of physical illnesses. Postoperative psychoses, more frequent in elderly patients than in younger ones, usually resemble those of toxic-exhaustive and infective states and therefore present features of delirium. Puerperal psychoses, even those that are fundamentally affective or schizophrenic in nature, often show characteristics of delirium in their onset. Delirious reactions are most frequent with excessive use of bromides and other drugs.

Dream States

Presenting a somewhat similar but more exaggerated symptom complex is the disturbance known as *dream trance* or *twilight state*. Such a state does not, like delirium, arise from toxic-organic conditions, but is of affective or other psychogenic origin. Consciousness is usually disturbed, in some cases being so clouded or confused that the patient is not aware of his real surroundings. Visual and auditory hallucinations occur, in response to which the patient may perform complex acts, such as running away or committing acts of violence. These dream states may last from several minutes to a few days.

When normal consciousness is regained, the patient may report that during the twilight state he felt as if he were dreaming and he has little or no recollection of events that occurred during its existence. Such dream states occur for the most part in dissociative reactions and in epilepsy. In dissociative reactions they represent escape from unpleasant reality or the gratification of frustrated wishes. In epileptic dream states the behavior is motivated by more deeply unconscious factors.

Stupor

Stupor is identified as existing when the patient is akinetic (motionless) and mute but with relative preservation of consciousness. Movement of the eyes and respiration occur. However, the eye movements generally appear purposeful. Subsequent to the stuporous state, there is often ability to recall events, although total amnesia may result. Stupor is to be differentiated from sleepiness, loss of consciousness as in coma, and organic motor paralysis.

Stupor may occur in a diversity of physical and mental conditions, from toxic states, organic brain disease, intense apathy, profound depression, blocking, epilepsy, and dissociative reaction to overpowering fear. In neither toxic-organic stupor nor psychogenic stupor does the patient move. In toxic-organic stupor, conscious thought processes are suspended; in catatonic stupor, there is intense preoccupation of thought which is often dereistic in nature, with a loss of reality sense but no real suspension of consciousness. A sudden change from stupor to activity, often impulsive or excessive, occurs in psychogenic stupor only.

DISORDERS OF ORIENTATION

The process by which one apprehends his environment and locates himself in relation to it is known as *orientation*. If a person knows his position in reference to time, appreciates his situation as to both space and circumstances, and understands his relationship to other individuals, he is said to be oriented. If he does not recognize and locate himself in respect to any one of these matters, he is said to be disoriented in the particular sphere in which he has an inadequate grasp. The development of personality identity, which commences with the early exploration of one's body and that of the mother, as well as the exploration of space and the growing awareness of time, established through the periodic experiencing of emerging needs and their satisfaction, lays down the individual's orientation in these spheres.

Disorientation may occur in any mental disorder in which there is extensive impairment of the patient's memory, of the extent or accuracy of his perceptions, or of his attention. Disturbances of orientation are the significant symptomatology of acute cerebral insufficiency, by which are designated the organic brain syndromes (delirious states) in which the physiological functions necessary for memory, perception, and attention are impaired. Less frequently, disorientation is caused by acute conflicts, intense affective factors, distractibility, or lack of interest or attention.

DISORDERS OF MEMORY

The function by which information that has been acquired and presented to consciousness through the observations of attention is stored, later to be summoned and again presented to consciousness, is known as *memory*. For the purpose of description, it may be considered as consisting of three processes: the reception and *registration* of a mental impression; the *retention* or preservation of the previously acquired impression; the reproduction or *recall* of the impression. Memories are defined now as recent or remote. As discussed earlier, permanent registration to establish the long-term memory trace is believed to involve complex electrochemical events within the brain. Memory is purposive and tends to promote adaptation with the minimum of effort by virtue of its role in assisting the individual to profit by his experience. Largely as a result of the investigations of abnormal psychology, it is known that memory is influenced by affect, the tendency being to modify it in the interests of the emotional needs of the individual.

Forgetting, too, is purposive in that it may be regarded as the result of the organizing process of memory. Those sensory impressions which are generalized or subordinated, or have come to be conceptualized as a means of retaining larger banks of information or memory or condensed and fused to maintain an efficiently operative working memory, tend to be forgotten. It is believed that everything registered as a memory persists, barring impairment of brain structure and function. Yet many sensory impressions may not be recorded within the brain as permanent memory. Psychologically repressed memories are not forgotten; they remain available when the affective states inducing repression are modified. Generally, forgetting may be thought of as a function of reorganizing of memory; newly recorded experiences have the potentiality of reorganizing existing memories.

The disorders of memory are three: abnormally pronounced memory, or *hypermnesia;* loss of memory, or *amnesia;* and falsification of memory, or *paramnesia.* Today, combinations of the latter are sometimes denoted the *amnestic-confabulatory syndrome.*

Hypermnesia

Hypermnesia is occasionally seen in mild manic states, paranoia, and catatonia. This excessive mnemonic capacity is largely limited to specific periods or to specific events and experiences that are connected with particularly strong affects. Impressions arising from emotionally colored events are registered with more than the usual intensity; with the result that the patient has a vivid recollection of details.

Amnesia

Amnesia may be produced either by organic or by psychogenic factors. In *organic amnesia,* physiological disturbances of neurons, through chemical alterations, trauma, or degenerative changes, interfere with associative processes. Organic loss of memory is caused by impairment of both registration and retention, especially the latter. In *psychogenic amnesia,* recall, for psychologic reasons, is inhibited. Strictly speaking, forgetting in psychogenic amnesia is not a passive loss of memory trace. The absence of memory is an active defense against experiences which have proved unbearably painful or anxiety producing. Psychogenic amnesia may provide escape not only from the memory of intolerable experiences but also from the consequences of an act. If anxiety is severe, a dissociative reaction may occur with a resulting fugue or flight automatism, in which the patient experiences a loss of memory of both his past experiences and his identity. By this escape, the patient's symptoms supply him, without awareness on his part, with a seeming solution for his difficulties.

Another and more frequent form of psychogenic amnesia is that for intended action. This is a result of conflict of wishes. We "forget" to perform some task or keep some appointment because the proposed act conflicts, perhaps unconsciously, with some wish or interest.

The differential diagnosis between organic and psychogenic amnesia is important. To differentiate between these two forms the psychiatrist must determine the cause. Often this is obvious, but if not readily apparent, a careful history should be secured and a searching examination of the nervous system be made before concluding that the amnesia is of psychogenic origin. Such an origin should not be accepted unless a psychological need for its occurrence is discovered.

If there has been no disturbance of consciousness and no impairment of intellectual functions, the amnesia is probably psychogenic in origin. A selective amnesia in which inconvenient events or topics are forgotten is of psychogenic origin. A sudden and complete recovery of memory is common in cases of psychogenic amnesia but does not occur if the amnesia has been caused by organic factors. Any recovery of memory which has been lost through organic causes takes place gradually and is often incomplete. A fragmentary type of amnesia with a scattered loss of memory for unrelated details of experience, as noted in general paralysis or senile dementia, is of organic origin.

Amnesia for circumscribed periods of time may be either psychogenic or organic in nature. A generalized failure of memory for both recent and remote events denotes an organic degenerative disease of the brain. A patchy amnesia with a memory for isolated events in a period of confusion is frequent in delirium. An organic amnesia may be followed or widely overlapped by a psychogenic failure of recall, especially in head injuries.

Modern students of amnestic states

often classify them as transient or persistent. The amnesias associated with acute cerebral insufficiency due to drug or toxic states, as in delirium, generally are transient. Those resulting from progressive impairment of cerebral function are persistent and are known as dementias.

ANTEROGRADE AMNESIA. An anterograde amnesia is one that extends forward to cover a period following the apparent regaining of environmental contact. Anterograde amnesia is sometimes observed in boxers who have received a severe blow on the head. The pugilist is hit but continues boxing in an apparently normal manner. Retrospectively, however, he reports a gap in his memory extending forward from the time of the injury and covering the period to the end of the fight or even beyond.

RETROGRADE AMNESIA. In retrograde amnesia, there is a loss of memory extending back over a period prior to the time when the onset occurred. In cases of trauma to the head, there may be a retrograde amnesia reaching back over a variable period prior to the injury with its accompanying loss of consciousness. It may also follow many other forms of organic interference with cerebral function, such as suicidal attempts by hanging or gassing, or epileptic convulsions. It is often seen after treatment by electric shock.

Recovery from retrograde amnesia is chronological, those memories nearest the injury being the last to return. The amnesia in Korsakoff's psychosis is both retrograde and anterograde. Retrograde amnesia may also be of psychogenic origin and has been known to stretch back over a prolonged period. In psychogenic retrograde amnesia, an experience has been registered but is not recalled except through an association of ideas. As it is recalled in this manner, the recall is accompanied by an emotional response appropriate to the forgotten material.

As the result of precise surgical extirpations it has been found that bilateral lesions of the medial surface of the temporal lobe, particularly the hippocampi, are followed by severe memory defects, particularly in the ability of retention. Such operations are also followed by both anterograde and retrograde amnesia; early memories and technical skills remain undisturbed.

Paramnesia

Paramnesia, or falsification of memory, as well as distortions of memory, also serves as protection against intolerable anxiety. In the form known as *confabulation* the patient fills the gaps in his memory by fabrications, which are without any basis of fact, although, when relating them, he accepts them as actual occurrences. These fictions change from moment to moment and may often be suggested and directed by the person to whom they are related. Paramnesia is observed occasionally in the senile psychoses but particularly in Korsakoff's syndrome.

RETROSPECTIVE FALSIFICATION. Of different psychological significance are the retrospective falsifications, or illusions of memory, created in response to affective needs. We all tend to embroider the truth in accordance with these needs or unconsciously to select those memories that suit our interests. Two persons who have intense but different emotional attitudes relative to a certain event or experience will relate quite different accounts of the circumstances. Both persons may be honest but each will remember details in harmony with his emotional needs and forget those not consistent with his affects. In paranoid psychoses, one meets with exaggerations of this tendency. The patient misinterprets an actual event, appends imaginary details to it, or even relates experiences that have little or no basis of fact. Such falsifications of memory serve the purpose of supplying supporting evidence for the patient's delusions, which, too, are products of affective needs.

Defensive distortions of recall may serve to avert threats or to enhance self-esteem. Early childhood memories reported by patients sometimes represent such distortions. Whether distorted or not, they are worthy of note as are first and repetitive dreams. It has been reported that the early memories of psychotics are more frequently of being lost, being threatened with death, or losing control. The psychoneurotic more frequently reports self-images. Memories of sickness and death in the psychotic are often those of neglect; in the neurotic, of overdependency.

"Déjà Vu"

Mention should be made of the illusion of memory known as *déjà vu*. In this phenomenon, there is a feeling of familiarity on observing something—a new scene, for example—of which there has, in fact, been no previous observation, or of having previously lived through a current experience. It arises when the present situation has an associative link with some past experience or occurrence for which the patient is amnesic.

Various explanations have been offered for the phenomenon, but it seems to occur when the forgotten experience has been the center of psychological conflict and consequent repression. Several psychodynamic explanations have been offered. For instance, there is a drive for a repetition, a second chance to solve a conflict, so that the outcome of the incident may coincide with the wish. Again, the *déjà vu* both symbolizes and stimulates the revival of an anxiety-producing wish or fantasy which is then defensively dealt with as unreal and projected onto the current external situation offered as a substitute for the past. Thus repression is main-

tained. It may occur in normal people, especially in young people who are given to day-dreaming. In the phenomenon of *jamais vu* there is a false feeling of unfamiliarity with situations which have actually been experienced. These phenomena may occur in schizophrenia, psychoneuroses, lesions of the temporal lobe, including epilepsy, and states of fatigue or intoxication.

Functions of Psychogenic Memory Disturbances

It is apparent from what has been said that memory loss, in the absence of structural or toxic changes in the higher cortical neurons, is a selective process and not a matter of chance. It plays an important part in promoting the comfort and self-esteem of the individual.

Largely through the observations of Freud and of Brill it has been realized that slips of tongue and pen, such as use of a wrong word, or one opposite to that consciously intended, the loss or destruction of objects consciously valued, little forgettings, and various erroneous acts of everyday life that are ordinarily regarded as merely "accidental," are determined by unconscious motives. Since these apparently unmotivated errors resemble symptoms in their relation to repression, they are often spoken of as *symptomatic acts*.

DEMENTIA

In any structural disturbance or degeneration of the higher cortical neurons, such as those caused by prolonged intoxication or malnutrition, there results a permanent, irreversible loss of intellectual efficiency known as *dementia*. If of but slight degree, the impoverishment may be manifested by defective self-criticism and by impairment in capacity for fine discriminations, in decisions involving delicate moral issues, and in ability to employ abstract ideas.

As dementia progresses, there are an increasing poverty of initiative, a restriction of interests, and a blunting of concern; impressions are taken in and assimilated slowly, with difficulty, and often inexactly. There is therefore a failure to profit from experience. Aptitude and learning capacity are reduced. It becomes increasingly difficult or even impossible for the patient to understand and follow conversation. Questions are not answered or are answered only after several repetitions. Memory is defective and disorientation and confusion may exist. There is a poverty of the imagination necessary for productive thinking. The content of consciousness is reduced in both number and variety of associations, with the result that new ones are formed with difficulty, imperfectly, or even not at all. The individual's capacity for integrating his past experience with his present is reduced, and judgment becomes defective. Emotions are unstable or inadequate.

Care must be taken not to mistake for dementia the temporary inhibition of interest caused by preoccupation, or the dulling of consciousness caused by external or internal toxins. One must not mistake the acquired dementia of organic lesions for the innate oligophrenia of the feeble-minded.

The causes of dementia may be grouped as follows:

1. Atrophic changes of the brain resulting in senile dementia;
2. Vascular disorders of the brain, including arteriosclerotic dementia and hypertensive encephalopathy;
3. Inflammatory disorders of the brain, particularly syphilis and epidemic encephalitis;
4. Degenerative diseases of the brain, notably Alzheimer's disease, Pick's disease, and Huntington's chorea;
5. Deficiency diseases, including Korsakoff's psychosis, Wernicke's encephalopathy, pellagra, and pernicious anemia or vitamin B_{12} deficiency;
6. Neoplasm;
7. Trauma.

BIBLIOGRAPHY

General

Jahoda, M.: Current Concepts of Positive Mental Health. New York, Basic Books, 1958.

Motor Disorders

Buglass, D., and Heston, J.: The repetition of parasuicide: A comparison of three cohorts. Br. J. Psychiatry, *125*:168–174, 1974.

Carluccio, C., Sours, J. A., and Kolb, L. C.: Psychodynamics of echo-reactions. Arch. Gen. Psychiatry, *10*:623–629, 1964.

Chapman, J., and McGhie, A.: Echopraxia in schizophrenia. Br. J. Psychiatry, *110*:365–374, 1964.

d'Orban, P. T.: Women who kill their children. Br. J. Psychiatry, *134*:560–571, 1979.

Frederich, C. J.: Crises intervention and emergency mental health. *In* Johnson, W. R.: Health in Action. New York, Holt, Rinehart and Winston, 1977.

Jennings, C., Barraclough, B. M., and Moss, J. R.: Have the Samaritans lowered the suicide rate? A controlled study. Psychol. Med., *8*:413–422, 1978.

Kolb, L. C.: Control of violence. *In* Frazier, S. H. (ed.): Aggression. Vol. 52. Association for Research in Nervous and Mental Disease. Baltimore, Williams & Wilkins Company, 1974.

Lion, J. R.: Evaluation and Management of the Violent Patient. Springfield, Ill., Charles C Thomas, 1972.

Martin, J. P.: Violence and the Family. New York, John Wiley & Sons, 1978.

Phillips, D. P.: Motor vehicle fatalities increase just after publicized suicide stories. Science, *196*:1464–1465, 1977.

Rachlin, S., Milton, J., and Pam, A.: Counter-symbiotic suicide. Arch. Gen. Psych., *34*:965–967, 1977.

Schneidman, S. (ed.): Suicidology; Contemporary Developments. New York, Grune & Stratton, 1976.

Perceptual Disorders

Egdell, H. G., and Kolven, I.: Childhood hallucinations. J. Child. Psychol. Psychiatry, *13*: 279–287, 1972.
Havens, L. L.: The placement and movement of hallucinations in space: Phenomenology and theory. Int. J. Psychoanal., *43*:426–435, 1962.
Johnson, F. H.: The Anatomy of Hallucinations. Chicago, Nelson Hall, 1978.
West, L. J.: A clinical and theoretical overview of hallucinatory experience. *In* Siegal, R. K., and West, L. J. (eds.): Hallucinations; Behavior and Experience. New York, John Wiley & Son, 1975, pp. 287–311.

Thought Disorders

Connolly, F. H., and Gipson, M.: Dysmorphophobia—A long-term study. Br. J. Psychiatry, *132*:568–570, 1978.
Kolb, L. C.: Disturbances of the body image. *In* Arieti, S. (ed.): American Handbook of Psychiatry. 2nd ed., Vol. 1. New York, Basic Books, 1974.
Seeman, M.: Delusional loving. Arch. Gen. Psychiatry, *35*:1265–1267, 1978.

Affective Disorders

Frances, A., Sacks, M., and Aranoff, M. S.: Depersonalization: A self-relations perspective. Int. J. Psychoanal., *58*:325–331, 1977.

Consciousness

Gill, M. M., and Brennan, M.: Hypnosis and Related States. New York, International Universities Press, 1959.
Joyston-Bechel, M. P.: The clinical features and outcome of stupor. Br. J. Psychiatry, *112*: 967–981, 1966.
Plum, F., and Posner, J. B.: The Diagnosis of Stupor and Coma. Philadelphia, F. A. Davis Company, 1972.

Memory Disorders

Arlow, J. A.: The structure of the déjà vu experience. J. Am. Psychoanal. Assoc., 7:611–631, 1959.
Schlesinger, N. J.: The place of forgetting in memory functioning. J. Am. Psychoanal. Assoc., *18*:358–371, 1970.
Whitty, C. W. M., and Zangwill, O. L.: Amnesia. 2nd ed. London, Butterworths, 1977.

7

PREDISPOSING AND PRECIPITATING FACTORS FOR MENTAL DISORDER

"Our prayers should be for a sound mind in a healthy body."

— Juvenal

The Disorders of Personality Functioning

The mental disorders emerge by the interaction of a personality, predisposed on the basis of its structural anlage and dynamic evolutions, with the stresses imposed upon it. In earlier chapters, there were described both the known physiological processes and the related psychodynamic forces from which mature personality function-ing develops. These processes and forces operate upon the human anatomical structure through genetic and constitutional determinants. Each individual personality thus carries within itself various predispositions with which to react to the ongoing stresses of life. Stress may occur as the result of impinging and sometimes overwhelming physical forces. In most instances the major stresses of modern life occur within the framework of a person's own

149

social network, arousing within him affective responses, and their associated emotional and behavioral responses. Failure of ego functioning, or inability to adapt internally to the stresses of living, is most commonly the precipitating factor in the sudden or acute onset of psychiatric disorder.

Although stresses threatening life, in the forms of serious or mutilating illness or the catastrophic disasters of war or civil life, may overwhelm the stimulus barrier of the individual and lead to personality malfunction, in many such instances careful analysis will disclose that the affective response to rupture or loss of a significant personal relationship is an important, if not the most significant, factor.

Insidious onset of mental disorder occurs when those with impaired personality development meet, over time, the progressively demanding performances that occur as one matures socially. Fixation to behavioral patterns accepted socially in childhood and adolescence leads to recognition of maladaptation in adulthood. Inflexible personality structure may yield to overwhelming internal affect when one is confronted with the newly emerging social stresses of adult life in a new family or vocation, or with the complex nuances of existence in a cultural or ethnic group foreign to the exposures of the earlier developmental period.

Stress for man must thus be recognized as occurring as much by the affective experiences aroused from human transactions—interpersonal relations—as by changes induced internally as a consequence of disturbance of the biophysical sphere.

The symptoms and signs of mental disorders cannot be explained as simply the result of disorganization of cellular structure or physiological processes. Only those behavioral expressions directly expressive of impairment or loss of personality functioning caused by brain tissue damage—thus the memory failures which typify the syndromes consequent to brain insufficiency—may be so explained.

In each instance of impaired personality functioning, the psychiatrist attempts to define, as far as possible, both precipitating and predisposing factors. In many, removal or alleviation of the former may relieve the symptomatic expressions of personality dysfunction.

Communication theory provides a framework for considering the interrelationship between the structural organization of man and his immediate relationship to his environment as well as the continuing influence of past social forces and experiences upon him which allow for recognizing, selecting, and patterning response and therefore determine his later behavior. The brain then functions as a central integrating and communicating system, subserving contact with the inner organ systems, past experiences, and outer world. Today, contact with the outer world is largely contact with other people. Any disturbances of the brain or other bodily tissues that influence the capacity of man to receive and perceive information from his environment and integrate it with past information will lead to defective psychosocial functioning and thereby disturb personality functioning. Any physical disturbance which upsets man's capacity to communicate with others, again, will lead to ineffective communication that produces disturbing feedback. The latter, in turn, induces anxiety, conflict, and personality unrest.

Thus one may recognize as etiologic factors in disrupting the communicative activity between people the effects of constitutional defects in the perceptual receptive system, such as deafness or blindness, failures of development or acquired defects in the central nervous system, or the later dysfunction of the brain due to metabolic or toxic agents. Again, failures to learn language, to understand social codes, or to speak effectively, with resultant interference of ability to recognize and integrate psychosocial signals, or separations from those who maintain stability or provide guiding signs, may be seen as contributing factors to disturbance in communication and thereby lead to psychosocial illness. Viewed in terms of interpersonal communication, the arguments relative to the etiology of psychiatric illness as primarily physical or psychological become meaningless. One attempts to understand the totality of the personality functioning in a communicative relationship, with its potential for the teaching and learning of behaviors that bring about social competence, as well as personal satisfaction and self-esteem. The therapeutic task is then to correct or modify for more effective social adaptation any defects found, or to develop substitutive behaviors if the defect is clearly permanent.

This chapter considers the many factors in the wide range from the biogenetic to the experiential deprivations that may influence personality functioning adversely.

Prevalence of Mental Disorders

Various efforts have been made in numerous areas of the world to ascertain the percentage of persons who have developed mental illness requiring treatment, have been so treated in the past, or suffer such disturbances but remain untreated. Rates of prevalence vary widely from one survey to another; this variability is dependent undoubtedly on the methods of data collection, the sensitivity to occurrence of mental illness existing in both medical and nonmedical personnel in differing states and countries, and the criteria for establishing diagnoses.

Studies of the prevalence of mental disorder have progressed from surveys of hospital records to those of general practice records and, more recently, to community surveys. In the latter both questionnaires and diagnostic interviews have been used. For the first time, a community survey was conducted in which each interviewer employed a structured research interview guide, and thus the investigators (Weissman, Myers, and Harding) achieved rates of specific psychiatric disorders in a New Haven, Connecticut, community. This work differs from the majority of community surveys that have assessed the presence of symptoms of overall social impairment. Of this population, 15 per cent had a definite and 2.7 per cent had a probable current psychiatric disorder. Major depressive reactions, generally unipolar depression, are most frequent. The schizophrenia rate was 0.4 per cent. After depression, anxiety, minor depression, and alcoholism were most prevalent.

Early studies agreed on the prevalence rates for psychotic reactions. In a survey conducted in Baltimore in 1936, the prevalence rate for all psychoses in a local district was 6.7 per 1000 and for the psychoneuroses, 4.3 per 1000. A 1957 survey in the same city gave rates for the psychoses as 4.3 and the psychoneuroses as 5.26 per 1000. In England, a survey of the medical practitioners showed that 4.8 per cent of the population at risk had sought advice for a psychoneurotic condition within a 12-month period, while 0.4 per cent also were seen for a psychosis or some other personality disorder. In another study in a new English housing estate 22 per cent of the population at risk were estimated to have psychoneurotic symptoms but only a portion had sought medical advice.

Cooper et al., reporting from England, recently found the mean annual prevalence rate for psychiatric morbidity of persons visiting medical practitioners to be 60 per 1000 for males and 72 per 1000 for females—not unlike earlier findings from this country. See Table 7–1.

For generations, speculation had centered on the question of whether mental illness was increasing in the population. The major support for the

TABLE 7-1   Community Surveys of Psychiatric Disorder: Extent and Reported Prevalence Rates

| | | | | | RATE PER 1000 AT RISK | |
AUTHOR	PLACE	DATE OF SURVEY	PERIOD COVERED	AGE RANGE	*Mental Disorders*	*Psychoses*
Rosanoff	Nassau	1916	one day	all ages	36.4	–
Cohen and Fairbank	Baltimore	1933	one year	over 15	44.5	8.2
Lemkau et al.	Baltimore	1936	one day	over 10	60.5	6.6
Roth and Luton	Tennessee	1935–1938	one day	all ages	46.7	4.9
Bremer	Norway	1940–1945	five years	all ages	193.5	14.3
Lin	Formosa	1946–1948	one day	all ages	10.8	3.8
Eaton and Weil	Hutterite communities	1950	three months	15 and over	16.7	4.7
Trussell and Elinson	New Jersey	1951–1955	one day	all ages	138.0	2.0
Srole et al.	Midtown Manhattan	1952–1958	one day	20–59	233.0	–
Leighton et al.	Stirling County	1951–1962	one day	adult	234.0	–
Shepherd et al.	London	1961–1962	one year	15 and over	139.6	5.8

(Modified from Cooper, B., and Morgan, H. G.: Epidemiological Psychiatry. Springfield, Ill., Charles C Thomas, Inc., 1973, p. 53.)

affirmative argument rested upon the increasing number of persons in the United States certified to the state mental hospitals. Thus, in the United States in 1904 there were 183.6 persons out of every 100,000 in these hospitals, whereas by 1950 this number had increased to 381. Since the introduction of modern methods of treatment, such as the psychopharmaceutical agents, and also the adoption of changes in statutes pertaining to certification, as well as the humanization of hospitals with "open-door" policies, there has been a dramatic drop in the population of these hospitals. On the other hand, short-term hospitalization in the psychiatric services of general hospitals has risen rapidly, as has registration of psychiatric patients in outpatient departments and day and night hospitals.

Increase in rate of hospitalization cannot be accepted as an indication of a trend toward increase in the occurrence of mental disorders. With the provision of more adequate facilities for the care and treatment of the mentally ill, and also with a changing attitude of the general public toward revealing the existence of emotional disturbances, more individuals enter or register as patients in the various psychiatric facilities.

Mortality

Mortality studies of all those newly admitted to psychiatric hospitals worldwide have exposed a risk of death four to ten times that of the general population. Beyond the age of 20, people with a psychosis are said to have a life expectancy 70 per cent less than those without. In a study of patient mortality reported to a county psychiatric case register between 1960 and 1966 (including both those who were hospitalized and those treated in outpatient or nonhospital facilities), Babigian and Odoroff confirmed the higher risk of death for the psychiatrically ill no matter in what facility treatment was given. They found this risk, when corrected for age, sex, and socioeconomic status, to be three times that of the general county population. While the chronically ill, the aged, and the alcoholic contributed heavily to the element of risk, removal of these groups still left an increased mortality risk for others; this risk remains high even when suicides are removed. (Of the total of 40,454 deaths, only 408 were due to suicide.) This study suggests the relatively high vulnerability of those with psychiatric symptomatology to toxic influences, trauma, and serious illness.

As Table 7–2 from their report shows, the relative risk for deaths due to neoplasms, as compared to the mortality experience of the corresponding county general population, is considerable, and is considered more like that of the general population than other causes of death in the psychiatric population. Suicidal deaths are high, as expected, yet those listed in the Monroe County Psychiatric Register account for only 33 per cent of the total number of suicides occurring in the county during the time span of record. The majority of those who suicide are never treated psychiatrically; more visit general practitioners, who frequently fail to detect the suicidal intent.

Teft, Pederson, and Babigian, in a recent study of death among suicide attempers, a psychiatric population, and a general population, found that the suicide attempter group separates demographically and in terms of mortality rates from the other two. Through age 44 years, suicide is the leading cause of death for the "attempter" group and re-

mains one of the three leading causes of death in this group later in life. Additionally, accidents are a leading cause of death through middle life, with circulatory disturbances becoming the major cause after age 45 years. Teft and associates conclude that much of the increased risk of death among the identified psychiatric population is related then to the small group of suicide attempters.

PREDISPOSING FACTORS

Genetics

Genetic factors, which establish the constitution of each individual, interact throughout life with the environmental forces impinging upon each individual. As development proceeds, it becomes increasingly difficult to determine the predispositions established through genetics in terms of the many and variegated personality traits of the growing and maturing individual.

As Professor John Rainer has stated, "Human genetics has now become the science of human development." The complexity of the interaction between nuclear, cytoplasmic, enzymatic, and anatomic forces and those forces resulting from the changing neural, hormonal, and behavioral responses becomes increasingly difficult to identify. Nevertheless, over the last several decades there have been numerous technical advances that tend to make more concrete and clarify the relation of genetics to psychopathology. Today, the genetic code is understood; it is possible to visualize human chromosomes, to detect gene-producing enzymes in individual cells, and to apply more refined methods for genetic study to large populations. These technical advances have allowed the delineation of increasing numbers of pathological syndromes in which genetics plays a major role.

As related to psychiatry, the attempts to separate hereditary and environmental factors remain difficult, yet increasing sophistication is evident in the

TABLE 7–2   Relative Risks of Death by Cause of Death in a Psychiatric Population

| | WHITE MALES | | WHITE FEMALES | |
	Number of Deaths	Relative Risk	Number of Deaths	Relative Risk
Neoplasms	155	1.2	144	1.5
Nervous system	169	2.5	200	2.2
Circulatory system	971	2.6	1,137	3.5
Respiratory system	161	3.5	114	4.0
Digestive system	82	3.1	44	2.5
Accidents	71	2.9	49	3.4
Suicides	81	8.0	52	11.3
Other or unknown	134	3.1	130	3.3

(From Babigian, H. M., and Odoroff, C. L.: The mortality experience of a population with psychiatric illness. Am. J. Psychiatry, *126*:470–476, 1969.)

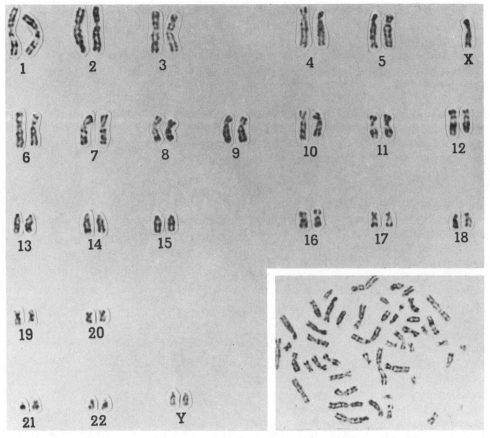

Figure 7-1 Chromosomal abnormality in XYY syndrome (by banding technique). (Courtesy of Professor John D. Rainer, Columbia University and Chief, Department of Genetics, New York State Psychiatric Institute.)

analytic processes now in use to determine the genetic loading as related to specific psychopathological entities.

It is now known that a large number of inborn errors of metabolism, which lead to cerebral maldevelopment and mental retardation, are directly attributable to genic influence. This fact has been established by classic familial studies over generations. Phenylpyruvic oligophrenia, attributable to a defect in the enzyme phenylalanine hydroxylase, is a prime example of such a condition. In recent decades, a large number of defects in amino acid, lipid, and sugar metabolism have been so identified.

In addition to the genetic defects determined by transmission of dominant or recessive genic factors, there have been identified through the visualization of human chromosomes a number of conditions that are due solely to anomalies of chromosomes. Such anomalies are divided into the autosomal and sex chromosomal types. These have been shown to be associated with improper splitting of the chromosomes during meiosis, leading to more than the usual number of chromosomes or to the distortion of certain of them. Of the former, trisomy 21 (Down's syndrome, formerly called mongolism), a major cause of mental retardation, is by far the most important. The genetically determined conditions described in the preceding two paragraphs that are important to psychiatry are discussed in Chapter 29 on mental retardation. Figure 7–1 illustrates the chromosomal abnormality in the XYY syndrome.

The determination of the effect of genetic loading on the major psychoses becomes more complicated as one attempts to discriminate it from interacting environmental forces. In order of increasing sophistication, the modern techniques being used are: 1) family studies, 2) twin studies, 3) adoption studies, and 4) longitudinal studies of twin, high-risk offspring.

As early as the mid-1930's, the twin studies conducted respectively by Rudin, Schultz, and Kallmann, and by Kallmann, Essen-Möller, and Slater indicated that there was a significant genetic contribution to the etiology of schizophrenia. These investigations emphasized that, while the genetic factor was necessary, it was insufficient to fully explain the evolution of the syndrome; environmental forces were also influential. The past decade has seen a number of additional reports on twin research in which the subjects were drawn from a wider population of patients than those used earlier who were largely confined to long-term mental hospitals. The results of these later studies confirm the earlier: concordance rates for schizophrenia in identical twins remain 3.5 times higher than concordance rates for fraternal twins.

Examination of schizophrenic patients reared in adoptive homes reveals that adoptive families do not demonstrate increased pathology in ways commensurate with that in biological families. Likewise, persons taken as children from schizophrenic mothers and reared in foster, nursing, or adoptive homes show a greater rate of schizophrenic and schizoid manifestations than similarly reared children of non-schizophrenic mothers used as controls. It is particularly important to note that the high risk for schizophrenia exists in paternal half siblings of schizophrenic adoptees; this finding diminishes consideration of the possible role of the intrauterine environment's influence.

Genetic studies now suggest a dichotomy of the affective psychoses into the *unipolar form* (with depressions alone) and the *bipolar form* (with manic and depressive episodes). Co-twins and family members have been found to be at higher risk for the psychoses than the general hospital population. There is increasing evidence that, in the bipolar form, dominant inheritance with x-linkage exists in many families. In the unipolar recurrent depression, the genetic mode of transmission remains unclear, with suggestions that autosomal or polygenic inheritance is possible. Such hereditary studies offer the potential not only for nosological clarity in the future but for clinical significance in treatment. Thus, the differing response to drugs is believed by some to be related to genetic variants of the psychosis.

As for the neuroses, the evidence of genetic factor remains much less clear. Before attributing a mental disorder to heredity, the psychiatrist should recall that parents frequently transmit their emotional difficulties to the next generation, not through their germ cells but through the influence of their neuroses on the child. In most cases of mental illness in a parent, one can presuppose a prolonged period of maladjustment with difficulties and inconsistencies in personal relationships which preclude the existence of a home atmosphere conducive to healthy emotional growth and future mental health. A failure to find gratification of psychological needs in one generation may also be reflected in the behavior of the next, with the result that difficulty of adaptation and social misbehavior may follow through several generations. Neurotic patterns have been communicated from one generation to another rather than inherited. A negative and hostile relationship toward parent or sibling may carry over and transfer negative, hostile psychopathogenetic feelings toward persons who stand in a parental or sibling role.

Chromosomal abnormalities are very

great at the time of conception. It is estimated that at least 6 per cent of conceptions are anomalous. Fortunately, spontaneous abortion apparently occurs in the majority of such unions of sperm and egg, and it is believed that as many as 50 per cent of spontaneous first-trimester abortions are associated with these defects. The autosomal trisomy most common at birth is that of chromosome 21 with a frequency of about 1 in 600, which probably represents an intrauterine survival of 40 per cent. The survivors of this defect have Down's syndrome. It is now believed that only the sex chromosome trisomies have no undue risk of abortion, and each has a birth frequence of the order of 1 to 1000 of the appropriate sex.

As Carter points out, any therapeutic measures that reduce the frequency with which fetuses with chromosomal anomalies spontaneously abort will bring about serious public health implications in the future. However, at this time there is little indication that spontaneous abortions due to chromosomal abnormalities are increasing because of any existing therapeutic measure. Effective therapies that increase the likelihood of transmission of genic strains predisposing to psychopathology in the general population do not exist although it is recognized that more schizophrenics now tend to marry and produce children than formerly.

As a result of the new knowledge regarding genetics, many questions of a social and ethical nature, important to physicians and psychiatrists, are emergent. For those concerned with the preservation of mental health and also the prevention of mental illness or retardation, the ethics of interfering with the drive for parenthood and for family interrelationships poses enormous issues in the provision of advice to those raised in families at high risk for mental disabilities, wherein the genetic loading is great. Social policies in regard to genetic screening are now being shaped.

Constitution

From the standpoint of psychiatry, constitution may be looked upon as that portion of the individual's physical organization derived from the genotype and prenatal and postnatal influences, but exclusive of the learning acquired through interpersonal influences. Representing as it does the reactive potentialities of the individual, constitution is important in determining modes of behavior considered basic to the personality. Constitutional factors and predispositions must, however, be regarded as highly complex and as yet poorly understood.

Constitution should be considered as in a limited dynamic flux in the light of studies in both men and animals that have demonstrated changing physiological functions as a consequence of adaptation to noxious and immunologic influences, as well as psychosocial stress.

Of major significance in the concept of human constitution is the accumulating evidence from animal research that prenatal stimulation by the mother, and such postnatal experiences as extensive handling in infancy and exposure to varying social groups, establish lifelong patterns of bodily resistance to stress by strengthened adrenal-cortical reactivity, and also determine to some extent the individual's emotionality.

Variations in constitutional makeup are apparent in the rhythms of daily activity and the temperament of individuals living under constant conditions. Recently, Lund has found that individuals who tend to be internally desynchronized physiologically—poorly maintaining a steady circadian rhythm when living under standard conditions—complained most of physical distress and displayed significantly greater indicators of neuroticism on psychological tests.

Constitution as related to temperament in mental illness has been a matter of interest since Greek and Roman times. Both Hippocrates and Galen proposed that those with certain body types were predisposed to particular disease processes.

Sheldon has carried out the most extensive studies in recent years of somatotypes as related to constitution. His basic types—endomorphic, mesomorphic, and ectomorphic—are similar to the earlier types described by Kretschmer as pyknic, leptosomic, and athletic. Sheldon's analysis of somatotypes goes much further than Kretschmer's with numerous, statistically delineated subtypes, well presented in *Atlas of Men* and other publications (Fig. 7–2).

He relates the endomorphic individual to such viscerotonic temperaments as relaxation, physical comfort, and sociability; the mesomorphic to the somatotonic characteristics of assertiveness, energy, and competitiveness; and the ectomorphic to an introspective tendency. Although various studies suggest that endomorphy is statistically related to the occurrence of the manic-depressive reactions, mesomorphy to the sociopathies, and ectomorphy to schizophrenia, the bodily constitution of adults does not achieve clinical diagnostic value.

From recognition of the long-continuing dynamic of personality evolution in the family and the local culture, we must recognize that the affectively toned perceptions and conceptions of one's body, that is, the body image, play the major role in determining individual psychopathological responses. Yet the variation in body build may correlate with as yet unknown, biologically determined, biochemical reactivity which predisposes to certain personality disorders.

Age

Psychoses are rare until adolescence, when their incidence rises sharply and continues to show a definite upward trend with the advance of age. This rate of increase is especially sharp at the older age levels. In proportion to the population, more than five times as many persons enter hospitals for mental disorders at the age of 80 as at the age of 20. As indicated, psychoses are uncommon among children. Those which occur at that age tend to be strongly influenced by situational and psychological tensions.

The critical points in development at adolescence, involution, and senility bring not only physical changes but also new psychological problems. The rapid increase of psychoses in adolescence has many causes. One is the new problem of integration of sex into the personality pattern. There are also social and employment problems and those of emancipation from parents. The involutional period brings an increase in mental disorders, due, in part, to declining activity of the endocrine and reproductive glands and to other degenerative involutional changes, but more often to the frustrations, threats, and other problems which the patient then meets. It has been suggested that the age at which a person develops mental disorder is an index of his frustration or conflict tolerance. After the age of 60, there is a distinct increase of emotional disorders, to which insecurity is apparently a contributing factor. The increase in mental disorder at the senium is largely due to the degenerative processes which may occur in the higher cortical neurons in old age; yet in some instances it is due to the fact that the changes in psychological situations that then arise cannot be met successfully. Sometimes, for example, the fact that an individual has to be supported by children, or by children-in-law, or by others arouses hostile feelings which are productive of psychosomatic or neurotic symptoms. Since one half of the population in America lives past the age of 65, the incidence of senile and arteriosclerotic mental disease is high. Omitting diseases of the senium, the occurrence of mental disorder reaches a peak in the 40s and then drops sharply.

A

B

Figure 7–2 Typical somatotypes. *A*, Polar ectomorphy; *B*, balanced midrange mesomorphy; *C*, balanced midrange endomorphy. (From Sheldon, W. H.: Atlas of Men. New York, Harper, 1954.)

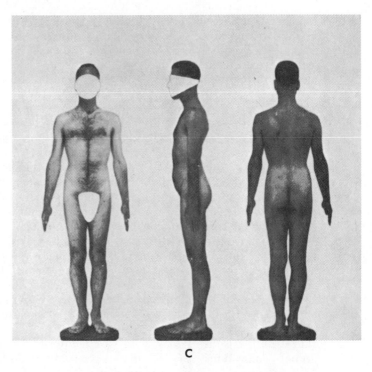

Figure 7–2 *Continued.*

C

Sex

More men than women are admitted to hospitals for mental disorders, the ratio among first admissions being six men to five women; however, because of the greater longevity of women, there are more women than men in public mental hospitals. As indicated earlier, more women than men with psychiatric disability contact physicians in office and clinic practice. General paresis, alcoholic psychoses, traumatic psychoses, psychoses with epilepsy, and psychoses with cerebral arteriosclerosis are more frequent in men. Manic-depressive psychoses, involutional melancholia, paranoia, and psychoses with somatic disease are more frequent in women. Schizophrenia appears to be a little more frequent in women.

Race

Although American studies that report rates of treated patients using beds in psychiatric hospitals have shown a greater utilization by blacks, Fischer and others emphasize the dubiousness of assuming that one may draw the conclusion of greater incidence of mental disorders among blacks than whites in this country or elsewhere. Such rates are derived only from known hospitalized and treated patients; the ratios to be derived from total populations remain unavailable. Also, rates require knowledge of available facilities for treatment. What is known today is the great disparity of such facilities in urban and rural areas where large black populations reside. In the former, many blacks are recent immigrants from backward rural areas. Also, the reported rates today vary as to whether prevalence or incidence is reported. Finally, studies of the processes of psychiatric hospitalizations and other institutionalizations have disclosed that those of lower socioeconomic status are less carefully examined and thereby more rapidly entered as admissions than are those in adequately staffed and readily available facilities. For the urbanized black in the U.S.A. this factor alone inflates admission rates to city and state hospital systems. When local facilities are available for diagnosis and immediate treatment, fewer are entered.

As to forms of mental illness, here again the various studies are highly divergent. Those from urbanized populations show that rates for psychoses among blacks—schizophrenic and alcoholic—are several times higher than among whites. Psychoneuroses are reported as less frequent, but again the less advantaged socioeconomic groups tend not to have available or to use facilities where such conditions are diagnosed or treated.

Definition of variable prevalence and incidence rates of psychiatric disorders in different races must await much more study, including extensive transcultural comparisons. Today, with vast internal migrations of populations worldwide to urban areas, the problem of relating rates of mental disorders to race alone has become exceedingly complex. Immigrant populations have been more subject to psychiatric hospitalizations than have stable populations. Such populations are usually disadvantaged in terms of communication and technical skills. Health, educational, and recreational services are limited. Family life is difficult owing to overcrowding, and malnutrition is frequent. Furthermore, such groups and other minority groups are exposed to exclusion from the majority culture. Often their self-perception becomes anxious and derogatory. Their self-esteem is low, thus placing them at higher risk for mental disorders in the face of additional stressful life events. Rosenberg and others have studied extensively these consequences of *contextual dissonance*.

Beyond that, interracial tension and derogation, now termed *racism*, play a significant role in impairment of stable personality development. The evidence suggests that the black minorities in largely white industrialized societies suffer most. The blacks are often as well educated as the neighboring white groups and other immigrant groups, but the derogatory attitudes of the majorities have produced discrimination in opening all aspects of society to the blacks to a greater degree. Thus they remain selectively deprived as regards social recognition, jobs, and equal opportunity to participate in all aspects of social life.

As a result of subjection to the long-continued attitudes of slave masters or their successors with racist attitudes, there may develop in the personality of some the variety of defenses against aggression described in the previous chapter: destructive or violent behaviors, or paranoid and regressive behaviors, including escapism into drug abuse. In others, reaction formations emerge, with undue compliance or passivity and, for men, failures in sexual identity, including homosexuality, promiscuity, or impotence. Affectively, chronic depression with hopelessness is common.

Upon personalities predisposed through cultural denigration and conflict to emergence of these personality features, additional stress is more likely to produce ego disorganization and emergence of frank psychiatric disability.

PRECIPITATING FACTORS

Environment: Familial, Social, and Cultural Factors

The environment in which an individual lives is much more than a physical world. It consists of the close interpersonal interaction within the family group and the support as well as the pressures imposed upon this group by the wider culture and its particular value systems. Socioeconomic forces, depending upon the class structure of the society in which the individual and the family live are also influential.

In recent years the family unit has become a subject of special study. Attempts to classify families have followed schemata related to styles of adaptation, family developmental stage, diagnosis of identified patient, and varieties of marital relationships. Recently Fisher devised a family schemata; his six types are (1) constricted; (2) internalized; (3) object-focused; (4) impulsive; (5) childlike; and (6) chaotic. The features of each are described in the chapter on Social Psychiatry.

It remains to determine whether there is a specific relationship between variety of family structure and forms of psychopathology. It is maintained that the attempt to understand personality development solely in terms of the interaction of the individual with past aspects of parents or others fails to provide the structure for a comprehension of the development of the social roles which each person plays in his adult life. The social self is expressed in group actions and modified by them; it may or may not reinforce the goals and values the individual has established for the personal self.

Nevertheless, the family forms the shaping influence in the development of the individual's personality. The family unit has a capacity to ameliorate the stresses and strains of everyday life for the various members. It passes on the mores of the culture in which it lives and provides as well, from the parents, emotional and nutritional support and the values to be transmitted to the children. If healthy, the family unit enhances interactions with others, providing excitement, pleasure, and joy, as well as aversive control for unacceptable behaviors. It is indeed a small group, in which each member interacts with the others. Thus, when a family role is vacated, usurped, or filled in a pathological or ineffective manner, the family homeostasis may be re-established only if others take on the activities of the lost or rejected member.

Crises in the family occur often: at times of pregnancy; with the onset of serious physical or mental illness; after the birth of a deformed, disabled, or seriously ill child; in the face of the terminal illness or death of one of the members; also, when the family undertakes a major change in its life style, such as a move to another social environment.

Loss or absence of mother has been referred to as maternal deprivation. Many recent studies have examined its effect upon infants and children admitted to hospitals or other residential institutions and have described the developmental retardation following impairment of the stimulating effect of maternal care. An association between delinquency and broken homes has been reported, as well as an affectionless psychopathy that may follow repeated experiences of separation.

Yet there is considerable variation in the ways in which children respond to maternal deprivation, particularly after the age of 4. The presence of other familiar persons or siblings tends to reduce the evidences of emotional disturbance in the younger child separated from the mother. The family bonding with others is important in maintaining the emotional stability of the young child during periods of maternal separation. It now appears from continuing study that the provision of social, tactile, and perceptual stimulation may modify the deleterious effects of the absence of mothering in developmental retardation. The conclusion must be reached, as Rutter has suggested, that this condition is the consequence of *lack* of stimulation and not *loss* of stimulation.

It is the provision of a stimulating environment that determines the intellectual development of a youngster. Intellectual competence tends to be greater in the first-born child and in those from smaller families. Last-born children, except for an only child, are more likely to be diagnosed as psychiatrically disordered.

Maternal deprivation alone probably is not causative, as has been shown with youngsters who are raised solely within their own homes but with little contact with others, such as canal boat children, those from isolated communities, or those who demonstrate poor verbal and intellectual ability in contacts with others. If the parents are capable of providing stimulation and allow contacts with others, verbal intelligence will evolve. Apparently, it is the presence of verbalization that is important to growth in verbal capacity. Even more important may be the clarity of the language environment rather than its complexity.

As for the effects upon family members of broken homes through death, separation, or divorce, it is usually considered that delinquency and later antisocial behavior commonly evolve from these family crises. Perhaps the internal family discord and disharmony preceding the break are more significant than the emotions engendered at the disappearance of the parental bond. Rutter suggests that the major issue in affectionless psychopathy is absence of the opportunity for the child to form an affectional bond, with its potential to evolve an affective relationship. This is particularly important in the period before age 3, when bonds develop readily.

The absence of the father (paternal deprivation) has been singled out as more definitely related to delinquency and antisocial behavior. Thus, the maintenance of the family with effective fathering appears to be of vital importance to the growing boy, particularly in the age period between 4 and 7, to establish the internalized control system of the superego.

The children of psychotic parents are exposed to an inconstant, often punitive, and irrational experience which contributes to their incapacity to develop social competence. The child living with a psychotic mother or father has the daily stress of adapting to the bizarre behavior and thoughts of the parents, develops uncertainty in regard to his own perceptions, and seldom has the capacity to reach out and accept the corrective associations available to him outside that milieu. Such children may develop psychopathology of any type later in life. They are at high risk for abnormal behavior and social incompetence.

From the earliest period of family interaction, parental expectations, wishes, and aspirations influence the younger members of the family in a variety of ways. Choosing a name for a child is an example. In a study of uniovular twins conducted by the senior author and his colleagues, prenatal preference for a youngster of one or the other sex led to feminizing or masculinizing naming and subsequent parental behavior toward the child, which eventually determined the sexual role in spite of the biological role. Such observations have been made by others more recently.

Families cope with their tensions in a variety of ways. They may share among the members; they may complement each other in their wishes, desires, and behaviors. There may be rebellious reactions by one or another or, indeed, the behavior of the parents may be seen as contagious. Where conflicts exist, often one or another member of the family may become the scapegoat and even be labeled "the patient" when, in fact, the problem rests elsewhere. Parents may develop defensive alliances against each other with one or another of the children, or members of the family may withdraw their affect from a particular member whose behavior distresses them greatly. Often a single member of the family may act as the supporter and healer of the family contact. In other instances, members of the family escape into lives with others or through leaving home. Repetitive fighting is observable in some family units. It is striking to some children to observe that parents who have fought each other for many years and seemed insufferable together remain inseparable later in life.

Overt *incest* is an example of tension-reducing "acting out" in a dysfunctional family which, while maintaining the facade of the family structure, often contributes to serious psychopathology in the involved minor. Thus the incestuous relationship between a father and daughter, the type generally reported, may go on for prolonged periods unreported by a mother. The latter, usually a rejected daughter herself, has married a weak and ineffectual man whom she despises and eventually rejects. The daughter, victimized in the family, becomes the mother substitute, supporting the mother in her housework but giving in to the father who she perceives has been turned away by her mother. In turn, the father, unrelieved in his sexual drives, sometimes seduced by the wife to incest, turns toward the daughter to maintain the family unity of importance to him. While the family unity may remain intact for considerable periods and the reporting of the act often occurs inadvertently when some outsider notes evidence of other maltreatment of children, the emotional consequences for the involved daughter as seen by psychiatrists are invariably those of guilty depression. Such daughters often have learning difficulties in school; they may become sexually promiscuous or develop psychosomatic symptoms. In their efforts to escape their guilt they deny the incestuous relationship, seek punishment through various masochistic drives, and overextend themselves to placate the mother to whom they are unconsciously hateful. When these psychological defenses are restricted the daughters may regress with psychotic behavior.

Incest taboo is pervasive in most civilizations yet incest occurs widely. The statistics of its occurrence in advanced countries range from a rate of 0.73 case per million population in Sweden to 1.1 cases per million in the United States in 1930. Incidence in total sex offenses varies from 2.4 to 6.3 per cent in various studies. Fathers who indulge in incest appear to be those in whom the act is a part of a pattern of indiscriminate promiscuity; in whom exists an intense craving for children as an expression of sexual psychopathy (pedophilia); or who are deprived and unable to cultivate sexual contacts outside the family.

Controversy exists as to whether repetitive and prolonged exposure of a young child to sexual activity between the parents is pathogenic. Most do not believe there are specific sequelae. Myers is of the opinion that within the American cultural milieu prolonged exposure is psychologically traumatic and leads later to sexual disturbances, learning inhibitions, and splitting of self representations.

The means by which couples come together to form the future family has bearing on understanding the etiology of mental disturbance. It appears that psychiatrically ill men and women find each other for marriage more frequently than by chance. Such matings are more likely to lead to mental illness in the children because there exists a greater potential for genetic predisposition or because a family transactional environment is established that is conducive to development of personality aberrations.

Gamer and his colleagues found that 1-year-old infants under the care of psychotic mothers demonstrated a lessened capacity for relations to others and more intense anxiety. As a consequence of the illnesses of their mothers, such infants experience maternal absence, care by a surrogate, or exposure to a strange environment.

In studying the family in relation to mental illness and health, it has been postulated that what goes on between the sick individual and his or her family takes place within a series of subsystems that include the individual, the family, the social network, the culture, and the value systems of each. Within this transactional system the interests center more on those processes between the individual and the family that are considered pathologic in the larger community, rather than on the narrower question of the interactions of the family members in relation to the pathology. Those working with the transactional method attempt to define strain as it exists in and between the culture, the family, and the individual and to relate each to the others. Much emphasis is placed on value systems and the conflicts that exist between those within the various units.

Beyond the family, the majority of persons have relations with others — they live in a social network which may or may not be emotionally supporting. Actual or threatened loss, either of the relationships within that network or of the values perceived within or among the social network, constitutes an emotionally stressful event to most individuals. Several life event scales have been devised to study correlations between the onset and occurrence of illness, including mental illness. These scales attempt to measure stressful life events within specific time periods. Recently Paykel has suggested a method of defining the relative risk of such events; he emphasizes that stressful events in the lives of the individual interact with a multitude of background factors that must be considered in the assessment.

Sociobiologists, the scientists now devoted to defining social behavior and its evolution and determining the processes that establish both behavior and social systems in all species as well as relating them to operations of biological systems, have collected data from various studies that support their predictions that individuals with access to kin support or friend support systems are at lesser risk for hospital admission for psychiatric disorder than are others without good access. Sociobiologists use the term *kin selection* to identify the existence of an active kin support system correlating to mental health. *Reciprocal altruism* refers to the existence of a similar friend support system and its relationship to mental health. As to social networks, healthy people have meaningful relations with approximately 25 others, neurotic and psychotic individuals with about 15 and 7, respectively.

Sociologists have propounded the theory of *labeling* and have called into question the concept that mental disabilities are more than behaviors that represent deviations from particular sociocultural norms. Deviant behavior is seen as eliciting societal reactions which aroused disapproval and stigmatization. The proponents of this theory believe that the label of mental illness applied to a person whose behavior is deviant tends to become fixed and the individual is thereby encouraged to learn and accept the role identity, which perpetuates the abnormal behavior pattern. Individuals stigmatized by labeling are considered followers in social groups generally and more vulnerable to the process than those accepted in the local society. The sociologists who foster these explanations for mental illness also suggest that the helping agencies of modern society contribute to the labeling process and, in fact, create problems for the very persons they treat.

While many of the points emphasized by social scientists interested in the labeling theory have a certain relevance, cross-cultural studies such as those recently done by Jane M. Murphy indicate that all nonindustrial societies identify the abnormal behaviors found in the Western industrial societies as major forms of mental illness. It is true that in some societies certain behaviors, such as the ability to be clairvoyant and to have visions and other preternatural experiences, are valued, but the phenomenal processes of disturbed thought and behavior found in schizophrenia are known to those living in other cultures and are sufficiently distinctive and noticeable that they have been named. On the other hand, psychoneurotic behaviors which have been listed as psychiatric disorders in Western culture only during the past century may remain without labeling, but most cultures tend to have a sense of estrangement or at least ambivalence towards those demonstrating even these behavioral traits. It is the nature of the individual's behavior that arouses the negativism across cultures rather than a pre-existing cultural set.

The argument made by certain psychologists and sociologists that psychiatrists and others may misidentify those who mimic mental illness hardly bears a relationship to the fact of the existence of such conditions. For centuries, able dramatic artists have had the capacity to note and act out the behavioral traits of many, including those who are mentally ill or retarded.

CULTURE. Those explicit and implicit patterns of behavior evolved and transmitted over generations by symbols, and particularly their related values, define a culture. Studies of cultures are significant to psychiatry as they assist in sharpening the definition of mental health, weighing the significance of variable child-rearing practices as related to personality development, and comprehending variant expressions of psychopathology, sex roles, alcohol and drug usage, forms of communication, and even therapy.

That cultural factors influence the etiology and psychopathology of mental disorders is generally agreed on the basis of studies by cultural anthropologists and by psychiatrists who have worked with persons ill in different cultural groups. Within a lifetime, the clinical phenomenology of various psychotic reactions has changed. As an example, the megalomanic delusions of being Napoleon, so common in the nineteenth century, are seen no longer. Now patients who have such a need fall

upon a character of this century or develop a messianic complex. In the United States the manic-depressive reactions are less prevalent than they were a quarter century ago, although they are common in Scandinavian countries. Conversion hysteria is thought to be less common in Western culture; alcoholic psychoses are frequent in the Irish and uncommon in those of Jewish faith.

Urbanization

The rapid, worldwide migration of recent decades from rural to urban areas has led to increasing urbanization. In 1900, two fifths of the population of the United States lived in central cities with populations of 50,000 or more. By 1950, three fifths were so located and by 1960, two thirds. Of this group, one third lived within the 25 largest metropolitan areas of the country. The effect of the urban environment on inducing mental illness is a matter of considerable speculation. Due to improving sanitary conditions, life in the central cities today in most Western cultures is less stressful in terms of recurrent disease, but on the other hand, as the result of the extraordinary technological advances, there is exposure to wider varieties of physical stresses in the form of traumas through vehicular and other accidents, excessive noise, multiplicity of extraneous stimuli, and the tenuousness of many social relations. For some, these various stimuli are provocative and lead to realization of full potential, while to others entering the city with high aspirations, the competitiveness and the failures to achieve result in inner affective and psychological distress, bringing mental maladaptation, ego failure, and the emergence of psychotic or neurotic symptomatology. As an example of the latter, excessive exposure of children to television programs depicting violence has been correlated with their increasing aggressivity. Dramatic newspaper reporting of suicides precedes an increase in the rate of suicidal behavior. The density of life in the central cities, with its potential for increasing aggressivity, has occasioned much discussion, particularly as experimental work in animals has shown that social behavior is disruptive in aggressively and increasingly crowded conditions.

One significant factor of the human condition noticed by social scientists is that the greater the density in the dwelling unit, the less the tendency for parents to maintain their children at home. As might be expected, the lack of parental control is conducive to impairment of superego development, related psychopathy, and also exposure of the children to social stimuli that may at times overwhelm their capacities. Dohrenwend and Dohrenwend, in their review of the studies of the effects of urbanization, believe the evidence suggests that overall rates of psychiatric disorder are higher in urban than in rural areas, particularly for the neuroses and personality disorders. The rates for psychoses do not change except among the lower social class. The various studies to date suggest, then, that from a psychiatric and mental health point of view, preventive and therapeutic programs should be directed predominantly toward those in the deprived socioeconomic groups.

It is known that more patients per unit of population are admitted to public hospitals from urban than from rural communities. This is due, in part, to the fact that admissions vary inversely with the remoteness of the community from an institution for mental diseases. Alcoholic psychoses, general paresis, psychoses due to drugs, manic-depressive psychoses, paranoia, and psychoneuroses are discovered more frequently in urban areas. Senile psychoses, psychoses with cerebral arteriosclerosis, involutional melancholia, and psychoses with mental deficiency are diagnosed with relatively greater frequency in rural regions. Schizophrenias occur with about equal frequency in urban and rural areas.

Socioeconomic Factors

One of the most consistent findings of social psychiatric studies has been that the prevalence of mental disorders (treated or untreated) is inversely related to socioeconomic status. Attention has centered on two alternative explanations; neither has achieved a consensus from the studies that have been undertaken. The first argues that more stressful life circumstances are found in those environments at the lower end of the socioeconomic structure, and therefore the greater prevalence of mental illness is a consequence of the individual's socioeconomic position. The second proposes that the mentally ill are placed in the lower socioeconomic strata as they are less effective workers and tend to drift downward in socioeconomic position owing to relative incompetence in contributing to the overall effort of the industrial societies. It is probable that both explanations are correct, although Brenner, who has conducted the most recent study of the relationship of economic trends to serious mental illness, suggests that large-scale, long-term economic changes are, in the main, responsible for downward mobility. To sum up, the stress that occurs by such economic changes falls most heavily on those in the lower socioeconomic strata. These people show the highest rates of mental hospitalization, as demonstrated in his studies over 127 years comparing the fluctuations in the country's economic status with the rates of hospitalization in New York State. At the same time, he recognizes that those with a history of psychiatric disturbance may often be the first to lose their positions due to their relative incompetence as workers.

In industrial societies those who have low levels of technological skill or are limited in the capacity for administrative responsibility become more expendable during periods of depression than those in positions of higher status. Furthermore, the latter are generally retained as more valuable to the various social and industrial organizations and have the potential of acquiring new positions more readily during periods of decline. Furthermore, those in the higher socioeconomic strata have available to them more extensive knowledge of differing opportunities and greater mobility, which allow readier acquisition of new positions and continuance of economic stability. While Brenner's statement that economic change is the single most important cause of mental hospitalization is disputed by some, the correlations detailed in his study are worth noting.

On the other hand, we must note that in socialized states, such as the U.S.S.R., the incidence of the psychoses and schizophrenia is recognized now as similar to that in the Western capitalistic countries where economic fluctuations have occurred widely for well over a century.

Hospitalization rates are dependent not only upon the incidence and prevalence of illness in the population but also upon the availability of beds, the prevailing attitudes of the community to their use as therapeutic asylums or as institutions for the isolation of those showing deviance in behavior, the availability of such institutions or alternatives, and the changing customs regarding tolerance of deviant behavior in communities. Acceptance of deviant behavior in Western countries has been greatly modified today with the early treatment of the behavioral disturbances, the availability of more effective therapeutic agents, and the realization of the effect upon the individual of prolonged isolation from family and friends in large institutions, with consequent social deterioration.

From 1910 to 1960, more than two thirds of the mentally hospitalized population in New York State were either foreign born or of foreign parentage. Migrant populations are exposed to stresses as they separate from their original cultures and are required to adapt to the changing culture of their new countries, and to seek new ways of personal and family support. For these reasons, their adaptation to life in the new countries and struggles with a strange language often place them among the economically disadvantaged. Too, they bring to their new homes differing social and economic aspirations, which are likely to be dashed under the severely competitive positions in which they find themselves. The relationship between long-term economic change and mental illness is exceedingly complex and must be understood in a dynamic framework. Economic stress forces change in personal self-esteem and the arousal of anxiety and depression, potential breaks in the network of supporting individuals within the individual's family and society, and disruptions of family life where that exists. Economic stress, too, may add an additional burden to already existing familial and social stresses and predispositions of the individual to mental illness.

In Hollingshead and Redlich's studies on the influence of social class upon the occurrence of mental illness in New Haven, schizophrenia was found more frequently in families in the lowest socioeconomic classes, as well as other disturbances indicative of superego defects. (Ninety-five per cent of persons in prison come from these classes.) On the other hand, obsessive-compulsive disorders are most common in the highest socioeconomic groups and oedipal conflicts in the middle group. Other studies have suggested, however, that the patient's social class is perhaps the consequence of the illness rather than evidence of influence of social class on its form.

One might expect that anxiety, open and often unopposed aggression (including sexual aggression), lowered self-esteem, and limited opportunities for emotional and cognitive growth are more often the ways of life in the personality development in those reared in the lower socioeconomic groups.

In the higher social classes, in contrast, demands for conformity presumably lead to the expression of compulsive patterns of living. One consequence of child rearing in families with superordinate wealth is the limited parental contact with their children. Children in such families, in which child rearing is delegated to servants, frequently develop without clear models for identification, and have low self-esteem and many of the features of pathological narcissism.

Marital Status

Statistics show that mental disorder is more common among the single than among the married. While this may be due in part to the more stable and regular mode of life led by the married person with the accompanying sense of domestic responsibility, this is probably only a minor reason for the better mental health among married persons. The marital association provides not merely for the satisfaction of sexual urges but for various important securities, the absence or loss of which may be very disturbing to the personality. The feeling that one is desired as a marital partner, that one is appreciated and is the subject of interest and affection, contributes greatly to a sense of security. The security from loneliness, the emotional satisfaction of parenthood, and frequently, in women in our culture, the added sense of economic security add wholesome satisfactions. With marriage the individual may be compelled to adjust to a very different type of environment and to personal relationships quite foreign to those in which that person was reared. Marriage and success in the responsibilities of marriage suggest great interpersonal adaptive capacities and personal esteem. The development of mental disorder before marriage naturally decreases the prospects of subsequent marriage; many whose affective and other personality limitations are so great that they are predisposed to mental disorders are never sought as partners.

Statistics show that there is a marked preponderance of mental disorder per unit of population among divorced persons. There are several reasons for the more frequent occurrence of mental disorders among this group. In many cases maladjustments representing early stages of mental disorder lead to domestic discord and divorce before the personality disturbances are sufficiently developed to be recognized as constituting mental disease. The same deep-seated mechanisms that tend to lead to marital discord also lead to psychosis or neurosis. Marriage is a relationship demanding a most highly sustained adaptation. The unmarried person may have been unable to achieve the adult toughness necessary to stand the give and take of adjustment to marriage and parenthood. Perhaps he or she may have been unprepared for this adjustment because his or her parents had not been healthy models for identification as mates and parents.

Mental illness may be precipitated by factors concerned with sexual functions, such as anxiety with motherhood or fatherhood, pregnancy, or abortion. Parenthood often rekindles conflicts over dependency or early sibling competitiveness, arousing anxiety, rage, and aggression.

A person who failed to reach a heterosexual level of development but remained, even though unconsciously, with a basic homosexual orientation may be unable to establish an abiding partnership with one of the opposite sex. Usually there will be no physiological interference in the exercise of sex functions natural to his or her sex, but the emotional, dispositional tendency of sex expression is directed to a homosexual partner. The attempt to meet this conflict between emotionally determined and biologically determined impulses may be made by projection or other psychopathological mechanisms, ending in mental disorder.

Pregnancy

Mental disorder may be associated with pregnancy or the postpartum period. There are, however, no specific mental disorders related to either of these periods. Latent or repressed psychological material may, under the stress of maintaining physiological homeostasis and of the emotionally significant situation, prove too great for the patient's ego resources with the result that psychopathological reactions occur. What her pregnancy unconsciously means to the mother is of significance, as is the birth of her child. Doubtless, it reanimates the patient's old attitudes toward her own mother and may revive old complexes of bodily harm or injury. Sometimes the patient expresses delusions indicating hostility for either the husband or the child, thus reflecting a conflict about married life or motherhood. Rejection of the child may be expressed by a delusion that it is dead, by abusive treatment of it, or by fear that something will happen to it.

Rosenwald and Stonehill have hypothesized differences in the personalities of those mothers who develop early postpartum psychoses from those with late postpartum psychoses. The birth event and the early demands of the infant are particularly taxing for the schizoid woman, who tends to withdraw and become autistic. Mothers with late postpartum psychoses have generally had histories of responding depressively to what they perceive as withdrawal of support and affection. They have been recognized as persons of ingratiating behavior, irritating to others, as shunning responsibilities, and having a need to compensate narcissistically. The pathology of the groups tends to differ. Those hospitalized shortly after delivery were preoccupied with thoughts of inner deadness, personal transformation, thought transmission, or supernatural forces, while those admitted many months after delivery presented persecutory ideas and obsessional fears of harming the infant.

Psychotic illness in association with pregnancy is rare; the expectancy is about 14 cases in 10,000 confinements. About 50 per cent of the mental illnesses associated with pregnancy or the postpartum period are schizophrenic, about 25 per cent are manic-depressive, and 20 per cent are psychoneurotic reactions.

The occurrence of such a reaction does not predispose to a similar reaction in a subsequent pregnancy. Almost one half of such illnesses occur with the birth of a second or a later child, and the outlook for recovery is similar to that of the general reaction type. These disorders occur with the same frequency in the postpartum setting as they do in any other setting.

Pregnancy, too, may induce psychophysiological symptoms in the father through arousal of anxiety. Trethowan has found that as many as 10 per cent of fathers report symptoms which in many respects are similar to those of the expectant mother: nausea, morning sickness, perversion of appetite, and, sometimes, abdominal bloating. These have been recognized in historical accounts of the *couvade syndrome*: the paternal identification with the maternal role.

Occupation and Work Load

As urbanization has increased and technology has expanded so rapidly, the methods and modes of transportation and communication are recognized as magnifying sensory and informational overloads. Except for research on the effects of high levels of noise with its potential for ultimate destruction of the auditory nerve and its distracting potential upon an individual's attention, relatively little investigation has been conducted upon these subjects. To a certain limit, feedback mechanisms within the nervous system protect man and other mammals from overload. Yet it is known that these adaptive processes may be overwhelmed and flooded under certain circumstances. The urban dweller is thought by some to be exposed to overload with resulting loss of efficiency in role performance. He is considered to have difficulty with social norms, cognitive functioning, and effective use of urban assets. Nevertheless, the urban dwellers adapt by limiting their exposure to the many available stimuli, by selecting information input and allowing less time for it, and by evolving behaviors that facilitate distancing, impersonality, and remoteness from the many social contacts which present themselves.

Work overload, per se, exists quantitatively—that is, the individual has more work than he can accomplish in a given period of time. It may occur qualitatively, when his position requires skills and knowledge exceeding those available to him. In the former situation an excess of information exists, while in the latter information input is too excessive or too complex to be mastered. Studies have shown that 44 per cent of male white-collar employees report some degree of work overload. Those with high aspirations tend to induce such overloads; consequently, impairment of behavior or emotional disturbance here would be linked primarily to personality factors.

Some degree of overload is generally not thought to be productive of personality disturbance. Job dissatisfaction and impaired job performance through criticism and lack of recognition have been discovered to increase anxiety. Such conditions bring about psychosomatic changes, such as elevation of cholesterol and heart failure, and must be distinguished from overload.

Some consider that the schizophrenic, with his high sensitivities to certain stimuli, has a defective filtering mechanism which makes him especially susceptible to information input overload. Thus, in childhood schizophren-

ics or in those acutely ill with this symptom complex, stimuli of ordinary intensity are often experienced as extraordinarily vivid and intense. Certain schizophrenic symptoms are thought to be protective reactions to reduce the informational overload—withdrawal, blocking of thoughts, paranoid delusions, or reduced spontaneity of movement or speech. The taking of psychedelic drugs tends to heighten sensitivity to low intensity stimulation, to increase arousal, and to allow a sensory and informational overload. Similar reactions have been observed in some experiments where work overload is produced.

The compulsive neurotic may work excessively hard, his job serving as a means of reducing anxiety and of support. Work may be the only outlet for an otherwise creative person. It may also in some instances serve as a neurotic outlet for aggression. It may give strong ego support through success or prestige to a person besieged with feelings of inferiority. For the withdrawn person, work may be his chief means of contacting others in a nonthreatening manner. Finally, satisfying work is important for mental health. It brings such healthy gratifications as creative expression, companionship, and a feeling of accomplishment.

Anxiety-inducing situations, such as inability to accept the authority of competent superiors or to suppress dependent longings and demands, often lead to breakdowns or failures at work in groups. The competition for advancement with the mobilization of envy, or the fear of others' envy by the dependent person who has been advanced to a position of responsibility, sometimes precipitates emotional disturbance; an example would be the case of a dependent vice-president advanced to the presidency and fearful of facing the envy and loss of acceptance by his former peers. Failures to receive advancement also mobilize aggressive fears that may precipitate disorder.

There is evidence that mental effort in the presence of emotional stress and tension can produce either neurotic or psychotic reactions. There is only limited justification for the pessimistic suggestion frequently made that the pace of modern life conduces to mental breakdown.

Retirement from an occupation is now known to produce anxiety in those who derived active satisfaction and self-esteem from their employment. With the giving up of work, stress arises from the loss of prestige and of being valued by others, and frequently from isolation from old companions. Those whose occupation was less satisfying accept retirement more readily and without affective distress.

Alcohol

The role of alcohol in the production of mental disease is complex. While in some respects our ideas are becoming clarified, there are still many unknown and variable factors. A direct relation between the amount of alcohol drunk in a community and the incidence of psychoses classified statistically in the alcoholic group is certain, as shown by experience in the United States during and following its experiment with prohibition. In 1920, immediately following the enactment of the Prohibition Amendment, the number of first admissions for alcoholic psychoses to New York State hospitals for mental diseases per 100,000 of general population fell to 1.2. This rate gradually increased to 7.1 in 1941, decreased until 1945, and has again continued to rise since World War II. During the three years (1919 through 1921) of relatively successful observance of the prohibition amendment to the Constitution there were 720 first admissions with alcoholic psychoses to all hospitals for mental disease in New York State. The total of such first admissions increased to 2013 in 1929 through 1931 and reached 3132 in 1939 through 1941, since which time there has been no appreciable change per unit of population.

The more carefully the history of a patient suffering from a chronic form of mental disorder is studied, the more frequently it will be found that any associated alcoholism is either a symptom of the psychosis or another method of dealing with the same personality problems that contributed to the mental disorder, rather than an essential cause of it. The role of avitaminosis in producing a psychosis in the chronic alcoholic must be borne in mind.

Chapter 26 discusses the alcoholic psychoses and alcoholism.

Physical Defects and Illnesses

Physical anomalies or disturbances not caused by endocrine dysfunction, yet ones which occasionally provoke resentment and other undesirable psychological reactions, particularly of a compensatory, aggressive, or other defensive nature, are congenital deformities, clubbed feet, scoliosis, kyphosis, and congenital defects of vision and hearing. Cleft palate, also, tends to create a sense of inability to meet social situations and to lead to feelings of inferiority and insecurity, again expressed in derogatory attitudes to one's self and body. Children with congenital or acquired defects develop feelings about the defects partly because of the way they see other people reacting to them. If others about them react with repugnance, revulsion, or abhorrence, so too will the child regard his deformity. Adolescence is the period in which physical defects are most apt to evoke unwholesome psychological reactions.

Where effective psychological compensatory mechanisms, including ego assets, are encouraged and evolve, serious personality abnormalities do not appear.

Acute physical illnesses with an associated toxic state frequently lead to an acute brain syndrome with an accompanying delirious state but are rarely directly responsible for neuroses or the so-called functional psychoses. Chronic illness, however, with its handicaps, frustrations, and unhealthy methods of attempting to surmount them, is a severe stress.

The patient with a physical defect or illness is confronted with two types of problems for which a variety of defenses and mechanisms of adaptation must be mobilized: (a) problems, largely conscious, related to the realities of the pain, inability to make a living, and handicaps imposed on or by family, and (b) problems arising from emotional needs and from the activation of hitherto repressed unconscious conflicts. These are discussed in a later chapter in the section on disturbances of the image of the body. A relationship will be noted between the psychological symptoms released by the ego-weakening effect of the illness and the premorbid personality of the patient. Physical illness, then, may precipitate or aggravate neurotic or psychotic trends in the personality. Thus recognition and correction of such illnesses or disabilities are of paramount importance in both prevention and treatment of the personality disorders.

General Cerebral Dysfunction

Mental symptoms arising from general dysfunction of the brain are dependent to a large extent on whether the brain disorder is of an acute or chronic nature, and, if chronic, whether the involvement is diffuse or circumscribed. The resulting symptom pattern tends, therefore, to fall into one of three types: an acute organic syndrome; a chronic syndrome due to a diffuse lesion; or a chronic syndrome due to a localized lesion. The acute organic reaction is the result of temporary, reversible, diffuse impairment of brain tissue function and is characterized by a disturbance of consciousness, difficulty of apperception, somnolence, coma, cloudy and delirious states, hal-

lucinations, and poorly organized transient delusions.

Chronic organic brain syndromes result from relatively permanent, usually irreversible, diffuse impairment of cerebral tissue function. The chronic brain syndrome may vary in degree of progress but usually some disturbance of memory, judgment, orientation, comprehension, and affect persists permanently. Frequently the organic syndrome is colored by the patient's individual personality with its particular conscious and unconscious impulses, fears, and wishes.

The causes of general brain dysfunction are trauma, infection, toxic states, metabolic disturbances, and various deprivational states.

Trauma

Trauma to any part of the body may result in a traumatic neurosis. But far more important to the precipitation of mental disorder than physical trauma is *psychic trauma*. Psychic trauma exists when individuals are confronted with unbearable affects of fright, pain, anxiety, or shame which they perceive subjectively as overwhelming their capacity to cope. A state of helplessness ensues, in which the defensive structure of the personality collapses and the individual "surrenders." Studies of major disasters of all types have shown that a stunned and bewildered response is the more likely general personality response than is panic—up to 25 per cent of people in some cases.

Psychic trauma suffered by infants and children differs from that of adults, for the psychological, cognitive, and perceptual powers of adults are much more fully developed. After a psychic trauma, children suffer a lifelong apprehensive dread of the recurrence of such an event associated with a continuing anhedonia. Adults exposed to horrifying experiences of life maintain some defensive capacity to repress or defend against affect flooding. In psychic trauma, it is emphasized that *psychic reality* is entirely subjective; the perception of unbearable threat rests completely within the individual.

Trauma of the head, with lesions ranging from a diffuse but minute separation of neuron structure through edema and hemorrhage to destruction of brain tissue with subsequent scar formation, may be followed by varying defects of mentation. The clinical picture is usually at first that of an acute brain syndrome. If the impairment of brain function is persistent, the clinical picture becomes that of the chronic organic brain syndrome with a permanent impairment of mental function.

Infections

Of all infections, it is probable that the viral encephalitides now play the most active part in causing mental disease. Formerly, the most common psychosis resulting from infection was that associated with syphilitic meningoencephalitis (general paresis), which accounts now for less than 2 per cent of all first admissions to public mental hospitals in the U.S.A. During the past 40 years there has been a constant decrease in the relative prevalence of active syphilis, with a resulting decrease in general paresis.

Toxic Agents

Certain chemicals and drugs may give rise to acute brain syndromes, frequently in the nature of a delirium of brief duration, although occasionally a delirious state of such an origin may continue for several weeks. The agents most frequently implicated in producing mental symptoms are barbituric acid derivatives, other sedatives, the hallucinogens, amphetamines, morphine, cocaine, marihuana, and lead.

Endocrine Disturbances

Abnormal functionings of the endocrine glands undoubtedly influence personality functioning through disturbing bodily functions. Such disorders, for example, may lead to changes in general efficiency of bodily functions with resulting feelings of frustration or insecurity. Occasionally neuroendocrine dystrophies produce biological defects, which make the individual conspicuous in physical appearance and lead to a disturbance in his body concept or image. The dissimilarity between the patient's concept and the change in his body induced by the endocrine disturbance contributes to self-consciousness, which favors the development of defensive and compensatory mechanisms that distort the personality and render adaptation more difficult. Certain endocrine deficiencies are known to lead to cognitive impairment. Thus cretinism is often associated with mental retardation, and hypothyroidism in midlife leads as well to impaired functioning and associated personality disturbance.

DEPRIVATIONS AND DEFICIENCIES

Lack of the basic bodily needs (oxygen, nutrition and fluids, sleep, perceptual stimulation), if sufficiently great or prolonged, may lead to serious constitutional deficits if they occur in the developmental period. Later in life such deprivations act as important etiologic factors in the determinations of various brain syndromes and in precipitating or complementing the primary psychogenic disorders.

Oxygen Deprivation

Beyond all other bodily organs and tissues the brain is the most susceptible to dysfunction and structural damage as the consequence of oxygen lack. Developmental defects and later behavioral changes are a regular accompaniment of hypoxia from whatever cause. Cerebral hypoxia in the perinatal period, inferred on the basis of clinical observation and now established by experimental studies, leads to profound defects in development from which result both mental retardation and personality disorders, as well as physical defects.

In later life, transient or chronic hypoxia as the consequence of acute oxygen lack at high altitudes, asphyxia, cerebral ischemia following arteriolar spasm, infarction or cardiovascular failure, chronic pulmonary disease such as emphysema, anemia, or poisoning by carbon monoxide and other cellular poisons, if severe, produces the symptomatology of general cerebral insufficiency (the brain syndrome).

A drop in arterial oxygen saturation to 85 per cent which persists over a period of two or three hours has been shown to lead in otherwise healthy persons to hyperpnea, fatigue, headache, and lassitude, followed by difficulty in concentration and impairment of emotional control. Depending upon the personality, oxygen-deprived individuals may become over-confident and elated and demonstrate judgmental defects in interpersonal contacts, expressed in undue irritability and aggressive behavior toward others, or become increasingly dull and depressed. Impaired emotional control is one of the finer indices of cerebral anoxia; evidence of it occurs long before difficulties in performance of routine tasks, psychological tests, or changes in the electroencephalogram. Under ordinary conditions of stress, healthy men exposed to hypoxia at the level of 85 per cent arterial oxygen saturation lose emotional control without warning and respond with unexpected truculence to verbal challenges directed to their superego values in the sexual or aggressive areas.

Prolonged ischemic anoxia is probably the major etiologic factor in the organic brain syndromes associated with arteriosclerosis. Whether the diminution of oxygen utilization found with the senile psychosis is representative of a primary anoxic defect or is secondary to the neuronal loss found with this condition is not known.

Cerebral hypoxia occurs with the use of convulsive therapy. It is known that the structure and probably the function of the most recently developed areas of the brain are most impaired through oxygen lack; thus the frontal lobe cortex often shows pathological damage when other areas appear healthy on examination with cellular stains.

Lack of Nutrition

Nutritional deprivation has profound effects on personality in terms of its development, drive states, mood, and performance. The consequences of primary nutritional deprivation may come to the attention of the physician as in those suffering malnutrition in childhood, those starved during wartime, or those suffering from brain syndromes as the consequence of vitamin deficiencies. More frequently encountered are the secondary states of semistarvation, which occur in depressions, some schizophrenias, and anorexia nervosa. Personality disturbances due to mild or moderate malnutrition appear, on the basis of current information, to be either slight or subject to reversal with later adequate nutrition.

Malnutrition during early brain development is known to curtail both protein synthesis and DNA synthesis. As a consequence, brain development is permanently stunted and the brain contains fewer cells of normal size. Malnutrition following cell division retards protein synthesis and results in an abnormal number of smaller cells in the brain. The latter changes are reversible with proper feeding. Thus, one may expect impairment of intellectual, cognitive, and motor development in children in whom deficiency has occurred as a result of severe and continuous malnutrition for an extended period of time without remediation, beginning in the first year. Extreme conditions of starvation or malnutrition affecting the mother during pregnancy or the child in the first year are associated with borderline or more severe mental subnormality, sometimes persisting into the preschool and early school years. If severe malnutrition of the child occurs during the first half year of life, and the child then is subjected to adequate nutritional remediation, the potential of reduction of intellectual functioning is unlikely.

The studies of experimental semistarvation in man have shown well the subjective changes this state induces, which may complicate the primary phenomenology of any illness. In addition to weight loss, fatigue increases steadily. There takes place an increasing preoccupation with food, including frequent simple wish-fulfilling food visions and dreams. Increasing appetite, muscle soreness, irritability, apathy, and sensitivity to noises gradually appear, with feeling of loss of drive and the ability to control oneself, associated with a diminution in attentiveness and ability to concentrate. The sexual drive becomes progressively weaker. Lack of interest in the attractive sex partner, disappearance of masturbation and seminal emissions, and diminution of the sperm count follow in men and amenorrhea in women. Recovery of these functions in previously healthy men semistarved on a 1600 calorie diet for 24 weeks has required a full six weeks of refeeding.

As observed during wartime, starvation leads to personality changes; meanness, secretiveness, and suspiciousness emerge, associated with social withdrawal. In the early period of starvation there are a general lowering of moral standards and a drive for other gratifications. Some wish to be cared for like children, become emotionally labile and impulsive, and develop enuresis and interest in feces and anal functions. If food deprivation continues, aggressive impulses, sucking activity, and oral interest appear to be subsequently superseded by apathy and eventually the symptoms of general cerebral insufficiency.

Specific vitamin deficiencies are known to produce encephalopathic syndromes resulting from metabolic or organic disturbances in the cerebrum. Pellagra and Wernicke's syndrome are among the most clearly recognized of the deficiency reactions. Brain syndromes rather than disorders of psychogenic origin usually occupy the foreground in personality disturbances associated with these deficiencies, although trends that have been developed for dealing with anxiety-producing situations may be revealed.

Sleep Deprivation

Continuous lack of sleep, as demonstrated by numerous studies on healthy young people, produces deterioration in personality functioning, expressed in unpleasant subjective experiences as well as changes in appearance, speech, mood, perception, and thought. Whether these changes are due solely to lack of sleep or to the associated muscular fatigue or even associated dream deprivation is not known. When a person is deprived of sleep, his prolonged attention to any task gradually diminishes and is associated with increasing restlessness, apathy, and inability to concentrate. Lapses of ongoing behavior or periods of extreme drowsiness or sleep take place in which delays or actual breaks occur in the performance of tasks, even though the situation is perceived by the nonsleeper as requiring action and a response. He may lose his contact with the immediate situation and confuse external and internal events. Thus a dream or intrusive thought becomes attached to the outward situation, and the faulty sleeper suffers a distortion of perception.

Over a period of time, lack of sleep leads to misperceptions which range from changes in the shape, size, movement, texture, or color of objects to misbelieving and misperceiving them. Such misperceptions at times appear to be hallucinations. Temporal disorientation gradually appears. Initially time seems to pass slowly, while later the sleep-deprived subject makes first occasional and then frequent errors in designating time to the point where eventually he is unshakingly deluded. His cognitive process suffers as well, as evidenced by infrequent lapses of thought or speech with limited lack of sleep; with further lack of sleep, these lapses extend to loss of the train of thought, incompletion of statements, forgetting, and eventually rambling and incoherent verbalizations, with inability to recognize errors or make corrections. Lack of sleep gives rise frequently to a bandlike sensation about the head, the "hat illusion," while there are often other subjective experiences reflecting feelings of change in the self or the body — feelings of not being oneself, of strangeness, which may be classified as depersonalization.

Associated with sleep lack, physiological depression takes place in muscle tone, body temperature, sweating, and capacity to respond to noxious stimuli. Increased pulmonary ventilation takes place as a means of removing the greater blood carbon dioxide and lactate. Some studies have demonstrated modest activation of the pituitary-adrenocortical system with disruption of its circadian rhythm, as well as a variable increase in catecholamine biosynthesis, as a result of sleep deprivation.

With increasing prolongation of sleep deprivation the electroencephalogram shows a progressive diminution in the alpha rhythm and the development of dominant slow wave activity. Nor does opening or closing of the eyes lead to enhancement of the alpha waves. Judging from the responses of organs controlled by the autonomic nervous system, sleep deprivation is associated with a progressive decrease in responsiveness to external stimulation but at the same time a persisting tendency to greater autonomic activity.

Prolonged wakefulness then may be interpreted as leading to decreased capacity for arousal and the emergence of a variety of psychopathological behaviors. It is evident that the sleep cycle must be preserved in order to sustain healthy behavior or to prevent the secondary complications due to oxygen deprivation with insomnia in the course of pulmonary illness.

During the recovery period after prolonged sleep deprivation there is an initial increase in both slow (nondreaming) and REM (daydreaming) sleep on the first night — a "rebound" effect. A relative increase in REM sleep may be noted for several nights thereafter.

In experiments performed by Dement in which the subjects were awakened briefly on four to seven consecutive nights when they were observed to show the eye movements and characteristic accompanying low-voltage, nonspindling electroencephalographic pattern noted only during dreaming, it was observed that the amount of dreaming increased during nights after dream deprivation. Also, the healthy experimental subjects became anxious and irritable and showed difficulty in concentration in performing daytime tasks during the period of nightly dream deprivation. Some were noted, as well, to develop an increase in appetite associated with weight gain during this period. Dreaming sleep may represent a physiological drive state that is significant in maintaining the psychological homeostasis of the organism. Vogel states from his review of the work done on deprivation of REM sleep that this experimental condition may not be equated with dream deprivation nor does such deprivation lead to harmful effects in schizophrenic, depressed, or healthy subjects. A sizeable literature has developed on the therapeutic effect of a single or several nights' sleep deprivation in the depressive states.

It has been suggested that the so-called toxic effects of drugs such as the amphetamines, which specifically suppress REM sleep, are due to the suppression of this portion of the sleep cycle.

Sensory Deprivation

A series of clinical investigations during recent years gives strong support to the hypothesis that a steady state of sensory stimulation or "input" is necessary to support the usual ego functions. As early as 1819 Dupuytren described delirious reactions with hallucinatory and emotional disturbance which occurred in the period following cataract extractions when the eyes were covered. It has been known for years that one factor causing senile nocturnal delirium is the loss of vision consequent to darkness.

The factor of lonely immobilization is thought to be responsible for the states of anxiety, disturbances in time sense, and delusional and hallucinatory experiences of some patients immobilized in respirators. It has been suggested that similar symptoms associated with alcoholism are caused, in fact, by isolation and reduction in sensory input. The factor of social isolation now is thought to contribute to "brain-washing" or "thought-reform" programs used by the Chinese with their war prisoners, to the prison psychoses, to the hallucinatory states of shipwrecked and lost persons, and perhaps also to the elaborations of the chronically hospitalized and isolated psychotic.

When healthy persons with no previous experimental experience are isolated, with vision and hearing diminished by the use of patches and ear plugs and with mobility limited after several hours, they experience anxiety and a desire for external stimulation and motor activity as well as difficulty in concentration, reduction in motivation, and progressive difficulty with directed thinking. After 72 hours in a few experiments they develop delusional and visual hallucinatory experiences. Following such experiences, visual disturbances continue for some time. They are reported as fluctuations, driftings, and swirlings of objects and surfaces in the visual field, associated with difficulty in fixing objects in space on eye or head movement, with distortions of margins, and exaggeration of contrasts and colors. During the deprivational experience, the electroencephalogram shows slower rhythms and slow wave activity.

During the deprivational experience the alpha rhythm of the electroencephalogram declines and there emerges increasing slow-wave activity, which parallels the progressive impairment in ego functioning. It appears from some studies that the degree of electroencephalographic change is greater after deprivation of patterned visual and auditory stimuli than after limitation alone of light and sound.

The perceptual phenomena and other ego disruptions seem less likely to occur when some meaningful stimuli are present and when the deprived subject is allowed kinesthetic and tactile stimulation through movement. Personality plays a factor in determining the characteristics of the response, with exaggeration of the usual adaptations and defenses.

Sensory deprivations during early life may impose permanent developmental defects that impair later learning. As far as perceptual and kinesthetic learning is concerned, the proposition seems well established for humans; the clinical observations on the children who failed to evolve good visual perception after corrections of congenital corneal defects by late transplantation of the cornea are fully supported by studies of artificial blinding of growing chimpanzees.

Studies of the congenitally blind, the congenitally deaf, and those youngsters who have been isolated and have suffered early deficiency of kinesthetic sensory experience support the contention that early sensory stimulation is necessary for healthy personality growth.

There seems to be evidence that in isolated youngsters gross and irreversible personality disturbances may evolve but if the impairment is lessened, development may advance through sensitization therapies. It is striking that some 25 per cent of the congenitally blind are later reported as autistic. Due to the inability to make eye contacts with their mothers, understimulation is common.

The congenitally deaf child who is behaviorally active and responsive during the early months of life seldom shows the degree of characterological deviation observed in the congenitally blind. The later development of the congenitally deaf is characterized more often by an increase in impulsive behavior rather than in other characterological or psychiatric disabilities found in the population at large, as Altshuler has pointed out. He has suggested that audition is necessary in the evolution of the internalization of rage. His hypothesis rests on the fact that language is delayed in these children and that their motor activity provides a means of discharge of this affect.

Social Isolation

Social or experiential deprivation in early life may well play a major role in many of the adult personality disorders. A mass of observations reported by child psychiatrists and animal psychologists shows that capacities for exploratory behavior, control of fear and anxiety, perception of pain and recognition of threat, somatic response to stress, effective sexual and child-rearing behavior, and affectional relations are impaired by isolation of the developing young. As yet undetermined for the growing child and the young of other species are the critical maturational periods during which appropriate experience must take place in order to allow maturation of structure and related function. There exists now a scientific void relative to such questions as the quantity of experience required to allow full evolution of function and the ultimate capacity of the growing or adult organism to repair deficiencies or develop them through later learning.

It has been suggested that autism in children is the consequence of a deprivation of tactile and kinesthetic arousal through inadequate mothering in infants who are born with a lessened capacity for arousal due to some impairment in the function of the reticular activating system. Mention has been made of the high incidence of autism in the congenitally blind—an observation that tends to support the view that sensory deprivation in the developing child is the basis for autism. In a family where parental fondling and body stimulation are limited, such infants presumably will develop with permanent deficits in their perceptual capacities. Also, the hypothesis has been offered that the primary deficit in the schizophrenias is lack of appropriate socialization during early life, causing a permanent incapacity to evolve mature patterns of interpersonal relations.

Poverty may be thought of as a form of social isolation, too. The relative lack of personal possession of material substances in itself does not necessarily predispose to or precipitate psychiatric illness. Many human groups live under materially deprived conditions as compared to others, yet there is little evidence that the forms or frequency of mental disease differ between the groups. When poverty is interpreted as limitation of emotional support in terms of the developmental process, even many children and others brought up in affluent families are disadvantaged.

Nevertheless, materially impoverished families in racial and cultural groups are exposed to a greater degree than others to the multitude of forces predisposing to and precipitating psychiatric disability. Malnutrition will affect maternal care, brain growth in the neonate, and physical development and susceptibility to illness of the infant and child. The various deprivations described heretofore probably operate to a greater degree for those in the often crowded, dirty conditions with limited access to education and intellectual stimulation in which the impoverished live. Such social conditions limit the potential for development of positive ego assets in trust, initiative, autonomy, and responsibility; at the same time, these conditions increase the affective drives which impair impulse control, allowing for continued expressions of aggression in destructive behavior to self and others, attitudes of mistrust, suspicion, hopelessness, and despair. The balance of the personality of those reared in conditions of poverty is likely to be warped negatively and predisposed toward personality disturbance.

Parenting Relationships

The parental relationship with the mother is the most determinative of the future mental health of the individual. A strangling, guilt-ridden overprotection by her may prevent her child from developing a mature, independent personality. Again, the maternal relationship may fail to give the warmth, security, and support necessary for the emotional and social growth of personality. For example, instead of providing a healthful emotional climate of affection, acceptance, and approval, the mother may to varying degrees reject or overprotect the child, with consequent misshaping of his or her developing personality.

Such attitudes, which exist particularly among mothers who have been damaged emotionally by their own life experiences, are usually unconscious ones. Other attitudes, often covert or ambivalent, which may also be manifested by psychologically important persons, are hostility, aggression, dominance, sadism, and dependence. Out of such relations are established patterns of personality culturally so unacceptable

that they are repressed and give rise to conflict and anxiety. Ambivalent attitudes, i.e., confusions of hostile and affectionate impulses, which had their origin in some childhood intrafamily relationship, often continue to influence the personality pattern throughout later life and constitute unconsciously a conflictual problem that cannot be met except by psychopathological methods.

The absent father deprives sons of a figure for identification and daughters of the opportunity to socialize over time with a member of the opposite sex. A domineering, aggressive, or exploitative father may interact with a son so as to inhibit his potential for developing an assertive self-confident esteem; an overly passive father may fail to provide the admired and loved focus for a mature masculine identification.

Divorce, too, serves as an emotional crisis for the growing child. The loss of one or the other parent precipitates anxiety, grief, or depression, often acted out in release of aggressively destructive behavior.

Much of adult behavior is determined to a considerable degree by events that took place in the preverbal age period or by later unresolved childhood conflicts. The *anlage* of many neuroses and of other personality difficulties and characteristics is found in the prolonged experiences of early childhood. Early tension-laden relationships with parents seem to be particularly apt to be pathogenetic. Interpersonal situations in later life awaken previous feelings and unresolved difficulties and lead to the re-enactment of problems generated in prior relationships. Difficulties in these relationships are therefore both expressions and sources of personality disturbances. Not only may aggression and hostility arise out of family relationships, but many other fixed emotional reactions, such as feelings of insecurity, rejection, guilt, dependency, overprotection, and jealousy, are acquired in response to repetitive early interpersonal experiences.

Bereavement

Through the close and intimate contact of the infant and young child with the mother, there is laid down the basic sense of security and trust through which the child is able to face separation and its attending loneliness and to seek an autonomous identity. Meeting the early dependent needs of the child through mothering lays the groundwork for a healthy personality.

GRIEF REACTION. A bereavement by separation or death is followed by a well-known train of events. Initially the young child protests by crying or other aggressive behavior, and after some hours passes through a phase of hopelessness, withdrawal, and inactivity. This is succeeded some time later by behavior characterized by detachment, with an unwillingness to resume the relationship if the lost person reappears. While detachment may be superseded in time, repeated separations lead to an effort at personal isolation from others, motivated, perhaps, as a protection from recurrent anxiety. In older children it is clear that the first phase of anxious protest is accompanied as well by rage. Children deprived of mothering early in childhood either suffer inordinately when separated from significant people, owing to paralyzing nostalgias, or later may be hungry for dependent relationships. They sometimes develop a protective, isolated defense as a form of pseudo-independence to prevent a repetition of despair and hopelessness.

Since the parent of the same sex offers the model for identification that establishes impulse control through superego formation, the ideals for aspiration, and the sexual role, it is not surprising then that statistical studies demonstrate the more frequent occurrence in adulthood of psychotic, neurotic, and psychopathic behaviors in children reared in families broken by death, divorce, separation, or abandonment. Death of the mother before the child was 10 is found to have occurred more frequently in the history of schizophrenics than in the general population. Death of the father before the child is 10 also exceeds the expected frequency in the histories of those with schizophrenic and manic-depressive psychoses and the neuroses. On the other hand, separation of parents is more frequent in the histories of psychoneurotic, sociopathic, and alcoholic patients.

Indications of impairment of healthy personality development through early parental deprivation have been found in studies of delinquency rates in adolescents. Thus both girls and boys who lose a father by parental separation or divorce are much more frequently involved in acts of delinquency. Boys who lose their father by death and girls who lose their mother by death appear as well to be detained more frequently for delinquency than their peers from intact families.

In adults *the grief reaction* may be delayed for hours or even several weeks following death or separation of the significant person. During this period the sufferer behaves as usual but may speak of feeling numb. Thereafter he or she undergoes periods of yearning and suffering associated with reminders of the deceased or lost person and accompanied by psychophysiological symptoms, most frequently gastrointestinal. Between such attacks of yearning the bereaved person is apathetic, has a sense of futility, and also may be depressed. There occur insomnia, anorexia, restlessness, and outbursts of irritability or even anger aimed at others or the self. Ruminative and over-idealized thinking about the separated person constantly recurs with thoughts that he or she is present. The reaction, common to all bereaved, continues with varying intensity, depending on the closeness of the relationship, for periods of one to six weeks, to subside in the healthy to minimal yearning after six months. Occasional and brief periods of yearning may erupt for several years thereafter. Often these are precipitated by events or other reminders of the lost relationship. The features of the grief reaction in the healthy must be known to the psychiatrist and distinguished from the distorted and exaggerated pathological variants which bring the separated or bereaved to him.

Parker has suggested that the specific grief reaction may be identified in typical, chronic, inhibited, and delayed forms from which one should separate out the nonspecific and mixed variants. In the latter he places those responses to bereavement capable of precipitation by other stressing incidents. Symptomatically one finds here the psychosomatic, neurotic, depressive, and manic responses and alcoholic episodes.

In chronic grief the bereaved undergoes an abnormal prolongation of the reaction often associated with ideas of guilt and self-blame and sometimes expressed as evidence of partial identification, or aggressive behaviors. Others seem to inhibit certain of the expressions and substitute other features. The young and very old more commonly inhibit their sense of bereavement. Finally, there are those who appear to repress the grief reaction for weeks, months, or years, yet its past representation is shown by attitudes of identification or by behavior not unlike that in chronic grief.

Bereavement caused by the death of a spouse is known to be followed by an increased mortality risk for the survivor. Young survivors and men are at the highest risk—the increased causes of death are due to such conditions as suicide, alcoholism, cirrhosis, heart disease, and the common respiratory infections.

Bereavement is also associated with losses other than that of death of a parent, spouse, or other significant person. The grief reaction and all other related personality disturbances may occur as the result of loss of part of one's body, as from limb amputations or mastectomy; through aging and change in appearance as a response to loss of a function such as sight, sexual function, or motility caused by paralysis or impairment consequent to arthritic processes; or from loss of one's possessions or economic status. It may follow the death of a pet.

For adolescents and adults the awareness of one's own impending death or that of another presents a life crisis attended by major emotional response. This awareness arouses the fundamental anxiety of life—the basic anxiety of fear of the unknown with its related deep sense of helplessness. Also, there emerge the fears of loneliness, of loss of family and friends, of loss of one's body and identity, and of loss of self-control.

Within the dying individual the crisis situation arouses all the anxieties of the past and mobilizes ego adaptations and the defenses evolved to cope with them: dependency, aggression, sexuality, and identity.

The acute and chronic traumatic reactions probably represent overwhelming responses to multiple losses and bereavement through exposure to the deaths of many others, threats to one's own life, as well as to disasters depriving the individual of personal belongings and the security of familiar surroundings. These are catastrophic events such as tornadoes, floods, earthquakes, or volcanic eruptions and, now, major airplane, automobile, train, or shipping accidents wherein many are killed or maimed. Long-continued exposure to losses, as in concentration camps, may produce the same behavioral changes.

Bereavement not only sets in motion a series of emotional and psychological processes but also leads to physiological effects. Elevation of 17-hydrocorticosteroid excretion has been found in parents following their children's death from leukemia.

ANNIVERSARY REACTION. Outbreaks

of anxiety or their symptomatic defensive expressions that occur regularly on specific dates often represent a symbolic re-enactment of an earlier important bereavement. Such reactions sometimes inaugurate the onset of a psychosis in which the emotional upheaval is observed to coincide with the patient's reaching a parent's age at death or sometimes when one of the patient's children reaches the same age as the patient when the parent was lost. Again, one occasionally sees recurrent attacks of anxiety coinciding with the date of death of a parent. Overbearing anxiety and grief appear to precipitate the ego break which manifests itself by the effort at restitution through emergence of pathological, neurotic, or psychotic defenses.

BIBLIOGRAPHY

Allen, M. G., Greenspan, S. I., and Pollin, W.: The effect of parental perceptions in early development of twins. Psychiatry, 39:65–72, 1976.

Altshuler, K. Z.: Studies of the deaf: Relevance to psychiatric theory. Am. J. Psychiatry, 127: 1521–1526, 1971.

Belmont, L.: Birth order, intellectual competence, and psychiatric status. J. Ind. Psychol. 33:97–104, 1977.

Bowlby, J.: Grief and mourning in infancy and early childhood. Psychoanal. Study Child., 15:9–52, 1960.

Brenner, M. H.: Mental Illness and the Economy. Cambridge, Mass., Harvard University Press, 1973.

Carter, C. O.: The treatment of genetically determined disease and the effect of current policies on population eugenics. In McLachlan, G. (ed.): Patient, Doctor, and Society: A Symposium of Introspections. London, Oxford University Press, 1972.

De Ajuriaguerra, J. (ed.): Désafférentation expérimentale et clinique. Symposium. Bel Air II, Geneva. George & Cie, s. a. Geneva, 1964.

Dohrenwend, B. P., and Dohrenwend, B. S.: Psychiatric disorders in urban settings. In: Arieti, S. (ed.): American Handbook of Psychiatry. Vol. 2. New York, Basic Books, 1974.

Essock-Vitale, S. M., and Fairbanks, L. A.: Sociobiological theories of kin selection and reciprocal altruism and their relation to psychiatry. J. Neurol. Mental Dis., 167:23–28, 1979.

Favazza, A. R., and Oman, M.: Overview: Foundations of cultural psychiatry. Am. J. Psychiatry, 135:293–303, 1978.

Fischer, J.: Negroes and Whites and rates of mental illness: Reconsideration of a myth. Psychiatry, 32:428–446, 1969.

Fisher, L.: On the classification of families. Arch. Gen. Psychiatry, 34:424–433, 1977.

Freedman, D. A.: Congenital and perinatal sensory deprivation: Some studies in early development. Am. J. Psychiatry, 127:1539–1545, 1971.

Gamer, E., Gallant, D., and Grunebaum, H.: Children of psychotic mothers. Arch. Gen. Psychiatry, 33:311–319, 1976.

Grinker, R. R.: The poor rich: The children of the super-rich. Am. J. Psychiatry, 135:913–916, 1978.

Henderson, D. J.: Incest: A synthesis of data. Can. Psychiatr. Assoc. J., 17:299–313, 1972.

Hilgard, J. R., and Newman, M. F.: Anniversaries in mental illness. Psychiatry, 22:113–121, 1959.

Hofer, M. A., Wolff, C. T., Friedman, S. B., and Mason, J. W.: A psychoendocrine study of bereavement. Psychosom. Med., 34:481–485, 1972.

Hollinger, P. C.: Violent death as a leading cause of mortality: an epidemiologic study of suicide, homicide, and accidents. Am. J. Psychiatry, 137:472, 1980.

Hollingshead, A. B., and Redlich, F. C.: Social Class and Mental Illness. New York, John Wiley & Sons, 1958.

Jacobs, S., and Ostfeld, A.: An epidemiological review of the mortality of bereavement. Psychosom. Med., 39:344–357, 1977.

Koranyi, E. K.: Fatalities in 2,070 psychiatric outpatients. Arch. Gen. Psychiatry, 34:1137–1142, 1977.

Krystal, H.: Trauma and affects. Psychoanal. Study Child, 33:81–117, 1978.

Landau, R., Harth, P., Othnay, N., and Sharfhertz, C.: The influence of psychotic parents on their children's development. Am. J. Psychiatry, 129:38–47, 1972.

Levine, S.: Maternal and environmental influences on the adrenocortical responses to stress in weaning rats. Science: 156:258–260, 1967.

Lipowski, Z. J.: Sensory and information overload: Behavioral effects. Compr. Psychiatry, 16:199–221, 1975.

Lund, R.: Personality factors and desynchronization of circadian rhythms. Psychosom. Med., 36:224–228, 1974.

Maddison, D.: Crises in the family—the family in crisis. Mental Health in Australia, 5:4–13, 1972.

McDermott, J. F.: Divorce and its psychiatric

sequelae in children. Arch. Gen. Psychiatry, 23:421–427, 1970.

Murphy, J. M.: Psychiatric labeling in cross-cultural perspective. Science, 191:1019–1028, 1976.

Myers, W. A.: Clinical consequences of chronic primal scene exposure. Psychoanal. Q., 48:1–26, 1979.

Paykel, E. S.: Contribution of life events to causation of psychiatric illness. Psychol. Med., 8:245–253, 1978.

Plaut, S. M., Åder, R., Friedman, S. B., and Ritterson, A. L.: Social factors and resistance to malaria in the mouse. Psychosom. Med., 31:536–552, 1969.

Rainer, J. D.: Genetics and psychopathology. In Wolman, B. B. (ed.): International Encyclopedia of Psychiatry, Psychoanalysis and Psychology, 1977.

Rosenberg, M.: Contextual dissonance effects: Nature and causes. Psychiatry, 40:205–217, 1977.

Rosenfeld, A. A., Nadelson, C. C., and Krieger, M.: Fantasy and reality in patients' reports of incest. J. Clin. Psychiatry, 40:159–164, 1979.

Rosenwald, G. C., and Stonehill, M. W.: Early and late postpartum illnesses. Psychosom. Med., 34:129–137, 1972.

Rubin, R. T., Kollar, E. J., Slater, G. G., and Clark, B. P.: Excretion of 17-hydroxycorticosteroids and vanillylmandelic acid during 205 hours of sleep deprivation in man. Psychosom. Med., 31:68–79, 1969.

Rutter, M.: Maternal deprivation reconsidered. J. Psychosom. Res., 6:241–250, 1972.

Rynearson, E. K.: Humans and pets and attachment. Br. J. Psychiatry, 133:550–555, 1978.

Schiele, J., and Brozek, B. C.: "Experimental neurosis" resulting from semistarvation in man. Psychosom. Med., 10:31–50, 1948.

Schoenberg, B., Carr, A. C., Peretz, D., and Kutscher, A. H. (eds.): Loss and Grief: Psychological Management in Medical Practice. New York, Columbia University Press, 1970.

Sheldon, W. H.: Atlas of Men. New York, Harper & Row, 1954.

Teft, B. M., Pederson, A. M., and Babigian, H. M.: Patterns of death among suicide attempters, a psychiatric population and a general population. Arch. Gen. Psychiatry, 34:1155–1185, 1977.

Trethowan, W. H.: The couvade syndrome—some further observations. J. Psychosom. Res., 12:107–115, 1968.

Vogel, G. W.: A review of REM sleep deprivation. Arch. Gen. Psychiatry, 32:749–755, 1975.

Wender, P. H., Rosenthal, D., Kety, S. S., Schulsinger, F., and Welner, J.: Social class and psychopathology in adoptees. Arch. Gen. Psychiatry, 28:318–323, 1973.

Willie, C. V., Kramer, B. M., and Brown, B. S. (eds.): Racism and Mental Health. Pittsburgh, University of Pittsburgh Press, 1973.

Winick, M.: Cellular growth during normal and abnormal development of the brain. In Hemwich, H. (ed): Biochemistry of the Brain. Vol. 2. New York, Marcel Decker, Inc., 1974.

8

EXAMINATION OF THE PATIENT

"I keep six honest serving-men
(They taught me all I knew);
Their names are What and Why and When
And How and Where and Who."

Rudyard Kipling

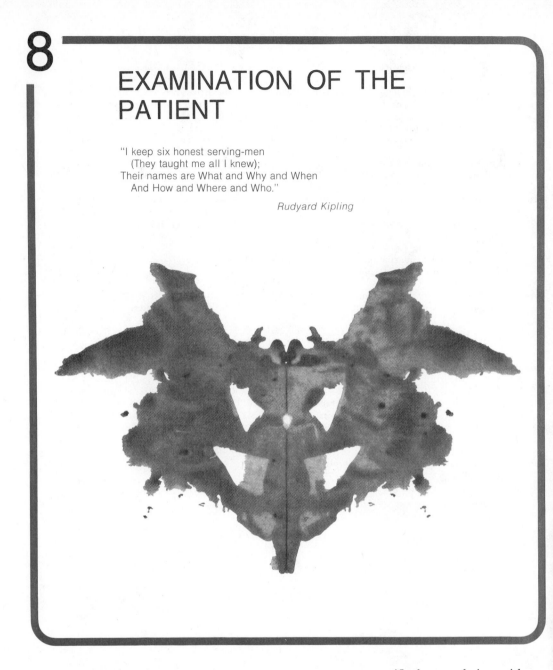

PURPOSE OF EXAMINATION

The purpose of the psychiatric examination is to discover the origin and evolution of such mental disorders as may be interfering with the happiness, satisfactions, efficiency, or social adjustment of the patient. One seeks, therefore, to secure a biographical-historical perspective of the personality, a clear psychological picture of the living person as a specific human being with individual problems. It will be found that there is a logical continuity in any personality manifestations, whether the manifestations be those that are called normal* or those that are called abnormal. The fundamental dynamic laws of

---

*Normality is, of course, a vague concept, since everyone projects his own ideal of perfection into it.

184

behavior and of personality development are the same for both. By securing the maximum knowledge possible concerning the personality of the patient, the forces that have determined it, and the problems of living found to be anxiety-laden, it should be possible to understand the function of the illness and the meaning of the symptoms.

All phenomena of behavior, including those of mental disorders, are natural events and should be studied like any other object of natural history investigation. This requires that an attempt be made to reconstruct the patient's behavior, to unravel the story of his neurosis or psychosis in the light of the fullest information possible concerning physical, chemical, anatomical, physiological, pathological, social, psychological, cultural, and educational factors and influences. It will be seen that the mental examination should be a clinical study of personality aiming at a comprehensive appraisal of the patient.

After an analysis of the concrete circumstances of the individual's life and of the complicated forces that have entered into the organization of the personality, the examiner will reformulate the patient's particular difficulties and behavior and reconstruct his or her inner life history. This formulation will include statements about the significant personal relationships during various periods of the patient's life, with special emphasis on the patterns laid down during childhood. The formulation should include experiences that have been important in the development and persistence of personality traits, types of conflict present, and the development of various adaptive processes and defense mechanisms. The formulation of the patient's clinical picture is in the form of probable facts and not in diagnostic labels. These facts must be orderly and intelligible. The formulation will include a discussion of the processes responsible for the behavior of the individual patient, will trace the complicated but significant sequences of cause and effect, and will, through their dynamic relationship, reconstruct past and present events and to a considerable degree predict future ones.

Although the elucidation of symptoms is important in establishing the evidence of psychopathology, symptoms should be looked upon as surface phenomena, and one should attempt to determine the needs, feelings, and motivations manifested in them. On the other hand, study of the personality will reveal certain themes or recurrent life issues or conflicts running through the individual's life history—topics or problems to which one may at times respond in the patterns known as mental disorders. An examination of the patient's history usually will show that the same anxiety-relieving mechanisms, the same psychological themes that are revealed in the illness, have been active in determining the personality type and character traits long before the illness appeared, going back usually, in fact, to early life.

THE PATIENT-PHYSICIAN RELATIONSHIP

While much has been said of the importance of the history in arriving at a diagnostic formulation, it needs to be emphasized that the psychiatric interview consists of significantly more than the verbal account by the patient of his illness and the sought-for elaboration of his developmental history by the physician. From the beginning, the patient's behavior in relation to the physician is revealing in terms of his personality functioning, and its careful observation in connection with the verbal statements made and questions applied is most important. The relationship to the physician influences to a large extent the patient's motivation to reveal the nature of his problems and their sources in his past experiences. If the physician is perceived as helpful and tolerant, the course of history taking and personal revelation will be facilitated. When the patient thinks of the physician as uninterested, hurried, critical, hostile, or demanding, he will be unlikely to unburden himself and will not reveal his innermost thoughts.

The majority of patients conceive of physicians as persons with whom they discuss their physical ailments, although in Western culture today a growing number recognize the psychiatrist as someone to whom one attempts to reveal feeling states, thought processes, and personal intimacies, subjects generally of less interest to the practicing physician.

Conventionally, it is not customary for most persons to discuss openly their intimate relations and thoughts with strangers in the first meeting, nor should the interviewing psychiatrist expect such a full revelation. Much is withheld and perhaps distorted on first contact with the patient, and one should consider as abnormal too open and precise details of usually suppressed and repressed information during an initial interview.

Largely determining the patient's behavior and the attitude he exposes in his relationship to the interviewer are the patterns of behavior he has learned in his relationships with parents and other persons significant to him earlier in life. Thus, he often projects his expectations of how others respond to him to the physician and perceives him or her in a distorted manner. In other words, from its inception the relationship is shaped by a transference, and such transference distortions vary considerably from person to person. The psychotic person is most likely to misperceive the physician, while the person with a neurosis respects more closely the reality role of the psychiatrist.

With the concept of role misperception or transference available to him, the interviewer should carefully notice the attitude of the patient toward him throughout the course of their contact. Does the patient deal with him, openly and frankly, as an ill person seeking aid? Is the patient unusually dependent, requiring magic reassurance from the beginning or soliciting support for his actions and thoughts? Is his approach one of surliness or suspicion, or is there a seductive, provocative, or exhibitionistic trend in the contact? On some occasion, the patient may attempt to ingratiate or bribe the physician for special attention or, on others, openly attack him or become sarcastic, jocular, or tearful. The type of behavior and the immediate sequence of verbal interchange in which it occurs are the important correlations that the skilled physician duly notes.

From these observations, the psychiatrist should infer similar behavior on the part of the patient in the past, an interpersonal approach perhaps revealing evidence of the personality disturbance, and he should question as well in what family setting and circumstance this behavior was learned and from what early sources of identification.

An awareness and appreciation of the dynamics of the patient-physician relationship and its potentialities for transference distortions of the physician by the patient are of major value in allowing the physician to maintain a necessary objectivity and detachment. From such a position, he may remain patient, tolerant, and sufficiently free from personal anxiety so that even the most suspicious and frightened patient will sooner or later perceive him as a nonthreatening aid. To put it more concretely, the physician, knowledgeable of the transference, will not be misled by unwarranted flattery in the initial interview or later nor will he respond either with guilty defensiveness or hostile rebuff in the face of bitter criticism presented by an embittered and suspicious newcomer to his office. He will not succumb to requests for immediate reassurances or provide promises to the magic-seeking dependent person and, in the face of a seductive approach, his information of the transference will hold him aloof since he knows that the same deceptive contact, covering hostility, has been applied to others before him.

It is the function of the psychiatrist, uninvolved in the nuances of the patient's behavior, to arrange and conduct the interview in such a way that the patient, who finds himself in a strange and unaccustomed situation with an individual who often fails to meet his expectations of the role of a doctor, is relieved of as much anxiety as possible. The success of this endeavor to ease the patient's discomfort determines the potentiality of the examiner to provide the information needed to reconstruct and understand the patient's illness.

THE CONDUCT OF THE INTERVIEW

When the patient is accompanied by a family member or friend, it is preferable at all times to interview the patient first. Furthermore, the patient should be advised of the psychiatrist's wish to discuss his illness with the accompanying person. By this means the relationship with the patient is benefited. He is provided the dignity of the responsibility of presenting his history prior to conversations with others who he may feel are motivated to distort his story. To be interviewed first may, too, allay a suspicion which sometimes exists that the physician is an enemy or is submissive to the wishes of a hostile family. The accompanying family member or friend should be seen on all occasions and, if additional information is provided that the patient has failed to present, he may again be interviewed to determine his conception of the unreported events or factors. The discrepancies between the report of the patient and of any other informant should be carefully noted.

The relative usually brings with him certain fears, misapprehensions, and feelings of guilt concerning the patient's illness. His attitude, too, may vary from acceptance and understanding to intolerance. He may be protective, demanding, condemnatory, or unrealistic. Often the relative, in an attempt to be helpful, may unwittingly contribute to the patient's illness.

It is important that the initial interview be conducted under circumstances that prevent the conversation with the patient from being heard by others. This makes for fairness and also leads to further investigation, as the patient often speaks more freely at this time than subsequently. The ease of a patient and his capacities for communication depend to a considerable extent on the manner of the physician's approach. The psychiatrist must be frank and courteous, show that he is genuinely interested in the patient, and, by the implicit elements of his character, be able to command the patient's respect. Rarely does the patient talk revealingly unless the psychiatrist shows signs of interest and understanding. The patient must be made to feel that he is being taken seriously, is being treated with dignity and as an equal, with due consideration for his opinions and statements. Also the psychiatrist must scrupulously seek to maintain the patient's self-esteem and allow him considerable initiative in relating his history.

In order that the optimum rapport and maximum information may be secured, the examiner must be flexible and the interviewing situation must be characterized by spontaneity. A patient's spontaneous account of himself will usually expose more informative material than the patient realizes. The psychiatrist will gradually seek to gain the confidence of the patient so that he will not hesitate to mention life experiences and desires which are so private that he has not mentioned them to his intimates. The patient usually feels that he is understood and his point of view appreciated if the physician permits him to tell his own story, with only an occasional tactful, courteous, and guiding question. Judicious questioning of a patient with an emotional disturbance in such a way that psychopathological mental content will become manifest is a fine art.

A physician who has placed his patient on the defensive has usually blundered in his technique and has perhaps greatly impaired his future usefulness as a counselor. This does not mean that a sense of delicacy should prevent a search sufficient to determine what is going on behind the scenes; rather, after the confidence and cooperation of the patient have been gained, the questions should be put with discretion and with respect for the patient's feelings and intelligence. Care should be taken not to frame questions in such a way that they will be interpreted as accusations. Skillful questioning should enable the interviewer, without arousing undue anxiety, to touch upon the most intimate aspects of the patient's life and open up subjects for exploration that might otherwise remain untouched. Often the patient is not able to respond affirmatively to certain topics suggested by the questioning. However, the fact that the psychiatrist has intimated through his questioning his acquaintanceship with and availability for discussion of such problems is of utmost importance. The patient has been made aware that he has available to him a person to whom he may reveal himself at an appropriate time.

The psychiatrist will never permit himself to become involved in an argument with a patient. The beginner is apt to think that the principal object of the examination is to ascertain the existence of abnormal ideas and to forget the significance of the social circumstances under which symptoms became apparent. He is often more interested in gross disturbances of behavior or in delusional material, with the result that he overlooks deviations in affect and mood, not to mention those of the sensorium.

The patient is initially often eager to discuss his symptoms, complaints, and present illness. While it is the custom in many hospitals and clinics to record these data at a later stage in the formal documentation of the patient's history, it will be found most satisfactory to allow the patient and the relatives to discuss these matters spontaneously and initially. To insist on a presentation of material relative to the patient's family and his life history is often regarded by patient and family informant as irrelevant and irritating.

Although the diagnostic interviews with the patient and his relatives and friends are to be conducted in a flexible manner, the recording of the data for analysis or future reference is best done in accordance with a definite schema. Such a schema is followed in describing the psychiatric examination, and the information to be considered or arranged is detailed under the various headings. In examining a patient, the error is often made of following such a schematic history with its various subdivisions in an obsessive manner, drilling the patient for information on each point. Such an effort is bound to be unrewarding, as patients are usually too anxious initially to provide pertinent material and therefore will respond to a routine staccato type of questioning only by withdrawal or irritation.

There follows a schematic representation of the headings, that are customarily contained in the recorded history. Under these headings are mentioned appropriate areas of life experience of which the psychiatrist should, at some time, gain knowledge. It is as imperative to realize what has not been mentioned and discussed in a spontaneously flowing interview, and the extent and affect attached to each area, as to record what has been gained. One may then question the existence of some special suppression or repression of experience or even a deprivation that has particular significance to the patient. Later these "missed" areas may be covered either through direct probing, or spontaneously, when the patient's anxiety has lessened.

THE PSYCHIATRIC HISTORY

A brief initial description of the patient's status is to be obtained, which will include a statement as to age, sex, marital status, racial background, and occupation. His address and means of direct communication with him (telephone) are also obtained.

Reason for Consultation or Commitment

With the widespread extension of psychiatric services into the areas of private practice, outpatient clinics, courts of law, welfare agencies, schools, and the general hospital, as well as the private and state institutions, a patient with a psychiatric disorder presents himself for examination under a variety of circumstances. The patient may come personally for examination or be referred to a private office or clinic by a physician or by a social agency or school. In other instances, he may be required by a decree of court or by certification to be examined or admitted to a hospital. Under all these circumstances, a brief statement of the manner and circumstances which led to examination or treatment should be obtained. This should include a record of the referring physician or agency and the reason for requesting the examination, if this is offered or is available. In the private office or clinic, the patient often comes alone, and the account of his illness, as he sees it, and of his life history is available only through him. This may also be the circumstance when a patient is committed to a hospital.

The Problem

A clear statement of the complaints and problems of the patient should be obtained from the patient. If possible, it is best to record statements made by the patient in verbatim form.

Present Illness

A detailed account of the development of the present illness of the patient should be obtained. This account should include not only the patient's statements in regard to the symptoms he has observed but also the acute or insidious changes in character, interest, mood, and attitude toward others, as well as modifications in his dress, personal habits, and physical health. It should provide, as well, a careful description of the social circumstances in which the symptoms evolved. The psychiatrist should attempt to ascertain what relationships with others may have been significant. He should seek to learn what has taken place in the lives of these persons and in their contacts with the patient which may have had an effect upon his emotional and psychological state. The psychiatrist should ascertain whether there have been deaths, separations, conflicts, or losses suffered by the patient in relation to his parents and other members of his immediate family or to relatives or friends who are not initially identified. The interweaving of these data and the patient's emotional responses to changes in his relations with others, as chronologically related to the development of his symptoms, often provides major clues to the psychodynamic factors influencing the illness and its prognosis.

The relationship of symptom development to periods of stress induced by interpersonal conflict or significant loss is seldom to be obtained by direct questioning. It is necessary for the psychiatrist to define the potential temporal relationship and then elaborate the problem.

While the search for the emotional disturbance has been emphasized as one of the most important parts of the story of the present illness, the patient and the family or friends usually tell their story by describing the preoccupying symptoms. It is important to obtain a clear description of each symptom, when it was first noticed, whether it is episodically observed or persistently present, its severity, the circumstances that influence each symptom for better or worse, and their effect on the patient's life. His social, sexual, and vocational adaptations must be explored.

The psychiatrist should seek to ascertain what changes were first noticed in the patient's behavior and how they developed and progressed. He should secure information concerning changes in emotion and mood and when undesirable emotional and other personality attitudes were first overtly expressed, and determine whether the patient has appeared increasingly tense and anxious or displayed obsessive or compulsive symptoms. Details of changes in work efficiency, degree of activity, conduct, attention, speech, and memory are important as indicators of illness. Inquiry should be made about whether the patient grasps questions and new situations as quickly as formerly and whether his judgment is impaired. Specific instances are necessary. Has he mentioned peculiar experiences? Has the patient said or done anything that suggests that he has heard imaginary voices or has had other sensory deceptions? Has he had expansive or depressive ideas, ideas of sin, unworthiness, persecution, jealousy, or infidelity? Have suicidal or homicidal tendencies existed?

All accounts of the current illness must consider the general areas of necessary biological functioning. Therefore, an exploration must be made of the changes in the patient's zest for life, his social drive, and the physiological indications of general anxiety exposed in his sleeping and eating habits, his bowel functions, and his usual sexual activities and gratifications.

Equally rewarding in the account of the present illness will be inquiries concerned with the patient's concept of the origins of his illness, its meaning and significance, both now and in the future, for himself and his important relations with others. Is the illness one to which he responds with overt anxiety or sadness, or does it provoke shame or guilt?

The attitude toward the illness is revealing as well. Does the patient deny its significance and seem to be gratified by the symptomatology and its effects on those upon whom he or she is dependent? In other words, is there an emotional gain from the illness? In some instances, the matter of material gain demands inquiry when insurance payments or litigation may be pending.

In contrast to the gain from illness, one will wish to consider as well the urge to recover. Some understanding of this urge may be ascertained by studying the patient's response to his previous illnesses. The duration of the dependency induced by illness in the past in relation to the specific disease and his understanding of his present illness and his expectations for its outcome may give clues to his drive for improvement.

All accounts of the present illness should contain a statement as to the reason for the request for help at the particular time that it is sought. Often patients give histories of long-continuing and unchanging symptomatic disturbance without medical consultation. The precipitating event is unrelated in some cases to symptom change and, frequently, is found in some sudden change in the interpersonal life situation. An inquiry must be made of previous illnesses of the same kind, of treatment given for the current illness and any preceding attacks, and of those who provided therapy so that additional information may be obtained from them, and also an estimate made of the value of the therapy. In some instances, it will be of value to explore the patient's collaboration in previous treatment regimens.

From the present illness, the psychiatrist should distinguish as far as possible the precipitating stress situations from those that predispose. For the most part, the latter will be discovered in the account of the family and personal life of the patient.

Family History

From the family history one may obtain information as to the genetic, familial, economic, and social forces to which the patient was exposed throughout his life. In addition to an account of the parents and siblings with whom the patient lived, which should provide a picture of their personalities, ills, strivings, and any defects, it is important to learn as well of the other persons who resided in or frequently visited the home. By inquiring as to the patient's impression of his parents and other family members and associates, their methods of rearing, and the social mores of their group, the examiner may infer much of the familial customs, conflicts, emotional control, and opportunities for identification offered in early life. The methods of enforcing obedience used by the parents and their substitutes are particularly revealing in this aspect.

A careful account of the reactions of the family and the patient to illnesses in other family members may reveal the sources of reactions to illness or patterns of symptom expression used by the patient and others. The influence of a powerful or domineering grandparent who has set certain ideals for the family, or even of the offsetting factor of training by some domestic helper, is worthy of note. The patient is usually able to indicate whether he or some sibling was the favored child of either parent and to comment upon his emotional reaction of pleasure, fear, envy, or jeal-

ousy relative to his position in the family as compared to that of his siblings.

Here one should note the response of the patient to events such as loss of a parent by death, divorce, or desertion. The age of the patient at the time that the separation took place is much more important to note from the psychiatric viewpoint than the age of the parent at the time of death or desertion. Whether mourning—or a sense of relief—took place should be learned, as well as the duration of this response to the loss and the response of other family members to the same event.

Specific information should be obtained about the occurrence of mental illness, suicide, alcoholism, delinquency, or eccentricity in direct or collateral lines, and whether the patient was of legitimate birth, adopted, or a foster child.

Throughout, it will be found that information is more easily elicited by making an effort to obtain specific descriptions of action and interaction with related reports of the concomitant emotional response, rather than by attempting to elicit responses to questions framed in terms of adjectival descriptions of behavior.

Personal History

It is convenient to think of the personal history as a record of the maturation of the individual and thereby to divide the written report into areas concerned with infancy, childhood, adolescence, and maturity. A report only of maturational development will be inadequate; again, the able historian attempts to define the concomitant interpersonal reactions and their possible influence on the growing person.

INFANCY.   Infancy poses a particular problem, since much of the available material is beyond the range of the patient's conscious memory and thus represents hearsay or the reports available from other family members or observers. Here one wishes to learn whether the patient was a wanted or unwanted child and what expectations the parents might have held for his sex and future development. If he was born with a physical handicap or failed to conform to the family expectations and hopes, the parents' response should be a matter of interest. The nature of the birth itself and the mother's reaction to it often determine mothering attitudes for long periods thereafter and are worthy of discussion.

An account should be obtained of the ages at which sitting, walking, talking, and bowel and bladder control took place. This information provides indications of maturation of functions of the nervous system. One should determine the mother's response to delay in these events and failure of the child to live up to her beliefs in evolving such activities. Important information may be elicited here, too, about the patient's infantile patterns of eating, sleeping, and playing and the parents' methods of participation in such activities.

CHILDHOOD. Childhood as a developmental period offers the opportunity to review the earliest aspect of the patient's active relationships with others. It is usually possible to obtain some expression about his reported personality traits at this time of life. Was he thought of as affectionate, trusting, generous, and active, or as shy, irritable, distant, easily frightened, suspicious, selfish, or aggressive? The capacity of the child for playing and sharing with others should be studied.

Here an account of the patient's earliest memories and dreams, particularly if repetitive, offers an opportunity to discern a wealth of material concerning his early fantasy and emotional life. Since the major interpersonal growth at this time is concerned with the issue of dependency or autonomy, the history should describe the interplay of forces toward independence or dependence. The patient's early efforts at self-expression and assertion should be sought, as well as the parental attitudes

and reaction to such actions. An evaluation should be made of the response to separations from the parents, such as homesickness. Particularly to be noted are the childish responses toward parental discipline and the accompanying or related emotional responses of fear, shame, or guilt. If the patient had feelings of inferiority early, their source should be sought, and if there occurred attitudes of self-compensatory grandiosity, they should be noted. The early expressions of hostility, anger, and aggression and their chief targets, as well as the methods of coping with stress (flight, fight, or immobilization), should be observed.

Sometimes, one may obtain only reports of symptomatic disturbances in childhood, of maldevelopment expressed in speech disorders or stuttering, enuresis, somnambulism, nightmares, or special phobias.

Since schooling commences in childhood and offers an opportunity of defining not only the early intellectual growth but also the initial socialization over periods of time outside the family, the patient's experiences in this milieu are of particular interest. Thus, one wishes to know the ages of entrance and leaving, the occurrence of grade failures or evidence of unusual ability, the child's attitudes toward his teachers and classmates, as well as indications of disturbance expressed in school phobias, truancy, or poor deportment.

Again, the historical study of childhood illnesses and injuries with their duration, complications, and residuals must be conducted, as it reveals the origin of important deficits and later character traits.

ADOLESCENCE. Adolescence holds the potential for re-experiencing at this later period of maturation many of the stresses of the earlier periods of life, as well as those that are uniquely characteristic of this developmental phase. Once again, the responses to illnesses, relations to seniors and peers, and schooling as experienced in adolescence should be reviewed. The patient's adaptations and reactions to such events should be noted. Of particular importance for the inquiry into the period of adolescent behavior is the response to pubescent development. The family's preparation of the growing boy and girl for such events as seminal emissions and menstruation needs to be known, as well as the adolescent's response to their occurrence. His emerging sexual interests and his reactions to those of his peers should be noted. Signs of failure to develop a clear psychosexual identity usually are evident by this life period.

Other questions of importance are those related to the reaction of mother to sexual curiosity and experimentation of early childhood; strong, persistent, dependent attachment to the parent of either sex; preparedness for and reaction to sexual differences; guilt concerning adolescent masturbation; persistence of "crushes"; heterosexual or homosexual attitude toward sex; frankness, prudishness; overt homosexuality.

Since adolescence is a period of emerging personal identity with evident struggles for autonomy and independence, the nature of the patient's adolescent friendships must be ascertained, as well as his participation in or rejection by adolescent groups, his predominant sources of idealized identifications, and his complacent or defiant attitudes to authority. In this period, special capacities or talents may be discerned and ascertained.

ADULTHOOD. Adulthood brings the special stresses of marriage and child rearing, in addition to those of vocational adaptation, plus the problems of establishing effective relations with persons in authority and peers, and of establishing adult social relations. The history should contain information pertaining particularly to these areas.

To assess the sexual adaptations of the adult, the historian will include an account of the courtship, the roles played by patient and partner, and their areas of agreement and disagreement. As the more common areas of disagreement in marriage center on sexual relations, the rearing of children, relations to in-laws, and the spending of money, detailed information will be sought in all these areas. Attitudes toward contraception, emotional reactions to infidelity, illegitimate pregnancies, abortions, or impotence should be looked into. If divorce has occurred, there should be special inquiry into its sources. If the patient has failed to marry, the sources of this lack of adult experience may be looked for in the possible overfixation on a parent, homosexual drives, aversion to the opposite sex, or some physical or social disability preventing the establishment of a heterosexual relationship.

In considering the occupational adaptation and perhaps the military experiences of males, the most significant areas of inquiry are those concerned with the aspirations he has held, the motivations leading to selection of a vocation, the perseverance and performance of the task, and the ongoing relations with work associates. The patient's ability to accept the direction of competent authority or his defiance of it will indicate in some measure his level of emotional maturity. His emotional response to his advancement or that of his peers is also to be carefully searched. Undue fear or envy or incapacity to adapt to the envy of others should be of particular interest. Other revealing areas for study are the various occupations entered, positions held, wages received, reasons for changing, periods of idleness and the reason for same; stationary condition or progress in efficiency and in responsibilities; attitude toward work; satisfaction from work; anything in the present position that is especially difficult, threatening, or inadequate in providing satisfaction; habits of saving or spending money; whether life aims were achieved.

LATE MATURITY. The later years of

life bring their special problems. Here one should examine reactions to the menopause, the emerging independence of and separation from children, retirement, and death of others. One will wish to know of the existence of special interests and avocations, athletic or other recreations, social and community activities. The satisfactions or stresses they produce represent important facets of the patient's personality functioning. These should be ascertained, as well as the need for alcohol and other drugs to relieve tension. An account should be given of the patient's religious interest and practices and the satisfactions gained thereby. It is often useful to have the patient describe a typical 24-hour day. One should also inquire about his current dreams, daydreams, and plans for the future; this information gives clues to his aspirations, ideals, and hidden drives.

Personality

On the basis of the developmental history, the interviewer may arrive at estimates of the social adaptability of the patient, his general activity, and his personality traits and characteristics. These estimates may be derived both from the patient's own comments about himself and those made by his relatives and friends, as well as the inferences obtained from the personal history. These statements and inferences should be recorded as a part of the personal history, with references to their source.

Particularly important here are the references to the prevailing mode of interpersonal relations. Have relations with others been satisfying to himself and them? If not, why not? Has his inner feeling for others seemed to have been one of hatred or of liking? Has the patient enjoyed a degree of affection and respect from others that provided emotional security and self-assurance? Since interpersonal relationships with their positive and negative feelings may be of much significance, inquiry should be made concerning any special attitudes toward parents, siblings, spouse, or others closely associated with the patient. Has filial devotion to either parent been extreme?

GENERAL ACTIVITY AND INTERESTS. Assessment should be made of the degree of initiative and of activity, the fluctuation of activity, the industry or the indolence; intense and poorly balanced devotion to special activities in work or recreation; range of interests; use of leisure; preoccupation, alertness, talkativeness, taciturnity. What have been the patient's dominant interests and activities? What satisfactions and dissatisfactions are experienced from work and environment?

EVALUATION OF PERSONALITY TRAITS AND CHARACTERISTICS. One wishes to have an opinion about whether the patient is given to emotional fluctuations; cheerful, light-hearted, optimistic; gloomy, pessimistic, worrisome; daring or timid; overconfident or cautious; self-reliant or dependent. Does he seek support, reassurance, and approval from others? Is he demonstrative or stolid, outgoing or shut-in, frank and open or reserved and reticent, bashful or at ease in the presence of strangers, talkative or taciturn, aggressive or submissive? Has aggression been constructively or destructively expressed? Is he generous or stingy, honest or deceitful, suspicious, given to misinterpretations, easily offended, prone to feel slighted, resentful, hostile, cynical, inclined to blame others, argumentative, stubborn, envious, cruel? Is he self-conscious, self-blaming, meticulous, perfectionistic, excessively orderly, overconscientious, overscrupulous, or boastful, overbearing, resentful, arrogant, calm or irritable, preoccupied with bodily complaints? Are his opinions and habits rigid, adaptable, characterized by special prejudices? Does he accept or shrink from responsibility? Does he have feelings of inadequacy? Is he given to daydreaming? What is his attitude toward authority? Does he have a sense of humor? What are his characteristic ways of handling stresses, failures, and frustrations? What is his tendency to evade reality and what methods does he employ? With what sets of reactions and patterns of behavior does he respond to new situations? What tension-relieving devices does he habitually use? It is also helpful to ascertain the persons toward whom the patient manifests any of the special personality characteristics described.

Information concerning the patient's personality organization will be secured by ascertaining the type of interpersonal relationships he has tended to develop, e.g., those marked by a predominance of hostility or of affection, of aggression or of submission, of projection or of incorporation, of independence or of dependence. What type of emotional disturbance has the patient most characteristically manifested when defenses have broken down, e.g., anxiety, depression, elation, rage, or others?

Expression of the patient's attitude toward himself and his body and an indication of his ideals, goals, aspirations, and the sources of his chief identifications, if obtainable, should be ascertained. In addition, there should be a statement about his superego function, with a note on the person or persons after whom he has modeled his conscience. Also included should be any past indication of the manner in which he placates feelings of guilt, whether, for example, by penitence, mourning, physical suffering, deprivation, or bribery.

Emotionally Disturbing Experiences

Special attention should be paid to respects in which life has not been psychologically satisfying. Was the need for affection in childhood adequately met? Were there frustrations of hopes and wishes or wounds of pride, vanity, and self-esteem? Were love and sex experiences of emotional significance? What experiences produced pent-up emotional tension or domestic, economic, or social stress? Have family or environmental entanglements been anxiety-producing? The patient should be encouraged to express freely his associations with significant life events and his feelings about them.

Either at this point or in the account of parental relations, the age of the patient at the time of death of a parent or other significant person should be noted. Furthermore, the patient's response to this loss in terms of sadness, depression, guilt, anxiety, or failure to respond emotionally, as well as the duration of the emotional response and its effect on his various activities, should be determined.

PSYCHIATRIC EXAMINATION

An examination must include a thorough physical and neurological examination, together with all indicated laboratory examinations. These investigations, which must be sufficient to discover all structural, functional, somatic, and metabolic factors, need not be discussed in this textbook. It should be borne in mind that psychotic patients may utter no word of complaint even though they are suffering from serious organic illness.

General Appearance, Overt Behavior, and Attitude

One will observe how the patient enters the room and responds to the conventional introduction to the examiner. The patient's facies and the various psychomotor tensions through which emotions are expressed will be noted. The initial interview affords opportunity to observe any obvious physiological signs of anxiety, such as moist hands, mopping of perspiration from the forehead, restlessness, tense posture, strained voice, wide pupils, or guarded vigilance. Attention should be paid to dress, gait, posture, gesture, or voice, and personal care and clothing. Dress often reveals much concerning personality.

Note should also be made of whether the patient is accessible, frank, evasive, self-defensive, suspicious, ingratiating, superior, disdainful, irritable, or otherwise characterized in manner and bearing and in his attitude toward the examiner and the environment. Is he or she assertive and aggressive, or meekly submissive? Is he superior and condescending in speech and manner, or self-depreciatory? Is he critical, sarcastic, and verbally abusive? Is he irritable and irascible? Is he opinionated or indecisive? Is he arrogant or obsequious? The patient's general reaction to examination may be significant. Does he welcome, tolerate, or refuse the interview? It will be remembered that surface attitudes are often compensatory or otherwise protective. Aggressiveness or a rugged and rough surface attitude, for example, may be a chronic defense against internal anxiety.

In regard to overt behavior, does he act in a reality-adjusted way?

The physician should note the patient's general *level of activity*. Is he ready for effort or does he avoid it; is he overactive and energetic or slow and retarded and perhaps unable to initiate action? Is he restless, agitated, impulsive, or assaultive? What, if any, activities does he spontaneously initiate? Distinction should be made between pressure of occupation with its eager output of energy and a mere undirected restlessness. Other disturbances of activity are reduction, stupor, negativism, stereotypy, catalepsy, mannerisms, tics, posturing, grimacing, silliness, automatic obedience (*flexibilitas cerea*, echopraxia), playfulness, impulsiveness, combativeness, and destructive tendencies. The apparent stupors,

which do not include those caused by an extreme clouding of consciousness, are those associated with deep depression, those resulting from negativism or resistance, and those resulting from resentment. Note should be made of any compulsive acts or ceremonials. Any evidence of a compulsive personality, as shown by scrupulosity or by excessive emphasis on orderliness or cleanliness, should be described.

Considerable information can often be obtained by having the patient write a simple sentence from dictation. The handwriting may show tremors, as in the paretic. In the same disease, various elisions are common. The manic frequently writes in bold characters, underscoring many words or adding spontaneous productions. Negativism, retardation, or pressure of activity may be demonstrated by the manner in which the patient approaches the task. Note should be made of the patient's degree of alertness, whether he is mute, whether he eats or refuses food, and the presence of bizarre postures or the sustained immobility of catalepsy.

Note should be made concerning sex attitudes or habits observed, including flirtatiousness, hypereroticism, anaphrodisia, exhibitionism, homosexuality and overt or covert masturbation.

Disturbances of attention, in the form of distractibility, preoccupation, excessive tenacity of attention, and absence of attention, should be included in this topic.

While many of the data under this heading may be noted and recorded at the beginning of the interview, they may frequently be modified or enlarged at its conclusion.

Affectivity and Mood

The prevailing mood is often suggested by the patient's facial expression, muscular tensions, and bodily attitude. One usually also inquires of the patient about his emotional state. The question should not be of a leading or inappropriate type. Frequently, the inquiry "How are your spirits?" will evoke the desired description. Discreet questions designed to bring out the patient's estimate of self may elicit not only a reply suggesting his mood but one containing other significant information. When the patient has indicated his mood, he may be asked the reason for his feelings, although the reply frequently represents the rationalization of factors not consciously recognized.

In addition to the important observations of the intensity of affect, its appropriateness, modulation, responsiveness, and oscillation, such states as euphoria, elation, exhilaration, exaltation, ecstasy, depression, gloomy irritability, apathy, or incongruity are noted. The patient who is euphoric or exhilarated will often be optimistic, self-assured, friendly, and buoyant. The depressed patient is usually quiet and restrained, often dejected and hopeless in attitude and manner. Affective states readily influence attention, concentration, memory functions, and thinking processes. Somewhat more complex states marked by disturbed affective components are fear, panic, hypochondriasis, apprehensiveness, worry, despair, chronic dissatisfaction, irritability, suspiciousness, anger, hate, and silliness.

If the patient is depressed, a careful effort should be made to ascertain any possible inclinations toward suicide. Inquiry should be made about whether the patient considers life worth living. If his response is in the negative, he may then be asked more specifically whether he has considered doing anything about it and what thoughts and plans he has constructed.

Associations and Thought Processes

In this field of examination the examiner observes not the content of thought but the tempo of associations and the characteristics of thought processes. Note should be made of any unusual rapidity of associations, as in flight of ideas, also of any slowness in associations, as in retardation. Disorders in the logical progression of thought will be shown by the patient's associations as he talks. The examiner should therefore note such disturbances as circumstantiality, incoherence, blocking, or irrelevance. Record should be made of any distortions of thought processes, such as neologisms, word salad, perseveration, echolalia, or condensation.

Thought Content and Mental Trend

A spontaneous development of the patient's mental content should be encouraged, and the narration should be interrupted with a minimum of guiding questions. Such questions as are asked should be carefully individualized, and be pertinent to and in logical relation to content that has already been expressed.

In the investigation of this important field, an error is often made by confining it to a search for delusions. The patient's dreams, the content of his fantasies, his ambitions, fears, and identifications afford significant glimpses into his preoccupations and personal problems. The psychiatrist will note the extent to which the patient misinterprets facts and reality in his unrecognized effort to meet his emotional and personality needs. The psychiatrist should be on the watch for a trend or general theme that runs through, correlates, and tends to determine beliefs and conducts. Some patients are eager to express any beliefs that center on such a trend, while others are evasive or suspicious.

In patients who are otherwise accessible but who are reluctant to divulge such content of thought as they fear will be considered disordered, much depends on the experience of the physician and the rapport established with the patient. Usually, while giving the story of his life and of his recent experiences, the patient will have divulged whether he has resorted to delusional beliefs in his efforts to deal with personality problems and difficult situations. If, up to this point, the patient has made no references to material which suggests that it may be delusional, its existence and an intimation of its nature may sometimes be secured by asking him if he has recently had any unusual, strange, or troublesome experiences. If it is suspected that he has resorted to projection as a protective device, the patient may be asked if people have been spreading lies about him or if ill-disposed people have attempted to harm him. Efforts to solve given personality needs are often met not only by projection and delusions of persecution but also by the mechanism of compensation. For this reason, inquiry may be made about self-flattering beliefs designed to magnify the patient's estimate of self. If the patient's mood is one of depression, he may be asked if he has done anything that is wrong or if he has sinned more than other people. Escape from intolerable reality may be provided by delusional consolations.

As the patient reveals his conscious ideational content, the examiner seeks, by the type of delusion, to ascertain what is being symbolically told him, as well as the relationship of its specific content to the patient's emotional needs and why at this particular time he has had to have the protection and support of his delusion. It will frequently be observed that the conscious content of the delusion is the converse of the true meaning. Statements made by the patient are often clues to the psychological realities they conceal. Motives ascribed to others, too, may represent the patient's own wishes and urges. Grandiose delusions often give a clue to previous frustrations.

If the patient is requested to write an account of his life, he will frequently disclose a trend or express material of psychopathological significance. Mental content previously undiscovered is at times revealed in letters or other writings.

Perception

In deeply toxic and in organic states, consciousness may be so seriously disturbed that the mental processes necessary to complete perception are impossible, with the result that imperception exists. In suspected mental disorder, particularly in delirious or in strongly affective states, the examiner should scrutinize the accounts of the patient's perceptual experiences and his observed reactions to them in order to discover any indications that they are illusionary in nature. Illusional misinterpretations not of psychopathological origin are usually, in the face of reasonable evidence, recognized by the individual as erroneous. If, however, the illusions have arisen from a deepseated anxiety or other personality basis, they are not amenable to reason.

The ease with which the occurrence of hallucinations is ascertained varies greatly. One looks first for auditory hallucinations, the method of inquiring for which will depend upon many factors, particularly upon the apparent integrity of the patient's personality and the extent to which he recognizes that hallucinations are mentally pathological. If the patient's evaluation of reality is considerably disturbed, he may be frankly asked if he hears voices. The subject may often be approached somewhat more indirectly by asking the patient if he has observed that he has been called derogatory names, or if unpleasant remarks have been directed to him. Frequently some remark of the patient affords a lead which, if pursued, will indicate whether hallucinations exist. Often the patient will describe hallucinatory experiences if he is asked whether he has had any "imaginations." The same inquiry may occasionally reveal delusions when the patient has some realization that his mental content is abnormal. This is not surprising, since the unitary reaction of the individual frequently uses both perception and mental content for the same purpose. Indeed, ideational and hallucinatory content are so intimately reciprocal and complementary that in a guide for mental examination they might properly be considered under the same heading.

In Chapter 6 attention was called to the fact that both hallucinations and delusions represent an inner falsification of the outside world, in accordance with the needs and wishes of the personality. The psychiatrist seeks, therefore, to determine what function the patient's hallucinations are serving in his total psychological experience. When the patient denies hallucinations, a suspicion that they exist may sometimes be confirmed by others, who may observe him in listening attitudes or responding to his hallucinations. Since, in disguised and projected form, the hallucinations express mental material that intimately pertains to his personality needs and problems, the patient is usually much preoccupied during his hallucinatory experience. In toxic states, the patient's behavior may suggest reactions to visual hallucinations; in other instances, an inquiry if he has had any visions may furnish information. For diagnostic purposes, it is a matter of great importance to determine whether hallucinations, irrespective of the type of sense expression, occur in a setting of clear consciousness. If consciousness is not clear, it is probable that toxic or organic pathology exists.

SENSORIUM

Consciousness

Under this heading one notes the sensorium, or functional state of the special senses, especially as it is related to the condition of consciousness, which may be clear or clouded to varying degrees. Deeper states of impairment are confusion, stupor, and unconsciousness. If necessary, the patient is questioned to determine his *orientation* to time, place, and person. He should be asked the date, where he is, and the names and roles of those in his presence. It is of great importance to determine whether symptoms are presented in a setting of mental clearness or one of clouding.

In addition to his state of orientation, special attention should be directed to his memory function, fund of information, arithmetical capacities, judgment and insight. Impairment of the sensorium is common in those conditions associated with both acute and chronic cerebral insufficiency (the acute and chronic brain syndromes). With other psychosis, some impairment may be suggested because of hyperactivity, lack of attention, and distractibility. Patience on the part of the examiner usually discloses that real deficits in these functions do not exist.

Memory

It is frequently desirable to determine the patient's memory for remote events. If he is asked as part of the general mental examination to give a chronological account of his life, a reasonably correct estimate of his remote memory can be determined by his success in giving dates of entering and leaving school, the places and dates of employment, and the names of employers. Special attention should be paid to whether the stated activities and dates are properly correlated. The patient's memory concerning events of somewhat less personal interest may be tested by asking about local or national events known to have occurred during the patient's life, which any person in the community would ordinarily know. Frequently, one should ascertain whether there is a hiatus of memory for a circumscribed period of time, particularly if there is a history of head trauma, delirium, epilepsy, fugues, or other dissociative reaction.

Recent memory can easily be tested by asking the patient when he came to the hospital, from what place, by whom he was accompanied, or about other events in the immediate past.

If the patient shows impaired memory for recent events, note should be made of any tendency to fill the gaps of memory with pseudoreminiscences (confabulation). Sometimes alleged activities and incidents can be suggested. In paranoid psychoses, especially, it should be determined whether the accounts of any incidents are elaborated with details, really fictitious but believed by the patient to be facts. In more exaggerated cases, the entire account of alleged incidents may be a retrospective falsification of memory.

Retention and recall ability may be tested by giving a series of four or five nonconsecutive numbers and asking the patient to repeat them in the same or in reverse order. Another frequent test is to give him a street address or the names of a few objects, with instructions that they be remembered. After a given period, e.g., five minutes or an hour, the patient is asked to repeat what he was enjoined to remember.

The subtraction of serial sevens (the patient is requested to subtract 7 from 100 and then subtract 7 from each succeeding answer) has been regarded as particularly useful in detecting impaired brain functioning. Milstein and his colleagues have recently re-examined this test and found that approximately 65 per cent of individuals, in both patient and presumed healthy groups, will respond without error. Performance on this test is complexly related to the disability of the patient, his intelligence and social class, as well as to his attentiveness, comprehension, and concentration. As the latter quali-

ties generally are disturbed in seriously impairing acute and chronic cerebral insufficiency, it would be expected that the examiner will detect more errors in serial seven subtraction in those with severe disabilities of this type.

Fund of Information

This will be indicated by the patient's replies to questions concerning current events, matters of common knowledge, and retention of knowledge acquired in school. The character of the questions will depend upon the opportunities the patient has had for acquiring information.

Judgment

By judgment is meant the ability to compare facts or ideas, to understand their relations, and to draw correct conclusions from them. The correctness of the patient's estimates and interpretations of external objective matters and the degree to which he recognizes the interrelation of significant factors and incidents are indexes of the quality of his judgment. Judgment is integrated in all personality functions but is particularly influenced by the patient's general grasp and by emotional factors. It might readily be extended to include the patient's estimate of his mental disorder, but his subjective judgment in this respect is so important that under the designation "insight" it is considered as a special field for examination. If objective judgment is impaired, one seeks to ascertain whether the defect is caused by a toxic disturbance of the sensorium or by degenerative or inflammatory involvement of higher cortical centers, or whether it is distorted by emotional influences and confined to matters conflicting with delusional trends and affective needs. In estimating the patient's judgment, an attempt is made to learn whether the patient's business affairs are conducted with prudence and his family obligations met.

Insight

Insight refers to the extent the patient is aware that he is ill, recognizes the nature of his illness, and understands the special dynamic factors that have been operative in producing illness. It refers to the patient's ability to observe and understand himself — the extent of his self-knowledge. One seeks to learn the patient's estimate of how personality difficulties are interfering with his social adjustment and the successful performance of his usual duties. An endeavor is made to ascertain whether the patient recognizes his adaptive limitations.

The patient is asked the reasons for the psychiatric consultation. If he is in a hospital, inquiry should be made about the cause for his admission, whether he wished to come, his need of treatment, whether he considers himself to be suffering from a mental illness or has so suffered in the past. Frequently it is well to ask him whether he has noticed any change in himself or in his outlook on life, or whether there has been any change in his feelings, interest, memory, or thinking. One seeks to learn whether the patient desires to be helped and what attempts he has made to adjust himself to the situation. Many patients state that they are or have been "nervous" or have suffered from a "nervous breakdown," and yet have no actual realization that they have suffered from a mental disorder.

Many patients, on recovering, have what might be described as a verbal insight but are quite lacking in any psychological insight, i.e., an appreciation of the presumed motives associated with the illness and the genesis of their symptoms. They are unable to reflect retrospectively on their feelings and experiences or to understand how the past interferes with present functioning. They may readily admit that they have suffered from mental disorder, yet they have little realization of what their symptoms have been, none as to the significance of their experiences, and no recognition of the factors that were operative in the production of their mental disorder.

Absence of an understanding insight is not surprising, since there is usually great resistance to the uncovering of dynamic tendencies that have been operating beyond the sphere of awareness. The patient is not emotionally prepared to face clearly and appreciate fully the existence of conflicts or the nature of the problems against which his symptoms constitute a defense. He is blind to their meaning since he needs his blindness. The patient must, too, avoid realizing that he has adopted delusional beliefs or otherwise disregarded reality in order to attain his ends. Asking the patient whether he has had any imaginations will often reveal the extent of his realization of his entertainment of delusional ideas or whether he has had hallucinatory experiences. In hospitalized patients, significant information can often be secured by asking the patient why he has been detained so long in the institution.

The extent to which the patient recognizes any continuing disabilities may at times be learned by inquiring what he expects to do when he leaves treatment. It is often well to ask the patient what the various psychopathological phenomena discovered mean to him and the reasons for his abnormal behavior. While it is unlikely that he can or will give the real explanation, his rationalizations may at times betray significant factors or psychological areas that require defenses. At its best, insight is usually a mixture of self-knowledge and of rationalization.

The goal of psychotherapy, frequently not attained, is that the patient gain such insight into and understanding of the unconscious roots of his problems, their genesis and dynamics, that changes in the dynamic structure of his personality will be promoted. Insight alone, however, does not cure; it must be applied.

Personality Maturity

As the psychiatrist continues his study of the patient's personality through successive interviews, he makes an evaluation of the emotional and personality maturity. He will note whether the patient's interpersonal and other attitudes are appropriate to a stage of personality development consistent with his chronological age. The degree of maturity of personality may be suggested by the perspective in which he sees his life and work. The psychiatrist will observe the patient's pattern of securing satisfaction, also the roles which he unconsciously demands from others. As a confidential rapport is established, the psychiatrist will study the patient's psychosexual development since, through the intimate and pervasive role which it plays in life, it becomes an important and sensitive indication of personality development. The evaluation of the maturity of the patient is important in assessing his capacity for various types of therapeutic endeavor.

While the levels of emotional maturity have been described previously, they are noted again in the following schematic manner. *Infantile attitude* is evident when the patient expects from others infinite service and tolerance and responds with petulance when his desires are not immediately gratified. *Childish emotional maturity* is signified in those in whom the psychiatrist finds a limited degree of responsibility with the expectation that, when required, his parents or those upon whom he is dependent will assume his care or excuse his defects. Such individuals also demand a complete trust in another as the basis of any acceptable relationship. The *early adolescent stage* is epitomized in youths concerned with the problem of independence from parents by their tendency to admire and be devoted to extrafamilial figures. They may be much interested in social organizations and mystic rivalry. Here, then, are con-

sciousness and awareness of sex. In the *late adolescent stage,* emotional drive at the adult level is for self-advancement through growth and learning. There are strivings for independence that are often challenging to parents and other adults.

It is important to recognize that the individual's emotional development may not have advanced equally in all respects or in all relationships. An individual may function at different levels of maturity in relation to members of one or the other sex, to those in authority, or to group activities.

PSYCHOLOGICAL TESTING

When administered by an experienced clinical psychologist, the varieties of psychological tests may be of major assistance in clarifying the diagnostic impression, disclosing various aspects of personality function inaccessible in the initial interview with the patient, and assessing the patient's potential for engagement in a psychotherapeutic relationship and/or his potential for ego-adaptive or regressive movements in the face of the anxiety of such treatment.

There are now available a wide variety of tests suitable for examining the intellectual and cognitive abilities of individuals of various ages and for examining aspects of personality functioning in terms of reality-testing ability and impulse control. Also revealed may be evidences of depression and guilt, major dysfunction, psychological defenses and symptoms, interpersonal conflict, affect, and self-concept.

The personality tests are classified into objective and projective. The *objective tests* are usually pencil and paper devices, in which questions with factual answers provide numerical scores and profiles subject to easy mathematical or statistical analysis. Such tests generally do not demand much experience or sophistication on the part of the user and come supplied with interpretive manuals. The *projective tests*, on the other hand, present visual or verbal stimuli of some ambiguity which lead the subject to expose his own fantasies into the unstructured stimulus through the psychological mechanism of projection. With the latter type of test, the greater the knowledge and experience of the examiner, the richer is the potential for interpretation of personality function.

In general, the clinical psychologist uses a battery of psychological test devices. His interpretations are derived from the responses made by the individual, as well as from the divergences elicited between his various responses to the several instruments.

Tests may be administered either individually or in groups. It is generally believed that the most valid evaluation is obtained through individual examination with a battery of well chosen tests. Such testing is both time consuming and expensive.

The administration of the Wechsler Adult Intelligence Scale usually requires only an hour but three or four times that amount of time may be necessary to subject the patient to a test battery. An almost equivalent period of time must be devoted to the scoring and interpretation. Today, aside from simple screening procedures, psychological testing is seldom done routinely. The psychologist wishes to have available salient questions that are to be answered to assist the psychiatrist or mental health team in the future disposition and treatment of a patient. He needs to know the condition of the patient in clinical terms, whether his brain functioning may have been modified through the use of psychopharmaceuticals or other hypnotic or sedative drugs, or as a result of electroshock therapy. Such testing is most likely to prove useful where the patient has been brought to understand the purpose of the testing as helpful for his future relief from distress and capacity to cope with living. Thus, distorted and poor performance may be expected from those patients who fail to comprehend the meaning of the test, are suspicious of its significance, or are forced to participate.

In the following sections are described the psychological tests of intellectual and cognitive functioning and personality functioning most widely used at present.

Tests of Intellectual and Cognitive Functioning

The modern tests of intelligence and cognitive abilities examine a wide variety of functions. Thus, one may determine the immediate capacities of the individual to assimilate factual knowledge, to recall recent or remote events, to use logical reasoning, to handle numerical or verbal concepts, to move from the abstract to the literal or vice versa, and to analyze and synthesize forms. These various abilities have been recognized for centuries and vary in their value from culture to culture. They were brought to a formal, quantitatively capable test realization in 1905 through the work of Alfred Binet, a French psychologist, and Théodore Simon, a French psychiatrist, in their study of the clinical problem of assessing the educable capacity of mental retardates. Binet and Simon were responsible for the concept of *mental age*, which represents the level of achievement in children that is characteristic of each age level. No matter what his chronological age is, a child may be said to have a mental age of 5 years when, on the basis of test performance, he completes successfully those items expected of a general range of 5-year old children.

Later, W. L. Stern (1912) described the intelligence quotient (I.Q.) as a ratio between mental age and chronological age times 100 (I.Q. $= \frac{\text{m.a.}}{\text{c.a.}} \times 100$).

In instances where the mental age

increases in proportion to the chrono-logical age, this index provides a clue to the developmental process of the individual. It has been discovered to be meaningful in the assessment of children's intellectual abilities and it influenced the development of the American revisions of the original Binet scale.

The various aspects of cognitive functioning develop over differing spans of time in individuals and, furthermore, certain individuals may perform remarkably well in particular areas but demonstrate a much reduced capacity in others. In the course of development, a leveling off of the differing functions may take place. It is recognized now that intelligence, as measured by tests early in life, should not be regarded as fixed. It is perhaps best to regard the evolution of the individual's cognitive capacities as a hierarchical process in which learning progresses through a series of increasingly complex steps.

Holding this view of the evolution of intelligence, it is evident that those who have specific defects may suffer from particular deficiencies in the physiological organization that inhibit evolution at a rate similar to that of others. Examples are the deficiencies in intellectual and personality development of the congenitally blind or deaf, discussed in Chapter 7. Modern psychologists are undertaking experimental studies of the differential learning of individuals with particular deficiencies. Some hold that it is necessary for information acquired largely through stimuli perceived through one sensory system to be integrated centrally with that perceived through other sensory modalities. O'Connor's experimental work suggests that for certain functions brain coding occurs independently of the presence or absence of a higher level of mental functioning, whereas in certain forms of spatial interpretation there must exist higher levels of integrative visual schemata. In the first instance,

memory coding occurs without transfer to other modalities of sensory experience, while in the second there is evidence that such transfer does take place.

The long continuing opinion of some that intelligence is set at birth and remains constant throughout life is incorrect. Furthermore, it is now known that mental abilities may not be predicted from performances noted in infancy. The study of consecutive mental test scores of individuals shows that there are variable rates of growth during the first three or four years. The experience of successive testing in individuals does demonstrate that as one approaches the chronological age of the early teens the rates of such growth become limited yet scores may continue to increase even up to the age of 50, particularly in the area of verbal facility and knowledge. Other abilities tend to peak in the early twenties and remain stable thereafter.

High scores in psychometric tests are not incompatible with serious mental disorder; in fact, patients suffering from paranoia frequently have a high intelligence quotient. On the other hand, some mental disorders are accompanied by an impairment of the original capacity for mental functioning, the deterioration being particularly manifested by difficulties in forming new associations, in making correct associations, in retaining recent memories, and in fixing attention. Certain functions may become impaired more rapidly than others, with the result that there may be a wide variation or "scattering" in the extent of the loss when one compares mental functioning in one area against that in others. The use of the intelligence test extends far beyond simply stating the intelligence quotient of the individual. Modern tests are devised to examine a wide range of functions and mental deterioration as inferred from the variations exposed in the capacities of the patient to perform in the various subjects. A brief description of the most commonly employed test of intelligence follows.

Wechsler Adult Intelligence Scale (WAIS)

This test, now the most frequently applied to test general intelligence, is also the best standardized. In contrast to the earlier tests of intelligence, which were largely verbal, the intelligence scale constructed by David Wechsler performs its measurements on suitable verbal and performance material in such a fashion that the age of the subject is taken into consideration. This is an individually administered scale, which consists of eleven subtests applicable to adolescents and adults. The *verbal scale* consists of six subtests, which examine general information, general comprehension, digit span, arithmetic, similarities, and vocabulary. The *performance scale* includes picture arrangement, picture completion, block design, object assembly, and digit symbol. In the verbal subtests, the responses to verbal stimuli are given orally by the patient. The performance scale includes certain subtests in which manipulation by the patient is important and others in which this element operates minimally. In scoring, items of each subtest are scored separately and the sum of these items yields a raw or unweighted score for particular subtests. These scores are scaled and converted into an I.Q. in accordance with the average of the individual's own age group. The test is an advance over earlier examinations, since it is standardized by actual examination of individuals in seven separate age groups ranging from 16 to 64 years, chosen as representative of the general population of the United States of America.

The use of the numerous subtests provides an opportunity for differentiating an individual, for studying the "scatter" pattern of individuals with various types of personality disorder. From an examination of the scatter patterns, certain diagnostic impressions are obtained, although experience has shown that much overlapping exists between the various groups.

All intelligence tests have certain deficits as they fail to allow for cultural variations. Thus, within the Wechsler scales psychologists recognize that certain subtests are more culture-bound than others. Yet it is likely that the cultural variables are much less important than are generally stated.

THE WAIS SUBTESTS. The *information* subtest is perhaps the least culture-free. Those who are exposed to cultural deprivation, language difficulties, or other experiences that inhibit new learning will test as high on this subtest as will those who rely on massive repression as a defense. On the other hand, overachievers and the obsessive-compulsive intellectualizers do well.

On the *comprehension* subtest, the examiner perceives the use of conventional social judgment. Those who are dependent upon the social structure and early learning score high here, while the obsessive person and those who are less aware of conventional behavior perform at an inferior level.

Arithmetic. Arithmetical ability is thought to be related to attention, concentration, and the analytic process.

Similarities. Verbal abstraction is examined, as well as the capacity of a person to discriminate essential and superficial likenesses in terms of psychopathology; those with mental retardation and schizophrenics may do poorly here. The former respond concretely while the latter offer bizarre or peculiarly personal abstraction.

Memory for digits. Immediate memory is examined in this subtest. In general, the majority are able to recall approximately two fewer digits backward than forward. Brain disorders and anxiety tend to limit performance on memory for digits.

Vocabulary. All global measures of intelligence tend to be correlated well with vocabulary. Vocabulary responses stand up to the impairment of aging, as well as to personality disturbances. Vocabulary responses are important, nevertheless, in terms of personality, as they may expose pedantic behaviors, disturbances of formal thinking, or superior intellect.

Capital digit symbols. This subtest examines the individual's ability to substitute nonverbal symbols for the appropriate digit. Psychomotor retardation in depression or agitation in depression, as well as aging, adversely affects the responsiveness. In contrast to the performance of the brain damaged, the majority of the subjects tend to improve their scores with practice.

Picture completion. Through inserting the missing part in 21 different pictures, the testee's perceptual and conceptual abilities are examined. Reality testing, too, is exposed; a schizophrenic often makes errors in easy items.

Block design. By requiring the subject to match visual designs with colored blocks, the ability to analyze totality into parts is demonstrated. Those with a limited capacity to defend against confusion often show difficulty on this subtest.

Picture arrangement. In requiring a subject to arrange pictures so as to establish a story, social intelligence is examined, as well as capacity for humor. Those weak in empathy perform less well on this subtest than those with good capacity for role playing.

Object assembling. This subtest requires the ability to deal with part-whole relationships and provides a demonstration of the thinking and working habits of the testee as he attempts to put pieces together to make familiar pictures.

Similar tests have been developed by Wechsler for children (4 to 6½ years; 6 to 16 years). In addition, those examining children have available the following: Gesell's Developmental Schedules; Cattell's Infant Intelligence Scale; Bayley's California First-Year Scale; Bayley's Infant Scales of Development (for age groups 2 to 30 months of age); Griffith's Scale for Babies. Those interested in the use of scales will find them described in the article by Bayley.

Personality Tests or Assessments

Although a knowledge of the individual's intellectual endowment often gives the psychiatrist useful information concerning the patient, the tests utilized for this purpose provide only limited information on personality functioning and psychodynamics. Therefore, they are supplemented by a variety of *projective* personality tests. The most widely applied are described below.

Much thought has been given to the development of probing techniques whereby one may investigate factors existing in the deeper levels of the personality and uncover unconscious needs and aspects that have been important in determining its structure and the individual's behavior. Such methods are known as projective since in them the subject interprets ambiguous stimulus situations according to his own unconscious dispositions, i.e., he reads into his perceptions and fantasied creations covert personality tendencies and processes. He projects out onto the external world the pattern of his own psychological life. The subject's performance patterns and responses, being projections of himself, reveal the personality structure and its underlying dynamics. The tests can also tell much about the subject's assets and liabilities. The projective tests have done much to close the gap between psychoanalysis and general psychology.

Rorschach Personality Assessment

This "test," published in 1921 by Hermann Rorschach, a Swiss psychiatrist, furnishes some information concerning the patient's intellect but is more valuable as a means of detecting fundamental personality characteristics. It indicates tendencies within the patient that

Figure 8-1 Rorschach card Number IV. (Reproduced courtesy of Hans Huber Verlag, Switzerland.)

may come to overt expression once the effectiveness of his defenses is diminished. In its application, the patient is shown ten cards, on each of which is a complex standard "inkblot" picture with two symmetrical halves (Fig. 8-1). Five of the ten cards are dark gray but with many different shadings; two are in dark gray and red; three are multicolored. The inkblots show a great variety of form, shading, and color, so chosen that they may have suggestive value for the responder. In the test procedure, the patient is asked to state what he sees in the relatively formless blot, what it looks like, what it makes him think of, or what it suggests to him.

By creating meaningful forms out of the apparently meaningless material, he unknowingly reveals fundamental traits and dominant trends in his personality. What the patient perceives becomes an expression of himself. In telling how the inkblots look to him, he tells the examiner about his own attitudes, feelings, conflicts, and significant aspects of his personality. In the apparently meaningless inkblot, the free-running fantasy of the patient discovers and reveals content that symbolizes significant and emotionally charged elements and problems of the personality. Authority figures and attitudes toward them, identifications, suppressed cravings, the quantum of aggression, conception of the life role, sexual identification, the psychosexual level, and specific anxiety-arousing factors and stresses are among the contents disclosed.

By this projective technique, the examiner obtains a psychological portrait of the personality and may discover pointers to underlying psychopathology. The patient's responses are scored and evaluated by means of an elaborate system in which location determinants and content of responses have been correlated empirically and logically with certain personality traits. In general, the present scoring system continues to rely on the recommendations of Rorschach but many of his successors have modified or refined their interpretations on the basis of their experience. The test is scored in terms of the frequencies of a variety of determinants.

LOCATION DETERMINANTS. The location determinants relate to areas on each card to which the subject responds. The subject may be stimulated by the whole (W), a sizable detail (D), a small detail (d), or the white spaces (S). Good orientational ability and intelligence are correlated with high W per cent scores while high D per cent scores are made by those with more pragmatic interests. Attention to minor detail is usually conspicuous in the responses of the obsessive or paranoid person and suggests oppositional and resistive tendencies. When overly frequent, the correlation is with paranoid potential.

SHAPE, FORM, AND COLOR DETERMINANTS. These responses are scored to include form (F), shading (K), texture (t) or (c), color (C), movement, either of people (M) or animals (FM), inanimate movement (m), or combinations. Fantasy is generally related to human movement responses and is associated with form accuracy. Fantasies are thought of as unrealistic or autistic, but if occurring in the context of good form are considered as related to affective reality testing. Availability of impulses to immediate gratification is related to the animal movement (FM) responses as well as spontaneity, but, if in excess, to immaturity. Tension and conflict are interpreted with occurrence of inanimate movement (m) responses—such arising from forces outside one's control. Overemphasis on form (F) suggests personal rigidity and constriction, while form accuracy [(F)-plus per cent] provides a measure of reality-testing ability and ego strength. The latter is often found high in depressive people and the intelligent, but low in manics, schizophrenics, and the retarded. An excessive amount of shading responses (KF, K) indicates profuse anxiety, while shading which is struc-

tured but three-dimensional (FK) is thought to show efforts to manage affectional anxiety by introspection. If excessive, strong inferiority feelings are suggested.

Texture responses (c, cF, Sc) correlate with awareness of needs for affection and dependency, while achromatic color responses (C', C'F, FC') indicate artistic inclinations and, when in excess, depression. Color responses, too, correlate with the emotional reactions of the subject in response to social and interpersonal contacts, as well as affective control. Scores relating the balance between M responses to total C responses suggest the degree of introversion or extroversion within the individual.

CONTENT DETERMINANTS. Whether the responses to the inkblots are described in human, anatomical, sexual, feeding, or natural terms, they are scored as content. The content area indicates breadth and range of interests. Human responses are considered to suggest interest in and awareness of others, yet not necessarily interpersonal involvement. Excessive animal responses are interpreted as immaturity in thought or lack of cultural breadth. Bodily harm, preoccupation with physical function, and defense against hostile destructive impulses are suggested by many anatomical responses. The food responses are seen as the expression of the need for nurture—a regression. The capacity to think along usual conventional lines is related to the number of popular (P) responses.

EGO BOUNDARY. The Rorschach test has been used to define the definitiveness of the ego boundaries of the individual. Thus, percepts in which body boundary is emphasized, such as the response "man in tank," have been labeled as barrier responses, whereas others emphasizing broken aspects of the body have been designated as penetration responses. Research findings have suggested that many barrier responses are associated with personality characteristics that are self-directive; a weak barrier index is correlated with psychosomatic disturbances that have an external bodily site.

PROGNOSTIC INDICATORS. Well-perceived and active human movement responses, animal movement responses, and good form, shading and color responses suggest to the psychologist a good prognosis, as these indicators disclose the ability to empathize with others; to control impulses; to test reality; to have sensitivity, the desire for affection, and responsivity to the environment; and to be productive and diverse. Human responses give excellent indicators of the individual's interest in others, as well as providing insights into his sexual identity.

The Rorschach test should yield information concerning "basic personality configuration," intellectual aspects, and emotional aspects of the personality. The psychological aspects as well as the personality strengths and adaptive tendencies of the patient are tapped by this test. His conflicts and defenses are revealed as well as his major affects, his fantasies, his capacities for interpersonal relations and ego adaptation, and his regressions. It affords much insight into the personality structure, although its critics say it is difficult to tell where the test results leave off and the personality of the examiner begins. Table 8–1 demonstrates how the Rorschach test may be used in differentiating abnormality.

TABLE 8–1   Schizophrenia vs. Organic Brain Syndrome as Differentiated by the Rorschach Test

	SCHIZOPHRENIA	ORGANIC BRAIN SYNDROME
General Test Characteristics	Variability in tempo, sequence, and accuracy of response. Distortions in thinking: may be highly symbolic or overly personal, autistic, unconventional, idiosyncratic, morbid, peculiar language. Disturbances in ego boundaries: loss of distance.	Decrement in ability to respond reflected in long reaction times, fewer than average responses, expressions of confusion and perplexity, inability to improve on performance, memory disturbances, automatic and perseverative phrases.
Example of Patient's Response to Rorschach Card 1	(5 minutes) "This is two dog-pigs eating the carcass of a raccoon, and they're brother dog-pigs. Their stepsister is a raccoon. They both like her equally, so it's bisected in half. They're going to eat her. It could be because I'm hungry." (Inquiry) "The sister is the middle part. . . . I was just thinking of the spine and heart. . . ." (Eating?) "Because their nose is in her face."	(45 minutes) "Doctor, you know this is hard. . . . It doesn't look like much of anything to me. . . . What is it supposed to be?" (Patient rotates card.) "Wings? Just wings? One, two. I really don't know, doctor. . . . I don't remember."
Psychologist's Interpretation of Patient's Response	Absence of usual ("popular") response suggests lack of adequate conventionality of thinking. Interpretation illustrates assumption that spatial relationship implies an actual one (dog-pig "eating" the carcass). Response is illogical, idiosyncratic, personalized and morbid. Primary process thinking in evidence. Most consistent with schizophrenia.	Reaction time is unusually long; patient appears unable to integrate whole blot into usual perception. Expresses dissatisfaction with his performance but is unable to improve it, while showing maximal effort. Raises question of possible organic brain syndrome.

(Modified from Dr. Arthur C. Carr, Professor of Medical Psychology, Columbia University College of Physicians and Surgeons, New York.)

Thematic Apperception Test (TAT)

Another projective test is the Murray Thematic Apperception Test, which was devised by Professor Henry A. Murray of Harvard University on the theory that the need is father to the fantasy and on the well-recognized observation that pictures are significantly provocative in stimulating projective expression of the content aspects of the personality. An analysis of the content will reveal the areas around which the patient's major problems revolve. In this test, the patient is shown, one at a time, twenty pictures of persons in various rather ambiguous but dramatic situations (Fig. 8–2).

Psychologists now frequently select fewer than the entire 20 pictures, depending on the subject matters they wish to explore. Among the most commonly used are the following:

1) A young boy viewing a violin.

2) A young woman holding books, a man working in a field, and an older woman looking on.

3BM) Model form of a boy with his head bowed.

3GF) A young woman standing with downcast gaze, her face covered with her right hand.

4) A woman with her hands on the shoulders of a man who appears angry.

6BM) A perplexed-looking young man facing the back of an elderly woman.

6GF) A young woman seated on a sofa looking at an older man.

7BM) A gray-haired man looking at a younger man.

7GF) An older woman seated on a sofa near a girl with a doll on her lap.

12M) A young man seated on a couch with an elderly man leaning over him.

13MF) A young man with downcast gaze standing beside a seminude woman in a bed.

16) A blank card.

From his or her imagination, the patient makes up a story about each picture, telling how the depicted scene came about, the relation of the individuals in it, what has happened to them, how they feel about it, and what the outcome will be. The patient usually identifies himself with a character and projects an image of himself and of the significant people in his life. He imagines situations and motives that represent projections of his own predispositions, impulses, feelings, thoughts, frustrations, conflicts, and situations. The fantasies evoked reflect inner feelings and states, latent and repressed material, and covert layers of the personality. The test yields information about the patient's attitudes and opinions in respect to his parents, death, violence, sex, and the like. The stories he tells furnish clues as to his level of intelligence, the range and type of his interests, and his unconscious directional tensions. To some degree, at least, the patient's stories represent a projection and expression of his own present or past personality. Not all the elements and incidents are significant personal references, and so care must be exercised in selecting those that are relevant. The stories, like dreams, may be used as points of departure for free associations.

Bender-Gestalt Test

This is a drawing test consisting of nine geometric designs chosen by Lauretta Bender from patterns first devised by Wertheimer in his study on perception. The nine patterns are presented to the subject one at a time and he is asked to copy what he sees. A frequent modification in the administration of this test is to ask the subject, after a short interval, to recall as many patterns as he can. The organization of the drawings, the page placement, the distortions and elaborations in the form of the individual drawings, any relative differences in pattern size, and other miscellaneous factors are used by an experienced interpreter to make inferences about personality functioning.

Figure 8–2 Thematic Apperception Test card Number 12F. (Reproduced courtesy of Harvard University Press, Cambridge, Mass.)

Test figures adapted from Wertheimer.

A

Figure 8–3 Bender Visual Motor Gestalt Test. A, Test figures (adapted from Wertheimer). B, Summary of responses for each year of age in developing children. This chart may be used for evaluating maturational norms and levels of retardation and regression. (Reproduced courtesy of the American Orthopsychiatric Association and Lauretta Bender, M.D.)

Because of its dependence on visual-motor functions, the test is often helpful in detecting organic pathology of certain kinds. Although it was conceived of by Bender as a "maturational" test, many workers have in recent years found it more useful as a general pro-jective technique and assign certain symbolic meanings to individual patterns.

The capacity of children of different ages to reproduce these designs has been examined, as Figure 8–3B demonstrates. Usually children below the age

	Figure A	Figure 1	Figure 2	Figure 3	Figure 4	Figure 5	Figure 6	Figure 7	Figure 8
Adult.	100%	25%	100%	100%	100%	100%	100%	100%	100%
11 yrs.	95%	95%	65%	60%	95%	90%	70%	75%	90%
10 yrs	90%	90%	60%	60%	80%	80%	60%	60%	90%
9 yrs.	80%	75%	60%	70%	80%	70%	80%	65%	70%
8 yrs.	75%	75%	75%	60%	80%	65%	70%	65%	65%
7 yrs.	75%	75%	70%	60%	75%	65%	60%	65%	60%
6 yrs.	75%	75%	60%	80%	75%	60%	60%	60%	75%
5 yrs.	85%	85%	60%	80%	70%	60%	60%	60%	75%
4 yrs.	90%	85%	75%	80%	70%	60%	65%	60%	60%
3 yrs.	--------Scribbling-------------------------								

Summary of responses for each year of age in developing children. It may be used for evaluating maturational norms and levels of retardation and regression.

B

Figure 8–3 *Continued.*

of 3 are unable to produce any of the designs. By the age of 12, a child should show an accurate and well-organized copy.

Sentence Completion Test (SCT)

In this test, the psychologist requests the subject to complete sentences in which certain sections are deleted. The subject is requested to write down the first response that comes to mind. Between 75 and 100 sentence stems are provided, in forms such as "I like. . . ." "Sometimes I wish. . . ."

A variety of scoring methods are used in interpreting this test. Generally, however, psychologists simply inspect the responses to note those indicative of major affective tone, those given repetitively, or those that appear idiosyncratic. So, too, omissions, factual reports, or blandness are of interest as they suggest denial.

This test elicits more conscious data than other projective techniques. Often the psychologist will use direct quotations from SCT data to illustrate the subject's idiosyncratic responses, as well as his most pressing anxieties or drives for achievement. A variety of sentence completion tests have been designed, of which the FORER Structure Sentence Completion Test provides a method of scoring that is useful in terms of affect. Responses to this test relate more easily to those of the other projective techniques. They examine the individual's reactions to aggression, rejection, failure, responsibility, sexuality, and love.

Word Association Techniques

This technique, often associated with Jung, is now less used than in the past. A number of variances presently exist, including lists particularly suitable for individuals with psychiatric disabilities.

Affective response to the request that the subject immediately provide a word related to that given is indicated by long reaction time, blocking in providing responses, repetition of stimulus word, its apparent misunderstanding, and idiosyncratic responses. Note is usually made of unusual comments or behaviors that accompanied the responses to the various words. On occasion, the list is repeated, with the examinee requested to respond as on the previous occasion. The discrepancies between responses sometimes bring to light additional evidence of affective blocking and association.

Draw-a-Person Test

One of the more recent but now widely used projective techniques for personality analysis is the Draw-a-Person Test. The theory upon which this test rests is the assumption that the body or the self, because of its intimate relation to the individual, serves as a natural vehicle for the expression of his needs, interests, and conflicts when projected by him into his drawing of a "person." In the application of the test, the patient is first merely asked to "draw a person." The examiner may then ask certain questions about the drawing in order to secure associations

to the drawing. The patient's concept of body image with its peculiar significance to himself is therefore elicited. This self-projection, arising necessarily out of personal experience, manifests itself in the attention to and emphasis on certain parts of the body or in the difficulty in handling them in the drawing. Correlations of clinical observations with analyses of material secured by this technique appear to substantiate it as a legitimate testing device. It is now used to supplement other projective techniques.

Minnesota Multiphasic Personality Inventory (MMPI)

Unlike the projective techniques discussed above, this test is a questionnaire of 550 items designed to provide scores on all the more important phases of personality and personality adaptation. As such, it ranges across the areas of investigation explored in the psychiatric interview. Both individual and group forms of the test are available, as well as a shortened research version. The questions are distributed into some 26 different categories. From this usage, nine clinical scales have been developed. These are hypochondriasis, depression, hysteria, psychopathic deviation, masculinity-femininity, paranoia, psychasthenia, schizophrenia, and hypomania. This questionnaire has the special features of additional validating scales which identify the test-taking attitude and provide an index of the degree to which the subject has been guarded and evasive, or overly frank and self-critical; a "lie scale"; and finally, a set of items indicative of gross eccentricity, carelessness in responding, or deliberate simulation.

Other studies, empirical in nature, have provided additional scales for social introversion, academic achievement, social satisfaction, and social tolerance. When used, a careful study of the item analysis in conjunction with the patterning scales may yield many unexpected insights concerning the individual. Computer scoring and interpretation now are available through various commercial services.

Examination of the Inaccessible Patient

The student often feels at a loss about how to secure significant clinical data when confronted with a patient who is unable or unwilling to speak or otherwise cooperate in the mental examination. The beginner may not realize that the various stuporous states are characterized by more or less well-defined features possessing much differential value clinically, or that the patient who fails to utter any word, as well as the one who declines to discuss certain subjects, unwittingly reveals much of psychological significance. The inaccessible states existing when the patient is first seen by the psychiatrist are usually rather acute manifestations and yield data of great value both in themselves and when considered in connection with subsequent symptoms observed at a later stage in the evolution of the mental disorder.

Since the clinical reactions of the inaccessible patient are in certain respects less well defined than in the cooperative patient, their detection and interpretation require a systematic method of study. The following plan of examination may serve as a guide to a study of personality expressions in the inaccessible patient.

GENERAL REACTION, MOVEMENT, AND POSTURE. After having described the patient's reactions in accordance with the plan noted in the paragraph entitled General Appearance, Manner, and Attitude, the following may be noted: Nature and degree of response to greeting: Will the patient shake hands with examiner? Is there any spontaneous speech? Are questions at times followed by replies? Is there apparent effort to reply by vocalization or by whispers, lip movements, or movements of the head? Are replies confined to impersonal questions? Are there special topics that the patient refuses to discuss? If he or she will not speak, will the patient write when offered pencil and paper?

Does the patient appear suspicious, on his guard, preoccupied, inattentive, evasive? Is the patient ever observed talking to himself? If so, what is the accompanying emotional state?

Are bodily positions assumed voluntarily or passively? Are they natural, affected, comfortable, or constrained? Describe any sustained, unnatural postures. Does the patient resist change of posture? Are muscles found to be relaxed or tense as extremities are passively moved? Are responses to suggested or passively attempted movements characterized by negativistic resistance or by movements in the opposite direction? What does the patient do when placed in an uncomfortable position? Any spontaneous activity and its amount and rate should be noted.

Does the patient obey commands? Are reactions influenced by distraction or command? Are movements of defense evoked by painful stimuli?

What are the patient's habits as to eating and dressing? If food has been refused, is it subsequently eaten if left near the patient? Is attention given to excretory needs?

Are the various characteristics of attitude, speech, and behavior constant, or do they vary from time to time? If variable, by what do they seem to be influenced?

FACIAL EXPRESSION AND EMOTIONAL RESPONSIVENESS. Should the patient's facial expression be described as alert, apathetic, vacant, placid, stolid, scowling, sullen, surly, morose, discontented, angry, or apprehensive? Does his face express aversion, hatred, bewilderment, perplexity, or distress? Is there any play of facial expressions? Are there tears, smiles, or other signs of emotion? On what occasions do they appear? Does the patient appear worried, anxious, fearful? Is grimacing noted? Describe any mannerisms observed.

Is the gaze fixed? Are furtive glances observed?

Is feeling manifested when the patient's family is mentioned? Is it shown when certain topics or certain experiences are mentioned? If so, what are they?

What reaction is shown to visits of the family? Describe any striking reaction to visits from particular members of the family or to those from certain other individuals.

Examination Under Narcosis

If, because of mutism, amnesia, or difficulty in establishing rapport, one is not successful in securing significant mental material from the patient, accessibility can often be increased by narcosis technique. Various forms of barbiturates may be used for the induction of narcosis, but one of the slow-acting forms, such as sodium amytal, is most frequently employed in this type of uncovering technique. A freshly prepared 10 per cent solution of sodium amytal is injected intravenously at the rate of approximately 1 ml. per minute. The injection is continued until the patient becomes drowsy, but care must be exercised that he does not become stuporous. Usually after the patient has received 200 to 400 mg. he will begin to respond to questions. In this lowered state of consciousness, midway between being awake and being asleep, inhibitory processes are released, rapport is produced, and suppressed and conflictual material is brought into consciousness.

Drugs may also be used on the patient who is accessible in order to bring repressed material to consciousness and to find underlying conflicts. The occasion can also be used for psychotherapeutic purposes. Since overdoses of sodium amytal produce a fall of blood pressure and respiratory de-

pression, it is wise to have appropriate respiratory stimulants available.

While accessibility is not increased in patients with organic brain damage and toxic states, the narcosis technique, as shown by Weinstein and Malitz, may be utilized diagnostically if the patient's attitude toward and recognition of illness and hospitalization are examined. Patients with brain damage explicitly deny their illness, become disoriented for place, and misidentify the examiners. Those without brain damage do not respond in this manner.

Diagnostic Formulation

A comprehensive psychiatric diagnosis is analogous to the diagnosis the internist aims to construct in order that his treatment may be rationally directed. As a result of the various studies of the patient's organs and their functioning, the internist makes an etiological, anatomical, and physiological diagnosis. Through the techniques of his specialty, the psychiatrist makes a comprehensive study of his patient's personality and formulates a genetic, a dynamic, and a clinical diagnosis. In his efforts to reach a *genetic diagnosis,* he searches both for any constitutional factors which may well have precluded the construction of a functioning personality and for emotionally significant and anxiety-producing experiences which made successful personality functioning difficult or impossible without resorting either to reparative or psychopathological measures. These inherent limitations to personality development, its arrests in the maturational process, and the emotionally disturbing impulses and events experienced, particularly in early life, establish the primary source or determinant of the mental illness or, in other words, constitute a genetic diagnosis.

Through a study of the mechanisms and techniques the individual has unconsciously employed to manage anxiety and enhance self-esteem, it is discovered how psychological forces have operated to produce personality characteristics and how those pathological functionings of personality called symptoms have been formed; i.e., a *dynamic diagnosis* that traces the human transactions and resulting intrapsychic changes that laid down psychopathological processes and their effects is formulated.

Finally, the general pattern of reaction that has resulted from the operation of genetic and dynamic factors is noted and classified in accordance with accepted clinical nomenclature. The *clinical diagnosis* conveys to the psychiatrist useful connotations concerning the reaction syndrome, the probable course and prognosis of the disorder, and often the methods of treatment that will probably prove most beneficial.

The formulation of the case may be schematized in the following way:

1. Summary of patient's problems.
   a. Behavioral disturbances, including character traits and interpersonal attitudes.
   b. Psychological disturbances, including conceptual and perceptual activities, thought, awareness, attention, et cetera.
   c. Affective disturbances.
   d. Physiological (somatic) disturbances.
2. Salient features of genetic, constitutional, familial, and environmental influences as revealed by the history and the various medical, neurological, and psychological examinations.
3. Psychodynamic explanation. Here an attempt should be made to reconstruct the origin of the various problems of the patient in terms of the interplay of the genetic and constitutional backgrounds and the impact upon the growing organism, and the influences of the family life and other environmental contacts upon his emotional and psychological development. It will not be possible to provide a complete explanation of the intricate processes of the individual's life. However, where gaps are noted or explanations may not be made, a statement to this effect should be included for further reference.
4. Diagnostic classification. The classification of psychiatric disorders as provided by the American Psychiatric Association should be utilized.
5. Treatment plan. A concise statement should be provided about the forms of treatment considered most effective, their availability and source, the needs for indicated adjuncts such as vocational, occupational, or recreational therapies, and the role to be played by the social worker in treatment. The desirability of inpatient or outpatient treatment, the need for certification, and the need for a guardian if the individual is considered incompetent to manage his personal or financial affairs should be stated.
6. Transference relationship. The expected repetitive attitudes of the patient toward the physician should be indicated if this can be ascertained from the developmental history. If psychotherapy is recommended, an additional statement should be provided in regard to the expected countertransference responses of the treating psychiatrist toward the patient.
7. Prognostic statement. A statement should be made concerning the expected modification of the patient's problems as a result of the therapy suggested above.

NOMENCLATURE AND CLASSIFICATION OF MENTAL DISORDERS

Following the practice of other branches of medicine in which pathological entities are ordinarily demonstrable, psychiatry, usually basing its attempt either on similarity of descriptive facts or on prognosis, formerly endeavored to classify personality disturbances as if these, too, were distinct entities. Unfortunately, in such an attempt one may easily err in mistaking reaction-sets for disease entities.

From a descriptive standpoint, the problem is simplified if mental disorders are divided into groups based on clinical and behavioral differences. Although classifications are necessary for statistical and other purposes, there has perhaps at times been too great a disposition in psychiatry to consider that its objective was attained when a classificatory diagnosis had been made. The principal value of classification is not in the categorizing of a disease entity but in the quick elimination of those considerations that will be least useful in understanding the patient and in directing attention to those likely to be relevant.

Except in organic disorders, a classificatory diagnosis is less important than a psychodynamic study of the personality. *The psychiatrist should be interested in process, not in labels,* and should remember that a particular pattern of behavior may stem from widely varying psychobiological causes. A diagnosis on a purely descriptive level without regard to the patient's affective states, thought content, and inner life will fail to provide the management outline necessary to relieve the patient of distress.

Since a medical nomenclature has the function of providing a list of generally approved terms for recording clinical and pathological observations, it must be extensive so that opportunity is afforded to record any pathological condition. With increase of knowledge, the nomenclature, too, must expand to include new terms that both allow recording and improve accuracy. Thus any morbid condition that is specifically described will need a specific designation in a suitable nomenclature.

Owing to their effort at completeness, nomenclatures do not serve well for statistical classifications. Statistical compilation of data is made to furnish quantitative data useful in providing answers about groups of cases; the interest is not in individual occurrences. The statistical classification then is more likely to be limited to a number of categories encompassing the entire range of conditions and chosen to assist the statistical study of disease. Titles of specific disease entities are warranted in such a classification when they occur frequently or when importance as a morbid condition justifies isolation as a separate category. The construction of a statistical classification, then, particularly of international scope, involves numerous compromises between efforts at classification based on etiology, circumstances of onset, and pathology and the forms and quality of medical reporting. The classification must also be varied to suit the demands of differing vital statistics offices, governmental institutions involved in health practices, insurance agencies, and so on.

DSM-III

The Third Edition of the Diagnostic and Statistical Manual (DSM-III) of Mental Disorders has been developed by the Task Force on Nomenclature and Statistics of the American Psychiatric Association. DSM-III includes many new features, such as a multiaxial approach to evaluation and specific criteria necessary to make a diagnosis.

The multiaxial system for evaluation that is outlined in DSM-III allows the recording of clinical information on each of five separate axes. The first three of these axes constitute an official diagnostic evaluation. Axes I and II include all the mental disorders (see the Table on pages 220–223). Personality disorders and specific developmental disorders are assigned to Axis II. All the other mental disorders are assigned to Axis I. In some instances a patient will have a disorder recorded on both axes.

Axis III permits the clinician to list current physical disorders. These may or may not be relevant to the mental disorders listed under Axes I and II. Axis IV permits the clinician to code the overall severity of stress that is judged to have been a significant factor in the development of the patient's mental disorder on a scale ranging from one (no apparent psychosocial stress) to seven (catastrophic stress). Axis V permits the clinician to record the individual's highest level of adaptive functioning during the past year on a scale ranging from one (superior) to seven (grossly impaired). The clinician may record a zero, indicating that no information is available for Axes IV or V.

The diagnostic criteria specified to make an Axis I or II diagnosis in DSM-III are quite specific and account for the improved diagnostic reliability over DSM-II in field trials.

Diagnostic Agreement and Quantification

Studies of agreement between psychiatrists in the detection and assessment of symptoms and signs of psychopathology and of diagnosis have revealed high reliability for the former and complexity in diagnoses. The problem of reliability of psychiatric diagnosis, reported in earlier studies, rests largely upon the failure to apply uniform methods for collecting data in the interview process, as well as a similar deficiency for quantification of the principal signs and symptoms recorded by different interviewers.

Spitzer has reported high diagnostic reliability among psychiatrists for categories of mental deficiency, organic brain syndrome, and alcoholism. For psychosis and schizophrenia, the level of reliability was low using DSM-II. Reliability has improved with DSM-III, as demonstrated in recent field trials.

For other categories (neuroses and personality disorders), diagnostic variability among psychiatrists derives from great variability in training across the world. The increasing realization of the limitations of diagnostic reliability has led to the development of specific inclusion and exclusion criteria of psychopathological symptoms to establish diagnoses, as developed in DSM-III.

In Chapter 7, criticisms of the use of a classification scheme by sociologists interested in labeling theory were mentioned. As reported there, transcultural studies have shown that behavioral abnormalities generally defined in Western societies as psychotic are recognized across all cultures and denoted linguistically. On the other hand, those abnormalities associated with the conditions termed neurotic or personality disorders, while recognized, are less clearly defined in nontechnological societies—the situation that existed in Western cultures less than 100 years ago.

In recent years numerous rating scales, inventories, and forms have been extrapolated from study of the process of the psychiatric interview. From such forms, which enforce on their users standardization of the interview procedure, there have been developed quantitative assessments of bits of psychopathology as well as aspects of personality. A number of them now are so constructed that their analysis on a large scale may be conducted using computer technology. The latest revisions of instruments such as the Psychiatric Status Schedule developed by Spitzer and his associates allow, in addition to the detecting and recording of psychopathological signs and symptoms, subsections designed to "evaluate (1) impairment in role function; (2) impairment in efficiency and conduct of leisure time activity and daily routine (e.g., handling of money, traveling, personal hygiene); (3) impairment in interpersonal relationships (e.g., friendship patterns, visiting); (4) the

Text continued on page 224

DSM-III CLASSIFICATION: Axes I and II Categories and Codes

All official DSM-III codes and terms are included in ICD-9-CM. However, in order to differentiate those DSM-III categories that use the same ICD-9-CM codes, unofficial non-ICD-9-CM codes are provided in parentheses for use when greater specificity is necessary.

DISORDERS USUALLY FIRST EVIDENT IN INFANCY, CHILDHOOD OR ADOLESCENCE

Mental retardation

Code in fifth digit: 1 = with other behavioral symptoms (requiring attention or treatment and that are not part of another disorder), 0 = without other behavioral symptoms.

317.0x	Mild mental retardation, _____
318.0x	Moderate mental retardation, _____
318.1x	Severe mental retardation, _____
318.2x	Profound mental retardation, _____
319.0x	Unspecified mental retardation, _____

Attention deficit disorder

314.01	with hyperactivity
314.00	without hyperactivity
314.80	residual type

Conduct disorder

312.00	undersocialized, aggressive
312.10	undersocialized, nonaggressive
312.23	socialized, aggressive
312.21	socialized, nonaggressive
312.90	atypical

Anxiety disorders of childhood or adolescence

309.21	Separation anxiety disorder
313.21	Avoidant disorder of childhood or adolescence
313.00	Overanxious disorder

Other disorders of infancy, childhood or adolescence

313.89	Reactive attachment disorder of infancy
313.22	Schizoid disorder of childhood or adolescence
313.23	Elective mutism
313.81	Oppositional disorder
313.82	Identity disorder

Eating disorders

307.10	Anorexia nervosa
307.51	Bulimia
307.52	Pica
307.53	Rumination disorder of infancy
307.50	Atypical eating disorder

Stereotyped movement disorders

307.21	Transient tic disorder
307.22	Chronic motor tic disorder
307.23	Tourette's disorder
307.20	Atypical tic disorder
307.30	Atypical stereotyped movement disorder

Other disorders with physical manifestations

307.00	Stuttering
307.60	Functional enuresis
307.70	Functional encopresis
307.46	Sleepwalking disorder
307.46	Sleep terror disorder (307.49)

Pervasive developmental disorders

Code in fifth digit: 0 = full syndrome present, 1 = residual state

299.0x	Infantile autism, _____
299.9x	Childhood onset pervasive developmental disorder, _____
299.8x	Atypical, _____

Specific developmental disorders
Note: These are coded on Axis II.

315.00	Developmental reading disorder
315.10	Developmental arithmetic disorder
315.31	Developmental language disorder
315.39	Developmental articulation disorder
315.50	Mixed specific developmental disorder
315.90	Atypical specific developmental disorder

ORGANIC MENTAL DISORDERS

Section 1. Organic mental disorders whose etiology or pathogenesis is listed below (taken from the mental disorders section of ICD-9-CM).

Senile and presenile dementias arising in the senium and presenium.

Primary degenerative dementia, senile onset,

290.30	with delirium
290.20	with delusions
290.21	with depression
290.00	uncomplicated

DSM-III CLASSIFICATION: Axes I and II Categories and Codes (*Continued*)

Code in fifth digit: 0 = uncomplicated, 1 = with delirium, 2 = with delusions, 3 = with depression.

290.1x Primary degenerative dementia, presenile onset, _____

290.4x Multi-infarct dementia, _____

Substance-induced

Alcohol

303.00 intoxication

291.40 idiosyncratic intoxication

291.80 withdrawal

291.00 withdrawal delirium

291.30 hallucinosis

291.10 amnestic disorder

Code severity of dementia in fifth digit: 1 = mild, 2 = moderate, 3 = severe, 0 = unspecified.

291.2x Dementia associated with alcoholism, _____

Barbiturate or similarly acting sedative or hypnotic

305.40 intoxication (327.00)

292.00 withdrawal (327.01)

292.00 withdrawal delirium (327.02)

292.83 amnestic disorder (327.04)

Opioid

305.50 intoxication (327.10)

292.00 withdrawal (327.11)

Cocaine

305.60 intoxication (327.20)

Amphetamine or similarly acting sympathomimetic

305.70 intoxication (327.30)

292.81 delirium (327.32)

292.11 delusional disorder (327.35)

292.00 withdrawal (327.31)

Phencyclidine (PCP) or similarly acting arylcyclohexylamine

305.90 intoxication (327.40)

292.81 delirium (327.42)

292.90 mixed organic mental disorder (327.49)

Hallucinogen

305.30 hallucinosis (327.56)

292.11 delusional disorder (327.55)

292.84 affective disorder (327.57)

Cannabis

305.20 intoxication (327.60)

292.11 delusional disorder (327.65)

Tobacco

292.00 withdrawal (327.71)

Caffeine

305.90 intoxication (327.80)

Other or unspecified substance

305.90 intoxication (327.90)

292.00 withdrawal (327.91)

292.81 delirium (327.92)

292.82 dementia (327.93)

292.83 amnestic disorder (327.94)

292.11 delusional disorder (327.95)

292.12 hallucinosis (327.96)

292.84 affective disorder (327.97)

292.89 personality disorder (327.98)

292.90 atypical or mixed organic mental disorder (327.99)

Section 2. Organic brain syndromes whose etiology or pathogenesis is either noted as an additional diagnosis from outside the mental disorders section of ICD-9-CM or is unknown.

293.00 Delirium

294.10 Dementia

294.00 Amnestic syndrome

293.81 Organic delusional syndrome

293.82 Organic hallucinosis

293.83 Organic affective syndrome

310.10 Organic personality syndrome

294.80 Atypical or mixed organic brain syndrome

SUBSTANCE USE DISORDERS

Code in fifth digit: 1 = continuous, 2 = episodic, 3 = in remission, 0 = unspecified.

305.0x Alcohol abuse, _____

303.9x Alcohol dependence (Alcoholism), _____

305.4x Barbiturate or similarly acting sedative or hypnotic abuse, _____

304.1x Barbiturate or similarly acting sedative or hypnotic dependence, _____

305.5x Opioid abuse, _____

304.0x Opioid dependence, _____

305.6x Cocaine abuse, _____

305.7x Amphetamine or similarly acting sympathomimetic abuse, _____

304.4x Amphetamine or similarly acting sympathomimetic dependence, _____

305.9x Phencyclidine (PCP) or similarly acting arylcyclohexylamine abuse, _____ (328.4x)

305.3x Hallucinogen abuse, _____

305.2x Cannabis abuse, _____

304.3x Cannabis dependence, _____

305.1x Tobacco dependence, _____

305.9x Other, mixed or unspecified substance abuse, _____

304.6x Other specified substance dependence, _____

DSM-III Classification Table continued on following page

DSM-III CLASSIFICATION: Axes I and II Categories and Codes (*Continued*)

304.9x Unspecified substance dependence, _____
304.7x Dependence on combination of opioid and other non-alcoholic substance, _____
304.8x Dependence on combination of substances, excluding opioids and alcohol, _____

SCHIZOPHRENIC DISORDERS
Code in fifth digit: 1 = subchronic, 2 = chronic, 3 = subchronic with acute exacerbation, 4 = chronic with acute exacerbation, 5 = in remission, 0 = unspecified.
    Schizophrenia,
295.1x disorganized type, _____
295.2x catatonic type, _____
295.3x paranoid type, _____
295.9x undifferentiated type, _____
295.6x residual type, _____

PARANOID DISORDERS
297.10 Paranoia
297.30 Shared paranoid disorder
298.30 Acute paranoid disorder
297.90 Atypical paranoid disorder

PSYCHOTIC DISORDERS NOT ELSEWHERE CLASSIFIED
295.40 Schizophreniform disorder
298.80 Brief reactive psychosis
295.70 Schizoaffective disorder
298.90 Atypical psychosis

NEUROTIC DISORDERS: These are included in Affective, Anxiety, Somatoform, Dissociative and Psychosexual Disorders. In order to facilitate the identification of the categories that in DSM-II were grouped together in the class of Neuroses, the DSM-II terms are included separately in parentheses after the corresponding categories. These terms are acceptable alternatives to the DSM-III terms that precede them.

AFFECTIVE DISORDERS
Major affective disorders
Code major depressive episode in fifth digit: 6 = in remission, 4 = with psychotic features (the unofficial non-ICD-9-CM fifth digit 7 may be used instead to indicate that the psychotic features are mood-incongruent), 3 = with melancholia, 2 = without melancholia, 0 = unspecified.

Code manic episode in fifth digit: 6 = in remission, 4 = with psychotic features (the unofficial non-ICD-9-CM fifth digit 7 may be used to indicate that the psychotic fea-

tures are mood-incongruent), 2 = without psychotic features, 0 = unspecified.

    Bipolar disorder,
296.6x mixed, _____
296.4x manic, _____
296.5x depressed, _____
    Major depression,
296.2x single episode, _____
296.3x recurrent, _____

Other specific affective disorders
301.13 Cyclothymic disorder
300.40 Dysthymic disorder (Depressive neurosis)

Atypical affective disorders
296.70 Atypical bipolar disorder
296.82 Atypical depression

ANXIETY DISORDERS
    Phobic disorders (Phobic neuroses)
300.21 Agoraphobia with panic attacks
300.22 Agoraphobia without panic attacks
300.23 Social phobia
300.29 Simple phobia
    Anxiety states (Anxiety neuroses)
300.01 Panic disorder
300.02 Generalized anxiety disorder
300.30 Obsessive compulsive disorder (Obsessive compulsive neurosis)
    Post-traumatic stress disorder
308.30 acute
309.81 chronic or delayed
300.00 Atypical anxiety disorder

SOMATOFORM DISORDERS
300.81 Somatization disorder
300.11 Conversion disorder (Hysterical neurosis, conversion type)
307.80 Psychogenic pain disorder
300.70 Hypochondriasis (Hypochondriacal neurosis)
300.71 Atypical somatoform disorder

DISSOCIATIVE DISORDERS (HYSTERICAL NEUROSES, DISSOCIATIVE TYPE)
300.12 Psychogenic amnesia
300.13 Psychogenic fugue
300.14 Multiple personality
300.60 Depersonalization disorder (Depersonalization neurosis)
300.15 Atypical dissociative disorder

PSYCHOSEXUAL DISORDERS
Gender identity disorders
Indicate sexual history in the fifth digit of

DSM-III CLASSIFICATION: Axes I and II Categories and Codes (*Continued*)

Transsexualism code: 1 = asexual, 2 = homosexual, 3 = heterosexual, 4 = mixed, 0 = unspecified.
302.5x Transsexualism, _____
302.60 Gender identity disorder of childhood
302.85 Atypical gender identity disorder

Paraphilias
302.81 Fetishism
302.30 Transvestism
302.10 Zoophilia
302.20 Pedophilia
302.40 Exhibitionism
302.82 Voyeurism
302.83 Sexual masochism
302.84 Sexual sadism
302.89 Atypical paraphilia

Psychosexual dysfunctions
302.71 Inhibited sexual desire
302.72 Inhibited sexual excitement
302.73 Inhibited female orgasm
302.74 Inhibited male orgasm
302.75 Premature ejaculation
302.76 Functional dyspareunia
306.51 Functional vaginismus
302.79 Atypical psychosexual dysfunction

Other psychosexual disorders
302.00 Ego-dystonic homosexuality
302.90 Psychosexual disorder not elsewhere classified

FACTITIOUS DISORDERS
300.16 Factitious disorder with psychological symptoms
301.51 Chronic factitious disorder with physical symptoms
300.19 Atypical factitious disorder with physical symptoms

DISORDERS OF IMPULSE CONTROL NOT ELSEWHERE CLASSIFIED
312.31 Pathological gambling
312.32 Kleptomania
312.33 Pyromania
312.34 Intermittent explosive disorder
312.35 Isolated explosive disorder
312.39 Atypical impulse control disorder

ADJUSTMENT DISORDER,
309.00 with depressed mood
309.24 with anxious mood
309.28 with mixed emotional features
309.30 with disturbance of conduct
309.40 with mixed disturbance of emotions and conduct
309.23 with work (or academic) inhibition

309.83 with withdrawal
309.90 with atypical features

PSYCHOLOGICAL FACTORS AFFECTING PHYSICAL CONDITION
Specify physical condition on Axis III.
316.00 Psychological factors affecting physical condition

PERSONALITY DISORDERS
Note: These are coded on Axis II.
301.00 Paranoid
301.20 Schizoid
301.22 Schizotypal
301.50 Histrionic
301.81 Narcissistic
301.70 Antisocial
301.83 Borderline
301.82 Avoidant
301.60 Dependent
301.40 Compulsive
301.84 Passive-Aggressive
301.89 Atypical, mixed or other personality disorder

V CODES FOR CONDITIONS NOT ATTRIBUTABLE TO A MENTAL DISORDER THAT ARE A FOCUS OF ATTENTION OR TREATMENT
V65.20 Malingering
V62.89 Borderline intellectual functioning (V62.88)
V71.01 Adult antisocial behavior
V71.02 Childhood or adolescent antisocial behavior
V62.30 Academic problem
V62.20 Occupational problem
V62.82 Uncomplicated bereavement
V15.81 Noncompliance with medical treatment
V62.89 Phase of life problem or other life circumstance problem
V61.10 Marital problem
V61.20 Parent-child problem
V61.80 Other specified family circumstances
V62.81 Other interpersonal problem

ADDITIONAL CODES
300.90 Unspecified mental disorder (non-psychotic)
V71.07 No diagnosis or condition on Axis I
799.91 Diagnosis or condition deferred on Axis I

V71.08 No diagnosis on Axis II
799.92 Diagnosis deferred on Axis II

use of drugs and alcohol, and illegal or other antisocial activity."

Another example is that developed by Gurland and his associates. The Structured and Scaled Interview to Assess Maladjustment (SSIAM) includes 45 items which assess deviant behavior, friction with others, and subjective distress in the five fields of work, social, family, marital, and sexual relations. An additional 15 items explore the degree of environmental stress, prognosis, and positive mental health. To administer this interview requires approximately 45 minutes.

In detection and quantification of severity of psychopathology the reliability between individual psychiatrists using such methods is high. Agreement as to diagnostic classifications is high as well when psychiatrists in the United Kingdom and the United States are exposed to televised psychiatric interviews with patients interviewed in either country, excepting certain subgroups. Thus, as Gurland and his colleagues observed, psychotic patient subgroups with marked mood disturbance and little disorganization tended to be diagnosed as schizophrenic in New York and affectively psychotic in London. Such differences in diagnostic tendency have been noted before—between psychiatrists resident in different states or attached to different institutions. Most likely the diagnostic variability represents the consequence of the differing educational exposure of psychiatrists, differences which are likely to recede as international communication and agreement increase between educational institutions.

Other Types of Records

The psychiatric interview—conducted in accordance with the advice and descriptions provided in this chapter, supplemented with the skilled observations of others involved with the patient and with appropriate diagnostic testing, and then subjected to a thoroughgoing diagnostic formulation as described—will provide a broad assessment of the social and adaptational problems facing the patient, his comprehension of the motivations, and the developmental processes with which to establish both pathology and social adaptation. From this, the psychiatrist is in a position to outline the appropriate therapeutic program.

It is unlikely that one may effectively apply the more recently devised short record keeping devices, such as the Problem Oriented Record (POR), unless he has first become thoroughly expert in the interviewing technique and developed the capacity for careful observation of both overt and covert behaviors, including the verbal and nonverbal aspects of the patient's transactions with him. The POR, devised first by Weed for medical record keeping, has developed as a result of the demand for accountability in both medicine and psychiatry. The intent of such a record is to explicitly expose the covert, branch-logic system of psychiatric decision-making.

The POR demands that each problem be explicitly stated initially, that the measures to be taken be recorded then, and that similar statements with comments on progress be made with each follow-up note. The attempt to involve the patient in problem identification is emphasized; this is thought to increase the potential for the patient's recognition of the issues to be addressed in treatment and to maximize the likelihood that the patient will be able to generalize therapeutic gains from treatment when in the home environment. It allows analysis of a patient's progress as subsequently monitored, in terms of change of problem status or approximation to correction of the identified treatment goals. Follow-up notes become more directed toward identifying that progress rather than interpretive in the sense of the changing psychodynamics, as is frequently the case. The POR has been developed for reporting the interview with both adults and children.

In their research, social psychiatrists have also been intent upon the development of skills that might allow a quantification of social stress as related to the evolution of psychiatric disability. Probably the best known of these scales is the Social Readjustment Rating Scale (SRRS) developed by Holmes and Rahe. Listing 43 life events apparently derived from clinical experiment, the questionnaire provides for a quantification of the exposure to stressful life events. The scale contains two categories of items: those descriptive of the life style of the interviewee and those indicative of events that have involved him. The events include those that have occurred in the family, marriage, occupation, economics, group and peer relations, education, recreation, and health. These events have been rated and given a quantified rank order. The SRRS has been used to study the similarities and differences among cultures, the recall of life events, and the relationship of life changes to the occurrence of disease. This approach and the critiques of its use are found in the various reports in *Stressful Life Events*, edited by Dohrenwend and Dohrenwend. Axis IV of DSM-III allows the clinician to score the overall severity of stress related to the development of the patient's mental disorder. The development of this axis was related to the excellent reference data derived by Holmes and Rahe using the SRRS.

BIBLIOGRAPHY

Bayley, N.: Development of mental abilities. *In* Massen, P.H. (ed.): Carmichael's Manual of Child Psychology. 3rd ed. New York, John Wiley & Sons, 1970.

Buschke, H., and Fuld, P. A.: Evaluating storage, retention, and retrieval in disordered memory and learning. Neurology, *24*:1019–1025, 1974.

Carr, A. C.: Psychological testing of personality. *In* Kaplan, H. I., Freedman, A. M., and Sadock, B. J. (eds.): Comprehensive Textbook of Psychiatry. III. Baltimore, Williams & Wilkins Company, 1980.

Conference on Normal Behavior. Arch. Gen. Psychiatry, *17*:257–325, 1967.

Diagnostic and Statistical Manual of Mental Disorders, Ed. 3 (DSM-III). Washington, D.C., American Psychiatric Association, 1980.

Dohrenwend, B. S., and Dohrenwend, B. P. (eds.): Stressful Life Events: Their Nature and Effects. New York, John Wiley & Sons, 1974.

Gurland, B. J., Fleiss, J. L., Cooper, J. F., Kendell, R. E., and Simon, R.: Cross national study of diagnosis of the mental disorders. Am. J. Psychiatry, *125*:30–38, 1969.

Gurland, B. J., Yorkston, N. J., Stone, A. R., Frank, J. D., and Fleiss, J. L.: The structured and scaled interview to assess maladjustment (SSIAM). Arch. Gen. Psychiatry, *27*:259–267, 1972.

Hilf, F. D.: Non-nonverbal communication and psychiatric research. Arch. Gen. Psychiatry, *27*:631–635, 1972.

Holmes, T. H., and Masuda, M.: Life change and illness susceptibility. p. 45–72. *In* Dohrenwend, B. S., and Dohrenwend, B. P., (eds.): Stressful Life Events: Their Nature and Effects. New York, John Wiley & Sons, 1974.

Holmes, T. H., and Rahe, R. H.: The social readjustment rating scale. J. Psychosom. Res., *11*:213–218, 1967.

MacKinnon, R. A., and Michels, R.: The Psychiatric Interview in Clinical Practice. Philadelphia, W. B. Saunders Company, 1971.

McLean, P. D., and Miles, J. D.: Evaluation and the problem-oriented record in psychiatry. Arch. Gen. Psychiatry, *31*:622–625, 1974.

Milstein, V., Small, J. G., and Small, I. F.: The subtraction of serial sevens test in psychiatric patients. Arch. Gen. Psychiatry, *26*:439–441, 1972.

Murray, H. A.: Uses of the thematic apperception test. Am. J. Psychiatry, *107*:577–581, 1951.

O'Connor, N.: The psychopathology of cognitive defects. Br. J. Psychiatry, *128*:36–43, 1976.

Spitzer, R. L.: More on pseudoscience and science and the case for psychiatric diagnosis. Arch. Gen. Psychiatry, *33*:459–470, 1976.

Spitzer, R. L., and Wilson, P. T.: Nosology and official psychiatric nomenclature. *In* Freedman, A. M., Kaplan, H., and Sadock, B. (eds.): Comprehensive Textbook of Psychiatry. Vol. 1. Baltimore, Williams & Wilkins Company, 1975.

Spitzer, R. L., Williams, J. B. W., and Skodol, A. E.: DSM-III: The major achievements and an overview. Am. J. Psychiatry, *137*:151–164, 1980.

Weed, L. L.: Medical Records, Medical Education and Patient Care. Cleveland, Press of Case Western Reserve University, 1969.

Weinstein, F. A., and Malitz, S.: Changes in symbolic expression with amytal sodium. Am. J. Psychiatry, *111*:198–206, 1954.

Whitehorn, J. C.: A working concept of maturity of personality. Am. J. Psychiatry, *119*:197–202, 1962.

Zubin, J., Eron, L. D., and Schomer, F.: An Experimental Approach to Projective Techniques. New York, John Wiley & Sons, 1965.

9

DISORDERS CAUSED BY OR ASSOCIATED WITH IMPAIRMENT OF BRAIN TISSUE FUNCTION

"The diseases of the mind are more and more destructive than those of the body."

Cicero

HIDEYO NOGUCHI
His research confirmed the existence of *Treponema pallidum* in paresis.
(From Scientific Monthly, *26*:90, 1928.)

This chapter will focus on the symptom complexes now designated as brain syndromes but formerly known as toxic-delirious reactions or dementias. In succeeding chapters of this section on brain syndromes, these are referred to in relation to their induction by specific etiologic agents. These symptom complexes are induced by a general derangement of cerebral metabolism, which produces a diffuse dysfunction of brain tissue and thereby impairs those functions most expressive in human beings of brain action—the positive functions of awareness, retention, memory, and comprehension.

Particularly for the psychiatrist practicing in general hospitals, the disorders designated as brain syndromes are among those for which consultation is most frequently requested. The diagnosis of the psychotic brain syndrome approximates 5 to 10 per cent in the medical departments of general hospitals; some report the evidence of delirium on admission to hospitals at 40 to 50 per cent among people over age 60.

Although they are critical conditions, indicating serious impairment of cerebral functioning, the acute brain syndromes (deliria) often go unrecognized by physicians, particularly in their earliest stages. Nursing staffs are usually much more sensitive to the presenting symptoms of the condition, and in most well-organized hospitals the behavioral evidence is well recorded in their notes. The consulting psychiatrists will frequently obtain many more data from this source than elsewhere about the existence of the behavioral indices of the brain syndromes, both acute and chronic.

DEFINITIONS

The term *general cerebral insufficiency*, discussed as an etiologic factor in Chapter 7, probably best designates these brain syndromes since this term draws attention to the basic etiology of all such states and relates them to the more familiar concepts of medicine, such as renal insufficiency, hepatic insufficiency, and cardiac insufficiency. Thus, with failure of the metabolic processes, there occurs a general lowering of the function of the organ or loss through death of the cellular units, or both, so that the activity of that organ is impaired. It may be recognized, then, that dysfunction of the brain caused by disturbance of the metabolic processes may evolve into permanent impairment of function if the cerebral metabolism is disrupted to such an extent as to kill a sufficient number of cells. In other circumstances, the condition may be reversible when the metabolic defect is insufficient to lead to cellular necrosis, or it may become permanent if the metabolic defect is sufficiently severe or prolonged.

The designations of *acute brain syndrome* or *delirium* are associated customarily with the reversible picture of cerebral insufficiency, while the designations of *chronic brain syndrome* or *dementia* are associated with persisting damage to brain tissue. As one may surmise, it is possible to have symptomatic expressions of both states simultaneously. When symptoms occur which are consequent to both ongoing metabolic disturbance and the effects of permanent damage to brain cells, it is customary to speak of the *organic syndrome*.

The terms *acute* and *chronic* are hardly useful, since it is possible to produce a widespread irreversible necrosis of cerebral cells—e.g., after a blow on the head—which will give the picture of delirium but end with a persistent defect later to be termed dementia. On the other hand, some types of cerebral insufficiency, such as those associated with prolonged illnesses, e.g., pernicious anemia, may develop slowly and last for weeks or months and yet be largely reversible when the proper treatment is provided.

Lipowski has suggested that a more useful classification of the psychopathological effects of cerebral disorders is one which recognizes both global and selective cognitive impairment and the behavioral and personality disturbances that present the features of the now-defined nonorganic psychiatric disorders. This general classification is shown in Table 9–1. In Lipowski's scheme, there is an intermediate condition between delirium and dementia, called the subacute amnestic-confusional state. Disturbance of consciousness is less apparent but various degrees of perceptual, memory, or cognitive impairment are evident to the close observer.

In addition to the symptoms directly expressive of impairment of function-

TABLE 9–1 Psychopathological
Presentations Related to States of
Cerebral Insufficiency

ORGANIC BRAIN SYNDROMES
  With global *cognitive impairment*
    Delirium
    Subacute amnestic-confusional state
    Dementia
  With selective *psychological deficit or abnormality*
    Amnestic syndrome
    Hallucinosis
    Affect, motivation and behavior disorders
    Other circumscribed cognitive, psychomotor
      and perceptual disorders
  Symptomatic functional psychoses
    Schizophreniform
    Paranoid
    Depressive
    Manic

PSYCHIATRIC DISORDERS REACTIVE TO ORGANIC
DISEASE AND/OR ITS TREATMENT
    Psychotic syndromes
    Neurotic syndromes
    Personality disorders

DEVIANT ILLNESS BEHAVIOR

(From Lipowski, Z. J.: Compr. Psychiatry, *16*:
105–124, 1975. By permission Grune & Stratton.)

ing of brain tissue and identifiable as the psychotic manifestations of this impairment, early loss of functioning induces various neurotic or other behavioral defenses in those so predisposed. We identify then the psychotic symptoms and nonpsychotic reactions to cerebral insufficiency. In the following chapters concerned with the brain syndromes, both psychotic and nonpsychotic expressions will be considered.

Pathophysiology

While it is probably correct to state that the brain derives most of its energy from those cerebral oxidative processes which require glucose as the major substrate, there is reason to believe that this statement is not completely accurate. There is evidence to suggest that some brain function can take place at times in spite of inadequate glucose supply. For this operation and maintenance of proper cerebral oxidative processes there must be available also ade-

quate quantities of oxygen and the necessary enzyme systems. Recent studies have demonstrated an active amino acid and protein metabolism in the brain, in which the glutamic acid cycle may act as a maintenance mechanism controlling carbohydrate metabolism. There is good evidence to show that ammonia, which is known now to be produced in the brain, may act toxically in excessive quantities to alter energy metabolism through depression of adenosine triphosphate (ATP) and creatine phosphate in the brain stem. Ammonia, apparently, is removable through the glutamic acid–glutamine system. Therefore, the syndrome of cerebral insufficiency may be expected to occur in circumstances wherein there is a lack of oxygen or glucose; an interruption of actions by toxic means; a deficiency in the enzyme systems related to carbohydrate metabolism and those of certain of the amino acids; or the presence of excessive amounts of ammonia owing either to excessive absorption or production, or to ineffective removal from the brain itself. Other processes also may be involved. (See Table 9–2). Invariably, lowered or impaired states of consciousness are associated with depression of the cerebral metabolic rate.

TABLE 9–2 Pathophysiological and
Biochemical Processes Inductive
of Cerebral Insufficiency

Deficiency in fuels for oxidative metabolism
Impairment in mechanisms of release, conservation, or utilization of chemical energy
Disruption of synaptic transmission or neurohumoral functions
Disturbance of ionic movement through excitable membranes
Major alterations in electrolytes, water content, osmolarity and pH
Impaired macromolecular synthesis necessary for renewal of cellular elements
Anatomical disruptions or disequilibriums in functional relations of neural subsystems involved in integrative actions

(Modified from Sokoloff, L.: Exp. Biol. Med. *4*:15–33, 1971.)

In association with the progressive impairment of cerebral functions, there occurs a slowing of the electroencephalographic brain waves. It appears that the degree of slowing is more significant in giving evidence of cerebral insufficiency than is the absolute frequency of the wave forms. Therefore, it is possible to have an electroencephalogram show a frequency generally considered to be within normal range in an individual whose premorbid frequency was 11 to 12 per second. A slowing to 8 to 9 per second will occur in such a person during a moderate delirium, yet both values would be considered within the accepted normal range for the adult population. As an aid in following the course of a case of cerebral insufficiency, the electroencephalogram may be most useful when successive recordings taken over time are examined. On the other hand, the single electroencephalogram has considerable limitations as a diagnostic method to establish the existence of cerebral insufficiency. Since the normal frequency count for the individual is seldom known beforehand, a slowing of frequency may not be surmised.

A much wider understanding is needed of the complex biochemical activities underlying the normal metabolic activity of the cerebral cortex, of the disruption of normal metabolism by toxic substances of chemical or microbial origin or by trauma, and of the various substrates and their related enzyme systems and interactions involved in carrying out the specific functions of particular components of cells. As we come to know more of the necessary substrates for the brain's metabolic activity and the associated enzyme systems and metabolites, it is possible that the effects of the various toxic substances upon the metabolic cycles and activities within different parts of the cortex will become understandable. This knowledge may lead to more rational therapy for the delirious reactions.

Symptomatology

Under the heading of Delirium and Dementia, the symptoms of cerebral insufficiency have been described in Chapter 6. The characteristic symptoms of the delirium usually associated with the acute brain syndromes are fearfulness, clouding of consciousness with bewilderment, restlessness, confusion, disorientation, and impairment in thinking, sometimes with delusions and hallucinations. Thus the acute brain syndrome differs from the so-called functional psychosis in the marked impairment of cognitive functions. It must be emphasized that the recognition of the cerebral insufficiency should not wait until the full appearance of the previously mentioned symptoms. Long before gross cognitive disorganization takes place, the acute observer will note failures in cognition. In the earliest stages, in which the condition might be likened to the mild intoxication experienced by many persons when drinking, there is a blurring or haziness of perception so that the sufferer notices a limitation in the accuracy of identification and apperception of sensations. He has difficulty in focusing attention on important percepts and in screening out interfering percepts. Again, one with incipient delirium will note a difficulty in thinking clearly and coherently; he may complain of inability to bring forward desired memories and associations. In the milder stages of the delirious process, such difficulties can sometimes be overcome by heightened attention and effort on the part of the affected person. Unless complained about, they may be quite inapparent to the clinical observer, who may note only some vagueness, uncertainty, and hesitancy on the part of the patient.

At a further level of impairment of consciousness, the affected person has difficulty performing correctly in spite of personal effort, and there now is evidence of confusion and bewilderment. In addition to hesitation in responses to questions, it is possible to expose defects in memory, retention, and recall. The heightened effort is sometimes revealed by the knitted brow and a tendency to glance up and around when asked simple questions. At this level of impairment, the patient usually has some difficulty in dealing with abstract concepts; the earliest expression may be in disturbance of time orientation, initially expressed for days of the week and later expanding to confusion concerning the month and the year. Furthermore, an examiner will note problems in retention of instructions, grasping their meaning, and carrying out directions. The patient may complain of inability to read as he cannot retain what has been put before him. At a still later stage of cerebral insufficiency, orientation as to place fails, and misidentification of perceptions with a development of illusions is noticeable. At this time, language difficulties appear, and there develops a defect in a coherent train of expression. Eventually, there takes place a deterioration in motor activity with problems in writing, eating, and grooming, and finally, incontinence of urine and feces may take place. In the later stage of delirium, complete disorientation exists, with delusory and hallucinatory experiences and severe impairment of motor control. Grasping and groping movements may occur. Delirium of this degree represents a *critical impairment* of cerebral function and should be recognized as diagnostically serious for life if it proceeds without arrest. The final stages of progressive cerebral insufficiency are stupor and coma.

It may be seen that impairment of cerebral functioning leads to progressive loss of the more differentiated and elaborated cognitive functions, and reappearance of more primitive activity. To put it in other terms, there exists a progressive impairment of ego functions of the individual, with interference in the ability to integrate new and current stimuli with the impressed patterns of older experience and bring them to proper thought and action.

The clinical expressions of cerebral insufficiency vary, depending on the nature of the past experience and the variety of ego defenses available to the ill individual, as well as the type of support received from the environment. Some delirious patients experience much anxiety because of their frightening thoughts and fantasies; these individuals will present, in addition to the evidences of ego disruption and cognitive impairment, the physiological expressions of anxiety. Others, due to their personality makeup, are able to minimize their concern over the progressive impairment of their faculties through such methods as withdrawal, denial, sleep, or a confiding relationship with their attendant. Some utilize the staff of the hospital for support and present denial with an unusual façade of cooperativeness, humor, and pleasantry, while those few individuals with limited ego development react to cerebral insufficiency with gross anxiety, panic, and periods of hallucinatory and delusional presentation. The individual prone to depressive responses to frustrations in the past may react to impairment of his mental faculties by an affective withdrawal of the same kind. Others respond with shame when they are unable to maintain their ordinary standards of performance. Yet others may act out aggressive and sexual impulses and respond to these with guilt. Such individuals may have suicidal drives.

One of the important characteristics of the delirious state is the variability in the symptoms over short periods of time. Even in one day the evidences of impaired cerebral functioning are often much greater at one time than another. Frequently, the most serious disturbances are seen at night, when the patient has available to him fewer sensory cues to aid his orientation in the absence of other persons and when there is lack of light. Thus his disability is aggravated by isolation and deprivation of sensory stimuli, as well as by the associated mounting anxiety.

Differential Diagnosis

It is most important to distinguish the acute organic brain syndromes with the delirious state from other psychiatric disturbances. In view of its threat to both life and future cerebral functioning, it is imperative to arrive at early recognition and immediate treatment. Schizophrenic reactions, although confused with them frequently, may usually be distinguished by the patient's clear orientation and ability to retain and recall past events, thus demonstrating an effective memory. In acute schizophrenic excitement, in which the patient has been heavily sedated, the diagnosis may be difficult. However, a brief period of observation usually leads to clarification. Table 9–3 lists some sensorial manifestations for each condition.

Depressive psychoses with retardation in thought do not lead to disturbances of orientation or mentation. In patients with hysterical amnesia, the memory defects are usually either too gross or spotty, with great clarity in certain areas. Amnesia for personal identity is not found in delirium. In all the functional psychoses and neuroses, the electroencephalogram will not show the slowing of frequency as in the acute brain syndromes.

TABLE 9–3   Differential Diagnosis in Brain Syndrome and Schizophrenia

Sensorium	ACUTE BRAIN SYNDROME	ACUTE SCHIZOPHRENIC REACTIONS
Fearfulness	+	0
Alterations of consciousness	++	0
Confusion	+	+†
Disorientation	+	0
Memory defects	+	0
Arithmetic ability	+	0
Illusions	++*	+†
Hallucinations	+*	+†
Delusions	+†	+
Judgment	Variable	+
Insight	Variable	+

*More often visual
†More often auditory

BIBLIOGRAPHY

Eichler, M.: Psychological changes associated with induced hyperammonemia. Science, *144*:886–889, 1964.

Lipowski, Z. J.: Psychiatry of somatic diseases: Epidemiology, pathogenesis, and classification. Compr. Psychiatry, *16*:105–124, 1975.

Posner, J. B.: Delirium and exogenous metabolic brain disease. *In* Beeson, P. B., McDermott, W., and Wyngaarden, J. B. (eds.): Cecil Textbook of Medicine. Philadelphia, W. B. Saunders, 1979, pp. 644–651.

Sokoloff, L.: Neurophysiology and neurochemistry of coma. Exp. Biol. Med., *4*:15–33, 1971.

Wohlrabe, J. C., and Pitts, F. N.: Delirium and complex electrolyte disturbances. Dis. Nerv. Syst., *26*:44–47, 1965.

10

PRIMARY DEGENERATIVE DEMENTIA

"He who is of a calm and happy nature will hardly feel the pressure of age."

Plato

SENILE BRAIN DISEASE
(Courtesy of the National Association for Mental Health, New York, N.Y.)

Through man's increasingly successful control of his environment, and particularly his progress against the inroads of infectious diseases and nutritional deficiencies, he has in this century vastly extended his longevity. Yet as a result many more people are exposed to the impairing processes of aging, of which progressive neuronal degeneration undoubtedly is the most distressing. Both cognitive deterio-

ration and the emotional reactions to this and to other losses contribute more heavily each year to the total of psychiatric disabilities.

In 1900, 1 in 25 living persons was over the age of 65; in 1978, this ratio had changed to 1 in 9. The total population of the United States more than doubled between those years, but the number of persons of 65 years or over almost quadrupled and is said to be increasing at the rate of 1000 per day. This has naturally been reflected in the number of aged people who develop mental disorders. Now, the total morbidity risk for the senile psychoses, referred to in DSM-III as Primary Degenerative Dementia, Senile Onset, is estimated to be approximately 0.6 per cent for men and 0.8 per cent for women (up to 80 years of age).

Aging

A gradual wearing down of energy, a decline in responsiveness, a waning of initiative and of creative imagination, a narrowing of interests, an increase in egocentricity, and a certain warping of personality must be looked upon as a normal involutional process operating with the passage of time. With advancing age, there is a progressive loss of physical and mental resources, a loss that tends to arouse feelings of helplessness. These feelings serve to create anxiety that the individual tries to overcome by mechanisms that he has long employed in making his adjustments. More specifically, with aging, the ability to respond to stimulation is retarded. Learning in unfamiliar contexts is more difficult than for younger persons and responses to tests of intelligence which involve time limits are poorer.

Beginning in the 40s, there takes place in healthy persons a decline in hearing and vision. Older persons have a particular deficit in their ability to adapt visually to darkness and to distinguish various intensities of light. Color vision is impaired in that the yellowing of the lenses filters out shorter wavelengths and thus retinal sensitivity to blue light is reduced. The loss of nerve cells in the inner ear causes a reduction in hearing, a loss which appears to affect background noises that are vital to understanding. Thus it has been suggested that the elderly do not need, as often has been thought, "peace and quiet" but, rather, more light and sound. At age 60, the majority of persons have suffered a 50 per cent loss of

their taste buds. Perception in the gustatory field is thus also reduced.

At least a third of those over 60 years of age also develop an abnormal electroencephalogram. The abnormality consists of focal slow waves, usually maximal over the anterior temporal area. While more often noted on the left side, it is unrelated to cerebral dominance as demonstrated by handedness. This abnormality starts in the middle years, when 20 per cent of the population show it.

The stress of increasing physical and mental limitations, loneliness resulting from the loss of friends and relatives, and perhaps rejection by children produce an anxiety that may evoke various protective mechanisms. Among the most frequently encountered responses are the depressive and hypochondriacal. Busse considers that the aging person tolerates more easily the loss of love relations and prestige than the onset of physical disabilities, particularly those disabilities that limit his mobility or disturb his communicative processes with others.

Depressive episodes increase in frequency and depth in the advanced years of life. In contrast with the psychodynamic constellations that induce depression in the young and middle-aged—that is, the guilty inward-turning of hostile impulses—the depression of the elderly is more frequently the consequence of loss of self-esteem through impairment of functioning, associated with feelings of personal derogation, shame, or helplessness.

Other personality reactions are a turning to and perhaps embellishment of the past, a paranoid projection, or a self-assertiveness to the point of being domineering. Other elderly persons, through feelings of insecurity or inadequacy, become ill-natured and contentious or regress to a dependent state. Both biological and sociopsychological factors contribute, therefore, to the personality changes of old age.

The more immature and maladjusted have been the adaptations of earlier life, the smaller is the stress required in old age to produce disorganized or disturbed behavior. That social activities and a wholesome variety of mental occupation may retard mental senility has long been recognized. In one of his dialogues, Cicero said, "Old men retain their intellects well enough if they keep their minds active and fully employed." It will therefore be seen that, although of great importance, organic disease of the brain is not the only factor in the development of primary degenerative dementias.

Pathology

It has been estimated that the brain of the healthy young adult contains over 12 million neurons and that in the latter half of life several thousand die daily. There is a progressive loss of brain size and weight; at age 75 the brain weight is approximately 55 per cent that of the healthy young adult.

The gross pathology of the brain in senile onset primary degenerative dementia is typically characterized by cerebral atrophy, but frequently this is not easily demonstrated. If atrophy is apparent, it will be greatest in the frontal lobes, where wide sulci and narrowed gyri may give the brain a wrinkled appearance (Fig. 10–1). In extreme cases, the ventricles are widened and the ependyma presents granular excrescences. On section, the gray matter may be less atrophied than the white.

One of the most significant histopathological changes, if demonstrable, is the reduction in the number of cells. The pathological process involving the nerve cells is usually one of shrinkage, but necrobiosis is seen as well. Other characteristic changes are the intraneuronal neurofibrillary condensation and distortions. But the most striking feature of senile onset primary degenerative dementia is the presence throughout of "senile plaques," small areas of tissue degeneration, roundish in shape and consisting of a granular or filamentous detritus. They are scattered throughout the cortex, but the frontal lobes and Ammon's horn are sites of predilection. Electron microscopy has shown such plaques to contain a core of extracellular amyloid fibers, large dendrites, and axons containing excesses of neurofibrils, dense and altered mitochondria, and lipofuscin bodies. Studies of the plaques have shown them to have a largely polyamide structure but with small amounts of carbohydrates. The amino acids in the structure are glutamic acid, glycine, leucine, and alanine. Sulfur and phosphorus are also found in the plaques, more so in those with cores.

Recent studies demonstrate lower concentrations of homovanillic acid in the brains (putamen and caudate nucleus) of those dying of senility, particularly dementia, than in the brains of others. Gottfries et al. argue from these findings that there must exist a diminution of release from dopaminergic nerve endings, and suggest that disturbance of this system is specific to senile dementia. They conclude that senile dementia is not a variant of aging but a specific disease.

Since these pathologic changes are not invariably related to the severity of the clinical expressions of senile dementia, pathologists have disagreed as to their pertinence to the disturbance. The interrelationship of the clinical and pathologic states has been more certainly established by recent studies; however, such a correlation is not crucial in view of the dynamic psychologic defensive and adaptative processes which, varying from individual to individual, are responsible for personality vagaries in the face of stress.

Mental Symptoms

The transition from usual old age to senile dementia is ordinarily gradual, and any decision as to when the imaginary line is passed must often be an ar-

Figure 10-1 Senile psychosis. *A,* Lateral view of the brain demonstrating pronounced atrophy: narrowing of the gyri, widening and deepening of the sulci. There was also reduction in size and weight. *B,* Three senile plaques in various stages of evolution. Braunmühl method. Magnification: 352×. *C,* Astrocytic reaction over a senile plaque. Cajal method. Magnification: 800×. *D-H,* Neurons from various regions of the cerebral cortex displaying different degrees of Alzheimer's type of neurofibrillary degeneration (tangles). Hortega method. Magnification: 920×. (Courtesy of Professor L. Roizin, M.D., Department of Neuropathology, New York State Psychiatric Institute, New York.)

235

bitrary one. A dislike of change, a reduction in ambition and activity, a tendency to become constricted and self-centered in interests, an increased difficulty in comprehension, an increase in time and effort necessary for the performance of familiar duties, an increasing difficulty in adapting to new circumstances, a lessened sympathy for new ideas and views, and a tendency to reminiscence and repetition are scarcely signs of senile dementia, yet they pass imperceptibly into mental destitution and personality regression. Many elderly people have little capacity to express warm and spontaneous feelings toward others.

As mentioned earlier, during relatively early stages and before mental impairment is advanced, periods of reactive depression following some specific event are common. Physical illness or severe emotional disturbance may quicken mental deterioration. Rarely are the symptoms of waning mental capacity sufficiently marked to warrant the diagnosis of senile dementia until after 60 years of age. The decreased impressionability, impaired registration, and declining interest in environment and in present affairs predispose to the loss of memory for recent events that often serves as the earliest clinical criterion for the diagnosis. Limitation of ideas and impairment of capacity for abstract thought usually appear early, as may also an indifference to the ceremonies and courtesies of social life. The patient resents what he considers interference by younger persons and may complain that he is neglected. Some show a hostile but anxious and fearful dependence. Natural affections become blunted and may turn to hatred.

A certain tendency to isolation occurs. This tendency to self-isolation and to hostility toward some living person is most frequent if some close member of the family has been lost. Altruistic sentiments are usually lost early, while egoistic, selfish ones are intensi-

fied and, like the instinctive ones, may be crudely manifested. Irritability, either as an expression of egocentric trends or a defensive reaction to the impairment of memory, is common. Exaggerated sexual activities or sexual indecencies may be exhibited, in which case they usually represent not merely a weakening of inhibitions but a defensive effort at psychological compensation for the waning of a fundamental function. Some senile dementia patients become careless in habits of toilet and dress; pride of appearance is forgotten. At times there is a tendency to be distrustful, prying, and suspicious. Hoarding and delusions of theft, of poisoning, of poverty, or of not being wanted are common.

Exaggerations and caricatures of the previous personality betray its earlier tendencies. Anxiety, irritability, timidity, and other personality changes frequently seen in senility are not attributable solely to changes in the brain. Many of them are caused by the fact that the individual has been shoved into a position that frustrates his wishes and deprives him of his usefulness and of his status as an autonomous person. A failure to find the satisfactions necessary to replace those the elderly person had when he felt needed, important, and productive tends to lead to regressive changes.

Psychodynamically the pathology of the patient with senile dementia may be understood as a series of ontogenetically related ego regressions. Thus, as the patient becomes aware of the gradual impairment of his capacities, there is at first an intensification of already existing character defenses—he "grows more like himself." As the character defenses fail to protect from anxiety, then depressive, persecutory, and hypochondriacal symptoms emerge as means by which the personality defends against fears of death and impending loss of functions and satisfactions. The senile patient undergoing a protracted course is much less likely to manifest depression; the anxiety over loss of functions or death is projected and demonstrated in his paranoid accusations. Later, with further progression of the illness, withdrawal occurs; the hypochondriacal preoccupation with his bowels and constipation or other organ discomfort demonstrates introjection of the fear. These symptomatic expressions of regression are not specific for senile dementia; they may be seen in other progressive brain syndromes as well as in deteriorating schizophrenia. These symptoms are brought into play with the continuing loss of gratification and represent, as well, the weakening functional capacity of the brain to deal with emotional arousal.

More constant and more characteristic are the evidences of progressive *impairment of cognitive functions* due to the ongoing cerebral degeneration. Accompanying, or even preceding, the amnesia is a tendency to reminiscence, the theme being characteristically personal. As memory for recent life sinks further away from recollection, the limits of recall are forced back further and further until the patient, with the loss of his ability to assimilate new ideas and experiences, comes to live in the distant past, often in the period of his childhood. The patient may speak of parents or grandparents as still living, and persons are often misidentified. Any recollection for the simplest events of recent life may be lost. This retention of memory for remote events and loss for recent ones seem reasonable in view of the theory that the hypothetical neuronal circuit patterns responsible for memories become more strongly established with time. The longer, then, the pattern has been established, the more strongly does memory resist degenerative states such as those of senility.

Orientation becomes defective, and in his confusion the patient may wander away and become lost. Judgment becomes impaired; the personal hazards of traffic or other situations are not recognized. Frequently, the patient forgets where he has placed articles and accuses other persons of having stolen them. He may leave the gas burner turned on and is careless with matches and fire. He may become the victim of unscrupulous persons, particularly if their technique involves an appeal to the patient's vanity, in matters of either competence or sex.

Many are restless at night and either wander about the house or engage in some aimless, perhaps destructive, activity in a confused manner. This nocturnal delirium is due apparently to the limitations of vision in darkness. Those with senile states become disoriented within an hour when placed in darkened rooms owing to failure to retain their spatial location; they then become anxious and more confused.

During the day, on the other hand, the patient may sleep much of the time. Hoarding articles of no value is common, quantities of worthless objects being carried in the patient's pockets or jealously guarded in some cherished hiding place. The *aged recluse,* living alone or with a close relative or associate, often may be recognized as one afflicted with senile dementia. The majority of those who have come to public notice seem to have been seclusive from early life, and perhaps of schizoid or compulsive personality. Often thought to be poverty stricken, living in a house of shambles and uninterested in ordinary pleasures, the recluse is discovered at death or following an accident to have hoarded and accumulated large sums of money. Many are victims of crimes of violence when their hoardings become known; others become a menace because of demented carelessness with fire and explosive hazards or because of an ill-kept collection of dogs, cats, and other animals.

Physical Symptoms

Physically, the patient usually exhibits conspicuous signs of senility. The skin is often thin, atrophic, and wrinkled. In advanced forms the special senses lose in acuity, weight is lost, and the muscles are wasted; the gait becomes unsteady and shuffling, the voice harsh, and the speech slow. The handwriting becomes tremulous, while tremors of head and hands are common. Coexisting sclerosis of the cerebral arteries frequently gives rise to headache, dizziness, and the episodic and focal disturbances incident to vascular accidents.

Clinical Types

Different clinical types, such as simple deterioration, delirious and confused, depressed and agitated, paranoid, and presenile are described, but there is frequently so much overlapping that assignment to any particular group is an arbitrary matter.

SIMPLE DETERIORATION. This is the most frequent form of primary degenerative dementia; it is characterized largely by progressive memory defect, at first for recent events but later for remote ones, a narrowing of interests, loss of initiative, sluggishness of thought, apathy, irritability, and nocturnal restlessness. Contact with the environment becomes less and less, and a vegetative, mildly stuporous state may finally develop.

A talented artist was referred by his wife; he had become anxious and mildly depressed when his first symptoms emerged. In many respects he was very fortunate. At the age of 65 he had achieved a national, even international, reputation as an illustrator. His talents were such that he had devised a special process used to produce color covers and prints. His illustrations were sought by many periodicals. He was employed for his talents as an artist to do some of the highest grade illustrations in the commercial art world. Recognition of his work gained him election to one of the distinguished clubs of artists in the city.

There had been some beginning failure in his memory. He complained of some difficulty in the use of his hands and arms, a clumsiness and lack of precision that did not exist before. When first seen, he advised that his father had become senile before his death and had had a slowly pro-

gressive course of increasing mental impairment, which the patient feared for himself, abhorring the thought. He was accompanied on his first visit by his wife, who had been his model. They had been married 30 years and had two daughters, both married.

She declared that at home he had become critical and querulous. He seemed to avoid going out to meet his artist friends. Furthermore, in contrast to his usual self-assurance at his work he seemed anxious and upset when requested to take on a new contract. His concern over his abilities, his doubts, and even refusal of work were reflected in his relations with his wife. Over the succeeding months it was learned that she had been nagging him. He complained that she had commenced to drink and did not seem as interested in the care of the house. Also, he said his daughters were hounding him. Although he was able to talk most interestingly of his past work and life, it was clear that he had difficulty in recalling his earlier visits with his physician, when they occurred, or what had been discussed. The course was slowly progressive. As time went on, the tension and near panic he felt over inability to perform, on the recognition of his slowly progressive impairment of perception and skill, accompanied by much anxiety in meeting his business and social acquaintances, continued to increase.

The therapeutic efforts were devoted to discussion of the events of the recent past, prescribing medication (Thorazine), which most effectively damped his mounting anxiety, explanation of the probable course of his illness to his wife, and the ways in which she could respond most helpfully. She had to know that he could not be held responsible, that the course would be progressive, that he would become increasingly unable to care for himself, even to the point of being unable to understand where he was, to dress, or to maintain his cleanliness. She was assured that her feelings of frustration and anger were justified, and that their control required that she be relieved at times and get away. Hospitalization was discussed. Contrary to the positions of many who have had intense attachments and perhaps live in less spacious rooms—theirs were by no means spacious—she wished to maintain the patient at home.

The failure in his mental functioning proceeded slowly. Periods of disorientation were first noticed at night when he arose to go to the bathroom. Some six years after onset he became seriously disturbed, had the delusion that men were attempting to kill him, and hallucinated voices. By increasing the dose of Thorazine and reducing other medication, this acute and overtly psychotic paranoid reaction subsided and hospitalization was avoided, but only through the warm and understanding attendance of his wife and his daughters in her relief.

The periods of anxiety and panic with breaks went on for another year or so, to be succeeded by increasing apathy and disinterest. He could no longer tell his wife of the difference between Picasso and Braque. He tried to draw, attempting to improve old sketches, but without creativity. He would talk to her of planning a Christmas card, but would forget that his daughters were married. His death, in a local general hospital, occurred quickly from cardiac arrest seven years after he was first seen.

DELIRIUM AND CONFUSION. The nature of the delirious and confused type is indicated by its name. The onset of this delirious and confused reaction is comparatively acute and may accompany a variety of physical illnesses. Among them are alkalosis, anoxia, hypoglycemia, and urinary infection. An incautious use of bromides, morphine, barbiturates, or other drugs may precipitate an attack. The reaction may be associated with dehydration occurring in fever or following a surgical operation (such as prostatectomy) requiring general anesthesia. Less frequently, it may be caused by vitamin deficiency. In milder cases the patient is perplexed, disoriented, and perhaps inaccessible. Insomnia is marked, and hallucinations are frequent. In more severe cases, the patient is restless, resistant, noisy, and may become exhausted. Strictly speaking, such a reversible process is not a part of primary degenerative dementia but represents a reaction to which the elderly person is particularly prone. Some senile subjects, however, present a chronic confusional state. Such a person may present a bewildered expression, move about in a vague and aimless fashion, and be only dimly aware of his whereabouts.

DELUSIONS. The paranoid type is distinguished by the conspicuousness of delusions, most frequently of a persecutory nature. Sometimes helplessness is used as an effective means of securing and wielding power. Many paranoid senile individuals are irritable, quarrelsome, hostile, and demanding. Complaints of bad treatment are nearly always expressed. This type of behavior usually occurs in persons whose life personality pattern has been characterized by dissatisfaction, projection, and

other defensive mechanisms. As its physical substratum suffers the degenerative changes of senility, the personality is no longer able to cope with its problems, its former defensive and compensatory mechanisms are exaggerated, and delusional beliefs falsify reality to protect the personality and maintain its self-esteem. Memory loss may be absent or comparatively insignificant for a long time. As memory defect appears, delusional extension and further defensive emotional reaction may take place in an attempt to repair the additional psychobiological defect. Similarly, as judgment fails, the delusions become more absurd, partly because beliefs are no longer subject to any critical scrutiny, and partly because the damaged personality requires more fantastic beliefs for its support.

Hallucinations and illusions occur more frequently than in any other type of primary degenerative dementia. Consciousness is not disturbed, and orientation usually remains unimpaired. Of the various types of primary degenerative dementias already mentioned, the form with delusion stands out most clearly as a special type. Transitions and admixtures of the various types described are common.

The following case history abstract illustrates primary degenerative dementia with delusions — a not uncommon association.

H. S. was admitted to a public hospital for mental disorders at 72 years of age. When 6 years old she sustained a fracture of the hip. Four years later an operation was performed in an effort to correct the deformity and disability. The functional results of this operation were disappointing, and the patient was always self-conscious concerning the considerable degree of disability that persisted. She always felt that people did not wish to mingle with her because of this infirmity, and she did not seem comfortable in the presence of others.

Five years before the patient's admission her adopted son, with whom she resided, noted that she was becoming forgetful, especially concerning her usual household duties and recent incidents. She hoarded articles and sometimes said that someone had stolen them. She remembered events of her childhood quite well and at times was somewhat boresome in her accounts of early experiences. Her adopted son noted that she became increasingly neglectful of her personal appearance. For many months prior to her admission she would not bathe unless reminded to do so. Recently she often went to bed without removing either clothing or shoes. At times she put on her clothing inside out. For four years prior to admission she seemed to find it difficult to prepare meals at accustomed times.

On many occasions she completed the preparation of the midday meal at 8 a.m. and insisted that the family should eat at that time. In preparing coffee she often put sugar instead of coffee in the coffee pot but failed to recognize her error. In a few instances she wished to pay bills that she had already paid. She was restless at night but often slept during the day. The patient became increasingly confused in surroundings with which she had formerly been quite familiar. Often, when crossing the street, she paid no attention to approaching automobiles. At times she wandered away from home.

There were periods during which she constantly packed and unpacked her clothing. She often failed to recognize friends, became increasingly suspicious, said that neighbors were talking about her, spoke of them in extremely derogatory terms, and maintained that her son lied to her and had tried to poison her, and that her neighbors had threatened to kill her. She claimed that her son and an elderly woman who had been employed to give her protective care had been secretly married. She complained that everyone was trying to control her activities and threatened to commit suicide if not permitted to do as she wished.

When the patient was brought to the mental hospital, she rose to meet the admitting physician, shook his hand, asked him where he was and if there was anything she could do for him. She knew her name but could not give her address or other identifying data. She claimed that her son, who had really been extremely devoted to her, had ejected her in order to secure possession of her house, which was located "down the hill." After her admission, affectless and placid, she sat in a rocking chair all day, paying little or no heed to her environment.

DEPRESSION AND AGITATION. The depressed and agitated type presents not merely the memory loss and intellectual impoverishment of primary degenerative dementia but also a marked egocentricity; persistent agitation; and melancholic, hypochondriacal, and nihilistic delusions.

Prognosis and Course

The prognosis of primary degenerative dementia of senile onset is for continued deterioration of all personality and cognitive functions. No well-defined remissions are to be expected, although in the depressed and excited types subsidence of symptoms may occur. The course is progressive; the patient gradually becomes more demented, although life may continue for 10 years or even longer before death supervenes.

Diagnosis

In well-developed primary degenerative dementia, the age of the patient, the progressive egocentricity, and the characteristic memory loss, particularly for recent events, make the diagnosis easy. In the form with delusion, the memory loss and evidences of dementia may be comparatively slight. Since these senile paranoid patients usually have had a life pattern of a defense, paranoid type, the matter of deciding when this exaggerated pattern crosses the psychotic line will be determined largely by social criteria and by the interpretation and values accorded to reality.

When arteriosclerotic changes in the brain, rather than the histological ones of senility, are the basis for such paranoid psychoses, the patient usually suffers from easy mental fatigability, dizziness, or slight confusion, suggestive of changes in the smaller vessels of the cerebrum. Some depressed and agitated types of symptoms suggest major depression, but it must be noted that depressive symptoms are more common in multi-infarct dementia. The differentiation must be based largely on the age of the patient and particularly on the presence or absence of deterioration.

A restricted diet in the aged may lead to avitaminosis suggestive of senile psychosis. Toxic psychoses are frequently mistaken for primary degenerative dementia. It should be remembered that, in the aged, mental disturbance may be caused by uremia, anemia, decompensated heart disease, or pulmonary disease rather than by senile dementia.

Treatment

The discussion in the early part of the chapter has already suggested the importance of prophylactic factors in the prevention of primary degenerative dementias. It is highly desirable that the aged person maintain a feeling of emotional security and a sense of dignity. One will accordingly attempt to see that the old person's needs for affection, for a feeling of belonging, for achievement, and for recognition and approval are met. Equally important are the maintenance of nutrition and careful management of health, with early treatment of any illness.

The milder forms of primary degenerative dementia should be cared for in the home. It is there that the patient's roots are deeply imbedded. Unless circumstances are such that either the safety of the patient or that of the family is endangered, it is well to attempt to care for him or her in the usual and familiar environment. The patient is ordinarily happier there than in the unaccustomed and rather rigid routine of an institution, where the habits of a life-time have to be reconstructed. It is true, however, that the patient's inability to recognize failing physical and mental vigor may present a serious problem to the family.

Hospital or nursing home care is necessary when there evolve excessive nocturnal restlessness, disturbing response to paranoid delusions, marked irritability, assaultiveness, sexual play with children, exhibitionism, or ill-considered plans for marriage. Impaired judgment in business affairs may make the appointment of a legal guardian necessary. Care must often be exercised to prevent the confused patient from setting fire to clothing or furniture, to prevent wandering from home or falling with resulting fracture of the neck of the femur. It is particularly important to maintain the visual orientation of the senile patient at night. This may be done by having adequate night lighting available if she or he awakens. During the day, the presence of familiar objects also supports the patient's orientation. Also, hearing impairment should be corrected, even if minor, by the appropriate audiophonic prostheses.

Psychotherapy wherein the physician or agent plays a supportive role is often useful in the earlier stages of the illness to sustain the patient's increased dependency needs. Advice to the family on the need to provide avenues of gratification is important, as well as advice on changing the home environment so as to ease the burden of the deficits of the elderly.

If appetite has been poor or diet restricted, it is advisable to prescribe ascorbic acid, thiamine chloride, niacin, and glutamic acid. Preparations are now available in which glutamic acid is supplied in its utilizable form, monosodium L-glutamate. Vitamins are frequently of value in confused and delirious senile states. In the depressive forms, electroshock therapy can often be used safely and with great success.

For insomnia, a mild hypnotic is advisable. Barbiturates often are tolerated poorly. A phenothiazine before bedtime may prove most effective.

For those with depression, trials should be made with the antidepressant agents. It should be kept in mind that the elderly are often unusually sensitive to these agents. Hypotension and urinary retention are common complications in their administration. When the antidepressants fail, electroshock is indicated. For restlessness, irritability, confusion, or delirium, chlorpromazine or another phenothiazine should be prescribed.

ALZHEIMER'S DISEASE

In 1906, Alois Alzheimer (1864–1915) described the case of a woman who had died at age 51 following a rather rapidly progressing dementia and whose brain tissue showed the development of tangled, threadlike structures occupying much or all of the body of many cortical ganglion cells. These agglomerated neurofibrils are stained black with silver stains. This degenerative change may involve even one fourth of the ganglion cells. It is now known that they are not limited to this disease but may be observed in senile dementia and even in the brain in normal senium. There are accompanying diffuse gliosis and an abnormal amount of fatty pigment in the nerve cells. Another histopathological change that practically always exists is the presence of senile plaques with their amorphous and homogeneous core. Plaques are most frequent in the frontal cortex and in the cornu Ammonis. In Alzheimer's disease the cortical degeneration is diffuse and involves the outer layers of the cortex, especially those of the frontal and temporal lobes.

Recent electron microscopic and histochemical studies have shown that the characteristic neurofibrillary tangles are composed of large numbers of closely packed hollow neurofilaments which have displaced cytoplasmic organelles. Within the senile plaques are cores of amyloid fibrils in extracellular positions. Neighboring enlarged dendrites and axons contain excesses of neurofibrils and electron-dense altered mitochondria. Lipofuscin bodies and astrocytic processes make up the other constituents of the plaque (Fig. 10–2). The brain in Alzheimer's disease contains increased amounts of acid polysaccharide and reduced amounts of an unknown neutral polysaccharide, perhaps glycogen. Conflicting accounts are now given regarding lessened amounts of brain lipid and cerebroside.

Recently, Crapper and his colleagues reported high brain tissue concentrations of aluminum (9 to 11 μg. per gm.) in Alzheimer's disease and suggested that this substance may play a role as an etiologic factor. So, too, they have induced neurofibrillary changes experimentally in cats by injection of aluminum chloride.

Symptoms

The onset of Alzheimer's disease is usually between 50 and 60 years of age, although earlier appearances have been reported. The disease begins insidiously, with a reduction of spontaneity, progressive intellectual deterioration, and alterations in behavior. There is no characteristic pattern in either the intellectual impairment or the behavioral disturbances. Disorientation, memory impairment, defects in calculation and general information, emotional lability, and decrease in concreteness in thinking are present in varying degrees and combinations. Pronunciation is difficult, spoken language is comprehended poorly, and errors are made in reading and writing. The patient makes mistakes in the routine details of his everyday life, words are forgotten, and speech disorders are common. A frequent disturbance is speech in the form of logoclonia. In advanced stages of the disease, speech becomes an incoherent jargon without sentence formation. Prolonged periods of restless overactivity, anxiety, and depression may occur. Agnosia, apraxia, and temporary hemiplegic or paraplegic weakness may exist. Syncopal and epileptic attacks are common. A Parkinson-like difficulty in gait is often seen. Facial paresis and hypertonicity of muscles are frequent, and in late stages there may be contractures of the extremities. At this stage the patient becomes extremely demented, is entirely out of touch with his environ-

Figure 10–2 Presenile psychosis. Cerebral biopsy. Lipofuscin degenerative products undergoing different stages of lipolysis and digestive degradation associated with marked glia fiber proliferation. Uranyl acetate and lead citrate counterstains. Magnification: 25,200×. (Courtesy of Professor L. Roizin, M.D., Department of Neuropathology, New York State Psychiatric Institute, New York.)

ment, and becomes reduced to a mere vegetative existence. The usual duration of the disease is five to ten years, but the course may be characterized by remissions.

The following is a rather typical clinical history of a patient suffering from this disorder.

W. M. was admitted to the hospital at the age of 52. The patient's early life, including medical history, does not appear to have been significant. The onset of his mental disorder was so insidious that his wife was able to give only an approxi-

mate date. About five or six years before his admission, he began to show less affection toward his family. His wife added that at about the same time "he grew lazy and his interests gradually dulled. He had a habit of just sitting around the house. For years he has not mentioned the payment of the interest on his mortgage or his taxes." About three years before admission his wife noticed that he could not tell time correctly and that he would make errors in writing a check. "He would set out for the store to buy feed for his cows and forget to do so. One time he wanted to walk to his father's place, thinking that it was just down the road, whereas it was a matter of 60 miles. He grew confused, and on one occasion he stopped the car in the middle of an intersection.

He would put on his trousers backward and his overalls inside out. Sometimes, when a dish of food was put on the table for the whole family, he would eat the entire amount himself."

The preadmission history is obviously that of an insidiously developing and progressive dementia. On admission the patient appeared to be older than he actually was. He was completely disoriented for time and place. He did not know whether his home was in Pennsylvania or New Jersey. On the day of admission he said he was 34 years of age; on the following day he gave his age as 25 and a few weeks later, as 80. He was careless and untidy in dress and wandered about the ward in a confused and bewildered manner, often mistaking the nurse for his wife.

General hyperreflexia was noted, but there were no other neurological abnormalities. Prior to his death his extremities showed spasticity. The patient became incontinent of urine; he gradually grew weaker and even more demented. Nearly two and one-half years after admission, he suffered a rather typical epileptic seizure. Shortly thereafter he became comatose and died nine days later.

At autopsy the brain weighed 1250 gm. A coronal section through the frontal lobes showed pronounced cortical atrophy, with enlargement of the sulci. The island of Reil was also atrophic. On microscopic examination, a marked cortical atrophy was found; there was also a decrease in the amount of subcortical white matter. In some convolutions the white matter was reduced to a narrow band. The subcortex showed moderate general demyelination. Sections through the plane of the substantia nigra showed this to be depigmented. A section further caudad showed the posterior horns of the ventricles to be considerably enlarged at the expense of the white matter. Stained sections showed a focal and general loss of ganglion cells, the presence of ghost cells, severe degenerative changes in the cells that remained, and a uniform gliosis. Special silver stains demonstrated numerous senile plaques and neurofibrillary degeneration of many ganglion cells. These showed thickening and agglutination of the neurofibrils, their displacement to the periphery of the cells, and their bizarre arrangement within the cells.

Diagnosis and Treatment

When there is a history of slowly progressive impairment in cognitive function taking place in the patient's late 40s or 50s, Alzheimer's or Pick's disease should be considered. Serial psychological tests are helpful in indicating the progressive nature of the condition. Air encephalograms show ventricular dilation and increased cortical markings.

Since the etiology remains obscure, treatment should be directed to maintaining the general health of the patient and protecting him from the vagaries of his increasing impairment while supporting his dependent needs and increasing demands.

It is most important to recognize the susceptibility of the progressively senile to all drug therapies. It is easy to produce delirium by dosages of drugs that are readily tolerated by younger persons. This is particularly true when sedatives and hypnotics are prescribed. Alcohol generally is poorly tolerated. Metrazol and ribonucleic acid have been prescribed to assist memory functions. Their value is uncertain.

The senile are subject to many other illnesses, whose detection and proper management are required for provision of care that alleviates the major problems of impaired brain functions.

PICK'S DISEASE

This uncommon chronic brain syndrome, first described by Arnold Pick of Prague in 1892, is characterized pathologically by atrophy and gliosis in the associative areas. The motor, sensory, and projection areas are relatively unchanged. Several reports of multiple cases in one family suggest that the disease may be a heredodegenerative disorder, but it does not show any simple mendelian pattern. The involvement is of cortical areas which are relatively younger phylogenetically, areas concerned with higher associative functions. The mechanisms of speech and of thinking are therefore especially impaired. It has been suggested that the disease is a premature and localized neuronic aging. The frontal lobe may look as if a constricting band had been applied to it. The clinical symptomatology is the result of a combination of the diffuse and focal processes. The majority of cases have been in persons between the ages of 45 and 60 years; the youngest person to have the disease was 31.

Local areas of the brain, particularly the frontal and temporal lobes, may be severely atrophied, and the total weight of the brain may be reduced to less than 1000 gm. (the average normal male Caucasian brain weighs 1340 gm.). The whole depth of the cortex may be involved. Microscopically the lesions are found to be degenerative and not inflammatory. Usually, there is distortion in the arrangement of the cytoarchitectural layers of the atrophic convolutions. Chromatolysis of the nerve cells is marked, there is a progressive disappearance of the chromatic substance, the nucleus becomes pale and is displaced to the periphery, and the granulations are lost. Ballooned cells, not found in Alzheimer's disease, are regularly seen in Pick's disease. The loss of ganglion cells becomes marked, and many of those remaining are swollen and show argentophilic granules. There is hypertrophy of the neuroglia, and the microglia present a swollen appearance, with relatively numerous fatty granules. Senile plaques and Alzheimer fibrillary changes, frequently found in senile dementia and Alzheimer's disease, are rarely found. The white matter atrophies early. Changes in the basal ganglia are regularly found in Alzheimer's disease but are rare in Pick's disease.

The affliction occurs twice as frequently in women as in men. Among the earliest symptoms are lack of spontaneity, loss of memory, difficulty in thinking and concentration, and a blunting of emotions. The patient becomes taciturn, indifferent, and bewildered and is unable to deal with new situations. The memory for the execution of normal, concrete tasks is relatively well preserved, but the capacity for abstract behavior is more seriously impaired. Dementia is usually well established within a year. Some patients show a euphoric contentment, while others are irritable, depressed, and suspicious. Common focal symptoms include apraxia, alexia, agraphia, or aphasia until such time as their charac-teristics are obscured by general dementia. The patient may have difficulty in naming objects, although he may remember their use and properties. A rather important characteristic of these aphasias is that they are of gradual rather than of sudden onset and the spontaneous logorrhea often found in aphasia due to vascular disease is not present. Echolalia and stereotyped reactions are not infrequent. The pupils, other reflexes, and spinal fluid are not disturbed.

As the disease progresses, the patient becomes asthenic, is confined to bed, and scarcely moves. Dementia becomes extreme, sphincter incontinence develops, the capacity for speech practically disappears, and cachexia becomes marked. The patient usually dies in four to six years of some intercurrent infection.

Diagnosis

Clinical differentiation of the disease from Alzheimer's disease is extremely difficult. Many clinicians believe that this differentiation can be made only on post-mortem examination of the brain. The age period, slowly progressive course, and intellectual impairment are similar in both diseases. Convulsions, facial paresis, and muscular rigidity, common in Alzheimer's disease, are rare in Pick's disease. Aphasic disturbances with perseveration and logoclonia are frequent in Alzheimer's disease but rare in Pick's. Motor impulsiveness and aggression are more common in Alzheimer's. Indifference is common in Pick's disease and anxiety in Alzheimer's disease. Defects of memory seem to occur earlier in Alzheimer's disease, and in late stages memory may be practically obliterated, whereas some retention of it continues in Pick's disease. Delusions, hallucinations, and confabulations, rather frequent in the former disease, are not common in Pick's disease. Hyperactivity is common in Alzheimer's disease; in Pick's disease the patient tends to be underactive.

Many believe that deterioration of emotional factors, and especially of habit, progresses more rapidly in Pick's than in Alzheimer's disease. In the former, neurological signs are more frequently focal than in the latter. Finally, Pick's disease occurs much less frequently than does Alzheimer's.

Cerebral arteriosclerosis can usually be differentiated by the antecedent history of headache, dizziness, apoplectic phenomena, and other evidences of vascular disease.

CREUTZFELDT-JAKOB DISEASE

This rare form of presenile onset primary degenerative dementia is considered now to be caused by infection with a "slow virus." Such agents remain undetectable with the electron microscope, yet through their retention on filters with pores of known dimension they should be observed with this instrument. They are apparently lacking in antigenic capacity. Creutzfeldt-Jakob brain tissue contains a transmissible agent now considered to be in the slow virus group, which has been shown to infect chimpanzees and other primates.

BIBLIOGRAPHY

Busse, E. W., and Blazer, D. (eds.): Handbook of Geriatric Psychiatry. New York, Van Nostrand, 1980.

Crapper, D. R., Krishnan, S. S., and Dalton, A. J.: Brain aluminum distribution in Alzheimer's disease and experimental neurofibrillary degeneration. Trans. Am. Neurol. Assoc., 98:17–20, 1973.

DeBoni, U., and MacLachlan, D. R. C.: Senile dementia and Alzheimer's Disease: A current view. Life Sciences, 27:1–14, 1980.

Marx, J. L.: Slow viruses (II): The unconventional agents. Science, 181:44–45, 1973.

Nikado, T., Austin, J., True, B. L., Hutchinson, J., Rinehart, R., Stuckenbrok, H., and Miles, B.: Isolation and preliminary characterization of Alzheimer plaques from presenile and senile dementia. Trans. Am. Neurol. Assoc., 95:47–50, 1970.

Simon, H.: Physical and socio-psychologic stress in the geriatric mentally ill. Compr. Psychiatry, 11:242–247, 1970.

Slaby, A. E., and Wyatt, R. J.: Dementia in the Presenium. Springfield, Ill., Charles C Thomas, 1974.

Yesavage, J. A., Tinklenberg, J. R., Hollister, L. E., and Berger, P. A.: Vasodilators in senile dementias; A review of the literature. Arch. Gen. Psychiatry, 36:220–223, 1979.

11

BRAIN SYNDROMES ASSOCIATED WITH CEREBRAL ARTERIOSCLEROSIS AND OTHER CEREBROVASCULAR DISTURBANCES

"It is not a divinity but the mystery of arteriosclerosis that shapes the earthly endings of most lives."

Walter Alvarez

Atherosclerosis, more commonly called arteriosclerosis, is an occlusive disease that affects the nutrient vessels of the brain, heart, or kidney. By progressively choking off the flow of blood and disrupting the integrity of the vascular wall, it produces leakage and at times frank bleeding. These changes lead to functional alteration, disability, or death. When the term arteriosclerosis is used in this chapter, it should be borne in mind that the real nature of the pathological vascular process is an atherosclerosis with its distinctive morphological feature of stainable lipid within the atheromatous lesions.

The Dynamics of Cerebral Circulation

Through the use of angiography, surgical explorations, and, more recently, anatomical studies, a greatly expanded appreciation of the vascular supply of the brain has emerged, particularly as it depends upon the functional integrity of the major extracerebral arteries and their capacity for expanding anastomotic connections.

In man, the internal carotid artery is the major arterial supply to the brain. Yet extensive anastomoses exist between the branches of this vessel and those of the external carotid. The vertebral artery provides a significant contribution to this circulation as well. These anastomotic changes, the *rete mirabile*, are known now to expand widely when the main channels of the internal carotid system are narrowed through occlusive disease such as atherosclerosis. Impingement upon the lumen of the great vessels of the arch of the aorta or at the bifurcation of the common carotid by atheromatous plaques, thrombosis, or other constricting lesions may critically influence the blood supply to the brain and produce periodic ischemic crises that impair brain activity and personality functioning just as decisively as focal ischemic crises due to reduction of blood flow by the terminal cerebral arterioles.

In man, each hemisphere is supplied by the ipsilateral carotid artery, while the cerebral structures contained in the posterior fossa of the skull receive their blood from the basilar artery.

It appears that the circle of Willis, that anastomotic link at the base of the brain between the carotid and basilar arteries, customarily brings up little interchange of blood between the two arterial supplies. In emergencies, with sudden occlusion of one of the major arterial channels to the brain, it provides an immediately available anastomotic channel. Thus, it is known that in young persons, ligation of one of the internal carotid arteries does not reduce the total circulation of the brain. However, in the elderly, in whom component vessels of the circle of Willis

may be partially occluded by an atheromatous plaque and incapable of full dilatation, the same procedure reduces cerebral blood flow and produces extensive signs of impairment of brain function.

While the cerebral cortex has an extensive capillary supply, varying from 1000 capillaries per millimeter of cross section in the gray and 300 in the white matter, its minute vascularity is much less than that of the heart. Occlusion of blood flow for two minutes in any area leads to cellular ischemia and necrosis.

Cerebral blood flow and cellular oxygenation are held steady in health through the many homeostatic mechanisms which control cardiac output, maintenance of blood pressure, and pulmonary ventilation, as well as the special receptors that influence the flow to the head, such as the carotid sinus. Constriction and vasodilation of these blood vessels are mediated by the intrinsic nervous supply of the carotid and vertebral plexi. Thus the sympathetic vasoconstrictors derive from the superior cervical ganglion while the fibers subserving vascular dilatation enter the plexi via the branches of the greater superficial petrosal nerve.

Humoral influences, too, are known to produce narrowing or widening of the brain arterioles. Dilatation occurs with high blood carbon dioxide tensions and constriction follows increase in blood oxygen tension. In pharmacological experiments in which the arterial blood pressure is raised 20 per cent with intravenous injection of norepinephrine, the cerebral vessels constrict with lowering of blood flow, while epinephrine injection brings about little change. Alcohol prescribed for the elderly patient with arteriosclerosis has little effect on brain vascularity. The same is true for nicotinic acid, which brings about dilatation of the external carotid system without modifying cerebral blood flow. While histamine dilates the cerebral vessels, its associated effect of lowering blood pressure also obviates change in that blood flow.

Pathophysiology

While in aged healthy people cerebral blood flow approximates that of younger persons, a gradually progressive decline in the cerebral circulation has been found in the majority of studies involving those from the fourth and fifth decade of life onward. With progressive arteriosclerosis there occurs a significant diminution in cerebral circulation, associated in some instances with increased vascular resistance to values twice those noted in healthy persons. With the resulting hypoxia there follow disturbances in cellular metabolism and eventual death of cells. Although it is true that some individuals with cerebral arteriosclerosis associated with markedly diminished general cerebral blood flow appear to show good personality and cerebral function and to withstand well sudden additional lowering of that flow, it must be kept in mind that the presently used techniques of measuring flow do not determine levels in localized subcortical areas, but rather present quantitative changes only in the circulation of the brain as a whole.

The part played by age in the genesis of atherosclerosis has been discussed at great length by pathologists. Although it is now generally agreed that atherosclerosis is not a necessary result of age, it is indirectly related to the aging process. With the progressive lengthening of the life span during the present century, there has been a great increase in the number of persons suffering from arteriosclerosis. There is perhaps no better evidence of this fact than the striking increase in the number of admissions to public mental hospitals of persons suffering from mental disorders incident to this disease.

With the progressive diminution in caliber of the relatively narrow vessels of the brain, the flow of blood is slowly throttled and the nutrition of the parenchyma affected. Ganglion cells gradually deteriorate and areas of atrophy develop around the constricted arterioles (Fig. 11–1). Hemorrhage or thrombosis and embolism with infarction may occur. Thrombosis is much more frequent and probably accounts for 85 per cent of vascular accidents.

While there are many case histories which suggest that those with cerebral arteriosclerosis are subject to episodic attacks of transient ischemia due to localized vasoconstrictions, the evidence for such spasms is inconclusive. An equally plausible explanation is the occurrence of transitory periods of hypotension which reduce oxygenation in an area supplied by a critically narrowed arteriole.

Symptoms

The principal organic mental disorder associated with cerebral arteriosclerosis and other cerebrovascular disturbances is multi-infarct dementia. The age of onset of this dementia varies widely, but in general it is between 50 and 65 years. Prodromal symptoms in the form of fatigue, headache, dizziness, diminution of capacity for prolonged concentration, drowsiness in the afternoon or evening, and an insidious impairment of physical and mental abilities are common. Frequently, latent character features are revealed or previous trends become pathologically exaggerated. Any apparent change in character in a person over 50 years of age should suggest the possibility of cerebral arteriosclerosis if syphilitic meningoencephalitis is excluded.

In somewhat more than half of the cases, a sudden attack of confusion is the first obvious mental symptom. Episodes of confusion or of excitement or, particularly, of their combined associa-

A

B

C

Figure 11–1 *See legend on opposite page*

tion constitute a frequent symptom of multi-infarct dementia. During such episodes, there are clouding of consciousness, incoherence, and restlessness, sometimes extreme. Recurrent episodes of this type, as well as transitory attacks of hemiparesis, hemianopia, or aphasia, should suggest the presence of occlusive atheromata in the major extracerebral arteries.

In other cases the onset is insidious, with stepwise deterioration in intellectual function, and represents what has been descriptively characterized as "a slow dying at the top." Among such symptoms are easy mental fatigability, a lessening of initiative, an impairment of attention, emotional instability with outbursts of weeping or laughter, and perhaps a tendency to depression. Some patients are irritable, aggressive, meddlesome, quarrelsome, obstinate, jealous, and paranoid. Finer sentiments, such as affection, may be destroyed. Some patients become garrulous. Memory is impaired to varying degrees. At first it may consist merely of difficulty in recollecting names, but later it may become general. The facies may become increasingly immobile and inanimate. Nocturnal attacks of bewilderment, of delirious, anxious states, or of violence may occur. As the illness progresses, the arteriosclerotic patients become neglectful of their personal appearance, their clothing may not be clean, and they may fail to bathe.

Delusions may be expressed and are particularly apt to be of a persecutory nature, although ideas of ruin and hypochondriacal delusions are not uncommon. Patients may be distressed by ideas of jealousy concerning their spouses or other members of their families. Their ideational content, like other expressions of their psychosis, is influenced largely by former types of mental mechanisms and other patterns of personality expression. Occasionally a patient is noted who expresses ideas of grandeur representing a compensation for failing sexual capacity. As in senile dementia, defective judgment and decreased inhibition may result in sexual indiscretions or offenses.

Characterological changes representing alterations in adaptive mechanisms and personality defenses may occur. Defenses against feelings of dependency may, for example, be replaced by acceptance of these needs. Hostile impulses that were previously suppressed may be released. Premorbid defensive drives, such as perfectionism, may be relaxed.

Among persons with more advanced cerebrovascular disease are those subject to "the little strokes." Such individuals may become intermittently psychotic or subject to periods of delirium. Vertical headaches that are worse in the morning, giddiness, short periods of confusion, fleeting loss of power in arm or leg, or momentary aphasias or apraxias usually give warning of subsequent, more serious focal lesions. Station becomes insecure, its base wide; the gait is uncertain, and the steps short and spastic. Pupillary inequalities are common, although recent studies have shown that there is no close relationship between retinal atherosclerosis and sclerosis of the small arteries supplying the brain. Coarse tremors may appear, and the patient may finally experience much difficulty in feeding himself.

Cardiovascular disease in the form of cardiac hypertrophy, coronary sclerosis, or chronic valvular disease is common. Numerous paralytic lesions appear—evidence of focal destruction of

Figure 11-1 Arteriosclerosis of the central nervous system. A, Lateral view of the brain presenting a cavitation within an old softening, affecting predominantly the territory of the superficial branches of the right middle cerebral artery. B, C, Cross sections of cerebral arteries revealing various degrees of degenerative changes and thickening of the elastic membrane, intima and media. Note distortion and narrowing of the vascular lumen. Elastic tissue technique counterstained with hematoxylin and eosin. Low power magnification. (Courtesy of L. Roizin, M.D., Department of Neuropathology, New York State Psychiatric Institute, New York.)

nervous tissue by occlusion or by rupture of a vessel of considerable size. Upper motor neuron paralyses and various aphasias and apraxias are most frequent. Paraphasia, or confusion of words, may occur.

Deterioration and dementia are hastened by these focal lesions, especially by those that result in serious speech disturbances. Certain intellectual functions may be much impaired while others remain comparatively intact. Epileptiform attacks, either jacksonian or general, may take place, caused, some believe, by temporary anemia or edema.

Patients with multi-infarct dementia are peculiarly apt, on the occasion of a mild infection, to suffer from episodes characterized by confusion, disorientation, misidentification of persons, anxiety, fear reaction, suspiciousness, and delusional trends.

In contrast to those with primary degenerative dementia, patients with multi-infarct dementia recognize, at least in the early stages of their deterioration, that there is a decline in the quickness and accuracy of their mental functions. They often feel keenly their difficulty in finding a word, their weakness of memory, and the diminution of physical and mental capacity.

The following abstract of a patient's clinical record illustrates some of the more frequent symptoms resulting from the physiological disturbances of brain function through arteriosclerotic changes.

W. B., aged 66, a bookkeeper by occupation, suddenly suffered an attack of vertigo and severe headache lasting for about 20 minutes. He then resumed his daily tasks although he felt weak and tired. On the following day, "for no reason that he can explain, as he claims he was not dizzy," his brother reported, "he just lost his balance and fell downstairs." He was then referred to the hospital for study and diagnosis.

The patient's brother added that 18 months previous to this episode the patient first showed a change in behavior. He talked much less and "would often sit and look at absolutely nothing for long periods. For the past year he had been saying rather peculiar things. He became silly, flighty, and confused." While in the general hospital to which he had been admitted, he was constantly worrying over loss of his money, although there was no basis for such a belief. The brother described the patient's behavior in the general hospital as follows: "He was very confused. He would remain in bed, and instead of getting out of the side of the bed, he would crawl over its foot to get out."

Upon arrival at the hospital, the peripheral and retinal arteries were found sclerotic. He said he had come from the B. General Hospital and had never heard of the Ab. Hospital. When asked the dates when he became ill, he maintained that he had not been ill. He gave his age, his birth year, and the current year correctly, but when asked the present date he replied, "The New York Giants won the first game, Brooklyn won the second game, and the third game was going home when I went." A month after admission he conversed freely and usually rationally with other patients and showed concern about the condition of the feeble ones. He continued, however, to manifest difficulty in concentration, in apperception, and in memory for recent events. He was then fully oriented as to time and place and recognized that his memory was impaired. He remarked to his physician, "I don't know. If I have to keep on this way, maybe the good Lord ought to take me." Four months after admission he was described as having periods of memory loss. Although the United States was then intently preoccupied with World War II, he took no interest in the world situation and important events. At times he showed difficulty in choosing the proper word and occasionally became quite irritated at himself for having this difficulty. Although he had completed three years of college, he was unable to answer simple mathematical questions and failed in an attempt to subtract seven serially from 100. Under the simple routine of hospital life and freedom from responsibility, the patient improved. Five and a half years after admission he was described as discussing his business affairs intelligently, showing an interest in hospital activities, and well informed on current events. Three years later there developed periods of 24 hours' duration during which he became excited, screamed at any who approached him, and often became quite threatening, although he never did violence to them. At such times he was somewhat confused.

Prognosis

The course is not always uninterruptedly progressive. It frequently happens that a patient, particularly if he also has cardiac and general vascular disease, is seen in a confused, perhaps excited, state, so that he appears to be quite demented. After rest and several days or a few weeks of the simple regimen of hospital life, the patient may become clearly conscious and apparently recover from the acute symptoms.

With early recognition by appropriate arteriography of cerebral insufficiency due to occluding atheromata of the extracranial arteries supplying the brain, it is now possible by means of appropriate surgical endarterectomy or angioplasty to alleviate immediate symptoms and also maintain improvement over long periods of time in two thirds to three fourths of those so treated.

There is constant danger, however, that an apoplectic stroke or another confused episode may occur at any time. Many patients, nevertheless, retain considerable, although impaired, capacity for several years before dementia or physical helplessness removes them from the scene of activity. In many cases death is hastened by general arteriosclerosis associated with cardiorenal disease.

Those who suffer transient attacks of cerebral ischemia before the age of 65 have a significantly poorer outlook for life than those whose symptoms present after this age. Later complications and death are due to both cardiac and cerebrovascular disturbances. The coexistence of hypertension does not seem to modify the mortality rates.

Diagnosis

In the early differential diagnosis of cerebral insufficiency due to atherosclerosis, it is of great clinical importance to distinguish between the type due to atheromata in the major extracerebral vessels and that due to intracerebral occlusive arteriolar disease. In most instances of the former condition, there occur transient episodes of cerebral ischemia which range in severity from bouts of minimal dysfunction in mentation or weakness to apoplectiform hemiparetic attacks. Such symptoms last momentarily or for days. One of the few signs suggestive of

extracranial arterial occlusion on physical examination is the presence of murmurs detectable over the great vessels, although the absence of murmurs is without significance. With incomplete occlusion of the internal carotid, systolic murmurs may be heard in the neck at the angle of the jaw; with partial occlusion of the vertebral arteries, they may be heard in the supraclavicular region. With partial occlusion of the great vessels in the chest, murmurs may be heard at the base of the neck or in the supraclavicular region, and the pulses in the arms and neck vessels are diminished or absent. Arteriography is, of course, diagnostic and may be done with low risk of complications.

The mental disorder from which the differentiation of multi-infarct dementia is most frequently required is primary degenerative dementia (See Table 11–1.) Since the two forms of deterioration are often associated and the manifestations of both are about equally prominent, differentiation may be difficult or im-

TABLE 11–1 Differential Diagnosis of Brain Syndromes Due to Multi-Infarct Dementia and Primary Degenerative Dementia

	MULTI-INFARCT DEMENTIA	PRIMARY DEGENERATIVE DEMENTIA
Occurrence	Greater in men	Greater in women
Onset	Early	Late
Headaches	+	0
Dizziness	+	0
Syncope	+	0
Convulsions	+	0
Confusional States (Transient)	+	0
"Strokes"	+	0
Physical Signs Cardiac Dysfunction	+	0
Renal Dysfunction	+	0
Retinal Dysfunction	+	0
Intellectual Impairment	Lacunar	Global

possible. Multi-infarct dementia occurs somewhat more frequently in men than in women, while primary degenerative dementia occurs more frequently in women. Headache, dizziness, or apoplectic phenomena occur in about half of the cases of multi-infarct dementia. Fainting attacks, convulsive seizures, or attacks of cardiac dysfunction likewise suggest an arteriosclerotic origin. Sudden attacks of confusion often occur.

In arteriosclerosis the intellectual impairment is lacunar; there is good preservation of the personality and the course is fluctuating. In primary degenerative dementia there is first a defect in recent memory, then disorientation, going on to progressive dementia. Signs of coronary disease, of retinal arteriosclerosis, and of kidney involvement, with associated changes in the urine and an increase in the blood nonprotein nitrogen level, suggest cerebral arteriosclerosis.

Perhaps one of the most significant and also most frequently overlooked factors in the differential diagnosis of multi-infarct dementia is that of the complicating depressive reaction or the depressive reaction of aging. The latter diagnosis is made much more frequently in England than in the United States. Obviously, the recognition of these depressive states is highly important now that impressive therapeutic measures may be initiated. Awareness of declining faculties establishes for the individual with the symptoms of either arteriosclerosis or aging the sense of loss with depressive affect and/or anxiety, limited drive and interest in activities and friends, and the sense of hopelessness and helplessness that characterizes these states. Suicidal ideation may be noted and, in those so predisposed, a depressive episode or a manic-depressive illness may erupt, with self-reproaches, nihilistic and somatic delusions, and reduction in psychomotor activity. The correct diagnosis of these affective states, either primary or secondary to the arteriosclerotic condition, provides the indication for often gratifying antidepressant therapy.

Finally, acute brain syndromes (delirious states) due to drug intoxications, infarctions, or states of malnutrition must be discriminated from the sudden episodes of cerebral ischemia so common with cerebral arteriosclerosis. Here, the clues are most likely to be given by the history of drug administration, excessive use of alcohol, recent illness, or poor feeding habits.

Treatment

Since our knowledge concerning the causes of cerebral arteriosclerosis is so limited, little can be done to prevent its development. In any case, a carefully regulated mode of life is a fundamental requirement in treatment. Although neither heavy manual labor nor mental tasks involving burdensome responsibilities or emotional stress should be permitted, an agreeable occupation of simple type should be continued as long as possible, due attention being paid to recreation and physical rest. It should be borne in mind that suicide is not rare in arteriosclerotic depressions. The arteriosclerotic patient will be wise to refrain from alcohol. Any inadequacies of nutrition should be improved, and attention should be directed to any associated cardiorenal or other pathological condition. The value of low-cholesterol, low-fat diets, estrogens, heparin, choline, or inositol as a means of influencing the presumed disturbed lipid metabolism remains controversial. Hydrotherapy in mild forms, carefully supervised, may be employed, but measures that are too long or too vigorous may be harmful.

Chlorpromazine has been helpful with some patients in reducing nocturnal insomnia and restlessness, confusion, excitement, and aggressive, destructive behavior, but care must be taken in the case of the arteriosclerotic patient because of the possibility of a hypotensive reaction following administration of the drug. For this reason, oral administration is preferred, commencing with small doses (10 mg. three times daily) and gradually increasing the amount. The use of other sedatives often may be discontinued. The dosage needed and tolerated is highly variable. Psychotherapy should not be forgotten in the anxious patient. Barbiturates will sometimes aggravate the confusion associated with multip-farct dementia and hypertensive encephalopathy. The dizziness, headache, insomnia, confusion, and delirious confusion occurring in these disorders are often relieved by the administration of aminophylline in doses of 250 mg. each four times a day.

Pentylenetetrazol (Metrazol) given orally in doses ranging from 4.5 to 12 gm. over prolonged periods is credited by some with improving the sense of well-being and relieving the general symptoms of debility.

The therapeutic value of vasorelaxant agents acting on smooth muscle of the vessel walls is unclear. Isoxsuprine (20 mg. by mouth three times daily) has been tried with reported success in relieving headaches and reducing symptoms suggestive of recurrent cerebral ischemic attacks. This pharmacologic agent with nylidrin also stimulates the myocardium and increases cardiac output without producing general vasodilation. Young and his colleagues report that patients given cyclandelate, 400 mg. daily, deteriorate at a significantly slower rate than others untreated with this agent.

Surgical treatment with endarterectomy or angioplasty is indicated in instances of occlusive disease of the extracranial cerebrovascular supply, particularly in early and incomplete obstructions. With thrombosis superimposed on atheromata, lesions of the innominate, subclavian, and common carotid are almost always amenable to such treatment, but operability is more difficult when the common carotid or vertebral arteries are involved. When both carotids are stenosed, but the clinical symptoms may be ascribed to major disease in one of the two vessels, effective intravascular surgery may provide relief for periods of three to five years before contralateral stenosis or occlusion occurs.

BIBLIOGRAPHY

DeBakey, M. E., Crawford, E. S., Morris, G. C., and Cooley, D. A.: Arterial reconstructive operations for cerebrovascular insufficiency due to extracranial arterial occlusive disease. J. Cardiovasc. Surg., 3:12–35, 1962.

Ehrentheil, O. F.: Differential diagnosis of organic dementias and affective disorders in aged patients. Geriatrics, 12:426–432, 1957.

Goldner, J. C., Whisnant, J. P., and Taylor, W. F.: Long-term prognosis of transient cerebral ischemic attacks. Trans. Am. Neurol. Assoc., 94:20–24, 1969.

Gurdjian, E. S., Darmody, W. R., and Thomas, L. M.: Recurrent strokes due to occlusive disease of extracranial cerebral vessels. Trans. Am. Neurol. Assoc., 94:11–14, 1969.

Kety, S. S.: The cerebral circulation. In Handbook of Physiology. Vol. 3, pp. 1751–1760. Washington, D. C., American Physiological Society, 1960.

Simonson, E., and McGavack, T. H. (eds.): Cerebral Ischemia. Springfield, Ill., Charles C Thomas, 1964.

Whittier, J. R.: Vasorelaxant drugs and cerebrovascular disease. Angiology, 15:82–87, 1964.

Young, J., Hall, P., and Blakemore C.: Treatment of cerebral manifestations of arteriosclerosis with cyclandelate. Br. J. Psychiatry, 124:177–180, 1974.

12

BRAIN SYNDROMES ASSOCIATED WITH INFECTION

"As man, perhaps, the moment of his breath,
Receives the lurking principle of death,
The young disease, that must subdue at length,
Grows with his growth, and strengthens with his strength."

Alexander Pope

JULIUS WAGNER: JAUREGG
(From Roback, A. A., and Kiernan, T.: Pictorial
History of Psychology and Psychiatry. New York,
Philosophical Library, 1969, p. 263.)

GENERAL PARESIS

The brain syndrome associated with syphilitic meningoencephalitis, known as general paresis, general paralysis of the insane, or dementia paralytica, is a disorder produced by progressive syphilitic meningoencephalitis leading to a degeneration of brain parenchyma with an infiltration of interstitial elements. Clinically, general paresis is characterized by a comprehensive, but variable, syndrome of neurological and mental disturbances associated with fairly constant serological changes.

HISTORY

Although Haslam of Bethlehem Hospital, in a monograph entitled "Observations on Insanity," described in 1798 the associated mental and physical symptoms that occur in general paresis, the credit for its recognition as a clinical and pathological entity belongs to the French psychiatrist A. L. J. Bayle, who published his thesis in 1822 at the age of 23. An opinion that paresis was caused by syphilis was first expressed in 1857 by Esmarch and Jessen. At first this theory received little credence. The development of the Wassermann reaction indicated the existence of syphilis in practically all cases of paresis. Any remaining doubt that syphilis is the sole determining cause was dispelled in 1913, when Joseph W. Moore at the Central Islip (New York) State Hospital and Hideyo Noguchi of the Rockefeller Institute demonstrated the *Treponema pallidum* in the brains of paretics. It is now possible to demonstrate treponemata in fresh paretic brains taken at necropsy and studied by darkfield illumination. They may also be discovered in brain tissue obtained by puncture in living paretics.

In 1917 Wagner-Jauregg of Vienna found that artificial fever induced by inoculation with malaria resulted in an arrest of the paretic process and an improvement of the patient. In 1943 penicillin was found to be an active spirocheticidal agent and has since then proved to be the effective means of treating both general syphilis and neurosyphilis.

Frequency and Pathogenesis

Prior to 1920, 8 to 10 per cent of the patients committed to public hospitals in the United States were suffering from general paresis, whereas at the present time less than 1 per cent of the patients admitted for the first time are suffering from this disease. This decline in admissions is probably a result of both a decrease in syphilis and earlier, more adequate treatment.

The *Treponema pallidum* is one of the few microorganisms that can penetrate the blood-brain barrier with ease. It is now believed that during the period of generalized spirochetemia this invasion of the neuroaxis occurs in most, if not all, patients infected with syphilis. In the majority of cases, this original invasion never produces symptoms, physical signs, or changes in the cerebrospinal fluid; the organisms that have penetrated the nervous system are spontaneously eliminated by obsure immune processes not yet understood. The reason for the development of paresis in some luetic individuals while others remain free from the disease is not known, but perhaps the incidence is determined by the virulence of the infection and by immune factors in the host. There probably is not a special neurotropic strain of treponema.

Paresis occurs four times more frequently in men than in women. The cause for this strikingly higher incidence in men is uncertain, since the probable ratio of primary syphilis infection among men as compared with women is not greater than 2 to 1.

Pathology

The basic pathology of paresis is a chronic syphilitic meningoencephalitis in which two pathological components—inflammation and degeneration—are at work. The process, with its progressive degeneration of nerve cells, begins largely in the frontal region, but as the disease progresses, any part of the cortex, cerebellum, or bulb may become involved.

Microscopically the perivascular lymph spaces of the vessels are crowded with proliferated endothelial cells, occasional mast cells, and, most important of all, lymphocytes and plasma cells. The pia mater is similarly infiltrated with lymphocytes and plasma cells. A sprouting of the capillaries produces increased vascularity, while the "cuffing" of these capillaries by the perivascular infiltration mentioned gives rise to one of the important histopathological features of paresis, although it is not confined to general paralysis but occurs also in epidemic encephalitis and in trypanosomiasis. The ganglion cells are cloudy and suffer degeneration, and many disappear, particularly in the middle layer of the frontal cortex. It has not yet been determined whether the degenerative changes are caused by the action of the spirochetes themselves or by their toxic products. The usual cortical architecture, with lamination and column formation of the neuron cells, is disorganized. The glia is proliferated. Scattered about through the cortex are numerous cylindrical-appearing cells known as rod cells or "Stäbchenzellen," first described by Franz Nissl.

Another constant finding in the brain of the paretic subject is the presence of iron pigment in the walls of the blood vessels and in the cortical microglia. Many pathologists consider that the presence in the rod cells of a substance giving a Prussian blue reaction is to be considered as characteristic and pathognomonic of general paresis. Spirochetes are found in about 80 per cent of the untreated cases.

Incubation Period

General paresis develops from 5 to 30 or more years after the primary infection with syphilis. In one half of the cases, the incubation period is from 10 to 20 years; in one fourth, the period is under 10 years; and in one fourth, it is over 20 years. The peak in the curve of incidence occurs between the ages of 35 and 45.

Invasion of the nervous system by *Treponema pallidum* is first manifested by a rising cell count in the *cerebrospinal fluid*. Three to six months later the protein becomes elevated, and this is then followed by the development of positive Wassermann and colloidal reactions. If the nervous system has not been invaded by the end of the second year of the disease, it is unlikely that it will ever be involved.

It is established that there is a preclinical period during which the only evidence of the condition consists of spinal fluid findings characteristic of the disease. During this period the patient may be said to be suffering from *asymptomatic paresis*, the forerunner of clinical paresis.

Symptoms and Signs

Syphilitic meningoencephalitis may conveniently be considered under the following headings: personality disturbance, physical and neurological signs, and serological changes.

PERSONALITY DISTURBANCE. Changes in personality and disturbed mentation commonly are the first noted signs of the illness. The clinical findings often fail to reflect the extent of the pathological process. Frequently, the mental symptoms develop so insidiously that the patient's family has not recognized that a deteriorating change in personality has been taking place. The early symptoms consist largely of an extension and exaggeration of previous personality traits. Other early symptoms may be irritability, fatigue, difficulty in concentration, depression, periods of confusion, disturbed sleep, and headache. The early paretic individual is often opinionated and perhaps quarrelsome. Frequently he becomes neglectful of his dress, unkempt in appearance, inconsiderate of others, and forgetful of social amenities and proprieties and manifests an insidious breakdown of higher ethical and cultural sentiments and standards. The moderate user of alcohol may become dissipated; sexual activities may become excessive. The person whose previous life has been quite exemplary not only may suddenly show some surprising defect of character but also may feel no concern for his dereliction.

Early in the disease there is often an impairment in professional skill or in craftsmanship. Unaccustomed slips and failures in the discharge of ordinary duties occur. The consequences of errors are not foreseen. The patient may conceive ambitious schemes of an extremely impracticable and extravagant nature. The businessman may no longer show his former capacity for successful management and, because of failing judgment, may dissipate the resources upon which the livelihood of his family depends. There is often a contented indifference—an apathy and unconcern that at first may be mistaken for laziness. Frequently there is a tendency to drowsiness. The patient becomes incapable of submitting his impressions and conclusions to a critical examination, nor does he recognize the insidious deterioration that is going on in the intellectual, feeling, and social aspects of his personality. The man previously regarded as possessing an acute and well-trained mind and sound judgment surprises his acquaintances by his failure to grasp the finer shades of meaning or by some puerile, inept remark. Associations are characterized by their slowness, superficiality, and poverty.

A change of mood is common in the early stages, the frequent mood being apathy or depression. Sometimes the early stages are characterized by anxiety. In some cases, euphoria and expansiveness exist from the beginning, but more often these mood trends appear somewhat later. Momentary periods of confusion or an inability to grasp a situation and to act promptly and correctly lead to automobile accidents in early paretic patients whose mental disorder has not yet been detected.

Delusions occur at some periods of the disease in a majority of the patients. It has usually been emphasized that the delusions are grandiose, yet not more than 50 per cent of the subjects express delusions of this nature. Expansive delusions may reach the height of absurdity. The patient may declare, for example, that he owns a trucking company, each car of which is loaded with million-dollar treasury notes. Ideas of boundless benevolence may be expressed, including fantastic schemes for the welfare of all mankind. However, delusions often are depressive, self-accusatory, nihilistic, or persecutory. Hallucinations occasionally occur but are not of diagnostic significance.

In the very early stage of the paretic process, individuals who, before the development of the psychosis, showed a definite tendency to schizoid or cyclothymic manifestations frequently exhibit at the onset of the mental disturbance features suggestive of schizophrenia or manic-depressive psychosis.

The dementia of general paresis, even at a comparatively early stage, tends to be of a diffuse type, involving memory, judgment, emotional life, and conative expressions. Intelligence tests show a mental deterioration with defective reasoning and an impairment of social ability, memory, and learning. Unlike the dementia of senility, it is not at first limited largely to memory. As the disease advances, the dementia becomes progressive. Affectivity and emotional response suffer impoverishment, inadequacies of perception prevent contact with the environment, memory fails, associations become slow and limited, apperception is destroyed, spontaneous activities cease, and finally, the mental processes, devoid of conscious participation, are reduced to those at the reflex and vegetative level.

PHYSICAL AND NEUROLOGICAL SIGNS. As numerous and varied as are the mental symptoms that may exist in paresis, the physical and neurological symptoms are equally so. During the stage of onset, the patient may become easily fatigued and may lose weight. Numerous somatic complaints referred to the various bodily systems are frequent. The diagnosis in many paretic patients has been neurasthenia. Many patients complain of headache. Because of the loss of tone in the facial muscles, the lines of expression become smoothed out. This relaxation of the facial muscles, together with the blunting of emotional response, gives the facies a vacant, fatuous appearance.

Disturbances in the eye, or in its innervation or reflexes, almost always occur at some period; these disturbances vary greatly in degree. Papilledema, syphilitic retinitis, or primary optic atrophy may occur. Complete optic atrophy occurs in 2 per cent of the cases and incipient and intermediate stages of atrophy occur in 62.5 per cent. More frequent than optic atrophy are the disturbances of the pupils, which may be unequal in size, irregular in outline, much contracted, or widely dilated. Reaction to light is often sluggish or lost, as may also be the convergence reaction. The type of pupil first described by Argyll Robertson in 1869 will be found in over half of the paretic patients. This is a miotic pupil that contracts when the eyes converge and accommodates for near vision, but does not contract when strong light is suddenly thrown on the eye. It is to be distinguished from Adie's myotonic pupillary response, which also is seen to be associated with absence of deep reflexes. The myotonic pupil is never miotic but is dilated, sometimes oval, and after a period in the dark it slowly contracts with exposure to light. Occasionally, there may be some degree of ptosis of one lid or weakness of one of the external muscles of the eye, especially the external rectus.

A progressive weakness and incoordination of all voluntary muscles occur. There is tremor of the facial muscles, first observed in the lips when the patient attempts to speak or show his teeth. As enunciation becomes more difficult, there is an overactivity of all the facial muscles when speech is attempted. The tremor of the tongue is coarse and is best demonstrated when the tongue is protruded. This muscle weakness and incoordination lead to a disturbance of speech, which, when associated with the blandly inane facial expression already noted, constitutes a syndrome so characteristic that the experienced psychiatrist can often make a diagnosis as the patient speaks. At first this speech defect is often manifested in the form of a hesitation, drawl, or slurring. Later there is omission, reduplication, or transposition of syllables. The speech disturbances are often best demonstrated by asking the patient to repeat polysyllabic words or phrases containing labial or dental types of consonants (as "electrical artillery brigade"). As the disease progresses, the speech may become quite unintelligible. Transient, incomplete aphasic attacks may occur, at times rather early in the disease.

Deterioration in handwriting is often an early clinical symptom. Because of loss in delicate muscular coordination, it is often tremulous. There may also be reduplication or elision of letters in syllables. Later the patient may become unable to write at all from dictation, and if he attempts to form characters, he produces only an unintelligible scrawl.

Muscular incoordination gives rise also to many other symptoms. Among early ones is a tremulous incoordination of finer movements of the hand. Later the patient is unable to button his clothing or even to dress himself. Station and gait then become uncertain, all movements are clumsy, and finally, because of his weakness and ataxia, the patient is confined to his bed. The muscles of deglutition do not escape involvement, with the result that difficulty in swallowing may occur.

Disturbances of the deep tendon reflexes are the rule. More frequently these are exaggerated, in which case ankle clonus and spasticity are usually present, but if, as frequently happens, a tabetic process coexists, the knee jerks are absent. Disturbances of the rectal and vesical sphincters are common in the terminal stages. The bladder may become greatly distended, resulting in a dribbling of urine caused by an overflow of retention. Rupture of such a bladder may occur upon receipt of slight trauma. Trophic changes may occur in the bones, causing them to be easily fractured.

It is not uncommon for the paretic subject suddenly to develop a marked rise in temperature without evidence of infection or of additional somatic disease. These fevers are probably a result of disturbances of the heat-regulating centers.

About three fourths of patients suffer from convulsions at some time during the course of the disease. Occasionally a convulsion, particularly of an abortive type, may be the first symptom to attract attention to the illness.

Another form of episodic attack is apoplectiform in type. These attacks are sudden in onset, are accompanied by disturbances of consciousness, and are followed by hemiplegia or more localized paralyses. These paralyses are usually temporary in nature, often clearing up without residuals in a few days. Less frequently a hemorrhage occurs, leaving a permanent paralysis.

SEROLOGY. Serological changes supply important diagnostic evidence of the existence of general paresis. The spinal fluid changes provide the best guide to the activity of a syphilitic infection of the central nervous system and to the effect of treatment. In nearly all cases of untreated paresis, the blood serological tests for syphilis are positive. In general paresis, the cerebrospinal fluid pressure may be increased, and in approximately 8 per cent of the cases it will exceed 200 mm. H_2O.

Spinal Fluid Reactions. In untreated syphilitic meningoencephalitis, the serologic tests for syphilis O in the cerebrospinal fluid are positive in 90 per cent of the cases. A positive serologic reaction does not signify that the neurosyphilis is of the paretic type, nor does it necessarily indicate that the process is active. An increase of protein to 50 to 150 mg. per 100 ml. (normal, 25 mg.) with a disproportionate increase of globulin is the rule in paresis. The total protein and the amount of globulin are greater in general paresis than in any other type of neurosyphilis except acute meningitis. The more active the paretic process, the larger the amount of these substances. In paresis, the number of cells in the spinal fluid may remain normal or may reach 100 per cubic millimeter, the average being 25 to 50. An excess of this number indicates that a syphilitic meningitis also exists. The cell count affords the most valuable information about the activity of the infection. It is also the first abnormality to return to normal as a result of treatment.

Colloidal Gold Test. Given a positive Wassermann reaction of the spinal fluid and other evidence of neurosyphilis, one of the most valuable tests in determining its type is the colloidal gold test described by Lange in 1912. The test depends on the precipitation and varying degrees of decolorization of a solution of gold chloride by a series of dilutions of the cerebrospinal fluid. Degrees of precipitation show as changes from the normal salmon-red color of the solution and range through a slight change to deeper red, to lavender, violet, and red-blue, the colorless solution representing complete precipitation of the gold. An intense paretic reaction might be 5555554432; a less marked reaction might be 55432111000.

In multiple sclerosis, Schilder's disease, and other types of neurosyphilis, the decolorization curve with colloidal gold may follow that of general paresis. The colloidal gold reaction is an indication of an abnormality of the protein content of the fluid. It does not reflect the activity of the disease. This, as previously stated, is best indicated by the cell count.

Clinical Types

Because of the conspicuousness of certain presenting symptoms, different clinical types of syphilitic meningoencephalitis are usually described. These are the simple, expansive, depressed, and circular types. Some cases do not fit into such classifications, and in others the symptoms may shift during the course of the disease. The *expansive form* is the most important, although no longer emphasized as distinctly characteristic. Our discussion will be limited to it.

In the early stages, the patient is self-satisfied and has a superficial good humor, but becomes easily irritated. If handled with good-natured and tactful suggestion, he is quite amenable, but if interfered with, his resentment may lead to violence. Although his grandiose ideas may be most absurd, the paretic patient sees nothing incredible in them.

The following report illustrates the defective judgment and grandiose ideas of the expansive type:

M., aged 41, a roofing salesman, was transferred to a state hospital from the jail to which he had been sentenced for violation of the motor vehicle laws. The prodromal symptoms of the patient's oncoming disease were apparently slight. The informant, his sister, who had seen him but infrequently, stated that she had not noticed any change in him except that for a year he had seemed somewhat "worried." While driving his car, he disregarded the collector at a toll bridge and drove across the structure at high speed. When overtaken by a police officer, the patient was found to have no license to drive an automobile, the permit having been revoked several years previously. Three days later, while awaiting trial for this offense, he was again arrested for driving an automobile without a license. He was given a short sentence in jail, where a physician soon recognized the patient's disorder and had him committed to the hospital.

On arrival at the admission office of the hospital, he told the office attendant that he was going to give her a million dollars because she was "a nice lady." As he was being questioned for the usual admission data, he began to boast of his wealth, claiming that he had three automobiles, thousands of dollars in the bank, a "diamond watch," and much other valuable jewelry. His son, he said, was lieutenant governor of the state, was soon to be governor, and later would be president of the United States. After having expressed various absurdly grandiose plans, he added, "I have another plan, too. I'm going to the wardens of the prisons in this state and all the other states and I'm going to buy the prisoners. I'll have an agreement with the wardens to take their prisoners and put them to work on farms, and I'll charge each prisoner $300 for doing it and for getting him out of jail. I made $105,000 with prisoners just last week, and when I get going, I'm going to make plenty of money." The neurological signs were all consistent with syphilitic meningoencephalitis, and the serology was in all respects typical of the disease.

TABOPARESIS.   Patients with neurosyphilis show not only evidence of the parenchymatous involvement of the brain seen in general paresis, but also symptoms and signs of involvement of the posterior columns met with in tabes dorsalis. The coexistence of both of these diseases is known as taboparesis. The symptoms of tabes usually precede those of paresis.

The taboparetic patient manifests not only the mental symptoms of general paresis, but also the ataxia and other physical evidence of tabes. Frequently there is a history of difficulty in walking in the dark, of "shooting" pains in the legs. The knee jerks are absent. Romberg's sign is present, and there is a loss of sense of position in the lower extremities. Primary optic atrophy may occur. The colloidal gold curve may be of the second zone type.

JUVENILE PARESIS.   This form, which occurs in the child or adolescent suffering from congenital syphilis, was first described by Clouston in 1877. Infection is transmitted from the mother to the offspring by the transplacental route after the fifth month of pregnancy. It is estimated that rather less than 1 per cent of the cases of congenital syphilis develop general paresis. The age of the juvenile paretic subject at the time of the onset of symptoms corresponds approximately to the length of the incubation period in adult paresis. The child will generally, therefore, be from 5 to 20 years of age at the time of onset of symptoms. In about one third of the cases, there is retardation of physical development. Many, perhaps 40 per cent, are found always to have been mentally retarded.

The child's history may reveal that he had attended school and had acquired knowledge with fair success until 8 to 14 years of age, when insidious dementia began to develop. Because of the impairment of intelligence and the appearance of convulsions, many of the cases are diagnosed as epilepsy or idiocy with epilepsy. Trophic and other neurological disturbances are often conspicuous.

Optic atrophy is common. The average duration of the disease is four to five years. Treatment is less effective than in adult forms.

The following is a fairly illustrative case of juvenile paresis.

J. C. was admitted to a hospital when 17 years of age. The first pregnancy following his parents' marriage terminated at seven months, the child dying almost immediately. The patient was the next child in order of birth. His early development was said to have been normal. He attended school from 6 to 13 years of age and is said to have been promoted each year. The first symptoms appeared in October, when, as his father explained, the boy "became draggy and droopy" and "didn't want to serve his paper route as before." In December, the teacher reported that he was failing in school. In the spring, the patient "began to talk funny and was thick-tongued." At practically the same time, the parents noticed a weakness of the left leg and arm. His difficulty in walking increased, his speech became almost unintelligible, and he occasionally soiled himself.

On admission to the hospital, the patient was found to be of rather small stature but fairly well nourished. He walked somewhat in the manner of a mechanical doll, with his elbows pressed close to his ribs, his forearms extended straight before him and his fingers separated. His steps were short and shuffling, with his feet widely separated as if to maintain his balance. His pupils were widely dilated (the right more than the left), were irregular, and did not react to light, but showed a little contraction on convergence. Both nerve heads were found to be somewhat atrophic. His tendon reflexes were exaggerated, there was a bilateral Babinski reaction, and he showed tremor of the fingers. Coordination in fine movements was defective. Attempts to secure the finger-to-nose tests were unsuccessful, as the patient could not be made to comprehend the instructions. The Wassermann reaction was positive on both blood and spinal fluid. The latter contained 19 cells and an excess of globulin and showed a colloidal gold curve of 5555422210.

Mentally, the patient's manner suggested severe retardation. His facial expression was smoothed-out, and he frequently exhibited a silly grin. He cooperated in the eager, ineffective manner of a mentally defective and responded to all questions with "Huh?" He could not utter a single intelligible word but obeyed simple requests, such as "Shut your eyes," "Close your mouth." The Wassermann reaction on the father's blood was found to be positive.

Because of the active effort now made to ascertain if pregnant women are infected with syphilis and the efficacy of treatment with penicillin, cases of congenital syphilis are relatively rare. Juvenile paresis is therefore now an uncommon disease.

Course and Prognosis

If not treated, syphilitic meningoencephalitis leads inevitably to dementia and death. If not arrested within a reasonable period, it produces a permanent but varying degree of dementia and economic dependence. In the absence of treatment, death usually occurs from two to five years after the first appearance of symptoms. The course may be interrupted, however, by spontaneous remissions in slightly over 10 per cent of the untreated cases. Remissions are more frequent in those cases in which the onset has been comparatively sudden and stormy. The duration of the remissions is quite variable, extending from one or two months to five or six years. The average life expectancy in the untreated patient is four years.

The prognosis in the treated patient depends upon the promptness and thoroughness of treatment. Active treatment with adequate doses of penicillin during the asymptomatic stage should prevent the development of clinical symptoms in at least 85 per cent of the cases. If treatment is begun in the early clinical stages, 60 per cent or more of the patients will improve sufficiently to return to work. It is generally believed that a spinal fluid that is negative after three years from the date of infection will not become positive. In hospitals where patients are admitted in all stages of the disease, the number recovering rarely exceeds 30 per cent, the death rate is 20 to 30 per cent, and further progress is arrested in 30 to 50 per cent of the patients.

Diagnosis

Paresis has been confused with Alzheimer's disease, Pick's disease, multiple sclerosis, senile dementia, cerebral tumor, or other diseases producing cerebral damage, particularly to the frontal lobes. The spinal fluid findings constitute the most important differential criterion.

Treatment

Penicillin is the treatment of choice for syphilitic meningoencephalitis. A course of penicillin, repeated if necessary, is effective in a large proportion of both symptomatic and asymptomatic forms of the disease. Recommended is the use of procaine penicillin G in aqueous suspension, 600,000 units daily, for not less than 15 days or benzathine penicillin G (Bicellin), 2.4 million units intramuscularly at seven-day intervals for four doses. If the patient is allergic to penicillin, the use of doxycycline hyclate in the dosage of 100 mg. every 12 hours for 30 days should be tried.

Following the initial injection of penicillin, many patients develop therapeutic shock (Jarisch-Herxheimer reaction), usually lasting no longer than a few hours. For relief, acetyl salicylic acid (aspirin) alone is sufficient. Prior advice about this potential reaction generally offsets the anxiety that the treated patient may develop.

The results of the spinal fluid tests serve as a guide for both the activity of the paretic process and the effect of treatment. The spinal fluid should be examined six months after the completion of treatment. The first change in the cerebrospinal fluid following penicillin therapy is a reduction in the number of cells, which usually reach normal limits within six months. This is followed by a drop in total protein level. If the increased cell count has reverted to normal or near normal, the amount of protein has decreased, and the patient seems improved, no further treatment is needed. The complement-fixation reaction and results of the colloidal test may not revert to normal for several months or years and cannot be used to gauge adequate treatment. If the cell count and protein value remain high, a second course of treatment is mandatory. The second course should be the same as, or more intensive than, the first one. When the response is favorable, the spinal fluid should be examined at intervals of four to six months for the first year after treatment, then yearly until the spinal fluid is no longer abnormal. Less reliance is placed upon clinical features than upon spinal fluid changes as a guide to further treatment.

In greatly overactive patients, as well as in those with prominent affective components, it is often well to precede the administration of penicillin by a course of electroshock treatments.

SYPHILITIC MENINGITIS

The differentiation of the meningovascular forms of syphilis from meningoencephalitis is clinically important, as the symptoms, course and prognosis are quite different in the several conditions.

It is customary to divide syphilitic meningitis into three types, depending on the site of selective involvement.

BASILAR MENINGITIS. In this form, the inflammatory process is concentrated around the base of the brain. Basilar meningitis, which is one of the commonest forms of neurosyphilis, usually develops from one to three years after the primary infection. Thickening and infiltration of the pia mater occur in the cerebellopontine angle and in the interpeduncular space. With the infiltration of the former region, the sixth, seventh, and eighth nerves are affected, and as exudative processes occur in the latter space, the second and third nerves are involved.

Headache and perhaps dizziness appear; the patient shows mental hebetude, impairment of memory for recent events, sleepiness, difficulty of comprehension, clouding of consciousness, confusion and delirium, and occasionally stupor. The degree of disturbance of consciousness and of impairment of the more strictly intellectual functions varies roughly with the extent to which intracranial pressure is increased, as well as the degree to which the cortex is involved. The mental symptoms, if present, are usually so clearly of an organic type, are so obviously associated with neurological signs, and yield so quickly to treatment that comparatively few patients reach the mental hospital. Signs resulting from involvement of the optic nerve and of the nerves controlling the extrinsic muscles of the eye appear early and are perhaps fluctuating and inconstant at first. Ptosis, diplopia, strabismus, pupillary disturbance, papilledema, and choked disc are therefore present. Loss of corneal reflex, facial anesthesia, peripheral facial palsy, deafness, or signs of involvement of other cranial nerves may occur. Even in the absence of treatment, the mental symptoms may disappear, only to reappear shortly.

VERTICAL MENINGITIS. This type of cerebral syphilis usually occurs later than the more focal forms of syphilitic meningitis and involves the meninges of the convexity rather than of the base of the brain. Severe paroxysmal headache, often worse at night, is common. Dizziness is frequent. Sometimes the mental symptoms are so indefinite and are combined with such an ineffectiveness of personality that the patient is thought to be neurasthenic. More frequently there occur irritability, loss of ability for sustained effort, progressive hebetude, slow thinking, inertia, amnesia, and other signs of intellectual impairment. There is often much irregularity in the impairment of intellectual functions, some being retained much better than others. The nucleus of the personality is less impaired than in syphilitic meningoencephalitis. Retarded speech, brief attacks of aphasia, and other speech difficulties occur. Generalized or jacksonian convulsions may appear, and hemiplegia is not uncommon. Confusion, delirium, and stupor may be present in relatively acute cases. Paranoid reactions may exist, but here,

as in the other types of nonparenchymatous forms of brain syphilis, there is less disturbance of behavior, judgment, and social reactions, and fewer delusional trends, than in paresis.

ACUTE SYPHILITIC HYDROCEPHALUS. This is a relatively rare form of neurosyphilis and is not characterized by selective involvement. Signs and symptoms include headache, nausea, vomiting, choked disc, stiffness of the neck, and Kernig sign. The symptomatology is caused by an excessive formation of cerebrospinal fluid and an impairment of the absorption of the fluid resulting from the inflammatory reaction.

Diagnosis

Syphilitic meningitis is accompanied by a positive Wassermann reaction in both blood serum and cerebrospinal fluid. Cells are markedly increased, there is an excess of albumin, and globulin is present. Typically, the precipitation of colloidal gold is greatest in the second zone, giving what is called the "luetic curve" (0123443210).

Treatment

The treatment of meningeal and vascular forms of neurosyphilis is the same as that of the meningoencephalitic form, i.e., with penicillin. Treatment with this antibiotic is usually followed by excellent results unless vascular or meningeal inflammation has already caused permanent damage to the nervous tissue. Routine laboratory examinations of both blood and cerebrospinal fluid should be made every six months.

THE ENCEPHALITIDES

Behavioral disturbances occur both during and after the acute phases of certain viral encephalitides. Glaser and Pincus have suggested that there may exist a predilection of certain forms to affect mainly the temporal lobe and, particularly, its medial portion associated with the limbic system. Thus, both acute and subacute inclusion body encephalitides, presumably due to herpes simplex, measles, and rabies, have such a predilection. It is thought that the unique histometabolic features of the limbic system render it susceptible to such infectious processes.

The symptoms are affective, with anxiety and apprehensiveness associated with outbursts of rage or terror and their behavioral concomitants. So, too, one may note any of the exaggerated ego defenses, described earlier, to protect against such affective arousal.

While not occurring widely today, the best studied of the encephalitides is Type A, von Economo's epidemic encephalitis.

EPIDEMIC ENCEPHALITIS

An infectious disease of the brain which appeared in Rumania in 1915, but was first described and identified in 1917 by Constantin von Economo of Vienna, spread to America in 1919 and subsequently attracted much attention both because of its devastating epidemiological features and because of its remarkable symptomatological polymorphism. Von Economo termed the disease lethargic encephalitis, but as it was not always characterized by lethargy, it has become generally known as epidemic or Type A encephalitis. No cases of the acute form have been reported since 1925, but the disease continues to have clinical interest, since chronic forms are still seen.

ETIOLOGY AND PATHOLOGY. It seems to be clearly established that the etiological agent was a filterable virus, although its mode of transmission is not known. The common pathological lesion was characterized by a cuffing or infiltration of the perivascular spaces in the brain with lymphocytes. Ganglion cells degenerated and many disappeared. In the chronic cases, findings were loss and degeneration of neurons,

especially in the substantia nigra, which was grossly pigmented, and gliosis.

SYMPTOMS. The acute forms tended to fall into two ambitendent types: the hypersomniac-ophthalmoplegic and the irritative hyperkinetic.

In the first or negative type, the most conspicuous symptoms were drowsiness with gradations to lethargy, stupor and coma, slowness of intellectual function, paralytic phenomena of cortical origin, aphasia, agraphia, astereognosis and loss of limb sense caused by paralytic lesions in the parietal cortex, ptosis, strabismus, and other disturbances of the ocular apparatus, as well as other paralytic phenomena indicative of localization in the brain stem. The lethargy and other sleep disturbances were often the most striking symptoms of the acute form. The patient might remain in a deep sleep for days or weeks. If aroused, he promptly fell asleep again.

In the irritative hyperkinetic or positive type were restlessness, irritability, excitability, insomnia, jacksonian or generalized convulsive seizures, and other irritative phenomena. Hyperkinetic phenomena resulting from involvement of the basal nuclei occurred in the acute form of the disease and were of a great variety. Among them were tremors, myoclonias, and athetoid and choreiform movements.

Chronic Phase. Following the great epidemic mentioned, many patients who had survived the acute phase continued to show symptoms that at first were ascribed to residual lesions. Other patients who had supposedly recovered began, after intervals of months or years free from symptoms, to develop parkinsonism or other evidence of a continuing process.

The symptoms of a chronic encephalitis of the von Economo type are varied and depend upon the areas in which the progressive inflammatory-degenerative changes take place, although the extrapyramidal basal motor nuclei are the most frequent sites. The most common syndrome is parkinsonism (cf. Chapter 17). Tremors, tics, myotonias, and athetoid and choreiform movements are frequently observed. In addition to these dyskinesias and hyperkinesias, there may be paroxysmal symptoms such as disturbances in rate or rhythm of respiration and gasping or yawning. One of the most frequent paroxysmal phenomena is oculogyric crisis in which the eyes are spasmodically turned upward owing to the periodic activity of certain neural mechanisms. Narcolepsy and epileptic attacks may occur. Excessive flow of saliva, seborrhea, and obesity are not uncommon.

The psychic manifestations of the acute phase of epidemic encephalitis presented the general characteristics of an acute organic type of mental reaction of toxic infectious origin, viz., clouding of the sensorium and impairment of the capacity for apprehension, for elaborating impressions, and for activating memories.

Behavior Disorders. In children the chronic stage of epidemic encephalitis was often associated with serious alterations in character and behavior, the severity of which bore no relation to that of the acute stage. In some cases, in fact, it was difficult to obtain any clear history of an acute attack. The restless overactivity, emotional irritability, and impulsiveness of the early period were followed in a certain number of cases by lying, stealing, running away, cruelty, gross sexual offenses, and other behavior comparable in many outward manifestations to that exhibited by the psychopathic child. The troublesome behavior disorders shown by the encephalitic child were of every variety and usually in a setting of constant hyperactivity. The behavior or the adequacy of the social adjustment showed no correlation with the neurological signs. The child's personality, too, might be completely changed, yet his intellectual functions might not be affected.

DIAGNOSIS. The most common manifestations are tremor, rigidity, and slowness of voluntary movements, which combine to form a neurological picture resembling in some ways the hepatolenticular degeneration of Wilson and, in others, paralysis agitans. Chronic epidemic encephalitis does not, of course, show the corneal pigmentation (Kayser-Fleischer rings), a mixed static and intention tremor, and the evidence of liver disease seen in Wilson's disease.

In degenerative parkinsonism, one does not see the bizarre postures and gaits, the muscular spasms such as those of oculogyric crises, the coarse tremors, or the behavioral peculiarities frequently seen among the sequelae of epidemic encephalitis.

PROGNOSIS. From 10 to 50 per cent of the patients died during the acute phase of epidemic encephalitis, usually from respiratory paralysis. Of the survivors, roughly 75 per cent, within a period varying from a few weeks to six years, developed neurological, endocrine, or metabolic disturbances, or personality disorder.

TREATMENT. Atropine, stramonium, and scopolamine have long been used for postencephalitic parkinsonism. Artane (trihexyphenidyl) and other antiparkinsonian agents may also be used. The initial dose of Artane should be 1 mg. the first day, the amount being gradually increased, according to response, to 6 to 10 mg. daily. These drugs are more effective in relieving rigidity and associated asthenia than in controlling tremor. Today, L-dopa is prescribed for patients with severe postencephalitic parkinsonism. Its use is detailed in Chapter 19. Benzedrine sulfate, administered orally two or three times a day in doses of 25 mg., is useful in reducing oculogyric crises and for asthenia.

OTHER ENCEPHALITIDES

There are other forms of neurotropic virus infections that may cause such mental and neurological symptoms as drowsiness, confusion, stupor or coma, and other focal symptoms such as convulsions, hemiplegia, aphasia, ataxia, cranial nerve palsies, tremor, chorea, athetosis, and rigidity. Among such forms of encephalitis are St. Louis encephalitis, equine encephalitis, and the occasional cases of encephalitis associated with measles, infectious mononucleosis, various enteroviruses (Coxsackie, ECHO, polio, mumps, and herpes), and vaccination against cowpox. Residual psychiatric effects of infection with both eastern and western types of equine encephalomyelitis have been reported in the United States and Canada; also, residuals have occurred following Japanese B encephalitis contracted by United States military personnel in Japan and Korea since 1950.

In both eastern and western forms of equine encephalitis, infants and children have been more prone than adults to infection. In the former, sequelae have been virtually universal and most severe in infants under one year of age, who suffered persisting mental retardation, spasticities, and hemiplegias. Similar residuals have been observed with the western type in infants as well. In one series approximately 25 per cent of adults affected who were followed over time showed impairment of higher intellectual functions with difficulty in abstract thinking and planning.

Additional progressive chronic degenerative diseases of the brain have been attributed to viral infections, including subacute sclerosing panencephalitis, progressive multifocal leukoencephalopathy, Creutzfeldt-Jakob disease, and kuru (Gajdusek, 1977). The latter two dementias have been shown to be associated with a transmissible virus. In the case of kuru, the virus was shown by Gajdusek to be transmitted through ingestion of infected brain tissue in cannibalistic funeral rituals.

ACUTE BRAIN SYNDROME ASSOCIATED WITH SYSTEMIC INFECTION

In the mental disturbances resulting from, or associated with, the infectious diseases that have thus far been mentioned, the infecting organism is located in the brain or its coverings. In many instances, however, mental disturbance may be associated with infections in which the infecting agent does not invade the central nervous system. Such temporary disturbances may result from many severe infections, such as typhoid fever or pneumonia, and appear especially during the febrile period and most frequently in the form of delirium.

Systemic infections with herpes simplex virus have been shown to produce encephalitis that is responsive to vidarabine, a drug responsible for lowering the mortality rate in this illness from 70 to 27 per cent (Taber, 1977).

MENINGOCOCCAL (EPIDEMIC) MENINGITIS

Probably the most important form of meningitis encountered by the psychiatrist is epidemic cerebrospinal meningitis. Actually the meningitis is but part of a septicemia caused by infection by meningococci. Delirium with confusion, muttering, rambling talk, disorientation, and restlessness usually occurs early in the course of the infection, but the acuteness of the mental symptoms depends on whether the disease is fulminating, acute, subacute, or chronic in type. At first the delirium may be nocturnal or exist only when the patient is undisturbed. In the acute cases, the patient is usually restless or even noisy and violent. In unfavorable cases, a terminal coma develops, appearing very early in the fulminating forms. In the subacute case, drowsiness, confusion, and mild delirium occur. Recovery may be complete or there may be special sense deprivations accompanied, perhaps, by various types of motor paralysis and a varying degree of mental defect. The resulting mental change may consist merely of moroseness, inability to concentrate, impairment of memory, and irritability, or there may be a serious arrest of intelligence, especially when the disease occurs in infants.

The diagnosis is established by the existence of the above-mentioned signs of diffuse cerebral dysfunction with the presence of signs of meningeal irritation, including a stiff neck and Kernig and Brudzinski signs. Often a purpuric rash, hyperesthesia, and hyperalgesia are noted. Spinal puncture shows a purulent fluid under increased pressure with a predominance of leukocytes. On Gram staining, the meningococcus may be cultured or tentatively identified as a diplococcus. The sugar and alkaloids of the cerebrospinal fluid are decreased.

Penicillin G, given in divided doses at two hour intervals to 20,000,000 units, may be given intramuscularly. If the patient fails to respond, chloramphenicol is indicated, in doses of 100 mg. per kg. at four- to six-hour intervals. If there is inability to use these agents, sulfonamide should be tried. The drug prescribed should be continued for four or five days after the patient becomes afebrile.

TUBERCULOUS MENINGITIS

In both children and adults, the onset of tuberculous meningitis is usually insidious. The previously active child begins to tire easily, appears weary, is irritable, peevish, and disinclined to talk or play. Sleep is often restless and disturbed by mild delirium. As the intracranial pressure increases, difficulty of grasp, clouding of consciousness, and confusion begin to appear, and headache increases. For a time, the patient, if roused, may for a short period be fairly well in touch with his environment, although he usually resents any disturbance. Some adults exhibit an agitated confusion. As the lethargy increases, the patient is no longer capable of recognizing friends and sinks into coma.

A diagnosis of tuberculous meningitis is made in the presence of signs of diffuse cerebral dysfunction as described above, with clinical evidence of meningitis indicated by a stiff neck, Kernig or Brudzinski responses or both, hyperreflexia, patellar and ankle clonus, and Babinski reflexes. Later, such signs may disappear with deepening coma. Cerebrospinal fluid is usually clear, with slight increase in pressure. A thin coagulum will develop if the fluid is allowed to stand. Tubercle bacilli may be found in the coagulum. The cells in the fluid are increased to 25 or more per cubic millimeter. Protein is elevated while glucose content is diminished.

Current treatment with streptomycin and isoniazid has been most gratifying. Intrathecal medication is unnecessary. With adults, streptomycin in the dosage of 1.0 gm. may be given intramuscularly in two divided doses in conjunction with 8 to 10 mg. per kilogram of body weight of isoniazid by mouth. This regimen should be continued for periods of six months or more after obvious clearing of the infection. The isoniazid may be decreased by 5 mg. per kilogram as improvement ensues. The clearing of the infection is indicated by the rise in the glucose content of the cerebrospinal fluid. Para-aminosalicylic acid may be given as well. In children, 1 gm. of streptomycin is given intramuscularly with isoniazid 10 mg. per kilogram daily in divided doses. When the cerebrospinal glucose has increased, the same dose of streptomycin is given twice weekly for one or two months, followed by sulfone (Promizole) by mouth for several years (0.25 to 8 gm.). Corticosteroid in the form of prednisone, 80 mg. per day in four divided doses, should be given but after a few days or a week a stepwise reduction in dosage is indicated, depending upon the clinical course and changes in the spinal fluid. The use of intrathecal corticosteroids is advisable in those cases in which the diagnosis is made later, in order to prevent the development of fibrinous inflammatory exudates which would hasten the blockage of flow of the cerebrospinal fluid.

Close observation is required to detect signs of intoxication with isoniazid and streptomycin. The symptomatology of toxicity with isoniazid is described in Chapter 18. Deafness and other disturbances have been observed with streptomycin. It has been shown that the prognosis for survival is related to the time of initiation of therapy and the severity of the illness. The state of consciousness, the degree of abnormality detected in the electroencephalogram, and the increase in cerebrospinal fluid protein with decrease in glucose provide indicators of the severity.

ACUTE (SYDENHAM'S) CHOREA

Sydenham's chorea is now regarded as an infectious encephalitis involving both the cortex and basal ganglia. It is thought that it results from the factors which produce rheumatic fever or from similar factors. It is probably a rheumatic encephalitis and represents an exudative stage of cerebral involvement similar to the exudative changes that may be observed in the joints and heart. It seems certain that a streptococcus is involved in the process. The involuntary, jerky movements, the muscular incoordination, and the grimaces are important symptoms of the disease, but only its mental aspects will be considered here.

SYMPTOMS. In addition to an easy mental fatigability, many psychic symptoms may be associated with chorea. One of the most constant of these is an emotional instability. The choreic child becomes preoccupied, sensitive, irritable, restless, quarrelsome, and resentful of correction. Insomnia, night terrors, and sleepwalking may occur. Heedlessness and impairment of attention and concentration are frequent; there is also an apparent inability to remember. The majority of these children are tearful, cry at the slightest provocation, and are peevish and fretful. Many show a lack of concern for ordinary duties and obligations. Occa-

sionally there may be considerable depression. The facies is sometimes described as wistful in expression. Selfishness and disobedience are common, and many feel that the somewhat frequent association of behavior disorders and delinquency with the disease is more than a coincidence. Sometimes the behavior disturbances are like those following encephalitis or trauma of the head. Delirious episodes may occur. Unfortunately, the family may fail to appreciate the seriousness and significance of the disease and therefore may scold and punish the child for the emotional and other rather trying behavior characteristics. Such ill-advised treatment tends to aggravate the emotional behavior and reactions. At best, the disease often leads to undesirable defense reactions. Chorea sometimes occurs for the first time, or recurs, in young women, associated with their first pregnancy.

DIAGNOSIS. A history of rheumatism or of repeated attacks of tonsillitis and the presence of heart disease or of high fever may be helpful in establishing the diagnosis. It must be differentiated from hysteria, tics, athetoid movements, and from a restless, general hyperactivity. Sydenham's chorea usually continues for two or three months and occasionally for longer periods. Relapses are common. The disease occurs much more frequently in girls than in boys. There is much to suggest that a postinfectious encephalopathy may exist following chorea and that it is accompanied by permanent personality changes in the form of hyperkinetic or neurotic symptoms and peculiarities of character or temperament.

TREATMENT. One of the most essential requirements of treatment is physical and mental rest. The earlier the child is put to bed, the shorter, usually, will be the course of the disease. The disturbing presence of other persons should not be permitted. Treatment in a hospital away from disturbing home influences is often wise. Sodium salicylate and aspirin have long been used, the latter given in doses of 100 mg. per kg., in six divided doses by mouth in milk or after meals to decrease stomach irritation. The total daily dose should not exceed 10 gm. per day. Such sedatives as bromides, chloral, or sodium amytal may be required if restlessness is marked. Since the chorea is merely a symptom of the rheumatic infection, the treatment of the latter must be continued until all criteria indicating its arrest are satisfied.

DELIRIA ASSOCIATED WITH FEVER

Depending on their temporal relation to the febrile stage of the infection, the deliria with infectious diseases are known as prefebrile (initial) delirium, febrile delirium and postfebrile delirium.

PREFEBRILE DELIRIUM. Initial or prefebrile delirium rather infrequently develops during the incubation or prodromal period of infectious diseases, before there has been any rise in temperature. The cause of the delirium naturally cannot be ascertained until symptoms diagnostic of the infection appear. Such deliria may be marked and often imply a serious prognosis.

FEBRILE DELIRIUM. The delirium occurring during the febrile period of an infection is often spoken of as febrile delirium. The intensity of the symptoms is dependent less upon the height of the fever than upon the integration of the personality and the importance of psychogenic factors. The forms of this, as of other delirioid reactions, are determined largely by individual personality factors. In milder degrees, there may be merely restlessness, sensitivity to light or noise, and disturbing dreams. In the more severe cases, there will be hallucinations, confusion which may become extreme, indistinct muttering, stupor, twitching, carphologia, coma, and death.

POSTFEBRILE DELIRIUM. Postfebrile delirium may be merely the continuation of a previous delirium into the postfebrile period of an infectious disease, or it may be a delirium making its first appearance after the temperature has returned to normal. Consciousness is clouded to a variable degree, sometimes even to the point of stupor.

In cases showing great prostration after the fall of the fever of infection, the symptoms may be of an extreme severity, constituting what H. Weber in 1866 described as collapse delirium. In this there is clouding of consciousness or a stuporous state, and sometimes marked confusion and great motor excitement that appear to be motivated by fear and may increase even to violence and destructiveness. The stream of talk may be an incoherent flight of ideas. Emaciation and exhaustion progress rapidly, and stupor and coma may develop. Death occurs in a few days in most of these malignant types of delirium, although a few patients recover after a prolonged sleep.

Treatment of Delirium

The treatment of delirium is primarily the treatment of the infection, toxic state, or other disturbing factor that led to the reaction. This does not mean, however, that the delirium itself should not be actively treated. Occasionally a beginning delirium may be aborted by reducing environmental stimulation, applying an ice-cap to the head, the reassurance of the nurse, or the administration of chlorpromazine or a hypnotic, such as paraldehyde. Precautions should be taken to prevent accidental injury or suicide. Unless carefully supervised, the delirious patient, usually disoriented and in some cases in intense fear, may unknowingly wander into danger or may attempt to escape imaginary enemies by suicide. Measures which tend to support his contact with his environment will lessen his fearfulness and anxiety. Such measures are the presence of close family members or familiar articles from his home in the room and a quiet environment with continuous light in the room day and night. Changes of environment or of physicians or nurses are apt to be disturbing.

The patient should receive an abundance of nourishment, which should include a liberal amount of proteins and carbohydrates. Chlorpromazine given by mouth or by intramuscular injection is often effective and may be used in a single large dose before sleep. Other phenothiazines may be used as well. Multivitamin preparations are usually advisable. Sodium chloride or other salts, and glucose, administered orally or intravenously, should be given liberally, if needed, to restore normal acid-base equilibrium. Caffeine may be advisable as a cardiac stimulant. The administration of sedatives should, if possible, be limited to the night. Bromides and the barbiturates should be avoided.

POSTINFECTIOUS MENTAL DISORDERS

These disorders differ somewhat from the postfebrile deliria just described. Delirium is not usually a conspicuous symptom, consisting, when it occurs, of a mild confusion and fleeting hallucinations. Rather more typical of the postinfectious mental disorders are states of easy exhaustion, reduced attention, restless irritability, difficulty in thinking, suspiciousness, anxious depression, and hypochondriacal ideas. The patient is frequently easily frightened, over-sensitive to light and noise, morose, complaining, and preoccupied with his physical sense of weakness and debility. A state of physical exhaustion and prostration exists and is doubtless an important factor in the development of the disorder. If there has been a prolonged subvitaminosis, there may be a retrospective falsification of memory suggesting Korsakoff's syndrome, which may be complete even to the existence of polyneuritis. On rare occasions, some degree of mental enfeeblement follows.

Although the outstanding symptoms in the post-infectious disorders may be mental, their cessation depends upon the recovery of the patient's physical health.

ACUTE VIRAL HEPATITIS. With the increased recognition of acute viral hepatitis in recent years, the occasional association of mental disturbances with this infection has been observed. In some instances, this is a coincidence, as has been noted in public mental hospitals in which mild epidemics of infectious hepatitis have occurred. Occasionally, however, the infection releases a psychotic disturbance in poorly integrated personalities.

TRICHINIASIS. Trichiniasis is scarcely comparable to the infections that have just been discussed, yet mention may be made of the fact that occasionally mental disturbances occur in this disease if the young nematodes invade the cerebrum. The symptoms are those of the toxic-organic syndrome— confusion, cloudiness, disorientation, delirium, hebetude, and, at times, confabulation. Occasionally, signs of focal neurological disturbances are noted.

BIBLIOGRAPHY

Gajdusek, D. C.: Unconventional viruses and the origin and disappearance of kuru. Science, 197:943–947, 1977.

Glaser, G. H., and Pincus, J. H.: Limbic encephalitis. J. Nerv. Ment. Dis., 149:59–67, 1969.

Hurdle, E. S.: Neurosyphilis. In Conn, H. F. (ed.): Current Therapy 1976. Philadelphia, W. B. Saunders Co., 1976.

Infections of the Nervous System. Proceedings of the Association for Research in Nervous & Mental Diseases. Vol. 44. Baltimore, Williams & Wilkins Co., 1964.

Merritt, H. H., Adams, R. D., and Solomon, H. C.: Neurosyphilis. New York, Oxford University Press, 1946.

Mulder, D. W., Parrott, M., and Thaler, M.: Sequelae of western equine encephalitis. Neurology, 1:318–327, 1951.

Taber, L. H.: Herpes simplex encephalitis treated with vidarabine. Arch. Neurol., 34:608–610, 1977.

Von Economo, C.: Encephalitis Lethargica. Its Sequelae and Treatment: Translated by K. O. Newman. New York, Oxford University Press, 1931.

13

BRAIN SYNDROMES ASSOCIATED WITH CONVULSIVE DISORDERS (EPILEPSY)

"As for this disease called divine, surely it too has its nature and causes whence it originates, just like other diseases, and is curable by means comparable to their cure."

Hippocrates

J. HUGHLINGS JACKSON
(From Roback, A. A., and Kiernan, T.: Pictorial History of Psychology and Psychiatry. New York, Philosophical Library, 1969, p. 87.)

The term *epilepsy*, derived from the Greek word meaning to seize or fall upon, has been applied to a group of explosive reactions formerly believed to constitute a disease *sui generis*. The name has persisted, although it is now generally agreed that epilepsy is not a disease entity but a symptom complex characterized by periodic, transient episodes of alteration in the state of consciousness, which may be associated with convulsive movements or disturbances in feeling or behavior, or both.

PATHOPHYSIOLOGY

Physiologically, epilepsy may be regarded as a disturbance in the electrophysiochemical activity of the discharging cells of the brain, a disturbance that may be produced by a variety of irritative stimuli impinging upon them from within or from without. This physiological disturbance may be expressed in the form of (1) a change in electrical potential as recorded in the electroencephalograms, (2) varied disorders of consciousness, (3) disordered functioning of the autonomic nervous system, and (4) convulsive movements or psychic disturbances. The nature of the disturbance of the internal milieu which, in so-called idiopathic epilepsy, alters the activity of the cortical neurons or of basal gray matter and precipitates an abnormal discharge of electrical energy in the brain remains insufficiently elucidated.

The capacity of the neuron to respond to external:internal stimuli, that is, its irritability, is transformed into a functional discharge when a stimulus reaches the nerve cell from a surrounding region. Under certain circumstances, cells may respond spontaneously. In general, excitation of neurons has been classified into those that are gradual and expressive of local excitation, which may be graded and signify a polarized membrane potential, or those that hyperpolarize to an explosive depolarization leading to a discharge to other cells. The resting membrane potential of a nerve cell is now known to be related to the ionic compositions of intra- and extracellular fluids. An abundance of potassium ions exists within the cell, but very few sodium ions are found; the reverse relationship exists in the intracellular fluid. As for anions, sulfate and protein exist within the cell and the chloride outside.

It is generally believed that the distribution of ions (polarization) remains fairly constant, yet the asymmetric arrangement of this distribution endows the nerve cell membrane with the property of storing electrical energy. Changes in membrane permeability for particular ions may raise or lower the capacity of the ionic battery within and without the cell. Thus, potassium chloride acts to produce a negative charge on the inside of the membrane. It is postulated that an ionic pump exists. So there is a high electrochemical gradient, which has the effect of a driving force for sodium ions concentrated on the exterior of the membrane; the sodium pump mechanism drives out surplus sodium ions that penetrate the cell. At the same time, there is thought to exist a potassium pump to maintain the equilibrium as this ion moves outwards.

It is the opinion of many that epilepsy occurs only when nerve cell membrane is damaged. At the synapses—the interfaces between the neurons—the explosive discharge may occur either as an excitatory postsynaptic potential (epsp) or as an inhibitory postsynaptic potential. Synaptic inhibition may take place directly through the discharge of inhibitory postsynaptic potential or through discharges in the central nervous system by inhibitory interneurons, which function as reversing pole changers. So, too, indirect synaptic inhibition may occur when excitatory impulses are blocked by opposing impulses and voluntary inhibition. Thus, in some epileptics, attacks may be prevented by competitive inhibition.

It is now postulated that pathophysiological processes affecting the inhibitory neurotransmitter gamma-aminobutyric acid (GABA) may be the significant element in leading to the explosive epileptic discharge. It is known that convulsive hydrazides inhibit glutamic acid decarboxylase and the enzyme synthesizing GABA in the brain; that the dietary deficiency of B_6 in infants is related to deficiencies of pyridoxal phosphate, as coenzyme glutamic acid decarboxylase; and that such convulsive drugs as picrotoxin and bicuculline block the inhibitory action of GABA at the postsynaptic membrane sites. Furthermore, some drugs that inhibit the later metabolism of GABA tend to have anti-epileptic actions.

Meldrum has reviewed in detail the data and the theoretical postulates relating to potential inhibition of gamma-aminobutyric acid as causative of the convulsive discharges. He makes the point that it is presently not possible to explain the precise site of action of the drugs most widely used clinically as anticonvulsants (now classified into some six groups) in relation to change in membrane potential, modification of explosive discharge, or inhibition by GABA in the synaptic cleft.

Nor have any explanations been given in the past for brain damage that takes place after repetitive seizures. Wasterlain has suggested, from his studies of those with epileptic seizures without motor manifestations, that cerebral protein synthesis is inhibited.

Precipitating Factors

Clinicians tend to recognize two major etiological categories of epilepsy: the idiopathic and the symptomatic. The idiopathic category contains the vast majority of individuals denoted as suffering from epilepsy. Both appear to arise spontaneously and to occur in the absence of other disorders of the nervous system. The idiopathic epileptic sufferer usually gives a history of commencement of the disorder in childhood or adolescence; a family history of the condition may be discovered. Therefore, it is thought that a genetic predisposition exists for the convulsive state.

Symptomatic epilepsy is the term used to denote seizure disorders in which an identifiable irritant lesion in the nervous system exists—either a current or previous tumor, previous encephalitis, or an existing metabolic disorder.

Many factors may precipitate the convulsive seizure in susceptible individuals. (See Table 13–1.)

Although it appears that, in the majority of patients, the attacks are not precipitated by obvious external stimulation, in some they are always induced by a specific type of physical or perceptual stimulation. The arousal of anxiety, either through some immediate interpersonal conflict or through fantasy of such a conflict, often acts as a precipitating factor. In patients whose attacks originate this way, psychiatric management may be helpful.

TABLE 13–1 Factors That May Precipitate Epileptic Seizures in Susceptible Individuals

Hyperventilation
Sleep (usually within the first 30 minutes or shortly before awakening)
Sleep deprivation
Sensory stimuli
Flashing lights
Reading-speaking, coughing
Laughing, touch, pain
Sounds (music, bells, etc.)
Trauma
Hormonal changes
Menses, puberty, adrenal steroids
ACTH
Fever
Emotional stress
Drugs
Phenothiazines, analeptics
Tricyclic mood elevators, butyphenones
Antihistamines, alcohol
Excessive anticonvulsants

(From Pincus, J. H., and Tucker, G. J.: Behavioral Neurology. New York, Oxford University Press, 1974.)

In other cases, specific sensory stimuli act as the precipitants.

Sudden sounds, occasionally listening to music, or flickering lights (as when driving through an avenue of trees in sunlight, watching sunlight on water or television, rapidly moving the hands before the eyes) may induce seizures. Seizures induced by flickering lights are now designated as *photogenic epilepsy.* In some instances, only complex visual stimuli prove excitatory. Prolonged reading has initiated an attack, which commences with "clicking" or movement of the jaws. Some patients are able to terminate such an attack if they discontinue reading upon initiation of the jaw "clicking."

In female epileptic patients, the occurrence of a seizure in association with the menstrual period is common, but it is not known how the premenstrual hormonal interplay acts to precipitate attacks. The final metabolic derangement that results in a seizure is probably not the same in all patients or even the same at all times in any one patient. If the equilibrium of the internal milieu is in delicate balance, an attack may be precipitated by a minor physiological disturbance, such as that produced by hyperventilation.

Electroencephalography

Although the occurrence of an abnormal discharge of energy in the cerebral cortex coincident with epileptic attacks has only relatively recently been proved by electrical methods, Hughlings Jackson (1834–1911), the father of clinical neurology, conceived the idea nearly 100 years ago that such a discharge must be the basis of epilepsy. In 1929 Hans Berger of Jena discovered that by perfecting technical methods of amplification he could record through the intact skull the changes in electric potential already known to accompany cortical activity. The electroencephalogram (EEG) indicates alterations in electrical, and thus physiological, activity within the brain. Further study showed that normally about 10 electrical impulses originate in the brain every second, and that when these currents are recorded in the electroencephalogram they show a pattern of voltage and frequency (height and rate of the waves) more or less characteristic of the individual.

In epilepsy there are paroxysmal bursts of abnormal cortical activity, with resulting changes in the rhythmic pattern of the EEG, indicating abnormalities in both rate and voltage of these currents. For this reason Lennox introduced the term "paroxysmal cerebral dysrhythmia" as applicable to epilepsy. Although abnormalities are to be observed in the electroencephalogram in many conditions other than epilepsy, in this disorder these abnormalities tend to assume certain patterns. Further, these patterns are distinctive for certain types of seizures. The electroen-

cephalogram reveals the presence of these dysrhythmic discharges but fails to reveal their pathogenesis. When the focal discharging lesion is in the parietal, occipital, or frontal lobes, the symptomatology is largely neurological; if the disorder is in one or both temporal lobes, the symptomatology is largely psychiatric or that of psychomotor epilepsy.

Electroencephalographic studies of cerebral epileptic foci indicate that occipital foci are most common in infancy, rolandic between the ages of 3 and 6, and temporal between the ages of 5 and 12. The clinical course varies with each type. In children, bilateral and multiple foci are frequent and the discharges synchronous. Such foci may remain stable over time, migrate, or spread. It is often difficult to relate the clinical phenomenology to the observed electroencephalographic foci. The morphology of the electrical discharges also may change over time. Thus, poorly organized "spike-and-wave" forms present at birth become more clearly evident after a few months of life. Tonic-clonic discharges become organized later, clonic between the ages of 3 and 6 months and tonic between 18 months and 2 years.

It is generally estimated that 5 to 10 per cent of normal persons exhibit abnormalities of their electroencephalograms, similar to those seen in epileptics. It is believed that such persons are predisposed to epilepsy, although the disturbance in cortical electrodynamics as represented by the EEG is not so serious as to result in seizures, unless the cerebrum suffers some pathological alteration. It has also been found that about 85 per cent of persons with a history of epilepsy show abnormalities of electroencephalographic rhythm during a 15-minute recording in the interval between convulsions, as compared to 10 per cent in the average population. When such abnormalities of the EEG exist in the interparoxysmal period, they tend to be of the same general type as those observed in the form of seizure from which the patient usually suffers. These types will be described later. There are, however, undoubted epileptics in whom abnormal tracings have never been obtained, even by repeated examination, using the techniques of recording available today.

It will thus be seen that the electroencephalogram has its limitations. Although the finding of seizure discharges creates a presumption that clinical seizures have occurred or will occur, a negative report (no seizure discharges) does not rule out epilepsy. This is because (1) seizure discharges can be present in the depths of the brain and not appear in standard recordings from the surface of the head, and (2) discharges may occur so infrequently that there is almost no likelihood of one occurring during the relatively short period of recording required in a routine examination. In the waking state, but more so during sleep, seizure discharges occur, as evidenced by the electroencephalogram, that are not immediately associated with clinical symptoms. Eighty per cent of patients with a history of convulsive epileptic seizures have nonconvulsive seizure discharges while asleep. When not asleep, only 35 per cent of this group have subclinical seizure discharges.

Frequency of Epilepsy

It is generally estimated that the incidence of epilepsy in the United States is 1 in 200 of the population. Because of the development of new drugs in recent years for the treatment of the disorder, fewer patients than formerly require institutional care. The incidence in males is slightly greater than in females, probably because of the greater frequency of head trauma in the male both at birth and in adult life.

Age of Onset

Idiopathic epilepsy may develop at any age, but a majority of the cases appear between the ages of 10 and 20. Not a few occur before 10 years of age, but the first appearance of a seizure after 20 requires study by all known methods before the conclusion is reached that it is idiopathic. Infantile convulsions appearing without obvious cause should be regarded with apprehension. It is reported that infantile convulsions associated with fever or other physical disturbances increase the chances of epilepsy five times.

Inheritance

The exact degree to which heredity influences the development of seizures is controversial. The prevailing opinion today is that the inheritance of epilepsy is multifactorial (polygenic) across the whole series of cases. In some instances the genetic role is significant; in others exogenous factors provide the predominant factor in predisposition and precipitation of the cortical convulsive discharge. It is now thought that the genetic factor is expressed principally in the tendency to produce spontaneous paroxysmal cerebral electrical discharges with an inclination for spreading of such discharges. Epilepsy is more common among relatives with nonfocal electroencephalographic abnormalities than those with focal distortions. An electroencephalographic examination of parents of epileptics revealed that these parents had abnormal brain waves much more frequently than did control persons. The presence of abnormal brain waves in the parents of epileptics is presumably evidence that the cerebral dysrhythmias associated with epilepsy are inheritable and that parents who show such cortical dysrhythmias are "carriers" of the disorder. Sixty per cent of the near relatives of noninstitutionalized epileptics had dysrhythmia and 2.4 per cent of them had a history of seizures. Of the controls, 10 per cent showed dysrhythmia. Of course, none had seizures.

It has been found that, among identical twins, idiopathic epilepsy occurs eight times more frequently in both individuals than it does in both of fraternal twins. It is estimated that epilepsy occurs about five times more frequently among near relatives of idiopathic epileptics than it does in the general population. The existence of a predisposition to the disease in the child of an epileptic is often demonstrable in the form of cerebral dysrhythmia. There is also a striking likeness of brain-wave abnormalities in epileptics with the same heredity. A person afflicted with epilepsy who marries a nonepileptic may, however, expect only one child in 50 resulting from the union to suffer from convulsions.

The psychiatrist is frequently asked about the advisability of marriage for the epileptic, or the probability that his or her children may inherit the disease. The following factors tend to minimize the chances of the disease in the child of an epileptic: a family history devoid of epilepsy or migraine for the spouse as well as the patient, a minimal abnormality of their electroencephalograms, some acquired condition that is at least partially responsible for seizures, late onset of the illness, and a normal mental endowment. The genetic factor in epilepsy is probably no greater than it is in many other common diseases.

Types of Seizures and Their Symptoms

Three major types of clinical seizures are usually described: grand mal, petit mal, and psychomotor seizure or psychic equivalent. Heredity is of importance in determining the pattern of seizure. The seizures of all types are irregular and unpredictable. There are many variants of epilepsy which, because they depart so far from the "usual" forms of seizures, are apt to escape recognition.

Loss of consciousness with or without convulsive spasm is the criterion of epilepsy. It is probably not sufficiently appreciated that in many attacks consciousness is not lost but is merely disturbed. The patient may be aware of all that is going on around him, may hear and understand what is being said, but is for the time being unable to collect his thoughts or reply to a question.

The occurrence of a major epileptic fit may suddenly render clear the meaning of obscure minor events that may have existed for years. These may have been myoclonic, local muscle spasms, defects of attention, "absences," dreamy states, or brief periods of mental inhibition when mental processes seemed to be arrested and the mind a blank. The form that epilepsy takes depends not so much on the pathological features of the lesion as on its site and the violence of the neuronal discharges in the neighborhood of the lesion and the extent of their spread to the rest of the brain.

GRAND MAL. The grand mal seizure with its intense spontaneous neuronal activity is the most dramatic of the epileptic manifestations. Seizures of this type tend to be accompanied by an increase in speed and voltage of brain waves, which are recorded in the electroencephalogram as sharp spikes, often at the rate of 25 per second.

Aura. From a moment to several seconds before the loss of consciousness, about half of the patients with a grand mal type of attack have an *aura,* or warning, that a seizure is immediately imminent. The aura is not really a premonition but the first manifestation of the neuronal discharge. The form of the aura depends primarily upon the site of the epileptogenic focus. Lesions of the precentral region generally give rise initially to motor phenomena and of the post-central region to sensory phenomena. The aura may consist of numbness, tingling, or uncomfortable sensations, of a feeling of distress in the epigastrium, perhaps passing up toward the head, or of a hallucination of the special senses, such as flashes of light, certain noises, or olfactory hallucinations. The aura is usually affectively unpleasant. Sometimes the aura is motor in nature and consists of a twitching or stiffness in a certain group of muscles preceding the loss of consciousness.

Tonic Phase. The loss of consciousness is sudden and complete. The patient falls at once, and, as he rarely has any opportunity to protect himself, he may sustain serious injuries. As he falls, the entire voluntary musculature goes into a continuous contraction, remaining in this *tonic* phase from 10 to 20 seconds. The muscles of the chest often contract at the same time as do those of the larynx; air is thereby forcibly expelled and results in the peculiar sound known as the epileptic cry. At first the face is pale, but as the muscles rigidly contract, the superficial veins become engorged. At the same time the chest becomes fixed and the aeration of the blood ceases, thus adding to the cyanosis of the face. During this tonic phase and for a variable period afterward, the pupils are dilated and do not react to light, and the corneal reflex is absent. The Babinski reflex is present and the tendon reflexes are absent or decreased. During the general muscular contraction, the bladder is often emptied and occasionally the rectum.

Clonic Phase. The tonic stage is followed by intermittent or *clonic* muscular contractions, at first rapid but gradually growing less frequent. If at this time the tongue happens to fall between the teeth during a relaxation, it may be bitten when a clonic contraction follows. As respiration returns, the saliva, which could not be swallowed, may become intermixed with air and thus appears in a foam, perhaps tinged with blood.

Coma. In the *postconvulsive coma*, the pupils are rigid, tendon reflexes are absent, respiration is stertorous, the face is congested and covered with perspiration, and the lips are cyanosed. If an arm or leg is lifted and then released, it drops heavily as in a state of flaccid paralysis. If left undisturbed, the patient may sleep for an hour or two, complaining of headache, fatigue, and perhaps of a painful tongue on awakening. As the patient emerges from the coma, he is often bewildered and may perform semiautomatic acts, move aimlessly about, exhibit chewing movements, fumble at his clothing, or attempt to remove it. Sometimes clouded states persisting for a few days may develop after several successive convulsions. They are more frequent in men than in women.

Some patients have convulsions during sleep as well as in their waking hours, while in some patients the convulsions are always nocturnal. Many have their seizure just as they are falling asleep. It should be remembered that occasionally an epileptic who is subject to nocturnal seizures is suffocated by burying his face in a pillow during a convulsion.

Status Epilepticus. Sometimes a patient may pass from one seizure into another without intervening recovery of consciousness. This condition, known as *status epilepticus,* always involves danger to life. It is sometimes precipitated by abrupt withdrawal of medication, particularly if the patient has been receiving phenobarbital. It may follow alcoholism or excessive fatigue, but frequently no precipitating factor is evident. It is not rare after cerebral operations on epileptics. If preventive measures are not taken, the temperature may rise to dangerous heights. The patient may become profoundly exhausted, lapse into coma, and die from cardiac dilation or pulmonary edema.

PETIT MAL. Abortive seizures of various degrees and types occur, in all of which there is usually some disturbance of consciousness. The most frequent of the minor forms is that of petit mal, which is characterized by a transient interruption of the stream of consciousness. The electroencephalogram of petit mal consists of a slow, round wave followed by a quick, sharp spike. Groups of these alternately slow and fast waves occur three times a second. It is the most distinctive of any of the epileptic brainwave records. The details of these minor attacks differ widely among individual patients, but the most frequent form consists of a loss of consciousness lasting from 5 to 30 seconds. They begin and end abruptly and are without warning or sequel.

The patient does not fall. He may become pale, with his posture fixed, his eyes staring and expressionless; his attention cannot be secured; he may suspend his occupation and, through loss of muscle tone, drop whatever article may be in his hand. Usually there is a little rhythmic twitching of eyelids, eyebrows, or head. After a few seconds, consciousness abruptly returns and the patient resumes his activities. Most patients recognize that an attack has occurred, but some remain unaware of this "absence."

The onset of petit mal is usually between 4 and 8 years of age. After 18 years of age it tends to disappear or to be replaced by other types of seizure. Petit mal attacks usually occur much more frequently than grand mal seizures. From one or two to a few hundred attacks may occur in a day. The two forms frequently coexist. Two of every three children with petit mal subsequently develop grand mal.

Many children with petit mal are often socially and emotionally maladjusted. This maladjustment often appears to be explained on the basis of an impaired parent-child relationship, which affects the child's personality formation. The impaired relationship apparently grows out of a conscious or unconscious parental rejection. The lack of basic security occasioned by the impaired parent-child relationship tends to extend and pervade all relationships. Sometimes the child, believing that all adults are like his parents, and that all experiences will be frustrating, develops a pattern of antagonism and rebellion.

Usually included in the petit mal form are myoclonic twitches in which single contractions of the flexor muscles of the arms occur without loss of consciousness, as well as *akinetic attacks* in which there is a sudden falling with muscular hypotonia. Like the classic petit mal, the latter two forms show a three per second spike and slow-wave rhythm of electrical discharge. Formerly the term pyknolepsy was given to what was believed to be a special type of seizure allied to petit mal. It is now considered to be a true petit mal. The name should therefore be dropped.

In recent years a significant increase in excretion of urinary amino acids has been found in many with petit mal.

PSYCHOMOTOR EPILEPSY. Of greatest importance to the psychiatrist is psychomotor epilepsy, since it is characterized by trancelike attacks and confusional episodes which often lead to its misdiagnosis as schizophrenia or psychoneurosis. It is much more common in adults than in children, although in minor forms of the condition the attacks are very similar to those of petit mal. They differ from petit mal, however, in various ways. The attacks last longer, from one-half to two minutes, and are frequently associated with movements of the muscles concerned with mastication, swallowing, or speech, so that the patient may smack his lips, chew, or make incoherent verbalizations. Also, the clouding of consciousness is greater than in petit mal, with amnesia persisting for one-half to several minutes after the attack. In other instances, brief episodes of automatic thought formations of a delusional nature and auditory or visual hallucinations may take place. With the former, the patient may report only an amorphous repetitive and ill-defined thought, a crystallized thought percept, or an internally located voice, usually in the head but sometimes in the abdomen or elsewhere or placed in the external environment. The visual hallucinations also may be apprehended either internally or externally. Finally, the electroencephalographic record is not similar to that of petit mal and its focus is the anterior pole of the temporal lobe.

Some patients describe brief affective

states of fear, vague alarm, terror, rage, and occasionally well-being or pleasure. The patient's behavior is appropriate to his mood. Other episodic but sustained moods may be in the form of extreme irritability, depression, ill humor, or bad temper. Sometimes the psychomotor seizure takes the form of a clouded state characterized by confusion, bewilderment, excitement with hallucinations, outbursts of violence, or, occasionally, ecstatic moods with religious exaltation. Clinically, the clouded state suggests a delirium with liberation of aggressive and, occasionally, self-destructive impulses. Acts of violence may be committed in these automatisms and may be of a strikingly brutal nature, the patient pursuing his crime to a most revolting extreme.

Epileptic furors are characterized by their suddenness, absence of premeditation and precaution, and amnesia for them. The extraordinary degree of discrimination and judgment displayed in the psychomotor attack often gives the patient's acts a misleading appearance of deliberation. It may be difficult to accept the fact that the author of the crime was not responsible for his acts. Usually these psychomotor seizures continue for only a few minutes, but they may go on for hours or even days. Sometimes the seizure may assume the form of a fugue. Occasionally the patient may report feelings of loneliness, strangeness, or typical "déjà vu" phenomena as if he had undergone the same experience in the dim past. Psychomotor seizures may occur in pure form, but in many cases grand mal seizures may also be present. Their frequency increases with age.

Rodin recently studied a large number of patients with psychomotor epilepsy in regard to the aggressive behavior. Of 700 such patients, only 34 were found who had committed aggressive acts. The profile he discovered of the aggression-prone individual with psychomotor epilepsy was of a young man, with lower than average intelligence and a long history of behavioral difficulties dating back to school age,

when this person generally did not have religious interests. To Rodin, psychomotor epilepsy did not appear to be the significant variable relating to the aggressive acting out. The question needs further study.

Many children with temporal lobe epilepsy exhibit outbursts of catastrophic rage. In a recent study of children with this behavioral expression, it appeared that such rage attacks had beginnings in three separate age periods. Those associated with hyperkinesis commenced before the fourth birthday. The majority of children without hyperkinesis but with the episodic rage attacks had onset between 7 and 11 years of age. Onset after that was not usually associated with outbursts of rage. In the first group, many remitted until late adolescence or early adulthood. It seems probable that disappearance of this type of behavior with epilepsy may be related to increasing inhibition due to cortical control and to superego development.

In most patients with temporal lobe discharge, sex behavior tends generally to be marked by a lack of libidinal and genital arousal, although a few have episodic expressions of excessive drive.

The episodic behavior disturbance of many with temporal lobe convulsive discharges has been likened to the schizophrenic reaction. Yet serious affective disturbances do occur as well. From his studies of a series of cases, Flor-Henry suggests that temporal lobe epilepsy of the dominant lobe predisposes to psychotic behavior; this is most likely to be schizophrenia-like. That of the nondominant lobe is more likely to be associated with affective reactions. Yet frequent psychomotor attacks seem to suppress such abnormal behavior.

Probably to be included among the psychomotor epilepsies is the syndrome known as *epilepsia cursiva* ("running fit"). This is an episodic alteration of awareness associated with running. Consciousness may be clouded to a variable degree. Sometimes the running fit occurs immediately after a grand mal seizure. There may or may not be an aura. The duration of the running is brief. Frequently one finds a history of conflicts with members of the family that seem to have acted as precipitating factors.

The distinguishing feature of the electroencephalogram in the psychomotor seizure is the presence of spike seizure discharges at the rate of four to eight a second. It is believed that the focus of electroencephalographic activity is the anterior part of the temporal lobe. There is an increasing tendency to use the term *temporal lobe epilepsy* as a synonym for the psychomotor type, or to refer to the seizures characterized by hallucinations, memory disturbances, and automatisms as "temporal lobe" in preference to "psychomotor." By stimulating the cortex of the temporal lobe in patients with temporal lobe epilepsy, complex hallucinations, vivid memories, and dreams that were often identical with the content of the seizures were produced.

A 10-year-old girl was brought to the clinic by her mother after she had suffered a number of episodes of loss of consciousness. These were described by the mother in the following way.

She awakened with a headache, seemed listless, and then was noticed by her mother to develop a twitching movement of the left side of her mouth and eyes. Her arms assumed an "odd," stiff position and became unresponsive. This condition persisted 5 minutes, to be followed by another similar episode 10 minutes later in which she urinated and defecated. These attacks were followed by five others preceded by an aura of "fear"—as the child stated, being "scared." The patient had total amnesia for the attacks.

Physically, no abnormalities were noted. An electroencephalogram showed a right occipitotemporal focus of high voltage, 31 per second activity aggravated by hyperventilation. Other studies were negative. Psychiatric and psychological examinations at this time showed no pathology. She was treated with phenobarbital and Dilantin in increasing doses, with reduction in the occurrence of attacks and in their intensity.

For years she reported only daily brief episodes of "scary feelings." It was necessary to increase the dosage of the anticonvulsant medication, and Mebaral was prescribed as well. At age 14 she was admitted to the hospital with an acute delirious state due to barbiturate overdosage. Following this hospital admission, her mother noticed a character change in that she became resentful and hostile, expressed the atti-

tude she was disliked, and seemed depressed. Then "slow spike waves" were observed over the left temporal region during periods of sleep.

At this time she commenced to have episodes of loss of consciousness, occurring without warning and with subsequent amnesia, in which she suddenly rushed away from her place of work, walking rapidly and aimlessly through the streets, impulsively removing her stockings and placing them in her purse or suddenly staring blankly, smacking her lips, giggling foolishly, and then mumbling incoherently. High-dosage combinations of various anticonvulsants failed to control these seizures. Due to her progressive social disability and withdrawal, in spite of medical therapy, a craniotomy with resection of the right temporal lobe was performed when she was 20 years old. Following the operation she was free of seizures and resumed her work on treatment with Dilantin alone.

Other Forms of Epilepsy

Much rarer, yet of importance to the clinician, are those unusual forms of epilepsy manifested by alimentary symptoms, which present as attacks of violent abdominal pain, followed by loss of consciousness and incontinence although on occasion loss of consciousness does not take place. Episodic attacks of pain, lateralized to one or the other side of the body, may sometimes be the only manifestation of the epileptic discharge. In some instances, the painful convulsive disorder has been associated with dysphasia, right-sided sensory extinction, dysgraphesthesia and poor touch localization. In others, the lateralized pain in the limbs may be associated with muscular spasms. The majority of such unusually painful convulsive discharges are symptomatic of an underlying tumor, generally localized in the parietal lobe.

It now appears that breath-holding spells associated with alteration of consciousness and postural tone and sometimes with loss of sphincter control, postictal exhaustion, and sleep also are frequently associated with electroencephalographic abnormalities. As Pelc found, children with such attacks developed syncope 18 per cent of the time, temper tantrums 43 per cent, and seizures 20 per cent.

Behavior Disorders with Cerebral Dysrhythmias

Some children without clinical evidence of the classic forms of epilepsy, but with cerebral dysrhythmia on encephalogram suffer behavior disorders. Such children may complain of headaches, be moody, have temper tantrums or attacks of rage, scream or cry unreasonably, and appear distractable, overaggressive, fearless, or lacking in shyness. Their attention span is often limited, and in formal psychologic tests wide scatter is often seen—a finding common in the brain damaged. Children with such symptoms should be examined electroencephalographically. They respond well to treatment with d-amphetamine, methsuximide (Celontin), or acetazolamide (Diamox).

Narcolepsy

The term *narcolepsy* was introduced in 1880 by Gélineau to describe a "rare neurosis characterized by an invincible need for sleep, ordinarily of short duration, occurring at longer or shorter intervals of time, often several times a day, forcing the subject to fall to the ground or to lie down in order to avoid falling." Gélineau's tetrad of symptoms includes narcolepsy, cataplexy, sleep paralysis, and hypnagogic hallucinations. It has been described as a variant of epilepsy. However, this is not the case, and it should be considered as a special clinical type in a group of sleep disorders. The syndrome narcolepsy is more common than originally thought and has been reported as occurring in an incidence of 0.03 per cent. Seven per cent of patients with the narcoleptic syndrome have cataplexy, 24 per cent have sleep paralysis, and 30 per cent have hypnagogic hallucinations. Only 30 per cent have all four of the symptoms. The syndrome has not been seen before the age of 7, but its onset may occur after the age of 30.

Narcolepsy is characterized by a sudden, irresistible desire to sleep. Regardless of the situation in which he may be placed or of the activity in which he may be engaged, the patient falls fast asleep. The sleep is apparently natural; the patient may be awakened, but the period of sleep usually lasts from seconds to 30 minutes. After he has awakened the patient usually states that he feels refreshed. Nocturnal sleep may be very deranged, with muscle twitching, cardiorespiratory irregularity, frequent awakening, and many shifts in sleep phases. The condition is most frequent in young male patients. Sexual impotence, obesity, and lymphocytosis are often associated symptoms. It is generally believed that some anatomical pathologic condition, the result of localized encephalitis, trauma, or neoplasm, exists in the gray matter surrounding the third ventricle at the level of the ocular nuclei or in the hypothalamus. Lesions of the hypophysis may be secondary.

Cases supposed to be psychogenic have been reported. Psychometric studies in certain groups of patients with the narcoleptic syndrome have shown a common background of emotional conflict. The individuals felt themselves to be caught in a life pattern they resented, but felt obligated to conform to it. Frustrated in their efforts to achieve an autonomy in another pattern of their own choosing because of their dependent emotional attachments, those affected develop the narcoleptic complex which relieves the anxiety of open conflict.

Many consider narcolepsy as a syndrome that may occur in several pathological states (see Table 13–2). It is probably not a disease *sui generis*. Electroencephalographic records do not show the cerebral dysrhythmia of epilepsy. When the individual is alert, the electroencephalogram appears normal. On the other hand, a large proportion of patients with the syndrome demonstrate the electrical patterns of REM (rapid eye movement) sleep in connection with narcoleptic attacks and at the beginning of nocturnal sleep, suggesting that the attack represents an aber-

TABLE 13–2   Causes of Pathological Sleepiness

SYNDROME	DISORDERS	EEG
Narcoleptic syndrome	Narcolepsy	Early onset of REM in night sleep
	Cataplexy	
	Sleep paralysis	
	Hypnagogic hallucinations	
Narcolepsy alone	Single symptom of the narcoleptic syndrome	Normal REM distribution in night sleep
	Psychogenically determined	
	Myxedema	
	One extreme of vigilance	
Secondary narcolepsy	Encephalitis (lethargica)	Focal features
	Cerebral tumors	
	Cerebrovascular disease	
	Other pathologies	
Kleine-Levin syndrome	Somnolence for prolonged periods	During sleep phase I-II NREM
	Hyperphagia	
	Males predominantly if not wholly affected, onset in adolescence with eventual recovery	
Pickwickian syndrome	Obesity	Waking EEG or phase I-II NREM
	Apnea	
	10–15 seconds sleep with CO_2 retention	
South African trypanosomiasis	Persistent somnolence with disturbed sleep rhythm in terminal illness	

(Modified from Parkes, J. D., and Marsden, C. D.: Br. J. Hosp. Med. *12*:325, 1974.)

rant diurnal expression of paradoxical sleep. Since REM sleep is specifically inhibited by *d*-amphetamine, it is not surprising that this drug is the treatment of choice. Because of the EEG findings, some regard narcolepsy as a reversible dysfunction of the pontine system and not as a paroxysmal convulsive disorder.

Yoss et al. have reported that the pupillographic studies of those with narcolepsy show characteristic spontaneous changes. In darkness the untreated narcoleptic has smaller pupils, which frequently change in size as waves of pupillary constriction and dilatation occur. In contrast, the nonnarcoleptic presents large pupils that seldom change in size. It is thought that these pupillary changes reflect decreased wakefulness. They are reversed when patients are treated with the am-

phetamines. Pupillography may be used to assess the appropriate therapeutic dosage of such agents.

Narcolepsy does not respond to bromides, phenobarbital, or other sedatives, but, as mentioned, it is controlled by *d*-amphetamine sulfate (10 to 60 mg. twice daily) or racemic amphetamine sulfate (10 to 80 mg. twice daily). Methylphenidate hydrochloride (Ritalin) given in 5-mg. doses also has been useful. If taken after midday, such drugs may produce insomnia.

DIFFERENTIATION FROM HYPERSOMNIA. Since this disorder may have psychogenic determinants or may be confused with hypersomnia as a symptom of an emotional disturbance, careful psychiatric evaluation is indicated in all suspected cases. Psychogenic hypersomnia differs in that the patterns of drowsiness or sleepiness last for several hours rather than for 15 to 30 minutes and are often associated with a history of disturbed nocturnal sleep, obesity, and the personality characteristics of passivity, with anxiety aroused by any situation threatening expression of criticism or anger to others. Such situations, particularly when the emotional outburst might be directed toward the person to whom they hold a strong dependent relationship, are the usual precipitant of the hypersomniac period. In hypersomnia, in contrast to narcolepsy, the amphetamines are unlikely to be useful, but their use may enhance the possibility of working out psychotherapeutically the psychodynamic conflict. Psychotherapy is reported to be helpful in certain instances. The variants of hypersomnia are discussed in Chapter 28, Disorders Usually First Evident in Infancy, Childhood, and Adolescence.

Cataplexy

Apparently related to narcolepsy are the paroxysmal attacks known as cataplexy in which, under the influence of emotional excitement, there are paralysis of voluntary movements and postural collapse of the whole body. The patient suddenly loses power and tone of all skeletal muscles, his knees give way, and he sinks helplessly to the ground. Many patients are unable to speak during the episode, although consciousness is fully preserved. Laughing, in particular, appears to provoke an attack, although anger, anxiety, or annoyance may act similarly. Narcolepsy and cataplexy are probably allied reactions, since cases of a transitional nature, including narcoleptic attacks provoked by emotion, are observed. The attacks of narcolepsy and cataplexy constitute what is often spoken of as the narcoleptic-cataplectic syndrome.

Recent studies of cataplectic attacks have shown that the electroencephalogram may remain similar to the normal baseline awake EEG, but that there occur short periods in which it is impossible to distinguish between REM sleep and cataplexy. At the same time, the electromyographic tracings show an abrupt drop of muscle tone during the cataplectic attack, involving both agonist and antagonist muscles. On the other hand, electrooculographic recordings demonstrate that patients are able to move their eyes during a cataplectic attack (see Fig. 13–1).

Treatment of cataplexy is similar to that of narcolepsy. Cataplectic seizures

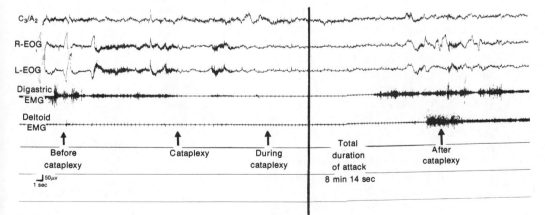

Figure 13–1   Recording of a cataplectic attack. EMG activity was completely suppressed during cataplexy. There was no change in the EEG from the precataleptic record. No EEG abnormality has ever been seen during any type of cataplectic attack. (From Guilleminault, C., Wilson, R. A., and Dement, W. C.: A study on cataplexy. Arch. Neurol., 31:255–261, 1974.)

will disappear when the amphetamines are given in sufficiently large dosage to render the pupillogram similar to that seen in normally alert persons. Shapiro has reported, however, that clomipramine in doses of 25 to 75 mg. a day totally eliminates all attacks of cataplexy, as well as the other symptoms of the Gélineau tetrad. This tricyclic compound is more effective than imipramine.

Epileptic Deterioration

Although the mean intellectual functioning of those with idiopathic epilepsy tends, as a group, to be less than that of their unaffected relatives, their intellectual functioning still falls within or close to the average. In fact, a third of the group exceed the performance of their unaffected relatives on appropriate tests. Nevertheless, continued and uncontrolled seizures are considered to impair intellectual functioning.

In a certain number of epileptics, the range of interests narrows as the convulsive reaction continues. A psychic slowness develops; attention, intellectual processes, and emotional responses become increasingly dull; and comprehension and memory become impaired. The patient suffers from a poverty of ideas, shows a tendency to stress the trivial as much as the important, to become circumstantial in his ideational expression, to disregard the interests of others, and to become selfish, affectively self-satisfied, boastful, lazy, and careless in appearance; his facies is characterized by expressionless vacuity. His speech comes to be slow and monotonous, with but little variation as to accent or tone, and his vocabulary becomes limited.

The degree to which dementia progresses, if it occurs, varies greatly. In extreme cases this dementia is great, the patient existing at a purely vegetative level, having no interest in, and no intelligible communications with, his social environment. Dementia is a much more frequent outcome in those who develop epilepsy in early childhood than in those in whom it appears in later years. Deterioration occurs less frequently if the patient was mentally normal at birth and if his seizures are of the petit mal or of infrequent grand mal types. It is more frequent in institutionalized patients than in the noninstitutionalized ones. Of the latter, about one third show some degree of mental impairment, although in only about 10 per cent is it so gross as to be immediately evident.

It is possible that deterioration may, in fact, be the result of the repeated anoxia and increased intracranial pressure that accompany repeated convulsions. In part it may be the result of the prolonged toxic effect of drugs; in considerable part it may be a response to the problems and situations which the very nature of the disease creates. The social and intellectual ostracism from which the epileptic often suffers, the deprivation of normal educational advantages, his feelings of inferiority, and his discouragement and hopelessness lead to a contraction of interests and to an impoverishment of personality.

The following case is fairly illustrative of the type of epileptic that enters institutions for mental disorders:

T. C. was admitted to a state hospital at the age of 31. He was described by his family as having a rather bad temper, being somewhat stubborn and inclined to boast. At 17 he began to suffer from mild seizures with loss of consciousness but without generalized convulsive movements. Not until age 27 did seizures occur more than two or three times a year. At that time they began to occur once or twice a month. At age 29 the seizures became more severe, with marked convulsive movements and longer periods of unconsciousness. Because of a seizure at his place of employment, he lost his position in an ice factory. Unable to find other employment, the patient became somewhat depressed, worried, irritable, and "hard to get along with." His seizures became more frequent and severe.

One day following a period of moody preoccupation, during which he seemed unaware of his wife's presence, he said to her, "Catherine, I've done good today. I've made my fortune." He then added, "Call the doctor and the priest, I'm afraid I am going to die." That night he walked about all night, talking constantly about becoming rich, quoted passages from the salesmanship instructions issued by a concern for which he had recently attempted to canvass, and paid little heed to his environment.

The following night he became so uncontrollable that, at his family's request, he was taken to the police station, and on the following day, he was committed to the state hospital. When he was brought to the institution, he shouted in a loud tone, "I drank a lot. I don't need that fellow. I thought an awful lot of that fellow. I think an awful lot of my mother. I told them plenty. I said, 'No! No!" At intervals he struggled violently to escape from the two officers who were holding him. When asked any questions he would shout, "None of your business."

On examination at the hospital, he was noted to be a tall, ungainly individual, his large ears standing out prominently nearly at right angles to his skull. The conformation of his facies suggested that he was a biological variant. He remained clouded for about six weeks, at times apparently hallucinated, sometimes preoccupied, mute, and having to be tube-fed, again talking in a loud, angry tone. He was usually to be found in his room, frequently with his prayer beads hanging from his mouth, often nude, and when approached would spontaneously make such remarks as "I'm—I'm trying to solve the problem. I'm trying to find the solution. Irish! Irish! Captain I, an eye for an eye, and a tooth for a tooth. I've tried to save my soul."

After this prolonged clouded state, the patient remained clear for two months, occasionally suffering from a convulsion. Four months after admission he again became cloudy. At times he was stuporous, at times excited, and on several occasions attempted suicide. Nine months after admission he was returned to his family, and for seven months he remained well except for occasional light convulsions. At the end of that period, while attending church, he suddenly arose during the services and began to pray loudly. He held a crucifix high above his head, and when led from the building, seemed much confused. The patient then returned to the hospital, where the clinical course was much like that of the first residence.

DIAGNOSIS

If the attack is witnessed by the physician or by a trained observer, the diagnosis of the typical grand mal, with its unconsciousness and sequence of tonic cramp, cyanosis, clonic convulsive movements separated by intervals of gradually increasing length, stertorous breathing, perhaps automatic activity, stupor, and hebetude, is comparatively easy. In the case of petit mal or of an atypical and incompletely developed seizure, the diagnosis may be difficult. One should inquire for a history of migraine and of fainting attacks, and ascertain if any disturbances of consciousness have been accompanied by biting of the tongue, relaxation of the sphincters, or injury to self. If observed by the physician, the discovery of fixed, dilated pupils, of loss of the corneal reflex, and the presence of a Babinski reflex may confirm suspicion as to the epileptic nature of the paroxysm. The diagnosis of epilepsy is, however, not always easy. Attacks of loss of consciousness, of muscle twitching, of feelings of faintness, or of unreality will usually suggest epilepsy, but often a diagnosis must be based on retrospective facts found by careful questioning of the patient and observers.

The electroencephalogram is of assistance in establishing a diagnosis, but the evidence supplied by it must be supplemented by clinical observation. It must be remembered that about 5 per cent of the persons who never suffer from seizures of any kind show minor dysrhythmia in the EEG, and occasionally the EEG in such normal persons may be characteristic of the records made in epileptics between attacks. This is particularly true in the relatives of epileptics. In rare instances an epileptic with definite clinical seizures may in intervals between convulsions show an entirely normal EEG. It is estimated that the chances are nine in ten that any disturbances of consciousness occurring in a person with a positive EEG are epileptic. Activation of the abnormal electrical potentials may be induced occasionally by hyperventilation, or by small doses of metrazol intravenously. It is of interest that mescaline and diethyl lysergic acid diethylamide (d-LSD-25) are incapable of activating the attacks or the typical electroencephalographic abnormality in those who have temporal lobe seizures.

Hysterical patients with attacks resembling epilepsy usually have normal electroencephalograms. The seizures of the hysteric occur in the presence of others, and there is often some fairly obvious gain or domination to be secured by the paroxysm. The hysterical person rarely injures himself in a seizure. It is important to remember the makeup of this type of individual, with his tendency to histrionic poses and simulation of symptoms. Although there may be a history of an emotional disturbance just prior to an epileptic convulsion, any dramatic staging of a seizure points strongly toward hysteria. The hysterical seizure is usually grotesque in its manifestations, lacks the characteristic "march" of phases seen in epilepsy, and is not accompanied by ocular signs indicated in the previous paragraph, by sphincter incontinence, Babinski sign, or so deep a loss of consciousness. In hysteria there is never any biting of the tongue as in epilepsy.

There may be difficulty in the differential diagnosis of temporal lobe epilepsy and hysterical amnesic periods with automatism. The presence of psychogenic factors and the absence of the psychomotor type of electroencephalogram will point to the latter. It is often said that no epileptic attack is "motivated" and that no motivated act is epileptic.

Also to be differentiated from the temporal lobe or psychomotor seizure are acute anxiety attacks manifested in the *hyperventilation syndrome*, particularly common in those with anxiety phobic neurosis. The hyperventilation syndrome and its diagnosis are described fully in Chapter 24.

Syncopal attacks associated with progressive slowing of the electroencephalogram may be induced in a high proportion of healthy adults by the Weber or Valsalva maneuver. In this maneuver the subject inhales deeply and then strains against a closed glottis as forcefully and long as he is able. This syncopal attack appears similar to others induced in situations of acute hypoxia that have been observed experimentally in low-pressure chambers; such attacks

might occur in airplane travel with sudden decompression. They differ from grand mal in that the subject suddenly loses consciousness and muscular tonus, sliding to the floor. Then there occur several bilaterally synchronous coarse clonic movements, generally in the upper limbs. With more severe attacks there may be extensor thrusts of the legs, but there is no *tonic phase*.

The diagnosis of syncope versus epilepsy is often complex. The loss of consciousness in epilepsy is primarily caused by paroxysmal discharges within the brain, while in syncope it results primarily from a fall in blood pressure. In syncope a cause—postural, emotional, or physical—seems apparent. In syncope there is a fairly long warning. The patient often comments "I feel faint," and adopts some protective action, such as sitting. Pallor and hot or cold sweating are apparent. Consciousness usually returns without any confusion or sequel except sweating. The epileptic's loss of consciousness is usually followed by drowsiness and frequently associated with headache. In a Stokes-Adams attack, syncope and a convulsion may be closely linked. Here a rapid fall of blood pressure caused by cardiac arrest produces convulsions through cerebral anemia.

COURSE AND PROGNOSIS

Today the average epileptic enjoys an incomparably brighter prognosis than he did 25 years ago. Credit belongs mainly to the widespread availability of the electroencephalograph for diagnosis, to an ever expanding group of nonsedative drugs that in many cases suppress epileptic phenomena, and to an increasing education of the public concerning the disorder with resultant lessening of the rejection and social stigma from which the epileptic suffers.

With temporal lobe epilepsy, the outlook for improved clinical, social, and psychological adaptation in those resistant to drug treatment is best following temporal lobectomy. In such cases, as

Taylor and Falconer report, the best outcomes were associated with pathological evidence of mesial temporal sclerosis in which there had occurred early onset of epilepsy associated with febrile convulsions. Overall, improvement relates most closely to relief from seizures.

Most epileptics are intelligent and normal persons apart from their attacks and are quite able to earn a living. In a large percentage of the patients seen by the private physician, deterioration does not occur at all; if it does, it is but slight. The prognosis is least favorable if the onset is in childhood. The prognosis for recovery is worse in petit mal than in grand mal, but, contrary to general opinion, the mental life does not suffer as much in petit mal.

To a considerable extent, the prognosis is dependent upon the promptness of diagnosis and treatment. Both rate and extent of deterioration vary greatly, but tend to be influenced by the age of onset, the frequency of seizures, and the effort made to maintain wholesome, constructive, satisfying, unselfish interests and constant employment. The emotional handicap produced through faulty attitudes such as shame or overprotectiveness on the part of the patient's family may operate against recovery. In its more malignant forms, the deterioration may proceed until the patient lives at an essentially vegetative level. A few epileptics become psychotic and require psychiatric care. However, with the anticonvulsant drugs now available, complete control or total abolition of grand mal seizures can be secured in 80 per cent of the patients.

TREATMENT

General Management

One of the fundamentals of treatment is the maintenance of optimum physical health. Physical and mental activities should be encouraged, especially those that afford a combination of muscular exercise, intellectual interest, and pleasure. It should be remembered that conscious or unconscious parental rejection may seriously warp the developing personality of the child. He should not be the object of oversolicitous fear and overprotection. Petit mal attacks, even if frequent, should not prevent attendance at school, nor should infrequent major attacks. The epileptic patient should be employed, but at a job where his own safety or that of others would not be jeopardized should he suffer a seizure. If possible, safety should not be purchased at the cost of active participation in life.

Although it is usually necessary to raise the seizure threshold through medication, psychiatric treatment should not be omitted, particularly when there is evidence that emotional arousal precipitates repeated seizures. Recently, behavioral therapy in the form of an "extinction technique" has been successful in the treatment of a case of "musicogenic" epilepsy. Emphasis should be placed upon the relief of emotional or other psychic stress and upon the promotion of a normal life within the limits of the patient's psychobiological equipment. He should be given an opportunity to preserve his self-respect, develop his abilities, and maintain social usefulness. Many epileptics tend to daydream and to indulge in idle dissipations that increase the frequency of their seizures and hasten deterioration. The epileptic should be encouraged to plan his own work, studies, and activities. Sustained work is often a difficult habit for him to establish but one of great importance.

There has often been an unnecessary restriction of the epileptic's diet. Ordinarily he should eat the same food as other members of the family, but attacks may be precipitated by hypoglycemia. The patient should therefore not go too long without food. The ingestion of an abnormal amount of fluid at one time may precipitate an attack. Food should be moderate in amount, and alcohol should be avoided.

Each state has enacted legislation to control the issuance of licenses to drivers with epilepsy.

Drug Therapy

The aim in treatment is to give medicine that will counteract the explosive tendency of the brain cells. For over 60 years bromides, first suggested in 1857 by Sir Charles Locock, constituted the principal form of medication. They have now been largely displaced by newer drugs.

There are now six groups of drugs most widely used clinically as anticonvulsants: the hydantoins (diphenylhydantoin); the barbiturates (phenylbarbitone, primidone); the oxazolidinediones (trimethadione); the succinimides (ethosuximide, phensuximide); the sulfonamides (acetazolamides); and the benzodiazepines (diazepam, nitrazepam). Today, the actions of these various agents in terms of the effects on neurotransmission remain unclear. Table 13–3 lists the commonly used anticonvulsants, the epileptic phe-

---

TABLE 13–3 Commonly Used Anticonvulsants

1. *Diphenylhydantoin* (Dilantin, phenytoin) is one of the most commonly used drugs, particularly in adults, for the control of grand mal, focal, and psychomotor seizures. It is essentially ineffective in petit mal and myoclonic seizures. Determination of the serum level of diphenylhydantoin in medical centers where the test is available provides a valuable guide to the adequacy of therapy; levels between 10 and 20 μg./ml. are usually considered to be within the therapeutic range. There is considerable variation in the dosage necessary to achieve this — in some adults 200 mg. is sufficient, others require 600 mg.
2. *Phenobarbital* is the most commonly used of all seizure medications and is one of the most effective. It may be effective in all types of seizure disorders, including petit mal. The therapeutic serum level for phenobarbital is usually the same as for diphenylhydantoin though tolerance is demonstrated by some patients who have been receiving the drug for long periods of time, by which time they can tolerate much higher levels. Most hospitals are equipped to perform determinations of serum barbiturates routinely in their laboratories.
3. *Primidone* (Mysoline) is a barbiturate-like compound which has its greatest use in the control of psychomotor seizures. Though many neurologists feel it is more efficacious than phenobarbital in controlling psychomotor seizures, there is little published evidence indicating that this is so.
4. *Ethosuximide* (Zarontin) is the drug of choice in petit mal. It has little other use but may occasionally help out in minor motor seizures.
5. *Acetazolamide* (Diamox) is a carbonic anhydrase inhibitor and may be effective in all seizure disorders, especially in minor motor and petit mal seizures. High doses (30 mg./kg.) are often necessary for seizure control.
6. *Diazepam* (Valium) has been effective in some minor motor seizure disorders when taken orally, but is most useful when used intravenously in the treatment of status epilepticus. It has become the drug of choice to be used if intravenous barbiturates fail in treating status epilepticus.
7. *Trimethadione* (Tridione) is a fairly toxic compound useful for the same disorders as is ethosuximide.
8. *Quinacrine* (Atabrine) is an antimalarial drug, which is sometimes effective in petit mal and minor motor seizures. Although very safe, it turns the skin yellow and thus makes the patient look "different."
9. *Paraldehyde, Chloral Hydrate, Amytal,* and the short-acting barbiturates are sedatives useful only in status epilepticus.
10. *Steroids and ACTH* are useful in infantile spasms and juvenile minor motor seizures at times. In other seizure types and at other ages, these are epileptogenic.
11. *The Ketogenic Diet* is useful in difficult cases of minor motor seizures, although it is somewhat complicated and unpalatable. It may completely stop seizures in 50 per cent of cases in which all other drugs have failed.

(From Pincus, J. H., and Tucker, A. J.: Behavioral Neurology. New York, Oxford University Press, 1974.)

nomena for which they have proven most useful, and some of the doses in which they may be given.

In addition to these drugs, in recent years there have been successes in the use of imipramine, given in a dosage of 1 to 3 mg. per kilogram for patients with petit mal and minor motor seizures, who had failed to respond to conventional anticonvulsive medications. Earlier it was mentioned that clomipramine is a useful agent in the treatment of the narcoleptic syndrome and, particularly, cataplexy.

Also, clonazepam has been found to have potent anticonvulsant effects on patients with temporal lobe epilepsy. This new benzodiazepine has been found to be effective in noncontrollable cases of petit mal. The optimal anticonvulsive dose ranges from 0.1 to 0.2 mg. per kilogram, while the maximum tolerable dose is 1.5 to 2 mg. per kilogram.

Phenobarbital, or phenylethylbarbituric acid, first recommended by Hauptmann in 1912, is one of the drugs most widely used for raising the convulsive threshold of the epileptic. In persons 12 or more years of age, one may begin with a dose of 0.1 gm. once a day. In adults this may, if necessary, be increased to 0.3 to 0.4 gm., administered in divided doses. In children under five, 0.05 gm. may be used. If the seizures are nocturnal, it may be given at bedtime. If they are diurnal, it may be taken in the morning. Should seizures be frequent and severe, the patient may receive the drug three times a day. Even ordinary doses may produce drowsiness at the beginning of its use, but this effect usually disappears in a few weeks. Toxic doses may produce apathy, slow mental reactions, ataxia, slow speech, and muscular weakness. A sudden discontinuation of its use usually leads to an increase in the number of seizures and even to status epilepticus. Phenobarbital, nevertheless, is usually the most effective drug in alleviating grand mal seizures and least frequently produces toxic symptoms. It is of little value in petit mal, which should usually be treated by Tridione. Methylethylphenylbarbituric acid (Mephobarbital or Mebaral) acts similarly to phenobarbital but is more effective with certain individuals. For adults the dosage is 0.3 to 0.6 gm. daily.

In 1937 Merritt and Putnam introduced sodium diphenylhydantoin sodium, generally known as Dilantin, an anticonvulsant that has proved of great value. Not being a hypnotic, it does not cause drowsiness, as is so often the case with phenobarbital. The usual dose is a 0.1-gm. capsule three times a day. The maximum amount that adults tolerate is approximately 0.6 gm. daily. As Cocks and his colleagues have found, it is possible to give the total necessary dose of phenytoin once daily, preferably before sleep. If necessary for the control of seizures, the dose may be increased somewhat. In psychomotor seizures, it is the most efficacious of the antiepileptic drugs and in grand mal may be effective in some cases in which phenobarbital has failed. There· is apparently a synergy between phenobarbital and Dilantin that makes the combination more effective than when either drug is used alone. In toxic amounts, Dilantin causes gastric distress, a symptom that usually ceases after one or two weeks of treatment. Less frequently, it causes dizziness, ataxia, tremors, nystagmus, diplopia, drowsiness, and hyperplasia of the gums. Its sudden, complete discontinuance may induce status epilepticus.

Continued usage of phenytoin may be associated with folic acid deficiency, particularly in hospitalized epileptic patients receiving anticonvulsive drug therapy, as Kariks and his colleagues have shown. They recommend that repeated serum folic acid and phenytoin estimations be made in all epileptic patients receiving prolonged anticonvulsive therapy with this agent.

Initially all patients with this form of convulsive disorder should undergo trials on phenobarbital and Dilantin and the combinations of the two. In instances where seizures remain uncontrolled or where several forms of seizures occur, other drugs and their combinations may be tried.

Another anticonvulsant now rather extensively used is Mesantoin. The usual doses are 0.1 gm. three times a day for children and 0.2 gm. for adults. Since it may be toxic, blood counts should be made once a month. Combined with Dilantin or phenobarbital, it may be effective in cases resistant to other drugs. Its combination with Tridione is to be avoided.

Trimethadione, introduced in 1945 under the trade name Tridione, has been found to produce gratifying results in the treatment of petit mal but may aggravate other types. The starting dose of trimethadione is 0.3 gm. three times a day for adolescents and adults. Gradual increases in dosage are carried out until a therapeutic effect is obtained, the optimal dosage being usually between 1.5 and 2.7 gm. daily. In children under two years of age, 0.15 gm. two or three times is the initial dosage, with increments of 0.15 gm. Toxic symptoms in the form of skin eruptions, "glare phenomenon," a photophobia in which objects appear to shimmer and vision is blurred, drowsiness, dizziness, and headache may occur. Toxic action on the blood-forming elements of the bone marrow followed by death has been reported. For some persons, paramethadione dimethylethyloxazolidine dione (Paradione) is more effective than Tridione. N-Methyl-α-phenylsuccinimide (Milontin) may also be used for petit mal, though it is less effective than the diones. For adults, the dose is 0.9 to 3.0 gm. daily, and for children, 0.6 to 1.8 gm. daily.

Another drug which has been increasingly employed in therapeutically resistant convulsive disorders since 1949 is Phenurone (phenacetylcarbamide). This may be used in both grand mal and psychomotor seizures, but seems to be more effective in the latter type. It may be given in 500 mg. doses three times a day. After the first week of treatment, an additional 500 mg. may be taken on rising. One half the adult dose is recommended for children from 5 to 10 years of age. It seems to be especially useful in combating drowsiness and lethargy in patients who are affected in this manner by phenobarbital and other drugs. Patients receiving Phenurone should be watched carefully for the possible development of serious damage to the hematopoietic system and to the liver.

Primidone (Mysoline) is safer than Phenurone and is reported to be of much value in the treatment both of psychomotor epilepsy and grand mal. Dosage range is from two to eight 250-mg. tablets a day.

Acetazolamide (Diamox) has been reported useful for all convulsive forms. The initial dosage is 0.25 gm. three times daily by mouth. This dosage then is gradually increased by a similar increment up to 1.0 gm. daily. Since hematuria and agranulocytosis have been observed during its administration, urinalyses and blood counts should be made recurrently.

It should be kept in mind that the phenothiazines and the aminodibenzal antidepressants (imipramine and its analogs) may activate epileptic foci and probably are contraindicated in the treatment of those with convulsive disorders even when there are severe behavioral accompaniments.

Patients with all types of seizures show some improvement under anticonvulsant therapy, and those with focal and grand seizures respond best. Phenobarbital and Dilantin usually give the best results in seizures of those types.

Because of the danger of status epilepticus, anticonvulsive drugs should not be withheld abruptly. The occurrence of status epilepticus constitutes a medical emergency and is best handled in a hospital. Prolonged status epilepticus may lead to irreversible cerebral changes and even death.

The patient must be placed under heavy sedation and kept in that condition for 24 hours. Diazepam (Valium) has been recommended recently as a highly effective drug for this condition. It may be administered in one or more intravenous or intramuscular injections of 10 mg. in 100 ml. In some instances 100 mg. has been given in a slow intravenous drip daily.

Others prefer to use a solution of amobarbital sodium, 1.0 gm. in 20 ml. for injection, given slowly intravenously at the rate of 1 or 2 ml. per minute until the seizure stops and deep sleep results. Sleep is maintained with a continuous intravenous drip of 0.5 gm. amobarbital sodium (Amytal) in 500 ml. of isotonic saline solution. The patient should be turned every half hour to prevent hypostatic and aspiration pneumonia. Mild Trendelenburg position is maintained, and mechanical aspiration of secretions is often necessary. Oxygen is given through a nasal catheter when indicated. Additional sedation may be obtained without depressing respiration with the use of paraldehyde suppositories, each containing 4.5 ml. of paraldehyde, repeated every four hours.

Surgical Therapy

In those patients with severe temporal lobe epilepsy difficult to control by pharmacological agents, consideration should be given to surgical excision of the convulsive focus. These operations have little likelihood of success when electroencephalographic studies show approximately equivalent seizure discharges in both temporal lobes. The best outcome from temporal lobe excisions occurs when epileptiform activity is delimited by the EEG to one temporal lobe or appears in the opposite side only as synchronous, lower-voltage transmitted waves. Following the operation, patients customarily are continued on medication for at least one year. If control is maintained, an attempt is made then to reduce dosage gradually. Postoperative mortality in patients with uncomplicated epilepsy

has been less than 1 per cent. Large excisions accompanied by vascular complications occasionally are followed by quadrant defects in the visual fields, or occasionally by hemiplegia or aphasia. Approximately two thirds of patients treated in a large series had satisfactory results, the majority being free of seizures and the remainder suffering only isolated attacks.

BIBLIOGRAPHY

Clinical Features

Ferguson, S. M., Rayport, M., Gardner, R., Kass, W., Weiner, H., and Reiser, M. F.: Similarities in mental content of psychotic states, spontaneous seizures, dreams, and responses to electrical stimulation in patients with temporal lobe epilepsy. Psychosom. Med., 31:479–498, 1970.

Flor-Henry, P.: Schizophrenic-like reactions and affective psychoses associated with temporal lobe epilepsy: Etiological factors. Am. J. Psychiatry, 126:400–404, 1969.

LaPresle, J., and Sicard, J. P.: L'épilepsie digestive. Sem. Hôp. Paris, 48:2231–2238, 1972.

Millechap, I. G., Jones, J. D., and Etheridge, J. E., Jr.: The abnormal aminoaciduria in petit mal epilepsy. Neurology, 16:569–572, 1966.

Needham, W. E., Bray, P. F., Wiser, W. C., and Beck, E. C.: Intelligence and EEG studies in families with epilepsy. J.A.M.A., 207:1497–1501, 1969.

Pelc, S.: Contribution á l'étude des spasms du sanglot. Rev. Neurol., 123:29–41, 1970.

Rodin, E. A.: Psychomotor epilepsy and aggressive behaviour. Arch. Gen. Psychiatry, 28:210–213, 1973.

Scott, D. F.: Psychiatric aspects of epilepsy. Br. J. Psychiatry, 132:417–430, 1978.

Wilkenson, H. A.: Epileptic pain: an uncommon manifestation with localizing value. Neurology, 23:518–520, 1973.

Pathophysiology

Jovanovic, U. J.: Psychomotor Epilepsy: A Polydimensional Study. Springfield, Ill., Charles C Thomas, 1974.

Meldrum, B. S.: Epilepsy and gamma-aminobutyric acid-mediated inhibition. Int. Rev. Neurobiol., 17:1–36, 1975.

Pincus, J. H., and Tucker, G.: Behavioral Neurology. New York, Oxford University Press, 1974.

Wasterlain, C. G.: Inhibition of cerebral protein synthesis by epileptic seizures without motor manifestations. Neurology, *24*:175–180, 1974.

Narcolepsy and Cataplexy

Goldstein, N. P., and Giffin, M. E.: Psychogenic hypersomnia. Am. J. Psychiatry, *115*:922–928, 1957.

Guilleminault, C., Wilson, R. A., and Dement, W. C.: A study on cataplexy. Arch. Neurol., *31*:255–261, 1974.

Parkes, J. D., and Fenton, G. W.: Levo (−) and dextro (+) amphetamine in the treatment of narcolepsy. J. Neurol. Neurosurg. Psychiatry, *36*:1076–1081, 1973.

Parkes, J. D., and Marsden, C. D.: Narcolepsy. Br. J. Hosp. Med., *12*:325–329, 1974.

Shapiro, W. R.: Treatment of cataplexy with clomipramine. Trans. Am. Neurol. Assoc., *99*:99–102, 1974.

Yoss, R. E., Moyer, N. J., and Ogle, K. H.: The pupillogram and narcolepsy. Neurology, *19*:921–928, 1969.

Treatment

Cocks, D. A., Critchley, E. M. R., Hayward, H. W., et al.: Control of epilepsy with a single daily dose of phenytoin sodium. Br. J. Clin. Pract., *2*:449–453, 1975.

Forster, F., et al.: Modification of musicogenic epilepsy by the extinction technique. Trans. Am. Neurol. Assoc., *90*:179, 1965.

Fromm, G. H., Amores, C. Y., and Thies, W.: Imipramine in epilepsy. Arch. Neurol., *27*:198–204, 1972.

Kariks, J., Perry, S. W., and Wood, D.: Serum folic acid and phenytoin levels in permanently hospitalized epileptic patients receiving anticonvulsant drug therapy. Med. J. Aust. *2*:368–371, 1971.

Masland, R. L.: A controlled study of clonazepam in temporal lobe epilepsy. Acta Neurol. Scand., *60*:49–54, 1975.

Taylor, D. C., and Falcone, M. A.: Clinical, socioeconomic and psychological changes after temporal lobectomy for epilepsy. Br. J. Psychiatry, *114*:1247–1261, 1968.

14

BRAIN SYNDROME ASSOCIATED WITH INTRACRANIAL NEOPLASM

"... in the human brain the parts are not equipotential and even the defect of intelligence does not, as is sometimes stated, depend only upon the quantity of cerebral tissue removed or destroyed."

Percival Bailey

TREPHINED NEOLITHIC SKULL
(From The Bettmann Archive, Inc.)

Brain tumors with accompanying mental disorder are more frequent than indicated by the diagnostic statistics provided from hospitals. Summaries of the total incidence of intracranial tumors found at autopsy in patients in mental hospitals in the United States give a figure of 3.7 per cent, against that of 2.35 per cent for patients without diagnosed psychiatric disorder in general hospitals. Men-ingiomas are found much more frequently in autopsies performed on patients in mental hospitals than in the general hospitals. The number of brain tumors discovered at necropsy is much larger than the number diagnosed correctly ante mortem. Probably in only a minority of early cases of brain tumor are the mental symptoms so pronounced as to form a conspicuous part of the clinical picture of the neoplasm, although there are few cases that remain entirely free of manifestations of mental disorder. There is need to recognize that the initial symptoms of tumor may be masked by pre-existing or concomitant mental and emotional disturbances. There is a great statistical disparity in both the frequency and the nature of mental symptoms in brain tumor. Clouding of consciousness and disturbance of memory occur most frequently. There is, however, no symptomatic picture considered characteristic of a brain tumor.

Symptoms

The genesis, pathological structure, neurological signs, and electroencephalographic records of brain tumor will not be discussed. Generally speaking, the symptoms and signs of brain tumor fall into three groups: (1) signs of increased intracranial pressure; progressive impairment of consciousness and energy with headache, vomiting, and papilledema; (2) focal neurological symptoms and signs determined by the location of the tumor; (3) psychiatric symptoms, which tend to fall into two types.

The psychiatric symptoms of the first type, which often appear early, perhaps before those caused by increased intracranial pressure or focal neurological symptoms determined by the site of the tumor, are psychogenically determined by the characteristics of the patient's premorbid personality structure and the particular stresses, conflicts, and defenses. In some cases the first and, perhaps for a time, the only symptoms may be psychiatric and consist of accentuations of personality tendencies. Some patients show a loss of inhibitions with blunting of social or moral sense, egotistic tendencies, shamelessness, and even gross sexual or other misbehavior.

Psychiatric symptoms of the second group stem from cerebral damage incident to the tumor and to increased intracranial pressure.

Among early symptoms may be absent-mindedness, later becoming an obvious memory defect, especially for recent events, easy fatigability, a raising of the threshold of consciousness, disturbances of sensorium, difficulty of grasp, impairment of calculation and of reasoning abilities, defective attention, hebetude, drowsiness, confusion, and disorientation. Psychomotor retardation is not uncommon. Fluctuations of consciousness may occur. Sometimes the patient may confabulate, as in Korsakoff's psychosis. Loss of libido is common.

Temporal lobe tumors are frequently mistaken for schizophrenic disorders. Often they present paroxysmal motor, affective, and perceptual disturbances. These may be crude and disagreeable olfactory or gustatory hallucinatory experiences. The disturbances are characteristically repetitive, and although the patient is absorbed in, and may suffer anxiety with, the experience, he is usually capable of perceiving the existence· of both the present environment and the hallucination. Either then or later he is able to distinguish the experience as ego alien—outside his usual personification of self-functioning. "Déjà vu" phenomena occur with such tumors, but more frequently patients describe emotional reactions and transitory experiences of strangeness, loneliness, or dreamy states. Also noticed are episodic and short-lived affective states consisting of feelings of dread, terror, or overwhelming fear. Some patients have reported either unexpected angry affect or feelings of well-being.

Motor automatisms may take place in which the patient may carry out sudden aggressive or assaultive actions or other complex performances for which he has no memory.

Frontal lobe tumors are particularly likely to produce symptoms affecting the functioning of personality over time. Slow-growing meningiomas compressing the frontal lobe are among the most frequently undiagnosed tumors of the brain that produce symptoms of a psychiatric nature. Tumors in this area produce insidious and subtle changes in personality functioning.

A flattening of affect, coupled with a growing apathy concerning personal and business affairs, is frequent. Other emotional disturbances are instability, irritability, depression, and anxiety. Euphoria and facetiousness ("Witzelsucht" of Oppenheim) are probably a little more frequent in tumors of the frontal lobe but are not specific for any one location in the brain. It well may be that this lightness of spirit and tendency to be witty are merely a defense reaction against the threat to the integrity of the organism by the destructive growth.

Occipital lobe tumors are associated more frequently with unformed simple visual hallucinating experiences, which consist of flashes of light or of colored lights. Moving objects may be hallucinated. Complex visual and auditory hallucinations are more frequent in tumors of the temporal lobe. Olfactory hallucinations in the form of disagreeable odors may occur in the case of tumors on the undersurface of the hemispheres.

Parietal lobe tumors may produce sensory and agnostic disturbances, particularly related to body recognition, left and right discrimination, acalculia, and other symptoms included in the Gerstman syndrome. Horton has emphasized that, as a part of minor parietal lobe dysfunction, the careful examiner will discover as well a transitional deficit to relate—that is, failure to use other persons or objects for emotional support and, in fact often a denial of this need and even resentment of the object or person. This symptom should be recognized as a representation of lack of awareness (anosognosia) and psychologically is often identified as "denial."

It is generally agreed that tumors of the *corpus callosum* are accompanied by intellectual impairment, difficulty in concentration and in thinking, and failure to respond to stimuli, particularly to auditory stimuli.

The conspicuousness of the symptoms and, to some extent, their nature are determined by the rate of growth of the tumor. In the case of slowly growing meningiomas, there may be simply a slowly developing mental deterioration. In rapidly developing gliomas (spongioblastomas), there may be an active delirium suggesting a toxic state, with confusion, disorientation, and perhaps stupor. In those that develop unusually rapidly, both the mental and neurological signs may suggest an inflammatory lesion.

Diagnosis

If increased intracranial pressure appears suddenly and develops rapidly, mental symptoms are usually produced and may be severe. If pressure increases slowly, there may be no mental symptoms. Many tumors, because of their site and the particular structures they injure, produce neurological signs of great localizing value. Mental symptoms by themselves have, however, little or no value in localizing a tumor of the brain. It is stated that mental symptoms are nearly twice as frequent in the case of supratentorial tumors as in infratentorial growths. If the brain tumor causes convulsions, difficulty may arise in evaluating the mental symptoms, with the result that they may be attributed to idiopathic epilepsy. Convulsions occur in about 8 per cent of the cases and may be either of grand mal or petit mal type. Seizures are rare in cerebellar tumors and most frequent in those of the parietal and temporal lobes.

Difficulty in diagnosis may also arise if the patient suffered from cerebral arteriosclerosis prior to the appearance of the mental symptoms. If the patient suffers from sensory or motor aphasia or from apraxia by reason of the location of the tumors, the resulting inability of the patient to communicate his ideas adequately may make it difficult to determine the presence or extent of mental symptoms. In the terminal phase the patient may be stuporous and lose control of both rectal and vesical sphincters.

The electroencephalogram is an invaluable aid in detecting those tumors present in "silent areas" or not productive of increased intracranial pressure early in their course. The use of the electroencephalogram has been recommended as a routine procedure for patients admitted to mental hospitals. However, its serial application is necessary in many instances to insure detection of tumors. Metrazol for activation of the electroencephalogram is valuable, particularly for the diagnosis of temporal lobe tumors.

More recently, cerebral arteriography and the use of radioactive scanning devices have expanded the diagnostic potential of the neurosurgeon, particularly in determining the localization and extent of the tumor mass. The use of computed axial tomography (CAT) scanning in particular, promises to extend current knowledge of neoplastic growth and its diagnosis.

Treatment

The decision about the appropriate therapeutic regimen depends upon the proper diagnosis of the tumor type and its site. Neurosurgical exploration and excision, radiotherapy, or chemotherapy or combinations of all three are the current choices.

BIBLIOGRAPHY

Bailey, P.: Intracranial Tumors. 2nd ed. Springfield, Ill., Charles C Thomas, 1948.

Horton, P. C.: Personality disorder and parietal lobe dysfunction. Am. J. Psychiatry, *133*:782–785, 1976.

Patton, R. B., and Sheppard, J. A.: Intracranial tumors found at autopsy in mental patients. Am. J. Psychiatry, *113*:319–324, 1956.

Soniat, T. L. L.: Psychiatric symptoms associated with intracranial neoplasms. Am. J. Psychiatry, *108*:19–22, 1951.

Weisberg, L. A., Nice, C., and Katz, M.: Cerebral Computed Tomography. Philadelphia, W. B. Saunders Company, 1978.

15

MENTAL DISORDERS CAUSED BY OR ASSOCIATED WITH HEAD TRAUMA

"It is strange that men can see beauty in the ruins of old castles and churches and can't see the tragedy in the ruin of a man."

G. K. Chesterton

ALEXANDER LURIA WITH A PATIENT WHO SUFFERED BRAIN DAMAGE AS A RESULT OF A WAR WOUND
(From Calder, N.: The Mind of Man, New York, Viking Press, 1971, p. 97.)

With the mounting occurrence of accidents incident to industry and traffic and with the enactment of industrial compensation laws, there has been a marked increase in traumatic mental disorders and their medicolegal importance. For these reasons, the relationship of head trauma to the development of mental disorders often presents an important and difficult problem. Frequently, the difficulty is accentuated because the clinical picture may be complicated through the personality response activated by loss or impairment of mental functioning following brain injury, with appearance of psychogenic symptoms, or by exaggeration or overdetermination of symptoms expressive of impaired brain function.

In order to arrive at an accurate diagnosis, it is necessary to make detailed mental and neurological examinations and to obtain a precise history of the patient's mental status prior to his injury. The opinion popularly entertained that injuries to the head are a frequent cause of mental disorders is an error. Undoubtedly severe trauma to any part of the body may occasionally serve as a contributing or precipitating agent in schizophrenia and manic-depressive psychosis in persons predisposed to these respective reactions. At times, too, trauma of the head, without recognizable injury to the brain, may activate an asymptomatic paretic process and lead to clinically active syphilitic meningoencephalitis. Such psychoses, however, are not included among the traumatic mental disorders.

The mental disturbances associated with head trauma are divided into those caused by acute brain disorder and those caused by chronic brain disorder. This classification will be explained as these disorders are considered.

ACUTE DISORDERS CAUSED BY, OR ASSOCIATED WITH, HEAD TRAUMA

The acute (at times subacute) disorders following trauma of the head tend to fall into the following syndromes:
- (a) Concussion
- (b) Traumatic coma
- (c) Traumatic delirium
- (d) Korsakoff, or amnesic-confabulatory, syndrome

Concussion Syndrome

In concussion, there is a momentary physiological interruption of cerebral processes because of head injury, but there are no histological changes or clinical signs. Recovery is rapid and complete. There is not only amnesia for the moment of injury but also for a period, usually seconds or moments, before the injury. Concussion follows the impact of a severe, functionally paralyzing force upon the head, especially of a force that causes abrupt acceleration or deceleration. In recent years it has been suggested that concussion may be the result of the cavitation phenomenon in the cellular fluids. Experiments show that an impulse applied to the skull by a severe mechanical blow or by an underwater explosion produces first a momentary positive pressure wave followed by a negative one. Although this negative wave is sustained for only an infinitesimal period of time, it apparently causes minute bubbles to form momentarily in the cellular fluids. This phenomenon of cavitation, with its molecular disrupting action, produces a momentary generalized cortical electric discharge that renders the patient unconscious. This discharge is followed by a depression of function.

Brains of animals subjected to concussion and examined by fine techniques several days after the trauma have disclosed histological changes in nerve cells. These suggest that some of the remote symptoms following concussion may develop on the basis of nerve cell changes taking place some time after the concussion. The period of unconsciousness may be momentary or may continue for hours. Many patients vomit as they regain consciousness. There is apparently no relationship between the severity of the concussion, as measured by the duration of unconsciousness, and the severity of the psychiatric sequelae. In regaining consciousness, the patient may wake up suddenly or may pass through a state of clouded consciousness and confusion. He will subsequently have a loss of memory (post-traumatic amnesia) for this period, even though he seems alert and able to carry on a conversation. Usually recovery is complete in a short time, but occasionally a chronic personality disorder may follow.

Contusing and lacerating injuries do not in themselves produce concussion, although they may be associated with it. On the other hand, a severe injury may be sustained without concussion. The diagnosis of uncomplicated concussion can be made only in retrospect. Only after the regaining of consciousness can one be sure that no organic sequelae will follow. Although cerebral concussion is an acute syndrome, there is frequently an aftermath of variable, even prolonged, duration.

Traumatic Coma

Severe concussion without injury, or, more frequently, concussion accompanied by contusion (a mechanical disruption of tissue usually accompanied by minute capillary hemorrhages) or by laceration (a gross tearing of tissue) may produce prolonged coma. Coma is, of course, characterized by absence of response on stimulation. It may last for hours or for several days, the duration depending upon the degree and extent of the injury. In the absence of localizing signs of laceration or of pressure (as by subdural hemorrhage), coma for more than 24 hours usually means a major contusion. Following coma there is a period of stupor, restlessness, and clouding of consciousness, from which the patient may emerge into clear consciousness or at times pass into traumatic delirium. Coma is often interrupted by intervals of semistupor. Prolonged coma is frequently followed by a period of delirium succeeded by a longer period of amnesia or by the amnesic-confabulatory syndrome known as the Korsakoff syndrome.

Traumatic Delirium

If delirium follows the suffering of head trauma, it usually begins during the gradual emergence of the patient from traumatic stupor or coma. The underlying cause may be concussion, contusion, laceration, hemorrhage, or increased intracranial pressure. In a majority of cases, delirium is mild and consists of haziness, irritability, dreamy fabrications, restlessness, and mild disorders of the sensorium. The patient does not grasp the finer points of situations and events of his surroundings. Although most of the time he may realize that he is in a hospital, he does not remember how he came to be there, may not recognize persons about him, and may not understand why he is detained. Other patients may be definitely bewildered. Many are apprehensive and fearful. In some cases the delirium is concerned with the patient's occupation. Others are resistive, noisy, irritable, uncooperative, and verbally abusive, while some are belligerent, demanding, and aggressive. If hallucinations occur, they are usually visual. In the more severe cases, there may be such confusional excitement and a tendency to wander about that restraint becomes necessary. Violent, impulsive outbursts making the patient dangerous to himself or others may occur. As their noisy delirium subsides, some patients remain talkative and show a perseveration of words. At times, after the stage of irritability, the emotional state may be characterized by a childish elation and happiness. As in delirium resulting from other causes, the course may be characterized by fluctuations between relative clearness and confusion. In some instances, the syndrome may be that of a twilight or dream state instead of delirium. With or without preceding delirium, various degrees of post-traumatic defect may follow major contusions with their diffuse degeneration of ganglion cells.

Delirium continuing for more than a week suggests considerable damage. An estimate of the final residual defect should not be given for at least six months. Delirium or coma of more than a month's duration usually means serious tissue destruction. An estimate of the final deterioration and other results of tissue destruction should not be made until 12 to 18 months after the injury. The final mental defect will usually not be as serious as early symptoms suggest.

Amnesic-Confabulatory Syndrome

A relatively frequent syndrome following head trauma is that first described by Korsakoff as associated with chronic alcoholism. The most striking feature of this syndrome is confabulation, although this is accompanied by disorientation and impairment of perception and recent memory. The fabrication of memory may be a mixture of truth and fiction or purely new fabrications. Suggestive questions may often elicit contradictory statements. The patient may superficially appear alert but on closer examination it will be found that perception is greatly deranged. Many patients with the Korsakoff syndrome show serenity and mild euphoria or even facetiousness but readily become irritable on questioning.

In practice it will be found that the acute and subacute symptoms of traumatic mental disorder do not usually occur in such distinct classificatory types as have been described. In severe cases one often observes mixed and transitional reaction types. Delirioid and Korsakoff symptoms are particularly apt to be associated.

Treatment of Acute Traumatic Mental Disorders

Except for the surgical procedures required in the case of definite injuries to the head, operative interference is to be avoided. The patient should be closely watched for any signs of increased intracranial pressure, and also for the occurrence of any complication.

The initial objective is to quiet the patient. Rest in bed and as limited a use of sedatives as possible are important. Narcotics are contraindicated. In the acute stages, careful note should be made of the state of awareness and the presence or absence of signs of injury to the cerebral substance. Vital signs should be recorded at intervals of two to four hours. Fluids and a soft or liquid diet may be administered if the patient is conscious and able to swallow.

With the presence of coma, either feeding by a nasal tube or the administration of parenteral fluids is indicated. Fluids and salt should be restricted but not to the point of leading to dehydration and acidosis. The fear of cerebral edema should not lead to their overrestriction. Patients with simple concussion require at least 24 hours of observation and may then return to their usual activities. The period of bed rest and convalescence of patients with more severe injuries is determined by the patient's reaction to the treatment. It is important that the severity of the injury not be overemphasized or the period of hospitalization unduly prolonged. There should be a gradual increase of activity with continuance of convalescence at home through the medium of graduated exercises. Active work should be deferred for two to three months following discharge from the hospital. Patients should be advised that alcohol tolerance is diminished following head injury.

Of utmost importance in the treatment of the acute traumatic mental state is the continued awareness of the possibility of severe complications. Such changes in the vital signs as slowing of the pulse and respiration, fluctuating states of consciousness, or the development of signs of focal disturbances of the brain, including paresis, suggest strongly the possibility of serious pathology. In particular, the possibility of *subdural hemorrhage* must be kept in mind.

Subdural Hematoma

Following injury to the head, subdural hematoma is said to occur in 1 to 10 per cent of individuals. In a series of 3100 consecutive autopsies of psychotic patients, 8 per cent showed evidence of subdural hemorrhage. Subdural hematoma may be associated with any variety of psychotic reaction, but occurs particularly in the senile, epileptic, alcoholic, and paretic individual. Such patients are especially prone to head injury.

Subdural hematoma consists of a collection of blood between the dura and arachnoid in the subdural space. The bleeding in this space is of venous origin and follows tearing of small veins reaching the subdural space. The fluid in the space may be admixed with cerebrospinal fluid if the arachnoid tears. Blood extravasated into this area fails to be absorbed and eventually is organized and encapsulated by the dura. Fibroblasts proliferate from the inner surface of the dura and invade the clot when in contact with the dura. Capillaries extend into the clot and gradually absorb the liquefied fluid. If the clot is small, it may become completely organized, but if large, fibroblasts may form an encapsulating membrane by growing both along the inner surface of the clot and on the surface adjacent to the dura.

Subdural hematomas may occur either acutely following the head injury or at later periods. In either case the symptomatology may be brought to the attention of the psychiatric consultant. Headache is invariably present. Perhaps most important is the variable state of consciousness. Following recovery from the initial coma, the patient becomes irritable or confused. His mental status frequently changes from day to day or even from hour to hour. Focal signs of cerebral damage are not present in more than one half of the cases. The most frequent signs are hemiplegia or central facial weakness. In chronic cases the symptoms are similar, but in addition, slight to severe intellectual impairment is usually noted. The initial trauma may not be remembered.

Cerebrospinal fluid is usually bloody and under increased pressure. Roentgenologic examination of the skull may or may not show evidence of a linear fracture. The brain scan is often helpful in defining an abnormality on one or the other side of the brain. The diagnosis is firmly established only by placing bur holes on both sides of the skull with discovery of the characteristic hematoma.

Other complications that may follow head injury in the acute phase are extradural hemorrhage, intracerebral hemorrhage, subdural hygroma, and cerebral thrombosis. When a subdural hemorrhage or other traumatic vascular lesion is suspected, neurological and neurosurgical consultations are immediately indicated.

CHRONIC MENTAL DISORDERS CAUSED BY OR ASSOCIATED WITH HEAD TRAUMA

A definite classification of mental disturbances caused by, or associated with, head trauma into a group of acute disorders and a group of chronic disorders is somewhat arbitrary, but in general there are two groups of syndromes both in respect to their temporal relation to the trauma and in respect to clinical features. The chronic disorders may also be divided into two subgroups. One subgroup consists of those disorders presenting symptoms that are the direct result of the trauma, and the other, those in which the syndrome is only a secondary result of the head trauma. The following classification of the chronic traumatic disorders is therefore suggested:

I. Caused primarily by head trauma: Post-traumatic personality disorders
   a. of adults
   b. of children
   Post-traumatic defect conditions
   a. traumatic encephalopathy of pugilists (punchdrunk)
   b. traumatic convulsive disorder (traumatic epilepsy)
II. Caused secondarily by head trauma: Psychoneurosis with head trauma

Psychopathology that occurs following lesions of the brain is now regarded not only as an expression of changes that the patient's personality undergoes as the result of cerebral lesions, but also as an expression of the efforts of the brain-damaged personality to adapt to these defects and to the demands that can no longer be met because of these defects. The various types of symptoms must be evaluated and understood in this context if a rational therapy is to be applied in the treatment of individuals with chronic disorders resulting from head injury.

Symptoms

The effort of such patients to find the new adjustment necessary because of the head injury results in three types of symptoms. The first expresses the conflict that the individual faces. The second reflects the tendency to build up substitutive performances to adapt to the demands of the environment. A third group of symptoms is the direct result of the impairment of the brain functioning itself. Here, the defect may be ameliorated by training, and it is here in particular that the impairment of the "abstract attitude" described by Goldstein is to be found.

Among the symptoms exposing the patient's defect is that now commonly known as the *catastrophic reaction.* Confronted with a problem he cannot solve, the brain-injured individual becomes suddenly anxious and agitated and may appear dazed. A change in his color may appear, he fumbles at the task, and he may present other evidences of autonomic disturbances, such as irregular pulse and changes in respiratory rate. If he was initially in good spirits, he now becomes evasive, sullen, irritable, and even aggressive. The catastrophic reaction develops simultaneously with the attempt to perform the task in which he fails, and not following the performance. Thus it does not represent the patient's response to the awareness that he has failed. As a consequence of such catastrophic reactions, a definite behavior pattern evolves in many of those with brain injury. Some, when confronted with tasks they cannot solve, lose consciousness. Others avoid exposing themselves to

such situations by isolating themselves from individuals, or by avoiding tasks through apparent inability to understand directions. Some brain-injured individuals attempt to prevent upsurges of anxiety by continuous activity, which exposes the patient's inability to adopt a reflective attitude, to take himself for granted, or to place himself in the position of a detached spectator. The over-activity may be of the type commonly spoken of as "occupational delirium" and seen in patients with dementia. Certain patients appear to be unable to follow directions and carry out tasks. Essentially they avoid the task in the anxious expectation of precipitating the unpleasant catastrophic response. Others adapt themselves through an excessive orderliness. This may express itself in a meticulousness not only in relation to one's own property but also to that of others in the home.

The brain-injured person tends to suppress knowledge of his disability. Such denial, according to Goldstein, is more easily achieved in the patient with complete destruction of some function than in the individual with incomplete disturbance.

In addition to the efforts of the brain-injured person to avoid the catastrophic reaction by restricting his environment, his brain defect expresses itself through evidence of increase in the threshold of excitability, with the result that greater stimuli are required to bring forth responses. At the same time, the patient may appear unusually susceptible to exposure to various external stimuli because of his easy distractibility. Owing to his difficulty in discriminating between the object to which he is exposed and the background or setting in which the object is presented, the brain-injured patient suffers doubt and anxiety in his perceptions of common objects presented under ordinary circumstances. Thus his capacity for solving problems is impaired as a consequence of this perceptual weakness.

Goldstein has described what he terms the *abstract attitude*. He defines this as the capacity to assume a mental set voluntarily; to shift from one aspect of a situation to another; to retain simultaneously several aspects of a situation; to break up and isolate the whole into its constituent parts; and to abstract common properties, plan ahead ideationally, and think or behave symbolically. The *concrete attitude*, on the other hand, is a form of thinking fixed and unable to proceed beyond the stimulus of an immediate experience or object. To him, the brain-injured person is impaired in his ability to assume the abstract attitude and has difficulty in moving easily from the abstract to the concrete.

Post-traumatic Personality Disorders

Although these personality disturbances are primarily a result of injuries to the cranial contents, psychological factors usually participate to a varying degree. A decision about the relative importance of the brain injury, of environmental factors, and of the previous personality pattern of the patient is not always easy. Sometimes the impression is gained that the patient has always had an immature attitude or, as a result of the accident, has reverted to such an attitude, accompanied by a reluctance to face former responsibilities. Again, the mental symptoms appear mainly or entirely psychogenic and merge into a neurosis secondary to the trauma (accident neurosis).

In adults this primary post-traumatic personality syndrome may assume two forms: a milder and more frequent form known as postconcussion syndrome or postconcussional neurotic state, and a more serious disturbance to which the name post-traumatic personality disorder is applied in a narrower and more specific sense.

POSTCONCUSSION SYNDROME. Whether the injury that preceded this syndrome was mild or severe, the presenting symptom is anxiety. Other symptoms are headache, dizziness, fatigability, oversensitivity to strong sensory stimuli, insomnia, impairment of memory and of ability to concentrate, a narrowing of interests, a lessening of spontaneity, aggravation of symptoms by heat, excitement, or exertion, and a reduced tolerance of alcohol. Headache and vertigo are aggravated by quick movement, by stooping, or by psychological tension. Many patients are emotionally labile, irritable, and easily moved to tears. Many complain of decreased sexual potency. Some become "head-conscious." This is perhaps to be expected, since the head is the most significant part of the body image. Head injury, therefore, is more commonly experienced as a form of psychic trauma than injury to almost any other part of the body. If the injury occurred under conditions of discontent or dissatisfaction, psychogenic symptoms are particularly likely to follow.

Diagnosis and Prognosis. The chief problem in the diagnosis of the postconcussion syndrome is to determine when a postconcussional headache and other symptoms having an organic basis cease to be a result of organic causes and are carried on by psychological influences. The relative importance of psychogenic and physiogenic factors is often difficult to determine. If the headache is paroxysmal, throbbing, and aggravated by postural alterations or physical exertion, it may be that it persists from an encephalopathic rather than from a neurotic state. The same is true if mental functions tend to be sluggish and if the emotional status is sanguine and not characterized by gloom, ready annoyance, and apprehension. If the symptoms are definite and constant and are not modified by suggestion, and if the patient's interest is in rehabilitation and not in indemnification, they are probably not of psychogenic origin.

While many clinicians consider that most, but not all, patients with the postconcussion syndrome recover if complications of psychoneurotic symptoms do not occur, Merskey and Woodforde recently reported a followup of patients with minor head injury (either no loss of consciousness or unconsciousness lasting less than 15 minutes). They found that symptoms had lasted for a median period of 4 years after the accident, with the range extending from 6 to 14 years. Over a third of the patients never sought financial compensation.

Treatment. In certain respects, the most important aspects of therapy are careful and adequate surgical and medical treatment at the time of injury, combined with subsequent discreet management in adjusting the patient to his symptoms and to the general situation with which he is confronted. Too early return to strenuous labor should be discouraged, yet too long a rest may lead to a secondary neurotic syndrome. Nearly every patient with concussion should have supportive and suggestive psychotherapy.

POST-TRAUMATIC PERSONALITY DISORDER OF ADULTS. In some instances, the most conspicuous sequel of head trauma is a change from the original personality makeup of the patient. The amiable, placid individual may become irascible, irritable, and impulsive. He may become quarrelsome and subject to outbursts of rage, aggression, and motor excitement. Family and other obligations and responsibilities are disregarded. Ambition and initiative are lost. The patient becomes petulant, resentful, self-centered, willful, and selfish. Some become morose and tend to develop paranoid reactions toward persons about them. Others lose all interest in activities and withdraw from social contacts. Not uncommonly, some degree of organic mental deterioration accompanies these changes in the psychological structure of the personality.

POST-TRAUMATIC PERSONALITY DISORDERS OF CHILDREN. In general, children withstand head injury better than adults. However, brain-damaged children may present serious behavior problems. Children without serious destruction of brain tissue may show much disorganization of behavior. The previously normal child becomes disobedient, distractible, impulsive, aggressive, destructive, cruel, quarrelsome, and antisocial. Constant restlessness and overactivity are the rule. There may be some degree of intellectual deficit. The child is dominated by instinctive and emotional impulses and shows no regard for the welfare of others. Although there is little impairment of original intellectual capacity, the child does not concentrate, shows little interest in school work, and does poorly in the classroom, where he is intolerably disruptive. The usual methods of training and discipline are ineffectual, and eventually the most seriously impaired require institutional care.

Because of his handicap, the child is in need of emotional support. Parents' feelings and their attitude toward his handicaps may greatly influence his behavior. Some parents may manifest a smothering overprotectiveness and others may be unsympathetic and rejecting. An impatient attitude and unjustified blame by the teacher increase the child's anxiety and result both in more disturbed behavior and in less ability to learn. Environmental pathology becomes, therefore, the crucial determinant of the disturbances in behavior.

Post-traumatic Defect Conditions

Mental deterioration (dementia) following severe head trauma may or may not have been preceded by traumatic delirium. It frequently happens that, as consciousness returns following delirium, an impairment of former mental capacity becomes manifest. In milder forms, this may consist only of loss of initiative, mental slowing, loss of sense of responsibility, and impairment of ability to recognize abstract relationships. In somewhat more serious disturbances, memory is impaired, attention is reduced, reaction time is slowed, and defensive confabulations may be expressed. Judgment is impaired and finer affective feelings are blunted. Social values are not appreciated. Tasks that were formerly performed easily become difficult or impossible. The patient may consider himself normal, although it is apparent to his intimates that he has never been the same since his injury. The degree of dementia varies greatly according to the site of the lesion, the nature and extent of the injury, and its secondary results (atrophy, meningoencephalic adhesions, distortion of ventricles). A permanent mental deterioration to a degree requiring institutional care is uncommon after contusion. If laceration has been extensive, the dementia may be great and associated with epileptiform seizures, paralyses, aphasia, deafness, and other neurological signs.

In the elderly, difficulty sometimes arises in differentiating post-traumatic mental deterioration from psychoses of arteriosclerotic origin complicated by head injury. Careful inquiry should be made as to any symptoms of arteriosclerosis existing before the injury. The possibility that the confusion of arteriosclerosis or of a cerebral attack may have led to the injury should be kept in mind.

Severe, chronic dementia is hopeless, yet caution should guide the therapist in expressing a prognosis in acute or subacute cases, since with time many patients show a surprising improvement.

Traumatic Encephalopathy of Pugilists (Punchdrunk)

A chronic post-traumatic personality disorder first described by Martland is that to which he gave the name "punchdrunk." This syndrome occurs among pugilists who have sustained repeated severe blows on the head over a period of at least a few years. The more skillful the fighter, the greater is the probability that he will either escape the causative injuries or remain relatively free from them for a considerable period of time. The disorder probably results from successive and accumulative petechial hemorrhages and foci of necrosis deep in the cerebrum. The patient shows an insidious impairment of skill, a slowing of muscular action, a little uncertainty in equilibrium, slight confusion, and deterioration in attention, concentration, and memory. Speech becomes thick and hesitating. The patient "continuously simulates a person who is just a little drunk." Most patients are voluble and euphoric. Confusion and defects of memory become more marked, and intellectual impairment continues to a disabling degree. The tremor, propulsive gait, and masklike facies of the parkinsonian syndrome may appear. The symptoms progress for approximately a year, then become stationary. The degree of deterioration depends upon the extent and degree of brain injury.

Traumatic Epilepsy

One of the sequelae of brain injury is epilepsy. There is so wide a variation in statistics as to the incidence of epileptic seizures following head injury—4.5 per cent to 34 per cent—that they are probably of little value. Study of 279 American personnel who sustained wounds of the brain in World War II showed that 36 per cent developed seizures within two years after injury, and 41.6 per cent within three years after receipt of penetrating brain wounds. The incidence is greatest in patients who suffer a penetration of the dura. The most frequent epileptogenic lesions in post-traumatic convulsive states are cerebrodural or cerebral cicatrix and focal atrophy. Epilepsy is therefore more common after penetrating than after closed injuries and is not the result of generalized damage to the brain. Seizures do not develop after a simple concussion.

A lesion causing the convulsive state does so as a result of irritation of adjacent areas of the brain. The pattern of the attack and the march of motor phenomena during the seizure may betray the epileptogenic point of origin. Electroencephalography may be of much value in localization of the lesion. In the typical focal or jacksonian seizure, consciousness is not lost. Clonic twitches develop in one part of the body and spread consecutively to other parts of the same side. In a large percentage of cases, however, consciousness is disturbed in the manner of either the petit mal or grand mal seizure. There may also be the same paroxysmal periods of depression, exaltation, or fugues. Mental deterioration may be slight or extreme.

CHRONIC MENTAL DISORDER SECONDARY TO HEAD TRAUMA: PSYCHONEUROSIS

Although a later chapter will be devoted to a description of the psychoneuroses, those associated with head trauma have features sufficiently significant to justify special mention of them in a discussion of mental disorders following head injury. It is not generally considered that traumatic neuroses are the direct result of anatomical or physiological changes produced by the trauma, yet a subjectively disturbing postconcussion syndrome or other post-traumatic symptoms may facilitate or become the nucleus for neurotic attitudes. In some individuals the traumatic incident sets off a stress reaction, with the typical symptoms described later in this book. If the trauma occurred at a time, or in a setting, in which anxiety-producing factors such as economic insecurity, occupational dissatisfactions, family tensions, or inability to secure work existed, the neu-

rotic response is more likely. The circumstances under which the trauma was sustained—such as compensable accidents, in contrast to accidental falls in the home or injuries in sports—may have a significant etiological relation. If the injury is followed by dizziness and headache, or if other physical symptoms are associated with it, a sense of insecurity and an associated anxiety may readily develop.

Complicating situational stresses arising from, or relating to, the injury tend not only to create but also to perpetuate the neurotic symptoms. Feelings of discontent or of grievance predispose to their development. Fear, suggestion, and wishful thinking may all be important psychological factors in the production of symptoms.

Diagnosis

The onset of psychoneurosis associated with head trauma occurs not at the time of injury but at a variable period after it. Frequently, there is a history that the patient recovered from the organic symptoms produced by the trauma and was about to return to his usual employment, or even resumed work for a brief period, when a return of headache, dizziness, and other symptoms rendered employment impossible. This period between the time of the injury and the appearance of neurotic disability is often described as one of "incubation and contemplation." The patient who has had a resentful, dissatisfied attitude toward his work and was protected from resuming former responsibilities by reason of the acute physical symptoms that followed the head trauma is prone to the development of a neurosis. With the loss of the protecting physical disability, other means of avoiding a return to a distasteful situation must be sought. This means is readily provided by a return of headache, vertigo, impairment of memory, fatigability, irritability, and other symptoms. Likewise, both the person who is fundamentally covetous and indolent, or who was harassed by debts or other financial obligations before the injury, and the apprehensive, suggestible person fearful of losing compensation by return to work may develop similar psychoneurotic symptoms to assure a continuation of compensation. The sympathy and solicitude of friends, lack of occupation and interest, suggestive examinations, misdirected treatment, continued compensation, and other subconscious motivations tend to fix the symptoms. Various factors, such as fears related to the injury, head-consciousness, and accentuation and elaboration of pre-existing conflicts concerning occupational and financial problems, contribute to the development of anxiety, which is often a conspicuous symptom. Other symptoms are physical and mental fatigability, depression, apprehension, neurasthenic and hypochondriacal reactions, and a volubility and elaboration in expression of complaints. Symptoms tend to be vague, numerous, and inconstant.

Undoubtedly, the organic concussion syndrome, with disturbance of consciousness, subsequent dizziness, and the feeling of insecurity connected with it, facilitates the production and suggests the nature of neurotic symptoms. It tends, therefore, to acquire an overlay of psychoneurotic symptoms. Frequently, indeed, the post-traumatic concussion syndrome becomes the basis for psychological elaborations of a hysterical type. As a result, psychogenic symptoms coincide or may be interwoven with organic sequelae of head injuries. Combinations of physiologically determined and psychiatric symptoms may, in fact, exist.

Treatment

Since the pretraumatic personality and the setting and circumstances of the accident are often more significant than the severity of the injury in producing post-traumatic mental disability, apprehension should not be manifested either by the physician or the patient's relatives. Prolonged rest in bed after head injury suggests that the injury is serious, engenders anxiety, and predisposes to the development of the post-traumatic syndrome. The stay in a hospital should not be prolonged, and the patient should return to his work as soon as practicable. Planned activity even before return to regular employment is desirable. Reference has already been made to the fact that occupational and home worries and concern for compensation favor the persistence of symptoms. Gain from the injury in any way deters recovery. A speedy settlement of any compensation question is advisable. Since the association between head injury and psychiatric factors is close, the "preneurotic interval" between the injury and the development of the neurosis is one in which preventive psychotherapy is advisable.

Rehabilitation of the brain-injured should commence immediately after the patient has become conscious. Such patients are often highly fearful and suggestible. Explanation as to the nature of the injury and reassurance as to outcome should be given. Efforts should be made to avoid inquiry concerning symptoms that are not spontaneously presented. As soon as the patient is able, he should move about, and a carefully planned program of progressive activity should be established. Such a program should not overtax his capacities intellectually, emotionally, or physically.

Those with chronic defects require more than a regimen of occupational therapy, games, and exercises, even though such activities assist in restoring self-confidence and an awareness of capacity for performance. Treatment is most effectively managed in hospitals with well-established departments for rehabilitation, including occupational, recreational, and vocational therapies.

Many advances have been made in the methods used in the re-education of those with chronic brain damage, particularly of those who manifest, in addition to disturbances of the abstract attitude, specific defects in the field of language, motor disabilities, and perception. Such patients require a careful psychological evaluation and then re-training by skilled persons. There is a continuing need for the insight of the psychiatrist and his assistants in dealing with the emotional problems of patients. However, in addition to this type of therapy, the utilization of the psychologist and other special educators trained in the pedagogy of the brain-injured, and also of the social worker if there are particular family needs, must be considered.

The outcome varies according to the severity of the lesion and the pre-traumatic personality of the individual. In some cases, intellectual tests may fail to reveal serious disturbances, yet when the patient has returned to work his impairment in judgment and capacity for work may be demonstrated. Here the well-established rehabilitation center, with the opportunity for testing per-formance in a workshop, is most useful in determining the eventual capacity of the individual for an occupation and the proper type of vocation for the future. In those rare cases of dementia with severe personality change, the prognosis is grave.

BIBLIOGRAPHY

Critchley, M.: Medical aspects of boxing. Br. Med. J., 1:357–364, 1957.
Denny-Brown, D.: Disability arising from closed head injuries. J.A.M.A., 127:429–436, 1945.
Eisenberg, L.: Psychiatric implications of brain damage in children. Psychiatr. Q., 31:72–92, 1957.
Goldstein, K.: After-effects of Brain Injuries in War. New York, Grune & Stratton, 1942.
Ingram, T. T. S.: A characteristic form of overactivity behavior in brain-damaged children. J. Ment. Sci., 102:550–558, 1956.
Logue, P. E.: Understanding and Living with Brain Damage. Springfield, Ill., Charles C Thomas, 1975.
Merskey, H., and Woodforde, J. M.: Psychiatric sequelae of minor head injury. Brain, 95:521–528, 1972.
Strauss, A. A., and Lehtinen, L. E.: Psychopathology and Education of the Brain-Injured Child. New York, Grune & Stratton, 1947.
Walker, A. E., and Erculer, F.: Head-Injured Men. Springfield, Ill., Charles C Thomas, 1968.

16

BRAIN SYNDROMES ASSOCIATED WITH ENDOCRINE, METABOLIC, NUTRITIONAL, AND TOXIC DISTURBANCES

All substances are poisons. The right dose differentiates a poison and a remedy.

Paracelsus

ACROMEGALIC SKULL
(Courtesy of Dr. T. Skillman, Ohio State University College of Medicine.)

Interactions between emotional and metabolic processes may produce endocrine disturbances, and these, in turn, may affect cerebral functions and mental reactions. The psychological consequences of a given hormonal action are not uniform. A certain hormonal change may or may not have a psychological effect. If it does produce an effect, it is not necessarily the same in all cases but will depend upon the previous personality organization of the individual and upon all the other influences acting upon the personality.

It is not clear, however, whether endocrine abnormalities will in themselves produce a psychosis. Some endocrine disturbances produce changes in brain function by influencing brain metabolism, but this is no indication that such changes are related to disturbances in behavior. This is well illustrated when thyroid function is considered. Although psychotic and other types of reaction occur in association with hyperthyroidism, it has been shown by recent work that the cerebral metabolic rate is not elevated from normal in this condition. On the other hand, in myxedema there are a reduction of oxygen consumption by the brain and a retardation in expression at the psychological level.

In the evaluation and management of the personality disorders associated with metabolic and endocrine disturbance, the degree of stress consequent to the metabolic shift and the rate of change of bodily functions secondary to that shift must be weighed against the constitutional and experiential development of the specific individual. The time in development at which such changes take place is highly significant.

Preceding the onset of personality disorder, there exist chemical, metabolic, physiological, and sometimes anatomical changes. This is in contrast to what is now known of the functional psychoses and neuroses. Such changes are perceived, and must be adapted to, by the specific individual in his or her own environment.

When endocrine disorder produces gross changes in the body, creating psychological and social stresses which vary from one person and culture to another, the adaptation is particularly difficult because the body image is disturbed. Thus the patient may see himself as deformed, inadequate, or sexually misidentified and may, in turn, suffer ridicule or attack. He then develops feelings of shame and inadequacy. His responses may be anxiety, hostility, guilt, or social withdrawal, or all of these.

In those instances in which the metabolic change induces largely subjective perceptions, there is often induced a shift in the affective life and the level of the drive. It is clear that the symbolic significance of change induced by the metabolic shift depends on the ego attitude toward the body and its functions,

derived during psychosocial development. Thus young women exposed to the masculinization resulting from an adrenal tumor develop anxieties as to their sexual role and functions, associated with activation of sexual fantasies and doubting, an attitude that would not be observed in the young child who has suffered since birth with the symptom complex due to adrenal hyperplasia.

ADRENAL DISORDERS

Cushing's Syndrome

In his original descriptions in 1932 of what has come to be known as Cushing's syndrome, Harvey Cushing called attention to the frequent coexistence of mental symptoms. It is now recognized that these occur in approximately a fifth of those with the syndrome. Originally thought to be associated with a basophil adenoma of the pituitary gland, Cushing's syndrome now is regarded generally as the result of adrenocortical hyperfunction, with either neoplastic or hyperplastic expression in the adrenal glands. It may also be caused by autonomous secretion of nonpituitary tumors, such as the small or "oat cell" carcinomas of the lung, or may be iatrogenic (from excessive administration of natural or synthetic ACTH or its analogues, usually given in the course of treatment of asthma, arthritis, chronic hepatitis, ulcerative colitis, or other "autoimmune disorders.")

The diversity of the associated personality disturbances indicates that they represent the individual's defensive adaptations to the endocrine imbalance and also, to a considerable extent, to the disfiguring alterations in appearance. Thus, as the illness progresses, the patient may change from an attractive young woman to an obese and bearded lady whose activities are restricted by weakness and easy fatigability.

A reactive depression is the most frequently encountered response. In relatively few patients it is associated with psychomotor retardation. Other patients, without depression, are anxious and have crying spells, or are agitated or stubborn in their behavior. Irritability, paranoid ideation, and, rarely, a florid schizophrenic response are seen. Less than a fourth of those with associated personality disturbance suffer serious personality decompensation with psychosis. Obviously, this syndrome presents symptoms similar to those induced by the administration of cortisone, other adrenal steroids, and corticotropin, as discussed in an earlier chapter.

DIAGNOSIS. This is made with observation of the complaints of marked weakness and easy fatigability and an often painful adiposity, which may develop rapidly, with characteristic distribution of fat in the areas of the face and neck (moon face) and trunk. The combination of supraclavicular fat pads and dorsal kyphosis due to osteoporosis sometimes gives a humped posture. There may be depressed purple streaks over the abdomen, thighs, and upper arms, with increased susceptibility to bruising. There is a diminished carbohydrate tolerance due to increased gluconeogenesis from protein, sometimes with diabetes. Hypertension and peripheral edema may occur. Women, the most frequently affected, are usually amenorrheic and show masculinization, with deepening of the voice, hirsutism, growth of the clitoris, and acne. Men are often impotent. The definitive diagnosis is established by laboratory evidence of increased excretion of 17-hydroxycorticoids in the urine. Also helpful are the findings of an eosinophil count below 50 per milliliter, lymphopenia, neutrophilia, polycythemia, and glycosuria, and evidence by x-ray of osteoporosis.

TREATMENT. The therapeutic efforts are directed toward reducing ACTH secretion, or cortisol secretion in spite of high levels of ACTH. These aims may be accomplished by megavoltage pituitary irradiation, which is effective in almost 50 per cent of patients. Children respond much better than adults to this treatment.

Abolishment of the adrenal hyperfunction by subtotal resection of the adrenal gland or removal of an adrenal tumor is the best and most certain method of treatment, but leaves the patient dependent upon daily replacement administration of glucocorticoids and mineralocorticoids.

The return to health is not immediate and requires time. Those who develop hypoadrenalism after adrenal surgery, and in whom substitution therapy proves inadequate, often have persistence of the personality disorder. Others, particularly young women who have suffered severe disfigurement due to hirsutism, bony deformities, and the scars of acne also are apt to have a stubborn perpetuation of symptoms.

Adrenogenital Syndrome

The virilizing effects of excessive secretion of adrenal androgens, whether due to bilateral hyperplasia at birth or an adrenal tumor (often carcinomatous) occurring later in life, have serious consequences for personality development. The condition is frequently associated with psychosis.

When the syndrome develops in women after puberty with the physical deformity resulting from overgrowth of sexual hair, deepening of the voice, absence of breasts, enlargement of the clitoris, and amenorrhea, it leads to marked anxiety. Female patients particularly are preoccupied with their masculinized appearance, develop doubts as to their gender and sexual role, often become depressed and withdrawn socially, and are obsessed with thoughts of homosexuality or guilt about masturbation.

DIAGNOSIS. This is established definitively by demonstration of increased secretion of adrenal androgens and 17-ketosteroids. Other forms of precocious sexual development and hermaphroditism may be distinguished by special differential analyses of steroid secretions.

TREATMENT. Small doses of cortisone suppress the virilizing activity of the adrenals. If this treatment is given in early life, the female patient develops normally and at puberty matures and menstruates regularly. With persisting amenorrhea, dexamethasone, 0.5 mg. daily, or prednisone, 5 to 7.5 mg. daily, may be prescribed. Removal of a tumor or partial adrenalectomy is the treatment of choice for those late in life.

Pheochromocytoma

Accompanying this rare medullary tumor of the adrenal or of other chromaffin tissues are many symptoms suggesting the existence of anxiety neurosis. These symptoms are due to increased secretion of norepinephrine and epinephrine by the gland.

Symptoms, which may exist for a few weeks or years, appear in some instances to be precipitated by emotionally charged incidents, and in others by physical exertion or changes in posture. They are variable in frequency, duration, and severity, and are spoken of as occurring in attacks by over half the sufferers. During such acute episodes, the patients suffer apprehension, pounding headaches, sweating, palpitation, tremulousness, pallor or flushing of the face, pain in the chest, nausea or vomiting, and paresthesias in the extremities. High levels of hypertension with hyperglycemia and glycosuria occur during such acute paroxysms.

The differential diagnosis from primary psychiatric disturbance is made in the presence of hypertension, either transitory or persistent, the palpation or radiographic visualization of a tumor in the adrenal areas, and the patient's response to provocative and blocking pharmacologic tests. Histamine phosphate given intravenously provokes a rise in blood pressure within two minutes with some of the symptoms of the paroxysm. The adrenergic blocking agent Regitine, given to patients with sustained hypertension, will lead to a fall of blood pressure to within normal limits within three or four minutes. Such tests must be administered with care; their indications vary with the nature of the accompanying hypertension.

THYROID DISORDERS

Hyperthyroidism

In the mental disorders associated with hyperthyroidism—an association in which there is a striking interaction between emotional and metabolic processes—it has long been noted that a special type of personality seems usually to have existed before the clinical signs of Graves' disease were apparent. This disease arises largely in sensitive, impressionable persons who react keenly to life, have a marked feeling of insecurity, and an unusual sense of responsibility. The general hypermotility, emotional excitability, and alertness to every sound and impression, the tendency to walk, talk, and eat rapidly, and the mild anxiety, apprehensiveness, and irritability commonly observed in Graves' disease and characterized by the laity as "nervousness," represent in many ways but an exaggeration of a previously existing pattern of response to ordinary life problems. In other words, these persons have been anxious individuals with psychiatric problems giving rise to tension. In them it is frequently impossible to tell where anxiety stops and hyperthyroidism begins.

Psychiatric studies have shown that, usually long before the onset of the clinical symptoms of hyperthyroidism, patients who succumb to this illness have suffered emotional and psychological maladjustment. The majority of those who have examined groups of patients indicate that the basic need of such patients is for the satisfaction of an exaggerated dependency relationship. With chronic frustration, their response is aggressive and leads to the welling up of death wishes toward the person from whom they had hoped to obtain gratification. As a means of adapting to such wishes, the patient may respond by an overdepressed relationship to the significant person or turn away from this person and attempt a striving at self-sufficiency which is often premature. Women with the illness have many conflicts and fears in relation to childbirth; yet at the same time they manifest a strong desire for children. The dependency needs are satisfied while the child is small, but when the time comes for the child to seek its own independence, the mother responds often with anxiety and anger or with the reaction formation of anxious overconcern. These psychological defenses are not specific for the hyperthyroid patient and may be seen in many other conditions. Nevertheless, the strivings of individuals with this type of personality structure relate well to those observations which show that the psychiatric problem frequently precipitating the hyperthyroid activity is the loss of a key person in the patient's life.

Although the usual mental symptoms associated with hyperthyroidism are those of tension, overactivity, and emotional instability, as mentioned, in many untreated, acutely thyrotoxic patients a psychotic reaction appears. In extreme cases a fairly typical manic excitement may develop as if in accordance with the increased tempo of all organic processes. In other instances there may be an acute hallucinatory delirium accompanied by great restlessness and insomnia. Other patients present depressed, anxious, agitated reactions. Paranoid states with systematized delusions may occur. In general, the symptoms manifested are exaggerations and carica-

tures of the previous personality. It will usually be found that persons with recurrent hyperthyroidism after thyroidectomy are still struggling with serious and unresolved personality difficulties.

The treatment of hyperthyroidism is often a joint task for the psychiatrist and the internist. The internist directs his efforts to the restoration of the metabolic rate to normal limits. The function of the psychiatrist is to aid patients who are disturbed emotionally in accepting the need for therapy through bringing insight to their denial of symptoms. Continued psychotherapy is indicated for those hyperthyroid patients who present clear evidence of psychological maladjustment prior to the onset. Here psychotherapy is an important adjunct in bringing about a permanent euthyroid state with reduction in emotional and psychological symptomatology.

Myxedema

Although Ord, in 1877, first proposed the term "myxedema," Gull, four years earlier, had presented a paper entitled, "On a cretinoid state supervening in adult life in women." Accompanying mental changes were noted in the early descriptions of the disease. Among the most frequent mental symptoms are slowness and difficulty in apprehension, thought, and action. These retardations, together with indecision and listlessness, may suggest depression. Memory may be impaired, the defect being more marked in respect to recent events. Speech is frequently slow, and changes in articulation may occur. Recently these clinical findings have been interpreted as the result of impairment of the level of awareness leading to defects in attention, concentration, endurance, and conceptual use without sensory activation. In cases showing such manifestations, there is associated an electroencephalographic abnormality with diminution in mean frequency and voltage, resulting from impaired cerebral metabolism. The serial subtraction test is said to expose the defect in awareness most effectively. Associated with their hebetude, many patients show an unusual fretfulness, irritability, and a paranoid trend. The clinical picture is determined largely by individual emotional and personality factors. There may, therefore, be paranoid characteristics, delusions of persecution, and hallucinations. Mild degrees of thyroid insufficiency are frequently seen in middle-aged persons who complain of fatigue, pains, and headache and are pessimistic.

Treatment with desiccated thyroid extract not only relieves the symptoms but also corrects the electroencephalographic disturbance in those without permanent cerebral damage. Treatment with the extract should be initiated with caution; such treatment is best carried out in a hospital under careful observation and should be commenced with low dosages of 15 mg. daily. The dosage may be increased to 0.1 to 0.2 gm. of thyroid extract daily. The sudden changes in metabolism are particularly dangerous for those with cardiovascular disorders.

PARATHYROID DISORDERS

Hypocalcemia

The most common cause of hypocalcemia is the removal of or damage to the parathyroid glands during thyroidectomy. Psychological symptoms are observed in such patients in addition to the characteristic clinical signs of paresthesia, cramps, carpopedal spasms, tetany, or laryngeal stridor. The most common symptoms are depression, memory loss, disturbance of deep reflexes, and emotional lability. Such symptoms may persist for years, yet are often quickly relieved by correction of the hypocalcemia with the administration of calcium salts orally and with vitamin D; the dosage is carefully controlled by regular determination of the serum calcium. Parathyroid hormone has not been effective for such control.

Hyperparathyroidism

Although uncommon, psychiatric symptoms do occur in patients with hyperparathyroidism owing to adenomatosis of these organs. Usually the presenting picture has been that of an acute brain syndrome (delirium) or evidence of a behavioral change expressed with depressive or paranoidal psychotic manifestations. Initially, the patient's history of illness is one of anorexia or listlessness. Later there occur apathy, weakness, insomnia, anorexia, nausea, and vomiting. A useful clue to the primary etiology is a history of previous renal calculi or peptic ulcer. The diagnosis will be made by evidence of hypercalcemia, abnormally low phosphatemia, and the electrocardiographic changes of prolonged P-R interval. Recovery follows, after surgical removal of tumor, in those without existing personality abnormality.

Several medical methods of control now exist that may be used when surgery is contraindicated. Their relative values require the careful assessment of a skilled endocrinologist for each case.

PANCREATIC DISORDERS

Hypoglycemia

It is now recognized that spontaneous—in distinction from therapeutically induced—hypoglycemic states may occasionally exist. At times the clinical picture of such hypoglycemic attacks may be dominated by mental symptoms, usually transitory in nature. There is no single psychic syndrome characteristic of the condition. Among the many mental phenomena that may be prominent are apathy, irritability, restlessness, anxiety, negativism, somnambulism, confusion, disorientation, fugue states, delirium, syncope, stupor, or coma. Thinking may be confused and retarded and speech may be disturbed. Grasp may be impaired and emotions unstable. Hallucinations and delusions may be present. The patient may complain of weakness, fatigability, and hunger. He perspires and may suffer from tremor, unsteadiness of gait, diplopia, and convulsions. There is no recollection of the attack. There is a tendency for the symptoms to appear after exertion or when the patient is hungry. Complete relief from the symptoms follows the administration of sugar. Hypoglycemia should always be suspected as the cause of any mental symptoms appearing in a diabetic who is receiving insulin.

DIAGNOSIS. The diagnosis of spontaneous hypoglycemia is made on evidence of depression of the blood sugar level. Since the periods of the condition are transient, it is often difficult to establish its presence by simple study of the fasting blood sugar. A definitive diagnosis is evident if the blood sugar level during an attack falls below 50 or 60 mg. per 100 ml. If the attack is convulsive in nature, the blood sugar may be elevated following the seizure. Glucose tolerance tests have limited value but may suggest the diagnosis if the blood sugar level falls to 50 mg. per 100 ml. three to five hours after the stimulating dose of glucose. When hypoglycemia is not demonstrated by these means, a 24- or 48-hour fast should be instituted and blood sugar determinations made at periods of 12, 18, and 24 hours. With the onset of symptoms and their prompt alleviation by the use of intravenous glucose, the diagnosis is established. Electroencephalographic changes occur in association with such attacks and show local or widespread dysrhythmias, which again are relieved on ingestion or intravenous administration of glucose.

ETIOLOGY. Once the diagnosis of hypoglycemia is established, its etiology must be determined. Although the majority of such patients will be found to suffer from hyperinsulinism caused by islet cell tumors of the pancreas, the functional cases with an associated neurosis are of particular interest to the psychiatrist. It has not been determined whether this type of condition may occur as a somatic manifestation of a psychoneurosis or whether the majority of these cases fall into the group of *induced hypoglycemic states* symbolic of a sadomasochistic neurotic conflict. A number of such cases of induced hypoglycemia have been observed, usually in women and most frequently in nurses who have had experience with the utilization of insulin. The diagnosis was established on occasion by tagging the insulin used by the patient with radioactive phosphorus and then detecting the excretion of the radioactive material in the urine the following day. In some instances the patient suffered from diabetes and had numerous unexplained attacks of hypoglycemia, though denying the use of insulin.

The following case history illustrates such a problem and its management:

The patient, a 44-year-old married nurse, with a history of episodic attacks of hunger, weakness, sleepiness, sweating, vertigo, and occasionally unconsciousness, was referred for study. The attacks were always aborted by eating. They were so severe that six months previously the patient had to give up a fast. Another physician had diagnosed an islet cell pancreatic tumor and advised surgery. The patient refused operations, stating that she had gained weight and was not suffering any pain. She consulted other physicians in an attempt to obtain a different diagnosis. She expressed her fear to these physicians that if operated upon she would become diabetic and require insulin.

A careful medical examination failed to reveal any evidence of tumor. The patient sustained a fast without the development of hypoglycemia. In view of previous experiences with patients who had induced hypoglycemia, the patient's room was searched while she was having a diagnostic test and several bottles of insulin and a syringe were found. At this point a psychiatric examination was requested.

In consultation the patient reported that her

mother, who had died two years previously, had been a diabetic and had been nursed in her terminal illness by the daughter. The patient had lived a restricted life and had entered nursing to relieve her loneliness. Some four years previously she had undergone a hysterectomy by a physician who had advised her that she had an islet cell tumor.

Following the initial psychiatric interview, the patient stated that she proposed to sign out of the hospital. Since it was considered that her condition was dangerous in the sense that she was exposing herself to a potentially major surgical procedure, the psychiatric consultant concluded that it was advisable to suggest the possibility of induced hypoglycemia to the patient. This was done by informing her of the conclusions reached by the medical service after finding the bottle of insulin and of the previous experience with others with similar conditions. The patient was gently told that, if this was the case, she must have some underlying emotional problems which had led her to the desperate expedient of the self-administration of insulin and that she might therefore wish to solve the major conflicts which had driven her to such action. The suggestion was met by immediate denial. When seen the following day, the patient asked assurance that any information given by her would be considered inviolate. When this was given, she broke down, cried, and gave the following information.

She stated that her drive for the self-administration of insulin began about four months previously, during the period of a fast when she felt weak and unable to continue her work. Believing that she might obtain a dispensation from a religious fast from the physician who had removed her uterus some years earlier, with whom she worked and toward whom she had a strong positive attachment, she asked if he would assist her in securing a dispensation for medical reasons. He replied that he would do so if he found her to be suffering from hypoglycemia. Shortly before blood was to be drawn for the determination of its sugar content, the nurse, without the knowledge of the physician, took her first injection of insulin. Naturally, hypoglycemia was found. The physician therefore gave her the desired recommendation that dispensation be granted from the obligation of fasting before communion.

The nurse then revealed that she had developed a feeling of depression after her hysterectomy. She feared that she had not healed properly and wondered whether she would develop a cancer. Her father had died of cancer and had suffered from fears relating to mental disease. He was given insulin to relieve his depression. The patient herself had given insulin in mental hospitals and recalled her anxiety on being shown the brain of a patient who had died during insulin shock therapy. Throughout her life she had felt hungry, had been an extremely heavy eater, and had felt weak when she fasted. The patient had always devoted herself to the care of her mother and an aunt and had spent months at home each year nursing them for their various ailments. The mother had written her that she should provide nursing services not only for herself and the aunt but also for her brothers, if she really loved her family. She always seemed fearful of losing the love of her relatives. Perhaps it is not surprising that upon the death of her parents she expressed the sentiment that her brothers "beat her out" of her patrimony.

The nurse declared that she had devoted the same amount of attention to the care of her physician's patients as she had to her own family. She admitted that her response to his insistence on evidence of hypoglycemia by blood test prior to supporting her request for a medical dispensation had been one of anger and resentment. On the other hand, she felt so anxious concerning the possibility of losing his respect and good will and so guilty in relation to the church that she felt obliged to continue the self-administration of insulin when faced with another medical examination. Following these revelations, which were responded to with sympathetic interpretation of her emotional reactions and their origin, the patient returned home to her profession and made a satisfactory adaptation, with no recurrence of the hypoglycemic attacks.

Acute Pancreatitis

A high proportion of patients who suffer recurrent bouts of acute pancreatitis in the course of a continuing relapsing disease of the pancreas develop an acute psychotic brain syndrome with these attacks. The majority of such patients are confirmed alcohol addicts. Their symptoms are most frequently hallucinatory, either auditory or visual, with memory deficits, difficulty in concentration, agitation, fearfulness, and, in some, confabulation. Often confused with delirium tremens, this toxic delirious state may be identified by the principal complaint of abdominal pain, usually associated with vomiting. The patient invariably has an elevated serum amylase level. Although associated with chronic alcoholism, the condition may occur in periods of long abstinence and is found in those with cirrhosis of the liver, diabetes, calcification of the pancreas, or malabsorption syndromes.

There is some reason to believe that impairment of pancreatic activity affects brain and associated mental functioning through metabolic mechanisms that are altered in an unknown manner. Supporting this possibility is the reported occurrence in some patients of severe depression that has antedated other symptoms of pancreatic carcinoma by months.

The hallucinatory brain syndrome associated with acute pancreatitis resolves rapidly over a 10-day period as the pancreatitis subsides.

Carcinoma of the Pancreas

Symptoms of depression, anxiety, and premonition of serious illness are among the most frequent presenting complaints of patients with carcinoma of the pancreas. From 10 to 20 per cent of patients have such symptoms. These symptoms are often noted before other signs and symptoms, which may present from one to four years later. A six-month interval is common. The insomnia associated with the depression has often proved unresponsive to prescription of ordinary hypnotics. The majority of patients with carcinoma of the pancreas, studied by Fras et al., tended to repress their rage responses and also suffered more significant loss of object relations in the immediately preceding months than did patients with other abdominal tumors. The relationship remains unclear between the physiological effects of this tumor growth as contrasted with others, the personality of the patient, and the potential precipitating factor of object loss.

PITUITARY DISORDERS

Acromegaloid Personality

Manfred Bleuler has called attention to the fact that, while acromegaly does not in itself lead to a psychosis, it is quite regularly accompanied by an alteration of personality. This change consists mainly of a lack of initiative and spontaneity and a change in mood. Some patients show brief periods of moodiness without apparent cause, sometimes alternating cheerfulness, self-satisfaction, and elation with passivity and indifference. Again, the mood may at times be anxious, resentful, tense, and unpleasant. In advanced acromegaly, even without increased intracranial pressure, there are slow reactions and a slowness in the stream of thought. There is no intellectual impairment except that referable to apathy and slowness of thought and action. The patient's social attitude is usually characterized by egocentricity, lack of consideration for and interest in other people, impatience, irritability, and oversensitivity during social contacts.

Bleuler does not mean that this type of personality is specific to acromegaly, but he speculatively raises the question whether the endocrine disturbance of acromegaly and the emotional and other psychological disturbances may not, as in other fields of psychosomatic medicine, be merely different aspects of a single life process. To support this hypothesis, Bleuler calls attention to the fact that it is now conceded that psychogenetic factors are of importance in many forms of hyperthyroid disorders, in Cushing's disease, and in other endocrine derangements.

METABOLIC DISTURBANCES

Porphyria

This condition, first described in 1911 by Günther, is a constitutional metabolic disorder resulting in the production of abnormal types of porphyrins, which appear in the urine. Porphyria is classified as the erythropoietic (congenital) type and the hepatic type. Of the latter there have been described acute intermittent, cutaneous, hereditary and mixed, latent hereditary, idiosyncratic cutaneous, and acquired forms. The congenital type is seen only in childhood, and the mixed has mostly dermatological symptoms. The acute intermittent type is the one with which mental symptoms are most frequently associated. In this form, acute attacks are precipitated often following prescription of such agents as the barbiturates, sulfonal, trional, chloroquine, or the taking of alcohol. Hexachlorobenzene, a fungicide, has been implicated as a causal agent in one acquired form.

The acute intermittent type is commonly familial and thought to be inherited through a mendelian dominant trait. Congenital porphyria, on the other hand, appears to be transmitted as a mendelian recessive.

Biochemically, it has been suggested that inhibited synthesis of purines with overproduction of porphyrins and their precursors takes place as a consequence of poisoning of the succinate glycine cycle. In this cycle, α-amino levulinic acid is the common precursor of both porphyrins and purines. Inhibition of the oxidative deamination of this acid may block purine synthesis and lead to overproduction of the porphyrins. The biochemical explanation remains to be confirmed. In the acute intermittent type the urinary porphobilinogen and α-amino levulinic acid levels are thought to continue high for years, in contrast to the mixed or variegate form. On the other hand, coproporphyrin and protoporphyrin excretions in the stool are raised only during the acute attack, in contrast to the condition in the mixed form.

Pathologically, the changes in the nervous system consist of patchy areas of demyelination with or without the destruction of axis cylinders, particularly in the spinal nerves. Retrograde degeneration of the motor cells occurs in the central nervous system and the sympathetic ganglia. These findings are inconstant and nonspecific. In rapidly fatal cases no changes may be evident in the central nervous system. The liver may show fatty degeneration, cirrhosis, or cell injury. In the hematopoietic type the bone marrow is hyperplastic and normoblastic. Splenomegaly and hemolytic anemia exist. The teeth may be reddish brown, as are the bones, as a result of uroporphyrin deposit.

An experimental model of porphyria has been produced in animals by allylisopropylacetamide.

Symptoms and Signs

Porphyria occurs much more frequently in women than in men. The disease may be suspected in a patient who presents a combination of abdominal, neurological, psychiatric and, at times, dermatological symptoms. The acute attack often starts with colicky abdominal pain, sometimes associated with nausea, vomiting, and constipation. The gastrointestinal symptoms often suggest appendicitis, with the result that laparotomy is performed. The patient continues to complain bitterly of abdominal pain and becomes anxious, irritable, argumentative, and perhaps obviously psychotic. As the disease progresses, the patient loses much weight and may become quite cachectic.

Psychiatric manifestations are varied and may be the most prominent presenting symptoms. They are probably due to a direct, possibly reversible, metabolic effect of the disease. They usually precede the neurologic symptoms. Agitation, depression, and disturbances of memory and of the sensorium, with delirious and psychotic-like hallucinatory and delusional experiences, are among the most common symptoms.

The neurological manifestations are greatly varied. Perhaps the most frequent are motor weaknesses, which may be irregularly distributed but are most frequent in the extremities and less so in the muscles of the trunk and abdomen and in the muscles innervated by the cranial nerves. Of the latter, the facial and oculomotor muscles are most often involved. The motor weaknesses may be accompanied by severe pain and paresthesias, but there is usually little or no objective sensory disturbance. The paralysis is flaccid, and tendon reflexes are usually absent or depressed. Convulsions may occur. Cases of both receptive and expressive aphasia have been reported. Bulbar involvement with dysphonia, dysphagia, tachycardia, and respiratory and vasomotor dysfunction may occur.

Tachycardia develops in some cases within a few days of onset of the initiating psychiatric and abdominal symptoms and precedes usually by several weeks the onset of neuropathy. When the latter occurs, the tachycardia increases as the neurological signs expand, disappearing as they subside. It has been suggested that the tachycardia may be due to autonomic cardioneuropathy.

The following case report illustrates the acute intermittent form.

A woman registered for examination at a medical clinic at the age of 40 with a history of five attacks of pain in the right upper quadrant of the abdomen during the previous eight months. The attacks of pain were described as continuing from a half hour to two hours. Results of the general physical examination were essentially normal. A cholecystogram made at this time was reported as disclosing nothing abnormal. A brief note by the medical consultant suggested the existence of an emotional disturbance associated with an unsatisfactory marital relationship. The diagnosis of porphyria was not made at this time.

A history was obtained of brief attacks of pain in the right upper quadrant of the abdomen recurring periodically over a period of 11 years. The present attack began 10 days before the patient's visit to the clinic. This attack was more severe than usual, was accompanied by fever, and persisted much longer. The severity of the pain was such that for the first time the patient allowed her physician to administer narcotic agents by hypodermic injection. These consisted of one tablet of scopolamine and morphine administered nine days before admission and 100 mg. of meperidine hydrochloride (Demerol) on the following days, when she was placed in a hospital elsewhere. No further sedatives were administered. Penicillin was given and plans were made to remove her gallbladder after the fever had subsided. The patient and her family, because of their religious beliefs, were opposed to this or any surgical procedure. Four days before her clinic visit her family noticed that she wrote unusual letters and displayed peculiar, incessant

to-and-fro movements of her hands and arms to the extent that she had no rest. She withdrew from contact with others. The day before her admission to the clinic she refused to accept food or fluids.

At the time of her registration, the patient held herself in a rigid position, with her right arm stiffly raised in a cataleptic pose. Her hands were clenched tightly, and her eyes were closed, and she muttered incoherently. When she was spoken to, she closed her eyes more tightly and repeated in a rhythmic way, "Are they laughing at her?" She resisted attempts to change her position by strong muscular contractions wherever she was touched. When she was left alone, she opened her eyes; occasional jerky, sucking movements of her mouth were observed. Results of the neurological examination were essentially negative. With great difficulty she was examined by a surgeon, who found no evidence of an acute abdominal lesion.

The patient's history was obtained from the husband. She was the eighth of 11 children. The father was alcoholic until 15 years before his death at 85 (four years prior to the time of this report). The parents' attitude toward surgical treatment had always been, "What God put there was meant to stay." The patient had repeatedly refused cholecystectomy. She had been in good health except for the repeated attacks of pain in the right upper abdominal quadrant previously mentioned. Information about the patient's relatives indicated that in general they had lived to advanced age and had been free of abdominal complaints and mental symptoms.

During her first seven days in the hospital, repeated physical examinations failed to disclose abnormalities except for the behavior disturbance. The patient's temperature remained persistently elevated between 99.6° and 102.8° F. Oliguria was present. The specific gravity of the urine was 1.030. Grade 4 albuminuria was noted. The value for urea nitrogen was 68 mg. per 100 ml. of blood. After the subcutaneous administration of fluids, the output of urine increased and there occurred a decrease in the content of albumin in the urine and a rapid decrease in the level of the blood urea nitrogen. On the third hospital day, qualitative study of the urinary porphyrins showed no uroporphyrins, but the presence of coproporphyrin. On the fourth and fifth hospital days, the patient was mute. On the sixth day she was either crying out incoherently or whispering and muttering unintelligibly. On this day the diagnosis of porphyria was established by the detection of porphobilinogen in the urine. (Quantitative porphyrin test, 24 units; uroporphyrin, none; porphobilinogen, 2.6 Ehrlich units; coproporphyrin, 333 μg.)

The patient's rectal temperature reached 105° F on the seventh hospital day. She remained withdrawn, mute, and uncommunicative until the twelfth hospital day, when she began to talk irrelevantly. Visual and auditory hallucinations occurred on the fourteenth hospital day. She sang and talked incoherently and screamed for long periods. She soiled and smeared herself with feces. She spoke of being crucified, of sinning so terribly that she would never be forgiven, and of committing sexual misdemeanors. On the nineteenth hospital day, results of qualitative tests for urinary porphyrins were reported negative. The behavior disturbance remained unchanged.

Electroshock treatment was initiated on the twentieth hospital day. Immediately after this treatment, the patient inquired as to where she was and what she was doing. She declared she wished "to get better." Following the second electroshock treatment she began to eat without assistance. She declared that she had burning sensations (paresthesias) and complained of pains in the distal portions of her extremities. Her verbal production still indicated suspicion and misinterpretation of her environment.

Six electroshock treatments were administered between the twentieth and thirtieth hospital days. After the fourth treatment the patient's temperature again became normal. She was oriented and was able to recall recent and past events except for the period of acute illness, although she did not recall her fright and some of the hallucinations which occurred in this period. At this time there was slight increase in the sensitivity of her feet to touch and pinprick. She was returned to her home 33 days after admission.

DIAGNOSIS. The diagnosis depends upon the finding in the urine of uroporphyrin or porphobilinogen, or both, in excess. Porphobilinogen is found only in patients showing combined abdominal and nervous manifestations. With the excretion of large amounts of uroporphyrin, the urine attracts attention because of its characteristic red, port wine color. Spectroscopic examination readily permits identification of the uroporphyrin. It is important to stress the fact that the presence of reddish urine is by no means a general rule. Frequently, a fresh urine specimen is nearly normal in color, while in other instances it is light yellow or dark amber. When porphyria is suspected, it is unwise to discard a sample of urine merely because it fails to show the characteristic port wine color. Such specimens should be kept in the light; they will then darken, and appropriate laboratory tests for uroporphyrin may be performed. Porphobilinogen may be detected in fresh urine by means of the Ehrlich aldehyde test. Excessive copro-

porphyrin may be found in such urines. Recently α-amino levulinic acid has been found also.

The triad of variable abdomen pain, gradually increasing paralysis of the arms and legs, and toxic-organic mental symptoms should suggest the possibility of this rather uncommon and frequently misdiagnosed disease. It is important to know that lupus erythematosus and porphyria may occur together in the same individual. Cram and his colleagues have collected a number of such cases and describe the special issues of diagnosis and management in the face of these dual pathologic processes.

PROGNOSIS. The outlook for life is relatively good in the erythropoietic and in the dermatological or photosensitive types; in the intermittent acute variety the mortality is relatively high, particularly in those with symptoms referable to the bulbar nervous system.

TREATMENT. Chlorpromazine is the most helpful remedy thus far available in the treatment of acute porphyria. It does not affect established paralyses, may not prevent fatalities from bulbar or respiratory paralyses, and does not appear to influence porphyrin metabolism directly. At the outset it may be necessary to give as much as 100 mg. four to six times in 24 hours intramuscularly; however, it is usually possible to reduce this dose quite rapidly and often to discontinue it entirely. There are some cases in which a small maintenance dose is necessary.

Electroshock therapy has been tried in several patients with psychotic symptomatology, and the response has been variable. Vitamin E has been shown to control porphyrin urinary excretion in the cutaneous form of this disease. Propranolol has been used with apparent success. The single case report requires verification through further therapeutic trials. Conflicting reports have been expressed concerning the effectiveness of cortisone and of corticotropin (ACTH).

Alcohol, barbiturates, and other toxic

agents should be avoided. It is important also that emotional stresses be alleviated, as these are often decisive in precipitating attacks.

Hepatolenticular Degeneration

This rare condition, described by S. A. K. Wilson in 1912, is associated almost invariably in its later course with evidence of personality disorder. In some instances, emotional lability or even gross behavioral deviations are the most prominent early symptoms. It has been, and is, most likely to be confused with schizophrenia, with paranoid, hypomanic, and depressive psychoses, and with hysteria.

Hepatolenticular degeneration is the result of chronic copper intoxication. It is caused by an inherited metabolic defect causing abnormal storage of copper in the liver, brain, and kidneys. The inheritance occurs as an autosomal recessive with gene frequencies computed at 1/200 and 1/500. Within the liver, the metal-binding protein metallothioneine has a copper-binding capacity four times that of the healthy person. It is associated with a deficiency of the copper-containing globulin ceruloplasmin in the blood. Ceruloplasmin does not appear to be a transport protein for the metal.

Characterized by degenerative changes in both brain and liver, it is associated in over half of those affected with a characteristic greenish-yellow ring seen on the undersurface of the cornea near its margin (the Kayser-Fleischer ring).

SYMPTOMS. The illness may occur in a rapidly progressive form, which commences most commonly in childhood and early adolescence, terminating in death after a few months or several years. Emotional lability of the pseudobulbar type (forced crying and laughing), thought of as childishness, and behavioral disorders occur with the development of dysarthria and dysphagia, slowing of voluntary movements, rigidity, and dystonic movements. The acute type is often associated with fever.

Those cases developing in later adolescence or early adulthood more frequently run a prolonged course, without fever, and are characterized by tremulousness, titubation, later contractures, and sometimes convulsive seizures, with eventual evidence of general cerebral insufficiency. These are the patients whose personality disturbances resemble the schizophrenic, hypomanic, and hysterical reactions. Untoward expressions of hostility, temper tantrums, antisocial behavior, and delusional and hallucinatory experiences may occur. The tremor is characteristic, most often involving the distal portion of the extremities. It becomes progressively more violent. When the arms are extended, it appears as though the patient were waving his hands (wing beating).

There is usually little evidence of hepatitis, although occasionally jaundice may precede the illness. The liver is seldom enlarged.

DIAGNOSIS. In addition to the various clinical symptoms and the presence of the Kayser-Fleischer corneal ring, there exist an increased urinary excretion of copper and amino acids and a diminution in serum ceruloplasmin. While a concentration of less than 20 mg. per 100 ml. is almost always diagnostic of the disorder, occasional patients with severe liver disease have normal ceruloplasmin concentrations.

So, too, a biochemical diagnosis of Wilson's disease may be made in asymptomatic members of families carrying the pathogenic gene. This diagnosis allows the institution of early preventive therapy, as Sternlieb and Scheinberg have reported. Determination by whole body reactivity for three or four weeks after intravenous injections of 60 Cu of prolonged retention of the metal, in the absence of cirrhosis, has been demonstrated as evidence of the carrier status. Combined external probe radioactivity studies of uptake of copper in liver and muscle have been suggested as a means of determining whether the individual is a homozygote or heterozygote carrier.

Minor symptoms of nausea and anorexia may precede or accompany the neuropsychiatric disturbance. More recently it has been found in x-ray studies that many patients with Wilson's disease have osteomalacia with pseudofractures and marginal bone fragmentation resembling the changes in the Fanconi syndrome.

PATHOLOGY. There is gross degeneration of the lenticular nuclei, particularly in the putamen and caudate nuclei. Histologically, neuronal degeneration with loss or pathological changes is found not only in the cells of the basal ganglia, but also in those of the cerebral cortex and cerebellum. There are generally nodular cirrhosis of the liver and splenomegaly. Excessive deposition of copper is found in the brain, liver, Descemet's membrane of the cornea, and other organs.

It appears that an excessive absorption of copper takes place from the intestinal tract. Evans, Dubois, and Hambridge postulate that the increased binding affinity of the abnormal liver protein metallothioneine changes the usual copper pool equilibrium in the liver. The liver excretes less copper and less is incorporated into the blood ceruloplasmin. With progression of the disease, the liver binding sites saturate and unbound plasma copper increases. It has been suggested that the excessive copper is toxic due to a blocking effect on coenzyme A or a related enzyme that leads to disturbed pyruvate metabolism.

TREATMENT. The preferred treatment today is by penicillamine (cuprimine), a chelating agent that promotes excretion of copper. It should be prescribed as D-penicillamine in divided oral doses totaling between 1 and 4 gm. daily. It is necessary to maintain an effective negative copper balance in order to bring about continuing therapeutic improvement. This requires repetitive copper balance studies at six- to twelve-month intervals to determine necessary changes in dosage of penicillamine and intake of copper. On carefully regulated regimens with continued penicillamine therapy and reduction of copper intake, a recession of psychiatric, neurologic, and hepatic symptoms takes place, along with a rise in capacity to perform in psychological tests. Since this agent sometimes causes fever, cutaneous eruptions, and, less commonly, hematological and renal reactions, close medical supervision is needed. With continued penicillamine therapy there are a regular recession of neurological symptoms and a variable response in the psychiatric and hepatic disturbances. Goldstein and his colleagues have found that with long-term treatment, as described, the liver slowly increases uptake of copper, suggesting a greater capacity to trap the metal. The Kayser-Fleischer rings recede and the cupriuria diminishes.

For patients sensitive to penicillamine, one may prescribe weekly intramuscular injections of 2,3-dimercaptopropanol (BAL or British antilewisite) in doses of 1.0 to 1.5 ml. of 10 per cent solution in peanut oil, to be given indefinitely. In order to reduce the absorption of copper in the diet, 20 mg. of enteric-coated capsules of potassium sulfide should be given with each meal, in association with a diet low in copper-containing foods.

VITAMIN DEFICIENCY SYNDROMES

In recent years it has been recognized that there is a common factor operative in various mental and neurological phenomena which had been previously regarded as unrelated entities. This common factor is a vitamin deficiency, particularly a deficiency of vitamin B. The localization of the pathological process produced in different parts of the nervous system by the deficiency determines the neurological signs and releases the mental symptoms. The nature of the symptoms or syndrome depends upon the particular member of the B complex in which the deficiency is relatively greatest and upon the part of the nervous system predominantly affected by the deficiency. If the deficiency of nicotinic acid is greatest, the clinical picture produced is that of pellagra. If, because of chronic alcoholism, the patient suffers from thiamine deficiency, he may suffer from a painful thiamine neuropathy, or "alcoholic neuritis." If at the same time there is a nerve cell degeneration in the cerebral cortex resulting from deficiency of another member (or members) of the B complex (probably niacin), the patient will present an alcoholic Korsakoff syndrome.

Wernicke's Syndrome

In 1881 Wernicke described a syndrome consisting of ophthalmoplegia, memory loss, confabulation, apathy, progressive dementia, ataxia, clouding of consciousness, and even coma. It is now known that it is invariably associated with thiamine deficiency and that usually there is a deficiency of niacin also. Because of the thiamine avitaminosis, there is an impaired oxidation of pyruvic acid, which is formed during the breakdown of glucose. As a result, pyruvic acid accumulates in the blood.

Wernicke's "encephalitis" mainly affects chronic alcoholics, but has also been described in pernicious anemia, hyperemesis gravidarum, and gastric cancer, and in prisoners of war. Delirium usually precedes its development. The Wernicke syndrome, formerly observed occasionally in pernicious vomiting of pregnancy or after abdominal or pelvic operations when solutions of glucose were administered in considerable amounts, is now seen much less frequently, apparently because thiamine is given with the glucose as a usual procedure. This syndrome has almost disappeared since 1942, ascribed to the fact that enrichment of bread and flour began in that year.

The pathological changes are mainly in the brain stem and involve the mammillary bodies and the regions adjacent to the aqueduct and to the third and fourth ventricles. The lesions are characterized by various degrees of necrosis of both nerve cells and nerve fibers, together with reactive changes of microglia and astrocytes, alteration of small blood vessels, and in some instances, petechial hemorrhages.

The ocular disturbances take the form of horizontal and vertical nystagmus and various degrees of paralysis of conjugate gaze and of the external recti.

H. B., aged 62, a chronic alcoholic who had been arrested many times for drunkenness, was taken to a general hospital because of confusion and difficulty in walking. There was a history that following a long alcoholic debauch he had been taken into custody by the Salvation Army. For several days the supervision of this organization made it impossible for him to secure alcohol. He then remained at its hotel for several days more, performing light duties until his physical disabilities made employment impossible. Soon after entering the general hospital he became confused, restless, demanding, and was noisy at night. He was then transferred to a psychiatric hospital where the confusion soon subsided. On neurological examination, he showed marked bilateral ptosis, his pupils reacted very slightly to light, and he was totally unable to follow a light in any direction. His speech was thick and slurred; there was a great defect in coordination of his extremities; all tendon reflexes, except the biceps, were absent. The calves of both legs were tender, and he was unable to walk unaided. A diagnosis of Wernicke's syndrome plus peripheral neuritis was made. He was at once placed on large doses of thiamine. He soon began to improve, but the evidence of ophthalmoplegia did not completely disappear for seven months.

If the thiamine deficiency produces peripheral neuropathy, cardiac hypertrophy, myocardial weakness, and edema, the clinical manifestation is that of beriberi, a form of deficiency without mental accompaniment. Beriberi may, however, be associated with

Wernicke's encephalopathy. An uncomplicated thiamine deficiency without any associated neurological phenomena may produce a neurasthenic syndrome characterized by feelings of weakness, easy fatigue, emotional instability, irritability, moodiness, quarrelsomeness, forgetfulness, apathy, mild depression, and vague fears. These symptoms soon disappear after the intake of thiamine is increased.

In nutritional encephalopathy, there is almost never a single vitamin deficiency. In the same individual one may see delirium tremens (the cause of delirium tremens is uncertain, but it is probably a result of a disturbance of cerebral metabolism incident to vitamin deficiency), Korsakoff's psychosis, nicotinic acid encephalopathy (pellagra), and the Wernicke syndrome. There may also be a neuropathy in the form of an "alcoholic neuritis."

Pellagra

Pellagra was first described in 1735 by a Spanish physician, Gasper Casal, under the name *mal de la rosa.* He attributed the disease to a poor diet, but not until 1915 was its dietary origin conclusively demonstrated by Goldberger. In 1937 it was discovered that nicotinic acid (niacin) is the pellagra-preventive vitamin. The principal deficiency, therefore, is in nicotinic acid, although it appears that the disease may also result from a deficiency in the amino acid tryptophan. Usually there are also other associated deficiencies, particularly of thiamine and riboflavin. Often, too, there is a deficiency of ascorbic acid. Many of the neurological symptoms in pellagra are presumably a result of the associated thiamine deficiency.

Pellagra occurs most frequently in communities where the prevailing low economic status leads to extensive nutritional deficiencies. Isolated cases occur among chronic alcoholics whose food has consisted largely of alcohol and has therefore been deficient in vitamin B complex. It is not rare in aged, destitute people who, living alone and in deprivation, suffer from vitamin deficiency. Sporadic cases may also occur in persons suffering from intestinal lesions that interfere with the absorption of food.

It should not be forgotten that pellagra may develop in persons who are already psychotic. This was formerly common in institutions for mental diseases. With more abundant and better-balanced diets, such institutional cases are no longer common.

NEUROPATHOLOGY. There is little experimental evidence indicating that uncomplicated niacin deficiency results in injury to the nervous system. In well-developed cases, neuronal and capillary changes are found distributed throughout the neuraxis, usually most marked in the cerebrum. In the frontal lobes and in the hippocampus, the ganglion cells lose their Nissl substance and may eventually disappear. There may be proliferation of glial cells and of capillary endothelium. The similarity of these changes to those of Meyer's "central neuritis" and Wernicke's syndrome has long been noted.

SYMPTOMS. The early mental symptoms of pellagra are often regarded as psychoneurotic and consist of vague headache, irritability, difficulty in concentration, forgetfulness, restlessness, apprehension, and a feeling of inability for mental or physical effort.

After some months, these are followed by stomatitis and glossitis; the tongue is red and painful and the papillae are atrophic. Digestive disturbances with achlorhydria and diarrhea are common. An early erythema of the skin is followed by coarse scaling and a deep red-brown pigmentation. The dermatitis occurs characteristically on the extensor surfaces of the extremities and on the vulva and inner surfaces of the thighs.

These early symptoms are followed by those of an organic syndrome and consist of memory defects, confusion, disorientation, intermittent delirium, Korsakoff's syndrome, and dementia. Some patients show a manic excitement, while others may be depressed, anxious, apprehensive, or paranoid. Although organically released, the particular type of such reactions will be determined by the patient's previous personality pattern. Later in the disease there may be evidence of irreversible neurological impairment resulting from advanced encephalopathy. This may be in the form of stupor, convulsions, incontinence, muscular rigidity, irregular involuntary movements, hypertonia, defective sensation, and muscle paralysis.

PROGNOSIS. If treatment is begun early, before irreversible neuronal changes have taken place, the prognosis is good, but in neglected cases, permanent impairment of memory and persistent dementia result.

TREATMENT. Mild, ambulatory cases of pellagra are relieved by 100-mg. doses of niacin or niacinamide given three to six times a day. In extremely severe cases the patient should receive 1200 to 1500 mg. a day for several days. Sodium nicotinate may be given intravenously or intramuscularly in 100-mg. doses. Parenteral liver extract given intramuscularly in doses of 20 cc. three to five times daily is indicated in severe cases. Since a thiamine deficiency usually coexists, this vitamin should also be given. The patient should receive from 40 to 200 gm. of powdered brewers' yeast daily, best tolerated in iced milk. The diet should be liberal and include a quart of milk daily, wheat germ, lean meat, liver, and such vegetables as lettuce, spinach, asparagus, fresh peas, cabbage, and tomatoes. Diets high in carbohydrate and fat are contraindicated. The patient should receive and maintain a well-balanced diet of approximately 4000 calories daily.

Pernicious Anemia

Although Addison in his original descriptions of pernicious anemia in 1849 and 1855 spoke of the occasional "wandering of the mind," the mental disorders associated with the disease have received less attention than have the associated neurological disturbances incident to the accompanying degeneration in the spinal cord, first recognized by Lichtheim in 1886. Mental symptoms of depression, anxiety, loss of libido, irritability, poor concentration, and impaired memory range from moderate to severe and have been noted in as high as a third of untreated patients. In Shulman's recent study of those depressed with pernicious anemia, there occurred a high incidence of personal or familial history of depression. These symptoms are probably secondary to disturbances in cerebral metabolism. With the effective and early treatment now available, these symptoms are encountered less frequently. Mental symptoms may be present alone or in association with cord disturbances.

NEUROPATHOLOGY. Areas of degeneration occur in the gray and white matter of the brain. The pyramidal cells undergo disintegration, with the presence of rod cells, an increase in glia, increase in lipoid products in cells, swelling and proliferation of intimal cells in cerebral blood vessels, and miliary hemorrhages. The pathological changes, both in their location and in their nature, are suggestive of those found in Wernicke's encephalopathy.

SYMPTOMS. The time of onset of mental symptoms in relation to the course of pernicious anemia is variable. Although any associated psychosis was formerly thought to be a terminal condition, it is now recognized that mental symptoms may also occur early, even before the typical blood picture of pernicious anemia is established. Except sometimes in the case of confusion, there is no relationship between the degree of anemia and the intensity of the mental symptoms. Although there is no mental syndrome characteristic of pernicious anemia, the mental picture tends to fall into one of the following groups: acute delirioid state, paranoid condition, affective reaction, or organic deterioration. Probably the organic changes release a psychosis, the type of which is predetermined by previous psychogenic factors and psychological mechanisms.

Organic Deterioration. In patients with the organic deterioration syndrome, there is a gradual disintegration of intellectual functions, with impairment of memory and judgment and, at times, periods of confusion.

TREATMENT. Symptoms of delirium and memory impairment improve with liberal doses of liver extract or with vitamin B_{12}. Both should be administered parenterally. During the first week of treatment, 30 μg. of vitamin B_{12} or its equivalent as liver injection USP should be given intramuscularly each day. Thereafter the same dose is given twice weekly. After two months, if the response is satisfactory, a single injection every other week is sufficient.

The depressive states with pernicious anemia are unrelated directly to vitamin B_{12} deficiency, but recovery from the physical effects of the illness leads to relief of the affective reaction.

Acute Vitamin Deficiency Syndrome

Chronic mental syndromes frequently accompany cases of chronic avitaminosis, particularly in thiamine deficiency, but acute mental syndromes are quite uncommon. Jolliffe, however, called attention to what he named "acute nicotinic acid deficiency encephalopathy." This syndrome is characterized by delirium, sucking and grasping reflexes, cogwheel rigidities, and irregular jerking movements of the extremities. This readily disappears after treatment with niacin.

EXHAUSTION DELIRIUM

At times, acute, confusional, delirioid reactions accompany marked states of exhaustion. Since such reactions are not associated with infection, they may best be considered in a discussion of acute syndromes resulting from disturbances of metabolism. Exhaustion delirium occurs occasionally, associated with hemorrhage, unusual and extremely prostrating physical exertion, starvation, prolonged insomnia under conditions of stress or emotional tension, and debilitating effects of emotional tension and effects of a chronic wasting disease such as carcinoma. The symptoms are those of the acute brain syndrome described heretofore (delirium).

This confusional toxic-exhaustive state may continue for several weeks, but recovery finally takes place except in the instances associated with the terminal stages of illness, such as carcinomatosis. After his recovery, the patient may be able to give considerable retrospective interpretation of his delusions and hallucinatory experiences.

TOXIC SUBSTANCES

Toxic substances may interrupt the multiple processes of general cerebral metabolism in a variety of ways. The associated clinical syndrome is that of cerebral insufficiency with various symptomatic expressions, depending upon the degree and suddenness of interruption of ego functions, the extent of permanent cellular damage, and the varieties of adaption to loss of function peculiar to the individual personality.

Such brain syndromes are frequently complications of modern medical therapy or represent the secondary effects of suicidal attempts, self-medication, or industrial poisoning. Again, in this day of heavy pollution of the environment through open disposal of industrial wastes, the syndrome may result from intake of toxic quantities of substances through inhalation, ingestion, or absorption.

Cortisone and ACTH

These agents may produce a wide variety of mental disturbances, resulting, apparently, from their direct effect upon the central nervous system, although the precise pathogenetic mechanisms are not yet determined. The total energy exchange of the brain as measured by cerebral metabolic rate does not seem to be altered by ACTH or by cortisone, yet these hormones disturb enzymatic reactions by altering the electrolyte and water patterns of the body. In general, the mental reactions do not exhibit the type of confusion, disorientation, and sensorial disturbance characteristic of toxic psychoses. Nearly all patients receiving the drugs show an increased joviality and optimism. Among the common disturbances are affective ones varying from depression to hypomania, also from apathy to panic, and even inappropriateness of affect. Feelings of depersonalization, or a sense of detachment or strangeness in awareness of one's body image, may occur. Disturbances of speech are frequent and may vary from mutism to flight of ideas. Illusions and hallucinations may occur, also delusions of depressive, grandiose, or persecutory types. A wide variety of motor disturbances may appear, including immobility, pressure of activity, and regressiveness. In general the type of mental disturbance produced by the drug seems to be determined by the basic pattern or structure of the patient's personality. Complete, spontaneous recovery occurs upon discontinuance of the drug. In prolonged cases, lucid intervals of gradually increasing frequency and duration may be observed until a normal state is fully established.

Experience has shown that the development of psychiatric disturbance with use of the corticosteroids does not indicate that a similar disturbance will take place if the steroid is withheld and then administered again at a later date. Nor is there clear evidence that these reactions are related to dosage.

Isoniazid

With the use of this drug for the treatment of tuberculosis, a number of cases of mental disturbance have been noted. The clinical picture is that of an acute, toxic, confusional disorientation for time, place, person, and situation; also, restlessness, and auditory or visual hallucinations. It is usually preceded by muscular twitching, hyperreflexia, difficulty in micturition, constipation, and sometimes convulsions. Occasionally, this toxic state is followed by signs of an organic cerebral impairment of the Korsakoff type. It has been stated that the toxic mental symptoms are related to the plasma level of the drug and that the majority of psychotic reactions occur in patients receiving more than 8 mg. of isoniazid per kilogram of body weight daily. Pyridoxine in large doses may prevent the appearance of isoniazid neuritis. This agent is not effective in reversing symptoms once they are established.

Lead

ETIOLOGY. Of the various metallic poisons, lead is the one with which mental symptoms are most frequently associated. Both the source of intoxication with lead and the clinical picture differ considerably in adults and children.

With adults the inhalation of toxic lead compounds is the major means of intoxication. The history of exposure in industry or building to paint spraying, burning of lead in salvage operations, oxygas cutting of red lead, painted steel, and older structures during dismantling, as well as vocational employment in bronze, solder, or type metal, or in the modern industries of enameling and glass manufacture, should suggest the possibility of exposure to poisonous, lead-containing vapors. The necessity of considering lead encephalopathy as a complication of chronic alcoholism has been suggested by discovery of this condition in individuals consuming large quantities of illicitly produced alcohol in communities of the southern United States. For the most part, patients with the lead encephalopathy–alcohol withdrawal complex have come from the lower socioeconomic black groups in these communities.

In infants, poisoning occurs through the eating or chewing of lead-containing paint, often picked up in flakes peeling from woodwork or painted surfaces. The occurrence of *pica* in children is frequently associated with mental deficiency, but it occurs also in children of good intellectual endowment who show some emotional disturbance.

Golter and Michaelson recently reported that daily lead administration to newborn rats increases brain norepinephrine, but does not modify brain dopamine levels. The finding suggests a relationship between the increased motor activity and other evidences of impaired cerebral functioning in the infant and child exposed to lead and abnormality in brain norepinephrine–mediated systems.

SYMPTOMS. Mental symptoms associated with lead poisoning tend to be of two types: (1) acute delirious episodes; (2) progressive mental deterioration. The delirious type may occur in either acute or chronic poisoning. It is of sudden onset and is characterized by confusion, insomnia, restlessness, tremors, fear, outbursts of violence, visual hallucinations, and delusions which are frequently persecutory in content. Convulsions may occur and may be accompanied by a delirium in which the patient experiences terrifying visual hallucinations. In the chronic form, apathy or depression, speech defect, forgetfulness, and at times confabulations suggesting the Korsakoff syndrome are frequently observed. The progressive mental deterioration may suggest general paresis. Occasionally the clinical picture is one of neurasthenia; the patient is irritable and depressed and complains of weakness, fatigability, and dizziness. In association with the mental disturbances, there is usually a history of colic, constipation, and vomiting. Colic is frequently more severe in adults than in children. In adults, black deposits may be seen around the gum margins of pyorrheic teeth. This is seldom visible in children. There is usually an associated hypochromic anemia with basophilic stippling. In children there may be a mild renal glycosuria. Coproporphyrinuria commonly accompanies intoxication with lead. Roentgenograms will demonstrate dense radiopaque bands going into the shafts of long bones in children. The spinal fluid protein content is increased to levels between 15 and 200 mg. per 100 ml.

The chronic encephalopathy of children is characterized largely by failure of cerebral maturation and demonstrates itself in defects in attention, judgment, self-control, and visual learning. For those children who survive, a high proportion suffer irreversible brain damage that limits maturation. The major threat to the life and mentality of the children is increased intracranial pressure. Such children may be verbally facile but find it difficult to learn the techniques of reading, writing, and arithmetic. In both adults and children, a characteristic peripheral neuritis is frequently seen. The most used muscle groups are affected rather than those supplied by individual nerves. Thus weakness of the extensors of the wrist occurs in adults and of the dorsiflexors of the feet in children. All tendon reflexes are lost, but sensation remains intact.

Determination of δ-aminolevulinic acid dehydratase (ALA-D) in red blood cells has been found to be a reliable indicator of occupational exposure to low lead concentrations.

TREATMENT. Treatment commences with removal of the patient from exposure to and absorption of lead. Since there is no antidote to lead, therapy must be directed to relief of the symptoms and elimination of lead from the body. Increasing the output of water is the simplest method of increasing the output of lead. Treatment with calcium disodium versenate (ethylene-diamine-tetraacetic acid, EDTA), a chelating agent that has the capacity to form stable, water-soluble complexes with metals, is now recommended to promote the loss of lead from the body. Combined treatment with BAL is said to be more effective. It may be given intravenously and by mouth, 1 gm. to 15 kilograms of body weight per day. One-half the 24-hour dose can be administered at intervals of 12 hours in 250 to 300 ml. of 5 to 10 per cent glucose solution. A test dose of 10 per cent of this amount is recommended. Treatment should be continued for three to four days, followed by an interval of three days, and a total of three or four courses should be given. The level of lead in the blood should then be determined. If the concentration of lead is excessive (0.08 mg. or above per 100 gm.), the course of treatment should be repeated. These interrupted courses of therapy should be repeated until the blood level of lead has fallen below 0.06 mg. per 100 gm. Recently, penicillamine (Cuprimine) has been reported as also effective, but its usage must still be regarded as experimental.

Since lead is stored in the skeleton and may be released later at dangerously high levels, it is recommended that levels of lead in the blood be determined subsequently at intervals of four to six weeks and that further courses be given when dangerous rises are observed. Neurosurgical decompression of the skull may be required in patients with evidence of medullary compression.

In addition to the specific therapy described above, patients with lead encephalopathy will require the general measures used in the care of the delirious states. Those with neuropathy should receive orthopedic protection of the weakened muscles and ligaments. In chronic lead poisoning, alcohol is to be avoided; a high-calcium diet supplemented by vitamin B is indicated.

Mercury

Among the mental symptoms manifested by patients suffering from chronic mercury poisoning are irritability, timidity, discouragement, loss of self-confidence, fear, and occasionally outbursts of extreme anger. Less frequent are apathy, drowsiness, and impairment of memory. Chronic mercury poisoning results from the inhalation of volatile mercury for long periods of time. The hazardous trades are those concerned with the production of mercury and its derivatives, the manufacture of scientific apparatus, preparation of hatters' fur, felt hat making, the extraction of gold from silver by amalgamation, and the application of antifouling plastic paint to the hulls of ships.

Minimata disease—poisoning by methyl mercury—has led to serious brain damage in those exposed to this substance in effluent discharges picked up by fish.

There is usually a moderately fine but later coarse jerking tremor of the orbits, lips, tongue, fingers, and limbs. Sometimes contractions of the limbs occur. The tremor is often intentional and subsides during rest. Weakness of both flexor and extensor muscles of the hand and forearms has been reported. No specific therapy is available for chronic mercury poisoning, although dimercaprol (BAL) has been used in those with acute poisoning. Recovery follows withdrawal from exposure.

Manganese

Workers with manganese may suffer from permanently disabling mental and neurological symptoms. Among the principal neurological symptoms are those of extrapyramidal involvement, including the basal ganglia. Gait and speech disturbances usually exist. Also present are tremors of the tongue and extremities and muscular weakness. About 20 per cent of the cases·show mental symptoms, including restlessness, elation, and uncontrollable laughter or crying. There is no specific therapy available for manganese poisoning.

Carbon Monoxide

The gas that most frequently produces mental disturbances is carbon monoxide. The deleterious effects of this substance, which is inhaled either intentionally or by accident from the exhaust fumes of automobiles or, more infrequently, in illuminating gas or gas produced through the defective combustion of coal in stoves or furnaces, are caused by anoxemia of the brain. Carbon monoxide combines with hemoglobin to form carboxyhemoglobin, a stable compound that prevents the blood from absorbing oxygen. In those patients who die after several days, the central nervous system shows ischemic changes of the nerve cells, as well as areas of softening, particularly in the cerebral cortex and the basal ganglia. Serious mental sequelae of carbon monoxide poisoning are infrequent in relation to the number of acute intoxications.

Mental symptoms following acute poisoning occur only in cases in which the intoxication has been extreme and unconsciousness complete. Of persons developing mental symptoms, about two thirds pass directly from the comatose condition into states of confusion and delirium. In the remainder there exists a clear period of a week or more between emergence from the coma and the appearance of mental symptoms, among which are apathy, lack of initiative, and indifference to duties and responsibilities. Some patients continue to show confusion, bewilderment, and impairment of memory, with Korsakoff-like confabulations. Amnesia lasting from six to nine months may occur. In extreme cases, the patient sinks to the level of vegetative existence, with incontinence, unresponsiveness, and in-

ability to carry on any voluntary activity. Occasionally a patient suffers from auditory aphasia. At times neurological complications may occur, owing usually to degenerative changes in the putamen or globus pallidus. Frequently, therefore, there is a modified parkinsonism, with stiffness of extremities caused by muscular hypertonia. Most patients with mental sequelae of carbon monoxide poisoning begin to improve within a few weeks after exposure and completely recover within two years. Those who have not recovered within that period of time remain in a state of mild or severe mental enfeeblement.

Attention has been called to the immediate and the delayed forms of mental sequelae arising from acute carbon monoxide anoxemia. Persons repeatedly subjected to moderate or minimal toxic amounts of the gas for periods ranging from several months to many years may develop mental and nervous symptoms. Among these manifestations are emotional instability, depression, agitation, anxiety, impairment of grasp and of memory, and at times confusion. Other symptoms are headache, vertigo, neuromuscular pains, digestive disturbances, dyspnea, and palpitation.

Carbon Disulfide

The extensive use of carbon disulfide in the manufacture of rayon has resulted in the production of toxic psychoses through its destructive effect upon the lipid content of neural tissue. Among the most commonly observed early symptoms are insomnia, bad dreams, fatigue, impotence, listlessness, and loss of memory. Neurologically there may be symptoms referable to almost any part of the central and peripheral nervous system. Among them are tenderness of nerve trunks and areas of hyperesthesia followed by loss of touch and pain sensation. Signs of irritated motor nerves include fibrillary twitching and spasmodic contraction of nerves. Among motor signs are early fatigue, weakness, and flaccid paralysis. Basal ganglia symptoms may include parkinsonism, thalamic syndrome, and choreoathetosis. Diminution and loss of corneal and pupillary reflexes are common.

Other Drugs

Several other drugs may occasionally produce delirium, particularly belladonna, chloral hydrate, and paraldehyde. Of these, belladonna probably leads most frequently to toxic symptoms. Occasionally patients, especially children, may develop delirium following the introduction of atropine into the eye. In addition to the usual physiological symptoms, the patient manifests a delirium marked by fear, excitement, and visual and auditory hallucinations. Prolonged use of chloral hydrate may lead to a delirium lasting two or more weeks.

Recently, there have been noted both acute and chronic symptoms of cerebral insufficiency in individuals exposed to organic phosphorus insecticides, which may irreversibly inhibit cholinesterase.

BIBLIOGRAPHY

ENDOCRINE DISORDERS

Brodie, H. K. H.: Central Control of Endocrine Systems. *In* Usdin, G. (ed.): Psychiatric Medicine. New York, Brunner-Mazel, 1977.

Adrenal

Hellman, L., Weitzman, E. D., Roffwarg, H., et al.: Effect of o,p'-DDD on cortisol secretory pattern in Cushing's syndrome. J. Clin. Endocr., *31*:227–230, 1970.

Moorhead, E. L., Caldwell, J. R., Kelly, H. R., and Morales, A. R.: The diagnosis of pheochromocytoma. J.A.M.A., *196*:1107–1133, 1966.

Trethowan, W. H., and Cobb, S.: Neuropsychiatric aspects of Cushing's syndrome. Arch. Neurol. Psychiatry, *67*:283–309, 1952.

Thyroid

Flagg, G. W., Clemens, T. L., Michael, E. A., Alexander, F., and Wark, J.: A psychophysiological investigation of hyperthyroidism. Psychosom. Med., *27*:497–507, 1965.

Parathyroid

Denko, J. D., and Kaebling, R.: The psychiatric aspects of hypoparathyroidism. Acta Psychiatr. Scand., *38*, Suppl. 164, 1964.

Reilly, E. L., and Wilson, W. P.: Mental symptoms in hyperparathyroidism. Dis. Nerv. Syst., *26*:361–363, 1965.

Pancreas

Fras, I., Litin, E. M., and Pearson, J. S.: Comparison of psychiatric symptoms in carcinoma of the pancreas and those in some other intra-abdominal neoplasms. Am. J. Psychiatry, *123*:1553–1562, 1967.

Rynearson, E. H.: Hyperinsulinism among malingerers. Med. Clin. North Am., *31*:477–480, 1947.

Schuster, M. M., and Iber, F. L.: Psychosis with pancreatitis. Arch. Intern. Med., *116*:228–233, 1965.

METABOLIC DISORDERS

Porphyria

Cram, D. L., et al.: Lupus erythematosus and porphyria. Arch. Dermatol., *108*:779–784, 1973.

Lesse, H., and Wetterberg, L.: Learned behaviour and limbic system activity in experimental porphyria. Arch. Gen. Psychiatry, *27*:119–124, 1972.

Nair, P. P., Mezey, E., Murty, H. S., et al.: The effect of vitamin E on porphyrin metabolism in man. Arch. Intern. Med., *128*:411–415, 1971.

Ridley, A., Hierons, R., and Cavannaugh, J. B.: Tachycardia and neuropathy of porphyria. Lancet, *2*:708–709, 1968.

Schwarz, D., and Mertin, J.: Die Anwendung von Propranolol bei der akuten intermittierenden Porphyrie. Nervenarzt, *44*:648–651, 1973.

Hepatolenticular Degeneration

Evans, G. W., Dubois, R. S., and Hambridge, K. M.: Wilson's disease; Identification of an abnormal protein. Science, *181*:1175–1176, 1975.

Goldstein, N. P., Tauxe, W. N., McCall, J. T., Gross, J. B., and Randall, R. V.: Treatment of Wilson's disease (hepatolenticular degeneration) with penicillamine and low copper diet. Trans. Am. Neurol. Assoc., *94*:34–37, 1969.

Goldstein, N. P., Tauxe, W. N., McCall, J. T., Randall, R. V., and Gross, J. B.: Wilson's disease (hepatolenticular degeneration). Arch. Neurol., *24*:391–400, 1971.

O'Reilly, S., Weber, P. M., Pollycove, M., and Shipley, L.: Detection of the carrier of Wilson's disease. Neurology, *20*:1133–1138, 1970.

Sternlieb, I., and Scheinberg, I. H.: Prevention of Wilson's disease in asymptomatic patients. N. Engl. J. Med., *278*:352–359, 1968.

Tauxe, W. N., Wellvonseder, R., and Goldstein, N. P.: Body retention of injected $^{67}C_4$ in patients with homozygous and heterozygous Wilson's disease and in normal subjects. Mayo Clin. Proc., *49*:386–389, 1974.

Walshe, J. M.: Wilson's disease. Biochem. J., *111*:8P–9P, 1969.

NUTRITIONAL DEFICIENCIES

Shulman, R.: Psychiatric aspects of pernicious anemia: A prospective study. Br. Med. J., *3*:266–269, 1967.

TOXIC SUBSTANCES

Cheatham, J. S., and Chobot, E. F., Jr.: The clinical diagnosis and treatment of lead encephalopathy. South. Med. J., *61*:529–531, 1969.

Cummings, J. N.: Heavy Metals and the Brain. Springfield, Ill., Charles C Thomas, 1959.

Gilbert, G. J., and Glaser, G. H.: Neurologic manifestations of chronic carbon monoxide poisoning. N. Engl. J. Med., *261*:1217–1220, 1959.

Golter, M., and Michaelson, I. A.: Growth, behavior, and brain catecholamines in lead-exposed neonatal rats: a reappraisal. Science, *187*:359–361, 1975.

Jenkins, C. D., and Mellins, R. B.: Lead poisoning in children. Arch. Neurol. Psychiat., *77*:70–78, 1957.

Karpinski, F. E., Rieders, F., and Gersh, L. S. Calcium disodium versenate in the therapy of lead encephalopathy. J. Pediatr., 42:687–699, 1953.

Pleasure, H.: Psychiatric and neurologic side effects of isoniazid and iproniazid. Arch. Neurol. Psychiatry, *72*:313–320, 1954.

Ritchie, E. A.: Toxic psychosis under cortisone and corticotrophin. J. Ment. Sci., *102*:830–837, 1956.

Tokuomi, H.: Comparison between the cerebellar signs of organic mercury poisoning and those of other neurological disorders. (Japanese). Adv. Neurol. Sci., *19*:706–713, 1975.

Tomokuni, K.: δ-Aminolevulinic acid dehydratase test for lead exposure. Arch. Environ. Health, *29*:274–281, 1974.

17

CHRONIC BRAIN SYNDROMES ASSOCIATED WITH DISEASES OF UNKNOWN OR UNCERTAIN CAUSE

"When the mind is in a state of uncertainty the smallest impulse directs it to either side."

Terence

Dr. George Huntington
(From Am. J. Anat., *39*(3):(front.), 1927.)

DEMYELINATING DISEASES

Although demyelinization within the nervous system occurs as the consequence of vascular lesions, infectious illnesses, and nutritional and toxic disturbances, this type of pathological lesion is not the primary phenomenon in these disorders. Multiple sclerosis and the various forms of diffuse sclerosis (encephalitis periaxialis diffusa of

Schilder, encephalitis periaxialis concentrica of Balo, and the several forms of progressive cerebral sclerosis) form the group of primary demyelinizing disorders. The etiology of these structural disturbances of the nervous system is unknown. Their importance to the clinical psychiatrist springs from the concomitant personality disturbance noticed in the course of the illness, or the behavioral abnormalities

335

often confused with other disturbances of personality. Their differentiation is important for therapeutic and prognostic reasons.

MULTIPLE SCLEROSIS

Despite the fact that multiple sclerosis is definitely a structural disease of the nervous system, in a considerable percentage of patients personality problems are present at the onset or during the course of the disease. Both in multiple sclerosis and in Parkinson's syndrome, enough concomitant psychiatric symptoms may be present to mask the organic picture, with the result that a psychiatric instead of a neurological diagnosis is made. Psychotic symptoms are, however, rare.

There is no characteristic syndrome determined by the organic pathology of the disease. The general nature of the symptoms tends to be dependent upon the personality makeup of the individual patient. Frequently, therefore, we see paranoid, depressive, hypomanic, or expansive reactions. Previous personality patterns of these types may, through the damage sustained by the personality at the organic level, become exaggerated. As a compensating psychological reaction to the disorganizing, destructive effect of the disease, one often observes a pathological complacency, cheerfulness, and even euphoria. These symptoms occur so frequently that they have often been erroneously regarded as a particular feature of the disease process itself.

Sometimes the patient's reaction to his disability is marked by an irritability or emotional instability that seriously disturbs interpersonal relationships. Impaired control over the expression of laughter and of crying resulting from bilateral upper motor neuron defects is often a significant feature. The emotional instability is associated with the clinical impression of intellectual impairment. If the explosive and forced laughing or crying occurs, the patient does not feel any affect such as the emotional signs suggest. A few patients manifest serious behavior disorders. These are occasionally observed in patients who are impotent but nevertheless have an increase in sex urge. Emotional lability and intellectual impairment are often found in patients with marked neurological disability.

Examination of cerebrospinal fluid will reveal some abnormality in cell count, total protein, or colloidal reaction in a majority of the cases. The electroencephalogram is abnormal in half of the patients, although there is no pattern specifically diagnostic.

Therapy today is directed to symptomatic relief and restoration or maintenance of social and motor skills.

DIFFUSE SCLEROSIS

The most common type is that known as Schilder's disease, which occurs as a rapidly progressive disorder productive of various mental symptoms, convulsions, loss of vision, and motor or sensory defects. Fatal cases show extensive demyelinization of the cerebral hemispheres. The signs and symptoms are inconstant from patient to patient and depend upon those areas of the cortical hemispheres involved. Headache, vomiting, and vertigo are common. Memory defects, apathy or irritability, personality changes, or confusion with disorientation and dementia may occur. The neurological signs are extensive. Cortical blindness is common. Hemianopsia, optic atrophy, and choked discs have been observed. All varieties of motor and sensory disturbances, with the associated defects in neurological examinations, may occur. Occasionally these conditions are confused with brain tumors caused by the increase in intracranial pressure. Early in the course of these illnesses they have been confused with hysterical or schizophrenic reactions. The spinal fluid shows no consistent changes. In the majority of instances, these illnesses are clinically progressive and terminate fatally following the development of dementia and quadriplegia with decerebrate rigidity. Remissions occasionally occur. Treatment consists presently of providing symptomatic care and nursing.

PARALYSIS AGITANS

In his "Essay on Shaking Palsy," published in 1817, James Parkinson, himself a victim, described the disease of late middle life now known as paralysis agitans. With its degenerative lesions of the extrapyramidal system, particularly of the corpus striatum and substantia nigra, the neurological symptoms are the conspicuous features of the clinical picture. A similar symptom complex may be induced by viral infections (encephalitis), trauma, or such toxins as manganese, carbon monoxide, and the phenothiazines. In almost all instances, toxin-induced parkinsonism is reversible.

The chronic progressive muscular rigidity, the immobile facies, the posture of flexion of neck, trunk, and extremities, the poverty of movement, and the slow, rhythmic tremor affecting the extremities to varying degrees constitute a striking syndrome. In many cases there are no mental symptoms. Most patients present a good-natured complaisance, but some, in reaction to their disability, are irritable, peevish, and dissatisfied.

Depressive reactions with obsessive-compulsive features are among the most frequently observed personality responses to this disorder. It remains unclear whether the depressive reactions that occur so frequently with parkinsonism are initiated and maintained by the now known defects in brain catecholamine metabolism, represent psychological reactions to the increasing impairment of motor function, or are a complex combination of the pathophysiological and psychosocial forces. Robins' study supports significantly the pathophysiological component in determining the higher incidence of depression in those with this illness. The fact that the patient finds himself in a continuously contracting environment in which he becomes more and more dependent on other members of the family creates many emotional problems.

With the discovery by Hornykiewicz of diminution of dopamine in the corpus striatum and the substantia nigra, where norepinephrine is absent, there was initiated a large number of studies that support the contention that abnormalities in brain catecholamine metabolism and, particularly, those functions dependent on dopamine transmission, represent the fundamental issues leading to this disease. The accumulated evidence relating abnormalities and brain catecholamine metabolism is summarized in Table 17–1.

Levodopa, $(-)$-3-(3,4-dihydroxyphenyl)-L-alanine, has been discovered

TABLE 17–1   Evidence Relating Brain Catecholamines to Parkinson's Disease

Human Brain	↓ Striatal dopamine correlated with cell loss in substantia nigra and with akinesia
	↓ Homovanillic acid, norepinephrine, serotonin
	↓ L-Dopa decarboxylase
Human CSF	↓ Homovanillic acid
Human Plasma	↓ Dopamine β-oxidase levels
Human Urine	Low homovanillic acid
Drug Effects	Therapy with L-Dopa, amphetamine, monoamine oxidase inhibitors, apomorphine: production of akinesia or rigidity by reserpine or dopamine receptor blockers
Animal Models	Midbrain lesions ↓ dopamine in basal ganglia, produce tremor, hypokinesia, rigidity: L-Dopa or ET-495 reverse lesion-induced signs

(From Wurtman, R. J., and Moskowitz, M. A.: Trans. Am. Neurol. Assoc., *99*:148–159, 1974.)

TABLE 17–2   Major Psychiatric Side Effects of Levodopa
Among 908 Reported Patients

| | | INCIDENCE |
SIDE EFFECTS	NO.	%
Confusion, delirium	40	4.4
Depression	38	4.2
Overactivity, restlessness, agitation	33	3.6
Psychosis, delusions, paranoia	33	3.6
Hypomania	14	1.5
Hypersexual behavior	8	0.9
Miscellaneous	14	1.5
Total	180	20.0

(From Goodwin, F. K.: J.A.M.A., *218*:1915–1920, 1971.)

to be the most effective agent for the relief of the parkinsonian syndrome, modifying rigidity and bradykinesia in particular. In some it reduces tremor, postural instability, dysphagia, and sialorrhea, as well as depression, dementia-like symptoms, and impotence.

The optimal therapeutic dose of levodopa for each individual must be carefully assessed through gradual administration of increasing dosage. It is usual to commence administration with 0.5 to 1 gm. daily in divided doses, increased by 0.125 to 0.75 gm. every three days to tolerance. The average daily therapeutic level is 1 to 6 gm. given three or more times with food.

The common side effects are nausea, vomiting, anorexia, postural hypotension and cardiac arrhythmias, and involuntary movements. Some patients develop severe agitation and hallucinations as well as restlessness and insomnia, which are relieved by withdrawing the medication. The variety and frequency of psychiatric side effects of levodopa are shown in Table 17–2 from Goodwin. Sacks and his colleagues warn that parkinsonian patients with dementia are prone to respond to this therapeutic agent with serious and prolonged adverse reactions and caution that its prescription to such individuals be given with utmost care. Table 17–3 lists some actions of levodopa on brain metabolism.

The drug should not be given when a sympathomimetic amine is contraindicated. Concomitant treatment with monoamine oxidase inhibitors is contraindicated, but the tricyclic antidepressants have been used effectively with levodopa to treat depression with parkinsonism. The dopa decarboxylase

TABLE 17–3   Some Effects of L-Dopa on Brain Metabolism

Increases *dopamine* levels transiently (within both dopaminergic and nondopaminergic cells)
Increases *norepinephrine* levels transiently
Releases stored *serotonin* and *norepinephrine*
Depletes S-adenosylmethionine, thereby slowing the O-methylation of catecholamines (and potentiating their physiologic effects)
Causes brain to accumulate 3-O-methyldopa
Competes with other *neutral amino acids* for transport into the brain
Disaggregates brain *polyribosomes*, thereby transiently suppressing *protein synthesis*
May increase requirements for B_{12}, *folic acid*, and *pyridoxine*

(From Wurtman, R. J., and Moskowitz, M. A.: Trans. Am. Neurol. Assoc., *99*:148–159, 1974.)

inhibitor carbidopa, combined with levodopa, should be tried when patients develop nausea, anorexia, and vomiting on prescription of levodopa alone.

Pyridoxine, in small doses, has been used to relieve the torsion dystonias and choreoathetoid movements sometimes induced by levodopa. Levodopa may be given with the solanaceous drugs and the synthetic antispasmodics.

Drugs of the solanaceous group have been used for over 80 years in the treatment of this disease. Hyoscine hydrobromide in doses of 0.3 or 0.6 mg. three times daily by mouth is the most commonly prescribed medication.

Of several synthetic antispasmodic drugs, trihexyphenidyl (Artane) is now widely employed. The initial dose is 1 mg. on the first day, increased to 1 to 2 mg. daily up to a total of 4 to 8 mg. divided into three or four doses. Elderly patients usually can take only 1 to 2 mg. daily. Toxic effects of these drugs are dryness of the mouth, excessive mydriasis, gastrointestinal upsets, and, rarely, a delirious reaction. In cases of severe muscle rigidity, contracture, and spasm, the powerful muscle-relaxant action of benztropine mesylate (Cogentin) may prove helpful. It is longer acting than other antispasmodics and can be taken in doses of 0.5 to 1 or 2 mg. in older patients and 1 to 4 mg. in younger patients, usually once a day on retiring. Procyclidine hydrochloride (Kemadrin) combines antirigidity action with a strong cerebral-stimulating action that is helpful in patients with somnolence and depression. The initial dose is usually 2.5 mg. three times daily, gradually increasing to 5 mg. three times daily. Another antiparkinsonian drug which has been increasingly employed is orphenadrine hydrochloride (Disipal). The average dose is 50 mg. three times a day. It is a harmless preparation with minimal side reactions. Its chief drawback is the tendency for the good effects to wear off in the course of months.

For those patients with an associated depressive reaction and its related symptoms, imipramine (Tofranil) or its analogues should be prescribed in doses of 25 to 50 mg. three or four times daily. This agent not only is effective in relieving the affective complications but also has proved useful in modifying rigidity and bradykinesia. It contrasts with agents of the phenothiazine group, then, which may induce parkinsonian-like states.

As Boshes and his colleagues have observed, patients capable of being maintained without complications on levodopa retain almost all the functions over many years (six in their study) that they had when this treatment commenced. The only impairments observed over time were in logical memory (ability to deal with complex input) and in the visual search mechanism.

HUNTINGTON'S CHOREA

Huntington's chorea is a degenerative disease of the central nervous system resulting from a dominant mutation. The first distinctive description of the disease was given in 1872 by Dr. George Huntington, whose father and grandfather had practiced medicine at East Hampton, Long Island, for a period conjointly covering 78 years. They had observed families in which an incurable chorea had existed for generations among the adult members. No person not descended from a progenitor so tainted has ever been known to develop the disease. It is inherited as a pure mendelian characteristic. It behaves as a dominant, with the result that there is a probability of 0.5 that the offspring of a sufferer will develop the disease. Over 1000 cases in the United States have been traced to three individuals who emigrated from an English village in 1630. Its organic basis was demonstrated by Alzheimer. The essential pathology consists of a slow degeneration of the cells of the caudate nucleus, the putamen, and the cerebral cortex.

Symptoms

The onset of Huntington's chorea is insidious and, generally speaking, occurs between the ages of 30 and 45 years. Frequently a change of character antedates or accompanies the appearance of the choreiform symptoms. The patient may be irritable, obstinate, and moody and lack initiative. In other cases the picture may be one of fatuous euphoria. Esthetic and ethical senses are blunted. Many patients become fault-finding, spiteful, irascible, and even destructive and assaultive. These emerging personality traits adversely affect their relations in marriage, their family, and their vocation. There is an increasing lack of spontaneity in activity, of concern as to the disease, and of solicitude as to obligations of conscience, affection, or ideals. Suspiciousness, jealousy, and paranoid trends, even to the extent of well-developed delusions of persecution, appear. Some patients experience hallucinations. With the increasing emotional deterioration, there is a coincident impairment of attention, memory, and judgment. Interest in life becomes progressively narrower. There is also a poverty of ideas and a disorderliness of thought. The dementia may become extreme.

Before the choreiform movements are clearly manifest and as muscle tone increases, with twitching, bobbing movements, and inability to remain still, accidents are frequent, owing to falls or collisions with objects. Complaints of soreness and stiffness of joints, weakness, and arthritis are common at this age.

The choreiform movements usually appear first in the upper extremity, neck, and face. These involuntary movements are clumsy, irregular, jerky, stretching ones. In the early stages it appears as if the patient were merely inattentive or careless in his movements, which gradually increase in intensity and incoordination. The contractions of the facial muscles result in grimaces while those of the tongue, lips, and respiratory muscles lead to a hesitating, explosive, poorly articulated type of speech which, in advanced cases, is difficult to understand. The choreiform movements result in a shuffling, dancing type of gait associated with irregular movements of the trunk. The movements usually cease during sleep. As the disease progresses, there is interference with swallowing, walking becomes impossible, and the patient may become bedridden. The tendon reflexes are increased. Suicide is not uncommon.

The diagnosis usually remains undetermined from onset of symptoms for from one to over ten years.

R. A. was admitted to a mental hospital at the age of 56. The familial incidence of Huntington's chorea was striking. The maternal grandmother, a maternal uncle and his daughter, the patient's mother and four of the patient's siblings exhibited definite symptoms of Huntington's chorea. Two members of the family committed suicide after they had developed the disease. Prior to her illness the patient was apparently an attractive, well-adjusted person. She was a Girl Scout leader and took part in community affairs. Shortly before she was 35 years of age she began to show an insidious change of personality. She discontinued her church, Girl Scout, card club and other activities; she lost interest in her family and at times wandered away from home, returning at night but giving no information as to where she had been. In this same period she began to drop articles and to show twitching of her hands.

The patient became neglectful of her personal appearance, refused to comb her hair, bathe, or change her clothes. She refused to launder soiled garments and would hide them in closets or corners. The choreiform movements increased in extent, and she occasionally fell. At times she showed temporary alertness and interest in anticipation of a visit from her daughter, but after one or two days she drifted back into her former seclusiveness and deteriorated habits.

On many occasions she threatened and even attacked her husband, sometimes with a knife, and on one occasion inflicted a four-inch scalp wound. She became profane and her favorite term in addressing her husband was "You G– d– fool." She was subject to tantrums in which she would threaten to jump from a window. She came to be known to the children in the neighborhood as "the old witch on the third floor." Finally, the choreiform movements became so extreme that it was difficult for her to go up and down stairs and she often fell.

On arrival at the hospital, her facial expression was vacant and she showed such uncoordinated and choreiform movements of her legs that she had difficulty in walking without assistance. There were gross choreiform movements of the head and all extremities. Her constant grimacing, blinking of her eyes, and twitching of her fingers were quite striking. The coordination of her hands was so poor and the movements of her head were so extreme that she had difficulty in eating. Her speech was explosive and difficult to understand. Although somewhat irritable, demanding, and distrustful, she adjusted to the hospital environment without serious difficulty.

Treatment

Treatment is directed toward relief of symptoms and emotional support. Oral fluphenazine given in increasing daily doses until the initial toxic symptoms of parkinsonism disappear (usually 6 to 8 mg. daily) will reduce the choreic activity and improve the mental status in the majority of patients. Some report this drug more effective in treatment of women than of men. Haloperidol has had similar therapeutic effect.

The average duration of life is 15 years.

LUPUS ERYTHEMATOSUS

The psychiatrist practicing in the general hospital now frequently encounters lupus erythematosus disseminata as a condition with various reaction formations, or with delirious and psychotic manifestations. This condition, once considered rare, is now frequently diagnosed on the medical services because of the increasing awareness of the symptomatology and a better knowledge of the tissue and cellular pathology, including the existence of the now well known "LE cells."

Lupus erythematosus disseminata is one of the group of conditions now known as diseases of the collagen tissues. In lupus the primary damage is to the subendothelial connective tissue of capillaries, small arteries, and veins, and the endocardium and synovial membranes. Approximately 85 per cent of all clinically recognized cases occur in women. The onset of the illness usually takes place in childhood but is most commonly recognized dur-

ing adolescence and early adult life. The pathological changes are found in the ground substance and collagen that serves as a matrix and binding substance for the capillaries and small blood vessels in various parts of the body. Gross thickening is found in the endocardial and pericardial tissues, while the small arteries and arterioles of various organs, including the brain, show a fibroid degeneration and necrosis in the connective tissue matrix of the vessel wall. In certain of the affected areas of connective tissue, the intercellular ground substance shows deep metachromatic staining or the presence of eosinophilic masses, thought to be a result of the swelling and fibroid degeneration of collagen fibers. Certain deep purplish staining material found in some of the affected areas has been identified histochemically as desoxyribonucleic acid. This is apparently the abnormal chromatin material found in the so-called LE cells of the blood and bone marrow on dry smears.

In one series of cases, 50 per cent presented delirious or psychosis-like phenomena at some time during the course of their illness. Another small group developed neurosis-like symptoms, while a considerable number had neurological signs at one time or another.

The early symptoms of the condition are easy fatigability, malaise, and fever. The so-called butterfly rash that occurs across the bridge of the nose and on the cheeks, often considered a traditional lesion of the disease, is not present or necessary for the diagnosis of systemic lupus erythematosus. Commonly, the initial signs are those of migratory reactions of joint and fibrous tissue simulating rheumatic fever or rheumatoid arthritis. Examination sometimes discloses anemia, lymphadenopathy, and edema, or signs indicating pathology involving the pleura, lungs, heart, pericardium, or gastrointestinal tract. The differentiation of the illness from rheumatic fever or rheumatoid arthritis is suggested on finding hematuria. The LE cell is found in stained blood of bone marrow smears, particularly those made from clotted blood or the buffy layer of heparinized blood. They consist of phagocytes containing masses of chromatin material, which stain deep purple with Wright's or Giemsa stain. When the LE cell test, the fluorescent antibody test, and complement-fixation tests are employed, almost every case will show a positive reaction to one of the three. Usually there are leukopenia, elevation of sedimentation of the erythrocytes, and occasionally intermittently or falsely positive serological reactions for syphilis.

At the onset of the illness, anxiety is often evident, and the patient may manifest personality changes that are frequently considered to be reflective of the personality structure. Phobic, depressive, and schizophrenic pictures have been seen, as well as delirioid reaction. The psychiatric disorders have been thought by many to be related to the use of steroid therapy in the course of this illness. The psychotic reactions are usually apparent some 12 days after the institution of steroid therapy, with a maximum of 30 days and a minimum of 2. It must be concluded, however, that the steroid therapy per se is not related to the occurrence of the disturbance of mental functioning. In one group of patients, a large number recovered from the initial delirioid psychotic reaction only to have an active recurrence of lupus at a later time. The majority, when placed on an equivalent dose of ACTH or cortisone, did not again present the mental aberration. Exacerbation of the lupus erythematosus itself, rather than the usage of the steroids, appeared to increase the possibility of the occurrence of psychiatric disturbances.

Although remissions may occur, and cortisone and ACTH have proved effective in inducing prompt improvement, most sufferers ultimately die from renal insufficiency and intercurrent pneumococcal or streptococcal infection. The majority who present psy-chotic disturbances have characteristic lesions in the cerebral hemisphere at autopsy.

The behavior disturbances associated with this illness often require protective hospitalization and careful nursing. Cortisone and ACTH should be administered. The former is usually given in dosages of 0.025 gm. every six hours intramuscularly. Cortisone may be administered orally 0.15 to 0.30 gm. in four divided doses during the day. Following seven to ten days on this dosage, the agents may be gradually reduced each succeeding two or three days until a maintenance level is reached, below which evidences of clinical activity are observed to recur. The majority of the patients require a small maintenance dosage for indefinite periods. The careful collaboration of a psychiatrist and the internist is often indicated in the treatment of disseminated lupus erythematosus.

J. M.: Five months before her admission to a general hospital, this 18-year-old girl noticed fatigability, sore throat, and fever associated with pain on movements of the ankles, fingers, and joints. These symptoms improved. About four weeks before admission she suffered nausea, loss of appetite, and intermittent vomiting. Eleven days before admission she developed double vision on lateral gaze, at first intermittent, but later constant. A few days later her vision was blurred. On admission her temperature was 98.8° F., pulse 82, respiration rate 14. She had lost 10 pounds in weight.

At this time her behavior and mental status were not unusual. She appeared thin, showed some unsteadiness in standing, and had double vision on lateral gaze, but otherwise there seemed to be no conspicuous physical disturbances. Her urine contained albumin; there was evidence of liver dysfunction with a positive cephalin flocculation test. Electroencephalogram was abnormal with disorganization and slowing in the temporal areas and periods of low voltage, 4 to 7 per second activity. At this time the sedimentation rate equaled 82 mm. per hour. Bilateral papilledema developed. A medical consultant suggested that the patient had either rheumatoid arthritis or possibly disseminated lupus erythematosus. An internal carotid arteriogram was normal. Treatment was commenced with cortisone. The spinal fluid contained 460 mg. of protein per 100 ml. The patient's symptoms increased, particularly those referred to the joint pains. When she finally received 100 mg. of cortisone daily two months after admission, her symptoms subsided quickly.

She was then discharged to her home on cortisone, 75 mg. daily.

She remained well at home until three months later, when she became very elated and overactive. She spoke of her body and brain shrinking; she said that she was becoming a baby again and would shortly die. Her return to the hospital was precipitated by a series of convulsions. She then seemed quiet and rather suspicious, but occasionally she called out for help in a loud voice. She failed to recognize certain physicians who had treated her before. The cortisone dosage was reduced from 125 to 75 mg. and her symptoms remitted.

Later the patient recounted that the psychotic disturbance occurred when she had the impression that she "was getting much better on the cortisone. I was getting stronger. About 8 p.m. when I was watching television I suddenly got the feeling that I was going to change into a baby. Previously I had talked to my relatives about this, but they didn't pay any attention to it. I felt that I was going to be bald, that all my hair was inside of my head, and that they couldn't operate to let the hair out. I felt that I was cramped up and couldn't move." (At this point she assumed the fetal position.) "I felt that I was going to die like a girl that I knew while in the hospital. I was in a dream." She declared that she felt that, when blood was being drawn from her arm, the purpose was to drain every drop of blood from her. "I felt that all the people in the ward were German spies. One of them had an Irish accent, but I felt it was a German accent. They were trying to electrocute me. When my mother came to visit me, I tried to push her off the bed so that she would not be electrocuted, but she didn't understand this. I felt that all the nurses were traitors—German spies." She seemed to interpret the slightest remark or facial expression as something of significance to her; she was frightened when the doctors approached her. Her sensorium was clear.

Some five days later the psychotic picture disappeared. A blood smear showed LE cells. The encephalogram performed at the time of the behavior disturbance revealed an increase in the abnormality. The patient was discharged on 75 mg. of cortisone daily.

Because of increased weakness, joint pains, and general debility, she was readmitted to the hospital seven months later. At this time no psychotic disturbance was evident, although she was carefully followed by a psychiatrist. She was from time to time preoccupied by a fear of death and freely called for psychiatric help when most anxious. No recurrence of psychiatric symptoms took place on elevation of the daily dose of cortisone to 87 mg. Following another period at home, she returned to the hospital two months later with hemiparesthesia and expired shortly thereafter. Necropsy disclosed the typical pathology of lupus erythematosus.

BIBLIOGRAPHY

Demyelinating Diseases

Ross, A. T., and Reitan, R. N.: Intellectual and affective functions in multiple sclerosis. Arch. Neurol. Psychiatry, 73:633–677, 1955.

Paralysis Agitans

Boshes, B., Arbit, J., Dolkert, M., et al.: The sixth year after L-dopa. Quality of life and insights derived. Trans. Am. Neurol. Assoc., 100:166–168, 1975.

Goodwin, F. K.: Psychiatric side effects of levodopa in man. J.A.M.A., 218:1915–1920, 1971.

Hornykiewicz, O.: Dopamine (3-hydroxytyramine) and brain function. Pharmacol. Rev., 18:925–964, 1966.

Lieberman, A., Goodgold, A., Jones, S., and Leibowitz, M.: Comparison of dopa decarboxylase inhibitor (carbidopa) combined with levodopa and levodopa alone in Parkinson's disease. Neurology, 25:911–916, 1975.

Parkinson, J.: An Essay on the Shaking Palsy. London, Sherwood, Neely & Jones, 1817.

Robins, A. H.: Depression in patients with parkinsonism. Br. J. Psychiatry, 128:141–145, 1976.

Sacks, O. W., Kohl, M. S., Messeloff, C. R., and Schwartz, W. F.: Effects of levodopa in parkinsonian patients with dementia. Neurology, 22:516–519, 1972.

Wurtman, R. J., and Moskowitz, M. A.: Brain catecholamines in neurological disease. Trans. Am. Neurol. Assoc., 99:148–159, 1974.

Huntington's Chorea

Enna, S. J., Bird, E. D., Bennett, J. P., et al.: Huntington's chorea: Changes in neurotransmitter receptors in brain. N. Engl. J. Med., 294:1305–1309, 1976.

Huntington, G.: On chorea. Med. Surg. Reporter, 26:317, 1972.

McCaughey, W. T. E.: The pathologic spectrum of Huntington's chorea. J. Nerv. Ment. Dis., 133:91–108, 1961.

Whittier, J. R., and Koreny, C.: Effect of oral fluphenazine on Huntington's chorea. Int. J. Neuropsychiat., 4:1–3, 1968.

Lupus Erythematosus

Heine, B. E.: Psychiatric aspects of systemic lupus erythematosus. Acta Psychiatr. Scand., 45:307–326, 1969.

Malamud, N., and Saver, G.: Neuropathologic findings in disseminated lupus erythematosus. Arch. Neurol. Psychiatry, 71:723–731, 1954.

18

SCHIZOPHRENIC DISORDERS

"Though this be madness, yet there is method in it."

Shakespeare

SCHIZOPHRENIA
(Courtesy of the National Association for Mental Health, New York, N.Y.).

Although the variety of behavioral expressions designated as the schizophrenias are relatively easily described and, in their grosser expressions, recognized with ease, even by the inexperienced, neither their definition nor the etiologic factors predisposing to them or precipitative of them have been universally agreed upon.

While avoiding a position that tends to emphasize the chronicity of schizo-

phrenia, as did Kraepelin, the writers of the third edition of the Diagnostic and Statistical Manual of the American Psychiatric Association (DSM-III) exclude from this diagnosis illnesses of less than six months' duration, as well as all conditions without gross psychotic behaviors and those previously labeled as latent, simple, or borderline. Other exclusions in this manual are patients who present schizophrenic features after age 45 years and those whose illnesses have affective components. Certain sections of this chapter have been reordered to fit DMS-III classifications, but the reality of long clinical experience does not bear out the narrow time-limited concept of schizophrenia presented by the American classifiers, which is not accepted internationally.

Symptomatically, the schizophrenias, are recognizable through odd and bizarre behavior apparent in aloofness, suspiciousness, or periods of impulsive destructiveness and immature and exaggerated emotionality, often ambivalently directed and considered inappropriate by the observer. The interpersonal perceptions are distorted in the more serious states by delusional and hallucinatory material. In the most disorganized forms of schizophrenic living, withdrawal into a fantasy life takes place and is associated with serious disorder of thought and profound habit deteriorations in which the usual social customs and personal care are disregarded.

It is generally considered that schizophrenic patients are incapable of effectively harmonizing their drives and inhibitions through mature adaptations and defenses. They have failed to develop a satisfying concept of the body and a clear or stable self-concept. They are often unclear in their goals, or their aspirations are so demanding or inflexible that they exceed the patients' talents, persistence, and drive to mastery. Thus they are deficient in their capacity to assess clearly the realities of the world. Interactions with others are characterized by immature processes of communication, affective control, thought, and adaptation.

In psychoanalytic terms, schizophrenic patients represent those who have failed to evolve the ego integrative processes or strengths necessary to flexibly resolve conflicts between their (id) drives and overdemanding superego attitudes and the aspirations of the ego ideal. They are thus defective in the capacity to adapt to the social demands confronting them and to their own drives. They thereby lack a harmonious self-concept and ego ideal with clear goals and motivations. Much of their adaptation is made, instead, through partially satisfying regressive or fixated infantile behavior.

Evolution of Concept

Although not so called, the clinical picture we now know as schizophrenia has long been recognized. In 1849, John Conolly (1794–1866) of Hanwell Asylum in England, the champion of "no restraint," stated in his Croonian Lectures: "Young persons not infrequently fall into a state somewhat resembling melancholia, without any discoverable cause of sorrow, and certainly without any specific grief; they become indolent or pursue their usual occupations or recreations mechanically and without interest; the intellect, the affections, the passions, all seem inactive or deadened and the patients become utterly apathetic."

The term *dementia praecox* (démence précoce) was first used by the Belgian psychiatrist Morel in 1860 in the case of a boy of 14 who previously always had been "first in his examinations, and that without effort and almost without study. . . . Unconsciously he lost his cheerfulness and became sober, taciturn, and showed a tendency to solitude." The boy showed a "state of melancholy depression and a hatred of his father even with the idea of killing him. . . . The young invalid progressively forgot all that he had learned, and his brilliant intellectual faculties entered into a very disturbing period of arrest. A kind of inactivity bordering on stupidity replaced his former activity and when I saw him again it looked as if a transition into an irrecoverable state of dementia praecox was taking place."

Morel interpreted this disorganization of personality as an arrest of development, to be included with mental deficiency as a "variety of intellectual, physical and moral degeneracy" resulting from heredity.

The next event in the history of dementia praecox was Hecker's description in 1871 of *hebephrenia,* although the term had previously been used by Kahlbaum. "The characteristic features of hebephrenia," wrote Hecker, "above all are: its appearance in connection with puberty, the succession or changing appearance of various forms (melancholia, mania and confusion), the very quick termination in a psychic enfeeblement, and a characteristic form of final deterioration, the evidences of which can be seen in the first stages of the disease." He considered hebephrenia to be a progressive disease of puberty and adolescence.

Another step in the development of the dementia praecox concept was the description of *catatonia,* or *"tension insanity,"* by Kahlbaum in 1874. He described catatonia as "that condition in which the patient sits quietly or completely mute and motionless, immovable, with a staring countenance, the eyes fixed on a distant point and apparently completely without volition, without any reaction to sensory impressions, sometimes with a full-fledged cerea flexibilitas as in catalepsy." Kahlbaum assumed that catatonia was the symptom of a structural brain disease.

Conceptions of Schizophrenia

Earlier conceptions of schizophrenia are based largely upon the formulations of Kraepelin, Bleuler, Meyer, and Freud; a brief presentation of their respective formulations is in order.

In 1896, Kraepelin, through his keen observations, gave an excellent clinical description of the disorder and classified it into types (hebephrenic, catatonic, and paranoid). Bleuler and Meyer, on the other hand, greatly advanced the psychiatric understanding of schizophrenia by their interpretation in dynamic terms of the symptomatic manifestations observed.

KRAEPELIN'S FORMULATIONS. Kraepelin brought together varied mental syndromes that he concluded were manifestations of a single disease entity. To these he gave the name *dementia praecox,* a term previously having a more limited application. He thought these clinical syndromes arose from the same disease process, since they had in common a beginning in adolescence or early adulthood and a progression toward a similar state of "dementia." Similar morbid processes were, Kraepelin assumed, the causes of the various clinical features. These causes, he believed, might be either a degenerative disease of the brain or metabolic disturbances that produced autointoxication. He believed, too, that injury to the germ plasm might be of significance in its development. Kraepelin was of the opinion that the clinical results of these processes consisted of a weakening of emotional and volitional reactions and a loss of harmonious connections among emotional, volitional, and intellectual reactions. He gave a comprehensive and lucid description of the clinical features of dementia praecox but was critical of any attempt to explain the behavior of a patient on a psychological basis.

BLEULER'S FORMULATIONS. Bleuler came to the conclusion that it was misleading to compare even the extreme deterioration of what Kraepelin called dementia praecox with the state of mind of the mentally defective or with that of organic deterioration caused by severe brain atrophy. Therefore the label "dementia praecox" was unsatisfactory. He pointed out that the patient's psychological reactions to the environment are complicated and differentiated, quite different in kind from the elementary, simple reactions of retarded persons and those with organic brain disease. Bleuler believed, therefore, that the disease was not one of *dementia,* a state of diminished mind, but a disharmonious state of mind in which most contradictory tendencies, thoughts, and potentialities existed together, so that the harmony of the personality was *split.* According to this conception, the outcome of the disease was not necessarily one of deterioration, as Kraepelin had maintained, and the diagnosis had nothing to do with the course.

Bleuler was the first to emphasize that it was not only interesting but extremely important to consider seriously and from a scientific point of view the content of patients' thoughts, their trends, their instincts, and everything that they did. Bleuler noticed that if patients' hallucinations and delusions were thoroughly studied, they could be connected with life histories, with early hopes and fears, and with early relationships with parents and siblings.

Bleuler distinguished between primary and secondary symptoms. He designated as *primary signs* those that he considered were the direct manifestations of a hypothetical somatic morbid process; these included a peculiar loosening of the associational links in thinking, a morbid ambitendency and ambivalence that dominated the affective life of the patient, and a tendency to replace reality by fantasy, a quality that was responsible for the various manifestations of autism. Among the *secondary symptoms*, or those that he believed were of psychic origin, were delusions explainable by the patient's frustrations and hopes, a part of the hallucinations, the mannerisms, the catatonic muscular symptoms, and a large part of the complicated attitudes that others had called deterioration or dementia. He believed that the secondary symptoms were attempts at adaptation to the primary disturbance.

After Bleuler had become convinced of the importance of psychological influences in the morbid picture of schizophrenia, it became clear to him that the disorder should be treated by psychotherapy. He stressed that a sound, strong, and personal relationship between nurse and patient and between physician and patient would exercise a beneficial therapeutic influence.

MEYER'S FORMULATIONS. Meyer's dynamic conception of schizophrenia and his naturalistic behavioral approach in its formulation appeared earlier than Bleuler's work. He emphasized the concepts of habit deterioration and of reaction types. The schizophrenic reaction, he believed, can best be understood as a habit disorganization resulting from a progressive maladaptation, in which there takes place "a substitution of inefficient and faulty attempts to avoid difficulties rather than to meet them by decisive action." The result is disorganization of the personality and final withdrawal from reality. Many of the clinical symptoms represent abortive and "twisted" attempts at balance and reconstruction. While he expressed the opinion that the failure to find any structural or physiological changes in neurons seemed to exclude an organic etiology, he believed that an inferior constitution, as well as a great variety of pathological conditions of a physical nature, may add to the individual's load of handicaps.

Meyer was one of the first to emphasize that the interest should be not so much in a classificatory diagnosis as in the facts and factors at work in the individual patient and in his assets. He did not subscribe to Kraepelin's invariably unfavorable prognosis of a progressive intellectual deterioration.

At the present time, the concepts of Kraepelin, Meyer, Bleuler, and Freud and his followers are all considered inadequate. Yet they contribute to an understanding of the evolution of schizophrenic behavior. A number of new working hypotheses will be discussed in the section on etiology.

Epidemiology

The schizophrenic psychoses are recognized in all cultures in which mental disorders have been subjected to thorough study. Cultural forces appear only to modify the clinical phenomenology of these reactions in terms of the content of delusional and hallucinatory material. Thus in Western society, religious and sexual delusions were more common a century ago than in the present. These psychoses occur in all socioeconomic strata, although several epidemiological studies have suggested a correlation between higher prevalence of illness and lower socio-economic status.

At this time the schizophrenias are the most prevalent of the major psychoses. In a recent examination of the existing material on prevalence and incidence, Mishler and Scotch conclude that at any moment 0.3 per cent of the general population is suffering the disturbance, 0.15 per cent of the population is likely to experience its development, and 0.02 per cent is admitted to hospitals with schizophrenia for the first time. Calculations made from various epidemiological surveys give the morbid risk for the syndrome as 1 per cent. Morbid risk is defined as the total risk of becoming manifestly ill for all persons surviving the age period of 15 to 45 years, when the disease is customarily recognized.

Deming, working with data derived from the annual statistical reports of the state of New York, applied to the 1960 data a recursion formula which hypothesized that (1) for every schizophrenic recognized in the hospitals of the state of New York there were three living in the community; (2) the proportion of males living in the state who had a first hospital admission as a schizophrenic is 1 in 68 and of females is 1 in 62; and (3) the proportion of people of all ages from birth on who have already had an admission as schizophrenic or will live long enough to have one is 1 in 46 for males and 1 in 39 for females.

Deming's calculations are based on experience in New York where diagnoses of schizophrenia by psychiatrists are recognized as exceeding those elsewhere in the U.S.A. as well as abroad, judging by various transcultural studies.

While the number of schizophrenic patients in the public mental hospitals of the United States of America rose steadily during the early part of the century, it leveled off at the rate of approximately 150 per 100,000 population in 1955. Since then, the numbers of hospitalized schizophrenics have declined continuously. Likewise, the first admission rate to mental hospitals of schizophrenic patients rose from 18 per 100,000 in 1950 to almost 20 in 1962. By 1964, the decline had reached 17 per 100,000. There occurred at the same time the introduction of more effective treatments and the tendency to treat in the community at the time of the initial diagnosis, as well as the development of psychiatric units in the general hospitals. In the public mental hospitals, the stay of patients showed a rapid decrease in length. In the state of New York, the length of hospitalization fell from 8 months in 1955 to just over 40 days in 1976. Few schizophrenics remain in the psychiatric units of general hospitals more than 17 days. This drop has occurred at the same time that the death rates were falling in mental hospitals.

The questions that have been raised by epidemiologists and others in regard to the effect upon the social system as a whole of the modern treatment for schizophrenics are of some significance today. There are those who inquire whether the shortened hospital stays indicate shortened schizophrenic episodes and thus a low schizophrenic prevalence in the population. Some suggest that the change is due only to provision of early treatment or outpatient treatment to replace the former hospital care. Others suggest that the shift of the burden of care for those with serious social incompetence due to schizophrenia has taken place merely as a reflection of the reaction formation to what has been termed the *social breakdown syndrome* or the institutional neurosis. Still others believe that the change is due to the effectiveness of the phenothiazine medications. In my opinion all these factors are relevant. There have been no decisive studies to provide a clear-cut discrimination of the importance of one or another of the social or therapeutic measures. Nevertheless, the major shift did occur at the time of the introduction of the powerful new medications—notably, the phenothiazines, while at the same time changes in the direction toward the open hospital were already taking place.

The age group of schizophrenics with the highest first admission rate falls between 25 and 34 years. This group has twice the overall rate for first admissions to hospitals.

Etiology

Personality development and maldevelopment are dependent upon the genetic and constitutional endowment of each individual. Impinging upon that endowment are the early maternal and later family transactions that dynamically bring about the unfolding of various ego and superego functions and the ego ideal of each individual. As the personality growth of each individual ensues over time, social opportunities and stresses must be met. These act upon the growing individual and may serve as precipitants of disorder.

THE GENETIC FACTOR. Over half a century of research into the genetics of schizophrenia has brought forward sufficient replicable evidence to leave little doubt of the existence of an inherited predisposition to the condition.

The interest in the genetic factor in schizophrenia commenced with the extensive statistical studies of Franz Kallmann. He found that if the disorder existed in one monozygotic twin, it also occurred in the other twin in 85.8 per cent of his cases. Kallmann's work has been repeated many times with different cohorts and patients. His colleague and successor, John D. Rainer, has recently reviewed the various genetic studies of schizophrenia in detail. Since Kallmann's work, evidence has accumulated from increasingly sophisticated analyses of studies of families, twins, adoptees, and high risk children. It is now recognized that, given the fact of genetic predisposition, the questions that remain unanswered are of the nature of the method of inheritance of this predisposition, its effects upon the biological constitution, and its expression during development and interaction with the environment. From a variety of family studies, it has been discovered that the risk of schizophrenics' immediate siblings also suffering the disorder runs about 15 per cent more than for individuals in the general population from families without schizophrenia.

From numerous twin studies that have now been performed (see Table 18–1), it may be concluded that (a) the concordance rate of monozygotic twins for schizophrenia runs three to six times as high as that for dizygotic twins; (b) the concordance rate for monozygotic twins lessens when the index cases are considered to suffer fewer disorganizing disturbances; and (c) among discordant pairs the schizophrenic twin has usually, from birth onward, been psychologically or physically less well developed than his or her twin sib.

In a variety of studies comparing the schizophrenic with the schizo-affective and the manic depressive, a clear dichotomy appears between schizophrenia and the manic-depressive psychoses. From the extensive examination of almost 16,000 pairs of twins by Cohen and his colleagues, the monozygotic pairwise concordance rate for schizo-affective disorders was discovered to be more than two times higher than that of schizophrenia, yet not significantly different from that of manic-depressive illness. This study and others have assisted in confirming nosology and also in the examination of the clinical heterogeneity of these conditions. Thus, in the Cohen study, schizo-affective psychoses had a mean age of onset earlier than both the manic-depressive and schizophrenic psychoses. Furthermore, the schizo-affective twins had a much higher suicide rate than those with the manic-depressive disorder and the schizophrenic group.

For schizophrenia alone, the twin concordance studies do not differentiate the subtypes (hebephrenic, catatonic, paranoid, simple).

TABLE 18–1   Summary of Studies on Concordance Rates of Schizophrenia in Twins

INVESTIGATOR	MZ PAIRS (NUMBER)	PERCENT MZ CONCORDANCE*	DZ PAIRS (NUMBER)	PERCENT DZ CONCORDANCE*	MZ/DZ RATIO	SAMPLING**	DIAGNOSED BY
Luxenburger, 1928 1930 1934	17 21 27	60–76(W) 67 33	33 37 —	0 — —	—	R, C	Author
Rosanoff, Handy, and Plesset, 1934	41	61	101	10	$\frac{61}{10} = 6.1$	R	Hospital
Essen-Möller, 1941	11	55–64(A)	27	15(A)	$\frac{64}{15} = 4.3$	C	Author
Kallmann, 1946	174	69–86(A)	517	10–15(A)	$\frac{86}{15} = 5.7$	R, C	Author
Slater, 1953	41	68–76(A)	115	11–14(A)	$\frac{76}{14} = 5.4$	R, C	Author
Inouye, 1961	55	60(W)–76(A)	17	12–22(A)	$\frac{60}{22} = 2.7$	R	Author
Tienari, 1963	16	6(F)–31(W)	21	5	$\frac{6}{5} = 1.2$	B	Author
Harvald and Hauge, 1965	9	44	62	10	$\frac{44}{10} = 4.4$	B	Hospital
Gottesman and Shields, 1966	24	42–65(A)	33	9–17(A)	$\frac{65}{17} = 3.8$	C	Hospital
Kringlen, 1967	55	25–38(W)	172	4–10(W)	$\frac{38}{10} = 3.8$	B	Author
Hoffer and Pollin, 1970	80	14–15(A)	145	4–4(A)	$\frac{15.5}{4.4} = 3.5$	B	Hospital
Allen, Cohen, and Pollin, 1972	95	27	125	5	$\frac{27.4}{4.8} = 5.7$	B	Hospital, author

*Abbreviations: W = "wide" concept of schizophrenia used, A = age-corrected, F = 1967 follow-up on 1963 series (16).
**Abbreviations: R = resident hospital population, C = consecutive hospital admissions, B = birth registry.
(From Allen, M. G., Cohen, S., and Pollin, W.: Am. J. Psychiatry, 128:939–945, 1972.)

Cadoret has summarized the studies of abnormal individuals in the families of schizophrenics examined by others in earlier years. Among such abnormal individuals are those with antisocial character traits or those with polyneurotic symptomatology. From his review, he has recently concluded that monozygotic twins discordant for schizophrenia have a high proportion of individuals with significant character abnormalities or neurotic symptoms; males are more likely to show the former, and females the latter. Character abnormality seemed to be associated more with nuclear schizophrenia. Cadoret has provided a table (Table 18–2) summarizing the presence of such characterological or neurotic characteristics found in other members of families with schizophrenics, in the course of either twin or family studies.

Studies of the biological families of adoptees who have developed chronic or borderline schizophrenia have shown that there is a higher prevalence of schizophrenia and related disorders in these families than in the biological relatives of control adoptees without schizophrenia. However, the biological families of adoptees with acute schizophrenia did not show this increase in one study. In another study of over 5500 persons matched to the adoptees, the investigators Kety, Rosenfeld, Winther, and Scholfinger, quoted by Rainer, discovered the same number of schizophrenic patients, thus indicating that the adoption itself is not predisposing to schizophrenia.

Another type of adoptee study is of schizophrenic parents who gave their children for adoption to others. In two such studies, higher rates were found for schizophrenia and related pathology in the children of the schizophrenic parents than in the children of nonschizophrenic parents, even though both groups were raised by other than their biological parents in adoptive homes. Furthermore, in the Japanese studies by Inouye where the culture dictates that twins be separated, with one reared by someone other than the mother, the

TABLE 18–2   Presence of Schizoid Types in Good and Poor Prognosis Schizophrenia Families

| | | | Schizoid Type | | | |
| | NUMBER OF FAMILIES | | NEUROTIC SYMPTOMS | | CHARACTER ABNORMALITIES | |
	Good	Poor	Good	Poor	Good	Poor
Twin studies						
Inouye (1970) (M-Z twin)	7	51	0	5	0	15
Guggenheim *et al.* (1969) (parents of discordant M-Z twins)	2	11	0	3	—	—
Kringlen (1967) (M-Z twin)	11	23	4	6	1	5
Family studies						
Alanen (1958) (mothers)	41	54	13	12	12	27
Kety *et al.* (1968) (adoptees)	7	16	0	4	1	3
Fowler and McCabe (unpublished) (1° relatives)	28	25	2	9	1	6
Winokur *et al.* (1967) (1° relatives)	48	59	5	5	0	0
Kant (1942) (families)	50	50	14	21	—	—
Kurosawa (1962) (1° relatives)	33	38	0	5	—	—
Total	227	327	38	70	15	56
% of Total			17%	21%	7%	17%

(From Cadoret, R. J.: Br. J. Psychiatry, *122*:679–685, 1973.)

frequency of the occurrence of schizophrenia in both monozygotic twins remains higher than in the dizygotic twins separated from birth.

As Rainer emphasizes, one of the goals of family genetic studies is that of identifying specific environmental factors that may limit, modify, or evoke the genetic potential. It has been found that lower birth weight is one of the most consistent attributes of a twin who will later become schizophrenic. Furthermore, in examining the dimension of communication in a population of persons deaf since birth or childhood, the schizophrenic expectancy rate has been found to be over 2 per cent higher than in those with other impairments in the general population. Rieder and his colleagues recently examined the offspring of schizophrenics and discovered an increased incidence of fetal and neonatal deaths, as compared to a closely matched control group. In some instances, major neurological malformations were found. Whether these findings can be entirely related to the genotype of the child or whether they represent adverse intrauterine environment or the toxicity of medications given is unclear.

At any rate, birth risk for schizophrenia for the children of parents with this condition approximates 15 times that of the general population. When both parents are schizophrenic, up to a third of the children have been found schizophrenic.

Various criticisms have been given to studies of twins. It has been pointed out that such studies lack information on the early biological and family experiences of the twins and have not weighed the psychodynamic forces in twin development that are believed to tend toward mutual identification between twins rather than for the growth of separate identities.

Thus a shared fetal cross-circulation may be found in monozygotic but not in dizygotic twins. Sufficient emphasis has not been placed upon studies of those factors that protect one of a monozygotic twin pair from schizophrenia in at least 15 per cent of the cases. It may be expected that important insights would come from examination of the supportive environmental factors useful in reducing the risk of the reaction in the spared twin.

In one sample of monozygotic twins, almost half had never been separated more than a single day, whereas three quarters of the dizygotic twins had this experience. So, too, monozygotic twins are often dressed alike, and even their parents mistake the individual identities.

In genetic research on schizophrenia, one must consider the schizoid but nonpsychotic person as well, because 45 per cent of the siblings, parents, and children of schizophrenics are found to be either schizoid or schizophrenic. From computations it is estimated that about 4 per cent of the general population will be affected by the schizoid–schizophrenic personality complex. This would explain this distribution on the hypothesis of a defect in a single autosomal dominant gene. The majority of geneticists have supported genetic transmission of predisposition to schizophrenia as polygenic, the illness being regarded as a threshold trait.

BIOLOGICAL PREDISPOSITION. That constitutional weaknesses exist is suggested by data indicating that schizophrenic mothers have a higher incidence of deviant fetal growth in terms of perinatal mortality and malformations in the newborn than mothers from the population at large. Also, careful physical and psychological investigations of groups of children considered to have childhood schizophrenia have shown that a majority present in their motor, postural, sensoriperceptual, and conceptual performances indications of delayed or uneven functioning. These impairments are described in greater detail later in this chapter in relation to childhood schizophrenia. Whether these impairments are due to delays in maturation as a consequence of a defect in genetic endowment or to unrecognized brain damage in early life has not been ascertained. Some would exclude from the schizophrenic reactions all children showing such defects.

Consistent physical abnormalities are not associated with schizophrenia; yet in the past clinicians have suggested that there existed instability in function of the autonomic nervous system. Largely, such inferences arose from observation of the pupillary dilatations and presumed vasomotor phenomena of the extremities usually seen in certain catatonics with coldness and cyanosis of limbs. So, too, it has been reported by Maricq and others that there is an abnormal subpapillary capillary plexus clearly visible in the nail folds of schizophrenics exceeding the findings of mental defectives and the healthy. The sweat of schizophrenics has been thought to give off a peculiar odor. The substance causing the odor has been identified as trans-3-methyl-2 hexenoic acid. Gillin and Wyatt have found that most actively ill schizophrenics fail to have a normal REM sleep rebound following deprivation of REM sleep. However, others with psychiatric disability show the same abnormality. There exist today no specific biological tests that discriminate the schizophrenic from others.

PATHOPHYSIOLOGY. The numerous experimental studies directed toward the finding of constitutional, metabolic, endocrine, and other physiological defects have yet to produce any significant data that have been subject to verification. These findings then remain irrelevant to clinical practice, as they offer, as yet, no useful theoretical, diagnostic, or therapeutic tools.

Perhaps the most attractive hypothesis currently extant to account for the biological basis for schizophrenia, and the subject of studies in many laboratories today, is the one suggesting disorder in the central catecholamine synapses that establishes the crucial vulnerability for schizophrenia and may explain many of its symptoms. It is referred to often now as the *dopamine hypothesis*. Thus, amphetamine has the ability to produce a toxic psychosis in many individuals who receive it in large doses that is difficult to distinguish from paranoid schizophrenic reactions. This agent releases dopamine and norepinephrine at catecholamine-containing nerve endings. It also potentiates the action of these transmitters at their synapses of the brain. There is also the knowledge that both the phenothiazines and the butyrophenones, highly effective therapeutic agents in this disorder, are thought to produce a blockade of dopamine receptors in the brain. It is of interest that amphetamines and norepinephrine, both of which produce stereotyped behavior, stimulate the dopamine receptors. Yet there are certain symptoms of the schizophrenic process that are little modified by the phenothiazines and butyrophenones. Notable among these are the flatness of affect, the anhedonia, withdrawal, and autism.

Kety mentions that in animal experiments alpha-methylparatyrosine, which blocks catecholamine synapses, produces animal models not unlike the catatonic states of schizophrenia. To him, this suggests that a defect leading to overactivity of dopamine and underactivity of norepinephrine might more readily account for more of the manifestations of this illness than a simple modification in the dopamine system itself. Therefore, he suggests that some abnormality in the functioning of the enzyme dopamine-beta-hydroxylase (DBH) (responsible for the conversion of dopamine to norepinephrine) might be involved. If this enzyme regulates the ratio of norepinephrine to dopamine, the balance in the synaptic transmissions due to the several transmitters might be affected. Recently, Wise and Stein discovered a 40 per cent reduction in the activity of this enzyme in the brains of schizophrenics at autopsy.

Dopamine has been found to be increased and glutamic acid decarboxylase (GAD) decreased in the nucleus accumbens of schizophrenic patients. A study made of the brains of schizophrenics treated over time with antipsychotic drugs has shown significant increases in homovanillic acid, a dopamine metabolite. While there are many defects in such post-mortem studies, it is now known from other investigations that monoamine oxidase is significantly reduced in the platelets of schizophrenic patients and in the schizophrenic and nonschizophrenic members of monozygotic twin pairs discordant for the illness. A reduction in monoamine oxidase in the brain, if it exists, could result in dysfunctional balances of central amine metabolism of the type mentioned.

An earlier theory postulated by Hofer suggested a defect in the metabolism of circulating epinephrine leading to the accumulation of adrenochrome. However, later studies failed to support any abnormalities in the metabolism of circulating epinephrine in schizophrenia. Also, there were hypotheses regarding the presence in the blood stream of certain plasma proteins, such as ceruloplasmin or "taraxein" and other putative neurotransmitters; none of these are supported or replicated by further experimental work.

Perhaps the most entrancing of the alternative hypotheses, beyond that concerning the imbalance of the neurotransmitters dopamine and noradrenaline, concerns transmethylation. It has been suggested that, in the schizophrenic, methylated hallucinogenic substances accumulate. Supporting this hypothesis is the fact that methionine, which is believed to increase brain levels of S-adenosylmethionine and favor transmethylization, does exacerbate a schizophrenic psychosis in some. Yet methionine produces no suggestion of a psychosis in normal volunteers.

Another enzyme, discovered by Axelrod and known to convert tryptamine to dimethyltryptamine, is a powerful hallucinogenic substance, and there have been reports that during administration of a methyl donor schizophrenic patients may show exacerbation of their illness while excreting increased quantities of the hallucinogens in their urine.

There have been numerous reports of the urinary excretion of abnormal metabolites, a recent one being that of a mescaline-like derivative. Yet it is now known that this substance, dimethoxyphenylethylamine (DMPE 4), is also nonspecific—in fact, the metabolites of chlorpromazine and other phenothiazines will produce "pink spots" in chromatographic procedures, and so will the urine of healthy individuals who drink tea.

Areas of investigation now most actively pursued are concerned with the intermediate metabolism of cerebral glucose. It is hypothesized that schizophrenics are deficient in their capacity to utilize available energy in reaction to stress, owing to metabolic defects in the Embden-Meyerhof scheme. It is reported that an abnormality exists in schizophrenic plasma which leads to abnormal production of pyruvate. Attempts to isolate and characterize this plasma fraction go on in several laboratories. Also, it is suggested that the presence of a malcontrolled protein in the blood contributes to the illness by selectively altering neuronal transmission.

Heath and Krupp proposed that there exists a structural abnormality in the septal region of the brain, the area shown in animal experiments to be concerned with alerting and repetitive activity assumed to be pleasurable. They described a spike and slow wave electroencephalographic discharge as consistently recurrent in the septal area of some schizophrenic patients during periods of abnormal behavior—an abnormality tending to disappear as the patient seemed to improve. But similar EEG activity has been recorded from the septal area in patients with other conditions, as well as from the brains of various animals.

At the moment enthusiastic speculation upon biological forces related to schizophrenia is rampant and centers on the possible role of the opiate peptide neuronal system (β-endorphins and enkephalins) and the prostaglandins. Solid evidence linking either to schizophrenia is so far lacking.

Arguing from the point of view of disturbance of cognitive functioning with loosening and fragmentation of associations as the central clinical feature of schizophrenia, Elkes has hypothesized that there co-exists a disturbance of information processing by the brain. He has suggested that the defect exists in the integration of the subsystems subserving attention and motivation in the selective organization of sense data. The interaction between sensory information and stored, affectively charged memory traces suggests to him that the limbic system as a first order monitoring group for sensory data in pleasurable or aversive control may be involved, as well as the highly discriminating, inhibiting processes concerned with specific altering and attention mediated by higher brain stem structures and defections. So, too, his hypothesis suggests that such defective subsystem functions must be interpreted in terms of biochemical or pharmacological abnormalities, which presumably would operate in terms of brain mechanisms (synaptic transmission) and, particularly, the neuronal integrating nets.

Developmental Psychodynamics

Whatever biological abnormality the future schizophrenic may bring with birth, his or her personality unfolds over the years of infancy, childhood, and adolescence as the consequence of the ongoing transactions between him and his parents and those others who relate with him and thus influence his emotional and cognitive maturation.

The range of such impairments in the conditions designated as childhood schizophrenia is wide; a considerable number show very little evidence of early retardation in development of sensorimotor, perceptual, and conceptual deficit. However, in cases in which studies have been made of the family unit and its functioning, it appears that gross personality disturbances in parents are more likely to be associated with minimal impairment of physiologic growth of the child, and minimal pathology in the parents is found to be associated with maximal physiological retardation in the schizophrenic child.

The family transactions induced by the interplay between the child's capacities, determined by his physiological equipment, and the expectations of the parents then appear to play an important role in the achievement of a healthy unfolding of personality and in the arrest or inadequate development of ego attitudes and functions. Thus a child who, as the result of delayed maturation of motor development, fails to acquire ease in relating to others, as well as skill in language, walking, and other coordinated movements may set up anxieties in certain parents with high expectancies and investment in his future. These developmental lags or delays are reflected in the parental relationship, with the parents pushing the child beyond his capacities while, at the same time, overprotecting him. In other children without evidence of physiologic deficit, it has been postulated that the parental investment in the child is disturbed from the beginning, as the child represents an expected source for emotional satisfaction, or the living out of gratifications not obtained in life by one or other of the parents.

Psychoanalytic theory has held that the earliest periods of mother-infant relationship must be deficient, since the adult pathology of the schizophrenic patient suggests a regressive withdrawal in the face of insurmountable automatic anxiety to infantile omnipotent behavior and rage reactions, associated with inability to perceive reality. Noted also is employment of primary process thinking; use of the infantile defenses of denial, idealization, and projective identification; and splitting.

In partial support of this hypothesis, the several direct observational studies of mothering of their infants by schizophrenic women seem to show that the mothering process was impaired by their affective depression. Such women did not play with and fondle their infants as do other mothers, although they did carry out well the usual procedures for nurture and bodily cleanliness of the child. Their infants, in turn, appeared irritable and depressed. It is probable that the restriction of affective and playful stimulation of the infant impedes the development of those early sensations that establish the body percept and the beginnings of ego attitudes of security, trust, and aggressiveness, upon which must unfold the capacities for self-control and later autonomous independence.

That deprivations of early mothering may bring about enduring defects in capacity to socialize and even to carry out sexual activities effectively now has received strong support from studies in primates and mammalian species. The animal experiments suggest that the timing and duration of the important mother-infant interaction may determine a permanent deficit in capacity to socialize—in other words, a fixation from which one may surmise only unstable substitutions or restitutive adaptations may be made. If the effects of early maternal deprivations are indeed significant to evolution of the schizophrenic process, such questions demand solution, as they hold the clues to both rational prevention and treatment.

If the early infant-mother relationship is so critical to the establishment of these ego assets, of necessity one must seek an explanation for the occurrence of schizophrenia in one or several children mothered by the same woman while others of her children show little evidence of psychopathology. In families in which some children became ill and others were spared, there was evidence of intense family crises at the time of birth or in the ensuing months which affected the mother and her relationship with the newborn and later ill child. Such crises were identified as: the development of depression in the mother with feelings of guilt owing to her hostility toward the new child, the birth of another sibling within two years, dislike of the child's physical characteristics, or the projective identification of the child in terms of certain unpleasant characteristics of the parents.

The consequence of the lack of early constancy in the mothering process, according to Burnham, is to impair the child's capacity to maintain a stable mental representation of the needed person in the latter's absence. The need for the mother is intensified and yet there is fear of her loss—the need-fear dilemma. The schizophrenic patient thus develops a special vulnerability to separation, which becomes the crucial factor in failure to establish and maintain satisfactory interpersonal relations.

Childhood shyness and the later shut-in life with limitation of friendships, characteristic of the preschizophrenic, perhaps have their origins in the seeking of security in early clinging, coupled with fearfulness of loss. It remains as an undifferentiated perception of relations to others and stems from the child's failure to develop trust and certainty in his autonomy. The later social relations with others are thus permeated by intense ambivalence, with inability to integrate this perception of need-fear with the consequent love-hate affects.

It is unlikely that disturbances in the early mothering process alone are capable of explaining the full range of schizophrenic psychopathology, such as the impaired sense of identity often associated with a confused sexual role, the use of primitive processes of thought and communication, the lack of ability to discriminate fantasy from reality, and the defects in establishing and maintaining object or interpersonal relations. These failures of development are more likely to rest on later deficiencies or distortions in the process of personality development.

From the various studies of family dynamics of the past decade, it has been found with significant frequency that schizophrenic patients have spent their childhood in seriously disturbed family groups in which both parents gave evidence of personality disturbance. In the Lidz studies, two thirds of the families contained one parent who was found to be schizophrenic. Such family groups are unintegrated and relate through conflict in which the parents oppose each other by derogating and defying the wishes of the spouse and by efforts to win the children to their side to obtain from them the emotional support not found in the spouse. In other families, the parental relationship is disordered in that one parent has a serious personality deficit, shown in domineering, brutal, aggressive, or alcoholic behavior, while the other passively accepts the behavior or is absent when the child is exposed to an unwholesome environment. Such parents often are doubtful of their own sexual roles; some have been homosexual, and others were in conflict over control of incestuous desires.

Caught in such family groups, the children are unable to find those conflict-free periods of personal interactions and play that establish a sense of personal security, an ability to share, and an ability to repress effectively hostile, aggressive, and sexual drives. Nor do they find the sources of sound personal or sexual identification. But most important for the understanding of the schizophrenic reaction are the series of events that impair the evolution of mature communication and thought.

Bateson and his colleagues put forward the hypothesis that the origins of the schizophrenic defects in communication rest upon a "double bind" transaction between two persons. Thus the schizophrenic may be seen as fixed in an intense emotional relationship with a parent who, by the contradictions between verbal remarks and behavior, makes it impossible for the child to discriminate properly or even to ask for clarification, as questioning is treated as a threat to the needed relationship by the parent. A concrete example is a schizophrenic adolescent who, tied to his mother verbally, is encouraged to use initiative in his school work, yet when he attempts to leave home to visit the library, he is told he must not as the parent needs him and will become ill in his absence. Such a double bind restricts and confuses the development of clear communication, since the parent's position is inconsistent. It also limits the son's helpful socialization with others, from which he might learn progressive social discriminations and develop the potentiality for evolving other healthy relations.

Whether the double bind is characteristic of schizophrenic families alone or has special features for such families is not known. Sluzki and Veron have suggested that the double bind hypothesis has a much wider application. What has not been done to verify its usefulness in this and other psychopathological states is to define and reconstruct the specific learning contexts of the various clinical expressions. This requires definition of a precise connection between the initial paradox and the resulting pathology.

Others have also been struck by the family milieu as the source of the irrationality of thought of the schizophrenic. Of particular interest in terms of the thought disturbances are the studies of Wynne, Singer, and their associates, who have offered new proposals as to their classifications and have studied family transactions through the medium of conjoint family therapy as they relate to the specific defects. Their work is reported later in the section on Psychopathology, Thought and Communication.

The process takes place dynamically, in that the growing child repeatedly has been the recipient of intrafamilial hostility and at the same time has identified with parents who themselves excessively use projection, denial, or conscious lying in their relations within the family. Upon this background there are often found discrete assaults upon the child or aggressive or sexual acts that the child must deny and repress in order to preserve his dependent relationship with the parent. Later the parent reinforces the child's fear and guilt by utilizing subsequent incidents to establish the child's responsibility for the earlier trauma and to escape from his own culpability. Thus the mounting denial and repression of the child's internalized rage leads eventually to breakdown, with psychotic withdrawal or impulsive sexual and murderous aggressive acts.

Failure to acquire social skills early narrows the probability of acquisition of emotional relations with extrafamily members in adolescence and adulthood; this again limits the probability of enhancing the personal skills and perceptual discriminations and sense of personal autonomy demanded for an effective social and heterosexual adaptation in adult life.

Onset

The age of onset is from late childhood to late middle age, although the most frequent age is adolescence and early adult life. Although uncommon, it is not as rare in children (3 to 13 years) as was formerly believed. The more fully the previous history is taken, the more frequently there will be found a previous manifestation not merely of schizoid traits, but even of phenomena that were nearly or quite psychotic in nature. The high incidence during adolescence is not unnatural.

There is probably, however, no specific relationship between schizophrenia and puberty, which is normally a period of emotional cross-currents and of struggle to adapt emergent, maturing urges to the demands of a restraining world. At that time, individuals are

precipitated into a critical emotional period without preparation or understanding. They are perplexed by new problems, particularly those pertaining to sex, religion, vocation, and social relations. They may be plagued by a desire for independence or crippled by a too prolonged dependence. Simultaneously they yearn for a close relationship with a peer or peers and respond to others' actions with sensitivity and anxiety, including moodiness, vague yearnings, sudden outbursts, defense attitudes, and the tendency to indulge in strange fancies, to project inadequacies, and to be irritable.

Although there is a striking contrast between a normal, well-integrated individual and the person reacting with a malignant form of schizophrenic psychosis, there is frequently no abrupt transition from the schizoid type of personality to the manifest psychosis. In adolescence there is a tendency to loneliness and perhaps to slight depressions.

Early indications of thought disorder often emerge as anxiety mounts. Adolescents may report that they are incapable of the mental work demanded at school, even though they have worked many hours each night and tried various stimulants, sedatives, exercises, and other diversions. Later, they have to devote more energy to maintain the coherence of their thoughts—to keep out personalized instrusions. They abandon recreation and report that their thought processing seems disturbed; their "mind wanders" though they may be able to learn precise factual subjects. As further deterioration takes place, they appear distractible and impulsive as they process their thoughts. They may seek retreat in relaxation through watching television or other passive activities requiring little personal mental involvement.

Even the person in the so-called "early" stage of schizophrenia has frequently been mentally sick for a considerable period before his personality disturbance is diagnosed as such. The patient's family has not usually appreciated the nature or significance of any personality change. The *mode of onset*, except in the catatonic type, is often a gradual evolutionary process, and there may be a transitional "preschizophrenic" phase of a year or two.

A variety of subjective experiences, associated with and/or induced by mounting anxiety and terrifying fears of personal dissolution, precede the earliest observed behavioral changes and oddities that bring the schizophrenic to treatment. He becomes aware of increasing tension, confusion, and distractibility in conversations with others and of his inability to maintain a train of thought in such human transactions. Outwardly this will be noticed as blocks or breaks in conversation, sometimes related by the closely observant to the introduction of abstract materials. At such times the schizophrenic may not speak or respond appropriately to his companions; he may look fixedly away, or he may appear to stare, as he does not regularly blink his eyes in his attempts to hold his attention. At the same time his sensitivity to extraneous sights or sounds may seem magnified, and his responses thereto intrude into these transactions, producing a degree of distractibility. If he is questioned then or later, he may speak of having a "temporary blackout," a "trance," a "blank spell," or a division of attention that he cannot control. These episodic periods of blocking have been dubbed as "microcatatonic" periods.

Many express, puzzle about, or are preoccupied with bodily concerns; they are undergoing a body image disturbance. There is difficulty in maintaining perceptual constancy as concerns both their own body and the external world. They may sense their body and its parts changing in size or shape, or shrinking or swelling, or they may visually record such variability in their perception of the bodies of others or of inanimate objects. They attempt to establish constancy by building up pictures or fantasies. Auditory perceptions, too, are uncertain—too loud, too removed, too undifferentiated and thereby frightening, uninformative, or confused.

Their perceptions from inside their body become preoccupying: borborygmi, flatus, muscular aches and pains, and the variable constancies and changes in the genitalia preoccupy and frighten them. They often attempt to deal with them by hypochondriacal complaining requests for assistance or by attempts at denial. In the later stages of the illness the concern over their bodies may lead to an impulsive rejection through mutilation. They may spend much time staring into a mirror or may alternatively undertake strenuous efforts to build up their bodies through exercise or dieting.

The schizophrenic then misperceives his body and its parts as repulsive, ugly, or threatening. His gender is felt as uncertain, and, if he dares sexual explorations, they often become polyperverse as a means of attempting to identify his proper role. It is the mounting and terrifying anxiety, the defects in attentions, and the perceptual distortions that perhaps lead to the increasing uneasiness in his interpersonal contacts. The uneasiness, in turn, produces in the members of his family, his few friends, and even strangers that uncanny and eerie response which experienced clinicians often refer to as the "praecox feeling."

During the early stage there may be no single feature that is pathognomonic of the disease. In some instances, the early symptoms are more suggestive of a psychoneurosis than of a psychosis. A common early symptom is an aloofness, a withdrawal behind barriers to an area in which, if access to it could be gained, would be found loneliness, hopelessness, hatred, and fear. Frequently, the patient seems preoccupied and dreamy; his friends may speak of him as appearing "far away." He does not empathize with the feelings of others and manifests little concern about the realities of his life situation. His plans for his future are often vague and unrealistic.

The schizophrenic suffers from a feeling of rejection, an intolerable lack of self-respect, and a dreadful lack of self-esteem. The characteristic way he protects himself against insult is by withdrawal from emotional involvements with other people. The resultant isolation is a protection against painful human relationships, but the loneliness contributes further to his feelings of rejection and hence to further withdrawal. The patient no longer trusts or confides in anyone. Instead of mingling with others, he remains at home, where he may sulk in his room and show an increasing indifference to members of his family, to accustomed interests, and to the demands and opportunities of his environment. It seems as if a fear of interpersonal contact had driven the patient into a state of regression and withdrawal. There may be an unexplainable deterioration in work, related first to inability to focus upon his subject matter because of the distractions of his personal emotional preoccupations about self and others; later a progressively hopeless lack of motivation to cope with a human world occurs. His withdrawal from contact with others leads to shallowness of affect, a paucity of emotional responsiveness, and an impairment in the richness and variety of emotional expression.

Acquaintances may attribute to laziness the patient's listlessness and loss of spontaneity, of ambition, of interest in competition with his group, and of sustained effort in pursuit of former goals. An irritable discontent is common. The patient easily feels slighted and may begin to believe that others are talking about him. He may become ill at ease, restless, taciturn, and unapproachable as he wonders what interpretation others are putting on his behavior. There is a lack of pleasure and satisfaction in his accomplishments, an *anhedonia*. The degree of anhedonia generally is much greater in the chronically ill than in the acutely ill.

A superficial attitude of superiority is not uncommon. Less heed is paid to social amenities and social requirements, while former loyalties and affections become blunted. The patient becomes disregardful of, and even resistant to, conventionality. Frequently he becomes neglectful of personal care and cleanliness. Ruminations on sexual topics are usual. The patient may feel that something wrong or unusual is going on in his environment. Mysterious meanings are discovered until finally misinterpretations and suspicions may cause him to move from place to place. For a few weeks or months the new environment may be free from any suggestion of hostility; then the patient begins to feel that people are watching him or conspiring against him. Odd mannerisms or ways of acting may appear, but they cause the patient no concern.

The early schizophrenic is often preoccupied with abstract speculations or with metaphysical ponderings on such subjects as creation and causality, or with religious doubts, mysticism, and meaningless problems. A young truck driver with a seventh grade education wrote an essay entitled "The Imperative Mind." In the very early stages, a few patients recognize that their ideas of reference and other abnormal mental experiences are unnatural; they may wish to know the meaning of their experiences and to understand their problems. Occasionally they may have some appreciation of the causes that have led to their illness. At this time they may be willing to discuss their problems. Later this desire is lost and the patient becomes inaccessible, while in many the desire never existed. During these early stages, before the construction of an elaborate symbolic system that becomes accepted as reality, the conflicts are much less disguised, and it may often be possible to discover the problems that the patient is living out in the drama of his psychotic behavior. Occasionally, the patient may show some sensorial confusion during the first few days of an acute episode. Both age and time disorientation are common in the chronic schizophrenic population.

In that group of schizophrenics now designated as "ambulatory," these indications of social withdrawal are less evident. Their dubious relationship to life is expressed in doubts about their aims, difficulties in making decisions about their future, the means to get on or to find a central interest. Although at times they may appear to be driving and busy, their actions are performed to prove themselves. The adolescent may date to "prove" that he can gain the attention of others as his peers do. Marriage becomes a means of "proving" that one is a man or woman or that one can "love." The relationship with children is a means of establishing the fact that one can be a parent. All activity is representative of an autistic dramatization without full affective contact with the realities of life, as though there were a continuous screen between the inner person and those with whom he relates. The existence has an "as if" quality; it is split from reality.

Sometimes the onset is sudden and precipitate. During adolescence, the loss of an only friend often precedes the gross indications of schizophrenia. Such a friend may have been the only outlet from a turbulent home life. The loss of the friend forces the future patient again to seek satisfaction in the family. This arouses increasing anxiety, and eventually panic ensues when the adolescent considers, or is unable to control, his hostility, sexuality, or his deepening despair because of being forced backwards into an isolated, lonely, unhappy life of daydreaming, hating, and fearing.

DISTURBANCES OF AFFECT. As we pass from this initial, and what might be called premonitory, stage, or stage of incubation, to the manifest psychosis, an apparent *poverty* and a *disharmony of feeling tone* appear. The dulling of finer feelings and an insidious narrowing of interests noted in the incipient stages become progressive.

The patient is unable to feel and regulate emotions properly. There is a withdrawal of feeling or affect from external realities back into the self. As the disease progresses and the emotional impoverishment increases, the patient becomes indifferent, not merely to those sentiments and subjective values that make life worth living for the person in mental health, but, apparently existing at a vegetative level, to fundamental comforts and needs. A few patients show not a burned-out affectivity, but a definite, prevailing one, such as euphoria or depression. These feelings, however, usually lack depth or focus. The persistent mood, or emotional rigidity, has little relation to external circumstances or experiences.

Anhedonia, an incapacity for pleasurable affect, first emphasized by Rado, does indeed exist in many schizophrenics. Yet recent studies indicate that anhedonia is not unique to the schizophrenic complex but is a prominent feature of those chronically disturbed by mental or other illness.

Another disturbance of affect is one in which emotional expression is unrelated to reality. This is manifested by an emotional disharmony, often first exhibited by inappropriate smiling or laughing and silly giggling. At times experiences and ideas that should evoke a certain emotional response will produce its opposite—an emotional disconnection or dissociation. The patient, for example, may with a silly laugh speak of the death of a beloved parent. Whenever there is a display of affect by the schizophrenic, it seems unnatural and stilted, lacking in any infectious quality, and often it arouses feelings of uneasiness or estrangement in the observer. At other times one notes capricious, fitful, apparently causeless changes in affect and mood. The impoverishment of emotional expression and the inappropriate emotional responses to situations constitute one of the important ways in which the personality is disorganized or split.

One of the most generally accepted

hypotheses advanced as an explanation of this serious disturbance in the affective life of the patient is that the affect, contrary to first impression, is not lost or destroyed but is withdrawn from the conscious, perceptive aspects of the patient's life, from matters of objective reality, and is attached to complexes and other material in the unconscious. The affect is hidden because it is fixed to highly personalized subjective constellations of ideas. According to this theory, the disorganization of affect appears all the greater because it is associated with and determined by not one constellation of unconscious ideas, but many complexes, among which there may be active conflict and discord. Since the affect is attached to and determined by material that is inaccessible, the emotions appear out of harmony with the contents and expressions of consciousness, although they are really in harmony with the psychic material to which the affect is attached and by which they are governed. The emotional disturbance in schizophrenia is more a displacement than a deterioration.

The emotional apathy of the schizophrenic individual has been the subject of earlier comment. To that we may add its defensive character; patients defend themselves by building a wall of indifference. Although this blunting of feeling may have arisen as a mechanism of defense against a troublesome situation in the inner world of a patient, it irradiates and becomes a general behavior pattern of the personality.

When interest and affect are withdrawn from the conscious familiar material with which they were formerly connected and are attached to the content of the unconscious, a state known as *depersonalization* may exist. The patient has feelings of vagueness, of unreality, of detachment, or of being a spectator of life instead of taking part in it. He feels himself changed throughout in comparison with his former state. As a result, he no longer acknowledges himself as a personality. His actions seem mechanical and automatic. The patient does not believe he is another personality (transformation of personality) but has rather a sense of loss of the limits of his own personality with its directive ego. The identification of one's own personality may become indistinct or confused. It seems to the patient that he no longer has any internal self to which he can refer forces and influences. In his attempt to rationalize this sense, the patient may come to feel that parts of his body or his mind seem strange and as though they do not belong to him. He may develop more nihilistic ideas and believe that he no longer has a body, that there is no world, or that he is dead. In addition to this change of self, the environment may seem unnatural and appear to have lost its character of reality. States of unreality are probably closely related to thought block, feelings of stupidity, fugues, dream states, and other involuntary withdrawals.

Among the disturbances of affect in schizophrenia, *hypochondria* is occasionally met. This preoccupation with the body and various subjective feelings provides a meaningful purpose as the schizophrenic loses contact with others in his social environment. The patient may then express toward his own body the same attitudes he has held toward others and use the same ego defenses. Feelings of guilt, due to sexual drives, can be centered on his genitals and lead to preoccupations with defects in genital functioning. He may express these preoccupations in such bizarre terms as "electric currents" in the genitals or as a sense of shrinking of the body. As mentioned earlier, modification of the body concept is common in the schizophrenic reaction in the early stages. In some instances, other body parts come to represent the genital areas through the process of displacement. Later, in some instances the patient's guilty anxiety becomes so great that he is led to carry out mutilative actions against his own body in those occasional fantastic acts of personal castration or other dismemberment.

ATTENTION. One result of the schizophrenic's loss of capacity for attachment of energy and interest to external objects and reality and of his autistic preoccupations is a *narrowing of attention*. Interest, and therefore attention, is centered on subjective creations, on matters within and not without the patient. This lack of attention and of concentration gives rise to the misleading impression that the patient is intellectually impaired, whereas he is intellectually inert. The replies of the schizophrenic individual are often trivial and uninformative because interests and energy are directed toward material not accessible to ordinary questioning. *Paralogia,* a condition in which the patient's reply shows that the question has been understood, but in which the answer is erroneous, is caused by the dereistic thinking to which the schizophrenic patient is particularly given.

Although active attention (concentration), as just indicated, is often disturbed, passive attention is much less affected, with the result that, even if the patient is living in a world of fantasy, he is still able to maintain a contact with reality sufficient for certain practical needs, yet often too inadequate for a socialized adjustment. Schizophrenics may be perplexed but rarely suffer from disturbances of the sensorium and therefore from confusion in the correct sense of the term.

THOUGHT AND COMMUNICATION. Normally, *associations of ideas* follow one another with a definite logical connection, progressing to an ultimate completeness of thought, but in schizophrenia they may be shortened, fragmented, and otherwise so disturbed as to lack logical relationship. Although the disturbances of associations in schizophrenia do not become particularly marked until serious disorganization of the personality has taken place, frequently one finds that long before any manifest psychosis developed the patient showed a loosening of the associational links in thinking. Later the patient may speak in generalities and abstractions that are difficult to grasp—a dereistic type of verbigeration rather than communicative talk. The use of eccentric, metaphorical expressions is not uncommon. Doubtless the communications of the schizophrenic patient are nearly always self-meaningful, although often their significance is not grasped by others.

In the more disorganized schizophrenic reactions, there is a tendency for associative connections to become more involved, incongruous, and at times so broken or incomplete that the patient's utterances become fragmentary, disconnected, illogical or even unintelligible. The train of thought may not be pursued to its logical goal, with the result that thinking becomes diffuse and disorganized. Cause and effect may be interchanged. If aware of his disordered thinking, the patient may say that his thoughts are suddenly taken out of his head. Irrelevance in replies to questions, a feature that, when consciousness is clear, is particularly suggestive of schizophrenia, may be quite striking. Probably, however, irrelevance is not irrelevant to the patient and would be relevant to the listener who had clues to the semantic significance of the patient's autistic productions. Set phrases may come to be used repeatedly as stereotypes. The thought productions of the schizophrenic person often become characterized by vague and unusual symbolism. It is believed that the disordered thought productions tend to express, by condensation, the various problems that concern the patient. Speech may show a curiously distorted use of language, varying from a stilted and formal phraseology without apparent substance to a "word salad" of nouns and verbs having practically no articulated structure or even without apparently meaningful connection. Doubtless there was earlier a significance that became lost. Affectations in manner of speech are often observed. The patient may show a "flight into intellectualism." The following is taken from a schizophrenic production entitled "Equalitized Metabolic Demention Metabolism."

"Improper wave length—wave length changes, later visible death. That is a moving trollysis similar to circulation of life action. Born high focussating action may die through wave length charge and still live until visible death takes place.

"Education comes from radiation of action. Anyone can study all science in a compositive way. It takes a compositive mind to be able to understand. Can tell compositive minds by stromonized conception. The mind at birth takes on a birthification, becomes environmental by the radiation to it. Metabolism to dimension differ in every person is of actions of metabolism and dimension balancing. . . ."

How the thinking of a formerly well-trained mind may become disorganized in schizophrenia is illustrated in the following intellectualized rumination taken from a letter written by a man who had had a scholastically brilliant college career and after graduation had spent two years at Oxford as a Rhodes scholar.

"I'm too utterly weary from battling with my financial-religious and general-religious problems to be able to survive any shock of learning that unhintably hard-won progress supposed to have been earned in the fraternal-religious problem is illusory. For that would wreck me—in my critically exhausted condition—with horror lest humanity—contrarily from being faith-imbued joy-multipliers of Revelations All Embracing God or Unfathomably Progressive Universe—are duped victims of God's opposite faith deluding us—with illusions of immortality, a Heavenly Father and of progress—into accommodation as evil-absorbers of His unconvertible and endless agonies and struggle."

Many schizophrenics appear to show a poverty of associations and of ideas, presumably because of preoccupation with material having its source largely in the unconscious and also because of the accompanying narrowing of attention. To be ascribed to these two conditions, as well, are the casual and trivial remarks and replies of the schizo-

phrenic so peculiar to the disorder as to have important diagnostic significance.

Elements in repressed constellations of ideas may produce various ellipses, short-circuitings of ideas, and even neologisms. These words of his own making are condensations and symbolizations of complexes with affect. Within their concealed meaning are compressed the condensations of words that refer to persons or things intimately related to the individual's particular conflict or psychic experience. The use of neologism by the mental patient always suggests a schizophrenic psychosis.

In connection with disturbances of associations, mention should be made of the fact that in early schizophrenia a fairly typical flight of ideas may occur, which later tends to develop into incoherence.

Blocking may occur as associations approach painful conflict material. It results, perhaps, from a threat that repressed material is approaching awareness. It tends to arise largely in connection with special topics, whereas neutral topics may be handled as usual.

The thinking of the schizophrenic seems directed from the unconscious. Associations and symbols are molded and directed by affective constellations and instinctive undercurrents. They rise into consciousness as a type of thought much like that of dreams, in which one finds active the processes of symbolism, displacement, and condensation. *Dereistic thinking* is of the pleasurable "primary process" type of early life that tends to falsify reality, to disregard realistic, logical, and scientific thought. It is not corrected by the logic of experiences or by the demands of the external world.

To put it another way, the explanation for the disorders in the thinking of the schizophrenic is found in the great extent to which associations are directed by internal perceptions and associations unrelated to occurrences in the immediate environment—that is, reality.

Harrow and Prosen suggested from their recent studies of bizarre schizophrenic language that much of it results from patients *intermingling* material from past and current experiences. Because of their origin in the unconscious, associations are broken, are led into bypaths, are fragmented, are incongruous, do not progress, or are joined through common affects rather than through conscious, logical connection, with the result that various forms of incoherence follow. When the connections appear particularly loose, we speak of the schizophrenic's thought as being "scattered." This means that the unconscious connection of ideas is unusually marked.

From their analysis of communication in the transactions of families with a schizophrenic member, Wynne, Singer, and their colleagues have proposed a classification of forms of thinking, descriptions of the types of parental communications as they appear to relate to these forms, and also descriptions of their methods of rating styles of communication. They, too, conceive of the family culture and its transactions as the means by which role structure, communication, perceiving, and thinking are experienced and psychically internalized by the growing child. Proceeding from the developmental principles of Heinz Werner that maturation moves from lack of differentiation through progressive states of increasing differentiation, articulation, and integration, Wynne and Singer have postulated a global, predominantly undifferentiated form of schizophrenic functioning, designated as *amorphous;* a more organized but incompletely differentiated form of thought, designated as *fragmented;* and a continuum between these two in terms of thought process, described as *mixed.* Those schizophrenics classified as *amorphously organized* communicate in sequences, broken by gaps, brevity, vagueness, and indefiniteness. Their affect is dull and apathetic and the developmental histories are associated with

evidence of defects and continued failure rather than indications of repressed loss. Those considered to have *mixed thinking* qualities show areas of perceptual and cognitive clarity and have functioned fairly well periodically in certain areas of life. Their premorbid background is found to have been poor. Patients with *fragmented forms* of thought, who would generally be classified within the borderline or pseudoneurotic groups, present preponderantly difficulties in integration and articulation of experience, which under nonstressful circumstances they appear to have differentiated. They are, however, vulnerable to emotional stress and in conflict over control of powerful impulses and thoughts. Their style of thinking approximates the normal, yet there is a lack of coherent and meaningful patterns in it and in their lives; opposing impulses are held together by constricting defenses of paranoid, obsessional, and other neurotic types.

In their transactions, the families of the "amorphous" schizophrenics seriously failed to communicate attention, role structure, and forms of interpersonal relatedness and affects. The parents were vague in their expectations of each other and of others, their verbal exchanges were seldom meaningful or relevant emotionally, and they appeared out of contact with each other as well as lacking in efforts to control their own or their offspring's behavior. In some instances one or the other parent showed these features or vacillated. On the other hand, parental transactions of "fragmented" schizophrenic patients were found to be vigorous and manipulative, with intensive interactions in which blame placing was frequent. There were common spurious agreements and fights with many shifts in position. While the parental role seemed well differentiated in some aspects, performance over time suggested poor integration, shown through shifting standards, idiosyncratic word usage, and even directfulness. Their expectations of others were shifting, so that they transmitted confusion and perplexity.

Since these various studies suggest that the genesis of schizophrenic disorders is in pathological family acculturation, their significance in terms of prevention and therapy is enormous. One wonders about the potential wisdom of placing children—as a preventive health measure—from the high-risk schizophrenic family with others. Still too limited and too global, lacking controls based on sufficient observation of parental transactions of those with other personality maldevelopments and of the healthy, these studies nevertheless pioneer a promising new area of exploration in the understanding of the genesis of schizophrenia.

DELUSIONS. The dominant *ideational content* of the schizophrenic is often delusional in nature. Because the satisfactions sought by his beliefs are so highly disguised by their symbolism and because the needs in response to which the *delusions* have been created are often not apparent, the delusions of the schizophrenic often appear grotesque and meaningless. His delusions are never meaningless, but are specific and adapted to his peculiar psychological needs and situation and are in keeping with his particular life experiences, although they are conspicuously disregardful of reality. In referring to symbols, attention may be called to the fact that if he has artistic ability, he may show symbolic condensations in his drawings or paintings, which may be used through therapeutic sessions to reveal the nature of his conflicts.

Messianic delusions are common in this disorder, expressing as they do the wish to avoid affective thoughts and experiences through ascetic self-elevation and exalted mystical states, thus defending against deep-seated and repressed feelings of inadequacy. They are common in the paranoid. In these days of countercultural movements, many with such psychopathology are found among the converts or even leaders of the movement. Messianic delusions, how-ever, reveal the patient's withdrawal into self and separation from others, which may be ambivalently reflected in that he wishes to give but secretly hopes to be loved or admired.

The schizophrenic patient's delusions tend to be grotesque, to be loosely organized, and to center on themes of persecution, grandiosity, sex, bodily functioning, and control by others. He may believe that his thoughts are withdrawn and others inserted from outside and that they are being broadcast, are very loud, or are different from those he believes his own. He may subjectively believe that his will is replaced by that of others, that he is forced to move or act or have wishes which he disowns as his own, and that even his spoken words and handwriting are controlled from outside. Such delusions are emphasized as "first rank" by Schneider and included as nuclear in certain international diagnostic schemes. That they arise from autistic sources and yet are expressed in a relatively clear setting is shown in the following letter addressed by a patient to one of the male physicians connected with the hospital in which she was under treatment:

"Dear Dr.——
    "My Plan." or as mother used to call you, "The Little Plant," or else one little Plant for I was the other Plant, called "Tant." Will you please see that I am taken out of this hospital and returned to the equity court so I can prove to the court who I am and thereby help establish my identity to the world. Possibly you do not remember or care to remember that you married me May 21, 1882, while you were in England and that I made you by that marriage the Prince of Wales, as I was born Albert Edward, Prince of Wales, I am feminine absolutely, not a double person or a hermaphrodite, so please know I am England's feminine king—the king who is a king.
    Your first duty is to me, and if you do not intend to do the right thing, helping me to get out of here, stop the thefts of clothing, money, jewelry, papers, letters, etc., etc.; you will please let me know so I can make some absolute change and further demand of the nations my release.
    1874 Building was to have been a palace for my mother, father, myself and you, that is, if you are the one I married—so why not get busy and furnish it up as such when I go abroad. Make my trips (our trips?) short and return to America on important matters and have the right place to

hold court. You and Dr. Black can take me to the equity court when I prove up my individuality and this must be done.

Sincerely,

"Tant"

Queen of Scotland, Empress of the World, Empress of China, Empress of Russia, Queen of Denmark, Empress of India, Maharajahess of Durban, "Papal authority" as a Protestant.

In the early stages of schizophrenia, the delusions may not be fixed, and the patient may at times be in doubt about his ideas of reference or the hostility of his environment; later he becomes convinced that his delusions are real facts. Both delusions and hallucinations often are concerned with others. The young adult is fixed upon a friend, relative, or work-related acquaintance, while the adolescent patient's person (object) fixation tends to be more diffuse and less well known to the patient. At the onset of his psychosis, the schizophrenic may have obsessive ideas that prove to be the early stages of a process that later becomes frankly one of externalization and projection.

Delusions in the schizophrenic often serve rather effectually in subjectively reorganizing his life situations and in dealing with such problems as thwarted trends and drives, frustrated hopes, biological inadequacies, feelings of insecurity, disowned qualities, gnawing feelings of guilt, and the affective constellations and other contents of the unconscious. In no other type of mental disorder are the patient's problems, wishes, and conflicts so thoroughly dramatized and symbolized in fantastic form. This fact and the schizophrenic's impaired ability to appreciate and test the reality of his fantasies tend to the creation of extravagant and bizarre delusions. The role of fantasy was well expressed by Macfie Campbell: "Fantasy is called on to supply what real life has denied, but the fantasies are not woven into a structure which is compatible with a normal social adaptation." There is a tendency to a reversion to belief in magical cause and effect.

Some patients in their schizoid withdrawal show no evidence of delusional ideation.

PERCEPTUAL DISORDER. Clinicians have remarked upon the hypersensitivity of the childhood or early schizophrenic to auditory and visual stimuli, as well as upon the apparent behavioral indifference of the chronically ill to all environmental stimulation. The paradox in these clinical observations is paralleled in the extensive research on the perceptual function in schizophrenics as compared to others. Wider deviations have been recorded on dimensions of sensory and perceptual behavior among the schizophrenic population than among others, but also there has been recorded high interindividual variability and difficulty in replication of findings between various observers. The necessity of evaluating the various laboratory findings differentiating the various subtypes of the schizophrenic reaction, as well as its duration, has been emphasized. The numerous findings may be interpreted, provided one accepts the concept, described in earlier chapters in this book, of a stimulus intensity control system within the central nervous system variously operative to reduce the input of excessive stimulations under different cognitive conditions. Attention, which defines the area of perceptual scanning, will also be modified. Thus the nonparanoid schizophrenics are both acutely aware of sensory stimulation and hyperreactive to aspects of the sensory fields generally regarded by others as marginal or irrelevant.

It is postulated that the hypersensitive long-term nonparanoid schizophrenics have developed stimulus intensity reduction defenses. Also, this group, in contrast to paranoid schizophrenics, demonstrates little scanning behavior. The chronic nonparanoid and/or premorbid schizophrenics are characterized by greater attention to the sensory aspects of perceptual-ideational inputs and less to the connotative attributes—particularly so if the input stimulation is psychologically threatening or affectively unpleasant. At such times they exclude these aspects of the awareness of fear in the stimulus situation. Thus situations to which others respond with psychological and physiological awareness lead in these schizophrenic subgroups to hyporesponsivity, highly variable responses, inattention, and disturbances of set and association.

Through failure of the schizophrenic to build up constant and realistic perceptions of himself, his parents, and others, he reveals during his illness his shifting perceptions of those to whom he relates. Searles has written poignantly of the schizophrenic's experience of his world — of his frequent and changing misperception or misidentification of even his closest associates as he attributes to the others a series of personal attributes derived from some characteristic — physical or psychological — of his parents.

HALLUCINATIONS. In no other form of mental disorder do *hallucinations,* or the projection of impulses and inner experiences into the external world in terms of perceptual images, occur in the presence of clear consciousness so frequently as in schizophrenia. Their mechanism is not unlike that of hallucinations in other abnormal states, but they tend to be more highly disguised in nature and to constitute a primitive form of adjustment and therefore are of much more serious significance than is their presence in delirium or in dissociative states. It is not difficult to conceive of highly significant material in the schizophrenic's inner life as assuming hallucinatory vividness. It is but a step from the figurative "voice of conscience" to its audible perception. Unconscious material and unadjusted tendencies break through and create sense perceptions, perhaps highly symbolized, in response to psychological needs and problems.

It is not surprising that olfactory and gustatory hallucinations, rare in general but most frequently discovered in the schizophrenic, are so commonly associated with delusions of sexual change, as Connolly and Gittleson report. These sensory, perceptual experiences, after all, are so closely related, both physiologically and psychologically, to differentiation of oral-anal-genital functioning and development.

Disowned desires and feelings of guilt are projected as auditory hallucinations that, as the voice of conscience, accuse and criticize. The patient, incapable of recognizing the origin or significance of his hallucinations because of his disorganized ego, believes in the reality of these projected images, accepts them at face value, and reacts in accordance with what he has accepted as reality. He can no longer distinguish between subjective and objective experiences, with the result that he tends to alter reality with hallucinations and delusions. Disruptively, the patient may identify his auditory hallucinations either as originating within his own body or from outside as voices talking about him, commenting upon or repeating his thoughts or even the material he might be reading.

Not all the hallucinated material of the schizophrenic is accusatory. Often, the auditory perceptions are comforting and provide companionship, advice, judgments, and even sexual gratification. These hallucinated perceptions may be identified frequently by patients as representing the voices of significant persons in their lives (parents, lovers, friends) and appear to serve as a substitute for those persons. The accusatory and affectional components thus appear to represent both the actual and the desired elements in the lost personal relationship. Frequently, the onset of hallucinatory experience takes place when the individual actually has lost a significant relationship or, through the isolation of the illness or hospital, is deprived of that relationship.

The schizophrenic may find his hallucinations so serviceable that he is unwilling to relinquish them, with the result that they come to constitute one of his cherished means of adjustment, and he becomes occupied not with a real but with a hallucinatory world, protected from the disturbances of reality. His hallucinations may be said to collaborate with delusions in the development of the same theme, the one by means of image symbols, the other by ideas.

Little need be said in description of hallucinations in schizophrenia. They are more frequently auditory than of any other sense. Olfactory and kinesthetic hallucinatory experiences often are overlooked. Visual hallucinations are not particularly frequent and tend to be limited to acute phases of the psychosis. During their early occurrence, hallucinations are often accompanied by considerable emotional tension and may have a disturbing and disquieting influence on the patient. As time passes, they may cause but little concern and exert less influence upon behavior.

IMPULSE AND ACTION. Many of these odd, unexplained, and impulsive activities of the schizophrenic grow out of a lack of harmonious association and integration of strivings, affects, and wishes—the existence of incompatible and frequently, also, of changing objectives.

The capricious, impulsive behavior of the schizophrenic is to be looked upon as a result of an ambivalence of impulse. The concept of ambivalence, or contradictory manifestations of impulse, idea, or affect, was stressed by Bleuler and considered by him to be a fundamental symptom of schizophrenia. It rests upon the principle that the true meaning of an idea, impulse, or affect is to be found in the exact opposite of that manifestly expressed. The conscious rejection and denial of expression of a desire, notwithstanding its indirect and unrecognized expression through projection in the form of hallucination or delusion, is a manifestation of the principle of ambivalence. At any rate, in schizophrenia there is a peculiar association of contradictions in mental or personality expressions. Ordinarily,

behavior represents a compromise, a working harmony among diverse desires, a result of the contrasting considerations, forces and motives prompting us. In schizophrenia, on the contrary, the two conflicting impulses—one of conscious origin, the other of unconscious origin—control behavior in erratic sequence or even struggle simultaneously to direct it.

AMBIVALENCE may be manifested by a grossly fluctuating blending of love and hate behaviors, with sudden unaccountable shifts in affection and hostility, leading sometimes to impulsive episodes. Occasionally, unpredictable suicidal impulses result in the unexpected death of a patient.

At times a schizophrenic patient may consciously resist a certain impulse, but he may nevertheless carry it through into action. Unconscious and dissociated tendencies acting in this way give the patient a feeling of being forced or controlled. This feeling of being forced permits the entertainment of thoughts or the indulgence in behavior that the socially determined standards of the individual would not permit, but for which the patient no longer recognizes responsibility.

ANERGIA. A common disturbance of activity in the schizophrenic is an avoidance of concrete or spontaneous activity, a loss of initiative and purpose, and the development of a state of inaction sometimes designated as anergia. This progressive limitation of habits of activity may perhaps be considered as a loss of interest and a retreat, one of the means adopted by the schizophrenic in renouncing the world with which he cannot cope. His behavior tends to become autistic and regressive.

NEGATIVISM AND SUGGESTIBILITY. Another disturbance is negativism, which may manifest itself in a perversity of behavior in the form of antagonism to the environment, in opposition to the wishes of those about him, and, in more marked cases, in mutism, rejection of food (even its rejection after eating by vomiting), refusal to swallow, or even to void urine. The patient may feel that negativism is a "safe" way of expressing hostility even though such actions may eventually threaten his life through impairment of biological homeostasis.

Although it is quite the opposite of negativism in certain of its objective manifestations, one occasionally meets with a *pathological suggestibility* that seems to have for its object the same purpose as negativism — a lessening of disturbing contacts with reality. It is less disturbing for the reality-evading patient blindly and passively to accept and follow whatever the environment suggests than it is actively either to oppose or to initiate contacts with reality. He may, therefore, show an automatic obedience to verbal directions without reference to their appropriateness or significance. Instead of answering a question, he may repeat it in a parrot-like manner — *echolalia*. Again, he may at once imitate the movement of a person in his immediate environment — *echopraxia*. Obedient following of the suggestion of the environment involves neither initiative nor responsible contact with others and often seems to express a mocking hostility toward them. The *waxy flexibility* of the catatonic represents this passive acquiescence to suggestions to a degree that may lead the patient to ignore physical discomfort or pain, accompanied usually by a marked disregard of his environment.

Among the disturbances of activity, *mannerisms* and *stereotypies* occupy a large place in the clinical picture. Schizophrenic mannerisms are of a wide variety. They may consist of affectations of manner, speech, gait, and so forth. Others consist of grimaces, sniffing, blowing out the cheeks, wrinkling of the forehead, ticlike movements, or elaborate methods of performing certain activities constituting a sort of ritual. Some patients assume certain postures for years. Sometimes the lips are puckered and held protruded in what is known as "snout cramp." In general,

the schizophrenic's attitudes, gestures, and actions, like many of his verbal communications, appear unintelligible. The bizarre behavior of the schizophrenic has, however, a meaning for him, although its purpose and value are often obscure to others because of condensation and symbolization.

CONSCIOUSNESS AND INTEGRATION. In schizophrenia there is relatively little impairment of consciousness, orientation, or memory, although, because of lack of interest, it is sometimes difficult to test these functions. The *time sense* of schizophrenics appears impaired. Many are unable to estimate units of time with accuracy, and others state their age as that when their illness or hospitalization first occurred. One often secures incorrect replies in answer to questions about orientation but these are because of negativism, the habit of giving casual replies in order to avoid troublesome reality, or occasionally a lack of attention associated with a certain falsification by hallucinations and delusions. Forgetting, inattention, distraction and imaginative thoughts are used by normal persons as expedients to overcome a disappointment; these are used by the schizophrenic patient not as substitutive reactions, but as if he were in a rut of least resistance.

Because of the disturbance in the integrative functions of the personality, leading, as it were, to a disturbance in fusion of cognitive, affective, and conative mental elements, the schizophrenic patient is often described as demented. This is not correct, as there is no irreparable impairment of cognitive and intellectual functions. This does not mean that judgment, the capacity for making conceptual inferences, is not impaired. Rather there has occurred a disorganization of personality or a failure of development of the personality. Not only does the patient have no appreciation of the disorganization that his personality has suffered, but also his concepts of personal welfare, social relationships, and purpose are rendered faulty and unreliable by introverted tendencies and distortion of both physical and social reality through delusions and hallucinations.

RESPONSE TO PSYCHOLOGICAL TESTS. Test devices provide the means of examining a variety of responses under conditions which may be held constant and varied to allow the examiner to study the variables influencing response. Tests also provide an index of how the patient functions in situations of varying degrees of structure or ambiguity. In the projective techniques, for example, only limited cues are provided for what is an appropriate response. It is well to remember that social situations, like test situations, vary in the degree to which they provide cues for appropriate social response. Some patients can function in an apparently adequate way until they are placed in a situation in which cues for appropriate action are not clearly specified. It is then that their weaknesses become highlighted.

Variability in functioning, distortions in thinking revealed in poor reality contact, overgeneralizations, unconventional and idiosyncratic thoughts, and peculiarities of language, as well as the affective disorders and disturbances of ego boundaries, are revealed in performance on the generally applied battery of psychological tests: WAIS, Bender Gestalt, Rorschach, and Thematic Apperception Tests. The performance on Stanford-Binet and similar intelligence tests by disorganized schizophrenics differs both qualitatively and quantitatively from that of subnormal persons of the same mental age level. In normal persons and in the mentally deficient, the age levels at which failures and successes are intermixed are grouped fairly closely around the determined mental age level, but in disorganized schizophrenics, as in persons suffering from many other psychoses that have led to deterioration, there is usually a spread of failures and successes at a number of age levels above and below the determined one. This phenomenon is known as *scatter*.

The detection of distinctive schizophrenic features in the responses to a Rorschach test is a complex procedure because of the many variations in the schizophrenic syndrome itself. There is no set or definite pattern, and a diagnosis of schizophrenic characteristics is largely made from inference. Variation in form of responses, contamination of ideas, bizarreness, withdrawal, environmental rejection, and poor affective control are revealed with the Rorschach test. Thus, poor form responses (F+%) indicates weakness in reality testing, the overutilization of small details reveals the trends to make unwarranted generalizations about the whole, and limited popular (P) responses reveal the unconventional or idiosyncratic. Complete rejection of the color cards suggests apathy or emotional blunting, while impulsiveness is equated with response determined solely by color. The disturbance in ego boundaries may be reflected in the ability of the patient to apperceive movements in the inkblots while his empathic defect is shown by the few percepts of human movement, as are his wariness and withdrawal from human transactions.

PHYSICAL CHANGES. The more disorganized and disturbed schizophrenics sometimes show certain *physical concomitants*. One of the most frequent of these is general disequilibrium of the autonomic nervous system. This is shown by cold, bluish hands and feet, blotchy skin, and widely dilated pupils, which, when tested by a strong light, may contract momentarily but quickly dilate again. Sometimes patients in a catatonic stupor who persist in standing about in an immobile manner develop a striking edema of the lower extremities. Attacks of vertigo and of hysteriform and epileptiform seizures may occur, more frequently in the early stages. Many patients lose weight during the acute phases of the disease. Those who enjoy a favorable outcome of a schizophrenic episode often show a marked increase in weight during convalescence; however, an increase in weight without a coincident mental improvement usually denotes an unfavorable prognosis.

Malnutrition and tuberculosis have been accompaniments of chronic hospitalization of schizophrenics. With improved hospital management, active screening and segregation of the tubercular, and the use of appropriate chemotherapy, these complications now are prevented.

Types of Schizophrenia

In formulating his concept of dementia praecox, Kraepelin classified his cases into different varieties, depending on the predominant symptomatology. Although classification according to reaction type continues to be made, it must be recognized that numerous patients show at one time or another psychopathology considered characteristic of the individual groups. More is to be gained by studying each patient, evaluating his central pathology, the deficits in his life experience, and the dynamic forces inducing his particular psychopathology, and by erecting a pertinent and individualized therapy, than by attempting to categorize his illness in a vague classificatory division. Since these types or divisions are widely used, they are delineated in this section.

The recently published third edition of the Diagnostic and Statistical Manual of Mental Disorders (DSM III) separates arbitrarily the schizophrenic from the schizophreniform disorders, largely on the basis of a duration of behavioral and symptomatic expressions enduring over a six-month period. It will be rediscovered clinically that the majority of so-called schizophreniform disorders continue over time or recur to be identified later as schizophrenic per se. The essential clinical phenomena are similar and are described in full in this chapter. The new American classificatory system has dropped the description of the simple type recognized for years by many experienced clinicians. We have retained a description of this type, which continues to be diagnosed elsewhere.

However, to follow the new classification, a separate chapter on Psychotic Disorders not otherwise classified (Chapter 21) has been inserted, which includes the schizophreniform and schizoaffective disorders of that scheme. The borderline or pseudoneurotic schizophrenias are described in Chapter 25, Personality Disorders.

DISORGANIZED OR HEBEPHRENIC TYPE. The onset of this type of schizophrenia is insidious and usually occurs in early adolescence. The sufferer is customarily single and unemployed. There is a family history of schizophrenic disorder. Occasionally the onset is subacute and is characterized by a depression that suggests a flattened affective reaction. Usually, however, affective reactions are shallow and inappropriate. Silliness, giggling, and incongruous or inappropriate smiling and laughter are usual. Hallucinations are frequent. The ideational content tends to take the form of fantasy or of fragmentary bizarre delusions rather than of elaborate or systematized beliefs. Associative processes are loose, speech is incoherent, neologisms are common, and posturing and mannerisms are frequent. Regressive features are prominent, wetting and soiling are common, and the patient eats in a ravenous, unmannerly fashion. The patient comes to lead a highly autistic life; he becomes bafflingly inaccessible and greatly introverted and withdrawn. The final disintegration of personality and habits is perhaps the greatest of any of the types of schizophrenia.

One of five children, Theresa was her mother's favorite. Greatly petted and babied by her mother, she always remained dependent upon her. She was described as having been a pretty child with a rosy complexion. She early became aware of this fact and enjoyed dressing up and strutting about to display her good looks. In spite of these signs of vanity, she was timid and shy and would blush in a self-conscious way when she realized that people were noticing her. In childhood she did not play freely with other children: "she thought herself above other children," and is described by her sisters as having in later years "a rather good opinion of herself and her abilities," and by her neighbors as "high-hat."

Soon after leaving school at age 16, she began to work in a bleachery, where she remained until shortly before her commitment. She never had any girl chums and did not participate in the activities of other girls at her place of employment. Her attitude was one of "proud distance." While she was still in school there were several boys who were quite friendly toward her, but her sister said she could not remember any instance when the patient had any male callers or associates after she grew up, although she gave much attention to her clothes and personal appearance, obviously, in the sister's opinion, in an effort to attract the attention of young men. Her family described her as devoid of humor, sensitive, jealous, stubborn, willful, and easily angered. She became more seclusive, had "melancholy spells," became preoccupied, and paid less attention to her environment. When addressed she would ask in an indifferent way, "What did you say?" She also became irritable and critical, particularly of the wife of her brother, with whose family she lived.

About six months before commitment to the hospital at age 32 she "began to grow thin and nervous" and became careless about her work, which deteriorated in quality and quantity. She believed that other girls at her place of employment were circulating slanderous stories concerning her. She complained so indignantly that X., an attractive young man employed in the same industrial plant, had put his arm around her and insulted her that her family demanded that the charge be investigated. This showed not only that the charge was without foundation but that the young man in question had not spoken to her for months. The family, however, had not suspected mental disease until six days before her commitment, when she returned from her work. As she entered the house that evening, she laughed loudly, watched her sister-in-law suspiciously, refused to answer questions, and at sight of her brother began to cry. She refused to go to the bathroom, saying that X. was looking in the windows at her. She ate no food and the next day declared that her sisters were "bad women," that everyone was talking about her, and that X. had been having sexual relations with her, that although she could not see him he was "always around." In her hallucinatory experiences she heard X. say, "Aren't you going to fire her? I've had her. She don't know it." The patient became resistive, was afraid of being killed, and at times said, "I'm dead." She stated that she was being poisoned, saw her dead mother, and heard her speak.

As the patient became noisy, did not sleep, and ate but little and then only when spoon-fed, she was committed to a private institution. Here she was uncooperative and silly, grimaced and whiningly repeated, "Oh, mama! Mama! I want to see my father before I die." She heard voices outside her window and at night would come to the door of her room several times saying, "What is it all about? Oh, mama!" Her associations became loose; she took no interest in the care of her person or in other patients but would stand for hours with her back against the wall, her head thrust forward, fingering her hair, and unobservant of her environment

After a residence of four months in the private institution, the patient was transferred to a public hospital. As she entered the admitting office, she laughed loudly and repeatedly screamed in a loud tone, "She cannot stay here; she's got to go home!" She grimaced and performed various stereotyped movements of her hands. When seen on the ward an hour later, she paid no attention to questions, although she talked to herself in a childish tone. She moved about constantly, walking on her toes in a dancing manner, pointed aimlessly about, and put out her tongue and sucked her lips in the manner of an infant. At times she moaned and cried like a child but shed no tears. As the months passed, she remained silly, childish, preoccupied, inaccessible, grimacing, gesturing, pointing at objects in a stereotyped way, usually chattering to herself in a peculiar high-pitched voice, little of what she said being understood. At an interview 18 months after her hospitalization, she presented an unkempt appearance, was without shoes, sat stooped far over, smiled in a silly manner, and presented a picture of extreme introversion and regression. During the attempted interview, she rarely spoke, although she occasionally replied, "I don't know" in an entirely indifferent manner and apparently with no heed to the question. The nurse reported the patient as seclusive, resistive, idle, and with no interest either in the activities of the institution or in her relatives who visited her.

CATATONIC TYPE. According to Guggenheim and Babigian, the catatonic type of schizophrenia remains very prevalent. A seven-year study in a single county in the U.S.A. exposed one instance per 1000 population. It comprised 5 per cent of all first diagnoses of schizophrenia. The condition is much more frequent in lower socioeconomic levels (two to eight times the upper). The death rate for this type is, with other psychiatric disabilities, 2.6 to 3.6 times greater than that for the normal population. A significantly greater number of women have the condition.

The catatonic type is characterized by phases of stupor or of excitement, in both of which negativism and automatism are prominent features. There may be alternation between little or no movement to an explosive overactivity. Frequently, however, a given catatonic episode may present but one phase, either stupor or disorganized overactivity, throughout its course. Again, there may be an admixture of symptoms usually thought of as belonging characteristically to one or the other phase. The majority display predominantly retarded motor activity; about 30 per cent will demonstrate both stuporous and excited behavior; and 25 per cent, predominantly excitement.

The most frequent age of appearance is between 15 and 25. Of the various types of schizophrenia, catatonia most frequently has a somewhat acute onset and is most frequently precipitated or preceded by an emotionally disturbing experience. The prognosis for a recovery with reintegration of personality after a catatonic episode is more favorable than in other types of schizophrenia, although after a period, perhaps after several episodes, there is a tendency for the catatonic type to pass over into states approaching the hebephrenic or paranoid, with permanent disorganization of the personality.

Catatonic Stupor. Catatonic stupor, or the stupor phase, is often preceded by depression, discontent, or emotional fermentation. The patient is inclined to be uncommunicative, and his reactions become increasingly characterized by failing interest, inattention, preoccupation, emotional poverty, and dreaminess. Mute, stuporous, and with mask-like facies, the catatonic may occasionally keep his eyes closed but more frequently he stares fixedly and blankly downward. He may stand almost immobile, seldom shifting his position during the whole day. The skin of his feet may become turgid and engorged, with swelling of unsupported parts. Another catatonic may spend the day sitting on the edge of a chair or crouching on the floor. With his implicit loss of reality sense, he denies the world and actively resists the environment. He opposes any effort to move him from attitudes and positions, often constrained and peculiar, that he has assumed and may maintain for months. The patient refuses to dress or to eat, although occasionally, if he thinks he is unobserved, he will eat greedily. Saliva, urine, and bowel contents are often retained. He may not only soil clothing but even exhibit an apparent purposefulness in his annoying disregard of all cleanliness in his habits of excretion.

Gestures, grimacing, and grinning are common. The hands may be held tightly clenched and other muscle tensions may be maintained. Occasionally the physical manifestations of catatonia show some points of similarity to parkinsonian akinesia and rigidity. Catalepsy, either flexible or rigid, may be present. In this state, the patient initiates no spontaneous movements but maintains the postures into which he is passively impressed. Through automatic obedience, the patient may carry out any verbal instructions, regardless of their absurd or even dangerous nature. He shows no avoiding reaction to feinting motions before the eyes, to pinpricks, or to other painful stimuli. Although giving no indication whatsoever that he is at all aware of what is going on about him, the patient really registers the events of his environment, and when he begins to speak again, he may give a surprisingly full account of incidents occurring while he was in his stupor.

In spite of the apparent ideational poverty, there seems to be every reason to believe that ideas and representations are by no means absent, but rather are centered on a dominant ideo-affective constellation. Perhaps an analogue to catatonic stupor may exist in the unapprehending, impassive response with which profound, overwhelming bereavement or catastrophe may at times be met. Both this reaction and the catatonic stupor of the schizophrenic may serve as methods of meeting situations too difficult to be met by active, resolute measures. The stupor may be thought of as a protective withdrawal from contact with surroundings that seem threatening. Again, the stupor may be compared to a retreat into an intense, trancelike preoccupation or reverie.

After a period of extremely variable duration, the patient may slowly, or at times suddenly, emerge from this profound generalized inhibition. Occasionally, catatonic rigidity and negativism may terminate in response to affective stimuli. The opposite occurrence, the sudden sinking into a stuporous akinesia following an apparently trivial physical or mental event, is more frequent. Interest, affect, and behavior may return more or less closely to normal, or the patient may pass into a state of catatonic excitement.

Catatonic Excitement. Catatonic excitement is characterized by an unorganized and aggressive motor activity. It is not accompanied by emotional expression and is not influenced by external stimuli; it is apparently purposeless and stereotyped and is usually confined to a limited space. Of all schizophrenics, the excited catatonic most frequently shows impulsive and unpredictable behavior. Without warning or apparent cause, he may suddenly attack an inoffensive bystander or break a window. He destroys his clothing, remains nude, and disregards all excretory cleanliness. Negativism is usually marked. The flow of speech may vary from mutism to a pressure suggesting a flight of ideas. Attitudinizing, mannerisms, stereotypies, and grimaces are frequent. The patient may react to terrifying or ecstatic hallucinations of sight or hearing. Mystical experiences are not uncommon. Hostility and feelings of resentment are common. The patient may be sleepless, appear delirioid, refuse food, and become dehydrated and exhausted. There is often a rapid loss of weight. On rare occasions the acutely and extremely excited catatonic may collapse and die. Usually no pathologic condition sufficient to explain the cause of death is found at necropsy. In such cases, therefore, the death is ordinarily said to be a result of "exhaustion syndrome."

Probably acute catatonic excitement is often the same as the reaction that Kempf termed *acute homosexual panic.* The great activity is often accompanied by fearfulness and auditory hallucinations that accuse the patient of homosexual practices or inclinations. As previously noted, he is often assaultive.

Many psychiatrists look upon catatonic stupor as a profound regression, a dramatization of death. Attention is called to the similarity between catatonia and the instinctive immobility reaction exhibited by certain animals when confronted with a life-threatening situation. Arieti has suggested that the immobility of the catatonic has its origin in family transactions wherein criticism is directed toward action tendencies of the growing child and is accepted by the compliant child. Catalepsy then is an expression of compliance to the demands of others. As mentioned earlier, it may symbolize an ambivalent negativism and be used to discharge hostility in a passive way.

The case of A.C., aged 32, will illustrate many of the features observed in both the excited and the stuporous phases of catatonia.

The patient's father was stubborn and self-willed; his mother was excitable and temperamental. At 7 years of age he went to live with his grandparents. The grandfather, whose "word was law," suffered from epileptic seizures and subsequently died in a hospital for mental diseases; he had no understanding of the child's point of view. His seizures greatly frightened the boy. The patient was a seclusive, day-dreaming, timid, shy, and sensitive, but stubborn and self-willed, child. He still remembers with resentment how his father whipped him before another boy whom he would not thank for an apple. He was uninterested in the play of other children and spent his time either in the town library or in his own room, where he made various toys that he guarded jealously from other children, allowing only his sister, his sole confidante, to share them. At age 17 he was graduated from high school, where he had learned easily but had taken no part in extracurricular activities.

His occupational history was without significance except that his early promise of success as a draftsman and designer of airplanes and motors had not been sustained and that for eight years prior to his commitment he had earned practically nothing. At age 20 he married.

Two months before commitment the patient began to talk about how he had failed, had "spoiled" his whole life, that it was now "too late." He spoke of hearing someone say, "You must submit." One night his wife was awakened by his talking. He told her of having several visions but refused to describe them. He stated that someone was after him and trying to blame him for the death of a certain man. He had been poisoned, he said. Whenever he saw a truck or a fire engine, the patient stated that someone in it was looking for him in order to claim his assistance to help save the world. He had periods of laughing and shouting and became so noisy and unmanageable that it was necessary to commit him.

On arrival at the hospital, the patient was noted to be an asthenic, poorly nourished man with dilated pupils, hyperactive tendon reflexes, and a pulse rate of 120 per minute. In the admission office he showed many mannerisms, lay down on the floor, pulled at his foot, made undirected, violent striking movements, struck attendants, grimaced, assumed rigid, attitudinized postures, refused to speak, and appeared to be having auditory hallucinations. Later in the day, he was found to be in a stuporous state. His face was without expression, he was mute and rigid, and paid no attention to those about him or to their questions. His eyes were closed and the lids could be separated only with effort. There was no response to pinpricks or other painful stimuli.

On the following morning an attempt was made to bring him before the medical staff for the routine admission interview. As he was brought into the room supported by two attendants, he struggled, grimaced, shouted incoherently, and was resistive. For five days he remained mute, negativistic, and inaccessible, at times staring vacantly into space, at times with his eyes tightly closed. He ate poorly and gave no response to questions but once was heard to mutter to himself in a greatly preoccupied manner, "I'm going to die—I know it—you know it." On the evening of the sixth day he looked about and asked where he was and how he came there. When asked to tell of his life, he related many known events and how he had once worked in an airplane factory, but added that he had invented an appliance pertaining to airplanes, that this had been stolen and patented through fraud and that as a result he had lost his position. He ate ravenously, then fell asleep, and on awaking was in a catatonic stupor, remaining in this state for several days.

He gradually became accessible, and when asked about himself, he replied that he had had a "nervous breakdown following the physical breakdown." He referred to his stuporous period as sleep and maintained that he had no recollection of any events occurring during it. He said, "Everything seemed to be dark as far as my mind is concerned. Then I began to see a little light,

like the shape of a star. Then my head got through the star gradually. I saw more and more light until I saw everything in a perfect form a few days ago." Two days later he admitted that he could remember having seen the examiner while in the stupor. He rationalized his former mutism by a statement that he had been afraid he would "say the wrong thing," also that he "didn't know exactly what to talk about." From his obviously inadequate emotional response and his statement that he was "a scientist and an inventor of the most extraordinary genius of the twentieth century," it was plain that he was still far from well.

PARANOID TYPE. The features that tend to be most evident in this type or phase are delusions, often numerous, illogical, and disregardful of reality, hallucinations, and the usual schizophrenic disturbance of associations and of affect, together with negativism.

Frequently, the prepsychotic personality of the paranoid schizophrenic is characterized by poor interpersonal rapport. Often he is cold, withdrawn, distrustful, and resentful of other persons. Many are truculent, have a chip-on-the-shoulder attitude, and are argumentative, scornful, sarcastic, defiant, resentful of suggestions or of authority, and given to caustic remarks. Sometimes flippant, facetious responses cover an underlying hostility.

The paranoid type tends to have its frank appearance at a somewhat later age than the other forms. It is not common until after adolescence and occurs most frequently after 30 years of age. More often the patient is married and has been employed. The evidence of familial illness is scanty. The patient's previous negative attitudes become more marked, and misinterpretations are common. Ideas of reference are often among the first symptoms. Disorders of association appear. Many patients show an unpleasant emotional aggressiveness. Through displacement, the patient may begin to act out his hostile impulses. His grip on reality begins to loosen. At first his delusions are limited, but later thay become numerous and changeable. In the early stages, too, their character usually indicates more clearly the particular psychological needs or experiences that they are created to meet. Occasional remarks may supply fragmentary disclosures of the patient's preoccupations. Rejected tendencies are ideationally projected instead of undergoing repression.

Delusions of persecution are the most prominent occurrences in paranoid schizophrenia, but expansive and obviously wish-fulfilling ideas and hypochondriacal and depressive delusions are not uncommon. With increasing personality disorganization, delusional beliefs become less logical. Verbal expressions may be inappropriate and neologistic. The patient is subjected to vague "magical forces," and his explanations become extremely irrational. Imaginative fantasy may become extreme but take on the value of reality. Repressed aggressive tendencies may be released in a major outburst; some inarticulate paranoids may manifest an unpredictable assaultiveness. Many paranoid schizophrenics are irritable, discontented, resentful, and angrily suspicious and show a surly aversion to being interviewed. Some manifest an unapproachable, aggressively hostile attitude and may live in a bitter aloofness. Auditory hallucinations usually occur, and the voices are most frequently threatening or accusatory in nature. The patient may show varying degrees of tension and may be subject to upsurges of rage that he seems unable to control.

As personality disorganization proceeds, affective responses become increasingly flattened. Mannerisms, apathy, and incoherence are common. In general, paranoid schizophrenia may be regarded as a projective, regressive, defensive type of reaction. In contrast to parental transactions thought to induce catatonic behavior by criticizing action, Arieti postulates that the future paranoid is exposed to accusations of malignant intentions, deceit, and lying. Action tendencies are fostered.

The following is in many respects a rather typical case of paranoid schizophrenia.

A.B., a physician, 38 years of age, was admitted to a hospital following his arrest for disturbing the peace. Specifically, he had frightened his neighbors by hurling objects at imaginary people who, he said, were tormenting him, by beating the air with ropes and by breaking glass in the apartment that he and his wife occupied.

The patient was born in the Ukraine. Little is known of parental characteristics. His mother is described as being "sweet and good-natured as long as things went her way, but she would have violent outbursts of temper, during which she would throw dishes and break glasses when aroused." The patient, the youngest son, is said to have been "the favorite of the whole family. He was spoiled, given his own way, and invariably the other children would be whipped for the misdemeanors of which he was guilty."

When 16 years of age, the patient came to the United States, where he continued his studies. After graduation from college, he entered medical school. His medical course continued satisfactorily until the third year, when he failed to pass a pathology course, which until that time had been one of his best subjects. For some reason, not stated in his history, he was dismissed from the first medical school he entered, but later was admitted to a second one, where he repeated the third year and was graduated.

Upon his commitment to the hospital, his wife described his personality traits as follows: "He has always been a deep thinker. Lately, however, he cannot concentrate. He is rather aggressive and is the type who insists upon imposing his own ideas on everyone else. He thinks that people have to agree with him. He is stubborn and argumentative. This trait was even referred to in his college yearbook. He is an independent thinker and is very bright. He had big plans for the future. He was formerly quite extrovertive until the last few years, when he refused to go out and mingle with people."

Soon after beginning his internship, trouble developed between the young physician and the chief resident. The former was compelled to resign but secured appointment in another hospital and completed an internship. Following this, he went to Vienna to pursue graduate work in ophthalmology, otolaryngology, and bronchoscopy. After his return to the United States, he entered private practice and was apparently successful for the first four years, although, because of various difficulties, he changed locations on several occasions. For some reason not stated in the history, the patient gave up his practice and became a medical officer in a government service. He soon began to complain that the commanding officer was "against" him. He made frequent applications of cocaine to his nasal mucous membrane, not, he said, because he was a cocaine addict but in order to neutralize the effects of chloral hydrate, which was being sprayed upon him. After a few months he was released from his appointment. He then began practice in another city, but as he believed that the spraying of chloral hydrate continued there, he remained but two months and then returned to his original place of practice. He met with but little success, as the same ideas of persecution persisted. According to his history, too, "He became forgetful and neglected his cases. He had lapses of memory and seemed to be preoccupied with his own thoughts."

The patient's wife described him as having usually preferred the company of men, "but he has quite a history as far as the opposite sex is concerned." While studying in Vienna, he became involved with a widow and married her. Two weeks after their marriage he discovered, he alleged, that his wife was unfaithful to him and was "a member of a gang of dope peddlers who tried to involve young medical students in their racket." He then returned to the United States. The following year he married again, but the couple lived together for only three months. Three years later the date was set for his third wedding, but he did not appear at a party scheduled to precede the wedding. A quarrel with the expectant bride followed, but finally the wedding took place. Soon he began to object to his wife's talking with other men and accused her of infidelity. On two occasions when she had not even been absent from home, he insisted he had seen her on the street with other men.

Four months before his commitment the patient awoke his wife and told her she must leave the house permanently the following day. He insisted that she was not his wife any longer and the next day asked if she had made her plans to leave.

In view of the failure of three marriages, his accusations of infidelity in at least two of them, and his preference for the company of men, the probability at once suggests itself that at least some of the patient's personality difficulties arose from unrecognized homosexual tendencies. Further support to this assumption is added by the fact that, during the psychiatric examination after his hospital admission, he remarked that certain physical complaints from which he was suffering suggested sexual perversion. Doubtless, too, the fact that for several years he had consumed a half pint or more of alcohol daily may be of corroborative significance.

As the patient's mental disorder progressed, he developed a great wealth of delusions. He stated that he was "the link between the living and the dead," that he was a "universal medium," that a certain physician called on him by mental telepathy for added strength and skill in surgical opera-

tions. He believed that someone was hiding in a trunk in his house and so he fired several bullets into the trunk. He accused his brother of spraying him with chloral hydrate from the third floor of his house. He therefore sat behind a closed door waiting for his brother, and upon hearing a noise, shot through the door. He grew a beard because his face, he said, was being changed in subtle ways by outside influences, adding that if he wore a beard, his true identity would be known. Following his admission to the hospital, he often spent long hours in his room where he could be heard pacing the floor, moaning, or making a noise like a dog, striking his head with his fist, or pounding the wall. When asked the reason for his behavior, he explained that he was suffering tortures because people abused their powers of mental telepathy and were directing those powers toward him. He spent nearly all the day in his room where, during the fourth and fifth years of his hospital residence, he would frequently be heard shouting, screaming, and uttering noises that the attendants described as resembling the howling of a wolf. In explanation of these noises, the patient stated that there was a woman spiritualist who, in some way through persons in the hospital, was exerting a peculiar spell on him, and that by making these noises, he could drive the spirits away. His thought processes became progressively disorganized.

Thirteen years after his admission to the hospital, he wrote his ward physician a 10-page letter which he concluded as follows: "In view of the facts and their significance, and in view of the connection of tendencies and the contingent and pertinent effects, and in view of my physical condition brought about by the connected and sustained tendencies and actuating reasons behind them, I shall not consider it a mere negligence, or merely a form of criminal negligence, or merely an ethical vice, but I shall consider your interference with the anatomical and physiological requirements of my health as an outright, deliberate, well-accounted for and reasoned out criminal and dastardly endeavor at homicide."

As the years passed, he was rarely to be seen on his ward but remained in his room, where most of his days were spent in writing and reading. When approached, he was hostile and resentful in attitude. He was, however, less aggressive and less abusive in speech. As frequently happens in the paranoid schizophrenic, his prolonged institutional residence had produced a lessening of tension but little or no modification of thought content.

UNDIFFERENTIATED TYPE. As mentioned earlier, over the course of the schizophrenic illness many patients may present the behavioral, affective, thought, or intellectual aberrations of the three differentiated types—the disorganized, the catatonic, or the paranoid. When the patient exhibits conspicuous delusional thinking, hallucinations, incoherent communication, or grossly idiosyncratic and socially aberrant behavior that does not easily fit the differentiated forms, it has been the custom to classify the case as *undifferentiated.*

SIMPLE TYPE. Not included in the new American classification but recognized elsewhere, this type shows marked disturbances of emotion, interest, and activity. If hallucinations occur, they are rare and fleeting, and delusions never play an important role. The disorder is usually gradual in its onset and assumes the form of an insidious change and impoverishment of personality, the significance of which is not understood by the patient's friends. In adolescence, young people who perhaps have shown much promise begin to lose interest in school or occupation and become moody, irritable, and indolent. Their goals are no longer realistic. Shallowness of emotions, indifference or callousness, absence of will or drive, and a progressive meagerness of inner resources betray the withering of personality that constitutes the most prominent feature of this type. Neither criticism by others nor the chagrin of parents appears to cause concern. Appreciation of esthetic and moral values is lost. The required period of training or apprenticeship in preparation for a profession or a skilled occupation is not completed. Many become irresponsible idlers, vagrants, tramps, prostitutes, or delinquents. In the milder cases, the social maladaption is less serious, but the patients are considered to be neighborhood eccentrics and, although intellectually unimpaired, are capable of performing only some simple routine task under supervision. The patients remain uninterested in their environment and unimpressed by responsibilities.

While the classification of this subtype has been questioned in recent years, V. Levit studied 1429 schizophrenic individuals from a single district in Moscow and found the incidence to be only 1.5 per cent (the lowest rate of all forms). Syndromes with continuing apathy were rare. With time, however, the clinical picture changed so that within ten years of the original diagnosis, over four fifths of the patients manifested behavioral disturbances and psychopathology more characteristic of the other subtypes.

A.R. was committed to the hospital when 21 years of age following his arrest for windowpeeping. In describing his childhood characteristics, the patient's family stated that he "was always a little hard to understand," but he was a quiet boy who never entered into rough games. His school record was excellent and he always stood high in his class. At age 17 years, when in the fourth year of high school, he was obliged to leave school and secure gainful employment because of a long illness of his father. He secured work with a large manufacturing company, where he soon came to be considered the second best operator on a certain type of machine. For two years he worked steadily, seemed ambitious, and appeared to have a normal and wholesome, but not marked, interest in girls. At age 19 years, he gave up his position, showed no interest in securing another, and, when asked if he worked, replied, "What do I want to work for? I have a father and sister working, and they are enough." He appeared quite self-satisfied and felt that he should have a position of importance.

About this time, he was arrested for the first time for peeping into women's bedrooms. Through the influence of his father, the charge was dropped. He became careless of his personal appearance and remained unoccupied except for occasional periods when he set up pins in a bowling alley. A year later, he was arrested but again was released on the intercession of his father. He came to say little unless addressed and grew antagonistic toward his father and sister. He would remain out until midnight and then come home, eat a large meal, read until 2 A.M., and sleep until noon. Finally, after his third arrest for peeping, he was committed to a hospital for mental disorders.

At the institution, the patient was found to be of asthenic physique and slightly effeminate in appearance. His emotional responses were shallow and inadequate. He showed no concern over his situation, laughed about it in a silly manner, and referred to his offense as "just a foolish idea." His hospital residence was characterized by apathy, preoccupation, and inactivity. During the summer he would at times take part in the patients' baseball games, but in winter he refused ground privileges. He never expressed any delusions and denied hallucinations. At times he would be seen, apparently much preoccupied, walking alone about the hospital reservation, laughing to himself.

This case illustrates how an individual is unable to complete the transition from adolescence to maturity, with its heterosexual and social adjustments. A certain innate limitation to the personality was observed. The patient's interest became largely withdrawn from the actual world, energy was absorbed by the subjective life, and there was a diminished response to social demands.

RESIDUAL TYPE. Following a simple or several well-defined schizophrenic episodes, a recession of symptoms may occur in some so that the prominent psychotic manifestations in bizarre behavior and abnormal thought and perceptual processes are scarcely evident. Yet the existence of the illness is evident in social withdrawal, some eccentricities of behavior, apathy or other affective unresponsiveness, and occasional indications of illogical thinking or loosening of associations.

Those cases with duration of less than two years — the period below which expectations of social recovery remain good — now may be classified as *subchronic*. The persistence of residual symptoms beyond two years of initial recognition should be termed *chronic*. From time to time, those with residual symptoms may show acute exacerbations of flagrant psychotic behavior. A very few may progress to a full remission of symptoms, with or without the continuance of treatment. These patients should be classified as chronic or subchronic as an aid to understanding their course in the future.

Schizophrenia in Childhood

There has been much controversy about whether childhood schizophrenia is related to or coterminous with adult schizophrenia, and the mounting evidence from genetic, developmental, and follow-up research increasingly supports the viewpoint that it is. Furthermore, Fish and others have collected clinical data and observed infants and children born of schizophrenic parents as well as a variety of neurobiologic antecedents of the childhood form. She and others believe that a genetically determined neurointegrative defect exists in such children. The childhood form of schizophrenia appears to have a higher degree of genetic penetrance than the adult form and to run a course more impairing and persistent than the latter.

As for the influence of mothering upon the evolution of the childhood schizophrenic, at this time one may conclude that the genetically vulnerable infant is more likely to respond poorly to emotionally depriving early transactions in comparison with other children at less risk. Yet certain of the early *developmental lags* may improve when such children are exposed to emotionally stimulating environments.

Goldfarb and others have found that the range of children diagnosed as schizophrenic includes several general clusters. On the one hand are those with predominant evidence of neurological or neurophysiological disturbance who were brought up in families found by psychosocial studies to provide adequate sources for identifications and skill in communications and social awareness. On the other hand, there is a cluster of such children showing little evidence of neurological defect who were reared in disturbed families that provided inadequate roots for the growth of personal identification, communication, and perceptual and conceptual clarity.

Diagnostically, these children show impairment in ego functioning. The development of a clear body image, sexual identity, and ability to conceive time and space clearly is impaired. They tend to prefer the sensory information available from the contact receptors — touch, taste, smell — rather than the distance receptors — hearing, vision; then their capacities for anticipation and generalization and their ability to find a personal identity remain limited. It is probable that a goodly proportion of the small children classified as schizophrenic more properly might be considered to be suffering from the personality disorders associated with organic brain damage. Some so classified undoubtedly fall into the group of mental deficiencies.

DIAGNOSIS. The diagnostic criteria specific for childhood schizophrenia are not definitely established. Undoubtedly a wide variety of clinical pictures exists. Bender points out that some schizophrenic children are regressive, retarded, blocked, inhibited, mute, autistic, withdrawn, physically asthenic, unsocial, and unable to relate. Others develop overfast, appear to present intellectual brilliance, and are overactive, advanced in language development, and excessively abstract in their thinking. In her experience, any severe psychoneurotic symptomatology in a child before puberty, whether obsessive-compulsive, so-called hysterical, or severe anxiety, is a reactive response to a deep, inherent, threatening disorder, most often schizophrenic in nature.

Goldfarb has summarized in Table 18–3 a diagnostic variety of impairments in social relations, communica-

TABLE 18–3 Diagnostic Criteria for Schizophrenic Children

LEVEL OF IMPAIRMENT	DEFINITION	RATING
Very severe	No differentiation of important persons, e.g., mother from others; makes no contact with anybody; no speech or gestural communication; total or near total avoidance of looking and listening; indiscriminate mouthing and smelling; near-total absence of self-care; no educability.	1
Severe	Human preferences observable but mis-identifications of important persons occur often; limited contact; speech and gestural communication below level of 3-year old (echoic, pronouns confused, comprehensibility below 90%); mouthing and smelling still prominent; self-care below that of 3-year old; minimal educability (at preschool level).	2
Moderate	Recognition of and responses to important persons, contacting behavior (approaching, talking to others); speech and gestural communication above that of 3-year old; responds to school education above grade 1; yet gross distortions of reality (body image, capacities, etc.) and psychotic behavior.	3
Mild	Mild eccentricity and no friends but functions acceptably in relation to school (including community school and with or without special adjustment such as un-graded class or special tutoring) and in relation to the external environment; or no longer manifestly outlandish or bizarre relationship to people, school, and the external environment but neurotic defenses present (e.g., obsessional or phobic).	4
Normal	By ordinary observation.	5

(From Goldfarb, W.: Growth and Change of Schizophrenic Children: A Longitudinal Study. New York, John Wiley & Sons, 1974.)

tion, interpersonal contacts, and ability to care for oneself. Interpersonal relationships may vary from a mild eccentricity with limited friendships to impairments that vary from recognition of other significant persons and ability to converse or make gestural communications, though with reality distortion, to conditions in which human preferences are noted but misidentifications of important persons occur, to the inability to discriminate others, including the mother. Confusion about the diagnostic feature in childhood schizophrenia has led a British working group to outline nine major criteria considered significant to establish the diagnosis:

1) Gross and sustained impairment of emotional relationships with people;

2) Apparent unawareness of his own personal identity to a degree inappropriate to his age;

3) Pathologial preoccupation with particular objects or certain characteristics of them without regard to their accepted functions;

4) Sustained resistance to change in the environment and a striving to maintain or restore sameness;

5) Abnormal perceptual experience (in the absence of discernible sensory abnormality);

6) Acute, excessive and seemingly illogical anxiety as a frequent phenomenon;

7) Speech either lost, or never acquired, or showing failure to develop beyond a level appropriate to an earlier age;

8) Distortion in motility patterns;

9) Background of serious retardation in which islets of normal, near normal or exceptional intellectual function or skill may appear.

The older the child, the more the clinical picture resembles that seen in adults. In such a child, therefore, we may see not only withdrawal and loss of contact and affect, but also hallucinations and delusions. The last two symptoms do not occur before eight years of age.

Dewdney has pointed out that the vast majority of the childhood schizophrenics he has seen expressed sensations of depersonalization of such intensity that the sufferer feels a threat to the very existence of his body and himself. In association with the sense of depersonalization, the youngsters frequently attack others to obtain contact perception to reassure them of the existence of their bodies. In addition, such children report that staring in conjugate gaze with another often produces a specific, frightening distortion of the other's face. In many instances, the child describes the distortion as though the frightening change were to "a zombie," "a werewolf," or "a living corpse." The distorted figure is that of a persecutor. Dewdney contrasted this distortion of the face from staring to the unknown identity of the double in the Capgras phenomenon.

In general, the change in the face stared at consisted of enlargement of the whole eye, a change in the sclerato-iris ratio, the illusion of the lengthening and thickening of the scalp, and diminution of depth perspective. Dewdney postulates that the persecutory and illusional change is defensive against the frightening sense of self-extinguishment and depersonalization by maintaining even a frightening object relationship. Several of his illustrations taken from children's drawings are shown in Figure 18–1.

In the older patient, the onset of symptoms may be insidious or acute, the insidious type being more frequent. It may be difficult to date the beginning, although retrospectively it is often remembered that peculiarities may have been noted. It is characterized by a general reduction of interests in play and other activities. There is a gradual loss of affective contact with people, accompanied by regressive phenomena. Some patients show a tendency to brooding or to obsessive rumination on some topic ordinarily not of interest to a child. Some patients become aggressive and destructive. Self-mutilation is a common behavior seen in these children. In some instances this is expressed indirectly as accident-proneness or masochistic provocativeness. In children with these behaviors will be found a significant history of physical abuse by the parents in the first two years of life. Many appear to be feeble-minded and are committed to an institution for mental deficiency.

Children with an acute onset have usually not been previously regarded as abnormal. Shortly before the appearance of acute features, there may have been an impairment of ability to concentrate, with an accompanying drop in quality of school work. The child may then begin to mumble to himself, sleep poorly, maintain odd postures, show diminished or rigid affect, become inaccessible and extremely rest-

less, and perhaps scream and kick. Usually, improvement takes place after several weeks but with a reduction of emotional and ideational expression. Subsequent acute episodes are usual, each one followed by increased personality disorganization.

The psychological problems that the child is attempting to meet with his schizophrenic reaction are those naturally accompanying, or appropriate to, childhood and are therefore different from those of adolescence or adulthood. They are also appropriate to the particular developmental period within childhood at which the onset of the disorder occurs. The symptom formation will therefore be related to the problem that has created the anxiety. In other words, much of the symptom

Figure 18-1 Schizophrenic children's drawings of distortions of faces from staring. (From Dewdney, D.: A specific distortion of the human facial percept in childhood schizophrenia. Psychiatr. Q., 47:82–94, 1973.)

formation is determined by the way in which the child deals with his anxiety.

The principal problems, particularly in the small child, are those of self-identity, relating to the rest of the world and to body function, and of relating to objects—for example, to play material, food, or clothes. In somewhat older children, there may be the problem of relationship to a parent, particularly the mother or siblings, or early childhood sex problems. Mental mechanisms that are normal for early childhood become points of fixation, exaggerated by repetition, and mingled with other mechanisms. They are carried into later periods of personality development, where they constitute the psychotic symptoms of the schizophrenic child.

PROGNOSIS. In spite of intensive therapeutic efforts, the vast majority of psychological, psychiatric, social and neurological findings show little change over time. In the intensive studies conducted by Goldfarb, there were slight improvements in a wide variety of characteristics, but none whatsoever in the deficiencies of either hypertonicity or hypotonicity of muscle tone, in the activity level of the children, in the children's capacity to respond to auditory startle, to modify their speech as a result of delayed auditory feedback, or to improve their detection on the double-stimulus stimulation test. These findings led him to conclude that there exists a persistent deficiency in auditory self-monitoring of speech with erratic attention to appropriate accepted views, which constitutes a deficiency of perceptual information. These deficiencies lead the schizophrenic child either to excessive trial or error responsiveness or attenuation of effort, and deprive him of the automatic, purposeful, and reflective adaptations to the varying demands of his inner and outer experiences.

EARLY INFANTILE AUTISM. In 1943, Kanner described a syndrome beginning as early as ages 2 or 3 years, characterized by an extreme withdrawal and obsessiveness. To this syndrome he gave the name "early infantile autism." Because of its similarities to, and its differences from, childhood schizophrenia, its categorical place presents a challenging problem. It is considered more fully in Chapter 28, Disorders of Childhood and Adolescence.

Psychodynamics of Schizophrenia

Those infinitely variegated expressions of disordered personality that constitute the schizophrenic reaction are the expressions of maldevelopment of ego and superego functions. Thus there are abnormalities in perception, thought, and action, including communication, affect, and the capacity to evaluate, make judgments, solve problems, and thereby adapt to reality. Such desirable ego attitudes as a capacity for trust, autonomy, initiative, and persistence are deficient and overshadowed more often by suspicious mistrusts, personal doubting, apathetic or indifferent efforts, and their consequences in uncertainty about sexuality and the adult role. There is evidence, too, of oppressive inhibitions and restrictions as regards expressions of aggression and of sexual and dependency drives.

While much of the psychopathology may be understood as the result of deficiencies, failures, or distortions in family transactions that impair the establishment within the incipient schizophrenic of dependable and meaningful models of personality functioning, this explanation alone of the weakness of development is insufficient. Inordinate aspirations, with attending feelings of deep shame at lack of achievement, and excessive burdens of guilt attached to high expectations for repression of anger, love, or tenderness attest to learning experiences that exaggerate social demands. In many schizophrenics the arousal of rage, the physiological pressures of the sexual drive and its expressions, and the needs for dependent support, all subjected to intensive repression, are tenuously checked but from time to time are discharged impulsively and then widely disrupt other functions.

Ping-Ni-Pao has formulated five steps in schizophrenic ego disorganization. The initiating step occurs with arousal of overwhelming organismic panic (automatic primitive anxiety), whether the onset appears acute or gradual. Conflict leading to the panic state generally derives from aggressive drives unacceptable to the future schizophrenic patient but also may be aroused by sexual or dependency demands. The future patient then utilizes such available infantile defenses as denial, introjection, projection, and splitting or fusion with the idealized. As the schizophrenic patient's ego functioning stabilizes from the initial stages of panic, primitive psychological defenses, and more regressive perceptual-cognitive-motor processes come into action, which give rise to the gross and bizarre symptomatology of the condition. This regression in ego functioning is the best immediate adaptation for the overwhelmed person.

Quiescent periods in the illness, now frequent with the use of antipsychotic medication owing to its capacity to reduce affect arousal, are interrupted when anxiety is rearoused. In the quiescent period, hallucinatory phenomena are usually agreeable and wish fulfilling. Attempts at development of new object relationships lead to insecurity. At such times, often hallucinatory content once again becomes persecutory.

The psychodynamic explanation for these two types of hallucinations, as Freeman posits, is concerned with patients' sense of identity and self-autonomy. Agreeable hallucinatory content is reported on the basis of "primary identification"—that is, a magical child-like identification with a loved object—a helpful mother substitute. While patients may recognize members of their family or hospital staff, at the same time they may declare themselves to be one of these persons or state that they are being addressed as one of them in a respected, loving way or recognized for their accomplishments.

In the paranoidal development, the libidinal drive is directed at the loved object, but love is transformed to hate. By projection, the patient has delusions of being hated and hallucinates persecutory attacks. Freeman has described in great detail the psychodynamic interpretations of shifting hallucinatory affect as it relates to reconstitution of self and object relations.

COURSE AND PROGNOSIS OF SCHIZOPHRENIA

Faced with a schizophrenic patient, the clinician invariably is confronted by worried parents, other family members, and friends wanting a prediction about the outcome of this disability. With an acute psychosis, the interest of both the clinician and the significant relatives may be in the *disappearance of the symptoms and signs* of the disorder. More significant, however, is the future potential of the sufferer to re-establish *social relations, employment,* and *independent living* in the community. To be sure, the symptomatic behavior is significant, but many patients are capable of partial or complete resumption of all these functions, despite the persistence of certain personality characteristics and symptomatic expressions of schizophrenia.

Inadequate or poor ability for social relationships is a strong predictor of the continuance of similar patterns in the future. Individuals with low self-esteem in their adolescence and those who have given evidence of difficult intrafamilial relations earlier by running away or dropping out of school more often have continuing symptomatic experiences of schizophrenia. Finally, a poor employment record prior to symptoms of disorder leads one to foresee a similar employment experience in the future, in spite of treatment.

Many attempts have been made to find the significant prognostic indica-

TABLE 18–4   Prognostic Features for Long-Term Outcome in Schizophrenia

INDICATIVE OF A GOOD PROGNOSIS	INDICATIVE OF A POOR PROGNOSIS
Good premorbid adjustment	Poor premorbid adjustment (schiz-oid/paranoid personality)
Precipitating factors	No obvious precipitating factors
Sudden onset (less than six months)	Insidious onset (greater than six months)
Absence of a family history of schizophrenia	Family history of schizophrenia
Family history of affective disorders	Absence of a family history of affective disorders
Dreamlike or altered state of consciousness on admission	Clear sensorium
Prominent symptoms of affectivity	Blunted affectivity
"Paranoid" symptoms (delu-sional mood and notions)	

(From Robins, E., and Guze, S. B.: Am. J. Psychiatry, *126*:938–987, 1970.)

tors of the eventual social outcome over the long term in this disorder. Table 18–4 lists the series of specific prognostic features that Robins and Guze have claimed successfully predict the long-term outcome in approximately 85 per cent of individuals diagnosed as schizophrenic. From their studies, they distinguished discrete populations, one of which probably classifies according to older terminologies as "process" schizophrenia and the other as "reactive." The former consists of patients whose disorder was persistently evident and who seldom, if ever, made an adequate social adjustment. The latter displayed the features in their life histories and social adaptation defined in Table 18–4.

In Europe, much emphasis is placed upon "first rank" symptoms, described by Kurt Schneider. It is his opinion that when any such experiences are present in the absence of a physical illness, a decisive clinical diagnosis of schizophrenia might be made. Schneiderian first rank symptoms include thought broadcasting; feelings by the patient that his impulses, thoughts, or actions are not his own (experiences of alienation); thoughts by the patient that his feelings, impulses, or actions are imposed upon him (experiences of influence); auditory hallucinations speci-

fically defined as coming from outside the patient's head, content-directed toward the patient's actions, thoughts, or repetitions of his thoughts; and delusional perceptions. Various studies in the United States suggest the Schneiderian system neither is diagnostically superior to others nor has more significant prognostic value. Both the Robins and Guze prognostic listing and the Schneiderian first rank symptoms probably identify generally the same patients.

Although the onset of gross schizophrenic disorganization often appears to occur suddenly, careful study of the patient's developmental history shows that there have been many indications of personality disturbances in earlier years. Usually, the diagnosis is made at a time when family members no longer are capable of adapting to the progressive disturbance in behavior of the newly identified patient that has proceeded insidiously over a number of years. Earlier, the indicators of childhood schizophrenia have been described.

In the O'Neal and Robins follow-up of children seen in one clinic, those who became schizophrenic had more infectious diseases during the first two years of life, more hearing problems, difficulties in locomotion, and physical disfigurements than normal children have. The boys were often spoken of as having a feminine appearance. Also, the presence of antisocial behavior antedated the schizophrenic reaction in half of those who were later so diagnosed. They were physically aggressive, incorrigible, and given to vandalism and pathological lying; they also had more phobias, feelings of depression, unhappiness, and paranoid trends than other children.

Schizophrenia once was regarded as a special type of maladjustment that usually showed a tendency to be progressive and was therefore looked upon with apprehension, but a permanent disorganization of the personality does not invariably follow. Indeed, it is now the opinion of many of the closest students of schizophrenia that acute, rather clearly psychogenic schizophrenia may at times disappear completely, without leaving any injury to the personality. Formerly, its incurable nature and progressive course were implied in the definition of the disease, and a favorable outcome was considered presumptive evidence of an error in diagnosis. Of course, the occurrence of an obviously schizophrenic reaction should make the physician exceedingly careful in predicting that a permanently inferior type of adjustment will not be sustained. In recent years, too, there has been an increasing recognition that the episodic nature of a psychosis and the occurrence of symptom-free intermissions may not exclude its schizophrenic nature.

Occasionally, one observes a schizophrenic episode of a mild, fleeting nature, with no subsequent recurrence. In many instances, however, the favorable outcome should be characterized as "social recovery" rather than as "cured" or as full recovery. This means that the patient is able to return to his previous social environment and to previous or equivalent occupation, but with minor symptoms and signs, such as irritability, shyness, or shallowness of affective responses.

From what has been said, it is evident that in any given case the effect of the appearance of a schizophrenic reaction upon the personality and future adjustment may be quite uncertain. As mentioned in the infantile case, the expectation of social adaptation is minimal if mutism continues until the age of 5. In some cases the course is continuously progressive; in others it is intermittent. More frequently it is a question of remissions and relapses in which, although from the beginning interests and habits tend to be undermined insidiously, there occur periods of adjustment at a lower level for a considerable period of time.

Over 80 per cent of patients who require admission to hospital will be discharged in the first year of residence. The hospital readmission rates run from 40 to 60 per cent of those discharged; many are readmitted more than a single time each year. Characteristic of the treatment of the schizophrenic today has been the remitting course of the illness, leading to periodic returns to hospital with recurrence of symptoms. Many studies have been made of the factors that induce an exacerbation of the psychotic process. The failure of the patient to be continued in treatment and to maintain phenothiazine medication often provokes an exacerbation. In a number of studies it has been shown that the use of long-acting, parenterally injected phenothiazines is effective in avoiding hospital readmissions of those who are not motivated to take their medication.

Perhaps of more significance in understanding the reasons for hospital readmissions is the information made available by Brown, Birley and Wing from their studies of the influence of family life on the course of schizophrenic disorders, and their review of the studies of others. Those schizophrenics with close emotional ties with parents or wives are likely to relapse with gross symptoms and return to hospital, as are those who were discharged from the hospital to understimulating social milieus. To define more precisely the "emotional involvement" of relatives with patients, these investigators found that critical comments made by the relatives about the patients were the most significant factor in inducing relapse, whether the parent or spouse was "warm" or "hostile." A high degree of emotion noticed in relatives at the time of the patient's admission was often associated with symptomatic relapse following discharge.

It is interesting to note that the emotional reactivity of the schizophrenic patient who is returned to his home might be mitigated by avoidance of excessive contact with the highly emotional relative. If the patient was exposed to relatives or spouse more than 35 hours per week, Brown and his colleagues discovered that the chances of symptomatic relapse were greatly increased. Regarding other social factors related to outcome, Astrachan and his colleagues have found that social class is strongly related to symptomatic outcome. In this instance, high social class generally was inclined to be associated with better symptomatic outcome than low social class.

The expectancy of recovery falls with each year of continued hospitalization. Roughly, about one third of those patients who are hospitalized during the first year of their illness make a fairly complete recovery; one third improve and become able to return to outside life but remain damaged personalities and may have to return to the hospital from time to time. The remaining third will require indefinite care and of these perhaps 10 per cent need protected institutional care. The introduction of the modern pharmaceutical therapies has not brought about a reduction in the number of schizophrenic patients requiring hospital care whose illness pursues a chronic course.

The age of onset is not of prognostic significance except that relatively late age offers a less favorable prognosis. Sex has no prognostic significance. Since onset in adolescence sometimes has seemed to occur after loss of a friendship, a study done to examine such relations suggests that one indicator of prognosis for the adolescent schizophrenic is the range and quality of his friendships. It has been found that those who pursue a course of chronic deterioration and hospitalizations have either none or very few adolescent friends. Such friendships are seldom lengthy and, if severed, are infrequently replaced. Usually the friend is either much older or younger, and the interaction between the patient and the friend is infrequent and is limited to a single form of activity. A lack of participation in group activities also expresses the same deficit in establishing interpersonal contacts beyond the family.

Such factors as psychotic or schizoid pathology in the mother, no separations from the pathogenic family, and little "acting out" of pathology in the community recently have been correlated with chronicity. A slow, insidious withdrawal is apt to lead to an irreversible disorganization of the personality. To put it in structural psychodynamic terms, if the ego was not strong enough to withstand routine difficulties of living, the prognosis is not good. If it broke only after overwhelming stress, the prognosis is better.

The prognosis is not influenced by the intelligence or previous education of the patient. Those with high personal aspirations often do poorly. An apparently "mild" case need not be an early one or of favorable prognosis.

As for psychopathologic determinants, the behavioral expressions of mutism, negativism, echolalia and inappropriate affect are more frequently correlated with continuing illness and limited social adaptation and economic productivity. Confusion and looseness of association do not have such a negative connotation. The presence of a well-marked, affective element is of hopeful significance, although hypochondriasis, particularly if it is predominantly self-accusatory, is usually associated with a long-term ineffective social adaptation. Self-condemnatory hallucinations have a more favorable connotation and seem related to the patients' willingness to accept some responsibility for their behavior. The persistence of hallucinations after an initial emotional tension has subsided is not a favorable indication. If the psychosis has existed for a year without clear-cut signs of improvement, a favorable outcome is scarcely to be expected, although it is by no means unknown.

Previous remissions should lead one to expect that a given episode will be followed by improvement. The longer the interval between attacks, the better the prognosis. In many cases of schizophrenia, regression is an important mechanism, so attempts are often made to base a prognosis on the depth of regression manifested by the patient. Infantile posture and behavior, although often of unfavorable significance, should not outweigh other considerations in forming an opinion about prognosis. It may be parenthetically noted that the physician whose psychiatric experience has been confined to institutions tends to develop an unwarranted pessimistic attitude in prognosis.

A word should be said about the prognosis in the different types. In catatonia, the prognosis is relatively good if the onset has been stormy and the episode is still acute. Morrison finds that the predominantly stuporous or retarded catatonic tends to have a more dubious outcome than the predominantly excited. Many of the latter are probably better diagnosed as having an affective disorder. Many of these patients are restored to their prepsychotic level of adjustment for varying periods, at times for several years.

The question as to whether the paranoid type of schizophrenic ever recovers is sometimes raised. The reply to this depends somewhat on a definition of terms. Undoubtedly remissions occur, and these may be looked upon as social recoveries, but they are rarely to be judged as psychological recoveries, even though the patient's adjustment during the interval is well socialized and there are no distortions of reality in response to subjective needs. In general, surly and bitter attitudes indicate the presence of a malignant process.

The prognosis in the simple form, with its insidious marasmus of the personality developing in the absence of unusual environmental and experiential stresses, is poor. A certain number, sheltered by some normal member of the family, maintain a colorless, uneventful existence, while others become paupers, hoboes, or petty criminals. The course of the hebephrenic form tends to be one of dereistic regression and of progressive disorganization, although occasionally remissions occur before the final disorganization of personality.

According to Shore, Anderson, and Cutler, self-mutilation, while uncommon, is more likely to occur in patients giving histories of previous self-injuries, in those with tyrannical superegos often associated with religious preoccupations, in those experiencing auditory command hallucinations, and in those with delusions of control from outside.

The mortality rate among schizophrenic patients is estimated to be twice as high as in the normal population. This increased risk of dying has been found largely due to "unnatural deaths" (suicide, violence, accidents) and infectious diseases.

Diagnosis

To establish the diagnosis of the schizophrenic reaction, the examiner must attend particularly to the quality of the interpersonal contact and to the perceptual and cognitive organization of the personality. Important in the contact will be the patient's ease in the interview, his ability to establish an affectively toned rapport vis-à-vis the examiner, and his capacity for sustaining attention and concentration. The examiner will note as evidence of schizophrenic organization the intrusive injection of irrelevant remarks or phrases, or blocks in the interchange. Important will be indications that the patient has difficulty in discriminating one person from another and in maintaining an affective constancy; that he tends toward overt expressions of hatred or love, mistrust or dependency; that he transfers and condenses into currently related persons the features of significant individuals from his past.

He may disclose problems in discrimination of auditory and visual percepts and in evaluating his social and sexual role and his bodily perceptions. Thought processes may be revealed as too concrete, with weak conceptual ability. While often difficult to discern, disorganization of percepts and thought in the form of bizarre hallucinatory or delusional experiences with an intact sensorium will strongly suggest the diagnosis. The general sense of the examination may arouse a subjectively eerie reaction sometimes referred to as the "praecox feeling." (Table 18–5 presents the criteria for diagnosis of a schizophrenic disorder from the Amer-

---

TABLE 18–5   Diagnostic Criteria for a Schizophrenic Disorder

A. At least one of the following during a phase of the illness:
  (1) bizarre delusions (content is patently absurd and has no possible basis in fact), such as delusions of being controlled, thought broadcasting, thought insertion, or thought withdrawal
  (2) somatic, grandiose, religious, nihilistic, or other delusions without persecutory or jealous content
  (3) delusions with persecutory or jealous content if accompanied by hallucinations of any type
  (4) auditory hallucinations in which either a voice keeps up a running commentary on the individual's behavior or thoughts, or two or more voices converse with each other
  (5) auditory hallucinations on several occasions with content of more than one or two words, having no apparent relation to depression or elation
  (6) incoherence, marked loosening of associations, markedly illogical thinking, or marked poverty of content of speech if associated with at least one of the following:
      (a) blunted, flat or inappropriate affect
      (b) delusions or hallucinations
      (c) catatonic or other grossly disorganized behavior
B. Deterioration from a previous level of functioning in such areas as work, social relations, and self care.
C. Duration: Continuous signs of the illness for at least six months at some time during the person's life, with some signs of the illness at present. The six-month period must include an active phase during which there were symptoms from A, with or without a prodromal or residual phase, as defined below.
    Prodromal phase: A clear deterioration in functioning before the active phase of the illness, not due to a disturbance in mood or to a substance abuse disorder.
    Residual phase: Persistence, following the active phase of the illness, of at least two of the symptoms noted below, not due to a disturbance in mood or to a substance use disorder.
    Prodromal or Residual Symptoms
  (1) social isolation or withdrawal
  (2) marked impairment in role functioning as wage-earner, student, or homemaker
  (3) markedly peculiar behavior (e.g., collecting garbage, talking to self in public, or hoarding food)
  (4) marked impairment in personal hygiene and grooming
  (5) blunted, flat, or inappropriate affect
  (6) digressive, vague, overelaborate, circumstantial, or metaphorical speech
  (7) odd or bizarre ideation, or magical thinking, e.g., superstitiousness, clairvoyance, telepathy, "sixth sense," "others can feel my feelings," overvalued ideas, ideas of reference
  (8) unusual perceptual experiences, e.g., recurrent illusions, sensing the presence of a force or person not actually present.

   As presented in the Diagnostic and Statistical Manual of Mental Disorders, Third Edition (DSM-III), American Psychiatric Association.

ican Psychiatric Association's Diagnostic and Statistical Manual of Mental Disorders.)

At times, perplexing symptomatic similarities are observed between schizophrenia and the psychoneuroses, and between schizophrenia and other biogenetic major psychoses, particularly the manic-depressive ones, but rarely between schizophrenia and organic mental disorders. Neurotic defenses have long been recognized as early signs of this disorder and as characteristic in the borderline state. Again, the distinction between schizophrenic disturbances of the personality and those of the psychopath or character neurotic may be very difficult.

Many of the differential points among schizophrenia, hysteria, and dissociative reactions are discussed in Chapter 22. In addition to what is mentioned there, attention should be called to the fact that the onset in hysteria is usually more sudden and that a psychological motive is more apparent. In schizophrenic stupor, one does not discover the expression of an emotional state. In dissociative stupor, on the other hand, one may note an expression of perplexity, fear, elation, or some other affective state. The history of an insidious change in interests points toward schizophrenia. Not only are the symptoms of hysteria and of dissociation more sudden in onset, but they are more paroxysmal. The symptoms of hysteria are influenced more obviously by certain persons in the environment. Whereas the hysteric desires attention, the schizophrenic is more apt to have periods when he is preoccupied, detached, and apathetic. The hysteric uses conventional, intelligible symbols, while the schizophrenic uses odd and idiosyncratic symbols. One can feel himself into the psychic life of the hysteric and of some persons with dissociative states, but with difficulty, if at all, into that of the schizophrenic.

In the early stage of schizophrenia, the differentiation from obsessive neurosis may be difficult. In schizophrenia there is usually more rumination and less tension than in the obsessive neurosis, as the patient who suffers from the latter has a strong conscious resistance to his or her obsessions and compulsions, a resistance that is lacking in the schizophrenic, who is not particularly disturbed by them. Often the schizophrenic, in the early phases of the disorder, expresses hypochondriacal complaints. The hypochondria lacks, however, the dramatization seen in the psychoneuroses.

Frequently, one of the most difficult differentiations in mental disorders is between schizophrenia and manic-depressive psychosis. Doubtless this is a result of the fact that many people are not pure schizoid or pure syntonic types but rather are personality alloys and are characterized by admixtures in their personality. In addition to what is said in Chapter 19 on affective reactions, it may be noted that the onset of schizophrenia tends to be more insidious. The excitement in schizophrenia is more frequently paroxysmal, while that of the manic is more sustained. The mood of the schizophrenic patient rarely possesses the infectious quality seen in the manic-depressive. The delusions of the depressed schizophrenic are more grotesque than those of the depressed manic, and the patient is less distressed by them. Illogical remarks and incongruous statements suggest schizophrenia.

The catatonic state may be diagnosed in the affective psychoses. Greden and Carroll have recommended the use of an overnight dexamethasone suppression test to separate out the latter. The test consists of determining the plasma cortisol levels the day before administration of 1 mg of dexamethasone. Patients who show two or more abnormal cortisol levels the following day are considered to have an affective illness.

The difficulty in differentiating between these two disorders arises largely in the earlier stages of schizophrenia. With recurring episodes, the schizophrenic nature of symptoms becomes more apparent, with the result that confusion with manic-depressive symptomatology no longer exists. It rarely happens that a psychosis apparently schizophrenic in its early phases proves subsequently to be of a manic-depressive reaction type. The reverse, however, is common. There are, nevertheless, cases of mental disorder of which the recurring episodes continue to show a mixture of schizophrenic symptoms and of affective ones, especially depression and anxiety.

In the acute schizophrenic disorganizations the differential diagnosis of the acute brain syndrome (delirious reactions) is important. The schizophrenic usually presents a clear sensorium. On examination of his mental status he is oriented in all spheres; his fund of information, capacity to calculate, memory functions, and retaining ability remain intact when one examines him with patience and forbearance. However, today, with the increasing frequency of drug abuse — particularly of the hallucinogens, barbiturates and other hypnotics, amphetamines, and alcohol — many young schizophrenics are brought to treatment with the symptoms of an acute brain syndrome. Only after the symptoms and signs of that condition have subsided under treatment may one be certain of the existence of the major underlying psychopathology — schizophrenia. In these instances, the immediate therapeutic task is treatment of the toxic delirium; the next, the recognition and therapy for the schizophrenic process.

There is usually no difficulty in distinguishing schizophrenia from epilepsy, except in the instance of psychomotor attacks associated with temporal lobe convulsive foci. Occasionally, nevertheless, the schizophrenic suffers from epileptiform or syncopal attacks that to the inexperienced observer strongly suggest the seizures of epilepsy. In that case, careful inquiry should be made whether the seizures or the

mental symptoms appeared first, and the nature of the seizure should be observed; in schizophrenia it lacks the definiteness in type and the genuine disturbance of consciousness occurring in epilepsy. Careful history and the use of the electroencephalogram should make the proper differential diagnosis.

In discussing the diagnosis of schizophrenia, mention should be made of what is often spoken of as *chronic alcoholic hallucinosis*. The permanent persistence in the chronic alcoholic of auditory hallucinations in a setting of clear consciousness, frequently with systematized delusions, was formerly considered as a symptom of an alcoholic psychosis. Many psychiatrists now believe that such cases are really schizophrenic reactions.

Posterior aphasic patients sometimes are confused with schizophrenic patients because of their incomprehensible speech, vagueness, loose associations, and apparent confusion. Gerson and colleagues point out that aphasics are usually 40 years or more of age; the length of their verbal responses is shorter; they are aware of a communication problem and attempt to enlist the examiner's aid; substitutions in language (paraphasias) are used, which are uncommon in schizophrenia; and bizarre content is absent. Such aphasics may show no neurologic abnormality but usually may be identified by electroencephalographic or CAT scan evidence of lesions in the dominant hemisphere.

Adolescent psychoses do not belong in any special classification of their own, yet their capacity for variation in duration, intensity, and form frequently causes them to present difficulties in diagnosis. At that period one may alternatively see phases of anxiety, behavior disorder, affective disturbance, or schizophrenia. In retrospect, truancy and other forms of delinquent behavior have preceded the onset of a disorder that is subsequently diagnosed as schizophrenia. The adolescent schizophrenic frequently shows a more lively emotional response than is usual in the adult and also less incongruity of affect.

The symptomatic emphasis in adolescent schizophrenia is usually on social withdrawal, on disorders of activity, interest, and speech, and on peculiarities of manner. It must be acknowledged, however, that it is not always easy to differentiate the emotional disorders of adolescence from incipient schizophrenia. That period is normally one of emotional turmoil and instability. Much that would be regarded as pathological in later life may then be but a temporary exaggeration of normal tendencies. The adolescent, with his self-questioning and perturbing heart-searching, may verbalize his disruption of emotion and impulse without being schizophrenic. Adolescent maladjustments among shy, withdrawn personalities with feelings of inadequacy or inferiority, with evident internal conflict and family tensions, particularly with one or the other parent, are not uncommon. Poor socialization, lack of motivation, and a brooding sense of inferiority may be merely a retarded ability to integrate the new emotional drives and experiences of adolescence. Such symptoms may, however, be those of an incipient schizophrenia.

Childhood schizophrenia must be differentiated from the forms of mental deficiency, other chronic brain disorders in early years, severe childhood neuroses, behavior disorders, and familial dysautonomia. Here, the history, the physical status of the patient, biochemical and electroencephalographic data, and responses to psychological testing usually will discriminate the various conditions. Katrina de Hirsch points out that although both schizophrenic and aphasic children have limitations of visual and auditory events, the latter have specific difficulties in interpretation of spoken and printed language. In both, auditory thresholds for speech are higher. In the schizophrenic this is due to the inability to integrate meaningful material; in the aphasics it is due to problems of decoding.

Auditory memory span is very short in the aphasic as contrasted to the schizophrenic children. The latter may be able to reproduce long and complicated television commercials—a task impossible for the former. Auditory feedback is distorted in both groups.

When it comes to language as communication, the schizophrenic child is lacking in communicative intent, as evidenced clinically in his impoverished and inappropriate gestural abilities and limited verbal output. Also, the echolalia of the schizophrenic is characteristic in its high-pitched "birdlike" quality. This differs from the occasional echolalic productions of the brain damaged, which more often occur as simple repetitions of words or phrases for clarification, enunciated in generally normal pitch and inflection. The speech of schizophrenic children is understood and given in idiosyncratic concrete terms with intent of immediate magical power and condenses much emotionally; that of aphasic children does not demonstrate looseness of associations.

Treatment

The treatment of schizophrenia, particularly in its early stages, is undertaken with far less pessimism than formerly. Its success depends to great degree upon the therapeutic initiative, energy, and effort of the treatment team.

PREVENTION. If it is correct that the family provides a pathogenic milieu for the incubation and development of those ego weaknesses that evolve in an individual predisposed through genetic and/or constitutional processes, clearly early separation from the pathogenic milieu would be desirable, provided there were means to identify with certainty those at high risk. This potential does not now exist. Only in Japan, where culture dictates that a mother may not rear both of her twins, has one of a high-risk pair had the privilege of separation and rearing in another family. Here, as Inouye has found, even if the disorder evolves, one of the twins is less severely impaired as regards pathology than is the other. In Western countries, certain high-risk children born out of wedlock are adopted. The extent of protection provided by rearing other than parental remains unclear.

As noted, schizophrenia is regarded now as an ego disorder. Discriminative functions have failed to develop evenly. The patients have difficulty in perceiving themselves as separate from others and separating aroused internal sensations from external sensations. Their adaptive functions are undeveloped, so that they are at a disadvantage in melding constructively their affects and thoughts in relation to the reality of outer social events. Their integrative functions deny them an instant percept of others or a steady value system to which they may commit themselves and dedicate their energy. There are impairments in evolution of ego assets (capacity for trust, curiosity, courage, flexibility, commitment, perseverance, responsibility, empathy, humor, and likeableness).

All the socializing experiences that strengthen ego functions may be regarded as preventive or therapeutic. Such experiences may occur through broadening social contacts outside the family, outside the immediate community or culture, in individual or group associations, or in therapy. They may be taken successfully when the potential or actual patient either has sufficient ego autonomy to risk separating from the family circle or is supported in his or her struggles by the relationship to a therapist who perceives that need.

Separation—prolonged social isolation in an institution, whether hospital or prison or another residential home wherein the schizoid person is not afforded a stimulating contact with others, may lead to further ego disorganization and regression. Gruenberg has termed this effect, produced by prolonged and nonstimulating hospital care, the "social breakdown syndrome."

Yet, as pointed out earlier, too intensive contact with a critically intrusive and overly involved family member or other associate may also lead to ego disorganization.

The values of hospital care, beyond its early functions of providing the diagnostic milieu and medical therapies, repose precisely on exposure to a stimulating yet nonintrusive perceptive social environment. Effective hospital care takes place when the staff affords healthy models for identification and offers opportunities for clear verbal communication, learning of new skills, and development of positive ego attitudes through the support of pleasurable and rewarding relationships.

EARLY STAGES. Ideally, treatment of the schizophrenic should have begun before obvious symptoms of a mental disorder are manifest. Unfortunately, this rarely occurs. The patient only occasionally seeks treatment himself, and his family, unable or unwilling to recognize that he is mentally ill, does not refer him to a psychiatrist.

Following the initial examination, decision usually must be made as to whether the patient should be treated in an outpatient department or office or admitted to a hospital. If behavior has been disturbed and promises to threaten later social acceptance, prompt admission for hospital treatment is indicated. Again, some form of hospital care is advisable when the patient is living in a home in which the family attitude is argumentative, critical, domineering, or rejecting. Social isolation at home or in a lodging and lack of vocational and social skills may suggest the advisability of day or night hospital care.

PHARMACOLOGICAL THERAPY. Whether the decision is to commence treatment on an outpatient or a hospital basis, the first therapeutic move is to provide relief of anxiety and its attendant reflections in the psychotic symptom-complex.

Phenothiazines. The psychiatrist has available today a number of potent neuroleptics for prescription. Among the groups of phenothiazines, thioxanthenes, and butyrophenones, there are a variety of analogues. From this grouping of drugs, which are available both for prescription orally and in the form of long-acting agents that may be given intramuscularly, potential exists for finding an appropriate agent individualized to the particular patient.

Deniker suggests that clinicians recognize the neuroleptics as having differing sedative or stimulant effects. He finds the aliphatic phenothiazines to be the most sedative and anti-excitatory, the piperazine derivatives to be the most stimulating, and the butyrophenones the most effective in control of hallucinatory phenomena.

The initial selection of a neuroleptic should be determined on the basis of the observed state of the patient when first seen, the principal complaints such as restlessness and insomnia, indications of suspiciousness, impulsivity, or agitation, or elicited tendencies toward suicide or violent aggressiveness to others.

The low-potency neuroleptics (re-quiring large milligram equivalents per unit of body weight; see Table 18–6) are more likely to induce central, autonomic, and peripheral side effects aside from parkinsonism than the high-potency agents such as haloperidol, fluphenazine, thiothixane, and trifluoperazine. Today the comparative tendency of drugs of varying potency to induce tardive dyskinesia is not known.

For the mildly disturbed schizophrenic patient, chlorpromazine probably is the preferred drug. Initial oral dosages of 25 to 50 mg. three to four times daily may be tried for several days to ascertain the patient's tolerance and idiosyncratic responses. The drug may then be administered in doses of 100 or 200 mg. given in a single dose before bedtime if the patient's condition seems to indicate this amount. Many patients may be maintained on a dosage of 400 mg. daily for indefinite periods. Some have received total daily doses of 1000 mg. or more without ill effect.

If the patient is acutely disturbed when first seen, rapid neuroleptization is often the preferred treatment, by prescription of either intramuscular or intravenous haloperidol. This method is indicated particularly for those who exhibit belligerent and agitated behavior when admitted to a hospital. Over two thirds of such patients become stabilized

TABLE 18–6 Molar Potency and Potency Ratios of Neuroleptic Drugs

	MOL. WT.	EQUIVALENT DOSE (mg.)	MOLAR POTENCY (mM. equiv.)	RATIO (CPZ = 1)
Chlorpromazine HCl	355	100	.282	1.0
Thioridazine	370	100	.270	1.0
Chlorprothixene	316	100	.316	.89
Clozapine	327	100 (?)	.306	.92
Molindone HCl	313	10	.0319	8.8
Loxapine Succinate	522	10	.0191	15
Perphenazine	404	10	.0248	11
Trifluoperazine 2HCl	484	5	.0103	27
Thiothixene	444	3	.00676	41
Haloperidol	376	2	.00532	53
Fluphenazine 2HCl	510	2	.00392	72

(From Zavodnick, S.: A pharmacological and theoretical comparison of high and low potency neuroleptics. J. Clin. Psychiatry, *39*:334, 1978.)

behaviorally with initial intramuscular administration of haloperidol, 2.5 to 10 mg. repeated at hourly intervals until the behavioral symptoms subside. The patient usually requires one to three or four injections before control is achieved; oral medication is then prescribed.

Rapid neuroleptization may be induced in other, less disturbed acute schizophrenics by oral prescription.

The phenothiazines are indicated for all types of schizophrenia. They are of particular value in the treatment of those patients who show tension, psychomotor overactivity, agitation, impulsiveness, aggressive outbursts, destructiveness, and antagonistic, paranoid reactions. Administration to the acutely ill schizophrenic patient frequently results in the disappearance of hallucinations and delusional ideas within the first two weeks of treatment.

High-dosage chlorpromazine therapy (2000 mg. per day), reported earlier as more effective than low-dosage regimens in the treatment of younger patients with chronic illnesses who have not been hospitalized for lengthy periods is no longer so considered. High-dosage regimens produce a greater number of serious side effects including tardive dyskinesia. In comparisons of various dosage regimens of haloperidol, rapid increases of oral medication against standard daily doses of 10 mg. have shown no advantage over time with a high initial loading dosage.

The longer the schizophrenic has been ill and hospitalized, the less chance there is that the use of the phenothiazines will be followed by recovery. The best results are secured with patients who have not been ill for more than two years. Among these, the results will depend largely on the clinical manifestations, the degree of improvement being much greater in the overactive, disturbed patient, who often becomes amenable to occupational and other activity therapies and to some degree of psychotherapy. Although most overactive schizophrenics who have been hospitalized for long periods of time show some improvement, not more than 5 to 10 per cent of those who have been hospitalized for more than five continuous years become well enough to leave the hospital, and an appreciable number of these will have to return at a later time.

Of those youthful patients who fail to improve in hospital on all dosages of the neuroleptics, as well as those who are discharged and then show a frequently remitting course, it is now recognized that the use of the parenteral forms of phenothiazines may prove effective. Of these, fluphenazine enanthate or fluphenazine decanoate is the agent usually used. It may be possible with some patients to obtain a response with the long-acting, newly tested, and orally administered drug penfluridol. This agent has been used effectively in the treatment of the schizophrenic when first seen.

The problem of the care of the chronically ill, overactive patient who does not improve sufficiently to leave the hospital has been greatly eased by the use of the neuroleptics. Delusions and hallucinations may persist, but usually they are no longer disturbing to the patient. The sullen, sarcastic, and antagonistic patient is less irritable and frequently becomes quiet, cooperative, and accessible.

Because of the risk of development of tardive dyskinesias, neuroleptic regimens should be established at the lowest possible dosage that allows control of symptoms. Drug-free holidays should be tried—up to 30 days—to determine whether the patient reques continued medication. Some will be found to improve on its withdrawal; for others returned to these agents substantially lower doses may suffice. Regular weekend drug holidays are in order.

Of the various types of schizophrenia, the acute paranoid forms appear to respond to the neuroleptics most favorably, followed by the acute catatonic. The behavior of the chronic catatonic patients and the hebephrenics is less modifiable, although lessening of aggressive and impulsive actions usually follows the use of this drug.

Certain other phenothiazines are reported to be more effective in modifying some forms of disturbed behavior than chlorpromazine. Thus trifluoperazine (Stelazine) is said to be particularly beneficial for the withdrawn, apathetic, and depressed schizophrenic. It is administered by giving initially oral doses of 5 mg. three or four times daily; this dosage may be increased to total daily levels of 60 to 80 mg. Thioridazine (Mellaril) serves as effectively as the other phenothiazines but is less likely to produce the general run of toxic side effects. Perphenazine (Trilafon) is indicated for those patients likely to be exposed to the sun, since its usage has not been associated with the skin photosensitivity noted with chlorpromazine and other derivatives.

For patients who gain weight on the phenothiazines, molindone may be indicated, as it has anorexigenic properties and may induce weight loss.

More complete descriptions are given of the pharmacological actions, dosage ranges, and side and toxic effects of these agents and others, in Chapter 32, Pharmacological Therapy.

It must be recognized that certain of those patients with schizophrenia respond with an increase in psychopathology following the usage of the neuroleptics, particularly when side effects are produced. To a large extent these increases in intensity of symptoms take place in those patients in whom the body concept is poorly developed. The somatic side effects of the drug increase the individual's anxiety regarding his own personal integrity. A wide variety of psychopathological phenomena occur, including mutism in some patients. In such instances, the agent should be withdrawn; trials might be made with a neuroleptic of another series or another analogue within the same series.

PSYCHOTHERAPY. A number of well-designed researches indicate that the combination of pharmacotherapy with psychotherapy and other sociotherapies is most likely to bring about the greatest degree of improvement of social adaptation in the form of resumption of social relations, employability, capacity for avocational activities, and increase in self-esteem, as well as prevention of relapse. For this reason, a thoroughgoing knowledge of the psychotherapeutic processes applicable in the treatment of schizophrenia is most important. In addition to the relief of anxiety and its attendant symptoms, the psychiatric therapist will be concerned with the establishment of a treatment regimen that provides opportunity for development of a more stable and adaptive personality with time. The therapist will be particularly mindful of those weaknesses of ego identity and function that characterize the schizophrenic patient and will attempt to ascertain through growing knowledge of the patient's development whether these defects are due to lack of socializing experiences or are the consequence of isolation and withdrawal as the result of psychological conflict and associated emotional turmoil.

It is necessary, then, to consider, in the long-term planning of treatment, the schizophrenic patient's day-to-day social milieu, as well as needs for specialized individual and group psychotherapies, and to assess the extent and quality of the patient's social network. Measures must be taken to strengthen the ego through restructuring the environment so that the schizophrenic patient comes in contact with other healthy persons whose interpersonal contact provides a ground in which to develop trust, assurance, and some personal autonomy. The possible identifications with others than family members will clarify confusion about the patient's own social and sexual identity.

The therapeutic milieu must be stimulating physically so as to provide an increasing awareness and perception of the schizophrenic's own body and its functions, upon which may be established a satisfying and realistic concept of the body and its actions. Furthermore, this environment must provide a structured and stimulating social world so that there may be ingrained the sense of time and satisfactions in completeness of action, and so that the patient may avoid the inevitable consequences of isolation. It must be emphasized that isolation leads to reduced awareness of perceptual stimulation from within and without and results in re-experiencing and becoming preoccupied with thought processes divorced from ego control, followed by regressive infantile thinking processes and hallucinatory satisfactions.

Therefore, if the patient is to be treated as an outpatient, arrangements should be made for the psychiatrist to see him on a regular schedule of appointments, with a clearly understood recognition that improvement with insight will not be quickly gained. Constancy in the relationship is a major factor in establishment and maintenance of a therapeutic bond. The psychiatrist should help the patient decide whether to continue to work or attend school, or to limit strivings in other directions. The patient should be cautioned about the toxic side effects of the pharmaceuticals prescribed. He should be advised also of the danger of usage of any of the hallucinogens (including marihuana) and of alcohol.

Many psychotherapists believe that the primary problem of the schizophrenic is not his anxiety about others and a consequent narcissistic withdrawal, often dating back to childhood, but fear of his own hostile, destructive tendencies. Although preoccupied, suspicious, and anxiety-ridden because of the negative impulses he feels in himself, the schizophrenic can often, at least in the early stages of his illness, be helped to relate himself to people. Frieda Fromm-Reichmann stressed that, although the schizophrenic longs for interpersonal contact, he equally fears such a closeness. Thus in office psychotherapy, careful

consideration must be given to the extent and readiness of each patient to engage in social relations with others. In many instances, aid must be provided to the withdrawn patient through planning with social service agencies and workers. Attendance at a day hospital, or at other facilities fostering social and vocational rehabilitation, should be arranged if the patient tends to isolation where he resides. If the patient lacks a home, or is residing with impatient, critical relatives, the therapist should seek a more congenial residential placement for the patient in a halfway house, hostel, or other setting.

The therapist must be ever mindful of the transference distortions of the schizophrenic patient. The capacity of these patients to misperceive the therapist in transient roles as recapitulations of the past identification he has made with parents has been described earlier. Searles' descriptions of the multiple misperceptions the patients project upon the same treating person explain much of the difficulty of establishing a constant relationship with the patient. So, too, the early lack of object constancy which Burnham and colleagues have emphasized affords the explanation for those defensive maneuvers used so effectively as resistances to establishing the therapeutic relationship in fear of the potential betrayal by the therapist. These defenses may vary from anxiety-producing clinging, which some therapists have difficulty accepting, to the avoidance maneuvers through withdrawal, noncommunication, violent counterattacks, or the use of substitute persons through acting out as a means of escaping the anxiety of the need-fear dilemma.

For those in acute episodes, and seriously disturbed, hospital care is advisable. The good hospital not only protects the patient from a threatening family, social, or vocational environment but provides healthy substitutes for erecting new identifications and sources for resolving conflicts, as well as learning social and vocational skills previously weak or defective.

As Artiss has described in discussing *milieu therapy*, the expectancies and attitudes of the treatment staff are central to bringing about social rehabilitation. For each patient there must be a known goal for the various treatment efforts, and the patient must be educated in the rudiments of successful social behavior wherever he exposes weaknesses, particularly through active participation in groups. The individual patient must be placed in a situation where he has a regularly recurrent opportunity to interact with a healthy group and a responsibility to do so.

Thus, the hospital psychiatrist and many other special therapists and patients of both sexes offer opportunities to the patient for testing and establishing less anxiety-ridden relations with others. In turn, these opportunities allow the potentiality for reducing the confusion of personal and sexual identity so characteristic of these patients. The well-regulated and structured activity of a therapeutic institution provides arrangements for the re-establishment of the patient's ego, allowing him to make clear-cut discriminations between himself and the environment and to refix his concepts of time and space. In the active and well-staffed hospital, opportunities for ego development through social interactions are made available through patient government and through group and family therapies. The use of recreational aids and physiotherapies is dynamically important in stimulating bodily activity that underlies the development of sound and satisfying body ego.

One attempts to stimulate the patient's interest and redirect it to things outside himself, detach his emotions from subjective material, inculcate healthful, socialized habits, and abstract him from his spiritual isolation. Among important aids to these ends and to the gaining of satisfaction from adaptive behavior are forms of occupational therapy chosen to meet his emotional needs. Recreation, games, music, and congenial companionships all have a common objective of promoting interpersonal relationships. Occupational therapy not only helps to re-establish contacts with reality, but through personal contact with the therapist frequently brings a therapeutic emotional relationship. Probably, in fact, the most important tools that the occupational or other auxiliary therapist brings to the treatment situation are a genuine warmth, understanding, flexibility, and objectivity.

With a therapeutic staff trained to understand the dynamics of behavior, each aspect of the patient's pathology may be examined and each member of the staff brought to support his assets and also to confront his distortions of reality so as to assist in more effective and alternative methods of solving his social difficulties. The hospital offers a milieu in which the patient may expose his deficits and test new methods of adaptation in a setting of trust and collaboration and without criticisms, thus fostering ego growth. In such a therapeutic milieu patients may be seen to pass through several stages of change, comprised initially of adjustment to the new environment, then exposure of the adaptive responses to the emotional stresses of interhospital transactions, and finally evolution of new and more effective techniques for coping with reality.

Although many patients become permanently isolated in their own autistic lives in spite of every effort at treatment, the degree of improvement is, broadly speaking, directly proportional to the attention and treatment that they receive.

Stanton and Schwartz have made interesting contributions to the concept of schizophrenic deterioration as a psychosocial adaptive pattern. They found it was possible to discern meaningful patterns in the occurrences in a mental hospital. They studied, for example, the symptoms of soiling and wetting, so common in chronic deteriorated schizophrenics. They pointed out that the term "incontinence" is a misnomer if by that term is meant loss of sphincter control. The so-called incontinent schizophrenic patient, Stanton and Schwartz discovered, discharges his excreta in a highly controlled manner. There are some situations in which wetting and soiling rarely, if ever, occur. On the other hand, they may take place in a specific constellation of circumstances under the pressure of an emotional need. One patient, for example, who was extremely fearful of human contact found that people left her alone when she had soiled. Another patient who craved the attentions of a mother figure soiled herself to compel attentions from a nurse.

Special Forms of Treatment

INTENSIVE PSYCHOTHERAPY. Although psychoanalytical techniques such as are usually employed in the neuroses have never been satisfactory in the treatment of schizophrenia, modifications have now been evolved that may successfully maintain many patients at a functioning level of social adjustment.

The establishment of a working relationship with the patient is essential to successful therapy in the schizophrenic. The relationship of the patient to the therapist is of a different quality from that seen in neuroses. It is exceedingly fragile and is subject to withdrawal on the basis of any suspicion or indication that there is a limitation of interest on the part of the physician. Breaking through to obtain the trust of the suspicious, withdrawn, highly sensitive, and perhaps disturbed patient requires infinite patience and tolerance. Rarely can the physician confine his contacts with the patient to set office hours. He must be available whenever periods of great anxiety occur. In the early stages of treatment, the patient's verbal communications may be incomprehensible to the physician, and some form of communication between the two must be established. At this stage, the therapist does not attempt to have the patient form an association with the verbalizations he is producing as would be done with the neurotic. Instead, the therapist listens and tries to relate the patient's verbalizations to the feeling-tone of the particular interpersonal events that are reported to have preceded the distorted communications or are observed to occur in close temporal relationship. Then, when particular communications are heard, the therapist may interpret the patient's feeling directly and make it possible for him to appreciate that he is understood and will not be hurt. The patient must find in the therapist a sustaining source of security on the emergence of anxiety and hostility.

The therapist must be constantly alert to his own behavior and its possible meanings to the patient. For this reason, the therapy is conducted with the patient facing the therapist. The patient has a continuing need to check his reaction through visualizing the gestures and moves of the therapist. The latter must see himself as an active participant with his patient and must be free to disclose his own feelings and the meanings of his actions in order to clarify the patient's frequent distortions of the situation.

Contrary to the usual custom in the analytical therapy of the neuroses, the analysis of dreams is not advised. Preoccupation with dream analysis perpetuates the schizophrenic's propensity for withdrawal into fantasy living. What he needs is to face continually the emotionally toned events of everyday living and to learn socially adaptive methods of accepting them. Usually, too, the primitive impulses of the schizophrenic are so evident in their overt pathology that dream analysis will provide but little additional information. In contrast with earlier attempts to resolve delusional and hallucinatory experiences through analysis of their content, this is now recognized as unsatisfactory procedure in the therapeutic process. Rather, efforts are made to derive an understanding of the interpersonal situations that precipitate the patient's expressions of delusional and hallucinatory material and the significance of the psychopathology in terms of the affect produced in such situations. Frieda Fromm-Reichmann described this technique in some detail.

It should be remembered that there are limitations in the psychotherapy of the schizophrenic patient. Complete resolution of the schizophrenic process, fixed through indelible deprivations or traumas of early life, is rarely obtained, even by therapists of the greatest experience and patience. If, in an effort to reach the ideal, the enthusiastic psychiatrist presses his patient beyond his capacity, he may do him incalculable harm. The therapist must, of course, continue indefinitely a supportive, though distant, therapeutic relationship when the patient indicates the need.

In some schizophrenics, a "spontaneous" remission or recovery occurs. In such cases, the therapeutic agent usually remains unknown. In many instances it would appear that improvement followed because, for some years, the patient was able to make contact with some individual—perhaps a nurse, aide, or even some other patient—in his environment, and this interpersonal relationship became a bridge toward reality.

Group Psychotherapy. Group psychotherapy has proved useful for many schizophrenic patients. It has been administered in conjunction with individual therapy or as the sole psychotherapeutic measure. It is most likely to have value for the schizophrenic with major deficit in group living and for those inhibited in individual psychotherapy.

SOMATIC THERAPIES. The history of the therapy of schizophrenia has been characterized by the use of various methods that temporarily had enthusiastic proponents but failed to stand the test of time. Insulin, electroshock, and prefrontal lobotomy as therapies have been largely superseded by the phenothiazine drugs in recent years. These treatments are discussed in Chapter 33.

BIBLIOGRAPHY

Concepts

Arieti, S.: Interpretation of Schizophrenia. New York, Basic Books, 1974.
Beck, S. J.: The Six Schizophrenias. Research Monographs, No. 6. New York, American Orthopsychiatric Association, 1954.
Bleuler, E.: Dementia Praecox or the Group of Schizophrenias. Translated by J. Zinkin. New York, International Universities Press, Inc., 1950.
Kraepelin, E.: Dementia Praecox. Translated by R. M. Barclay. Edinburgh, E. & S. Livingstone, 1919.
Winters, E. (ed.): The Collected Papers of Adolf Meyer. Vol. II. Baltimore, Johns Hopkins University Press, 1951.

Epidemiology

Deming, W. E.: A recursion formula for the proportion of persons having a first admission as schizophrenic. Behav. Sci., *13*:467–476, 1968.
Gruenberg, E. M.: Epidemiology of schizophrenia. *In* Arieti, S. (ed.): Handbook of Psychiatry. 2nd ed. New York, Basic Books, 1974.
Guggenheim, F. G., and Babigian, H. M.: Catatonic schizophrenia: epidemiology and clinical course. J. Nerv. Ment. Dis., *155*:291–305, 1974.

Etiology

Allen, M. G., Cohen, S., and Pollin, W.: Schizophrenia in veteran twins. A diagnostic review. Am. J. Psychiatry, *128*:939–945, 1972.
Cadoret, R. J.: Toward a definition of the schizoid state: Evidence from studies of twins and their families. Br. J. Psychiatry, *122*:679–685, 1973.
Cohen, S. M., Allen, M. G., Pollin, W., et al.: Relationship of schizo-affective psychosis to manic depressive psychosis and schizophrenia. Arch. Gen. Psychiat., *26*:539–546, 1972.
Dunham, H. W.: Sociocultural studies of schizophrenia. Arch. Gen. Psychiatry, *21*:206–214, 1971.

Elkes, J.: Schizophrenic disorder in relation to levels of neural organization: the need for some conceptual points of reference. *In* Folch, P. J. (ed.): The Chemical Pathology of the Nervous System. London, Pergamon Press, 1961, pp. 648–655.

Gillin, J. C., and Wyatt, R. J.: Schizophrenia: Perchance a dream. Int. Rev. Neurobiol., *17*:297–342, 1975.

Heath, R. G., and Krupp, I. M.: Schizophrenia as a specific biologic disease. Am. J. Psychiatry *124*:1019–1024, 1968.

Kety, S. S.: Progress toward an understanding of the biological substrates of schizophrenia. *In* Fieve, R. R., Rosenthal, D., and Brill, H. (eds.): Genetic Research in Psychiatry. Baltimore, Johns Hopkins University Press, 1975.

Lidz, T.: The Origin and Treatment of Schizophrenic Disorders. New York, Basic Books, 1973.

Rainer, J. D.: The genetics of schizophrenia. *In* Wolman, B. (ed.): International Encyclopedia of Psychiatry, Psychoanalysis and Psychology. New York, Van Nostrand Reinhold Company, 1977.

Rieder, R. O., Rosenthal, D., Wender, P., and Blumenthal, H.: The offspring of schizophrenics. Fetal and neonatal deaths. Arch. Gen. Psychiatry, *322*:200–211, 1975.

Sluzki, C. E., and Veron, E.: The double bind as a universal pathogenic situation. Family Process, *10*:397–410, 1971.

Wing, J. K.: The social context of schizophrenia. Am. J. Psychiatry, *135*:1333–1339, 1979.

Wynne, L. C., and Singer, M. T.: Thought disorder and family relations of schizophrenics. Arch. Gen. Psychiatry, *9*:191–198, 199–206, 1963.

Diagnosis

Gerson, J. N., Benson, F., and Frazier, S. H.: Diagnoses: Schizophrenia versus posterior aphasia. Am. J. Psychiatry, *134*:966–969, 1977.

Greden, J. F., and Carroll, B. J.: The dexamethasone suppression test as a diagnostic aid in catatonia. Am. J. Psychiatry, *136*:1199–1200, 1979.

Morrison, J. R.: Catatonia, retarded and excited types. Arch. Gen. Psychiatry, *28*:39–41, 1973.

Pathology

Bruch, H.: Falsification of bodily needs and body concept in schizophrenia. Arch. Gen. Psychiatry, *6*:18–24, 1962.

Burnham, D. L., Gladstone, A. I., and Gibson, R. W.: Schizophrenia and the Need-Fear Dilemma. New York, International University Press, 1969.

Connolly, F. H., and Gittleson, N. L.: The relationship between delusions of sexual change and olfactory and gustatory hallucinations in schizophrenia. Br. J. Psychiatry, *119*:443–444, 1971.

Easson, W. M.: The early manifestations of adolescent thought disorder. J. Clin. Psychiatry, *40*:469–475, 1979.

Feinberg, I., Braun, M., Koresko, R. L., and Gottlieb, F.: Stage 4 sleep in schizophrenia. Arch. Gen. Psychiatry, *21*:262–266, 1969.

Harrow, M., Grinker, R. R., Sr., Holzman, P. S., and Kayton, L.: Anhedonia and schizophrenia. Am. J. Psychiatry, *134*:794–797, 1977.

Harrow, M., and Prosen, M.: Schizophrenic thought disorders: bizarre associations and intermingling. Am. J. Psychiatry, *136*:293–296, 1979.

Schneider, K.: Clinical Psychopathology. Hamilton, M. W. (ed.) (trans.). New York, Grune & Stratton, 1959.

Searles, H. F.: The schizophrenic individual's experience of his world. Psychiatry, *30*:119–131, 1967.

Shakow, D.: Psychological deficit in schizophrenia. Behav. Sci., *4*:275–315, 1963.

Stevens, M., Crow, T. J., Bowman, M. J., and Coles, E. C.: Age disorientation in schizophrenia. Br. J. Psychiatry, *133*:130–136, 1978.

Tsuang, M. T., and Winokur, G.: Criteria for subtyping schizophrenia. Arch. Gen. Psychiatry, *31*:43–47, 1974.

Childhood Schizophrenia

Bender, L.: The life course of children with schizophrenia. Am. J. Psychiatry, *130*:783–786, 1973.

Bennett, H. S., and Klein, H. R.: Childhood schizophrenia: 30 years later. Am. J. Psychiatry, *122*:1121–1124, 1966.

de Hirsch, K.: Differential diagnosis between aphasic and schizophrenic language in children. J. Speech Hear. Disord., *32*:3–10, 1967.

Dewdney, D.: A specific distortion of the human facial percept in childhood schizophrenia. Psychiatr. Q., *47*:82–94, 1973.

Fish, B.: Neurobiologic antecedents of schizophrenia in children. Arch. Gen. Psychiatry, *34*:1297–1313, 1977.

Geller, J.: Development of behaviour therapy with autistic children: A review. J. Chronic Dis., *25*:21–31, 1972.

Goldfarb, W.: Growth and Change of Schizophrenic Children: A Longitudinal Study. New York, John Wiley & Sons, 1974.

Green, A. H.: Self-destructive behavior in physically abused schizophrenic children. Arch. Gen. Psychiatry, *19*:171–179, 1968.

Treffert, D. A.: Epidemiology of infantile autism. Arch. Gen. Psychiatry, *22*:434–438, 1970.

Psychodynamics

Freeman, T.: A Psychoanalytic Study of the Psychoses. New York, International Universities Press, 1973.

Freeman, T.: On Freud's theory of schizophrenia. Int. J. Psychoanal., 58:383–388, 1977.

Pao, P-N.: On the formation of schizophrenic symptoms. Int. J. Psychoanal., 58:389–401, 1977.

Prognosis

Astrachan, B. N., Brauer, L., Harrow, M., and Schwartz, C.: Symptomatic outcome in schizophrenia. Arch. Gen. Psychiatry, 31:155–160, 1974.

Bland, R. C., and Orn, H.: Prediction of long term outcome from presenting symptoms in schizophrenia. J. Clin. Psychiatry, 41:85–88, 1980.

Brown, G. W., Birley, J. L. T., and Wing, J. K.: Influence of family life on the course of schizophrenic disorders. Br. J. Psychiatry, 121:241–258, 1972.

Hogarty, G . E., Goldberg, S. C., and Schooler, N. R.: Drug and sociotherapy in the after care of schizophrenic patients. Arch. Gen. Psychiatry, 31:609–618, 1974.

O'Neal, P., and Robins, L. N.: Childhood patterns predictive of adult schizophrenia: a 30-year follow-up study. Am. J. Psychiatry, 115:385–391, 1958.

Pitt, R., and Hage, J.: Patterns of peer interaction during adolescence as prognostic indicators in schizophrenia. Am. J. Psychiatry, 120:1089–1096, 1964.

Preiser, M., and Jeffrey, W.: Schizophrenic patients and Schneiderian first-rank symptoms. Am. J. Psychiatry, 136:323–326, 1979.

Serban, G., and Gidynski, C. B.: Differentiating criteria for acute-chronic distinction in schizophrenia. Arch. Gen. Psychiatry, 32:705–712, 1975.

Shore, D., Anderson, D. J., and Cutler, N. R.: Prediction of self-multilation in hospitalized schizophrenics. Am. J. Psychiatry, 135:1406–1407, 1978.

Silverstein, M. L., and Harrow, M.: First-rank symptoms in the post-acute schizophrenic. Am. J. Psychiatry, 135:1481–1486, 1978.

Strauss, J. S., and Carpenter, W. T., Jr.: The prediction of outcome in schizophrenia. II. Relationships between predictor and outcome variables: A report from the WHO international pilot study of schizophrenia. Arch. Gen. Psychiatry, 31:37–42, 1974.

Tsuang, M. T., Woolson, R. E., and Fleming, J. A.: Causes of death in schizophrenia and manic-depression. Br. J. Psychiatry, 136:239–242, 1980.

Treatment

Artiss, K. L.: Milieu Therapy in Schizophrenia. New York, Grune & Stratton, 1962.

Behrman, S.: Mutism induced by phenothiazines. Br. J. Psychiatry, 121:599–604, 1972.

Choirnard, G., and Annable, G.: Penfluridol in the treatment of newly admitted schizophrenic patients in a brief therapy unit. Am. J. Psychiatry, 133:820–823, 1976.

Deniker, P.: Impact of neuroleptic chemotherapies on schizophrenia. Am. J. Psychiatry, 135:923–927, 1978.

Donlon, P. T., Hopkin, J. T., Tupin, J. P., Wicks, J. J., Wahba, M., and Meadow, A.: Haloperidol for acute schizophrenic patients. Arch. Gen. Psychiatry, 37:691–695, 1980.

Edelson, M.: Sociotherapy and psychotherapy in a psychiatric hospital. In Redlich, E. (ed.): Social Psychiatry. Res. Publ. Assoc. Res. Nerv. Ment. Dis., 47:196–212, 1967.

Fromm-Reichmann, F.: Psychotherapy of schizophrenia. Am. J. Psychiatry, 111:410–419, 1954.

Gardos, G., and Cole, J. O.: Weight reduction in schizophrenics by molindone. Am. J. Psychiatry, 134:302–304, 1977.

Grinspoon, L., Ewalt, J. R., and Shader, R. I.: Schizophrenia Pharmacotherapy and Psychotherapy. Baltimore, Williams & Wilkins Company, 1972.

Hagarty, G. E., Schooler, N. R., Ulrich, R., Mussare, F., Ferro, P., and Herron, E.: Fluphenazine and social therapy in the aftercare of schizophrenic patients. Arch. Gen. Psychiatry, 36:1283–1294, 1979.

Kolb, L. C.: A new look at psychotherapeutic evolution. In Talkington, P. C., and Bloss, C. L. (eds.): Evolving Concepts in Psychiatry. New York, Grune & Stratton, 1969.

Marder, S. R., van Kammen, D. P., Docherty, J. P., Rayner, J., and Bunney, W. E., Jr.: Predicting drug free improvement in schizophrenic psychoses. Arch. Gen. Psychiatry, 36:1080–1083, 1979.

May, P. R. A.: Treatment of Schizophrenia. New York, Science House, 1968.

Mosher, L. R., and Keith, S. J.: Research on the psychosocial treatment of schizophrenia: A summary report. Am. J. Psychiatry, 136:623–631, 1979.

Zavodnick, S.: A pharmacological and theoretical comparison of high and low potency neuroleptics. J. Clin. Psychiatry, 39:332–336, 1978.

AFFECTIVE DISORDERS

"Moody madness, laughing wild."

Thomas Gray

"Melancholy is the nurse of frenzy."

Shakespeare

Paintings by an English artist, Louis Wain, an eccentric bachelor who specialized in portraits of his 17 cats before suffering a breakdown in middle life. The cat becomes more horrifying and the background more bizarre and abstract until finally the cat disappears entirely. (© Guttmann Maclay Collection, Institute of Psychiatry, University of London.)

AFFECTIVE DISORDERS

The group of affective disorders constitutes those behavior disturbances characterized principally by increased or decreased activity and thought expressive of a predominating mood of depression or elation. Although at the ranges of disturbance the behavioral change is conspicuous, it is seldom bizarre. The abnormalities of activity, affect, and thought seem often to the casual observer to have a plausible relationship to the immediate social environment.

While one group of individuals suffers from the direct behavioral expressions of depressive affect, modified according to the weighting of guilt, shame, anxiety, or helplessness that is induced as response in the specific personality make-up, in others the affective expression is obscured through the use of psychological mechanisms of denial or projection. In some, the underlying depression is covered by a paranoidal picture in which the guilty affect is assigned by projection onto others. In another group the depression is masked or may alternate with phases of elation. These several major variants are found in the involutional and the manic-depressive psychoses, respectively. In still others depression is masked by various neurotic symptoms or by psychophysiological responses, particularly those expressed in excessively driven oral behavior, such as overeating and obesity, alcoholism, or drug dependency.

In this chapter consideration is given to the affective disorders and the specified variants, as expressed in the standard nomenclature, of bipolar disorders and major depressions occurring during and outside the involutional period. (See Table 19–1.)

Within the past decade, genetic, clinical, pharmacological, and physiological studies have tended to indicate that the affective disorders might better be classified as *bipolar*—relating to the well-defined cyclical manic-depressive psychosis—and *unipolar* or *major depression*. In the latter category, one would place all those who have only depressive psychosis, whether it is single, recurrent, or determined by onset during specific age periods, such as the involutional in

women. Since the bipolar disorder is the most easily diagnosed over time, its various features are described first in this chapter.

Prevalence

It is now said that depression is the most undertreated of the major diseases. It is estimated by the National Institute of Mental Health that, in any given year, 15 per cent of adults between the ages of 18 and 74 may suffer serious depressive symptoms. Less than 5 per cent of those in need of treatment find their way to psychiatric care. Many are treated by general practitioners and other specialists, judging from analysis of prescription writing. Approximately 33 per cent of psychotropic drug prescriptions are written by specialists other than psychiatrists and neurologists. Approximately 8 per cent of new prescriptions and 9 per cent of refills are for depression.

Of admissions to mental hospitals, 23 per cent are for depression while the psychiatric units in general hospitals admit 30 per cent for the same condition. The total of depressive disorders discovered in general hospital practice is as great as or greater than all other diagnostic categories.

In an analysis of inception of mental illness in an English city, Adelstein et al. found that the rate of 97 per 100,000 for depressive psychosis was

---

TABLE 19–1   Classification and Sub-classification of Major Depressions

Diagnostic Criteria for Major Depressive Episode

A. Dysphoric mood or loss of interest or pleasure in all or almost all usual activities and pastimes. The dysphoric mood is characterized by symptoms such as the following: depressed, sad, blue, hopeless, low, down in the dumps, irritable. The mood disturbance must be prominent and relatively persistent, but not necessarily the most dominant symptom, and does not include momentary shifts from one dysphoric mood to another dysphoric mood, e.g., anxiety to depression to anger, such as are seen in states of acute psychotic turmoil. (For children under six years of age, dysphoric mood may have to be inferred from a persistently sad facial expression.)

B. At least four of the following symptoms have each been present nearly every day for a period of at least two weeks (in children under six years of age, at least three of the first four).
   (1) poor appetite or significant weight loss (when not dieting) or increased appetite or significant weight gain (in children under six years of age, consider failure to make expected weight gains)

Table continued on following page

    (2) insomnia or hypersomnia
    (3) psychomotor agitation or retardation (but not merely subjective feelings of restlessness or being slowed down) (in children under six years of age, hypoactivity)
    (4) loss of interest or pleasure in usual activities, or decrease in sexual drive not limited to a period when delusional or hallucinating (in children under six years of age, signs of apathy)
    (5) loss of energy; fatigue
    (6) feelings of worthlessness, self-reproach, or excessive or inappropriate guilt (either may be delusional)
    (7) complaints or evidence of diminished ability to think or concentrate, such as slowed thinking, or indecisiveness not associated with marked loosening of associations or incoherence
    (8) recurrent thoughts of death, suicidal ideation, wishes to be dead, or suicide attempt

C. Neither of the following dominates the clinical picture when an affective syndrome (i.e., criteria A and B above) is not present, that is, before it developed or after it has remitted:

    (1) preoccupation with a mood-incongruent delusion or hallucination (see definition below)
    (2) bizarre behavior

D. Not superimposed on either Schizophrenia, Schizophreniform Disorder, or a Paranoid Disorder.

E. Not due to any Organic Mental Disorder or Uncomplicated Bereavement.

Fifth-digit Code Numbers and Criteria for Subclassification of Major Depressive Episode

(When psychotic features and Melancholia are present the coding system requires that the clinician record the single most clinically significant characteristic.)

6– In Remission.   This fifth-digit category should be used when in the past the individual met the full criteria for a major depressive episode but now is essentially free of depressive symptoms or has some signs of the disorder but does not meet the full criteria.

4– With Psychotic Features.   This fifth-digit category should be used when there apparently is gross impairment in reality testing, as when there are delusions or hallucinations, or depressive stupor (the individual is mute and unresponsive). When possible, specify whether the psychotic features are mood-congruent or mood-incongruent. (The non-ICD-9-CM fifth-digit 7 may be used instead to indicate that the psychotic features are mood-incongruent; otherwise, mood-congruence may be assumed.)

Mood-congruent Psychotic Features.   Delusions or hallucinations whose content is entirely consistent with the themes of either personal inadequacy, guilt, disease, death, nihilism, or deserved punishment; depressive stupor (the individual is mute and unresponsive).

Mood-incongruent Psychotic Features.   Delusions or hallucinations whose content does not involve themes of either personal inadequacy, guilt, disease, death, nihilism, or deserved punishment. Included here are such symptoms as persecutory delusions, thought insertion, thought broadcasting, and delusions of control, whose content has no apparent relationship to any of the themes noted above.

3– With Melancholia.   Loss of pleasure in all or almost all activities, lack of reactivity to usually pleasurable stimuli (doesn't feel much better, even temporarily, when something good happens), and at least three of the following:

    (a) distinct quality of depressed mood, i.e., the depressed mood is perceived as distinctly different from the kind of feeling experienced following the death of a loved one
    (b) the depression is regularly worse in the morning
    (c) early morning awakening (at least two hours before usual time of awakening)
    (d) marked psychomotor retardation or agitation
    (e) significant anorexia or weight loss
    (f) excessive or inappropriate guilt

2– Without Melancholia

0– Unspecified

(From the Diagnostic and Statistical Manual of Mental Disorders, 3rd ed. Washington, D.C., American Psychiatric Association, 1980.)

the highest of any diagnostic category. The rate increased with age for both sexes, but women had an earlier and higher peak in the 30 to 39 year period, which was in excess of the rates between 40 and 59 in the same sex. Widowhood was associated with the high rates in the 30s. This lack of association of high rates in women during the menopausal period is surprising. In this study the diagnostic analysis did not provide discriminations of the varieties of affective psychosis. One may only conclude that in this city the rates for the involutional psychoses were lower than for the depressive psychoses.

BIPOLAR DISORDER

Although the contrasting affective states of depression and elation had been recognized for many years to occur in the same patient, it was not until 1896 that Emil Kraepelin designated the condition as manic-depressive insanity. He observed the periodicity and favorable outcome of the seemingly opposite stages of disordered affect and concluded they were variations of a single morbid process based upon physiological determinants.

Today, it is known that many patients may have only recurrent depressive reactions without elation; few present the alternation between the two affects. For these reasons, these conditions are subclassified in the nomenclature as manic-depressive reaction, "manic type," or "depressive type," or manic-depressive "circular." In the "circular," existence of one or another state is denoted as manic-depressive, circular, or manic-depressive, depressed.

It is reported that bipolar illness is apparently discoverable only in descendants of families in which there is a record of its occurrence in previous generations. Parental deprivations by death or divorce also characterize this group, suggesting that manic episodes are destructive to the family relationship. Phenomenologically, the bipolar patients exhibit lower levels of physical activity and overt expressions of physical complaints than the unipolar group.

Prevalence

There are striking differences in the reporting of manic-depressive psychoses in various countries. The admission rate of manic-depressives to hospitals in England and Wales exceeds that for the public mental hospitals in the United States by 18 times (36 per 100,000 population versus 2 per 100,000 population) and by 9 times when admissions in the United States are computed for both public and private mental hospitals. The recorded rate of first admissions of those with manic-depressive psychoses in New York State fell steadily from 1930 to 1950. They were as follows: 177 per 100,000 in 1920; 174 in 1930; 111 in 1940; and 71 in 1950. The explanations for these variations are numerous. It has been suggested that constitutional or genetic differences determine higher rates in northern European countries; that increasing immigration of southern Europeans to the United States has led to dilution of the older northern European population, with the diminished frequency of illnesses characteristic of northern populations; and that the diagnostic criteria vary from country to country and generation to generation. Also, the admission rates of the manic-depressive to the private psychiatric hospitals in the United States, which cater largely to the wealthier families of older stock, greatly exceed rates for the public mental hospitals serving the more deprived economically and representing largely waves of immigrants from southern Europe. Another reason for the decline in hospital admissions of this group perhaps rests in their increasingly successful treatment through clinic or office therapy.

Genetics

The rather common occurrence of manic-depressive psychoses in the same family suggests that a biogenetic factor may be a contributory cause, but this can scarcely be proved or denied. Rudin has stated that the incidence of manic-depressive psychosis is 25 times as high among the siblings of manic-depressive patients as in the average population. If it occurs in monozygotic twins, both of them will be affected in more than half of the cases. (See Table 19–2.)

In a German psychiatric clinic to which patients are admitted irrespective of social position, Luxenberger found manic-depressive psychoses to be nearly three times as frequent in the highest social class and four times as frequent in the professional classes as in the general population. This distribution of incidence seems to be similar to that observed by American psychiatrists. In World War II, manic-depressive psychoses were three times as frequent among officers of the American army as among enlisted men.

The terms unipolar and bipolar, now widely used, separate those patients with clear episodes of mania or hypomania and depression from others having only depressive illnesses without evidence of mania or hypomania. It has been found that relatives of the unipolar patients show a high prevalence of unipolar illness and depressive personalities, as well as a low prevalence of bipolar illness. Also, it is now known that relatives of bipolar patients have a higher prevalence of bipolar illness and cyclothymic personality than unipolar patients.

It has been found difficult to distinguish whether a proband with unipolar illness belongs to the unipolar or bipolar genetic population. Computations suggest that 25 per cent of monozygotic twins concordant for affective illness are discordant for other types of illness, leading to the conclusions that the genes predisposing to bipolar illness have incomplete penetrance and that some of the unipolar relatives of bipolar patients may carry the bipolar gene.

If the unipolar and bipolar conditions are distinct entities genetically, they should differ in other aspects as well. A corroborating fact is that the median age of onset for bipolar patients approximates 30 years while that for unipolar patients is about 45. Additionally, there seems to be an excessive mortality in bipolar patients from causes other than suicide, with a considerable shortening of life expectancy.

These two types of disturbance vary in their response to pharmacological treatment as well. Depressed bipolar patients appear to respond to lithium carbonate as a preventive while this does not occur with the unipolar patients. Bipolar but not unipolar patients are likely to develop episodes of hypomania when treated with the tricyclic antidepressants or with L-dopa.

Other differences exist. Evoked cortical potentials vary between the two

TABLE 19–2   Heritability of Affective Disorders*

INVESTIGATOR	MONOZYGOTIC PAIRS	MONOZYGOTIC % CONCORDANT	DIZYGOTIC PAIRS	DIZYGOTIC % CONCORDANT	HERITABILITY
Luxenberger (1930)	4	75.0	13	0	1.74
Rosanoff (1935)	23	69.6	67	16.4	1.08
Kallmann (1954)	27	92.6	55	23.6	1.16
Slater (1953)	7	57.1	17	23.5	0.70
Da Fonesca (1959)	21	71.4	39	38.5	0.56
Harvald & Hauge (1965)	10	50.0	39	2.6	1.23

*Twin data adapted from Zerbin-Rudin; calculation of heritability by twin method of Jensen. Data not corrected for age.

(From Gershon, E. S., Dunner, D. L., and Goodwin, F. K.: Arch. Gen. Psychiatry, 25:1–15, 1971.)

groups, as well as excretion of urinary hydroxycorticosteroids. In women, the erythrocyte-soluble catechol-O-methyltransferase has been reported to be lower in the unipolar group.

The inheritability of the condition (inheritability referring to a relative contribution of existing genetic and environmental factors in the particular population studied) has been difficult to estimate. Relatively few investigations have been reported of monozygotic twins reared apart in unrelated environments, which is conceptually the best way of arriving at such an estimate. The technique of making an estimate by calculating inheritability as a function of the difference between the incidence of the disorder in the population and the incidence in relatives of the probands suggests that the disorder is inheritable and that a nonadditive genetic factor such as dominance, the presence of a single major gene, or assortative mating is present. The evidence does support the role of environmental (dynamic) influences in expression of these disturbances. Presumably, the experiences of bereavement or loss have greater emotional significance to the predisposed individuals than to others.

The studies of the mode of genetic transmission have not provided a clearcut determination as to whether one is dealing with a simple dominant or polygenic gene expression.

It has been suggested that the genetic factor responsible for the effectiveness of lithium in the treatment of bipolar disease expresses itself through modifications in membranes. Thus, Schless and his colleagues have found that two groups of sheep with genetically determined differences in their cation concentrations selectively differ in their management of the lithium ion. The low red blood cell–potassium ion sheep concentrate the lithium ion in the red blood cells to a higher degree than the high red blood cell–potassium ion sheep group. This experiment of nature may have relevance to the clinical observations, in that depressed patients who respond to lithium carbonate have significantly higher erythrocyte lithium ion than depressed patients who do not so respond. In other words, the distribution of lithium ion across the erythrocyte membrane was significantly different between the responders and the non-responders. Furthermore, the majority of depressed patients who responded to lithium carbonate were bipolar patients.

Another genetic marker for the affective disorders appears to be erythrocyte catechol-O-methyltransferase (COMT). Patients with affective disorders tend to have higher activity levels of COMT and, furthermore, this activity positively correlates with activity in the erythrocytes of relatives. COMT is the enzyme responsible for the initial enzymatic inactivation of released catecholamines. The enzyme is found in erythrocytes and in other tissues in both membrane bound and soluble states.

It is suggested that a dominant X-linked factor is primary for the transmission of manic-depressive illness when one limits the definition to families in which one or more members have had manic episodes as well as depressions. Thus, affected maternal relatives in families with affective illness are found twice as frequently as paternal. So, too, association of color blindness as a sex-linked genetic marker with manic-depressive illness is being sought.

The recent research by Fieve, Mendlewicz, and Fleiss has uncovered the fact that manic-depressive illness and the Xg blood group, a genetic marker located on the X chromosome, exist as co-related, inherited linkage in successive generations of six families. These data support the earlier studies that a dominant X-linked factor is involved in the transmission of predisposition to manic-depressive illness within the families studied.

Certainly, until there has been established international agreement on diagnostic criteria for all the psychoses and evidence has accumulated that clinical observations and diagnosis in differing geographic areas are highly reliable, the differences in prevalence rates and their interpretations offer dubious support to any theories on etiology.

The bipolar disorders occur about twice as frequently in women as in men, and the average age of onset in women is younger. The aggressive woman with masculine strivings seems to be especially predisposed. Although these reactions are most frequently recognized during early maturity, more recent clinical observations have shown initial periods of depression with crying commencing in early childhood. The nuclear facets of the personality characteristics defined in the adult patients are then already evident.

Pathophysiology

From the accumulation of evidence on the action of drugs that influence the affective states and the growing understanding of their pharmacological effects, there has emerged a hypothesis relating changes in catecholamine metabolism to states of depression or elation. Those drugs that potentiate the action of brain norepinephrine also stimulate overt behavioral expressions, including excitement, and function in man as antidepressants, while those that inactivate or deplete norepinephrine centrally predispose to sedation and depressions. It has been suggested then that some depressions, and perhaps all, are associated with a deficiency of catecholamines, and especially norepinephrine, at the significant adrenergic receptor sites in the brain, while an excess of these amines exists with behavioral states of elation. This hypothesis, based on indirect evidence, has been reviewed by Schildkraut.

However, in the light of other data, the catecholamine hypothesis is now recognized as too simplified. In his recent review Maas has elaborated the original catecholamine deficiency hypothesis by suggesting that there are several depressive disorders. In one there exists a norepinephrine disorder without modification of dopamine metabolism and in another the major metabolic abnormality is related to the serotonin system. The evidence for his position is that a group of depressed patients excrete significantly less premethoxy-4-hydroxyphenethylene glycol (MHPG) in urine than do healthy groups of persons. The quantities of urinary normetanephrine (NM) and metanephrine (M) excreted by both groups seem to be similar. MHPG is considered the principal metabolic process of brain norepinephrine (NE). Any considerable fraction of urine MHPG is derived from the metabolism of brain while urinary NE, NM, M, and possibly vanillylmandelic acid (VMA), are derived from pools external to the central nervous system. Inspection of the data from a number of studies reexamining this original finding shows that many depressed patients excrete normal and greater than normal quantities of MHPG. The possibility is raised, therefore, that those who excrete less than normal amounts of MHPG may represent a particular subgroup with special biochemical and pathophysiological characteristics.

There is now evidence that the "low MHPG" group may be identified on differential clinical criteria. It is now known that patients who excrete less than normal quantities of MHPG prior to treatment with imipramine hydrochloride or desipramine hydrochloride have favorable responses to treatment with these drugs. Other depressed individuals who excrete normal amounts of MHPG do not respond well to treatment with either drug. Furthermore, those who respond well increase excretion of urinary MHPG after four weeks of drug treatment.

It has been found also that depressed patients who respond with mood elevation following the administration of dextroamphetamine have favorable responses to treatment with the tricyclic medications mentioned before with the exception of amitriptyline. These are the same individuals who initially excreted less than normal quantities of MHPG. On the other hand, the individuals who are normal or high excreters of MHPG respond favorably to amitriptyline hydrochloride. This group does not show a favorable treatment response when given dextroamphetamine and, in addition, demonstrates decrements in urinary MHPG following treatment with imipramine, desipramine, or dextroamphetamine.

In light of the fact that the agents effective in treating the low MHPG individuals block norepinephrine uptake and have little effect on the serotonin system, the assumption may be made that an abnormality exists in the noradrenergic systems centrally related to their depressive state. Their lack of response to amitriptyline may be related to the fact that this agent is not effective in blocking the re-uptake of norepinephrine as it is demethylated slowly into nortriptyline, which does bring about blockade. Presumably, there is a delay in raising the plasma level of norepinephrine to effective therapeutic levels with the use of amitriptyline.

It is possible that beyond the noradrenergic systems other brain amine systems may be involved. The argument for this possibility lies in the fact that tricyclic antidepressants have significant peripheral anticholinergic properties. The effects of these drugs on central cholinergic systems may combine to make them the effective agents they are in contrast to dextroamphetamine, which fails to produce a long-term therapeutic change in the treatment of depression. Thus, the above data argue the possibility that manic-depressive illness is a function of abnormal metabolism of the adrenergic-cholinergic balance.

On the other hand, in another group of patients, the possibility of alternation of the serotonin system is supported by the data that certain depressed patients have less than normal increments of 5-hydroxyindoleacetic acid—5-HIAA—following probenecid administration and that this group will respond with a favorable therapeutic response when given hydroxytryptophan. Furthermore, it has been found that patients with cerebral spinal fluid 5-HIAA concentration above 15 mg. per milliliter have favorable responses to treatment with nortriptyline, but below that level they do not.

Other biogenic amines are concerned in synaptic transmission, and perhaps their relative participation in this or that brain subsystem determines the effective integrative fusing within the brain. Thus the regular induction of hypomania by L-dopa in bipolar manic-depressive patients has been reported. Coppen and colleagues have found that the average urinary excretion of tryptamine during depression is half that of the normal, and other studies have shown that the concentration of 5-hydroxyindoles in the cerebrospinal fluid is lower than in the nondepressed. The indoleamines (tryptamine and serotonin) are involved as well. Much additional research is required before a clear comprehension is achieved of the relationship of biogenic amine metabolism to manic-depressive illness. Nevertheless, the evidence for such a relationship is very powerful.

So, too, it appears that electrolyte disturbances may be associated with bipolar disorders. During depression, sodium retention occurs and sodium distribution may be altered. Potassium and water excretion varies with the mood, being increased during depression and decreased during elation. This assumption gains support from the fact that lithium salts effectively inhibit the manic phase of the illness. Additional endocrinological abnormalities have been reported in the affective disorders. Sachar and associates found that unipolar depressed patients (postmenopausal women) secrete significantly less growth hormone (GH) than do healthy persons or the bipolar depressed patients.

Others have reported changes in adrenocortical function judged from studies of the circadian variations of excretion of plasma and urinary steroids and high plasmin lipid values in manic-depressives.

Hartmann has found that the sleep dream cycle of manic-depressive patients, examined electroencephalographically, differs from that in health. Total sleep time is always lower during manic phases, but varies in depression from unchanged to increased. Total rapid eye movement (REM) and dream time (D-time) are also less in the manic phases and tend to be higher during the depressions. So, too, D% is low in the manic stage and high during the depressions, but less so in the absolute D-time. D latency (amount of sleep before the first D period) varies with manic phases but is low during depressions. The findings differ from those of other depressed patients. They suggest that the manic-depressives have a need or pressure for dreaming time. Hartmann suggests that the shifts in the physiological stages of sleep may be related to catecholamine metabolism. His suggestion receives support from other researches, such as that of Iskander and Kaebling, who demonstrated that experimental reduction in catecholamine levels brings about increase in REM sleep.

The sleep abnormality may persist for months after treatment, as may indications of other disturbed biological functions. Thus Haure and his colleagues found that remitted, presumably unipolar depressives continue to suffer delayed sleep onset and show more stage 1 sleep, less delta sleep, and a slower sleep cycle. There occurred too a greater variability in sleep patterns in remitted depressives than in those never suffering depressions. This variability suggests once again less bio-

logical homogeneity. The group may have contained some subjects with bipolar illness.

Other changes reported to persist in remitted depressives are increased muscular tone and low levels of 5-hydroxyindoleacetic acid.

The "sedation threshold," defined by Shagass and colleagues as the amount of amobarbital sodium in milligrams per kilogram of body weight required to produce a specific inflection in the amplitude of frontal lobe electroencephalographic activity during intravenous injection, is lowered in those with psychotic depressive reactions, again in contrast with other types of psychosis. The threshold for each individual is reproducible over time, and it is not modified greatly by moderate doses of phenothiazines.

Shagass and Schwartz also report a significant increase in the mean recovery time of the cycle of cerebral cortical potentials following stimulation of the ulnar nerve in the psychotic depressive, the schizophrenic, and those with personality disorders. The techniques of defining and measuring the sedation threshold and the cycle of cortical excitability are given in various papers cited by Shagass and his coworkers.

In light of the clinical evidence that the initiation of the affective disorders is often associated with actual or fantasy loss leading to the emotional states associated with bereavement, the evidence that an activation of adrenocortical function occurs following bereavement is worth noting. Hofer and his colleagues have described increases in 17-hydroxycorticosteroid excretion in parents shortly after the death of a child due to a serious illness. The change may persist for many months following the bereavement. It seems that the initiation of the affective change—either depressive or manic—may be regarded as triggered by an event that induces diffuse and widespread psychoendocrine and metabolic dysfunction. In fact, then, the affective psychoses might be regarded as one of the forms of psychosomatic disorder.

Studying the switch process from depression into mania, Bunney et al. reported that urinary norepinephrine is significantly elevated prior to and during the manic episodes. It is not known whether psychological processes precede the change in behavior and shift in metabolism or whether the latter precipitates the manic attack. The psychodynamic explanation for the switch will be described in a later section of this chapter.

Psychopathology

There are two well-defined types or phases of the bipolar disorders: a manic, or hyperactive phase, and a depressive phase.

Although the disorder typically assumes the form of psychotic episodes separated by intervals of mental health, a person may suffer only from one episode, or, again, the disorder may become continuous. These episodes may be in the nature of a manic or of a depressive reaction; there is no constant sequence or alternation of these reactions. The swings from one phase to another seem to prove the homogeneity of the bipolar disorders.

MANIC PHASE. In personality make-up, the patient whose episodes are of a manic type has usually been a self-satisfied, confident, aggressive, effervescing extrovert, at ease with other people. He or she has been inclined to scatter energy over a wide field of interests. His affective attitude has been one of emotional expression and responsiveness. The manic phase or reaction is usually preceded by a simple depression. This depression is of brief duration and mild in degree, often lasting for only a few days and either not noted by the patient's family or not considered significant. This brief period is followed by exhilaration or mild excitement.

Sometimes the attack remains in this attenuated form known as *hypomania.* In this hypomanic state there are increased assertiveness, an air of self-assurance, careless gaiety, breezy affability, self-satisfaction, buoyant self-confidence, and boundless energy. No matter how inhibited the patient may normally have been, he is now irrepressible, demanding, uninhibited, effusive, and often astonishingly unconventional in speech and manner. He is narcissistic, childishly proud, and quite intolerant of criticism. Glib of tongue and genial of hand, the patient is socially aggressive, witty, boastful, flippant, argumentative, spends his money extravagantly, pawns his belongings, is full of ambitious schemes and starts enterprises that soon fail or that he soon abandons.

Excessive indulgence in alcohol colors and confuses his behavior. Today, as Reich, Davies, and Himmelhoch report, it is only the excessive use of alcohol that distinguishes the manic who requires hospital care from those who do not. Alcoholic abuse is consciously determined as a means of providing relief from the manic symptoms and, particularly, to assist in gaining sleep. Of those bipolar-polar patients who drink to excess in both the manic and depressive phases of the illness, the increase in consumption generally is greater and more sought for in the manic phase.

Often striking is the frequency of use of direct and indirect quotations, particularized references, and adverbs of degree ("absolutely," "much," "never"). His conversation is directed principally to a recital of events, circumstances, and meetings with others, but it seldom contains statements about their inner affective meaning to him or his personal evaluation of the interactions between himself and others. Thus there is little evidence of introspection but more that of comparing, weighing, and evaluating the performances of others and himself. From this trend, coupled with the many indications of denial and over-compensatory self-references, there emerges a self-image toward which the patient appears to be striving.

His excuses and arguments contain a superficial but specious plausibility. His disregard for the truth may carry great conviction to those not previously acquainted with him. The patient is bored with routine, lacks a sustained interest in any activity, and is too busy to submit his impressions to critical examination. Attention is often easily distracted, thought processes are accelerated, and the stream of thought is prone to wander. His manner of speaking has an undertone of emphasis and exaggeration.

Many hypomanic patients are mischievous, boisterous, and full of pranks, indulge in risqué remarks and coarse and unseemly jokes, and make facetious comments about some object, or especially some person, in the environment. They are superficial in their relationships with other persons and insensitive to the latters' needs and feelings. Some hypomanic individuals delight in joking efforts to tease the physician. Unbridled criticism and bluntness of speech, even to the point of impudence, are common. Without constraint, the manic patient blurts out what he has doubtless long wished to say but has previously been afraid to express.

The usual good humor, which is often infectious in nature, frequently continues as long as every whim of the patient is gratified. When denied his requests and demands, his good humor quickly tends to be replaced with anger, caustic speech, and verbal abuse. In place of this good humor, one occasionally meets with a sustained anger, argumentativeness, irritability, haughtiness, arrogance, sarcasm, and querulousness. Open hostility to members of the family is common.

Extrapunitive hostility characteristic of the manic phase disappears with recovery. After her recovery, one woman whose hypomanic attacks were characterized by a great outburst of hostility described her psychotic episodes as seeming "like a prolonged spell of anger." In her normal periods, she was a friendly person, anxious to help others, and took great pride in her love for them. (One suspects that this desirable personality characteristic was a reaction formation that served as a defense against a deep-seated hostility.)

Sudden oscillations of emotion are common. In the midst of an exuberance of manner and spirits, the patient may suddenly burst into tears and give expression to some depressive idea, but after a moment be as cheerful as ever. He may likewise change rapidly from irritability to affability. The hypomanic patient may work with great, but capricious, enthusiasm and energy, but his stimulation and expansiveness impair his judgment. He is often so officious and meddlesome that he becomes an annoyance to those about him. He declares that he needs no rest. Although under a constant pressure of activity, he feels no sense of fatigue. He writes numerous letters in which he underscores many words and passages and introduces various parenthetical remarks. The style of composition may be flowery and witty and the script large, flowing, and perhaps graceful. No sooner, perhaps, has he posted a letter than he decides that the mail is too slow for his urgent business so he dispatches a telegram to his correspondent. He discusses with strangers and without reserve matters of an intimate, private nature. The hypomanic is often erotic and, if a man, may indulge in sexual excesses, while a previously chaste and modest young woman may become sexually promiscuous. Although from custom and convenience the symptoms just described are designated as hypomanic, any attempt to divide the imperceptible gradations of hyperactivity occurring in bipolar patients into clinical groups is entirely arbitrary.

In a well-developed picture of mania

the *affective tonality* is one of eagerness, exaltation, and joyous excitement. The tempo of the whole personality is quickened. The patient's patterns of thinking and behavior reflect his mood. He sings, dances about, whistles, and may be exhilarated to the point of noisy hilarity. He shows an unrestrained playfulness and mischievousness. His elation stimulates ideas of grandeur and perhaps fleeting delusions of wealth and power. The exhilaration may be punctuated with anger, irritability, and even with combativeness if the patient is denied some request or privilege, a granting of which his disturbed state forbids.

Again, a well-developed *paranoid trend* may exist, and the patient may be verbally abusive to the person toward whom, for the moment, he may feel most resentful. Patients with this impure affect are often haughty, demanding, revengeful, sarcastic, and arrogant. They may seem to delight in an unbounded expression of aggressiveness and hostility.

The *stream of thought* is characterized by loquaciousness and rapid association of ideas. Frequently, the patient speaks with a crispness and vigor of articulation, with emphatic accents and frequent changes of pitch. His style of phrasing may be pompous, and his speech may assume the character of theatrical declamation. As the hypomanic state passes into acute mania, the pressure of speech develops into a flight of ideas with rhyming, play upon words, and "clang" associations of words having similar sounds but no relation in meaning. Superficially the therapist receives the impression of a great variety of ideas, but if he carefully observes the manic patient's associational products, he discovers that their range is really limited. As a matter of fact, the manic individual evades thinking and is occupied with rhetoric and phonetics rather than meaning. Associations that remind the patient of some overvalued idea or egocentric interest are particularly apt to divert the stream of thought. Although the patient's racing flow of ideas appears illogical and directed by such stimuli as similarity of sound and environmental objects and events, beneath these superficial associations may often be discovered an underlying but limited range of topics toward which associations tend to flow. Without realizing their significance, the patient often makes remarks that afford a hint as to the unconscious motivation of his ideas, since, although apparently devoid of motivation, they are not so in fact. In both sequence and significance, they approach the character of free associations and therefore, like them, are prompted by unconscious and instinctive agencies.

The third of the mental fields in which it has been customary to describe disturbances as taking place is that of *psychomotor activity*. There is an overactivity, ranging from the pressure of occupation described in hypomania to the violent motor excitement of acute mania. In the hospital the patient meddles with ward activities and with other patients; he has numerous suggestions about how the institution should be conducted. He decorates himself with trinkets and improvised badges and medals. In more excited states, he tears his clothing into ribbons with which he decorates himself in a grotesque manner. He sings, shouts, and assumes dramatic attitudes. He may destroy bed and personal clothing, an activity usually prompted not by malice but by an urge to be busy. A woman ordinarily refined and modest may disregard all former sense of propriety, make indecent sexual proposals, and be obscene in speech. The overactive manic sleeps little and yet does not appear fatigued. He sustains cuts and abrasions to which he pays no attention and for which he will permit no treatment. Infections may occur and complicate the clinical picture. Rarely the patient shows such a pressure of activity that he does not eat and requires tube feeding, although in the usual degree of excitement the patient may bolt large quantities of food with complete disregard of manners.

The attention of the manic is usually much disturbed, the disorder being caused not by any defect in vigilance but by lack of tenacity, as a result of which attention is easily distracted. Environmental noises and activities constantly divert his attention. Commonly, he misidentifies persons, being particularly prone to identify a stranger as a former acquaintance because of the fact that he discovers some slight point of similarity but fails to scrutinize the points of dissimilarity. The patient usually remains well oriented, but at times his grasp of his environment may be faulty because of an absence of sustained and discriminating attention.

Hallucinations may occur in manic excitement but are not common; they are usually more in the nature of illusions.

Delusions are usually expansive or wish-fulfilling in nature, are fleeting, and not systematized. Ideas of persecution are not rare.

As may be implied from the foregoing description of overt behavior, judgment is markedly impaired. While manic, the individual regards himself as sociable, trusting, pleasant, and unaggressive. Those whom he contacts perceive him as barely acceptable socially, impulsive, rebellious, and aggressive. On recovery from the manic state, the same individual assesses his ill behavior much as do those who have contacted him while ill.

Physically, the patients classed as milder cases appear in excellent health. The eyes are bright, the face flushed, the head erect, the step quick. Weight may be gained. In extreme excitement, the patient may lose weight because of great expenditure of energy. In greatly overactive states, the patient is usually dehydrated. Pneumonia, acute nephritis, and other infections may be unrecognized because of the difficulty in making a physical examination of a

patient so extremely excited. In such cases, the real nature of a superimposed delirioid state may escape recognition. Any real clouding of consciousness in a patient who has been greatly excited should suggest the possibility of a complicating infection.

Among women with the bipolar affective disorder, the likelihood of a postpartum episode is much greater than in the unipolar form of the disturbance, as computed by Baker and his colleagues. Furthermore, the manic-depressive (bipolar) women have a significantly higher rate for the development of subsequent postpartum affective episodes if they have once occurred.

The following, taken from the records of a man who first entered a public institution for mental diseases when 54 years of age, illustrates many of the typical behavior reactions of manic excitement:

At ages 35, 41, and 47, the patient suffered from depressed episodes, each attack being from four to six months in duration. In January he became restless and talkative. Early in February he began to send checks to friends, sometimes even to strangers who, he said, might be in need. Ten days later he was sent home from the office where he was employed with the explanation that he was becoming overwrought. A few days after his suspension from work he was admitted to a private institution for mental disorders, where he pretended to commit suicide by mercury poisoning. He then drew a skull and cross bones on the wall of his room. After three weeks he was taken home, but a few days later he was committed to a public institution where he bustled about the ward, giving the impression that he had important business to which he must attend.

Occasionally he was seen lying on a bench, pretending to sleep, but in a few minutes he resumed his usual activity. He talked quickly, loudly, and nearly constantly. He was interested in everything and everyone around him. He talked familiarly to patients, attendants, nurses, and physicians. He took a fancy to the woman physician on duty in the admission building, calling her by her first name and annoying her with letters and with his familiar, ill-mannered, and obtrusive attentions. On his arrival he gave five dollars to one patient and one dollar to another. He made many comments and asked many questions about other patients and promised that he would secure their discharge. He interfered with their affairs and soon received a blow on the jaw from one patient and a black eye from another. He wrote letters demanding his release, also letters to friends describing in a circumstantial, inaccurate, and facetious way conditions in the hospital. His letters were interlarded with trite Latin phrases. He drew carcicatures of the physicians and the nurses and wrote music on toilet paper. He drew pictures on his arms; on one occasion he secured a bottle of mercurochrome and painted the face of another manic patient. When permitted to play the ward piano, he played piece after piece without stopping, improvising a great deal. A doctor rarely passed through the ward without being called by the patient, who would slap the physician on the back or shake hands effusively and talk until the door closed. At times during an interview his voice became tremulous, tears came to his eyes, and he sobbed audibly with his face buried in his arms. A moment later, however, he was laughing—a manifestation of the bipolarity of emotion so markedly illustrated in this disease.

Course. Modern treatment methods tend to obscure the various stages of the manic illness as described by Kraepelin and to blur the development of its symptomatic expression and personality disorganization as were frequently seen in the past. Yet the untreated or mistreated patient may go through a series of phases, as observed by Carlson and Goodwin. Initiating the onset of a manic attack is the appearance of psychomotor activity, expressed in the increasing rate of speech and physical activity, a rising sense of euphoria, the initiation of expansive and grandiose ideation, and overconfidence. At this stage the thought expression tends to be coherent. During the next, or second, stage the majority of patients have a further pressure of speech and psychomotor activity. Euphoria continues, broken now by dysphoria and evidence of depression. The irritability sometimes observed in the initial phase progresses to open hostility and anger of an explosive and assaultive expression. The flight of ideas is evident and there is increasing disorganization in the cognitive state. It is at this time that the earlier grandiose trends appear as frankly delusional; paranoid ideation is seen.

In the final stage, the patient's behavior becomes panic-stricken, hopelessly distraught, with frenzied and bizarre psychomotor activity. At this time there may be a definite loosening of associations with bizarre delusions and hallucinations, which might lead to confusion with the schizophrenic reaction if one is not aware of the extent of disorganization occurring in this illness. For the clinician concerned with making the appropriate diagnosis and providing the indicated treatment, the extent and breadth of the psychopathology must be recognized over these various phases. Table 19–3 indicates the frequency of the so-called classical and atypical symptoms in manic patients.

Observation of a series of individuals who had not received treatment indicates that the sequence of symptom progression is very consistent but the acceleration is variable. Some patients moved to the final stage within a few hours while others progressed over a number of days. In the recovery phases, as mood returned to normal, delusions and hallucinations tended to remit.

DEPRESSIVE PHASE. Although a larger percentage of the episodic depressions of this disorder occur in persons who have also a history of manic episodes, in some bipolar patients the psychotic episodes are confined to those of a depressive type. In such cases one often finds a rather characteristic type of prepsychotic personality. Many of these individuals whose psychotic episodes are limited to depressive reactions have always been friendly, unobtrusive, timid persons with an underlying sense of insecurity and overdependency and they manifest sensitive and appreciative emotional responses. Others have been scrupulous persons of rigid ethical and moral standards, meticulous, self-demanding, perfectionistic, self-depreciatory, prudish, given to self-reproach, and sensitive to criticism. Their obsessive-compulsive tendencies have doubtless been defensive mechanisms for handling hostility, which characteristically they cannot express externally. Frequently, they have had fixed opinions and set

TABLE 19-3   Classic and "Atypical" Symptoms in Manic Patients

SYMPTOMS	PATIENTS MANIFESTING SYMPTOMS, %
Hyperactivity	100
Extreme verbosity	100
Pressure of speech	100
Grandiosity	100
Manipulativeness	100
Irritability	100
Euphoria	90
Mood lability	90
Hypersexuality	80
Flight of ideas	75
Delusions	75
Sexual	(25)
Persecutory	(65)
Passivity	(20)
Religious	(15)
Assaultiveness or threatening behavior	75
Distractibility	70
Loosened associations	70
Fear of dying	70
Intrusiveness	60
Somatic complaints	55
Some depression	55
Religiosity	50
Telephone abuse	45
Regressive behavior (urinating or defecating inappropriately; exposing self)	45
Symbolization or gesturing	40
Hallucinations (auditory and visual)	40
Confused	35
Ideas of reference	20

(From Carlson, G. A., and Goodwin, F. K.: Arch. Gen. Psychiatry, *28*:221–228, 1973.)

ways of doing things and are habitually apprehensive and fearful. Often they have been hesitant and without courage, yet have sought and achieved worthwhile accomplishments. Frequently, their greatest emotional need seems to have been love, respect, and belonging.

Just as in the manic type of bipolar disorder all degrees of overactivity are found, so in the depressive type one meets with varying degrees of depression. If arbitrarily we describe three degrees of activity—hypomania, acute mania, and delirious mania—in the excited phase, so mild depression, acute depression, and stupor may be said to represent the different degrees of the depression. One should remember, however, that these arbitrary divisions merge imperceptibly into one another.

Because of the absence of striking disturbances, the real nature of *mild depression* is frequently not recognized. In fact, it should be borne in mind that various moods that are called normal pass imperceptibly into the different forms of bipolar disorder. Mild depressive phases tend, roughly speaking, to assume one of two general forms: either a period of fatigue, staleness, and inertia, or one during which the patient has physical complaints for which no organic basis can be discovered. Affective depression exists in both forms but does not constitute the chief complaint and consists of a mild downheartedness. Occasionally the onset is characterized by obsessive features. If the depression stands a bit to the fore, the patient's friends may speak of his episodes as "blue spells." The patient lacks confidence in himself, loses his zest for living, feels inadequate and tired, shows a growing aversion to activity, likes to be left alone, and finds it difficult to perform his ordinary duties. Color and joy are gone out of life. Every task seems a burden, and in many cases the patient gives up any attempt to continue his employment. He has doubts and fears, is frequently overanxious about his family, states he has not provided amply for their future welfare, and has mild ideas of unworthiness.

Thinking may be difficult, ideational content becomes confined to a few topics, spontaneous speech is limited, replies to questions are delayed and condensed as much as possible, and the patient is disinclined to reveal his private thoughts. Social contacts are not sought, and the patient may even show an obstinate unwillingness to meet people. Many show a marked indecisiveness, probably indicative of their apprehension of further failure, rejection, and retaliation.

Less frequently encountered are those who tend to be morose, gloomily irritable and sensitive, often stubborn and inconsiderate of others, and inclined to project in the form of dissatisfication or fault finding. Sadness is little evidenced.

Others are openly hostile, angry, and punitive. They resent efforts to assist them and deny the existence of their illness. These persons usually have manifested domineering and outwardly aggressive personality traits prior to their illness and they become depressed when their sense of self-sufficiency and ability to control their environment is frustrated.

In the second group of mild depressions, physical complaints are among the most conspicuous symptoms and may mask the depression. There is not merely the loss of weight, coated tongue, disturbed and unrefreshing sleep, and poor appetite observed in depressive states, but the patient has various hypochondriacal ideas. He feels weak and fatigued, worries over trifles, and suffers from insomnia, headache, and debility and perhaps from precordial or epigastric distress. Any bodily sensations that may arise on a physical, tension, or anxiety basis become the principal object of the patient's attention. He therefore believes, as often do his friends, that the real disorder is physical and that his downheartedness is the natural result of ill health, whereas the physical complaints are really but the rationalization of a primary affective distress. To the inexperienced practitioner, these depressive episodes may appear to be neurasthenic. Occasionally there is a history of laparotomy or pelvic surgery without a discoverable pathologic condition having been revealed.

The onset of a *severe depression* may resemble the mild depressive states just described, but the initial downheartedness soon passes into a profound affective distress. Posture, muscle tensions, and various physical signs and symptoms present a composite picture indicating depression. The body is stooped, the head flexed, the facies immobile, the forehead furrowed, and the patient looks fixedly downward. Deep vertical wrinkles appear between the eyebrows, the nasolabial folds are marked, and the down-turned angles of the mouth constitute a picture of dejection. The face may have a troubled, perplexed expression. The patient loses weight and appears ill. Perspiration and other secretions are decreased. Muscle tone is decreased, the bowels are constipated, sexual desire is decreased, and the male patient is usually impotent. The sleeping pattern is disturbed in a characteristic way. Although there is usually little delay in falling asleep, the patient awakens much earlier than when he is well. The diurnal severity of his depressive affect also varies in a customary way in that it is usually most severe in the morning and relents as the day wears on. As the depression becomes more profound, everything is interpreted in terms of hopelessness and despondency.

Occasionally a patient says he has no feeling. Others complain that things seem strange and unnatural—feelings of unreality. They usually recognize that the change, caused by the influence of the depressed feeling-tone on perceptions, by the loss of interest in external phenomena, and by their altered affective relationships, is in themselves and not in the fundamental nature of environmental objects. Many patients have an indefinite dread or a sense of impending disaster, frequently accompanied by an attitude of submission to their fate. Efforts at reassurance make no impression, and the patient shows no response to appreciative and sympathetic counsel. A sense of fear is not uncommon and, if it is intense, consciousness may be clouded and the patient may be confused.

In the *retarded depression* there is an inhibition of the stream of thought and of psychomotor activity. The retarded patient speaks slowly and seems at a loss for words. His replies are brief, frequently monosyllabic, and expressed in a low tone. Not rarely he begins, but never completes, the reply to some inquiry, or else he finishes it only as the examiner moves away. Perhaps he may merely move his lips but fail to utter any intelligible response. Efforts to make decisions result in vacillation or perplexity.

In the psychomotor field, externally directed behavior becomes progressively retarded and inhibited. There is slowness both in initiation and in execution. The patient complains of an inability to carry out suggested activities, and every attempt requires great exertion. Retardation may be so pronounced as to amount to stupor.

In depressive states the patient's ideas tend to represent a projected expression of his inner feelings and a rationalization of his affects. The delusional content of the depressive patient is characterized by self-depreciation, ideas of guilt, remorse, self-accusation, and hypochondriasis. Frequently, there is a suspicious, paranoid, complaining, and persecutory trend to the patient's ideas. This is particularly the case when the patient's prepsychotic personality was characterized by sensitiveness and feelings of inferiority.

Hallucinations are not conspicuous symptoms in the depression of manic-depressive psychosis, and although they may occur, a persistent falsification of reality in this way should raise the question of a more malignant psychosis, particularly if the hallucinations do not clearly represent the projection of affective distress. Illusionary misinterpretations are frequent—a pounding in the basement is that of workmen constructing the patient's coffin.

Dream life of the depressive tends to change as he moves from the phase of severest suffering to that of recovery. During the former period, as Miller has found, dreams tend to be bland and pleasant, denying the anguish of the illness. As recovery ensues, the dream content shifts to reveal concern over being hurt by others; that hurt is delivered largely through coercive interaction. Coercion by others plus the personal inability to cope effectively with it may be a central problem in depression. It deserves much study.

The patient usually remains well oriented unless from his affective distress he becomes so preoccupied that attention is impaired. As already indicated, he may be confused if his fear is intense. Depressed patients usually have little or no appetite, and some would starve if not encouraged or forced to eat. Spoon or tube feeding is sometimes necessary. This failure to eat may result from the profound psychomotor inhibition, or from the patient's belief that he is unworthy to receive the food, or from a desire to diet. This feeling of unworthiness and the desire for self-punishment often lead to suicidal attempts and occasionally to self-mutilation.

The most intense form of the depressive phase is depressive *stupor*. It was probably this type of stupor to which Esquirol gave the name "acute dementia." In this profoundly inhibited state, there is practically no spontaneous motor activity. There is a complete, or almost complete, immobility, with a minimal response to external stimuli. The patient is mute, his sensorium is clouded, and he is intensely preoccupied, often with ideas of death and with dreamlike hallucinations. The face is either masklike or rigidly anxious. Many patients have to be tube-fed; some soil and wet themselves.

Elderly, depressed patients may manifest organic mental symptoms such as confusion, disorientation, and memory defects, which are alleviated or may even disappear with recovery from depression. Sometimes a depression terminates with a brief hypomanic reaction.

Crimes of violence may be associated with bipolar disorders. Such crimes are more frequent in depressed than in manic states, probably because depression may be a result of a weakening in the repression of hate and aggressive strivings. It is reported that, of 90 patients confined to the Broadmoor, England, Criminal Lunatic Asylum because of murder committed during affective psychoses, 62 were suffering from depression and 28 from mania at the time the homicides took place. More homicides are committed by depressed women than by depressed men. Usually the victim is not only a member of the patient's family but the one who has apparently been the most loved. It has been suggested that the homicide may be regarded as an extension of the suicidal impulse. As suicide is an act of aggression against self, then the homicide (in depressive patients) might be considered an extension of aggression to include not only the self but those nearest the self, the victim being almost a part of the self. An example of this psychopathology is manifested when a depressed mother kills both herself and her child.

The following case report is of a severe depression unaltered by modern therapeutic measures. It is presented because such pathology continues to be seen.

E. D., aged 60, was admitted to the hospital because he was depressed, ate insufficiently, and believed that his stomach was "rotting away." The patient was described as a friendly, sociable individual, not quarrelsome, jealous, or critical, and with a sense of humor. He was considered even-tempered, slow to anger, tender-hearted, and emotional.

At 51 the patient suffered from a depression and was obliged to resign his position. This depression continued for about nine months, after which he apparently fully recovered. He resumed his work but after two years suffered from a second depression. Again he recovered after several months and returned to a similar position and held it until two months before his admission. At this time he began to worry lest he was not doing his work well, talked much of his lack of fitness for his duties, and finally resigned. He spent Thanksgiving Day at his son's in a neighboring city, but while there he was sure that the water pipes in his own house would freeze during his absence and that he and his family would be "turned out into the street." A few days later he was found standing by a pond, evidently contemplating suicide. He soon began to remain in bed and sometimes wrapped his head in the bed clothing to shut out the external world. He declared that he was "rotting away inside" and that if he ate, the food would kill him. He urged the family not to touch the glasses or towels he used lest they become contaminated.

On arrival at the hospital, he appeared older than his years. He was pale, poorly nourished, and dehydrated, with his lips dry, cracked, and covered with sores. His facial expression and general bearing suggested a feeling of utter hopelessness. He was self-absorbed and manifested no interest in his environment. When urged to answer questions, there was a long delay before he attempted to reply, but he finally spoke briefly, hesitatingly, and in a low tone. He occasionally became agitated and repeatedly said, "Oh, doctor, why did I ever get into anything like this? Doctor, I am all filled up! I can't get anything through me—what am I going to do? Oh, dear! Oh, dear!" In explaining his presence in the hospital, he said he realized he had been sent by his

family because they believed he would be benefited by the treatment, but added, "I don't know
how they sent me here when they had not the
means. My wife cannot pay for me, and by this
time she must have been put out of the house."

After several months the patient began to improve, although hypochondriacal ideas persisted
for a considerable period. Finally, when the matter of freedom of the hospital grounds was considered, he seemed in a normal mood and indicated that he was beginning to think somewhat
differently concerning his gastrointestinal tract. At
that time he commented, "There's a good deal of
life in the old horse yet." A month later he became alert, animated, talkative, exuberant in
spirits, and confident in manner. This state continued for about two months, when he settled
down into what seemed to be his normal mood
and state of activity. After a few weeks he was
discharged, but several months later he again
showed signs of depression and hanged himself
before arrangements for readmission had been
made.

CIRCULAR TYPE. For a few bipolar
patients, the episodes suffered are
always manic or always depressive, while
those of most patients are of irregular
sequence in respect to the mood disturbance. The episodes of still other patients may be characterized by an alternation of manic and depressive
reactions. In some patients there may
be no appreciable interval of normality
between the alternations; in other cases
there may be variable periods free
from symptoms.

The following case illustrates the cyclic tendency and its influence in preventing successful adjustment during a
large part of the patient's adult life.

M. M. was first admitted to a state hospital at
the age of 38, although since childhood she had
been characterized by swings of mood, some of
which had been so extreme that they had been
psychotic in degree. At 17 she suffered from a
depression that rendered her unable to work for
several months, although she was not hospitalized. At 33, shortly before the birth of her first
child, the patient was greatly depressed. For a
period of four days she appeared in coma. About
a month after the birth of the baby she "became
excited" and was entered as a patient in an institution for neurotic and mildly psychotic patients.
As she began to improve, she was sent to a shore
hotel for a brief vacation. The patient remained at
the hotel for one night and on the following day
signed a year's lease on an apartment, bought
furniture, and became heavily involved in debt.
Shortly thereafter Mrs. M. became depressed and

returned to the hospital in which she had previously been a patient. After several months she
recovered and, except for relatively mild fluctuations of mood, remained well for approximately
two years.

She then became overactive and exuberant in
spirits and visited her friends, to whom she outlined her plans for re-establishing different forms
of lucrative business. She purchased many
clothes, bought furniture, pawned her rings, and
wrote checks without funds. She was returned to a
hospital. Gradually her manic symptoms subsided, and after four months she was discharged.
For a period thereafter she was mildly depressed.
In a little less than a year Mrs. M. again became
overactive, played her radio until late in the night,
smoked excessively, took out insurance on a car
that she had not yet bought. Contrary to her usual
habits, she swore frequently and loudly, created a
disturbance in a club to which she did not
belong, and instituted divorce proceedings. On
the day prior to her second admission to the hospital, she purchased 57 hats.

During the past 18 years this patient has been
admitted and dismissed from the hospital on
many occasions. At times, with the onset of a
depressed period, she has returned to the hospital seeking admission. At such times she complained that her "brain just won't work." She
would say, "I have no energy, am unable to do my
housework; I have let my family down; I am living
from day to day. There is no one to blame but
myself." During one of her manic periods, she
sent the following telegram to a physician of
whom she had become much enamored: "To:
You; Street and No.: Everywhere; Place: the remains at peace! We did our best, but God's will
be done! I am so very sorry for all of us. To brave
it through thus far. Yes, Darling—from Hello
Handsome. Handsome is as Handsome does,
thinks, lives and breathes. It takes clear air,
Brother of Mine, in a girl's hour of need. All my
love to the Best Inspiration one ever had."

In the last year Mrs. M., now 59, has been making an excellent home and community adjustment. Her husband has had several cerebrovascular accidents and has required considerable
nursing and assistance. She has efficiently met
the various responsibilities and family emergencies that have befallen her and has supplemented her husband's pension by baby-sitting. It is
altogether probable, however, that she will experience returns either of excitement or of depression.

MIXED TYPES. Psychomotor activity,
flow of thought, and affectivity were
formerly thought of as independent
and more or less separable functions of
the mind, which in their positive or
negative variations could be combined
in various ways as may the letters of the
alphabet. Basing his ideas on this conception of a coexistence of manic and

depressive elements, Kraepelin described special clinical forms. These he designated as the "mixed" types of bipolar disorders. He described such "mixed" forms as agitated depression, manic stupor, unproductive mania, depressive mania, depression with flight, and inhibited mania. The present tendency is to discontinue such artificial classifications.

Of these groups, *agitated depression* most nearly deserves a special recognition, yet this group is really a depressive reaction in which the agitation is simply an expression of anxiety—a persistent expression of the apprehension, tension, and feeling of prospective harm arising from threatening factors deep in the mental life. The great internal uneasiness produces a psychomotor agitation.

Psychodynamics

Various psychoanalytic studies have suggested that the pathologic affects of the depressive state associated with helpless anxiety occur in those who must compulsively maintain goals or personal attachments (object-relations) to maintain a sense of security. Unlike those who are capable of passing through a healthy mourning process as the result of realistic perception of a loss, the patients with major affective disorders are unable to give up their wishes even though they are beyond attainment. Three sets of aspirations and hopes that must be maintained and are not necessarily exclusive are the wish to be worthy and therefore loved and respected—and thus not to be inferior and disrespected; the wish to be strong, superior, and secure—and not to be weak and insecure; and the wish to be good and to love—and not to be aggressive, hateful, or destructive. It is in the conflict and tensions between these hopes and aspirations and their opposite potentials in reality or fantasy that the depressive complex arises.

It is now recognized that the helpless anxiety of the patient with a major depression is of a different kind from that which occurs in the anxiety disorders. The repetitive and constant demands for support and the clinging have suggested that the anxiety of involutional melancholia and other psychotic depressions is less differentiated and more primitive than that observed in the healthy or psychoneurotic individual. It suggests the dependent infant; thus depressive behavior and its associated affects are considered by many psychoanalysts as regressive to behaviors characteristic of the infantile state. They take place in those who have failed to develop the necessary defenses against the affective states induced in early life through the stress of partial separations or limited experiences of affect deprivations and in those who through the persistence of the infantile defenses of denial, projection, or obsessive reaction formations have warded off the socially maturing capacities of response to loss.

These views are in contrast to the early psychodynamic explanations of the depressive states, wherein the central pathology was considered to be a sense of pathological guilt, derived from a distorted development of the superego through excessive internalization of critical and punishing attitudes. Thus, fearful of expressing rage toward loved objects, the depressed patient turned this emotion upon himself as a means of atoning for his guilt.

It would seem that in patients with major depression, one may discern in varying degrees in different patients both the regressive move to states of anxious infantile dependency and its associated physiological concomitants in sleep and eating disturbances, as well as evidence in the thought disturbances of internally directed rage expressed in the atoning delusions of guilt, shame, and self-punishment.

The bipolar state has certain psychopathology in common with other depressive reactions. There is the depressive complex itself, composed of various combinations and intensities of the affects of sadness, anxiety, rage, shame, and guilt. To these affects are added a profound sense of helplessness associated with a diminished self-esteem and the general inhibition of personality functioning.

According to modern psychoanalytic theory, there evolves during the early developmental period a basic mood of elation as the infant commences to practice and involve himself in the various human and psychomotor activities characteristic of that period. Thus the elation of the manic may be regarded as an affective regression taken in reaction-formation to the loss that has precipitated the psychotic reaction. As an affective regression and a reaction-formation, it should be recognized as differing from the basic mood of the infant and as pathological.

The capacity for warm and responsive social relationships that exists in the manic-depressive perhaps rests on a satisfying early infantile mothering contact during which the child commences to evolve the early nucleus of personal identity and sense of security. Yet for reasons poorly understood, the capacity to accept separation, with the limitations it imposes thereby and the attendant affective arousal, is not fully mastered. Those who respond with pathologic depression maintain a presenting and often compulsive fixation on the significant and wished-for object relationship or its symbolic representation in some goal that will assure love, respect, or power and provide escape from isolation, humiliation, and a sense of weakness. Thus, even in the depressive, there is a persistent denial of loss, and projection may be utilized as a defense to escape the realization of personal limitations imposed as the consequence of the loss, whether actual or fantasied. Such denial is conspicuously present in the manic and hypomanic states.

The dynamics of all the aggressive states, including the bipolar, revolve around the personality. Malfunctioning of the attempts to control aggression in the form of hostility has been a central explanation of these conditions for numerous decades. Thus, depression and its obverse may be postulated as caused by the inhibition of regressive responses to frustrations. This fundamental hypothesis has received considerable support from the recent epidemiological reviews of Kendell. He points out that studies of cultural variations of the incidence of depression in relation to the attitudes of the differing societies toward tolerating aggressive behavior, as well as the information from examination of the occurrence of depression in various age groups, the sexes, the social class, and ethnic minorities, would seem to support the hypothesis.

These psychodynamic theories, relevant to all depressive reactions, add to the earlier theories, which emphasized that depression should be regarded as a result of anxiety in a person who experienced severe loss, real or fantasied, at an early stage of development. The loss is perceived as rejection, which precipitates anger. Since the feeling of anger cannot be tolerated, it is repressed and turned inward on the self. Although these feelings of anger and hostility are repressed, they cause the individual to feel guilty, unworthy, and depressed.

There remains to be formulated a psychodynamic explanation for the recurrent episodes of affective disturbance and the cyclic shifts from depression to mania which give this psychosis its nominal designation.

It well may be that the shift from depression to elation takes place in association with vacillating processes of identification with parental figures. During depression the patient identifies with the maternal figure in a submissive role. At the initiation of the period of elation, he denies the submissive, maternal identification and acts out an intense, acquisitive, sadistic drive with fantasies of strength in which he becomes emancipated, elated, and overaggressive, in imitation of the paternal figure, with whom he is now identified. With the failure of his aggressiveness to accomplish the fantasied aim of revenge, the patient again has to renounce the paternal identification and to deny his aggressiveness, and so he becomes depressed and helpless. These aggressive and assured personality characteristics of the manic are not necessarily related to the parental sex, as in some instances the mother is identified as the striving person who provided the child the ideal of strength in times of family stress. As one woman manic patient expressed it,

"When our family and its fortune were falling apart during the depression, my mother laughed and made light of it—my father withdrew. I have always admired her and sought to be like her when things were bad."

The manic's behavior is essentially a defense of massive denial against the underlying depression. Although he may appear confident and occupy the role of a leader, the manic is basically overdependent. Although he appears outgoing and friendly, he is self-centered, actively controlling, and manipulating. These attitudes are based on an emotional need for a dependency relationship. When his demands are frustrated, hostility is generated, which must be repressed so that it does not further imperil the dependency relationship. The imperfectly repressed hostility may, in turn, produce depression.

To interpret his behavior in a psychosocial or transactional sense, the manic would seem to perceive threat and danger in accepting his dependent needs to be cared for by others. To maintain his self-esteem and to defend himself, to maintain his key perception of power and strength, he appears to use those transactions which control others to whom he looks for emotional support. He must appear extraordinarily independent, needing no one; he thus develops a repertoire of behaviors in which he suggests that he will care for others—his grandiose schemes. He repeatedly attempts to test, manipulate, and overcommit others so that he in-

volves others around him to care for him. As Janowsky and his colleagues interpret this behavior, he obtains the needed dependent role while challenging external constraints under the guise of an aggressive pseudoindependence.

Sometimes an important source of conflict for the manic-depressive patient seems to be strong hostility connected with envy, which is repressed and avoided. He is often the best-endowed member of the family and has been expected to provide the prestige for the group. This position places great responsibility on him, yet exposes him to the envy of his siblings, or even to envious competition with his parents. The future bipolar patient has grown sensitive to envy and competition, and to counteract the potentiality of suffering the hostility of envy due to his own abilities, he has unconsciously developed the pattern of disparaging himself in order to conceal his full capacity.

Feelings of guilt and reflected depression springing from them arise in various ways. Some repressed wish, for example, is occasionally granted by accident, such as by the death of a parent whose continued existence had prevented the fulfillment of a greatly desired wish. In such a case, a depression may sometimes result because of the feeling of guilt that follows the gratification of the consciously repudiated desire. In general, as already indicated, feelings of guilt giving rise to depression arise not so much from what one has done as from what one has unconsciously wished to do. Depression represents a penance for repressed hatred, aggressiveness, and other repudiated tendencies and impulses that have given rise to feelings of guilt. Guilt, too, may be expressed in terms of self-punishment.

There is much to suggest that hostility is the denominator common to both manic and depressive phases. Because of his rigid superego, the depressed patient does not permit himself to live out his hostile, aggressive tendencies against others, but redirects them

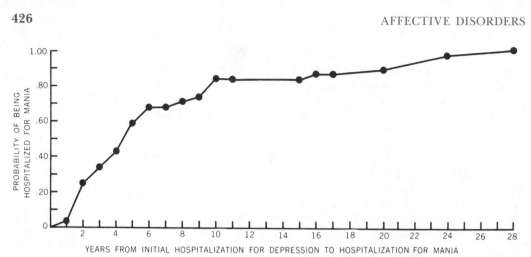

Figure 19-1   Probability of being hospitalized for mania for 32 patients who were initially hospitalized for depression and followed over time. (From Dunner, D. L., Fleiss, J. L., and Fieve, R. R.: The course of development of mania in patients with recurrent depressions. Am. J. Psychiatry, *133*:907, 1976.)

against himself or expresses them in projected form. The influence of pathological feelings of guilt and of hostile impulses turned against the self may therefore find expression in suicide. The fact that feelings of guilt and self-accusation may be assuaged by attaching to others the motives that created them contributes to the paranoid features that may accompany depression. If the release of repressed impulses is particularly threatening, the depression may be accompanied by manifest expressions of anxiety.

The easiest and most natural way by which an ill-defined sense of guilt or of remorse may be rationalized and thereby find the required sense of reality in the consciousness of the patient is by linking it up with some trifling indiscretion of earlier life. This indiscretion is usually found to have been really trivial, although it never enjoyed full approval of the individual's socially determined conscience. All the energy of the affect, tied up with the repudiated wishes and material that have been repressed, usually with difficulty and for a long period, is displaced to this lapse and its ideational representation. This idea receives the displaced affect that both rationalizes and renders concrete the vague feeling of guilt arising from disowned strivings and desires.

Differential Diagnosis

It has become important, in view of the regimen to be described, to differentiate between unipolar and bipolar depressive attacks. In the latter, lithium is the agent most likely to be effective over time; with unipolar attacks, the tendency will be to treat with the tricyclic compounds, monoamine oxidase inhibitors, and as a last resort electroshock therapy in the most severe cases. As Dunner, Fleiss, and Fieve have analyzed the course and development of mania in patients with recurrent depression, almost 80 per cent of bipolar patients initially are hospitalized for mania. On the other hand, the chance of a patient with recurrent major depression to be later diagnosed as bipolar approximates only 5 per cent.

Of those patients who were initially hospitalized for depression and were later rediagnosed as manic-depressive (bipolar), the probability of being hospitalized for mania within ten years of the initial hospitalization was 0.84 per cent (Fig. 19–1). Figure 19–2 demonstrates the probability of being hospitalized for mania of those initially hospitalized for depression, followed through other depressive episodes. The vast majority of the manic-depressives will have a manic attack early in the

Figure 19–2 Probability of being hospitalized for mania for 32 patients who were initially hospitalized for depression and followed through other depressive episodes. (From Dunner, D. L., Fleiss, J. L., and Fieve, R. R.: The course of development of mania in patients with recurrent depressions. Am. J. Psychiatry, *133*:907, 1976.)

course of the illness. A study of the histories of the remainder indicates that most of this group will experience a manic attack within ten years of onset.

That the validity of the diagnosis of bipolar disorder is very high indeed has been demonstrated in a prospective study with a five-year follow-up by George Murphy and his colleagues. By specifying explicit diagnostic criteria for this condition, they found that interrater diagnostic reliability equals 100 per cent initially for the presence or absence of affective disorder and that at the end of the follow-up agreement exceeded 80 per cent. (See Table 19–4.) Nevertheless, certain clinical ex-

pressions of the bipolar illness or one of its phases often present the clinician with difficulty in assuring the correctness of his or her diagnostic impression. Since the modern therapies are so effective and the appropriate diagnosis must be discovered early in order to bring the quickest relief to the sufferer, the clinical conditions most commonly confused are discussed here.

The most difficult problem in the differential diagnosis of bipolar disorder is its distinction from *schizophrenia*. In the typical case, this presents no difficulty, but in many cases there is doubt as to how symptoms should be interpreted. In general, the disturbance

TABLE 19–4 Criteria Differentiating Bipolar and Unipolar Affective Psychoses

	BIPOLAR	UNIPOLAR
Family history	+	−
Age of onset	Younger	Older
Sex	Equal in both	Female, Male
Manic attacks	+	0
Manic response when administered tricyclic antidepressants or L-dopa	+	0
Therapeutic and preventive response with lithium	+	0
Urinary 17-OHCS	Decreased	0
Growth hormone	0	−
RBC Sodium	+	0
RBC COMT	0	Lower in female
Platelet MAO	−	0
Plasma tryptophan	?	−

+ = Increased; − = Diminished; 0 = None or normal.

in personality in bipolar disorders seems to be a quantitative one, a matter of "too much" or "too little," rather than a lack of organization of personality, as in schizophrenia. There is not, moreover, complete agreement among psychiatrists about how much temporary disorganization of the personality may be considered consistent with the diagnosis of bipolar disorder, or how much diagnostic weight should be assigned different symptoms. Behavior may be equally disturbed in the manic excitement of an affective psychosis and in the catatonic excitement of schizophrenia.

In approaching the problem of differentiation, it is necessary first to secure as full a knowledge as possible of the prepsychotic personality of the patient, to determine whether cyclothymic or schizoid characteristics have predominated, and whether energy has been directed into extroverted channels and marked by objectivity and realism, or whether it has been introverted and characterized by subjectivity.

In general, the interpersonal contact with the manic or depressive is more conventional and initially is perceived as a close one by the psychiatrist. With the schizophrenic, the interview is felt to be an uneasy one of distance, unfamiliarity, and suspicion. The presence of flight of ideas and of psychomotor activity in the early phases of a mental disorder may not constitute unequivocal diagnostic criteria, since both may exist in reactions that end in schizophrenia. In schizophrenia, there tend to be more incoherence and greater poverty of ideas. The excitement of the schizophrenic lacks the depth of emotional expression that is usually observed in the excitement of the manic-depressive, is less influenced by the reality of the environment, is more episodic and impulsive, and tends to be undirected, stereotyped, confined to a limited space, and determined more by hallucinations, delusions, and autistic processes. The more grotesque, and therefore the more primitive or highly

symbolized, the ideas, the more are they to be looked upon as schizophrenic.

The mood of the schizophrenic lacks both an infectious element and that component causing one to feel empathy with the patient, who, in general, is less accessible than the manic-depressive. The greater the harmony between mood, ideational content, and behavior, the more is a bipolar disorder suggested. The less the mental processes remain integrated, the more is schizophrenia denoted. Even though it may at first be temporary, with more disorganization of the personality—as shown by absence or inappropriateness of affect, hallucinations, soiling, and apparent noninterpretability of behavior—one expects an ultimate, and for the most part permanent, schizophrenic disorganization. The clinical picture of some young patients initially considered to be suffering from a manic phase of a bipolar disorder changes to one that is clearly schizophrenic in nature.

Many hypomanics in whom the emotional exaltation is replaced by anger, resentment, irritability, irascibility, litigious tendencies, and perhaps paranoid delusions were formerly diagnosed as having acute *paranoia*. Such hypomanics lack the solitary and asocial tendency usually exhibited by the true paranoid, who presents a more sustained, brooding, sensitive, suspicious pattern. Persons in whom these impure affects replace an exaltation were characterized by a tendency to defensive projections prior to their psychosis.

This well known clinical confusion has been reaffirmed by Abrams et al., who found that very few of a group of patients originally diagnosed as paranoid schizophrenics fitted that categorical diagnosis when he and his colleagues carefully analyzed diagnostic criteria for the several conditions. Those rediagnosed as manic tended to be older at admission, had a longer duration of illness, fewer Schneiderian first rank symptoms (FRS), and nonauditory hallucinations. Their family histories contained a greater loading for affective illness and alcoholism.

The sense of inadequacy, abnormal fatigability, depressive ideas, and apprehension that may accompany mild forms of the depressive or mixed types, particularly in the early stages, are often misinterpreted as symptoms of *neurasthenia,* of a *compulsion neurosis,* or of an *anxiety state.* An obsessional personality, as previously reported, is found frequently in the depressive states, whose personality type is not exclusive, and is found to be more significantly associated wtih lessened apathy and greater agitation. Obsessions per se in depression exclusive of personality type, according to Vaughan, are associated with rapid changes of mood, anxiety, agitation, overactivity, and little retardation.

In the bipolar disorders, sluggishness of thought and action is more common, patients are more reticent about their feelings, and they do not show the eagerness to interview the physician usually seen in the psychoneuroses. Also, the severe disturbance or inhibition of physiologic functions in areas of sleep, alimentation, and sexual functioning do not occur in these neuroses. Psychogenic causes and processes are usually more easily ascertained in psychoneuroses. Mild but often unrecognized forms of the depressive type are frequent, with the result that the number of bipolar patients in extrainstitutional life probably exceeds those under treatment in hospitals for mental disorders.

Masked depressions often present in the form of episodic alcoholism, drug addiction and drug abuse, or "acting-out" behavior, including antisocial behavior. The latter type of behavioral expression of depression is more common in the young.

In the depressive phase, there occurs the customary disturbance of the sleep pattern, with early morning awakening and the morning aggravation of de-

pressive affect, anorexia, weight loss, amenorrhea, and impotence. The physiological diminution of the rate of salivation and the low sedation threshold may be used as differential points.

In early *syphilitic meningoencephalitis,* the presenting symptoms may reflect previous personality trends and therefore suggest a manic-depressive psychosis. Neurological signs and serological tests will at once make a diagnosis possible.

Prognosis and Course

It has already been indicated that the prognosis for a single affective episode is usually to be regarded as good but that recurrences are not uncommon. That for the illness over time is also favorable, as several recent reports have confirmed. Only one fifth did not recover fully, and less than one tenth became chronically ill. Women did less well than men, both those with mania alone and those with the bipolar form.

Perhaps there has been too great a tendency to stress the frequency of recurrence. Of admissions to state hospitals because of bipolar disorders, 55 per cent are first admissions, about 25 per cent second admissions, and 9 per cent third; the remainder of the patients have had more than three admissions.

Another important feature of bipolar disorders is the fact that even repeated episodes usually leave the mind unchanged in its intellectual, affective, and conative aspects, and that a disorganization of the personality does not follow. Many highly productive and socially respected individuals have suffered this personality disorder. Much of Ruskin's best work was done during his hypomanic states. Occasionally, after a series of attacks, the patient shows impairment of initiative and of judgment and becomes less able to deal with everyday affairs of life.

The most frequent age for the first manic episode is between 20 and 25 years. The average age of onset for first depressive attacks is about 10 years later. The earlier the onset of either type, the worse the prognosis for the occurrence of further episodes. If the first attack is manic in type, it almost certainly will not be the only one; if it is of a depressed type, it may not be followed by a recurrence. Some recent studies give indication that the prognosis is worse when the precipitation of illness is related directly to an actual loss (exogenous cause) than when it is due to covert experiences or factors (endogenous). This information is contrary to previous viewpoints and differs from data on the outcome of schizophrenic psychoses.

The patient's prepsychotic personality traits influence the prognosis of both duration and outcome. If he has shown himself to be flexible, tolerant, conciliatory, without defensive or compensatory traits or other signs of a deep sense of insecurity, and has had varied and wholesome interests, the prognosis is more favorable than if his personality patterns have been of the opposite type. As age increases, there is some tendency for attacks to be depressive rather than manic, perhaps because of the changing outlook on life. (See discussion of etiological factors in involutional psychotic reactions.)

The duration of manic and depressive episodes is extremely variable. The average duration of untreated manic attacks may be estimated at six months and of depressive episodes at nine months. There is a tendency for depressions to increase in length with advancing age. Many depressions terminate with a brief hypomanic elation. The duration in individual cases may be either much shorter or much longer. One is never safe in predicting the probable duration of a given episode. Some patients may never have more than a single episode; in others a large part of the time may be occupied with recurring psychotic periods. The more frequent the attacks, the poorer the prognosis. The more chronic the illness, the less severe the symptoms.

Depression is much more likely to become chronic than is mania. Chronic mania is uncommon before the age of 40. The prognosis is considered less favorable in depressions manifesting a nihilistic hypochondriasis, particularly if accompanied by anxiety or when associated with paranoidal trends.

Treatment

Depending upon the severity of the depressive or manic reaction and its influence upon the patient's capacity to function in his accustomed vocational and social life, initial therapeutic judgments must be made about the wisdom of urging continuation of work or advising withdrawal, and whether to provide treatment at home or in a hospital environment.

DEPRESSION. The treatment of mild depressions may, in certain respects, constitute a greater problem than does the treatment of the deep depressions. The friends of the patient suffering from a mild episode of a bipolar disorder often refuse to believe that he or she is suffering from a major mental disorder or may have suicidal tendencies.

Today, the mildly depressed bipolar patients preferably should start on pharmacological treatment with an antidepressant agent, usually one of the tricyclic aminodibenzol derivatives, and lithium. For those patients with unipolar (major) depression, tricyclic compounds alone are effective in over 70 per cent. For unipolar patients who do not respond to tricyclics, monoamine oxidase inhibitors should be considered.

The use of tricyclic antidepressants, monoamine oxidase inhibitors, and lithium and the complications attending their administration are described more fully in Chapter 32.

With office or outpatient treatment, the patient should be seen on a schedule of fixed appointments at frequent intervals. A favorable response is seen usually in a lessening of self-deprecatory and accusatory statements and hypochondriacal complaints, improvement in the sleeping pattern, increased activity, and interest in socialization. Many patients with mild depression may continue their normal activities owing to treatment with the antidepressant pharmaceuticals.

In more severe cases, in which psychomotor retardation is of such a degree as to impair or make impossible the patient's usual vocational activities, the issue of hospitalization becomes immediately primary. Many families may be unwilling to accept the physician's opinion and advice to hospitalize; if there is little danger of suicide and the family is cooperative, treatment may be attempted at home. However, with the more severely ill, treatment at home is inadvisable unless skilled nursing services are available. An attempt on the part of the relatives to care for the patient is generally unwise, if for no other reason than that they usually either argue with him concerning his fears, constantly attempt to distract him, or urge the patient to rouse himself. With such patients, an organized program that fills the patient's day is desirable. This should be of a type which will not require spontaneity, close concentration, or strenuous activity. The program may include handicraft, walks, reading, games, social and recreational activities, and the encouragement of special aptitudes and interests. Although the patient should not be idle lest he become unduly preoccupied with his problems and with self-examination, it should be borne in mind that a depressed patient, prompted by his lifelong rigid requirements of self, may undertake too much and become more depressed when he finds he falls short of expected accomplishment. Many depressed patients complain of fatigue, but since this type of fatigue is really an expression of mood, it is not relieved by rest. One should remember that the depressed patient's tendency to hypochondriasis has at times led to unnecessary surgical operations. Unless carefully supervised, the depressed patient may not receive sufficient food.

In cases of severe depression, treatment in a hospital is wise. In nearly all cases resistant to pharmacotherapy, the use of electroshock therapy is accompanied by a gratifying improvement. Treatments are usually given three times a week. With many patients, 10 or 12 treatments are effective; others require 20. Approximately 90 per cent of the depressed patients recover with this form of treatment.

It is extremely important that the depressed patient receive a high caloric diet. Usually it is desirable that he receive milk or additional food between meals. Refusal of food should not be permitted for long. Sometimes after one feeding the patient will, with a little assistance, eat voluntarily.

Occasionally the hospital physician finds that for a considerable period before admission a patient has not been receiving sufficient food or water. His tongue is dry and leathery, his breath is foul, he appears dehydrated, and has a slight tendency to acidosis. In these patients, special effort must be made to have them receive an abundance of fluid. In depressive stupors, attention should be paid to the condition of the bladder and the bowels.

Among the early signs of recovery are a return of interest in eating, increase in weight, bowel function, and restful sleep. Interest in others, initiative, and self-confidence follow. As convalescence proceeds, there should be a gradually increasing participation in occupational and recreational activities. The patient should be relieved of the necessity for making decisions until he is well on the road to recovery. An early resumption of usual duties and responsibilities is to be discouraged. The question of when the convalescing depressed patient may be dismissed from the hospital is not always easy. The usual opinion is that he should remain in an institution with its simple routine until convalescence is well established. It must be remembered, too, that, because of the increased danger of suicide during convalescence, the patient may require closer supervision during that period than is possible at home. On the other hand, a return home before the depression is entirely cured may sometimes hasten the patient's recovery. He should not resume full duties for several weeks.

MANIA. The decision as to whether the mild forms of excitement or hypomania should be treated in a hospital is difficult. In the case of the hypomaniac, it is often evident to the psychiatrist that prudence requires more control of the patient's activities than is possible in the home. Since, however, there is nothing "unpsychological" in his behavior, the patient's relatives frequently fail either to accept the statement that his exuberance of spirits, pressure of activity, and volubility are evidence of mental disorder, or to appreciate the embarrassment to themselves and the aggravation of the psychosis that may result from the absence of restraining measures. For these reasons, they are frequently averse to the patient's admission to a mental hospital. They often believe that the only required treatment is a change of scenery or an urging of the patient to rouse himself.

The apparently inexhaustible energy of the hypomanic may suggest that an outlet for it should be provided. The physician should remember, however, that fatigue produces not tranquility but excitement. The usual desire for almost constant activity must therefore be curbed, although with the production of as little irritation as possible. The hypomanic patient must be protected from his tendency to enter into unwise business or financial schemes. Careful supervision of the patient who is not hospitalized may be necessary, as alcoholic abuse, ill judged spending, or, often, increase in sex drive may lead to regrettable indulgences. Frequently, the prepsychotic personality of the manic has been characterized by a sensitive pride. The physician will therefore carefully guard against the contradictions and arguments that the hypomanic's irritability, unrestrained speech, activity, and resentment at interference with his wishes are prone to provoke.

Pharmacological control of the manic overactive is best initiated with lithium and a neuroleptic, preferably haloperidol (see Chapter 32).

Cooper, Bergner, and Simpson have described a technique of determining the appropriate daily lithium administration to effect therapeutic response by administering a 600-mg. priming dose and measuring the serum lithium level in a sample collected 24 hours later. The recommended dosages on the basis of the 24-hour serum level after the single loading dose are shown in Table 19–5.

In his review of the use of maintenance therapy in the affective disorders, John Davis has marshaled impressive evidence that the continuance of lithium therapy effectively prevents recurrence of both mania and depression in the bipolar disease and depression in the unipolar disease. Lithium is the agent of choice in the bipolar disease. Maintenance therapy with the tricyclic compounds is also preventive of the recurrent attacks of unipolar depression. In the latter condition, the clinician would wish to determine whether preventive therapy with either of these agents should be undertaken, particularly if the intervals between the attacks are unusually long (several years or more).

Because of its high toxicity for kidney function, lithium is contraindicated when the function of this organ is impaired, and in heart disease, epilepsy, and elderly people. The most common minor toxic symptom is a fine tremor of the hands. (Propranolol may be administered an hour before a steady hand is required if the tremulousness affects the occupation of the patient.) The drug should be withdrawn if diarrhea or vomiting ensues or if tremulousness is very severe and associated with drowsiness, ataxia, or dizziness. Other symptoms of intoxication are thirst and a large output of urine. T wave changes in the electrocardiogram may occur.

Lowering of protein-bound iodine has been reported with long-term lithium maintenance therapy. If this treatment is instituted for preventive therapy, there is merit in assessing thyroid function periodically through palpation of the thyroid and determining of the T-3 and T-4 levels. Polyuric side effects may occur after a single lithium dose during chronic treatment. It has been determined that this diabetes insipidus–like condition is mediated by renal vasoconstricting–sensitive adenylcyclase.

Other complications are likely when patients are placed on diuretics or low salt diets, or in conditions that increase sodium loss, as when the patient is fed well or the temperature is high. A further discussion of lithium and its pharmacologic properties is given in Chapter 32.

Manic patients who respond poorly to lithium treatment are those in whom there existed continuing anxiety-provoking situations in their lives — particularly conflict. Those with paranoid symptoms do less well than those with principally grandiose symptoms. In reviewing the manic defense, Aranoff and Epstein suggest that in some poor responders a psychological shift occurs

that may affect metabolic processes adversely. Good response in an early phase of lithium treatment is not always correlated with similar response during prolonged treatment, in which adverse emotional reactions to interpersonal events may not be avoided.

PSYCHOTHERAPY. This form of treatment has been employed successfully in the treatment of the mild depressive and hypomanic states. It has been demonstrated that even with the effectiveness of the currently used tricyclic antidepressants and other agents, psychotherapy improves the social adaptation of depressed patients, as estimated by their work performance and their ability to communicate, reduce interpersonal tension, and avoid continuing rumination.

Efforts have been made in the past to treat bipolar patients by classic psychoanalytical techniques. It usually has been found that neither retarded nor hyperactive patients seem suited to the rigid routine of the customary psychoanalytical process. New efforts have made it evident, however, that modified, analytically oriented psychotherapy is possible for some patients and seems to be beneficial.

Experience indicates that it is not advisable for the psychotherapeutic interviews with the depressed patient to be held four or five times a week, as is fre-

TABLE 19–5   Lithium Dosages Required to Achieve a Serum Level of 0.6 to 1.2 mEq./liter*

24-HOUR SERUM LEVEL AFTER SINGLE LOADING DOSE	DOSAGE REQUIRED
Less than .05	1200 mg. three times a day
.05 .09	900 mg. three times a day
.10 .14	600 mg. three times a day
.15 .19	300 mg. four times a day
.20 .23	300 mg. three times a day
.24 .30	300 mg. twice a day
More than .30	300 mg. twice a day**

*The regimen selected minimizes fluctuation in the plasma level while maintaining a schedule the patient can adhere to. Variation in this regimen can be made at the choice of the clinician, but the total daily dose must remain the same. All "steady state" values are collected just before the next medication is to be taken.

**Use extreme caution.

(From Cooper, T. B., Bergner, P. E., and Simpson, G. M.: Am. J. Psychiatry, *130*:601–603, 1973.)

quently to be recommended in the case of the schizophrenic or often with the neurotic. Interviews, with their implied insistence that the patient be productive, if held more frequently than once or twice a week seem to cause him to exaggerate his shame and guilt. Because of the high personal standards that the depressive requires of himself, and because of his feelings of impotence and incapacity, therapy may be very difficult if the psychiatrist urges productiveness. Because of his feelings of guilt and shame, the patient is unable to express his underlying sadness and rage. Since he is unable to meet the demands that he feels the therapist exerts, pressure by the latter arouses additional feelings of hatred and shame. The therapist does not, however, adopt the passive role usually followed in a more classic form of psychoanalysis.

Other features of this modified analytical psychotherapy are a constant reassurance of the patient that he will recover and a certain directness and openness in dealing with his problems. It will be remembered that in his depression the patient is over-reacting emotionally to an actual or fantasied loss of a love object. He is therefore seeking another, or substitute, love object. The process of calm reassurance fits this need symbolically. The patient has also a need to escape from the feelings of guilt caused by his repressed rage in his depression. If, therefore, he reports events that seem to be conducive to the production of rage and anger within himself but has not expressed their emotional connotation, the therapist may verbalize such feelings and state their relationship to other persons involved in the patient's situation. In this way the patient is relieved of the burden of stating his rage or anger and is not exposed to subsequent feelings of guilt for expressing the forbidden emotions. With this elastic, nondemanding, and at the same time, active, interpretive approach, it is at times possible to abort

depressions. Some therapists suggest it is better initially to have the depressed patient focus on an experience of recent loss rather than to encourage him to recall the earlier events and interpersonal experiences in his life that determined or reinforced his depressive symptomatology. Dream productions in the depressed patient are often helpful in breaking through to deep-seated associations that give a clear understanding of his basic longings and conflicts.

Psychotherapy with the hypomanic or manic is difficult. Since such a patient usually identifies with a covertly aggressive, sadistic, and successful member of the family, the therapist must constantly guard against the provocation of rejecting a patient whose behavior seems designed for such a purpose, i.e., of embarrassing significant object relations. It is generally agreed that the conversion of manic or hypomanic symptoms to depressive ones is desirable. Sometimes this is effected simply by the therapist's indicating his doubts of the soundness of the patient's presumption that he has reason to behave as if he were successful or in control of the situation.

Psychotherapeutically, the aim of treatment of patients with bipolar disorder is to bring them to the point where they can consciously face periodic loneliness and separation without resorting to either submissive depression or revengeful overactivity.

PSYCHOSES OF THE INVOLUTIONAL PERIOD

The involutional psychoses tend to fall into two types. One is characterized largely by depression, the other by paranoid ideas. In spite of the feature of depression common to both bipolar and involutional reactions, special physiological and psychological factors in the involutional reaction are such that it is no longer considered to be a modified bipolar reaction occurring at a particular physiological epoch. Both conditions, as well as the neurotic depressions, are precipitated, as are healthy grief reactions, through the perception of a loss by the sufferer. That loss may be the death of or separation from some loved person or the disruption of an important bodily function, a desired social or economic status, or even a cherished ideal or hope for the future. Such a precipitating loss may be discovered in an actual event or apprehended in fantasy. While often obscure on casual examination, the existence of the precipitant in some interpersonal incident or its apprehension in fantasy may be discovered on closer and more penetrating study.

Loss as it pertains to those with involutional psychotic reactions is discussed later in this chapter in the section entitled Predisposing Factors. Its general and psychodynamic consequences are subjects of comment in both this and succeeding chapters concerned with varieties of depressive reactions.

MAJOR DEPRESSION DURING THE INVOLUTIONAL PERIOD

The incidence of the depressive type of involutional psychosis is two to three times greater in women than in men. In diagnosis of first hospital admissions for mental diseases, it is exceeded in frequency only by schizophrenia, senile dementia, and syndromes associated with cerebral arteriosclerosis.

Age Factors

Although subject to considerable individual variation in the age of incidence, the involutional psychoses occur most frequently in women during their late 40s and in men during their late 50s. It will be noted that this is the period when the endocrine and reproductive glands begin to suffer a decrease in functional activity—the age generally known as the involutional period. As the activity of these glands declines, there are extensive changes in the metabolic and vegetative activities of the body. With the cessation of ovarian activity there may be a change in functioning of other parts of the endocrine system, involving an increased irritability of the sympathetic nervous system. Just what part these changes in essential physiological functions play in the genesis of the psychosis is uncertain, but there is much to suggest that they are not so important per se as are their psychological implications. The threat to the personality through the loss of prized biological functions and the imminence of the aging process, with all it connotes, may be more disturbing to the personality than endocrinological changes. The period is one of psychophysiological stress, in which increasing threats to an insecure personality are likely to elicit anxiety, depression, and paranoid reactions or all of these; a period that threatens the security that has been established at a time when the individual can least afford to lose it. It is a period that, in women, has often been anticipated with exaggerated fear.

Prepsychotic Personality

In a significant number of cases of the involutional depressive reaction, there is found a certain general type of personality makeup and of habits of life. Usually the patient was an anxious child with a background of early fundamental insecurity. A review of the patient's previous personality and temperament often shows that he or she has been a compulsive, inhibited type of individual with a tendency to be quiet, unobtrusive, serious, chronically worrisome, intolerant, reticent, sensitive, scrupulously honest, frugal, and penurious. Usually, the patient has been of exacting and inflexible standards, lacking in humor, overconscientious, and given to self-punishment. Such persons have been mild, submissive, and sensitive to the moods and feelings of others. They have never been boastful but have depreciated their own worth, which often has actually been high. Frequently they have been exploited by the selfish. The prepsychotic personality has been marked by a rigidity that represented a neurotic defense, and the patient has been perfectionistic, prudish, and prone to feelings of guilt. The personality has been superego dominated. Many involutional patients have been self-effacing and self-sacrificing and have had an exaggerated need for, and dependency upon, the approval of others.

Often the patient's sex life has been suppressed or unsatisfactory. Her interests have been narrow and her habits stereotyped; she has cared little for recreation, has not sought pleasure, and has had but few close friends. Frequently, the patient has been a loyal subordinate, meticulous as to detail, rather than an aggressive, confident leader. Some have been fidgety, fretful, apprehensive persons. Others have been characterized by caution or indecision.

Undoubtedly, involutional depression evolves out of a masked neurosis of earlier life. In some instances, hostile and aggressive impulses have been repressed with difficulty. The prepsychotic personality of the involutional depressive type has been developed as a reaction-formation against aggression.

Predisposing Factors

The age at which the psychosis develops is one at which adjustments to new situations and circumstances are no longer easily made. Perhaps life has not brought either the success or satisfaction that hope had cherished. At this period there is a more or less conscious recognition that early dreams and desires cannot now be fulfilled, that the zenith of life has been passed, and that ambition and life's forces are waning. The fact that opportunity no longer exists for repairing old errors or achieving new success creates a sense of frustration and increases the feeling of insecurity. In women, loneliness or fear of a loss of physical attractiveness may be a contributing factor. The high value placed upon youth, beauty, and sex in our culture contributes to the drastic reorientation that must be made. The patient may feel that she is no longer attractive. At this period of life, some women have a deeply seated resentment, which may be expressed in depression and self-hate.

A rebellion against aging may also tend to promote depression. The transition to another stage of life with its new and difficult problems, both psychological and biological, is not easy. Regrets and a sense of failure contribute to the prevailing mood. Perhaps friends are beginning to die, or children to whom the patient has devoted her life are leaving home and becoming preoccupied with their own lives and families. The patient may feel that she is no longer needed. In some cases, aged parents who formerly represented security, but are now dependent on the patient, constitute a problem.

The realization by the woman that her most highly prized biological possession, that of childbearing, perhaps long frustrated, is now a lost capacity, is for the patient more than the loss of one of the most fundamental of functions—it is a symbol that both the sources and ends of energy have failed. Sometimes sexual desires, which have previously been suppressed, are perturbingly aroused. Previous reaction-formations prove inadequate, and acquired compensations and other protective mechanisms begin to fail.

As the flush of maturity fades, thoughts of death are suggested and contribute to the anxiety so common in the disorder. With the decrease of physical strength, unconscious forces and old conflicts become relatively stronger and return to threaten and torment. This threat to the ego is ceaseless, and since the source of the danger is hidden and within, any escape from it is impossible. As a result, the apprehension, tension, and unrest of anxiety are intensified. In a certain number of cases, retirement from business means the renunciation of long-cherished interests and a withdrawal of psychic energy. Sometimes a real economic stress or the possibility of becoming dependent upon someone is added to other problems. It is not surprising, therefore, that in the event of some disturbing experience, such as the breaking up of the home or other threatening change in the life situation, the loss of position, or the death of one upon whom dependence was felt, the psychosis, with its pathological depression, apprehension, ideas of death, and nihilistic and hypochondriacal delusions, is precipitated.

Symptoms

As with all the affective disorders, the major component in the disturbance is the development of an unpleasant affective state. This state is compounded of a number of subjective components, of which grief and sadness represent only a part. Those others are varying degrees and combinations of intense anxiety, shame, and guilt. To these affects are added, as major components of the state, ego attitudes of profound helplessness and diminution of self-esteem, with severe inhibitions of previous personality functioning.

The manifest symptoms of the psychosis are often preceded by a period of several weeks or a few months during which the patient exhibits hypochondriacal trends, becomes irritable, peevish, pessimistic, suffers from insomnia, is perhaps suspicious, shows a disinclination for effort, and may be given to spells of weeping. She is unable to concentrate and shows doubt and indecision. Frequently there are a narrowing of interests and a shrinking from the environment. The patient complains of distressing sensations in the head, eats poorly, loses weight, worries about health or finance, and becomes apprehensive and restless. In a more or less typical case, the most conspicuous symptoms are profound depression, anxiety, agitation, hypochondriasis, and guilty delusions of sin, unworthiness, disease, and impending death.

The patient's appearance becomes one of extreme misery. The fear, apprehension, and agitation increase; the patient wrings her hands, paces back and forth, weeps, may beat her head against the wall, picks at her face, bites her nails, and tears at her handkerchief or clothing. She moans, and in a whining voice constantly repeats, "Why did I do it?" "Oh, God, what will become of me?" or some other stereotyped expression indicating hopelessness and affective distress. The patient may constantly besiege doctors and nurses with inquiries, complaints, or requests for reassurance, literally clinging to them and reiterating the demand that they help her or that they not abandon her.

Some patients present a morose depression or a depressive hostility. Misinterpretations and delusions are almost constantly present. Feelings of guilt explain in part both the great emotional depression and many of the delusions. Trifling indiscretions of youth or unformulated sins become the "unpardonable sin." The patient holds herself responsible for the fate of others. She has infected, disgraced, or harmed her family. She is about to be horribly butchered, a fate that she says she deserves, but awaits with intense fear and with pleas for mercy—indicating her ambivalent desire both for death and for life.

The delusion that she is about to be destroyed may be the patient's rationalization of her sense that life forces are declining. Inner distresses and dissatisfactions are rationalized as physical disease and thus produce the hypochondriasis so frequently observed. In this way the patient comes to believe that her intestines are obstructed, that she has no stomach, or that her brain is "dried up." Hallucinations, although less frequent than illusions, may occur. She hears preparations for her torture. Consciousness remains clear, and the patient is oriented, although in some cases the subjective absorption of attention is so great that she may appear to be confused and not thoroughly in touch with her environment.

Some patients are perplexed and bewildered. Depersonalization with feelings of unreality may exist. Food is often refused, sometimes because of a desire for death; at other times this occurs when, because of self-accusatory ideas, the patient believes she does not deserve food; again refusal may be caused by a belief that the food is poisoned, or by nihilistic ideas that she has no stomach or intestines. There is no other mental disorder in which suicidal attempts are so common. There is great danger that previous unsuccessful suicidal attempts will be repeated.

Although the patient never has a discriminating insight, she nevertheless usually realizes that matters are not as usual with her mentally. Early in the disorder the poorly understood sense of apprehension and the affective distress are so great, and are recognized as constituting such a contrast to her previous feeling-state, that the patient often expresses the fear she is going to lose her mind. She remains, nevertheless, thoroughly convinced as to the correctness of the idea she expresses.

Most patients lose weight and in severe cases become seriously dehydrated. The hands are usually cold and cyanotic. The pulse is rapid and the respirations are shallow. The bowels are constipated and the urine scanty.

Another group of middle-aged patients are less disturbed yet appear dismal and hopeless and suffer as well from a loss of self-esteem. Behaviorally, they appear withdrawn and apathetic and are isolated in social groups, owing to their attendant retardation in speech and thought. Such patients, too, may suffer delusions reflecting their sense of guilt and shame. But the clinging helplessness, agitation, hypochondriacal complaining, and somatic symptoms of insomnia, anorexia, and constipation are absent or much less conspicuous than in the most seriously disturbed group. Premorbid adaptation has usually been that of a well-adapted compulsive personality with the depressive state coming on as the result of physical illness and aging.

The following summary illustrates many of the common features of involutional melancholia.

E. M., a single woman in her early 50s, was admitted to a hospital following a suicide attempt. She was described as having been a shy, sensitive, and affectionate child. Although in early life she attended dances, she was never known to have had any male friends. She always said she wished to "live alone and not be bothered by a man's company." After coming to America from Ireland at age 23, she secured employment as a domestic. She apparently was well regarded by her employers, to whom she became quite attached and with whom she usually remained for many years of continuous service. She was described as always using all her spare time in "doing little things about the house, darning stockings, cleaning something, and doing ironing." She was conscientious, likeable, ambitious, and affectionate, but stubborn and difficult to convince. She was carefully observant of what she considered to be her religious duties and attended church regularly.

On arrival at the hospital, her facies denoted fear and apprehension. Although agitated, she supplied the usual admission data, and when asked if she was married, she at first replied in the affirmative, but a moment later stated that she was not married. Shortly afterward, when seen in the ward, she repeatedly inquired if the place was a jail. Upon being asked the reason for such a question, she replied, "Because jail is the safest place. I hope I won't be killed." She became increasingly anxious, agitated, and apprehensive, and on the day following her admission, she attempted to thrust her head through a closed window. Whenever a physician entered the ward, she approached him and with but little variation constantly repeated: "I am afraid, Doctor. Oh, my God! I am afraid of those men upstairs!" (There were no men in that section of the building.) "Look at those big snakes! Look at those big dogs!"

The patient had always lived frugally and had methodically deposited her savings in a bank, where she had accumulated several thousand dollars. She maintained, however, that her money was all lost and that she was destitute. Several days after her admission the patient was brought before the staff for diagnosis. At that time she showed the same anxious depression and agitation that had characterized her entire hospital residence. Soon after entering the staff room, she asked whether the door leading to an anteroom where patients of both sexes were waiting was locked. When asked the reason for the question, she replied, "I am afraid of the men."

Many of the factors that resulted in this woman's psychosis are comparatively simple and evident. The rigid environment in which she had been reared discouraged a normal interest in those of the opposite sex. That she had repressed any instinctive interest in men was betrayed by her statement that she did not want to be "bothered by a man's company." She became a faithful, conscientious servant, scrupulous as to detail but with an increasing limitation of external interests. Matters continued in this simple but hardly satisfying manner until physical capacity began to decline. The fact that life had not brought all that was desired became more or less vaguely realized; she was also aware that strength was waning and that whatever life had not already brought could never be attained. As physical energy declined with the involutional changes, the repression of material that had formerly been maintained, although with difficulty, began to fail. With their repression weakened, instinctive tendencies that had always been scrupulously denied any conscious recognition began to threaten from within.

With no escape possible, anxiety, depression, fear, and apprehension followed. This fear was projected as one of men, since it was the patient's repressed interest in them which she feared. This sense of danger was rationalized as one of threat to life, while affective and subjective material came to possess the vividness the patient had always associated with sensory experiences, with the result that she heard voices saying she was to be killed. Doubtless the patient's anxiety and depression represented much more than a weakening in the repression of instinctive tendencies of a psychosexual nature; the approach of an age when physical vigor and means of livelihood were declining, a sense of isolation, and vague feelings of disappointment and failure and perhaps of guilt all contributed to a sense of insecurity that added to the affective tension and apprehension.

Prognosis

Before the introduction of electric shock treatment, about 40 per cent of the patients with involutional melancholia recovered. Convalescence, however, was slow, and those who recovered were frequently ill for two or three years. With the use of electric shock, more than 50 per cent of the involutional melancholia patients showed prompt recovery. Now more than ninety per cent of patients are restored to health as the antidepressant pharmaceuticals have come into use. The more closely the general manifestations of the reaction approach those usually seen in the depressive phase of bipolar disorders, the better the prognosis. The prognosis is worse to the greater degree of deterioration of personal habits, grotesque delusions or hypochondriacal ideas, hallucinations, marked poverty of thought, and tendency to aversion, depersonalization, or rut-formation with its meager affect reaction. Whining, surliness, and seclusiveness are not favorable symptoms. The more narrow and rigid the prepsychotic personality, the poorer the prognosis.

Diagnosis

Psychiatric disorders that may present features requiring a consideration of differential diagnosis from major depression in the involutional period are bipolar disorders, cerebral arteriosclerosis, and anxiety disorders occurring in the psychoneuroses.

In bipolar disorders, the question of major depression in the involutional period need not be considered unless the age of the patient is compatible with the latter diagnosis. In that case, there is usually a history of previous attacks either of excitement or of depression. Frequently, the bipolar patient has been of a cyclothymic temperament, whereas the involutional depressive has a compulsive type of personality. In the depression of a purely affective psychosis, there is typically a retardation in the flow of thought and in activity. The presence of agitation, hypochondriacal and nihilistic ideas, peevishness, and hallucinations points toward an involutional depressive reaction. In this, fear, apprehension, and ideas of impending destruction are more marked. Stereotypes of behavior or speech and admixtures of other schizophrenic symptoms are more consistent with major depression in the involutional period.

Occasionally the *arteriosclerotic* patient is apprehensive and agitated, but he lacks profound and sustained fear. If the involvement is principally in the smaller vessels, the headaches and unpleasant cephalic sensations may suggest the hypochondriacal ideas of major depression in the involutional period, but the easy mental fatigability, occurrence of confused periods, slight delay in comprehension, a lessening of initiative rather than a preoccupation, and a slight memory loss should indicate the organic source of the mental disorder.

Among the psychoneuroses, the anxiety and depressive reactions must be differentiated occasionally from the involutional psychotic reactions. While a sustained apprehensiveness associated with phobias occurs with the anxiety neuroses and may be confused with the agitation and the obsessive delusional state in the involutional condition, the episodic attacks of acute anxiety with hyperventilation and its physiological concomitants of breathlessness, palpitation, sweating, and paresthesias characteristic of the former condition are not seen in the psychotic state. The patient with an anxiety neurosis contacts others easily and is voluble and capable of speaking at length of his or her life problems. There is no psychomotor retardation nor does the patient suffer from the somatic symptoms of insomnia, anorexia, or constipation.

The history of depressive affect immediately reactive to an evident loss, without significant impairment of capacity for interpersonal transactions, motor retardation, anorexia, or disturbance of libido, but with some degree of intermittent insomnia, distinguishes the neurotic depressive. The latter may also manifest acute anxiety attacks with hyperventilation. In these conditions there is no general inhibition of personality functioning.

Treatment

The patient suffering from a major depression in the involutional period should usually be cared for in a hospital, particularly since there is no other type of mental disorder in which so large a percentage of patients attempt suicide. The general lines of treatment are the same as those employed in the treatment of other major depressions, but severe untreated cases require particular stress on improving the physical state of the patient, which frequently becomes weakened and impaired. On arrival at the hospital, many patients are badly dehydrated and nearly always undernourished. There must be assurance, therefore, that the patient receives an abundance of liquid and food. Because of fear and apprehension, the purpose of any procedure or change from routine should be carefully explained to these patients. If treatment with the antidepressant pharmaceuticals fails to effect change within a month, recourse should be made to electroshock. The technique of its application is discussed in Chapter 33. The patient should usually receive from 12 to 20 treatments. If the patient is greatly agitated, chlorpromazine may be used for its tranquilizing effect.

PARANOID DISORDERS IN THE INVOLUTIONAL PERIOD

A certain number of persons develop a paranoid disorder during the involutional period. Although never previously psychotic, nearly all such patients are found to have been persons whose prepsychotic personality was characterized by projective defensive patterns. Usually it will be found that she has been critical and inclined to blame others for her failures and has seen slights where none were intended. By her associates she was probably regarded as obstinate in opinion, jealous, unforgiving, secretive, unhappy, dissatisfied, given to nursing of grievances, resentful, and suspicious. These defensive character traits prove sufficient support for the personality until the involutional period when, with the added physiological and psychological burdens previously mentioned, they are no longer adequate, and resort is made to the more extreme defensive and compensatory measures provided by the paranoid psychosis with its delusions and misinterpretations. The delusions usually revolve around ideas of persecution and are well organized, but they lack the fantastic content observed in schizophrenia. Many patients show much bitterness and hostility. The prognosis is less favorable than in melancholia. Electroshock treatment is of limited benefit. The aggressive and disturbed patient may be helped by chlorpromazine.

The following case illustrates many of the features often seen in paranoid involutional psychosis.

A. S. was admitted to the hospital at the age of 59. The patient was born in Latvia. Little is known concerning her childhood experiences and the emotional climate of the home. She came to the United States at the age of 19 to marry a man who had preceded her to this country. She and her husband returned to Latvia, where the husband took over his father's farm and attained considerable success and status. At this point the farm buildings were destroyed by fire, and the patient was so seriously burned that she required hospital care for three months. They returned to the United States and the husband established an upholstering business in which the patient assisted until this business failed. The husband then began to drink, and he committed suicide by hanging, a casualty discovered by the patient.

When she was approximately 54 years of age, the patient began to complain that people were talking about her, that her son-in-law was maritally unfaithful, that nearly all persons, especially the clergy of a different religious faith, were sexually immoral. She expressed a fear that she would be "signed away for experimental purposes." She stated that a physician who had treated her at the menopause had given her cancer. Finally, after having complained to the police on several occasions that her food was being drugged and that a "society of science" was plotting against her, she was committed.

Following the patient's admission to the hospital, her daughter, in describing her mother's personality pattern, reported that she had always been a meticulous, hard-working person who was critical, suspicious, stubborn, uncompromising, and domineering. The daughter described her mother as an immaculate housekeeper who also did "beautiful sewing."

On arrival at the hospital, her sensorium was clear, and she was fully oriented. She was suspicious, and when her abdominal reflexes were tested, she asked if the physician was going to operate on her. At times she became quite agitated and hostile and insisted that she be permitted to leave. Someone, she said, was trying to secure possession of her home and to kill her; she must therefore appeal to the police to help her. She complained that the nurses were trying to compel her to perform unpleasant tasks because they were members of a religious organization that was persecuting her.

Because of an electrocardiogram suggestive of coronary involvement and myocardial damage, it was decided not to give the patient electroshock treatment. After seven months of hospital residence, the patient became much less tense, was pleasant and cooperative, and was regarded as one of the most faithful and capable workers in the hospital cafeteria. Within a year after her admission, she was given freedom of the hospital grounds and was free to spend weekends with friends. Unless questioned, she expressed no delusional ideas. Upon inquiry, however, it was found that there had been no fundamental change in her paranoid ideation. Fifteen months after her admission the patient was permitted to leave the hospital. A year later her employer wrote: "Mrs. S. is cheerful and pleasant and I am very satisfied with her work."

MAJOR DEPRESSIVE EPISODE WITH PSYCHOTIC FEATURES

Such depressions arise when the patient has been confronted with a personal situation of great stress. Environmental factors and personal experiences have been cruelly frustrating, have aroused intense feelings of guilt or remorse, or have painfully wounded pride. In these disorders, the reaction to the current situation is a definitely pathological depression, at times associated with gross misinterpretation of reality in the form of delusions, frequently but not always somatic; suicidal ruminations or attempts; intense feelings of guilt; and retardation of thought and of psychomotor activity.

In four-fifths of the life histories of bipolar patients, definite disturbing events are discoverable, which may be assumed to precipitate the emotional disturbance through psychodynamic force activated in the personality. This, in turn, mediates the related psychophysiological disturbances through aroused mechanisms within the central nervous system. In middle or late life one finds, in addition to loss of significant personal relationships, the threats to social, economic, and physical security as precipitants to the recurrent episodes of the illness.

BIBLIOGRAPHY

General

Kraepelin, E.: Manic-depressive Insanity and Paranoia. Translated by E. Barclay. Edinburgh, E. and S. Livingstone, Ltd., 1921.

Prevalence

Adelstein, A. M., Downham, D. Y., Stein, Z., and Susser, M. W.: The epidemiology of mental illness in an English city. Social Psychiatry, 3:47–59, 1968.

Genetics

Allen, M. G., Cohen, S., Pollin, W., and Greenspan, S. I.: Affective illness in veteran twins: A diagnostic review. Am. J. Psychiatry, 131(11):1234–1239, 1974.
Fieve, R. R., Mendlewicz, J., and Fleiss, J. L., Manic-depressive illness: Linkage with Xg blood group. Am. J. Psychiat., 130:1355–1362, 1973.
Gershon, E. S., Dunner, D. L., and Goodwin, F. K.: Toward a biology of affective disorders. Arch. Gen. Psychiatry, 25:1–15, 1971.
Gershon, E. S., and Jonas, W. Z., Erythrocyte-soluble catechol-O-methyltransferase activity in primary affective disorder. Arch. Gen. Psychiatry, 32:1351–1356, 1975.

Marten, S. A., Cadoret, R. J., and Winokur, G.: Unipolar depression—a family study. Biol. Psychiatry, 4:205–213, 1972.
Schless, A. P., Frazer, A., Mendels, J., et al.: Genetic determinant of lithium ion metabolism. II. An in vivo study of lithium ion distribution across erythrocyte membranes. Arch. Gen. Psychiatry, 32:337–340, 1975.

Pathophysiology

Baer, L., Platman, S. R., and Fieve, R. R.: The role of electrolytes in affective disorders. Arch Gen. Psychiatry, 22:108–113, 1970.
Brandrup, E.: A controlled investigation of plasma lipids in manic depressives. Br. J. Psychiatry, 113:987–992, 1967.
Bunney, W. E., Murphy, D. L., and Goodwin, F. K.: The "switch process" in manic-depressive illness. Arch. Gen. Psychiatry, 27:295–309, 312–317, 1972.
Coppen, A., Eccleston, E. G., and Peet, M.: Total and free tryptophan concentration in the plasma of depressive patients. Lancet, 2:60–63, 1974.
Hartmann, E.: Longitudinal studies of sleep and dream patterns in manic-depressive patients. Arch. Gen. Psychiatry, 19:311–329, 1968.
Haure, P., Chernik, D., Hawkins, D., and Mendels, J.: Sleep of depressed patients in remission. Arch. Gen. Psychiatry, 31:386–391, 1974.
Hofer, M. A., Wolff, C. T., Friedman, S. B., and Mason, W.: A psychoendocrine study of bereavement. Part II, Observations on the process of mourning in relation to adrenocortical function. Psychosom. Med., 34:492–504, 1972.
Iskander, T. N., and Kaebling, R., Catecholamines; a dream-sleep model and depression. Am. J. Psychiatry, 127:83–90, 1970.
Maas, J. W.: Biogenic amines and depression. Arch. Gen. Psychiatry, 32:1357–1365, 1975.
Mendels, J., Stern, S., and Frazer, A.: Biochemistry of depression. Dis. Nerv. Syst., 37:5, 1976.
Sachar, E. J., Frantz, A. G., Altman, N., and Sassin, M.: Growth hormone and prolactin in unipolar and bipolar depressed patients: Responses to hypoglycemia and l-dopa. Am. J. Psychiatry, 130:1362–1367, 1973.
Schildkraut, J. J.: The catecholamine hypothesis of affective disorders: A review of supporting evidence. Am. J. Psychiatry, 22:507–522, 1965.
Shagass, C., Naiman, J., and Mihalik, J.: An objective test which differentiates between neurotic and psychotic depression. Arch. Neurol. Psychiatry, 75:461–471, 1956.
Shagass, C., and Schwartz, M.: Cerebral cortical reactivity in psychotic depressions. Arch. Gen. Psychiatry, 6:235–242, 1962.

Psychopathology

Arieti, S., and Bemporad, J.: Severe and Mild Depression. New York, Basic Books, 1978.

Baker, M., Dorzab, J., Winokur, G., and Cadoret, R.: Depressive disease: The effect of the postpartum state. Biol. Psychiatry., 3:357–365, 1971.

Carlson, G. A., and Goodwin, F. K.: The stages of mania. Arch. Gen. Psychiatry, 28:221–228, 1973.

Dunner, D. L., Fleiss, J. L., and Fieve, R. R.: The course of development of mania in patients with recurrent depression. Am. J. Psychiatry, 133:905–908, 1976.

Kramer, M., Baldridge, B. A., Whitman, R. W., Ornstein, P. H., and Smith, P. C.: An exploration of the manifest dream in schizophrenic and depressed patients. Dis. Nerv. Syst., 30:126–130, 1969.

Miller, J. B.: Dreams during varying stages of depression. Arch. Gen. Psychiatry, 20:560–565, 1969.

Reich, L. H., Davies, R. K., and Himmelhoch, J. M.: Excessive alcohol use in manic-depressive illness. Am. J. Psychiatry, 131:83–86, 1974.

Vaughan, M.: The relationships between obsessional personality, obsesssions in depression, and symptoms of depression. Br. J. Psychiatry, 129:36–39, 1976.

Psychodynamics

Birthnell, J.: Depression in relation to early and recent parent death. Br. J. Psychiatry, 116:299–306, 1970.

Gibson, R. W., Cohen, M. B., and Cohen, R. A.: On the dynamics of the manic-depressive personality. Am. J. Psychiatry, 115:1101–1107, 1959.

Janowsky, D. J., Leff, M., and Epstein, R. S.: Playing the manic game. Arch. Gen. Psychiatry, 22:252–261, 1970.

Kendell, R. E.: Relationship between aggression and depression. Arch. Gen. Psychiatry, 22:308–318, 1970.

Lewin, B. D.: The Psychoanalyses of Elation. New York, W. W. Norton & Company, 1950.

Ping-Nie-Pao: Elation, hypomania and mania. J. Am. Psychoanal. Assoc., 19:787–798, 1971.

Spiegel, R.: Communications with depressive patients. Contemp. Psychoanal., 2:30–35, 1965.

Zetzel, E. R.: The predisposition to depression. Can. Psychiatr. Assoc. J., 11(Suppl.):236–249, 1966.

Diagnosis

Abrams, R., Taylor, M. A., and Gaztanaga, P.: Manic-depressive illness and paranoid schizophrenia. Arch. Gen. Psychiatry, 31:640–642, 1974.

Murphy, G. E., Woodruff, R. A., Jr., Herjanic, M., and Fischer, J. R.: Validity of the diagnosis of primary affective disorder. Arch. Gen. Psychiatry, 30:751–756, 1974.

Treatment

Aranoff, M. S., and Epstein, R. S.: Factors associated with poor response to lithium carbonate: A clinical study. Am. J. Psychiatry, 127:472–480, 1970.

Bratfos, O., and Havy, J. O.: The course of manic-depressive illness. Acta Psychiatr. Scand., 44:89–112, 1968.

Cooper, T. B., Bergner, P. E., and Simpson, G. M.: The 24-hour serum lithium level as a prognosticator of dosage requirements. Am. J. Psychiatry, 130:601–603, 1973.

Davis, J. M.: Overview: Maintenance therapy in psychiatry. II. Affective disorders. Am. J. Psychiatry, 133:1–13, 1976.

Glassman, A. H.: The clinical pharmacology of imipramine. Arch. Gen. Psychiatry, 28:649, 1973.

Murphy, D. L., and Beigel, A.: Depression, elation, and lithium carbonate responses to manic patients. Arch. Gen. Psychiatry, 31:643–648, 1974.

Shobe, F. O., and Brion, P.: Long-term prognosis in manic-depressive illness. Arch. Gen. Psychiatry, 24:334–337, 1971.

20

PARANOID PSYCHOSES

"Often suspecting of others comes of secretly condemning ourselves."

Sir Philip Sidney

DANIEL PAUL SCHREBER, DR. JUR.
The autobiographical account of his paranoid disturbances was analyzed by Sigmund Freud to formulate Freud's psychodynamic explanation of this condition. (From the book jacket of Niederland, W. G.: The Schreber Case. New York, Quadrangle Books, 1974.)

PARANOID REACTIONS (PARANOIA AND PARANOID CONDITIONS)

Paranoia is a chronic mental disorder of insidious development, characterized by persistent, unalterable, systematized, logically reasoned delusions. General demeanor, talk, and emotional and behavioral reactions remain unaltered except as they are influenced by delusional beliefs, which become the uppermost and guiding theme of the patient's life and may therefore seriously impair discretion and judgment. The term was first used in 1863 by Kahlbaum to designate various persecutory and grandiose states.

Etiology

There is convincing evidence that the causes of paranoia and paranoid conditions are psychological. Among these psychological causes may be ambitious but frustrated strivings; a need for defense of the personality against undesirable tendencies and repudiated impulses; feelings of shame, or other anxiety-producing factors; a continued failure to achieve overvalued goals; or a need for enhancing prestige or self-esteem. Specific traumatic life experiences may serve as contributory factors. In a significant number of cases it will be found that the paranoiac comes from a family that has been severely authoritarian, demanding, harsh, and cruel. Frequently a parent, usually of the same sex, has been a hostile, controlling person who, through accusations, produces fear, anxiety, feelings of inadequacy, and a self-image of the "bad" child, which, however, he or she does not accept. In many, perhaps in most, cases there has been an early overidentification with the parent of the opposite sex. As a result of the emotional experiences and frustrations, patterns of hatred and aggression are frequently established; these, however, the child must endeavor to repress because of fear of the parent.

As is frequently observed, parents whose personalities were warped through distorting attitudes and relationships with their parents may affectively distort those of their own children. Often the child has been involved in, observed, or come to knowledge of parental or family transgressions that, if revealed, would have seriously damaging social consequences for him or the significant person. On occasions the parent or other person may deny the transgression and threaten the child, insisting that he hold the secret. Thus the use of denial and rationalization is enhanced by the child. Simultaneously the child must repress his own rage toward the parental figure with whom he is involved. In other instances, fantasies of parental or family transgressions function in the same manner. The nature of the behavior then may lead the child or young adult to withdraw from social contacts and come to feel rejected. This may stimulate resentment and contribute a paranoid element to the developing personality that may finally culminate in the paranoid psychosis. Sometimes self-pity or sibling rivalry seems to facilitate the establishment of paranoid tendencies.

Another train of events has been suggested by Artiss as a means of development of the paranoid personality. When high expectations for outstanding achievement are fostered by the parent, the doubtful child may develop secret longings and also subterfuges to attain the desired goals. When these secretly elaborated fantasies, resorted to as a means of maintaining respect within the family group, are frustrated, there follow a sudden and terrifying anxiety and depression, compensated for by the erection of the defensive internalization and projections so characteristic of the paranoiac.

Even as a child, the future paranoid individual usually shows troublesome trends that make it difficult for him to participate in congenial play with other children for more than brief periods. He is often a lonely, unhappy, brooding, insecure child, lacking friends with whom he can share confidences and exchange perspectives. Frequently, he is suspicious, stubborn, secretive, obstinate, and resentful of discipline. When crossed, he is apt to be sullen, morose, peevish, and irritable. As adult life is approached, the early personality characteristics become accentuated. The future patient becomes increasingly sensitive about the attitude and behavior of others, "builds mountains out of molehills," and may believe that others wish to do him injury. He is lacking in a sense of humor and impresses others as egotistic, sarcastic, derogatory, querulous, embittered, and resentful. Usually the paranoid person has always been demanding, inflexible, biased, mistrustful, impatient, and often defiant of conventions. Characteristically, he has been argumentative, uncompromising, and aggressive. Interpersonal relationships are difficult. He approaches others with a "chip-on-the-shoulder" attitude. The drive for achievement may be intense and may impel him to seek goals that are beyond his capacity. Intolerant of criticism and unable to accept suggestions, he readily criticizes and belittles others. Meticulous and precise, he is in some respects highly efficient but is jealous and unadaptable. He needs to demonstrate his superiority. If in a position of authority, he may be a petty tyrant.

At times one meets persons handicapped by such *paranoid personality* characteristics which, however, never develop further. In other people these characteristics become gradually and insidiously intensified until the patient is clearly psychotic. In the same problems and factors are found the sources of both the paranoid personality and the paranoid psychosis. The latter represents a progressive, developing continuance of the former. In some instances, repressed homosexual impulses seem to be the source of the psychopathology.

The mental mechanisms and reactions observed in paranoia are exaggerations of ones noted constantly among persons who are not thought of as psychotic. In everyday life, fear and insecurity are expressed in such disguises as pettiness, oversensitiveness, irascibility, never-ending bickering, overcompensation, seclusiveness, selfishness, or cynicism. Even caution may develop into suspiciousness. Many people are at times inclined to feel slighted, to think that their merits are unrecognized, to blame their environment for what are really dissatisfactions with self, or perhaps in part to fulfill their wishes in fantasy. Daily we meet those who are unable to recognize and admit their faults and defects. Real or imagined injuries to pride tend to result in feelings of resentment and bitterness of variable duration. The well-defined paranoid personality often seems to display a remarkable genius for detecting in the ordinary run-of-life situations just those tiny slights, inadvertencies, or trifling disparagements that others overlook but that he builds up into crucial issues, not altogether imaginary but vastly overemphasized.

One must agree with the English psychiatrist Crichton-Miller: "For every fully developed case of paranoia in our mental hospitals there must be hundreds, if not thousands, who suffer from minor degrees of suspicion and mistrust; whose lives are blighted by this barrier to human harmony; and who poison the springs of social life for the community."

The paranoid personality may be overaggressive as he sees an aggressor in everyone around him. This makes him feel that his war against the world is waged in self-defense. A rebellious, superior attitude may serve to bolster self-esteem and prevent a realistic but intolerable self-evaluation. Thus the paranoid individual treats others as projections of certain of his own unconscious trends. As a result, his statements, manner, and behavior alienate friends and create enemies. The fact that he thereby incurs the hostility of others and is therefore often rejected and isolated adds more fuel to the psychopathogenic fire.

As we study the behavior of individuals and the methods by which they meet conflicts within and blows from without, we often find it difficult to say when the expressions of a paranoid personality become the symptoms of a paranoid psychosis. Anomalies of character become continuous with the psychosis, both, to a large degree, going back to the needs and problems of the personality and to the habitual techniques or patterns that the individual has adopted in attempting to meet such irregularities.

Formerly there was a tendency to subdivide the permanent paranoid reactions into definite disease entities. Kraepelin looked upon paranoia as a fixed type of disease resulting exclusively from internal causes and characterized by persistent, systematized delusions, the preservation of clear and orderly thinking and acting, and the absence of hallucinations. He recognized an entity intermediate between paranoia and paranoid schizophrenia that he called *paraphrenia,* differing principally from paranoia by the fact that the delusions lack paranoia's logical systematization. The delusions are more apt to be extravagant and, in addition, hallucinations are present at times. Not for many years, if at all, is there any deterioration of general interest or of personality.

Psychopathology

As noted, there is no clearly defined point at which the personality marked by the characteristics previously described should be called psychotic. The paranoid tendencies rarely become so extreme as to justify a diagnosis of paranoia before the age of 30. The disorder is more common in men. The presenting symptom of paranoia and of paranoid states is a rigid, persistent system of delusions. At times the patient's delusions may take their origin in some actual fact. On cross section, his behavior and thought content may be deceptive, and a severe disorder camouflaged by a seemingly normal surface. On longitudinal section, however, the paranoid theme is discovered. The content of paranoid ideas varies widely and is determined primarily by the particular psychological needs they are created to fulfill, and secondarily by the type of rationalization that will appeal to the ideas and beliefs current in the patient's environment.

The patient's own inclinations are mirrored in the particular motives and intentions attributed to others. His rationalizations are vigorously defended, and he exhibits a convincing earnestness in his efforts to win others to his delusional beliefs. The patient may rationalize so plausibly that his friends accept his allegation that specific individuals, rather than he, are responsible for his difficulties. His superior intellectual endowment may remain unimpaired. Some paranoiacs become aware that the credibility of their delusions is questioned and therefore attempt to hide them. The patient's judgment may be defective only in relation to his delusional system, which often develops slowly and ultimately becomes intricate and complex. The dominating ideas tend to be those of persecution, of expansive grandiosity, or of both themes.

As *persecutory* trends develop, the patient attributes hostile or aggressive motives to others, nurses his grievances, and becomes increasingly secretive. In the earlier period of his psychosis, he may be hypochondriacal and uneasy. He may become depressed, gloomy, spiteful, vindictive, and given to morose rumination. Frequently, he manifests a self-righteous resentment against others. Misunderstandings and misinterpretations develop into delusions of persecution.

The tendency of the paranoiac to seek ulterior motives of others or to misinterpret events is illustrated by the case of a woman who, soon after graduation from a law school, sued the school for damages. The faculty had awarded her the annual prize for the greatest improvement in scholastic work during the course. She alleged that the awarding of such a prize was for the purpose of representing her as having been more poorly fitted than her associates for the study of law. (Doubtless the same sense of insecurity that led to her psychosis determined also her choice of law as a profession.)

In an effort to control his hostile impulses in which the genesis of his paranoid reaction is often to be found, the patient projects them and experiences them as being directed against himself. Filled with hate, he feels and believes that he is the victim of persecutors, who, in fact, are but the objects upon whom he has projected his own hate.

The mood of many paranoiacs is one of sustained sullenness. Ideas of reference appear: there is a hidden meaning in what is taking place in his environment; cryptic significances are read into casual remarks and events; slights and indignities are imagined; far-reaching significance is attached to trivial details in the behavior of others. Vague feelings of fear tend to increase suspicion and the patient's malevolent trend of thought. Although in the case of the "normal" person incredulity, indignation, and anger often help to prevent the individual from becoming aware of qualities, strivings, and tendencies that offend self-esteem, these defensive reactions are used much more by the paranoid patient.

Delusional ideas extend: the patient believes that people spread lies about him; persons tamper with his mail; accusing remarks are overheard; hostility and jealousy are observed on every hand; business plans are thwarted; he is the victim of a conspiracy, and the agents of malevolent social organizations pursue him, persecutors who seek to conceal their identity by various disguises. He may become depressed and even suicidal because he feels overwhelmed by an environment with which he cannot cope.

In the persecutory as well as in other forms of paranoia, there is a central delusional theme that pervades the whole life of the patient, who is quite incapable of criticizing the pseudologic he employs in supporting this dominant idea. His premises are not scrutinized, and present events, regardless of their relevancy to the prevailing idea, are interpreted wholly with reference to it. Affect determines the patient's logic. Incidents of the past receive a new interpretation and are fitted into the framework of present persecution—a process known as retrospective falsification. As a result, the delusional system constantly extends, and the most commonplace incidents, because of their affective interpretation with reference to the prevailing idea, become events of the greatest importance. In all paranoid reactions, the patient, always confident that he is right, clings obstinately to his opinions, since his inner sense of insecurity cannot permit him to feel otherwise. He maintains his delusional misinterpretations, too, by continually overemphasizing the inferred or implied meaning and by discarding the obvious and real content of a statement or action.

A common form of paranoia is the *litigious* type. Although it will usually be found that this type of paranoiac individual was always stubborn and insistent upon his "rights," with many defensive mechanisms, the litigious activities frequently do not appear until after some legal experience that ended less satisfactorily than the patient desired. Because of his dissatisfaction, the patient initiates further but ill-advised legal action. He always fails to see that he has not proved his case. Every new litigation brings further controversies and new grievances for which the patient feels prompted to seek redress. His attempts to secure it, however, result in fresh feelings of injustice. Fundamentally, it is often not a question of law and justice, as the patient insists, but of attempts to put others in the wrong, to show that he was right, that he is superior, in order that thereby his sensitive insecurity may be strengthened and the weak points of his personality may be protected.

In the *exalted* type of paranoia, the ideas of grandeur may appear after a long preceding stage of feelings of persecution, or at times the grandiosity may be present practically from the beginning of the psychosis. Ideas of invention constitute a frequent form of grandiosity. Patients with such beliefs usually neglect their usual method of livelihood and devote their time to the drawing of plans and the construction of models. At times the patient claims that models are completed but that enemies prevent him from securing a patent; again, he is on the point of perfecting the machine. In either case, the patient frequently claims to utilize some force or to attain some objective contrary to the accepted laws of science. In this type of disorder, the patient may have a sense of mission and pursue his impracticable goal with more zeal than discretion. Others have expansive ideas of noble birth. Frequently the grandiose patient attempts to play the role that his ideas have assigned him. If, for example, he believes he is a religious leader, he may affect an air of humility —an air that often poorly disguises a repressed hatred.

The exalted beliefs in some paranoid states are of a religious nature. The patient is the chosen one of God, is Christ, prophesied the war, has supernatural powers. Some establish new religious sects and secure adherents; others proclaim themselves leaders of a new order but are so bizarre in belief and behavior that they fail to secure followers.

Occasionally paranoia assumes an *erotic* form. The patient believes that some woman of title or wealth whom he may have casually seen or met is in love with him. He writes her affectionate letters and perhaps poems. Her failure to reply to them is intended solely to test his love. Items in the newspapers, the flight of the birds, and various events are disguised recognitions of her presence and acknowledgments of her love. Such patients may become annoyingly persistent in their attentions and threatening in their manner. De Clérambault described a similar condition, now carried informally under his eponym, in which a woman holds the delusional belief that a man, usually well known due to his position as a prestigious actor, politician, or wealthy figure, is madly in love with her. Often the condition has a sudden onset. The patient's real relationship with the object of passion either was momentary or never existed in fact.

The paranoid psychoses have been studied in much more detail among men than among women. Modlin describes a group of premenopausal married women between 30 and 45 years of age who had established adequate sexual relations within marriage but became acutely psychotic with paranoid ideation. None had extramarital relations, and all had exhibited stability and considerable ego strength before the illness. Precipitating the illness in each instance was a change in the husband-wife relationship which led to a reduction in frequency of or cessation of sexual intercourse. In some instances other family members moved into the home; in others the husband became ill or overly preoccupied with the demands of his employment, with a consequent drop in the amount of attention and time formerly devoted to the relationship with the wife. In some illnesses the initial phase of the psychosis was marked by depression in which the patients feared they were losing their husbands. Suspicious attitudes and ideas of reference were followed by a florid paranoidal delusional system. In this series the illness had lasted, with remissions, from over one to seven years.

A particular form in which a delusion of infidelity is the predominantly psychopathologic element is sometimes referred to as the "Othello syndrome." In its pure form, it is generally categorized as a special variety of paranoia. Psychotic jealousy, as in this syndrome or other paranoid states, may lead to acts of violence against the spouse or lover who is the subject of the delusional system.

More recently, Freedman and his colleagues have suggested from their clinical studies that one may separate paranoid patients into two groups: those who are socially isolated, nonbelligerent, and with an undifferentiated cognitive function, the latter defined according to various responses to the Rorschach tests and human figure drawings; and those who are socially active, aggressive, and demonstrate in psychological test behavior a differentiated cognitive style. The two groups respond variously to treatment; those in the first are likely to remit, whereas those in the second are unlikely to do so.

Among common causes for the commitment of paranoid patients are homicidal or suicidal attempts, the writing of anonymous letters to persons in authority, litigation, or persistent statements that they are the victims of a conspiracy.

Psychodynamics

Although disparity between achievement and ambition, early experience heavily loaded with affect, vague or subconscious feelings of dissatisfaction or irritation with self, and injuries to self-evaluation, as well as various other needs for defense, may act as dynamic agents and lead or contribute to a fixed paranoid reaction type, there is much to suggest that repressed homosexual impulses may be a genetic factor. The persistence of homosexual impulses, unrecognized consciously, may doubtless be caused by more than one factor, but, characterized as the homosexual is by his mother imprint, there seems good reason to believe that if, at puberty, an inhibitive maternal overpossessiveness impedes the maturation of the psychosexual aspects of her son's personality, these may remain fixated and never attain a mature heterosexual development.

Contrary to the theory that repressed homosexual drives contribute to the genesis of paranoid delusions are the clinical observations that in many instances the paranoid symptomatology does not reflect a homosexual reference. Also, in some cases patients appear to accept an existing overt homosexuality without conflict. From the standpoint of psychoanalytic theory it is pointed out that manifest and latent homosexuality are dissimilar in that they occupy different levels in the psychic apparatus and operate independently. Thus, as Carr indicates, a patient may consciously accept and engage in homosexual practice but deny the unrecognized and unconscious murderous and sadistic homosexual fixations derived from his or her early infantile and childhood attachment to a punitive and aggressive parent. What is overlooked commonly in the paranoid homosexual fixation is the competitive and hostile aggressive component of the attachment, with overemphasis placed on the libidinous attachment to a member of the same sex.

According to Ovesey and many other recent theorists, another factor much underemphasized is the "power anxiety" of the paranoid, which essentially should be regarded as the primary motivating force in the development of his pathological defenses. Consciously and unconsciously perceiving himself as weak, defective, or inadequate, whether he evaluates his performance socially, vocationally, or sexually, he builds up a structure of projective defense – the paranoid system.

An elaboration, perhaps, of this point of view is Colby's shame-humiliation theory. To avoid the negative affect of humiliation-shame, those who become paranoid develop a series of strategies to avoid shame and assign blame to others for any failure or wrongdoing. Thus they escape initially a sense of self-inadequacy but often suffer from the retaliatory moves of others whom they blame.

Assuming that there is a relation between this fixation, or incomplete evolution of the personality, and homosexuality, how does the latter lead to paranoia? According to Freud, it is through the mechanism of projection by which the original but repressed and therefore consciously rejected affect is reversed and transferred to the homosexual object. Because it is consciously inadmissible, the patient's "I love him" is changed to "I do not love him; I hate him," which, to be acceptable, requires projection as "He hates me" and is elaborated into "I am persecuted by him."

An abnormally high percentage of paranoids do not marry, while many others are divorced. This is not only because of a basic homosexual orientation but also because of the fact that their chronic hostility and anger make them undesirable as partners. If the paranoiac does marry, the marital life is so full of discord that it frequently ends in divorce.

The "true" paranoiac is often a person of superior intellectual endowment, but one whose energy is so largely expended in repudiating desires that the paranoiac does not wish to recognize that social relations become disturbed, and constructive achievements are nil. The fact that life has failed to bring the success and satisfactions to which the native intelligence of the patient would ordinarily have entitled him undoubtedly tends to aggravate his defensive reactions. The more promptly and passively an individual gives up the struggle for self-esteem and for recognition, the more nearly will the reaction approach the schizophrenic, regardless of the native intelligence, while the more active and sustained the struggle, the more likely is the result to approach paranoia.

The following case presents many of the characteristic features of paranoia:

P. G. was committed to a hospital for mental diseases because of his peculiar religious ideas and rites, one of them being the practice of going about nude. The patient's parents were strict in their moral principles and rigid in discipline. All the paternal siblings were teachers except the patient's father, who was a farmer and who was always dissatisfied with his lot, often expressing the wish that he could "get away where he could read and study and reform the world." The patient had one sister, also a brother who was older and stronger and who used to "lord it over" the patient. His association with his sister was close, and shortly before leaving home as a young man he suggested to her that if she would not get married, he would not do so either, and they would live together.

As a child he was described as sensitive and fearing criticism. "Because he was not strong, he was somewhat of a sissy," the sister stated. At school he was a ready scholar and completed the equivalent of two years of high school work. If he received less than 90 in his grades, he felt disgraced. Prior to his marriage at age 26 he had paid little attention to persons of the opposite sex. At that age he married his landlady, a woman of 66, "as a humane act"; this was his characterization of the match when he entered the hospital. When questioned concerning his sex life, he stated that men had aroused him sexually more than women, for whom he had no sexual desire. He took part in homosexual practices on only a few occasions. When asked if he thought his religion had helped him in repressing his homosexual tendencies, he replied, "I do not think so, I know it." He acknowledged that he derived pleasure from exposing himself to other men, although he claimed that his practice of going about nude was a health measure permitted by his religion and not for the purpose of satisfying exhibitionistic impulses—doubtless a rationalization of socially prohibited inclinations. When questioned concerning his social life, he had, he said, "a distinct aversion to secret organizations"—perhaps an unconscious defense against his homosexual tendencies, since such organizations, made up as they usually are of individuals of one sex, serve to provide a sublimated and socialized outlet for homosexual trends, although the psychological basis of these bodies is also one of narcissism and compensation.

During his early adult life, the patient became interested in various unusual religious cults (probably an effort to obtain a feeling of security), although this striving did not result in such a serious disturbance in thought and behavior as to lead to his being considered psychotic until after he was 40 years of age. He described himself as suffering at about that period from "lack of initiative, inability to concentrate, general weakness, anxiety about the future, irritability, and hypopotency of the heart." Doubtless this represented a stage of subjective analysis often occurring in the disease. He addressed a prayer to the "Deity" asking for aid and threatening to commit suicide if it were not forthcoming. Almost immediately it was "revealed" to him, not through a voice or visible signs but "simply through thought process," that he was to establish a new religion to take the place of Christianity, one that would be more comforting and satisfactory. He called his new religion "Omnivitism" and spent day after day writing "a set of mottoes instead of commandments, a set of actions and ideals, prayers, verse, comment on principles, affirmations and denials, suggestions regarding services, and miscellaneous dissertations." When questioned about the specific teachings of his religion, little but vague generalities was secured. "It teaches," he said, "that all forms and phases of existence are essential factors of one all-sufficient existence that is called 'Omniad.'" He had tracts printed and distributed them widely, setting forth "the rule of Omnivitism, which is to teach according to his needs."

About this time he began to go to isolated spots and to walk about nude, explaining that he was taking "sun baths." Gradually he made fewer attempts to retire from sight when taking his "sun baths," particularly after he derived considerable enjoyment from the fact that he was seen by the occupants of two automobiles that passed while he was unclothed. Finally, after having been warned on repeated occasions by the local constable that he must not continue his exhibitionistic practices, the patient was committed to a hospital for mental disorders.

On arrival at the hospital, the patient was pleasant and smiling but obviously exalted, with an air of self-satisfaction and superiority. He was a small man of rather effeminate physique. His hair reached nearly to his shoulders, and his beard was long, his appearance strongly resembling the traditional picture of Christ. He accepted his detention philosophically, expressing the opinion that it was what one in his position must expect—a sort of martyrdom in a worthy cause. He had, he said, founded a religion "more up to date" than Christianity and one that would supplant the latter and dominate the world. Further, the patient was to have been President of the United States. This, he added, was in accordance with the prophecy of Sir William Hope made on the day of Washington's birth. On that day he foretold that a new nation would arise in America and the part that would be played by Washington, and that finally there would come a ruler whom he characterized as "six plus added six—great, good and wise," at the same time referring to "a star that on his way shall shine." This prophecy, the patient said, referred to him, since there were six letters in each of his names, while his sister was the star, since it was she who had invited him to come to their old home. In an old novel, too, the patient claimed he had found the following: "There will come in the western continent a greater man than this world has seen since this civilization began. It will not be through the ignorance of the people that this man will be carried into the White House. In some respects this man will be the intellectual and philosophical leader. He will be to the world what Mohammed was to Arabia, Columbus to the New World, Moses to the Jews, Plato to the Greeks, et cetera—yet he will be greater than all and more powerful for good." This, the patient said, referred to him.

On psychometric examination by the Stanford-Binet scale, the patient was found to have an I.Q. of 115. It is interesting to note that in ability to see logical relationships, language ability, and constructive visual imagery he attained an 18-year level, but on practical judgment in social situations he graded at a 9-year-and-1-month level. In describing his attitude toward the examination, the psychologist recorded that the patient seemed to enjoy the opportunity of demonstrating his intellectual endowment, that he frequently laughed in a superior manner, that he exhibited great precision of speech, and delighted in showing off his large and unusual vocabulary. On several occasions, in a tolerant and somewhat condescending manner, he criticized the examiner for her use of words.

The patient's paranoid system was associated with too great disorganization of personality and disturbance of reality evaluation to permit the diagnosis of paranoia, but may properly, we believe, be regarded as a paranoid state rather than paranoid schizophrenia. The patient was unable to secure a satisfying adjustment to a sense of biological and social inadequacy, to a fundamental homosexuality, and doubtless to other conflicts. However, instead of investing the external world with his own unrecognized but repudiated trends and feelings, he organized his emotional constellations into ideational systems that afforded a satisfying but unsocialized adjustment. The compensatory feelings of superiority developed to meet the subconscious feelings of inferiority and doubtless of guilt (arising from an imperfectly repressed homosexuality) were rationalized into grandiose delusions.

Other factors, too, presumably contributed to the life pattern of the patient's personality and his desire for high personal value. It may well have been that the dissatisfactions with self and the vaguely defined strivings owed their origin in part to absorption from the early family life, since we learned that his father was dissatisfied with his lot and wished to "study and reform the world." The fact that he was "lorded over" by a stronger brother presumably led to feelings of inadequacy and contributed to the psychological need for the artificially obtained feeling of security and self-esteem. To have been taught that school grades below an unreasonably high standard constituted a disgrace tended to lead the boy to form ambitions that, with his limitations of personality and opportunities for training, inevitably resulted in wounds to pride and vanity.

Among the traits of childhood were sensitiveness and fear of criticism. His slightness of physique called for compensation, and a certain degree of biological deviation and the failure to emancipate himself emotionally from his older sister, who perhaps served as a mother surrogate, served to fix the development of his personality at a homosexual level. His exhibitionistic practices are doubtless also to be explained on the basis of arrest in psychosexual evolution. His egotistic wishes prejudiced his judgment and led it to disregard the usual criteria of reality, thereby both preventing a correct perspective and destroying the capacity for self-criticism.

Shared Personality Disorder

Lasègue and Falret in 1877 gave the name *"folie à deux"* to this condition wherein a persecutory delusional system evolves in the close relationship of one person to another who has preexisting paranoid delusions. Identification is usually an important mechanism in its production.

Most frequently such a dual psychosis involves mother and daughter, two sisters, or husband and wife. The person suffering from the primary psychosis is usually the dominant individual, while the one who develops the secondary or induced psychosis is of a submissive and suggestible type, dependent upon and having a close emotional attachment to the infector. Misinterpretations, illusions, and ideas of persecution increasingly disturb the infector, who persuasively relates his or her convictions and psychotic experiences to the weaker person or infectee, who comes to accept and react to the systematized delusional ideas of the first.

It will often be found that both persons have been poorly adjusted individuals having a narrow range of interests, of the same general background and environment, and facing perhaps the same situation. The induced ideas must be acceptable and usually offer some satisfaction to the person infected. In nearly every instance the delusional ideas are dropped by the recipient if he is removed from association with the dominant person.

The usual setting of the disorder is one in which the two persons concerned live in comparative seclusion. It is more frequently found among women. This is probably because they tend to be more isolated within the domestic circle, and their outside interests and ambitions are more likely to be restricted or frustrated.

Diagnosis

At times psychiatric literature contains references to "acute paranoia." "Reactive paranoid psychosis" is a term also used. Although descriptively acute paranoia is a good term, it is somewhat misleading, since often it will be found that the episodes thus classified are fundamentally affective in nature, being hypomanic attacks of manic-depressive psychosis in which the usual emotional exaltation is replaced by irritability and anger. The patient is aggressive, haughty, hostile, and complaining. Psychodynamically, it is to be expected that projective paranoid states might be used to deny and deflect an underlying depression initiated by anxiety over a potential loss.

In paranoia there is a greater tendency to project and to rationalize one's affective state than in the usual manic episode. The true paranoiac is more restrained both in behavior and in speech, and his ideational content is characterized by a more sustained and dominant idea than is the more excited manic with his fleeting affective changes. As the affect subsides, the delusional ideas of the acute paranoid episode are dropped, but they are not corrected, and the manic patient remains without insight regarding the beliefs he formerly expressed with great conviction and feeling. (See Table 20–1.)

Concealed behind the symptoms of anxiety, erythrophobia sometimes, and a history of frequent spoiling of occupational success, there often exist the essential components of the paranoid. These patients, too, have overwhelming aspirations for success and desire for recognition, coupled with an intense but repressed capacity for guilt because of the association of success with aggression, symbolized as a murderous hostility. Among patients with this symptom complex and personality organization will be found some with a capacity for paranoid hallucinatory decompensation. Their discrimination from those with psychoneurotic personality is important before undertaking dynamic psychotherapy, as the course may be interrupted by sudden decompensation.

Often there is difficulty in deciding whether a person whose behavior is governed by, and indicates a thorough contact with, reality, who has suffered no dilapidation of affect or of personality, and who is not hallucinated, but who constantly employs projection and

TABLE 20–1   Diagnostic Criteria for Paranoid Disorder

A. Persistent persecutory delusions or delusional jealousy.
B. Emotion and behavior appropriate to the content of the delusional system.
C. Duration of illness of at least one week.
D. None of the symptoms of criterion A of Schizophrenia, such as bizarre delusions, incoherence, or marked loosening of associations.
E. No prominent hallucinations.
F. The full depressive or manic syndrome (criteria A and B of major depressive or manic episode) is either not present, developed after any psychotic symptoms, or was brief in duration relative to the duration of the psychotic symptoms.
G. Not due to an Organic Mental Disorder.

(From the Diagnostic and Statistical Manual of Mental Disorders, 3rd ed. Washington, D.C., American Psychiatric Association, 1980.)

other defensive measures, should be considered as suffering from paranoia or as a paranoid, but not psychotic, personality. In general, if the exaggerated reaction is continuous, if the beliefs through which it manifests itself cannot be corrected, if they disclose an inadequacy of logic, and particularly if they tend to spread and to reveal that the affective and conative forces are sustained and have great energy, then the reaction must be looked upon as psychotic. The psychiatrist will not forget that paranoid tendencies may be channeled and expressed in many eccentricities and fanatical ways.

West suggests that one must separate reactions of severe pathological jealousy from the group of chronic psychotic reactions. In discussing the "Othello syndrome," he emphasizes the fact that cultural factors, including racial prejudice, feed into and contribute to the development of such states.

Prognosis

It is doubtful whether a patient with traditional paranoia ever fully recovers. In those cases in the paranoid series that most nearly approach paranoid schizophrenia, a remission may rarely occur, but in these, also, the ultimate prognosis is poor. In true paranoia there is little or no general personality disorganization, and the patient's conduct usually remains within the bounds that society will tolerate. For this reason, a large proportion of such patients do not enter a hospital for mental disorders. In the community the individuals are often looked upon as "cranks," but, as they usually do not act without reflection, show a certain amount of self-control, and limit themselves to legal means of redress, they avoid commitment much more frequently than do those with paranoid conditions that approach the schizophrenic pole of the series. The latter are less sociable, less industrious, and less restrained by social custom and law.

An analysis of the causes of death in the psychoses shows that a larger percentage of paranoid patients than of any other group with biogenetic psychoses die of degenerative circulatory disease.

While clearly defined paranoid psychoses are uncommon, one may differentiate those in whom a paranoidal complex exists into acute or reactive forms, as well as a chronic from a schizophrenic paranoid. These differentiations may require long periods of observation to establish the appropriate classification with any certainty. Nevertheless, the differentiation does have prognostic import, as is well shown in Retterstol's personal long-term follow-up of a sizeable series of those so suffering and from a review of the literature.

Retterstol divided his series of 169 personally followed patients designated as reactive psychosis into three groups: cured with relapse, cured with subsequent relapse, and chronic. He relates his diagnosis of reactive paranoid psychoses to those that would now be classified in the *Diagnostic and Statistical Manual* as paranoid states, psychotic depressive reactions, and the schizo-affective psychoses. While the grouping is diverse, his long-term follow-up and method of study provide information on prognostic indicators related to later social adaptation and modification of psychopathology that deserve serious consideration. Related to favorable outcome in the reactive psychoses were married status, premorbid hypersensitivity (rather than schizoid), onset after age 30, identification of a precipitating event, associated depressive mood, ideas of reference, and good emotional contact while in hospital. Eighty per cent of the reactive group had a favorable course. Hallucinations, ideas of influence (rather than ideas of reference), and depersonalization were associated with an unfavorable long-term course.

Retterstol found that over two thirds of his reactive patients were supporting themselves. This social outcome was superior to that of his paranoid schizophrenics. Over time the ability to function outside hospital diminished so that almost two thirds required some form of care (brief or residential). Loose paranoid delusions vanished in 76 per cent of his cases and systematized delusions were reduced in 62 per cent. There were seven suicides.

Treatment

Unless his behavior is too disturbing socially, it is well for the patient with paranoia to remain in the community, since interference and restraint embitter him and lead to an extension of his delusional system and to a stimulation of his hatred. If the paranoiac is considered dangerous, commitment, of course, becomes imperative.

To determine when he has become dangerous is not always easy. A careful evaluation of the patient's history will usually indicate the extent to which delusions may be expected to control behavior. If delusions have exerted an important influence on behavior and if they are directed toward particular individuals, this estimate should be made. The willingness and the degree of objectivity with which the patient will discuss his delusions are important. The character and intensity of his emotional reaction will greatly aid in deciding the question of the hazard entailed in the patient's liberty; the greater the overt hostility, the more imperative is his removal from society. Many times the patient will discuss the extent to which he believes he is justified in protecting himself or his interests or in securing redress. An indication can thus be obtained about the probability of acts of violence.

Whether the patient is to be treated as an inpatient or outpatient, the therapist must keep clearly in mind certain expectations relative to the transference. The paranoid is generally suspicious and distrustful, considers himself unloved and incapable of giving affection, and has usually come to believe through long experience that what is conveyed by the spoken word does not reflect the actual intent of those with whom he has been closely related. He has a need to see himself as a center of interest and activity as a means to sustain a façade of importance that protects him from suffering hurt by his deep sense of personal inadequacy, shame, or humiliation.

Treatment, then, should initially be as permissive as possible. The physician should maintain an open, courteous, considerate attitude, coupled with scrupulous truthfulness and good faith. Recalling the essential pathology, attention should be paid to the patient's delusions, but no attempt should be made to criticize or convince the patient that he is in error as to his conclusions. Such efforts only produce a further lowering of self-esteem and arouse greater compensatory deficiencies or outright acts of destructive hatefulness. Nor should any efforts be made to convince him that he is among friends who are kindly disposed to him, or that he has a warm and attractive personality himself. All forms of ingratiation should be avoided, as they will be interpreted as evidence that the patient is again dealing with persons similar to those who he believes have betrayed him in the past. The physician's attitude to the delusions will not imply agreement, however. It will imply rather, "I can understand how you feel, but it does not seem so to me." The physician will make his role and his position clear and hold them firmly.

The patient's anxiety and tension should be relieved by the administration of a neuroleptic as described in Chapter 32. With these measures, many paranoid patients will, if allowed the opportunity, commence exploration of their problems in psychotherapy. Such a patient should be allowed to follow his own leads, and, when occasions arise, the physician may

offer tentative and alternative hypotheses about the determining factors that the patient provides to explain his delusional interpretations of his relations to others, his failures and successes. By such means, doubt may be created in the patient's concept of his relations with others. Later, more direct confrontations may be used, and realistic appraisal of his interpretations may be provided.

As for the homosexual trends, often these are regressive fantasies due to fear of rejection or lack of success in relating to the opposite sex. Sometimes they are representative of impotency, which is the outcome of the deep lack of security of the patient. Sexual fears will be dealt with, then, in terms of the patient's anxieties in relation to the opposite sex rather than by humiliating remarks or interpretations concerning homosexuality. The patient should be advised that from time to time he is likely to become suspicious or distrustful of the psychotherapist and also advised that he should speak of it when he has this experience so that the underlying reasons may be clarified.

This therapeutic approach, which consistently allows a deeper examination of reality without exposing the patient to shame and, at the same time, strengthens the patient's satisfaction in achievements within the limits of his capacities, has been of aid in bringing about satisfactory social adaptation.

As for the women described by Modlin who become paranoid when their sense of strength and power is undercut by the lessening sexual activity of their husbands, he recommends a treatment regimen of firm, authoritative control of the patient's behavior while in hospital, to cut through her tendency to misinterpret and react to the environment on the basis of her abnormal perceptions. He also emphasizes the usefulness of focusing on current realities and of avoiding expressive or supportive psychotherapeutic positions. Her delusional expressions should be accepted with little if any comment, except when she herself expresses some doubts as to her interpretations. At such times opportunity should be seized to provoke by questions further dubiousness of the abnormal ideation. The husband should be drawn into the treatment program, as well as any important family members.

BIBLIOGRAPHY

Artiss, K. L.: Paranoid thinking in everyday life. Arch. Gen. Psychiatry, *14*:89–93, 1966.

Carr, A. C.: Observations on paranoia and their relationship to the Schreiber case. Int. J. Psychoanal., *44*:195–200, 1963.

Colby, K. M.: Artificial Paranoia. New York, Pergamon Press, 1975.

Enoch, M. D., Trethowan, W. H., and Barker, J. C.: Some Uncommon Psychiatric Syndromes. Bristol, John Wright & Sons, Ltd., 1967.

Freedman, N., Cutler, R., Engelhardt, D. M., and Reuber, M.: On the modification of paranoid symptomatology. J. Nerve. Ment. Dis., *144*:29–36, 1967.

Freud, S.: Certain neurotic mechanisms in jealousy, paranoia and homosexuality. Int. J. Psychoanal., *4*:1–10, 1923.

Freud, S.: Psychoanalytic Notes upon an Autobiographical Account of a Case of Paranoia. *In* Collected Papers, Vol. 3. London, Hogarth, 1925.

May, R.: Paranoia and power anxiety. J. Per. Assess., *34*:412–418, 1970.

Michaud, R.: La folie à deux (ou folie communiqué). Lasèque, C., et Falret, J. Ann. Med. Psychol., *18*:321–355, 1877. English translation and bibliography, Amer. J. Psychiat. (Suppl.), *121*:1–23, 1964.

Modlin, H. C.: Psychodynamics and management of paranoid states in women. Arch. Gen. Psychiatry, *8*:263–268, 1963.

Novey, S.: The outpatient treatment of borderline paranoid states. Psychiatry, *23*:357–364, 1960.

Ovesey, L.: Fear of vocational success: a phobic extension of the paranoid reaction. Arch. Gen. Psychiatry, *7*:88–92, 1962.

Retterstol, N.: Prognosis in Paranoid Psychoses. Springfield, Ill., Charles C Thomas, 1971.

West, L. J.: The "Othello Syndrome." Contemp. Psychoanal., *4*:103–110, 1968.

Wolowitz, H. B., and Shorkey, C. T.: Power motivation in male paranoid children. Psychiatry, *32*:459–466, 1969.

21

OTHER PSYCHOTIC DISORDERS

THE NIGHTMARE
(By Fuseli, 1781; reproduced courtesy of the Detroit Institute of Arts, Detroit.)

Within the structure of the third edition of the American Psychiatric Association Diagnostic and Statistical Manual of Mental Disorders (DSM-III), a need occurred to recognize a range of psychotic manifestations excluded under the rigid and often arbitrary operational criteria established for the more frequently encountered psychotic disorders. These manifestations are categorized as schizophreniform disorder, brief reactive psychosis, and schizoaffective disorder. For others not easily diagnosed in any of the above categories, the clinician is advised to classify the patient as having atypical psychosis.

Schizophreniform Disorder

Since the diagnosis of schizophrenia under DSM-III is to be made only after identification of a six-month duration of symptoms, including those thought to be prodromal and residual as well as active, there is no question that the majority of the schizophreniform disorders eventually will be reclassified as schizophrenia. Since symptomatic expression of the two conditions is essentially similar and schizophrenia has been discussed at length in Chapter 18, a description of schizophreniform disorder here would be redundant. Reported within the category will be more cases with acute onset of gross disorganizations with confusions and more rapid disappearance of gross psychopathology and resumption of premorbid personality functioning. It is believed that among those in whom the schizophreniform diagnosis is retained, a prevalence of schizophrenia among family members no greater than that among the general population will be discovered.

At times a schizophreniform disorder is precipitated by ingestion of hallucinogenic drugs. Recently, Annitto and Layman have described its occurrence in athletes secondary to the use of anabolic steroids.

Brief Reactive Psychosis

In the DSM-III classification, this condition is discriminated from the schizophreniform. Onset follows an easily identified intensive and easily discovered psychosocial stress, and duration is less than two weeks. Many of those conditions heretofore diagnosed as hysterical psychoses or associated with psychotic-like symptoms in the acute posttraumatic state will be so classified. Such acute and transient psychotic episodes occur not only in those with histrionic personality but also in those with paranoid, narcissistic, schizotypal, and borderline personality disorders. It is usually encountered in late adolescence or early adult life. Hysterical psychoses have been diagnosed commonly but never directly recognized in various nomenclatures.

Usually the outbreak of this acute delusional-hallucinatory experience takes place dramatically after a period of mounting frustration in some important personal relationship. Often the precipitating event for the anxiety occurred in perception of a threat or loss of a significant relationship, a death, or some act of aggression. On analysis, the hallucinatory and delusionary experiences may be discovered as representing family themes, preoccupations, or persisting anxieties. They are, as Richman and White state, family syntonic. The condition resolves rapidly, particularly if the dynamic forces of the outbreak are brought into the open and the patient is led, through interpretation, to understand them. It is to be differentiated from acute schizophrenia; the personality of the hysterical psychotic is not schizoid, nor is the schizophrenic thought disorder evident.

The following case report has been provided through the courtesy of Doctor Hollander and Doctor Hirsch.

The patient, a 26-year-old married woman, was first admitted to the hospital at the age of 22, 12 days after giving birth to a child fathered by a man other than her husband. She was in the process of obtaining a divorce from her husband and planned to marry the father of her child. During the pregnancy she had been abandoned by her parents, who felt that she had disgraced them. She apparently did well until the time of delivery. Following her delivery, she began to feel extremely anxious. She did not know precisely how to care for her new baby; she received no support from her parents; and her paramour was becoming upset because of the total situation, but especially by her continual talking. He threatened to leave her. Her behavior became more hyperactive and disorganized. She began to spend much time reading the Bible. Feeling that she had no one to turn to, she decided to take her life two days prior to admission to the hospital. When she attempted to accomplish this with several pills, the result was only somnolence.

On admission, the patient appeared disheveled, motorically hyperactive, and agitated. She was very concerned that the relationship with the interviewer would be only temporary, and she expressed her desire for a continuing relationship. She was highly productive and spontaneous, but her stream of thought was difficult to follow since she would begin one subject and shift to another without completing the first. Despite its disorganization, her trend of thought seemed to deal with her effort to master the situation related to the birth of her child. She expressed the delusion that God was determining the course of events in her life and that she was able to transmit a kind of mystical energy from her eyes to the eyes of her sister.

The patient was placed on chlorpromazine and was given intensive supportive psychotherapy. She rapidly became calmer and was able to organize her thoughts and to gain some understanding of the problems that led to her hospitalization. Within ten days she had reconstituted and at the end of two weeks she was well enough to be discharged. Four months later, she married her former paramour. She described this marriage as "turbulent."

Four days prior to the patient's second hospitalization three years later, the couple had an argument during which the patient accused her husband of infidelity. He, in turn, assaulted her and banged her head against the floor. Later that night, the patient left the house and remained with friends for three days. She went to her parents' home one day prior to hospitalization. On the morning of admission, the patient was discovered by her mother lying limply in a partially filled bath tub, with her eyes closed and her face dry. On being "revived" (with artificial respiration), the patient announced that she had died from drowning but that God had made her invulnerable to further pain and even death, that she was now a form of God, and that while Jesus took care of men, she would take care of women. Once again, the patient reconstituted from her acute psychosis within ten days.

The patient's father, in his mid-fifties, had always insisted on high moral standards for his children. He stated that he and the patient were never very close. Her mother, aged 50 years, also had never had a close relationship with the patient. She had been permissive and had never discussed anything with her daughter. The patient's father indicated that there was always friction between his wife and daughter.

The patient had married for the first time at age 20, and separated from her husband after three weeks because of "incompatibility." She then worked for a time as a nightclub singer and travelled to New York with her agent. There she was picked up by a "bookie" who acted as her "sugar daddy," and the two lived together. During his absences the patient became acquainted with a musician. She invited him to her apartment and lived with him after the bookie threw her out. After returning to her home town, she became pregnant by the man who subsequently became her second husband.

Richman and White consider this psychosis occurs when, in the face of an affective crisis, repression fails. The patient then acts out a family fantasy. In all their cases, there was overwhelming anxiety related to death, aggression, and critical object loss. The majority of the patients were or had been suicidal.

TREATMENT. Treatment should be directed immediately to alleviation of the major affective arousal by prescription of neuroleptics as well as by psychotherapeutic and sociotherapeutic interventions to alleviate the psychosocial stress.

Schizoaffective Disorder

Less frequently seen are cases of mental disorder characterized by recurring episodes that continue to show admixtures of schizophrenic and affective symptoms. The mental content, for example, may be so reality-disregarding that it seems schizophrenic; the mood is one of pronounced elation or depression. Again, the affective features may stand out, but the patient's behavior may be so bizarre that it must be regarded as schizophrenic. In some instances, the prepsychotic personality may have been strongly schizoid or, on the other hand, outgoing and well socialized, yet the clinical features of the psychosis may be quite at variance or inconsistent with the early personality pattern. It is not uncommon to see depressions in schizoid individuals who, in addition to the depression, show a great deal of anxiety and many neurotic patterns.

Tsuang and others believe this condition is genetically heterogeneous with two subtypes: one a variant of affective disorders and the other of schizophrenia. Patients with this condition have a much better outlook than those with schizophrenia.

Atypical Psychosis

To be classified as such are patients with monosymptomatic delusions of bodily change without impairment of social functioning, transient psychosis with menstruation, postpartum conditions that do not classify easily in other categories, or those psychotic conditions in which information to establish a more precise diagnosis remains lacking or in which the behavioral expressions and symptoms remain confusing.

BIBLIOGRAPHY

Annitto, W. J., and Layman, W. A.: Anabolic steroids and acute schizophrenic episode. J. Clin. Psychiatry, *41*:143–144, 1980.

Hollander, M. H., and Hirsch, S. J.: Hysterical psychosis. Am. J. Psychiatry, *120*:1066–1074, 1964.

Kasanin, J.: The acute schizoaffective psychosis. Am. J. Psychiatry, *90*:97–127, 1932.

Richman, J., and White, H.: A family view of hysterical . psychosis. Am. J. Psychiatry, *127*:280–285, 1970.

Tsuang, M. T.: 'Schizoaffective disorder': Dead or alive? Arch. Gen. Psychiatry, *36*:633–634, 1979.

Tsuang, M. T.: Long-term outcome of major psychosis. Schizoaffective disorder compared with schizophrenia, affective disorders and a surgical control group. Arch. Gen. Psychiatry, *36*:1295–1301, 1979.

22

THE NEUROSES

"The fears we know are of not knowing."

W. H. Auden

Pierre M. F. Janet
(From Roback, A. A., and Kiernan, T.: Pictorial History of Psychology and Psychiatry. New York, Philosophical Library, 1969, p. 87.)

The neurotic personality disorders arise from an effort to deal with specific, private, internal psychological problems and stressful situations that the patient is unable to master without tension or disturbing psychological devices caused by the anxiety aroused. The affect of anxiety is the common dynamic source of the neuroses. The symptoms of these disorders consist either of a manifestation of anxiety as it is directly felt and expressed or of automatic efforts to control it by such defenses as repression, displacement, isolation, reaction formation, undoing, substitution, and conversion. Ordinarily repression, frequently aided by socially acceptable and useful reaction-formations, enables the individual to deal comfortably with feelings and situations that tend to create anxiety. In the neuroses, however, repression is never complete enough to prevent both the feeling and manifestation of anxiety and the formation of unconscious, repetitive techniques designed to control it. These feelings and manifestations of anxiety or the methods of adaptation (defenses) to it constitute the symptoms of the neuroses.

The methods of adaptation utilized by those with a neurosis, in addition to their repetitive and unchanging character, are considered to represent behavioral, affective, or psychological traits that proved satisfying at an earlier stage of development. In short, they represent either a regression to an earlier, more gratifying type of behavior, or a failure to develop beyond a fixation at a developmental level that proves inappropriate and inadequate in the face of the responsibilities of later life. Neurotic adaptations are never fully satisfying, since secondarily they lead to feelings of inadequacy, shame, and guilt. In the neuroses, therefore, the symptomatic clinical phenomena are usually not significant in and of themselves but merely indicate that anxiety-producing, meaningful situations are perturbing to the individual. Many times, the symptom may afford a clue to the nature of the underlying problem, but the understanding of a neurosis depends on a recognition of the unconscious, neurotic purpose it serves.

The form of the neurosis is determined largely by the type of defensive measure that the patient has learned for control of anxiety. Relatively few patients utilize a single defense. Many neurotics, therefore, show mixed features.

The patient does not recognize the relationship between emotional conflicts and conflictful situations and his or her disturbed personality functioning. For example, a person, without any apparent reason, may develop a panic-like reaction in a crowd or in an open place. Again, without any recognition of its face-saving function, the patient may develop an invalidism that provides escape from a difficult situation. Another patient may experience the persistent recurrence of an appalling or disgusting thought, or feel an overpowering urge for the repeated, ritual-like performance of some act that serves to ward off anxiety. Aggressive, hostile wishes may become so threatening that the patient has to employ some neurotic mechanism for handling them. These defenses are often so ego-hampering that they are burdensome. Many persons presenting a variety of symptoms are known to the laity by such terms as "nervous invalids." The term "nervous" is euphemistic and evasive, since there exists no known physiological disturbance of the nervous system.

Neuroses Versus Psychoses

Many criteria have been suggested to differentiate between psychoses and neuroses. Some designate the psychoses as "major reactions" and the neuroses as "minor reactions," the distinction being made on the extent of the involvement of the personality.

In general, the diagnosis of psychosis implies a greater severity of personality disturbance than occurs in neurosis. The neurotic's defenses against anxiety are largely substitutive or symbolic; the psychotic's defenses are more extreme, regressive, and disregardful of reality. In many instances, there is a difference in their outcome in regard to the integrity of the personality. In the psychoses, the distortion or disorganization of personality is often great, and its social functioning is greatly disturbed, whereas in the neuroses the personality usually remains socially organized. In the neuroses, inner experiences do not upset external behavior to the extent or in the abnormal manner that occurs in the psychoses. In the psychotic individual, the capacity for discriminating between subjective experiences and reality may be greatly impaired. In the neurotic individual, there is no grave interference with reality-testing; the ego remains sound. Any evasion of reality is partial and at comparatively little expense to the personality. As Freud put it: "Neurosis does not deny the existence of reality, it merely tries to ignore it; psychosis denies it and tries to substitute something else for it."

Psychotic patients create a new environment to which they impute the forces and properties of reality. They may distort or falsify reality in the form of delusions or hallucinations. The environment of neurotic patients remains unchanged, although certain elements may be invested with abnormal affective values. The thinking of the psychotic may be dereistic, a type of thinking not occurring in the neurotic. The content of thought in the neurotic may be temporarily restricted by overvalued ideas, yet true delusional formation does not occur. Associations are frequently disturbed in the psychotic but remain unimpaired in the neurotic. Desires and motives are often projected in the psychotic, but they are never so externalized in the neurotic, at least not to the extent of producing delusions. In the psychotic, repression fails to function effectively; the ego will tolerate repressed impulses or fantasies uncritically, or will fail to recognize that they arise from itself. In the neuroses, repression appears to be maintained, but nevertheless the repressed material returns, although in such a distorted form that it is acceptable to the ego.

Conation may be profoundly disturbed in the psychotic, but only to a slight degree does it suffer in the neuroses. In the psychotic the changes in affect may be great, and affective lability is often decreased, while the neurotic affective changes are slight, and lability is maintained. Any depression in the neuroses is determined more by evident environmental factors than is the case in psychoses and is accompanied by a greater degree of insight and by an absence of retardation. The neurotic usually well retains interest in

the outer world and remains sensitive to changes in the social atmosphere; the interest of the psychotic may be lost. Neurotics conform more nearly to the social norm in their relationships. The regression of the psychotic may be extreme, but it is not an important mechanism in the neurotic who never, if consciousness is clear, regresses to an infantile level with its excretory soiling.

Generally speaking, psychotic patients do not recognize that they are ill and therefore have no desire for change in their subjective status. Neurotic patients, on the contrary, usually feel keenly their subjective suffering and consciously want to get well, although it is known that their more powerful unconscious desire is to the contrary.

Neurotics, especially the hysterics, often exploit their symptom for *secondary gain*, whereas psychotics acquire no secondary gain from their illness.

Frequently, a reaction that would be classified as neurotic will later assume a form descriptively classified as psychotic. This does not mean that one type of mental illness is being superseded by another form fundamentally different in nature. It is, in fact, the opinion of some psychiatrists that if the life history of a patient suffering from a psychosis not associated with toxic or organic factors is fully known, evidence will always be found of an untreated or inadequately treated pre-existing neurosis-like syndrome out of which the psychosis grew.

Criteria differentiating the neuroses and psychoses are given in Table 22–1.

Classification of Neurotic Disorders

In the new American classification (DSM-III), the neuroses are defined in such major groups as affective, anxiety, somatoform, dissociative, and psychosexual disorders. These groups encompass all those heretofore recognized, as listed below. The grouping and ordering of DSM-III differs but will be followed in this edition of the text, except

TABLE 22–1   Criteria Differentiating Psychoses from Neuroses

	PSYCHOSES	NEUROSES
Behavioral syndromes	Overactivity Impulsivity Retardation Suspiciousness Idiosyncratic oddities Withdrawal	Apprehensiveness Anxiety attacks Phobias Obsessions Compulsions Conversion reactions Fugues Amnestic confabulatory states Repetitive
Psychological defenses	Denial Regression Introjection Projection Identification 　　(pathological)	Repression Displacement Isolation Reaction-formation Undoing Substitution Conversion
Affect	Elation Depression Apathy Ambivalence Inappropriateness	Responsive
Ego functions	Impaired Reality relation distorted Confused Idiosyncratic	Intact but constricted Reality oriented
Interpersonal relations	Object relations ambivalent or 　　seriously impaired Sexual relations confused	Object relations maintained Emotional lability Dramatization or constriction Impaired heterosexual relations

for the dysthymic disorder (depressive neurosis), which we place after the anxiety states.

Anxiety disorders
　Phobic (neuroses)
　Anxiety states (neuroses)
　Post-traumatic stress disorders
Somatoform disorders (hysterical neuroses)
　Somatization disorder
　Conversion disorder
　Psychogenic pain disorder
　Hypochondriasis
Dissociative disorders
Factitious disorders
Psychosexual disorders

The so-called "types" are not disease entities in genesis, mechanisms, or manifestations. The neuroses should be regarded as a series of varying types of reaction brought about by multiple causative factors that vary from case to case. The more carefully the reactions of the neurotic are examined, the more frequently it will be found that there are no sharply defined lines among the various types of neuroses. The classification schemes must be recognized as arbitrary; they seldom conform to clinical reality. It is rare, for example, to find a "pure" hysteria or "pure" obsessional neurosis. Frequently, the neurotic will, in varying degrees, show somatoform, obsessional, anxiety, and even psychosomatic manifestations. Overt anxiety, for example, although the most conspicuous and characteristic symptom in anxiety states, is frequently an important picture in other forms. Also, just as the distinction between the neuroses and the psychoses often is not sharply defined, neither is that between the psychoneuroses and many character traits of the so-called "normal" person who consistently uses the "neurotic process" to fend off anxiety. Far more frequently than is realized, outstanding character traits are really neurotic reaction formations that serve as defenses. Neurotic syndromes fit into the personality patterns of the individuals and are allied to the techniques they have employed all their lives in handling situations.

Causes

When we look for the causes of the neuroses, we must conclude that emotional, meaningful factors play a predominant and, in a broad sense, perhaps an exclusive role. Usually from early life the neurotic has shown personality traits that are so deeply rooted in the make-up of the individual that some refer to them as constitutional. These traits are acquired during impressionable years through close association with, dependence upon, and transactions with various members of the family. Most major neurotic patterns basically depend on conflicts and feeling-attitudes that arose in childhood; thus, in order to understand a patient's neurosis, an attempt should be made to connect the patient's present symptoms with some unresolved childhood experiences.

Often the childhood of the neurotic is punctuated by such disturbances as sleepwalking, crying out in sleep, enuresis, disturbances of speech, food idiosyncrasies, delirium accompanying slight rises in temperature, destructiveness, emotional excitability, temper tantrums, phobias, compulsions, shyness, nail-biting, and other disguises looked upon as constituting personality and behavior problems. These childhood symptoms generally are regarded as evidence that specific conflicts and situational factors produced anxiety and led to neurotic symptoms or character traits.

It is necessary, however, not only to examine the childhood background for scars that the special circumstances of early life have left, but to be alert for feelings of guilt; conflicts over unconscious needs; meaningful life events; recurrent, cumulative stresses and tensions of interpersonal relationship difficulties; and the everyday stresses of family living, including marital or sexual problems. The role that each plays in establishing the primary distortions in the neurotic process, the secondary affects of anxiety, guilt, and shame, and the tertiary defenses in denials in the style of life or in symptomatic defenses are only understandable in careful and detailed study of conscious and unconscious processes in the life of the individual patient.

Immediate reality factors serve as precipitants of emotional upheaval or psychic stress, but generally not as basic etiologic factors. An apparently smooth adjustment is often a cover for stormy problems that have long existed beneath the surface. This is why a neurotic reaction may become manifest suddenly, even in middle or late life. Thus the seemingly successful compulsive worker in our Western culture may become anxiety-ridden and depressed in the face of a mandatory retirement or the loss of those skills required to maintain his driven performance.

Whatever determined their personalities, there seem to be individuals who are unusually sensitive to tension and conflicts of life. Although the efficiency of most persons is impaired by neurotic tendencies, much of the best work of the world is done as an expression of neurotic disorder. This has been particularly apparent in art and literature.

Of the immediate causes for the development of the neuroses or the recurrence of neurotic symptoms, it may be said they are frequently to be found in the necessity to repress, distort, or displace emotions of hostility or rage or the drives of sexuality and dependency as they emerge and conflict with order and peace in the patient's personality. These and similar factors, often of a conflict-producing nature, create *anxiety*, which is the commonest and most important source of neurotic disorders. Anxiety, engendered by a too severe and exacting superego but perhaps stimulated by an external situation, mobilizes the defenses of the personality.

If the anxiety is felt and expressed directly, is "free-floating," and is not confined to definite situations or objects, the neurosis is spoken of as an anxiety state or anxiety neurosis. If the repressed wish or impulse causing the anxiety is "converted" into functional symptoms in organs or parts of the body, the clinical picture is that of somatization or conversion hysteria. If the anxiety overwhelms and temporarily controls the individual, the clinical picture is that of dissociation, as in hysterical stupor, fugue, or amnesia. In compulsion neurosis, the patient controls the anxiety by a repetitive activity. This activity or ritual protects the patient against the threat of repressed impulses. In phobias, anxiety is controlled by detaching it from some idea or situation and, by displacement, attaching the fear to some specific object or situation that serves as a symbol.

The neuroses are more frequently diagnosed in women than in men. This may be the consequence of societal demands that generally value more rigid repression of basic biological needs and instincts in women, with the result that anxiety defenses in the form of neurotic symptoms are more frequently required than in men. The psychosexual life, with its many taboos and social restrictions, is by no means, however, the only factor, since any fundamental urge or desire against the expression of which a defensive barrier must be constructed, or the gratification of which must be vicarious, may give rise to neurotic symptoms. Feelings of guilt, social situations, irritating relationships that strain the ability to adjust, and marriage with its new responsibilities are examples of the many factors that may contribute to a neurosis.

In a married woman, chronic marital dissatisfaction and disappointment may contribute to the development of a neurosis. The husband may not have proved to be the ideal mate that was expected, desired demonstrations of affection may have been lacking, or marriage may have failed to be the sustained romance that the wife ' had dreamed it would be. She may deny any dissatisfaction that may be consciously acknowledged only if she frankly faces her feelings. Other women, interested in a business or professional career, or hesitant to exhibit any interest in, or behavior toward, the opposite sex that would lead to marriage, may put it off until they reach an age when opportunities for marriage are infrequent. The sense of frustration and of a certain emptiness of life may lead to a neurotic reaction. Again, the involutional period, with its reluctantly acknowledged psychological implications, may be accompanied by anxiety, depression, or irritability that is readily converted into functional symptoms.

At times a neurosis may develop as an indirect result of long-continued physical illness. In such cases, the prolonged and perhaps severe illness may threaten the patients' sense of self as it compels them to give up activities and interests that have been highly prized and sustain their sense of self, or jeopardize their ability to function at their previous level. Such factors may stimulate an anxiety that had previously been handled without difficulty.

Most neuroses of adults develop between late adolescence and 35 years of age. This is the period when the individual becomes confronted with the problems of adult adjustments and responsibilities. It is the period when satisfying social, economic, and sexual situations should be established. Frustrations in these critically important fields may lead to conflict and anxiety that can be met only by neurotic mechanisms.

Elaborate disguises, including fears that have no obvious connections with immediate realities and make the neurotic's behavior more or less incomprehensible both to himself and others, are among the conspicuous features of neurotic behavior. A rational explanation for the apparently unintelligible behavior will be found, however, when its psychodynamics is studied. It will be observed that neurotic syndromes tend to fit into the established personality pattern of the individual and are allied to the techniques he has employed all his life in handling difficult situations.

In some psychoneurotic reactions, particularly in anxiety states, the patient often fears the existence of some serious physical disease, whereas the causes of the symptoms are in fact psychogenic. In such cases, the patient will usually not accept assurances of good physical health unless a physician has first made such a painstaking physical examination and has shown such open-mindedness and true interest concerning the possible existence of physical disease as to make the patient willing to accept the physician's statement that there is no organic basis for the symptoms. It should be emphasized, however, that a diagnosis of psychoneurosis cannot be made merely by the exclusion of organic factors. It can be made only on the discovery of positive factors in the psychological sphere sufficiently pertinent to offer a logical explanation for the symptoms.

The evidence for genetic or constitutional predisposition remains weak. For those interested in this evidence, the papers by Miner and Lund are recommended. Lund notes that those individuals who live under constant conditions (without time cues) and show variable rhythms of activity and temperature, whom he denotes as physiologically desynchronized (about 20 per cent of a small series studied), score high on neuroticism scales and tend toward complaints of physical ailments.

Prevalence

Certainly the neuroses are the most ubiquitous of the disorders that afflict human beings. The exact prevalence is uncertain, owing largely to the differences in definition that exist among psychiatrists, the varying cultural attitudes to certain neurotic character traits and symptoms, and the variable methods used to collect the data. Taylor and Chave, in a study of an English town, found neurotic symptoms insufficient to bring the sufferer to medical attention in 330 per 1000 residents. Eighty-one per 1000 sought help for such symptoms from a general practitioner, 44 per 1000 attended a psychiatric outpatient department, and 1.9 per 1000 were admitted to a hospital for a period of treatment. In various surveys of general hospital services and clinics as well as the practices of general physicians, upward of 30 to 40 per cent of patients who come for treatment have been considered to have a neurosis, either as the primary diagnosis or in conjunction with and complicating other illnesses. A study of the practice of internists in New York City found that approximately 10 per cent of patients examined on the first visit on referral from general practitioners had mental, neurotic, or personality disorders; probably the vast majority were neurotic.

Mortality

An increased relative risk of death in severe neuroses is apparent. Suicide and accidents contribute to this increased risk early in the course of the disorder. Later, various nervous, respiratory or cardiovascular conditions contribute, which suggests that the neurotic defenses alone are unable to protect the individual from stress.

CHARACTER NEUROSES

While the official schemes of classification of the neuroses designate the subvarieties in terms of the predominant psychological defenses, it is generally recognized by practicing psychiatrists that each neurotic patient has a distinctive character structure. This character structure, usually referred to as the *character neurosis,* has served as a means of containing anxiety—repressing it in the individual's ongoing interpersonal transaction. It is betrayed by his or her more or less fixed attitudes, affectations, and mannerisms; a variegated host of traits of relating to others; as well as by deeply rooted and persisting affects held over from infancy and childhood.

These characterologic manifestations of the neuroses are perceived with difficulty unless one has the opportunity of relating to the patient closely over prolonged periods. They are rarely the subject of complaint at the time the neurotic presents himself for examination; he is most likely then to state his problem in terms of symptoms expressive of anxiety or the psychological defenses against it. His family, close friends, and others whom he sees frequently and regularly usually have some recognition of the rigidities and peculiarities of his behavior that constitute the neurotic façade or character.

Some character traits serve to discharge drives or impulses, while others are reactive. The latter are sometimes referred to as "character armor" protecting the individual from arousal of conflict through attitudes of avoidance or opposition. Environmental situations that face the personality with unusual intensity or duration or unexpected expressions of stress are those that break through the ego "character armor." It is then that the personality responds with the open expression of symptoms recognized in the well-known varieties of neuroses.

Certain of the neurotic personalities and their expressions in characteristic attitudes and traits are described in the chapters on personality disorders, e.g., the histrionic and obsessive personality. In some the neurotic character fixations are seen in actions typifying excessive dependency or submission to others and often arise from a continuing feeling of personal insignificance which leads to overvaluation of others. Ingratiating and self-effacing behavior, coupled sometimes with demanding requests for affection and appreciation, represents one form of this character. Others may demonstrate their character defense in repetitive and persistent tendencies to mistrust or dominate their fellows, or to insist on their self-sufficiency; thus they become detached. Still others are masochistically self-sacrificing, constrained or inhibited in asserting their talents, or insistent on rigid ways of behavior under the guise of seeking an unrealistic or idealistic goal. Some are compulsively driven to activity, such as the compulsive gambler, others to a repetitive search for relief from anxiety through sensual means in long series of sexual or oral efforts. The need to dominate in order to suppress the anxiety of insecurity may be expressed in the drive to accumulate wealth or position, to excel others in giving or in spending, or to overvalue collections of facts and ideas. The "acting out" character neurotics tend to deny feeling through compulsive action. Thus they are difficult to bring to the verbal therapies.

ANXIETY DISORDERS

As previously indicated, anxiety may be described as a painful uneasiness of mind, a state of heightened tension accompanied by an inexpressible dread, a feeling of apprehensive expectation. It may arise with any situation that constitutes a threat to the personality. The emergence of repressed material is particularly apt to be anxiety-producing. Anxiety may arise when self-requirements and the security of the personality are threatened by the danger of a breakdown in the repression of forbidden sexual desires or attempts to ward off loneliness through dependency, or of unconscious hostile and aggressive feelings. Again, anxiety with its obsessive apprehensiveness may arise in association with frustrations or dilemmas occurring in some major life problem related to such topics as vocational, sexual, or marital adjustment.

In the other neurotic reactions, some specific, auxiliary form of psychological defense mechanism is devised to control anxiety. In anxiety reactions, however, there is no such specific method of defense. Repression alone is insufficient to control the anxiety. As a result the anxiety, not being displaced as in phobic reactions, not being "converted" into functional symptoms as in somatization or conversion, not being discharged by some gross personality disorganization such as dissociation, fugue, or amnesia, and not being automatically controlled by some repetitive thought or act, remains diffuse and uncontrolled, with the result that the patient is in a state of constant *anxious apprehension*. Anxiety reaction is therefore sometimes spoken of as the simplest form of neurosis.

If the diffuse anxiety is not too painful, it may be expressed or controlled through certain personality traits. Individuals who are constantly beset by pervading anxiety are characteristically tense, timid, apprehensive, sensitive to the opinions of others, and easily embarrassed and tend to worry. Many persons with such a constant sense of anxiety are self-distant and given to inferiority feelings, experience difficulty in making decisions, and are afraid of making mistakes. Usually they are scrupulous, overconscientious, and ambitious, and feel that they must live up to self-imposed high standards. Although such a person suffers moderate distress through apprehension and other tendencies previously noted, the tension is not usually intolerable. If, however, the anxiety becomes more disturbing, it may be expressed in such symptoms as depression, sleeplessness, irritability, restlessness, a paralyzing indecision, psychosomatic disturbances, outbursts of aggressiveness, attacks of weeping, and feelings of inadequacy and inferiority accompanied, perhaps, by a paranoid attitude. Usually the patient with an anxiety reaction feels chronically fatigued and complains of inability to concentrate. Some express the fear that they are "becoming insane."

The anxiety reactions are most frequently associated with phobic defenses that are often overlooked. Untreated, the phobic anxiety state, often designated "anxiety hysteria," may extend with either the development of obsessive ideation and disappearance of the acute anxiety reactions or progressive withdrawal associated with phobic diffusion that leads to a state of helpless isolation simulating a psychotic regression.

PHOBIC DISORDERS

While phobias are among the more common symptoms in populations of patients recognized to have a psychiatric disability, the phobic reaction *per se* is diagnosed relatively infrequently. A figure of approximately 3 per cent has been found in reports from psychiatric clinics in the United States of America. Perhaps the failure to report the phobic reaction more frequently is due to the common association of this symptom with anxiety, and also its occurrence in association with other psychoneurotic symptoms. Phobias are reported to be twice as common among women as among men.

Agras and his colleagues carried out a five-year follow-up study of a group of 30 phobic individuals who never received treatment. They found that 100 per cent of children's phobias disappeared during this time; 43 per cent of the adults were relieved or much improved, 20 per cent were unchanged and 33 per cent were worse. In the adults, broad generalizations of the original fearfulness were associated with poor outcome. Animal phobias are most likely to disappear, while agoraphobias have the poorest outlook.

As mentioned in the previous section of this chapter, phobias are present in a large number of the chronically apprehensive persons who suffer anxiety attacks. At one time this triad of symptoms, so well described by Freud in his original paper on the anxiety neurosis, was designated *anxiety hysteria.* Upon his study of "little Hans," reported in his paper "Analysis of a Phobia in a Five-Year-Old Boy," rests the psychodynamic understanding of phobic reactions. Freud interpreted Hans' fear of going into the street because he was afraid that a horse would bite him as a displacement of the boy's fear of his father. That fear was inferred to have its origin in expected punishment for his unconscious hostility toward the father in his competition with him for his mother's affection. The displacement of the fear to the horse avoided the exposure of his hostility and the fear of retaliation and permitted him to retain his love for his father.

Thus a phobic reaction is a defensive one in which the patient attempts to deal with his anxiety by detaching it from a specific idea, object, or situation in his daily life and displacing it to some associated object, situation, or idea in the form of a specific neurotic fear. Although the patient consciously recognizes that no actual danger exists, if exposed to the specific phobia-stimulating symbolic object or situation he is powerless to keep from experiencing an intense sense of fear. The intensely distressing sense of apprehension associated with the consciously feared object or situation is actually derived from other sources—sources of which the patient is unaware. A defense against the anxiety arising from this unrecognized source is provided through the mechanisms of displacement and symbolization. By these means, the anxiety is detached from its real source—unconscious, forbidden tendencies and impulses, for example—and displaced to some situation or object that is usually symbolic of the threatening tendency or wish.

A great variety of phobias have been described. Among them are fear of dirt, of bacteria, of certain animals, of travel by a certain type of vehicle. Many of them have Greek names attached to them, as *agoraphobia,* a fear of open places, or *claustrophobia,* a fear of confined spaces. Now they are subdivided into three types: agoraphobia, social phobia, and simple phobia.

Agoraphobia

The fear or being alone or in public places where one would find it difficult to escape is today the most frequently encountered and often the most socially impairing of the phobic states. Agoraphobia may occur with or without associated panic attacks; the several variants come about as follows.

When exposed to the specific situation that evokes his fear, the phobic becomes intensely anxious. He may then experience faintness, fatigue, palpitation, perspiration, nausea, and tremor. This is the typical acute *panic* or *anxiety* attack, the physical symptoms secondary usually to hyperventilation. He may be unable to continue with the duty at hand and be overwhelmed with panic.

Avoidance of the specific phobic object or situation brings him control of anxiety but at the expense of limiting the range of activities in which he may engage. Were the patient to carry out the feared activity, it would unconsciously mean to him that he was performing the forbidden activity that arouses the dreaded anxiety. He also constantly punishes himself for his unconscious tendencies and impulses by the distressing restrictions and sufferings imposed by his phobia.

A major component of the phobic reaction is the avoidance pattern. While avoidance of the feared situation, person, or idea allows a partial control of anxiety and for a time allays the fears, very often the phobic avoidance fails and the sufferer has a distressing outbreak of anxiety under situations other than the feared one. Then the displacement is generalized to new situations and additional phobias evolve. In some the generalization of the phobic reaction is so widespread that their activities eventually become circumscribed to a few rooms and they become socially isolated.

The maintenance of the phobia often depends upon the secondary gains obtained through the control the symptoms may exercise upon those with whom the patient lives. The phobic wife now leaves her home only in the company of her husband, and he may leave her alone only at the risk of a terrifying anxiety attack. It is this aspect of the phobic reaction that is so conspicuous in the school phobias of children, which require treatment for the participation of the family member or members engaged in the symbiotic perpetuation of the symptom. Many agoraphobics attempt to relieve their recurrent anxiety through the use of alcohol or drugs.

Social Phobia

Distinguished from agoraphobia are persistent fears coupled with a drive to avoid social situations in which an individual develops anxiety in expectation of unfavorable evaluation by others. He may anticipate misbehaving and the suffering of humiliation or embarrassment. This phobic condition is consciously recognized by the sufferer. Common types of social phobias are those related to appearing in public, and per-

forming or speaking before groups. There is some question as to whether this is a true phobia, since psychological displacement is not so clearly evident; it may represent a late manifestation of attachment behavior and separation. Usually evident in late childhood or early adolescence, it may be associated with other phobic states. The condition is usually persistent but seldom incapacitating. At times the phobic state exacerbates when the individual exposes himself socially and judges his performance adversely. Anxiety thus increases, leading to a greater tendency to phobic avoidance. Like the agoraphobics, those with a social phobia may abuse alcohol or sedative drugs to alleviate their anxiety.

Simple Phobia

These are the specific phobias in which the phobic object often is an animal, an insect, or a situation such as heights (acrophobia) or closed spaces (claustrophobia). The animal phobias usually commence in childhood; the majority remit. When the child has been exposed to a traumatic attack, an animal phobia is likely to persist throughout life. Such phobias are seldom impairing to social adaptation, particularly if easily avoided. Marks has pointed out those with specific phobias condition differently than others do. The animal phobic patient responds well to behavioral desensitization techniques, in contrast to the agoraphobic patient.

PSYCHOGENESIS

The phobic sufferer often comes from a family in which the mother is fearful of her aggression, is herself phobic, and is unable to exact conforming behavior from the children and even the father except through nagging insistence. If the father overtly complies with the mother's phobic insistence, even though he appears firm, some of the children may become phobic as well, as this becomes the dominant adaptation for control. Simple association is considered by many to determine the choice of the phobic object to which displacement occurs. Psychoanalytic theory, however, suggests that the choice of phobic object is made on the basis of its symbolic meanings.

The *success phobia* is a subtle expression of this reaction. Unconsciously fearful of retaliation for aggressive aspirations, men or women with this phobia suffer outbreaks of anxiety at those times when they verge on some personal success. In men, this phobic state is sometimes associated with retarded ejaculation. Later the partial avoidance of competitive success may be followed by periodic depressive reactions as a substitute for the anxiety which may occur when a desired position is achieved.

The *counterphobic defense*, while seemingly very different from the avoidance behavior of the usual phobic sufferer, nevertheless bears a dynamic relation. In this instance the sufferer attempts to master his anxiety by repetitive confrontation with the phobic object and may, if successful, evolve a drive to gratifying repetition. Its senseless and compulsive bravado distinguishes it from anxiety-free confrontation.

DIFFERENTIAL DIAGNOSIS

Phobias may occur in association with many other psychiatric symptoms and syndromes. These are discriminated from obsessive thoughts by the associated affect. With phobias, the affect is anxiety with obsessive guilt.

Phobias of internal stimuli, related to assumed illness such as cancer, heart disease, venereal disease, and the like, more frequently have an obsessive character and are discovered in the neurotic hypochondriacal states or as symptoms of incipient schizophrenia. Treatment of these phobic disorders is discussed following description of the anxiety states, including panic disorder and generalized anxiety disorder.

ANXIETY STATES

Panic Disorder

The patient suffers acute and terrifying, but episodic, attacks that apparently come on unpredictably. They may last for a few minutes or up to an hour. Rapid heartbeat, palpitation, precordial discomfort, nausea, diarrhea, desire to urinate, dyspnea, and a feeling of choking or suffocation may be experienced. The pupils are dilated, the face is flushed, and the skin perspires; the patient suffers from paresthesias and tremulousness, feels dizzy or faint, and often has a sense of weakness and of impending death. The psychophysiological mechanism of *hyperventilation* is the mechanism that causes these symptoms in the majority of acute anxiety attacks. The symptoms are reproducible by having the patient overbreathe for 90 to 120 seconds, as described later in the hyperventilation syndrome. Other physiological expressions of acute anxiety perhaps occur through activation of various segments of the autonomic nervous system and the adrenal medulla and its secretions. In an acute reactive anxiety attack, the clinical picture may be colored by a traumatic situation. This is well illustrated in the anxiety attacks of combat neurosis.

Generalized Anxiety Disorder

This diagnosis is now made in those with persistent tension lasting over a month, but not necessarily associated with phobic development or panic attacks. Yet many who are subject to acute anxiety attacks usually suffer also from a chronic anxiety state. They experience difficulty in falling asleep, are disturbed by fearful dreams, suffer from coarse tremors or "trembling," and complain of a "band around the head" or of a "quivering in the stomach." They are

TABLE 22–2   Symptoms of
Anxiety Neurosis

SYMPTOMS	60 PATIENTS %	102 CONTROLS* %
Palpitation	97	9
Tires easily	93	19
Breathlessness	90	13
Nervousness	88	27
Chest pain	85	10
Sighing	79	16
Dizziness	78	16
Faintness	70	12
Apprehensiveness	61	3
Headache	58	26
Paresthesias	58	7
Weakness	56	3
Trembling	54	17
Breath unsatisfactory	53	4
Insomnia	53	4
Unhappiness	50	2
Shakiness	47	16
Fatigued all the time	45	6
Sweating	42	33
Fear of death	42	2
Smothering	40	3
Syncope	37	11
Nervous chill	24	0
Urinary frequency	18	2
Vomiting and diarrhea	14	0
Anorexia	12	3
Paralysis	0	0
Blindness	0	0

*Healthy controls consisted of 50 men and 11 women from a large industrial plant, and 41 healthy postpartum women from the Boston Lying-In Hospital. (After Wheeler, E. O., White, P. D., Reed, E. W., and Cohen, M. E.: Neurocirculatory asthenia (anxiety neurosis, effort syndrome, neurasthenia). J.A.M.A., *142*:878–889, 1950.)

absent-mined and seem worried without knowing about what or why. They complain that their minds are in a constant daze and that they are unable to control their thoughts. They are apprehensive and afraid to be alone, yet do not desire conversation. They feel too tired to attempt anything constructive and continually seek a physical explanation for their distressing mental states.

The condition occurs frequently in relatives—up to 40 per cent in studies in which family interviews were done.

A listing of the frequency of occurrence of the various physical complaints typical of this neurosis is given in Table 22–2. Table 22–3 presents the diagnostic criteria for this disorder.

DIFFERENTIAL DIAGNOSIS.   These attacks are often considered to be due to heart disease, thyrotoxicosis, hyperinsulinism, or dysinsulinism. The condition is sometimes confused with the mitral valve prolapse syndrome and may be associated with it. This latter syndrome is caused by a midsystolic prolapse of one of the mitral leaflets, with or without regurgitation. On cardiac auscultation, a midsystolic click or a late systolic murmur is heard. The diagnosis is confirmed by echocardiography. Like panic disorder, anxiety disorder affects

TABLE 22–3   Diagnostic Criteria for
Generalized Anxiety Disorder

A. Generalized, persistent anxiety is manifested by symptoms from three of the following four categories:
   (1) motor tension: shakiness, jitteriness, jumpiness, trembling, tension, muscle aches, fatigability, inability to relax, eyelid twitch, furrowed brow, strained face, fidgeting, restlessness, easy startle
   (2) autonomic hyperactivity: sweating, heart pounding or racing, cold and clammy hands, dry mouth, dizziness, light-headedness, paresthesias (tingling in hands or feet), upset stomach, hot or cold spells, frequent urination, diarrhea, discomfort in the pit of the stomach, lump in the throat, flushing, pallor, high resting pulse and respiration rate
   (3) apprehensive expectation: anxiety, worry, fear, rumination, and anticipation of misfortune to self or others
   (4) vigilance and scanning: hyperattentiveness resulting in distractibility, difficulty in concentrating, insomnia, feeling "on edge," irritability, impatience
B. The anxious mood has been continuous for at least one month.
C. Not due to another mental disorder, such as a depressive disorder or schizophrenia.
D. At least 18 years of age.

As presented in the Diagnostic and Statistical Manual of Mental Disorders, Third Edition (DSM-III). Washington, D.C., American Psychiatric Association, 1980.

women more frequently than men, is familial, and occurs in up to 10 per cent of the population.

PROGNOSIS. While up to 5 per cent of Western populations suffer from the condition, the majority of patients function reasonably well through expressing dissatisfaction with their vocational adaptation. In a recent follow-up by Noyes and his colleagues of a group of patients treated largely by medication or psychotherapy (12 per cent had no treatment), only 25 per cent reported loss of job efficiency. Thirty-five per cent suffered marital dissatisfaction related to inhibited desire or excitement. One third of the patients reported social isolation. Those with a long duration of symptoms (more than six years) had a less favorable outlook than those with a shorter duration. There is a greater likelihood for hospitalization for those with panic attacks than for healthy persons; episodes of secondary depression occur in up to 40 per cent.

A 27-year-old woman entered the hospital complaining of multiple fears. She was too frightened to get on streetcars or buses, to go to the movies, and to go out to supper. She was also afraid that she would not live up to the expectations of her mother, was dubious about her own capabilities, and indicated that her marriage was in difficult straits and that she had previously been separated from her husband for 18 months. She stated that their only son was a bed wetter. In addition, she presented the symptoms of acute anxiety with palpitation, perspiration, dizziness, and shortness of breath. These symptoms were replicated when she hyperventilated, on request, for 90 seconds.

Brief questioning elicited the information that her mother had been a nagging, sadistic person, who unmercifully switched the patient and her brother whenever they failed to obey her command. The father, a mild, subservient individual, had seldom been at home. The patient was a quiet and obedient, though fearful, child, usually timid and retiring, who felt that she must always acquiesce to the wishes of others or be subject to their criticism and withdrawal of affection.

The diagnosis in this case was generalized anxiety disorder, associated with the hyperventilation syndrome and a phobic state. The anxiety attacks occurred regularly in situations in which the patient's husband, mother, or even the doctor did something or said something to arouse in her a fear of separation associated with a wish to retaliate angrily. She could not allow herself to express further criticism and rejections. Although the majority of anxiety attacks were relieved after several months of psychiatric treatment, she was not entirely free of her symptoms until after a year of regular visits.

TREATMENT. Two phases of an anxiety-phobic disorder require attention—one, the acute panic or anxiety attack and the other, the anxiety neurosis. During the attack, the rapid pulse and pounding heart lead the patient to believe that only a heart attack could have produced this distress. After an examination of the heart and other organs has been made and no physical disorder discovered, the patient should be confidently assured that there is no heart disease.

The cause of the symptoms may be demonstrated easily by simply requesting the patient to overbreathe for a period of two minutes, as described in Chapter 24 under the hyperventilation syndrome. Many patients may be trained to hold their breath when a panic attack ensues or to breathe into a small paper bag, though the patient should be advised that this maneuver will not suffice to correct the condition. He should be advised that such attacks do not endanger his life and that additional psychotherapeutic or psychopharmacologic treatment will be needed to prevent or block later panic attacks.

To effect permanent change and prevent dependence on drugs, a dynamic psychotherapy is in order. This is particularly important for young parents if prevention of the condition in their children is a therapeutic goal.

Further somatic complaints should be disregarded and the examination of the heart should not be repeated. The patient should not, through the use of drugs, be led to believe that his pathologic condition is physical rather than emotional, and rest should not be advised, nor should personal reassurance be repeated to a degree that the patient constantly feels the need for it.

Treatment of the basic neurosis may commence with an attempt to relieve symptomatic distress through the use of the anxiolytics. These alone are seldom sufficient unless the anxiety is produced by a transient social stress. For the patient with panic attacks, phobias, and generalized apprehensiveness, treatment with the tricyclic autidepressants is indicated. Agoraphobia and specific phobias do not respond to such treatment—here the behavioral therapies are in order. Up to 75 per cent of agoraphobics show improvement in the main symptom over a four-year period.

OBSESSIVE-COMPULSIVE DISORDER

In the obsessive-compulsive reaction, the patient's anxiety is automatically controlled by associating it with persistently repetitive thoughts and acts. The patient recognizes that his unwanted thoughts and ritualistic acts are unreasonable, but he is unable to control them. The obsessive-compulsive reaction may be expressed in three clinical forms: (1) the persistent recurrence of an unwelcome and often distressing thought; (2) a morbid and often irresistible urge to perform a certain repetitive, stereotyped act; and (3) an obsessively recurring thought accompanied by a compulsion to perform a repetitive act.

Obsessive ideation may be concerned with various topics. Frequently the patient must fight against thoughts that are repugnant to his conscious moral and esthetic feelings, such as thoughts of a blasphemous nature or fantasies of killing a beloved member of his family. Although horrified that he should entertain such thoughts, the patient is unable to rid himself of them. The intruding and constantly recurring thought may be pointless and absurd, such as the case of the well-educated patient who persistently wondered why a chair had four legs instead of one. Ruminative preoccupation and speculation on such topics as creation, infinity, or other philosophical or religious questions are common. The condition of being obsessively preoccupied with an apparently indifferent topic, with marked exclusion of other interests, is sometimes known as an obsessive-ruminative state. The greater the effort to dispel obsessive thoughts, the more stubbornly they return. Ritualistic activities may be performed in an effort to dispel or counteract the thoughts. Practically never do such patients carry out any recurring thoughts suggesting an immoral or violent act, although they may become very apprehensive lest they do so. The inability of the patient to free himself from the distressing thought may occasionally lead him to suicide.

Types of Obsessive-Compulsive Reaction

FOLIE DU DOUTE. Some obsessive thinking assumes the form of *folie du doute*, characterized by persistent doubting, vacillation, and indecision, usually with compulsive ruminations that lead to repetitive acts aimed at dispelling the irrational doubts. Because of them, the patient must check and recheck even the simplest acts. He may, for example, lock the front door at night, but no sooner has he reached his bed than he is in doubt about the security of the door. He must therefore return and try the lock. Even then his doubts may recur after he is again in bed and require further visits to verify that the door is locked. Obsessive doubts and indecisions often arise in cases of conflict between desire and counterdesire.

Insistent, obsessive thoughts are defensive in purpose. The persistent idea is not to be taken at face value, so to speak. It is a substitute for another idea and thereby serves an anxiety-preventing function. Other affects are concealed behind the apparent content. The real sources may be any impulse, tendency, or wish that would be consciously intolerable to the patient. A hidden feeling of guilt is the common source. The manifest and recurring idea is the result of an effort to keep something else out of the mind and is formed by the mechanisms of displacement, symbolization, and condensation. The process is much the same as that occurring in a dream, where the latent or true content is concealed by these mechanisms so that the idea, wish, or impulse appears in the conscious dream in distorted and symbolized form.

COMPULSIVE ACTS.   A second clinical type of obsessive-compulsive reaction is that of compulsive acts. In this there is the obligatory repetition of a certain act. The forces that produce the compulsive act are, of course, unconscious. Since the symbolic act cannot adequately satisfy the forces that produced it, the act is stereotyped and repetitive. When the patient is asked the reason for his behavior, he may either offer some explanation that he knows has no rational basis or he may admit that it is absurd and purposeless. Usually, the patient consciously experiences some rejection and resistance to the carrying out of his defensive, compulsive act, but tension and anxiety mount until the urge to repeat becomes irresistible. If the patient is prevented from carrying out his compulsive ritual, overt anxiety appears. One of the most frequent forms of obsessive-compulsive rituals is that of handwashing, which has for its purpose the warding off of anxiety.

Most obsessive-compulsive acts consist merely of such simple useless acts as touching or counting, or excessive ones, such as repeated handwashing. Some, however, become elaborate rituals or ceremonials. They superficially appear as meaningless formalities and are only recognized as neurotic ceremonials when a necessity for renouncing them is accompanied by discomfort and anxiety.

The ritualistic ceremonial described by Freud in one of his earliest papers (1896), entitled "The Defense Neuropsychosis," is often quoted and is an excellent illustration of the complexity that may be assumed by these compul-sive devices designed to protect against anxiety:

> "An 11-year-old boy had instituted the following obsessive ceremonial before going to bed. He did not sleep until he had told his mother in the minutest detail all the events of the day; there must be no scraps of paper or other rubbish on the carpet of the bedroom; the bed must be pushed right to the wall; three chairs must stand by it and the pillows must lie in a particular way. In order to get to sleep he must first kick out a certain number of times with both legs and then lie on his side."

The function of compulsive acts also is to allay or bind anxiety. The compulsive act that the patient performs has, it will be found, a symbolic significance. This symbolic act serves as a sort of magic ritual by which he undoes or annuls the possible effect of his unrecognized impulses and achieves a distorted satisfaction, self-punishment, and atonement. It temporarily dispels the dangerous situation; as long as it can be carried out, the intensity of the anxiety is reduced. If the performance of the ritualistic substitutive act is resisted or impossible, the effectiveness of the protective obsessive-compulsive defense is eliminated, and the forbidden wishes and impulses arouse anxiety. The need for ritualized behavior increases, since the unconscious striving threatens to erupt into consciousness; more and more symptoms must be constructed to provide defenses against the forbidden tendencies. In many respects, the defensive patterns of the compulsions resemble penances, atonements, and punishments, or serve as precautions, prohibitions, and restrictions. In many ways, they are closely allied psychologically to the ceremonies and taboos that primitive people devise as protections against demonological and other supernatural forces.

Compulsive acts are not uncommon in children and adolescents, in whom they originate as expiratory ceremonials or as means whereby, through attributing a certain magic-like power to an act, a particularly desired wish may be attained. The acts then become established through habit, but they normally disappear as repressed tensions subside and more adequate social adjustments are established.

DISORDERS OF IMPULSE CONTROL. Allied to the compulsive activities just described are the episodic, repetitive behaviors in which the individual cannot resist the drive to carry out some act which may be harmful either to himself or others. These recurrent compulsions, in contrast to those described before, intrude less into the daily life of the sufferer. They have achieved social notoriety because of the conspicuous destructive behavior to self and others. Before the episodes, the sufferer develops an increasing urge; at the completion, the affective experience is pleasurable and sometimes orgasmic. Later, the person may be self-denigrating, regretful, or guilty, but the action is repeated, thereby typifying it as neurotic.

Pathological gambling, stealing (kleptomania), firesetting (pyromania), and assaultive behavior toward others are included here. These behaviors may occur in schizophrenia, the antisocial personality disorders, or the conduct disorders of childhood. Psychodynamically, such actions have the same motivation as the usual compulsive behaviors, but superego controls periodically break down, allowing the acting out of wishful pleasurable but self-destructive behaviors.

PHOBIA WITH COMPULSION. In this reaction, a phobia or obsessively recurring idea is associated with a compulsion to perform a repetitious act. This association occurs when there exists an overpowering fear of intolerable impulses. Usually, considerable anxiety is observable. One of the commonest examples of this type of reaction is a repetitive handwashing, the result of an obsessive fear of dirt or uncleanliness. Whatever object the patient touches has, he is confident, left his hands contaminated. Since he can scarcely avoid touching objects, he must repeatedly wash his hands. As every object is a possible source of contamination, the patient may resort to complicated and troublesome means of avoiding the touching of objects. He may open doors with his elbows or handle articles with gloves or other coverings. One patient washed each Saturday the church pew she expected to occupy the following day. Because of this tension, preoccupation, and irresistible handwashing, the capacity for gainful employment may be destroyed.

Here, too, are found the same mechanisms of displacement and undoing. The real fear is, of course, not of dirt but of intolerable impulses or guilt-laden strivings that have been displaced and symbolized by constant preoccupation with fear of dirt. The anxiety to which they have given rise is temporarily alleviated by the compulsive washing, with its symbolic cleansing significance.

The following case illustrates many of the features of a mixed phobic and compulsive reaction.

S. K. was admitted to a mental hospital at the age of 29. The family history revealed no significant history. During the second and third grades of school "he was a problem to the nuns because of his stuttering. They would ask him to read a paragraph over two or three times." For a considerable period at this age "he felt he had to bless himself a certain number of times in the evening." When in the fourth grade and after an illness "he was afraid to go to sleep at night for fear he might die. He would call his mother two or three times before going to sleep. He would not go to sleep unless she reassured him that he would not die. This lasted for two or three months." He bit his nails until he was 16 years of age.

At the time of his admission, the patient's mother and wife were requested to describe his adult personality characteristics. He was, they reported, a quiet, serious, honest, thrifty, saving, stubborn, and somewhat worrisome person. "He was ambitious. He wanted to go through college and be more than an ordinary working man. In college he studied very, very hard, and was an honor student." When 18 years of age the patient drank excessively for a period of several months. He then suddenly stopped and became so opposed to liquor that, to quote his wife, "He wouldn't touch a drop, and I remember once when we were both young he walked out of a home where liquor was being served because he was so opposed to it."

He enlisted in the Marine Corps. When, after his

admission to the hospital, he was asked what prompted him to volunteer, he replied, "Well, I felt uneasy a little bit with my scrupulosity. I wasn't too uneasy, but I thought somehow the service would take it away." Asked what he meant by 'scrupulosity,' he said "I was doubtful about my confessions." Asked if he was doubtful that he didn't confess enough, he answer was, "That's right; I didn't have enough sorrow for my sins." When the admitting physician asked the patient about his duties in the military service, he replied, "I had a job cleaning urinals. I probably was very good. I tried to do a thorough job. I saw cigarettes, but I always kept on cleaning all the time. It could have been done in 2 or 3 hours, but I worked 8 or 9 hours. I volunteered for the job." Two years later he wrote his fiancée that he wished to break his engagement as he was going to study for the priesthood after discharge from service. Six months later he wrote again, saying he had decided not to become a priest and asked that their engagement be renewed. Twenty-four months later he was married but had no sexual relations with his wife until 17 months later.

After his discharge from military service, the patient entered college, from which he was graduated, although several months before graduation his neurotic reaction had become so disabling that he was unable to continue his studies for the final two months of his senior year.

Soon after the patient's admission to the hospital, his wife was asked to give a history of the patient's illness. She reported that he had exhibited a compulsive handwashing for several months but that it became more serious. "He used to wash his hands and keep the water running for 15 minutes at a time. After he had washed them, he would turn off the spigot with his elbow. He had to count and wash and rinse his hands a certain number of times. If he had touched the door or door knob, he would go back and wash his hands again. One time he began to wash his hands at 1 o'clock in the morning. After we moved into our own house, he refused to use the front door or to turn the knob on the door for fear there might be germs. He used to go to the back window and call me to go to the front door and open it for him. He reached the point where he would climb in and out of windows so that he wouldn't have to enter the doors at all." The wife described also the following compulsion: "He also had the idea that when he walked there was something under his shoe. He would stop and look on the sole of his shoe, but there would be nothing there. He also worried as to whether or not his shoe laces were tied. He would pick up his foot and look to make sure. He had to do that a certain number of times before he was absolutely sure they were tied. When he walked down a street, if he kicked a stone he felt that he should put it back in the same place. If he walked on a line, then he would have to walk on all the cracks in the sidewalk."

On arrival at the hospital, the patient stated to the admitting physician, "I like to wash my hands many times a day in order to get them good and clean." While talking to the physician, he stood with his arms folded in order to avoid touching anything. He readily acknowledged that he was worried about touching objects lest he give others disease. As he seemed somewhat depressed, he was asked about suicidal thoughts. He replied that he felt he would be better off dead than to be thinking of the things he did but added that he would "not really" commit suicide. He then added, "When I say things, they have to be said a certain way. If I don't say them properly, I must apologize. I do this all the time. This irritated my wife and was another reason why she couldn't live with me. I would leave my books to apologize to her. It was the apologizing that was bothering her—not being at peace. I thought if I rubbed my hands 88 times, shut the water off, and then went back again, it would be all right. Then I thought maybe it hadn't been 88 times."

A month after the patient's admission, his ward physician entered the following note in the clinical record: "This patient has become extremely disturbed over his obsessive-compulsive ideation during recent days. He stops his physician at every opportunity and repeatedly asks the same questions, which include the following: "Should I wash my hands after I go to the bathroom and just do number one? Should I wash my hands when I go to the bathroom and have a bowel movement? My penis touches the toilet seat. Do you think I should wash it off with soap and water so there won't be a spread of disease? I wouldn't want anyone to get this disease. There's a rash there. Do you want to look at it? I think it is some sort of disease. I'm afraid everybody will get it. I don't know, doctor, I'm afraid something is going to happen. I have a feeling that I might go crazy or something. Someone asked me if I thought these things were silly and I said, 'Yes,' but now that I think of it, they don't seem silly. I just can't quite explain them. They must not really seem silly to me or I wouldn't have to do them like I do." The patient manifested an interesting inability to make any definite statement or to take any decisive action. When discussing a point he would say such things as the following: "Well, doctor, it's just like this. Well, no, it isn't exactly like that. I should say rather that's a little on the order of—well, that isn't quite right either. Perhaps I should put it this way. It's more of—uh—well, no, that isn't it."

Under therapy, the patient gradually improved. Two years after his admission he left the hospital for employment in a brick plant. A report received a year later stated that, although not entirely well, he was successfully employed.

Prevalence

The condition is rare and is estimated at 0.05 per cent in the general population. Its incidence in psychiatric populations has varied from 0.1 to 4.6 per cent.

Psychodynamics

Psychogenetically, the origin of obsessive-compulsive behavior is believed to rest in the early struggle of the growing child between his drives for omnipotent self-assertion and the necessity to conform to the demands of his parents in order to maintain their love and respect. The early period of toilet training initiates the conflict. Often the later obsessive-compulsive individual is one brought up by a rigid, compulsive mother, who insistently demands compliance and threatens both loss of love and various forms of punishment for failure to behave properly. The growing child is then exposed to repeated arousal of rage through the insistent requirements for cleanliness and compliance but must repress them in order to retain his relationship with the parent. Very early he learns to regard his underlying thoughts of hostile reprisal to be taboo, and therefore subject to punishment and requiring penance. He may learn, by observing the parents, that his defiant behavior provides gratification in the attentions of the parent, yet at the same time he must then atone both by carrying out the parental desire as well as by an associated expiatory act. This train of behavioral responses, derived from the long-continued relationship with such parental figures, becomes internalized and unconscious so that each thought reflecting rage or hostility sets in action the psychodynamic train of ambivalently balanced action and counteraction symbolizing rage, gratification, compliance, and expiation.

In the following brief summary are the free associations of a compulsively neat and fussy young woman lawyer, given during psychoanalysis and following an observation by the therapist that she seemed to wish to be messy in the office, judging by the way she dropped cigarette ashes on the furniture there.

"It is hard to believe that I do something like being messy or neat to annoy somebody. Being messy was a way to annoy mother. It seemed to me that mother's cleaning up and criticizing me for not being neat was a way to annoy me and father, I felt I had no way to get back at her. I never felt more angry toward anyone than mother. Being messy was a way I learned of getting back at her, of rebelling. She once told me how upset she was when I broke something that was valuable. . . . I became like my mother in camp when I was with Ruth. She was so neat, shiny. Everyone liked her and admired her. She inflicted her standards on everyone. Recently I met her and thought she was a snob."

Prognosis

When the obsessive-compulsive state has onset in childhood or early adulthood, the course is usually chronic but variable, with many patients suffering episodic periods of severity although able to adapt socially. This reaction does not increase the risk of suicide, homicide, or drug abuse of any kind, or of prolonged hospitalization. The patient's compulsive needs frequently interfere seriously with his comfort and efficiency. In extreme cases his constant preoccupation with his protective rituals renders him socially impossible. Some psychiatrists characterize the obsessive neuroses as intermediate between neuroses and psychoses. The obsessive-compulsive states of children usually disappear with time if not taken seriously in the presence of the child. Such compulsions grow out of childhood anxiety, often a single one. The prognosis is much more serious if the onset is during adolescence or early adult life.

A summary of outcome in obsessional patients, from a number of sources, is shown in Table 22–4.

Diagnosis

A diagnosis between early schizophrenia and the obsessive-compulsive neuroses is at times exceedingly difficult. The obsessive thinking of the psychoneurotic may be like the subjective rumination of the schizophrenic, and the compulsive ritual of the former may suggest the mannerisms of the lat-

TABLE 22–4 Follow-up Studies of Obsessional Neurosis

| SAMPLE CHARACTERISTICS | | | | LENGTH OF FOLLOW-UP | CONDITION ON FOLLOW-UP (%) | | |
Author	Place	Pt. Source*	N†	(to nearest yr.)	Asympto-matic	Im-proved	Unim-proved
Balslev-Olesen et al.	Denmark	I, O	52	0–8	6	58	37
Grimshaw	England	O	97	1–14	40	24	35
Hastings	U.S.A.	I	23	6–12	13	40	47
Ingram	England	I	46	1–11	9	30	61
Kringlen	Norway	I	85	13–20	4	45	45
Langfeldt	Norway	I	27	1–11	26	41	33
Lewis	England	I, O	50	>5	32	34	34
Lo	Hong Kong	I, O	87	1–14	20	36	44
Luff et al.	England	O	49	3	39	27	34
Müller	Switzerland	I	57	15–35	28	50	22
Pollitt	England	I, O	66	0–15	24	48	28
Rennie	U.S.A.	I	47	20	36	38	26
Rüdin	Germany	I, O	130	2–26	12	26	61

*I = inpatient; O, outpatient.

†Excluded are lobotomized cases and patients dead on follow-up. The sex ratio differs from study to study, but approaches unity when all studies are combined.

(From Goodwin, D. W., Guze, S. B., and Robins, E.: Arch. Gen. Psychiatry, 20:182–187, 1969.)

ter. The symbolisms seen in the compulsive acts of the neurotic individual, as well as the substitutive nature of the phobias, are close both in resemblance and in relationship to the symbols seen in schizophrenia. It frequently happens that what is first thought to be the ruminative and obsessive tension state of a neurotic subsequently becomes an obvious schizophrenic reaction, usually of the paranoid type. In general, it may be said that the greater the rumination and the less the tension, the nearer does the reaction approach that of the schizophrenic. The patient's failure to regard his obsessions and compulsions as absurd and, particularly, ascribing them to external influences indicates a malignant schizophrenic origin. The compulsive neurotic never loses the capacity for discrimination between subjective experiences and reality, as is the case in schizophrenia. Finally, as Bleuler points out, the compulsive neurotic struggles *against* his obsession, whereas the delusional patient struggles *with* his idea.

At times the genuine depressions of manic-depressive psychosis may be accompanied by obsessive ideas. In differentiating such cases from compulsive states, one will inquire which appeared first, the depression or the obsessive idea.

Treatment

Fully developed obsessional and compulsive reactions are even more refractory to treatment than the milder psychoses. It is therefore important that treatment be early. The obsessive-compulsive neuroses usually develop in individuals who have been characterized by compulsive personality traits. The neurosis is in many ways an exaggeration and caricature of that pattern. Treatment, then, should be psychotherapeutic. Both dynamic and behavioral modification techniques are in use today.

Suess has reported that a short-term psychotherapeutic approach may be taken with obsessive-compulsive reactions. In this method, the therapist constantly attempts to have the patient verbalize his feelings, particularly in relation to reported current life events. Initially, he may have to assist the patient in identifying those feelings by suggesting the affective response from his analytic intuition of the described event, or from the patient's verbal expressions of affect as inferred from voice tones, facial expressions, or other bodily cues noted during the account of the event. In this way, the therapist provides an external superego permission. By this activity of the therapist, patients slowly tend to overcome their defenses of intellectualization, isolation, ambivalence, and undoing, used against forbidden affects, and become personally expressive and less cautious. As this happens, the defensive symptoms tend to subside.

If short-term dynamic psychotherapy fails, more intensive treatment of this kind may be tried.

Marks, Hodgson and Rachman have applied a behavioral model of "in vivo exposure" to treatment of these patients with some success, particularly in regard to compulsions. Their treatment required 4 to 12 weeks of inpatient residence, with a mean of 23 individual sessions per patient. No patient dropped out of therapy. In these treatments, the therapist and the patient prepared a hierarchical list of situations, from least to most distressful, of those that caused anxiety and consequent compulsive activity. The patient was then encouraged to enter gradually each situation which provoked the rituals. Trials were made of exposure to the least distressing situation, working up to the most disturbing, or vice versa; slow or rapid exposure was also tried. Each step was first demonstrated by the therapist in a calm and reassuring way.

All who showed improvement over two years demonstrated change within the first three weeks. It was noted that a good patient-therapist relationship was necessary to carry through the treatment and that the successful patients were those who were well motivated. Marks and colleagues noted that depressive episodes were common before, during, and after treatment and required prescription of antidepressant tricyclic medication. A recent study of chlorimipramine therapy showed that in a short time trial this tricyclic produced improvement in severity and occurrence of obsessions, anxiety, depression, and associated phobias. On the other hand, it did not modify obsessive ruminations, rituals, temptations, or doubts. Of over 125 obsessive-compulsives offered behavioral therapy over a four-year period, one fourth refused the treatment.

Prefrontal leukotomy has at times been followed by improvement. It should, however, be limited to cases so severe that the patient is practically confined to his home and incapacitated for any useful activity because of his compulsions. Results are better when there is evidence of persistence and drive and when the obsessional symptoms are accompanied by considerable anxiety.

DYSTHYMIC OR DEPRESSIVE DISORDER

In the neurotic depressions, anxiety becomes masked by self-depreciating behavior and depressive affect without, however, the gross affective, cognitive, or somatic disturbances associated with the primary affective disorders. As there has been little unanimity in the making of this diagnosis, some have argued discarding it to await a more certain clustering of symptoms. Others have indicated the behavioral variation found in the group, ranging from depression with anxiety to hostility. In a recent paper, Klerman and his associates review the literature and discuss these issues.

Such disorders include the many instances of pathological grief, the prolonged mourning that takes place following the death of a close family member. In most instances the onset of the reactive depression follows shortly after a significant and evident loss through death or separation or takes place subsequent to a defeat in social, economic, or personal life. These crises, then, may be the breaking of an engagement; a jilting; a divorce; the death of a spouse, lover, or parent; or the sudden loss of a fortune, a prized possession, or a valued function. Less commonly the depression follows the achievement of a wanted position—the so-called *success depression.*

In every instance the loss induces the affective state of sadness and also anxiety and frequently guilt or shame. The general response differs in no way from that described earlier for the affective psychotic reaction. With the neurotic depressions, however, the symptoms of profound somatic regression, such as anorexia, weight loss, constipation, sexual impotency, extreme retardation, and agitation, are not seen. On the other hand, other reactive character changes may take place, as well as the resort to oral gratifications. Crying appears to be more frequent in the neurotic than psychotic depressions.

The reactively depressed usually are drawn from those with one of the neurotic character structures. Thus there are the excessively timid and self-depreciating, the overbearing or arrogant, and the compulsively self-righteous. When such persons are faced with a loss, there is the expected sadness with mourning and self-depreciation, and in addition, there is often usually guilty anxiety due to surging up of unacceptable rage and aggression toward the lost object relation. Sometimes the depressed attempt to overcome the guilty anxiety and tension by taking alcohol or drugs. Others seek dependent support through hypochondriacal complaining. The reactively depressed are common in general medical clinics with their symptoms of aching pains, backaches, and preoccupation with various organ functions. A few others attempt to solve their rage and anxiety by impulsive acting out in various antisocial ways, such as promiscuity or indulgence in varieties of sexual excesses. The majority, however, complain of fatigue, lassitude, and difficulty in sleeping and in working. They deprecate their past, are pessimistic and self-pitying, but manage a precarious continuance of their general activities. In the instance of the loss of an ambivalently loved partner the virtues of the wife or husband are extolled, the rituals of mourning are prolonged, pictures and memories are displayed and conspicuously commented upon, while all recollections of disharmony are denied.

Depression that emerges after a presumed post of responsibility has been achieved accomplishes the aim of preserving the person with success phobia from the anxiety associated with assumption of a position of authority and acclaim, wherein the need for firmness and the acceptance of reward expose the sufferer to fears of retaliatory rage and envy, attitudes which he himself has held toward authority in the past.

Psychotherapy is the therapeutic method that most frequently provides the needed emotional support, and when coupled with psychodynamic understanding will bring about resolution of pathological guilt and shame. The anxiolytic drugs, as described in Chapter 32, should be tried in all cases.

POST-TRAUMATIC STRESS DISORDER

Following severe threat to life, whether as the consequence of stress in civilian life in the form of catastrophes such as automobile, airplane, or train accidents, floods, tornadoes, volcanic eruptions, or personal assaults such as rape, or of stress in warfare, combat, or the horrors of concentration camp existence, a well-defined personality disorder frequently results. This condition, known much earlier in the German literature as fright (*Schrek*) neurosis and in the English as traumatic neurosis, may occur as an isolated disturbance or may complicate pre-existing personality disorders. In the U.S.A., it probably occurs most commonly, and is most frequently unrecognized, after automobile accidents. Adler differentiates two types of post-traumatic states: those with immediate and those with delayed onset.

Stressful situations with threats or induction of fantasies of annihilation are not necessarily conducive to the ego-disorganizing neurotic stress syndromes. Under certain conditions stress-inducing situations lead to personality growth and increased ego potential for emotional control. The exposure to either an acutely terrifying event or catastrophe or prolonged or repeated threats that overwhelm the perceived capacity of the individual to defend himself against death, annihilation, or mutilation leads to the psychic trauma that causes the post-traumatic stress disorders. The emotional arousal is unbearable; repression fails; an affective storm occurs in which the individual fears he can no longer cope effectively or control the intensity of the affective state. Collapse occurs when he perceives he is helpless; beyond that, he gives up to the inevitable ending either in a frantic trancelike flight or a catatenoid state. It has been reported that, following major civilian catastrophes, between 10 and 25 per cent of survivors appear acutely stunned and immobile. It must be stressed that the perception of catastrophe is subjectively judged by the individual; it may not be perceived by others. (See Table 22–5 for diagnostic criteria.)

Krystal has discussed the differing effects of psychic trauma upon children as opposed to adults. The responses of adults vary because of their development of capacity to block emotion and constrict cognition. For the child, the intense affective arousal alone is overwhelming.

In a series of studies of the immediate reactions to acute stress of differing kinds, Janis described obsessional staring initially as a response to disaster. Such staring is also observed in those who converge on the disaster scene. Both victims and observers are preoc-

TABLE 22–5   Diagnostic Criteria for Post-Traumatic Stress Disorder

A. Existence of a recognizable stressor that would evoke significant symptoms of distress in almost everyone.

B. Re-experiencing of the trauma as evidenced by at least one of the following:
   (1) recurrent and intrusive recollections of the event
   (2) recurrent dreams of the event
   (3) sudden acting or feeling as if the traumatic event were re-occurring, because of an association with an environmental or ideational stimulus

C. Numbing of responsiveness to or reduced involvement with the external world, beginning some time after the trauma, as shown by at least one of the following:
   (1) markedly diminished interest in one or more significant activities
   (2) feeling of detachment or estrangement from others
   (3) constricted affect

D. At least two of the following symptoms that were not present before the trauma:
   (1) hyperalertness or exaggerated startle response
   (2) sleep disturbance
   (3) guilt about surviving when others have not, or about behavior required for survival
   (4) memory impairment or trouble concentrating
   (5) avoidance of activities that arouse recollection of the traumatic event
   (6) intensification of symptoms by exposure to events that symbolize or resemble the traumatic event

As presented in the Diagnostic and Statistical Manual of Mental Disorders, Third Edition (DSM-III). Washington, D. C., American Psychiatric Association, 1980.

cupied by thoughts and fantasies about what might have happened to them during the disaster, or of what might happen in the future. When suffering or threats of death or annihilation extend over months, as with prolonged illness or in sadistic prison camp experiences, the process of *working through* is prolonged, and profound attitudinal changes may be noted. As Janis reviews the evidence, working through, that is, the "work of worrying," seems to be a means of increasing the level of tolerance for subsequent threat or signals of danger. In a series of experiments he found that the more thorough the preliminary and anticipatory fear, apprehension, and worrying have been, the more reality-tested the individual's self-reassurances are likely to be and the more emotional control he is likely to exhibit under actual stress of life threat or deprivation. When the stressful event is so sudden as to eliminate the potential for worrying, when adequate prior warning of disaster or stress is not obtained, when the individual is given false reassurance, or when he is given to suppression of anticipating anxiety by means of the defense of denial through overoptimism or avoidance of warnings, the subsequent stress-induced reaction will be much more profound than in those prepared through anticipatory fear.

Perhaps the most closely related experimental model of the traumatic neuroses is the conditioned emotional response (CER) induced in animals. In this model, the emotional response is greater to the conditioned than to the unconditioned stimulus; that is, to put it in terms of human thinking, any perceptive thought or other associations to the traumatic event both continue and magnify the response disruptive to ego functions.

Working from the earlier conditioning theories of Watson, Mowrer and others, Eysenck has advanced modification of learning theory which he believes is capable of verification by experimentation. He attempts to explain the neurotic paradigm of behavior as quoted from Mowrer — the paradox of behavior simultaneously self-defeating and self-perpetuating! Originally, Watson proposed that there existed three primitive emotional reactions: fear, rage, and love. Fear is reproducible by such simple stimuli as loud noises, loss of support, and physical constraint.

The Eysenckian theory replaces the classic law of extinction with one that allows for incubation effects of exposure to conditioned stimuli only and for extinction effects. It holds that either a single traumatic exposure to a fear-inducing stimulus or repeated subtraumatic exposures provide the unconditioned stimuli that are linked to various associative conditioning stimuli and conditioning responses. Fear and anxiety acquire drive properties through incubation that lead to establishment of conditioned responses equivalent to the unconditioned responses and thereby reinforce the conditioned stimuli presentation. The stimuli are frustrative and non-rewarding. While non-reinforced conditioned stimuli that do not acquire drive properties through arousal of fear and anxiety may extinguish if presented frequently enough, conditioned stimuli with such acquired drive properties enhance the conditioned responses and expand and perpetuate the neurotic process.

Avoidance behavior develops secondarily to protect from the conditioned stimulus, since the response is reinforced by prevention of the unconditioned responses and by termination of the conditioned stimulus. Eysenck postulates that conditions favoring the incubation of fear-anxiety responses are short as opposed to long, and strong as opposed to weak, presentation of the unconditioned stimuli. Pre-existence of neurotic or introverted personality traits favors the development of the neuroses. How they develop is left unexplained. There are now identified *acute*, *chronic*, and *delayed* post-traumatic stress disorders.

Investigation of the survivors of concentration camp experiences, where on a mass scale men and women were exposed over years to the imminent threat of death, repeated brutalities, separation and loss of emotional support from family and friends, and physical deprivations of the most extreme kinds, supports the existence of the chronic stress state. This was identified earlier in studies of older veterans of World War I.

Lifton and Olson, from study of a group of survivors of a major civilian disaster, delineate the response of each individual survivor as first, that of *death imprint* and *death anxiety;* second, *death guilt;* third, *psychic numbing;* fourth, *impaired human relations,* especially with conflict over need for nurturing and suspicions of counterfeit support from others; fifth, *the meaning of the disaster* to the individual and the necessity to structure the death encounter significantly in relation to one's own existence.

As the response to combat in war has been the most thoroughly examined of the acute stress disorders, it is given extended discussion as the prototype. The concentration camp syndrome, similarly, is described as the prototype of the chronic syndrome. The delayed stress disorder is treated separately but, again, is best defined from clinical experience with Vietnam veterans.

Combat Reactions

Combat neuroses have long been associated with warfare, although their real nature and psychopathology were not recognized until World War I. During the Civil War, DaCosta described the "Irritable Heart of Soldiers." This was undoubtedly a neurosis induced by the stress and anxiety of combat and closely resembled the "Disordered Action of the Heart," 80,000 cases of which, it is said, occurred among British soldiers during World War I. It is of interest that this high incidence was not reported in World War II, presumably because the condition had become recognized as a neurosis.

In modern warfare, air attack, bombing, and artillery fire reached a new intensity, with a fear-producing potential probably never before attained. With terrifying shell-fire, combined with fear-inspiring air attacks, soldiers developed a striking variety of symptoms, including paralysis, gross tremors, mutism, blindness, confusion, or intense anxiety. In apparent absence of other etiological factors, it was at first concluded that the brain must in some undetermined man-

ner sustain damage by a blast concussion attending the nearby explosion of a shell. The term "shell shock" was therefore applied to these psychiatric casualties and prolonged hospitalization was prescribed for their treatment. Gradually, it was recognized that shell shock was primarily a psychological problem. It became apparent, too, that prolonged hospitalization merely fostered and fixated the mental symptoms, which, because they prevented return to combat and even brought a compensation pension, provided a considerable secondary gain.

In World War II, functional disability was much less likely if the patient with an acute, battle-induced neurosis was treated near the front lines and returned to duty as soon as possible. It was noted that the percentage of recoveries was greater if the attitude of the psychiatrist indicated that no organic damage had been sustained and if the name by which the neurosis was known to the soldier implied that the disability was transient.

Figures on the incidence of post-traumatic stress reactions are sparse. The psychiatric casualty rates among troops do not relate entirely to combat stress. Levie and colleagues, in a recent study of combat reactions during the Yom Kippur War, used an "epidemiological triangle," defined as agent (intensity of fire), host (age, rank and sociophysiological grading), and environment (corps and military assignment) to study the various factors that influenced rates of *acute* combat reactions seen beyond the immediate front line. He found, as others have, that rates for psychiatric casualties between combat units relate directly to the number of killed and wounded in any action. Soldiers in close logistical or support units appear to be at higher risk than fighting men. As to the individual host, the very young and those with low rank and low ratings on sociopsychological gradings are at greatest risk.

This relationship is demonstrated by

studies of neuropsychiatric admissions correlated with battle injuries. (See Figure 22–1.) Physical exhaustion alone is not sufficient to produce the neurosis, but it does serve to lessen resistance so that psychodynamic forces are more easily released. However, the greater the element of decreased physical efficiency resulting from fatigue, lack of food and sleep, or intercurrent illness, the more easily does emotional breakdown occur and the greater is the possibility of the soldier's not returning to active duty.

Personality factors predispose to the combat neuroses. It is not easy to select the man who will maintain emotional equilibrium in combat and eliminate the one who will prove inadequate for the stress. It is not always the unstable and neurotic man who, as might be supposed, lacks resistance to the terror that accompanies long and intense combat. In general, it is the timid and passive person or those with demanding and

rigidly held ego ideals, who cannot mobilize and externalize their anger and react aggressively toward the enemy and thus discharge their tensions, who are prone to develop a combat neurosis.

Most men, although wishing to meet the demands of their country during wartime, are induced into the armed forces without strong, conscious desire for military life or for combat experience. Many, at the time of induction, remain emotionally dependent on their families, perhaps overprotected by their mothers and intimidated by cruel fathers. An unduly large number of combat neuroses occurred in individuals from broken or distorted homes unfavorable for the development of a well-integrated and mature personality. Induction into military service is accompanied by the abrupt loss of emotional support provided by family and friends, the deprivation of female companionship, and the loss of individuality and privacy. Frequently, the unseasoned

Figure 22–1 Correlation between surgical and psychiatric casualty rates over six weeks of active service. (From Glass, A. J., and Bernucci, R. J. (eds.): Neuropsychiatry in World War II. Washington, D.C., Office of the Surgeon General, Department of the Army, 1966.)

soldier has a feeling that he is not appreciated and nurses resentment resulting from the change from the relatively flexible and permissive civilian pattern of living to one of subjection to strict discipline, regimentation, and subordination.

The stresses and conflicts to which the soldier is exposed during his training period are relatively mild; they are handled by most trainees without the development of protest symptoms in the form of neurotic or psychotic syndromes. Even though the period of training is not accompanied by the hazards of combat, normal gratifications are renounced, allowing release of hitherto destructive aggressive drives. New relationships that would meet the soldier's emotional needs in the strange and abnormal state of affairs have to be established. Under these circumstances, the most constructive relationship is the soldier's identification of himself as an integral part of his unit, and his unit as a part of himself. He must have confidence in his unit and in the character, capability, and bravery of his leader. With the formation of deep emotional relationships with his leader and his buddies, the soldier's feelings of security and power are increased and his morale, or those attitudes, feelings, and beliefs that promote participation in a united effort, is promoted.

Fear is an emotion experienced in response to a stimulus having actual reality, one that either constitutes a present threat to the individual or portends real danger. Anxiety, on the other hand, is an expectation of danger, an emotional state of apprehensiveness, uncertainty, and insecurity, that may be produced either from situations symbolic of external danger or from internal conflicts and tensions present in the unconscious. Frequently, anxiety springs from internal threats of repressed hostility, aggression, or resentment. Although this distinction between fear and anxiety can be made, in war situations they operate jointly. Their feeling-tones and their accompanying physiological expressions are the same. Although anxiety arises from internal threats, it is attributed to (projected upon) some real external source. In the war neuroses, this projection is upon a dangerous external situation that is also provocative of fear. Both fear and the feelings of apprehension and insecurity characteristic of anxiety may therefore seem to have a common source.

FACTORS CONTRIBUTING TO WAR NEUROSES. As indicated, fear and an impairment of the ability to repress fear reactions are highly provocative of anxiety. A breakdown of group morale or an attitude of defeatism within the combat unit greatly increases the psychological strain. Such a loss of morale is particularly prone to exist in case of lack of faith in commanding officers, in the absence of identification with one's unit, or during a retreat. The quality of leadership is one of the most important factors in the incidence of neurotic breakdown in any given unit.

Prolonged periods of enforced inactivity during which men are exposed to danger predispose to an anxiety reaction. So does the loneliness of foxhole fighting. Repeated narrow escapes, high combat losses, and repeated exposure to the mutilation and death of close friends increase apprehension and stimulate guilt and anxiety. Fear of being a coward or of losing one's self-control, a realization of the responsibility for the lives of others, and an insufficient understanding of war or a lack of conviction of the need to fight, all predispose to war neuroses.

Feelings of guilt provoke anxiety as well. Such feelings may arise from the soldier's thought that he has been responsible for the death of someone else, perhaps a civilian as well as an enemy. The death of a comrade toward whom the soldier entertained ambivalent feelings or whom he had identified with a sibling rival may create feelings of guilt with anxiety or depression. An unconscious hostility may lead to the soldier's conviction that he has actually caused the death of a comrade. Following the death of a buddy, a man may develop a feeling of guilt through a belief that he failed to take care of his friend. Frequently, the loss of a buddy or of a respected officer, by creating the feeling that one is being left alone, helpless, and deserted, deprives the soldier of emotional support and leads to an unendurable anxiety.

PREVENTIVE FACTORS. One of the most important mechanisms in strengthening the ego against factors productive of anxiety and other neurotic reactions is the soldier's identification with his unit. By this mechanism, he transfers a considerable share of his personal self-love to affection for and pride in his outfit. Thus his feelings of obligation and loyalty overrule personal interests and provide strong motivations for combat and effective protection against any expression of his conflicts.

The group relationship and its emotional bonds are among the most constructive and integrative forces for the individual. Similarly, an intense loyalty between individual men and the immediate leaders promotes morale and raises the threshold against anxiety. Other factors that aid in warding off anxiety are the desire to avoid loss of the esteem of the group by any failure in courage or in other demands of military tradition and also the habit of obedience and the disciplined behavior established by military training.

An additional factor in the prevention of war neuroses is education concerning the nature of fear. The trained soldier has been taught that fear is a normal emotion of battle and to experience it should not be considered an occasion for censure or self-depreciation. He is given simple information concerning its physiological manifestations and the nature of the nervous reactions it produces. His recognition of fear and his effort to deal with it on a conscious level tend to minimize its anxiety-stimulating influence.

NORMAL BATTLE REACTION. To protect itself from an overwhelming threat to its existence, the organism becomes completely and continuously alert. This leads to severe and continuous emotional tension. In spite of the various factors that aid in the prevention of combat neuroses, such stresses as exhaustion, excitement, and mortal terror inevitably produce reactions that would be considered abnormal in a civilian setting, yet are not so incapacitating as to demand removal from combat. Unless extreme, such reactions must be considered within the range of normal. Many reactions represent psychosomatic responses to stress and fear: sensations of pulling or pressure over the back of the head and neck, muscular tension, and shaking and tremor. The soldier may be transitorily immobilized. Excessive perspiration is common, and some experience anorexia, nausea, vague abdominal distress, mild diarrhea, and urinary frequency. Tachycardia, palpitation, breathlessness, and a sense of thoracic oppression and of faintness, together with generalized muscular weakness and lassitude, often exist. Many soldiers experience difficulty in sleeping and have repetitive nightmares of battle and "startle" reactions to threatening noises. Irritability is usual in the soldier subjected to long-continued battle, and resentment is common among those who have lost friends and withstood privations and dangers.

An 18-year-old Navy radioman was admitted to a hospital with symptoms of anxiety and depression.

The patient was the youngest son in a happy family of four children. He was the favored child and throughout his early life gave no indications of instability. At school he was an average student and later was president of his high school class and an outstanding football player. At the outbreak of World War II, he enlisted in the naval service with the consent of his parents, and immediately after completing his recruit training was detailed aboard a destroyer, where the morale was high. He made many close friends, and with the personal assistance of the communications officer, who helped him with the radio work, made a rapid advancement in rate.

The destroyer was part of the screen of an aircraft carrier engaged in the Coral Sea Battle, the raid on the Gilbert and Marshall Islands, and later the Battle of Midway. At the onset of each engagement, the patient felt apprehensive, but once firing commenced, he became entirely composed and attentive to his duties. While the destroyer was lying alongside a stricken aircraft carrier following a bombing attack during the Battle of Midway, the patient saw "torpedo wakes" approaching the ship; he resumed his post, until suddenly he was thrown out of his seat when the torpedo exploded beneath him. He plunged overboard, reached a nearby raft, and was later taken aboard another destroyer where he collapsed. He knew that his best friend, his immediate chief and the communications officer had all been killed. Following his return to the naval base, it was learned that he had suffered blast injury to the chest and abdomen that eventually necessitated intestinal resection. During convalescence from this operation, he first had terrifying nightmares in which various scenes related to the sinking of the destroyer were continually repeated, during which he awoke in a state of anxiety. Sudden noises also produced unusual apprehension.

There was no evidence of physical disease, but insomnia, anorexia, constipation, and fatigue were observed and psychiatric study was requested. The patient was listless, dejected, and emotionally labile. Discussion of his battle experiences was distressing to him, and he described in detail his sensitivity to sounds and various combat scenes in motion pictures. The latter stimulus invariably led to anxiety. After one month of treatment on the psychiatric service, he became more energetic and content, slept well, commenced to eat, gained some weight, and again desired to return to duty. Nightmares were infrequent and sounds were less disturbing to him.

Acute Form. The most frequent form of the post-traumatic reaction is the *anxiety state.* This constitutes over 75 per cent of acute war neuroses. In moderate or mild anxiety states, the patient shows tension, tremor, apprehension, weeping, depression, feelings of guilt, dizziness, tinnitus, urinary frequency, insomnia, and repetitive nightmares and dreams of battle trauma. In those men with impaired personality development, *conversion reactions* may consist of paralyses, sensory losses, aphonia, deafness, partial or total blindness, speech defects, astasia-abasia, a fixed stooping posture known as camptocormia, and, occasionally, a persistent amnesia. Such patients exhibit little visible anxiety and may manifest "*la belle indifférence.*"

Some cases of combat neurosis assume the form of *depression,* usually preceded by anxiety. The depression may not be particularly obvious until after the effort to control anxiety has failed. The depression is frequently precipitated by the death of a comrade to whose loss the soldier was unable to reconcile himself. The conscious mental content is dominated by ideas of failure, guilt, and self-condemnation. The patient is convinced that he has let his buddies down or that in some way he has been responsible for their deaths. Frequently, such depressions arise in cases in which the patient has had ambivalent feelings directed toward a comrade. Upon the death of his buddy, the unconscious hostility that existed in these feelings stimulates the conviction that he actually caused the death of his comrade. This evokes guilt, depression, and self-punishment. The clinical symptoms are characterized by a rigid, masklike face, by paucity of movement, and by ideas of self-accusation and self-depreciation.

A 17-year-old seaman had seven months' active duty in World War II prior to admission to the hospital with a tentative diagnosis of intracranial injury.

He was the third of four boys in a family of six. His father was a "shell-shocked" veteran of World War I, now alcoholic and a chronic complainer. The mother was migrainous. The home was kept discordant by parental quarrels; nevertheless, the patient, though of a retiring and quiet nature, adjusted well at school, was accepted by his classmates, and was not considered temperamentally unstable.

Following his enlistment in the naval service, he received three weeks of basic training and was detailed aboard a transport for drill in amphibious operations. The patient had hoped for duty aboard a combat ship of the line. Three weeks prior to the departure of the convoys for the North African engagement, he was transferred to another ship. There he was barely acquainted with his new shipmates when the engagement opened. His immediate chief was regarded by him with little respect as an "old man." The seaman was extremely apprehensive as his landing boat approached the beach during the opening operations, but he quickly regained composure when not exposed to fire. The following day he was frightened to the point of believing his legs were paralyzed when an enemy plane strafed the ship and he threw himself on the deck. The fourth day the ship was suddenly torpedoed. He was blown against the bulkhead and struck his head but was not injured and quickly climbed down a net into a tank lighter below. While throwing out lines to men struggling in the water, he was fascinated by their cries and amazed to see some cast aside their life jackets. After helping one man aboard, the patient felt so weak that he lay upon the deck and later had to be assisted ashore. The following day a plane killed a French woman in town, and he morbidly examined her body and the leg wounds of a sailor wounded in the same raid.

He then realized how tense and anxious he felt, and in the following weeks had difficulty in sleeping, being repeatedly awakened by dreams in which his ship was torpedoed or he was shot in the leg. While aboard the transport returning home, he and the men in his division were quartered in a forward compartment. During a prolonged storm, the group repeatedly rushed to the boat deck in panic when a loose hatch cover slammed above them. He was given a 30-day leave after arriving in this country, but the change in his personality was so conspicuous to his family that his mother shortly sought medical advice concerning his symptoms.

On return to duty, the patient complained of headaches and dizziness and was transferred to the hospital for study. As there was no evidence of organic disease, psychiatric examination was requested. His extreme restlessness, amounting to agitation, and his inattentiveness and irritation were immediately apparent. He was unable to concentrate, expressed death fears, and presented the history of nightmares and sensitivity to sounds reminiscent of combat. His sleep was broken almost nightly by terrifying dreams. With sedation and psychotherapy there was some diminution in the restlessness, the insomnia, and his response to startle. He put on weight but continued to complain and insisted upon his inability to return to duty. It was evident that he would not again adjust in the service and, accordingly, he was recommended for discharge.

This youthful seaman, who was reared in a discordant home by a neurotic, alcoholic father and a high-strung mother, presented no evidence of emotional instability prior to his traumatic combat experience. He then developed nightmares, a startle reaction, and a personality change marked by agitation, anxiety and preoccupation, with the complaints of headaches and dizziness. The case study illustrates the importance in determining the neurotic reaction of a disturbed home life with the possibility of neurotic identification, and the contributing factors of inadequate training, indifference to leadership, and low morale. The repeated panics during the voyage home probably further served to deepen the patient's anxiety by the process of conditioning.

PSYCHOTIC-LIKE STATES. In some cases of overwhelming anxiety, panic is so great that ego organization fails. The man appears out of contact with reality and so confused and dissociated, with such bizarre behavior, that he appears psychotic. The onset is usually sudden; the clinical picture is schizophreniform. Many patients are disoriented and fail to reply to simple questions. Some behave as in a catatonic stupor; others suggest a catatonic excitement.

In the most severe reactions, the onset is acute and sudden. A coarse tremor is not uncommon. It may be difficult or impossible to establish contact with the patient. Even though no longer under fire, the man may believe himself still in battle and behave accordingly. He may, with expressions of terror, call to his friends to look out for the shells. Some show highly dramatic reactions and excessive startle patterns in response to slight stimuli. In extreme cases, the soldier's behavior is one of panic with complete disruption of personality organization. His uncontrolled, catastrophic reaction may vary from wild, impulsive flights to "freezing," or primitive protective withdrawal, with stupor, catatonia, or mutism.

These psychotic-like pictures occur in individuals who have not been psychotic in their previous reactions or in their basic personality structures. Such short-lived "three-day" psychoses usually disappear when the patients are removed from the traumatic situations.

TREATMENT. In treatment of the acute neuroses in the armed forces, emphasis is placed on preservation of discipline, early and vigorous treatment, the shortening of the period of hospitalization, the avoidance of unnecessary hospital atmosphere, and the promotion in the patient of the expectation of return to full duty. Care is exercised to preserve the patient's identification with the combat group, to minimize the secondary gain of neurotic illness, and to avoid any suggestion of illness and disability. It is a basic principle in the attainment of these objectives that treatment should be as far forward toward the battle lines as possible. So far as practicable, soldiers who show symptoms of becoming psychiatric casualties on the battlefield receive what may be called psychiatric first aid from members of their own combat units. Here company officers promote morale by counsel, reassurance, exhortation, and leadership. Soldiers with relatively minor complaints may frequently be prevented from entering medical channels where the dissolution of group ties and the factors of secondary gain and suggestion tend to fix their symptoms.

If his motivation has been reasonably good, the patient responds well to proper therapeutic handling. If formal medical treatment is required, the patient is evacuated to the battalion aid station. Here most patients are those suffering from mild to moderate anxiety states, complicated by physical exhaustion and the effects of exposure. They are usually wet, cold, dirty, and physically worn out.

If the anxiety state is no more than moderate, the patient is kept at the aid station for 24 hours, where he is cleaned up, dried, adequately fed, and given sedation. By his manner and remarks, the battalion surgeon indicates that he expects an early return to duty of the soldier after he is rested. Many of the patients evacuated to the battalion aid station are simply suffering from normal fear reactions, with the somatic and psychological manifestations of that state. The patient has usually become alarmed by these symptoms that he has interpreted as those of cardiac, gastrointestinal, or other physical disorder. A careful physical examination is made. If no organ involvement is found, the cause of the symptoms is carefully explained to the soldier, who is assured that there will be no lasting effects or disability. After 24 hours of rest and psychotherapy consisting of reassurance, support, and exhortation, many patients are so greatly improved that they may be returned directly to duty.

Those with the more severe psychotic-like reactions are unsuited for management in the battalion aid station and are therefore transferred to the division clearing station. Upon arrival, active psychiatric treatment begins. Sedation is given at once to those who have not already received it, and they are placed in adequately heated tent wards, are provided with cots for sleeping, and are given an abundance of hot food.

The psychiatrist combines attitudes of respect and sympathy for the patient, yet he also permits no doubt to arise in the patient's mind that he will return to full duty after a brief rest. If the patient is allowed to ventilate his fears, hopes, and resentments, prompt symptomatic relief often follows. An attempt is made to avoid any suggestion of illness in the organization and atmosphere of treatment stations and in the attitude and action of the psychiatrist. As much care is used to avoid suggestion of serious psychiatric illness as of physical disease.

For those who fail to respond to these immediate treatment efforts and remain withdrawn or behaviorally disturbed, early treatment using the narcosynthetic technique or hypnosis often brings a quick resolution of the grosser symptomatology.

Delayed Stress Disorder

That many exposed to catastrophic experience present themselves for care months later has been recognized for many years but emphasized recently, particularly in the United States, as a consequence of clinical experiences with combat veterans of the Vietnam experience. Increasingly, those soldiers, rapidly discharged into the civilian population that often projected its rage and blame for the wasteful conflict upon the returned soldier, have presented themselves for care. They do so through medical services owing to resurgence of panic attacks; through inpatient psychiatric services owing to transient states of dissociation, often associated with violence; through outpatient services owing to marital and family difficulties, problems at work, or insomnia; and through drug abuse services owing to secondary alcoholism or other drug abuse. The diagnosis of delayed stress disorder is made customarily if the delay in recurrence of symptom expression comes six months or more after the traumatic event.

A high majority of individuals experience the acute symptoms described earlier in this chapter following a traumatic event. The senior author examined 90 survivors within two weeks of the sinking of a destroyer during World War II. Ninety per cent had the acute symptoms of hyperalertness, restlessness, insomnia, repetitive nightmares of the sinking, and the startle reaction to sounds. Two months later, these same men were re-examined after rest at home. Only five had persisting symptoms.

That such symptoms may persist for much longer periods in large numbers of traumatically shocked persons can be seen from DeFazio's examination of combat veterans from Vietnam five years after their exposure. None had presented themselves for psychiatric help. DeFazio found that 67 per cent had frequent repetitive nightmares, 41 per cent were short tempered, 32 per cent had difficulty relaxing, 35 per cent had difficulty with intimacy with others, 35 per cent remained fearful, approximately the same percentage reported the symptoms of fatigue, and 28 per cent spoke of nervousness.

PSYCHODYNAMICS. After the traumatic incident, the individual attempts to restore ego functioning by aversive behaviors and re-erecting his psychological defenses. He attempts by all means to avoid the intrusion of memories and the overwhelming related affects pertaining to the catastrophic incident. Nevertheless, the repetitive nightmares continue to occur; some have thought these are attempts at resolution but others believe they evidence ego failure. During the day, intrusive thoughts of the event break through. These are triggered by external stimuli, such as loud noises reminiscent of sounds associated with the traumatic event, by questions or conversation regarding it, or by auditory or visual stimuli coming from dramatic presentations involving scenes of violence. The sufferer generally takes aversive actions to avoid such stimuli. He does not go to movies or view television shows reminding him of his experience. He shies away from those who pry into his experiences with questions and generally feels most at ease with other persons who suffered the same type of traumatic experience.

Such external stimulation being capable of re-arousing intensive anxiety is characteristic of conditioned emotional states. Recently, in the course of pentobarbital narcosynthesis, the senior author discovered full emotional abreactions of fear, rage, shame, and anger, with immediate time regression to the traumatic scene, on exposing Vietnam veterans with the clinically diagnosed post-traumatic stress disorder of ten years' duration to 30 seconds of tape-recorded combat sounds.

Other avoidance behaviors are observed in the social withdrawal of many or the so-called "psychic numbing" in which the individual is unable to commit himself to an intimate or responsible relationship with another in the fear of re-arousal of the emotions suffered when he lost comrades earlier in combat.

Close relations, with the inevitable ambivalence, arouse rage, which also threatens the defensive shell erected to avoid memory-affective re-arousal. The individual lives in a continual state of dread of recurrence of the event, as well as fear that it will so occur. As a husband, parent, or employee, he cannot face arguments or criticism because of the expectation that his internalized rage, which he foresees as overwhelming, may break out.

Continuing anhedonia is common, as the sufferer cannot commit himself to others, gives up many activities as potentially threatening, and suffers an enduring survivor's guilt.

Unfortunately, the aversive defensive structure often breaks down. Exposure to conflict with family members or supervisors or to external noises often generates intense internalized stress. Panic attacks ensue, which often are thought to be owing to cardiac disease. Attempts are made to desensitize one's self by alcoholic or narcotic numbing. At times the emotional upheaval is so great that ego integration fails and trance states ensue, with eruption of violence or development of late conversion symptoms. Continuing depression or its equivalent in painful, complaining behavior is seen in many. Insomnia often occurs as a major symptom because of night terrors. The individual then fears going to sleep. Little is known about the neurophysiology of the sleep disorders, so that rational therapy is precluded.

DIFFERENTIAL DIAGNOSIS. Adjustment disorders are differentiated, as the stressor is less severe and re-experiencing the trauma as intrusive thoughts or dreams does not occur. Panic and phobic and anxiety states occur because of conflict, not exposure to catastrophe. In the phobic disorder, there is displacement of anxiety from the threatening object. In the stress disorders, a true phobia does not exist; the threatening situation is recognized. What is derived is the fear of annihilation of control.

TREATMENT. Treatment should be directed initially to decreasing the occurrence of the distressing symptom expressions. Appropriate antidepressant medication often relieves the symptom and blocks the occurrence of panic attacks. Dalmane or other benzodiazepines may assist in treatment of the sleep disorders. Excepting in those with related schizotypal personality, the neuroleptics are contraindicated.

To bring about long-term improvement in social competence, group and/or family therapies are indicated. Individual psychotherapy may be required for those with predisposing person-ality disorders, but it is difficult for the patient to enter or maintain treatment because of the sufferer's inclination to avoid close human relations.

Chronic Stress Disorder

Chronic stress reactions are suffered by veterans of combat, released prisoners of war, hostages, and survivors of massive catastrophes—devastating earthquakes, violent storms, tidal waves, erupting volcanoes. Drifting in a lifeboat for days or weeks may be a cause. Survivors of the concentration camps of World War II are today the largest group of sufferers of chronic stress reactions. As the most widely recognized clinical example, *concentration camp syndrome* will be used for illustration.

Those millions confined to concentration camps were exposed to differing kinds of stress. The threat of imminent death or permanent incarceration was suffered by all. The intensity of the threats was variable. Those exposed to the open brutalities and killings and executions of other prisoners and who were required to participate in prison camp persecutions and burials, while surviving separation from family members and friends, suffered differently from others incarcerated and deprived physically owing to severe shortages of food, clothing, housing, activity, and opportunities for needed human contact, emotional support, and stimulation. The vast majority of those survivors who had symptoms impairing their personality functioning experienced the full range of terrifying and despair-creating stresses: personal assaults of all kinds, perceptions of brutality and killings of others, desecration of bodies, separation from families and friends, and physical illness and deprivations. Many became "living corpses" in the concentration camp.

Those who survived did so through the mobilization of a variety of psychological defenses and adaptations—as well as through being among the group fortuitously saved by circumstances. Fantasy, identification with the aggressor by privileged prisoners, and sublimation through some form of intellectualization have been noted as common defensive maneuvers. Political, but not religious, group activities seemed supportive. The mobilized adaptations and defenses are considered to have been called into play while the established ego and superego attitudes were eroded under a continuing barrage of exhausting challenges.

The sufferers of the concentration camp syndrome complained of increased fatigability, impairment of memory, difficulty in concentration, emotional lability, bitterness, depression, lack of pleasure in any effort, apathy and indifference to others, persisting disturbances of sleep, recurrent nightmares and daytime preoccupations and fantasies of these past experiences, irritability, restlessness, and headaches.

Restlessness, tension, and chronic anxiety with inability to forget or put aside memories of the concentration camp persecutions often led the sufferer to isolate himself socially from his environment as a means of cutting off associations that intensified these symptoms. The numerous physical symptoms represented the psychosomatic expressions of anxiety. Concentration camp survivors are more subject to those conditions associated with specific tissue damage, such as peptic ulcer.

Others who lost their families, homes, and vocations were apathetic, indifferent, depressed, and guilty. Enduring and burdening guilt responses followed as the sufferer realized that he was the sole surviving member of a family or group or even a single relationship. The guilt often was in response to a sense of implication in the death of others. Those with a predisposition to psychoses or with previous psychoses expressed their symptomatology in the defenses characteristic for their personality make-up. Some evolved paranoid persecutory attitudes. Those who were exposed to the concentration camp early in life often expressed their personality restrictions in antisocial behaviors. Yet the psychiatrist will note the surmounting symptoms expressive of the chronic stress reactions. These emerged in the perpetual preoccupation with the past, the terrors of the experience, the recapitulating nightmares and either restlessness, irritability, and irascibility or apathy, hopelessness, and indifference.

As Krystal has analyzed the variety of responses to trauma in his studies, the juvenile survivors have afterwards a higher rate of psychosomatic disorder (75 per cent) than the adults (30 per cent). Among the juvenile psychosomatic responses, 10 per cent had demonstrable peptic ulcer, and another 60 per cent had gastric psychophysiological symptoms.

Psychodynamically, these symptom expressions have been interpreted as an erosion of ego and superego functions. With the threat to self and the loss of relations with others, the sense of personal identity was impaired and depersonalization occurred. This was followed by eruption of intense anxiety and terror which evoked in turn the primitive psychological adaptations and defenses such as passivity, sadomasochistic traits, and identification with the aggressor. These infantile modes of adaptation and defense remained even after removal from the camp. The capacity to redevelop defenses and adaptive processes seemed impaired or permanently damaged. There was a loss of more mature volitional, cognitive, and affective processes.

The personality breakdown appears to affect adversely later parental functioning of survivors. Sigal reports that the parents have difficulty in controlling their children and that, in families with more than one child, the overt sibling rivalry is excessive. Either the children are overvalued and parental firmness is lacking, or any deviation from parental expectations is punished.

So, too, the parents' preoccupation with the unending mourning process leaves them communicatively remote from the children. The overreverence for the child given by many as a means of living out their own hopeful fantasies impairs children in finding their own identities. Thus the second generation of those suffering from the chronic stress reaction appear to endure a form of parental deprivation. Their adult adaptations remain for future study.

There is reason to believe that this form of personality disruption is irreversible in many, particularly those who suffered head injuries and other cerebral or general physical disability as the result of deprivations. Prolonged psychotherapy has had only limited success in such patients. Those who have attempted psychotherapy with the sufferers of the concentration camp syndrome have noted their frequent reluctance to enter treatment. This stems in some from their unwillingness to once again establish an emotionally intense relationship with another, which might be betrayed through loss of that person and lead to overwhelming re-arousal of rage, sadness, and guilt. In others, treatment threatens their uniqueness— their sense of omnipotence in survival which seems to serve as a defense against terrifying anxieties of loss and abandonment and/or death.

In those who enter treatment it is necessary to work through the anxieties associated with abandonment and death At first such patients may express their disappointment with their present situation and accuse their physician of a lack of understanding and warmth. Such patients will not be concerned with their losses and the associated guilt until late in treatment. Some are concerned early with the working through of grief and guilt, others with projections of destructiveness to the therapist.

The major therapeutic problem for all is the fear of a new close human relationship. Avoidance of therapy represents this anxiety, as does the frequent aggression toward the therapist used as a defense against involvement and the anxious helplessness of potential abandonment.

For psychotherapy to be successful, many believe the patient must be offered or have available opportunities to express realistically his aggressive strivings. This is in keeping with the finding that presumed successful life adaptation of survivors of Nazi concentration camps often has been based upon aggressive single-minded drives toward outward attainment. In many of these untreated persons the outwardly successful aggressive drive state obscures the underlying anxiety, depression, and hostile defenses against others.

Treatment for many then will remain directed at amelioration of symptoms through emotionally supportive management and use of appropriate drugs.

SOMATOFORM DISORDERS

This new categorization includes within it all those conditions known as hysterical neuroses in earlier editions of this work, except the dissociative states. The latter are now separated into a new major category. We now find the earlier hysterical states subclassified independently under DSM-III as Somatization Disorder, Conversion Disorder, Psychogenic Pain Disorder, Hypochondriases, and Atypical Somatoform Disorder. In the belief that the psychogenic processes determinative of dissociative disorders, as well as the factitious disorders, are similar to those of the above, we include these categories within this chapter.

Considered under the somatoform disorders are a wide variety of symptomatic expressions suggestive of physical disease, in which one does not discover through physical examination evidence of structural organic abnormality or physiological dysfunction.

SOMATIZATION DISORDER

Those patients with multiple somatic complaints are frequent visitors to physicians and clinics, vague in their descriptions of troubles, often dramatizing their distress or appearing to exaggerate their symptoms. The symptoms and dysfunction range across the organ systems, as Table 22–6 demonstrates. The patient presents as possibly having neurological, gastrointestinal, psychosexual, and cardiopulmonary disorders. Anxiety and depression frequently may be present in some, as are evidences of antisocial behavior.

Onset is usually during late adolescence. In women, menstrual difficulties may be the presenting complaints, but headache, abdominal pain, and depression are common. The condition is found in approximately 1 per cent of women. Panic disorders may co-exist. It is the combination of symptoms pro-

duced through the processes of conversion and pathological identification, as well as the physical manifestations of anxiety such as hyperventilation with panic attacks, that accounts for the polysymptomatic expressions of this disorder. This disorder is more common among family members than in the general population. Its polysymptomatic expression and tendency to occur in other family members separate it from the now-designated conversion disorders.

Course

The symptom expressions fluctuate over time, with periods of remission. Such patients pass from physician to physician and sometimes consult several simultaneously. They are prone to overmedicate, become drug abusers, and often are subjected to unnecessary surgical procedures. Often there are suici-

TABLE 22–6   The Frequency of Symptoms in Hysteria

SYMPTOM	%	SYMPTOM	%	SYMPTOM	%
Dyspnea	72	Weight loss	28	Back pain	88
Palpitation	60	Anorexia	60	Joint pain	84
Chest pain	72	Nausea	80	Extremity pain	84
Dizziness	84	Vomiting	32	Burning pains in	
Headache	80	Abdominal pain	80	rectum, vagina, mouth	28
Anxiety attacks	64	Abdominal bloating	68	Other bodily pain	36
Fatigue	84	Food intolerances	48	Depressed feelings	64
Blindness	20	Diarrhea	20	Phobias	48
Paralysis	12	Constipation	64	Vomiting all nine	
Anesthesia	32	Dysuria	44	months of pregnancy	20
Aphonia	44	Urinary retention	8	Nervous	92
Lump in throat	28	Dysmenorrhea		Had to quit working	
Fits or convulsions	20	(premarital only)	4	because felt bad	44
Faints	56	Dysmenorrhea		Trouble doing anything	
Unconsciousness	16	(prepregnancy only)	8	because felt bad	72
Amnesia	8	Dysmenorrhea (other)	48	Cried a lot	60
Visual blurring	64	Menstrual irregularity	48	Felt life was hopeless	28
Visual hallucination	12	Excessive menstrual		Always sickly	
Deafness	4	bleeding	48	(most of life)	40
Olfactory hallucination	16	Sexual indifference	44	Thought of dying	48
Weakness	84	Frigidity		Wanted to die	36
Sudden fluctuations in		(absence of orgasm)	24	Thought of suicide	28
weight	16	Dyspareunia	52	Attempted suicide	12

(From Perley, M. J., and Guze, S. B.: Hysteria—the stability and usefulness of clinical criteria. N. Engl. J. Med., *266*:421–426, 1962.)

dal attempts and threats, but death by this means usually is the result of accidental overdosage by drugs. The outlook for significant improvement is limited.

Symptoms

The symptoms of the somatization disorder are many, as Table 22–6 illustrates. Panic attacks cause the majority of the cardiorespiratory symptoms. Conversion, with site determination usually based on pathological identification, explains the majority of the symptoms, often compounded with disorders of the central or peripheral nervous system. In women, psychosexual dysfunction so common to those with this condition is expressed in menstrual complaints, dyspareunia, and frigidity as well as other genitourinary symptoms. Tension, anxiety, depression, lack of self-esteem and security with feelings of hopelessness are often ongoing symptoms that usually precede the more dramatic presentations of impaired functioning. The latter are particularly prominent in terms of gross conversions leading to motor and sensory function or painful complaints. (See Table 22–7 for diagnostic criteria.)

Etiology

In these disorders, anxiety is translated into functional symptoms in organs or parts of the body innervated by the sensorimotor nervous system instead of being consciously experienced, either diffusely as in anxiety reactions, or displaced as in phobias. The symptoms serve to prevent or lessen any conscious, felt anxiety and usually symbolize the underlying mental conflict that is productive of anxiety. The reaction usually meets some need of the patient and therefore serves not merely as a defense against anxiety but also provides some more or less obvious "secondary gain," a phenomenon discussed in this chapter.

Viewed a little differently, the symp-

TABLE 22–7   Diagnostic Criteria for Somatization Disorder

A. A history of physical symptoms of several years' duration beginning before the age of 30 years.

B. Complaints of at least 14 symptoms for women and 12 for men, from the 37 symptoms listed below. To count a symptom as present, the individual must report that the symptom caused him or her to take medicine (other than aspirin), alter his or her life pattern, or see a physician. The symptoms, in the judgment of the clinician, are not adequately explained by physical disorder or physical injury and are not side effects of medication, drugs, or alcohol. The clinician need not be convinced that the symptom was actually present, e.g., that the individual actually vomited throughout her entire pregnancy; report of the symptom by the individual is sufficient.

Sickly: Believes that he or she has been sickly for a good part of his or her life.

Conversion or pseudoneurological symptoms: Difficulty in swallowing, loss of voice, deafness, double vision, blurred vision, blindness, fainting or loss of consciousness, memory loss, seizures or convulsions, trouble in walking, paralysis or muscle weakness, urinary retention or difficulty urinating.

Gastrointestinal symptoms: Abdominal pain, nausea, vomiting spells (other than during pregnancy), bloating (gassy), intolerance (e.g., gets sick) of a variety of foods, diarrhea.

Female reproductive symptoms: Judged by the individual as occurring more frequently or severely than in most women: painful menstruation, menstrual irregularity, excessive bleeding, severe vomiting throughout pregnancy or causing hospitalization during pregnancy.

Psychosexual symptoms: For the major part of the individual's life after opportunities for sexual activity: sexual indifference, lack of pleasure during intercourse, pain during intercourse.

As presented in the Diagnostic and Statistical Manual of Mental Disorders, Third Edition (DSM-III). Washington, D.C., American Psychiatric Association, 1980.

tom may be regarded as expressing a conflict or an idea in symbolic form. It may, for example, "convert" a mental concept into a significant body symptom, as when hysterical paralysis of an arm expresses a wish to do a forbidden act, yet ambivalently prevents its accomplishment. The form of the symptom is determined by some feature of the situation it was designed to meet.

If a person were consciously to counterfeit some physical sign or symptom of some mental disturbance for the purpose of attaining a particular objective, we would say that he or she was *malingering*. Conscious recognition of its intent is not necessary, however, in order that behavior may be purposive. In the somatoform disorder, the symptoms, without awareness on the part of patients, provide some form and extent of solution for their problems and afford them a certain relief from the anxiety involved. Some hysterical phenomena are on the borderline between psychoneurotic reactions and simulation and therefore come close to malingering. Just where, as to awareness, the line between simulation and hysteria should be drawn is therefore arbitrary. In both there is a subtle interweaving of conscious factors. Both are related to some definite purpose, usually protective or wish-fulfilling in nature. It is not surprising that the difference in the hysteric's mind between reality and fantasy is often vague.

Causes

The immediate factor in the production of these disorders is some anxiety-producing situation. With the frequent exception of the post-traumatic hysterias, we find that the conversion reactions of civilian life tend to develop on a certain personality background characterized by immaturity in the psychosexual and emotional fields. The most common personality type subject to expression of such symptoms is the histrionic, but those with passive-aggressive personality disorders also are prone to such symptom development, as well as certain obsessive and schizoid individuals. Thus today, the diagnosis of "conversion reaction" is not thought synonymous with the designation of "hysterical personality," although the majority of sufferers of conversion symptoms have such a personality make-up.

Accepting somatization as occurring in many personality reactions other than the histrionic and even applying diagnostic criteria as demanding in terms of symptom expression as those required to establish the diagnosis of hysteria, prevalence of 2 per cent among a general female population has been found.

Puberty is a favorite period for the appearance of such reactions. What may be called the normal psychic characteristics of that period are often found to persist in the mental life of the adult who is subject to conversion. Maturing drives, for example, may remain in an arrested or infantile state of development, a state to which a failure to attain an emotional independence from a parent sometimes contributes. Impulses, sentiments, and other bases of the personality are not well integrated. Some, with their immature personality development, are basically hostile and aggressive persons.

Further mention may be made of some of the personality characteristics frequently observed. It will often be found that evasions and mechanisms of retreat have been habitual since early life. The narcissism that tends to characterize arrested personality development makes one prone to a self-display that is often expressed in childish and dramatic ways. Persons of the histrionic type of personality desire an immediate gratification of their wishes but avoid effort to gain their goal. They are self-engrossed, offended by trifles, and dependent in attitude; they bid for sympathy and attention and are given to suicidal "gestures." Such acts are not with intent to die. The threat or shock of the apparent attempt is used by them to control the environment, to gain attention, to arouse sympathy, or to frighten others into submission. Many seek to rule their environment by being sick, pitiful, and appealing. Such persons exaggerate any existing physical symptoms and even precipitately develop those of a critical or unique nature. Attention-getting, secondary-gain complaints are common. Hysterics, with their immature personalities, rarely react with awe, reverence, wonder, or pity; they may exhibit self-depreciation, remorse, or grief, but if so, it is because those emotions are the ones that gain them the greatest attention or best obtain a desired domination over their environment. These are the characteristics that often make such patients "special" in hospitals.

Such patients are notoriously suggestible, and their symptoms tend to follow the fashion of their particular period. One now rarely sees the dramatic posturings that were common in Charcot's clinic or the astasia-abasia of Victorian women. They are frequently, however, imitations of actions or disabilities either seen or read about. If such a patient, confronted with some difficult and unpleasant situation, observes the successful evasion of a similar situation by another person, that patient may develop the same symptoms as a means of escape.

In ordinary civil life, wishes, struggles, and disappointments associated with the sex life form, especially in women, one of the most important groups of experiences that produce the major forms of hysteria. The sexual impulse, although often active, may fail to develop toward a natural goal and is gratified in fantasy and autoerotic habits. A confused admixture of sexual desire and aversion, of erotic feelings and prudish attitudes often exists. Erotic fantasies often contrast with conscious expressions of fear and disgust in regard to sexuality. Among the problems that in women may give rise to hysteria are an unsuccessful love affair; jealousy, perhaps arising from the marriage of a sister; an undesired marriage; fear of pregnancy; difficulties in intercourse; or an unhappy marriage. Many such women are sexually frigid.

The developmental histories of such women make evident the sources for the disordered psychosexuality. In contrast to the earlier concept that the disorder resulted from disturbances in the oedipal period, it often commences in the initial maternal relationship. In many instances the mother, of hysterical make-up herself, has been rejecting, arousing in the child retaliatory fantasies that have been repressed. The mother often has been recognized as hypocritical about sex, dependent herself, and subtly clinging to the child for whom she has special ambitions. The father of such patients is inadequate, repressing this through either alcoholism, antisocial behavior, or passivity and is usually derogated by the mother.

This family situation forces the child to perceive her mother ambivalently — as "good" or "bad" — often "good" in the sense of offering concern during illness and as setting idealistic standards for repression of sexual and aggressive activity. She, however, is "bad" in lacking in tenderness, and her interest, even though denied, in the father and other siblings exaggerates feelings of jealous rivalry in the child. The latter, rejected herself, both turns to the father as a substitute mother and envies the father or males siblings, who she considers receive preferential treatment from the mother. Fixed on and desirous of maternal attention, she seeks it from the mother through early identification with the father and brothers. She displays tomboyishness, enuresis, difficulty with menstruation, and later, difficulty in acceptance of the feminine role, which is shown in frigidity, vomiting in pregnancy, or hostile seductiveness with men. In all these reactions, the symptoms symbolically express her conflicts and confusion in regard to her sexual identification.

Cloninger and Guze have confirmed recently the higher prevalence of somatization disorder in women who had been convicted of felonies and were fathered by sociopathic men.

In men, threats to self-esteem, to economic success, or to self-preservation more frequently present situations from which escape is sought through the hysterical symptoms. Many men are of immature personality with a strong dependent attachment to a mother.

The cognitive style of the hysteric personality tends to limit persistent or intense concentration and analysis, with much potential for distractibility and impressionability. The patient often acts on impressions and inspirations of transient interest. This style disallows curiosity or interest in factual information and its significance.

Frequently, the factor or event that precipitated a conversion reaction may have been trivial, but had some special meaning to the patient. Sometimes the precipitating situation may have some special similarity to a previous occurrence. It is therefore well to ascertain what the setting was at the time of appearance of the conversion reaction and also what the patient's emotional state was at the time. The nature of the earlier experiences that give special meaning to the precipitating event and the patient's predisposition to respond with a selective conversion mechanism may usually be determined only by psychoanalysis, although much recall may emerge in hypnotic or narcosynthetic states.

CONVERSION DISORDERS

Conversion Disorder (Hysterical Neurosis: Conversion Type)

In this condition, the individual is seen with a predominant dysfunction, more often than not a single expression of disturbance. In this sense, it differs from the somatization disorders. The loss of function is beyond voluntary control. The first expression generally occurs in late adolescence or early adulthood, but may be seen initially in middle or late life.

COURSE. It is often short, with abrupt onset and rapid resolution. Episodes may recur. Symptom expressions impair social functioning if continued for long and when persistent may lead to serious complications, such as seen in those with conversion paralysis. Rapid resolution of symptoms often occurs with appropriate management.

SYMPTOMS. The nature of the conversion symptoms is often determined by some need or feature of the situation that produced them and the type of disability that will be most useful in satisfying the subconscious purpose they are designed to meet. Physical symptoms may be sensory or motor. The motor disturbances in hysteria are various. In all cases, function is disturbed without demonstrable physiological or anatomical change. Paralyses may be in the form of monoplegia, hemiplegia, or paraplegia and may be either flaccid or spastic. The deep reflexes are not lost in flaccid forms; they may be exaggerated in the spastic forms, but there are not true clonus and no Babinski reactions. In hemiplegia, the paralysis of the proximal muscles is greater than that of the peripheral, being in this respect the contrary of that existing in organic hemiplegia. The forearm is extended instead of being somewhat flexed, as in organic hemiplegia; the leg is dragged instead of being swung in circumduction. There is no appreciable wasting of the paralyzed extremities. The maintenance of normal electrical reactions in flaccid paralysis is diagnostic, as is an absence of bladder symptoms or of tendency to bedsores in paraplegia. Contractures are common if the paralysis has been longstanding. A fairly frequent form is that of a tightly clenched fist. In hysterical paralyses, the muscles in question may be used in one voluntary movement and not in another. An attempt to exercise the paralyzed function is accompanied by a display of excessive effort.

A common symptom in women is that of urinary retention. Patients with this symptom are notoriously lacking in knowledge of urogenital anatomy and functions, have much guilt over early sexual exploration, and often have identified with other family members with urinary symptoms due to either a psychogenic or a physical cause.

Tics, tremors—usually coarse in nature, and choreiform and clonic movements occur. Aphonia, in which the patient cannot phonate speech but continues to cough as formerly, is not rare. Whereas in aphonia the patient finds no difficulty in communicating in whispers, the patient with hysterical mutism can utter no word, although he or she communicates freely and correctly in writing—a point of differentiation from aphasia. One patient who developed hysterical mutism in prison dreamed that the institution for mental diseases to which he had been transferred was on fire, whereupon he screamed and thereafter talked normally.

The occupational neuroses, such as writer's cramp, usually belong among hysterical reactions. The hysterical tic consists of a spasmodic, coordinated twitching movement of a small group of functionally related muscles. It may take the form of twitching of the facial muscles, blinking of the lids, sudden turning of the head, or a gesture-like movement of the hands. Such tics may represent dramatization of psychic experiences. Because of the suggestion of defense that they manifest, they may appear purposive. Care must be taken not to confuse hysterical tics with the more complex, coordinated, ticlike movements observed after epidemic encephalitis and certain other organic diseases of the brain.

Sensory symptoms, like other physical disturbances, are usually those of functional incapacity. Among the more frequent ones are anesthesias, paresthesias, and disturbances of special sense organs, such as blindness or deafness. Hysterical anesthesia does not follow the distribution of a nerve but involves an extremity up to a sharply defined line above which sensation is normal. It follows what the patient believes to be

the distribution of the nerve, which is represented in the patient's mind as a functional unit. One half of the body may be anesthetic, in which case the special senses—hearing, smell, taste, and sight—may be lost on the same side. Hysterical anesthesia may be extended in area by the suggestive and repetitious procedure of the physician in examination. Anesthesia probably cannot be produced de novo by the physician's examination, although this was believed by Babinski. The area and degree of the anesthesia may vary from one examination to another. While the evidence is conflicting, largely because of variations in the research techniques employed, it appears that the averaged evoked response (A.E.R.) by electroencephalography is reduced from the contralateral brain sensory area when stimulation is applied to the anesthetic site.

Hysterical disturbances of vision are of various forms, the most frequent being blindness and "gun-barrel" narrowing of the visual fields. Hysterical blindness usually has a sudden onset. The pupils continue to react to light, and usually, but not always, the patient avoids objects that would injure him if he came into collision with them. The onset is usually either closely related to some distressing visual experience or has a fairly obvious symbolic relation and significance.

A striking conversion is pseudodementia, recently re-emphasized by McEvoy and Wells. In an elderly person, the sudden occurrence of a memory impairment may be confused with a senile or arteriosclerotic state. The nature of the patient's complaints of memory deficit and his or her behavior in unstructured situations often provides the clue that the symptom is due to conversion. Its resolution is prompt with appropriate treatment.

A 70-year-old man was admitted to a hospital in the expectation of undergoing an operation for hip replacement to correct bilateral deformities that were preventing his walking. After exhaustive medical study, the staff decided his physical status precluded the risk of surgery. His wife visited infrequently and did not push for his return home.

The patient became increasingly fractious and commenced to shout, "I can't remember. I can't remember!" He gave this response to all inquiries about himself and his family. Seen in psychiatric consultation to determine whether he had a senile psychosis, the diagnosis of pseudodementia was entertained. A pentothal narcosynthesis produced immediate recall to all questions put to him and a touching reunion with his wife, who was present at the time of the treatment. He expressed the impression that she did not want him back. On recovery, his behavior underwent an abrupt change and he again collaborated with the staff in the long-term nursing unit.

Psychodynamics

The many theories evolved to explain conversion symptoms have been influenced by the concepts that have prevailed during different periods relative to natural phenomena in general, and human behavior in particular. Among these theories are the teaching of Hippocrates that hysteria is caused by the wandering of the uterus through the body in search of humidity, the belief of the 17th century that its striking manifestations seen in that period were a result of witchcraft or demoniacal possession, and the conviction now generally accepted that it is an adjustmental technique to which the personality may resort.

Among those who have contributed most to our understanding of conversion and dissociative reactions are Charcot, Janet, Bernheim, Babinski, Morton Prince, and Freud. Although his point of view was entirely neurological, Charcot was the first to demonstrate that the dramatic manifestations of hysteria could be produced and allayed by hypnotic suggestion. He thus demonstrated that psychological influences could affect bodily mechanisms, although, with his lack of aptitude for psychological investigation, he assumed that a hereditary degeneration was an essential prerequisite for hypnotic or hysterical phenomena. His discovery did, however, lay the foundation for investigative work by others.

Bernheim expressed the opinion that all hysterical symptoms are the result of suggestion. Babinski added the opinion that not only could all such phenomena be produced by suggestion but they could be removed by persuasion.

It is now universally agreed that conversion and dissociative disorders are of psychogenic origin. The greatest influence in creating this point of view is to be found in the contributions of Freud. Most psychogenic theories of the nature of conversion hysteria go back to the concepts of conflict and of repression. According to Freud, the wish or other repressed material, although not permitted frank expression, obtains release in disguised form through the mechanism of conversion, by which the psychic conflict is transformed into a physical or mental symptom. Freud explained the hysterical symptoms as caused by a conflict between the superego and some wish that, because of its consciously objectionable nature, is repressed by the superego. This repression is not, however, entirely successful, and the wish therefore obtains disguised expression by its "conversion" or transformation into the symptom. The nature and localization of the symptom thus produced are such that it symbolizes or provides disguised expression of the repressed wish and at the same time provides some degree of its fulfillment or of relief from the emotional conflict. Many psychiatrists who accept the role of repression in the production of the hysterical symptom hesitate to accept Freud's belief that a repressed Oedipus complex is an essential condition for the development of hysteria.

At the present time, the most widely accepted explanation of the mechanism known as conversion is that repressed impulses in the personality, highly charged with emotion, are productive of anxiety. The anxiety is then mitigated or dispelled by being "converted" into functional symptoms manifested in the voluntary musculature or in special sense-organ systems. The exact process involved in this "conversion" is uncertain.

The symptoms may be conceptualized in terms of modern communication theory, as well. Thus the conversion mechanism represents a nonverbal communication presented in a particular setting of the doctor-patient relationship. Again, it may be explained in game theory terms as a device to transmit a signal of distress to an appropriate individual through the socially acceptable symbols of the sick roles. The person using such communicative messages may have weaknesses in verbal skills. In our opinion, these explanatory models are weak because there is no provision for the hypothetical tools needed to analyze and tease out the reasons for the specific impairment of function.

The manner in which conversion, or the transformation of anxiety-producing emotional conflict into a specific symptom, can alleviate the anxiety caused by the patient's conflicting desires, and at the same time yield a secondary gain that enables the patient to escape from an extremely unpleasant situation, is illustrated by the following case.

M., a young man who had been a dancer and an acrobat in a circus, enlisted in the army during peace time. Here he found the discipline rigid, his duties irksome, and his experiences monotonous. He longed for travel, excitement, attention, and the opportunity for exhibition enjoyed in his former life. The situation became quite intolerable, but to leave meant that he would be treated as a deserter. A conversion reaction, induced by two conflicting motives, the one to conform to the requirements of military life, the other to secure escape from a hated situation, provided a solution that permitted him to gain his own end, i.e., to obtain immunity from unpleasant experiences and tasks, and at the same time alleviated his anxiety and enabled him to maintain his self-respect. On arrival at the mental hospital to which he was transferred, he could neither walk nor stand, and his legs were anesthetic to even vigorous prickings by a pin. At the same time, he displayed a significant attitude of unconcern (la belle indifférence) as to his disabilities, although, as far as he was consciously aware, they were complete and incurable. His absence of concern is to be explained by the fact that the penalty was less than the gain, although one must not conclude that this weighing of advantages and disadvantages was at all a matter of conscious reflection. A few months later, the man was discharged from the army on a surgeon's certificate of disability. Soon the suspended motor and sensory functions began to return. Persistent efforts to walk met gradually with success, and in another three months he left the hospital practically well.

In the case of this soldier, it can be seen how a psychological mechanism "converted" the anxiety stemming from his repressed hostile drives against those in authority and his wish for release from military service into an overt and incapacitating symptom that, however, yielded a definite secondary gain.

The conversion reaction may provide patients with a defense against anxiety, enable them to maintain their self-respect, and at the same time accomplish some purpose, the achievement of which would otherwise have been forbidden. It may make possible an escape from an intolerable situation; it may afford an exoneration for oneself, an excuse for one's failures, serve as an attention-getting device, or enable one to evade some duty, shun a responsibility, express some spite, or realize some purpose that would not bear the scrutiny of consciousness.

In connection with conversion reactions such as the one cited, it should be kept in mind that several factors usually play a role in determining the specific nature of the neurotic reaction. This concurrence and integration of adaptive functions unconsciously served by the symptoms is known as *overdetermination*. Through this process, a single symptom or neurotic reaction may be a complex compromise formation, to the production of which several needs have simultaneously and unconsciously contributed. If an overdeterminative process is analyzed, it will be found that in many neuroses there are anxiety-relieving values that have been produced by the symptom, together with further advantages that the patient secondarily derives from his illness, once it is established. Two or more birds are killed with one stone, so to speak.

Two sets of values derived from the neurosis, primary and secondary, are often spoken of as gains. The *primary gain* is the defense against anxiety supplied by the symptom. The *secondary gain* is a material advantage that is contributed by the symptom. In the case of the soldier just mentioned, the conversion symptom (hysterical paralysis) relieved him from the anxiety incident to his ambivalent wishes. It also afforded what was to him a very important secondary gain: it rendered him unable to perform military services and therefore made his discharge necessary. Conversion reactions usually meet some immediate need of the patient and are therefore associated with the less obvious "secondary gain." The secondary gain is not always material but may be emotional or social, e.g., the extraction of love, sympathy, or consideration from other people. Usually the element of "secondary gain" secured from the disturbing conversion symptoms seen daily in the general practice of medicine is less apparent than in the case of the soldier. Frequently, in fact, when symptoms of anxiety are also present, the element of secondary gain may be slight.

In the case of the soldier, comment was made concerning the attitude of unconcern manifested toward his disability. This satisfied indifference and pathological tranquility, characterized by Janet as *la belle indifférence,* is of diagnostic significance in a conversion reaction, representing as it does the characteristic use of denial as a means of defense. The conflict having been solved and anxiety having been relieved through conversion of the repressed impulses and wishes into a functional symptom, an outward calm follows, even though the symptom produced is so disabling that it would presumably be a source of great concern.

Accident or Compensation Neurosis

Industrial and automobile accidents, in which a question of indemnification for a real or presumed disability may arise, are frequently followed by a definite psychoneurotic reaction. The presenting features of this reaction may be anxiety, hypochondriasis, conversion, or mixed types. Frequently, the conversion symptoms are sufficiently prominent so that compensation neuroses are often classified among the somatizations. It was formerly considered that a desire for what the patient considered adequate compensation was the principal, if not exclusive, factor in the production of neuroses following industrial accidents. In recent years, closer studies of the patient's personality have shown that other factors also are usually dynamically important.

Persons of a paranoid tendency, those who are insecure, and those who crave sympathy and attention are predisposed to compensation neurosis. The same is true of the individual who finds himself in an employment situation that is becoming progressively more unbearable. The necessity, because of financial obligations, for continuing work beyond mental or physical capacity, or the failure to derive satisfaction from one's work may predispose to a traumatic or compensation neurosis. Some incidental gain resulting from an injury, such as escape from dreary or wearisome conditions of employment, may be an important contributing factor.

Oversolicitude on the part of the patient's family or an injudicious remark by the physician in the first days or weeks after an injury concerning its severity may create fear in the mind of the patient and predispose to the development of a neurosis. Experience connected with bodily helplessness, disturbance of business resulting from the accident, or worry about cure may conduce to its development. Not only a desire for financial gain but the conviction on the part of the patient that he has the right to expect indemnification may be motivating factors. Social custom and public opinion tend to encourage the development of accident neuroses by their attitude toward the question of responsibility.

The probability of developing a compensation neurosis following a relatively slight injury is greater than if the injury is so disabling that it is obviously compensable. Mild traumatic residuals may become heavily overlaid with hysterical elaborations. The traumatic or accident neuroses rarely occur when the victim of the injury must bear the brunt of the financial responsibility for the accident, as in the case of injuries sustained in sports. There is usually an incubation period between the injury and the appearance of the mentally determined symptoms. This interval before the development of the chronic disabilities is of value in excluding an organic source. It is usually occupied with vague ruminations that tend to be of an imaginative, affective, resentful, wish-determined, and suggestive nature.

SYMPTOMS. The symptoms of the accident neuroses are various, but these neuroses differ in no essential feature from others except in the matter of compensation. Frequently, the symptoms include irritability, stubbornness, argumentativeness, crying spells, anxiety, depression, sleeplessness, headache, and dizziness. The patient is garrulous in describing his feelings and may complain of poor memory and inability to concentrate. If the foreman, "company doctor," or insurance adjuster questions the genuineness of his symptoms or the validity of his claim that the injury was sustained while at work, the patient frequently reacts with an indignation and resentment that aggravates and prolongs his symptoms. The fact that a hysterical reaction may be superimposed on an organic injury that has escaped attention should not be forgotten. Sometimes the neurotic symptoms do not become seriously troublesome until after the patient has returned to his employment, when they become so aggravated that he gives up work.

Tremors, paralyses, and other motor and sensory conversion symptoms occur. At times the necessary form of treatment for the original injury may be instrumental in suggesting a disability to a person of a hysterical type. Immobilization by splints of an injured extremity, for example, may be followed by its paralysis. As in other psychoneuroses, symptoms may be firmly fixed by overexamination or by overtreatment based on wrong premises. The development of symptoms through suggestion is, of course, in no way limited to accident neuroses involving the matter of compensation. A repetition of physical examinations may aggravate symptoms when organic disease exists and produce them when no disease exists.

The fact that the physician's words and acts may have a suggestive effect upon the patient imposes a special responsibility upon her or him. In those cases in which indemnification is a participating motive, the patient remains unaware of such an influence and denies that he desires compensation, declaring that he would gladly forgo any financial satisfaction could he be restored to health. He complains of his symptoms, but he rarely asks how he may get rid of them. Underlying feelings of guilt may be overcompensated and experienced as self-pity.

Workmen's compensation acts and industrial accident insurance have greatly increased the incidence of compensation neuroses. The effect on the worker of the general practice of awarding compensation for injury is to create a receptive mental state so that, when injury occurs, there follows an unconscious wishing for compensation. This does not at all mean that a worker who, following an industrial accident, complains of symptoms without organic basis is a malingerer or that compensation is not merited. The disability, it is true, would not have occurred had the results of the injury not possessed potential benefits in some form. The misfortune is that the injury in the "damage-suit" hysteria occurred in a person who was psychologically predisposed to a neurotic reaction. The existence of litigation tends to maintain the patient's focus on his injury, particularly if legal processes are prolonged. Contrary, however, to a frequent belief, the end of litigation does not always terminate the symptoms promptly. A termination does usually, however, have a salutary effect on the symptoms by removing one factor that has tended to keep the patient's attention focused on himself.

Mention should be made of the *occupation neuroses*, a large proportion of which, particularly those characterized by spasms, are to be looked upon as hysterical. In these neuroses, the patient, on attempting to execute some specialized movement in an occupation requiring the coordination of groups of muscles, suffers from a spasm of the muscles involved in this act. Their function remains unimpaired when an attempt is made to employ the same muscles for the performance of some other act.

DIFFERENTIAL DIAGNOSIS

In addition to differentiation from the other neurotic reactions, features of which it often shares, conversion reactions are to be differentiated from organic disorders, malingering, schizophrenia, and the psychophysiological reactions.

A conversion reaction may simulate an astonishing variety of organic symptoms. The frequency of misdiagnosis of conversion reactions and the overlooking of physical disease is high. In a 10-year follow-up file study of patients initially diagnosed as suffering conversion reactions, Watson and Buranen found the false-positive rate to be 25 per cent. One should ascertain whether sensory and motor disturbances are consistent with known anatomical and physiological facts regarding the distribution and function of the central and peripheral nervous system. Conversion symptoms often change from time to time and with suggestion. Reflex and trophic disturbances do not accompany hysterical disturbances, aside from the changes that may come from chronic disuse following a paralysis. Before deciding that a physical sign or somatically expressed symptom is of psychogenic origin, one should carefully attempt to ascertain whether a setting of affective dissatisfaction existed before the appearance of the sign or symptom. DSM-III diagnostic criteria are presented in Table 22–8.

The patient's attitude of satisfied indifference toward his disability and the circumstances under which the disorder arose are often significant. The

TABLE 22–8 Diagnostic Criteria for Conversion Disorder

A. The predominant disturbance is a loss of or alteration in physical functioning, suggesting a physical disorder.

B. Psychological factors are judged to be etiologically involved in the symptom, as evidenced by one of the following:

   (1) there is a temporal relationship between an environmental stimulus that is apparently related to a psychological conflict or need and the initiation or exacerbation of the symptom

   (2) the symptom enables the individual to avoid some activity that is noxious to him or her

   (3) the symptom enables the individual to get support from the environment that otherwise might not be forthcoming

C. It has been determined that the symptom is not under voluntary control.

D. The symptom cannot, after appropriate investigation, be explained by a known physical disorder or pathophysiological mechanism.

E. The symptom is not limited to pain or to a disturbance in sexual functioning.

F. Not due to somatization disorder or schizophrenia.

As presented in the Diagnostic and Statistical Manual of Mental Disorders, Third Edition (DSM-III). Washington, D.C., American Psychiatric Association, 1980.

coincidence or immediate sequence of an acute emotional state and the appearance of physical phenomena are suggestive, especially if the connection between the psychological event and the sign is unrecognized by the patient. In actual physical disease, the patient readily accepts or even suggests the statement that his disability is of mental origin. On the other hand, the patient whose disability is psychogenic eagerly seeks a physical basis. Both patients, of course, are really attempting to avoid the truth. It is always well for the physician to ask himself whether the signs and symptoms serve a purpose in the life of the patient (secondary gain) and not let the apparent loss or suffering exclude conversion from consideration. In making the diagnosis of conversion hysteria, too, one should not rely solely on the presence of conversion symptoms but should also consider whether the patient is an emotionally immature type of person. It must be remembered that organic disability and a conversion reaction are not mutually exclusive. Organic neurological disabilities may be complicated by superimposed conversion phenomena.

The confusion of a conversion reaction with malingering is most apt to be made by persons who consider all hysterics as malingerers and mistakenly believe that the hysteric could control his symptom if he wanted to. Discrepancies, contradictions, and exaggerations of symptoms are more frequent in malingering; also, the malingerer usually expresses much concern about his symptoms. The use of appropriate psychological tests, such as the Minnesota Multiphasic, may suggest the tendency to lying and deception. In the classic form of major conversion hysteria, the patient manifests little concern about symptoms. Because, however, of the considerable component of anxiety often accompanying a recently established conversion reaction, the patient may show signs of concern. Surprise examinations or observation of which the patient is unaware may reveal the deception in malingering. Conversion reactions and malingering have much in common. The difference is largely one of the relative degree to which consciousness participates in the reaction. In malingering there is a subtle interweaving of conscious and unconscious factors.

Since there may be reactions in schizophrenia strongly resembling hysteria, the diagnosis is not always easy. The native temperament of the patient may be somewhat indicative, that of the hysteric person having been characterized by more easily shifting emotions. In hysteria a dominant affect usually exists, there are no inconsistencies in symptoms and no disturbance of associations, there is a greater response to any emotional reaction on the part of nurse or relative, and there is no deterioration in habits of dress or cleanliness. In hysteria there is an apparent desire to be the center of attention, and it will usually be found that either parent or mate has been accustomed to exhibit a sympathetic and exaggerated emotional reaction to any illness on the part of the patient. Here the aid of the clinical psychologist may be most helpful, particularly as the usual diagnostic interviewing with the hysterical patient is distorted through his unwitting use of denial and the force of repression.

Attention is called in Chapter 24 to the fact that conversion reactions should be distinguished from psychophysiological reactions, in which tension and anxiety arising from psychological conflicts and emotional stresses are allayed, not by channeling them through voluntary muscular and special sense systems (conversion), but through the vegetative nervous system into visceral organ symptoms and complaints. Yet many patients show combinations of both varieties of reaction.

PROGNOSIS

The degree to which somatization can be eliminated depends to a considerable degree on the extent to which evasions become habitual in early life and on the maturity and independence of the personality pattern. The prognosis depends, too, upon the strength or weakness of the patient's personality resources in relation to the environmental demands and to the other stresses that he will be called upon to face. If the patient's capacity for social adaptation has been limited, if it has been his habit to deal with minor difficulties by evasive methods, or if he has led an aimless existence without apparent social drive or ambition, it is probable that further conversion defenses will be employed. Symptomatology alone is a poor guide to the future. If the patient was formerly well adjusted and the conversion reaction was brought on by unusual stress, the prognosis is favorable, provided return to the precipitating situation is not required.

The somatoform reaction, in many instances, is engrafted upon a basically schizoid personality structure. With such persons, the psychotic reaction eventually becomes apparent. This is particularly so in groups of patients diagnosed as hysterical and followed for years after their initial admission to a mental hospital. On the other hand, similar follow-up studies over a period of a decade on patients who presented a monosymptomatic conversion in a general hospital or outpatient clinic made it clear that, even with treatment by measures designed only to modify the symptoms without restructuring the personality, the majority remained well and made excellent social adjustments. The outlook is best in the monosymptomatic hysteria that occurs in adult life rather than adolescence. Presumably here the response takes place in the face of a severe stress.

TREATMENT

In the treatment of the somatoform disorders, the psychiatrist attempts to ascertain the purpose of the symptom and to discover the factors causing anxiety so great that it could be handled only through the mechanism of conversion with functional physical symptoms. Since the patient's disorder arose through mental causes and through the operation of mental mechanisms, the treatment should basically be that of psychotherapy.

The nature and energy of the dynamic factors that have led to the patient's symptoms are concealed from his recognition, and any explanation of the underlying mechanism is often received with resistance and protest. The patient's conversion reaction may, too, appear so remote from his emotional problem that only a searching analysis can uncover the relationship between the two.

Before beginning psychotherapy, the physician should first make a thorough physical examination. If no evidence is found that there is physical disease, no more physical examinations should be made, even though new symptoms occur. Continued examinations and long hospitalization may cause new symptoms to appear and old ones to become fixed.

Psychiatrists should remember that they must deal with two distinct although related problems: one, the removal of the symptom; the other, that of enabling the patient to apprehend the source of his anxiety and the significance of his symptom in order that he may form a more constructive method of action for the future. It is much easier to dispel a conversion than to help the patient to achieve further emotional growth.

It is important to make a correct estimate of the patient's personality stability, maturity, and intellectual resources. If the personality limitations are relatively minimal, the treatment may be psychotherapeutic and based on analytical principles, with an investigation of the dynamic factors of repression. In the person of low intelligence and in the unstable individual who develops a conversion reaction in a relatively uncomplicated situation, the principal therapy will be limited to symptom removal and re-education. In no case must the patient be accused of dishonesty or of a lack of desire to get well.

When the conversion symptom presents as a major disability incompatible with return to social and vocational activities, consideration must be given to its rapid reduction. In making this clinical judgment, the psychiatrist keeps in mind the defensive nature of the symptom and should evolve a concept of what the symptom defends against. With its rapid removal, the therapist must be aware that there will occur either overt anxiety or substitution by another symptom with equivalent symbolic significance. Either of these alternatives may be more suitable than major paralytic symptoms, blindness, choreiform states, or astasia-abasia. However, in those instances in which rapid symptom removal is likely to induce a serious disruption of self-esteem with anxiety, shame, and guilt, associated with regressive phenomena, this judgment is avoided. Serious regressions of this type are likely in those in whom the personality is essentially schizoid or there exist other symptoms indicative of an underlying schizophrenic reaction.

Persuasion, narcosynthesis, or hypnosis, as described in Chapter 30, are the therapeutic measures of choice for rapid removal of symptoms. Not all patients with symptoms of the somatoform disorders are open to trance induction and suggestion by the hypnotic technique. This potential may be tested easily, using the Stanford Hypnotic Induction Scale or the Spiegel Scale. Narcosynthesis is the indicated treatment when hypnosis cannot be used. Once the acute symptomatic disability is modified, the psychiatrist will then determine the potential for character change through the use of a dynamic psychotherapy. If this potential is considered to exist, dynamic psychotherapy is recommended as a means of avoiding further symptomatic recurrences. These methods of treatment are described also in Chapter 30.

Evidence for the presence of a schizophrenic disturbance may be gained by careful assessment of the developmental history. Family history of psychotic disturbance or pre-existing information of a dependent, withdrawn, and isolated life with resort to fantasy or other disordered behavioral traits should arouse suspicion. Often, because of denial by the hysteric in presenting his life history initially, valid information is not obtained. Many consider that the aid of psychological tests, particularly the projective methods, should always be sought in such instances before treatment goals are determined and therapy is initiated. Such tests may provide clues of the potentiality of severe regressions that will require hospital treatment if sudden removal of symptoms appears to be the method of choice. The author has been impressed with the frequency of such regressions in patients who present numerous pure color reactions in their Rorschach responses.

In the treatment of *accident neuroses* there are certain factors that require special attention. In case of injury any suggestion that it is serious should be carefully avoided. If possible, the injured person should be kept at work, and, if his condition does not permit this, he should return as promptly as possible. Care should be exercised that the treatment of any physical complication is not prolonged. The attitude of the physician toward a patient suffering from such a neurosis should never be one of suspicion or antagonism. If he approaches the patient with a biased, skeptical attitude, disregards his complaint, and makes but a superficial examination, he destroys the possibility of any therapeutic rapport and may even contribute to further psychological elaboration.

A hope for indemnification on the part of the injured employee makes it impossible for him to disregard unpleasant sensations or unpleasant subjective experiences or to adjust himself to them. In contrast to an athlete similarly injured, the workman is prompted to magnify rather than ignore the discomforts resulting from his injury. The harshness and disregard of complaints by representatives of insurance companies, a ready assumption of intent to swindle, and the delays and technicalities of court procedure tend to stimulate untherapeutic patterns of reaction. Such attitudes engender resentment and discouragement and may force the injured person to resort to a primitive (conversion) mode of response. Whether a compensation award granted to the workman suffering from a traumatic neurosis is paid in a single sum or extended through a number of installments makes little difference so far as the neurosis is concerned. It is important, however, that a settlement be made promptly and that any litigation be terminated.

Psychogenic Pain Disorder

When the predominant clinical picture is one of complaining of pain, not associated with signs of physical illness and with evidence of psychological disturbance, this diagnosis is to be made.

The siting of the pain complaint either is inconsistent with the known distribution of the nerve supply or, if it resembles a recognized disease, the entity cannot be accounted for by evidence of structural or functional pathology.

Often a temporal relationship between the onset or exacerbation of the pain complaining and the occurrence of some personal loss or an actual, threatened, or fantasied interpersonal loss will be discovered.

Painful complaints may sometimes be hallucinatory as well as representing an affective state, such as anxiety or depression or a symbol expressive of bodily derogation. Painful complaining may

also be used to evoke social responses directly. The diagnostician must determine the meaning or meanings of the complaint in order to effect an appropriate therapeutic plan. This conversion symptom is perhaps the commonest expression of the illness at the current time and is frequently misdiagnosed and mistreated. As with other hysterical symptoms, the patient presents a bizarre or unusual account of the symptoms that is not easily recognizable as a result of the usual physical illnesses, or he may exaggerate the pain of a relatively minor physical disturbance. In spite of his insistence on the severity and disabling nature of the symptom and his demands for medication and care, he may be observed frequently to appear indifferent and undisturbed by the symptom. Placebos may relieve the symptom. There is often an intermittent history of its occurrence, and exacerbations may be found related to incidents arousing emotional conflict.

In taking the history, the examiner may induce many hysterical patients, apparently indifferent to the symptom, to complain at the point where the psychiatrist touches upon the emotionally disturbing relationship or incidents in his life. If the psychiatrist is easily dissuaded from the task of history-taking in an effort to provide immediate relief of a sudden complaint of pain offered by the patient during the interview, a valuable opportunity and a significant clue pertaining to the emotional connotation of the symptoms are missed. Reintroduction of the anxiety-ridden topics or associated themes often gives rise again to painful complaining. The arousal of painful complaining may be regarded as perhaps hallucinatory. It may occur in the course of psychotherapy when the patient associates pertinent information symbolizing the conflicting needs that underlie the symptom.

The determination of painful complaints appears to rest on any one of the following parent-child interactions.

Oversolicitude by the mother following minor painful experiences may establish the predisposition to obtain gratification, in the face of conflict, by means of painful complaining in later life. Envious observation of the attention given to another sibling or home member sometimes arouses fantasies of suffering that are repressed until the later conflictful period and are then aroused as a substitute means of allaying anxiety. Of greatest importance are the childhood experiences of pain that lead to *masochistic* suffering in order to obtain gratifying affectional responses. In some instances, parents suffer guilt on punishing the child for misdeeds and then lavish affection following punishment as a means of assuaging their own anxiety. If this is the means by which the patient as a child repetitively obtained emotional satisfaction, a pattern for later masochistic pain and suffering is established. Another method, described by Freud, has to do with the guilt suffered by a child after secretly enjoying the punishment offered an envied brother or sister. To assuage this guilt, he must then suffer some distress. In all these instances, the basic issue is the wish for the affection and acceptance by the parent or parental substitute. With the masochistic expression, pain or distress must be expressed in order to obtain the wished-for affection and acceptance denied in reality.

Organic Factors and Conversion Reactions

The existence of organic symptoms does not exclude the presence of conversion ones also. Symptoms of organic disease that still exist may be exaggerated, or symptoms may persist after the organic basis for them no longer continues. In such cases, the symptoms produced by the disease were found to serve some psychological purpose, to be of value in themselves. Because of their usefulness in providing protection, escape, or advantage, they are uncon-sciously exaggerated or prolonged. Hysterical symptoms of this nature occur particularly in industrial, insurance, and traumatic neuroses, but they are by no means confined to them, since there are many situations in which physical symptoms may serve some useful function. At times the organic disease may impose sufficient additional stress so that emotional problems can no longer be dealt with in a realistic manner. Exhaustion, whether a result of fatigue or of anxiety resulting from prolonged indecision or from emotional conflict, may predispose to a hysterical retreat from a situation that would otherwise have been met with ease. The person already having some organic disease will often, if his situation does not demand some other special symptom, select one related to the organic disorder with which he is already familiar. The organic symptoms may merge imperceptibly into the hysterical one.

HYPOCHONDRIA

The term *hypochondria*, or hypochondriacal reaction, is one that has been long applied to a group of psychoneurotic symptoms. The reaction is characterized by an obsessive preoccupation and concern of the individual about the state of his health or the condition of his organs. Often he expresses a multiplicity of complaints about different organs or body systems, which, the patient reiterates, must be incurably diseased. The hypochondriac is not only aware of various sensations that most persons disregard, but he also perceives and is preoccupied with normal sensations such as fatigue and others in an intensified way. Hypochondriasis seems to be a displacement of anxiety onto the body, with the resulting somatic complaints. Some hypochondriacal reactions may become excessively and persistently obsessional, and associated compulsions may develop.

DISSOCIATIVE DISORDERS

At times anxiety may so overwhelm and disorganize the personality that certain aspects or self-functions become dissociated from each other. In some instances, the personality may be so disorganized that defense mechanisms that govern consciousness, memory, and temporarily even the total individual break down and behavior occurs with little or no participation on the part of the conscious personality. When this sudden change in the integrative function of personality occurs, memories of significant events may be lost if consciousness is impaired. Again, if the sense of identity is threatened, a new identity may be assumed and the individual's sensory reality may be impaired. In such cases, the patient may appear psychotic. Formerly the dissociative reactions were classified as a type of conversion hysteria.

Psychogenic Amnesia

One of the commonest anxiety-stimulated and defensive dissociative reactions is amnesia. Forgetting is a simple expedient. Amnesias obliterate recollections and memories of circumscribed events. Amnesia may be *selective, generalized,* or *continuous.* Such states are rare and follow a major psychosocial stress. The amnesia generally terminates as abruptly as it started and has a good prognosis. It is more common in the young.

Dissociative amnesia is not a mere forgetting. It is an active process, a blotting out of awareness of unpleasant features. Periods of stupor or of twilight state may precede such an amnesia, which then tends to become selective and limited to the particular element or experience that evoked it.

Among experiences that suspend the ability to bring pertinent factual data to consciousness are those involving great terror, as in war, or covering periods and behavior with which shame, guilt, or other intense feeling-tone is connected. How satisfactorily an amnesia exercises its protective and escape purpose is shown by the unperturbed manner in which the patient accepts the loss of memory.

Although most dissociative amnesias are of brief duration, they sometimes blot out long periods, sometimes even the patient's entire previous life. In some instances, there is a reversion to an earlier period of the patient's life, with retrograde amnesia for events subsequent to that period.

In differentiating between an organic and a dissociative amnesia, it will be found that a sudden return of memory is indicative of its dissociative loss. The onset, also, of the dissociative amnesia will have been sudden. It is to be differentiated as well from acute alcoholic stupor, the "blackouts" of chronic alcoholism, the amnesias following head trauma and epileptic seizures, catatonic stupors, or malingering.

Frequently, the various forms of twilight state suggest delirium. Such psychogenic delirious states are usually preceded by marked emotional experiences or displays and consist of dream states accompanied by more or less confusion, dramatic posturings and activities, and an excessive flow of speech appearing nonsensical, but in which occur references to strongly affective experiences. Dissociative delirium often represents the dreamlike realization of a wish or the dramatic reliving in fantasy of an affectively traumatic experience. Its clouding of consciousness and the presence of illusions and hallucinations may exclude the reality of the outside world and falsify it in accordance with deep-seated motives and unsatisfied wishes. Occasionally the patient spins fantastic stories. Such instances usually represent an effort to supply romance and drama to a life devoid of emotional satisfactions.

Psychogenic Fugue

At times a psychic escape may be in the form of a dissociative *fugue.* In this there is a sudden change in state of consciousness, during which the patient may be impelled by unconscious forces to perform complicated activities, involving sudden and unexplained travel over long distances. Throughout this period, the patient may appear quite normal to the casual observer. In some instances there is a loss of personal identity. In the fugue the patient indulges in acts or fantasies that are in conflict with his superego, and the function of the fugue is to permit the carrying out of these acts or fantasies. A further defense mechanism becomes necessary, however, and so the patient attempts to protect his ego by forgetting his name and past history, that is, by losing his identity. In other instances there is not a loss in personal identity but a change in it. In such a case the patient assumes a false name and identifies himself with the person whose name he takes. The assumption of the false name is associated with the unconscious fantasies responsible for the genesis of the fugue.

After the termination of the fugue, the patient may have a complete amnesia for his journey until the memory of it is restored by hypnosis or other psychic means.

Examination of the patient, either by narcosynthesis or hypnosis, usually reveals the personal, emotional factors that prompted an escape mechanism in the form of an automatic, unconscious, uncontrollable withdrawal. In certain studies, it has been found that the fugue state is preceded by depression and may be regarded as an attempt to ward off this affect. The model for a number of fugue states apparently has been supplied by a previous head injury with a resulting amnesia, or amnesic states induced through alcohol, or identification with others who suffered dissociative reactions.

Multiple Personality

This rare behavioral aberration is less frequent than the preceding forms of gross dissociation. It is thought that as anxiety repeatedly accelerates in psychosocial conflict, the individual transits from one personality type to another. Each personality configuration represents an aspect of his own personality, which he cannot integrate as a totality. In short, the patient's self-system has failed to develop securely. One of the presenting personalities may be the socially acceptable and proper person, a protector of others; another the acting out, promiscuous, and socially defiant aspect of the person; while the third represents the idealized personality. Thus the patient with multiple personalities accomplishes through transitions over time expression of superego and ego ideals as well as id impulses.

Sometimes one of the sub-personalities is of the opposite sex, or of a different race or age or family origin. In one or other of the sub-personalities, the patient may admit or provide awareness of existence of the other personalities and talk with or indicate participation with the other or others in some actions.

Multiple personality has been observed in childhood but generally is recognized in early adulthood. It tends to be chronic. It has been suggested that severe physical abuse or other psychic trauma predisposes to the occurrence of this dissociative state. Some have related the condition to rapidly alternating manic-depressive swings.

Differential diagnosis must include amnestic states as well as schizophrenia.

Treatment may be by hypnosis or narcosynthesis. Electroshock therapy followed by psychotherapy has proved successful in resolution of the dissociation in some refractory cases.

A 28-year-old married woman was admitted to hospital following a suicidal attempt. She was then depressed and retarded. Several days after admission, she became angry, attempted to assault the nurse, and claimed that it was her fault that she was depressed. She then stated that Mary was the depressed person; she was Cynthia. As Cynthia, she reported leaving home, picking up sailors and lesbians, and acting in a loose and lascivious manner. As Mary, she was a dutiful, quiet, submissive housewife, angry and depressed over her husband's poor relationship with her. Periodically, she abruptly assumed the character of Cynthia and became loud, boisterous, and sexually uninhibited.

Psychodynamically, in the depressed character she accepted the dictates of her superego, repressed the rage toward her husband, and dutifully attempted to assume her responsibilities as a housewife. When overwhelmed by rage, she acted out through defiance her aggressive and sexual urges as Cynthia.

This patient's dissociation was resolved only after electroshock treatment.

FACTITIOUS DISORDERS

As a grouping, the factitious disorders constitute those conditions in which the individual undertakes actions that lead to the simulation of physical illness or psychological or emotional disorder. The actions are voluntarily known to the individual but the goal goes unrecognized and the motivational drive is uncontrolled. Often the factitious disorders carry a compulsive quality; the sufferer is unable to refrain from his acts, which are often self-destructive in spite of shaming by discovery.

Malingering is to be differentiated from factitious illness. In the former, the patient has a clearly defined goal in mind and will desist from simulating when his goal is accomplished, provided there is no necessity to continue. He seldom mutilates himself nor exposes himself to unnecessary or painful diagnostic or surgical procedures.

The variety of factitious symptoms and illnesses is enormous. Factitious fevers; kidney stones; hematuria and urinary diseases; dermatitis, including ulcerations; nausea, vomiting and diarrhea sometimes productive of serious metabolic disturbances; anemia; ecchymoses; meningitis; convulsive seizures; hemoptyses; hypoglycemia; and lymphedema have all been reported.

Often illnesses are produced by ingestion of medication to toxic levels. Some have feigned bereavement. Hereafter follows a case of factitious hypoglycemia.

The patient, a 44-year-old married nurse, with a history of episodic attacks of hunger, weakness, sleepiness, sweating, vertigo, and occasionally unconsciousness, was referred for study. The attacks were always aborted by eating. They were so severe that six months previously the patient had to give up a fast. Another physician had diagnosed an islet cell pancreatic tumor and advised surgery. The patient refused operation, stating that she had gained weight and was not suffering any pain. She consulted other physicians in an attempt to obtain a different diagnosis. She expressed her fear to these physicians that if operated upon she would become diabetic and require insulin.

A careful medical examination failed to reveal any evidence of tumor. The patient sustained a fast without the development of hypoglycemia. In view of previous experiences with patients who had induced hypoglycemia, the patient's room was searched while she was having a diagnostic test and several bottles of insulin and a syringe were found. At this point a psychiatric examination was requested.

In consultation the patient reported that her mother, who had died two years previously, had been a diabetic and had been nursed in her terminal illness by the daughter. The patient had lived a restricted life and had entered nursing to relieve herself of her loneliness. Some four years previously she had undergone a hysterectomy performed by a physician who had advised her that she had an islet cell tumor.

Following the initial psychiatric interview, the patient stated that she proposed to sign out of the hospital. Since it was considered that her condition was dangerous in the sense that she was exposing herself to a potentially major surgical procedure, the psychiatric consultant concluded that it was advisable to suggest the possibility of induced hypoglycemia to the patient. This was done by informing her of the conclusions reached by the medical service on the basis of finding the bottles of insulin and the previous experience of the hospital with others with similar conditions. The patient was gently told that, if this was the case, she must have some underlying emotional problems which had led her to the desperate expedient of the self-administration of insulin and that she might therefore wish to solve the major conflicts which had driven her to such action. The suggestion was met by immediate denial. When seen the following day, the patient asked assurance that any information given by her would be considered inviolate. When this was given, she broke down, cried, and gave the following information.

She stated that her drive for the self-administration of insulin began about four months previously during the period of a fast when she felt weak and unable to continue her work. Believing that she might obtain a dispensation from a religious fast from the physician who had removed her uterus some years earlier, with whom she worked and toward whom she had a strong positive attachment, she asked if he would assist her in securing a dispensation for medical reasons. He replied that he would do so if he found her to be suffering from hypoglycemia. Shortly before blood was to be drawn for the determination of its sugar content, the nurse, without the knowledge of the physician, took her first injection of insulin. Naturally, hypoglycemia was found. The physician therefore gave her the desired recommendation that dispensation be granted from the obligation of fasting before communion.

The nurse then revealed that she had developed a feeling of depression after her hysterectomy. She feared that she had not healed properly and wondered whether she would develop a cancer. Her father had died of cancer and had suffered from fears relating to mental disease. He was given insulin to relieve his depression. The patient herself had given insulin in mental hospitals and recalled her anxiety on being shown the brain of a patient who had died during insulin shock therapy. Throughout her life she had felt hungry, had been an extremely heavy eater, and had felt weak when she fasted. The patient had always devoted herself to the care of her mother and an aunt and had spent months at home each year nursing them for their various ailments. The mother had written her that she should provide nursing services not only for herself and the aunt but also for her brothers, if she really loved her family. She always seemed fearful of losing the love of her relatives. Perhaps it is not surprising that upon the death of her parents she expressed the sentiment that her brothers "beat her out" of her patrimony.

The nurse declared that she had devoted the same amount of attention to the care of her physician's patients as she had to her own family. She admitted that her response to his insistence on evidence of hypoglycemia by blood test prior to supporting her request for a medical dispensation had been one of anger and resentment. On the other hand, she felt so anxious concerning the possibility of losing his respect and good will and so guilty in relation to the church that she felt obliged to continue the self-administration of insulin when faced with another medical examination. Following these revelations, which were responded to with sympathetic interpretation of her emotional reactions and their origin, the patient returned home to her profession and made a satisfactory adaptation, with no recurrence of the hypoglycemic attacks.

Münchausen Syndrome

This uncommon syndrome bears a relationship to hysteria and malingering. It is of particular importance to physicians in hospital practice. Those with the syndrome are repeatedly admitted to hospitals for treatment of presumably acute illnesses. They are dramatic in presentation of their symptoms, are often knowledgeable of medical terms, tend to sexualize their relation with physicians of the opposite sex, prevaricate skillfully, and wander from one institution to another seeking care from physicians. The variety of simulated illnesses is extensive. Often they are subjected to unnecessary medical and surgical procedures.

The name of the syndrome derives from the similarities of behavior of these repetitive care-seekers to the fabrications of the mythical Baron Münchausen.

Individuals whose behavior classifies them into this syndrome psychodynamically seek a repetitive relationship with a physician to act out a desired dependent-maternal relationship in which the medical care given substitutes for the maternal role. There are elements of identification with the physician as in the hysteric. An early satisfying relationship with one as a parent or friend may be demonstrated by the use and knowledge of medical terms, or even in vocational activities, such as nursing. The ambivalence in the relationship emerges with discovery of the malingering; the presumed patient may then leave the physician and hospital in a hostile mode.

Ganser Syndrome

This rare syndrome, with its combination of instinctive, rational, purposeful, and deceptive elements and theatrical behavior, is an alteration of consciousness allied both to simulation and to dissociative dream states. In this syndrome, first described as occurring among prisoners under detection while awaiting trial, the patient, being in a situation that would be solved or mitigated by irresponsibility, desires, although not consciously so acknowledged, to appear irresponsible, and accordingly without being aware of it, actually does develop mental disturbance. The conspicuous features of this disorder consist of a childish, ludicrous performance of simple acts, the correct procedure for which is fully known by the patient. The patient's responses to questions are wrong but are not far wrong and bear an obvious relation to the question. His replies show that he understood the meaning of the questions, but they are beside the point and are in the nature of approximate answers—a phenomenon known as paralogia, or "Vorbeireden." Thus, if asked how long he has been in the hospital, he might reply, "I could have come just now, couldn't I?" Or if asked the color of his shirt, he might reply giving a color other than the correct one. The purpose of the patient's behavior appears so obviously irresponsible that he may seem to be malingering.

Since the circumstances under which the Ganser syndrome occurs are such that the advantages to be gained by a mental disability are greater than those obtained by physical disorders, the reaction takes place in terms of the former rather than of conversion hysteria. As in other dissociative reactions, the protection from a full realization of his situation affords the patient a relative freedom from the anxiety that might otherwise be intolerable.

In Whitlock's recent review of the reported cases and a study of some six additional patients whom he considers to fit into the Ganser syndrome, he suggests that one should more properly regard the condition as psychotic. In many of the cases reported, classic paralogia or "Vorbeireden" has followed acute cerebral trauma or has appeared in the course of an acute psychosis of schizophrenic nature. Also, its occurrence has been noted often in those other than prisoners. Whitlock concludes that the basic element is disturbance of consciousness, which separates the condition from hysterical pseudodementia. He would restrict the diagnosis to patients who develop clouding of consciousness with paralogia following head trauma or with acute or psychotic reactions in which one may note a number of hallucinations and conversion symptoms. So, too, the condition must terminate abruptly.

BIBLIOGRAPHY

General: Etiology and Prevalence

Eysenck, H. J.: The learning theory model of neurosis—a new approach. Behav. Res. Ther., *14*:251–267, 1976.
Fenichel, O.: The Psychoanalytic Theory of Neurosis. New York, W. W. Norton & Company, 1945.
Freud, S.: Collected Papers (5 Vols.). London, Hogarth Press, 1924–1925.
Freud, S.: The Ego and the Id. London, Hogarth Press, 1927.
Freud, S.: The Basic Writings of Sigmund Freud. New York, Modern Library, 1938.
Gray, M.: Neuroses: A Comprehensive and Critical View. New York, Van Nostrand–Reinhold, 1978.
Kubie, L. S.: The relation of psychotic disorganizations to the neurotic process. J. Am. Psychoanal. Assoc., *15*:626–639, 1967.
Lund, R.: Personality factors and desynchronization of circadian rhythms. Psychosom. Med., *36*:224–228, 1974.
Miner, G. D.: The evidence for genetic components in the neuroses. Arch. Gen. Psychiatry, *29*:111–118, 1973.
Sims, A., and Prior, P.: The pattern of mortality in severe neuroses. Br. J. Psychiatry, *133*: 299–305, 1978.
Taylor, S. J. L., and Chave, S.: Mental Health and the Environment. Boston, Little, Brown & Company, 1964.

Character Neurosis

Borriello, J. F.: Patients with acting-out character disorders. Am. J. Psychother., *27*:4–14, 1973.

Anxiety Disorders

Crowe, R. R., Pawls, D. L., Slymen, D. J., and Noyes, R.: A family study of anxiety neurosis. Arch. Gen. Psychiatry, *37*:77–79, 1980.

Freud, S.: The Problem of Anxiety. New York, W. W. Norton & Company, 1936.

Fry, W. F.: The marital context of an anxiety syndrome. Family Process, *1*:242–245, 1952.

Noyes, R., Clancy, J., Hoenck, P. R., and Slymen, D. J.: The prognosis of anxiety neurosis. Arch. Gen. Psychiatry, *37*:173–178, 1980.

Phobic Disorders

Agras, W. S., Chapen, H. N., and Oliveau, D. C.: The natural history of phobia. Arch. Gen. Psychiatry, *26*:315–317, 1972.

Emmelkamp, P. M. G., and Kuipers, A. C.: Agoraphobia: A follow-up four years after treatment. Br. J. Psychiatry, *134*:352–355, 1979.

Enoch, M. D., Trethowan, W. H., and Barker, J. C.: Some Uncommon Psychiatric Syndromes. Bristol, John Wright & Sons, 1967.

Friedman, M.: Success phobia and retarded ejaculation. Am. J. Psychother., *27*:78–84, 1973.

Kantor, J. S., Zitrin, C. M., and Zeldis, S. M.: Mitral valve prolapse syndrome in agoraphobic patients. Am. J. Psychiatry, *137*:467, 1980.

Marks, I. M.: The classification of phobic disorders. Br. J. Psychiatry, *116*:377–386, 1970.

Ovesey, L.: The phobic reaction; A psychodynamic basis for classification and treatment. *In* Goldman, G. S., and Shapiro, D. (eds.): Developments in Psychoanalysis at Columbia University: Proceedings. New York, Hafner Publishing Company, 1966, pp. 41–68.

Zitrin, M. S., Klein, D. F., and Woerner, M. G.: Treatment of agoraphobia with group exposure in vivo and imipramine. Arch. Gen. Psychiatry, *37*:63–72, 1980.

Obsessive-Compulsive Disorder

Ananth, J., Solyom, L., Bryntwick, S., et al.: Chlorimipramine therapy for obsessive-compulsive neurosis. Am. J. Psychiatry, *136*:700–701, 1979.

Goodwin, D. W., Guze, S. B., and Robins, E.: Follow-up studies in obsessional neuroses. Arch. Gen. Psychiatry, *20*:182–187, 1969.

Marks, I. M., Hodgson, R., and Rachman, S.: Treatment of chronic obsessive-compulsive neuroses by in-vivo exposure. Br. J. Psychiatry, *127*:349–364, 1975.

Stern, R. S., and Cobb, S.: Phenomenology of obsessive-compulsive neurosis. Br. J. Psychiatry, *132*:233–239, 1978.

Suess, J. F.: Short-term psychotherapy with the compulsive personality and the obsessive-compulsive neurotic. Am. J. Psychiatry, *129*:270–275, 1972.

Tan, E., Marks, I. M., and Marset, P.: Bimedial leucotomy in obsessive-compulsive neurosis: A controlled serial enquiry. Br. J. Psychiatry, *118*:155–164, 1971.

Dysthymic (Depressive) Disorder

Davis, D., Lambert, J., and Ajan, Z. A.: Crying in depression. Br. J. Psychiatry, *115*:597–598, 1969.

Klerman, G. L., Endicott, J., Spitzer, R., and Hirschfield, R. M. A.: Neurotic depressions: A systemic analysis of multiple criteria and meanings. Am. J. Psychiatry, *136*:57–60, 1979.

Post-Traumatic Stress Disorders

Adler, R. H.: Psychotropic agents in the management of chronic pain. J. Human Stress, *4*:13–17, 1978.

Bluhm, H. O.: How did they survive? Mechanisms of defense in Nazi concentration camps. Am. J. Psychother., *2*:3–32, 1948.

Figley, C. R. (ed.): Stress Disorders Among Vietnam Veterans; Theory, Research and Treatment. New York, Brunner/Mazel, 1978.

Furst, S.: The stimulus barrier and the pathogenicity of trauma. Int. J. Psychoanal., *59*:345–352, 1978.

Janis, L.: Some implications of recent research on the dynamics of fear and stress tolerance in social psychiatry. Res. Publ. Assoc. Res. Nerv. Ment. Dis., *47*:86–100, 1969.

Krystal, H.: Trauma and affects. Psychoanal. Study Child, *33*:81–116, 1978.

Levar, I., Greenfield, H., and Baruch, E.: Psychiatric combat reactions in the Yom Kippur War. Am. J. Psychiatry, *136*:637–641, 1979.

Lifton, R. J., and Olson, E.: The human meaning of total disaster: The Buffalo Creek experience. Psychiatry, *39*:1–18, 1976.

Moses, R.: Adult psychic trauma: The question of early predisposition and some detailed mechanisms. Int. J. Psychoanal., *59*:353–363, 1978.

Sigal, J. J.: Second-generation effects of massive psychic trauma. Int. Psychiatry Clin., *8*:55–56, 1971.

Somatoform (Hysterical) Disorders

Breuer, J., and Freud, S.: Studies in Hysteria. Translated by A. A. Brill. Washington, D.C.,

Nervous & Mental Disease Publishing Company, 1937.

Chodoff, P.: The diagnosis of hysteria: An overview. Am. J. Psychiatry, *131*:1073–1078, 1973.

Cloninger, C. R., and Guze, S. B.: Hysteria and parental psychiatric illness. Psychol. Med., *5*:27–31, 1975.

Hafeiz, H. B.: Hysterical conversion. A prognostic study. Br. J. Psychiatry, *136*:548–551, 1980.

Janet, P.: The Major Symptoms of Hysteria. 2nd ed. New York, The Macmillan Company, 1920.

Levy, R., and Mushen, J.: The somatosensory evoked response in patients with hysterical paralysis. J. Psychosom. Res., *17*:81–84, 1973.

Raskin, M., Talbott, J. A., and Meyerson, A. T.: Diagnosis of conversion reactions. J.A.M.A., *197*:530–534, 1966.

Richman, J., and White, M.: A family view of hysterical psychosis. Am. J. Psychiatry, *127*:280–285, 1970.

Watson, G. G., and Buranen, C.: The frequency and identification of false positive conversion reactions. J. Nerv. Mental Dis., *167*:243–247, 1979.

Wells, C. E.: Pseudodementia. Am. J. Psychiatry, *136*:895, 1979.

Psychogenic Pain Disorders

Engel, G.: "Psychogenic" pain. Med. Clin. North Am., 1481–1496, 1958.

Hilgard, E. R., and Hilgard, J. R.: Hypnosis in the Relief of Pain. Los Angeles, William Kaufman, Inc., 1975.

Kolb, L. C.: The Painful Phantom; Psychology, Physiology and Treatment. Springfield, Ill., Charles C Thomas, 1954.

Kolb, L. C.: Symbolic significance of the complaint of pain. Clin. Neurosurg., *119*:248–257, 1963.

Sternback, R. A.: Pain Patients: Traits and Treatment. New York, Academic Press, 1974.

Szasz, T. S.: Pain and Pleasure. New York, Basic Books, 1957.

Dissociative Disorders

Alexander, V. K.: A case study of a multiple personality. J. Abnorm. Psychol., *52*:272–276, 1956.

Berrington, W. P., Liddell, D. W., and Foulds, G. A.: A re-evaluation of the fugue. J. Ment. Sci., *102*:280–286, 1956.

Ludwig, A. M., Brandsma, J. M., Wilbur, C. B., Bendfeldt, F., and Jameson, D. H.: The objective study of a multiple personality. Arch. Gen. Psychiatry, *26*:298–310, 1972.

Factitious Disorders

Cramer, B., Gershberg, M. R., and Stern, M.: Münchausen syndrome; Its relationship to malingering, hysteria, and the physician-patient relationship. Arch. Gen. Psychiatry, *24*:573–578, 1971.

Shafer, N., and Shafer, R.: Factitious diseases, including Münchausen's syndrome. N.Y. State J. Med., *80*:594–604, 1980.

Snowden, J., Solomons, R., and Druce, H.: Feigned bereavement: Twelve cases. Br. J. Psychiatry, *133*:15–19, 1978.

Whitlock, F. A.: The Ganser syndrome. Br. J. Psychiatry, *113*:19–29, 1967.

23 PSYCHOSEXUAL DISORDERS

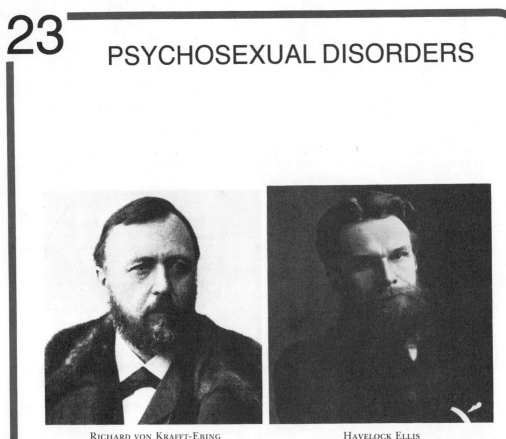

RICHARD VON KRAFFT-EBING

HAVELOCK ELLIS

Pioneers in the study of human sexuality. (Photographs courtesy of The New York Academy of Medicine.)

As a consequence of the prolonged exposure of the growing child to conflicting biological drives and the attitudes of the child's family and society to sexual behavior, it is no wonder that disturbances of sexual identity and function are so common. During development, ideas pertaining to sexual role, sex, and sexuality often become associated with feelings of shame, disgust, guilt, fear, and hatred. Although such attitudes are often caused by faulty and deficient education, in many instances they represent a symptomatic expression of a general personality disorder that requires skilled psychiatric treatment for its resolution. Even though urologists and gynecologists have become increasingly aware that the majority of disorders they treat are the consequence of personality maldevelopment and educational defects, far too many men and women continue to be subjected to unnecessary surgical and physical procedures that usually only serve to fix a conviction of physical illness, thus impairing the potential effectiveness of the indicated forms of treatment.

Studying the records of 96 patients who were seen for treatment of dysfunctional sexual disorders, O'Connor and Stern discovered from developmental histories that such individuals are more disturbed than are those in other patient groups. Fifty-seven per cent of the patients had at least one parent with a history of alcoholism; abnormal sexual behavior, incestuous experience, exhibitionism, psychosis, some form of obsessional activity, or expression of excessive brutality was noted. A third of the patients had been partners in some form of bizarre sexual activity within the family structure, while another third had been reared in an atmosphere of excessive prohibition of sexuality. A death had occurred within the immediate families, and there was prolonged separation from one or both parents before the patients became 16 years of age. Many had been exposed to an early and traumatic initial sexual experience within their family.

Included in this chapter is discussion of those conditions that result from inhibition in sexual desire or response and from developmental faults that lead to psychologic impairment in gender identity; also the paraphilias, in which the individual responds to other than normal sexual objects or obtains arousal by means that impede affectionate sexual relations. We describe ego-dystonic homosexuality in conjunction with disorders of gender identity.

PSYCHOSEXUAL DYSFUNCTIONS

Disturbances in the total sexual act lead to a variety of symptoms. In men, the common symptoms are impotence and premature ejaculation. Frigidity, dysmenorrhea, dyspareunia, premenstrual tension, and the quest for castrating operations are common expressions of psychopathology in women.

Sexual dysfunctions may take place in the initial phase of active sexual engagement, occur after initial successful coital contact, or be intermittent in expression. While choice of partner and acceptance by partner are important for arousal, more often sexual dysfunctions relate to the sufferer's own concepts of sexual adequacy or relate to attitudes pertaining to the partner. Attitudes of repressed hostility, anxiety, shame, or guilt in the interpersonal relationship frequently underly the inhibiting factors.

Depression, particularly, impairs both desire and function. Women of histrionic (hysterical) personality frequently have inhibitions of sexual excitement as well as orgasm. The same holds for men of compulsive make-up. Chronic anxiety relates frequently to premature ejaculation.

Impotence and Premature Ejaculation

One may classify impotence as (1) total impotence, in which a man has never been able to achieve satisfactory coitus associated with orgasm, although such individuals may be able to masturbate with normal heterosexual fantasies, and (2) partial impotence, in the following behavioral subgroups: those who complete satisfactory intercourse with subtotal erection; those with subtotal erection without ability to complete intercourse; those who have satisfactory erection with some women but not with others; those who have experienced impotence only following an anxiety-provoking change in their life situations (often the commitment to marriage or the birth of a child). There also occur premature ejaculation; retarded ejaculation (a rare phenomenon occurring in less than 0.15 per cent of men), and retrograde ejaculation, a phenomenon frequently discovered in diabetics or following vasectomy.

For the successful completion of the sexual act in men, needed are a certain sexual drive (libido), an attracting partner, and a situation that provides freedom from distraction and anxiety, allowing in turn erection, penile insertion, and the muscular activity that provides penile friction and stimulation.

Impotence, then, may follow either when there is lack of attraction to the partner or when the coital environment is threatening or distracting. Much more common, however, are those often unconscious and conflictful loves, due either to persisting infantile attachments to the mother, sister, or some other important succoring woman in early life, or to latent homosexual attachments. Again, anxiety may prevent potency owing to underlying hostilities toward women stemming from childhood experiences in which the opposite sex is perceived as critical, punitive, and capable of damaging the male genitals. Guilt, anxiety, or shame may lead to impotence in which the sufferer fears disapproval by parents or society, has unconscious wishes to damage the partner, or considers exposure of his body or his sexual performance subject to ridicule. Also, fears of contracting venereal disease or of dying sometimes inhibit potent behavior. Impotence is a common accompaniment of the depressive reactions, in which it often is obscured by the symptom of backache serving to prevent initiation of coitus.

To establish the diagnosis of psychogenic impotence, a careful history must be taken that will determine the situations in which failure at intercourse has occurred. Particular attention should be paid to the attitude toward the partner, the environment of the coital acts, the frequency of sexual relations, attitudes toward and desires for various forms of precoital stimulation, and the attitude of the partner. Note should be made of any fantasies that take place during intercourse. Some men undertake relations while thinking of another partner or are dis-

satisfied because of the belief that their partner will not allow precoital stimulation of various kinds when they desire it; others find themselves impotent only with certain women. As an example, a man may be unable to have satisfying sexual relations with his wife, yet may be potent with prostitutes or in extramarital affairs. Those who use intercourse as a means of defense against unconscious homosexual fears are likely to fail.

The attitude of the partner is most significant. If the woman is domineering or competitive with men, her persistent derogation of her husband or lover may not only induce but also perpetuate the impotence. On the other hand, the female partner may be sexually inhibited and thus too submissive. As Friedman has pointed out, others are narcissistic and regard the sexual act as a gift to be rendered to them. Without an erection, the man may be regarded as unreasonable or derogatory and therefore the rightful subject of criticism and outright anger. Such women show little interest in their partner's genitals and tend to avoid the penis.

Impotence due to such illnesses as multiple sclerosis, syphilis, diabetes, or other disorders involving the sacral segments of the spinal cord, the lumbar parasympathetic outflow, or the lumbar sympathetic chain should be excluded by general medical and neurological examination. In psychiatric patients treated with phenothiazines, impotence may be a toxic effect of drug administration.

Aside from those occasional instances in which the symptoms may be rectified by simple advice concerning disturbing situational conditions, such as attempting intercourse in the parental home or bedroom or avoidance of an unwanted partner, the indicated treatment is psychotherapeutic and preferably with psychoanalytic orientation. In most cases of failure of erection, the patient should be advised initially to avoid in-

Figure 23–1 Effectiveness of treatment of human sexual dysfunction by psychological methods. (From O'Connor, J. F.: Clin. Obstet. Gynecol. *19*:449–464, 1976.)

tercourse and failure as a means of preventing futher lowering of self-esteem. Such advice is probably unnecessary and unwise for premature ejaculation, in which more frequent attempts may reduce the anticipatory tension. When impotence is a symptom of depression, the patient may be advised that the symptoms will disappear with relief of the affective disorder. Relief of the symptom is less likely in the elderly or in those cases in which the sexual partner is consistently intimidating or threatening. In the majority of instances in which impotence occurs in marriage, the partner should be involved in the treatment.

O'Connor reports 74 per cent of men improved by either psychoanalysis or psychotherapy, with the former more effective. Failures were associated with the coexistence of more severe forms of psychopathology. This investigator compared the response to various forms of psychotherapeutic intervention, including the processes recommended by Masters and Johnson. Findings are shown in Figure 23–1.

Frigidity, Dyspareunia, and Infertility

In considering the response to sexual intercourse, it must be kept in mind that the climax of coitus in women is not analogous to orgasm in men. Even the anatomical structure of the female genital tract differs from that of the male. Sensory cells similar to those found in the glans penis are confined largely to the clitoris, with some located in the labia minora and lower vaginal muscles. The vagina is homologous with the penile shaft and therefore cannot respond to sexual stimulation in the same way as the phallus. The widely held notion or expectation of rapid and climactic orgasm in women similar to that of men is probably incorrect. It is now generally accepted that possibly 30 per cent of the general female population fail to achieve orgasm during their first experience of intercourse, but up to 90 per cent are experiencing orgasm after ten years.

For satisfactory sexual relations, women must have a desirable partner, be devoid of anxiety and guilt, and must then be provided with appropriate stimulation in order to achieve a slower but more enduring gratification. Many women believe they are frigid due to misconceptions about feminine arousal. Much has been learned of sexual arousal in women through the work of Masters and Johnson; this knowledge is imperative to all psychiatrists concerned with evaluation of symptoms indicative of sexual dysfunction.

Frigidity often is related to fear of injury in intercourse or of pregnancy and may spring from envy of and hostility to men. Unfulfilled expectations of their response arouse in some women feelings of shameful inadequacy or rage at their partner. Less anxious women and those who accept a more giving and passive role are often gratified even without full clitoral stimulation and orgasm. Dyspareunia and vaginismus are the consequence of the same anxieties and fears that impair sexual satisfaction in women. It appears likely that infertility also has its origins in suppression by central mechanisms of ovulation through persisting anxieties and doubts of pregnancy and childbearing.

When it is evident that emotional factors are the primary factor determining the existence of these conditions, psy-

chotherapy is the indicated treatment. It is more likely to prove beneficial in those whose inhibitions are due to unconscious feelings of guilt, disgust, or repressed hostility than in women with a strong maternal fixation and infantile personality make-up. Women with frigidity treated by psychoanalysis or dynamic psychotherapy experienced less improvement than men. Nevertheless, as O'Connor found, 25 per cent were relieved of their symptoms while another 36 per cent improved. These results are less impressive than those for men treated for the varieties of impotence and are independent of the duration of frigidity.

GENDER IDENTITY DISORDERS

Persons whose biological sex urges are directed toward a normal heterosexual goal, but who, because they are segregated from the opposite sex and seek sexual satisfaction through various perversions, are scarcely to be considered as sexual deviates. In the true deviate, the offending sexual act is the surface symptom of a more profound personality disturbance.

In the opinion of many psychiatrists, the term sexual deviate should be limited to the individual whose sexual impulse, through defects in the step-by-step development of personality, either has remained immature or has undergone deviation in the course of its maturation. The arrest or deviation in development is not, of course, in the anatomy or physiology of sex organs but in the psychosexual, i.e., the emotional, dispositional aspect of sexual expression. Psychosexual maturation may lag behind biological maturation or be so blocked that mature heterosexual impulses are not established. Satisfaction of the sex impulse is therefore sought through such expressions as voyeurism, exhibitionism, homosexuality, rape, pedophilia, masochism, sadism, and other means.

If the family and social environment are not favorable to a healthy, mature psychosexual development, the drive toward mature heterosexuality will be blocked or deviated. Thus a boy held closely by his mother through his growing years and deprived of close association with a father, through the latter's absence, indifference, or hostility, is likely to have homosexual relations as his preferred form of sexual gratification in adulthood. There is much evidence from both the clinic and the laboratory that effective heterosexual development in man and animals depends upon continuing contacts with members of both sexes throughout growth.

Through the recent work of Money, Stoller, and others and from the extensive clinical experiences of those suffering various forms of sexual maldevelopment, the tendency has been to distinguish between sex and gender. Much of the research on sex is related to the biological make-up of the individual and overlooks the vast areas of the developmental processes concerning sexual behavior, the fantasies it causes, and the feelings of those concerned. The developmental task for mankind is the establishment of *gender identity*. The primary determinants of gender identity are psychological, as clearly established by clinical investigation, study of hermaphrodites and transsexuals, and the differential sexual behavior of certain sets of identical twins. This is in no way at odds with the findings of Brodie and his colleagues, who have reported that the levels of plasma testosterone in a group of young male homosexuals were significantly higher than those of a matched group of heterosexual men.

It is the individual's own self-designation as male or female that the workers in the general area of sexual development refer to as gender identity. *Core gender identity* refers to the individual's biologically determined sex; that is, male or female. *Gender role identity* designates the individual's personally perceived social role as masculine or feminine. It is within the framework of identification as a boy or girl or a man or woman that the early developmental process is crucial. The assignment of the gender occurs as a result of the attitudes of the parents before and after birth and the transactions to which the child is exposed in relation to the subsequent fantasies, wishes, and desires of the parents.

Even though the core gender identity is clear and the parental transactions occur without ambiguity, the individual may nevertheless have defects in the gender role. Core gender identity is established early in life and is fixed, but gender role evolves over time, influenced as it is by the attitudes of parents and others. It contains within it the behavioral traits identified as masculine or feminine. Gender identity, which determines the range of overt and fantasied sexual behaviors, develops through the ongoing flow of personal experiences in living, and is constrained in expression only by the rigidity of the personality structure.

Transsexualism

Transsexualism is not to be confused with transvestism. The term has come into use since the introduction of gender transmutation by surgical or endocrinological means. A transsexual is a biologically normal person with an unalterable conviction that he is a member of the opposite sex. He argues that throughout life he has so regarded himself. Such persons often attempt now to join the desired sex through requests to reshape their genital organs by surgical or endocrinological means. By so doing it is their hope to achieve their enduring fantasy in reality.

In those requesting transsexual change, Person and Ovesey have defined a primary group, whom they classify as a special syndrome, and a secondary group, whom they regard as transsexuals deriving from homosexuals and transvestites. Person and Ovesey believe that all three disorders arise from unresolved separation anxiety during the early phases of infantile development. Primary transsexualism is regarded as the most infantile fixation, with transvestism and homosexuality arising through later experiences. In male transsexualism, a fantasy of symbiotic fusion with the mother is used to prevent the anxiety of potential separation, which would first appear before the age of 3. Such fantasies differ from those used by the transvestite and the homosexual, who develop a clear, if distorted, core identity as a male.

In another account of the early development of the future transsexual, Stoller reports the maternal relationship as one of close emotional contact extending for years, uninterrupted by other siblings, which fosters the wish to remain a part of the mother. The parents of the transsexualists he examined generally had a loveless, sexless marriage; the mothers were commonly depressed, with a sense of emptiness. The fathers, on the other hand, were detached, passive, and often handsome.

Many male transsexuals are reported to show an early displeasure in boyish pursuits of a competitive nature and some had preferences for girls' activities and girls as playmates. Feminine behavior was common; they were often thought of as sissies by their peers. On the other hand, Person and Ovesey found less evidence of feminine behavior early in life and discovered that future transsexuals were generally withdrawn and spent vast amounts of time alone with hobbies and watching television, or were preoccupied and depressed. They were envious of girls and fantasied being girls. None actually believed that he was a girl. They detested their male physical characteristics, including the genitalia, their musculature, hair distribution, and absence of breasts. The primary desire is to rid themselves of the penis. All engaged in cross-dress-

ing early in life, but struggled in the postadolescent period to make a major effort to act out their biological sex by engaging in distinct masculine activity. This effort fails and leads them to seek sexual transformation through the surgical and endocrinological techniques now available.

Those who request surgical transformation generally are poor candidates for psychotherapy. The primary transsexual is obsessed with gender-related matters, even after successful surgery. This is evident in his preoccupation in gaining perfection as a woman through additional physical procedures, such as facial plastic operations or breast augmentation. Many secondary transsexuals have already sought and failed in psychoanalytic or behavioral therapies, or their encounters with psychiatrists have led to unfavorable judgments that they are psychotic.

The existing follow-up studies of those who have undergone sex reassignment by endocrinological and surgical processes generally indicate subjective satisfaction with the change but little or no modification in social competency. The primary transsexual would be expected to make the best candidate for sex reassignment. Careful psychiatric and psychological study, such as is done in the major clinics undertaking surgery, should be performed by the people who are recommending the procedure. In some clinics, surgery is not undertaken until the individual has lived the reassigned sexual role for a year or more.

Gender identity disorder is recognized in childhood by a deep rejection of the usual feminine or masculine role. The girls associate generally with boys, are interested essentially in sports and physical activities while rejecting playing house or "dolls." They may declare they will become a man, that they will not develop breasts, and will have a penis. Boys with this condition prefer to dress as girls and engage in girls' games and occupations while avoiding the pastimes of their boyhood associates. In some instances they speak with disgust of their genitals and suggest they will disappear. Both sexes may refuse to attend school where they are teased for their difference.

Cross-dressing in such boys occurs before the age of four years in about three-fourths of the group. In adolescence, for both girls and boys, there is a tendency to concealment of the patterns of behavior of the other sex, yet homosexual arousal now emerges.

Homosexuality

There is a wide range of homosexual behavior in both men and women. Some live an exclusively homosexual life and receive all adult sexual gratification from a partner of the same sex; others are predominantly but not exclusively satisfied in this way. In a large number of adolescents and adults, the major sexual expression is heterosexual, yet occasionally or incidentally these individuals have homosexual contacts. Such incidental contacts may take place when the person is deprived of heterosexual contacts, after alcohol debauches or head injuries, or in situations of homosexual license.

As a matter of concern for psychiatry, homosexual behavior productive of conflict between the sexual drive and the individual's ego ideals and superego may lead to anxiety, depression, shame, or other neurotic defensive activities. Therefore, the condition is ego-dystonic.

Diagnostically, homosexuals are not disgusted with the anatomic evidence of their sex, as is the transsexual, nor do they usually cross-dress, as does the transvestite. However, cross-dressing may co-exist with homosexuality.

The term homosexuality is often used in ways other than to indicate a personality disorder wherein the predominant mode of sexual expression is with a member of the same sex. "Latent homosexuality" refers to the existence of a personality make-up similar to that of the overt homosexual, and associated even in some cases with fantasy formation of homosexual activity, but without overt homosexual activity. Unfortunately, homosexuality is now used frequently as a derogatory designation, and some neurotic patients designate themselves as homosexual owing to their feelings of failure and inability to express and utilize successfully their aggressive drives to mastery.

Among the groups of men charged with homosexual behavior in courts, one finds the female impersonator, as well as the isolated and dull person who has not had a loving relationship in the past, the resentful antisocial, those generally compensated individuals who are apprehended after an overt act while drinking in later life, and those whose homosexual behavior is a single component in a more serious psychotic disorder, most frequently schizophrenic or mentally defective.

There are many homosexuals whose personality development and ego functioning appear intact and who conduct themselves both effectively and constructively in society. These individuals show certain common features in the personality. They have difficulty in reconciling dependent and assertive drives, an ambivalent maternal relationship, and a high frequency of being reared in a broken home.

Homosexual behavior is determined on the basis of defect in psychosexual maturation. A study of a number of identical twin pairs showed one to be heterosexual and the other homosexual. In such twin pairs the opportunity was optimum to examine the differing psychogenetic forces that relate to the several forms of sexual behavior; the findings of these studies gave strong support to earlier psychodynamic formulations.

For a healthy psychosexual development, the child should form an identification with the parent or a member of his or her own sex. The future homosexual male has an inordinate attachment to his mother, fostered by her and leading to identification with her.

This attachment flowers in the absence or indifference of a father or when the child fears or hates this parent or derogates him as the mother often does. The homosexual who has identified with the mother as the dominant person seeks out males as sexual companions, motivated either through fear of incest or loss of the maternal relationship that is threatened in his contacts with women. Then there are underlying castration fears, and resentments toward women derived from the repressed hostilities toward the mother. The homosexual relationship may express also his hostility to men.

In a few instances, male homosexuality arises when the child has been separated from women and reared by men throughout life. Here he is deprived of the experience of heterosexual contact and also fears women.

Female homosexuality has been much less studied than male homosexuality, in spite of the fact that surveys of sexual behavior have indicated that 28 per cent of women in Western societies report homosexual contact, approximately half leading to orgasm. The vast majority of the female homosexuals are only children who became emotionally attached to other women before the age of 14 years and had their first direct homosexual experience before the age of 20 years. In general, confirmed *lesbians* differ from healthy women in giving histories of exposure to severe abusiveness and alcoholism, the development of indifference toward men, the lack of gratifying relations with others, and loneliness. A considerable percentage become involved in health care work. Many tend to be depressive and have strong suicidal tendencies.

PARAPHILIAS

These disorders are characterized by the fact that sexual arousal requires indulgence in imagery or acts of an unusual kind. These actions are compulsively repetitive, may require the presence of other than a human being for arousal, involve suffering or personal debasement, or require the use of nonconsenting partners — human or animal.

Transvestism

Transvestism is the impulse to dress in the clothing of the opposite sex and thereby attain sexual gratification. Formulations of the psychopathology of fetishism and of transvestism are still largely speculative. Transvestism occurs more frequently in men than in women. Usually, the patient's mother wanted a girl and literally reared her son to be one.

Transvestism is not to be confused with homosexuality. Most transvestites are oriented to heterosexual relations, as well as to social relations with the opposite sex. They often marry.

Transvestism usually commences between the ages of 5 and 14, in the association of articles of feminine clothing with sexual gratification through masturbation. The behavior is reinforced if the growing youngster's potential for heterosexual development is impeded through passivity or opposing family or social forces which he cannot overcome.

Stoller suggests that transvestism contains motivations of revenge, the excitement of risk, and also mystification. Many transvestites report having been humiliated as youngsters by being dressed by women in feminine clothes. At the same time and as part of the humiliating experience, they obtained a sense of gratification in the pleasure it gave the women who so encouraged them; the sense of being male and masculine was aroused. Thus dressing as a transvestite provided a sense of sexual excitement, in which the boys evolved fantasies to sustain their gender roles against the attacks of the women who pressured them this way early in life. Women's clothes and the appearance of femininity provided excitement as well as revenge through filling the obverse role. The transvestite act is associated with the risk of discovery, stimulating the individual toward perversity and eventual satisfaction in orgasm. By the late teens the transvestite pattern becomes fixed.

The term transvestite has been used often to refer to others who derive satisfaction from cross-dressing. Thus there are other heterosexual and homosexual persons who find gratification in this act, although they do not have the developmental history or the psychodynamics of the transvestite as just described. It has been used to label transitory cross-dressing in children who later may or may not become homosexuals. Also erroneously designated have been males who adopt a ritualistic fetish of wearing special articles of female clothing openly or concealed beneath male clothing, as well as male homosexual "drag queens" who periodically cross-dress.

Pedophilia

Pedophilia, or a pathological sexual interest in children, is regarded as a variant of homosexuality in which homosexual strivings are directed toward children. It occurs largely in weak and impotent persons, the immature, and often those with mental retardation or the isolated elderly. Another, and perhaps more logical, explanation of the pedophil's behavior is that he functions on an immature psychosexual level because of his fearfulness and doubt concerning himself. As a result of these feelings, he expects rejection and failure in adult, heterosexual advances. His sexual expression is therefore released toward children. This expression may represent the wish he had for himself as a child, the narcissistic choice, or its obverse, and lead to harm or violence to the seduced child. Certain pedophils also indulge in voyeurism, exhibitionism, and homosexuality.

Pedophils who engage in violence or other criminal activity have been found to have hyperactivity problems in the past and to have records of other antisocial activity.

Fetishism

Fetishism is a perversion peculiar to men. The fetishist is unable to love a real person but becomes attached to some object having a feminine association, such as a lock of hair or an undergarment. This object attains a highly exaggerated value and becomes a special source of erotic gratification, a reliever of both psychic and sexual tension, as contact with it leads to orgasm. The fetish always has a genital meaning; it serves the purpose of denying the anatomical difference between the two sexes, discovery of which caused an overwhelming genital fear.

Fetishism has usually been considered a substitutive genital drive attendant on fears of castration. Some psychoanalysts consider the fetishistic attachment an effort to gain an ego identification through contact with a substitutive satisfying object, and point to the fetishistic attachment of little children to blankets, toys, or other objects as a means of satisfaction in the absence of the mother. Thus, the fetish may be seen as satisfying a pregenital wish.

Zoophilia

Here the preferred or only method of deriving sexual excitement is through the use of an animal. The action may be one of intercourse or the animal may be trained to lick or rub the sexual organs of the zoophilic. Most frequently, the animal is one with which the person has lived—often a pet. The types of persons so inclined are similiar to the pedophils.

Exhibitionism

In exhibitionism, one of the commonest sexual deviations, one usually finds that the offender is a son of a dominant, aggressive mother who resents her feminine role and tries to live her life through her children, especially the sons. The father is frequently a weak and ineffective person who has exerted little influence in shaping the son's emotional development. Because of the mother's spoiling and showering the boy with unusual affection, he comes to identify himself with her. Incestuous wishes develop as well. With a strong taboo against such insistent but consciously forbidden wishes, the boy must build compulsive, but unconscious, defenses. The symptom of exhibitionism with genital exposure to others functions to reassure him against castration.

While the exhibitionist tends to be seen as socially passive, Rooth's study disclosed that their outward timidity contrasted with bullying behavior at home with family members. In general, they had difficulty in effecting and adapting well to their aggressive impulses. A few exhibitionists also had indulged in pedophilia in adolescence; of this group a limited number exposed more regularly only to prepubertal children. Thus, the relationships between pedophilia, hebephilia and exhibitionism are often blurred. Some have been voyeurs and indulged in homosexuality as well.

Voyeurism

This perversion is related to the pleasure in looking (scoptophilia), but the voyeur obtains his sexual gratification through attempting to repeat visually the anxiety-arousing, yet exciting scenes of early childhood. In a sense, the effort required to watch a member of the opposite sex undress or to visualize the sexual act offers a repetition of this anxiety and excitement. The voyeur often has a sense of fearfulness in regard to looking and cannot accept the gaze of the other person. In one case the voyeur who went on to attempt rape covered the eyes of his victim.

The voyeur has often been exposed, in an aggressive way, to the nudity of his mother. In his adolescence, he attempts to regain this sexual excitement through surreptitious visualization of other women undressing or through observation of the sexual act, in which he himself may be impotent because of those fears that commenced as he looked at the mother in early childhood. The voyeur may entertain aggressive, murderous fantasies against women. He suffers the fear of merging and fusing with the mother. The act functions to reinforce his masculinity through visual experience. He generally masturbates during the voyeuristic acts, although on some occasions, as mentioned in the section on exhibitionism, he may startle the visualized person by exhibiting his penis. This perversion can proceed from looking to touching, seizing, and later to actual assault and sadism.

Sadism and Masochism

Through the autobiographical writings of the Marquis de Sade, the association of sexuality and cruelty attracted the interest of psychopathologists and led to the introduction to psychiatry of these pathological behaviors by Krafft-Ebing in 1882. *Sadism* is defined as the experience of pleasurable sexual sensations, including orgasm, when inflicting acts of cruelty oneself or witnessing such upon others or animals. In order to experience the sexual pleasure, the sadist must humiliate, wound, harm, or even kill another. The sadistic acts that give pleasure may occur after coitus that is not gratifying, prior to coitus to increase desire, or solely to induce orgasm without intercourse in those sadists who are impotent.

For the most part, men have been identified as sadists, but sadism is not exclusively a male sexual perversion. The varieties of action are wide and include the most vicious of physical attacks, including strangling, disemboweling, or cutting a body to pieces, often with concentration upon removal of the breasts and genitals. The odor and taste of blood often provide the necessary stimulus; in some instances, the sadistic act may be limited to defecation, urination, or other defilation on the sexual object.

From early observations of cruelty to others to which the future sadist experienced sexual arousal, fantasies then evolve associated with masturbation, which are later succeeded by infliction of the cruel or humiliating acts upon the selected object. Krafft-Ebing viewed power as the motivating force—the wish to subjugate the other. Many psychoanalysts perceive the sadist as acting out his desires on a victim to whom he has transferred his ambivalent feelings about sexuality. The victim is perceived as one who threatened punishment for sexual activity, who aroused internally prohibited sexual desires, or who expressed inexcusable submissiveness. The sadist experiences then the complex of affects of anxiety, rage, vengeance, and ecstatic relief as he acts out aggressively towards the other. The sadist is rarely encountered by psychiatrists today.

Masochism, named for Sacher-Masoch, who was a masochist, is the obverse of sadism. The masochist gains sexual pleasure by being subjected to the aggression of the opposite person—by being hurt, abused, or humiliated to induce the orgastic pleasure. In some instances, masochistic pleasure is gained through association with disgusting fetishistic attachments, such as licking or smelling body or clothing soiled with excrement, or other bodily filth. The masochist often enjoys biting, striking, or flagellation by the partner, and during the sexual act the masochist may become increasingly unaware of personal bodily damage as sexual arousal takes place.

Masochism's origins may lie in a child's identifying with someone being punished while at the same time experiencing sexual pleasure and arousal

as the pain is inflicted by a loved one—as, for instance, the child enjoying the beating of a sibling rival. It may arise as an alternative method of gratification in the face of anxiety over possible suffering or greater harm. Thus, parental spanking relieves the guilt of punishment for sexual fantasies. Finally, by suffering, some exercise power through inducing guilt in the desired love object, who then offers them sexual gratification.

Other masochists whose major pathology is dependency eroticize power. In these masochists, the wish is to gain power through support of the partner, rather than to obtain sexual satisfaction. This type of masochism may express itself in many forms, such as self-infliction of injury, or pseudo-illness by taking medications, or in accident proneness. Masochistic behavior is often observed in the obsessive, the depressive, or those with success phobias. These may use behavior destructive of acceptance by others, to whom they then relate in a paranoidal manner.

PATHOGENESIS OF PARAPHILIAS

A characteristic common to all forms of sexual perversions is their repetitive, compulsive, patterned nature. Such behavior represents the expression of an uncontrollable urge, committed without logic or rationale and apparently for the purpose of securing relief from an unbearable tension. The satisfaction derived from the commission of the sexually deviated and compulsive act is symbolic and substitutive; it is therefore temporary and requires repetition. These characteristics constitute the criteria of the neuroses. There is, in fact, an increasing tendency to regard the true sexual perversions as basically psychoneurotic in their psychopathology and therefore as a kind of mental illness. As in the case of compulsive handwashing, the apparent motive is not the real, or at least not the only, motivating factor. The real motive is to satisfy aggressive or various other immature and deviated aspects of the psychosexual component of the personality.

A majority of serious sex offenders are unable to comprehend the reasons, the inner compulsion, for their actions. The sexual deviate's behavior is not a substitute for normal heterosexual relations. It is a form of sexual activity that satisfies some very specific need ungratified by normal sexual activity.

Studies in the pathogenesis of the sexual deviations make it appear that overt antisocial misbehavior may be caused by often unwitting parental seduction. In infancy, nudity, fondling, and virtual absence of privacy are appropriate and even necessary. If, however, such evidences of kindly parental affection persist until childhood or adolescence, they become pathological. Under the guise of "motherly" or "fatherly" affection, boys and girls may be bathed by parents, often of the opposite sex, until adolescence. Sleeping with children of the opposite sex may be prolonged into the teen-age period. Undressing may habitually occur in the presence of children. Sometimes legitimate parental embraces of affection extend into the sphere of frank bodily petting of adolescent children. Stimulated by parental behavior, the child finds no outlet for the aroused sexual impulses. Eventually, mounting frustration and anger force him or her to follow one of two courses. One is regression to the safety of more infantile attitudes of sexual behavior. The other is sexual aggression toward the opposite sex. In girls, of course, this leads to further repression. Neither course resolves the rage or dissipates the overstimulated unconscious sexual drives. The result may therefore later be a direct, sexual, destructive acting out of the conflict.

In contrast to the direct, hostile act-ing out stemming from the repeated seduction and frustration incident to the child's intimate association with the parent of the opposite sex, such sexual aberrations as exhibitionism, voyeurism, and transvestism may be traceable to the unconscious tendencies of the parent. In such cases, the instinctual sexual development of the child seems to represent or constitute an acting out of the unconscious wishes of the parent.

TREATMENT

Before considering therapy, the matter of prevention of such maldevelopment needs consideration. Prevention requires a knowledge of its origin. It requires also a recognition and emotional acceptance by the public of the fact that true deviation, in contrast to methods of sexual gratification adopted in the absence of opportunity for the satisfaction of a biologically normal heterosexual impulse, is a manifestation of a developmental fault in the mental life that originated in the early formative years of childhood. Progress in reducing sexually psychopathic behavior has been exceedingly slow. The most hopeful approach is prevention through more and proper sex education in childhood, the establishment of identifications consonant with the child's sex, and assistance in a constructive sublimation of sexual and aggressive impulses that may be misdirected by the vicissitudes of childhood.

The child's sexual development will occur through identification with a parent or parent substitute of the same sex. Being reared by a single parent, and without exposure to family members of both sexes for observation of their preferential behaviors limits the potential for establishing clearly defined sexual identity. Use of the child by parents to relieve their own ungratified sexual impulses through unnecessary sexual exposure, sexually motivated physical contacts, incest, or verbal or physical abuse for the child's innocent personal sexual explorations or masturbatory activities set the stage for the evolution of later sexual maldevelopment, or perversions, or both. Therefore, in cases of potential transsexualism, male children or adolescent boys should be treated by a male therapist and associate with those who demonstrate a male sexual role. Parents who have tended to treat their child's effeminate behavior as "cute" or to deny it will need treatment as well.

Psychotherapy utilizing psychoanalytical principles is the rational treatment for the sex deviate. Some sexual psychopaths have no conscious desire to be cured of their behavior. Ideal conditions for therapy exist when the deviate has not been guilty of offense against the person, has therefore not committed a serious social offense, and has voluntarily sought therapy. If his offense has been so serious that the community must be protected, the deviate must be confined. The prison environment and routine are not, however, conducive to successful therapy. The personality factors and emotional conflicts that led to the crime will not, of course, be worked through by simply spending a certain amount of time in prison. If the offender has not been guilty of violence, it is usually desirable that he be confined in a hospital atmosphere in which the therapist may supervise the surroundings in accordance with the needs of the patient as the therapy progresses. Through therapy and subsequent parole, some offenders, if their desire for improvement is strong, may be enabled to channel their impulses into constructive activities.

Behavioral therapies have been attempted in recent years, but long-term results remain to be assessed. As Abel and Blanchard point out, increasing use of fantasy as the important independent variable substituted for the deviant fantasy relates these therapies more to the psychoanalytic therapies.

BIBLIOGRAPHY

General

Ford, C. S., and Beach, F. A.: Patterns of Sexual Behavior. New York, Paul B. Hoeber, 1951.

Psychosexual Dysfunctions

Friedman, H. J.: An interpersonal aspect of psychogenic impotence. Am. J. Psychother., 27: 421–429, 1973.
Hastings, D. W.: Impotence and Frigidity. Boston, Little, Brown & Company, 1963.
Masters, W. H., and Johnson, V. E.: Human Sexual Response. Boston, Little, Brown & Company, 1966.
O'Connor, J. F.: Effectiveness of treatment of human sexual dysfunction. Clin. Obstet. Gynecol., 19:449–464, 1976.
O'Connor, J. F., Shelley, F. M., and Stern, F. M.: Behavioral rhythms related to the menstrual cycle. In Ferin, M., et al. (eds.): Biorhythms and Human Reproduction. New York, John Wiley & Sons, 1974, pp. 309–324.
O'Connor, J. F., and Stern, L. O.: Developmental factors in functional sexual disorders. N.Y. State J. Med., 72:1838–1843, 1972.

Gender Identity Disorders

Green, R.: Sexual identity of 37 children raised by homosexual or transsexual parents. Am. J. Psychiatry, 135:692–697, 1978.
Green, R., and Money, J.: Transsexualism and Its Management. Baltimore, Johns Hopkins Press, 1969.
Green, R., Newman, L. E., and Stoller, R. J.: Treatment of boyhood "transsexualism." Interim report of four years' experience. Arch. Gen. Psychiatry, 26:213–217, 1972.
Hunt, D. D., and Hampson, J. L.: Follow-up of 17 biologic male transsexuals after sex-reassignment surgery. Am. J. Psychiatry, 137:432–488, 1980.
Meyers, J. K., and Reter, D. J.: Sex reassignment. Arch. Gen. Psychiatry, 36:1010–1015, 1979.
Pauley, I. B.: Female Transsexualism. Arch. Sexual Behavior, 3:487–526, 1974.
Person, E., and Ovesey, L.: The transsexual syndrome in males. I. Primary transsexualism. II. Secondary transsexualism. Am. J. Psychother., 28:4–20, 174–193, 1974.

Homosexuality

Bell, A. P., and Weinberg, M. S.: Homosexualities. New York, Simon & Schuster, 1978.
Bieber, I., et al.: Homosexuality. New York, Basic Books, 1962.

Brodie, H. K., Gartrell, N., Doering, C., and Rhue, T.: Plasma testosterone levels in heterosexual men. Am. J. Psychiatry, *131*:82–89, 1974.

Kolb, L. C., and Johnson, A. M.: Etiology and therapy of overt homosexuality. Psychoanal. Q., *24*:506–515, 1965.

Paraphilias

Abel, G. G., and Blanchard, E. B.: The role of fantasy in the treatment of sexual deviation. Arch. Gen. Psychiatry, *30*:467–475, 1974.

Bieber, I.: Sadism and masochism; Phenomenology and psychodynamics. *In* Arieti, S. (ed.): American Handbook of Psychiatry. 2nd ed. Vol. II. New York, Basic Books, 1974, pp. 316–333.

Johnson, A. M., and Robinson, D. B.: The sexual deviant (sexual psychopath) — causes, treatment, and prevention. J.A.M.A., *164*:1559–1565, 1957.

Krafft-Ebing, R. von: Psychopathia Sexualis. (Translated from the 12th German edition by F. S. Klaf.) New York, Stein & Day, 1965.

Marks, I., Gilder, M., and Bancroft, J.: Sexual deviants two years after electric aversion. Br. J. Psychiatry, *117*:173–185, 1970.

Rainer, J. D., Mesnikoff, A., Kolb, L. C., and Carr, A.: Homosexuality and heterosexuality in identical twins. Psychosom. Med., *22*:251–259, 1960.

Rooth, G.: Exhibitionism, sexual violence and paedophilia. Br. J. Psychiatry, *122*:705–710, 1973.

Stoller, R. J.: Sex and Gender. New York, Science House, 1968.

Swanson, D. W., Loomis, S. D., Lukesh, R., et al.: Clinical features of the female homosexual patient. J. Nerv. Ment. Dis., *155*:119–124, 1972.

Yalom, I. D.: Aggression and forbiddenness in voyeurism. Arch. Gen. Psychiatry, *3*:305–319, 1960.

24

PSYCHOLOGICAL FACTORS AFFECTING PHYSICAL CONDITION

"The sorrow which has no vent in tears may make other organs weep."

Henry Maudsley

IVAN P. PAVLOV AND WALTER B. CANNON
Pavlov, a Russian physiologist and experimental psychologist,
discovered the conditioned reflex; Cannon, an American
physiologist, introduced the concept of homeostasis.
(From Psychological Review, *53*:137, 1946.)

The reactions included in this chapter comprise those that are more frequently referred to as "psychosomatic disorders." In the language of general systems theory, these disorders relate particularly to the malfunctioning of those two critical subsystems found in all living states: the organs functioning to process matter to energy, and those directed to the same purpose but also processing generational biological in-formation. Malfunctioning takes place, however, owing to failure on the part of a third subsystem, the informational system of the brain, to effectively process the incoming symbols from all sources and integrate the operations of all three systems.

To put it in human terms, the affects of depression, anxiety, and/or fear or their derivatives in guilt and shame are aroused and maintained to levels of intensity that break through the usual psychological defenses. Anxiety or depression leads to disturbances that are expressed predominantly through physiological processes rather than symbolically. The expression of affect being through viscera, its feeling or subjective part is repressed and therefore largely prevented from becoming conscious. Nor is its expression under full voluntary control or perception.

As the result of the stress of long-continued and exaggerated physiological expression of the affect, malfunction or even eventual structural change may take place in the organ or viscus through which it is expressed. The physiological and the organic are secondary to vascular disturbance, smooth muscle dysfunction, and hypersecretion or hyposecretion of glands, innervated largely by the sympathetic and parasympathetic divisions of the autonomic nervous system.

The concept used here is to classify as psychosomatic all those disturbances involving the organs of internal economy, of instinctual function, and of the body image as a whole. It is evident that the internal organ systems located within the body cavities are largely controlled through the connections of the central nervous system and various metabolic and hormonal feedbacks. The organ systems that have direct contact with the external environment are used for the intake and elimination of needed bodily substances and for procreative activity (respiratory, gastrointestinal, and genital apparatus) and are controlled in part at their orifices by the voluntary nervous system and also by the autonomic through the integrative activity of the central nervous pathways. Here is seen initiation of the functions by utilization of the voluntary nervous system, followed by increasing degrees of automatization through the sympathetic and parasympathetic innervations.

In the instances of the body image disturbances, the total organism is involved, not a single organ or series of organs. Excluded, then, from the area of the psychosomatic disorders are dysfunctions of the central nervous system subserving the external relations of the individual, his perceptual and conative activities, communicative systems, orientations in space and time, and his capacity to organize and integrate the information provided him from the outside world. It is clear that the borderline between the disorders subsumed under the body image and those of the integrative functions of the nervous system in contact with the external world may not be sharply delimited and subtly merge with general personality functioning.

As Weiner and associates point out, the psychosomatic approach to illness postulates that social and psychological factors are significant in establishing the predisposition, inception, and maintenance of many illnesses. The psychosomaticist is concerned with adaption to change, its successes and failures, and the personal developmental forces possibly determinative of both. The therapist is interested in the antecedent conditions that establish individual differences in perception of illness and is inquisitive as to why some people are threatened and others are not.

Emotional Components of Physical Illness

The manifestations of a physical illness are frequently much colored by the patient's personality. Many persons who already have a well-defined chronic disease experience exacerbations or complications of it in relation to severe life stress. The course and outcome of the organic process may be greatly influenced by the mental attitude of the patient. Illness, therefore, of a clearly established physical nature is often attended by important psychological concomitants that, because of their importance in both prognosis and treatment, should be recognized by the physician. A patient suffering from serious and progressive physical disorder will develop some psychological responses to it. In addition to the anxiety he suffers about outcome, there always exists sadness (evident, suppressed, or repressed) if loss of function or bodily mutilation takes place.

Among psychological defences may be repression, denial, or perhaps exaggeration of symptoms through a desire for pity and attention. At times the damage suffered by the emotional life and mental health of the patient through somatic illness or disability may be more serious and permanent than are the physical results of the organic lesion. It is therefore not only illness or disability in itself that is of psychiatric importance, but also what a particular ailment means to a particular individual. The meaning of the illness or its symptoms often assumes paramount importance to the individual.

Many fears and exaggerations of the importance of disease arise from feelings of guilt, particularly from a sense of guilt concerning early sex activities or indiscretions. A slight indisposition may be attributed to a regretted lapse and may be magnified into disabling or fatal illness and regarded as a just desert.

As Lipowski summarizes, psychological dysfunction may occur in the course of physical illness: 1, as a consequence of the distressing meaning, either conscious or unconscious, of the illness for the patient; 2, through impairment of the individual's capacity to cope with his needs and goals; 3, to mobilize defenses against the aroused inner conflicts and secure the desired gratification; 4, by aggravation of previously unresolved conflicts and emotional states; 5, through impairment of ability to meet and achieve the social and economic satisfaction necessary to maintain general self-esteem; 6, in alterations of internal and external sensory input and feedback which will influence brain function either tempo-

rarily or permanently; 7 through disturbance of the body image; and 8, by disruption of the sleep-wakefulness pattern.

ATTITUDE TOWARD ILLNESS. The patient must adapt not only to the disability, but also to the idea of the disability. Faced with physical disease, the patient may readily accept or even suggest that the disability is of mental origin. Symptoms may be neglected or the patient may deceive himself or herself about their seriousness. On the other hand, the patient whose disability is of psychic origin often seeks a physical basis for the symptoms. Instances in which the patient consciously desires cure from a physical disability but unconsciously wishes that the symptom may continue are common. Patients sincerely believe that they desire to be cured but unconsciously cling to their disability with a tenacity that may defeat the physician's therapeutic efforts.

The motives that *delay recovery* may be various—a sense of helplessness or hopelessness or both, self-punishment, self-importance, revenge, or protest. For various psychological motives, certain patients may welcome or request surgical operations. With some patients, surgery may be an attention-gaining device; with others it may be a means of punishing themselves for feelings of guilt or of escaping responsibility or irksome drudgery. If psychiatric or emotional components accompany definite physical disease, a failure to treat them also often will tend to prolong convalescence or encourage a reaction of chronic invalidism. The physician who concentrates attention on symptoms without an adequate attempt to ascertain or remove their causes may aggravate or permanently fix them.

SOCIAL ENVIRONMENT. Factors arising from the patient's social environment or from interactions between the patient and his social setting may be important in the causation of illness and require consideration in its diagnosis and treatment. It is not always easy to determine whether the symptoms are to be attributed entirely to disease or in part or even largely to personality disturbance or to environment. A study of an unselected series of patients who consulted the outpatient clinic of a large general hospital showed that in 65 per cent of these patients there were adverse social conditions related to their illnesses. In 35 per cent of these cases, there were emotional reactions that were largely responsible for their illnesses.

MEDICAL STRESSES. The physician should remember that in the workings of the general hospital itself, conditions and situations may arise constantly that tend to produce various stresses and tensions and thereby promote unhealthy mental reactions or physical complaints, perhaps with visceral disturbance. Among them may be protracted convalescence, awareness of incurable or crippling disease, fear of death, conflicting medical statements or advice, or the misinformation and misguided advice of other patients.

Every medical specialty is accompanied by procedures or situations heavily weighted with elements potentially disturbing to emotional life or personality. In ophthalmology, for example, the bandaging of both eyes during a prolonged convalescence in a darkened room may precipitate a panic reaction of a delirioid nature. In gynecology, there may be problems connected with contraceptive practices, illegitimate pregnancy, or the occurrence of cystoscopy addiction. In urology, psychiatric problems connected with impotence, frigidity, dyspareunia, or premature ejaculations are common. In surgical disorders, a fear of mutilation or disfigurement or of loss of vital structure or capacity may threaten the patient's sense of security. Today, with the increasing resort to organ transplantation or reliance upon such synthetic organ substitutes as the artificial kidney, a host of new stresses has arisen for the patient and the family and associates, as well as for those in the health professions. These stresses, too, have been cause for precipitation of anxiety and/or other affects with arousal of pathological behaviors, psychological defenses, and further organ malfunctions.

Convalescence from a serious physical illness often constitutes a psychiatric problem. The patient may be reluctant to give up the luxuries of the sick room and the unconscious secondary gains of illness. He may be resentful as the warmth of feeling and interest previously manifested by his family seem to lessen. More frequently, the family may insist on continuing to be protective and the patient on being babied, with the result that regressive personality characteristics persist. He may even create new symptoms as they are needed. The longer the patient defers his return to his responsibilities, the harder it is to come back, and the more firmly are fixed any unwholesome personality reactions that have been established. His convalescence and rehabilitation may be largely dependent on his adjustment to an existing emotional problem.

PERSONALITY PATTERNS. Frequently, the manifestations of the patient's illness are determined more by his personality characteristics than by the nature of the etiological agent producing the disease; he experiences his illness in accordance with his personality makeup and established types of reaction to stress. These patterns are brought particularly into the foreground in the case of chronic disabling illness. Some patients accept their handicap in a spirit of apathy and refuse to make any active effort to overcome their handicap. They may regress to an infantile dependent state. In some instances, the reaction may be one of depression and anxiety; again, there may be a greater feeling of optimism and well-being than may rightly be expected. Patients who feel an implication of inferiority, abnormality, or incurability associated with their disease may, through brooding and resentment, develop various compensatory defensive reactions, often of an aggressive nature.

In the well-studied psychosomatic disorders, Sifneos has defined a number of psychological characteristics that seem to occur with great frequency under the term *alexithymia*. These include a striking limitation in fantasy and dream life, with drive to describe trivial environmental details; difficulty in articulating feelings; suppression of crying; inappropriate affect; a tendency to take impulsive actions as well as be action-oriented; dependency upon others or avoidance reactions to others, thus having poor interpersonal relations; and rigid posture.

Among the psychological concomitants of chronic illness, the physician should remember the potential impairment of the mental health of other family members that may result from the presence of a member suffering from prolonged disability, particularly if the patient reacts to his disease with irritability or aggressiveness or in some other unpleasant way, or if the responsibility for his care means the frustration of deeply cherished desires on the part of some other member. At times, too, chronic invalids suffer more from disordered family relationships that have grown out of the disability than from the disease itself.

Whatever the individual's physical disability may be, a certain amount of anxiety is added to the burden imposed by the disease or injury itself. The clinical picture may therefore be directly influenced by this anxiety and the particular reactions of the patient to it.

Diagnosis

Because chronic emotional states frequently associated with physiological malfunctions are often closely related to the everyday problems of living, the physician or psychiatrist must take a careful and extended look into the whole development and experience of the patient. The crisis diagnostic approach, described in Chapter 31, is the mode of approach to be preferred initially in examining most patients with a physical illness.

Home life and its jealousies and frustrations, as well as working conditions—which frequently involve the boredom of constant repetition or a perpetual striving for security or achievement, with the attendant drives for prestige or comradeship in relation to those in authority or to other persons—are common stressful problems, yet ones that may lead to a variety of symptoms that are unrelated to detectable pathological changes in organs or cell structure. Cumulative problems of interpersonal relationships produce a large share of the tensions and anxieties that beset the human being and upset his or her physiology. Lack of emotional satisfaction in one's life may act likewise. Anxiety reactions to situational difficulties and crises seem particularly prone to be expressed in psychosomatic symptoms. The psychiatrist inquires, therefore, for personal situations that may give rise to anxiety, hostility, aggression, guilt, bottled-up resentment, smoldering discontent, and other disturbing emotions that may act as the cause or as an aggravating factor in the production of much ill health manifested at the somatic level.

Sometimes a temporal relationship can be established between the onset of the symptom and some emotionally disturbing event. Again, it may be possible to identify experiences of early life that seem highly relevant to adult attitudes and diseases. Ruesch makes the observation that the psychosomatic disorders as organ reflections of psychological tension are most common in the middle class, with its greater burden of self-required striving, conforming, and repressing. There seems, also, to be a greater tendency for emotionally introverted persons to show somatic complaints than for those who are extroverted.

Physical symptoms are the presenting ones and so dominate the clinical picture that their mental source is not superficially recognizable. The patient rarely complains of his anxiety, depression, resentment, or sexual tension, but rather of his disorder of bodily functions, such as anorexia, vomiting, backache, headache, or palpitation.

Psychosomatic medicine deals with several groups of patients: (1) In the first group are those who suffer from various physical symptoms but who do not have a bodily disease that may serve as a cause for the symptoms. As the result of the failure to recognize that such illnesses are of emotional origin, they have often been called "functional." (2) In another group of psychosomatic disorders, a physical disease exists, but the original, causative factors were of an emotional nature. The pathological condition resulting from the action of the emotional causes reaches a point where it is no longer reversible. (3) In a third group of psychosomatic disorders, the patient does have actual organic disease, but certain of his symptoms arise not from this disease but from affective factors, such as anxiety. In disorders of this type, the disability is often out of proportion to the physical disease.

For purposes of diagnostic classification the physician should list first the organ disorder, if such exists, and then the nature of the related psychological diagnostic category as well as the presumed extent it may play in the illness behavior.

Psychological Stress and Physiological Functioning

Early in the century the physiological studies of Cannon demonstrated that various changes in secretions, muscle tensions, and circulation might be produced by arousal of emotions in animals. The research of Pavlov went further; it showed that, in animals, such emotional arousal with induction or inhibition of organ functions might be learned with a symbol acting as a conditioning stimulus, substituting for the original situational ("unconditioned") stimulus that produced emotion. More recent research on conditioning factors, as emphasized by Miller, shows that not only fear responses but also learning through reward (instrumental) influences visceral responses.

The influence of emotional factors on physiological functions was well demonstrated in a patient with a gastrostomy with herniated gastric mucosa. It was found that pleasurable emotions of appetite led to some increase in secretion and vascularity of the mucosa, with increased motility of the stomach wall. Sadness, discouragement, and self-reproach led to prolonged pallor of the mucosa and hyposecretion. Anxiety produced hyperemia, hypersecretion, and hypermotility. Aggressive feelings, including resentment and hostility, led to a great increase in secretion and vascularity and to some increase in motility.

In portions of exposed colons in persons with fistulas, it has been shown that situations productive of conflict, resentment and hostility are associated with hypermotility and hypersecretion of the enzyme lysozyme and of mucus. In some patients with sustained hyperfunction during anger and resentment, the appearance of petechial hemorrhages has been noted. Dejection and fear have been associated with hypofunction of most of the large intestine.

Learning by association to respond to specific cues in the environment, such as the presence of another person who may symbolize release of tension or its arousal, takes place very early in life. The differentiation of gut responses to such social stimuli was found by Engel and Reichsmann in their studies of an infant girl with a gastric fistula. After a time her stomach responded physiologically as though it were receiving and processing food whenever her physician was present.

It is on the basis of these experiments and a variety of clinical observations that Engel has hypothesized that the precipitation of psychosomatic disorders is largely on the basis of unresolved feelings of separation or loss of a significant human relationship, associated with profound feelings of helplessness. However, psychological stress, even in the animal world, is more complexly determined than by the threat or actuality of loss of a dependency relationship. Thus an "executive monkey" placed in a training situation where he could learn to work to avoid electric shocks developed gastric ulcers; his companion monkey who was not allowed to control the shock schedule remained without a somatic lesion.

These experiments and others suggest that inflexibly continuing activation or inhibition of organ systems, in a manner that is often inappropriate to the immediate environmental situation, is the culmination of a specific genetic makeup, the patterning by the nervous system, through a long-continued experiencing of responses, which in themselves contain poorly understood and critical variables that lead to their impress. Experiences arousing emotions of high intensity, owing either to their suddenness or unexpectedness or to their variable or sometimes prolonged recurrence, all have potentials for establishing disruptive patterns of physiological functioning, as both clinical and laboratory observations now show.

Sachar emphasizes that past research in psychosomatic medicine has suffered by lack of recognition of the complexities that determine these conditions. To understand the intimate relationship between brain function and function of the internal organs, the pathophysiological mechanisms by which affective states modify somatic functioning and the illness must be clarified. Many of the so-called psychosomatic disorders, such as peptic ulcer and ulcerative colitis, are beyond the realm of direct investigation from a psychosomatic viewpoint. Currently, general medical research has failed to clarify the nature of the primary disorders. Thus, Sachar points out that the physiological processes and pathways by which affective states lead to exacerbations of rheumatoid arthritis presently are unknown nor is there any acceptance of what system is disturbed in that illness. For this reason, investigators in the field have turned toward examining psychological effects on somatic systems in which responses can be measured.

The neuroendocrine apparatus offers just such an opportunity (Fig. 24–1). For instance, we now know that the vast majority of individuals exposed to stress—hospitalization, the death of significant persons, military training, facing a diagnostic procedure in the hospital—will physiologically show little, if any, elevation in 24-hour corticosteroid excretion. Yet, there are a number of studies that show concomitant increases in 24-hour corticosteroid excretion (usually 25 to 35 per cent of baseline values) for some. There are, then, those in the general population who respond to different stresses by a shift in endocrine function. It must be mentioned that cortisol influences electrolyte imbalance, carbohydrate metabolism, and immune responses. Evidence is also accumulating that psychological stress may reduce the secretion of testosterone and increase that of growth hormones. On the other hand, children suffering from maternal deprivation have been found to lack the usual growth hormone response.

ANIMAL MODELS. Research on the effects of affective arousal upon organ systems utilizes many animal models to work out the complicated neuroendocrine and other pathways resulting in the malfunctioning of the organism. Hypertension may be studied in rats that developed spontaneous systolic hypertension as a result of selected breeding, in rats subjected to repeated immobilization, and in mice

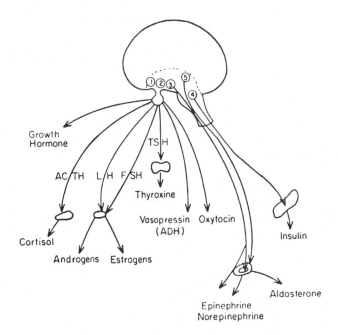

Figure 24–1 Points of anatomical contact between nervous and endocrine systems. *ACTH*, adrenocorticotropic hormone; *LH*, luteinizing hormone; *FSH*, follicle-stimulating hormone; *TSH*, thyroid-stimulating hormone. (From Mason, J. W.: The scope of psychoendocrine research. Psychosom. Med., 30:Suppl:565–575, 1968.)

subjected to psychosocial stress following early isolation. Experimentally induced hypersensitivity to disease of joints occurs in rats exposed to a single injection of Freund's adjuvant following sensitization. Bronchospasm with the clinical features of acute asthma has been induced in dogs and primates by passive transfer of human allergic serum. There seems reason to believe that lesions resembling ulcerative colitis occur in guinea pigs and rabbits following ingestion of high molecular weight sulfated polysaccharides. For many years it has been known that thyroidism occurs spontaneously in animals.

The complex interrelationship that is set up over time between the functions of component parts of the brain—the hypothalamus, limbic system, and cortex (described in Chapter 3, Brain and Behavior)—forms the neural pathways determinative of psychophysiologic expression of symptoms. The fact that emotions may influence physiological functions and dysfunctions is now well established by both clinical and experimental observation. That a patient suffering from physical disorder, especially if it is of a serious and progressive

nature, is very prone to develop some psychological response to it is equally well established.

Psychodynamics

The psychophysiological responses may be interpreted as the inappropriate perpetuations of organ reactions adaptive to, or protective against, some stress in human life experience. They are *not*, as some psychoanalysts once considered, direct symbolic expressions of neurotic conflicts in the same way as are the conversion symptoms in hysteria. Thus, no longer is heavy breathing interpreted as a disguised wish for coitus or vomiting as a rejection of oral sexual desires. The symptom expression is recognized primarily as an activation or deactivation of the organ or system on the basis of arousal of an affect. To be sure, secondarily, the act may have attached to it symbolic meanings, but the crucial clinical question is the primary affective state and the sequence of events that led to its precipitation.

As has been shown in previous chapters, stress reactions include not only those caused by assault by other organisms and physical agents, but also those consequent to man's capacity to interpret symbols as indicative of danger derived from his past experiences, including the threats resulting from necessary conformity to family and cultural mores that in themselves lead to deprivation of certain innately desired satisfactions. In response to the stress imposed by various threats and conflicts, organ reactions occur, in conjunction with various feelings and attitudes, to assist in adaptation or to prepare for emergencies to protect the individual. The perpetuation of the organ reactions beyond the period of stress leads to sustained responses that are inappropriate and may end in tissue damage.

The psychosomatic symptom represents the physiological concomitant of an emotional state. In the acute emotional state of rage, for example, it is a normal vegetative process for the blood pressure to be raised. This rise in blood pressure will subside if the angry man releases his emotional tension by physical or verbal attack on the object of his anger. If, however, a persistent, inhibited aggression (chronic rage) continues, the patient's emotional tension does not subside, his blood pressure does not become less, and he suffers from "essential" hypertension. In other words, a chronic emotional tension has activated bodily changes resulting in vascular hypertension. The physical symptoms of some cases of hypertension are therefore of psychosomatic origin. If a chronic emotional tension acting through the vegetative nervous system stimulates muscular or secretory activity of the gastrointestinal tract, then the psychosomatic symptom will be referable to that system. The physiological expressions of anxiety may then be interpreted by the patient as "stomach trouble." Through introspection, these self-diagnosed conditions may be exaggerated.

It is postulated that the psychosomatic symptoms represent physiological re-

gressions in much the same way as psychological symptoms often express recurrence of infantile behaviors as an attempt at solution of conflict. In these views, the physiological expression is due to the failure of the ordinary psychological defenses to maintain homeostasis. The symptoms are seen as analogous to the undifferentiated organ responses characteristic of the infant whose needs are frustrated.

The regression hypothesis does not provide any clues about the organ system selected for disturbance in the individual patient. Adler's early suggestion of organ inferiority as a means for determination of specific symptoms led later to other efforts. Most psychiatrists now agree that the conception of Dunbar of a personality constellation specific to each psychosomatic disorder has no sound foundation. Alexander and others stressed a *specific emotional conflict* as determining the disordered function in a specific organ. Thus, with hyperthyroidism, the specific emotional conflict thought to precipitate this organ disturbance centers on the arousal of death wishes toward one with whom the sufferer holds an exaggerated and gratifying dependency relationship. Among the objections to this hypothesis are the facts that similar conflicts may be discovered in patients who have other psychophysiological disturbances, and that many patients have symptoms referable to disordered function in several or multiple organs.

Rather than specific emotional conflicts, Engel emphasized as the initiating factor in many illnesses a generalized sense of loss (actual or fantasied) leading to attitudes of hopelessness and helplessness. As defined in earlier chapters, Holmes and Rahe, working objectively to obtain records of stressful life events preceding onset of illness, found such stress to have occurred in 80 per cent of patients in the two years preceding onset. Essentially, stressful events are perceived as producing or threatening loss of some kind.

In the phenomenon of *syndrome shift*,

one illness syndrome is sequentially replaced by another, as for example the occurrence of bronchial asthma in babies or young children as their infantile seborrheic eczema disappears. Such shifts may take place after apparently successful therapy of the initial symptom complex. They have occurred following the use of pharmacological and surgical measures, psychotherapy, and electroconvulsive treatment. Syndrome shift is a manifestation of the nervous system's ability to substitute one form of illness used adaptively for another. The phenomenon frequently involves a shift in the gross personality reaction, such as the neuroses and the psychophysiological reactions or vice versa. Such shifts may be seen as a means of maintaining a precarious homeostatic adaptation through illness, where the personality of the individual and the pre-existing stress which induced the reactive syndrome remain unchanged, while the reactive syndrome has been modified environmentally—a therapeutic intervention that has left uninfluenced the basic personality structure and the impinging and stressful threat.

Although many such shifts have been reported (agitated depressions to rheumatoid arthritis, compulsive and hysterical neurosis to duodenal ulcer, ulcerative colitis to schizoid and depressive psychosis, asthma to psychosis), the evidence for them is uncertain. It seems true, for instance, that the rate of rheumatoid arthritis is much less in hospitalized psychotic patients than in the general population. Yet O'Connor and Stern discovered only one instance of symptom alternation during treatment of over 300 patients classified as having psychosomatic disorders. In the overwhelming number of cases they reviewed, exacerbation of physical disease was associated with onset of psychotic and neurotic processes. On the basis of their findings, they warn against using the concept of symptom alternation in determining appropriate medical management.

Another view is that the organ system affected by the emotionally acting influences is determined not by psychological factors but by an inherited tendency to respond somatically to stress and conflict in a fashion consistent for each person. This view differs from the earlier ideas of inherited or acquired systemic or organic weaknesses. That some constitutional determinants exist for specific psychophysiological disturbance is supported by data that the pepsinogen and uropepsin levels in patients with peptic ulcers are significantly higher than in the population at large. Such levels are higher, commencing at an early age in some persons who are prone under particular psychosocial stress to develop symptoms and signs of ulcer.

The psychosomatic symptom alone, however, does not fully account for the patient's distress. More influential is the underlying affective state that gave rise to the symptom and threatens to break through failing defenses. In a way, therefore, the psychosomatic "functional" symptom may be considered an emergency measure to prevent the patient from being overwhelmed by anxiety. They may consciously want relief from their neurotic, defensive symptoms. The psychosomatic patient, like the neurotic, has an unconscious resistance to relinquishing measures that are partly or largely defensive. In the endeavor to stress a purely somatic origin of symptoms and to deny even the possibility of psychological causes, the patient may seem to protest too much. Conscious negation of such an origin amounts to an unconscious acknowledgment. One objective in therapy is to help the patient understand the relation of his or her symptoms to the particular personality difficulties and maladjustments that are a source of anxiety.

If the physician fails or refuses to recognize the importance of emotional factors in illness, or by a useless repetition of previously negative examinations continues to search for an organic pathological condition, the patient becomes even more convinced that his trouble is organic. The doctor's attitudes may also be important factors in perpetuating or provoking illness. By his tone of voice, words, and gestures, his own anxiety may readily be transferred to the patient. If some incidental pathological condition is found, the patient's anxiety becomes fixed on the system in which the perhaps unimportant pathological condition is found. Through emotional disorders misidentified and mistreated as organic diseases, the patient's troublesome symptoms, instead of improving, tend to become chronic.

Postoperative Reactions

The most frequent type of postoperative syndrome is delirium, with its confusion, disorientation, hallucinations, paranoid delusions, fear, apprehension, and restlessness. Similar disturbances may follow amputations of limbs and other external appendages. In these instances, the clinical picture is complicated by the patient's reaction to the "phantom phenomenon." A not uncommon postoperative mental syndrome is that which occasionally follows the removal of a cataract. The patient becomes suspicious and confused and manifests fear and panic-like excitement, particularly at night. The loss of familiar landmarks adds to the sense of insecurity. It is now thought that those psychotic reactions that occur due to the covering of the eyes after cataract removal are induced by deprivation of visual perception.

Manic states, depressions, and schizophrenic reactions determined by long-standing personality factors may be released by emotional, toxic, or other agents incident to the operation.

Surgery may be accompanied by trauma not only to the body but also to the personality. Psychological factors such as those mentioned may also act in the production of anxiety and occasionally of hysterical syndromes. In addition to these factors, ill-considered remarks by the surgeon or his assistants, technical bedside discussions, or the demonstration of charts or roentgenograms that create apprehension in the patient may produce alarm in the insecure personality. Hysterectomy or oophorectomy in the woman highly desirous of bearing children may prove so frustrating that a permanent neurosis results. Although scarcely pertinent to the present topic, it should be borne in mind that many a failure of surgery to relieve a disabling symptom occurs because an attempt has been made to remove surgically the somatic expression of an emotional illness. Postoperative anxiety and other neurotic states are, too, more frequent than postoperative psychoses. Their source is to be sought in emotional factors.

Physical agents, other than metabolic changes, causing disturbances may include the anesthetic and sedative drugs. Other factors may be toxic and infectious complications and also nutritional disturbances with associated dehydration, ketosis, or avitaminosis. Among psychological factors are fear and apprehension preceding the operation. The fear of mutilation, of loss of part of one's body, and of possible death is important. The strangeness of the setting, the sights and sounds in the operating room, and all the other preoperative procedures, including anesthesia with the fear of losing consciousness, contribute to the tension and apprehension. The importance to the patient of the particular organ operated upon affects the possibility of a postoperative psychosis and will influence the character and content of any psychotic ideas. There is usually a postoperative interval of three to ten days before the onset of the psychosis.

The long-term consequences of life-extending and cosmetic surgery are matters that involve personality factors. These are discussed in later sections of this chapter.

Prevalence

Epidemiological support is strong for a close association between physical and psychiatric disorders. There exist health surveys of random samples of general practice populations with independent assessments of physical and psychiatric status; surveys of the incidence of physical illness in psychiatric inpatients, outpatients and emergencies; examinations of the prevalence and incidence of psychiatric disorders in medical patient populations; incidence of indices of psychopathology—that is, anxiety and depression in particular medical setting populations, such as general medical wards, coronary care units, and cancer, cardiovascular, and gastrointestinal disease units; examinations of the incidence of inception of psychiatric symptoms following physical illness; and, finally, reports of the prevalence of behavioral disorders in children with chronic illness.

From the studies reviewed by Lipowski, it is evident that emotional disorders were diagnosed in 9 to 23 per cent of patients with various groups of somatic diagnoses seen in a number of general medical clinics in Monroe County, New York. This is the area where there exists today the outstanding register of psychiatric patients. Studies of large groups of medical and surgical inpatients, using either the clinical interview or completion of the Cornell Medical Index, indicate that anxiety occurs in the range of 20 to 25 per cent of such groups, while depression has been reported in the order of 20 to 64 per cent.

As we examine the studies of groups of psychiatric patients, it is clear that individuals in such groups tend to have a greater number of physical diseases of all kinds. The order of occurrence in several studies approximates 50 per cent, whether taken from a random sample of persons from group practices or from those found in outpatient departments of general hospitals. So, too, psychiatric emergencies are at high risk for medical disorders. When one examines the relationship between physical illness and psychiatric disability in children, up to 30 per cent have been found to show social and psychological maladjustment.

From these various epidemiological studies, one must conclude that a statistical association exists between physical and psychiatric disorders and symptoms, as well as between the onset of physical disability and the inception of neurotic illness.

TYPES OF PSYCHOPHYSIOLOGICAL REACTIONS

It has been pointed out that emotional conflicts produce anxiety that through prolonged action on the vegetative nervous system may seriously disrupt the autonomic regulation of the body, with resulting manifestations of symptoms referable to various visceral vegetative organs. These symptoms tend to be manifested in disturbances of certain systems, particularly the cardiovascular system, the gastrointestinal tract, the endocrine system, the respiratory tract, the skin, and the genitourinary system.

ALIMENTARY SYSTEM

It is hardly surprising that the gastrointestinal function provides the most frequent focus of psychosomatic syndromes. In life experience, one of the first contacts of the infant with another person comes in relation to the nursing process. The infant here experiences his first relief from physical discomfort and tension through the intake of milk. The satisfaction of relief from hunger through this experience becomes strongly associated with feelings of well-being in maturity. On the other hand, deprivation of food or its irregular presentation is associated with feelings of tension and rage. Compounded with the somatic disturbance and the attending emotions are the gradually developing perceptual processes in relation to contacts with the mother and mother surrogates.

Hunger, as a percept to which the individual responds, depends, too, on the learning reinforcement which comes in the transactions between child and mother. Central percepts of need or satiety in feeding as well as sensations of gastric motility seem to form the basis of this important percept. Hunger and satiety as percepts serve as a guide for the need to consume or to fast. The successful development of these percepts is a requisite for maintenance of food intake and the establishment of an internal homeostasis which regulates the healthy establishment of bodily reserves expressed in acceptable weight.

In addition to the growing awareness of the dependence on the mother with satisfactions and frustrations coming as they do through feeding, there is also the similar interpersonal conditioning that takes place through the eliminative activities of the lower end of the gastrointestinal tract. Here again the infant is brought to eliminate and retain fecal matter in terms of relating to the mother.

The satisfactions gained through the early sucking process are associated with the emotion of being loved and the development of feelings of security and satisfaction. On the other hand, the bowel training process again provides opportunity for feelings of approval through cleanliness or of stubbornness through retention and constipation. Frustration of the pleasures of feeding mobilizes aggressive activity in the form of biting, taking, greed, and envy. The process of eating is surrounded both in the family and in the culture with many opportunities for pleasure and conflict in interpersonal reactions. This is less apparent in respect to eliminative processes, which are usually solitary.

Symptoms of disturbance of the alimentary system are widespread, as they extend from those focused in the oral cavity and most frequently encountered by the dentist to the multitude of expressions of disordered function of the stomach, large and small intestines, and the related major secretory organs. The most common are anorexia, nausea, "nervous indigestion," vomiting, belching, distress from gas, pain, diarrhea, and constipation. Less common are burning sensations in the mouth, pain and clenching of the jaws, difficulty in fitting dentures, and canal tenesmus with pain. Frequently the abdominal pains and discomforts are attributed to "chronic appendicitis," and the patient is subjected to surgery. This is soon followed by a recurrence of symptoms. In other cases the gallbladder is removed. Spastic or mucous colitis with diarrhea and constipation represents another phenomenon of this disturbance of the gastrointestinal tract. In addition, obesity and anorexia nervosa may be considered psychosomatic expressions of this system.

Peptic Ulcer

Not only the clinician but also the lay person is aware that functional gastric symptoms commonly follow worry, business reverses, family quarrels, and other emotionally disturbing experiences. Similarly, for many years physicians have considered that psychogenic factors are of importance in the etiology of peptic ulcer. The evidence to support this clinical impression is impressive. It includes the early observations of the effects of emotional arousal on gastric functions as observed by William Beaumont through the fistulous opening into the stomach of Alexis St. Martin, the more precise but similar studies of Wolff and Wolf on their patient Tom, and most recently those of Engel and his colleagues upon the infant Monica.

It has been stated that ulcer in man is probably the classic example of psychosomatic disease. Many techniques have been devised for producing this gastrointestinal disease in animals; deficient nutritional states, administration of various drugs, brain stimulation, surgical procedures, and immobolization are all effective. Just as in man, it has been discovered that high plasma pepsinogen levels tend to indicate those who are susceptible to the development of ulcers. It seems then that the human or animal who develops a peptic ulcer has a biological predisposition. In man this predisposition may be aggravated by his personality organization, which determines his capacity to cope with the environment.

There is evidence that the predisposition for peptic duodenal ulcer is determined genetically. Peptic ulcers vary not only in anatomical site (gastric or duodenal) but also in duration and association with levels of secretion of pepsin, hydrochloric acid, and mucus. The specific local variables that produce ulceration remain unclear.

Anxiety and aggressive strivings increase motility, vascularity, secretion, and even the electrical activity of the stomach; sadness, depression, and discouragement equally depress these functions.

The ulcer syndrome is now among the most frequently encountered psychosomatic conditions. It is of interest that the incidence of peptic ulcer has significantly changed within the past half century in western European societies. At one time it was extremely prevalent in women, but now it occurs chiefly in men. The change in the sex ratio is unexplained. Recent pediatric studies have shown that such ulcers occur as well in children. Peptic ulcer is much more frequently seen in people subject to depressions and alcoholism; it is uncommon in the schizophrenic.

Peptic ulcer may occur under a number of circumstances. It may be seen as an acute transient reaction in the face of unusual stress. Such stresses may be the serious threats to life, or,

on the other hand, internal inhibition may lead to frustration, mounting tension, and consequent psychosomatic expression through the gastrointestinal tract. In addition, there is a group of individuals in whom dependency longings are so exaggerated that they may not be satisfied or are bound to remain ungratified because of the ordinary demands of living. These are individuals with essentially infantile personalities.

Alexander and his colleagues defined a specific emotional conflict determining the peptic ulcer psychophysiologic reaction. From psychoanalytic studies, peptic ulcer patients were found to have a persisting, strong, infantile wish to be loved and cared for, conflicting with the adult drive for independence. Thus the conflict, heightened often by adverse external circumstances, induces shameful anxiety. The drive to be cared for is equated with that to be fed and hence associated with gastric hyperactivity. This basic striving is held to be common to all peptic ulcer patients, no matter what the personality characteristics are — that is, whether they are overtly aggressive, ambitious, and driving or dependent, irresponsible, and inactive. In the former case the overt behavior is considered a reaction to the infantile wish. Weiner and associates are of the opinion that the Alexander hypothesis is strong for adult men with peptic duodenal ulcers.

Others, however, have suggested that any persisting conflict-inducing anxiety will lead to gastric hyperactivity and thereby ulceration. Studies of women with peptic ulcer have shown that the onset is often related to surgical procedures or other events that have threatened their sexual functioning in reality or in fantasy. Since threat to the sexual functioning may also simultaneously be seen as a threat to the dependency relationship of the patient, the production of ulcer symptoms may well be related to the conflict situation described above.

From the therapeutic point of view, the psychiatrist may seldom function successfully for these patients. It may be recommended that the repressed dependency needs of the patient be gratified directly or indirectly without inducing shame, guilt, or resistance. This can be done by environmental manipulation, including vacation, enlisting the support of key figures in the patient's environment, or strengthening the patient-physician contact through regularity and frequency of visits. In those individuals with an infantile personality, facing the conflict during psychiatric treatment may well lead to serious depression and a more disturbing personality reaction than that accompanying the primary ulcer symptomatology.

Irritable Bowel Syndrome

In this disease we meet with a group of symptoms into which anxiety-producing problems are frequently translated. Among these symptoms are constipation and the discharge of mucus-containing stools, hence the old term "mucous colitis." Shreds of membrane are discharged in masses or mixed with soft or liquid fecal matter. The patient complains of indigestion. Appetite is poor and capricious, and the patient resorts to an increasing restriction of diet in an attempt to find one that will not cause discomfort. Distention of the stomach, belching, flatulence, heaviness or pain after eating, nausea, and other gastric symptoms are common. Many patients are asthenic and show diminished output of energy. In many cases this physiological disturbance appears to be in response to anxiety, guilt, sensitivity, overconscientiousness, and resentment. It is common for the symptoms to be attributed to various alleged causes varying from chronic prostatitis to gallbladder disease. Too frequently the patient is advised to have colon irrigations or an operation. It has been stated that the irritable bowel syndrome is responsible for the removal of more undiseased appendices than any other cause.

The evidence, however, is that those with irritable bowel syndrome suffer from psychiatric disabilities and that these are frequently missed by the primary physician. In the recent study by Young et al., 72 per cent had such illnesses, with hysteria and depression as the most prevalent syndromes. Esler and Goulston found that the individuals with these symptoms who had predominant diarrhea were significantly more anxious and more neurotic than control populations, on the basis of examination by various psychological tests.

Ulcerative Colitis

A relationship between periods of emotional stress and the onset of exacerbation of symptoms has been recognized in those with ulcerative colitis. Quite frequently the attacks commence three or four weeks after a sudden, unforeseen threat to the patient's security, commonly in the form of bereavement through death, separation, rejection, disillusionment, loss of a part of the body, or changes in psychological status, such as graduation or failures at school or at work and other causes of diminished self-esteem. Although those patients who have been studied psychiatrically often appear to be highly intelligent, their emotional lives suggest impaired capacity for appropriate affective experiences. They attempt to maintain close relations to their mothers or other maternal surrogates through attitudes of deference and compliance. Thus they seem keenly perceptive and sensitive to the emotional responsiveness of others. They respond to loss of the dependency relationship with depression and rage, accompanied by disorganization of bowel function. Many patients whose primary affective need was the protective care of a maternal figure were disturbed through their early conditioning in relationship to dominating, hostile, or rejecting mothers, so that they expected humiliating rejection. Again, in the family setting physical symptoms often had signified preferential care. With emerging hostility or rage toward the wanted person, such patients frequently responded with guilty fear of retaliation. It has been noticed that both men and women with ulcerative colitis, when referred for psychiatric treatment, have shown considerable evidence of disturbance of psychosexual development.

Treatment of the patient with ulcerative colitis must generally be carried out by the physician or internist. The psychiatrist's·contribution initially is that of assisting in or advising the establishment of a solid dependency relationship that will again provide the patient with a feeling of mastery over himself and his environment. Dramatic interruption of attacks of colitis has been obtained by some psychiatrists through assuming a simple supportive and protective role for the patient and demanding little.

There is evidence from carefully controlled follow-up studies that those patients who receive intensive dynamic psychotherapy over time more effectively manage their symptoms and improve their social, sexual, and emotional functioning, compared with patients who receive little psychotherapy. Such treatment leads to improvement in physiological functioning of the bowel but does not modify significantly the lesions in the colon as visualized through the proctoscope. In this series of patients, a high proportion were schizophrenic, and the severity of the illness and ultimate prognosis for those with this personality disorder were much less hopeful than for those with other types of personality organization.

Obesity

Obesity has been understood largely from the standpoint of an increased drive to eat. Physiological and psycho-logical studies have been directed toward the unraveling of the source of this pathological drive. It now appears, from the physiological demonstration of two hypothalamic areas subserving separately the act of feeding and the accomplishment of satiation, that overeating must be recognized as much more complex than a simple increase in a drive to fill a need. In the laboratory, diminution in the capacity for satiation through specific brain lesions causes hyperphagia without increase in hunger. Those hypothalamic brain lesions which cause hyperphagia are believed now to result from alteration of both noradrenergic and serotoninergic pathways.

But other regulatory processes than those concerned with determination of hunger and its satiation determine lipogenesis (formation of fat). It has been shown that the storage of lipid increases when food is forced through intermittent heavy feedings, in contrast to unregulated and free patterns of ingestion. Much more attention has been directed to the processes that favor excessive eating, and too little to those that bear upon the patterning of eating habits. In all individuals, there is a tendency to obesity with aging in spite of unchanged food intake and exercise.

As our knowledge of the physiological processes underlying feeding behavior and satiation has enlarged, so also has knowledge of the parental influences on personality growth that affect the development of eating behavior. It is necessary that the growing infant and child stabilize within his personality an awareness of hunger as well as of satiety if his impulses for eating are to be controlled. There is some evidence that certain animal species (rats, monkeys) become obese if overfed as infants, although this has not been confirmed in other species (baboons).

Bruch and Voss contend that at birth a discriminating awareness of hunger does not exist. The discrimination comes about through the reciprocal transactional feedback patterns established in the relationship with the mothering person responsive to the infant's and child's demands. The same inference may be adduced for satiety. For the majority of patients, the satiety factors are probably the major determinants in the obesity syndrome. Without their recognition and consideration, the treatment of the overweight patient often fails and on some occasions leads to serious disruptions of personality functioning.

What constitutes obesity or overweight is not well defined. The changes and fluctuations in weight measured over a period of time provide a better index of weight disturbance than the percentage of weight excess computed from the standard height-weight tables. Stability in weight is recognized when the individual maintains a relatively constant poundage without concern over dieting. Some individuals maintain weight curves close to the average, but only through a life perspective fixed on maintenance of weight dieting, a measure that for them is abnormal. The study of the extended temporal weight curve provides important clues for the treatment of the obese person who is seeking help.

Among the obese, three groups may be defined: (1) those whose weight is stable or who have arrived at a stationary stage of obesity; (2) those who show dramatic fluctuations in weight; and (3) the hyperobese, with weights exceeding 136 kg. (300 pounds) and up.

With evidence of many fluctuations up and down, with or without medical supervision, it may be inferred that additional attempts at weight reduction will be unsuccessful, since the previous failures and successes have not been comprehended in their fullest meaning. Here a study of the weight changes in relation to the total personality functioning, which includes an estimate of the patient's sense of well-being and adequacy, becomes as important as the weight changes. Weight stability is a reliable guide for estimating whether the obese person is adapting well to his life experience, particularly during childhood and adolescence. A stable degree of overweight in these periods becomes disturbing only when the growing person is involved in a ceaseless weight-reduction struggle because of family and cultural pressures, enhanced in Western society in these times by our insistence that slimness is a desirable bodily trait.

The relationship between obesity and social class has been found striking in a study of New York City women. Obesity is six times as common among those in the lower social classes. The same correlation between obesity and social status is true during girlhood. Furthermore, obesity is less likely to be found in families upwardly mobile in socioeconomic status and less frequent the longer a family has lived in the United States. In some families and cultures, obesity is accepted and even encouraged. Psychiatric and psychoanalytic studies of the obese have been made for the most part on middle class individuals who were aware of some personality problems in connection with their somatic disturbance. If preventive measures are to be taken, the evidence of the patterning of overeating in children and adolescents suggests that education should be directed at the young.

In recent years the statistical evidence that overweight contributes significantly to increased death rates resulting from circulatory disturbance has been strongly challenged by new information and analysis. Yet the health emphasis on weight reduction continues. It is accepted in many medical circles that a weight 20 per cent above the standard for a particular age and sex constitutes pathological overweight. The concept, although useful in the clinic in detecting individuals at the extremes of the weight curves and providing clues pertaining to pathological disturbances and their changes, fails to take into account the genetic and constitutional differences in individuals. It is perhaps wiser to think of a "preferred weight" for the individual, as Bruch does.

The development of obesity often occurs in a family setting in which the parents compensate for their own life frustrations and disappointments through their attachment to the child. In most instances the mother is the dominant family member and holds the obese child by anxious overprotection, including pushing food. The mother frequently has high expectations for the child's achievement, to compensate for the failures of the parents. Often the mother's attitudes reflect her own early sufferings and hardships, coupled with resentments toward her family's and her own childhood experiences. Toward herself she appears self-pitying, yet intent on saving her children from similar experiences.

The child is not cared for as an individual with particular problems that require emotional support. As the aims of the parents are predominant, the child fails to develop personal independence or self-esteem. In many instances the obese child is not a wanted child, but one who has passively accepted the indulged role without rebellion because of his or her own demanding attitude, which cannot be fulfilled outside the home. On the surface, the obese individual, as a child and later as an adult, is most frequently seen as submissive and unaggressive. Yet this is not really the case. The child's demands in the family setting are balanced by the substitution of food for love and satisfaction.

The overweight adult often is unable to notice the existence of hunger contractions or to estimate as well as others the amount of his food consumption. Bruch has suggested that through the family feeding processes a distorted perception of the growing child's bodily sensations occurs, preventing him from properly identifying and appropriately responding to hunger and satiation.

This takes place by the parent telling the child how the child feels and forcing food as a means of alleviating the parent's anxiety, unrelated to the bodily demands of the child. This perceptive distortion is considered crucial by Bruch for understanding developmental obesity. Research by Bruch, Stunkard, and their colleagues has demonstrated that such a perceptual distortion exists in the obese, who fail to perceive changes in gastric motility associated with food limitation or intake as do others. Also contributing to the condition is the greatly limited physical activity of the obese person.

When exposed to social frustrations with their consequent arousal of hostility, the overweight person seeks satisfaction in overeating and by this means symbolically obtains an expression of his aggression, as if the food represents evidence that he is the best loved. Often the overeating is done at night in association with insomnia and is then accompanied by morning anorexia. There is some indication that the uptake of glucose by the tissues in the obese is accelerated in periods of anxiety. If this is the case, satiation might well not occur physiologically.

In time, the obese body image also comes to have high emotional significance, as it often represents the desire to be strong and powerful and actually, in life, provides satisfactions. The child is conspicuous and may receive attention through this source, even though denied it by other, socially more acceptable means. Loss of weight becomes difficult not only because of inability to face the physical discomfort of hunger, but also because of the symbolic loss of love and revenge that eating provided, and later because of fear of loss of the power symbolically represented by the obese frame.

During a 15-week period of hospital weight reduction produced by limiting the diet to 600 calories daily, quantitative observations by Glucksman and his colleagues on the behavioral changes of severely obese nonpsychotic persons revealed affective, perceptual, sexual, and feeding changes. Anxious and depressive symptoms occurred during and following weight loss, with the appearance of hostile aggressive actions only while undergoing caloric deprivation. Perceptual alterations in the period of weight loss were shown in concern over change in bodily size and "permeability of ego boundaries." Figure drawings then showed expanded waist diameters and total body areas. Subjectively, the patients reported feelings of obesity following weight loss. Also in this period there occurred augmentation of sexual psychopathology, dreams and fantasies of food and eating, as well as acting out in diet-breaking, and increase in interpersonal transactions.

With the concept of specialness and power that the obese child develops from the maternal association and later attaches to his size, the psychological life becomes filled with grandiose daydreams, particularly in those persons who daily suffer defeat in their major aspirations. These fantasies are usually conscious and not deeply repressed as in many with psychoneuroses. The fantasies differ from those of the psychotic because the obese person has awareness of their unreasonableness. Obesity at a later stage then becomes, in itself, the rationalization for failure. In some, the overweight is used as a means of escaping the anxieties requisite for the pursuit of a creative social existence. The overweight person's attitude toward himself is further complicated by his felt rejection by family and friends because of his obesity, particularly since he has a deep need to be accepted as he is.

Sexual maturation is complicated for both the overweight boy and girl. In many fat men, there is marked lack of interest in women and failure to establish heterosexual relations. Yet homosexuality seems rare. The clear concept of the man as a masculine personality is often lacking. Overweight women are usually outgoing with men and succeed in establishing marriage relationships.

The term "reactive obesity" has been used by Bruch to separate out those problems of overweight that occur suddenly after a psychologically traumatic incident in persons who have not previously been obviously stout. Yet indications from the study of such persons show they have previously reacted to stress with overeating, and the family patterns and personality development are very similar to those with "developmental obesity." Most frequently, the incident leading to reactive overeating has been either the death, or anxiety associated with the possible loss, of a close and significant person. Among those who may be considered as reactively obese are individuals who have for periods been deprived by starvation. Obesity has been frequently observed in those who have spent long periods in prison camps, deprived of love, happiness, and recognition and who have substituted eating for satisfaction.

The satisfactions of overeating appear protective in some with incipient psychoses. Such a person may develop a full-blown psychotic state when undertaking to lose weight by dieting. This is particularly so in the schizophrenic, while in the depressive individual we most frequently encounter anorexia with weight loss. A number of patients overeat and become overweight, sometimes with reversal of depressive mood to manic behavior.

The psychology of the obese person, as discussed, explains the usual failure of medical therapies to effect continuing change in the overweight state. Since simple loss of weight in those with developmental obesity threatens their psychological defenses, symbolized by the satisfactions of eating and the personal concept of strength in size, the failure to obtain gratifications either through fantasy or through becoming slender results in relapse. Before yielding to the wish of the overweight patient or of his or her parents for treatment, it is necessary to determine whether the desired change is likely to threaten the physical and psychological balance of the individual. The threat to physical health in terms of later cardiovascular disease appears to be overemphasized, and the physician and psychiatrist should take into account possible serious psychological and emotional disturbances that may result from efforts at weight reduction.

TREATMENT. Successful treatment of the obese person requires a knowledge of the total personality, also a recognition that the goal of treatment must be directed beyond the mere reduction of weight. With young people, these aims are not likely to be achieved unless the parent in the parent-child symbiosis that led to the overeating is also willing to participate in the treatment, even in some instances to the point of undertaking simultaneous psychotherapy. When psychotherapy is utilized, it is unwise to attempt weight reduction initially and then discontinue therapy at the point the patient has attained an ideal weight. The timing of the dieting, in association with psychotherapy, needs careful consideration. The nature of the diet and its palatability are important.

Anorexigenic pharmaceuticals, which suppress appetite by their action upon the neurotransmitter mechanisms, are of value for this purpose only. Mazindol (Sanorex), a phenylethylamine, is the latest agent of this type marketed in the U.S.A. Some compulsive overeaters who have abnormal electroencephalograms appear to respond well to treatment with the anticonvulsant phenytoin.

There is a growing appreciation that exercise, coupled with diet, is important in reducing weight and maintaining a slender figure. Since inactivity, like overeating, is often an essential facet of the personality of many obese individuals, a simple medical authoritarian approach is unlikely to increase the patient's exercise. In individuals in whom eating provides the major satisfaction in life and other gratifications are not available, psychotherapy is often not successful.

Many of the obese who will accept the social rewards and punishments of group therapeutic approaches, as in the programs of such organizations as "Weight Watchers" and "TOPS," do very well in effecting and maintaining weight reduction. In their experience with short-term follow-up, Levitz and Stunkard report that patient self-help given through such groups, combined with behavior modification techniques, results in greater weight loss and less patient attrition than either technique alone.

For some of the hyperobese unresponsive to all the previous therapeutic measures, surgical bypassing of the small bowel by use of jejuno-transverse colostomy has given good results in weight reduction, although fatty hepatitis has been reported as an occasional complication. Successful weight reduction in the hyperobese through this surgical procedure has been followed by increased self-esteem, diminished depression, and improvement in interpersonal relations and vocational and other activities. Some have recognized their essential character weaknesses and requested and worked in psychotherapy following the operation.

Anorexia Nervosa

A somewhat uncommon psychophysiologic gastrointestinal reaction is known as *anorexia nervosa*. The disorder was first described in 1868 by Sir William Gull and given the name anorexia nervosa in 1874. In a classic paper, he called attention to its neurotic peculiarities. The reaction occurs largely in young, single women. Most patients are intellectually superior and in personality characteristics are introverted, stubborn, selfish, perfectionistic, and overly sensitive, and manifest compulsive and self-punitive behavior.

PSYCHODYNAMICS. While disgust

for food or lack of appetite has been described as the cardinal symptom, the essential symptom appears to be a compulsive drive for *thinness,* often coupled with an antipathy to being fat. Bruch has suggested from her studies of a sizable patient group that the majority are relentlessly driven to maintain thinness and, while they often exhibit bizarre eating habits, the primary concern is not phobic avoidance of food per se. Many in this group indulge in episodic gorging, coupled with later guilt and sometimes induction of vomiting. In a second but smaller group, the primary drive is phobic avoidance of food and eating per se, and the act of taking in has symbolic representation in terms of disgust or various sexual meanings.

In addition to the loss of appetite, there is an extreme emaciation with a remarkable preservation of bodily vigor that, as Gull pointed out, cannot be reconciled with inanition caused by constitutional disease. Other symptoms are amenorrhea, constipation, low metabolic rate, dehydraton, dryness of skin, falling of hair, and restless activity. Roentgenographical gastrointestinal studies are negative, and no evidence of pituitary disease is demonstrable by roentgen ray examination.

TYPES. Dally has suggested that patients diagnosed as suffering from anorexia nervosa may be separated into three differing groups, when one examines their symptoms as regards hunger, appetite, attitudes to eating, food, treatment, the presence of overeating, vomiting, their activity, concern over physical health, sex and amenorrhea, prevalent mood, and compulsion to mirror gazing.

In the primary form hunger persists, as does appetite. The patient consciously fears eating because of possible weight gain and consciously restricts this activity. She may insist on eating alone. Paradoxically she often has an intense preoccupation with cooking, and reads or may collect cookbooks. Her attitude toward treatment is usually devious or negative, and she will employ subterfuges to avoid eating, although sometimes "surrendering." Overeating may alternate with periods of refusal to eat. Vomiting, sometimes voluntarily produced, often occurs after the excessive indulgence. In spite of the restriction of food, she is noted for her excessive activity and energy but often complains of exhaustion as a consequence. Fearful of sex, she is not concerned greatly about her amenorrhea nor about her health in general. Depression with shame are the prominent moods. Mirror gazing is common. The general character structure is obsessive.

To Dally, the second group tends toward a hysterical makeup. Here hunger and appetite are denied from the beginning. There is a phobic attitude to eating because of intestinal discomfort. Eating experiences are social, but there is no interest in cooking. This group does not overeat and vomits only occasionally. Overactivity is less obvious. Sex is abhorrent or avoided, and concern over amenorrhea is denied. Affective changes are denied, and there is little concern over body image as shown through mirror image gazing. These patients often remain amenorrheic after gaining weight.

The third group is composed of those with anxiety and conversion reactions, including the schizophrenic. Aside from those with anxiety, the prognosis is poor even if weight gain occurs. This group differs in that energy seems lacking and overactivity does not occur. The affect is depressive.

Anorexics also have been typed according to their method of weight loss. One group purges and induces vomiting and may develop serious metabolic disorders. In this group, which some wish to designate as a "bulimic" subgroup, patients frequently have been obese earlier, have a family history of obesity, and display many impulsive self-destructive behaviors, including suicide attempts, self-mutilation, and alcoholism. Another group achieves the desired end solely by dieting.

COURSE. Onset of anorexia nervosa is generally noted between 10 and 15 years of age at a risk of 5 to 75 per 100,000. The mortality rate is high (5 to 15 per cent). A variable morbidity rate of from 34 to 65 per cent is reported as concerns psychopathology and sexual functioning.

Anorexia nervosa does occur in males, although rarely. A study of anorexic boys by Taipale and his colleagues led them to conclude that psychodynamically the future anorexic boy adapts well to the developmental days of infancy and childhood. However, such boys perceive themselves as rejected by their fathers because of apparent weakness while favored by their mothers owing to certain feminine features. With the approach of adolescence, the boys become anxious as neither parent is able to support their aspirations toward growth and manhood. Fasting represents a regressive return to maternal care needed under these circumstances.

The patient, a married woman, was referred for consultation to determine whether lobotomy should be performed to relieve her serious condition of anorexia nervosa. Thirty-seven years old, she stated that she became nervous and excitable following her first pregnancy ten years ago. Her symptoms worsened during her second pregnancy five years later. Prior to her last pregnancy she began to lose weight. Following the termination of that pregnancy, she commenced to take laxatives. She could not recall whether she vomited or induced vomiting, but that vomiting occurred there was no doubt. She advised that she weighed only 65 pounds, a weight she was afraid to tell her husband.

The patient declared that her husband was very angry about the third pregnancy and stated that he was in no position to support more children. It was her impression that she resented the child at birth.

Before the last pregnancy, she commenced to see a psychiatrist regularly, one hour per week. He gave her tranquilizers, and she was entered in group therapy. She considered herself very amusing to others in the group; yet the experience did not help her condition. Following the pregnancy she became so weak that she was unable to stand. Multiple sclerosis was suspected. She

then entered a psychiatric hospital for a period of six weeks, where it was discovered that she had a potassium deficiency. In her treatment there she gained 5 pounds. The treatment consisted of psychotherapy two or three times a week, multivitamins, and necessary ions. One year later she was admitted to a general hospital, where 14 electroshock treatments were given but without improvement.

The patient stated that both her parents were living. Her mother, some 5 feet tall, had always been heavy, and now weighed approximately 150 lb. Her father was a big eater and a hard worker, and her mother was a "fantastic cook." The mother always bragged that she had enormous meals for her children and told her friends that when they were in school she arranged that they eat well by having the dinner at noontime. She urged her son and daughter to eat. Her famous expression at meals was: "Finish it." The children's threat toward their mother in defiance was to say, "I won't eat."

The patient declared that she was always overweight, but that this was fluctuant. At age 19 her poundage was 135. Her early development seemed to be normal. She was a good student and entered a university. Her marriage took place 12 years before the consultation. There was some loss of weight following the birth of her first child when she commenced to take laxatives during pregnancy to prevent gaining weight. There were two sons, aged 11 and 5, and a daughter, aged 2. The marriage had never been sexually satisfactory. She stated that she had never enjoyed sex and that she and her husband had not had intercourse since her last pregnancy.

Discussion of her eating habits disclosed that she would eat if her mother cooked for her, but at such times she forced all the food at one big sitting. Then, after taking a cathartic, she spent the rest of the day in the bathroom attempting to get rid of the food. In recent months she had advised her mother to discontinue giving her "goodies." Since then she did not remain up at night forcing food into herself or taking laxatives. She declared that mother always disliked her being overweight, and that her mother was domineering and aggressive. She hated her mother's way of managing money and spoke of it as "Jewish."

The patient declared that she was the one in the family who loved to go to restaurants and have fine food. Also, she collected cookbooks. She liked the taste, the smell, and the difference in consistency of food most of the time, but sometimes rejected all. An account of the eating schedule in her home indicated that she prepared a regular dinner for her husband and children but that all other meals were irregular. She no longer prepared breakfast for her children. When she had no taste for food, she ate eggs or Chinese food, as they went down easily. One time, food seemed to get stuck as she swallowed it.

Also, she had great concern over constipation.

Her mother always said that she could not leave the home until her bowels had moved. Her mother forced prune juice upon her, and gave her enemas and suppositories.

At times she attempted to discontinue the taking of cathartics. After stopping a day or two she would eat an enormous amount of food. If she had no laxative, she nibbled and got very hungry.

Her husband stated that she was a failure as a housekeeper and a mother. She did not perform her housework, did not take care of the baby, and gave no time to other members of the family.

A niece had entered a psychiatric hospital over a year previously and was treated successfully for anorexia nervosa.

Further hospital treatment was suggested by the consultant, but the patient died within 60 days. Her husband indicated that she had discontinued eating at home.

There is often a preceding history of obesity and over-eating, with a feeling of shame at being fat. Usually there are unhappy home relations, often taking the form of hostility between mother and daughter. The pursuit of thinness is used sometimes as an act of hostile and defiant compliance by the patient against the mother who has insisted on dieting to avoid obesity. Thus the illness often comes on suddenly in adolescence.

Psychodynamically it has been suggested that the syndrome arises from impairment of psychosexual development, arising from the early mother-daughter relationship. The adolescent girl, faced with the feminine individualization of adolescence and threatened by the loss of her family dependency, responds to the conflict by an aggressive regression to an infantile-maternal relationship with craving for the feeding experience denied in her bulimia.

The ambivalent relationship between the patient and the mother sometimes is strikingly demonstrated in the hospital where the mother refuses to part from her child. The latter in turn may reject all food or accept some only to be found inducing vomiting shortly thereafter. With removal of the parent, the patient commences to eat once again. There may also be sibling rivalry and jealousy. In a striking number of cases there is a history of frustration in heterosexual adjustment. In some cases, a pregnancy fantasy seems to have prompted the patient to begin to diet.

Halmi and Loney have discovered a correlation between anorexic patients and a high frequency of alcoholism in both their mothers and their fathers. They suggest that their findings are underestimates and recommend that efforts be made to document the existence of parental alcoholism during examination. The matter becomes particularly important when family therapy is undertaken.

Probably, however, the neurosis has many varied conscious and unconscious psychological roots. Some psychiatrists point out that the patient seems to achieve both primary and secondary neurotic gains through the reaction. They suggest that, through working out her hostilities and by provoking the environment to acts of punishment that alleviate a sense of guilt, a primary or internal gain is obtained. The illness brings, too, a secondary, but unconscious, gain in the form of desired attention, affection, and sympathy from the family. In some instances it seems to lead to diversion of family notice from a supposedly more popular sibling.

Care must be taken not to confuse anorexia nervosa with Simmonds' disease, which results from insufficiency of the anterior lobe of the pituitary, or Sheehan's acute pituitary necrosis, which occurs secondary to pregnancy and parturition.

Endocrinologists have been interested in anorexia for years due to the usual appearance of secondary amenorrhea as a feature of the disease. They have discovered a decreased excretion of gonadotropins. Neither thyroid nor adrenal functions are found to be abnormal. The presence of primary pituitary disease has never been established by pathological examination; while the possibility of hypothalamic disorder is entertained, the evidence is doubtful.

This evidence has been thoroughly reviewed by Robert S. Mecklenburg and his colleagues, who indicate that anorexic patients show the stigmata of hypothalamic dysfunction, but cannot be clearly proved to have it. Food deprivation may damage the hypothalamus and psychic stress may interfere with its function, or psychosomatic manifestations of anorexia may be relatively independent expressions of a primary hypothalamic disorder of unknown etiology. The arguments for the latter derive from the fact that hypothalamic effects in the sleep-wake pattern, water balance, thermal regulations, carbohydrate metabolism and gonadotropin secretion may be produced experimentally in animals following lesions in this area of the brain. It is also seen in patients with syndromes approximating anorexia nervosa.

TREATMENT. Treatment will depend upon the condition of the patient when first seen. If she is seriously starved, with evidence of vitamin deficiency and electrolyte imbalance, infusions and spoon and tube feeding may be necessary to preserve life. Hyperalimentation may be used. In this condition, efforts other than the establishment of a supportive, encouraging therapeutic relationship are unwise. The patient should be brought by suggestion to initiate intake of portions of food perceived by her as less than her capacity, slowly increasing these portions over days. When much transactional conflict is evident, she should be protected from intrusion of family members. In a few hospitalized patients, some have found that behavior therapy in the form of operant reinforcement, wherein the reward for eating was the privilege of physical activity, produced rapid weight gain.

In recent years, a number of anorexics regarded as having an affective disorder have gained weight when treated with amitriptyline or cyproheptadine.

Direct involvement of the family in the behavioral regimen, particularly after hospital discharge, has been found to promote the necessary family restructuring that must be gained to prevent relapse. The patient must be recognized as unique and in need of a long-term psychotherapeutic relationship, and fostered in all efforts toward personality growth and autonomy.

Later on, in those with psychoneurotic personality makeup, insight therapy may be undertaken. In many, over long periods of time, the outlook for social adaptation and even freedom from symptoms is good. Some with schizophrenic makeup may die or become permanently incapacitated.

Oral and Dental Conditions

Since the mouth is involved in the complex relationship between the dependent infant and the mother from the earliest period of life, and since the satisfactions and frustrations of both ingestion and denial of food are centered there, it is not surprising that it is the focus of many emotionally determined symptoms. The mouth and its teeth have significance through both use and symbolic representation as an orifice concerned with aggressive and sexual behaviors.

It is the dental practitioner who is confronted most frequently with complaints or actions symptomatic of emotional disturbance fixated in the mouth. Sometimes these expressions are in terms of either compulsive sucking or chewing movement or avoidance of these actions. Lack of chewing, in turn, may contribute secondarily to the development of such conditions as *malocclusion* or *periodontitis*. Some people avoid dental care or neglect needed assistance because they fear pain or loss of control and possible sexual attack under anesthesia, while others deny the presence of a defect by totally or repeatedly rejecting a prosthesis that is indicated for the correction of some dental abnormality.

Some patients have abnormal habits

of chewing, of which the condition called *bruxism* is the best known. This is the persistent grinding of teeth in adults even during sleep, associated with pain and trismus of the jaw. Its persistence may lead to damage of oral structures. Pain from abnormal habits of sucking and chewing may develop in the temporomandibular joints, as well. Dental and oral procedures occasionally are the precipitating external event for the development of the syndrome of atypical facial pain. Then there are the subjective symptoms of burning pain referred to the tongue and oral mucosa designated as *glossodynia* and discovered often in those with hysterical or obsessive personalities. *Xerostomia,* excessive dryness of the mouth, often is a source of neurotic complaint. This condition is to be differentiated from the dryness of the mouth secondary to administration of phenothiazine and antidepressant drugs.

The majority of patients with glossodynia seen in one dental clinic are chronically anxious and complaining. Cancerphobia is a major problem in many. Of the women, many have empty lives and are sexually dissatisfied, rigid, tight-mouthed, and often openly hostile.

Bruxism has been found in overly dependent individuals expressing much hostility. It seems to occur as a ticlike preoccupation in obsessive individuals as well; it is detected often in those with rigidly controlled facial expression owing to a tight-set mouth. Such conditions may relate to the habitual finger sucking of children. Olkinuora divides bruxists into those who are consciously able to relate symptom to strain and those who are not. Strain bruxists tend to have a greater tendency to other psychosomatic disturbances, while non-strain bruxists are discriminated by a greater familial predisposition to the symptom, accompanied by less defensive behavior and less verbal aggressiveness. Both groups tend to feel isolated, are easily insulted

by others, suffer from headache and muscular pain and yet are meticulous and striving and usually successful in academic achievement.

The psychiatrist called in to consult should recommend treatment based on analysis of the personality structure and situational factors confronting the patient. Antidepressant drug therapy has been used with success in certain patients when the symptoms have been expressive of a related involutional psychosis.

Colostomy

This surgical procedure, producing a mutilation of the abdomen, an unsightly open orifice, difficulty in control of fecal discharge, and sometimes sexual malfunction, is often productive of postoperative emotional reactions. Some depression is almost universal, even though the surgical removal of a carcinoma or relief from the symptoms of ulcerative colitis ensues. Many colostomy patients are shamed to the point of arranging personal isolation through their doubts of controlling fecal discharge or flatus. Men may suffer failure of ejaculation or impotence or both owing to damage to the sympathetic or presacral nerves during surgery.

Careful preparation by the surgeon and the nursing staff, for both patient and spouse, is helpful in alleviating the personality reactions attending this surgical procedure. Colostomy clubs, too, have done much to assist in adaptation. In serious personality reactions, psychiatric treatment is indicated.

CARDIOVASCULAR SYSTEM

For various reasons, perhaps largely because the heart is generally regarded as the most important bodily organ and because the idea of sudden death is often associated with it, anxiety may focus on the heart in conditions of prolonged tension. It has been demonstrated that stress-inducing anxiety tends to increase the heart rate, cardiac output, and blood pressure, as well as to cause changes in heart rhythm and the electrocardiogram. Dejection and despair are associated with diminution in the cardiac rate and output and lowering of the blood pressure. With anxiety and resentment, exercise tolerance is impaired. Such functional derangements may become the neurotic focus, particularly if associated with injudicious comment or procedure by the examining physician, or a suggestive but not significant symptom.

Without Structural Disease

The clinical picture known as *neurocirculatory asthenia*, or effort syndrome, characterized by breathlessness, easy fatigability, palpitation or heart consciousness, trembling, fainting, giddiness, headache, and fear of effort, is not of organic but of psychosomatic origin. The term "effort syndrome" is a misnomer, since the symptoms of the syndrome are not confined to effort. The term "effort intolerance" has been suggested as more appropriate. To a varying degree, the symptoms of anxiety coexist and assume the form of bad dreams, apprehensiveness, sweating, depression, trembling, and a tense restlessness. The symptoms described in many instances represent the physiological expression of the hyperventilation syndrome that is precipitated by situations that arouse acute anxiety or fear in the individual. This condition, although not always the physiological source of the "effort syndrome," is readily recognizable and is described later in this chapter under the heading of Respiratory System. It is to be differentiated from mitral valve prolapse.

The question of whether there is a predisposing potential to express symptoms of emotional arousal through the cardiorespiratory systems remains un-answered. In a group of cardiac "labiles" and "stabiles," the former exhibit much sinus arrhythmia and generally are sensitive to environmental cues. They are, therefore, more easily aroused. The cardiac stabiles exhibit little sinus arrhythmia and tend to ignore the environmental stimuli.

Sudden *cardiac arrhythmias* may be precipitated by strong emotional arousal, particularly in those with labile, intense, and histrionic personalities.

With Structural Disease

It is assumed generally from clinical data that stress-inducing emotional change contributes to the development of *coronary artery disease, angina pectoris,* and *myocardial infarction* and their expression in various forms of heart failure. These conditions are determined by multiple factors, including genetic and constitutional, which are reflected in biochemical predispositions (lipid metabolism), the latter probably modifiable through external stress. It should be recognized, however, that good validating support from carefully controlled studies is scant. Rosenman and Friedman describe a group of middle-aged men with behavior patterns of great drive, ambition, drive for recognition, competitiveness, a sense of urgency of time, with multiple activities that demand meeting "deadlines," and committed to executive positions. These men had a higher level of blood lipids than normal, as well as predisposition to coronary heart diseases (Type A). In these respects, they differed significantly from another group of men of similar age who were not under similarly urgent competitive stresses (Type B). These characteristics apparently are acquired through developmental processes and are not inherited; thus they are modifiable to some extent.

The Liljefors and Rahe study of coronary heart disease in identical twins demonstrated that those more severely ill devoted more time to work, were less able to use leisure time, and had a greater number of conflictive home interactions. These authors suggest that the most significant variable was the manner in which the individual perceives his work and other aspects of his life. Those who experience satisfaction and enjoyment from their work and their home life, in spite of work and conflict, may not be as vulnerable to coronary heart disease.

Fear and anxiety are common to all patients with angina pectoris and coronary heart and are complicated as well by pain in those with acute coronary occlusion. Fear and pain may subside with recovery from acute attacks of occlusion. In those with personality defects, adaptation to the illness is difficult and various neurotic defenses are mobilized. Sometimes excessive dependency needs or needs to control the environment may prolong an invalidism for secondary gain. As in the case of other disabling illnesses, the patient may use his invalidism to escape from some emotionally troublesome situation and may be reluctant to relinquish this defense as he improves physically. Again, the threat of his illness may be so intolerable to the patient that it may lead to an irrational and rebellious denial of its existence.

Cumulative evidence seems to support the contention that emotional stress precipitates attacks of congestive heart failure. Also, proper psychiatric attention to the anxiety-producing situations incurred by those admitted to coronary care units or returned home from such units seems to reduce mortality among those so attended and facilitates maximal adaptation on discharge.

With arousal of stress, it is postulated that the release of adrenergic catecholamine and glucocorticoids enhances the myocardial need for oxygen. In the normal heart the need is met by augmenting the coronary blood flow, but with coronary artery sclerosis or myocardial insufficiency the augmentation fails to occur, thus leading to myocardial hypoxia, depletion of cardiac magnesium and potassium, and increase in sodium, owing to the contributing action of the adrenal glucocorticoids. Cardiac hypoxia is again aggravated, establishing the vicious circle precipitating the congestive failure.

Cardiac Surgery

With the increase in the use of surgical procedures for correction of both congenital and valvular defects in the heart, numerous early and late postoperative failures in personality functioning have been reported.

In their extensive studies of the postcardiotomy reactions in patients, Kornfeld and his colleagues report that 25 per cent developed a postcardiotomy delirium following a lucid interval of about 48 hours. Six per cent displayed a typical brain syndrome promptly after awakening from anesthesia, characterized by anxiety, disorientation, transient disturbances of perception with illusions, visual and auditory hallucinations, and paranoid delusions, sometimes accompanied by episodic attacks of hyperventilation or auras. This reaction often confuses the evaluation of the postoperative state and impedes surgical recovery. Some patients so affected have attempted suicide, while others in their agitation attempt to pull out or upset tubes or other measures of medical support needed for their postoperative management.

This acute postoperative disturbance appears related to the duration of the operation and of cardiac bypass. The combination of the induced cerebral insufficiency, of environmental factors in the recovery room which prevent sleep and lead to a deprivational state, and of the intense anxiety associated with the threat imposed by operation on the organ, impairs ego functions.

Postcardiotomy delirium has declined in recent years, so that now up to two thirds of the patients operated on no longer so suffer. This has come about through correction of the contributing factors, such as prolonged time on the cardiopulmonary bypass pump, changes in the frightening and disturbing aspects of the recovery room, and reassurance through preoperative interviews with psychiatrists. The incidence of such postoperative delirium may be reduced by half when a psychotherapeutic team is available to the patient immediately or soon after recovery.

Beyond the recovery period from cardiac surgery, evidence of psychological maladaptation often appears when increased physical activity is possible, with less need for support from others. Those patients who have become dependent through long invalidism or who have utilized the illness to avoid anxiety-provoking situations are most prone to respond to the surgical procedure in this manner.

Overdetermined reactions of anxiety often are found to be related to pathological identification with a relative or important love object who has suffered presumed similar symptoms or illness. Distorted perceptions of the illness derived from childhood experiences or parental admonitions, or suppressed and repressed acts and thoughts related to prohibited rage or sexuality and conceived as shameful or sinful and therefore causative, often will be discovered to be readily accessible and to contribute directly to the emotional disturbance. Frequently, their verbal discharge rapidly allays the pathological affect.

In the instances of chronic invalidism and persistent inability to readapt even though cardiac functioning is restored, more often long-standing patterns of passivity and dependency are discoverable, which require continuing support and authoritative encouragement to effect improved social and physical functions.

Treatment

When cardiac function is greatly disturbed by a serious somatic lesion, a load of anxiety added from the psychic side may be sufficient to throw the balance in the direction of decompensation. If a patient is found to have frequent breaks in compensation when there is but relatively slight damage of heart muscle, a search should be made for complicating psychic factors, the elimination of which may determine the course of the illness. Frequently, the patient is deeply threatened by his symptoms and by the implications, often irrational, conveyed by the diagnosis. The physician should utilize his knowledge of psychopathology in dealing with the lowering of personality defenses that may occur in the face of fear of possible impending death. A strong, dependable, and constructive doctor-patient relationship should help the patient in handling both intrinsic and extrinsic tensions and the emotionally disturbing life situations that frequently exist.

In heart disease, particularly in coronary thrombosis, the physician should seek to dissipate the patient's fear of the disorder as an incapacitating or fatal ailment. Unwarranted fear is too often fostered by the gloomy predictions of the physician.

Treatment of coronary disease in Type A individuals is often very difficult. They wish to preserve their assumed independency, which is dependent upon the compulsive drivenness of their daily activities. The physician should suggest that the patient modify his or her intensive drives, ambitions, and time urgency, as well as assist in the expression of hostile feelings. Through the patient-physician relationship, the patient may learn to recognize his essential worth, substitute excellence of values for material acquisition, and develop avocational interests in which competition is nonexistent or dissipated. The executive might be helped by a Type B secretary to screen phone calls and appointments. If at all possible, his relations with others should focus on Type B individuals.

Since many with myocardial disease are depressed and anxious, treatment with the tricyclic antidepressants often is prescribed. Certain of these drugs prolong intracardiac conduction and have been thought to induce arrhythmias, particularly among the elderly. In every instance they produce some degree of orthostatic hypertension. More recent studies show that when given within the ordinary therapeutic range, imipramine suppresses atrial and ventricular premature contractions, acting like quinidine.

Hypertension

Vascular hypertension is not a specific disease; it is, rather, a systemic reaction induced by a variety of causes. Much more is known of essential hypertension now than in the past. It is thought that different physiological mechanisms may operate in differing individuals early in the disease. In early labile hypertension, β-adrenergic substances increase cardiac output while in other hypertensions there exists a variety of changes in the renin-angiotensin system that regulates aldosterone secretion. These various regulatory disturbances are known now to vary in different stages of the disease. Animal studies support clinical observation that social stress may lead to vasoconstriction and hypertension.

Predisposition to hypertension exists among such groups as the American black. Socioecological stress studies such as those of Harburg and his colleagues support the contention that those living under conditions of great stress are more prone to high blood pressure than those living under lesser stress.

The cases of primary interest to the psychiatrist are those in which a major factor is emotional tension operating through the vegetative nervous system to cause vasoconstriction. Some are of the opinion that the unrealized inner tension that often accompanies hypertension is to be attributed to the mobilization of excessive rage in the face of a threat to the dependent relationship of the hypertensive patient. This emotion is seen as partly repressed and suppressed and inadequately discharged through verbal or motor activities. The personality of many hypertensive patients is one of outward serenity and affability, but it covers conflicting attitudes of readiness for aggressive hostility with needs to conform in order to maintain often strong dependent attachments, particularly to those in positions of authority. Often the predisposed are overly sensitive to perceived criticism or contempt by others, or excessively concerned with threats of violence or danger. However, hostility is not peculiar to hypertension. Many hypertensives are neurotic, with strong perfectionistic and compulsive tendencies. It must not, of course, be assumed that psychodynamic factors are the only ones that contribute to essential hypertension.

Some patients with early hypertension suffer also from gastrointestinal symptoms, head discomforts, and fatigue. Such symptoms cannot usually be accounted for on the basis of the hypertension itself but are presumably a result of the same emotional factors that contributed to, but did not cause, the hypertension. With the patient's discovery of the hypertension, the "blood pressure phobia" may dominate the clinical picture. Investigation of the life situation and psychotherapy often will make the patient a more contented and effective person. Trials of biofeedback as a method of reducing hypertension as yet have limited success.

Increasingly effective control of

essential hypertension and its consequences in cardiac and cerebrovascular complications and deaths has occurred as the result of intensive efforts in the U.S.A. to educate the public about early detection and treatment by modern medical means. Education to modify illness-producing behavior as well as the use of various relaxation techniques has been helpful. The latter are apparently more effective than biofeedback.

ENDOCRINE SYSTEM

Diabetes Mellitus

Among the more striking examples of the influence of emotional disturbances on somatic functioning is that seen in some sufferers of diabetes mellitus. Personality factors and the consequent emotional responses to the treatment regimen of this condition affect almost all the issues pertaining to the therapy of diabetes. The psychiatrist may make a major contribution in the treatment and management of those difficult patients with "brittle diabetes." Psychosomatic investigations in recent years have elucidated the disturbances in glucose metabolism and variations in ketonemia resulting from changes in the emotional state of the individual. Such diabetics, untreated, are frequently the subject of attacks of diabetic coma or hypoglycemia and are at high risk of developing brain damage as well as other complications of the disease.

While it is known from twin and other genetic studies that a strong genetic predisposition exists in the development of diabetes, it has been suggested that the onset is often related to periods of severe emotional distress. Although study of the personality structure of the diabetic has failed to demonstrate a uniform personality picture, many psychiatrists have emphasized the passivity and immaturity. As with other psychosomatic disorders, loss or threat of loss of significant personal relations, with arousal of rage, anger, and feelings of hopelessness, lead to actions or inactions that impede the maintenance of the prescribed health behaviors.

On the physiological side, it has been shown that urinary and blood glucose levels are elevated following periods of emotional stress and that the glucose tolerance curves may be modified at such times. In general, the glucose tolerance test has been found to indicate a higher degree of diabetes when the individual is feeling more hostile and depressed, and it approaches the healthy curve when the patient feels accepted and cared for. It has been shown that an increase in ketone bodies in the blood stream may occur in similar situations; also, that with increasing diuresis, the diabetic may lose sugar, ketones, and chlorides, with depletion of fixed base and a rapid fall of glycogen in the blood stream. Such physiological changes, associated with the metabolic defect, lead to acidosis and may precipitate coma, particularly when the anxious or depressed patient neglects his diabetic regimen, as frequently happens.

Since the customary regulation of diabetes requires both control of the diet and the administration of insulin, management is often complicated because the symbolic significance of the feeding process and its relationship to providing emotional support through love may modify the therapeutic indications. It is particularly true that the giving and depriving of food become paramount in those homes where tension exists between parents and a diabetic child. The illness magnifies the difficulty between the child and the parents. Those parents with perfectionistic, aggressive attitudes may bring their children to good control of the diabetes but create a behavior difficulty. On the other hand, parents who pity themselves or blame the child and reject it may foster poor control of the diabetes.

The need to limit food often becomes a battleground between the child and parents and the child and physician. This is particularly so since the giving of candy or of food is often a token of approval in the family. The child has an excellent weapon that he can use against rigid punitive parents by refusing to eat when he is denied his wishes. Other children, finding themselves starved for food or affection, express their hostility through eating as they wish and then lying convincingly. Thus the rigid dietary management insisted upon by the physician and the family leads to serious emotional disturbance in the child, with concomitant change or modification of the glucose metabolism and probable ketosis, or to psychological conflicts that deter the proper acceptance of therapy. In such instances, the psychiatrist is needed to work through the emotional conflict of the child with the parents, to assist the parents to understand the child's problem, and occasionally to advise the internist of the personality reactions of the child and the need to modify the dietary regimen and insulin requirements.

Because this 16-year-old lad had been hospitalized nine times in a general hospital for diabetic acidosis or coma during the preceding six months, he was referred for psychiatric consultation. There was a history of diabetes commencing three years previously, when his mother noticed he had lost weight and suffered abnormal thirst and frequency of urination.

Previous to the onset of the diabetes the boy had been able to engage in all activities with friends of his age. He withdrew from his contacts with other children following the commencement of his treatment owing to their teasing of him as "diabetic kid" and "sugar blood kid." His physicians advised him that if he did not take care of his diabetes by diet restriction and proper use of insulin, he might lose a limb or his sight or be subjected to overwhelming infections if he were injured. His diabetic treatment proceeded well during the first year under the care of a firm, insistent, older physician. However, difficulties arose when this physician retired and the patient transferred to another, more permissive doctor In view of the inability to control him under general medical care and as the result of the psychiatric consultation, it was decided to hospitalize him in a psychiatric nursing unit.

On admission, the patient advised that his problem was simple. He stated he was a compulsive eater and that all he had to do was learn how not to eat. When his mother was consulted, she appeared anxious and expressed feelings of depression and hopelessness in regard to the pa-

tient. She described her deep feelings of guilt toward him but explained she was unable to cope with his rebelliousness. Her three other children were obedient. She stated that he seemed to awaken at all hours of the night and had taken to stealing food, frequently failed to give himself insulin injections, and strongly resisted the mother's attempts to administer them. He refused absolutely to perform the urinalysis, and he falsified reports to the clinic physician. He told his mother that he would rather have cancer and die than continue with the diabetes. He was openly aggressive toward her, and when angry he threatened to refuse to take insulin the next day. His relationship with his father was similar to that with the mother.

The mother admitted that she constantly argued with the patient to persist with his diet and to take insulin as prescribed. At the same time, she forbade mention of the diabetes at other periods. The father saw the patient's diabetes as a severe blow, as he had long hoped that the patient would be able to assume the financial support of the family. The father described his discontent in the marriage and accused the mother of forcing him into marriage. The patient was born as an illegitimate child. However, approximately 2 years later, the parents married following the mother's second pregnancy. The father spoke of his resentment toward his very active son because of his noisy play and admitted frequent beatings of the boy.

The developmental history revealed that the patient was a feeding problem from birth onward. He cried frequently at night and was awake for most of the day. Following an early circumcision, he developed projectile vomiting. Throughout his childhood he was a poor eater and required small feedings eight to ten times daily. His mother held and fed him until he was three years of age. With the birth of his sibling, there was evident rivalry and hostility. Since the father worked at night, this boy had slept in the mother's bedroom until the onset of the diabetes.

It was formulated that this young patient had suffered early affective deprivation that established an exaggerated need for a dependent emotional relationship. Also, the early feeding pattern had formed a demanding need for satisfactions that were not being met through the restricted and rigid diabetic dieting. In addition, it was considered that the boy was fearful of expressions of hostility due to the threatening relationship with the father and the threats provided him by the physicians in charge of his case. In reaction to his exaggerated dependency needs, he had developed an air of defiance. It was accordingly arranged that on admission to the hospital he would be allowed a permissive diet, with the privilege of controlling his own utilization of insulin, and that treatment should be conducted by a relatively firm male physician.

The patient was seen twice weekly in psychotherapy over a period of one year. Initially he was grandiose, defiant, and a braggart, both in relation to other patients on the ward and during treatment hours. Much anger was expressed toward his father, and he suffered mood swings. Some 10 weeks after admission, he burst into tears while describing an incident in childhood when his father had locked him in a room. At this point he verbalized the reasons for his hostile feelings toward his mother and also became defiant toward the nurses on the wards. Many fears were then expressed about mutilation and death, which were traced to the father's early threats of bodily harm.

Following a home visit, when he had an argument with the father, he developed a stuporous condition simulating a diabetic coma on return to the hospital. This was recognized as a hysterical dissociation; it was treated conservatively and later studied in psychotherapy. In the course of a succeeding therapeutic hour, he acted out his rage toward the father in relation to the therapist. When no harm resulted, there were no further recurrences of the dissociated activity, diabetic coma, or acidosis. He was discharged home to his family, continuing on the permissive diet and personal control of insulin.

Control of diabetes with improved relationships and understanding between the patient, parents, and siblings was evident in follow-up visits extending two years after his discharge from psychiatric hospitalization. The diagnosis was character neurosis with diabetes mellitus, juvenile type.

Adult diabetics who repeatedly go into acidosis are usually individuals who are seriously disturbed. Such individuals either give up all dietary control or cease taking insulin, to express their depressive and suicidal drives. Although this is the case in the majority of instances, other persons are precipitated into states of acidosis by serious transient emotional disturbances. Sexual difficulties are common in both men and women with diabetes. Diabetic women are concerned over child bearing, while diabetic men are frequently impotent. Childbirth itself may activate regressive cravings for care and affection in diabetics of either sex. The new child may be seen as a rival for the affection of the husband or wife. Thus the dependent cravings of the patient may be magnified, with resulting feelings of anxiety and depression that disturb the metabolic balance or lead to despair and diminished motivation for control of diet. Obese diabetics who are addicted to sweets or to over-eating are likely to over-eat when anxious in spite of threats of physicians concerning their future health if they fail to adhere to the diabetic regimen. Here, again, the need for psychiatric aid becomes important.

Hyperthyroidism

The most important of the endocrine glands as related to psychosomatic medicine is the *thyroid.* Although as early as 1803 reference was made to the occurrence of sudden fright preceding hyperthyroidism, not until relatively recently has the possibility that emotional troubles may play an important part in the cause and course of the disease received adequate attention in the treatment of thyrotoxic states. This recent knowledge is detailed in Chapter 16 of this book.

GENITOURINARY SYSTEM

Nonspecific urethritis, frequent in young men, in some instances probably represents a psychosomatic response to continuing sexual fantasies, perhaps associated with excessive secretion from the urethral glands. It may be complicated by a secondary nongonococcal infectious process.

Chronic prostatitis apparently may be in some instances induced by psychosomatic factors. Among a group of men whose symptoms of prostatitis persisted or became worse over a number of months during treatment with prostatic massage, Mendlewicz and colleagues found that over two thirds gave histories of family maladjustment, 80 per cent were unmarried, and the remainder were divorced or separated. These men complained of a diffuse, ill-defined discomfort in the urinary-genital region. A third had a family history of urological disease, usually in the father, suggesting the use of pathological identification as the determining symptom selection. As a group they were anxious and expressed strong feelings of guilt or self-reproach. Sexual intercourse was associated with anxiety and diminished self-esteem. Prostatic massage was experienced with much satisfaction. Mendlewicz and colleagues warn that prolongation of massage tends to increase the dependency and becloud the working through of the basic personality factors underlying the symptom expression.

In a few young women the history and recurrent attacks of *interstitial cystitis* were considered by Cohen to be similar to a migraine-like syndrome. He reported that ergotamine prophylaxis and psychotherapy led to remission of such symptoms.

Hemodialysis and Kidney Transplantation

Psychiatrists in general hospitals are now called upon to assist in decision-making in regard to the patients with renal failure most likely to successfully adapt to the stresses of prolonged treatment by the technique of renal dialysis, to treat those who developed neurotic reactions during therapy, and to assist in and aid the family, the donor, and others involved in that network when renal transplantation is planned.

Regarding renal dialysis, Viederman is of the opinion that for successful treatment by this method the candidate must have the capacity to adaptively regress to a state of dependence without conflict. Such regression allows acceptance of the machine, the varying personalities of the treating staff, an open willingness to follow dietary instructions, and acceptance of pain. To him the usual criteria for judging health and psychopathology do not serve as reliable indices of the individual's capacity to adapt to this treatment procedure.

Many patients selected for hemodialysis have demonstrated self-destructive drives, with an expression of suicidal behavior computed at a rate 400 times that of the general population. The suicidal behavior has been expressed through withdrawal from the programs, failures to follow the prescribed regimen of treatment, direct suicidal efforts, and numerous extraneous accidents.

With the great demand for renal dialysis and the limited supply of technical equipment, there has been increasing interest in defining those who will most benefit. Gloster and his colleagues discovered that those who survived over two years on renal dialysis had strong religious feelings (Roman Catholic), were bolstered by the continued presence of one or both parents, and demonstrated a mean low blood urea nitrogen level. They were capable of overcoming a sense of guilt in accepting treatment which deprived others, through the use of the psychological defense of denial; they demonstrated indifference to the plight of the deprived.

It is of interest that all patients on dialysis showed evidence of a mild dialysis-modified uremic encephalopathy. The evidence for this was indicated in diffuse slowing of electroencephalograms and interruption of sleep patterns. Symptomatically, the encephalopathy was demonstrated in behavioral changes such as irritability, fluctuating mood, poor concentration, and mental fatigability with associated physical symptoms of insomnia, anorexia, nausea, weakness, and impotence.

There are few dialysis patients indeed who sooner or later do not suffer some evidence of psychopathology. Each patient suffers constantly from the anxieties attending the enduring perception of eventual mortality, also from the pain that may not be escaped owing to continuing physical illness. Although the dialysis improves the subjective sense of well-being, it by no means restores the sense of health.

Just as the dialysis procedure affects

the individual patient, his experience and the change in his behavior usually bring about changes in the family homeostasis which may or may not be conducive to the maintenance of his precarious existence. Here, too, the psychiatrist is often the member of the hemodialysis team who must intercede to assist in maintaining the necessary family stability.

In kidney transplantation, there may be an initial need for the psychiatrist to investigate the unconscious fantasies of the donors—their expiatory, reparative, or rescue dreams—and their motivations as related to the recipient. Depending upon the attitudes and fantasies of the recipient toward the imagined donor, such psychological processes as hostility may be activated toward the transplanted organ, which the recipient may feel will reject him. Viederman reports this in a black man who distrusted whites and made remarks such as "The kidney will reject me." It was later learned that he thought the kidney was from a white man. Whether rejection of a transplant may in any way be related to a specific unconscious conflict selected psychosomatically is unknown and has not been researched.

On the other hand, there may be benevolent feelings relating to an introjection from early life or a tendency to identify with the imagined donor. The potential for identification has both positive and negative aspects. An individual with an insecure sexual identity may react negatively if subjected to a kidney transplant from the opposite sex. The transplant of a kidney from a man she admires to a woman with strong wishes for masculinity and competitive strivings against men may increase her adaptation generally.

Menstrual Disorders

With the regular fluctuation in hormonal control that maintains the menstrual cycle throughout the child-bearing period, there occurs parallel shifting in emotional state. At the onset of the cycle and coincident with the gradually rising production of estrogen, there occurs an active drive to heterosexual contact with the biological aims of copulation. This phase is commonly one of emotional well-being and may be recognized in the behavior, conscious activities, and desires of healthy women. If the drives of the phase remain ungratified, tension with irritability and restlessness betray the frustration. On the other hand, in the inhibited or immature woman the activated heterosexual drive of this period may be defended against by hostility toward men. With ovulation, there occurs readiness for conception, and the behavioral tendencies just commented upon reach their height.

Relief of tension takes place after ovulation, when both estrogen and progesterone are secreted simultaneously. There occurs a shift from the heterosexual to a receptive-retentive phase at this time which, in neurotic young women, may bring out infantile wishes to be cared for as a child. This may be expressed through increasing need for attention or dissatisfactions due to lack of care.

Coincident with the fall in hormonal production in the premenstrual period, there generally follows an increase in sexual behavior in the healthy. In the neurotic, this period more often is associated with a depressive mood, with inclination to bodily complaints, preoccupations, and emotional regression with less control. At the onset of menstruation, and associated with the sudden decrease in hormonal production, tension and excitability again decrease. Overdetermined responses to this recurring cycle of psychophysiologic preparation for sexuality and conception constitute the basis for many of the menstrual disorders.

Woman's traditional maternal and homemaking role is now being seen as but one possibility for a fulfilled personality. Many neurotic symptoms of menstrual disorders are no doubt connected with the conflict experienced by some women between their inner needs for accomplishment and self-fulfillment and the outward conformity demanded by society.

PREMENSTRUAL TENSION. The symptoms of the premenopausal syndrome consist of one or several of the following: irritability, depression, tension, headaches, energy loss, and sensations of swelling. It seems to occur in several forms. In one it is first noticed with menarche and persists throughout the menstrual period; in the second, it commences initially several years after the menarche. In the former, sexuality and menstruation have been presented to the developing girl in a derogatory way by her mother. The feminine role is derogated by her, sexual activity is presented as immoral or disgusting, and the menses are spoken of as illness. The menarche is experienced by girls identifying with these mothers as a messy, unwanted event that they complain about as sickness and for which they often demand excessive care. Such young women live in a hostile, dependent relationship with their mothers, who themselves are living in marital discord. With the delayed form of premenstrual tension, there is more likely to be found guilt over sexual temptations or transgressions in recent life experiences. However, there is a greater initial acceptance and pride in the female experience of menarche. Oral contraceptives have been observed to reduce premenstrual irritability and tension in most women; edema and headaches have not been much improved. There have been some recent efforts to modify the edema with lithium therapy. Symptomatic relief is now obtainable in some women with the prescription of non-steroidal anti-inflammatory agents.

DYSMENORRHEA. Severe dysmenorrhea and the less recognized condition of *pelvic pain*, which may be related to vascular congestion, seem to occur also in women ambivalent concerning their sexual and feminine role in life. This may be owing to early anxieties, doubts, and lack of healthy identification with successful role models in the home as a wife and mother, or in obtaining gratification as a single individual.

AMENORRHEA. Although amenorrhea may be the consequence of delayed sexual maturation owing to hypogonadism, it may also occur as a defense against sexuality. It is seen as well in depressions in women and, similar to the impotence of depressed men, disappears when recovery takes place. It is a common symptom of anorexia nervosa. Menses cease also with *pseudocyesis* when, influenced both by the wish for and fear of pregnancy, certain immature women present themselves for examination with many of the signs of the condition, including distended abdomen, changes in the breasts, and increase in weight. The majority of women with pseudocyesis are dependent hysterical personalities who seek to preserve a marriage in which they perceive themselves as unwanted unless they bear children. On some occasions, sexual relations have not occurred.

Amenorrhea then must be recognized as a multidetermined symptom. It seems evident that the hypothalamic regulatory system which influences the activity of pituitary, ovarian, and adrenal glands through the autonomic nervous system and direct hormonal action is itself subject to influence by the cerebral cortex, wherein are laid down the perceptions of childbearing and sexuality.

MENOPAUSE. Menopausal symptoms again represent a complex of physiological and psychological responses to which the mature woman usually adapts more effectively than those who have neurotic or psychotic personalities or in those whose sexual and maternal functions have been frustrated. With the diminution of hormonal secretions, neurovascular control becomes labile, and there result episodic periods of perspiration, flushings, tension, or moodiness. Associated may be increasing anxiety and agitation, with exaggerations of all personality defenses. The prescription of synthetic hormones will alleviate the physiologically determined symptoms but not those aroused as the consequence of growing awareness of fading opportunities to fulfill the primary biological functions of womanhood or those secondary to loss of parental responsibility, when grown children are separated from the home and deprive the mother of satisfaction in their immediate care.

Reactions to Abortion, Sterilization, and Contraception

Those medical and surgical procedures that prevent reproductive function in women and men are bound to produce psychological conflict and emotional disturbance in some. Since the ideal concept of healthy human growth includes, in the attainment of adult status, sexual maturity, with capacity to conceive and bear children, measures that prevent the realization of these aspirations are likely to arouse feelings of sadness, shame, inadequacy, envy, and hostility toward the more fortunate, including those who are seen as responsible for the frustration. Furthermore, anxiety and depression are mobilized, with their attendant defenses. Such emotional responses may be expected and do occur more frequently in those who have not attained the satisfaction of marriage and the bearing and rearing of children. Women are more frequently disturbed than men following surgical operations on the genitalia, since marriage and the maternal function have traditionally played a significantly greater role in the realization of a satisfying self-concept than the attainment of fatherhood.

The physician and psychiatrist today are ever more frequently called upon to make judgments pertaining to therapeutic abortions, sterilization procedures in both men and women, hysterectomies, and the use of contraceptives.

Along with the now ready availability of controlling conception by a multitude of techniques and concern over the need to control population, there are under way worldwide changes in human values regarding sexual activity and freedom and the traditional roles of men and women.

Medical and surgical skills have decreased the need of therapeutic abortion for such illnesses as heart disease, tuberculosis and diabetes. Although there is little difference in the recognized indications for therapeutic abortion on the grounds of physical disease, the range of indications on social-psychological grounds varies tremendously from country to country throughout the world. In some states and countries, therapeutic abortion may be recommended legally only when the life of the mother is threatened by the pregnancy's coming to term. In other states and countries, therapeutic abortion may be recommended for economic, social, and psychological reasons.

In these countries, there has been brought to light much information from the careful studies of the emotional responses of women who have been recommended for and denied abortions that they requested. In one early series, over a third of the women who were not sterilized at the time of abortion became pregnant again. A number do so consciously, and soon after the abortion. As many as a fifth of the women allowed therapeutic abortions later expressed regret for accepting the procedure, although in a tenth these personal reproaches were of short duration.

When one considers the advisability of allowing therapeutic abortions literally to all women, a group of women who will react with continuing psychopathology must not be overlooked. The majority in this group will be found to have had pre-existing personality disorders and unsatisfactory family relations during childhood and adolescence, to be unmarried, and to have undergone previous abortions. However, clinical experience has shown too that if the request for abortion is denied to this same group of women they are again most prone to unfavorable personality disturbance. The most recent evidence indicates that in women without prior major psychiatric disability, the risk of unfavorable personality reaction is no greater than among women studied in the general population.

Solution of the clinical problem confronting the psychiatrist called upon to determine whether abortion or any sterilizing procedure should be performed demands not only a full knowledge of the life experiences, expectancies, and personality weaknesses of the patient, but also awareness of the legal status of therapeutic abortion and sterilization in the community. From the study of many psychiatrically ill patients, the conclusion is inescapable that these women who do not wish to bring a particular conception to birth seldom make a satisfactory mother for that child. The experienced clinician, however, will not uncritically accept the initial verbal declaration of patients that they do not want to bear; in some instances these declarations are made to gain or regain love and attention or may be demands complying with the request or insistence of a consort who does not wish to bear his responsibility for the child.

Experience shows that pregnancy and birth do not influence adversely the course of schizophrenia, manic-depressive illness, or the majority of the psychoneuroses, but they may be precipitating factors for a period of serious ego decompensation. It is also true that women who have a postpartum psychotic reaction often go through later pregnancies without ego disorganization.

Suicidal threats are used frequently to force recommendation for abortions. Here again, experience has shown that execution of the threat is uncommon when the mother is allowed to go to term. If suicidal attempts have been made previously, if a psychotic disorder is known to exist, or if previous postpartum personality disorders have occurred, there exist grounds for psychiatric considerations for therapeutic abortion. The eventual psychiatric recommendation must rest not only upon the personality of the patient and the past sexual and maternal satisfactions, but on her needs for future stability. Allowing the birth of a child even in the face of a physical illness is indicated for the preservation of mental health for certain women. In such instances, however, all arrangements must be made to assure the needed medical and psychiatric care through term and beyond parturition.

Sterilization procedures for men, such as *vasectomy*, often are requested by those with pre-existing defects in personality functioning. In one early series of men followed after vasectomy, over 10 per cent were hospitalized for psychiatric illness within a year, and almost 25 per cent had been or were in the process of divorcing their wives. Multiple marriages were common in both members of the marital couple that decided on vasectomy. The operative procedure was followed usually by feelings of inadequacy, shame, or guilt. In only a few marriages did a better sexual relationship follow surgery. Too frequently the vasectomized male wished a reconstruction. Thus it is clear that the psychiatrist will undertake careful assessment of the personality and motivation of those men who either seek his or her advice or are brought to consultation before vasectomy. The following case report illustrates a psychodepressive reaction to a vasectomy.

The patient, an artist in his middle 40s who had been in treatment with a psychoanalyst, was hospitalized following an outburst of rage directed toward his wife. He struck his wife savagely a number of times. In describing this incident, he declared, "I wanted to kill her. All of a sudden I hated her guts." From there on, he used these precise words in describing his ambivalent relationship to his mother. He had been drinking heavily for some months and admitted that when he did so he became enraged and attacked his wife verbally and physically. He experienced depression, inhibition in completing paintings, and a sense of "growing impotence" in many areas of his life. He described particularly one canvas depicting a scene of a marina to which he had been compulsively attached but was unable to complete. He felt impelled to paint an erect phallus in the usual position of an outboard motor, as well as an intervaginal diaphragm in the sky. His feelings toward the painting were those of hatred. The inhibition went further: in the past he had been able to paint beautiful girls with pleasure, but now was unable to do so. His libido was much decreased and he was consciously aware that he used every possible excuse, including drinking, to avoid the act of intercourse with his wife.

The patient stated that he was "brought down" following the vasectomy agreed upon by him and his wife eight months before. About this same time, his mother underwent surgery for cancer and his father was hospitalized for senile dementia. Describing his impression of the vasectomy, he declared vehemently, "I really thought I was deballed!" In tears, he stated he had "invented guilt" and then recounted the drowning of a son several years ago which led him and his wife to decide to have another child.

Coincident with the onset of the symptoms, he suffered nightmares in which he awakened apparently suffocating (hyperventilating), with a perception of being in a narrow tunnel with only a small air hole.

Both his parents were unusually successful; the father was a professional man given to violent outbursts of rage; the mother came from an old and highly respected family and was active socially. He admired and idolized his father, who had a successful career and had been a combat pilot in World War II. On the other hand, his mother tended to continually complain and derogated his father for coming from a family with a lower social position than hers.

The patient was one of fraternal twins. His twin brother was always sickly and took much of his mother's attention. There was also an older brother. The brothers fought with their mother, who threw things and screamed, and treated them in a dictatorial manner or neglected them in favor of her civic activities. As time went on, she became increasingly alcoholic. Developmentally, the patient adapted well with his peers and was a better than average student, finishing college after an absence of two years to follow his artistic bent.

His sexual experiences started at the age of 13 with anal intercourse with his twin. His father at this time displayed an "aberration" in beating his sons violently over the buttocks. The patient was particularly humiliated when the father punished him in this way upon finding him urinating in the shower. He described his father as a prude on one hand, and promiscuous on the other, as he once discovered him in bed with a strange woman.

During his first marriage, his mother interfered frequently and constantly criticized his wife. After the breakup of that marriage and his divorce, he lived promiscuously for several years until remarriage five years previously. Once again, the mother behaved in the same manner toward his wife—a woman he had known before his first marriage and whom he desired even then to marry. He described his anxiety and passivity in not approaching her initially.

As a means of providing separation from the anxieties of direct family contact and to alleviate the intense feelings of anxiety, hatred, and guilt, hospital care was maintained for several months, with treatment by psychotherapy and anxiolytic drugs. The patient's symptoms progressively improved. He was discharged home to continue out-patient treatment, apparently with better insight into the ambivalent relationship toward his parents and the projection of this ambivalence toward the castrating mother onto his wife. The vasectomy acted as a precipitant of the depressive reaction in this individual suffering a basic sense of insecurity in terms of his masculine image, his vocational status, and sexual potency.

Although the use of *contraceptive devices* is increasingly accepted, sexual conflicts are complicated by this very fact for many. In assessing the sexual complaints of individual patients, the wishes and attitudes of each partner toward the use of contraceptives should be explored. In some instances, the type of contraceptive device may impair sexual gratification, as for example, in the limitation of frictional stimulation experienced by some men with the use of condoms or in the feeling of disgust or lack of spontaneity induced by the use of a diaphragm in certain women. Again, family or religious training may contradict the use of such devices, and yet fear of pregnancy may lead to their trial with resultant guilty anxiety. No less difficult are those interpersonal conflicts in which the responsibility for the use of the contraceptive is foisted upon an unwilling partner as a means of expressing hostility or neurotic dependent demands and as a means of intimidating the partner by denying sexual relations when he or she complains of or fails to accept this responsibility.

Both physician and psychiatrist should be fully acquainted with the various types of contraceptive measures that may be prescribed, as well as the commonly accepted views of various religious groups in their use. With the development of effective oral contraceptives it is possible to offer a safe method of preventing conception that has proved widely acceptable. These agents have physiologic actions similar to the natural estrogens and progesterone, which inhibit secretion of pituitary gonadotropins and thus prevent ovarian follicular maturation and ovulation. It is reported by Kane et al. that they also influence the metabolism of the biogenic amines. In the United States of America, at least ten different synthetic steroids are available. There are excellent reviews on their structure, biologic properties, mechanism of action, and side effects. The latter have consisted largely of headache, nervousness, abdominal pain, dizziness, nausea, and vomiting. No serious personality disturbances from their administration have been reported.

There have been several cases reported of psychotic reactions developing after withdrawal of an oral contraceptive. In these instances the patients have suffered previously from postpartum psychosis or a similar disturbance while taking other contraceptives.

NERVOUS SYSTEM

Disturbances of the Image of the Body

Although our modern conceptions of the body image derive from the studies of Schilder, the knowledge of phantom phenomena, which demonstrate so strikingly the validity of this concept, extends well back into medical antiquity. They were known to Ambroise Paré and surgeons before his time. They were the subject of study by Weir Mitchell over a century ago. It is now recognized that, with growth, the individual develops a total perception of his or her own body as well as certain attitudes toward the physical self that many consider the core structure in the development of the ego. The body percept slowly evolves through the multiple sensory experiences of the infant in the discovery of his body parts. The various sensory impressions conveyed by means of kinesthetic, visual, and tactile apparatus to the cortex lead to an expanding and growing perception of body awareness, presumably organized and integrated in the parietotemporal cortex of the brain.

In addition to this physiological substratum acquired over the years by postural, tactile, and visual percepts, each individual attaches to this appreciation of the body and its various parts attitudes with emotional overtones that derive from early experiences in the family and as a result of the parental evaluations of the person's physique. The attitudes are ingrained through verbal remarks, nonverbal indications, and the expressions of valuation pertaining to desirable physical traits and attainment. The comparison of one's own physique with that of parents and peers and the emphasis on the differences play a large role in the body image of the growing child. The parents imply that the child's body and its parts are good or bad, pleasing or repulsive, clean or dirty, loved or disliked. Thus, in some families in which physical strength and physical accomplishment are emphasized, a boy's attitude toward his body is determined to a large extent by the parents' feelings and attitudes toward development of his limbs and muscles. In a similar manner, the parents or the culture may overemphasize physical beauty or particular physical attributes in girls. The American cultural overemphases are evident in our advertising and writing.

It may be mentioned that certain families and ethnical groups tend to derogate various body parts that have sexual significance. This, in turn, reflects in part on both conscious and unconscious conceptions of body parts in certain individuals. The loss of a hand, for example, may have a very different meaning to a violinist than to a professor of history, and a resulting disturbance or disorganization of the personality would therefore be much more apt to result in the former. Lesions in parts of the body that psychologically represent organs of marked value for the personality—such as eyes, breasts, sexual organs—may be highly disturbing, even though the disease, objectively considered, is not serious. Disturbances of the personality rarely follow operations upon the appendix or other organs not invested with deep emotional value. On the other hand, psychiatric complications following operations upon highly valued ones, such as the reproductive organs, are not uncommon.

Disabling physical handicaps, such as crippling, blindness, and deafness, which put the person at a disadvantage with his fellows, may have profound effect upon emotional health. The sensitive, even paranoid, reactions of the deaf, at times more disturbing to the individual's social adjustment than the deafness itself, are familiar observations.

Because of the high evaluations traditionally placed upon their biological functions and because any conditions that adversely affect these functions may seriously jeopardize their personal, economic, and social security and happiness, women are particularly subject to fears and emotional conflicts when such functions are disturbed. Lack of attractiveness, or physical defects that preclude offers of marriage, an inability to bear children, the loss of financial security through unemployment because of age or disease, the presence of conditions that make discontinuance of marital relations necessary, or the approach of the involutional period may constitute problems to which emotional adjustment is difficult or impossible within the limits of mental health.

For the clinical psychiatrist, disturbances of the body image will be observed in association with many of the major psychoneurotic and psychotic disorders. However, there are certain expressions of primary body image disturbance of particular interest that may be recognized as separate entities. Among these are the various phantom phenomena and the efforts on the part of the individual to adapt to these phenomena, as well as such conditions as neurasthenia and hypochondriasis.

Phantom Phenomena

Phantom phenomena are considered the expression of the enduring concept of the individual's body image persisting after loss of a body part. It is significant that phantoms have not been noted in those with absence of a limb resulting from a congenital defect or from infantile amputations. The phantom is not explainable, then, on the basis of wish fulfillment or "gestalt" psychology. The observation of a phantom limb after amputation occurs in some 98 per cent of amputees. Such phantoms are initially perceived as consisting of the whole extremity. Usually the distal portion of the phantom, such as the hand or foot, is most conspicuous. As times passes, the phantom appendage tends to shrink and may eventually disappear into the stump. Movements of the amputation stump may induce the impression of movement of the phantom extremity provided kinesthetic sensation remains in the stump.

Three kinds of sensory phenomena may be noted in the phantom limb. In all patients with a phantom, there occurs a mild tingling, the basic phantom phenomenon, which may be regarded as dependent upon the function of the sensory-motor cerebral cortex. A stronger momentary pins-and-needles sensation may be provoked in the phantom by touching neuromas in the stump; this sensation is dependent upon functional activity of lower spinal centers. Also included under the second type of sensory phenomena are sensations referred into the phantom in the presence of disease of other organs, such as referred pain of cardiac origin. Referred sensations into the phantom may be elicited by deep pressure on the amputation stump, less often with algesic skin stimulation, and least by tactile stimulation.

The third type of painful sensory disturbance in the phantom is the common cause of the amputee's referral for psychiatric or neurologic consultation. Questioning usually reveals that the patient is concerned about sensations that he describes variously as "twisting," "burning," "pulling," or "itching." In most instances, the symptom is intermittent. It is more often annoying than agonizing. The introspective, observant amputee notes its aggravation by stimulation of the stump, sometimes by micturition in those who have lost a leg, by changes in weather, and in many instances by emotionally disturbing incidents.

Limb phantoms are common; mammary, penile, rectal, and nasal phantoms are rare. But Simmel's study has shown that mammary phantoms, after mastectomy, are much more frequent than was heretofore thought. About 50 per cent of women report no change in their body sensation following surgery; if subjected to a body sway test, the phantom breast sensation is more frequently and vividly noted. However, the phantom breast is less vividly presented as a hallucinated phenomenon than the phantom limb. Phantoms of the bladder and rectum have rarely been observed in paraplegic patients, while those of the flaccid penis and erect penis are more frequent. The existence of phantom images of other internal organs is not generally accepted as occurring, although it has been suggested that the occurrence of phantom pain in the abdomen may explain the recurrence of peptic ulcer pain in the patients who initially report the disappearance of such pain after vagotomy.

An amputee's admission that he has a limb phantom should be regarded as a healthy psychological response. Following amputation, the healthy individual slowly reorganizes his body image by means of the new sensory experiences related to the changed body form. The persistence of a physical defect irritating the afferent nerves from the amputated part will delay this reorganization and may cause pain.

The healthy amputee accepts his defect, resumes his family position, returns to his occupation, and, with an adequate stump, makes use of an appropriate prosthesis. On the other hand, a serious personality disturbance is usually being suffered by those who complain of persistent or intermittent pain in a phantom, incapacitating them for a return to life in society, in whom the painful symptom does not conform to the recognized descriptions of the sensations resulting from irritation of known structures, with referral into recognized areas of nervous distribution, and in whom there is resistance to a prosthesis or poor family, marital, or occupational adaptation. Such disturbances, though rare, occur as amputation brings an upsurge of anxiety owing to distortion of the patient's concept of his body and therefore of himself and his relations with others. Also, hostile feelings may emerge in the amputee toward those people with whom he identifies, on whom he is dependent, and whose rejection he now apprehends. The painful symptom thus may symbolize the need for dependency and apprehension about its possible loss.

In many instances the amputee with the painful phantom has identified in a hostile way with another amputee significantly related to him in his early life. In those amputees with a hysterical personality make-up and identification with another amputee, the fantasy life often discloses superstitious rationalization to explain the existence of the phantom phenomenon. The rationalizations are concerned with the loss and the fantasied disposal of the amputated part. In association with these fantasies, the amputee attempts to master his grief and mourning over the loss of the amputated part. He desires to have the part disposed of tenderly and respectfully as if the whole body were to be buried.

The neurotically overdetermined painful symptom has been relieved by a variety of psychotherapies, including suggestion, hypnosis, biofeedback, narcotherapy, electroshock, lobotomy, and more recently by the tranquilizing drugs. The therapeutic procedure of choice must be determined on the basis of the overall personality disturbance observed in the individual patient. The following report illustrates an acute emotional disturbance associated with the phantom phenomenon.

A 14-year-old boy came to clinic complaining of a "knot in his leg." He said he had bumped the lower part of his right leg against a step one month previously.

On examination a hard, fixed, tender mass was noted in the middle third of the injured part of the leg. Roentgenograms showed a primary malignant tumor involving the anterolateral cortex of the right tibia. Three days later, amputation of the right leg was performed through the lower third of the femur. The pathologist reported an osteogenic sarcoma of the tibia. The patient complained of pain in the phantom right leg shortly after recovery from the anesthesia. Within two days after operation, large doses of narcotic agents were being employed in an attempt to relieve him of pain. By the ninth postoperative day, the patient was complaining bitterly of a burning pain, was overactive, thrashed about in bed, and spoke of jumping out of a window. Special nurses were required at this time, and psychiatric consultation was requested. The patient was found to be fearful, disoriented, and confused. Administration of all drugs except morphine was discontinued in order to alleviate the mild toxic delirious state.

The next day the patient was rolling about in his bed, with his eyes closed, apparently oblivious to those about him. He cried out repetitiously, "Help me, help me. Do something for the pain." It was believed that frightening rationalizations as to the origin of the phantom contributed in part to the state of painful panic. The boy was therefore asked whether he was aware of the feeling of a phantom limb after operation. Surprisingly, the boy immediately became silent, opened his eyes, and responded affirmatively. Under questioning he stated that a year previously one of his school teachers had casually discussed amputations with his class. The teacher told the class a story of a man who had undergone an amputation, after which a severe stinging pain developed in his phantom limb. The story went that the limb was disinterred and that ants were discovered burrowing into and stinging the amputated part.

When inquiry was made as to what disposition the boy believed had been made of his own amputated extremity, he stated that he thought it was being burned. He was reassured and informed otherwise. The complaint of pain and his wild overactivity subsided to a large extent immediately after this interview. It was possible to discontinue the use of all morphine within 24 hours and to discharge the patient's special nurse shortly thereafter.

Complete relief of his pain, however, required four additional hours of psychotherapy. It was learned that the boy had been severely upset by his mother's death from cancer of the breast five years previously. The boy never spoke of his mother after her death but was morbidly inquisitive whenever anyone became ill and would inquire of his father whether the person was about to die. The mother had undergone amputation of the breast. The latter hours of treatment brought to awareness the boy's repressed hostility toward his mother, with whom he identified as an amputee, and his ambivalent feelings toward his father.

When he was dismissed from the clinic 25 days after operation, the boy had no pain, did not require medication, was active on crutches, and was eager to have a prosthesis fitted. A year later his stepmother wrote that he was without pain and was wearing a prosthesis. He had returned to school, was doing well in his studies, and had been elected to a class office.

Cosmetic Surgery

Castelnuovo-Tedesco points out that psychological reactions to surgery may differ considerably, depending upon whether a surgical procedure is *life saving* or *life-extending*. The variety of cosmetic procedures and organ transplants done now fits into the latter category. The meaning of the procedure or the special significance of a transplanted organ from another body is decisive in the capacity to integrate the surgical procedure effectively into the individual's perception of self and social adaptation.

The psychiatrist may be asked to advise on the propriety of carrying out a corrective surgical procedure for a deformity. In the vast majority of instances, corrective surgery leads to improvement of self-esteem and reduction of affective disturbance and negative personality traits. Druss has reported recently upon the positive changes in the body concept following breast augmentation surgery. He emphasizes that the improved bodily appearance appeased lifelong interpsychic doubts about the patients' femininity, which they sought to achieve through narcissistic identification with their mothers.

On the other hand, a 15-year follow-up study by Connolly and Gibson of individuals who underwent elective rhinoplasty for cosmetic reasons, compared with another group for whom this surgical procedure corrected defects of disease or injury, disclosed a high percentage of severe neuroses and psychoses in the former group. They concluded that dysmorphophobia carries a poor prognosis.

Penile implantation now is being undertaken for many men who have become impotent because of physical disease or trauma. When successful, it has been gratifying to the sufferer and has improved the mental health of families. It is urged by some for those whose impotence is due to neurotic processes, as described earlier in this text. Outcome, in terms of general social competence for these persons, awaits further study.

If it is evident that the person requesting corrective surgery tends to suffer the delusion that his or her incapacity in interpersonal relations is related almost totally to a single defect, the consulting psychiatrist will be wary of suggesting the procedure unless the defect is major. Those with minor deformities often have an underlying paranoid make-up and respond with outright paranoidal reactions following surgery when it becomes painfully apparent that the hoped for magical modification of their social and sexual adaptation has not occurred. Some have been known to assault the surgeon who performed the corrective procedure.

Athlete's Neurosis

Men and women whose senses of personal esteem rest largely upon their athletic abilities are high-risk subjects for neurotic reactions. These reactions often are long enduring and difficult to manage. They are not unlike the middle-aged neurotic reactions of those women whose ego strength has resided largely in the adulation given them for their earlier but now fading beauty. The conflict essentially is between the idealized physical self-concept and the currently perceived body concept. The usual precipitating causes are direct threat to physical well-being, injuries, and illnesses. In contrast to other neurotic reactions, the response must be seen as one of deprivation or loss of the overvalued body concept of physical prowess. There is, then, a strong, reactive-depressive element in the neurotic reaction, often obscured by the extroverted and sociable personality evolved by many successful athletes. Hypochondriasis and anxiety attacks are frequent symptoms, but any neurotic or psychotic constellation may develop in these athletes, who are vulnerable through their obsessive preoccupation with the gaining of love and acceptance, perceived by them only during the performance of their sport.

MUSCULOSKELETAL SYSTEM

Rheumatoid Arthritis

Psychiatric interest in rheumatoid arthritis stems from the repeated observation that the onset or exacerbation of the illness has been related to a period of emotional stress. The patient with rheumatoid arthritis often has been described as an individual who is composed emotionally, seldom expresses his feelings overtly, and appears to derive gratification from being of service to others. Usually active physically and intellectually, the patient is inclined to outdoor and competitive sports. His dependence on others is masked. The majority of such persons were brought up in families in which the mother was the domineering parent, while the father was gentle and compliant. This led to a strong dependency, with fear of the maternal figure and, in girls, a competitive relationship toward the father and brothers. Control of the intense hostility is accomplished through neuromuscular activity, domineering position, ability to control the environment, and overvaluation of physical functions.

The precipitating events leading to the arthritis generally have been loss or potential separation from another, such as the death of the mother and threat of the father to remarry, separation or rejection from the husband or other important figures, miscarriage, or disappointments in personal relations. It is believed that the common affective and subsequent personality response factor in these various events has been an unconscious increase in the feelings of resentment, rebellion, and hostility associated with guilt that had been previously handled through self-sacrificing activity and service to others. In a number of patients, exacerbations of rheumatoid arthritis have occurred following the suppression of feelings of grief on the loss of an important family member. Sometimes such exacerbations are seen as anniversary reactions to the loss, associated with feelings of depression.

There is a frequent association of rheumatoid arthritis with duodenal ulcer. It has been stated that individuals with psychoses seldom suffer from rheumatoid arthritis, yet in a study of a number of arthritic patients by psychoanalytical technique, covert psychotic defenses were noted and in the course of treatment several became overtly disturbed.

TREATMENT. At the onset of rheumatoid arthritis, or during emergencies, the therapy is essentially management of acute illness by the internist, with restoration of the patient's sense of security. The psychiatrist at this time is most effective as a consultant and advisor unless the patient has been in psychiatric treatment previously.

Patients with rheumatoid arthritis do poorly in the psychodynamic insightful therapies. They respond best to supportive treatment with actively verbalized advice or questioning clarification by the therapist and for a long time accept activity, rather than words, as security. Psychiatric therapy may be of assistance in those in whom the impairment of neuromuscular function exceeds the extent of the disability—that is, the functional incapacity is overdetermined, as with secondary gain.

Many patients with this illness deny their need for help, yet with the establishment of a regular regimen of therapeutic interviews arranged on the authority of a physician, they often do well over long periods of time on little more than supportive treatment. Only in occasional instances can the patient be freed from the often unrecognized hostile identifications with lost persons.

Backache

Complaint of pain in the lower back, heard so frequently by orthopedists, must be recognized as a frequent psychosomatic disorder. In one pain clinic, 70 per cent of the referrals presented this complaint, and, of this group, over a third were without any positive physical findings. The personality characteristics are those of depression, hysteria, and hypochondriasis. Generally, patients with persisting or chronic complaint of low back pain report that they have given up employment and are supported by welfare, social security, or disability income. Characteristically, they spend only a few hours daily on their feet, have few avocational interests, and are frequent visitors to physicians' offices. Their self-concept is that of an invalid.

Physical examination will reveal evidence of muscular spasm in some, but such findings are absent in others.

It is clear that their relationship to the clinical caretakers is ambivalent, consisting of both dependency and suppressed and repressed hostility reflective of transference from significant persons in the past. In examining those with the back pain complaint, the clinician tends to overlook the pervasive personality disorder.

The type of psychiatric treatment will depend on the assessment of the predominant personality traits, particularly the patient's defenses and assets. At times the low back pain complaint in psychotic depression is used as a defense against disclosure of sexual impotence or frigidity. In these instances, antidepressant medications will prove effective in addition to psychotherapeutic support. Biofeedback has been used with some success in treatment of those whose muscle spasm represents chronic tension.

OTHER PSYCHOSOMATIC PAIN SYNDROMES

The headache syndromes span a wide variety of psychophysiological disturbances. They represent the expression of chronic anxiety and tension exerted through neurovascular or neuromuscular structures, or both.

Migraine

Although the conspicuous feature of migraine is the episodic and usually unilateral headache, the syndrome consists of a widespread neurovascular dysfunction and other somatic symptoms, accompanied as well by disturbance of mood in individuals of a driving perfectionistic personality.

SYMPTOMS. Before the onset of headache, there exists for some hours or days evidence of mood change, associated with increased variability in the contractile state of the blood vessels, particularly of the head. Irritability or moodiness at this time is often associated with flushing or pallor of the face due to contraction or dilatation of the extracranial blood vessels. Visual phenomena, including scintillating scotomata and unilateral or homonymous hemianopia, occur in about 15 per cent of the patients in the hour or two preceding the headache, owing to vasoconstriction of the retinal vessels. As these symptoms disappear, the typical throbbing unilateral headache ensues, usually located opposite to the side of the perceived visual disturbance. The headache is due to vasodilatation of the common carotid and external carotid arteries and may be relieved by pressure upon them by the actions of vasoconstricting pharmaceuticals. With the persistence of vasodilatation for several hours, there occurs edema or tenderness in the vessels, which become incompressible and less amenable to the actions of vasoconstricting drugs. Also at this time, redness or tearing of the eye and swelling of the nasal mucosa, and, in some patients, painful contraction of the neck musculature follow. With some patients, nausea, vomiting, fluid retention, and other variant phenomena are associated or may represent minor variants of the migraine attack.

Total plasma serotonin falls sharply at the onset of the migraine attack to about 40 per cent of its former level. It remains depressed throughout the attack. Before the headache, plasma serotonin rises. During most attacks of migraine both serotonin and the urinary catabolic product of serotonin, 5-hydroxyindole acetic acid (5-HIAA) are excreted in excess. Serotonin in dosages of approximately 5 mg. has been reported to ameliorate migraine attacks when given intravenously. However, many side effects occur during such administration (faintness, flushing, nausea, hypernea, restlessness). Administration of reserpine will induce a headache and a drop of serotonin in plasma in those susceptible to migraine. Intravenous injections of heparin (150 to 175 mg.) will abort a migrainous attack shortly after onset.

ETIOLOGY. The migraine sufferers tend to come from ambitious, highly conventional families that attach great significance to attainment and in which children are required to conform to strict behavior patterns that limit the direct expression of aggression by either physical or verbal activity. Failure to conform threatens the family attachment. Thus hostile feelings toward parents or other respected or loved persons are repressed. Consequently, the arousal of rage or hostile wishes leads to conflict and anxiety, and this condition acts as precipitant for the pathophysiologic neurovascular response. Migrainous patients often disclose in psychotherapy hostile fantasies toward siblings and other family members. Frequently they have fantasied smashing the head of the person toward whom they have felt hateful. The arousal of sexual drives, which in turn are rejected by their overly strict superego, may lead again to the secondary emergence of rage and consequent precipitation of headache. The personality of the majority of those with migraine is one expressive of consideration to others, control, and outward calm, and the individual is often thought of as an effective driving and perfectionistic person. Just prior to the migraine attack, some personality traits and moodiness more directly expressive of the concealed rage may become evident. There is frequently a family history of migraine, and women are affected more often than men.

TREATMENT. Treatment for the acute migrainous attack is directed to symptomatic relief by providing a vasoconstricting agent. The administration by mouth of 1 mg. of ergotamine tartrate and 100 mg. of caffeine sodium benzoate (available in tablet form as Cafergot) repeated at 30-minute intervals up to six doses usually effectively relieves or aborts the headache. If the patient is nauseated or vomiting, a subcutaneous injection of 0.25 or 0.5 mg. of ergotamine tartrate may be given.

Many migrainous patients have depressive personality disorders. For such individuals, the tricyclic antidepressants have been successful in both reducing and preventing attacks.

As a preventive for migraine, methysergide maleate (1-methyl-D-lysergic acid butanolamide bimaleate), a serotonin antagonist, given in tablet form, 2 mg. three times daily, has been effective. It has no value in aborting the acute attack. Undesirable side effects have been noted in 10 to 15 per cent of patients. Its adverse side effects in order of frequency are nausea, dizziness, epigastric pain, restlessness, drowsiness, and leg cramps. The drug is contraindicated with pregnancy or in the presence of any vascular disease. Retroperitoneal fibrosis will develop in approximately 1 per cent of patients administered this drug over prolonged periods. It has been recommended that a urogram be obtained at the start of methysergide therapy and be repeated at six-month intervals to detect any evidence of silent ureteral obstruction owing to such a growth.

Psychotherapy is recommended when the migrainous episodes are so frequent or so disturbing as to affect the general life adaptation of the sufferer. Treatment should be directed to allowing more direct and constructive expression of the rage and aggressive drives and to reducing the exaggerated superego demands.

A 30-year-old married woman was referred for psychiatric treatment by another psychiatrist who was treating her son and daughter. The children were being treated for behavior problems on complaint of the mother that her 7-year-old son clung to her unnecessarily and that her 8-year-old daughter was depressed and listless.

At the first visit, she appeared reserved and distant. She smiled continually and seemed pleasant, but her tension was most apparent. Until directly confronted with her own difficulties, she focused her whole discussion on the behavior of the children. In response to inquiry about her own problem, she described a course of headaches which dated back many years. Within the past three years, coinciding with the appearance of what she regarded as her son's difficulties, the headaches became more severe. They tended to occur at night and frequently she experienced nausea with them. At times they persisted for a series of days and their occurrence was frequently associated with her menstrual period. The patient noticed that the headaches were particularly likely when she was in conflict with her son, especially when he refused to eat foods she considered proper.

During this visit she characterized the headache as a dull, aching feeling accompanied by blurred vision, slight nausea, and occasional spots before the eyes. She reported that the headache became severe and generalized although it usually disappeared after a short rest in bed. With the migraine attack the patient described the feeling that she must get away or that if she could scream she would feel infinitely better and the headache would disappear. It was evident that on some occasions she had screamed at her children with the onset of the headache.

On the patient's next visit the psychiatrist observed her in the waiting room with her children. It was noted that she was very critical toward them, made unfavorable remarks about their clothing, and seemed insistent that they be neat, quiet, and immediately compliant to her wishes.

The patient was seen twice weekly for a period of four months. Within this period there was a marked reduction in the frequency and intensity of the headaches. Therapy was directed to encouraging her verbal expression of rage toward others when frustrated, alleviating the guilt aroused by such affect through uncovering the punitive and depriving experiences which led to the evolution of the pathological and infantile superego. In her recounting of the transactional experiences in her parental and marital families, the therapist first voiced the expected related affects, which later permitted her to do so spontaneously, as illustrated in the following paragraphs.

The patient reported that when she was four years old her mother died following an abortion. The patient and her older brother went to live with the maternal grandmother, where the patient remained until the age of 8. At this time her father married a widow who had a son of her own. The patient was returned to the new household of her father and stepmother, but had difficulty relating to the latter.

The father was described as a hard-working man who the patient felt had no warmth for her as he had sent her off to live with relatives. While she denied any feelings of bitterness towards him, she intimated that these might have existed because of his behavior toward her at the time of the mother's death and later in the second marriage. The patient spoke of her stepmother as a woman who was continuously critical of her. In commenting on some difficulty with her mother-in-law, who lived with her and her husband, she was very guarded and disclaimed the matter as

having any great importance or significance to her problem.

She generally considered that boys were preferred, and in her first efforts to maintain a relationship with her mother, as well as later in her relations with her grandmother and father, she developed meticulous working habits which she had learned evoked their appreciation. With the pattern well established, she utilized this approach later in pleasing her husband, employers, and other significant adults. She admitted feelings of resentment and anger toward her stepmother, and later the mother-in-law, but she felt she could not express her feelings and wants to her husband as such actions would lead to altercation with him. Feeling deeply dependent on him as the one person who cared for her, she was unable to express any of her needs or disappointments. However, as it was eventually revealed in treatment, she felt much anger toward her husband for not arranging for the mother-in-law to live elsewhere and for failure to provide her with the attentions that she craved. The patient reported that while she was incapable of insisting upon her son's eating properly, she was compulsively driven to maintain the strict dietary regimen as suggested by her pediatrician. To complicate the disciplining of the children, the mother-in-law openly criticized the patient. The patient was conflicted between the impression that a good parent should not punish the children and her critical and hostile feelings toward her children. Following punishment or restriction of the children, she felt guilty and anxious.

She spoke of her shyness, lack of self-confidence, her compulsive meticulousness as a home-maker, and her occasional periods of depression.

The patient's sexual education was limited in the sense that she was not advised of the onset of menses. When she inquired of her stepmother, she was immediately warned that she should be careful of herself or she would become pregnant. Marriage for her was a means of attaining a home. Sexual relations with her husband were performed without gratification and through a sense of duty and with concealed resentment. She shunned expressions of affection because she was fearful of becoming emotionally involved and therefore hurt if her husband or others failed to respond to her advances. Her wish to have children was competitive and substantive, to prove that she was as capable as other women. With pregnancy, she was ashamed of the undeniable evidence of sexual relations, terrified of the birth process itself, and felt inadequate to give her children what they might need from her.

At the end of treatment (without drug therapy) the patient reported that she had become more relaxed, was freer in expressions of her own needs and feelings, and less conflicted in her management of her children as she came to understand the origin of her anxieties.

Cluster Headaches

Cluster headaches are probably related to migraine. They differ by episodes of excruciating pain around one eye, associated with excessive tearing and stuffiness of the ipsilateral nostril. Pain rapidly increases in intensity and generally persists around 45 minutes. The attacks of pain may erupt four to six times during a day and often in the middle of the night, and persist for a period of six to eight weeks. While many patients with cluster headaches will initially respond well to drugs such as methysergide, ergotamines, caffeine, propranolol and other sedatives, they later relapse. Recently, it has been reported that prednisone in a dose of 30 mg. provides immediate relief, with continued freedom from headache lasting several months in many. This drug has been given in 20 mg. doses on alternate days with breakfast in treatment directed to decreasing the frequency of attacks.

Tension Headaches

Tension headaches are precipitated in other individuals of essentially the same personality make-up by similar emotional conflicts, or they may complicate the migrainous state. The tension headache typically produces diffuse and sustained aching pain in the forehead, back of the head, shoulders, and neck. It is frequently encountered as the somatic component of a chronic anxiety state or in those whose personality characteristics and development are described in Chapter 22. Hence the pain is due to prolonged and sustained contracture of the cervical musculature.

Symptomatic relief from these headaches may be obtained with the use of drugs relieving anxiety and by muscular relaxants. The anxiolytics with muscle-relaxing properties are recommended, to be given at three- to four-hour intervals until relief is obtained. Again, the frequent or prolonged occurrence of such headaches indicates the prescription of biofeedback or dynamic psychotherapy to allow recognition of conflict and modification of the underlying pathological structure of the personality.

The following case report of tension headache also illustrates its successful resolution through psychotherapy.

The patient, an intelligent and attractive 29-year-old married woman with two children, was referred for psychiatric treatment after diagnostic study of her complaint of headaches, described as tension and pain in the back of the neck and radiating forward over the head to the forehead. These symptoms had occurred periodically for five years, but their frequency and pain had increased over the twelve months prior to the patient's seeking help. The pain usually persisted from one to four hours. There were no associated symptoms of scotomata, nausea, vomiting, or preceding aura. The headaches could generally be relieved by the use of aspirin or codeine. The patient linked their occurrence directly to the arousal of disturbing emotions.

The patient described herself as prone to generalized tension, anxiousness, moodiness. These mood states developed in situations in which she experienced anxiety in relation to the attitude of her parents, teachers, or husband toward herself. The patient spoke of her self-doubts, her consistent feelings of inadequacy, and her belief that she was less attractive and capable than others. She recognized herself as overly dependent on others and requiring constant approval and reassurance. When she was extremely tense, she retreated to reading, oversleeping, or periods of frantic work.

The patient first experienced the headaches at the age of 16 years. Initially they appeared as a mild feeling of tightness and pain in the neck and the base of the skull. When they became worse while the patient was a student at college, she was referred to a psychiatrist whom she saw weekly for 20-minute interviews over a period of months. The most severe attacks occurred when she became pregnant just prior to her marriage. The patient felt so doubtful of her capacity to be a mother that she was able to obtain a therapeutic abortion. While she had enjoyed sexual contact with her future husband in her premarital life, from the day of her abortion she had only markedly repugnant and resistant attitudes toward sexual relations. In spite of the fact that her husband was sympathetic and helpful in her periods of anxiety, she was frightened and repulsed. With her continual denial of her husband, arguments and quarrels had arisen between them. Recognizing her childishness and her role in the marriage difficulty, the patient suggested that perhaps she acted toward her husband as if he were a father substitute.

She was the eldest of five children. Her father was a prominent and outstanding internist of great prestige. Her mother had died from cardiac failure when the patient was 7 years old. The patient had one brother who was three years her junior, and three young sisters who were born of her father's second marriage, which took place when she was 10. The patient described her father as an ambitious and hard-working man who had little capacity for enjoyment of anything but his work. While she admired and respected him, she also resented him, feeling that he exerted pressure on her to follow his path of brilliance in the field of medicine. She described her attacks of abdominal pains when a child and the reactions of her father when she told him of these pains and others. In her recollections she saw him as taking a calloused attitude toward physical illness and treating her in an offhand manner. In treatment, the patient openly criticized her father for never having a close, warm, affectionate relationship with her. She expressed resentment that he always took credit for her accomplishments in social and school affairs.

Insofar as she could recall her family life before the loss of her mother, the patient had the impression that her parents were happy. On the other hand, she felt the relations of her father and stepmother were difficult or at best strained. The father married a younger woman 3 years after his first wife's death and had left the family almost immediately for a year while he was in military service. The patient had never become close to the stepmother, feeling that she was cold and distant. Toward her half-siblings she felt a responsibility to try to make their lives more happy, since she felt they were largely ignored by their mother.

Other data on the childhood years served to clarify the origin of the patient's symptoms. After the death of her mother the patient apparently suffered for several years from frequent and different injuries. She found it impossible to bring her childhood friends to her home. With respect to early sexual development, she reported that masturbation occurred infrequently and always produced feelings of guilt and anxiety. Her father advised her that any sexual activity such as kissing or necking was degrading and harmful. He had also warned her that premarital intercourse might make marriage impossible. The patient's engagement was announced within a half year of her meeting the compassionate medical student who became her husband.

The patient was seen twice a week in psychotherapeutic sessions for a total of some forty hours. During the course of this treatment, in which she ventilated her emotions regarding childhood deprivation and neglect after the loss of her mother, her bouts of headache disappeared. There was evidence, from her associations and her dreams, of strong dependency needs from which arose hostile drives when they were frustrated. A death phobia centering on her pregnancy was also evident, deriving from her conception of the sexual act as violent and aggressive, her memories of her mother's death, and the conflict between the demands of her own maternal activity and the competitive strivings with her own children.

The types of headaches discussed are to be discriminated from those due to other physical illness, as well as those symbolic complaints of head pain or peculiar head sensations seen occasionally in the schizophrenic that represent in some way derogatory inferences to intellectual functioning or doubts about social or emotional capacities. Patients with such a concept frequently speak of their complaints in a vague and bizarre manner, in contrast to the usual stereotyped descriptions of headache provided by those with an organ illness or neurovascular or neuromuscular dysfunction involving the head and neck.

RESPIRATORY SYSTEM

Emotional behavior involves the respiratory system, both in its expression and in its action. Crying and laughter, screaming, or speech involve change in respiratory action; overbreathing and its obverse typify responses in contrasting periods of action or relaxation. According to Dudley and his associates, one of the main factors in contemporary life that may determine the response to psychologic distress through either hypoventilation or hyperventilation is orientation toward action. Thus arousal of anxiety or anger leads to hyperventilation, as does exercise. Conversely, apathy and depression, like sleep, bring about hypoventilation. Dudley suggests that neural factors make the major contribution to hyperventilation in response to action, and his studies show this response in the majority of persons in the face of sudden or short-lasting life stresses. The experienced clinician has been aware for years that the hyperventilation syndrome is the most frequently encountered of the psychophysiologic disturbances. It is also the symptom complex most recurrently unrecognized and mistreated.

Hyperventilation Syndrome

Subjective symptoms resulting from overbreathing are frequently not recognized by either the psychiatrist or the internist. Hyperventilation is the common physiological means by which the subjective disturbance noted in the usual acute *panic* or *anxiety attack* takes place. It may be induced by any condition producing fear and not uncommonly occurs in the course of other personality disturbances when anxiety becomes manifest. Its recognition is important, since in the medical clinic the afflicted patient is often considered to have heart disease, angina pectoris, asthma or other respiratory disease, or even painful lesions presumed to be a result of spinal cord disease. Up to 6 per cent of patients attending specialty clinics present this symptom complex and even more are seen in the offices of general physicians. In the psychiatric clinic, many patients have been exposed to time-wasting therapy in which efforts were made to interpret the symbolic meaning of the subjective phenomena produced by overbreathing.

The sufferer usually does not recognize that he or she is overbreathing. The increase in the depth and rapidity of respiration may be so slight that it goes unobserved. It is well known that an irregular respiratory rhythm occurs in anxious individuals and is accompanied by sighing and yawning. Furthermore, these respiratory disturbances, if sufficiently prolonged, lead to reduction in the alveolar air and the carbon dioxide tension of the arterial blood with a fall in the blood bicarbonate. Consequently, many physiological systems are altered. The acid-base equilibrium is disturbed, the urine composition and volume are affected, circulatory changes take place, and neuromuscular and electroencephalographic alterations ensue. If the condition becomes chronic and repeated attacks occur, blood pH returns to normal, owing to compensatory mechanisms that maintain a lowered plasma CO_2. It is not surprising that subjective disturbances take place because of the pervasive effects upon the cardiovascular, neurological, respiratory, gastrointestinal, and musculoskeletal systems.

The initial subjective feeling resulting from overbreathing is lightheadedness or giddiness. If overbreathing continues, the individual has the sensation that he is about to faint; he may perspire profusely, and, if walking, his gait may seem unstable. There then follows a sensation of air hunger or shortness of breath and feelings of pressure in the thorax. Some patients speak of palpitation or of pain in the heart; others describe chest pains that Wheatley has defined as of three types: "sharp, fleeting, and periodic, originating in the hypochondrium or anterior left chest and radiates into the neck, left scapula, and along the inferior rib margins;" "persistent localized aching discomfort under the left breast;" or "a diffuse, dull-aching heavy pressure over the entire precordium or substernum." The senior author has heard complaints of a bandlike sensation around the chest.

With mounting anxiety over presumed lack of air, many consciously increase the depth and rate of breathing, thereby exacerbating the initial cause of the subjective symptoms. The more commonly taught symptoms of hyperventilation consist of tingling paresthesias in the fingertips, perioral region, or toes, followed by tetanic contractions, which are, in fact, rare. If overbreathing persists over a sufficiently prolonged period, disturbance of awareness may result, associated with pallor; vasomotor collapse; rapid, irregular, and weak pulse; and ending, in many instances, in loss of consciousness or in convulsions.

When the psychiatrist sees a patient who complains of attacks of breathlessness, palpitation, and dizziness or perspiration, episodic attacks of hyperventilation precipitated by acute situational anxiety should be considered. Such patients frequently are able to define well the initial and last situations in which the attacks occur and provide excellent descriptions of disturbing interpersonal contacts, with arousal of unbearable feelings of hostility, resentment, or sexuality. The attack of hyperventilation frequently takes place as the consequence of a disturbing dream or nightmare.

DIAGNOSIS. The diagnosis of a hyperventilation syndrome as the source of the symptoms of the individual patient may be easily determined by requesting the patient to overbreathe for a period of two minutes in a sitting position. To carry out this test effectively, it is frequently necessary to provide a brief demonstration of what is required, also strongly to encourage the patient to continue overbreathing, as many will attempt to desist after 30 seconds of hyperventilation. At the end of this test the patient may be asked to describe his or her subjective symptoms. If he is unable to elaborate them spontaneously, the psychiatrist should inquire about the presence of giddiness, breathlessness, palpitation, shortness of breath, perspiration, and pins-and-needles sensation. The patient then may be asked if he identifies the subjective sensations of overbreathing as those that he has suffered in the episodic attacks of which he complains. Sometimes the neurological symptoms that occur in the course of this disturbance are unilateral.

In general, the carbon dioxide–combining power of the blood and the blood calcium are unchanged. However, in chronic hyperventilation, venous alkalosis has in some instances been demonstrated. Occasionally, with chronic, persistent hyperventilation, a compensatory acidosis with reduction in blood carbon dioxide has been reported.

Hyperventilation may result not only from sudden emotional stress and anxiety but also in the course of febrile ill-nesses, high-altitude anoxemia, high external temperatures over a prolonged period, and occasionally in the course of encephalitis.

TREATMENT. In some sufferers, the duplication of the characteristic symptom complex by requested hyperventilation provides immediate and continuing relief of symptoms. On the other hand, in those individuals who have clear-cut evidence of chronic anxiety usually associated with phobic symptoms or with depressive or schizophrenic personality disorders, the demonstration of the physiological source of the symptomatology is effective only in providing an intellectual interpretation of the acutely disturbing symptoms, not continuing relief. Tricyclic antidepressants will block these panic attacks, yet leave the individual with continuing anticipatory anxiety. Psychotherapy is recommended, for it may modify the personality structure that predisposes to the eruption of anxiety repetitively in particular situations. In young parents, it will contribute to preventing similar symptomatology from developing in their children. The majority of hyperventilators suffer an anxiety neurosis with phobias, which they tend to perpetuate in some of their offspring.

A 57-year-old woman who had been under medical care since her menopause at the age of 50 was referred for psychiatric treatment. At the onset of the menopause she had complained of headaches, nausea, tremulousness, and cold sweats. Her blood pressure was usually about 180 systolic, 90 diastolic. She made regular visits to her physician, who treated her with diet and Theominal. The patient did well for a period of five years until her treatment by this physician was abruptly terminated by her husband.

The patient was brought for psychiatric treatment two years later by her husband, who stated in her presence that he could no longer stand her "huffing and puffing." In the intervening two years he had taken her to several other physicians for her increasingly frequent and severe attacks of apparent shortness of breath. The patient described these as occurring only in the morning upon awaking. She would then seem short of breath and soon become dizzy and weak. She next suffered from palpitation, followed by tingling and numbness about the mouth and tips of the extremities. The attacks had increased in frequency to one daily. Each morning they prevented her husband and daughter from going to work and kept her from preparing the breakfast and doing the housework. The patient had been advised to "snap out of it," and had been given sedatives and ammonium chloride without avail.

The only abnormality observed on physical examination was a slight elevation of blood pressure. She was requested to hyperventilate and it was demonstrated to her that her symptoms could be reproduced by this procedure. The patient was considered to have essential hypertension complicated by attacks of hyperventilation resulting from chronic anxiety.

From spontaneous remarks made by the patient at this time, it was learned that during the period of overbreathing she was concerned about dying—not the possibility of her own death, but the death of her husband. She spoke of the recent death of her brother from heart disease and cancer, and stated that her children had now grown up and no longer needed her. She commented that the family had threatened to place her in a hospital for mental disorders. Her past history indicated that the patient was a driving, energetic woman who had been completely immersed in her family. It was inferred from her remarks about death that she harbored repressed resentment toward her husband, who showed little sympathy with her during the initial interview. It soon became apparent that situations arousing repressed hostility toward her husband and family, feelings that were unacceptable to her as a conscientious person, and threats of separation from her family induced the acute anxiety attacks manifested by overbreathing.

It was learned that the patient had married her husband suddenly after having been jilted. At that time, too, she had given up an excellent job. Her own daughter had been jilted some six months prior to the consultation. The patient described her husband as self-centered, buried in his work, disinterested in social life, and disparaging in his attitude toward her church and recreational activities. He was seen and advised to spend more time with his wife.

In four subsequent visits she was encouraged to ventilate her unacceptable feelings concerning her family and husband. She commented on the fact that she wished to resume typing and playing the piano. She was frank in speaking of her anger toward her husband for his years of indifference, obstinacy, and ridicule, culminating when he forbade her to continue to attend the doctor who had helped her so well throughout the menopause. The patient was encouraged to plan activities outside the home that might help to make her less dependent on the family. She responded quickly. Within six weeks she was free of overbreathing attacks, did not require medication, and had returned to her housework. She then decided that further treatment was unnecessary, since her immediate symptoms had been relieved.

This case illustrates several important factors in the management of the hyperventilation syndrome. First, the patient was made aware of the physiological mechanism underlying the attacks by intentional hyperventilating. This test also made her realize that her symptoms were regarded as significant in themselves. Second, a series of simple psychotherapeutic discussions allowed the patient to express herself freely concerning her emotions and attitude toward her family. This discussion of her feelings, interspersed only with a few directional questions related to possible anger and resentment, relieved her of her symptoms. Third, this patient was an excellent choice for brief psychotherapy as she gave a history of previous satisfactory adjustment at home, at work, and in marriage.

Asthma

That a relationship exists between emotional arousal and the precipitation of an asthmatic attack has been a matter of comment since the time of Hippocrates. Although it is generally conceded that asthma occurs in individuals with a constitutional predisposition to bronchospasm, there are now on record many cases in which the attacks were initiated by events rather than by the presence of a specific antigen. The well-known instance of "rose asthma" represents this type of induction: the patient regularly had an attack when she came in contact with roses but also had asthma when she was shown a papier-mâché rose. Other similar precipitating instances are recorded in which patients have their asthmatic attack at a regular hour each day, when they hear a particular song or type of story, on hearing comments about a parent, or on visiting the parent's grave. Under such circumstances, the asthmatic attack is regarded by some as the conditioned response to the situational cue—that is, as a conditioned reflex to a conditional stimulation. Hyperventilation leads to bronchial spasm; its precipitation through induction of anxiety also may initiate the asthmatic episode. Freeman and his associates have reviewed critically the considerable literature on this subject. In some surveys of allergic patients, as many as 75 per cent were found to have an emotional component influencing their attacks.

The asthmatic personality often is one of irritability and quickness to respond, coupled with lack of confidence, submissiveness, and anxiety. Most clinical observers have noticed that there is an unusually strong maternal dependency that arouses conflict when aggressive or sexual drives threaten the relationship. The exaggerated dependency drive has arisen either through the relationship of the child to a rejecting mother or through too early urging by the parents that the child assume independence, a pseudo-independent façade thus being forced. Thus one group of asthmatic patients does better when close to the person or persons to whom they are attached; another group does poorly in such an instance as they fear the exposure of their dependency or the nagging such exposure produces.

The attack has been thought to represent symbolically a protest against separation from the mother and also the wish to re-establish this relationship through crying; thus it is considered equivalent to a repressed cry. Others have stressed the relationship of the asthmatic attack to arousal of repressed conflicts relating to bodily odors, particularly those concerned with excretions and secretions, therefore presumably involved in early childhood rearing relative to cleanliness, dirtiness, or sexuality. There is evidence that asthmatics show significantly greater blocking of associations upon exposure to various odors than do other groups.

In addition to medical care to prevent and also treat the acute seizure, many asthmatics may profit by psycho-therapy particularly directed to resolution of the dependency problem, which is often associated with repressed hostility. It has been found that children with asthma frequently respond promptly upon separation from their parents. Permanent improvement for such children requires, as well, effective counseling and psychotherapy for the parents.

SKIN

Since the skin is an organ subject to the direct influences of the autonomic nervous system and the indirect effect of endocrine activity, as well as subject on the body surface to compulsive contact or self-inflicted damage representing unconscious conflict, the means of expression of the psychological disturbance vary greatly from one type of lesion to another. In the past few years, with the increasing recognition of psychological factors in the genesis of somatic diseases, the dermatologists have emphasized a high degree of association between various skin diseases, such as pruritus, neurodermatoses, hyperhidrosis, and other reactions, and evidences of difficulties in adjustment of personality to stressful life situations. Some dermatology clinics have reported that psychiatric factors were found to be of significance in over 75 per cent of their patients.

There have now been carried out numerous experiments indicating that the skin inflammatory responses in the same individual are variable depending upon his mood and attitude and the situational stress. Depression is associated with low responsiveness. High responsiveness occurs in association with evidence of diminished adrenal cortical function.

In cases of the dry type of *neurodermatitis*, it has been considered that excoriation of the skin is more fundamental than the pruritus usually complained of by these patients. The itching often represents a voluptuous or tantalizing sensation. Events that produce the emotions of anger, with depression and feelings of guilt, generally precipitate the exacerbation of the cutaneous eruption. The family picture often shows a hostile, dependent, maternal relationship, in which itching and scratching symbolize anger at the mother figure, handled masochistically because of guilt.

In the exudative type of neurodermatitis of children (*atopic dermatitis*), there has been found evidence of maternal rejection. Here the emotional disturbance is thought to be expressed primarily through a psychophysiologic mechanism that induces vesiculation. In *urticaria* the psychodynamic explanation is very similar to that of asthma, with the lesions precipitated by situations that induce resentment and frustration resulting from a threat to an important dependency relationship. With *pruritus of the anogenital* area, repression of various sexual conflicts has been observed. *Dermatitis factitia* has been recognized for many years as psychologically determined. Sado-masochistic mechanisms associated with the need to maintain a gratifying passive dependency again underlie the self-infliction of the lesions in many such instances.

Various methods of treatment for the neurodermatoses have been devised. Frequently, separation from the significant family members brings about clearing, with recurrence noted on return to the family.

The patient, a 46-year-old retired policeman, was seen with the chief complaint of a skin rash. The onset of his dermatitis occurred 25 years previously when, shortly after his marriage, he noted the gradual appearance of a diffuse scaling eruption of the scalp. Some time later he developed redness and scaling in the groin, and a more or less generalized eruption, especially around the sides of his neck and in the creases of the knees and elbows. The rash was intensely pruritic, and the patient frequently scratched until he bled. Two years prior to admission, the eruption became generalized. No relief was obtained from steroid therapy and a multitude of other medications. Because of a lifelong history of emotional problems, he was referred for psychiatric consultation.

The patient was the second of six children. His father was described as a strict disciplinarian who beat the children regularly with a cat-o'-nine-tails. Until 17 years of age, the patient was not allowed to stay out in the evening without his father's permission, and if he arrived home late he was beaten.

The mother was described as a warm, understanding person who was affectionate with the children but showed little love toward her husband. The patient's older brother was a fireman, who had retired 10 years previously following an acute psychotic episode. The other four siblings appeared to be in good health. The patient explained their good fortune with the statement, "By the time they arrived, my father had mellowed."

The patient's early development was unremarkable and his progress at school was average. He remembered that he was never able to express anger and never disobeyed his father's detailed instructions.

As an adolescent the patient was a shy, sensitive boy who was self-conscious and avoided social relationships with girls. There were exaggerated guilt feelings over masturbation. When confronted with social situations that were threatening, he would turn to drinking. He stated, "I had a terrific inferiority complex and liquor helped me to overcome it."

Since a civil service position offered a secure position and pension, he joined the police force at the suggestion of his father. When 20 years of age, he married in the hope of getting away from home. From the first there was marital difficulty, and he began to drink a quart of liquor daily.

Fourteen years before psychiatric consultation, the patient, during a riot, was struck on the head and sustained a concussion necessitating a brief hospitalization. Following his discharge he became tremulous and complained of extreme nervousness. His alcoholic intake increased in an effort to alleviate the pruritus, his anxiety, and the constant fear that he was about to die. He was discharged from the police force with a pension and the diagnosis of post-traumatic psychoneurosis.

During the subsequent two years he separated from his wife and child, lost contact with his family, and lived with an alcoholic woman who suffering from cirrhosis. There were several episodes of delirium tremens, and he was hospitalized for alcoholic neuropathy, hepatic cirrhosis, and hematemesis.

Eight years prior to this consultation and following the death of his female companion, he was warned by a physician that if he continued drinking he would probably not survive another year. He discontinued drinking, was reconciled with his wife, and his dermatitis cleared, leaving only a few eczematous patches. He returned to work as a law clerk, attended church regularly and, in his own words, "became a model citizen." He maintained a rigid routine involving difficult hours of work. He dressed meticulously and attempted to do a perfect job at the office.

During the past two years his rash again became generalized and intensely pruritic. His wife informed him that, while asleep, he scratched as if he were intent on killing himself. He was admitted to a hospital in the hope that separation from his family and job would help in the treatment of his skin condition.

When seen in psychiatric consultation, he appeared as a well-groomed, neatly attired, middle-aged man, alert and accurate, who spoke of his past experiences with obvious embarrassment. His memory was good, and he was well oriented, with an average intelligence and a normal fund of knowledge. He seemed anxious to please the interviewer and stated that he needed psychiatric help. During consultation he scratched freely. He volunteered that scratching usually brought him great relief and, at times, a satisfaction not unlike that of sexual pleasure. When psychotherapy was suggested, he quickly agreed. It was explained that he would be seen once a week for a period of 10 weeks by the psychiatrist in the outpatient department and that immediately preceding the interview he would be seen by the dermatologist for a brief examination.

During the first two interviews, an anamnesis was obtained, with particular emphasis on his current activity. He discussed the present fear of his father and the avoidance of situations that would bring him in contact with him. His wife frequently accused him of being a coward because of this, but he could not admit his fear to her. He described his wife as a stubborn, outspoken woman who was usually the disciplinarian with his 17-year-old boy. When he attempted to punish his son, his wife became outraged and pointed out to him how good it had been of both of them to accept him back eight years ago. He nevertheless denied that there was friction in the household and stated that, in many ways, they were an ideal family. His son had recently been arrested on a minor charge, and it was suggested to the patient that perhaps he was failing as a father by not setting limits for the son.

During the third visit it was noted that the scratching had increased, and there was no improvement in the skin condition. He stated early in the interview, "I followed your advice and asserted myself with the boy but was careful not to become angry." His wife had been angry with him, but he pacified her by taking her out for a drive. He admitted that he dared not express anger toward her for fear she would leave him. Scratching was frequent, especially when his fear of expressing anger was discussed. His wife insisted upon knowing what was going on in therapy. He resented this but felt he could not refuse to tell her. He was told that it was not necessary to tell her, and he appeared to have considerable anxiety over this.

At work he was accused by a colleague of being a perfectionist; he admitted being angry at this criticism. When it was suggested that he deal more directly with the problems confronting him at work and at home, he scratched and talked of his extreme loneliness. When the patient attempted to discuss early experiences and relationships, he was referred back to current areas of conflict.

At the fourth interview, his skin condition was much worse, and he was unable to attend work. He had purchased two suits of clothing without consulting his wife, who usually accompanied him. He made some rather feeble attempts to tell his wife that he preferred shopping without her but felt that it was unsuccessful. He turned to the interviewer and asked, "Doc, tell me, what do you do when you become angry?" There was a fantasy of telling off a coworker, and he remarked that recently he felt resentful and angry, wondering if his increased scratching was related to this.

At the time of the sixth interview, his skin remained unchanged. He expressed his fear of losing control of his anger and appeared more aware of his current problems. He talked of his helplessness and became angry with the interviewer for not being of more help to him.

With the seventh interview, his skin looked considerably better. He had informed his wife that he was the boss around the house and, following a minor altercation with his son, had told him that he was "not yet dry behind the ears." He appeared surprised that his wife was "snapping to," and that his son was spending more time around the house.

In the ninth week, his skin improved remarkably. He related an incident with pride in which, when his wife refused to prepare breakfast for him, he had advised her that she had better behave herself, ordered her to the bedroom, and had intercourse with her. That evening he took her to the movies and noted that she was affectionate.

He remarked that during the previous week he had been able to tell his employer that too much of the work fell on him and that this should be changed.

Treatment was terminated after twelve visits. The patient was seen in dermatology clinic two months later. His skin had cleared completely except for a small area of dermatitis behind the knees. He was feeling well, had no difficulty sleeping, required no medication, and was much satisfied with the changes in his relations with his family and employers.

Schoenberg and Carr have found that patients who respond promptly with remission of neurodermatitis to this brief psychotherapy may be selected by their evident hostility during initial diagnostic interviews and by a high frequency of hostile content responses on the Rorschach test. The existence of overt psychotic symptoms did not preclude the active psychotherapeutic approach.

BIBLIOGRAPHY

General and Theoretical

Alexander, F., French, T. M., and Pollack, G. H.: Psychosomatic Specificity. Experimental Study and Results. Chicago, University of Chicago Press, 1968.

Cannon, W. B.: Bodily Changes in Pain, Hunger, Fear and Rage. 2nd ed. New York, D. Appleton Century Company, 1929.

Hofling, C. K.: Textbook of Psychiatry for Medical Practice. 2nd ed. Philadelphia, J. B. Lippincott Company, 1968.

Kubie, L. S.: The central representation of the symbolic process in psychosomatic disorders. Psychosom. Med., 15:1–7, 1953.

Lipowski, Z. J.: Psychiatry of somatic diseases: Epidemiology, pathogenesis, classification. Compr. Psychiatry, 16:105–124, 1975.

Mason, J. W.: The hope of psychoendocrine research. Psychosom. Med., 30:Suppl:565–575, 1968.

Miller, N. E.: Effects of learning on visceral functions: Biofeedback. N. Engl. J. Med., 296:1274–1278, 1977.

O'Connor, J. F., and Stern, L. O.: Symptom alternation. An evaluation of the theory. Arch. Gen. Psychiatry, 16:432–436, 1967.

Pavlov, I. P.: Experimental Psychology. New York, Philosophical Library, 1957.

Rahe, R. H., and Arthur, R. J.: Life change and illness studies. J. Human Stress, 4:3–15, 1978.

Ruesch, J., et al.: Chronic Disease and Psychological Invalidism. Berkeley and Los Angeles, University of California Press, 1951.

Sachar, E. J.: Some current issues in psychosomatic research. Psychiatric Annals, 2(8):22–35, 1972.

Sifneos, P. E., Apfel-Savitz, R., and Frankel, F. H.: The phenomenon of "alexithymia." Proceedings, 11th European Conference on Psychosomatic Medicine. J. Psychother. Psychosom., 28:45–57, 1977.

Titchener, J. L., and Levine, M.: Surgery As a Human Experience. New York, Oxford University Press, 1960.

Weiner, H., Hofer, M. A., and Stunkard, A. J. (eds.): Brain, Behavior, and Bodily Disease. Proc. Assoc. Res. Nerv. Ment. Dis. 59. New York, Raven Press, 1981.

ALIMENTARY SYSTEM

Ader, R.: Experimentally induced gastric lesions. Adv. Psychosom. Med., 6:1–39, 1971.

Bruch, H.: Eating Disorders: Obesity, Anorexia Nervosa, and the Person Within. New York, Basic Books, 1973.

Druss, R. G., O'Connor, J. F., Prudden, J. F., and Stern, L. P.: Psychologic response to colectomy. Arch. Gen. Psychiatry, 18:53–59, 1968; 20:419–427, 1969.

Engel, G. L., and Reichsmann, F.: Spontaneous and experimentally induced depressions in an infant with gastric fistula. J. Am. Psychoanal. Assoc., 4:428–452, 1956.

Olkinuora, M.: Psychosocial aspects in a series of bruxists compared with a group of non-bruxists. Proc. Finn. Dent. Soc., 68:200–208, 1972.

Schoenberg, B., Carr, A. C., Kutscher, A. H., and Zegarelli, E. V.: Chronic idiopathic orolingual pain. N.Y. State J. Med., 71:1832–1837, 1971.

Young, S. J., Alpers, D. H., and Norland, C. C., et al.: Psychiatric illness and the irritable bowel syndrome. Gastroenterology, 70:162–166, 1976.

Obesity

Bruch, H., and Voss, W. R.: Infantile obesity and later weight control in the baboon. Nature, 250:268–269, 1974.

Coscina, D., Godse, D. D., and Stancer, H. C.: Neurochemical correlates of hypothalamic obesity in rats. Behav. Biol., 16:365–372, 1976.

Glucksman, M. L., Hirsh, J., McCully, R. S., Baum, B. A., and Knittle, J. L.: The response of obese patients to weight reduction. Psychosom. Med., 30:359–373, 1968.

Green, R. S., and Ray, J. H.: Treatment of compulsive eating disturbances with anticonvulsant medication. Am. J. Psychiatry, 131:428–432, 1974.

Halmi, K. A., Long, M., Stunkard, A. J., and Mason, E.: Psychiatric diagnosis of morbidly obese gastric bypass patients. Am. J. Psychiatry, 137:470–472, 1980.

Kornhaber, A.: Obesity-depression: Clinical evaluation with a new anorexigenic agent. Psychosomatics, 14:162–167, 1973.

Levitz, L. S., and Stunkard, A. J.: A therapeutic coalition for obesity: Behavior modification and patient self-help. Am. J. Psychiatry, 131:423–427, 1974.

Nelson, R. A., Anderson, L. F., Gastineau, C. F., et al.: Physiology and natural history of obesity. J.A.M.A., 223:627–630, 1973.

Stunkard, A. J., d'Aquili, E., Fox, S., et al.: Influence of social class on obesity and thinness in children. J.A.M.A., 221:579–584, 1974.

Anorexia Nervosa

Cantwell, D. D., Sturzenberger, S., Burroughs, J., Salkin, B., and Green, J. K.: Anorexia nervosa: An affective disorder. Arch. Gen. Psychiatry, *34*:1087–1093, 1977.

Crisp, A. H., and Kalucy, R. S.: Aspects of the perceptual disorder in anorexia nervosa. Br. J. Med. Psychol., *47*:349–361, 1974.

Dally, P.: Anorexia Nervosa. New York, Grune & Stratton, 1969.

Garfinkel, P. E., Moldofsky, H., and Garner, D. M.: The heterogeneity of anorexia nervosa. Arch. Gen. Psychiatry, *37*:1037–1046, 1980.

Goldberg, S. C., Halmi, K. A., Eckert, E. D., Gasper, R. C., and Davis, J. M.: Cyproheptadine in anorexia nervosa. Br. J. Psychiatry, *134*: 67–70, 1979.

Halmi, K. A., and Loney, J.: Familial alcoholism in anorexia nervosa. Br. J. Psychiatry, *123*:53–54, 1973.

Liebman, R., Minuchin, S., and Baker, L.: An integrated treatment program for anorexia nervosa. Am. J. Psychiatry, *131*:432–436, 1974.

Lucas, A. R., Duncan, J. W., and Piens, V.: The treatment of anorexia nervosa. Am. J. Psychiatry, *133*:1034–1038, 1976.

Maloney, M. J., and Farrell, M. K.: Treatment of severe weight loss in anorexia nervosa with hyperalimentation and psychotherapy. Am. J. Psychiatry, *137*:310–314, 1980.

Mecklenburg, R. S., Loriaux, D. L., Thompson, R. H., et al.: Hypothalamic dysfunction in patients with anorexia nervosa. Medicine, *53*:147–159, 1974.

Palazzoli, M. S.: Self-starvation: From Individual to Family Therapy in the Treatment of Anorexia Nervosa. Translated by A. Pomerans. New York, Jason Aronson, 1978.

Taipale, V., Larkio-Miettinen, K., Valanne, E. H., et al.: Anorexia nervosa in boys. Psychosomatics, *13*:236–240, 1972.

CARDIOVASCULAR SYSTEM

Framkin, K., Nathan, R. J., Prout, M. F., and Cohen, M. C.: Non-pharmacologic control of essential hypertension in man: A critical review of the experimental literature. Psychosom. Med., *40*:294–320, 1978.

Harburg, E., Erfurt, J. C., Chape, C., et al.: Socioecological stressor areas and black-white blood pressure: Detroit. J. Chronic Dis., *26*:595–611, 1973.

Kornfeld, D. S., Heller, S. S., Frank, K. A., et al.: Personality and psychological factors in postcardiotomy delirium. Arch. Gen. Psychiatry, *31*:249–253, 1974.

Liljefors, I., and Rahe, R. H.: An identical twin study of psychosocial factors in coronary heart disease in Sweden. Psychosom. Med., *32*:523–542, 1970.

Rahe, R. H., Hervig, L., and Rosenman, R. H.: Heritability of Type A behavior. Psychosom. Med., *40*:478–486, 1978.

Rosenman, R. H., and Friedman, M.: Behavior patterns, blood lipids, and coronary heart disease. J.A.M.A., *184*:934–938, 1963.

ENDOCRINE SYSTEM

Bale, R. N.: Brain damage in diabetes mellitus. Br. J. Psychiatry, *122*:337–341, 1973.

Levine, M. (ed.): Endocrines and the central nervous system. Proc. Assoc. Res. Nerv. Ment. Dis. 63. Baltimore, Williams & Wilkins Company, 1966.

Stein, S. P., and Charles E.: Emotional factors in juvenile diabetes mellitus: Study of early life experiences of adolescent diabetics. Am. J. Psychiatry, *128*:700–704, 1971.

Tattersall, R. B., and Pyke, D. A.: Diabetes in identical twins. Lancet, 2:1120–1125, 1972.

GENITOURINARY SYSTEM

Brown, E., and Barglow, P.: Pseudocyesis. Arch. Gen. Psychiatry, *24*:221–229, 1971.

Calderone, M. S. (ed.): Abortion in the United States. New York, Hoeber-Harper, 1958.

Cohen, R. L.: The treatment of "interstitial cystitis" as a migraine equivalent: Report of four cases. Compr. Psychiatry, *4*:58–61, 1963.

Engels, W. D., Palter, C. J., and Wittkower, E. D.: Emotional settings of functional amenorrhea. Pschosom. Med., *26*:682–700, 1964.

Ewing, J. A., and Rouse, B. A.: Therapeutic abortion and a prior psychiatric history. Am. J. Psychiatry, *130*:37–40, 1973.

Foster, F. G., Cohn, G. L., and McKegney, F. P.: Psychobiologic factors and individual survival on chronic renal hemodialysis; a two year follow-up. Part I. Psychosom. Med., *35*:64–82, 1973.

Herzberg, B., and Coppen, A.: Changes in psychological symptoms in women taking oral contraceptives. Br. J. Psychiatry, *116*:161–164, 1970.

Jansson, B.: Mental disorder after abortion. Acta Psychiatr. Scand., *41*:87–110, 1965.

Kane, F. J., Lipton, M. A., Krall, A. R., and Obrist, P. A.: Psychoendocrine study of oral contraceptives. Am. J. Psychiatry, *127*:443–450, 1970.

Mendlewicz, J., Schulman, J. C., DeShutter, B., et al.: Chronic prostatitis: psychosomatic incidence. Psychother. Psychosom., *19*:118–125, 1971.

Peel, J., and Potts, M.: Textbook of Contraceptive Practice. New York, Cambridge University Press, 1969.

Viederman, M.: Adaptive and maladaptive regression in hemodialysis. Psychiatry, *37*:68–77, 1974.

Viederman, M.: The search for meaning in renal transplantation. Psychiatry, 37:283–290, 1974.

Ziegler, F. J., Rodgers, D. A., and Prentiss, R. J.: Psychosocial response to vasectomy. Arch. Gen. Psychiatry, 21:46–54, 1969.

NERVOUS SYSTEM

Annexton, M.: Treatment of impotence by penile implants. J.A.M.A., 241:13–17, 1979.

Castelnuovo-Tedesco, P.: Organ transplant, body image, psychosis. Psychoanal. Q., 42:349–363, 1973.

Connolly, F. H., and Gibson, M.: Dysmorphophobia: A long-term study. Br. J. Psychiatry, 132:568–570, 1978.

Druss, R. G.: Changes in body image following augmentation breast surgery. Int. J. Psychoanal. Psychother., 2:248–256, 1973.

Druss, R. G., Symonds, F. C., and Criklair, G. F.: The problem of somatic delusions in patients seeking cosmetic surgery. Plast. Reconstr. Surg., 48:246–249, 1971.

Kalick, S. M.: Toward an interdisciplinary psychology of appearances. Psychiatry, 41:243–253, 1978.

Kolb, L. C.: Disturbances of the body-image. In Arieti, S. (ed.): American Handbook of Psychiatry. Vol. IV. New York, Basic Books, 1975, pp. 810–837.

Little, J. C.: The athlete's neurosis—a deprivation crisis. Acta Psychiatr. Scand., 45:187–197, 1969.

Schonfeld, W. A.: Gynecomastia in adolescence. Personality effects. Arch. Gen. Psychiatry, 5:46–54, 1961.

Simmel, M. L.: A study of phantoms after amputation of the breast. Neuropsychologia, 4:331–350, 1966.

OTHER

Headache

Carroll, J. D., and Hilton, B. P.: The effects of reserpine injection on methysergide treated control and migrainous subjects. Headache, 14:149–156, 1974.

Frazier, S. H.: Complex problems of pain as seen in headache, painful phantom and other states. In Arieti, S. V. (ed.): American Handbook of Psychiatry. Vol. IV. New York, Basic Books, pp. 838–853, 1975.

Jammes, J. L.: The treatment of cluster headaches with prednisone. Dis. Nerv. Syst., 36(7):375–376, 1975.

Misch, K. A.: Development of heart valve lesions during methysergide therapy. Br. Med. J., 2:365–366, 1974.

Sjaastad, O.: The significance of blood serotonin levels in migraine. Acta Neurol. Scand., 51:200–210, 1975.

RESPIRATORY SYSTEM

Dudley, D. C., Martin, C. J., and Holmes, T. H.: Psychophysiological studies ot pulmonary ventilation. Psychosom. Med., 26:645–660, 1964.

Freeman, E. H., Feingold, B. F., Schlesinger, K., and Gorman, F. J.: Psychological variables in allergic disorders. A review. Psychosom. Med., 26:543–575, 1964.

Kalogerakis, M. G.: Role of olfaction in sexual development. Psychosom. Med., 25:420–431, 1963.

Missri, J. C., and Alexander, S.: Hyperventilation syndrome. J.A.M.A., 240:2093–2189, 1978.

Purcell, K., Brady, K., Chai, H., Maser, J., Molk, L., Gordon, N., and Means, J.: The effect on asthma in children of experimental separation from the family. Psychosom. Med., 31:144–169, 1969.

Wheatley, C. E.: Hyperventilation syndrome: A frequent cause of chest pain. Chest, 68:195–199, 1975.

SKIN

Ely, N. F., Veehey, J. W., and Holmes, T. H.: Experimental studies of skin inflammation. Psychosom. Med., 25:264–284, 1963.

Schoenberg, B., and Carr, A. C.: An investigation of criteria for brief psychotherapy of neurodermatitis. Psychosom. Med., 25:253–263, 1963.

25

PERSONALITY DISORDERS

"...and a sick soul is always astray and cannot either attain or endure, never does it cease to desire."

Cicero

JAMES COWLES PRICHARD
Author of *Treatise on Insanity;* credited with outlining the personality disorders. (From Smith, G. M.: A History of the Bristol Royal Infirmary. Bristol, Arrowsmith, 1917, p. 471.)

The group of personality disorders includes a wide range of cases in which malfunctioning is expressed in inflexible and limited patterns of behavior. At times these personality patterns and traits are compatible with social success and satisfaction when the particular features of the individual make-up are accepted and rewarded by the culture or vocation, or both. The inflexibility of the personality or its special vulnerability to particular stresses remains unnoticed, except perhaps in the form of a peculiarity or eccentricity, until the individual is required to adapt to another environment or is exposed to personal or environmental pressure previously avoided or escaped. In other personality disorders, difficulties in social and sexual adaptation are evident and occur repetitively throughout life, in spite of adequate intellectual capacity.

The personality disorders differ from those previously discussed in that the psychopathological manifestations seldom present themselves in the grossly regressive disturbances of the behavior, affect, or thought of the psychoses, nor in the exaggerated and fixed psychological defenses that characterize the psychoneurotic. Nor does the disorder present itself in the form of somatic symptoms due to an expression of anxiety or other affect through disruption of psychophysiological functions.

In this chapter, the authors have for the most part followed the categorical listings contained in the third edition of the Diagnostic and Statistical Manual of Mental Disorders (DSM-III). However, where the authors of that manual have made deletions or transfers that remain unrecognized worldwide, we have maintained the existing international recognition. Therefore, the cyclothymic personality disorders and their long recognized variants—the hypomanic and the melancholic—are included. Frances' commentary on the personality disorders section of DSM-III provides a perspective upon the decision-making that established the categories therein, as well as his perceptions of their strengths and weaknesses.

The cyclothymic, paranoid, schizoid, and schizotypal personality disorders are recognized as forms of personality organization similar to those found in patients with the various types of affective and schizophrenic reactions, but in the former, ego functioning and reality testing remain intact and allow a generally acceptable social adaptation. Presumably, the paranoid, cyclothymic, schizoid, obsessive-compulsive, and melancholic personalities form a reservoir of persons vulnerable to psychotic disorganization when exposed to a sufficiently severe and appropriate loss or frustration, with concomitant stress and affective arousal beyond the ego's capacity of containment.

Among those personality disorders demonstrating often histrionic emotional display, with erratic behavior frequently harmful to self and others and with evident and repetitive difficuly in controlling drives, are the histrionic, narcissistic, antisocial, and borderline subcategories. For the most part, this second group of personality disorders comes to medical or psychiatric attention through contact in or referral from social institutions such as courts, prisons, and special schools. They now constitute problems for large organizations such as the armed services and labor unions. This antisocial group of people was formerly termed "psychopaths."

A third group are those disorders in which patients have persisting, exaggerated, fearful behaviors. These are the avoidant, dependent, and compulsive disorders.

Etiology

It was formerly believed that the unmodifiable behavior patterns of such persons were matters of inborn disposition, constitutionally influenced or directed. The assumption of a constitutional basis has failed to yield any understanding of the behavior of such persons; it is only logical that such behavior disturbances should be explainable by theories analogous to those that have been so fruitful in illuminating other reaction types.

Thus the pathologic behavior of those with the personality disorders presumably has a psychogenetic origin. The major defect in the personality rests in failure to establish an identity with constructive and socially useful adaptations or to evolve those controls that allow the delay and repression of impulses to action often generated by anger. Loss or absence of parents and parental substitutes and limited contacts with other adults and peers often deprive the growing child, who later presents psychopathic features, of the experiences necessary to establish an ego identity through the process of identification. In some instances the behavior may be the result of frustration in efforts to achieve satisfaction of such fundamental needs as love, security, recognition, respect, and success. The child who was rejected may react by becoming resentful, rebellious, and antisocial, and thus establish a "negative identity" that brings some ego satisfactions.

The origin of these personality disorders can best be regarded as the expression of an arrested or deviated development of personality. Whether or not this behavior represents the consequence of a development fault—an experiential lack in the process of emotional maturation through deficiency of interpersonal contact or a character neurosis—it denotes the continuing activity of psychopathological forces set in motion very early in life. The persisting drive to or reaction to aggressiveness, passivity, frustration, or deviated sexuality gives a compulsive chronicity to the behavior.

From studies of children deprived of early parental care through loss, or placement in foundling or children's homes, and studies of animals exposed to maternal or peer deprivations at certain critical periods in early development, experiential deprivation often appears to lead to persisting defects in social and sexual behavior. Whether such behavioral pathology may be modified by substitutive experiences later in life remains uncertain. For the growing child, neither the critical periods for social experiencing nor their duration or intensity are established or fully defined.

It has been suggested from studies of "acting out" in children, adolescents, and adults in psychoanalytic therapy that the critical experiences that initiate impulse control take place during the second year of life. At this time the growing child undergoes those series of transactions with the mother or her substitute designed to establish control of activity and the somatic functions of bladder and bowel so that he or she may become socialized. At this same time he commences to evolve the highly complex motor activity concerned with speech. Impairment in development of language has been pointed to as a common finding in children and adolescents who display delinquent and antisocial behavior. Inconsistent or deficient mothering at this stage is thought to lead to limitations of those ego and superego functions which characterize the later behavior of the adult with a personality disorder. Here, future research promises to provide a more precise understanding of the deficits in family transactional processes which underlie later intrapsychic inadequacies.

DISORDERS OF PERSONALITY

Cyclothymic Personality

Kahlbaum introduced the term *cyclothymia* to designate the predisposition of the individual to alternating moods of cheerfulness, vivacity, and mild depression; cyclothymia also indicates the tempo of the personality, i.e., whether it is lively or retarded. While oscillations are not uncommon, mood and tempo continue to harmonize and the different components of the personality in their reactions and expressions function as a unit. Kretschmer characterized as *cycloid* those people who are subject to cyclic variations of mood, tending to swing between exhilaration and depression, but not to pathological extremes. As might be expected, the cycloids or cyclothymes are predisposed to the development of manic-depressive or affective psychoses. Christopher Smart (1722–1771), the English poet who on at least one occasion developed what was undoubtedly a manic-depressive psychosis, said of himself, "I have a greater compass both of mirth and melancholy than another."

Polar variants of the cyclothymic are the hypomanic and melancholic personalities.

HYPOMANIC PERSONALITY. The hypomanics are outgoing and cheerful enjoyers of life. They are free from internal inhibitions, many being vivacious and sprightly and showing a sustained buoyant, confident, aggressive, optimistic, perhaps exhilarated reaction. They are usually energetic, gregarious, pleasure-loving, unstable, given to fleeting enthusiasms, and easily swayed by new impressions. Some are blustering, domineering, argumentative, and hypercritical. Their judgment often appears superficial, and they have a ready excuse for their failures. The hypomanic cannot subordinate himself or herself, resents frustrations and disappointments, and is usually adept at talking the way out of difficulties. The hypomanic woman is often a chatterbox.

MELANCHOLIC PERSONALITY. Those cyclothymics at the melancholic pole are often kindly, quiet, sympathetic, good-tempered people, lacking in strained eccentricity but tending to be easily depressed. They feel little of the normal joy of living and are inclined to be lonely and solemn, gloomy, submissive, pessimistic, and self-depreciatory. They are prone to express regrets and feelings of inadequacy and hopelessness. They are often meticulous, perfectionistic, overconscientious, and preoccupied with work; they feel responsibility keenly and are easily discouraged under new conditions. They are fearful of disapproval and tend to suffer in silence and perhaps to cry easily, although usually not in the presence of others. A tendency to hesitation, indecision, and caution betrays an inherent feeling of insecurity. A few are irritable and paranoid. Many psychiatrists feel that the melancholic temperament develops as a reaction formation against aggression.

Paranoid Personality

Suspicious, stubborn, secretive, obstinate, and resentful of discipline, the paranoid individual is lonely, insecure, unhappy, and brooding. When his wishes are not met he tends to become sullen, morose, irritable, or threatening. He is strikingly sensitive concerning the attitudes of others, usually exaggerates their behavior, and misinterprets it as directed by wishes to harm him. Lacking in a sense of humor, he is often perceived by others as sarcastic, derogatory, querulous, embittered, or resentful. When his points of view or actions are questioned, he responds with arguments and with aggressive and uncompromising positions. Moreover, he belittles and criticizes others. His interpersonal relations, characteristically demonstrate a "chip on the shoulder."

His insecurity is often disguised by an intense drive for achievement which may impel him to strive for goals beyond his innate capacity.

While often highly efficient because of his striving, meticulousness, and precision — compulsive features — his interpersonal competence is impaired by his envy and jealousy of others. In positions of authority his behavior is often tyrannical.

Schizoid Personality

The schizoid (Bleuler) or schizothymic (Kretschmer) personality is marked by incongruities of the feeling-life coupled, characteristically, with a poorly socialized personality. In the schizoid personality the feeling-life lacks the resonance and responsiveness that characterize the cyclothymic. Its contrasting affective poles are sensitiveness on the one hand and dullness or coldness on the other. The sensitive schizoid feels lonely, imperfectly understood, and isolated. Timid, shy, self-conscious, often self-dissatisfied, perhaps stubborn, secretive, and suspicious, he is wounded constantly.

In childhood, he is often teased by his playmates who look upon him as "queer." In school or college, he rarely takes part in rough-and-tumble games but strives for a sense of security through superiority in school work. Silent and unsociable, his love of books is often a substitute for human companionship. He chooses subjects of an abstract, perhaps philosophical, nature rather than those of a concrete, objective type. He may be imaginative and idealistic, perhaps with vague schemes for bettering humanity. Many schizoids of this group attempt art or poetry. Some are successful in transmuting their daydreams into cultural values.

Many of these sensitive persons suffer from a sense of isolation. What their thoughts may be is often unknown, even to their friends, since others are rarely admitted into their confidence. Many have feelings of inferiority and of discomfort in interpersonal relations and are aloof to the opposite sex. In speaking of the sensitive schizoids, Kretschmer comments that they close the shutters of their houses in order to lead a dream life. Many have a genuine love of nature, while those who have had cultural opportunities often show a rare esthetic taste, gentle manners, and an uncommon avoidance of the coarse or vulgar.

Frequently, they are ambitious, conscientious, meticulous, and perfectionistic. The overconscientiousness of the schizoid tends, however, to exert a paralyzing effect on initiative or variation, with the result that he often performs his duties in a stereotyped, almost ritualistic manner. Some schizoids are overscrupulous, and by making a virtue of their repression become ascetics or prudes. To a certain number of these frail, sensitive individuals, the harsh realities and frustrating experiences of life become too painful and they retreat into a world of fantasy.

Many schizoids, while retaining an imaginative attitude toward life and its experiences, lack the finer sensibilities just described. Some members of this second group are kindly and honest, but they are also emotionally dull, taciturn, unsociable, and given to rites and cults. Because of a lack of spontaneity, they appear to be indifferent, indolent, colorless persons. Others are often cold, reserved, callous individuals, frequently jealous of those more happily adjusted. Some shrink unhappily away into themselves and become preoccupied with unwholesome ruminations. In adolescence they are usually willful, disobedient, headstrong, moody, passively stubborn, ill-tempered, easily offended, and resentful of advice, supervision, or correction. Such a schizoid may be described as a "lone wolf" who prefers to get along without strong ties to other people. Often his early relationships within the family are disturbed and unsatisfying.

The self-confidence that sometimes characterizes these unfeeling, distrustful individuals will be found to be of compensatory origin and to arise from a sense of insecurity which, in turn, stimulates defensive attitudes and reactions that tend to increase and complicate the problems of adjustment. They have to show the world how tough they are lest they betray their shyness, diffidence, and sense of insecurity.

The mistrustful schizoid who expects and detects disapproval and insult may feel safer to endure in silence with self-restraint and sullenness, retaliating, as it were, in daydreams, fancying how he may punish and destroy his alleged adversaries. In less marked types, the dearth of esthetic sensitiveness may be shown by a neglect of personal appearance, home, and family, or by a lack of tact and other evidences of social sensibilities and amenities. A rigid moral idealism expressed in inflexible rules of conduct and associated with a self-satisfied intolerance is common.

Actually, few schizoids belong to the purely sensitive or to the purely unfeeling type. In the majority of them we find characteristics from both groups. Often, to our surprise, we find a sensitive and tender nature hidden beneath a cold and unresponsive exterior. Similarly one must not conclude that the schizoid type always exists in pure form. Often it is not clearly differentiated from the cyclothymic type, in whom there is a sliding scale between the cyclothymic and the schizoid.

Bleuler preferred the term *syntonic* to Kretschmer's *cycloid* to describe a personality tendency opposed in characteristics to the schizoid. The syntonic person is in vital contact with his environment, is emotionally lively and responsive, and his affects are versatile in expression and appropriate to the occasion. Syntonic characteristics reach their greatest development in harmoniously adjusted persons, whereas schizoid elements reach their maximum development in the schizophrenic psychoses.

Schizotypal Personality

Those individuals whose personality functioning is typified by their idiosyncratic perceptions, thought processes, and behavior who yet may not be considered as clearly schizophrenic may be classified here. They may be identified through having bizarre fantasies or preoccupations in early life or magical thinking later, or through ideas of reference or some persecutory ideation. From time to time they experience illusory perceptions or a sense of depersonalization or derealization. Their speech may be odd or their word usage deviant, but they are never incoherent and never clearly demonstrate loose associations. As with the schizoid personality, they tend to be social isolates and their constricted and sometimes inappropriate affective interchanges make interpersonal relations problematic.

Evidences of anxiety and other affective disturbances may occur. The behavioral traits limit both social and occupational functioning. When serious disruptions occur in their lives, brief reactive psychoses may erupt.

The lack of odd behaviors differentiates the schizotypal personality and depersonalization disorders from the schizoid. Tables 25–1 and 25–2 differentiate the schizotypal personality from borderline personality disorders.

Histrionic Personality

More clearly defined for women than for men, this type of personality makeup is recognized by the traits of vanity, self-indulgence, and self-centered attitudes associated with histrionic behavior, dramatization, or exhibitionism. Affectively, the hysterical personality is labile, emotionally capricious, and prone to emotional outbursts. Sexual behavior in women of this type is provocative and coquettish, with erotization of nonsexual relations. In actuality there often exists sexual fear with frigidity in women who have a pronounced masculine protest. The provocative attention-getting behavior appears to overlie a driving dependent need, demanding in quality. There is reason to consider that many women of this type have been spoiled and overprotected in earlier years.

Thus the hysterical woman is actively engaged in the social world yet responds badly to frustrations in reality. Possible attainment of the wish-fulfilling fantasies arouses excessive excitability. Her active fantasy life is filled with distortions of the environment into sensual and sexual preoccupations which exaggerate her excitement and lead to tension due to her inner inhibitions against this drive. Her self-presentation is that of the child-woman.

Such women are fearful of their sexual drives, yet seek through seductive behavior to achieve security and power vicariously through the passionate engagement of a man to themselves. Se-

TABLE 25-1   Results of Questionnaire Study of Schizotypal Personality Items*

	FREQUENCY		FACTOR LOADING				DISCRIMINANT FUNCTION	
	Borderline (B) (N = 808)	Control (C) (N = 808)	B Only (N = 808) 1	2	B + C (N = 1,616) 1	2	B vs C (N = 808 vs 808)	Schizotypal vs Unstable (N = 222 vs 234)
Odd communication (*not* gross formal thought disorder); e.g., speech that is tangential, digressive, vague, overelaborate, circumstantial, metaphorical	58	11	08	**33**†	23	**56**	.35	-.55
Ideas of reference, self-referential thinking	58	16	-07	**58**	11	**66**	.23	–
Suspiciousness or paranoid ideation	59	17	-04	**50**	15	**62**	.21	-.28
Recurrent illusions, sensing the presence of a force or person not actually present (e.g., "I felt as if my dead mother were in the room with me"), depersonalization or derealization, not associated with panic attacks	33	5	02	**39**	12	**49**	.17	–
Magical thinking, e.g., superstitiousness, clairvoyance, telepathy, "sixth sense," "others can feel my feelings"	47	10	01	**49**	11	**58**	.24	-1.04
Inadequate rapport in face-to-face interaction due to constricted or inappropriate affect; e.g., aloof, distant, cold, superficial histrionic, effusive	66	23	05	**20**	26	**43**	.24	–
Undue social anxiety or hypersensitivity to real or imagined criticism	85	60	18	**25**	**35**	25	–	–
Social isolation; e.g., no close friends or confidants, social contacts limited to essential everyday tasks	58	29	-04	**17**	16	**33**	.12	–

*Judged applicable only if characteristic of long-term functioning and not limited to discrete episodes of illness.
†Highest loading is indicated by boldface type.
From Spitzer, R. L., Endicott, J., and Gibbon, M.: Crossing the border into borderline personality and borderline schizophrenia. Arch. Gen. Psychiatry, 36:18–19, 1979.

TABLE 25–2 Results of Questionnaire Study of Borderline Personality Items*

| | FREQUENCY | | FACTOR LOADING | | | | DISCRIMINANT FUNCTION | |
| | Borderline (B) (N = 808) | Control (C) (N = 808) | B Only (N = 808) | | B + C (N = 1,616) | | B vs C (N = 808 vs 808) | Schizotypal vs Unstable (N = 222 vs 234) |
			1	2	1	2		
Identity disturbance manifested by uncertainty about several issues relating to identity, such as self-image, gender identity, long-term goals or career choice, friendship patterns, values, and loyalties; e.g., "Who am I?" "I feel like I am my sister when I am good"	80	33	23†	13	43	34	.36	—
A pattern of unstable and intense interpersonal relationships; e.g., marked shifts of attitude, idealization, devaluation, manipulation (consistently using others for own ends)	80	30	45	–01	61	26	.36	1.39
Impulsivity or unpredictability in at least two areas that are potentially self-damaging; e.g., spending, sex, gambling, drug or alcohol use, shoplifting, overeating, physically self-damaging acts	78	34	44	–01	52	22	.24	—

Inappropriate intense anger or lack of control of anger; e.g., frequently loses temper, always angry	68	27	**39**	07	**47**	27	.19	—
Physically self-damaging acts; e.g., suicidal gestures, self-mutilation, recurrent accidents, or physical fights	53	16	**44**	−02	**48**	19	.16	−.28
Work history or school achievement unstable or below expected on basis of intelligence, training, or opportunities‡	75	38	**22**	−00	**41**	21	—	−.47
Affective instability: marked shifts from normal mood to depression, irritability, or anxiety, usually lasting hours and only rarely for more than a few days, with a return to normal mood	77	43	**45**	03	**52**	15	.12	—
Chronic feelings of emptiness or boredom	74	38	**26**	04	**44**	24	.13	—
Problems tolerating being alone; e.g., frantic efforts to avoid being alone, depressed when alone	58	38	**38**	−03	**42**	04	—	.47

*Judged applicable only if characteristic of long-term functioning and not limited to discrete episodes of illness.
†Highest loading is indicated in boldface.
‡Not included in final list.
From Spitzer, R. L., Endicott, J., and Gibbon, M.: Crossing the border into borderline personality and borderline schizophrenia. Arch. Gen. Psychiatry, 36:18–19, 1979.

cretly they are competitive—against men as a means of conquering them and against women as a method of exclusion. Their seductive behavior to men then covers both an aggressive element and a wish for a dependent childish relationship. Often they complain of shyness yet appear highly competent in actual social life, as they are lively and engaging. They avoid and are uncomfortable with the exact and precise. At home with their families their behavior is frequently regressive and thought of as childish and helpless. Some women of this type have been brought up closely attached to the mother yet also stimulated and treated seductively by the father, who, as they approach adulthood, then condemns their budding sexuality.

Another group of women have essentially similar personality traits but expressed in more blatant forms, with insistent competitiveness and dependency needs. These women demonstrate an exaggerated exhibitionism, sometimes coupled with lying and deceitful behavior or play-acting to attract attention or avoid shame. Here the affective responses may appear shallow or fraudulent. Their personal contacts, initially strong and idolatrous, usually dissipate, when their hopes are not fulfilled, into bitterness, isolation, and depression. These women with less well-structured personalities come from more inconsistent and disorganized families where there is often evidence of a greater degree of maternal deprivation due to illness or egocentricity. Evidences of emotional immaturity are seen early in life in such childish neurotic symptoms as enuresis, thumbsucking, and fetishism and a history of an early fantasy world peopled with imaginary companions to offset an actual isolation. They have seen themselves as isolated, alone, or different.

The "Don Juan" character represents this personality type in men. Again, there is the histrionic display. The drive for sexual conquest and exhibitionism often rests upon a hidden feeling of masculine inadequacy and is coupled with the need to deceive, outwit, and conquer. The Don Juan makes evident through the repetition of his conquests the lack of satisfaction in each successful affair.

Borderline Personality

Both Bleuler and Adolf Meyer recognized that the onset of the schizophrenic reaction was often concealed by symptom formations considered as neurotic. The obsessive-compulsive and hysterical façades are the most commonly recognized. Hoch and Polatin described what they termed "*pseudoneurotic schizophrenia*," a condition frequently seen in private practice and only occasionally in the mental hospital. As the name implies, the dynamics are psychotic in character, although the symptom picture, at least in the early stages, appears neurotic. The pseudoneurotic schizophrenics usually show a mixture of anxiety and of phobic, obsessive, depressive and hypochondriacal symptoms. The underlying schizophrenic disorder is hidden by a façade of neurotic manifestations. Hoch and Polatin spoke of the symptomatology as a pan-neurosis. A diffuse anxiety pervades all the patients' life experiences, and, although they try to force pleasurable experiences, they do not derive pleasure from anything. The neurotic manifestations constantly shift but are never completely absent. The true neurotics are usually anxious to describe their symptoms in minute detail and press their physician with their explanations. The pseudoneurotic schizophrenics' explanations are vague, indistinct, and often contradictory, and are repeated in a stereotyped manner without details. Sexuality is often chaotic. Some of these patients have brief psychotic episodes. About one third of the patients with this misleading neurotic overlay gradually go on to a frank psychosis, although with less regression than that observed in the usual schizophrenic.

Since these early phenomenological and descriptive clinical accounts, many others have reported on behavioral and symptomatic expressions, and given psychodynamic formulations and reports of psychological test findings.

More recently, Grinker and his colleagues have attempted an analysis of the borderline syndromes and have concluded that there exist four separate subgroups differing in behavior from those previously so classified.

The first, considered to have the least well developed ego functions and most closely related to the psychotic, expressed their abnormality in inappropriate and negative affect toward others whether in individual or group relations. Usually careless in their grooming, they were immature in their sleeping and feeding behaviors. Their spontaneity was limited, and toward others their affective expression, both in verbal and nonverbal communications, was negative and expressed in occasional impulsive angry eruptions.

Their second subgroup, considered the "core" borderline category, also displayed a pervasive negative affect. However, this was "acted out" in many ways. These patients seemed to have established a reasonable personal identity, but did not always act consistently with that individuation. They were depressed except when "acting out," participating in, or rebelling against the environment. This group may well be the same described by Hoch and Polatin as "pseudopsychopathic."

The third subgroup were indivduals with blandly adaptive behavior. What was missing was the presence of positive affect—love or affection for others. Also, their self-identity was uncertain. They resembled the "as-if" character described earlier in this book.

The smallest subgroup showed some behavior exhibiting positive affection toward others. But here the feeling was directed to females and resembled

that of a childlike clinging depression. Also, anxiety and depression were predominant in their affective life, associated with lack of self-esteem and confidence.

In the rage reactions, the borderline features will be found in the propensity for self-destructive behaviors, such as repeated efforts at self-mutilation, suicidal behavior, the impulsive quitting of jobs, or flare-ups in relation to presumed friends or close associates. Feelings of insecurity are pervasive, but often are coupled with grandiose fantasies of omnipotence, which lead the borderline patient to justify his feelings and desires to both be gratified by and exploit others.

In general the borderline syndrome has been found to be expressed in anger as the major affect, with infantile, dependent or complementary, but rarely reciprocal, adult transactions with others. All "borderlines" have an unclear self-identity, in which most characteristically they report themselves viewing or watching themselves "playing a role." Finally, depression reflected as a sense of loneliness and inability to relate to others—rather than caused by guilt or shame—seems a common element, although in the last group depression seems unassociated with anger.

For the psychodynamic development of the borderline state, Kernberg defines a series of "nonspecific" ego weaknesses, expressed in (1) the relative inability to face anxiety, (2) a deficiency in the control of impulses, and (3) a limitation of sublimatory channels (or, as the author puts it, ego assets). The borderline individual, in contrast to the fully developed schizophrenic, generally appears to have well-organized formal thought processes. Yet, on projective tests, in unstructured or strange social situations, or as a consequence of the use of hallucinogenic drugs (mescaline, LSD-25, etc.), there frequently occur infantile perceptions of others, the use of regressive ego defensive mechanisms especially expressive of "splitting" in the perceptual cognitive world — the inability to fuse or recognize the potential of coexistence in others of their good-bad aspects, and sometimes severe regression with refusal of self with maternal objects.

Psychodynamically, Kernberg suggests that the dissociative process occurs due to partial failure of the development of a sense of primary separation and autonomy, perhaps a constitutional defect in tolerating anxiety, or excessive real frustrations with consequent magnified, socially aggressive expressions. He discriminates between the repressive refusal of the psychotic self and the introjected images from the borderline organization, where there is a pathological intensification of all phases of "splitting." This mechanism protects the positive identifications and makes possible a better social façade and hope in the therapeutic relations. The individual divides others (images) into "all good" or "all bad" and holds the potential of shifting his relationship with each individual quickly from one percept to another, disallowing the potential of constancy evident in mature, interpersonal perceptions. This primitive idealization may occur with establishment of clinging relationships, as well as infantile, fearful, and devaluative projections of one's own aggressiveness. The feared, projected image must either be controlled or avoided. Denial of one or another aspect of human object relations thus is common.

Characteristically, individuals with such traits display a limited capacity for evaluation of others or empathy for them. Relations always are highly ambivalent. Their interpersonal relations are shallow, as they must protect themselves from their aggressive and positive affective drives toward others. There is limited capacity to experience anxiety as concern or guilt in relations with others, nor is there an ability to comprehend the potential emotional states of others. Such limited capacity evolves from the anxieties inherent in close and constant contact. The results might be infantile idealization of the other or rage engendered by frustration of their excessive demands.

Cattell reports that 60 per cent of a group of individuals diagnosed as pseudoneurotic and followed from 5 to 20 years never required hospital treatment. The remaining 40 per cent were periodically admitted to the hospital. Only one in five developed overt psychotic symptoms, and one half of these remitted. Thus only 10 per cent evolved the well-known classic forms of schizophrenia.

Narcissistic Personality

The narcissistic personality has been much discussed in the recent psychoanalytic literature. Those classified in this group by Kernberg and others are thought of as having a personality organization relating to the borderline psychotic. The superficial social functioning of these individuals appears reasonably competent. Yet they require a great degree of self-reference in their interactions with others. The major expectations they harbor, of being loved and admired by others, are a contradiction to their overtly perceived behavior, which is an expansive demanding of appreciation and tribute from others. The narcissists have little empathy for the feelings of others. Their satisfactions derive from the appreciation others give to them or from their own inner, grandiose fantasies. When these sources of gratification are lacking, they become bored and restless. Usually their interpersonal transactions are expressed by envy toward others, a tendency to idealize some from whom they expect tribute, and a tendency to treat with contempt those who are unlikely to admire them.

Kernberg emphasizes that their relations are both exploitative and parasitic.

In such relationships the narcissistic wish to control and possess others is often conducted with a façade of charm and engagement yet with coldness, ruthlessness, and absence of guilt. While on the surface they appear to be dependent, in fact they lack the capacity to trust others and have need to deprecate them.

This character organization appears to exist as a defensive operation against paranoidal traits, which have a tendency to project rage central to their psychopathology. Psychodynamically, interactions with others appear to reflect intense fantasied relationships filled with anxiety and deficient in internalization of relations affectively perceived as satisfying and good. Kernberg regards this group as a subgroup of the antisocial personality.

THE ANTISOCIAL PERSONALITY

The majority of patients now classified as antisocial personality were formerely designated "constitutional psychopathic state" or "psychopathic personality." The present term provides a more restrictive application and refers to those chronically antisocial individuals without the capacity to form significant attachments or loyalties to others, to groups, or to codes of living. Thus they seem callous and given to immediate pleasures, appear devoid of a sense of responsibility, and, in spite of repeated humiliations and punishments, fail to learn to modify their behavior. They lack social judgment, yet frequently are capable of verbal rationalizations that often convince them their actions are reasonable and warranted.

The essential defect in the character structure rests in the failure to develop a socialized superego and ego ideals. If these exist, they are directed to personal self-aggrandizement, acquisition of money and material goods, and the control of others for immediate pleasures and satisfactions.

Etiology

While past evidence for genetic and constitutional factors in the antisocial personality has tended to be weak, Schulsinger studied the parents and relatives of 57 psychopaths found among over 5000 adoptees and discovered a clear surplus of psychopathy among the biological relatives, compared with a matched set of controls. Of interest is that five times as many of the biological fathers of the psychopaths also suffered psychopathy as was found in the adoptive fathers or biological fathers of controls. However, Schulsinger points out that this finding may relate only to the fact that men tend to be classified as psychopaths much more often than women. His conclusions were that genetic factors play an important predisposing role in the etiology of psychopathy, hence, a consitutional difference is present.

In a conditioning experiment, Fenz, Young, and Fenz found that sociopaths showed resistance to developing anticipatory cardiac responses to signals of a forthcoming noxious event and also, after developing conditioning, demonstrated resistance to extinction. Their work tends to corroborate earlier studies of this type and they attribute the delay in responding to changes in environment to selective deficit in attention.

From a psychogenetic viewpoint, the family histories of antisocial psychopaths expose strong evidence of experiential deficit of the parental transactions likely to produce ego and superego organization. For example, the studies of female criminals carried out by Cloninger and Guze disclosed that the families of convicted women were characterized by very high rates of psychopathology—in particular, antisocial personalities, hysteria, alcoholism, and drug abuse. These findings are consistent with studies of male felons and their families. They lend support to the suggestion that the several conditions of antisocial personality development and hysteria have certain features in common, the origins of which are unclear.

The future antisocial personality is often a child born to parents who did not want him, and frequently he or she is of illegitimate birth. The mother's own early life and development have been unhappy, and her departure from her parents has been motivated by a wish to escape from them. She has few resources to offer others and thus comes to term feeling herself deprived. Any suffering with the birth or failures to realize her fantasies in the child serve only to increase her negative attitude toward the infant. Even when the parents have married, their relationship usually terminates in desertion or divorce. Thus the child may have been passed frequently between others or institutionalized. If he remains with the parents, he may have been exposed to violent tempers, abuse, and a variety of brutalities and sexual aberrations that occur frequently in parents addicted to alcohol and to promiscuity.

In this type of family, authority goals for the child are not clearly established and are never based on a foundation of mutual affection, tenderness, and trust. The attempts by school and other authorities to establish some control for the acts of the child are treated indifferently, openly defied, and fought off by the parents. The child is deprived again of other sources for establishing healthy identifications with those maintaining the social values of the community. Further, both the attitude of the parents to outside authority and the child's own resentments are often deepened and embedded.

Even in childhood, the future pathological personality usually shows signs of emotional maladjustment and unwholesome personality traits. Typically, he is characterized by an emotional immaturity reflected by his impulsive and instant response to his feelings. His personality seems to be dominated by primitive drives to the exclusion of rational behavior. Certain lines of con-

duct, particularly of a socialized nature, are never learned. Some of these children are sensitive, stubborn, and given to tantrums or to outbursts of rage; frequently these preadolescent psychopaths steal, run away, suffer from enuresis, are destructive, quarrelsome, sulky, deceitful, obstinate, defiant, boastful, shameless, and erratic. Antagonism or open rebellion against a dominating parent may be shown. This is often reflected or transferred to schoolteachers, who find them restless, challenging, or defiant. The adolescent resists the ideals and mores of his family and tends to socialize at a lower level. With approaching maturity and the weakening of the restraining forces of the home and with the increase of responsibilities and of environmental contacts and demands, the earlier tendencies become outspoken manifestations. These are elaborated in some as they obtain gratifications through cupidity, deceit, or sadistic acts as the few means learned in such family environments in response to their own needs and desires.

Many psychopaths, although not intellectually deficient, seem emotionally so. They lack keenness and delicacy of sentiment. The psychopath gives the impression of being affectionless, selfish, ungrateful, narcissistic, and exhibitionistic. He demands much and gives little. His excess of demand is, in fact, one of the outstanding characteristics. He has no critical awareness of his motives and is unable to judge his own behavior from another's standpoint. In spite of the fact that his conduct is so inadequate or so hostile from a social standpoint, the psychopath is satisfied with it. He demonstrates few feelings of anxiety, guilt, or remorse yet underneath these feelings do exist, as Vaillant has found, when the patient is confined and brought into a deep psychotherapeutic contact. Under such circumstances, the sociopath will be found to express anxiety and depression related to his dread of being hurt through surrender to close contact with another.

He lacks definite objectives, and his

usual state of restlessness may result from a search for the unattainable. Occupational application and efficiency are usually faulty; routine is intolerably irksome. He demands immediate and instant gratification of his desires, with no concern for the feelings and interests of others, with whom he forms few emotional relationships or stable affectional ties. He does not build up a sense of social values as normally should occur through the process of identification.

He is often plausible and talkative but absolutely unreliable. Frequently, the only environment to which he can adjust is the one that he can dominate. Surprising irregularities of ability and inconsistencies of behavior are constantly demonstrated. A certain number escape from a difficult situation by way of a psychotic episode, while others at the slightest stress resort to alcohol or drugs. Many psychopaths tolerate alcohol poorly and under its influence become noisy, quarrelsome, and destructive. The sociopathic personality projects his own insecurity by blaming others. Psychopaths range from those considered queer to criminals, with a large intermediate group made up of cranks, extremists, eccentrics, habitual delinquents, and other social misfits.

Sometimes one sibling in a family may manifest the behavior and personality characteristic usually associated with the sociopathic personality, while other siblings may present mature and well-adjusted personalities. Presumably, this difference in personality characteristics is because the effect of a particular emotional experience or social influence in the family was highly specific to the individual. This type of psychopathic behavior probably develops more often in upper or middle class families than that previously described. The superego defect or lacuna, as it has been termed, may be limited to a single form of behavior—such as stealing, running away, or promiscuity.

In this respect, concurrent studies of children exhibiting antisocial activity and of their parents provide insights into both the form of deviant behavior adopted by the child and its impulsion for gratification. Johnson and Szurek have found that the more important parent, usually the mother, has unconsciously encouraged the amoral or antisocial behavior in the child. Although the parent verbally protests such behavior both to the child and to others, yet it is accepted, either unconsciously or with a guilty permissiveness, by the parent. The permissiveness has appeared to gratify vicariously neurotic needs of the parent that derive from her own lack of current satisfactions or unmet needs of childhood, or both. Since the parent's permissiveness is uncertain and incomplete, the child, and later the adult, is inconsistent and confused. Healthy discipline is not administered by such a parent—discipline combining firm prohibition with reward for socially acceptable behavior. Through his own overt acts, inconsistencies, innuendoes in speech, or various nonverbal means of communication, the child has been found to recognize the partial permissiveness. But since the child is both partially gratified and encouraged in his action and partially frustrated by the parent, there are associated with the act feelings of hostility toward the parent and perhaps of guilt. In instances in which this variety of family interaction exists, the antisocial behavior is fixed unless the several participating persons can be brought to understand and modify their behavior or they are completely separated.

Psychopathology

These sociopathic individuals show a moral and ethical blunting, a lack of sympathy for their fellow men, and a behavior destructive to the welfare of the social order. As children they are often self-willed, play truant, commit petty thefts, are cruel and untruthful, and as they grow older they may be inaccessible, boorish, and without a sense of responsibility. Their emotional life is superficial and affectively cold. They seem incapable of mature emotional relationships. They cannot organize an acceptable, constructive expression of their aggressions. They appear to lack ambition, application, seriousness of purpose, and foresight. They are irritable, arrogant, unyielding, characterized by a brutal egoism, and rarely feel remorse for their most serious offenses against person or property. Frequently, they show a rebellious attitude toward authority and society. Changes in mood are sudden and often without apparent cause. They are cynical, devoid of a sense of honor or of shame, and are lacking in sympathy, affection, gratitude, and other social and esthetic sentiments.

When frustrated, they may be dangerous to others. Their offenses may constitute the whole register of crime — theft, embezzlement, forgery, robbery, brutal sex attacks, and other acts of violence. Many take pleasure in their struggle with the law and feel pride in their accomplishments. They are unable to identify themselves with society and its laws. Punishments are considered as expressions of injustice and have no deterrent effect.

It would appear that one may discriminate several types of violent offenders, the majority suffering antisocial personality disorders on the basis of their history. The habitual violent offender tends to be younger at the age of first arrest and at the time of arrest for the index crime. He has been incarcerated more frequently, both as a juvenile and an adult, and the history of his development is characterized by hyperactivity, fighting, and temper tantrums, with continual difficult social and sexual adaptation. Separating the habitual from the occasional violent offender is a history of earlier loss of one or both parents and rearing by persons other than his own family. Further, the habitual violent offender, who is often a repetitive murderer, generally describes poor relations with both parents, accompanied by physical aggression practiced

by their fathers towards them as well as parental abuse of alcohol, drugs, or expression of suicidal attempts, psychiatric disability, aggressiveness, violence and criminality.

To indicate the wide variety of behavior patterns that the antisocial personality may manifest, a description is given of a group formerly characterized as pathological liars and swindlers. In this group are egocentric individuals whose social maladaptation consists of extravagant, often apparently purposeless, lying, frequently combined with swindling. They exhibit a marked excitability of imagination combined with an instability of purpose. They are usually good-natured, of agreeable manners, optimistic, of a light-hearted geniality, and make social contacts easily. A glibness of tongue, and unusual aptitude for the use of language, a self-confident manner, a frequently assumed dignity, and a misleading appearance of knowledge readily enable them to convince the credulous of their statements. They acquire a smattering of art, literature, or technical parlance, which they employ to their own profit and to the expense and humiliation of their victims. They spin remarkable tales concerning past experiences and paint their future with a careless disregard for reality. Some are guilty of sex offenses and others obtain large sums of money under promise of marriage.

When discovered in their delinquencies, they profess amnesia, and if charged with offense, they often stage an emotionally affecting exhibition designed to impress observers and arouse sympathy. They are restless and unstable and are incapable of exertion or responsibility. They never learn to meet the struggle for existence with industry and perseverence, but live in a world of imagination and seek to acquire the necessities of life by deceit and fraud. They are unable to accept the limitations of reality. Their theatrical imitation, their tendency to daydream, to boast, to avoid realities, and to surround themselves with an imaginary world suggest a childish immaturity of personality, while their wish-fulfilling fabrications have much in common with the fantasies of childhood. Many times their flagrant lying is defensive in purpose.

On a less conscious level is the extravagant and often apparently purposeless romancing known as *pseudologia phantastica*. This egregious disregard of the truth seems to result from a pressing need to indulge in extravagant castle-building in order to make up for a reality that appears to be too onerous or prosiac. Inasmuch as the content of the fantasy is generated by unconscious forces, the patient is not entirely aware that his statement is a fabrication. His unusually rich imagination, stirred into active expression by acute emotional needs, enables the patient to live in a dream world. Psychometric tests usually disclose a normal or superior intellectual capacity, but as with other psychopaths, intelligence has little regulating influence on behavior. At times it would appear that such personality characteristics grow out of a feeling of inferiority, envy, or jealousy.

From the foregoing behavioral descriptions, it is evident that the character defenses of the sociopath are fantasy and projection combined with hypochondriacal and sadomasochistic complexes.

DIFFERENTIAL DIAGNOSIS. Not all delinquents and criminals, even though guilty of repeated offenses, are to be considered as antisocial personalities or psychopaths. In previous chapters mention has been made of criminal behavior as an incidental manifestation of the neuroses, the affective and schizophrenic reactions, and the mental deficiencies. However, the personality structure and its precursors in the constitutional and psychogenetic history differ from that of the psychopath. Also, it must be kept in mind that cultural, economic, and social forces may determine antisocial behavior and in some instances release it,

as, for example, in times of war, when the ordinary standards of social interaction are overturned or reversed even for those with well-established social values.

There exist in many societies subcultures that live through their adeptness in defying the usual social codes, the members of which constitute a separate criminal class. Persons in these groups differ from the psychopath or antisocial personality in their personality structure. As an example, in a study of a group of thieves. Medlicott concluded that stealing may be a symptom of a depressive illness. Among 50 thieves he found 14, all women, with depressions resulting from recent bereavement, many in the menopausal or postmenopausal period, who acted out their rage and frustration through presumably senseless thefts. In contrast to the antisocial personalities, individuals of this group are capable of warm and strong loyalities to others and to their group. To Jenkins and others they represent a criminal occupational group motivated as other citizens to gain, but through illegal means. They learn, plan, and adapt as do others without significant personality disorder. The major differences rest in their group loyalties and the nature of their early development, which has fostered the capacities for interpersonal contact and trust. Through continued existence in a delinquent or criminal subculture, behavior is limited to that acceptable to those groups. The antisocial adolescent gang activity, now widely reported but known for centuries, represents culturally determined antisocial behavior.

Particularly to be distinguished from the sociopathic group are the *neurotic characters*. Here the neurotic conflict is resolved through asocial or antisocial behavior rather than through a symptom neurosis; the psychopathology is expressed in antisocial behavior rather than in neurotic symptoms. In the antisocial neurotic character, compulsive "acting out" relieves anxiety that would otherwise be distressing. Often the acting out is motivated by a pathological sense of guilt due to an abnormal superego. It is performed to relieve the guilt through apprehension and punishment. Intellectually, such patients are aware of the potentialities for punishment and humiliation, but are unconsciously impelled to the repetitive antisocial act in order to assuage the unconscious guilty anxiety and need for punishment. The neurotic character, then, differs from the antisocial personality in that he has evolved an ego structure that allows for trust and attachment to others and has internalized social codes. Thus he has available superego structure, but this is distorted and creates a persisting unconscious irrational sense of guilt, shame, or unworthiness.

A characteristic of all antisocial psychopathological behavior is the fact that the drive or motivation behind it is intense and forceful. The immediate urges are stronger than any rational considerations. The pathological personality who repeatedly commits some antisocial act appreciates intellectually that he will doubtless be caught, and if so, will face severe punishment. His need for his customary means of anxiety-relieving nevertheless impels the compulsive continuance •of his behavior. He may make a genuine effort to "go straight" and yet find his efforts futile in the face of strong unconscious forces. At times this may be the result of a vicious circle. His dynamically motivated aggressiveness, for example, may generate anxiety, and his anxiety, in turn, may generate antisocial aggressiveness. Although from a psychopathological standpoint the sociopathic personality may be looked upon as not responsible for his conduct, from a legal point of view he is regarded in most American courts as accountable for any violations of the legal code.

The projective psychological techniques may yield significant information concerning personality structure and underlying psychopathology and reveal the areas around which the patient's major problems revolve. The Minnesota Multiphasic scales also are most revealing in assisting in this diagnosis.

Prognosis

There has been an impression that those with antisocial personality disorders slowly mature and become less involved in criminal and other disruptive behavior as they age. Maddocks' report of a five-year follow-up of social adaptation in a group of untreated psychopaths belies the complete validity of this impression. He discovered that conviction rates fall with increasing age, yet some three out of five psychopaths do not establish a satisfactory social adjustment in later life. Maddocks suggests that when they leave the circuit of detention in prisons as they age, many then enter the medical care system as an expression of their continuing maladjustment.

In another follow-up study Tölle addressed himself to the differing courses the antisocial personality takes in his attempt at "mastery of life." Some were found to do so by increasing social withdrawal and abnormality; others improved slightly in their capacity to utilize the opportunities for social improvement offered them; another group succeeded partially by limiting their range of activity. The mastery of others was highly successful in spite of considerable stress. About one third pursued the first two lines of adaptation; another third the second; and the remainder the last mode.

Treatment

One must not oversimplify the factors that have determined the behavior of the sociopathic personality. Pernicious social and cultural influences may contribute to the creation of the sociopathic personality, although they do not serve as the basic genetic agents. Often there is an interplay between psychological and social factors. If environmental influences are contributory, either their modification or the patient's removal from them is desirable.

The rational treatment of the antisocial and dyssocial must differ from that of those neurotics who perform delinquent or criminal acts. Essential to any effective therapy is placing the individual and retaining him sufficiently long, in an accepting and warm human environment where he may find it possible to develop a therapeutic relationship with some member of the treatment group whom he perceives as having his interests at heart and to whom he can give some trust. In dealing with delinquency of late childhood and adolescence, it is often found that one of the most effective corrective measures is a warm, authoritative father figure with whom boys can identify.

With the older psychopaths, this initial step becomes increasingly difficult and often is impossible owing to the inherent ego defect of basic distrust. Psychiatrists and others treating such patients must be highly motivated and endowed with a mature patience, combined with firmness, to effect the development of the therapeutic relationship.

When the treatment relationship is established, through either individual or group identification, pressure through personal and verbal behavior must be initiated toward certain goals and standards of social relationship. Usually, such efforts must be made continuously and slowly, and infractions should be treated by withdrawal of privileges and their reinstitution on improved behavior.

The treatment relationship, whether established through the medium of a single psychiatrist or a group, makes clear certain standards of behavior, and their abuse is managed by frustrating loss of satisfaction in other areas. A sense of authority is consistently and firmly maintained. This treatment regimen frequently cannot be attained without some type of institutional care. Placement in group homes with firm

surrogate parental figures offers an alternative now widely practiced. Treatment clearly differs from the continually permissive attitude necessary for the treatment of the neurotic child or adult. If such permissiveness is adopted for treatment of the psychopath, no focus will be established for superego growth, and the permissiveness may aggravate the antisocial behavior.

In this respect the use of group process through exposure to the "therapeutic community" has been on trial for many years. Whiteley has reported that of over 122 patients so treated and released during a two-year period, 40 per cent remained without conviction or psychiatric hospitalization. Those with good social adaptation had previously achieved some success in school, at work, and in interpersonal relations, as well as exhibiting a capacity for emotional responsivity and involvement with others. Whiteley suggests that for the more immature, persistently acting-out psychopath, the therapeutic community is both unbeneficial and sometimes harmful; for the egocentric, impulsive, thought-disordered, and aggressive psychopath, little benefit may be achieved.

When the antisocial behavior of a child or adolescent has its origins in the family interactions described by Johnson and Szurek, for treatment to succeed, in most instances, the parent of the patient must also be treated or, in the case of a child or young adult, separated during the course of psychotherapy. Such separations are resisted by parents whose major gratification comes from their dependent relations with the "scapegoat" child. In some instances, separation of the patient from the parent, or change in the behavior of the patient during treatment, has led to serious behavior disturbance in the symbiotic parent.

Treatment for those with a neurotic character of the antisocial type that has led to repetitive antisocial behavior should conform to the psychoanalytic model as described in a subsequent chapter. Here the hope of the therapist is to ventilate past conflicts that have led to a pathological sense of guilt and its expressive force in masochistic "acting out." Since the patient has already established a set of values, it is unnecessary to remove him to a setting that prevents actions and punishes failure to comply.

A prison environment is often a handicap to therapy. If the sociopsychopath's behavior brings him before court, the judge may be aware that ideally the treatment of the prisoner's behavior is by one of the several forms of psychotherapy. Like the psychiatrist, he may realize that punishment without recognition of the prisoner's emotional problems may intensify his social maladjustment. On the other hand, a person cannot be sentenced to therapy.

In general, the use of pharmaceuticals has proved ineffective in bringing about lasting change in the personality and overt behavior of those with antisocial behavior. Recent trials with lithium carbonate suggest a reduction in aggressive behavior while the individuals received the agent in a controlled environment. There exists no careful long-term follow-up, and no indication of willingness of those receiving the lithium to continue the treatment upon return to life in the community.

Frequently, in the case of the sociopath, psychiatrists are confronted with the question of criminal responsibility. As scientists, they should seek to ascertain whether the criminal behavior is susceptible of psychopathological interpretation, but they should also remember that it is not easy to prove or disprove such interpretations, that society cannot yet evaluate them, and that it cannot yet, and perhaps should not, establish them as criteria of responsibility. The matter of judgment of responsibility rests solely with the law. The only function of psychiatrists is to provide their opinion of the motivating forces for the criminal act and their origins as determined from the personality study.

Avoidant Personality

Sometimes confused with the schizoid due to the tendency to social withdrawal, those with this condition nevertheless are motivated by desire for the affection and acceptance of others. They are hypersensitive to social situations in which the expectation is for humiliation and shame or rejection by others. Their self-esteem generally is poor. Yet they may have a few friends who give them continual and unquestioning approval.

Affectively, they suffer from anxiety and depression associated with self-directed contempt. These personality features impair their capacity for social relations. In childhood, a similar disorder may have been noted as a social phobia, which is a predisposition for the adult condition.

Passive-Aggressive Personality

The passive-aggressive personality is thought to result from failure to attain mature emotional development, manifested in one of three ways.

PASSIVE-DEPENDENT TYPE. In this type there is a frank expression of absence of mature self-confidence and self-reliance. The individual is overwhelmed by feelings of helplessness and indecision. He is irresponsible and childish and may cling to others as a dependent child does, to a supporting parent. He requires approval and assurance. The clinical picture may include anxiety manifestations. The passive-dependent husband may depend on his wife for all major decisions. Individuals of this type shun overt expression of aggression and withdraw from any situation likely to arouse hostility. They are passive, timid, and fearful. The underlying hostility, covered by a rigid shell of timidity and passivity, is entirely unconscious.

PASSIVE-AGGRESSIVE TYPE. In this type of personality contains a considerable element of aggression, doubtless largely defensive in origin, expressed by passive measures, such as sullenness, stubbornness, procrastination, inefficiency, and passive obstructions. Some persons of this type complain and are dissatisfied. They usually work poorly with others and may have a demoralizing effect on a group. Some have been fearful of or have shown a covert hostility to their fathers, who have been dominant, rigid, unapproachable, demanding, and difficult to please.

AGGRESSIVE TYPE. In this type the outstanding manifestation is a persistent reaction to frustration with such immature measures as irritability, temper tantrums, and even destructive behavior. Sometimes there is resentment of pathological degree. Many persons of this type are hostile, provocative, antagonistic, competitive, and ambitious. They manifest a "chip-on-the-shoulder" attitude. They may be sharp and biting and aggressively resistant. They demand special attention and assume unwarranted authority. Frequently they attempt to lure those in authority into long argumentative discussion. Grandiose fantasies are common. Earlier in their lives these persons have been openly hostile to their fathers. A deep dependency can be discovered below the surface. The aggressiveness here originates in a reaction formation.

Obsessive-Compulsive Personality

Individuals of an obsessive or compulsive nature are those whose superego functions are severe. They tend to be punctilious, rigid, fastidious, formal, meticulous, may be in constant doubt what to do, and have to go over things again and again. They are overinhibited, perfectionistic, self-doubting, and are unable to carry on their work if under pressure. They lack a normal capacity for relaxation. They show a tendency to literal obedience, have an exaggerated sense of duty, are harassed by their responsibilities and scrupulosities, and cannot make decisions. If circumstances require a decision, regret is expressed for the choice made. The person of compulsive character is stubborn in his

convictions and manifests a tendency to hair-splitting. In contrast to the suggestible, demonstrative, extroverted personality of the hysteric, he is likely to be of a day-dreaming, introverted, self-centered type. The compliance and "correct" behavior of the compulsive personality are frequently a defense against hostile impulses.

If the individual is relatively free from anxiety, the existence in the personality of a certain degree of obsessive-compulsive drive and persistence adds a desirable quality. Compulsive personality traits are within the range of normal personality variants—as distinguished from symptoms of a compulsion neurosis, which are pathological exaggeration of these variants. Such traits impart a desire to succeed; the compulsive person, too, is a hard worker. A degree of compulsiveness adds to strength of character. The difference between a compulsive personality and a compulsive neurosis is therefore one of degree, of the amount of anxiety present and of the extent to which the personality habitually defends itself against chronic anxieties by ritualistic devices. Frequently the traits are safeguards against hostile impulses, unconscious aggression, and accompanying guilt. The chronic tension of the compulsive personality may as a result of stress lead to an obsessive-compulsive neurosis.

Other Types

EXPLOSIVE PERSONALITY. Individuals with this type of personality are characterized by the explosive intensity of their emotions in reaction to relatively slight external stimuli. Between their outbursts they are usually outgoing and friendly, happy, and likable. Their relationship to other persons, however, is constantly subject to fluctuating emotional attitudes because of strong and poorly controlled hostility, guilt, and anxiety. Their emotional tension is usually at a rather high pitch and may suddenly and unexpectedly burst out in uncontrolled anger or other disproportionate emotional display. At these times such persons may shout, bluster, threaten, or even become destructive and assaultive. In some, the excitability may be manifested in outbursts of despair, sulky irritability, or obstinate inaccessibility. Suicidal attempts in response to frustration or as an effort to relieve a situation regarded as intolerable are frequent. Jealousy and quarrels with those of the opposite sex are common.

Far from being the desired evidence of vigor and strength of personality, the outbursts of the excitable are often poorly concealed attempts to disguise an inherent weakness. Such reactions, characterized by fluctuating emotional attitudes, unstable and explosive feelings, and undependable judgment, are to be regarded as expressions of an immaturity of personality and probably may not be distinguishable from the passive-aggressive personality type.

INADEQUATE PERSONALITY. In spite of average educational and other opportunities and of normal intelligence as measured by psychometric tests, individuals of the inadequate type of personality fail in emotional, economic, occupational, and social adjustments. They are often good-natured and easygoing but are inept, ineffective, and unconcerned. Their judgment is defective; they lack initiative, may be dreamy, and seem to lack physical and emotional stamina. When it is clear that effort would be rewarded, they lack sufficient perseverence to achieve the results already in sight. They can neither work nor wait for deferred pleasure or reward. As a result, they are improvident and shiftless. Many of the ne'er-do-wells belong in this group.

DENIAL PERSONALITY. From certain clinical studies of patients with both organic brain syndromes and other psychotic processes, a *denial personality* reaction has been described. These people explicitly deny the presence of their illness or its symptoms, even if it is as grossly apparent as a limb paralysis caused by a brain lesion. They tend to be highly conventional in their behavior, perfectionistic, prestige-oriented, and limited in empathy as well as in introspective capacity. Their traits and their responses on the appropriate psychological tests are similar to those of the *authoritarian personality*. It has been suggested that, when psychiatrically ill, those with this constellation of personality traits respond more effectively to treatment with physiological therapies, such as electroshock, than to the psychotherapeutic approach. As yet, this conclusion remains unwarranted.

Also important for the clinical practice of psychiatry is the understanding of such personality traits as resignation, tranquillity, apathy, boredom, or gloating, traits that tend to defeat attempts to intervene therapeutically in spite of the existence of gross malfunctioning of the personality. The psychoanalytic literature contains what is known of the existing psychodynamic understandings of such traits. The bibliography of this chapter records the more recent references.

BIBLIOGRAPHY

General

Frances, A.: The DSM-III personality disorders section: A commentary. Am. J. Psychiatry, *137*:1054, 1980.

Schizotypal

Hoch, P. H., Cattell, J. P., Strahl, M. O., and Pennes, H. H.: The course and outcome of pseudoneurotic schizophrenia. Am. J. Psychiatry, *119*:106–115, 1962.
Spitzer, R. L., Endicott, J., and Gibbon, M.: Crossing the border into borderline personality and borderline schizophrenia. Arch. Gen. Psychiatry, *36*:17–24, 1979.

Histrionic (Hysterical)

Hollender, M. H.: Hysterical personality. Comments Contemp. Psychiatry, *1*:17–24, 1971.

Luisada, P. V., Peele, R., and Pittard, E. A.: The hysterical personality in men. Am. J. Psychiatry, *131*:518–522, 1974.

Borderline

Brinkley, J. R., Beitmar, B. D., and Friedel, R. O.: Low dose neuroleptic regimens in the treatment of borderline patients. Arch. Gen. Psychiatry, *26*:319–326, 1979.

Grinker, R. R., Werble, B., and Drye, R.: The Borderline Syndrome. New York, Basic Books, 1968.

Gunderson, J. G., and Kollar, J. E.: Discriminating features of borderline patients. Am. J. Psychiatry, *135*:792–796, 1978.

Kernberg, O.: Borderline Conditions and Pathological Narcissism. New York, J. Aronson, Inc., 1975.

Kohut, H.: The Analysis of the Self. New York, International Universities Press, 1971.

Masterson, J. F., and Rinsley, D. B.: The borderline syndrome: The role of the mother in the genesis and psychic structure of the borderline personality. Int. J. Psychoanal., *56*:165–177, 1975.

Reich, W.: The Spectrum Concept of Schizophrenia. Arch. Gen. Psychiatry, *32*:489–498, 1975.

Rinsley, D. R.: Borderline psychopathology: A review of etiology, dynamics and treatment. Int. Rev. Psychoanal., *5*:45–54, 1978.

Antisocial

Aichhorn, A.: Wayward Youth. New York, Viking Press, 1935.

Alexander, F.: The neurotic character. Int. J. Psychoanal., *11*:292–311, 1930.

Cleckley, H. M.: The Mask of Sanity. 5th ed. St. Louis, C. V. Mosby Company, 1976.

Cloninger, C. R., and Guze, S. B.: Psychiatric illness in the families of female criminals. A study of 288 first degree relatives. Br. J. Psychiatry, *122*:697–703, 1973.

Fenz, W. D., Young, M. J., and Fenz, H. G.: Differences in the modulation of cardiac activity between psychopaths and normal controls. Psychosom. Med., *36*:488–495, 1974.

Glueck, E. T.: Identifying juvenile delinquents and neurotics. Ment. Hyg., *40*:24–43, 1956.

Jenkins, R. L.: The psychopathic or antisocial personality. J. Nerv. Ment. Dis., *131*:318–334, 1960.

Johnson, A. M., and Szurek, S. A.: Etiology of antisocial behavior in delinquents and psychopaths. J.A.M.A., *154*:814–817, 1954.

Maddocks, P. D.: A five year follow-up of untreated psychopaths. Br. J. Psychiatry, *116*:511–515, 1970.

Medlicott, R. W.: Fifty thieves. N.Z. Med. J., *67*:183–188, 1968.

Rexford, E. N.: A developmental concept of the problems of acting out. J. Am. Acad. Child Psychiatry, *2*:6–21, 1963.

Schulsinger, F.: Psychopathy: Heredity and environment. Int. J. Ment. Health, *1*:190–206, 1972.

Tölle, R.: The mastery of life by psychopathic personalities. Psychiatr. Clin. (Basel), *1*:1–14, 1968.

Tupin, J. P., Maher, D., and Smith, D.: Two types of violent offenders with psychosocial descriptors. Dis. Nerv. Syst., *34*:356–363, 1973.

Tupin, J. P., Smith, D. B., Clanon, T. L., et al.: The long-term use of lithium in aggressive prisoners. Compr. Psychiatry, *14*:311–317, 1973.

Vaillant, G. E.: Sociopathy as a human process. Arch. Gen. Psychiatry, *32*:178–183, 1975.

Whiteley, J. S.: The response of psychopaths to a therapeutic community. Br. J. Psychiatry, *116*:517–529, 1970.

Other

Stokes, A.: On resignation. Int. J. Psychoanal., *43*:175–181, 1962.

Whitman, R. M., and Alexander, J.: On gloating. Int. J. Psychoanal., *49*:732–738, 1968.

26

ALCOHOLIC PSYCHOSES AND ALCOHOLISM

"In the bottle, discontent seeks for comfort, cowardice for courage, and bashfulness for confidence."

Samuel Johnson

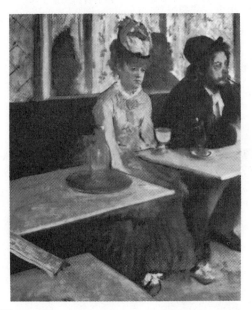

L'ABSINTHE
(By Degas, 1876; in Musée de l'Impressionisme, Paris.)

Over the centuries, people have indulged in a wide variety of drugs as a means of experiencing pleasure, enhancing social contacts, alleviating pain and, in some instances, dissipating physiological consequences of withdrawal from that same agent. There is an ever increasing recognition today that the use and abuse of drugs must be seen as a continuum. Control of the deleterious consequences of abuse of

any drug necessitates evaluation of a multitude of factors which not only motivate usage but also may contribute in some to predisposition to its physiologically destructive consequences. Taken in moderate dosages well within the limits of the physiological capacity of the individual to metabolize appropriately and to excrete, the majority of the drugs presently abused could be considered harmless. Nevertheless, there is

616

no question that all may produce temporary or irreversible physiological change that may lead to serious personality malfunctioning.

Of the various drugs actively pursued for recreation and nonmedical purposes, it is clear that the alcoholic beverages far exceed all other varieties. This is well demonstrated in Table 26–1, taken from the report of the National Commission on Marijuana and Drug Abuse.

Alcoholism and the disturbances of metabolism often associated with it may lead to both acute and chronic brain syndromes. A discussion of both of these syndromes is included in this chapter, as well as various other aspects of indulgence in alcohol.

Since the earliest recorded times in history people have consumed alcohol for euphoric purposes, to celebrate various festivities, to solemnize religious rituals, to grace social functions, and to provide surcease from immediate or continuing emotional stress. The widespread use of alcohol seems to have commenced with the beginnings of the Western industrial societies, although the consequences of its continual abuse were known many centuries earlier.

Feighner has made the point that one must differentiate between alcoholism per se and the alcoholic. Some define alcoholism as existing in one who demonstrates: 1) severe medical or psychological effects of repeated binge drinking, 2) the inability to control drinking, 3) dyssocial behavior while intoxicated, and 4) family, social, or personal dissatisfaction with the pattern of abnormal alcoholic intake. On the other hand, when one considers the drinking patterns inherent in certain cultures, including the American Indian and others, it is evident that alcoholism in the sense just defined is not easily separated from drinking excessively to maintain one's standing in the culture. Sexual or aggressive acts under the influence of alcohol acquire a distinctive value in terms of proving evidence of one's position in society, of masculinity, or perhaps of spiritual sensitivity. When it comes to giving a diagnostic label based on the above criteria, it is evident that one must consider the cultural standards in regard to the use of alcohol, just as one would correlate

TABLE 26–1   Psychoactive Drugs Used by Youth and Adults for Recreational and Nonmedical Purposes, 1973

DRUG	YOUTH[a]		ADULTS	
	%	Number	%	Number
Alcoholic beverages[b]	24	5,977,200	53	74,080,220
Tobacco, cigarettes[b]	17	4,233,850	38	53,114,120
Proprietary sedatives, tranquilizers, stimulants[c]	6	1,494,300	7	9,784,180
Ethical sedatives[d]	3	747,150	4	5,590,960
Ethical tranquilizers[d]	3	747,150	6	8,386,440
Ethical stimulants[d]	4	996,200	5	6,988,700
Marijuana	14	3,486,700	16	22,363,840
LSD, other hallucinogens	4.8	1,195,440	4.6	6,429,604
Glue, other inhalants	6.4	1,593,920	2.1	2,935,254
Cocaine	1.5	373,575	3.2	4,472,768
Heroin	0.6	149,430	1.3	1,817,062

[a]"Youth" refers to people aged 12 to 17. [b]Figures refer only to use within the seven days prior to the survey. [c]"Proprietary" means drugs sold over the counter. [d]"Ethical" means drugs intended to be sold only on a doctor's prescription. (From National Commission on Marijuana and Drug Abuse: Drug Use in America: Problem in Perspective (second report), Washington, D.C., U.S. Government Printing Office, 1973.)

varying ethnic and cultural groups with other types of drug abuse.

Prevalence

It is estimated that there are about nine million persons in the United States on whose lives drinking has an adverse effect in one way or another. Five out of six alcoholics are men between the ages of 30 and 55 — the most productive years. Hospital admissions for alcoholism rank now only behind those for schizophrenia and mental diseases of old age.

Those alcoholics admitted to hospital with psychoses or seriously impairing behavioral disturbances form only a small minority of the total who suffer from alcoholism in all parts of the world. In France, where a high proportion of the adult population derives its income from the production and sale of alcoholic beverages, there is much acceptance of wine drinking and little public expression of drunkenness. High rates of alcoholism and its complications exist among the Irish and Irish Americans, low rates among Orthodox Jews and Asians. These variations in degree of alcoholism seem related to usage and acceptability of drinking within the ethnic and cultural groups.

Those psychotic reactions secondary to alcoholism occur at a mean age in the forties. They are the consequence of drinking habits initiated many years beforehand. Usually, the alcoholic commences his or her habituation with social drinking. He or she enjoys relief from the usual stresses of life and learns that inner tensions can be alleviated by the intake of alcoholic drink. Over time increasing reliance is placed upon drinking as a means of reduction of anxiety.

Later the alcoholic's bouts of drinking are associated with amnesic episodes in which he or she does not seem to lose consciousness, but has little or no later recollection of actions or of events that took place, even though to others the amount of alcohol imbibed seems small. This is sometimes spoken of as a prodromal phase of alcoholism. As a habitual drinker, he has limited ability to control his intake. Once he commences to drink, he continues until comatose, unable to coordinate his actions for imbibition, or nauseated and vomiting. At this time in his course he may periodically discontinue drinking. However, once accepting another drink, his compulsivity reasserts itself. Criticized by his family, friends, and employers, who recognize his instability in action and thought, he offers various excuses, yet may indulge in surreptitious drinking, hiding his habit from others. Personal care declines, attention is blunted, and he neglects his work, family, and social relations. It is here that he may develop vitamin deficiencies through neglect of his regular eating, or, in the state of addiction, a withdrawal syndrome with psychotic or epileptiform convulsions.

Genetic Predisposition

While the evidence for a genetic predisposition toward alcoholism and its consequences is unclear, a number of recent clinical studies have demonstrated that individuals of Oriental birth (Japanese, Taiwanese, Koreans, as well as American Indians) are much more sensitive to the oral administration of ethanol in single dosage than those of Occidental ethnicity. This sensitivity exists in both adults and infants. It is demonstrated through facial and body flushing, elevation of blood pressure, increase in heart rate, and a sense of general discomfort. It is of interest that alcoholism is uncommon among those residing on the Asiatic continent yet occurs with high frequency among American Indians, who value the experience of intoxication as culturally important.

Another study, done by Goodwin and his associates, tends to support a predisposition to alcoholism derived from genetic factors. A group of men, who had been separated from their biological parents early in life and of whom one parent had a diagnosis of alcoholism, had a history of drinking problems and psychiatric treatment of an order significantly different from another group of matched control adoptees. The adoptive parents of both the index and control subjects had similar rates of alcoholism, other psychiatric disorders, and came from comparable socioeconomic classes.

Psychogenesis of Alcoholism

Continuing studies of the families and relatives of alcoholics reaffirm that experience of early parental loss through death, separation, or divorce is more common in the alcoholic than in others. Deprivation of both parents with subsequent institutional or foster home care for the children has been noted as significant in some series of studies. Large families with older fathers and predominantly male members generate more alcoholics in some countries. An earlier initiation of excessive drinking seems more likely in those who experienced parental loss than in those without such a loss. Alcoholism is more common among men than women. So, too, the recognition of its existence as a serious habituation or addiction takes place at a mean age almost a decade earlier in men than women. Many married women commence their drinking in middle age as their role of mother and wife is challenged with departure of their children from the home—the challenge of the "empty nest."

When one examines the families and relatives of alcoholics in relation to risk of associated psychiatric illness, it appears that primary affective disorders are discovered in a considerable proportion of the female alcoholics—in whom this term is used to mean a disorder present before excessive drinking occurred. A personality disorder, usually sociopathy, is the primary diagnosis most frequently made

in the males. Yet the morbid risk for affective disorder and alcoholism is greater, as Winokur and his colleagues have found, in relatives of both males and females, with a greater risk for alcoholism among male relatives and for affective disorders in female relatives. The affective disorder found in this series of relatives was usually depression alone: "unipolar depression."

As emphasized earlier, genetics, constitution, and the child's emotional experiences in its family transactions all contribute to the predisposition to alcoholism. Cultural influences reinforce the family patterns, establishing the predilection for alcohol abuse as the means of gaining relief from anxiety and depression. Later experiences of deprivation of emotional support may act, and sometimes act repetitively, as precipitants to bouts of drinking or return to alcohol in those who have given up the habit.

Often the family histories demonstrate that the future alcoholic was mothered by an overindulgent and overprotective parent who encouraged his infantile oral demands from the early periods of life so that eventually they were too excessive to be met. The outbursts of rage at frustrations of demands are met by such mothers with redoubled efforts which, in turn, intensify the infantile demands and dependency. The maternal overprotection often is brought about by conflict resulting from a remote, cold, or brutalized relationship with the marital partner or by his or her regular or intermittent absence due to a variety of causes. The conflicts with father and siblings are heightened for children reared in this way. In other families from which alcoholics emerge, the paternal attitudes also are alternately severe and over-indulgent; bewildered by such inconsistency, the child evolves into a passive-dependent adult who is either unable to express his needs and is thereby frustrated and filled with guilt and resentment due to the restrained and internalized hostilities, or else is subject to periodic outbursts of aggressions when released from his inhibitions. Social and sexual identities are inadequately established as the parental roles are confused. Since the growing child is protected from environmental demands through parental ambivalence and conflict, ego functions fail to evolve satisfactorily.

Alcohol is discovered as a release from the painful internalized emotions because the parents are permissive toward drinking. It has been found that there is an overrepresentation of the last-born (youngest) children among the population of male alcoholics. Thus the psychodynamic theories that suggest the relationship between the dependency conflict and alcohol abuse are in order. It is this open indulgence in alcohol in the family or in the adolescent society of the future addict which allows the superego defect that permits its repeated use. Secondarily, there evolves the psychological and pharmacological dependency on a substitute, which at first offers euphoria but which later, as ego frustrations mount, offers little more than relief from unbearable tensions.

The psychopathologic conditions leading to alcoholism vary with the individual alcoholic. Thus it appears in many instances that the addictive drinker may have been psychologically traumatized very early in life and his personality remained fixated at an early, oral stage of development. Again, alcoholism may occur in persons who, through the absence of a desirable identification figure, never developed a stabilizing superego. Assessment of the personality of the alcoholic particularly requires evaluation of superego maturation. In this respect, attempts should be made to determine from the history evidence of whether social controls have been internalized, and whether superego functioning is directed to regulate behavior in conformance with an ego ideal or to regulate self-esteem by self-condemnation. It is common in alcoholics to observe increasing difficulty in their ego capacity

to meet superego injunctions. The classic example is the alcoholic's inability to control his or her impulse to drink while at the same time desiring to stop.

Much of the influence of group therapeutic activities, such as that offered by Alcoholics Anonymous, lies in the group's ability to take over and provide new superego standards for the individual. The group's controlling superego is less demanding than the individual's; the member is judged by his performance in controlling drinking, but his other activities remain uncriticized. In this way, the guilty addict with a punitive superego, which demands beyond his capacities, is relieved. Hospitalization, group therapy sessions, and the use of drugs also offer the patient relief from his own responsibility for control. Here too, the superego authority is assumed by others and the alcoholic generally feels relieved from the internalized punitive attitudes. It is perhaps for this reason that alcoholics hospitalized following a suicidal attempt are so seldom observed as depressed.

There are among the shame-ridden and guilt-ridden alcoholics those who later project upon the therapeutic team their own personal superego standards. Then the program is perceived as punitive and the individual is likely to drop out. This is particularly true in the setting of individual psychotherapy.

The guilty obsessive alcoholic continues in treatment and may move from excessive internal superego control and from a position of overdemanding criticism to substitution of a more realizable ego ideal.

There is, however, the alcoholic who drinks to attain the ego ideal of masculinity. We have mentioned that this condition may exist among North American Indians. Here, if the individual behaves antisocially during drinking, he may suffer shame, guilt, or surprise, but this is related to the antisocial act and not to the drinking per se. These individuals are perhaps, as Gale and Frances have suggested, better treated with deteriorated alcoholics so that they may become aware of the ultimate consequences of excessive alcoholism. Such individuals are the traditional binge drinkers.

The superego of the sociopathic alcoholic differs in that the individual unconsciously, but maliciously, devotes his efforts to outwitting both his internalized controls and those that represent him in the outer world. The sociopathic drinker seldom profits from other than a lengthy residential treatment and peer pressure, which offer the external controls.

With the deteriorated alcoholic, regression in both ego and superego functioning is such that the individual essentially requires nurturance. Only with continual support and care may it be possible to re-establish certain ego ideals. Since the taking of Antabuse completely relieves the individual of the necessity to exert control, it is a useful adjunct for the majority of this group as it provides a concrete dependency gratification. At the same time, with each daily dose the individual is required to decide to exert control through taking the medication.

Age

While it is commonly thought that the incidence of alcoholism is at maximum between the ages of 35 to 40, it would be a mistake to believe that the condition is insignificant at other age periods, particularly among the elderly. As Zimburg has pointed out, mid and late adulthood are also periods of high incidence, but it tends to disappear beyond the age of 75. Among the elderly alcoholic are those who have been addicted throughout life, as well as others whose abuse of this substance was initiated in response to the emotional stresses and deprivations of the aging process.

Sex

It is generally stated that the ratio of male to female alcoholics is in the order of five to one, but it is recognized that insufficient attention has been given to the occurrence of this condition in women. The commonly accepted imbalance of alcohol abuse between the sexes is probably distorted, due to women's tendency to drink socially and privately at home. Belfer and his colleagues discovered that a high proportion of women (67 per cent of their sample) related their periods of drinking to menstrual cycles, and that the drinking began or increased in the premenstrual period. The alcoholic women generally were more anxious and depressed than nonalcoholic women; on psychological tests they scored similarly as regards femininity. It would appear that among the alcoholic women, the inability to accept traditional feminine role behavior, as well as the stress of the physiological change of the premenstruum, precipitated drinking as a means of relieving psychological anxiety.

Physiological Effects

While alcohol affects all cells of the body, its most marked effect is on the cells of the brain, therefore manifested in behavior. Since alcohol does not require prior digestion, it may be absorbed directly into the blood. The rate of absorption is much more rapid than its elimination, so with heavy indulgence a considerable concentration may occur. While there is an individual tolerance, it is generally accepted that a person showing a concentration of 150 mg. or more of alcohol in 100 ml. of blood, or its equivalent in urine, saliva, or breath, should be considered intoxicated. In the opinion of the National Safety Council Committee on Tests for Intoxication, this concentration so impairs judgment and performance in driving an automobile that operation of a car is unsafe.

The presumed stimulating tendencies of the drug, in terms of behavior, are due to loss of inhibition through impairment of the ordinarily present ego-superego controls. Thus alcohol reduces avoidance of behaviors generally inducing shame, guilt, or anxiety. It also has specific analgesic effects. The release of inhibition upon moderate use of alcohol is the major behavioral effect leading to a feeling of well-being, social ease, and sometimes increased capacity for creative work and effective drive. Creative thought probably results from the emergence of primary thought and its reorganization and integration with secondary thought processes. Such effects do not occur with heavy intoxication, when impairment of all perceptual, cognitive, and judgmental activities takes place. Alcohol tends to be sedating and to induce sleep, but even here its actions vary in moderate doses, depending upon the individual. Some become aggressive and noisy.

In the chronic alcoholic, Johnson, Burdick, and Smith have found long latencies for sleep onset. In alcoholic sleep, there are frequent awakenings and bodily movements and numerous shifts from one sleep stage to another, with marked diminution of stage 4 (slow wave sleep).

Alcohol is an energy-rich compound which is metabolized differently by and has widely dispersed and toxic effects upon a variety of bodily processes, according to Lieber. In contrast to other energy-rich compounds, such as carbohydrates and fats, which are synthesized in the body as well as ingested in the diet, alcohol is foreign to the body. Rapidly absorbed through the intestinal tract, it is an agent that must be metabolized through oxidative processes as it does not store in tissues and little is passed through the kidneys or lungs. The oxidative process takes place in the liver alone, making that organ the prime source for the toxic effects of the agent.

As alcohol has a high calorie value (7.1 calories per gm.), its intake in sizeable amounts offsets the requirement for other food. As a result, appetite may be diminished. Furthermore, as it directly leads to inflammation of the stomach, pancreas, and intestines when used to excess, it may impair the digestive processes and absorption of nutrients into the body. Consequently, malnutrition may evolve. Its effect on the intestines owing to the secondary consequences of inflammation further enhances potential malnutrition, as absorption of other foods may be diminished. Both alcohol and its primary conversion product, acetaldehyde, may interfere with the activation of vitamins by liver cells and the consequence of this action is to once more increase the potential for malnutrition.

Catalyzed by the enzyme alcohol dehydrogenase, ethanol is transferred from the agent to a cofactor, nicotinamide adenine dinucleotide (NAD), thereby converting the alcohol into acetaldehyde. The latter is next oxidized to form acetate, which in turn is converted into carbon dioxide and water. The major metabolic effects of ethanol are related to the acetaldehyde and hydrogen formed during its oxidation.

Due to the excess of hydrogen in the liver during alcohol metabolism, the metabolic processes in that organ are modified. The metabolic process whereby amino acids are reduced to pyruvate is deflected, in the sense that pyruvate in turn is reduced to lactate instead of glucose. This diversion of the process of gluconeogenesis leads to a lowering of the blood sugar (hypoglycemia).

The increase in lactate as a consequence of excess hydrogen produces a lactic acidosis, which in turn affects the kidney and interferes with the secretion of uric acid. As Lieber points out, the consequent hyperuricemia, secondary to excessive alcohol intake, may lead the individual predisposed to gout to acute attacks of that disorder.

The excessive hydrogen generated by the reduction of alcohol also affects the synthesis of alpha-glycerophosphate and fatty acids—the precursors of the triglycerides (lipids) which accumulate in the alcoholic fatty liver. So too, the excessive hydrogen absorbed into the cellular mitochondria blocks oxidation of fat and lipids which tend to build up.

The accumulation of lipids leads to excessive formation of lipoproteins. This is evidenced in the increase of a smooth endoplasmic reticulum in the cells. Adapted to the production of such lipoproteins, the liver of the alcoholic responds to food intake regularly by activating this process, thereby bringing about hyperlipemia. In addition to the development of hyperlipemia, the liver has to dispose of the excess fat by converting it into ketone bodies, which in turn may result in ketoacidosis in the alcoholic.

There is evidence to show that the proliferation of a smooth reticulum after chronic alcohol consumption increases its metabolic capacity in relation to degradation of drugs. Thus the chronic alcoholic will require higher dosages of barbiturates, meprobamate and perhaps other agents as well as anesthetics during surgical procedures in order to achieve the effect desired, as contrasted to those who are not addicted to ethanol. This is true, however, only when the individual is sober. When the chronic alcoholic has been drinking, the effect is the opposite as the increased activity of the smooth reticulum metabolizes alcohol itself by way of the accessory pathway and supplements the basic alcohol dehydrogenase system. This microsomal ethanol pathway commences to operate when ethanol reaches a particular level as it enters into competition with other drugs whose metabolisms share elements of the functioning of this system, thereby slowing down their degradation. So too, the increased activity of this system may explain the excessive liability to the toxicity of carbon tetrachloride which has been observed in the chronic alcoholic.

In addition to the direct effects of alcohol upon liver functioning, acetaldehyde, its degradation product, has major effects upon brain function. It has been suggested that acetaldehyde, rather than alcohol, may be responsible for the development of the dependence that occurs along with tolerance. The hypothesis is that acetaldehyde competes in the brain with the neurotransmitters and that unmetabolized neurotransmitter aldehydes accumulate to combine with the major neurotransmitters to form compounds similar to certain morphine derivatives. Another suggestion is that the acetaldehyde combines directly with amines to form isoquinoline derivatives that are known to be potent psychoactive compounds.

Ethanol tends to produce a hypoglycemia in fasting healthy persons, alcoholics, thyrotoxics, and decompensated diabetics. Fasted nondiabetic obese persons are refractory to the induction of hypoglycemia by alcohol.

It may well be that alcoholics who develop one of the encephalopathies are so predisposed by the defective metabolism of magnesium. Stendig-Lindberg has found that hypomagnesemia associated with delirium tremens tends to evolve toward an alcoholic encephalopathy more frequently than in those without such a condition. Ethanol ingestion appears to bring about urinary loss of the magnesium cation. Furthermore, on a long-term follow-up (five years), alcoholic patients whose magnesium replacement treatment was interrupted demonstrated low serum magnesium concentrations in spite of adequate diet and lenghty alcohol abstinence. Thus it is possible that the magnesium pool may be lower in alcoholic patients and that there may be continuing loss of magnesium cation.

Recent research produced evidence that hepatomegaly which occurs in alcoholism results not only in an increase of lipid in that organ, but also of protein. Furthermore, this protein accumulation takes place in the soluble fraction of the cell and probably is accounted for by intrahepatic retention of the export proteins.

As for the sterility which takes place

in the chronic alcoholic, Rubin and his colleagues found in animal experiments and also in human volunteers that a prolonged ethanol consumption increases remarkably 5-alpha-testosterone reductase activity and, therefore, may impair this major pathway related to testosterone metabolism. Related to the same matter, Van Thiel and his associates, working from a knowledge that testicular atrophy occurs in from one half to three quarters of male chronic alcoholics with cirrhosis of the liver and noting the atrophy of the testes on biopsies, found that ethanol inhibited metabolism of vitamin A in the testes. This, too, may relate to the occurrence of sterility in the 10 per cent of chronic alcoholics who develop this biological deficiency.

Administration of alcohol leads to a reduction in the blood of a norepinephrine-like substance that is elevated in association with anxiety, a cholinergic-like substance that is elevated with arousal of tension, and a substance regularly found in association with resentment. Alcoholics consistently were found to have greater amounts of the "resentment substance" than others, and alcohol was effective in reducing the action of all these substances in the blood of alcoholics.

Since alcohol reduces his anxiety, tension, and resentment, the alcoholic seeks its use more and more frequently. His addiction is manifested not only by this persistent use but also by the effects of its withdrawal. These results may be moderate, such as increased anxiety, a craving for alcohol, weakness, tremor, and perspiration, but may be serious and include anorexia, nausea, vomiting, fever, tachycardia, convulsions, hallucinations, and delirium tremens.

Socioeconomic Factors

Brenner has found that trends in the state of the economy are related to alcohol consumption and therefore to the ultimate effects upon the individual of alcoholism and its complications. With a long-term trend of increased per capita personal income in the U.S.A. an increase in per capita alcohol consumption is seen. On shorter fluctuations, the two variables are inversely related. Distilled spirits tend to be consumed increasingly with a long-term rise in income, as well as in short-term economic stress. On the other hand, the consumption of beer and wine has increased with both long- and short-term increases in per capita income. From the economic standpoint, it would appear that one population uses alcohol under conditions of general economic stability while another population indulges in distilled spirits when under major economic stress. The latter population, which is the smaller, tends to be the one most often in contact with the mental health or criminal justice system. They are also the chronic abusers, who suffer liver damage and increased mortality rates.

Alcoholism and Vehicular Accidents

In modern societies with their great dependence on high velocity transportation, acute or chronic alcohol intoxication—and through it impairment of perception, judgment, reaction time, and quality of response—contributes excessively to accidents. Alcoholic intoxication in Western societies is a major cause of death and morbidity due to traumatic accidents, particularly through automobile driving. In New York State, with a population of approximately 18 million, the Department of Motor Vehicles listed 2,663 persons killed and an estimated 295,000 people injured in automobile accidents in 1974. At least 50 per cent of the fatalities in pedestrian accidents involved individuals who had been drinking. Furthermore, arrest records in the state for driving while intoxicated reached 13,439 in 1974; in 1972, there were 38,014 apprehensions for driving while intoxicated. It is interesting to compare these figures with the 2,034 deaths caused by murders or nonnegligent manslaughter in New York State in 1973. We must recall that alcohol is implicated as the agent precipitating violence, which leads to assault and murder in a high number of instances, as well as being a major cause of self-directed violence through suicide or self-mutilative acts.

Blood alcohol levels of over 0.10 per cent have been found in large numbers of persons killed in auto accidents. Impairment of functioning as a driver occurs in many others at much lower concentrations of blood alcohol. Blood alcohol levels of 80 mg. per 100 ml. impair dark adaptation in the eyes. Also, at this level various investigations have demonstrated that car drivers show impaired judgment in passing other vehicles, in approaching caution lights, in interpretation of multiple sensory inputs, and in maintaining attentiveness when driving for long periods. Studies have shown that the risk of incurring an automobile accident increases appreciably when the blood alcohol level enters the range of 50 to 100 mg. per 100 ml. At the latter level the probability of an accident is ten times more than that for a sober driver.

In private aviation, 35 per cent of fatalities occur in drinking pilots. In one general hospital, 20 per cent of hospital admissions for home accidents were associated with intoxication.

Alcoholism and Crime

It was formerly stated that alcoholism was directly responsible for a large, perhaps a major, part of crime. There is now an increasing tendency to consider that alcoholism and criminalism are caused by similar social and psychological factors. Emotional instability and other expressions of a poorly integrated personality characterize both the recidivist criminal offender and the alcohol addict. The relation of alcohol to crime is more frequently one of a common cause rather than of cause and effect. It should be added, however, that the drinking of alcohol tends to be accompanied by a release of sexual and aggressive impulses.

Alcoholism and Suicide

As with other destructive acts, suicide is a common occurrence among alcoholics. Among those who attempt or accomplish suicide, Mayfield and Montgomery have defined several groups. A major group are those with a depressive reaction associated with chronic alcoholism, who make their attempt after weeks of excessive drinking. Preventive detection and therapy are most likely to lead to avoidance of the suicidal attempt in this group. In another group are those who act out their rage and aggression while drinking in the context of an interpersonal action with another—usually someone within the family. Under these conditions there is a high incidence of amnesia for suicide attempts, associated as well with later denial. Or the individual may initially admit inflicting an injury upon himself and later deny it. Many alcoholics who make suicidal attempts are remarkably relieved of significant depression, guilt, and shame following the attempt.

In their study of suicide, Barraclough and his colleagues listed the prominent features of those who take such actions (see Table 26–2).

Alcoholism and Personality Disturbance

Alcohol addiction is symptomatic of personality disturbance. Underneath the expressions of chronic intoxication with alcohol, and in spite of the conviction of most alcoholics that they would be quite normal if they ceased drinking, psychologically well-adapted personalities are seldom found during periods of sobriety. Some two thirds of chronic alcoholics fall outside the ordi-

TABLE 26–2   Leading Features of Alcoholic Suicides

(N = 15)	%
Heavy drinking, causing physical or mental illness, or social disability	80
Heavy drinking, not causing such disability	20
Informant says suicide drank too much	100
Family says suicide drank too much	93
Suicide said he drank too much	40
Frequency of drinking:	
Daily	67
Two to three times weekly	33
Bout drinking	80
Illness due to drink	47
Trouble at work	53
Arrested because of drunkenness	33
Heavy drinking at time of suicide	47
Recent change in drinking habits:	
Increase	40
Decrease	53
No change	7
Help to stop drinking	40
Duration of heavy drinking (in years):	
0–9	7
10–19	20
20–29	40
30–39	27
40–49	7
Age of onset of heavy drinking:	
10–19	33
20–29	47
30–39	7
40–49	7
50–59	0
60–69	7

(From Barraclough, B., Bunch, J., Nelson, B. and Sainsbury, P.: Br. J. Psychiatry, 125:355–373, 1974.)

nary classifications of the psychoses and psychoneuroses. The vast majority have character traits of the inadequate, passive-aggressive personalities. A lesser number are rigidly organized, compulsive individuals or dependent individuals with depressive affect and certain paranoidal personalities. The remainder of the addicted present the character traits and symptomatic expressions of the major psychoses, particularly paranoid and "pseudoneurotic" schizophrenia and the manic-depressive reactions, as well as the psychoneuroses and the antisocial personality disturbances.

Studies of chronically alcoholic men, the "skid row" alcoholics, have disclosed that they demonstrate as much or more psychopathology as do groups of psychotic hospitalized patients, particularly in such behavioral indices as bizarre appearance and behavior, speech disorganization, social isolation, and disoriented memory. These chronically habituated alcoholics are most conspicuous for their evidence of addiction, but they must also be recognized as predisposed to it through the existence of prior severe personality disorders.

Alcoholism and Psychoses

The relation between alcohol and the so-called alcoholic psychoses is not as simple as was formerly assumed. In many instances alcohol serves merely to release a reaction that is primarily psychogenic with factors intrinsic in the personality. In other cases there is such an interplay of psychogenic and metabolic factors that the picture becomes complex. In Korsakoff's syndrome and in chronic alcoholic deterioration, the psychosis is not, as was formerly believed, caused by the toxic effects of the alcohol itself but by thiamine deficiency. Even in this, the structure of the personality influences the picture. It is important to remember, too, that alcoholism may be a symptom—sometimes the most obvious symptom—of another personality disorder, such as depressive psychosis, schizophrenia, or paresis.

ACUTE ALCOHOLISM AND ALCOHOL WITHDRAWAL STATES

In the majority of instances, bouts of acute alcoholism may be terminated by establishment of a supportive, nonstimulating environment, with provision to insure adequate sleep and rest. In such circumstances, bodily processes quickly metabolize the excessive alcohol.

Much more complicated for therapeutic management are the acute withdrawal syndromes which erupt when long-continuing drinking bouts are terminated. After a few days of drinking, abstinence may result in tremulousness, nausea, and vomiting. If the individual resumes drinking and then abstains once more, as the signs of acute intoxication subside convulsive seizures or delirium with hallucinations may appear. The latter occurs only when the drinking bout has lasted several weeks.

Alkalosis regularly follows in the early stages of withdrawal, and other electrolytic disturbances, including hypomagnesemia, are frequent. For proper management, blood electrolyte studies should be performed. If deficiencies are noted in the fluid and electrolyte balances, they may then be corrected with administration of appropriate intravenous fluids.

To control the convulsions that may occur during sudden alcoholic withdrawal, Rothstein reports that chlordiazepoxide (Librium) administered with thiamine hydrochloride will successfully prevent such seizures. In a series of patients treated in a detoxification clinic, 50 to 100 mg. of chlordiazepoxide was administered orally or intramuscularly every few hours for the first 24 hours, maintaining the patients in a somnolent state. At the same time the patients received 100 mg. of thiamine hydrochloride. On the average, the individual patient received approximately 360 mg. of this drug in the first 24 hours. Patients treated in this way did as well as those in the control group receiving diphenylhydantoin (Dilantin). Chlordiazepoxide achieves the significant blood levels more rapidly than does diphenylhydantoin.

IDIOSYNCRATIC INTOXICATION

Occasionally, an individual of unstable personality may, on partaking of alcohol, suffer from a transitory mental state much more striking in the nature and severity of the symptoms than ordinary drunkenness, and known as idiosyncratic intoxication or pathological intoxication. The onset is dramatically sudden. Consciousness is impaired, and the patient is confused and disoriented and suffers from illusions, hallucinations of sight, and transitory delusions. Activity is exaggerated, impulsive, and aggressive, even to the point of destructiveness. The emotional disturbances are profound and may consist of rage, anxiety, or depression, perhaps with attempted suicide. The disorder lasts from a few minutes to a day or more and is usually followed by a prolonged sleep, after which there is an amnesia for the episode.

There is an increasing tendency to consider that such episodes, with their disturbances of consciousness and perhaps crimes of violence, are really instances of psychomotor epilepsy released by alcohol in persons predisposed to such seizures.

The behavior observed in idiosyncratic intoxication is in many ways illustrated by the following case:

N. W., aged 28, was seen in jail while awaiting trial on a charge of drunkenness and disorderly conduct. The patient's father had committed suicide as he was about to be sent to a hospital for mental diseases. The patient himself was described as being a friendly but quick-tempered and restless individual whose marriage had terminated in early divorce. He was said never to have been particularly alcoholic, but one July 4 he celebrated the holiday by drinking two bottles of beer and a glass of wine. Soon afterward he attempted to fling himself down an 80-foot embankment and was so greatly excited that he was taken to the police station for the night. The next morning he had no recollection of the affair. Ten months later the patient called late one afternoon to see friends who invited him to sample what they considered choice varieties of whiskey and gin. He accepted their invitation and drank somewhat more heavily than usual. Soon after leaving the home of his friends he was observed by a police officer to be acting strangely. As the officer spoke to him he attacked him. While the officer was calling for help, the patient disappeared. About 15 minutes later two women were startled to see a strange man thrust his head through a closed window of their living room, and shout "Help! Murder!" It was the patient, who then ran on to another house where he rang the doorbell insistently. As the occupant answered the summons he again screamed "Murder!" and ran to the street once more, where he broke the windshields and headlights of several parked automobiles and tore out the seats and pulled parts from other cars. At this point he was seized and taken to the police station where, on awakening the following morning, he had no recollection of his experiences of the previous night.

DELIRIUM TREMENS

This is an acute psychosis that may develop in the chronic alcoholic following an unusually severe or prolonged debauch. The term *delirium tremens* was first used by Thomas Sutton in 1813 in what is regarded as the classic description of this disease. The nature of the factors that operate in its production is uncertain. While it was long considered an acute psychosis developed during drinking, it is now generally thought to be a withdrawal syndrome precipitated in the chronic alcoholic suddenly deprived of alcohol. Delirium has been produced in the experimental laboratory by the sudden withdrawal of alcohol in those consuming 12 oz. or more of the agent for 48 or more days. The withdrawal may be associated not only with delirium and sometimes with convulsions, but also with abnormalities in the encephalogram. On the other hand, the disorder may arise from metabolic disturbances, including faulty carbohydrate metabolism, impairment of the detoxicating function of the liver, disturbed protein metabolism, acidosis, suboxidation of the brain, disturbed water balance, and various nutritional deficiencies, particularly of vitamin B, which the alcoholic usually takes in insufficient amounts and may not be able to absorb.

Delirium tremens or *withdrawal delirium*, the term used to describe this condition in DSM-III, is rare in a person under 30 years of age, or after less than three or four years of chronic alcoholism. The delirium is usually preceded by an aversion for food, restlessness, ir-

ritability, and disturbed sleep in which terrifying dreams occur. Occasional illusions and hallucinations are soon followed by more frequent ones, usually of a fleeting, terrifying nature. Figures on the wallpaper become menacing animate objects; inkspots become insects which the patient attempts to seize and destroy. The visual hallucinations are often of objects that appear to be moving and are particularly apt to represent loathsome animals of fantastic shapes, which terrify the patients and from which they may struggle to escape. These imaginary animals may be of diminutive size. At times hallucinations can be suggested; the patient, for example, may be handed an imaginary thread which, in response to instructions, he will carefully wind about his finger. Tactile hallucinations, probably associated with peripheral neuritis, are not infrequent. The patient feels as well as sees the insects on his skin. Olfactory hallucinations may occur. The patient may exclaim with terror that gas is being pumped into his room. While visual hallucinations are most numerous, auditory ones are not infrequently added.

As indicated, the mood is usually one of irritability, fear, apprehension, and even of terror. Occasionally, however, it is one of euphoria, amusement, good-natured silliness, or grim humor accompanied by the narration of preposterous confabulations.

Consciousness is clouded, and the patient may be greatly confused with disorientation for time and place. Speech is often incoherent. Persons about the patient may be misidentified. Attention is fleeting and impressions are retained but a moment. At times the delirium is of an occupational type. The motor restlessness is marked. The patient repeatedly gets out of bed to attend to some detail of his supposed occupation or to seize some imaginary object. Sleep is usually impossible.

On physical examination, the conjunctivae and face are ordinarily found to be congested. The pupils are dilated and often react slowly. A coarse tremor is an almost constant accompaniment. It is increased by muscular tension, such as extension of the fingers. The tongue is tremulous, as are also the muscles of the lips and face in well-developed cases. The pulse is rapid and often irregular and weak. The temperature is elevated and in some cases may be high. The skin is moist, the face often showing marked perspiration. The tendon reflexes are usually increased, although occasionally they are absent because of neuropathy. The nerve trunks and muscles may be painful to pressure. Albuminuria exists in about half the cases.

Differential Diagnosis

Delirium tremens is to be differentiated from other forms of alcoholic hallucinosis, as well as brain syndromes. Among the latter, and particularly pertinent to the group of alcoholic patients, is the delirious state associated with *acute hepatic insufficiency* and referred to sometimes as *impending hepatic coma.*

With the rise in incidence of alcoholism in the U.S.A., there has been a related increase in the incidence of cirrhosis of the liver. In 1974, cirrhosis outranked arteriosclerosis, influenza, and pneumonia as the most frequent cause of morbidity. It was seventh among the leading causes of death and in certain urban areas it was the third most frequent cause of death between the ages of 25 and 65.

Hepatic coma is considered dependent upon the accumulation of excessive amounts of ammonia in the bloodstream, which slows the Krebs' cycle in the brain, diverts alpha-ketoglutarate to glutamine and leads to excess amounts of the inhibitory neurotransmitter gamma-aminobutyric acid (GABA) and also accumulation of other false neurotransmitters. Fischer and Baldessarini have reported improvement in the mental status of patients with hepatic coma treated with L-dopa. It is their suggestion that this precursor of catecholamines, which is capable of entering the peripheral and central nervous system sites, increases neurotransmitter stores and thus replenishes the depletion that has occurred by the action of accumulated false neurotransmitters such as octapamine.

Alcoholic cirrhosis of the liver is the most common cause of the condition, although it may occur with other illnesses which lead to severe disturbance of the brain parenchyma. The importance of its discrimination rests upon the necessity of prescribing quite differing therapy; that for delirium tremens may lead to a fatal outcome in the patient with impending hepatic coma.

While both conditions may follow a period of heavy drinking, delirium tremens more often has its onset after cessation of drinking. The patient with delirium tremens is consciously responsive unless sedated, often aggressive and destructive, and his hallucinatory experiences are generally visual. The patient with impending hepatic coma more often is dull and lethargic, with diminution of psychomotor activity, and seldom has vividly formed visual hallucinations. Perhaps the most characteristic differential point is the irregular, "flapping" tremor which presents itself on extension of the arms in hepatic insufficiency. Speech is more often slowed, slurred, or monotonous, with perseveration, and a masklike facial expression may be seen. Both flexor muscle tonus and tendon reflexes are increased.

Those with impending hepatic coma usually subside into stupor with little indication of anxiety or fear, and there is more likely to be hypersomnia than the insomnia of the individual with delirium tremens. Hyperphagia exists with liver disorder, in contrast to the anorexia of the delirium tremens.

Also, the general medical examination in hepatic coma often shows evidence of jaundice, gross hepatomegaly, and fetor hepaticus, with elevation of 'the blood ammonia; these findings are absent in delirium tremens.

The electroencephalogram has been useful in the diagnosis of hepatic insufficiency in that a "triphasic wave" may be found in approximately 25 per cent of cases. Furthermore, a provocative dose of oral ammonium chloride (0.05 grain per kilogram of body weight) leads to an increase in EEG abnormality within 30 to 60 minutes in this condition.

Acute pancreatitis, another complication common in the chronic alcoholic, may also be associated with a hallucinatory psychosis that must be differentiated from delirium tremens. Here the symptoms of severe abdominal pain with abdominal tenderness, vomiting, tachycardia, leukocytosis, and particularly an elevated serum amylase level (over 300 Somogyi units) should establish the primary diagnosis.

Pathology

Changes both of a degenerative and of an inflammatory nature may occur. The brain is usually edematous. There are more or less liquefactive degeneration of nerve cells and an increase of glia with some round-cell infiltration. There is degeneration of myelin sheaths, especially in the cerebellum. Punctate hemorrhages occur and there is a mild degree of leptomeningitis.

Course and Prognosis

Delirium tremens usually runs an acute course, terminating in from three to ten days. Convalescence is frequently preceded by a prolonged sleep, after which consciousness becomes clear and the hallucinations disappear, although brief periods of delirium may occasionally recur at night for a short time. The prognosis depends largely upon the presence or absence of coexisting disease. The existence of myocardial degeneration, which is not uncommon in such chronic alcoholic patients,

makes the prognosis much less favorable. The mortality in the type of case that reaches a hospital has averaged in the past from 5 to 15 per cent, the two most frequent causes of death being heart failure and pneumonia. Occasionally, instead of terminating in death or recovery within the usual period, the psychosis may merge into a Korsakoff's psychosis.

Treatment

It has been customary to withdraw alcohol at once, but this practice is questionable. It is of great importance that care be taken to conserve the strength of a patient suffering from delirium tremens. The patient should be placed in bed immediately. As he is usually fearful, he should be constantly supervised and reassured concerning his fears and hallucinations. Many patients have died from exhaustion while struggling under mechanical restraint or from the depressing effect of sedative drugs. Restraint should therefore never be employed. Chlordiazepoxide should be prescribed orally in doses of 50 mg. every six hours. Any fluid or electrolyte imbalance or deficiency should be corrected by administration of appropriate parenteral infusion. Other sedation should be avoided. Morphine should never be given.

Cade emphasized the major importance of providing massive doses of thiamine in the treatment of acute alcoholic psychosis, as a means of preventing the cardiac failure that occurs. He believes that, regardless of the etiology of delirium tremens, many patients suffer a thiamine deficiency which, in turn, leads to a cardiomyopathy. Others have suggested that there exists as well a vagus neuropathy. Cade recommends that each patient receive not less than 200 mg. of thiamine immediately, to be repeated once or twice in the first 24 hours. Subsequent vitamin supplements should be given orally. Under such a regimen, he and his staff at the hospital in which he worked completely eliminated mortality in the acute alcoholic psychosis.

In those patients in whom delirium and marked tremor exist, the possibility of magnesium deficiency must be considered. With evidence of depression of the serum magnesium (normal 2.0 milliequivalents per liter), magnesium sulfate in a 5 per cent sterile solution may be given in doses up to 2.0 gm. four times daily for three days and then 1.0 gm. per day for an additional two or three days.

The patient has usually eaten little or nothing for several days. Since his gastrointestinal tract suffers from catarrhal inflammation because of his long indulgence in alcohol, he has little appetite and may even be nauseated. It is, however, exceedingly important that he receive an abundant, soft diet, particularly of carbohydrates. If possible, it should contain from 3000 to 4000 calories a day and should be rich in vitamins. The administration of the entire vitamin B complex is especially advisable as a preventive of Wernicke's syndrome or encephalopathy from nicotinic acid deficiency.

In contrast to the above treatment, alcoholic patients with the deliria of *impending hepatic coma* must be placed on a protein-free diet and fed with fruit juices and dextrose. Tranquilizers, sedatives, and methionine are to be avoided, while tetracycline, 1 to 2 gm. daily, and infusions of sodium glutamate (25 to 100 gm. daily in glucose solution) and L-arginine may be given to lower the blood ammonia. Fischer and Baldessarini have found that L-dopa is effective in reversing coma in this condition. Continuous plasma and whole blood transfusions have proved effective in relieving such conditions.

KORSAKOFF'S PSYCHOSIS

Sometimes it will be noted in what appears to be an ordinary case of de-lirium tremens except for the absence of the usual critical sleep, that the hallucinations and acute delirium disappear but the clinical picture merges into one characterized by amnesia, disorientation for time and place, and a falsification of memory, associated with the symptoms and signs of peripheral neuropathy. At other times the syndrome develops in the chronic alcoholic who has not suffered from a preceding delirium tremens but has indulged excessively in alcohol for several years. This syndrome was described in 1887 by the Russian psychiatrist, Sergei Korsakoff. Because of its frequent association with chronic alcoholism, Korsakoff's psychosis, or amnestic disorder as listed in DSM-III, has long been classified among the alcoholic psychoses. Strictly speaking, this syndrome should be classified elsewhere.

Etiology and Pathology

The condition is but one of several syndromes that result from vitamin B deficiency, a form of deficiency to which the chronic alcoholic is especially prone because of his impaired gastrointestinal absorption, his diet that is largely limited to vitamin-free alcohol, and his increased vitamin requirement resulting from the high caloric effect of alcohol.

Vitamin B deficiency may, of course, exist under various circumstances. Although a deficiency of other vitamin B constituents doubtless contributes to these syndromes, thiamine and niacin deficiencies are particularly responsible for them. The variations in these syndromes depend largely upon the parts of the nervous system in which the neuronal degeneration is localized. If this degeneration is largely in the cerebrum and the peripheral nerves, Korsakoff's syndrome results. If the degenerative changes occur in the long peripheral nerves of the alcoholic, the result is known as "alcoholic neuritis." If the greatest deficiency is in niacin and the degeneration is marked in the cerebrum, less in the spinal cord, and least in the peripheral nerves, the vitamin deficiency encephalopathy assumes the form of pellagra. If the brain stem is the site of the degenerative process, the syndrome is that of Wernicke's disease.

Frequently, these syndromes are not sharply defined but merge one into another, the pattern depending upon the vitamin in which the deficiency is greatest and upon the sites and extent of the degeneration. For example, symptoms of Korsakoff's psychosis and Wernicke's disease or of Wernicke's disease and pellagra may be associated. In fact, in nutritional encephalopathy it is possible in the same individual to see delirium tremens, Korsakoff's psychosis, niacin deficiency encephalopathy, and the Wernicke syndrome.

The nutritional encephalopathy is probably caused by the fact that in the absence of ample quantities of thiamine and nicotinic acid there is an impaired oxidation of pyruvic acid during the breakdown of glucose.

The histopathology of Korsakoff's psychosis consists of diffuse parenchymatous changes. Among these changes are axonal alterations, a deposition of excessive amounts of normal lipochrome pigment in the nerve cells, glia, microglia, and around the blood vessels in the prefrontal and motor cortex, and acute chromatolytic changes in the larger nerve cells in these areas, especially in the Betz cells.

Symptoms

The most conspicuous symptoms have already been indicated. Superficially, consciousness may appear clear and the seriousness of the mental disorder may not be apparent. On questioning the patient, however, one is often surprised to discover the extent of mental impairment. Although possessing a relatively good grasp of what is in sight, he or she is disoriented as to that which is beyond immediate observation and dependent on memory. At

first the memory loss is most marked for events occurring since the onset of the disease, but later the memory for remote events is lost also. The amnesia is anterograde, and frequently the patient cannot recall what has just been said to him and often misidentifies people about him. He usually presents a superficial cheerfulness and often evades inquiries by jocularities.

In his confabulation the patient relates fictitious memories which superficially conceal the actual amnesia. The pseudo-reminiscences, which usually vary from day to day, can often be suggested and guided by leading questions, with the result that the patient will narrate whatever fictitious reminiscence is proposed. Presumably the patient's confabulations serve as a defense against anxiety by concealing from him his defective functioning. Disorientation, especially as to time, usually exists. The polyneuropathy, which is sometimes absent, is most marked in the legs, with pain, tenderness over the nerve trunks, absent knee jerks, and, in severe cases, foot drop and wrist drop. The disease is relatively more frequent in women.

Course and Prognosis

Many cases clear up after six or eight weeks, with approximate restoration to mental health provided treatment is given. If the process is not fully reversible, the disease continues for several months, with a gradual improvement but without complete return of memory. In some cases there are a permanent impairment of efficiency and a certain degree of intellectual, emotional, and esthetic deterioration. The neuropathy usually improves rather rapidly and often completely disappears.

A Korsakoff-like amnesia with confabulations serving to fill in the losses of memory may occur in uremia, after brain trauma, in general paresis, and in other organic and toxic diseases of the brain—conditions in which the pathogenesis does not seem related to dietary deficiency. If irreversible changes have not already occurred, the active symptoms may rapidly disappear. Insight is not usually regained.

Treatment

The first step in treatment is the discontinuance of the use of alcohol. To correct the deficiency of vitamin B_1, 20 to 50 gm. of thiamine chloride may be given daily for a few days, to be followed by 20 gm. of powdered brewers' yeast in iced milk three times a day. Milk, fruit, eggs, meat, and other foods rich in vitamin B complex should be liberally provided. It is probably advisable to administer ascorbic acid also. If irreversible structural changes have already taken place, the symptoms are not affected by vitamins. When acute neuropathy exists, rest in bed is desirable. Care should be exercised to prevent permanent foot drop. As soon as pain and tenderness in the legs have disappeared, active physiotherapy with massage and appropriate exercises should be instituted.

ACUTE HALLUCINOSIS

Since excessive indulgence in alcohol occasions the symptom complex to be considered, it has usually been classified as an alcoholic psychosis. The present tendency is to look upon it as a psychogenic reaction liberated by alcoholic excess, rather than as a purely toxic expression. It seems reasonably safe to state that the clinical characteristics are determined by personality factors. Some cases lead one to believe that the disorder is a schizophrenic reaction released by alcohol. However, recent clinical studies have disclosed that the majority of individuals with this syndrome are cyclothymic or extroverted individuals, with a family and developmental history quite unlike that of the schizophrenic. Cases diagnosed as chronic alcoholic hallucinosis ultimately become obvious paranoid schizophrenic reactions.

From the histories of cases of prolonged inebriation with onset shortly after withdrawal of alcohol or restriction of intake, it appears likely that this acute condition represents a type of alcoholic abstinence syndrome, perhaps occurring in individuals with a constitutional predominance for auditory imagery or with some disturbance of the seventh nerve and the auditory pathways within the central nervous system predisposing to tinnitus, with subsequent auditory illusions or hallucinations. Thus tinnitus is reportedly found in a high proportion of patients with auditory hallucinations. Furthermore, in those with unilateral tinnitus, the hallucinatory experience customarily is ipsilateral. Pure alcoholic hallucinosis occurs much less commonly than does delirium tremens or hallucinatory states with both visual and auditory hallucinations.

Symptoms

As in the case of delirium tremens, acute alcoholic hallucinosis develops only after the prolonged and excessive use of alcohol, although usually it is precipitated by increased indulgence. Descriptively, the reaction may be summarized as one of auditory hallucinosis occurring in a clear sensorium accompanied affectively by marked fear. In the majority of cases, the hallucinations are usually accusatory, or threatening, or both. The voices are particularly apt to accuse the patient of homosexual practices and to call him indecent names. In women, as in men, the hallucinations are frequently accusatory and of sexual content. The voices, however, accuse the patient of heterosexual offenses rather than of homosexual ones as in men. The hallucinated voices often refer to the patient in the third person and threaten him with such expressions as, "Now shoot him"; "Let's cut him up tonight." The patient may hear the firing of pistols or other sounds suggesting a threat of attack. Frequently, in the case of the operator of some mechanical equipment, the hallucinations appear at first to come from his machine and to be synchronous with the rhythmical sound of its operation. In a few the vocal hallucinations are benign and may or may not affect the behavior of the patient. Olfactory hallucinations are frequently associated. Illusions of sight are not uncommon. Visual hallucinations may be intermingled to a slight extent but are rarely present in a typical case.

The patient's ideational content and his behavior are determined by the acceptance of his hallucinations as reality. Ideas of reference and misinterpretations are common. A delusional system is rapidly acquired, while additions and elaborations are quickly introduced. The patient may appeal to the police for protection or arm himself in self-defense.

In contrast to its disturbance in delirium tremens, consciousness remains clear in alcoholic hallucinosis and the patient continues to be oriented, projecting his hallucinations into a real environment. In another respect, too, acute hallucinosis differs from delirium tremens: after recovery there is no amnesia for events occurring during its course.

The disturbance in mood is usually pronounced, being characteristically one of fear and apprehension. Terror-stricken by the threats of his imaginary pursuers, or reduced to despair by the accusing voices and his panic state, the patient may attempt to end his own life. The fear may at times be accompanied by anger or depression. Frequently, there is an element of irritability, while during the temporary cessation of the hallucinations the characteristic alcoholic humor may be manifested.

Course

Recovery from alcoholic hallucinosis usually occurs in five days to a month. Recurrences are common if the patient again indulges excessively in alcohol. Unlike delirium tremens, alcoholic hallucinosis is never followed by the Korsakoff syndrome. Occasionally, the hallucinatory episode continues beyond the usual period and merges into a manifest schizophrenia.

Psychological Factors

Mention has already been made of the fact that acute hallucinosis is not always an uncolored alcoholic psychosis. There seems reason to believe that if a certain type of personality takes large quantities of alcohol over a considerable period of time, a psychogenic reaction of an acute schizophrenic nature may be liberated. The frequent history of unsuccessful heterosexual adjustment in the patient with alcoholic hallucinosis and the homosexual character of the hallucinations suggest that in some cases, at least, unrecognized homosexual tendencies may be the psychopathogenic factor which has both prompted the use of alcohol and determined the nature of the hallucinations. As to the psychogenic determination of the mood in alcoholic hallucinosis, one may speculatively suggest that the unconscious sense of threat to the personality in the biologically destructive and socially prohibited homosexual impulse is greater than the feeling of guilt which this repressed impulse sometimes arouses; hence the mood is usually one of fear rather than of depression. From the standpoint of self-respect, too, fear is psychologically preferable to shame. If the sense of guilt is relatively strong, then the patient exhibits the depression occasionally seen in the disease.

Treatment

The treatment consists in placing the patient under such supervision that he may neither commit an indiscreet act nor do harm to himself. All alcohol must, of course, be withdrawn. A neuroleptic is useful for relieving fear and anxiety. The administration of food is not so difficult as in delirium tremens, but it should be given regularly and in abundance. It is well to give large amounts of orange juice, also vitamin B complex.

ALCOHOLIC PARANOIA

It is convenient to describe alcoholic paranoia clinically, although its recognition as a true alcoholic psychosis is scarcely warrantable. Here, too, there may be a common factor — the repressed homosexual impulse — beneath both the alcoholism and the psychosis. Usually, the patient has never established a mature heterosexual relationship. In the prepsychotic life of the patient, we often find the same incomplete developments, fixations, traits of personality, and psychopathological processes as in other paranoid psychoses. In alcoholic paranoia, the use of alcohol, prompted by these tendencies, weakens repression and causes the vicious psychopathological circle of homosexual conflict, alcoholic indulgence, and paranoid delusion to continue without interruption. Psychologically, the conditions were favorable for the development of a psychosis before the use of alcohol became excessive. In some cases one might almost say that a latent psychosis already existed and that the alcohol did no more than hasten its appearance. The prior personality pattern has been characterized by stubbornness, suspiciousness, resentment, projection, and other defensive mechanisms. The history of the patient usually shows that he has accepted discipline poorly and that he has preferred the society of men.

Symptoms

This clinical manifestation is typically characterized by delusions of jealousy and infidelity. At first the patient is irritable, fault-finding, and distrustful. To these unpleasant defensive characteristics are later added accusations of marital infidelity, as evidence of which are cited the most insignificant and absurd arguments. With his jealousy motivated by an unrecognized sense of guilt and fear based on the odious trends and impulses of his own personality, the suspicious husband devises numerous schemes to entrap his wife and her supposed paramour.

A noncommissioned officer in the Army, whose enlistment had perhaps been prompted by an unrecognized homosexual interest, argued that he could not be the father of the child to which his wife had given birth inasmuch as it was born 279 instead of 280 days following marital relations with her. As evidence that the family physician was the father of the child, he cited the fact that on one occasion the doctor had not submitted his bill promptly. On several occasions, he threatened the life of the physician and finally actually attempted to shoot him.

Because of their incompletely developed and poorly integrated personalities, these patients are peculiarly inadequate for the sustained demands for social adaptation which marriage brings. By imputing to the wife, too, the interest which they fundamentally feel for other men, they secure an alleviation of anxiety. The ideas that follow are psychologically protective but adjustively disruptive. At times, with the increased use of intoxicants, impotence, produced by the toxic action of the alcohol on the central nervous system, increases the patient's sense of insecurity and incompetence. To prevent any recognition of this requires a further development of ideas of infidelity.

Prognosis

The prognosis in the alcoholic paranoid state is not good. With the decrease in demands for adjustment that follows removal to a hospital, the patient may improve and no longer entertain his delusional ideas. At other times, having observed that the expression of his ideas has resulted in a deprivation of his liberty, he may dissimulate and maintain that he now recognizes he was in error and that he no longer doubts the fidelity of his wife. At any rate, after the return to the old situation, the former delusions and threatening behavior usually soon reappear.

OTHER ENCEPHALOPATHIES

Wernicke's encephalopathy, resulting from a deficiency in vitamin B, may be associated with alcoholic addiction or with other conditions in which this deficiency exists. It is discussed in Chapter 16, Brain Syndromes Associated with Endocrine, Metabolic, and Nutritional Disturbances.

The chronic alcoholic may also develop a *nicotinic acid deficiency encephalopathy,* in which are seen typical pellagra-like symptoms with clouded consciousness, parkinsonian-like rigidities, and sucking and grasping reflexes. Improvement follows treatment with a high calorie, high vitamin diet and administration of nicotinic acid or nicotinamide.

Marchiafava's disease, with signs of aphasia, agnosia, and apraxia, is related to long-continued excessive use of cheap red wine. Pathologically there are found degenerative changes in the corpus callosum and multiple cortical and subcortical areas of encephalomalacias. Cerebellar ataxia may also develop in chronic alcoholics.

ALCOHOLIC DETERIORATION

A considerable number of persons who consume large amounts of alcohol over a prolonged period ultimately suffer a certain disintegration of personality, the change ranging from an impairment of emotional stability and control to a noticeable dementia. The principal organic damage that alcohol inflicts upon the human nervous system probably is caused by avitaminosis rather than by primary toxic injury itself. From the standpoint of anatomical pathology there is, in the more severe cases, a progressive, chronic parenchy-

matous nervous degeneration, sometimes affecting a considerable part of the neuraxis. As previously indicated, so-called alcoholic dementia is caused by progressive atrophy of the cortex of the frontal lobes.

Symptoms

One of the earliest mental symptoms of the abuse of alcohol is an increased tendency to act out impulsively in response to momentary affectivity. The alcoholic patient develops resentment, hostility, and feelings of guilt. Although for a considerable period a capacity for ethical sentiments remains, these are not sustained or applied, with the result that ethical purposes and strivings suffer, persistence and commitment to goals or tasks are impaired, perseverance of endeavor is lost, and the patient becomes untruthful and unreliable. The tendency to deceive and to gloss over whatever is discreditable in behavior or character represents a fundamental inability to face the facts of reality and of the patient's own situation. He blames others for failure and presents himself as abused or as the victim of circumstances for which he is in no way responsible, while at the same time he exaggerates his own achievements.

Affection is lost and ambition disappears. The confirmed alcoholic becomes careless of his personal appearance and neglectful of his family. With an increasing egocentricity, his former sense of social or other responsibility disappears, or rather is avoided by the process of evasively treating it facetiously and superficially. Usually the patient's mood is one of unwarranted euphoria and carefree good humor, but a word of implied reproval may evoke a violent and profane outburst of irritability. With his friends, the alcoholic may be a congenial and welcome companion who enters enthusiastically into their pleasures, but at home he may be brutal, surly, and without shame.

In nearly every instance, the patient's sex life is defective in some respect—with impotence, and evidence of either latent or overt homosexual expression. This failure in some instances serves as a cause of the alcoholism and in others represents a result. Frequently, this maladjustment operates to continue the vicious circle. A defensive attitude is assumed toward those who are not alcoholic in their habits, and the patient is touchy, irritable, and critical in the presence of those who he believes do not approve his excesses. There is an increasing poverty of ideas, with a growing incapacity for sustained attention and for more delicate discriminations. After a time, memory becomes impaired, and the insidious dementia finally becomes extreme.

A physician, whose practice had been ruined by his alcoholism, abused his children and accused his wife of neglect and infidelity. He was unable to remember how long he had been in the hospital or give the name of his ward physician who had seen him daily for months.

Course and Outcome

If the use of alcohol is discontinued as soon as any early character changes are noted, there may be a nearly complete restoration to former mental health which, however, must always remain precarious, since the alcoholic was never well-adjusted to life. Moreover, the alcoholic, in spite of his protests to the contrary, rarely is motivated to give up his addiction because alcohol provides the easiest way of escape from the difficulties which his inadequately integrated personality has precipitated. Deterioration of personality is permanent, and any actual dementia is, of course, quite irremediable.

Treatment

Unfortunately, alcoholism has been regarded as a moral problem, with the result that the complex contributing factors have not received the scientific attention they have merited, and atten-tion to therapy has not been commensurate with the extent of the social problem.

The excessive abuse of alcohol is symptomatic of a personality disorder. As in anxiety disorders, with which alcoholism has much in common, the patient is usually unaware of the particular personality problems from which he or she has sought relief through the escape and anxiety-relieving mechanisms which alcohol facilitates. Theoretically, therefore, treatment should be directed toward preventing the patient from desiring alcohol rather than toward restraining him from it. While it is exceptionally uncommon for an addictive alcoholic to become a moderate drinker, the goal of achieving total abstinence for those who come to treatment should not be regarded as the sole criterion of success. In some, total abstinence does not bring about overall improvement in social adaptation; it may result in social deterioration. A number of chronic alcoholics may learn to restrict their drinking within the framework of the social mores and successfully reinstate themselves in their family and social life. The personality characteristics that typify this group and the supportive forces that sustain this balance between limited abstinence and social functioning remain to be determined. For the most part, however, total abstinence has proved more effective in rehabilitation.

The patient should be approached with the attitude that his illness arises from a personality disorder for whose origins and functions he has not been responsible—an approach quite different from that of the moralizers who have attempted usually to deter his excessive usage of alcohol prior to his entrance into a treatment program. Psychiatric treatment should have a basic routine program of active physical exercise, constructive occupational work, agreeable social relaxation, and psychotherapy. The patient's mental life and experiences should be reviewed for the purpose of discovering the main factors which have caused him to become dependent on alcohol. One must, therefore, obtain a thorough understanding of the patient as a person and of his particular life situation. Psychoanalytic techniques are usually not practicable with the addictive drinker, as generally the emergence of suppressed and repressed rage deepens his suffering from the affects of shame and rage to an extent that is beyond his capacity to endure further self-relevation. Because of these characteristics, he usually resumes drinking whenever painful unconscious material begins to come to the surface. A constructive analysis of his personality difficulties must be accompanied by a prolonged re-educational effort.

The alcoholic is usually a dependent personality and therefore needs continuous support over a long period of time, frequently for years. Often, beneath his façade of genial affability he is a hostile, anxious, guilt-ridden person. Primitive or restraining measures that increase the patient's sense of being wronged and stir aggressive and resentful feelings should be avoided. The therapist should not condone the patient's alcoholic habits, yet he or she should not be critical. The attitude should be objective and impersonal. It should be remembered that the patient's reasons for his alcoholism are rationalizations.

Where there is a demonstrated dependent relationship upon a protecting person, often the mother, wife, or lover, who provides the alcohol and gives in to the insatiable demands of the alcoholic, this individual must also receive treatment in order to break the pathological bond that perpetuates the habit.

Psychotherapy is of course possible only in the addict whose intellectual equipment is still sound. If dementia has occurred, he must usually be committed to an institution.

Behavioral therapy has been tried in a number of programs for alcoholics. Miller recently reported on a behavioral intervention program with skid row alcoholics. Necessary services were provided as incentives, dependent on their sobriety. Withdrawal of supplies and services and a 5-day suspension were alternatives. He observed substantial diminution of alcohol consumption and public drunkenness and an increase in number of hours employed in a small group. In another study of the chronic deteriorated alcoholic, Gallant and his colleagues reported that compulsory inpatient treatment, followed by compulsory clinic treatment, has no advantage over voluntary or compulsory clinic treatment.

Group psychotherapy of alcoholics is employed with great frequency. The experience of being with other similarly afflicted people seems to make the alcoholic accept more readily treatment in the group environment. The interpretations offered by other members make the attainment of insight easier and less frightening.

ALCOHOLICS ANONYMOUS. Alcoholics Anonymous, established in 1935 in Akron, Ohio, and conducted by former alcoholics, has produced many temporary and even prolonged cures of alcoholic addiction. It was organized without psychiatric guidance and in its social-religious program it has constructively utilized many principles of group psychotherapy.

As a rule, members of Alcoholics Anonymous are above the average in intelligence, education, and social status, and their attitude toward the addict is tolerant and constructive. The organization offers the confirmed addict an opportunity to escape from his or her former psychosocial isolation, from the feeling that no one really understands or cares about him and that he can trust no one. In his group, the addict has a sense of belonging, of being understood and accepted, and of sharing common convictions. By means of his allegiance to the group, the member develops a religious fervor, and when he answers a call to aid another alcoholic at the cost of inconvenience and self-denial, his religious devotion is constructively internalized. An inspirational and mass-suggestion approach is an important feature.

By arousing a deep desire to help others and by creating a sense of responsibility for doing so, the organization contributes to the addict's cure. The opportunity to talk about himself in the group meetings affords the addict an opportunity for narcissistic satisfaction, for self-expression, and for therapeutic catharsis. The program of Alcoholics Anonymous ignores the cause of the alcoholic's addiction and focuses directly on the drinking itself.

Unfortunately, certain individuals addicted to alcohol are unwilling to join this organization. The reasons for their lack of motivation for this group affiliation remain unclear. Some do so as a denial of the addiction, while others appear to have competing loyalties, are perpetuating a defense of self-sufficiency against dependent strivings which would arouse shame, or are prone to develop intolerable anxiety in group situations. Some appear unable to accept the emphasis on obtaining spiritual aid from a "Higher Power."

Related to Alcoholics Anonymous are the Al-Anon family groups, consisting of nonprofessional self-help groups of spouses, relatives, and friends of alcoholics who come together to work through the common problems they have experienced in living with the problem drinker. Such groups are self-selected and a considerable majority of the members join after reading of the organization in a newspaper column. Many of the members of Al-Anon had alcoholic parents as well as having married an alcoholic. Many admit that they are as disturbed as the alcoholic family member. The Al-Anon groups identify an alcoholic personality, come to recognize how their own behavior often contributed to the drinking habit of the spouse, and develop insight through the sharing of the group experience, the group superego, and the didactic information made available. Members

learn that they cannot control the actions of the other, and must detach themselves from the attempt to do so. By so doing, self-esteem and independence are re-established, as well as personal reliance on spiritual support. The Alateen groups for adolescents in the alcoholics' families function similarly.

DISULFIRAM OR ANTABUSE THERAPY. In 1948 two Danish investigators, Jens Hald and Erik Jacobsen, in search of a vermifuge, tried disulfiram (tetraethylthiuram disulfide). They observed that persons who had ingested this substance prior to the consumption of alcohol showed symptoms that differed quantitatively and qualitatively from those in the common picture of alcoholic intoxication. The discomfort after alcohol consumption in persons taking this drug was so great that these investigators decided to use it as a remedy for alcoholism. It is believed that the discomfort is caused by interference with the excretion of acetaldehyde, an intermediary product in the oxidation of alcohol.

When a patient who has taken 0.5 to 1 gm. of disulfiram within the preceding 12 hours partakes of alcohol, he experiences within 5 to 15 minutes a feeling of heat in the face, soon followed by an intense vasodilation of the face and neck, the skin of which may assume a purple-red color. At the same time, the conjunctiva is injected, and the patient suffers from tachycardia. These symptoms are soon followed by headache, dyspnea, dizziness, chest pain, nausea, palpitation, and vomiting. There is an initial rise of blood pressure followed by a fall, perhaps to 80 mm. Hg. The discomfort following the imbibition of alcohol so long as disulfiram is in the blood is so great that the patient does not care to drink.

The dose of disulfiram should be individualized, but usually 0.5 gm. once a day, preferably in the morning, is sufficient. Rarely, 1.0 gm may be required. Initial treatment with a drug possessing such serious toxic potentialities should be under constant medical supervision.

Although it was originally believed that persons suffering from marked disease of the liver, coronary disease, arteriosclerosis with hypertension, or diabetes should not receive disulfiram, experience with a large series of patients suggests that the only important contraindication is cardiac decompensation. There have been reports of eruption of a psychotic reaction during the use of the drug.

Formerly, the administration of disulfiram was not begun until after an abstinence from alcohol for one week, but in recent years disulfiram has been given even when the patient is intoxicated. In such instances, the initial dose is one-half or less the usual one (7.5 mg. per kilogram of body weight) and is given with an antihistamine drug, such as 25 mg. of Promethazine, and 5 gm. of sodium chloride in one-half glass of water. There are now some patients who have been kept on moderate doses of the medication for as long as several decades.

Baekeland and his colleagues emphasize from their experience that those who tend to do better on disulfiram treatment are likely to be older, to have a relatively long history of heavy drinking, to have suffered delirium tremens, and to have had contact with Alcoholics Anonymous. Also, these individuals did not have a depressive make-up and were not depressed. Comparisons of groups of patients who had been given disulfiram with and without the opportunity for regular psychotherapeutic follow-up visits have shown that those motivated to maintain the continuing therapeutic contact respond most effectively when this drug is given.

Disulfiram therapy must be considered as a variation of the behavioral therapies of the aversive type. In contrast to other forms of conditioned reflex methods, the unpleasant effects not only are present each time the patient takes a small but adequate dose of disulfiram and drinks alcohol, but they actually increase with continued ingestion of the drug. If continued, it probably helps to overcome the craving for alcohol. For the treatment to be successful, however, it is necessary for the patient to have a real desire to be helped, to be willing to take the drug with consistency, and to cooperate in psychotherapy. Daily uninterrupted administration of disulfiram makes it physiologically impossible to continue to use alcohol as a defense mechanism. To remove this protection, however, without at the same time eliminating its need by psychotherapy can scarcely lead to a cure of the patient. As long as the basic difficulties which led to the alcoholism are not resolved, the desire for alcohol persists and, along with it, an unwillingness to take the medication.

Calcium carbamide (Temposil) has actions similar to disulfiram but appears to be excreted more rapidly so that its effectiveness is short lived following its ingestion. Calcium carbamide is considered a safer medication than disulfiram, because when taken with alcohol it produces fewer hypotensive and electrocardiographic changes. Furthermore it appears more acceptable to patients, because the associated side effects are less.

Other clinical experiments in the use of drugs in treatment of the alcoholic have shown that the antidepressants have some efficacy in those with depression. Akiskal and his colleagues report a clinical experiment in the use of a diuretic antidepressive combination in the treatment of a small group of alcoholic depressives. In this instance, the diuretic furosemide in doses of 40 mg. twice daily was prescribed for 24 days, combined with amitriptyline in a single dose of 150 to 200 mg. before bedtime. These clinicians suggest that the furosemide enhances the antidepressive action of amitriptyline and that the diuretic brings about a natriuresis to reverse the sodium retention which some have concluded is related to a depressive state.

BIBLIOGRAPHY

Akiskal, H. S., Beard, J. D., Fink, R. D., and Knott, D. H.: Diuretic-antidepressant combination in alcoholic depressives. Dis. Nerv. Syst., 35:207–211, 1974.

Arky, R. A., Abramson, E. A., and Freinkel, N.: Alcohol hypoglycemia. Metabolism, 17:977–987, 1968.

Arlon, J.: Al-Anon family groups. Am. J. Psychother., 28:30–45, 1974.

Baekeland, F., Lundwall, L., Kissin, B., and Shanahan, T.: Correlates of outcome in disulfiram treatment of alcoholism. J. Nerv. Ment. Dis., 153:1–9, 1971.

Barona, E., Leo, M. A., Barowsky, S. A., and Lieber, C. S.: Alcoholic hepatomegaly accumulation of protein in the liver. Science, 190:794–795, 1975.

Barraclough, B., Bunch, J., Nelson, B., and Sainsbury, P.: A hundred cases of suicide: clinical aspects. Br. J. Psychiatry, 125:355–373, 1974.

Belfer, M. L., Shader, R. J., Carroll, M., and Harmatz, J. S.: Alcoholism in women. Arch. Gen. Psychiatry, 25:540–544, 1971.

Blane, H. T., Barry, H. III, and Barry, H. J.: Sex differences in birth order of alcoholics. Br. J. Psychiatry, 119:657–667, 1971.

Brenner, M. H.: Trends in alcohol consumption and associated illnesses: Some effects of economic changes. Am. J. Public Health, 65:1279–1292, 1975.

Brod, T. M.: Alcoholism as a mental health problem of native Americans. Arch. Gen. Psychiatry, 32:1385–1391, 1975.

Cade, J. F. J.: Massive thiamine dosage in the treatment of acute alcoholic psychoses. Aust. N.Z. J. Psychiatry, 6:222–230, 1972.

Davidson, E. A., and Solomon, P.: The differentiation of delirium tremens from impending hepatic coma. J. Ment. Sci., 104:326–333, 1958.

Dott, A. B.: Blood alcohol levels and intoxication. J.A.M.A., 214:2196, 1970.

Ewing, J. A., Rouse, B. A., and Pellizzari, E. D.: Alcohol sensitivity and ethnic background. Am. J. Psychiatry, 131:206–210, 1974.

Feighner, J. P., Robins, E., Guze, S. B., et al.: Diagnostic criteria for use in psychiatric research. Arch. Gen. Psychiatry, 26:57–63, 1972.

Fischer, J. E., and Baldessarini, R. J.: False neurotransmitters and hepatic failure. Lancet, 2:75–80, 1971.

Gale, L., and Frances, A.: Superego factors in alcoholics. Am. J. Psychother., 29:235–242, 1975.

Gallant, D. M., Bishop, M. P., Monledoux, A., et al.: The revolving door alcoholic. Arch. Gen. Psychiatry, 28:633–640, 1973.

Gerrein, J. R., Rosenberg, C. M., and Manohar, V.: Disulfiram maintenance in outpatient treatment of alcoholism. Arch. Gen. Psychiatry, 28:798–802, 1973.

Goodwin, D. W., Schulsinger, F., Hermansen, L., Guze, S. B., and Winokur, G.: Alcohol problems in adoptees raised apart from alcoholic biologic parents. Arch. Gen. Psychiatry, 28:235–244, 1973.

Graw, R. G., Jr., Buckner, C. D., and Eisel, R.: Plasma exchange transfusion for hepatic coma. Transfusion, 10:26–32, 1970.

Gross, M. M., Halpert, E., Sabot, L., and Polizoes, P.: Hearing disturbances and auditory hallucinations in the acute alcoholic psychoses. J. Nerv. Ment. Dis., 137:455–465, 1963.

Isbell, H., Fraser, H. F., Wikler, A., Belleville, R. E., and Eisenman, A. W.: An experimental study of the etiology of "rum fits" and delirium tremens. Q. J. Stud. Alcohol., 16:1–33, 1955.

Johnson, L. C., Burdick, A., and Smith, J.: Sleep during alcohol intake and withdrawal in the chronic alcoholic. Arch. Gen. Psychiatry 22:406–418, 1970.

Kaim, S. C., Klett, C. J., and Rothfield, B.: Treatment of acute alcohol withdrawal state: Comparison of four drugs. Am. J. Psychiatry, 125:1640–1646, 1969.

Koller, K. M., and Castanis, J. N.: Family background and life situations in alcoholics. Arch. Gen. Psychiatry, 21:602–610, 1969.

Levy, M. S., Livingstone, B. L., and Collins, D. M.: A clinical comparison of disulfiram and calcium carbamide. Am. J. Psychiatry, 123:1018–1022, 1967.

Lieber, C. S.: The metabolism of alcohol. Sci. Am., 234:25–31, 1974.

Mayfield, D. G., and Montgomery, D.: Alcoholism, alcohol intoxication and suicide attempts. Arch. Gen. Psychiatry, 27:349–353, 1972.

Miller, P. M.: Behavioral intervention program for chronic public offenders. Arch. Gen. Psychiatry, 32:915–918, 1975.

Morse, R. M., and Hurt, R. D.: Screening for alcoholism. J.A.M.A., 242:2688–2690, 1979.

New York State Task Force on Alcohol Problems: Action against Alcohol Problems. Albany, N.Y., N.Y. State Department of Mental Hygiene, 1975.

Pattison, E. M.: Critique of abstinence criteria in treatment of alcoholism. Int. J. Soc. Psychiatry, 14:268–276, 1968.

Rothstein, E.: Prevention of alcohol withdrawal seizures: The roles of diphenylhydantoin and chlordiazepoxide. Am. J. Psychiatry, 130:1381–1382, 1973.

Rubin, E., Lieber, C. S., and Altman, K.: Prolonged ethanol consumption increases testosterone metabolism in the liver. Science, *191*:561–564, 1976.

Sokoloff, L.: Neurophysiology and neurochemistry of coma. Exp. Biol. Med., *4*:15–33, 1971.

Spitzer, R. L., Cohen, G. M., Miller, J. D., and Endicott, J.: The psychiatric status of 100 men on skid row. Int. J. Soc. Psychiatry, *15*:230–234, 1969.

Stendig-Lindberg, G.: Hypomagnesaemia in alcohol encephalopathies. Acta Psychiatr. Scand., *50*:465–480, 1974.

Van Thiel, D. H., Gaveler, J., and Lester, R.: Ethanol inhalation of vitamin A metabolism in the testes: possible mechanism for sterility in alcoholics. Science, *186*:941–944, 1974.

Victor, M.: Alcohol withdrawal syndrome: Theory and practice. Postgrad. Med., *47*:68–72, 1970.

Victor, M., Herman, K., and White, E. E.: A psychological study of the Wernicke-Korsakoff syndrome. Q. J. Stud. Alcohol, *20*:467–479, 1959.

Winokur, G., Reich, T., Rimmer, J., and Pitts, F. N., Jr.: Acloholism. III. Diagnosis and familial psychiatric illness in 259 alcoholic probands. Arch. Gen. Psychiatry, *23*:104–111, 1970.

Zimburg, S.: The elderly alcoholic. Gerontologist, *14*:221–224, 1974.

27

DRUG DEPENDENCE

"...his sense of happiness—was now. Nothing more than a thin cover beneath which anguish and the obsession of death were awakening."

André Malraux

(Courtesy of Office of Chief Medical Examiner, Baltimore, Maryland.)

Drug-seeking behavior, drug dependency, and addiction have increased markedly, particularly among the adolescent and young adult populations of the world. Many factors have influenced this trend. The number of new drugs produced synthetically has increased enormously. Some, notably the hallucinogens, have been advertised to the public as "mind-expanding" agents that are presumed to give the taker unexpected personal powers. Widespread communication of information regarding drugs between countries through radio, television, and other media, along with wide advertising of the general use of pharmaceuticals as a means of relieving pain, distress, or discomfort or enhancing well-being, has established an international cultural milieu of acceptance of drug taking. The vastly improved and

643

rapid means of transportation and supply and improved individual purchasing power have provided an availability of drugs to populations never before exposed. In contrast to the economic rewards of drug production, distribution, and sale which have facilitated usage, legal control measures throughout the world directed against abuse have proved incapable of effective application.

In countries where certain drugs known to be capable of producing physical harm, such as alcohol and tobacco, remain socially acceptable among older age groups, in adolescents esoteric drug taking may be motivated as a means of defiance and experimentation, to express dissent from the hypocrisy they detect in their society. Also, in certain sections of this age group, peer acceptance provides the force for experimentation with drug taking and even maintenance to habituation. To quote from Tart, "Experiences of ecstasy, mystical union, rapture, beauty, space and time transcendence, transpersonal knowledge — all common in altered states of consciousness — are attractive in themselves." These are the promises which stimulate curious exploration among the young and lay the groundwork for addiction or serious psycho-pathological reaction for those with biopsychological predisposition.

Also changed are the drugs abused and the styles in which that abuse is expressed between generations and cultures.

To comprehend the drug abuse problems today, the perspective must be one which includes all drug taking. Among those drugs used for euphoriant or anxiety-reducing effects which lead to habituation, addiction, or other physical disabilities, one must include those legally accepted by societies, in which production and distribution are sometimes supported by the state and even taxed by society, as well as those in which any aspect of production or distribution is prohibited. In the United States of America, alcohol represents a drug that is legally and socially accepted, in contrast to the narcotics whose distribution is legally prohibited except under government regulation.

In this chapter, consideration is given to the psychiatric consequences of dependence on opium, its alkaloids and derivatives; the synthetic analgesics with morphine-like effects; the barbiturates and other hypnotics and sedatives; cocaine; *Cannabis sativa* (hashish and marihuana); and other psychostimulants such as the amphetamines and the hallucinogens, A slang expression for the sedatives and hypnotics is "downers." Stimulants, or "uppers," are the amphetamines and hallucinogens. The latter have been termed "mind-expanding." In general, the majority of people who become habituated and addicted to these agents suffer from personality disorders. Others are neurotic and psychotic.

Definitions

The following definitions are those formulated by the World Health Organization in 1969. *Drug abuse* is persistent or sporadic excessive drug use inconsistent with or unrelated to acceptable medical practice. *Drug dependence* is a state, psychic and sometimes also physical, resulting from the interaction between a living organism and a drug, characterized by behavioral and other responses that always include a compulsion to take the drug on a continuous or periodic basis in order to experience its psychic effects and sometimes to avoid the discomfort of its absence. Tolerance may or may not be present. A person may be dependent on more than one drug.

By *habituation,* or habit-formation, is meant a psychological dependence on the use of a drug because of the relief from tension and emotional discomfort that it affords. By *tolerance* is meant a declining effect of the same dose of a drug when it is administered repeatedly over a period of time. As a result, it is necessary to increase the dose in order to obtain the original degree of effect. *Physical dependence* refers to an altered physiological state brought about by repeated ingestion or administration of a drug in order to prevent the appearance of a characteristic illness called an *abstinence syndrome.*

Dependence on narcotics is characterized, on their withdrawal, by autonomic dysfunction, such as yawning, lacrimation, rhinorrhea, gooseflesh, and symptoms reflecting general irritability of the central nervous system, and also twitching of muscles, insomnia, hypertension, and fever. Dependence on hypnotics and alcohol is manifested chiefly by the development of convulsions and delirium following withdrawal.

Physical dependence is a self-limited process. The symptoms appear in a definite time sequence following withdrawal of the drug, reach maximum intensity at a definite time, and decline at a definite rate. The symptoms that follow withdrawal of drugs with relatively short lengths of action, such as heroin and Dilaudid, appear quickly, become intense in a short time, and decline rapidly. Symptoms that follow withdrawal of a drug with a long length of action, such as methadone, appear slowly, are never intense, and decline more slowly. *Physical dependence capacity* (PDC) refers to the "ability of a drug to act as a substitute for another upon which an organism has been made physically dependent, that is, to suppress abstinence phenomena that would otherwise develop after abrupt withdrawal of the original dependence-producing drug."

Extent and Prevalence of Drug Abuse

A compilation of 38 studies of the extent of drug usage among university, college, high school, and selected graduate students, hippie groups, and adults reported by Berg in 1969 documents the widespread experimentation in drug usage then taking place in the U.S.A. *Extent* refers solely to an individual ever having used an illicit drug; thus it includes all such persons, and not necessarily current users, as well as regular users of one or more drugs. It contrasts with *prevalence*, defined as the number of current regular users of illicit drugs. That the rates of usage vary widely is apparent. Rates among high school students were surprisingly like those among the college students. Rates of extent of marihuana use varied from 5.6 to 34.9 per cent, amphetamines from 9.5 to 21.5 per cent, barbiturates and LSD from 1.7 to 15.7 per cent, and opiates from 1.0 to 4.7 per cent.

The rates for high school users were collected from institutions where a drug problem was known to exist. Also, in this group were many who tried a drug experimentally only once. Finally, the schools surveyed were located in metropolitan areas; available statistical reports on rural schools show generally low rates of illicit drug usage. Juvenile users of narcotics are usually those living in the urban ghettos; the increase is greatest among black and Spanish-speaking ghetto families.

In recent years, as the supply of heroin diminished in the United States of America, patterns of drug abuse changed. Polydrug abuse has increased and there has been a widening social tendency to accept usage of marihuana socially and legally in the U.S.A. The White Paper on Drug Abuse of President Ford's Domestic Council acknowledged that the attempt to totally eliminate such behavior is beyond the realm of possibility—an obvious conclusion for all who have examined world history in this regard. Because the destructive effects of the various drugs differ, the report suggests that those bent on control should perhaps concentrate their attention toward reduction of usage of the more dangerous. Heroin, cocaine amphetamines, and barbiturates were ranked as the drugs most likely to produce the most serious consequences when used in excess.

At the site of entry into psychiatric services where serious disability, including addiction, habituation, and personality disturbance coincide, the pattern of drug abuse is well described by Hekemian and Gershon. From over 100 patient admissions to a city receiving hospital of those improperly using drugs, the majority of the heroin users fell into the group of antisocial personalities. Emotionally disturbed but younger groups tended to use marihuana, amphetamines, and the hallucinogens. One half of this group were considered schizophrenic before taking drugs, and 40 per cent required prolonged hospitalization. The desire for euphoria, thought to be due to a wish to escape underlying depression, was the most frequently given reason for drug taking. Secondly blamed were the influences of friends or the need to escape the living environment. Almost all patients had taken more than one agent.

NARCOTICS ADDICTION

Extent

When the Harrison Narcotic Act was passed in 1914, there were 175,000 narcotic addicts, mostly women, in the United States of America, which then had a population of 92,000,000. The rate equaled 1.9 per 1000.

In 1969, the Bureau of Narcotics and Dangerous Drugs reported 68,088 narcotic addicts (95 per cent heroin) in the U.S.A., a number double that of 1968. However, using the dubious approach of computing the number of addicts from the number of heroin-related deaths, which in some states equal 1 per cent, the national total of addicts could have been above 200,000. This extrapolation fails to take into consideration the change in the pattern of heroin use with the greater frequency of "mainlining" (intravenous injection). The rapid increase in deaths from heroin usage is attributed in large part to this practice, as well as to drug-related infections such as septicemia. In 1970, in New York City, there were

1154 deaths as the result of narcotic addiction. Approximately 50 per cent of these deaths occurred in the young (aged less than 23), and the same percentage was due to overdosage. These high rates reflect the new patterns of narcotic use, as well as the highly variable dosages available in supplies provided through the illicit market.

If the total of narcotic addicts equals 200,000 today, this is equivalent to one per 1000, far below the rates of the 1920s. So, too, as described earlier, although the extent of heroin use may be rising, the degree of addicted users in this country is, for the most part, less. It has been noticed that the abstinence syndrome of many of the heroin users arrested for trading in this country has become much less marked in intensity on withdrawal. Also, those who have observed addiction in opium-producing countries, such as Laos, are impressed with the much greater severity of the individual addiction there than in the United States of America.

Etiology

Addiction to drugs and the extent of its occurrence result from a complex interaction of cultural and familial forces that determine the availability of the pharmacologic agent, the opportunities for initiation to its usage, and the individual predisposition to continue its usage. In China and other Asian countries where opiates have been readily available in the past, addiction was common. Where the drug traffic offers opportunity for large profits and its usage is pushed, as in those areas of the U.S.A. offering sites of entry and distribution, prevalence of narcotic addiction is higher. Here, again, the initiation to its use takes a daring and defiant attitude that appeals to the adolescent and the immature. In those Western European countries, such as England, where narcotic addiction is managed as a medical problem, where drug traffic is less profitable, and where the culture does not place prestige on its use by overemphasizing its significance, the number of narcotic addicts is much smaller.

Those who become addicted are for the most part antisocial personalities, but the neurotic and psychotic also are predisposed in view of their affective problems. Those seeking the use of an addicting drug are motivated by the wish to induce and perpetuate the most satisfying state of personal existence, even at the risk of impairment.

The largest group of addicts is composed of individuals with personality disorders who became addicted to drugs through contact and association with persons already addicted. The addict often seeks to recruit new addicts, hoping to secure funds to supply his own needs by selling to others. Most members of this group are emotionally immature, hostile, aggressive persons who take drugs in order to secure relief from inner tension. They have few healthy resources or interests and are motivated by immature drives for immediate goals. The addict-to-be finds in the drug a release from tension, felt as a restless need for pleasurable or exotic sensations, and the satisfaction of a longing for artificial elation or peace. Conscious discomfort is eliminated, repressed drives may be released, and responsibility is evaded. Another group consists of frankly neurotic persons with anxiety and obsessive-compulsive or psychophysiological symptoms that are relieved by drugs. A third group consists of persons who, in the course of physical illness, have received drugs over an extended period and after the termination of the ailment have continued their use. However, probably all persons who acquire addiction in this manner have some fundamental emotional problem that caused them to continue the use of drugs beyond the period of medical need. Many addicts were intemperate in the use of alcohol before they became addicted to drugs. In practically all addicts, the previous adjustment to life was marginal or unsatisfactory.

Physiological Theories

Possibly the most significant new information in regard to the physiological action of opiates is derived from the research on the endorphins--endogenous morphine-like substances. These substances appear to act similarly to heroin and morphine yet occur actually in the brain or the pituitary. There is reason to believe they may be a new class of neurotransmitters. With identification in the brain and other tissues of opiate receptors (the cellular components to which opiates attach), it is now known that at least seven substances bind to them. Several of these are structurally related peptides, one is a pituitary peptide of unknown structure, and one is a low molecular weight peptide in the blood and bladder. Smaller peptides have been designated as enkephalins; these contain two pentapeptides with similar amino acid sequences. Metenkephalin, isolated from the pituitary glands, appears in a polypeptide beta-lipotropin which is believed to be related to the beta melanocyte-stimulating hormone (MSH).

Whether enkephalins act as neurotransmitters or the larger peptides their precursors, or whether the larger endorphins are the physiologically active substance and the enkephalins the degradation products is now unknown. In vitro studies show that the enkephalins bind to morphine receptors less actively than does morphine. Their effects are blocked by naloxone and other specific antagonists of opiate action. Yet, to date, direct injection of enkephalins into the brain has not produced evidence of morphine-like analgesia.

It is now known that the receptors are located in the subcellular structures of brain cells containing synaptic membranes—areas paralleling that where opiate receptors exist. It has been found that the enkephalin content of rat brains increases when the animals are implanted with a slow-release pellet of morphine.

It has been hypothesized that exogenous opiate morphine inhibits, by a feedback mechanism, the firing of neurons that normally release enkephalins as neurotransmitters. Much more work is required to fully relate the action of the endorphins to opiates and to ascertain the possible relationship to their known physiological properties. Readers are referred to the 1976 articles in Science magazine by Goldstein and Marx.

Other research on the effects of short- and long-term administration of morphine on the serotonergic pathways in the central nervous system has shown that morphine administration produces in animals an immediate drop in the nerve-ending enzyme tryptophan hydroxylase, while long-term administration induces a rise. There is no change in the activity of this enzyme in the cell body. Furthermore, these changes are more evident in the forebrain (septal) areas than in the midbrain serotonin system.

In rat experiments on penetration of the blood-brain barrier, heroin is rapidly taken up for a short period of time, succeeded less rapidly by methadone, codeine, and morphine, respectively. The previously recorded findings do not provide potential as yet for a cohesive hypothesis for the addicting properties of the opiates.

Although there is no proved explanation for the phenomena of tolerance and of physical dependence, there are now a number of hypotheses. According to one, morphine has diphasic actions—excitation and depression. The excitant effects persist longer than do the depressant effects. For this reason, as doses of morphine are repeated, excitant effects are accumulated, larger and larger doses being required in order to obtain a sufficient degree of depression to mask the excitant effects. This is the suggested explanation for tolerance. Following withdrawal of the drug its excitant effects are released, thus accounting for physical dependence.

A second hypothesis advanced to explain the development of tolerance and physical dependence is known as the theory of cellular adaptation. According to this hypothesis, the administration of opiates stimulates compensatory homeostatic mechanisms that oppose the depressant effects of the drug. These homeostatic responses become strengthened upon repeated administration of the substance. More and more drug is therefore required to induce the original degree of effect, and when the drug is withdrawn, the enhanced homeostatic mechanisms are released from the brake imposed upon them by the continued presence of morphine within the body, thus giving rise to physical dependence. This theory is based largely on the observation that manifestations of abstinence are always opposite in nature to those of the direct effects of opiates. Thus in the nontolerant, nonaddicted person, morphine constricts the pupils, lowers body temperature, reduces blood pressure, and causes sedation. Following withdrawal of morphine from the addict, there are noted dilation of the pupils, fever, a rise in blood pressure, and insomnia. Still another theory with some support from animal experimentation is that the body develops immunity to the opiates and subsequent injections are progressively diminished in the "immunized" individual.

Social conditioning, too, appears to play a major role in narcotic abuse and addiction. There must first be a situation that conduces to trying drugs. Curiosity, rebellion against parents or other authorities, imitation, peer pressure, boredom, the wish to escape from some distress and the receiving of information about what the drug may do, or the expectation of ultimate pleasure motivates the individual to try a drug. Thereafter, he or she learns or is taught by others to identify the drug effect, as well as the various methods of administering it to regulate or maximize the desired effect, and then to connect this effect with the drug's use.

The user discriminates the response to the drug in terms of dosage and method of administration as miserable or relief-giving, even though this may not have characterized the initial experience. The acquisition of habituation, then, can be recognized as a process occurring in a social matrix. The personality characteristics of the individual define the extent to which the process is carried.

In Preble and Casey's study of the life of the heroin user in the modern urban American ghettos among blacks and Puerto Ricans, there are many social rewards for successful "hustling." In these deprived communities, where to sustain a mild habit requires the daily output of twenty or thirty dollars, the user aggressively expends his day in a career devoted to finding the monies to give him his fleeting moments of euphoria or surcease from distress and anxiety. The life of thievery to achieve his goals is active and may be seen as adventurous and challenging. The business demands liveliness and resourcefulness to hustle (rob or steal), seek victims, avoid police, find the dealers, purchase the heroin, adulterate it, and then cheat others. The competitiveness for monies is now so great that these users seldom associate other than in pairs. Then they steal and prey on each other, as well as their family members and those living in the neighboring communities. The successful hustler thus comes to be treated with respect by those in the "biz." The successive process of adulteration of heroin in the course of its passage through the lengthy chain of supply now has reduced the daily average to the bulk of heroin users to about 3 mg.—the estimated contents of one "bag." As Preble and Casey put it, "If they can be said to be addicted, it is not so much to heroin, as to the entire career of heroin user."

Still another process takes place as the narcotics user receives his drug from a peddler, injects it ("mainlining"), and responds with euphoria and relief of tensions. There is now good evidence, as in the demonstration that animals with implanted electrodes in areas of the midbrain and certain midbrain nuclei repeatedly stimulate themselves electrically as though receiving pleasure or a reward, of the drive of the nervous system to reinforce activities that provide satisfactions. It may be assumed that a conditioning process now takes place as well. Such a process, with the possibility of establishing as unconditioned stimuli the presence of another narcotics user, the offer of a drug, or a syringe, may well explain the propensity to relapse even long after a formerly addicted person has recovered from a state of physical dependence and perhaps has even been relieved of the painful affect that originally led to the pleasure in the drug.

Any theory concerned with drug dependence and addiction must account for individual repetitive motivation, habituation and later physical dependence, the symptoms of abstinence in development of physical dependence as well as the likelihood of relapse. Wikler has proposed a conditioning theory that addresses each of these phases of habituation to and/or dependence on drugs. He points out that both the pharmacological actions of the drug, early and late, as well as the social conditions attendant upon its use and following thereafter, may be regarded as reinforcers. He defines pharmacological reinforcement as direct if such sources of reinforcement have not been engendered by the drug itself, or indirect if the contrary is true. Direct pharmacological reinforcement may be intrinsically built into the nervous system structure or acquired developmentally in the course of the personality growth. The details of his hypothesis are shown in Table 27-1.

Wikler's hypothesis is that initiation of drug dependence occurs through social reinforcement which, in turn, is reinforced partly by pharmacological means as each successive dose depresses

TABLE 27–1 Reinforcing Processes in Opioid Dependence*

REINFORCING PROCESSES	SOURCES OF REINFORCEMENT	REINFORCING EVENTS	BEHAVIOR
I. Social Street corner society; slum big shots; cultist rituals and beliefs	Need to belong; boredom; anomie; hostility to establishment	Acceptance by deviant subculture	Drug-taking in accordance with rituals; affirmation of cultist beliefs
II. Primary Pharmacological A. Direct (nondrug engendered = psychic dependence)	1. Intrinsic (cerebral drug-sensitive reward systems?) 2. Developmental (personality): anxiety in particular situations	1. Relatively nonspecific drug effects (release or blockade of NE, DA, ACh, etc., in brain) 2. Specific pattern of agonistic actions of opioid drugs	1. Subjective: high; thrills (intravenous only) Objective: elated behavior 2. Subjective: content; coasting Objective: nodding; leveling of performance
B. Indirect (drug-engendered = physical dependence)	Early abstinence changes (manifest or detectable by subject's cerebral sensors); restlessness, etc.	Suppression of early abstinence by next dose of opioid. (NB, tolerance has developed to directly reinforcing effects of opioids)	Subjective: craving and satisfaction of craving Objective: hustling for opioids; increasing dose and frequency of opioid taking (appetitive reinforcement)
III. Secondary Pharmacological (conditioning of reinforcing processes to exteroceptive and interoceptive stimuli) A. Direct B. Indirect	Classically conditioned CNS changes (counteradaptive to agonistic effects of opioids) A. Conditioned inhibition of CNS reward systems B. Conditioned abstinence changes	Agonistic effects of opioids as in IIA & B, but after IIA and B, suppression of conditioned abstinence is more reinforcing	Subjective A. "Low," "disgusted" B. "Sick," "got the flu," "need a fix" Objective A. Depressive behavior B. Signs of opioid abstinence (conditioned); renewed hustling; RELAPSE

*Reinforcement is the consequence of interaction between sources of reinforcement and reinforcing events.
From Wikler, A.: Sources of reinforcement for drug-using behavior: A theoretical formulation. In Cochin, J. (ed.): Pharmacology and the Future of Man. Proceedings of the 5th International Congress on Pharmacology, 1972, Vol. 1. Basel, Switzerland, Karger, 1973.

the homeostatic need generated by counteradaptive changes. The latter applies unconditionally in response to the initial use of drugs. As to the counteradaptive pharmacological actions, it has been demonstrated that the abstinence syndrome can be conditioned in both man and animals. The continuing temporal relationship between pharmacological reinforcement and the recurrent social and physiological stimuli progressively increases the potential of occurrence of the mental and the socially counteradaptive reactions following the self-administration of psychoactive drugs, setting up a repetitive drive. This condition lasts long after simple detoxification.

On the basis of his theoretical proposition, he postulates that the prevention of relapse depends upon both extinction of the conditioned abstinence and the conditioned self-administration of the psychoactive drugs—which must be accomplished after detoxification. Within a practice deriving from the theory, Wikler perceives verbal psychotherapies as hastening extinction and directing the individual toward cognitive redefinition of the conditioned responses. Details of the therapeutic regimen derived from his conditioning theories, to my knowledge, have not been tested on any scale. They are quite complex and require knowledge of both social and pharmacological processes related to the continuing of habituation and the acquisition of dependence in those taking addicting substances.

Psychodynamics

The majority of the narcotics addicts are those with arrests in the ego and superego development and, for the most part, fixed to an ambivalent maternal figure. The latter is both possessive and rejecting—on the one hand encouraging the addicted child to give up the habit, and on the other often offering or smuggling the addicting agent to him.

As in other families where psychopaths are reared, there has been an absence of a strong and consistent father figure. The addict fails to develop internal controls, hopes for immediate gratifications of his needs, and yet is continually frustrated due to his exaggerated demands, his psychosexual immaturity, and his lack of ego capacity that might bring satisfaction by delay and insistent efforts toward his goals. Whereas the psychopath is deprived of pleasure and pained by his frequent failures socially, the neurotic and psychotic suffer from either anxiety or depression, or both. Narcotics, particularly, and other drugs as well, offer to such individuals both immediate reduction in the painful affects and the provision of a sense of pleasure or euphoria that provides a striking contrast to the usual state of those with personality disorders.

The narcotic agents also reduce hunger, pain, and the frustration of threatening yet unrelieved sexual urges. Thus they alleviate the anxieties and tensions attendant on continuing frustrations of oral and sexual drive states. The drug then substitutes for satisfaction of the basic biological drives. As the drug effect wears away, anxiety, depression, or the customary feelings of loneliness or hopelessness recur, compounded with a neurotic or psychotic sense of guilt. The drive to be relieved again becomes insurmountable, and additional doses are taken leading to addiction.

OPIUM ALKALOIDS AND DERIVATIVES

Morphine is the most common substance among the opiates. *Heroin*, taken both hypodermically and by snuffing, has great addiction liability. Many consider it the most difficult of all addictions to cure. *Codeine* has a definite, though low-grade, addiction liability. Both *Dilaudid* (dihydromorphine hydrochloride) and *metopon* (methyldihydromorphinone) have high physical dependence and habituation liabilities. *Demerol* (meperidine hydrochloride) is a synthetic analgesic that is not chemically related to morphine but is nevertheless addicting. It possesses considerable habituation liability, and after prolonged administration its addicts develop physical dependence. Any differences in the addiction liability of the new analgesic drugs from that of morphine are differences in degree, not in kind. The general features of the morphine abstinence syndrome are also characteristic of these drugs.

DeQuincey states in his "Confessions of an Opium Eater" that at one period in the history of his drug addiction he took 500 ml. of laudanum, or approximately 4.6 gm. (72 grains) of morphine, daily. Today, most addicts in the United States subsist on a much lower daily dosage. Many addicts tolerate, without unfavorable symptoms, several times the dose they are accustomed to receive. This tolerance is destroyed following disappearance of the withdrawal symptoms. Addicts usually do not realize how rapidly they lose their tolerance for opiates. Sometimes during the "cure," addicts have obtained access to an opiate and have taken, with fatal results, what was the usual dose before withdrawal was instituted.

After recourse to the drug, the addict feels a sense of relief and perhaps of exhilaration, together with an increase in efficiency. The sense of well-being is so great that, as its pleasant effect diminishes, the desire for the satisfaction that the drug affords can scarcely be resisted. Although the continued administration of small amounts of the drug will prevent the distressing withdrawal symptoms to be described, increasing amounts are necessary to obtain the desired exhilaration and sense of increased capacity. As a result, the quantity taken is gradually increased until enormous amounts are required.

The eventual effect of the habit is impairment of a higher ethical sense, that is, the ego ideals. This moral and social deterioration is not a result of the direct effects of narcotics, but rather, of social consequences of the life of addiction. When the narcotic is taken in large doses, ambition and physical energy are lessened, lethargy is produced, and the pleasurable feeling that all is well makes the addict contented. As a result, he pays less attention to work and becomes an idler. Those who depend upon an illegitimate source for their supply of drugs are sometimes unable to work because of discomfort and weakness resulting from inability to secure the usual dose. When such patients, after a short period of deprivation, secure a supply, they often take more than is necessary to keep them comfortable. As a result, they alternate between physical and mental instability and physical and mental lethargy.

Diagnosis

Frequently, the individual admits that he is addicted to and needs drugs. If he denies the habit, the diagnosis can at times be made on the basis of needle marks, indurations, and the scars of abscesses. Miosis is suggestive, but not definitive evidence. Periods of restlessness, irritability, and anxiety, followed rather suddenly by euphoria and apparent relief and contentment, should be suggestive of drug addiction.

At times the only method of diagnosis may be isolation of the patient from a source of drugs, followed by observation for signs of abstinence. The addict may be exceedingly clever in concealing a supply of his drugs. He may enter a hospital for the purpose of being cured of his addiction, yet at the same time have a supply craftily concealed in personal articles or even in body cavities.

A diagnostic test of considerable sensitivity has been developed that depends upon precipitating the abstinence syndrome by the parenteral injection of N-allylnormorphine (Nalline), a morphine antagonist. Before conducting such a test, it is advisable to obtain written permission of the patient or his or her guardian. This test is performed by injecting subcutaneously 3 mg. of N-allylnormorphine. In less than 20 minutes after injection, clear-cut signs of the abstinence syndrome will be noted in addicts using 60 mg. or more of morphine daily or equivalent amounts of heroin, dihydromorphinone, methadone, or Levo-Dromoran. Symptoms of the abstinence syndrome are described in the next section of this chapter.

If the response to the first injection is negative or doubtful, a second dose of 5 mg. should be given 30 minutes after the first, and again a third 30 minutes after the second. At this time, if abstinence symptoms have not become apparent and if the signs of the direct effects of the injected drug have appeared, the test may be read as negative. N-Allylnormorphine directly produces dizziness, pseudoptoses, mioses, and reduction in the respiratory rate, with a drunken experience. The absence of response to this test may occur in addicts who have been withdrawn from narcotics for as short as a week's period, or in addicts taking scattered doses. It is unreliable for meperidine (Demerol) addiction and contraindicated in the presence of serious organic disease.

In recent years, polydrug abuse has become more common. Alcohol, cocaine, and other agents, such as the hypnotics, may be taken. Of particular significance is drug detection in those under therapeutic programs of methadone maintenance. In such programs, some take heroin in addition to the methadone. Physical signs indicative of heroin use in the methadone-treated patient are the presence of a puffy face as well as evidence of edema elsewhere, general sluggishness, and arthralgia. One may suspect the alcoholic among those on methadone if the plasma alpha amino-n-butyric acid to leucine ratio is elevated above 0.2—a new indicator developed by Shaw et al. Simultaneous cocaine use may be detected by a simple thin-layer chromatographic process using cation exchange paper as described by Chambers and his colleagues.

Withdrawal Symptoms

Whenever opium or its habit-forming derivatives are abruptly withdrawn, a definite train of symptoms known as *abstinence* or *withdrawal symptoms* appears. If, within 12 to 14 hours after the administration of morphine, the dose is not repeated, the so-called withdrawal signs and symptoms begin to appear. Among the first are yawning, lacrimation, rhinorrhea, sneezing, and perspiration. These symptoms become more marked, and anorexia, dilated pupils, tremor, and gooseflesh are added. About 36 hours after the last dose, uncontrollable twitching of the muscles appears and cramps develop in the legs, abdomen, and back. The patient becomes intensely restless, is unable to sleep, and both pulse and blood pressure rise. Vomiting and diarrhea are frequent. These acute signs and symptoms reach their height about 48 hours after the last dose of morphine and remain at this height for 72 hours. They then gradually subside during the next five to ten days.

As the withdrawal symptoms develop, the patient becomes restless, pessimistic, surly, fault-finding, and irritable and exhibits an unpleasant, increased psychomotor activity. He has a marked subjective feeling of weakness, and considerable prostration may occur. He may curse, cry, be impulsively destructive, and make suicidal gestures. To quite an extent, the intensity of withdrawal symptoms depends on the amount of drug the patient has been receiving. To some degree, the extent of the symptoms can be controlled by the patient himself. Any patient who appears comfortable during the period of withdrawal should be suspected of illicit possession of the drug.

Treatment

On a rational basis, the preferable mode of treatment of the drug addict should be directed at relief of the distressing affective state that originally predisposed him to respond positively to the use of drugs. Such treatment would be directed to correction of the personality disorder or the psychoneurotic or psychotic state by the therapeutic process most applicable for the particular patient. Withdrawal of the drug then would not be undertaken until there had occurred the development of a firm dependent therapeutic relationship with a physician or other member of the therapeutic team. This relationship might sustain the patient through the period of abstinence and provide positive support to sustain withdrawal.

Unfortunately, therapeutic efforts today are directed largely to simple withdrawal of the drug, which must be undertaken in a facility where the activities of the patient and the sources of the drug can be controlled. The patient must remain long enough to be relieved of any physical ailments, to have opportunity to develop habits of living and working without drugs, and to be helped in discovering the source of his emotional difficulty.

WITHDRAWAL. It is not humane and it may be even dangerous to withdraw a narcotic abruptly. The narcotic may be withdrawn rapidly over a period of ten days, in which case 30 mg. may be given every six hours for two days, with continued reduction thereafter until withdrawal is complete by the end of 10 days. It is probably more desirable to begin with the withdrawal of the narcotic, then shift to methadone, which suppresses the withdrawal symptoms in persons addicted. In this method, one should first ascertain the least amount of drug that will prevent the appearance of withdrawal symptoms. This is termed the stabilization dosage and can usually be determined in two or three days. Once the stabilization dosage is known, 1 mg. of methadone may be substituted for every 3 mg. dose of morphine or 1 mg. of heroin.

After substitution of methadone has been effected, the calculated dosage should be maintained for two or three days. The total dosage can be adjusted upward or downward, depending on the patient's response. Thereafter, methadone should be withdrawn over the course of seven to ten days, depending on the patient's response. Although withdrawal symptoms should be expected near the end of treatment, severe manifestations of abstinence are never seen when this method of withdrawal is used. Neuroleptics are also useful in the tension states occurring in the withdrawal of opium and other narcotics. Great caution should be exercised in withdrawal of drugs from patients with evidence of myocardial insufficiency.

After withdrawal, with discontinuance of methadone and without substitution of other drugs, most former addicts experience malaise, insomnia, irritability, and restlessness for months. It is for this reason, as recommended later, that the detoxified patient should remain in a social rehabilitative program if he is not to be placed on methadone maintenance.

Sometimes the patient, without knowledge of the physician, has also been taking barbiturates before his admission. In that case the patient may develop an abstinence syndrome resulting from barbiturate withdrawal as well. This will usually be in the form of a severe convulsion in which fractures may occur, or sometimes a delirious psychotic reaction. The prevention of this additional abstinence syndrome is the continued but gradually decreasing administration of a barbiturate.

An effort should be made to establish rapport and positive transference between the patient and physician during withdrawal. The patient usually has a resistance to gaining insight into the real causes of his or her addiction. Psychotherapy should, however, be directed toward his motivations, defenses, and adaptations. Many heroin users are now under treatment in various therapeutic groups. The outcome of such treatment remains to be evaluated. The usual recognition of drug addiction as a crime rather than as a disease reacts unfavorably on success of therapy. The vocational and social discrimination experienced by the addict following his discharge tends to lead to relapse.

The discharged addict should be required to report regularly for a period of five years to a center staffed with internists, psychiatrists, and social workers who are specifically trained to help him meet his problems. If left to solve his problems unaided, he usually returns to the use of drugs. It is frequently helpful if he joins the organization known as Narcotics Anonymous.

NARCOTIC ANTAGONISTS. *Cyclazocine Treatment.* Cyclazocine, a long-acting, orally effective narcotic antagonist of the benzomorphan series, is sometimes useful as a therapeutic agent in the treatment of addiction. Like nalorphine, when given to an addicted person this drug will precipitate an acute abstinence state. In the previously addicted, the administration of this drug reduces or prevents the development of physical dependence on morphine-like drugs. Presumably, it does so by preventing morphine from fixating to the usual receptor sites in the bodily tissues, including the central nervous system.

From 48 to 72 hours after completion of withdrawal from the addicting drug with the help of methadone, patients may be given subcutaneously two successive doses of cyclazocine of 3 and 4 mg., separated by a 30-minute interval. If no signs of abstinence are noted, cyclazocine administration is commenced at 0.25 mg. twice daily. This dosage is elevated by 0.25 mg. daily if no side-effects occur, until the daily dosage reaches 1.75 or 2.0 mg. The patient may then be seen once or twice weekly outside the hospital. When the dose reaches 1.0 to 1.5 mg. per day, a single dosage may be given.

Initially, the drug produces in some a degree of motor incoordination and slowing of thought. These patients must be advised not to give the drug to their friends who are narcotics users, as a serious or fatal reaction may be induced. However, the patient will not have discomfort if he himself takes a morphine derivative. The drug, if taken regularly, allows the addict to return to his usual environment, but deprives him of the capacity to receive gratification from the use of narcotic-addicting substances. Presumably, then, the reinforcement of the habituating drive is voided. It is not yet known what group of addicts will continue the use of cyclazocine; its immediate acceptance as therapy by addicts apparently is less than for the methadone treatment.

Naloxone (*N*-allylnoroxymorphone), another narcotic antagonist, has been tried in treatment as well. Unfortunately, its effects are less enduring than those of cyclazocine, as administration is required more than once per day. Nor is it very effective administered orally.

Recently, a new narcotic antagonist, naltrexone, has shown promise as an effective treatment for heroin addicts. This compound has a longer duration of action than naloxone and is currently in large-scale clinical trials.

At this time the narcotic antagonists seem useful only in the treatment of the casual user of heroin with high risk for addiction, in the rehabilitation of the addicted who do not desire methadone maintenance, or in those entering treatment who reject attachment both to a therapeutic community and to a methadone maintenance program.

METHADONE TREATMENT. Maintenance treatment with methadone is based on the hypothesis that to achieve a homeostatic state, physiologically and psychologically, the confirmed narcotic addict must be freely provided with a medication to levels of narcotic tolerance that simultaneously protects him from the drive to obtain heroin or other addicting substances. The addict is considered to need the drug to obtain a comfortable physiological state that will allow social functioning. This addicted condition is considered analogous to that of the diabetic, who is deficient in substances needed to metabolize glucose and therefore physiologically in need and incapable of homeostasis unless receiving substitutes such as insulin.

Dole and Nyswander have placed confirmed heroin addicts on oral methadone, commencing with doses of 10 to 20 mg. dissolved in a fruit juice. The dosage is increased gradually over a four-week period to levels of 50 to 150 mg. daily in a single oral dose. Too rapid elevation of the dosage may lead to oversedation, urinary retention, or abdominal distention. Too little methadone leads to abstinence with symptoms of malaise, sweating, lacrimation, and restlessness. On the full stabilized dose, formerly refractory addicts with prolonged records of job instability, marital discord, and criminal recidivism have become socially productive. Others have maintained patients on much lower dosage levels than have Dole and Nyswander, but the patients' tendencies to relapse or substitute other drugs, including heroin, seem to be greater.

A longer-acting suppressant of the narcotic abstinence syndrome, *l-methadyl acetate*, is now in use as a substitute in methadone maintenance. This agent's suppressive actions appear to last up to three days. It may be given in doses of 40 to 80 mg. three times per week and has proved as effective as methadone in these trials.

Methadone maintenance programs have been the best evaluated of the numerous therapeutic procedures in use for the confirmed narcotic addict. The evaluations have been made by groups other than the administrators of the programs. It is evident that many former heroin addicts have become employable (some 25 to 40 per cent), or, in the younger age groups, have returned to educational programs in approximately the same numbers. They exhibit much less antisocial behavior and have maintained a perspective of social adaptation greater than during the periods of heroin addiction. However, there is a considerable dropout rate. Those who remain usually elected the program and are on high dosages of the maintenance drug. Many initial dropouts return to these programs at a later time.

Trials are now underway to determine whether those who have successfully adapted socially on a long-term methadone maintenance program may be withdrawn from the drug.

It must be noted that the polydrug users who enter such programs present a particularly difficult problem, as do the young. In the heroin addict who is also taking alcohol, it has been found that disulfiram may be effectively used for alcohol abstinence. This is best arranged when the daily administration of methadone is made contingent upon prior taking of the disulfiram.

CLONIDINE. Recently, Gold and colleagues have demonstrated remarkable reversal of opiate withdrawal symptoms using the antihypertensive drug clonidine. This compound is effective for withdrawing patients from methadone and may ultimately prove effective in the treatment of heroin addiction.

Prognosis

More addicts than is commonly realized are permanently cured. The United States Public Health Service Hospital, Lexington, Kentucky, an institution for the treatment of addicts, found that only 0.2 of 1 per cent of the patients who left the hospital in less than 30 days remained off the drug, whereas 24 per cent of those who remained for the recommended period were believed to have remained free from addiction.

Some addicts, pretending that they no longer have any desire for the drug, eagerly look forward to an opportunity to return to their habit and devise every imaginable pretext to hasten their release from the treatment program. Even those who believe they wish to be cured return to the drug on the slightest pretext after simple detoxification, the alleged occasion being actually but a rationalization of their emotional defects and their psychological need for obliterating reality and its problems. They feel lost without the narcotic and the sense of physical comfort it imparts. Many, too, feel that they are not understood, are in a constant state of mild dissatisfaction, and long to return to the accustomed companionship of other addicts, by whom they feel they are understood and with whom they feel a sense of security and comradeship.

Often other addicts, sometimes for the sake of self-justification, sometimes because, as vendors of morphine, they see in their unhappy companion a potential customer, urge the recently "cured" patient to share the alleviating agent. The profits from this "cured" patient will replenish their own diminishing supply of the drug, of course.

It is often the pattern for the narcotic addict to waver between periods of voluntary or involuntary withdrawal for a decade or more. Recent long-term studies have found that, by the age of 40, approximately three quarters of persons addicted in early adulthood have withdrawn from drug usage. Stable abstinence takes place in about 25 per cent, and frequent relapse does not preclude recovery. Yet, in a 20-year period, 25 per cent died of unnatural causes. In the group of former addicts who achieve abstinence, the outlook for social stability is high; thus as many as three quarters obtain full-time employment, support themselves and their families, and eschew abuse of other drugs and alcohol as well as criminality. Nor do they succumb to depressive or psychosomatic complaints.

As Table 27–2 shows, the most effective method of treatment for attaining long-term abstinence in a group of patients at the U.S. Public Health Service Hospital at Lexington was prison and parole, followed by methadone maintenance.

TABLE 27–2   Relative Efficacy of Five Modes of "Treatment" in Facilitating Abstinences of a Year or More

	1952–1964		1965–1970	
	"TREATMENT" EXPOSURES	PER CENT FOLLOWED BY ABSTINENCE	"TREATMENT" EXPOSURES	PER CENT FOLLOWED BY ABSTINENCE
Voluntary hospitalization	270	3	91	2
Short imprisonment (<9 mo.)	279	3	84	3
Long imprisonment (9 + mo.)	46	13	4	25
Prison and parole	30	67	4	100
Methadone maintenance	—	—	15	67

(From Vaillant, G. E.: Arch. Gen. Psychiatry, *29:*237–241, 1973.)

Prevention

Hughes and Crawford have suggested that in an outbreak of drug abuse in a community, public health authorities might intervene with a contagious disease model to prevent spread. This would involve detection of the individuals who were encouraging others, and bringing together the drug users in therapeutic programs. Such efforts have not been undertaken to any major extent and therefore their value remains speculative.

OTHER ABUSED DRUGS

BARBITURATE INTOXICATION AND ADDICTION

Incidence, Etiology, Symptoms

According to reports of the United States Public Health Service, there has been a great increase in recent years not only in acute barbiturate intoxication but also in barbiturate addiction. Acute intoxication with barbiturates accounts for about 25 per cent of all deaths from acute poisoning among admissions to general hospitals, and more deaths are caused by barbiturates, either accidentally ingested or taken with suicidal intent, than by any other poison.

As in alcoholism and in narcotic drug addiction, the important factor in barbiturate addiction is an underlying personality difficulty. Many psychoneurotics become addicted to barbiturates through prescription of the drugs for insomnia. Persons with character disorders ("psychopaths") begin the use of the drug to experience its intoxicating effect. Morphine addicts often use the drug when they are unable to secure morphine or in order to reinforce the effect of that narcotic. Alcoholics may begin the use of barbiturates to relieve the tension following a debauch and continue their use to induce toxic effects. In contrast to the situation in other narcotic drug addictions, a large proportion of the cases of barbiturate addiction results from administration by physicians. Special care should be exercised in prescribing them for emotionally unstable persons. Simple insomnia alone is rarely a valid indication for the use of barbiturates.

Not only do the barbiturates induce acute brain syndromes but also they cause chronic delirious reactions in those who use the drug in large amounts over periods of time. In the latter there may occur, on sudden withdrawal of the drugs, an *abstinence syndrome*, again characteristically delirioid but often with an associated convulsive state. It is necessary to differentiate the two conditions (that due to intoxication and that due to abstinence); they differ in their clinical manifestations and their treatment.

The "minor tranquilizers," developed several decades ago, quickly found widespread use, entered illicit markets, and became used as intoxicants, as did the barbiturates. Since their pharmacological actions are very similar, the psychiatrist now encounters acute states of intoxication, as well as withdrawal symptoms in periods of abstinence, in their users. The following are some of the more widely prescribed and abused of the 25 or more agents marketed in the United States of America: meprobamate (Equanil, Miltown), chlordiazepoxide (Librium), ethchlorvynol (Placidyl), glutethimide (Doriden), diazepam (Valium), and chloral hydrate (Sominos).

Acute barbiturate intoxication occurs frequently in those with suicidal intent and sometimes as an accidental occurrence in some who are using such agents for insomnia. In the latter instance, in partially confused states from previous doses that have failed to provide hypnosis, the patient automatically takes excessive amounts. Again, accidental overdosage may be observed in persons suffering severe anxiety who self-administer additional doses when the prescribed amount has failed to bring relief.

Diagnosis

With *acute intoxication*, there is impairment of cognitive functions, as with any form of cerebral insufficiency; lack of emotional control, shown in bursts of laughing or crying, garrulousness, and poor judgment; followed later by progressive drowsiness, stupor, and, finally, coma. While the condition often resembles acute alcoholism, there is no odor of alcohol on the breath. It is characteristically associated with certain cerebellar signs such as a gross dysarthria, a constant nystagmus, ataxia in both gait and stature, and adiadochokineses. With deepening intoxication, absence of the deep tendon reflexes, Babinski reflexes, and contraction of the pupils develop. Respiration is characteristically slow, and in severe intoxication is shallow or even periodic. Peripheral circulatory collapse may supervene.

In states of *mild intoxication*, the patient is confused or, if drowsy, is easily aroused, judgment is defective, and the nystagmus is transient, with at best reduction in the skin reflexes (abdominal). Neither respiration nor blood pressure is depressed. *Moderate intoxication* may be estimated in the presence of sleep, or drowsiness with arousal only on vigorous stimulation, constant nystagmus, and dysarthria. There is depression of tendon reflexes and respiration is slow. *Severe intoxication* is judged when the clinician observes unarousable coma, absence of all reflexes, including the corneal and pharyngeal, periodic respiration, and the symptoms of shock.

The diagnosis may be confirmed by the finding of barbiturates in the urine and blood. With mild and moderate states, the electroencephalogram shows a characteristic fast wave frequency.

Barbiturate addiction occurs when an individual is given eight or more times the usual therapeutic dose for three to six months. The addicted will suffer an abstinence syndrome upon abrupt withdrawal, which may manifest itself in convulsive activity or a frank psychotic reaction, in addition to anxiety, tremors, and weakness.

In the examination of a suspected barbiturate user, a meticulous search should be made of his belongings and his person. The chronic user often secretes drugs in his clothing or even in his person, in the mouth, rectum, or vagina.

A *"barbiturate test dose"* is sometimes useful in estimating tolerance and physical dependency in the suspected barbiturate addict. In the nonaddicted, 200 mg. of pentobarbital given orally, in a resting state and several hours after the last meal, should produce signs of mild intoxication after one hour. If the patient fails to show such signs, he is probably tolerant. The signs of acute intoxication are dysarthria, ataxia, pseudoptosis, and presence of Romberg's sign. Many nonaddicted individuals will be asleep one hour after receiving the test dose. The clinical observations made one hour following the test dose, as indicated in Table 27–3, allow an estimation of the daily barbiturate dosage required for stabilization of the patient.

Treatment

Treatment should be conservative for all patients with mild and moderate degrees of barbiturate intoxication, since only the severe grades of cerebral insufficiency threaten life. In acute intoxication, gastric lavage is indicated if the drug was recently taken. The patient should be kept awake by such measures as talking, walking, and the administration of caffeine sodium benzoate, 0.5 gm. intramuscularly, or 10 to 40 mg. of amphetamine sulfate by mouth or intramuscularly. The patient should not be allowed to sleep.

Comatose patients who may be aroused

TABLE 27–3   Determination of Degree of Tolerance and Daily Dosage
Levels of Barbiturate for Stabilization

PATIENT'S CONDITION ONE HOUR AFTER TEST DOSE	DEGREE OF TOLERANCE	ESTIMATED 24-HOUR BARBITURATE REQUIRED
Asleep, but arousable	Tolerance	None
Drowsy, slurred speech, coarse nystagmus,	Definite tolerance; marked intoxication	500 to 600 mg.
Rombergism. Comfortable, fine lateral nystagmus only drug effect	Marked tolerance; mild intoxication	800 mg.
No signs of drug effects, perhaps signs of abstinence persisting	Extreme tolerance; no intoxication	1000 to 1200 mg. or more

(From Jackson, A. H., and Shader, R. I.: Dis. Nerv. Syst., *34*:162–166, 1973.)

by manual stimulation may also be treated conservatively. If stupor deepens, adequate pulmonary ventilation must be maintained with the use of an automatic positive-pressure apparatus or a Drinker external respirator and circulatory collapse prevented by intravenous administration of a plasma expander. Oxygen is of doubtful value as it may further depress respiration. In some instances an endotracheal tube or tracheotomy is required. Supportive treatment of this type alone has given a better overall prognosis than use of a diuretic or dialysis.

It must be recognized that in the recovery phase from coma there again supervenes a delirious state that will require protective nursing until the patient fully recovers.

Addiction to barbiturates may develop; yet such hypnotics may be taken in doses of 0.5 gm. or less daily for prolonged periods without harm. Those who consume 0.8 gm. daily suffer definite impairment of mental functioning and will develop addiction as judged by the appearance of an *abstinence syndrome* if the drug is suddenly withdrawn after six to eight weeks of continuous ingestion. Those consuming amounts between these levels of 0.2 to 0.8 gm. daily show variable degrees of deficit.

Chronic cerebral impairment due to barbiturates produces signs similar to those described earlier for the mild states of intoxication, shown in fluctuations in intensity of the degree of confusion and in impairment in thinking, judgment, and motor activity. There exist persistent nystagmus and various degrees of dysarthria, dysmetria, and ataxia, with loss of the superficial reflexes. Often the condition of chronic intoxication is confused with multiple sclerosis. Again, the blood and urine will show evidence of barbiturates, and the electroencephalogram presents a characteristic fast pattern.

Treatment of the *chronic barbiturate user* requires careful evaluation of the extent of his habituation or addiction, which is often most difficult to assay. Here the word habituation is used to indicate psychological dependence on the drug, and the word addiction to indicate physiological dependence with propensity for development of the abstinence syndrome on withdrawal. In no instance should abrupt withdrawal of the barbiturate be attempted in the chronic user. Since such patients often distort the amount of drug they consume daily, their needs for stabilization should be determined as described earlier, on the basis of observation of response to the barbiturate test dose.

To initiate withdrawal, the patient should be maintained on the presumed stabilizing dose for 24 to 48 hours under careful observation to determine whether any kind of abstinence has occurred. In addition to short-acting barbiturates, it is recommended that the withdrawal be undertaken with phenobarbital; in long-acting barbiturates, a process similar to the use of methadone withdrawal with a heroin addict is recommended, by using the long-acting substitute methadone. Withdrawal of the barbiturate may be safely prescribed at the rate of approximately 10 per cent of the stabilization dose daily, administered in divided doses every six hours, day and night, except in those with minor degrees of addiction. In the latter, night-time sleep need not be interrupted. The last dose to be discontinued on such a schedule is the bedtime dose of phenobarbital.

An individual simultaneously addicted to heroin should be stabilized on both methadone and phenobarbital. The barbiturate should be withdrawn initially. Once this process has progressed well, methadone withdrawal may be initiated.

The appearance at any time of anxiety, tremor, insomnia or weakness or the development of slow-wave activity in the electroencephalogram heralds the onset of the abstinence syndrome. Such symptoms call for termination of withdrawal and support with additional barbiturates. If the abstinence syndrome appears, a dose of 0.2 to 0.3 gm. of pentobarbital orally usually is sufficient to prevent its full symptomatic expression. After a convulsion, 0.3 to 0.5 gm. of pentobarbital or amobarbital should be given parenterally or orally, followed by the oral administration of these drugs to the level of mild intoxication.

During withdrawal, patients require careful nursing and observation. With the withdrawal complete, it then is necessary to ascertain the motivating forces which led to dependence and arrange for appropriate treatment of the primary psychopathology of the individual.

COCAINE

For many years, cocaine addiction constituted one of the major drug problems, but, because of legislation, it is much less prevalent than formerly. At the present time, nearly all cocaine addicts acquired their habit through other addicts. Strictly speaking, cocaine is not a narcotic. It produces a marked stimulation, a sense of exhilaration, euphoria, and self-confidence, an increased flow of ideas, and a pressure of speech and activity. During this period of stimulation and sense of competency, there may be an actual increase in capacity for work. As the stimulus of the drug wears off, the patient feels weak, depressed, restless, morose, and irritable. Other abstinence symptoms are digestive disturbances, tremors, palpitation, specks in front of the eyes (muscae volitantes), muscular weakness, slight confusion, and impotence.

Frankly psychotic symptoms are common among those who continue the use of large doses of cocaine over a prolonged period. Such addicts may experience terrifying visual hallucinations, become suspicious, and perhaps show much excitement. Delusions of jealousy and of persecution are common and may lead to violence. A characteristic phenomenon is the frequent occurrence of formicative paresthesias. Associated with these may be the delusion that there actually are insects on the skin, and the patient may attempt to demonstrate them.

The moral deterioration in the cocaine addict is even greater than in the morphine addict. The prospects of any permanent cure of the habit are even less favorable than in the morphine addict. Withdrawal of the drug is not accompanied by the painful experiences and tendency to collapse that occur in withdrawal of opium derivatives.

AMPHETAMINES

Chronic intoxication with the sympathomimetic amines amphetamine (Benzedrine) or methamphetamine (Desoxyephedrine or Desoxyn) may be brought about by the continuing use of these drugs. It has been suggested that they produce chronic central nervous stimulation through accumulation of the biogenic amines norepinephrine and epinephrine, releasing the latter by occupying their binding sites in the brain. Of the amphetamines, the dextroisomer is the more potent inhibitor of catecholamine uptake by norepinephrine neurons in the brain. Behaviorally, it is ten times as potent as the levo isomer in enhancing locomotor behavior in animals. Both isomers are equally active in inhibition of brain dopamine.

The amphetamines physiologically are known to specifically block "fast" or REM (rapid eye movement) sleep, and their symptoms of chronic intoxication may thereby be similar in development to those seen with prolonged sleep deprivation. A sensitive and specific enzymatic assay for determining amphetamine concentration in human plasma has been developed.

Since these drugs bring about a sense of well-being and exhilaration, with relief from fatigue, their abuse is frequent among thrill-seeking adolescents and among those needing a "lift" from depression or from the aftereffects of other sedative agents and alcohol. Their stimulatory effect is succeeded again by fatigue and depression, and, as pharmacologic tolerance also occurs, increasingly larger doses are necessary to produce the desired euphoria. Some addicts of amphetamine have taken individual doses as high as 250 mg. and a daily dose equivalent to 1 to 1.5 gm.

There are a variety of methods of abuse. Some people take amphetamines sporadically to maintain alertness and to perform more effectively a particular intellectual or physical task. Others are recommended to the drug by physicians or friends to overcome fatigue or during treatment for obesity or depression. They then continue to use it compulsively. Some discover that inhalations ("snorting") or injections of the substance intravenously produce a sudden, intense "flash," termed a "speed run." Some women instill it into the vagina before intercourse ("balling"). Many inject amphetamine alone or in combination with barbiturates, heroin, or cocaine.

As much as 1000 mg. may be injected intravenously in a single dose. Some have taken 5000 mg. in a 24-hour period. The behavior of those who indulge in "speed runs" becomes overactive and impulsive, and demonstrates defective reasoning and judgment. They may develop paranoid ideas. Initially, they experience a feeling of high elation and a sense of being extraordinarily alert, powerful, and full of energy.

Poor impulse control in "speed freaks" is revealed by their involvement in numerous car accidents and the commission of homicides during drug intoxication. Chronic use may produce stereotyped behavior, such as skin-picking and bead-stringing and unstringing. Such stereotypic behavior may be reproduced in animals. Orgasms or ejaculations are delayed or impossible to achieve. Occasionally, the individual becomes unable to move or speak. Pulse is rapid, temperature is elevated, and invariably, there is elevation of blood pressure, sometimes associated with chest distress. The drug produces a strong psychic dependence, marked tolerance, and, on continuous large-dose administration, a mild physical dependence.

The symptomatology of chronic intoxication is very similar to that of cocainism. Although subjectively the users report a sense of increased assurance and decisiveness with greater energy, they also frequently recognize tension and irritability. Amphetamine abuse may be suspected when an appearance of restlessness and rapidity of speech are noted, associated with unusual cheerfulness or euphoria. The clinical evidence consists of irritability, anxiety, ataxia, and teeth-grinding movements. Physically, there occur dry mouth, tachycardia, brisk reflexes, dilated pupils, increased pulse pressure, and fine tremulousness of the limbs. Nystagmus, cardiac arrhythmias, and weight loss may be observed.

With severe intoxication, shallow respiration or circulatory collapse may be noted. Subjectively, the user may complain of sleeplessness, headaches, or nausea. Apprehension, tremulousness, and jerky muscular twitches ensue with time. Mounting insomnia and anorexia develop, and there is increasing motor activity with loquacity.

Amphetamine psychosis seems to be a distinctive entity with recurrent psychopathology unrelated to the personality makeup, aside from the reflection of it in the content of the hallucinatory and delusional material. It is characterized especially by vivid visual hallucinations, ideas of reference, and persecutory delusions, without the loosening of thought processes noted with schizophrenia or the impairment of sensorium diagnostic of the delirious syndrome (acute brain syndrome or acute cerebral insufficiency). It has been induced experimentally by intravenous injection of methamphetamine and it persisted six to twelve days after the divided dose injections. The rapid onset of the psychotic state after the single large doses of the agent has led Bell and Rozelle to suggest that the current hypothesis that relates this state to depletion of catechol amines and their metabolites may be inadequate.

Upon withdrawal of the drug this syndrome disappears within a period of ten days, but it may be seen recurrently in those who return to use of the drug. In those addicted individuals with a schizoid or schizophrenic premorbid personality, long-continued paranoid states have been precipitated. These differ from the simple psychotic state in the occurrence of other types of hallucinatory experiences (particularly auditory) and the usual disorganization of thought. Whether long-continued addiction leads to permanent personality disorganization and brain dysfunction, except in those with schizophrenic predispositions, is unknown. Other side effects of long-continued usage are malnutrition and cachexia; abdominal pain; dyskinesias, including jaw-grinding; hypertension; cerebral hemorrhage; and, in "speed freaks," a necrotizing angiitis.

Treatment requires immediate withdrawal of the drug and use of neuroleptics. The neuroleptics should not be used if anticholinergic drugs have been taken in addition to amphetamines. For the depression associated with amphetamine withdrawal, tricyclic antidepressants have been used with some effect. This depressive state is associated with altered electroencephalographic sleep patterns, including increased amounts of REM sleep and a decrease in excretion of 3-methoxy-4-hydroxyphenylglycol (MHPG—a metabolite of norepinephrine).

Psychotherapeutic measures are indicated, following recovery, to correct the motivational forces underlying the need for the drug.

HALLUCINOGENIC AGENTS

For centuries the plant-derived hallucinogens have been used by man in religious ceremonies, in the hope of divining a prophecy, to produce euphoria, or as aphrodisiacs. *Amanita muscaria*, the mushroom, is thought to have provided the substance inducing madness in the Norwegian berserkers and to have been the deified soma transported to India by the Aryans over three thousand years ago. It was used by the Koryak women of Siberia to stimulate their men. Mushroom cults exist in Central America and the mescal cactus peyote was used in Aztec religious practices. *Cannabis sativa*, or hemp, thought to be the most widely distributed hallucinogenic plant in the world, was known to the ancient Chinese and Assyrians and has been used as hashish in Asia Minor and Africa for centuries. Bhang is its designation in India. In South America, it is marihuana.

To commune with their gods, Aztec priests are thought to have eaten ololiuqui, the morning glory, which has psychotomimetic constituents similar to ergot, which in turn relates to LSD. The daturas of the Solanaceae family are so used by the Zuñi and Jivaro Indians of North and South America. Other ancient peoples discovered the hallucinogenic potentials of snuff prepared from leguminous trees, the hormala-alkaloid–containing plants, and certain mints, including catnip.

The Western world's current interest and concern over the use and abuse of such drugs represents no more than an expanded revival of practices existing throughout the ages. The revival of interest comes at a time when the hopes of personal security promised in the advances of science and technology seem delusional to many.

"Sniffing" by children and adolescents of gasoline fumes and a variety of volatile substances containing aromatic hydrocarbons as a means of producing euphoria, erotic fantasies, and a general sense of intoxication has been reported in recent years. Knowledge of the biological actions of the volatile euphoriants and hallucinatory stimulants is incomplete.

Marihuana and Hashish

The rapid and enormous popularity in use of the products of *Cannabis sativa* since the early 1960s represents the greatest shift in patterns of drug use and abuse in Western societies. The interest in marihuana, particularly among adolescents and young adults, has aroused great controversy about its potential deleterious effects on personality functioning and general health and has stirred heated debate about the need for legal control of its production and distribution.

Marihuana is a crude preparation of the whole plant, including flowers, leaves, seeds, and stems. Hashish is prepared by scraping resin from the tops of the hemp plant. Marihuana is five to ten times less potent than hashish and is by far the most commonly used preparation of cannabis. Tetrahydrocannabinol (THC) is the active ingredient in these drugs.

Cannabis derivatives are fat-soluble and have been found to be maintained in the brain and other human organs for as long as eight days after ingestion. They tend to concentrate in the frontal lobes and cortices of the brain. In human experiments, it has been shown that the smoking of a marihuana cigarette produces high amplitude and slow wave activity in electroencephalograms.

Among regular users of marihuana, smoking generally induces an enjoyable experience, consisting of a sense of exhilaration or euphoria, relaxation, calm, increased sensitivity, a sharper perception of sound, a perception that time slows, increased thirst, and dry mouth and throat. Some 6 per cent have unpleasant or aversive experiences, with symptoms of anxiety, memory impairment for object recognition rather than memory retrieval, or a sense of depersonalization. Many report pleasant and noticeable changes: they have floating sensations, become more talkative or laugh and giggle, have increased desire for sweets, or become sexually aroused. Conjunctival infection is noticed in about a third of regular smokers.

Studies of regular and heavy users of marihuana show that many come from a population at high risk for psychiatric problems—affective disorders and sociopathy, particularly—which usually preceded use of this drug. Polydrug use (particularly alcohol), acting-out behavior, and repeated homosexual experiences also characterize regular marihuana users.

Regarding the development of drug-related psychopathology, those who smoke three to ten times a week become apathetic and sluggish, lose interest in personal appearance, and have flattening of affect (which is sometimes confused with equanimity and well-being as the individuals appear to be at peace). Their activities are without direction and they avoid definite goals by calling socially aggressive behavior reprehensible. This façade of equanimity is easily interrupted when family members or old acquaintances are mentioned. A chronic marihuana abuser often displays irritability or outbursts of irrational anger.

Psychodynamically, Hendin has found from intensive study of a few patients that the use of marihuana appears to bolster the psychological defenses of the individual. It provides the illusion of compliance rather than submission to parental figures. Drugs sound attractive as a means of avoiding the anxiety of facing brutalizing or humiliating competitive situations. The need to avoid anxiety derives from early transactions with combative fathers. The abusers tend to respond with a wish to withdraw from competition, aggressiveness, and assertiveness. Living in a conflicted state, the impulse is to repress drives to bully others. In addition, the abusers usually had difficulty in relating to mothers who were lacking in love, warmth, and supportiveness.

In some doubtless predisposed individuals, heavy marihuana smoking appears to precipitate psychotic activity characterized by passivity and ideas of reference and influence, accompanied, at times, by delusions of grandeur. Hallucinosis has seldom been observed. In the few cases of this kind, it is not known that the individuals abused only

marihuana; they may have been taking other hallucinogens, as well. Use of the phenothiazines or haloperidol led to rapid clearing of symptoms. On withdrawal from heavy abuse of marihuana, restoration of socially adaptive behavior often is delayed for months.

The same clinical phenomenology is found among persistent users of the more potent agent hashish. Some believe that these individuals will, in time, suffer permanent brain damage. Uvular edema is reported as a diagnostic sign. Hashish users seem to be subject to various respiratory disorders, including bronchitis, asthma, and oropharyngitis. Diarrhea, hepatotoxicity, and acne also seem associated with its use.

Following exposure, the individual may sleep for one to six hours and awaken without exhilaration or other "hangover." There is no evidence that its usage leads to serious abuse of or addiction to the narcotics.

LSD-25 and Mescaline

As a consequence of the ill-advised dissemination of public information on the hallucinatory properties of these drugs and the unsupported and extravagant claims made that they expand psychic activity and thereby enhance creative processes, they have been eagerly sought by the same types of individuals who have attempted to find release from their personality disturbances through the use of amphetamines, barbiturates, alcohol, or narcotics. The more widely disseminated and known of these agents are the synthetic drugs d-lysergic acid diethylamide-25 (LSD), an alkaloid of the ergonovine type, and mescaline, the best known of the various active compounds of the naturally occurring cactus *peyotl*.

It is surmised from various studies that the hallucinogenic agents also affect the biogenic amines within the brain and thereby produce their now well-known modifications of perceptual and other physiological functions. Thus it is hypothesized that LSD-25 exerts its effects by release of norepinephrine with consequent activation of various neuroreceptors while binding serotonin and histamine.

Under experimental conditions, these agents produce vivid alteration of perceptions without clouding of consciousness, as well as certain symptoms caused by autonomic dysfunction, sympathomimetic in nature. The subjects report an impressive intensification of perceptions with kaleidoscopic visual hallucinations, hyperacusis, tactile paresthesias, and distortions of the body percept. The thoughts appear novel and illusory, are portentous, and are often interpreted in mystical terms. Feelings of estrangement and variations in mood take place. Psychodynamically, it has been suggested that a release of primary processes occurs or that primitive percepts emerge as the result of toxic impairment of ordinary ego operations. For the latter reasons, certain psychiatrists have employed these agents to assist in therapeusis with, however, no well-established evidence of their effectiveness.

In a study of college students using LSD, Hendin found that they differ from marihuana users. They are overly passive and constricted and feel cut off from their inner lives. The drug is used as a rebellious act against parents perceived as distant, as well as a means of breaking through their defensive intellectualizations and constricting obsessiveness.

Abused by those predisposed through personality defect, LSD-25 has been implicated in the precipitation of frank schizophrenic reactions. Others have been admitted to hospital in panic states, and those taking the drug over prolonged periods have had intermittent episodes of panic even in periods of abstinence. Those in panic report terrifying experiences, with the emergence of haunting experiences of loneliness, depression, depersonalization, and visual hallucinations. Both homicide and suicide have been acted out in states of LSD intoxication.

A 21-year-old woman was admitted to the hospital along with her lover. He had had a number of LSD experiences and convinced her to take LSD to make her less constrained sexually. About half an hour after ingestion of approximately 200 μg., she noticed that the bricks in the wall began to go in and out and that light affected her strangely. She became frightened when she realized that she was unable to distinguish her body from the chair she was sitting on or from her lover's body. Her fear became more marked after she thought she would not get back into herself. At the time of admission she was hyperactive and laughed inappropriately. Stream of talk was illogical and affect was labile. Two days later, this reaction had ceased. However, she was still afraid of the drug and convinced that she would not take it again because of her frightening experience.

These "bad trips" must be recognized as caused often by the taking not only of LSD but of other drugs simultaneously, as well as unknown and sometimes toxic adulterants and contaminants. It is important to recognize "the bad trip" sufferer who has also taken anticholinergic drugs, particularly the belladonna alkaloids.

Treatment of the "bad trip" is best carried out in the majority of cases by verbal reassurance repetitively defining reality and indicating that the frightening experience and the perceptual distortions are caused by the drug. Also, it has been helpful to maintain the patient's orientation by advising him of his identity, those who are with him, and his location. Assisting him to identify and examine concrete objects is sometimes helpful.

The recommended treatment of an LSD-induced crisis is administration of a phenothiazine. When adulteration with anticholinergics has occurred, the use of phenothiazines will enhance their action and may induce coma or cardiorespiratory failure. The differentiation should be made by attempting to obtain from the ill person or his or her friends a history of the drugs taken and their effects on others. Physically,

LSD and mescaline generally induce pupillary dilation and reflex hyperactivity, with a slight increase in pulse rate and blood pressure, sweating of palms, and tremor. The anticholinergic agents produce similar signs, but there is dryness of the mouth and absence of sweating.

If medication is indicated owing to the severity of the patient's anxiety or the inability to control his behavior, and there is no evidence of the taking of other drugs with anticholinergic properties, 50 mg. of chlorpromazine may be given intramuscularly. Pulse and blood pressure should be followed. This dosage may be repeated in 45 to 60 minutes if no symptom improvement has occurred, and again at similar intervals provided the circulatory system is maintained.

McGlothlin and Arnold's follow-up study of 247 persons who had taken LSD either in experimental situations or during psychotherapy did not reveal any permanent personality defects. However, these individuals were not among the group of compulsive users. Taken regularly, any hallucinogenic drug will lead to increasing tolerance, as well as to cross-tolerance to other members of the group. Physical dependence does not occur. On the other hand, in some persistent users of LSD, chronic psychotic reactions of a schizophrenic type have evolved. The psychotic state is egosyntonic in some, as it provides a rationalization of their drive to withdraw from interpersonal contact and its often related affective distress.

PHENCYCLIDINE

Recently, there has been a dramatic increase in abuse of the compound phencyclidine (angel dust, PCP, and HOG), a parent compound of the intravenous anesthetic ketamine. Phencyclidine produces a floating euphoria, which in some progresses to an acute toxic psychosis with outbursts of aggressive behavior and severe impairment of sensation and verbal communication. This state may progress to coma and death. Given the high levels of morbidity and mortality associated with use of phencyclidine, further research and educational efforts are required to develop appropriate treatment and preventive approaches to the abuse of this drug.

BROMIDES

Incidence and Etiology

If administered in toxic amounts, several salts of bromide may produce acute brain syndromes. With the development of methods of determining the bromide content of blood, it was found that mental disturbances resulting from bromides were more frequent than had been realized. Twenty-five years ago, in some psychiatric clinics, 4 per cent of all those admitted were found to be suffering from bromide psychoses. The condition is now seen infrequently. About 50 per cent of the cases arise through repeated refills of bromides prescribed by physicians. Many toxic states arise through self-medication, principally by the use of proprietary preparations containing bromides.

Symptoms of intoxication may be expected if the bromide content exceeds 150 mg. per 100 ml. of blood serum, although there is a wide variation in susceptibility to the drug. The mechanism of bromide poisoning is through the replacement of the chloride with bromide. Elderly or arteriosclerotic patients have a poor tolerance and may develop toxic symptoms even though the blood content may be relatively low. Bromides are excreted slowly, and a mental disturbance may develop within two or three weeks after one begins to use amounts as small as 45 to 60 grains a day. Malnutrition, dehydration, and arteriosclerosis render the patient more susceptible to the effects of bromides. Their use is at times associated with alcoholism.

Diagnosis

In mild intoxication there may be a feeling of tiredness or weakness, irritability, broken sleep, slowness of mental grasp, inability to concentrate, faulty memory, drowsiness, impaired attention, and perhaps even confusion. Physically, one notes a dry skin, coated tongue, digestive disorders, impotence or menstrual disturbances, ataxic gait, tremors of tongue and fingers, and hyperactive, sluggish, or absent deep reflexes. Dehydration is common. Protein elevation in the spinal fluid is frequent. Acne, considered an ordinary sign of bromidism, is often absent.

In more severe intoxication, the clinical picture is one of delirium with fever, confusion, clouding of consciousness, varying degree of drowsiness or stupor, disorientation, difficulty in grasp, misidentification, motor restlessness even to the point of extreme excitement, fear, and memory loss accompanied by confabulations. Speech is thick, muttering, hesitant, and slurred, and the face is masklike and expressionless. The mood is often one of fear or depression. In bromide as in other toxic psychoses, there may be a loss of the usual forces of repression, with a resulting appearance of hallucinations. The ideational content of the delirium may be colored by individual psychogenic factors. Paranoid ideas are common. Occasionally, a schizophrenic-like syndrome is observed. Bromide delirium may continue for ten days to two months. Remissions and exacerbations with sudden changes in the mental state are not uncommon.

Treatment

The treatment consists of stopping the drug, the forcing of liquids, and the administration of 2 to 4 gm. of sodium chloride every four hours unless gastric irritation forbids such large doses. Most patients can take a total of 4 to 6 gm. a day in divided doses if it is given in enteric-coated tablets. Bromides are ex-creted more rapidly following the administration of ammonium chloride than after the use of sodium chloride. Ammonium chloride not only furnishes a chloride for displacing bromide but acts also as a diuretic. In some instances intermittent peritoneal lavage or the use of the artificial kidney might be considered to increase bromide excretion. Cathartics are usually necessary for the obstinate constipation that often exists. An anxiolytic or other hypnotic may be advisable to correct insomnia during detoxification.

Clinical Report

C. M., aged 38, was transferred to a mental hospital on October 22 from a hospital to which he had been admitted five days previously. His history prior to the present illness was without particular significance, although apparently he was of a somewhat immature, unstable personality.

In September the patient became tense and greatly concerned because, after a brief and stormy marriage, his daughter had left her husband. About October 1 he began to drink heavily. Between October 9 and October 13 he consumed four "large bottles" of a proprietary drug product containing a large quantity of bromides. So far as was known, he took no alcohol during that period. On October 13 he appeared confused and showed a slurring of speech and an unsteadiness of gait. Soon, in addition to these symptoms, he stated that he would shoot his son-in-law, also other members of his family.

On October 17 he was admitted to the general hospital. There he was seen by a consulting psychiatrist. His blood bromide was found to be 600 mg. per 100 ml. The patient was confused, refused to stay in bed, showed poor motor coordination, and one night locked himself in a closet. He thought he had a gun in bed with him. He made such irrelevant remarks as, "I know who shot him. I was behind the curtain." He told his wife that the patient in an adjoining bed had "killed the little girl on B Street," located near his home. No such incident had occurred.

On October 21 he became much more confused; he was completely disoriented and his speech was quite incoherent. He heard gun shots in his room; he said there were dead bodies there and that his wife was sleeping in the hospital with other patients. He attempted to jump from a window, and it was necessary to place him in restraint pending his transfer to a mental hospital. He was restless and constantly responded to both auditory and visual hallucinations. When asked where he was he replied that he was at "Mom's and Pop's place." Upon being asked why he was in bed, he answered, "It seems to be a precaution to be parked here to smooch." He pointed to the bedcovers and said, "That's my wife there." He felt about the covers and remarked, "See that stone. It makes me G— d— mad." He turned and shouted over his shoulder, "Well, come on, you might as well take it off. Sure going to get hell over that. What do you think of buying that place out?"

By October 26 the patient was more cooperative, but still disorganized and restless. A physician introduced himself to the patient, who then said, "Yes, I heard about Hugh Pendleton. I better sleep pretty good tonight. He's got his offices at DeKalb and Jacoby Streets. Do you know it's him?"

On October 29 he knew where he was but gave the date as October 5 and had no recollection of having been in the general hospital. He stated that he had been depressed over his daughter's troubles and had taken triple bromides. For several following days there were periods during which he was noisy and restless and his verbal productions were incoherent and irrelevant. By November 9 his sensorium was fully clear and his apperception was intact. When asked about his experiences, he replied, "I must have caused considerable uproar at home with my antics. They thought I was drunk. I insisted I was not. I took it upon myself to take that bromide medicine for my nerves. My wife tells me I was in C. Hospital for four days. It's a blank wall. It seems I only really started remembering things from last Saturday, when my family saw me. My folks were telling me about some of the stuff that I did. I sure feel like an ass."

On November 10 the patient's blood bromide content had been reduced to 75 mg. per 100 ml. His convalescence continued without interruption and on November 20 he was discharged as recovered.

BIBLIOGRAPHY

General

Berg, D. F.: Extent of illicit drug use in the United States. Division of Drug Sciences, Bureau of Narcotics and Dangerous Drugs, United States Department of Justice, 1969.

Gossett, J. T., Lewis, J. K., and Phillips, V. A.: Extent and prevalence of illicit drug use as reported by 56,745 students. J.A.M.A., 216:1464–1470, 1971.

Holden, C.: Drug abuse 1975: The "War" is past; The problem is as big as ever. Science, 190:638–639, 1975.

Kolb, L.: Drug Addiction: A Medical Problem. Springfield, Ill., Charles C Thomas, 1962.

Krantz, S.: Deterrents to drug abuse. The role of the law. J.A.M.A., 206:1276–1279, 1968.

Musto, D. F.: Dangerous substance use: An uncommon history. Trial Magazine, Nov./Dec., 1974, pp. 59–62.

Report on drug addiction. II. New York Academy of Medicine, Committee on Public Health. Bull. N.Y. Acad. Med., 39:417–473, 1963.

Tart, C.: States of Consciousness. Science, 177:1203, 1972.

Wikler, A. (ed.): The Addictive States. Association for Research in Nervous and Mental Diseases, Baltimore, Williams & Wilkins Co., 1968.

World Health Organization: Technical Report Series. No. 407, WHO Expert Committee on Drug Dependence. Sixteenth Report. Geneva, 1969.

Opium, Its Alkaloids, and Related Synthetics

Berkowitz, B., and Spector, S.: Evidence for active immunity to morphine in mice. Science, 178:1290–1292, 1972.

Chambers, C. D., Taylor, W. J. R., and Moffett, A. D.: The incidence of cocaine abuse among methadone maintenance patients. Int. J. Addict. 7:427–441, 1972.

Dole, V. P., and Nyswander, M. E.: Methadone maintenance treatment: A ten year perspective. J.A.M.A., 235:2117–2119, 1975.

Demetrius, J. A.: Research and development of naltrexone: A new narcotic antagonist. Am. J. Psychiatry, 135:782–786, 1979.

Editorial: Narcotics addiction: Where will it end? J.A.M.A., 215:1661, 1971.

Freedman, A. M.: Clinical studies of cyclazocine in the treatment of narcotic addiction. Am. J. Psychiatry, 124:1499–1524, 1968.

Gearing, E. R.: Evaluation of methadone maintenance program. Int. J. Addict., 5:517–543, 1970.

Gold, M. S., Redmond, E. D., and Kleber, H. O.: Noradrenergic hyperactivity in opiate withdrawal supported by clonidine reversal of opiate withdrawal. Am. J. Psychiatry, 136: 100–102, 1979.

Goldstein, A.: Opioide peptides (endorphins) in pituitary and brain. Science, 193:1081–1086, 1976.

Hekemian, L. J., and Gershon, S.: Characteristics of drug abusers admitted to a psychiatric hospital. J.A.M.A., 205:125–130, 1968.

Hughes, P. H., and Crawford, G. A.: A contagious disease model for researching and intervening in heroin epidemics. Arch. Gen. Psychiatry, 27:149–155, 1972.

Jaffe, J. H., Senay, E. C., Schuster, C. R., et al.: Methyl acetate vs. methadone. J.A.M.A., 222:437–442, 1972.

Knapp, S., and Mandell, A. J.: Narcotic drugs: Effects on the serotonin biosynthetic systems of the brain. Science, 177:1209–1211, 1972.

Liberson, I., Bigelow, G., and Flamer, R.: Alcoholism among methadone patients: A specific treatment method. Am. J. Psychiatry, 130:483–491, 1973.

Marx, J. L.: Neurobiology: Researchers high on

endogenous opiates. Science, *193*:1227–1229, 1976.

Mason, P.: The mother of the addict. Psychiatr. Q. Suppl., *32*:189–199, 1958.

News and Comments: Narcotic antagonists: New methods to treat heroin addiction. Science, *173*:503–506, 1971.

Oldendorf, W. H., Hyman, S., Braun, L., and Oldendorf, S. Z.: Blood-brain barrier: Penetration of morphine, codeine, heroin, and methadone after carotid injection. Science, *178*:986–988, 1972.

Preble, E., and Casey, J. J.: Taking care of business—the heroin user's life on the street. Int. J. Addict., *4*:1–24, 1969.

Rado, S.: Narcotic bondage: A general theory of the dependence on narcotic drugs. Am. J. Psychiatry, *114*:165–170, 1957.

Seevers, M. H.: Psychopharmacological elements of drug dependence. J.A.M.A., *206*:1263–1266, 1968.

Tarail, R., and Dorn, W. D.: A sign of heroin use in methadone programs. J.A.M.A., *228*:283, 1974.

Vaillant, G. E.: A twenty-year follow-up of New York narcotic addicts. Arch. Gen. Psychiatry, *29*:237–241, 1973.

Wikler, A.: Dynamics of drug dependence: Implications of a conditioning therapy for research and treatment. Arch. Gen. Psychiatry, *28*:611–616, 1973.

Barbiturates and Other Sedative Drugs

A.M.A. Committee on Alcoholism and Addiction: Dependence on barbiturates and other sedative drugs. J.A.M.A., *193*:107–111, 1965.

Jackson, A. H., and Shader, R. I.: Guidelines for the withdrawal of narcotic and general depressant drugs. Dis. Nerv. Syst., *34*:162–166, 1973.

Matthew, H. (ed.): Acute Barbiturate Poisoning. New York, Excerpta Medica Foundation, 1971.

Shaw, S., Simmel, B., and Lieber, C. S.: Plasma alpha amino-*n*-butyric acid to leucine ratio: An empirical biochemical marker of alcoholism. Science, *194*:1057–1058, 1976.

Smith, D. E., and Wesson, D. R.: A new method for treatment of barbiturate dependence. J.A.M.A., *213*:294–295, 1970.

Wikler, A.: Diagnosis and treatment of drug dependence of the barbiturate type. Am. J. Psychiatry, *125*:758–765, 1968.

Amphetamines

Bell, D. S., and Rozelle, N. S. W.: The experimental reproduction of amphetamine psychosis. Arch. Gen. Psychiatry, *29*:35–40, 1973.

Cohen, S.: Amphetamine abuse. J.A.M.A., *231*:414–415, 1975.

Kreuz, D. S., and Axelrod, J.: Amphetamine in human plasma: A sensitive and specific enzymatic assay. Science, *183*:420–421, 1974.

Taylor, K. M., and Snyder, S. H.: Amphetamine: Differentiation by *d* and *l* isomers of behavior involving brain norepinephrine or dopamine. Science, *168*:1487–1489, 1970.

Watson, R., and Schildkraut, J. J.: Amphetamine withdrawal: Affective state, sleep patterns and MHPG excretion. Am. J. Psychiatry, *120*:263–269, 1972.

Hallucinogens

Ackerly, W. C., and Gibson, G.: Lighter fluid "sniffing." Am. J. Psychiatry, *120*:1056–1061, 1964.

Cohen, S.: Suicide following morning glory seed ingestion. Am. J. Psychiatry, *120*:1024–1025, 1964.

Glass, G. S., and Bowers, M. D.: Chronic psychosis associated with long-term psychotomimetic drug abuse. Arch. Gen. Psychiatry, *23*:97–103, 1970.

Hendin, H.: College students and LSD: Who and why? J. Nerv. Ment. Dis., *156*:249–258, 1973.

Isbell, H.: Clinical aspects of various forms of non-medical use of drugs. Part II. Anesth. Analg. (Clev.), *50*:897–905, 1971.

Jackson, B., and Reed, A.: Catnip and the alteration of consciousness. J.A.M.A., *207*:1349–1350, 1969.

McGlothlin, W. H., and Arnold, D. O.: LSD revisited. A ten-year follow-up of medical LSD use. Arch. Gen. Psychiatry, *24*:35–49, 1971.

Schultes, R. E.: Hallucinogens of plant origin. Science, *163*:245–254, 1969.

Showalter, C. V., and Thornton, W. E.: Clinical pharmacology of phencyclidine toxicity. Am. J. Psychiatry, *134*:1234–1238, 1977.

Taylor, R. L., Maurer, J. I., and Tinklenberg, J. R.: Management of "bad trips" in an evolving drug scene. J.A.M.A., *213*:422–425, 1970.

Cannabis Sativa (Marihuana and Hashish)

Abel, E. L.: Marihuana and memory: Acquisition or retrieval. Science, *173*:1038–1040, 1971.

Halikas, J. A., Goodwin, D. W., and Guze, S. B.: Marihuana use and psychiatric illness. Arch. Gen. Psychiatry, *27*:162–165, 1972.

Hendin, H.: Marijuana abuse among college students. J. Nerv. Ment. Dis., *156*:259–270, 1973.

Kolansky, H., and Morre, W. T.: Toxic effects of chronic marihuana use. J.A.M.A., *222*:35–41, 1972.

Marijuana and health: A report to the Congress. Am. J. Psychiatry, *128*:189–193, 1971.

Maugh, T. H.: Marihuana (II). Does it damage the brain? Science, *185*:775–776, 1974.

Meyer, R. E., Pillard, R. C., Shapiro, L. M., and Mirin, S. M.: Administration of marijuana to heavy and casual users. Am. J. Psychiatry, *128*:198–207, 1971.

Nahas, G. J.: Marihuana–Deceptive Weed. New York, Raven Press, 1973.

Tennant, F. S., Preble, M., Prendergast, T. J., and Ventry, P.: Medical manifestations associated with hashish. J.A.M.A., *216*:1965–1969, 1971.

28

DISORDERS USUALLY FIRST EVIDENT IN INFANCY, CHILDHOOD, AND ADOLESCENCE

"By human caring is meant that feeling of concern, regard, respect one human being may have for another. Its biological roots lie in the maternal and paternal behavior of all living things, and it is reinforced by environmental circumstances. Most important of these is the presence of caring in another human being.

"Upon it, along with aggression, rests our survival."

David E. Sobol

(Courtesy of Ken Heyman)

This and the following two chapters describe the personality disturbances recognized during childhood and adolescence. Described are the behavior disorders in which the major etiologic factors depend upon disruptions in the developmental process, often influenced by the transactions between the growing child and the parents or parental substitutes. Those special symptoms which bring children to the attention of physicians and psychiatrists—the speech and learning disturbances, tics, and disorders of sleep, alimentation, and evacuation also are described in this chapter. The succeeding chapter discusses mental retardation, including the various causes of impairment of cognitive development dating from the earliest period of human life.

672

EXAMINATION OF THE CHILD

The treatment of children's psychiatric disorders differs in many respects from that of adult psychiatric problems. In large measure, this is because children are living through the most active phase of the developmental process. Their personalities are less structured and formed, and from one stage of growth to another, they show rapid modifications in behavior.

Those who work in the field of child psychiatry must have a knowledge of the ever-changing patterns of healthy behavior at the various age levels, as a means of evaluating the existence of disturbance. Again, the environmental pressures leading to disordered personality functioning in the child may usually be discovered in the present or recent past. They contribute a continuing influence in the life of the child. Since at this age the child is dependent upon the parents emotionally and in all aspects of living, one must deal directly with the parents in the course of arranging the treatment and in determining future management. Children seldom come to treatment on their own; they are brought in by the parents or referred by community agencies, schools, or courts.

Still another difference is evident in the practice of child psychiatry: the means of obtaining information and evaluating the problem of the child. Of necessity, much of the history must be obtained from the parents and from others who relate to the child in school or other environments. Inferences in regard to emotional reactions and relations with others, particularly in the younger age periods, are derived from psychological testing and from play therapy, wherein the child acts out his or her fantasies. Therefore, the work of the child psychiatrist must be actively supplemented by the skills of the clinical psychologist and psychiatric social worker. Furthermore, in prescribing treatment, consideration must be given to the significant persons in the child's environment, as well as to the child. The outcome of a particular problem depends to a great extent upon the family structure from which the child comes. Some symptoms are fostered by the family. Efforts directed toward understanding and modifying the behavior of the child would remain unsuccessful unless the significant family members also entered therapy.

Although in recent years the tendency has largely been to consider the majority of behavior disorders as emotionally determined, there is a growing recognition of the great extent of brain injury concurrent with childbirth as contributing to many of these disturbances. The syndrome of *minimal brain dysfunction* is now diagnosed frequently. This condition appears to be caused by cerebral hypoxic lesions, thought by Towbin to be due to venous infarctions suffered by the fetus during or around parturition.

While the specific problems of the brain-injured, epileptic, and mentally defective have been discussed in other chapters, their recognition and significance for the developmental interactions of the child were not then specifically discussed. If one is to assess the existence of brain dysfunctions or delay in maturation, one must pay attention to those behavioral sequences that characterize emotional stability, attentiveness, integration of action, and all forms of sensory reception and perception at differing periods of maturation, rather than to consider only the simple aspects of sensorimotor and reflex functions tested in the ordinary neurological examination. Whatever the type of disturbance or its etiology, it must be recognized that troublesome trends in the development of growing children make it difficult for them to be accepted comfortably by those who care for them. The difficult and asocial responses of children, as well as the feelings of the parental figures, should be understood in this context and not from that of moralistic disapproval.

Sources of Referral

Today, in the U.S.A., schools, more than any other source, refer children to psychiatrists for examination because of behavior disturbances. Other important referral sources in this country, in order of frequency, are physicians, social agencies, courts, guidance clinics, and parents. The types of behavioral problems in referred children tend to vary, depending upon the source.

From the schools come largely the children who are difficult to manage in the classroom—the troublemakers—as well as those with academic problems arising from the reading and learning disorders. Physicians mainly send in the children with psychosomatic complaints and those in whom the behavioral response to impairing illness, either acute or chronic, is considered abnormal. For the most part social agencies request consultation for orphaned and neglected children. Because of their extensive responsibility in caring for such children, the patients they refer tend to have the most serious problems. The court referrals to psychiatrists generally consist of children charged with delinquent acts or neglected or abused children whose parents are charged as responsible. Guidance clinics have need from time to time of special diagnostic studies or wish placement of their patients in residential or day care centers staffed by psychiatrists. Parents may refer children for any of the aforementioned reasons; the fact that others prove to be the main sources of referral suggests the perceptual limitations of many parents for the social functioning of their children.

The Examination

The diagnostic process differs greatly from child to child. The examiner is confronted with overt behavioral problems much more frequently than in clinical assessment of the vast majority of referred adults. Physical and neurological examinations are in order if they have not been performed previously. Psychological tests are desirable in most instances, but in some cases are not necessary. In general, the parents, if they are available, will prove the major source of information, but that provided by the sources of referral is clearly of importance. When families and the referring agency are not ready informants, a social worker's evaluation will be necessary.

The examiner must be able to relate to those children who are brought in frightened and resistive, and learn to accept with patience whatever they may do in their initial visit: whether they scream, kick, bite, or tear and grab things from others; whether they are inattentive or aggressively social; whether they are silent, sullen, or stubborn and unwilling to communicate in any way.

The clinical examination of the child is more important in the overall assessment than the history. This is because the child is unable to provide the history and that given by parents will be incomplete, for only the patient knows his or her experiences and suffering. Consequently, the overt behavior and the inferences one may make from it take on significance in the diagnostic process.

Diagnostic Information

The child therapist will seek from the diagnostic study information on the child's behavior as it relates to the following points:

1. Motility and speech, including spontaneous productions and play.

2. Relationship behavior with others, as demonstrated in the interview and during spontaneous play.

3. Affective behavior, including that toward the examiner.

4. Attitudes toward family members, school, and playmates.

5. Stated interests and motivations toward them.

6. Self-evaluation and perception of

the problems for which he or she is referred.

7. Temperament, which will include the examiner's evaluation of general activity, intensity of reaction, tendency to approach or withdraw, adaptability, attention span and persistence, distractability, and threshold of responsiveness to various sensory stimuli.

In the infant and young child, the examiner must be fully cognizant of the changes in behavior that may be observed during the progressive sequences of early development. The knowledgeable examiner will assess five behavioral areas: adaptive, gross motor, fine motor, language, and social. The progressive changes that occur in these behaviors over the first five years of life are well described and illustrated in Gesell and Amatruda's Developmental Diagnosis, edited by Knobloch and Pasamanick.

To examine young children, it is necessary to create a situation for attracting the child's attention and providing pleasure, which has the potential for eliciting his repertoire of behaviors. The office furnishings most likely to provide this situation will include a play table; blocks; water colors; crayons; clay and plasticene; dolls representing adults, children, and babies in costumes attractive to children of the area; toy furnishings of various rooms of a home and school, including bathrooms; a punching bag; balloons; and some simple craft utensils.

For older children and adolescents, the diagnostic exchange alone may be sufficient to elicit the desired information. Variations with questioning, story telling, and play have been found more suitable for some.

Psychological Testing

Those tests in general use are described in Chapter 8. The use of psychometric scales, widely applied in Western countries, preceded the development of generalized tests of personality functioning. Interest in mental testing developed in the latter half of the nineteenth century, with the contributions of such workers as Sir Francis Galton and J. M. Cattell. In 1905, Binet, a French psychologist, and Simon, a psychiatrist, the former's associate on a commission appointed to study the matter of instruction of defective children, published the first scale of intelligence tests for children. They drew up a set of graded problems constituting a progressive scale arranged in steps of increasing difficulty, which, in 1908, was revised to include age levels. These problems constituted tests of imagination, attention, comprehension, suggestibility, logical memory, language functions, common information, and ability to discriminate concepts, detect absurdities, and solve problems. These tests, first introduced into the United States in 1910 by Henry Herbert Goddard of the Training School for Feeble-Minded Children at Vineland, New Jersey, were devised after studying the abilities of children of all ages up to 16 years. It was found that after age 16 there was little increase in native intelligence, as distinguished from knowledge.

The Binet scale was restandardized in the United States in 1916 by Lewis M. Terman of Stanford University, who first used the term "intelligence quotient" (I.Q.) for the relationship of mental age to chronological age, which in 1911 had been suggested by Stern as a more constant quotient than the developing mental age. This Stanford test was revised in 1937, when some shortcomings were eliminated, new problems were introduced, and the scale was extended for both the higher and the lower mental ages.

In the application of the test, the patient is given a standardized series of graded groups of tests, each successively more difficult. The tests are grouped according to the age at which they are usually passed. Each succeeding group should be solved by a child one year older than the child who solved the preceding one. One group of the series, for example, should be successfully solved by a child of 6, and the next most difficult group in the series by a child of 7. The mental age of the person examined is the average of the series of tests he can successfully pass. The lowest age group used in determining the average is that one in which all the problems were successfully solved, and the highest is that in which at least one problem was solved.

INTELLIGENCE QUOTIENT. In earlier forms of the Stanford-Binet scales, an I.Q. as the index to relative intellectual brightness was arrived at by dividing the mental age of the patient by the chronological age (after age 13, increasing fractions of successive chronological age increases were disregarded until age 16, after which 15 was used for all adults) and multiplying the quotient by 100 to eliminate decimals. In the latest revision (Form L-M), however, this ratio method has been corrected for deviations occurring at various ages and for the fact that recent retest findings indicated that mental growth, as measured by the test, extended beyond age 16, contrary to earlier assumptions. For adults, the chronological age of 18 is now used. The resulting standard score I.Q.s are presumably directly comparable at all age levels.

Because of the difficulties with the "mental age" concept as applied to adults, many authorities prefer to use the Wechsler scale for evaluating adolescents and adults, because on it I.Q.s are determined by separate norms for each age level through old age. Nevertheless, the Stanford-Binet scales are often considered preferable for children, particularly in evaluating mental deficiency.

It should be remembered that, because intelligence tests are expressed in terms of numerical findings, their apparent definiteness is apt to be misleading. It should be remembered, too, that an adult who is, say, 10 years old mentally but 40 years old chronologically is a very different person from a child of 10. He may not be able to do any more with his intellect than a 10-year-old child, but he has had 30 more years of experience in living, and his emotional experiences, conditionings, and maturity may be very different. The results of these tests will therefore be modified somewhat by the home environment and social status of the subject.

Qualitative features of the subject's limitations may offer the experienced clinician information on the role that cultural deprivation may be playing in his or her difficulties. They are useful as guides to educational policy and, to some extent, to the complexity of the social and occupational situations to which adjustments may be expected. If the subject's score gives him a mental age of less than 10 years, it is not to be expected that he will be both self-supporting and capable of an unsupervised adjustment in an urban community. Although we can scarcely identify the various attributes and qualities that enter into what we call intelligence, yet there appear to be a number of more or less distinct components in mental ability, each of which can be measured by appropriate tests. Aptitude tests have been devised to discover evidence of one's fitness for certain types of professions or occupations, but any conclusions based on them must be accepted with great discretion.

Frequently, in medicolegal matters the question arises about the responsibility of an alleged feeble-minded person. In general, it may be said that no limitation of responsibility should be recognized if the offender has a mental age exceeding 10 years.

The various intelligence tests fall into two groups so far as technique of application is concerned. Some, like the Stanford test, must be given to one person at a time. Others can be administered to groups. The individual examination has the advantage of better rapport, and the potential for examining and stimulating motivation and assessing cultural influences.

ETIOLOGY

The child is a changing personality, and in order for emotional growth to proceed in a natural and spontaneous way it is necessary that he or she receive affection, understanding, security, and discipline and be stimulated by achievement and social acceptance. It is necessary, too, that he feel satisfaction in his relation with his parents, that he develop a feeling that he is lovable, that his individuality be respected by his parents, and that he attain confidence in his own strength and capacity as a person in his own right. The maladjustments of childhood sometimes originate from a single cause, but more frequently they arise from the combined action of several types: emotional, situational, intellectual, and constitutional. Care must be exercised not to oversimplify the problem and explain it by one formula. From our earlier description of the importance of attachment, it is reasonable to assume that human relationships have acted as a significant etiological factor in many maladjustments of childhood, through their influence upon the developing personality. Of all these relationships, that of parent and child is the one in which the problem is most frequently rooted.

Disturbances and distortions in the personality growth process result in undeveloped phases of the child's personality. The undeveloped phases may have arisen through such factors as the striving of the mother to hold her child as an undifferentiated part of herself. Thus the child does not obtain the natural love, guidance, and direction necessary for his development into an independent personality, with fulfillment of his individual potentialities and responsibilities. Again, the failure of the personality development, with resulting inadequate capacity of the child to deal efficiently and realistically with the business of living, may result from the fact that he struggled to protect his dependency status against the demands of growth, against giving up his infantile relationship to the mother, and against an independent organization of his own powers and capacities. The child has been delayed or blocked in some aspect of his growth toward a normally functioning self and cannot handle his feelings in a way that permits those growing relationships with others that are essential for his development.

The affective state of well-being, induced and maintained through consistent and interested maternal care, so well described by Sandler and Joffe, may be interrupted at any stage of growth by deprivation, loss, or even the fantasied loss of those on whom the child is dependent. Its interruption leads the child to a subjective sense of loss, which may be of such a magnitude that the child responds with behavior characterized by helplessness and passivity, perhaps denoted best as *childhood depression*. Depression in the infant and child does not necessarily relate to feelings of aggression toward the lost parent or parent surrogate. The growing child responds to the distress of deprivation in one of the following ways: by angry protest and aggressive unacceptance; by denial through passivity; by reversal in clowning; by direction of the distress against himself; or by presenting psychosomatic symptoms. If deprivational states are worked through, normal growth and development can follow. The psychopathology of childhood depression is described later in this chapter.

In Chapter 4, on personality development, the transactional processes of general significance at various stages of growth were described. In Chapter 7, many variables were indicated that pathogenically interrupt those processes establishing the progressive sets of well-being and health on which successful maturity rests. The succeeding paragraphs will mention other pathogenic factors that were not emphasized earlier.

Early Mothering Experiences

Observation of infants seems to show that the need for mothering, sensory stimuli to skin and mucous surface, and instinctual emotional gratification is present from the time of birth, and that the lack of these may result in inhibition of personality development. Sudden weaning or attempts to establish toilet training at too early a stage of the child's development may indicate parental attitudes that pave the way for later emotional and behavioral disorders. At about the beginning of the third year, the necessity for growing into relationships with other people and accepting their values becomes definitely greater.

Other factors that may distort the parent-child relationship and disturb personality development are neurosis, psychosis, or psychopathic, antisocial, or aggressive tendencies of the parent. The psychological fate of the child is to a considerable extent determined by the emotional health of the parents and by the complex forces interacting within the family group. Many faulty parent-child relationships are related to the parents' own personality structure, their emotional conflicts, biases, and past experiences. To secure a clear picture of the influences to which the child is subjected, one should know how the parents feel unconsciously about the child, what conflicts disturb the parent-child relationship, even what conflicts have existed between the parents and their parents, and how these have affected the ability of the parents to relate themselves to the child. The emotional reaction of the parents to the behavior of the child should not be overlooked. Occasionally the behavior of the parents is a result of the child's behavior rather than the cause of it.

Early institutional care or other interruptions in the continuity of parent-child relationship are harmful and lead to defects in personality development expressed as emotional apathy or inadequacy in forming relations with others, inability to accept obstructions, failures, and separations, as well as perceptual, intellectual, and language disturbances.

Bernard and Crandell, from their examination of the available research on adoption and foster homes, give strong evidence of the necessity to avoid repeated disruptions for children through changing foster homes. The ultimate health of a child who is not to remain with his own parents may depend more on the later ameliorative mothering by the adoptive or foster parent or on his trauma-reinforcing attitudes than on the original parental separation. The latter has its major impact at that time in early life (from five to six months of age) when the infant is developing attachment behavior. Impermanence of care through repeated transfer from one foster family to another, as well as congregate foster care, provides a less effective means of preventing psychiatric and social disability among those children who lose parents.

Relations to siblings may be the source of personality problems. Parental favoritism and a feeling of being supplanted by the birth of a younger sibling at times arouses abnormal sibling rivalry and jealousy. It should be remembered that it is particularly difficult for some children to share an adult (especially a parent) with another child.

Parental instability with resulting shifts of attitude on the part of the child may prevent identification, one of the most important mechanisms in shaping character. Death of a parent or, more frequently, desertion or divorce, usually preceded by a long period of domestic unhappiness, may be important in the production of personality disorders. Attitudes experienced by the stepchild or the foster child may create personality maladjustments. Many school experiences are important in giving rise to personality problems. Failure in school and the factors that contributed to the failure, such as mental retardation or unhappy home conditions, faulty handling by teachers or difficulties in relations with classmates, often are sources of personality difficulties. Sometimes poverty and privation operate to produce neurotic traits or behavior disorders. In such a case, the deprivation has some special meaning to the child.

Belonging to a social group regarded as inferior or alien to the major environmental one, with the resulting conflicts in identification with one's own family group in ideologies and in accepted culture, may create many emotional problems. Difficulties in language and lack of social and educational privileges and experiences also contribute to the problems.

The child who feels rejected is often insecure and anxious, as a result of which he is hyperactive, emotionally unstable, has difficulty in concentrating, feels resentment toward the person who denies him the love he wants, and expresses his hostile feelings by temper tantrums and disobedience. He may cover up his need for affection by an air of bravado and attack. Students of child delinquency report that generally the delinquent has had an unhappy childhood characterized by feelings of rejection, inadequacy, and guilt and by lack of affection.

The attitude of the parents toward the child is greatly influenced by the degree of satisfaction and contentment they have been able to achieve in their own lives. Frequently, the mother carries over into her relationship with her child the unresolved conflicts that arose in her relationships with her own parents. Hostilities and resentments from such a source disturbing the relationship with her child may have a harmful effect on social and emotional growth and development. Conflict over hostile feelings is common in parents and much of the behavior expressed in troubled parent-child relationships derives from that source.

Parental oversolicitude is much more frequent than neglect and is equally pernicious in its results. Such overprotection in every phase of the child's life, including dress, health, food, play, and association with other children, prevents the development of independence, responsibility, and maturity of personality essential for successful adaptation. Such children, shielded from all the ordinary hazards of life, are rendered dependent, infantile, and frequently hostile. They lack the satisfying pleasures of childhood and are usually whining and deceitful. Oversolicitous parents, in their anxiety to protect the child against imaginary harm, usually nag, scold, and constantly admonish him. As he grows older, they continue to treat him as a child rather than as a responsible, or at least partially responsible, person.

Maternal overprotection is more frequent than is paternal oversolicitude. It may be manifested in the case of both the wanted and the unwanted child and for various reasons. The fact that the prospective child was unwelcome may have made the mother feel guilty for having entertained such a thought. A smothering oversolicitude then represents the denial and disguise of a hostile rejection of the child—a device for the denial of hate. The defensive reaction to her unconscious hostility to the child may lead her to extravagant measures of protection resembling an obsessional neurosis. The relationship to the father often has proved frustrating and she finds in her child a solution of her own emotional needs. Overprotection may take the form of continuing such activities as feeding, bathing, nursing, or dressing the child long past the usual time. It may be shown, too, by the mother's practice of sleeping with the child even in his teens, or by a desire to have the child constantly in her presence. Usually, also, there is oversolicitous protection against physical danger, illness, or the "bad influence" of other children.

In her training of the child, the overprotective mother is either indulgent or dominating. The child of the indulgently overprotective mother continues his infantile demands and expectations long after they should have been outgrown. He is often a disciplinary problem, and his behavior may be characterized by disobedience, impudence, tantrums, an aggressively demanding attitude, and varying degrees of tyrannical behavior. He may be selfish, conceited, and a show-off. His bossy and demanding attitude betrays the fact that maternal indulgence has stimulated the development of aggressive components of the child's personality. Feeding problems are common in the child of the indulgent, apprehensive mother. The problems of the dominatingly overprotective mother's child are largely anxieties, fears, shyness, and submissive behavior. In both cases, the overprotection operates against outside influences that make for growth in social adaptation. The child may use neurotic symptoms to control the mother and retain the infantile advantages of the emotionally intertwined mother-child relation.

Many instances of the overprotective relationship arise from the mother's insatiable hunger for love, a hunger based on a severe privation of love in her own childhood. To this impoverishment in the child of all those positive feelings implicit in parental love—recognition, security, affection and sympathy—Levy gives the term "affect hunger."

The emotional influences in a particular family are never identical for any two children. Probably, too, a mother's psychology is such that no two children can bear for her the same emotional meaning. Occasionally a mother may entertain a hostility toward a particular child, arising, perhaps, from a hatred that is directed primarily toward her husband and then transmitted to a child who resembles him. Again, disappointment concerning the sex of the child may create a maternal attitude that is traumatic to it.

The overstrict, punitive father may arouse disturbing tensions and such emotional reactions as fear, anxiety, resentment, and hostility, with consequent personality or behavior disorders. The tension of actively aggressive impulses evoked by the severity of a father who represents an object of frustration and fear may cause a child to erect defenses against aggression, perhaps in the form of an obsessional character or an obsessional neurosis.

The *child abuse syndrome,* also referred to as the "battered child" syndrome, has laid bare the dimensions of brutality directed at some young children, as these cases have come to notice in pediatric clinics. The majority of the victims are under 3 years of age and most are under 1 year. Alcohol is an important contributing factor in the parent. Psychoses in the parent have seldom been found. Parents frequently justify the physical abuse of the infant or child on the grounds of discipline, but the evidence of the gross physical injuries suffered shows this explanation to be, at best, a rationalization.

At issue in child abuse is the inability of immature parents to nurture their children with a balance of affection and kindness coupled with firmness—the indications of maturity. Studies of abusing parents have discovered some who show continual hostility and aggressiveness, uncontrollable in some throughout their lives. Such parents have also been the subject of violence from their own parents. Others are rigid, compulsive, and lacking in warmth, and readily rationalize their abuse of the child as a means of effecting proper social conduct. Some are passive, immature, and dependent, competing with their children for the attention of their spouse and responding when unrewarded by attacking the infant or child, whom they unconsciously perceive or sense as a competitor.

Statistical studies have shown that 70 per cent or more of all cases of serious child abuse are the result of actions of the mother. This is not surprising, as mothers spend the largest amount of time with their children. Few parents have the maturity to meet the demands of the young throughout the day and the night without some relief. The abused child, responding as he may with feeding problems or crying, presents in retaliation to the punishing parent his own behavioral aggression, such as demanding more attention, stealing, or lying, which then provokes further parental aggression.

Just as there has been a growing awareness of the extent of physical abuse of infants and children, sexual abuse has also been reported more frequently. Such assaults may occur in infancy: the adult masturbating the infant to pacify him, or, in a more covert way, persistently and repetitively taking the child's rectal temperature, inserting suppositories, smacking the child's naked buttocks, or sleeping in the same bed. Overt sexual attempts of an incestuous nature may occur, as discussed earlier.

In infancy, reactions to sexual assaults are often restlessness and feeding disturbances. In early childhood, common symptoms of anxiety such as thumb sucking, nail biting, enuresis, or conduct disturbances follow. The child may develop sexual fantasies to lay the groundwork for a later perversion. The outcome in late childhood and adolescence may be direct expression of a variety of behaviors.

While the forms of child abuse are seen in parents in all socioeconomic classes, it is not surprising that Rutter and his colleagues discovered much higher levels of conduct disorders, neuroses, and reading retardation in 10-year-old boys and girls living in the inner city of London compared to similar children in a rural area in England, the Isle of Wight. Within the inner city, family discord, parental deviance, social disadvantage, and corrective schooling were found much more frequently than in the rural areas.

Handicaps and Overambition

The child who is so retarded mentally that he cannot compete with his peers, the one who is small for his age but strives to compensate through his readiness to fight, the child who is deaf or who has suffered from a prolonged physical illness or from encephalitis may react with emotional or behavior disturbances. The brain-injured child must also be considered. Beneath this child's disturbed behavior there may be a rich and troubled inner life marked by anxiety, regression, and frustration. Neurological or orthopedic handicaps, obesity, or other physical abnormalities that attract attention require special consideration.

Factors that stimulate self-consciousness or an exaggerated feeling of difference in relation to those about the child also act as potentially pathogenic factors. Overambitious educational expectations sometimes evoke emotional and behavioral reactions of a neurotic nature.

One must not forget the emotionally deprived child who appears to be retarded in every field of personality development, including even intellectual functioning. Such children are most frequently found among those who were reared in institutions during infancy.

ATTENTION DEFICIT DISORDER

Hyperkinetic Syndrome

It was the description of the overactive behavior of children who had suffered definitive brain damage early in life that led to the definition of this syndrome. Because of this, unfortunately, hyperactivity in children is too generally equated with the existence of brain damage—even though minimal. Other children without such damage may also express themselves through overactivity.

In some, the hyperkinetic reaction may be based on a genetic predisposition. Some animal models of inheritance are known now. Morrison and Stewart suggest from their family studies that a polygenetic inheritance exists; they found double the incidence of alcoholism in families with secondary cases of the hyperactive child syndrome. Other children have a low level of arousal of functions, possibly due to limited capacity for inhibition within the nervous system, as the result of minimal brain damage. In still others, the syndrome represents the consequences of family transactions rewarding or permitting the expression of the symptoms, or some combination of genetic-constitutional predispositions and the dynamic of learning in the family.

The affected children are reported by parents and teachers as being excessively active. Their lack of attentiveness, restlessness, garrulousness, and impulsivity often disrupt classrooms and irritate their elders. Their short attention and concentration spans and subsequent distractibility make it impossible for them to maintain continuing direction or focus on the tasks or objects before them. Those who contact these children may refer to them as spoiled, undisciplined, badly mannered, or odd. Secondarily, such children may react to their social disability by such other behavior as clowning, negativism, withdrawing, or avoiding. Evidences of the condition are present in many children as early as 3 years of age. Its prevalence is estimated at 3 per cent of prepubertal children; it occurs ten times more frequently in boys than girls.

In those children with the minor signs of brain damage will be found evidence of impairment of fine movements and coordination; deficits in attention and affect; perceptual, intellectual, and memory faults; and central sensory impairment. In approximately 50 per cent of the affected group, the electroencephalogram is abnormal. Not necessarily all, but often only a few of these "soft" neurologic signs are used to support the contention of minor brain damage.

History of birth injury, encephalitis, or some other encephalopathic disturbance would support the contention of maldevelopment of the central nervous system with subsequent impairment in integrative function. In evaluating the symptoms it is important to determine whether the hyperactive child's problem is due to attentional or perceptual deficit, or to a combination of the two. In others the activity is due to impulsivity or failure to retain events well.

Treatment today is best effected by combining the pharmacologic approach with therapy of the child and parental guidance. The treatment program is directed and programmed best by initially establishing appropriate medication, then attending to the child's educational problems, providing parental guidance, and, often, psychotherapy.

Approximately 75 per cent of hyperactive children respond favorably to prescription of the central nervous system stimulants, particularly methylphenidate. Initially, 0.25 mg. per kg. may be given daily in divided doses before breakfast and lunch. This dosage schedule may be doubled during successive weeks of treatment, up to a level of 2 mg. per kg. If a change in behavior occurs, the drug should be continued for several months. It may be withdrawn slowly to determine whether its continuation is required. Other children may respond better to dextroamphetamine.

Imipramine has also been used in the treatment of this condition. However, comparative studies of those receiving methylphenidate and imipramine show that a higher rate of discontinuance of imipramine occurs than of methylphenidate. Both drugs given over time to boys decreased their rate of weight gain but had no significant effect on height.

Advice to teachers about the child's condition will be helpful. As the child's attention and concentration increase and distractibility decreases, the educational process generally improves. Psychiatrists should offer parental advice, too. For some children who fail to improve, psychotherapy should be undertaken.

Gardner has described well the process he utilizes in the treatment of those with secondary psychogenic problems consequent to minimal brain dysfunction. He hypothesizes that the therapist must recognize the impaired perception, poor retention, and social isolation that often contribute to the child's failure to learn. The therapeutic task is to attempt to bring the child to perceive reality more clearly, to relinquish both the use of denial as one of his primary defenses and expectation of the magical cure, to assess his fear of and withdrawal from involvement with others, and to concern himself with his tendency to regress and to act impulsively. Gardner advocates the use of play therapy with story telling. He has found it useful to have the mother attend throughout the therapeutic sessions so that she, too, may learn to manage the youngster. Also, he has advised the parent to make tape recordings of the sessions and replay it with the child between sessions. The playback is not only reiterative of the therapeutic communications, but assists both the attending parent and the absent parent in understanding the problems of the child.

Some children exhibit the features of attention deficit without hyperactivity. These are now classified separately.

CONDUCT DISORDER

Antisocial behavior in children is a frequent cause of referral to psychiatrists. Among child psychiatrists, sizable controversy exists over the categorization of conduct disorders in which the child repetitively and persistently disregards the basic rights of others and may physically attack them. While the four subtypes now specified in the American DSM-III (to be described hereafter) meet the demands for classification, many clinicians are of the opinion that more heuristic distinctions might be made on the basis of the forms of behavior exhibited, their frequency, and their antisocial seriousness.

Of the subtypes described, the socialized non-aggressive and undersocialized aggressive types are the most prevalent.

Unsocialized Aggressive Reaction

This is diagnosed in children with assaultive tendencies; they start fights, are cruel to other children and animals, defy authorities, and are maliciously mischievous. Such children, at best, have superficial relations with other children. Except for immediate personal gratification, they do not relate to others. Their actions are performed with little or no guilt. The youngsters come from rejecting parents who provide limited opportunities for association and through their indifference or absence fail to offer the opportunity for an attachment bond that would establish healthy identification and development of superego and ego ideal.

Undersocialized, Non-Aggressive Reaction

Children may be so classified who persistently run away from home and school or lie, destroy property, or set fires but do not commit acts of violence or stealing outside the home.

The predominant feature is running away from home. Such children often steal at home before running away. Often seclusive and apathetic, they admit their unhappiness at home. Parents complain of their staying out at night. Frequently, they seek solace in peers whom they perceive as stronger than themselves and as accepting of them. Some, through their passivity, are engaged in homosexual behavior, and others drift into companionship with various adolescent gangs, including the delinquent and antisocial groups. Such children, however, are generally deficient in the sense of loyalty necessary to establish them as acceptable members of well-knit adolescent groups, and often they are deceitful.

These children feel rejected at home because of unusual parental severity or inconsistency. Often physically slight, they are incapable of developing an aggressive adaptation to living. Their growth is associated with a derogatory self-image and a deep lack of self-confidence and esteem. Illegitimate children and only children often fit into this behavioral pattern.

Treatment of members of the family is necessary if change is to occur. When this is unlikely, children are served best if placed in a foster home or a treatment facility to gain the necessary corrective socializing experience.

Fire-setting behavior, because of its sometimes frightening and destructive consequences, is an important symptom complex that demands immediate attention. Watching fires and learning to light fires and extinguish them are exciting and pleasurable for most children, perhaps more so for boys than girls. Usually first experienced at an early age under supervision by parents and adults, many youngsters indulge in preparing, setting, watching, and extinguishing fires. This playful activity is not pathological. However, when the individual child indulges repetitively and his or her actions take on destructive overtones, the motivations are usually neurotically determined.

Fire setting occurs infrequently even among seriously disturbed children. One study found only 60 instances among 1755 disturbed children under age 15. The vast majority of fire setters are boys. The fire-setting child or adolescent is usually reported to have expressed other antisocial behavior; generalized aggression, stealing, and truancy are common. Also, he may have a learning disability or some physical handicaps.

Fire setting occurs among younger children and in adolescents, but the two groups are not distinctive, as some of the young fire setters once again indulge in adolescence. In the younger group, the act often has, as its dynamic, aggression as revenge against some significant person. Among adolescents, the same motivation exists, complicated by sexual motivations and fantasies of union or reunion. The majority of fire setters are diagnosed as psychotic or borderline.

In the younger group, the fire setters usually show evidence of acute anxiety. They have frightening nightmares and fantasies. Many seem to come from homes where the father is involved with the making or maintaining of fires; others have close associations with firemen. The children set fires near their homes, in association with fantasies of burning some family member who has seemed to reject or displace them from a favored role with the parents.

Among adolescents the act is more complex and the fires set often are dangerous and seriously destructive, thought through, and planned in advance. Often the fire setting is carried out by a pair of adolescent boys. One is the organizer and director and the more dominant; the other is passive. Between the two there exists a homosexual bond. The fire setter almost always remains to observe the fire and may assist those attempting its extinction. During the period of watching, they report sensing excitement, pleasure in power, and sometimes sexual arousal and discharge. Dreams of fire were noticed by Freud to occur in the enuretic, and enuresis has been noted as frequent in the history of fire setters, suggesting to analysts that fire setters should be regarded as urethral erotic.

As Macht and Mack emphasize, fire setting should be regarded as a complex syndrome in the adolescent, with different motivations attaching to various segments of the behavioral sequence. For the most part, the adolescent fire setters were schizophrenic and mentally retarded. In all their cases, the acts occurred when the patient's father was absent, arousing yearning, rage, and frustration owing to that absence. The patient identified with the father or his surrogates in fire departments, thus determining fire setting as a preferred act. Observing and extinguishing the fire, set to relieve anxiety related to the aggressive drive, seem to serve as a means of alleviating, mastering, and controlling the guilt attached to that drive.

TREATMENT.   Because of the seriousness of this symptom and its potential harmfulness to both the child or adolescent and the community, immediate decision should be made to bring the individual into treatment. Hospital treatment is indicated initially. Removal from the home usually brings about cessation of the fire setting.

M. L.,* a 16-year-old female high school student and only child, entered the hospital after having set five small grass fires in a park. One year prior to her admission, the patient's father, a merchant seaman who served as a fireman in the engine room aboard ship, had suddenly left home on a sea voyage. He had not been to sea in many years and had held fireman jobs (working in boiler rooms, stoking furnaces, etc.) on land. The patient had favored his going back to sea and had taken his side against her mother in the discussion leading up to his leaving. Subsequent to his leaving, Mrs. L. became depressed and withdrawn and developed intractable vomiting. The mother spent two weeks with a friend during which time the frightened girl lived alone at home. When Mrs. L. returned, she was still suffering from vomiting and the patient was forced to take care of her. This continued for some six months, during which time the patient became more anxious and unhappy. When Mrs. L. failed to improve and the patient continued to worsen, they decided to move in with the paternal grandparents. Both mother and daughter rapidly improved and two months prior to admission they moved into an apartment of their own near that of the grandparents. The patient became progressively more anxious, especially at night. Frequently, she would ask Mrs. L. to stay with her in her bed, which the mother would do. She began to attend school erratically, preferred to stay at home with her mother, and became increasingly angry at Mrs. L. for reasons of which the mother was unaware. The anniversary of the father's leaving on his voyage coincided with Mrs. L's receiving a letter saying that he would be home in a month's time for a short visit and would then return to sea. The patient felt happy at first that he was coming back, and then disappointed, angry, and despondent that he would be leaving again shortly. She talked at length with a girlfriend, felt very close to this girl, and was relieved. However, upon leaving her, she suddenly felt the urge to set a fire. She set five small grass fires in a park and then turned in the alarm and stayed to watch the firemen put them out. She told her mother of this behavior in hopes that Mrs. L. would have her hospitalized, but Mrs. L. did not believe her. Two

---

*This case is quoted, with gratitude for permission to use it here, from the paper by Lee B. Macht, M. D., and John F. Mack, M.D., as given in the Bibliography under Conduct Disorder.

days later she set fire to her coat sleeve, after which she was hospitalized. She was seen in intensive psychotherapy, two or three times a week, over the next several months in the hospital, and then as an outpatient for a total of two years.

Her past history contained the following pertinent data. When the patient was 5 years of age, Mr. L. (with whom the girl always spent a great deal of time and was very close) left for his first sea voyage since her birth. The mother observed that as soon as the father left, the patient became "extremely clinging and cried a great deal and was very sad." Mrs. L. stated that the patient would even follow her to the toilet and would not allow her to be out of sight. She noted that the patient "demanded to sleep in the same bed" with her, which was allowed. Mr. L. returned after an absence of three months, and the patient immediately "calmed down and was just like she was before" (according to the mother). The father did not go away again until the time we have already noted.

The patient recalled observing several fires during the years from 8 to 12. In particular, she recalled seeing a large grass fire while on a walk with her father. She remembered enjoying the scene and she remembered her own and also her father's excitement at the fire. She later recalled that he told her of lighting fires when he was a boy. Mr. L. corroborated his early history of fire setting, saying that he had set several "small fires in the woods as a teenager." He alluded to the fact that he still "loves fires" and will go out of his way "to see a good fire."

Observation showed the patient's behavior to be striking when her mother and father visited on the ward. The mother sat placidly watching as father and daughter paraded around the hospital arm in arm. She was virtually ignored—as was almost everyone else—by the twosome. This corresponded to interview material with the patient at that time having to do with wanting "to be with him and always close to him." She said she planned "to join him and live with him in Japan after his next trip." She added as an afterthought, "Mother will come along too, of course."

Mr. L. left for the sea again rather suddenly. The patient, who had been more outgoing on the ward during his visit, became quite withdrawn. She later described feeling progressively more and more "anxious and angry." She felt "like exploding, like setting a big fire or something." She asked a female attendant with whom she had been speaking to call a doctor to talk to her (she knew there was a male doctor on call). During the time she waited, she tried to play cards with some female patients but found she was "becoming more panicky" with them. She then tried to read but felt no better. Finally, in desperation she took a cold shower but still felt the same. She remarked that she "needed to cool off." Then, "as all else had failed," she set the shower curtain and some window curtains on fire and immediately "felt relieved." When the doctor arrived, she was already calm and in excellent control.

Interview material almost a year after the fire in the hospital revealed that she had felt "furious at him (father) for going again, and leaving me with Mother. I couldn't stand that again, it hurt too much. I like my mother, true, but to be alone with her . . . and have to take care of her . . . I'm sorry, that would have been too close." She continued, "I wanted him home. . . . I couldn't stand his going away again. I would have done anything to get him to stay. But he loved the sea . . . more than me and I hated him for that. I think I hated him so much that I wished he were there . . . in the fire."

* * *

Eight months later the patient wrote to the therapist from a distant city saying she wished to correspond with him. She reported that she was well and self-supporting but that she felt "ikky." To our knowledge, she has not resorted to firesetting since the hospital episode.

Socialized Non-Aggressive Reaction

When the child or adolescent does not act out violently against others or invade the basic rights of others, yet defies age-appropriate rules of conduct at home or school in such behavior as truancy, running away, lying, or stealing without confrontation of the victim and maintains peer relations, he may be classified as socialized non-aggressive. The conduct disturbance may represent the child's attempt to bolster feelings of inadequacy or inferiority, an effort to make himself feel courageous and superior by overemphasizing his independence in the form of aggressive and disturbing behavior. Sometimes it serves as defiance of authority or as a means of controlling the mother or of tyrannizing the household. Some forms of conduct disorder represent efforts to escape from anxiety-ridden situations. In others, the behavior disorder arises as a consequence of a desire for punishment created in response to marked feelings of guilt.

Socialized Aggressive Reaction

These children may be identified by the existence of several of the following overt behaviors: gang activities, staying out late, habitual truancy from school, cooperative stealing, vandalism, rape, fire setting, mugging and assault, and thefts outside the home with confrontation with the victim.

Here the family pattern is one of negligence, and the environment allows exposure to delinquent influences. Children gain their security through group identification and support. Many of these early behavior disorders represent transformations or reactions to aggression. Aggression may play a part in the very symptoms that at first sight seem to bear no relation to it. Frequently, in fact, the troublesome behavior of the child gives no clue to its real source. The conduct disorder may be an adaptation to submissiveness or may result from an effort through group identification and support to obtain substitute or compensatory satisfactions for those not received at home.

In Chapter 25 on personality disorders, the etiology suggested by Johnson and Szurek for such antisocial conduct disorders as fire setting, truancy, stealing, and unacceptable sexuality as it occurs in some children is discussed. Here the source for the antisocial behavior is believed to be in the parent's unwitting sanction or indirect encouragement of the child's behavior. In these instances, the child is healthy, not deprived emotionally, nor exposed to cultural patterns that encourage the pattern, but comes from an apparently "good" family. In such instances, the parent appears overtly to interdict the act that is the source of complaint. However, study of the parent-child interaction in the course of collaborative treatment has demonstrated that, through unconsciously driven behavior, the parent or both parents communicate their permissiveness to the child. The approval is often expressed in non-verbal forms by undue attention to the child's disturbing behavior, by the lack of consistent firmness, or in its management through unwitting and sometimes suggestive remarks, smirks, or encouragement. In such instances, to effect a change in behavior requires treatment of the permissive parent, who obtains a vicarious gratification from the child's misbehavior that acts out the parent's repressed impulses.

A 7-year-old boy was referred for psychiatric consultation from the Board of Education because of his inability to make a satisfactory adjustment in his classroom. The teacher reported that he was constantly aggressive toward other children and that much of his behavior seemed bizarre. He had been discharged from a class the previous year because of similar disturbances of behavior. The mother reported that she had had difficulty in controlling him at home. To her, he seemed very restless, blinked his eyes frequently, and masturbated constantly. She summed up her problem in one sentence: "I can't seem to get through to him." She dated the change in his behavior to the age of 2½, when he first was observed to be tense and seemed to joke about everything said to him. The boy was found to be pale, stocky, well developed, and with a husky voice. He frequently asked what would happen to him when he would return to the classroom. He seemed anxious about the possibility of bodily injury and became very apprehensive when feeling the cutting edges of carpentry tools in the play room. He did not talk spontaneously and was evasive in his replies. There was evidence of poor motor coordination and little patterning in what he did. Psychological tests showed him to be hesitant, suspicious, and interpretive of all remarks as hostile. He frequently evaded by apparent misunderstanding or not hearing what was said to him. It was felt the child needed assistance in a residential hospital setting.

In the discussion of the problem with the father, it was learned that on many occasions the father had beaten the boy severely. It seemed evident that the father was competing with his son in many ways, and he remarked in regard to games with him, "He can't lose, he wants to win the games we play. I usually win. It's hard for him to beat me. If he loses, he loses legitimately!" The father also indicated his resentment toward the son and spoke of his son's interests as silly. He expressed favoritism for a younger child. The mother was found to be an immature, dependent, and self-centered person, limited in her fantasy life, and depressed in mood.

When the boy was brought to the hospital, he first expressed much concern about "who is boss" on the ward. He frequently insisted that he was "the boss" and often attempted to engage in power struggles with other children and the doctor. He remarked, "Well, if you are strong, how come you haven't killed me yet?" Frequently, he talked of his own strength or expressed desires of being killed. In play sessions, he acted as the

father and behaved in an impatient, angry, and cruel way to a doll. The game often ended with the doll killing all other little dolls and destroying the furniture and the parents. With continuing treatment, he became destructive and aggressive in the hospital. This behavior subsided when he was provided the interpretation that apparently it was his wish to provoke the psychiatrist to respond as would have happened at home. He then made efforts to seek closeness to the psychiatrist.

Additional history disclosed that the patient was a planned child, and his early development had been quite normal. The mother reported that bowel training had been difficult and that she had had a constant struggle with the child. She stated that she had beaten him if he failed to excrete properly and admitted being constantly frustrated and angry in caring for him.

In the course of the treatment of the child, it became apparent that the problem was one of a hateful struggle for control between the boy and his chronically distressed mother. His only conception of existence seemed to be in fighting and attaining the position of "the boss." The father contributed to the child's hostility through his competitive feelings and his hostile aggression toward the child. The boy's behavior slowly but gradually improved in the protective milieu of the residential treatment center and with play therapy sessions in conjunction with special schooling. After 18 months he was discharged home. By then his parents had received some understanding of their problems through psychotherapeutic treatment.

ANXIETY DISORDERS

Separation Anxiety

Recognized for years as an excessive form of nostalgia or homesickness, the critical factor is the onset of a behavioral disturbance when the child is separated from his or her mother or other major attachment figure. Children subject to this condition often are uncomfortable when travelling away from home. At home they may refuse or dislike to visit a friend's home, school, or camp or to remain alone. Sometimes they cling to or "shadow" the parent. Frequently, when threatened or exposed to separation, psychophysiological symptoms erupt in stomachaches, nausea, vomiting, or headaches.

If separation from the significant person does occur, the child may speak of and be preoccupied with fears of accidents or illnesses involving that person as well as dread of being lost or abandoned. These types of fears vary with the age of the child and become organized around specific dangers as aging occurs.

Often children exhibiting separation anxiety are phobic about animals and imagine monsters or other potential attackers and become fearful taking trips on various conveyances. Fear of dying is common. Difficulty in going to sleep alone, insistence on parental presence, or requests to sleep with the parent often occur, as do nightmares. Fear of the dark is frequent.

Such children may be either demanding of attention and thus intrusive, or conforming and conscientious and thereby pleasing.

School phobias are probably misnamed. In most instances, the anxiety reaction on going to school is due to response to separation from the mother—a form of separation anxiety. A therapeutic regimen that directs the prompt return of the child to school has a high chance of success, particularly with younger children. A highly successful method for rapid resolution of acute school phobia has been reported in detail by Kennedy. The method is effective, without relapse over time, in children undergoing the first episode of refusal to attend school, which usually follows a weekend of physical illness. The child, usually a weak student, expresses concern about death. The mother's health has been in question. The parents communicate well, are well adjusted in most living areas, and are perceptive emotionally, but the father may be competitive with the mother in household activities.

Kennedy states that the treatment procedure necessitates a working relationship with the school, the avoidance of interest in the child's physical complaints, structured interviews with the parents, interviews with the child, and forced school attendance. The parents must be interviewed together, and the father is directed to take the child to school. The mother may be advised that she can go with the father or visit the school during the day—but not remain. The principal or teacher must participate by keeping the child in the classroom. The therapist must be confident, optimistic, and firm with the parents, advising them to avoid all discussion of the issue of school attendance with the child until it is required. They must be firm and matter of fact in preparing him or her for attendance in spite of complaints. After three or four days of being conducted to school, the child usually goes alone, without complaints or symptoms.

Such a method has been ineffective when failure in treatment has occurred several times or when the onset is insidious and not on the first day following a physical illness.

Older children with school phobia usually are found in families with highly disturbed parents who are incapable of mastering their own anxiety over aggressiveness and providing the firmness necessary to face the complaints of the child. Often parents of older children who have failed to enter school due to phobia are themselves severely neurotic or psychotic. Here therapy for the parent is necessary to effect change.

Another method that has proved successful in resolving school phobias in both young children and early adolescents is prescription of imipramine. The dosage is elevated slowly to 75 mg. daily during the first two weeks and then modified weekly to an effective level (100 to 200 mg.). With this successful therapeutic regimen, the child and parent are seen once weekly and given advice similar to that described earlier in this section. Over three quarters of the children on this regimen return to school within six weeks.

Pittman and his colleagues report that, in 9 of 11 cases of work phobia in adults, the patients had histories of overt school phobias or reluctance to attend school in childhood. Work phobias must be differentiated from the success phobias described in the earlier chapter on Neuroses. In the work phobias, the anxiety is related to concern over surrendering dependence and leaving home, in contrast to the success phobias in which inhibition of action results from anxiety over repression of aggressive assertion and success in competition.

OTHER PHOBIAS. These disorders, of a transient variety, are common in childhood, particularly fears of heights, the dark, animals, and other frightening figures. To be considered pathological, the response to the feared object must be overdetermined and lead to gross disturbance of behavior, with anxiety or panic. In contrast to the adult phobic reactions, childhood phobias are less frequently associated with acute anxiety attacks (hyperventilation). Nightmares are common.

Children who have been harmed by animals or by adults may be expected to have a generalized overreaction to them. In these instances the reaction may be thought of as a conditioned response; in other children, however, the phobia represents a displacement of fear to some other object and derives from aggressive drives directed toward one or the other parental figure. The dynamics of these phobic states are described in Chapter 22.

AVOIDANT DISORDER

Traits of seclusiveness, shyness, and sensitiveness characterize children with this condition. They shrink from and avoid strangers, hold to their family or caretakers, and seek support and affection from them. Worrying, apathy, and undue submissiveness are the expressions frequently noticed in this syndrome. The majority are reared in families in which punitive or critical suppression of activity is the general frame of transaction. Many of the children have some physical deficiency or inadequacy. Their affective life is one of shame for presumed failures in meeting the ego ideal.

Such children indulge in daydreaming. There is an absence of close friendships as well as affective relations of all kinds. They are frequently inarticulate with others and may give the impression of being mute. Often they have been deprived or suffered in their relations with parents and others and in reaction formation have turned to fantasy and social isolation. If withdrawal continues, impairment will follow in their capacity to effectively evaluate reality.

The sources for the child's frustration in human relations may stem from maternal ill health in the form of psychosis or neurosis, or a personality disorder.

Treatment requires the development of an emotional relationship with the child that allows the patient to express and be drawn away from the life of fantasy. From that relationship, further socializations may be encouraged.

Overanxious Reaction

Those youngsters whose predominant symptoms are persistent anxiety, excessive or overdetermined fears, particularly about future events—including school examinations—or about participation in social activities or meeting any expectations of others, restless sleep, nightmares, and other psychophysiological symptoms are classified as suffering the overanxious reactions. If not treated, the sources of such symptoms will establish the basis for the well-recognized anxiety states and neuroses and some of the psychophysiological states.

Children suffering these symptoms are seen often by parents as worriers—sensitive, shy, and aspiring. They feel inferior, are submissive to others, and cry easily. They are anxious to meet the expectations of others and to avoid criticism, as their major drive is to maintain security through pleasing.

Often the mother is herself ridden by anxiety, is fearful, and nags the child to meet social expectations. Frequently, these children are found in ambitious middle class families who promulgate high standards of achievement. The children come to recognize that their acceptance within the family is contingent on their continued outstanding performance, thus establishing for themselves strict superego and aspiring ego ideals.

Treatment for these children is best done by uncovering techniques. In such treatment, the sources of the driving effects of guilt and shame are alleviated by uncritical acceptance of the revelation of the child's anxiety and rage in relation to the parental figures and his or her identifications with the less punitive figure of the therapist.

OTHER DISORDERS

OBSESSIVE-COMPULSIVE TRAITS. In the past, doubt has been expressed over the existence of neurotically fixed obsessive-compulsive symptoms in children. Judd's study discovered such states in a group of children averaging about seven years of age. Often the symptoms appeared with dramatic suddenness in intellectually superior children. Never were there single compulsive acts. The most common were handwashing and touching compulsions or bedtime rituals, while the associated obsessional ideations usually were related to contamination or infection, right or wrong, or fears of harm and danger. A considerable number of symptoms invariably led to the child's conflict with his social environment.

As with adults with an obsessive-compulsive neurosis, the children so affected seemed rigid, with an overmoralistic superego, fearful of defying rules, and overcompliant to parental authority. Yet these children often had an active fantasy life. Within the family, one

or both parents were compulsive; the history showed that early bowel training was not punitive. Such children commonly were ambivalent, but usually with open aggression expressed toward one or both parents. They also often had transient phobic symptoms.

These states are differentiated from the compulsiveness usually found in healthy children, in whom it is not perceived as incongruous and does not require efforts at resistance. The healthy child is able to give up the ritualistic behavior or play and also carries it out with pleasurable affect; nor does it disrupt his ordinary relations or activities.

The outcome of such childhood obsessive-compulsive states is as yet not well documented. Some respond well to psychotherapy.

CONVERSION REACTIONS. Children exhibit conversion reactions as do adults. The symptoms are usually grossly evident and present as convulsive seizures of the tonic-clonic type, astasia-abasia, urinary retention, hemiparesis or hemianesthesia or both, aphonia, and blindness. Often the conversion symptoms may be associated with various psychophysiological expressions of anxiety conversion. As in adults, they may not be directly related to the existence of a hysterical personality structure.

Children who develop conversion reactions are usually found to have been exposed to a precipitating event, such as a bite by a dog or other animal, a minor injury or threat of injury, associated in time with some emotional stress within the family. They will have displayed evidences of overdependency, tendencies to control and demand parental attention in immature ways, fear of parental abandonment, and difficulty relating to their peers. Often they have tended to withdraw, to demonstrate aggressive phenomena with feelings of rejection by others, and to lack confidence or have poor self-esteem, as well as ideas of guilt.

Looff suggests from his study that

families of children with conversion re-actions have difficulty in verbal expres-sion of affects as related to sexual matu-ration and functioning. On the other hand, those with children exhibiting es-sentially the physiological symptoms of anxiety were inhibited in expressing this intense concern over separation.

These reactions and their develop-mental history and dynamics are dis-cussed in detail in the chapter on the neuroses.

DEPRESSION.   As mentioned earlier, childhood depression does exist. It is a reaction to deprivation or loss of affec-tional attachment, most often owing to adverse family relations. Those chil-dren so suffering appear sad or un-happy, often are withdrawn socially and, if questioned, speak of being un-wanted or unloved. The depressed chil-dren most frequently conceive of them-selves negatively. They describe themselves as "stupid" or "mean" or use some other derogatory term ex-pressing badness, failure, or disgust. Often there is difficulty in control of their aggressive drives. Many of the children display this in fighting, biting, or other destructive actions against per-sons or physical objects. Subtle expres-sions occur, too, in the form of teasing others. Public defecation or enuresis may accompany the depression, as may insomnia and excessive autoeroticism. Psychosomatic symptoms have been considered as depressive equivalents.

The parents, too, have personality difficulties expressed in outbursts of anger, temper tantrums, or criticism, as well as differing degrees of emotional distancing from the children. Depres-sion in one of the parents is common. Physical abuse is a common form of punishment in the family, and some of the mothers indulge in punitive measures in weaning and toilet train-ing. Scapegoating, depreciating re-marks because of either fantasied or ac-tual physical or mental disability, and bullying by both parents and older sib-lings subtract from the child's sense of personal worth and engender continu-ing hostility, reflected as described earlier. Divorce, separation, the ab-sence of parents for months with care provided by indifferent surrogates, death of the significant parent or parental substitute, or sudden with-drawal of interest in the child by a parent, are frequent in the families in which these depressed children are raised.

PSYCHOSES. These are described under the appropriate headings in previous chapters.

Here it should be mentioned that great care must be taken to discrimi-nate hallucinatory experiences of chil-dren in the context of neurotic or psy-chotic disorders or health. Many youngsters with anxiety states may de-scribe hallucinatory experiences as might be expected, since fantasy life is so commonly resorted to for protection from anxiety and depression. Lukiano-witz has described such hallucinations in nonpsychotic children, finding an in-cidence of 12 per cent in a selected group. Furthermore, the hallucinatory experiences were visual, auditory and tactile, with half the group experienc-ing both visual and auditory experi-ences. Childhood hallucinations oc-curred as undisguised expressions of hostile and aggressive feelings toward parents and others rejecting or abusing the child, from fear of guilt and fear of punishment, and, in some instances, as the reliving of traumatic events.

Reactive Attachment Disorder of Infancy

Infants with this condition are so diagnosed through evidence of lack of social responsiveness and general apathy. Indications of physical abnor-mality are lacking, and the essential etiologic factor appears to be lack of adequate caretaking.

Disturbances of behavior due to iso-lation or maternal deprivation in chil-dren reared in institutional homes dur-ing the first two years of life have been known since the 1920s. Schlossman coined the term "hospitalism" in 1926 to designate the condition. Levy defined the genesis of the condition in his paper, "Primary Affect Hunger," in 1937. Later, Spitz studied experimentally the withdrawal of the infant, apprehension at the approach of others, weepiness, sadness, loss of appetite and of weight, and insomnia that take place in the periods between six and twelve months as a consequence of separation from the mothering one.

The child may show a retardation of development, with inability to walk, delayed reaction to external stimuli, slowness of movement, and stupor if the separation is continued for a period of time. Earlier, at two months of age, visual tracking may not evolve. The smile response and reciprocal gaze with another may remain absent. Later, the infant may not engage in simple games with the caretaker, or attempt vocal responses, or reach out when others attempt to pick him or her up. If the mother returns, there is a rapid disappearance of the evidence of disturbance in behavior. Illness, tension, or anxiety in the mother may also lead to similar, though usually less severe, disturbances in the behavior of the infant. Prolonged maternal deprivation is productive of severe personality maldevelopment, as described elsewhere in this chapter.

OTHER DISORDERS

ELECTIVE MUTISM. Despite the ability to understand spoken language and also to speak, the child generally refuses to do so, but may communicate with others through use of gestures or sometimes by monosyllabic comments. Such children often have been noted to be shy and socially withdrawn and to display other difficulties in developmental controls, such as enuresis, encopresis, negativism, oppositional behaviors, and compulsive traits. The condition usually is noted on school entry and most often is transient, if the youngster is not exposed to excessive teasing.

OPPOSITIONAL DISORDER. In this condition, the behavioral expression of the child is continuous disobedient and provocative behavior in response to parental directions or those of other adults in authority. When thwarted, the child is likely to have a temper tantrum. The behaviors persist even though the child or adolescent suffers and is deprived thereby.

Children with oppositional behavior are designated often as stubborn or procrastinating. If these traits continue, the children are usually recognized as passive aggressive in adolescence. Problems at home as well as school are common. Erratic and authoritarian parental discipline usually typifies the transactional relations between children with this condition and their parents.

IDENTITY DISORDER. Children and adolescents may suffer severe subjective distress over sense of self or expose behavioral uncertainty as to their sexual identity, friendships, career choice, religion, loyalties, morals, and goals, yet do not clearly demonstrate the behavior of the psychoses or other personality disorders. Often the adolescent will admit to anxiety and depression, which is recognized as aroused by reflections and personal doubts about self. Reactive, oppositional, or "as if" identities may evolve and often are transient. Achievement levels are below those expected on the basis of the physical, intellectual, and educational assets of the individual.

While often transient, the identity crises often herald the most serious personality disorders in adulthood. The cause is lack of acceptable models of identification.

PERVASIVE DEVELOPMENTAL DISORDERS

Included here are those conditions in which children show distortions or lags in evolution of social skills and language.

Relations to others and attentional, perceptual, sensory and motor development have failed to progress as in the healthy child of comparable age; thus, reality testing appears impaired.

A variety of heretofore diagnostic terms have been used for such conditions in the past: childhood schizophrenia, symbiotic psychosis, atypical children and infantile autism. In this chapter we concern ourselves essentially with the recognized features of the latter. Childhood schizophrenia has been described earlier in the chapter on schizophrenia.

Infantile Autism

The prevalence of infantile autism in a general population of Great Britain is reported by Wing and his colleagues as 2.1 per 10,000 of the age group 8 to 10 years when determined on the basis of Kanner's essential features (autism and insistence on sameness). Another 24 per 10,000 have a similar syndrome but present only one of the two essential features. The male-female ratio was 2.75:1. More recently, in the U.S.A., Treffert found the combined prevalence rate for childhood schizophrenia and infantile autism as 31 per 10,000. Of these, 25 per cent were classic infantile autism, 57 per cent, psychoses of childhood with later onset, and 18 per cent, psychoses with demonstrated brain disease. To him the differences in the groups seemed less compelling than the similarities; he doubts that infantile autism should be considered as separate from childhood schizophrenia.

The striking disability in interpersonal relations and the severe obsessive-compulsive mechanisms are the pathognomonic features of autism, but the peculiarities of language and thought, although somewhat different, share the general features of schizophrenia. The amplitude of the electroencephalographic auditory averaged evoked response measured during REM sleep has been reported by Ornitz and his colleagues as significantly greater than in healthy children. Lowered excretion of urinary 3-methoxy-4-hydroxy-phenethylene glycol (MHPG) occurs in some children with this condition. In a few autistic children, Himwich and his colleagues found urine samples containing the hallucinogen bufotenin. These findings have not been confirmed by others.

The psychotic-like nature of the illness becomes apparent before the end of the first, and certainly not later than during the second, year of life.

Affective contacts with mother and other persons and the ability of the child to relate in the ordinary way to people and situations should normally be well established by 2 or 3 years of age. In early autism there seems to be an inability to form affective ties, with a resulting lack of responsiveness. The mothers of such children complain that "the child looks right through me—he does not see me." Almost invariably it is found that the parents of these children are intelligent and successful, often professional persons in good economic circumstances, but obsessively preoccupied with abstractions of a scientific, literary, or artistic nature. The family life is of a cold, formal type, and the child has received extremely little fondling, cuddling, or warm, genuine parental affection. The behavior of the mother toward the child is mechanical and does not convey love.

When a child with early autism is brought to a psychiatrist, the parents have usually assumed that he or she is severely feeble-minded. The autistic child 3 or 4 years of age usually does not talk, does not respond to people, and often has temper tantrums, if interfered with. He has little ability to empathize with the feelings of others. His autistic and impenetrable aloneness shuts out anything that comes from outside. If he attempts to form sentences, they are usually for a long time mostly parrot-like repetitions of word combinations that he has overheard, often long previously. He frequently refers to himself as "you" and to the person spoken to as "I." Although the child has no interest in people, he has a good relation to objects and may play happily with them for hours. He has an obsessive urge for a maintenance of sameness. Furniture must continue to be arranged in the same manner and the routine of life must be unchanged.

Although the extreme withdrawal and limited responsiveness of the autistic child suggest that he is mentally retarded, it will usually be found that he has average or even superior intellectual potentiality. The facial expression is often serious and perhaps tense but is usually strikingly intelligent. Frequently those who speak have an extensive vocabulary and a surprising rote memory.

Many of these children continue to function in an emotional vacuum and, for all practical purposes, function in a socially retarded manner all their lives. Some of them, through permissiveness and emotional stimulation, attain a normal intelligence quotient, become able to pay attention to persons, and to accept and return affection. They may even participate in environmental activities, although they often remain "peculiar."

Perhaps the primary psychopathological mechanism in infantile autism may be described as a disturbance in social perception, analogous to, but more complex than, perceptual difficulties at the sensory-motor level. The question has been raised whether there may not be a syndrome of affective inadequacy parallel to intellectual inadequacy. Since a quarter of the autistic children have I.Q.s in the normal range, Rutter and colleagues conceive of the condition rather as a central disorder of language development involving both language comprehension and its utilization, and the conceptual skills needed for thinking. Others emphasize the sensory-motor disorder or speak of multiple, high-level perceptual-cognitive-language maldevelopment, based on a neural failure of organization.

Treatment of the various social, behavioral, perceptual, and cognitive deficits requires a full range of therapeutic efforts directed first at establishing human contact with the child. Sensitivity training and behavior modification techniques often are the first methods of approach. Food has proven to be a most successful primary reinforcer with such children.

Follow-up studies of autistic children show that by 15 years of age one third have achieved a moderate social adjustment. About half of those who possess a meaningful language by the age of 5 show further improvement, whereas only rarely does the child without ability to communicate verbally by that age show significant subsequent improvement.

ADJUSTMENT DISORDERS OF CHILDHOOD

These are manifested in such simple repetitive activities as nail biting, thumb sucking, enuresis, masturbation, and temper tantrums. One group of these disorders concerns manipulations of certain parts of the body, such as thumb sucking, nail biting, nose picking, and tongue sucking. These conditions are generally differentiated from tics; they are felt to occur at a high level of awareness, are intermittently present, are variable in duration, intensity, and course, and the action in itself seems to be pleasurable. If they are interrupted at any stage of a single performance, they are recognized by the patient as actions for which he is responsible and that are subject to his control.

THUMB SUCKING. One of the earliest forms of body manipulation, this is usually either the consequence of deprivation in the early sucking activities of the infant or, in older children, a regressive act during periods of tension or fatigue. In the majority of the infants thumb sucking is a result of insufficient lip movements or incompleteness of the sucking phases of the feeding act, regardless of the type of feeding. Thumb sucking results not only from difficulties in feeding the infant and expressions of anxiety in the mother, but also from faulty techniques of nursing. Probably of greater concern are those anxieties in the parents related to the presumed effects of thumb sucking. In the past, various statements were made to the effect that distortions of personality, as well as malformations of the jaws and palate, resulted from thumb sucking. Management of this adjustment reaction is to be directed to the parental attitude rather than to the thumb sucking of the infant.

NAIL BITING. This is probably the commonest of the forms of habitual body manipulation occurring in both children and adults. It is usually first seen around the fifth year of life and increases in its occurrence up to the tenth or twelfth year, when children gradually relinquish the habit. Threats to prevent the child from carrying out this act are usually unsuccessful. The condition is now recognized as an expression of tension. Its removal may be attempted through understanding and relieving the source of the underlying anxiety.

MASTURBATION AND OTHER MANIPULATIONS. Masturbation, commonly practiced by children, requires treatment only if the parental or adult attitudes toward the act have instilled in the child anxieties and fears that affect his personality development adversely. More frequently, the problems of masturbation in a child involve clarifying parental misconceptions about the ill effects of the procedure and preventing radical efforts to thwart the act.

The other varieties of body manipulation, aside from hair pulling (trichotillomania), are relatively of little importance. Hair pulling calls for more careful attention and may be associated with serious problems within the family.

ADJUSTMENT PROBLEMS OF ADOLESCENCE

Considering the complexity of the developmental tasks that confront the adolescent, it is surprising indeed that there are not more demands for assistance in adjusting during this period of life. Where psychiatric and/or psychological counseling is available and accepted, as in many colleges in the United States, up to 20 per cent of the student body at one time or another request aid. The vast majority come for problems other than those described in the preceding chapters concerned with general psychopathology, but many do have neurotic and psychotic conditions.

The adolescent girl and boy must not only adapt to the rapid physiological changes taking place which herald biological and sexual maturity, but must also acquire those social skills which will insure the capacities for intimacy with another as well as to become part of a group. Personal decisions that will determine future careers must be faced. In this task, determination and persistence are needed once the decision as to one's life work is made, and in the daily competition of life he or she must be free to use aggressive drives along socially acceptable lines without paralyzing guilt or fear.

Adolescence is the period when exploration, trial, and effort are made in seeking the eventual decisions which establish the individual adult identity. Today in the affluent Western societies, where increasing numbers of adolescents and young adults are supported through college and graduate schools or through family support can postpone decisions, the period of adolescence tends to be prolonged. The potential for commitment as an independent and self-sustaining adult is delayed.

Doubtful and anxious in attempting differing tasks at home, school, or work; frightened over pent-up rage at those in authority in any of these settings; guilty, ashamed, or filled with despair in sexual explorations; accepted or rejected and accepting or rejecting others; envious of the success of friends or alarmed at their demands, the adolescent often seeks help today. The expressions of maladaptation are usually anxiety with tension, restlessness, and insomnia, occasionally compounded by minor depressive symptoms and the physiological expressions of these affective states.

With the rapidly changing value systems in our society expressed in more permissive attitudes toward sex and personal liberties, many are concerned over the defiant responses of the adolescent expressed in dress, speech, and clothes. The experimentations with drugs, sex, and violence and the "hippie cultures" are to be recognized in large part as indicative in the adolescent of the struggle for identity.

When these forms of acting out carry the adolescent to acts and associations imperiling himself, there is justification for referral for study and possible treatment. Not all, but many of the more persisting and destructive forms of adolescent acting out will be discovered to be neurotically determined and deserving of treatment as described in other chapters. However, often the offensive behaviors of the adolescent are aggravated by parental efforts at correction through authoritarian dominance. In such instances, parental counseling or family treatment is in order.

SPECIFIC DISORDERS

In addition to the varieties of general behavior disturbance described previously, many children are referred for psychiatric examination by parents or other interested persons as the result of difficulties they encounter owing to disturbances in establishing healthy alimentary, bowel, and bladder control; difficulty in motor activities, including

speech; and problems in particular areas of learning. If uncorrected, some symptoms may continue into adult life or influence health personality development adversely through persistence of anxiety, with secondary arousal of pathological, characterological, or symptomatic defenses.

Eating Disturbances

ANOREXIA NERVOSA. This disorder, generally first noticed in adolescence, is the most serious of the behavioral disorders related to development of habits of eating that assure good intake. As does the rumination disorder of infancy, it threatens general physical development through caloric limitation and often associated metabolic disturbance. A detailed description of anorexia nervosa appears in Chapter 24, Psychological Factors Affecting Physical Condition.

BULIMIA. Some separate the syndrome of bulimia from anorexia nervosa. The bulimic patient engages in episodic eating, fully aware that this eating pattern is abnormal. Following the "binge," the patient is generally depressed and suffers guilt for giving in to the impulse.

Often the binges of sweet foods are planned and end with the suffering of abdominal pain, vomiting, social withdrawal, and sleep. Those so indulging, like the anorexic, are concerned about their weight, undergo wide weight fluctuations, and attempt control not only by dieting but also through the use of cathartics or diuretics or the induction of vomiting. They may appear in general hospitals and be identified as suffering metabolic acidosis or other metabolic disorders, as well as a factitious disorder. Between binges, normal eating or fasting periods occur.

The bulimic patient is usually female and often has obese parents.

RUMINATION DISORDER OF INFANCY. This very rare condition usually is identified in infants between the ages of

3 and 12 months. Death from malnutrition occurs in about 25 per cent of sufferers. The infant, though hungry and eating, regurgitates food, which leads to malnutrition. This condition induces anxiety and depression in the mother, who then fails to make the effort to feed.

In regurgitation, the infant brings up partially digested food but shows no behavior indicative of nausea, disgust, or illness. A position of straining, with back arching, is adopted, which holds the head in retraction. Sucking movements of the tongue occur.

PICA. The craving, chewing, and eating of non-nutritive and sometimes poisonous substances is a frequent behavior pattern in children. It requires supervision over time by parents to bring about the discrimination required to direct the growing child's innate drive to mouth objects of all kinds so that he eventually chews and ingests foodstuffs only. Pica may be understood as the continuance of the infantile pattern of mouthing and thus may be regarded as a developmental immaturity, a fixation or regression to an infantile level of behavior. In other instances the mouthing continues as an expression of deprivation of parental supervision—a neglect of either attention or food or both. On occasions the behavior is determined as a familial or cultural expression, the child mouthing a specific object also chewed upon or mouthed by older family members or those in the community. Pica has been reported as occurring in about 20 per cent of populations of children seen in mental health clinics.

Since the etiologic factors leading to this mouthing disturbance are multiple, the primary sources will be found only in careful assessment of the child, his developmental state, and the family and cultural environment in which he has been raised. Hunger, neglect, brain damage, mental retardation, or cultural factors may singly or jointly be causative. One of the most serious consequences of pica, mentioned earlier in this book, is lead poisoning, in which children chew and eat objects covered with the old lead-containing paints.

Treatment must be directed to correction of the underlying forces leading to pica. In cases of neglect or retardation, training is necessary under constant but interested supervision of those capable of establishing a warm human contact.

Excretory Disorders

ENURESIS. This disturbance, the involuntary passage of urine, is common and is frequently referred to the child psychiatrist. In some psychiatric clinics, enuresis is the problem for which the majority of children are seen. At the age of 2 years, some 80 per cent of children have ceased to wet themselves. By the end of three years, the average child is usually able to keep his or her clothes and bed clean and dry. Enuresis occurs twice as frequently in boys as in girls; it is unrelated to intelligence, and in the majority of instances has been persistent. There is a group of children in whom the habit disappears only to recur at a later date during a period of tension.

By far the most frequent variety of enuresis is the nocturnal type, although diurnal enuresis and combinations of both have been noticed.

In the majority of instances, no physical disturbance of the nervous system or genitourinary apparatus is found on examination. Enuresis may occur as a matter of inadequate training, resulting either from parental attitudes or because of lack of opportunity for adequate training. In some infants, the mother is overprotective, and the child's continuing inability to maintain himself dry is accepted by her on the basis that he is too small or weak for training. The child is thus infantilized and retains an infantile lack of control. Lack of opportunity for training as a causative factor occurs only in children reared in rural homes or in crowded urban areas, where toilet facilities are inadequate and the child is not expected to visit the bathroom under conditions of cold or crowding. In other instances, enuresis occurs as an expression of revenge in which the child wets, a reaction to too rapid and punitive training.

A common type of enuresis is the regressive. In children suffering from this form of enuresis, wetting occurs as a means of again obtaining the gratification of maternal contact. Very frequently, regressive enuresis may be seen as a consequence of the birth of a younger child, with the loss of the mother's attention. The child now wets in order to obtain the care and personal attention and affection he misses because of the mother's preoccupation with the newborn. In such instances, the proper parental reaction leading to change is to allow the youngster more attention for a time, so he may grow beyond his childish needs. Punishment seldom leads to modification of regressive enuresis.

The series of studies by Gerard suggests that two thirds of the enuretic children have failed to identify with the parent of the same sex. The failure of sexual identification seems to take place in families in which the parent of the opposite sex has a passive personality, whereas the parent of the same sex is feared as more strict and rigid. Enuretic boys consequently tend to be passive and unassertive youngsters who are unable to compete actively, whereas girls with the wetting problem are found to be tomboyish and aggressive.

It is well to recognize that enuresis is often symptomatic of anxiety-arousing problems in the family. The symptom is often severe, prolonged, and not easily modified by therapy. It leads, if continued, to many additional conflicts in the growing child, depending upon the attitudes of people with whom he is in contact. As a result of punishment and shaming, the enuretic child develops secondary feelings of inadequacy. Many suffer from sleeplessness in their attempts to control the bladder. These children have feelings of embarrassment and lack of self-confidence that restrict their capacity to form easy relationships with others, as well as feelings of helplessness resulting from their inability to control the habit. They are often told repeatedly that they suffer from "weak bladders" or "weak kidneys," their personal conviction of physical weakness and disability thus being deepened. Exposed to the consequences of teasing when sent to camp or to school with other children, their sense of social inadequacy is again magnified.

The newer physiological and pharmacological knowledge has expanded the opportunities for treatment of enuresis. Enuresis usually takes place during deep sleep unassociated with rapid eye movements and their typical electroencephalographic recording of REM. Ritvo reports that about 40 per cent of enuretic periods take place during stage 2 sleep and over 40 per cent during stages 3 and 4. Two thirds of all wettings seem to be preceded by electroencephalographic arousal. Ritvo states that one may distinguish waking, arousal, and nonarousal types of enuresis. He concludes that when enuresis persists beyond age 3 or 4, the symptom may form a nucleus around which other neurotic formations occur. Ritvo found that children with arousal and waking enuresis had a history of sporadic wetting and several other neurotic symptoms, but no family history of enuresis, although the families exhibited much concern over the patient. The group of children with "nonarousal wetting" came from families with a history of enuresis. The children had a history of regular wetting and were indifferent to it. The mother is then instructed to awaken the child and have him evacuate the bladder. Regular repetitions of this act with avoidance of bed wetting often lead to inhibition of wetting.

A number of clinical trials with imipramine (Tofranil) have shown that this tricyclic compound with anticholinergic properties will interrupt enuresis in from 70 to 80 per cent of children. The drug may be given before the noon meal and prior to bedtime in 10 mg. doses for younger children and 25 mg. doses for adolescents. After a youngster is dry for a year, the drug should be terminated. Approximately a third of the children so treated continue to be nonenuretic. If enuresis recurs on withdrawal of imipramine, resumption of the drug usually relieves the symptom once again. Other tricyclics also have proved effective.

In those children refractory to such measures, psychotherapy should be attempted. The following is a case report of a child effectively treated in this manner.

A 12½-year-old girl was brought to the pediatric psychiatric clinic by her mother, who complained that she wet her bed, was very nervous and restless, bit her nails, and screamed while playing with other children. The mother recounted that her daughter had been enuretic since infancy. Initially, she wet her bed every hour or so during the night; at this time, she wet it once or twice a week. The mother awakened her twice during the night. She stated that if the children got her daughter to laugh in the daytime, she occasionally wet herself. The mother stated that the daughter had slept with her in the same bed for two years. Her daughter always liked exciting things and was admired by everyone around her, but she did not care for work about the house and wished to be a lady; nor did she wish to learn anything. When asked to help with the housework, she argued and became angry.

The daughter was the only child. The mother felt that the pregnancy was quite normal. The child was breast fed for 14 months and walked at one year but was slow in beginning to talk. Her dentition was completed at seven months, and bowel control at three years. The mother continued to feed the girl until the age of 8, since she would not take a spoon in her own hand. Her mother bathed her until she was 11 years old and reported that her daughter had dressed herself only for the past six months. She first allowed her daughter to cross the street alone within the same period of time. The explanation of this was that the mother had seen another child run over some time before. The girl had had no unusual illnesses, but was sick with teething and vomited a

great deal at that time. Her school work was good. She began school at six and a half and was regularly promoted with her class. On psychological testing, she was found to have an I.Q. of 113.

The mother described the father as a nervous man whose hands shook and who was preoccupied with palpitation of the heart. He was seen as impatient and easily upset. The mother considered herself a fairly healthy person, but nervous since an operation for appendicitis the previous year. She spoke of crying quite easily and complained about her marriage, stating it had not been happy in the early years as her husband was attached to his mother.

When the daughter was seen, she was found to be a tall, gangling, very talkative, "smart alecky" girl, rather restless, walking about uneasily. In discussing the problem of bed wetting, she stated that she used to have difficulty in sleeping because "I was afraid I couldn't wake up in time and then I couldn't get to sleep; then I would worry because I couldn't sleep and I wouldn't." She said she had slept better since her parents did not put her to bed so early. In discussing her parents, she said, "They have to love me, I'm the only one." She described her mother as "treating me like a baby. She won't let me go to the movies alone." She volunteered that she did not want to grow up but preferred to remain the same age she was. "It is more fun."

In subsequent treatment hours with the mother and child, it was learned that the daughter had been unwanted but always overprotected, the mother believing that some harm would come to her. Initially, she was a shy child, but later developed many friends, mostly among older children. Although she was at first distant with her father, she had become quite close to him since the mother became ill and was not available to do everything for her. She stated that her father was a mother to her. The child and her mother were seen only intermittently over the following three years, as they lived at a distance. She did better at school but continued to be enuretic, although with diminished frequency. After three years, the enuresis disappeared, but there was occasionally frequency of urination at night or during the day. In the meantime, the child worked out many of her conflicting feelings in regard to her dependent relationship with her mother and ambivalent attitude toward her father.

ENCOPRESIS. Much more uncommon, but more disturbing to parents and those associated with children, is the persistence of fecal soiling. This condition is usually evidence of serious psychopathology when its existence is unassociated with anatomical or physiological defect. Its presence indicates a more severe disturbance than enuresis.

Encopresis is to be differentiated

from fecal incontinence, which refers to soiling caused by a physical disorder, such as Hirschsprung's disease, defects of the rectum or anal sphincter, or impairment in neurologic control to the cerebral, spinal, or lower motor neurons. Encopresis denotes incontinence with constipation.

The term encopresis should be reserved for children who continue to soil after the usual age for establishing bowel control; over 90 per cent achieve this control by age 3. Any child who continues to do so frequently following the fourth year should be considered as possibly having this condition in the absence of demonstrable physical defect. The majority with encopresis will be found to be mentally retarded; others are brain damaged or psychotic.

Children with this behavior may soil continuously or episodically. The former have not been successfully trained to bowel control, whereas the latter usually have undergone such training but regress to soiling later. The two varieties of this condition generally occur with about equal frequency. In studies of large series of patients seen in psychiatric clinics, approximately 3 per cent presented this symptom.

In the instances of secondary or regressive encopresis, onset usually occurred following some family incident threatening the future patient's closeness to the parents. Such precipitating incidents have been birth of a sibling, the mother's going to work, parental separation, entrance of the child into school, or punishment.

Most of the children with this symptom tend to be passive and often appear depressed. In the Bellman study, 15 per cent of the fathers and 1.3 per cent of the mothers had a history of encopresis between ages 7 and 14.

One group of children soil from inadequate parental training, sometimes owing to parental guilt and passivity over their own earlier conflicts in learning bowel control. In the regressive group, soiling may be regarded as a counteraggressive act against loss or aggression on the part of parents or siblings. Soiling sometimes takes place when children are withholding defecation and represents fecal overflow around an impaction – a condition denoted as psychogenic megacolon. In this condition, the soiling is sometimes mistakenly considered a diarrhea.

Treatment is usually difficult in those children brought to psychiatrists. Since the symptom is expressive of a family conflict, the parents must be involved as well as the child. Help is needed to bring the parents to avoid expressions of critical disgust toward the child, which gives him the power to use the symptom as a counteraggressive expression to them. The family conflict or deficiencies in training inducing the symptom must be discovered and efforts made to bring about their correction. The mother must be discouraged from emphasizing the symptom by recourse to use of laxative and enemas. She must be assisted to bring the child to toilet regularly without recrimination or disgust, leaving him alone in the bathroom. It is helpful to give the child a peristaltic stimulant, such as lemonade, beforehand.

When the symptom has existed for years, it is usually necessary to separate the child from the family. This is best done in a child psychiatric unit, where a staff is available. Encopresis is seldom encountered beyond puberty.

Movement Disorders

Tics.   Tics occur as involuntary but apparently purposeless movements of interconnected muscles. They frequently involve the muscles of the eyelids, with blinking or squinting, but also occur as repetitive frowning, grimacing, sniffing, grunting, swallowing, head twisting or shaking, coughing, grunting, or explosive verbalizations. *Gilles de la Tourette's disease* or *maladie des tics* is a tic syndrome involving the upper body, including the face, shoulder, and arms.

It may be associated with coprolalia and sometimes echolalia and echokinesis. Often, tics are first noticed in childhood; they then disappear, only to recur at a later date at the time of some conflict.

Frequently, it will be found that the tic was first noticed after a frightening experience leading to a fear of injury and that it represents a defensive muscular withdrawal response of small muscle groups appropriate to the expected trauma. Although initially the defensive muscular contraction may have involved many muscles, the tic represents a rudimentary response of small muscle groups. Because of the persistence of the response beyond the particular time of the injury, the ticlike movement becomes inappropriate and involuntary. The use of the small muscle groups develops as a consequence of parental prohibition for the full movement. The tic then represents both the fear of injury and the attempt to maintain gratification by complying with parental wishes.

Children with tics are often restless, self-conscious, sensitive, or spoiled, or may be overambitious and overconscientious. Easy excitability and fatigability are observed. There are other children who are shy, seclusive, and embarrassed. The tics of psychogenic origin are to be differentiated from those that occur as a result of encephalitic disease affecting the basal ganglia. Treatment of the latter is difficult.

A six-year-old boy was brought to the clinic by his mother, who complained that he jerked his head and blinked his eyes frequently. She stated that he had begun this habit about four or five weeks previously. When the habit spasm began, she paid little heed to it, but later she slapped him in the face for it. At first she thought it might be caused by disease of his eyes. She became annoyed when he began to open his eyes with his fingers. The boy reported it was his feeling that his eyes were closing on him when the lids were heavy.

The mother went on to describe her son as restless, unable to sit in a chair, and very fidgety. She also reported that he had occasional headaches and had begun to suffer from asthma at 17

months of age. His last attack had taken place 12 months previously. Early in life he had played with younger children, but now he played only with those of his own age. The boy had been breast fed for six months and bottle fed until 1½ years. At five months of age, he had been able to sit alone and had stood up and taken some steps at 9 months. At the end of the first year, he had said a few words. She indicated that his bowel and bladder training had been completed in less than a year. The mother had dressed the boy until a year and a half ago and said that he wished her to dress him even now. It was only at this time that he had begun to wash himself. The story of his schooling showed that he had entered the first grade at 6, had done very well, and was advanced several classes. He was, at the time of examination, the youngest child in his class. It was the mother's impression that he felt uneasy. The father was described as a happy-go-lucky person who enjoyed his children. The mother thought of herself as being well. There were three children, the patient being the eldest. A sister was two and a half years younger and a baby was 18 months old.

When the boy was seen, he was found to blink, roll his eyes, and grimace about his mouth. He said that the trouble with his facial muscles came on after he had arrived home from school some weeks before and done his homework. He felt he could not stop the movements once they started. He also reported that he had been unable to sleep well and admitted some recent worries about masturbation. He saw himself as a sickly boy and described his fear of playing rough games with others. The matter of the boy's masturbation was discussed with the mother, who became overtly anxious in dealing with this subject. On returning home, she was able to talk to her son on the subject without threatening him. The mother discontinued bathing him and allowed him to go to bed later. During several additional hours, the matter of the sexual interests of the son was brought up for discussion by the mother. The physician worked with her and the boy, with gratifying results. The facial tics disappeared following a series of four visits. Treatment for the asthma was continued for several years.

Simple tics have a good chance of spontaneous disappearance, but the prognosis for the complex conditions such as seen in Tourette's disease is less favorable. Familial cases have been reported within the past few years, suggesting a hereditary determination for this and other chronic tic syndromes.

The butyrophenone haloperidol appears effective in relieving many sufferers. Shapiro and colleagues have reported a subgroup of patients with the

Tourette syndrome who can only be treated successfully with haloperidol when the dosage is slowly increased from 0.25 mg./day with increments of the same at two- or three-week intervals. Also, the parents and others must be assisted in their efforts to correct the child in attempts to suppress the movements, and to desist from other punitive and oppressive efforts at training. If psychotherapy is also required, the fears and anxieties that activate the tic should be uncovered.

Speech Disturbances

Disorders of speech are reflected in phonation, speech sound articulation, fluency and rate, or symbolic representation. They may result either from physiological disturbances in the organs of phonation, their innervation, or the brain processes concerned with speech, or as the result of interference through emotional instability. Johnson concludes that 4 per cent of children in the United States have significant problems. The majority of these lisp, about 16 per cent stutter, slightly fewer have speech defects associated with hearing loss, and the remainder have impairment owing to voice problems, fluency and rate problems, retarded speech development, complications of cleft palate and lip, those of cerebral palsy, and other neuromuscular defects. Usually considered to have a significant relationship to emotional disturbance is stuttering.

STUTTERING. This disturbance customarily has its beginning in childhood and, when persistent, seriously impedes the child's social adaptation and development. A differentiation has been made between "stutterers" and "clutterers." The former speak at a reduced rate and the "clutterers" speak at an increased rate, compared to normals.

It must be recognized that short periods of stuttering may take place between the second and fourth years, when the growing child's efforts at expression exceed his capacity to verbalize. Parents who have themselves been stutterers or have been related to a stutterer often become overly anxious and tend to emphasize the child's defect by their efforts at control through admonitions to speak more slowly and by their evident preoccupation with the speech difficulty. Many stutterers are made anxious by silence. Silence seems to "freeze them" and they may have difficulty commencing speech. Gould and Sheehan suggest that silence may become the conditioned cue for arousal of anxiety and therefore stuttering.

The persistent stutterer is considered to have a conflict between passive and aggressive drives, which is reflected in his speech. Such a child often tends to show other compulsive and ambivalent traits. His speech expresses his obstinacy in his forcing others to wait while he completes his efforts.

As to course, from 50 to 80 per cent of childhood stutterers recover spontaneously. About 1 per cent of all children continue to stutter to adolescence.

Treatment should be aimed to reduce interpersonal stress through family counseling, with the child exposed to methods of muscle relaxation, control in speech pace, prolongation of vowel sounds, and coordination of respiration and vocalization. These methods are best taught by a speech therapist.

Recently, haloperidol has been used for the elimination of stuttering, with some success.

Learning Disturbances

DEVELOPMENTAL READING DISORDER. Approximately 12 per cent of all children in the United States fail to learn to read as well as the average. As a group, they are not homogeneous. Difficulties in learning fall roughly into four categories: psychogenic, neurogenic, developmental lags or delays, and difficulties deriving from social and environmental deprivations.

One particular group are those children who have better than normal intelligence. Their social and vocabulary development is excellent, as well as their vision, but they suffer from the condition known as *dyslexia*, occasionally but not always associated with left-handedness and with difficulty in converting to right-handed writing. This disability manifests itself in a variety of ways: sometimes as confusion of one consonant with another, such as b for d, p for q, or t for f, or as a reversal of syllables, words, or entire sentences as mirror writing, with a complete failure to recognize words.

Among those with specific learning deficits, shown in poor attention span, reading, and spelling, impairment of audiovisual receptivity, and poor performance in arithmetic and language, are those with abnormal developmental profiles and electroencephalograms. The EEGs may show a 14-6 cycle per second record with spike-wave phantoms and paroxysmal activity. A group of children with developmental dyslexia have been found with a reversal pattern of cerebral asymmetry on analysis by computed brain tomography.

Another group of children suffer from an inability to learn as a consequence of particular methods of teaching reading. By these methods, children are taught to read whole words, phrases, and sentences, with the analysis of individual words into phonic sounds and letters undertaken only secondarily. Because of their particular perceptual capacity, some children are unable to learn to read or spell by this method of pedagogy. In such children the emotional expressions of fear and anxiety, caused by failure to meet the standards of the family or class and by hostility resulting from feelings of rivalry and jealousy, tend to imbue concepts of personal inferiority and encourage behavior disturbance.

These children first have a reading disability which, in time, becomes a learning disability. Early in life, if properly tested by psychologists, they show evidence of perceptual-motor and visual-motor weaknesses, as compared to other children of their age. By adolescence, many of the signs of such lags in ego functions have disappeared, and the early and often severe hyperkinesis has improved greatly. These children appear to have compensated, as they have an adequate intelligence and may read very well. Yet there are residual signs of reading disability. Their spelling capacity is very poor, owing to inability to retain verbal visual configuration. Handwriting is not rhythmic, and their organization of their school papers is poor. On multiple-choice examinations, their performance is often good, but essay examinations reveal their weaknesses. They are customarily inarticulate, and language is not used well in their communication. Their written compositions are unimaginative. Metaphors are understood poorly, and when they are asked to define them concrete responses are given— not, however, the egocentric and loose replies of the schizophrenic. The boys are able often in mechanical efforts and in sports. Emotionally, they are usually explosive and have a limited tolerance for frustration. With proper tutoring these youngsters are often able to proceed in school. Later they do better in technical or business colleges than in the formal academic institutions.

Many behavior disorders founded on such a basis disappear rapidly with improvement in the reading. The important element in treatment is recognition of the underlying incapacity to learn. Here the use of a remedial teacher is often the effective technique to bring about a satisfactory modification of the behavior disturbance. The following case illustrates this problem.

O. E. was an 8½-year-old boy referred for evaluation and possible treatment of emotional problems involved in his inability to read. The school teacher and psychologist felt that the patient had an emotional block that prevented his learning to read. The child was restless and unruly in school and a difficult problem in management. Physical examination was negative except for confusion in handedness. Past history was free of gross emotional disturbances. He was well liked by his many friends and had many interests. His parents had high academic aspirations for him and were distressed by his poor scholastic performance. He was compared unfavorably with his very bright 10-year-old brother.

During the psychiatric interview, he appeared friendly and cooperative and fully understood the reasons for his being in the doctor's office. He said, "I can't read and it gets me worried." He handled a pencil very poorly in either hand, and in printing reversed several letters and words. He could not read. Psychological tests revealed an average intelligence. He could not be tested in reading achievement, because this was so defective. Bender Gestalt designs were below his age level, but he showed difficulty in integration of the designs. A diagnosis of learning disability was made. It was felt that the problem of anxiety was secondary. A remedial reading teacher was engaged. Parents and teachers were encouraged to let him progress and learn at his own speed. He did well under special instruction, progressing slowly but quite satisfactorily in reading. His restlessness, tension, and disobedience subsided quickly.

De Hirsch points up the differentiations of these children, usually boys, from the group of scholastic underachievers whose difficulties stem from poor reading comprehension owing to preoccupation with their fantasy life, phobias, or depressive inability to focus attention. These children, in contrast to the previous group, are often highly verbal and their abstract competence is good. Later in school they do poorly, however, as they lack persistence and attentiveness. Usually rather schizoid, they develop learning difficulties in the context of conflicts over control of aggressive impulses, associated with anxiety and depression. Their major need is for psychotherapy rather than for tutoring in remedial reading.

Disorders of Sleep

Many children are referred for psychiatric care by mothers complaining of problems in the youngsters' patterns of sleep. The most common complaints center on restlessness, talking in sleep, nightmares, irregular sleep habits, night terrors, and sleepwalking. The majority of these complaints do not signify existence of psychiatric disorder, but rather the anxiety of the parent and her difficulty in establishing a satisfactory milieu conducive to induction and maintenance of steady sleep.

There are wide variations in sleeping patterns during the developmental period. While premature babies sleep almost continuously throughout the day and night, the sleep time of the infant gradually diminishes in relation to the waking time as he ages. The majority of the simple problems in relation to sleeping occur as the result of ineffective patterning of sleeping habits within the family. Babies who are regularly rewarded when they cry out by being quickly picked up and carried elsewhere, those who find they can terminate separation from the mother through their activity, restlessness, or crying when placed in bed, or who are visited frequently by parents during the night are those who develop patterns of restlessness, delay in initiating sleep, or restlessness in sleeping.

Late napping prevents others from falling asleep at night. Sleep difficulties in older children usually reflect some anxiety as the result of insecurity in family or school relations. Once poor sleep habits are established, they are difficult to modify. Early advice to the mother is important, then, in preventing those disturbances which continue into adulthood.

However, patterns of sleep are highly variable among all. From sleep research, Hartman found that some adults sleep less than six hours per night, others more than nine hours, and there are those whose sleep requirement is variable. The latter group relate variations in sleep time to various types of stress.

RESTLESS SLEEP. In most children with marked restlessness, the history generally discloses that they are equally overactive and excitable during the day. However, there are some active during the day hours who achieve quick and deep sleep easily. Specifically, the complaining mother may report jerking, rolling, and turning during sleep, periodic awakening, or rhythmic movements such as rocking or head banging. The latter expressions of restless sleep may represent either conflict with the mother, related to overdependence, or the existence of brain damage or retardation.

TALKING SLEEP. The majority of children express themselves occasionally at some time through sleep talking, heard as a few words or phrases. Sleep talking may indicate more serious and persisting anxiety, particularly if continued and associated with other manifestations of behavior disturbance. Teeth grinding (bruxism), too, may start in childhood.

NIGHTMARES. In contrast to the frightening dream, the child experiencing a nightmare (incubus) cries out while asleep and awakens with the physical expressions of an acute anxiety attack. He or she is perspiring and breathing heavily. His pupils are usually dilated and his facial expression expresses terror. He may complain of tightness or heaviness of his chest. He is, in fact, overbreathing. With a frightening dream, the child awakens but is not in an acute anxiety or panic attack. If the nightmare is repeated frequently, the child may become fearful of going to bed.

The majority of frightening dreams and nightmares occur physiologically during REM sleep and during the latter part of the sleep period. The child may be able to recount the contents of the nightmare or dreams as they are clearly represented. If so, inferences may be made about the sources of his fright and anxiety.

Those who continue to have nightmares as adolescents or adults tend to be apprehensive individuals, often overly concerned with death and generally fearful. They are generally thought to have significant psychopathology, as judged by profiles on psychological tests. Many such adults complain of insomnia. A familial association is common. Sixty per cent of somnambulists report nightmares.

Night terrors, referred to sometimes as *pavor nocturnus*, are severe reactions associated with frightened crying out or screaming. The sufferer usually gets out of bed, appears confused and unresponsive, and describes an enormous dread. A single hallucinatory recollection may be reported.

In contrast to anxiety dreams or nightmares, night terrors occur during non-REM sleep and almost two thirds take place during the first non-REM period—that is, shortly after falling asleep. The electroencephalogram shows an initial series of K complexes. Cardiac rate accelerates within a second, followed by a drop in skin resistance. Much less common than the frightening dream or nightmare, they have been observed, at the earliest, commencing at age two years. In contrast to the occurrence of nightmares, the suffering child cannot be consoled and appears to remain throughout in a semi-sleeping disoriented state from which he or she cannot be aroused. After 10 or 15 minutes, he then falls asleep, to awaken later with a complete amnesia for the occurrence.

The etiology of pavor nocturnus has been much discussed. Its source may be epileptic. It occurs more frequently in males. When severe, the frequency may increase to two or four attacks per week. A relationship exists between this condition, somnambulism, and enuresis. Many children with this condition have severe behavior disorders. In the night terrors, eruption of deeply repressed and intense anxiety probably occurs.

Diazepam, prescribed in a dosage of 5 to 20 mg. before bedtime, suppresses night terrors. Imipramine has been used successfully as a suppressant in a few patients.

A comparison of the dream anxiety

and the night terror attack is presented in Table 28-1.

SLEEP PARALYSIS. This condition is sometimes referred to as a nightmare but differs from it in taking place when the sufferer falls asleep or awakens. There is much anxiety during this episode; the sufferer cannot move, talk, or shout, even though trying to do so. Partially awake and also partially somnolent, he attracts attention to himself by moaning. Some try to break the paralytic attack by forcing a leg or arm off the bed. A touch generally leads to arousal. Frightening hypnagogic hallucinations accompany many attacks. The sufferer feels as though there is a heavy load on his chest and may speak of "someone sitting there." Sleep paralysis, often part of the symptom tetrad of narcolepsy, usually occurs associated with a sleep-onset REM period. Whether sleep paralysis exists unassociated with the narcoleptic potential is unclear. It differs from pavor nocturnus and nightmares in the sleeper's awareness of his location, his recollection of the event, and the paralysis.

SLEEP APNEA. In this condition, apneic episodes of 10 seconds or more occur recurrently during sleep. Such interruptions of respiration are associated with increased respiratory effort; when it is severe, patients have been subjected to tracheostomy. The associated episodes of violent behavior, anxiety, depression, and personality changes are important events for psychiatrists. The apneic episodes may occur in both REM and non-REM sleep. REM deprivation has been associated with a paranoid syndrome. Tricyclic antidepressants appear to ameliorate sleep apnea.

SOMNAMBULISM. Sleepwalking in childhood may continue into adolescence or adulthood. It appears to be related to a maturational defect in which action-oriented activity with imagery occurs during deep sleep, in contrast to the fantasy noted with dreaming sleep. It is now known that somnambulistic incidents take place in stages 3 and 4 sleep. Continuous electroencephalography during sleep shows that somnambulistic episodes commence shortly after a sudden burst of high-voltage slow-wave activity (S frequency). This type of cortical activity is found in the electroencephalographic records of 95 per cent of infants between the ages of 6 and 11 months. By the age of 10 years, only 3 per cent of children still show such activity during sleep. In contrast, sleep talking, like nocturnal enuresis, bruxism, and head banging, accompanies dreaming (REM) sleep.

Somnambulism is unrelated to specific personality organization, may occur with any level of intelligence, and often occurs in those with little evidence of emotional unrest. In many respects it appears related to psychomotor epilepsy.

HYPERSOMNIA. A variety of subtypes of hypersomniacs is now recognized, differing from the psychogenically induced, described in Chapter 13, and discriminated from narcolepsy. *Chronic hypersomnia* is expressed in periods of extended nocturnal sleep and also in frequent and prolonged sleep periods during the day. Many with this condition also complain of

TABLE 28-1   Summary Comparison of Dream Disturbances

	NIGHT TERROR/ NIGHTMARE SYNDROME	DREAM ANXIETY ATTACK
Stage of sleep	non-REM	REM
Time of night	early	late
Mental state on awakening	confused	clear
Autonomic activation	++++	+/−
Amnesia for event	yes	no
Dream content	+/−	++++
Treatment	Benzo-diazepine	Benzo-diazepine

(From Kramer, M.: Dream disturbances. Psychiat. Ann., 9:68, 1979.)

sleep drunkenness — a condition of confusion very similar to acute alcoholic intoxication — which occurs immediately after awakening and persists for 15 to 60 minutes. Falling asleep rapidly, these individuals do not awaken easily and often sleep for hours beyond the ordinary span unless awakened by others. The extended sleep is associated electroencephalographically with the ordinary patterns of REM and non-REM sleep. Many show higher cardiac and respiratory rates than other healthy, normal sleepers. Such hypersomniacs have been classified into idiopathic and symptomatic groups, the latter usually giving a history of skull injury or encephalitis. The diurnal hypersomniacs may be treated with the stimulants phenmetrazine hydrochloride, dexphenmetrazine, or amphetamine sulfate, in dosages of 10 mg. two or three times daily; or methylphenidate, 10 mg. three to six times daily.

A rare condition, the *Kleine-Levin syndrome,* in which excessive eating is associated with hypersomnia, has been found by Karacan et al. to be associated with decrease of both REM and stage 4 non-REM nocturnal sleep patterns.

The *pickwickian syndrome,* also uncommon, is an association of hypersomnia, periodic respiration, and obesity. The sufferer exhibits an unusual relationship between the sleeping and respiratory disorders following entry into sleep. Just before return of respiration, electroencephalographic arousal occurs. The etiology of these two syndromes is unknown.

As described earlier in this book, sleep disturbance may arise during later life as a symptom of a more profound personality disorder. This symptom, however, may be the complaint that brings the patient to medical care. Also, the sufferer may medicate himself and become drug-dependent by attempting to relieve this disruptive symptomatic expression of his illness.

A classification of the disorders of sleep is shown in Table 28–2.

TABLE 28–2   Classification of Clinical Disorders of Sleep

PRIMARY SLEEP DISORDERS
Insomnia
Narcolepsy
Chronic Hypersomnia
Kleine-Levin Syndrome
Pickwickian Syndrome
Sleep Paralysis
Nightmares

SECONDARY SLEEP DISORDERS
Schizophrenia
Depression
Chronic Alcoholism
Postpartum Emotional Disturbances
Chronic Renal Insufficiency
Nutritional Disorders
Thyroid Dysfunction
Neurological Disorders

PARASOMNIAS
Sleepwalking
Sleep Talking
Nocturnal Enuresis
Bruxism

SLEEP-MODIFIED DISORDERS
Cardiovascular Disorders
Respiratory Disorders
Epilepsies
Neuromuscular Disorders

(From Karacan, I., Sales, P. J., and Williams. R. L.: Psychosomatics, *14*:77–88, 1973.)

SLEEP MANAGEMENT

The psychiatrist will explore the ways in which the child has been trained and attended by the mother as regards sleeping behavior. Also, he or she will attempt to discover in the child's thinking the possible reasons for abnormal sleeping behavior. Usually there will be found anxiety over separation from the mother, being harmed, or dying during sleep, or losing control of bladder or bowels, eliciting criticism or punishment by the mother.

In those instances in which the sleep disturbances appear to be an expression of inadequate or anxious training on the part of the mother, she should receive appropriate counseling.

If the problem is one of bad dreams or nightmares, their content may reveal the sources of the anxiety in the day-time relations of the patient, thus allowing the psychiatrist inferences about the treatment method most likely to alleviate the source of the nighttime disruption.

Pharmaceutical control of sleep disturbances may be necessary if the preceding methods fail in relief. In severe disturbances, with interruptions by nightmares or pavor nocturnus, the choice of hypnotic or other drug may best be determined after electroencephalographic analysis of the child's sleeping pattern.

The Kales suggest as treatment for the primary insomniac encouragement of physical activity during the day, but no exercise near bedtime. Exercise several hours before sleep increases stage 4 sleep. The adult patient should be urged to regulate his day and night schedules. If, however, he does not fall asleep, he should be advised not to remain in bed. Thus he is to condition himself to go to bed when sleepy. Also, before bedtime he is advised to avoid stimulating mental activities, including games.

For difficulty in falling or staying asleep, the Kales recommend flurazepam. When insomnia is associated with depression, a tricyclic antidepressant medication may be given before bed—these agents increase stage 4 sleep and maintain sleep.

The REM suppressant drugs (the barbiturate hypnotics, glutethimide [Doriden], ethchlorvynol [Placidyl], methyprylon [Noludar], diphenhydramine [Benadryl]) are useful, particularly in those psychosomatic conditions in which sleep arousal with REM cycles is associated with symptom expression, such as pain of duodenal ulcer or nocturnal angina pectoris. Glutethimide is perhaps the best, owing to its long duration of action and continual suppression of REM. With improvement of the patient, these drugs must be withdrawn very slowly to minimize the REM rebound phenomenon.

Those drugs that suppress stage 4 sleep and do *not* suppress REM sleep (chloral hydrate, flurazepam hydrochloride [Dalmane], methaqualone [Quaalude], chlordiazepoxide hydrochloride [Librium], and diazepam [Valium]) are indicated for somnambulism and night terrors.

THERAPEUTIC MEASURES

The treatment of personality difficulties of the child must vary with the individual and his or her problems. The principal emphasis, however, is on "the child's needs, strivings, and growth tendencies in a social and cultural background." The fundamental objective is a healthy reorganization of the personality and an improved emotional adjustment. Many of the child's behavior problems and neurotic difficulties arise from emotional handicaps sustained through earlier relationship experiences that were not conducive to healthy emotional growth. One seeks, therefore, to acquire an understanding of the forces that have been operating in the early life of the child. Although the child cannot, of course, develop beyond the limits of his constitutional potentialities, it is the aim of therapeutic measures to remove or reduce his persistent and crippling emotional difficulties and to aid him in reorganizing those emotional attitudes and patterns of reaction that have been governing his personality functioning. In this way, growth of the patient's personality toward new and more spontaneous and satisfying patterns is made possible.

A growth-promoting therapeutic relationship must be substituted for the previous ones that produced insecurity, abnormal aggression, or hostility and that reinforced infantilization and prevented growth in the direction of self-reliance and social maturity. Into this relationship the child brings his resentments, anxiety, fears, and guilt, and the fantasies that have arisen from such feelings. The first essential is for the psychiatrist to establish a friendly, interested, and satisfactory relationship between the child and himself. He accepts the child as an equal and as a person in his own right. He neither stresses nor ignores the difference in age and maturity but assumes it as a matter of course and does not assume an artificially childish language. In the therapist the child finds someone who can help him as he is. The therapeutic approach must be gradual. To hasten it may defeat the relationship and cause the child to withdraw into evasion, indifference, or falsification. Any early reference to behavior disorders may stimulate hostility or tension. Early discussions may therefore deal with the child's interests and activities and in direct questioning about neutral matters. With the therapist-child relationship satisfactorily established, the patient may, in this friendly atmosphere, verbalize his conscious conflicts, opinions, ideas, and feelings, which can then be discussed.

Through this relationship, the child projects his anxiety and hostility onto the personality of the physician. By projection, the child may make use of the therapist to symbolize an unacceptable part of himself as he moves toward freeing himself of the unacceptable aspect. The child may also project onto the therapist desirable qualities that he hopes to attain. The therapist will not be critical of the child's behavior and will take his ideas seriously and as worthy of attention and consideration. He will seek to feel and understand just what problems the child is trying to solve which have brought him to the psychiatrist. His attitude will not be one of condescension. Within the security of the dependent relationship with the emotionally more mature therapist, whom he trusts and imitates, the child relives his emotional conflicts. The physician will aim to have the child feel that the therapist is a kindly adult, a helpful, protective parent figure who understands his feelings and is helping him.

Occasionally, if the problem is a simple and largely environmental one, talks with the patient concerning situations that are troublesome may be sufficient intervention. The patient may have reacted to a situation with confused apprehension and undesirable behavior through not·understanding the chain of circumstances that produced a given result. One must not, however, by merely attempting to have the child see what is wrong or undesirable about himself or herself, expect the patient to relinquish old ways or control them more effectively. Even with simple problems, there must usually be a reorganization of emotional attitudes and patterns of reaction. To secure this, the patient must be aided to obtain compensations and outlets and gain new ways of feeling—that is, change and grow.

Children are known to be better subjects for hypnosis than adults. There has been a resurgence of use of this technique to assist the uncovering necessary in treatment of conversion reactions, described and reviewed by Williams and Singh.

Family and/or group therapies are important in enhancing ego growth in many instances. The physician may wish to make use of *group therapy*, consisting of clubs, camps, dancing classes, boarding schools, or other activities, to enable the patient to make contacts with others and develop interests of his own. In some cases, separation for long periods of time from an overprotective mother may be desirable. In younger children, play techniques involving psychoanalytical principles are largely used.

Parental Therapy

Since the child's problem usually arises from the living relationship between himself and a parent and is interwoven with a parent's attitude, modification of parental attitudes toward the child is necessary to effect change. This is particularly so with the younger child.

Usually, a series of interviews either with both parents or with the mother is desirable before the child is examined, to discuss the problem that the child presents. By giving the mother—and sometimes both parents—an opportunity to express and relieve anxiety, the therapist gains her confidence, often secures revealing information about personality characteristics of the parents, and assists the parent in seeing the child's trouble in a truer perspective. The mother may explain the child's behavior as a result of heredity, but the therapist will usually discover that the mother's neurotic conflict has entered the child's handling. Her expressions of guilt, accusations, hostility, anxiety, and excuses may betray the nature of interpersonal relations that have been a source of difficulty.

Inquiry should be made about the onset of the child's difficulty, the mode and circumstances of its first appearance, and its development. The interview will presumably assist the physician in securing information concerning the child's cultural background, the family's ways of living, its intelligence, its beliefs and problems, the relationships between father and mother, and the child's group relations. Through a knowledge of the parents' past and present attitudes toward the child, the psychiatrist learns much about to what situations the child's behavior is an adjustment. As previously indicated, it will often be found that the mother is carrying over into her relationship with her child the unresolved emotional problems that arose in her relationships with her own parents. The aim is to uncover a dynamic picture of the experiences and emotions of the child in relation to those surrounding him.

Although the problem may have arisen from the father-child relationship, more frequently it arises from that of mother and child. Both require therapy; they are not, however, interviewed together. The psychiatrist and social worker collaborate in helping parents and child to resolve difficulties that have arisen through living together. Usually, the social worker sees the mother, while the child sees the psychiatrist. Through visits, the mother acquires a new understanding of her relation to the child and a realization that she has a part in the child's therapy. The simultaneity of these appointments, usually held weekly and lasting 45 minutes, assists mother and child to realize that the problem requiring help does not exist solely in the child or in the mother but in the relationship between them.

If the mother's feeling for her child is one of rejection, treatment of the latter's problems is often difficult. The mother, burdened with anxieties and fears, cannot emotionally accept or understand a direct interpretation of her unconscious feelings or her personality patterns. By indirect methods, therefore, the mother is helped to objectify the problem, to formulate her thinking, feeling, and behavior in relation to the child, and to allay her guilt and anxiety. She is assisted in establishing a satisfying relationship with the child that will permit a progressive and wholesome growth of her personality. No attempt should be made to make the mother recognize that she is coming for treatment for herself as a patient. If a favorable rapport is established with the therapist, the mother accepts this relationship as a search for causes for the child's difficulties, and in examining the family life, she may begin to examine herself. The mother's influence and behavior in relation to her child are partially dependent upon her own self-understanding. She may be helped to see family members in their respective relationships and, knowing their life experiences, may begin to find new meaning for their behavior. In this manner her understanding of, and her relation to, the problem child may become clearer. Any necessary manipulation of the environment will be carried out by the social worker.

Play Therapy

It is well recognized that free association is a valuable technique with adults for the investigation of significant psychological material below the level of consciousness. In children, however, play is a more normal mode of expression than are verbal forms. Play technique consists of introducing a child to a group of toys and permitting him to use them freely while the observer looks on. The toys represent all the common interests of childhood—animals, building blocks, and other objects of a creative type. Dolls often represent members of the family. Play being the medium in which the child expresses himself most freely, the use which he makes of the toys reveals his fantasies, offers insight into his mental mechanisms, and gives clues regarding his unconscious. Some play therapists engage the child in story telling; still others attract the interest of the child by demonstrating and teaching the child magical tricks while drawing him into revealing himself.

In the child, play may be regarded as the speech of the unconscious. He may use the imaginary characters of his play to express his own disturbed feelings. Being a projective technique, play may show human relations and problems arising out of them. It therefore sheds light on the family relationships as no other medium can. It illuminates the relation both of the child to his parents and of the parents to the child. Hiding behind the anonymity of a doll, he may tell of death wishes directed toward a parent or sibling. The child should be permitted to choose the toy and use it spontaneously, since he will select the medium of expression best suited to himself and therefore best adapted to

express his immediate problem or situation.

Drawing and painting may also be used as projective techniques, not only for securing clues about the child's problems and psychic dynamics, but also as therapeutic adjuncts. In his art sessions, the child may attribute various imaginary roles to parent or sibling and may use his products as a channel of release.

There are many interesting phenomena in play technique comparable to those observed in psychoanalysis. For example, the child may show an anxious care in excluding some toy from his play, or, on approaching some aspect of the play that he seems to find unsafe, not permissible, or unsatisfactory to the point of discomfort, he becomes upset and is unable to go on playing in peace. This is strikingly similar to the signs of emotional disturbance present when, in free association, conflicts and anxieties push too near the surface. In this way, the psychiatrist may secure clues to the sources of the child's difficulties. To be able not only to interpret the disruptions or interruptions of play such as those just described, but also to interpret the symbolic gestures and words that the child constantly presents, is of great aid in ascertaining the source of his difficulties. This requires experience, insight, and imaginative vision on the part of the psychiatrist. An effective elaboration of play therapy to assist the child in communicating his problems is through the use of mutual story telling.

Pharmacological Therapy

Pharmacological treatment with methylphenidate, amphetamines, and the tricyclic antidepressants is indicated particularly in those children with the hyperkinetic syndrome so often associated with evidence of brain damage or maturational lags. Methylphenidate and amphetamine have a so-called "paradoxical effect" in such children, acting as sedating agents particularly for those who are overactive, with a limited attention span, impulsivity, emotional lability, and erratic behavior. As mentioned earlier, controlled studies have shown that children receiving these drugs gain weight less rapidly than expected, yet growth in height is sustained. Learning capacity has been shown to improve when such children are treated with the stimulant agents.

BIBLIOGRAPHY

General

Bernard, V. W., and Crandell, D. L.: Evidence for various hypotheses of social psychiatry. *In* Zubin, J., and Freyhan, E. A. (eds.): Social Psychiatry. New York, Grune & Stratton, 1968.

Blumberg, M. L.: Psychopathology of the abusing parent. Am. J. Psychother., *28*:21–29, 1974.

Bowlby, J.: Attachment and Loss. Vol. 1. New York, Basic Books, 1969.

Chess, S., and Hassibi, M.: Principles and Practice of Child Psychiatry. New York, Plenum Press, 1978.

DeAjuraguerra, J., et al.: Le Choix Therapeutique en Psychiatrie Infantile. Paris, Masson et Cie, 1967.

Knobloch, H., and Pasamanick, B. (eds.): Gesell and Amatruda's Developmental Diagnosis, 3rd ed. New York, Harper & Row, 1974.

Levy, D. M.: Maternal Overprotection. New York, Columbia University Press, 1943.

Levy, D. M.: Capacity and motivation. Am. J. Orthopsychiatry, *27*:1–8, 1957.

Lewis, M., and Sarrel, P. M.: Some psychological aspects of seduction, incest and rape in childhood. J. Am. Acad. Child. Psychiatry, *8*:606–619, 1969.

Redl, F.: Controls from Within. Glencoe, Ill., Free Press, 1952.

Rutter, M., Yule, B., Quinton, D., et al.: Attainment and adjustment in two geographical areas. Br. J. Psychiatry, *126*:520–533, 1975.

Schlossman, F. E.: Zur Fragedes Hospitalismus im Sauglingsaustalten. Ztschr. Kinderheilk., *42*:31–38, 1926.

Sobel, D. E.: Human caring. Am. J. Nurs., *69*:2612–2613, 1969.

Spitz, R. A.: Anaclitic depression. Psychoanal. Study Child., *2*:313–342, 1946.

Williams, D. T., and Singh, M.: Hypnosis as a facilitating therapeutic adjunct in child psychiatry. J. Am. Acad. Child Psychiatry, *15*:326–342, 1976.

Attention Deficit Disorder

Barclay, R. A., and Cunningham, C. E.: The effects of methylphenidate on the mother-child interactions of hyperactive children. Arch. Gen. Psychiatry, *36*:201–208, 1979.

Denckla, M. D., and Rudel, R. G.: Anomalies of motor development in hyperactive boys. Ann. Neurol., *3*:231–233, 1978.

Gardner, R. A.: Psychotherapy of the psychogenic problems secondary to minimal brain dysfunction. Int. J. Child Psychother., *2*:224–256, 1973.

Loney, J., Prinz, R. J., Mishalow, J., and Joad, J.: Hyperkinetic/aggressive boys in treatment. Predictors of clinical response to methylphenidate. Am. J. Psychiatry, *135*:1487–1491, 1978.

Morrison, J. R., and Stewart, M. A.: Evidence for a polygenetic inheritance in the hyperactive child syndrome. Am. J. Psychiatry, *130*:791–792, 1973.

Satterfield, J. D., Cantwell, P. P., Schell, A., and Blaske, T.: Growth of hyperactive children treated with methylphenidate. Arch. Gen. Psychiatry, *36*:212–217, 1979.

Towbin, A.: Organic causes of minimal brain dysfunction. Perinatal origin of minimal cerebral lesions. J.A.M.A., *217*:1207–1214, 1974.

Weiss, G., Hechtman, L., Perlman, T., Hopkins, J., and Wener, A.: Hyperactives as young adults. Arch. Gen. Psychiatry, *36*:675–681, 1979.

Conduct Disorder

Jenkins, R. L.: Varieties of children's behavioral problems and family dynamics. Am. J. Psychiatry, *124*:1440–1445, 1968.

Johnson, A. M., and Szurek, S. A.: Etiology of antisocial behavior in delinquents and psychopaths. J.A.M.A., *154*:814–817, 1954.

Macht, L. B., and Mack, J. F.: The fire setter syndrome. Psychiatry, *31*:277–288, 1968.

Stewart, M. A., Cummings, C., Adams, B. S., and Meardon, J. K.: Unsocialized aggressive boys. J. Clin. Psychiatry, *39*:797–799, 1978.

Anxiety Disorder

Baker, H., and Wills, U.: School phobia: Classification and treatment. Br. J. Psychol., *132*:492–499, 1978.

Kennedy, W. A.: School phobia: Rapid treatment of fifty cases. J. Abnorm. Psychol., *70*:285–289, 1965.

Pittman, F. S., Langsley, D. G., and De Yoeng, C. D.: Work and school phobias. A family approach to treatment. Am. J. Psychiatry, *124*:1535–1541, 1968.

Other Disorders

Cytryn, L., McKnew, D. H., and Bunney, W. E.: Diagnosis of depression in children: A reassessment. Am. J. Psychiatry, *137*:22–25, 1980.

Himwich, H. E., Jenkins, R. H., Fujimori, M., et al.: A biochemical study of early infantile autism. J. Autism Child. Schizo., *2*:114–126, 1972.

Judd, L. L.: Obsessive-compulsive neurosis in children. Arch. Gen. Psychiatry, *12*:136–143, 1965.

Looff, D. H.: Psychophysiologic and conversion reactions in children. J. Am. Acad. Child Psychiatry, *9*:318–331, 1970.

Lukianowicz, N.: Hallucinations in non-psychotic children. Psychiat. Clin. (Basel), *2*:321–337, 1969.

McKnew, D. H., Jr., and Cytryn, L.: Historical background in children with affective disorders. Am. J. Psychiatry, *130*:1278–1280, 1973.

Ornitz, E. M., et al.: The auditory evoked response in normal and autistic children during sleep. Electroencephalogr. Clin. Neurophysiol., *25*:221–230, 1968.

Rock, N. L.: Conversion reactions in childhood: A clinical study of childhood neuroses. J. Am. Acad. Child Psychiatry, *10*:65–93, 1971.

Rutter, M., and Bartak, L.: Causes of infantile autism: Some considerations from recent research. J. Autism Child. Schizo., *1*:20–32, 1971.

Sandler, J., and Joffe, W. G.: Notes on childhood depression. Int. J. Psychoanal., *46*:88–96, 1965.

Treffert, D. A.: Epidemiology of infantile autism. Arch. Gen. Psychiatry, *22*:434–438, 1970.

Eating Disorders

Cooper, P.: Pica. Springfield, Ill., Charles C Thomas, 1957.

Excretory Disorders

Bellman, M.: Studies on encopresis. Acta Paediatr. Scand., Suppl. 170, 1:+, 1966.

Drooby, A. S.: A reliable truce with enuresis. Dis. Nerv. Syst., *25*:97–100, 1964.

Gerard, M. W.: Enuresis: A study in etiology. Am. J. Orthopsychiatry, *9*:48–58, 1939.

Mariuz, M. J., and Walters, C. J.: Enuresis in nonpsychotic boys treated with imipramine. Am. J. Psychiatry, *120*:597–599, 1963.

Oppel, W. C., Harper, P. A., and Reder, R. V.: Social, psychologic and neurologic factors associated with enuresis. Pediatrics, *42*:627–641, 1968.

Rapoport, J. L., et al.: Childhood enuresis. Arch. Gen. Psychiatry, *37*:1146–1152, 1980.

Ritvo, E. R.: Contributions of sleep research to understanding and treatment of enuresis. Int. Psychiat. Clin., *7*:111–122, 1970.

Silber, D. L.: Encopresis: Discussion of etiology and management. Clin. Pediatr., *8*:225–231, 1969.

Movement Disorders

Friel, P. B.: Familial incidence of Gilles de la Tourette's disease, with observations on etiology and treatment. Br. J. Psychiatry, *122*:655–658, 1973.

Gerard, M. W.: The psychogenic tic in ego development. Psychoanal. Study Child., *2*:133–162, 1946.

Golden, G. S.: Tics and Tourette's: A continuum of symptoms. Ann. Neurol., *4*:145–148, 1978.

Sanders, D. G.: Familial occurrence of Gilles de la Tourette syndrome. Arch. Gen. Psychiatry, *28*:326–328, 1973.

Shapiro, A. K., Shapiro, E., Bruun, R. D., and Sweet, R. D.: Gilles de la Tourette Syndrome. New York, Raven Press, 1978.

Speech Disorders

Barbara, D. (ed.): The Psychotherapy of Stuttering. Springfield, Ill., Charles C Thomas, 1962.

Gould, E., and Sheehan, J.: Effect of silence on stuttering. J. Abnorm. Psychol., *72*:441–445, 1968.

Johnson, W.: Problems of impaired speech and language. J.A.M.A., *170*:2102–2103, 1959.

Murray, T. J., Kelly, P., Campbell, L., and Stefanik, K.: Haloperidol in the treatment of stuttering. Br. J. Psychiatry, *130*:370–373, 1977.

Perkins, W. H.: Speech Pathology: An Applied Behavioral Science. St. Louis, C. V. Mosby Company, 1971.

Learning Disorders

de Hirsch, K.: Learning disabilities: An overview. Bull. N.Y. Acad. Med., *50*:459–479, 1974.

de Hirsch, K., Jansky, J. J., and Langford, W. S.: Predicting Reading Failure. New York, Harper & Row, 1966.

Goldberg, H. K., and Schiffman, G. R.: Dyslexia: Problems of Reading Disabilities. New York, Grune & Stratton, 1972.

Hier, D. B., Lemay, M., Rosenberger, P. B., and Perlo, V. P.: Developmental dyslexia: Evidence for a group with a reversal of cerebral asymmetry. Arch. Neurol., *35*:90–92, 1978.

Johnson, D. J., and Myklebust, H. R.: Learning Disabilities. New York, Grune & Stratton, 1967.

Rome, P. D., and Oshan, J. S.: Remediation: Procedures for helping the dyslexic. Psychiat. Ann., 7:73–111, 1977.

Smith, W. L., and Weyl, T. C.: The effects of ethosuximide (Zarontin) on intellectual functions of children with learning deficits and cortical brain dysfunction. Curr. Ther. Res., 10:265–269, 1968.

Sleep Disorders

Berrettini, W. H.: Paranoid psychosis and sleep apnea syndrome. Am. J. Psychiatry, 137:493–494, 1980.

Clark, R. S., et al.: Sleep apnea: Treatment with protriptyline. Neurology, 29:1287–1292, 1979.

Fisher, C., Kahn, E., Edwards, A., and Davis, P. M.: A psychophysiological study of nightmares and night terrors. The suppression of stage 4 night terrors with diazepam. Arch. Gen. Psychiatry, 28:252–259, 1973.

Hartman, E.: Sleep requirement: long sleepers, short sleepers, variable sleepers, and insomniacs. Psychosomatics, 14:95–103, 1973.

Kales, A., et al.: Personality patterns in insomnia. Arch. Gen. Psychiatry, 33:1128–1134, 1976.

Karacan, I., Sales, P. J., and Williams, R. L.: Clinical disorders of sleep. Psychosomatics, 14:77–78, 1973.

Kramer, M.: Dream disturbances. Psychiat. Ann., 9:50–68, 1979.

Schneck, J. M., and Fuselli, H.: Nightmare and sleep paralysis. J.A.M.A., 20:725–726, 1969.

Zung, W. W. K.: The pharmacology of disordered sleep: A laboratory approach. Int. Psychiat. Clin., 7:123–146, 1970. Also, J.A.M.A., 211:1532–1534, 1970.

29

MENTAL RETARDATION

"...It cannot too often be recalled for the encouragement of those entering into the work...that they will likely see advances in this field of humane endeavor much beyond the achievements of any previous period."

Friends Hospital
Annual Report

HYDROCEPHALY
(From Wechsler, I. S.: Clinical Neurology. 9th ed. Philadelphia, W. B. Saunders Company, 1963.)

Definition

There exists a large group of individuals whose personality limitations rest essentially upon failure to develop sufficient intellectual capacity to cope with the demands of their environment and thus to establish an independent social existence. This lack of intellectual capacity may derive from an innately imposed limitation in cerebral development due to genetic endowment, may be the result of malnutrition, disease, or injury to the brain before, during, or in the immediate period after birth, or may be the consequence of impaired maturation due to insufficient environmental stimulation from familial and cultural sources.

In the early years of developmental impairment, the rate of maturation or the acquisition of various sensorimotor activities most frequently provides the evidence for the diagnosis of mental deficiency. Thus delays or failures in the sequential evolution of motility, language, bladder and bowel control, and ability to interact with other children provide the clues. Inability to acquire and retain knowledge as the result of experience is an indication of a deficiency in *learning ability* and is best observed during the child's school years. If the mental defect is mild, the child may show little evidence of it until he enters school. Social adaptation becomes important as an indicator of mental retardation, particularly at the adult level, but is reflected earlier in the individual's capacities to relate to parents, teachers, and peers.

In terms of intellectual functioning, the mentally retarded appear to have difficulty in retention and recall and thus in the acquisition of information. These lacks, in turn, limit their capacity for analysis and synthesis of information and for other than relatively simple efforts at problem solving. Under circumstances in which their intellectual capacities are overtaxed, whether in clear-cut or complex intellectual tasks, including emotional and social factors, these individuals appear inept and deficient in planning and judgment. When not taxed beyond their capacities, provided their emotional development has been healthy, they perform well in accustomed social and vocational settings.

Prevalence

Owing to the differences in criteria for the diagnosis of mental retardation, as well as the varying cultural tolerances for and demands upon the subnormal and also the individual's capacity to relate to his peers, comparative estimates of prevalence are difficult to assess. That vast inequalities in mental capacity exist is well shown in the data summarized in Table 29–1. Thus, 1 to 4 per cent of the population are considered educationally subnormal in dif-

TABLE 29–1   Observed and Expected Distribution of Scores, U.S. Army General Classification Test, World War II

GRADE	TEST SCORE	OBSERVED FREQUENCY	EXPECTED FREQUENCY
I	130 and over	5.8	7
II	110–130	26.2	24
III	90–110	30.7	38
IV	70–90	28.5	24
V	Below 70	8.8	7

(From Bingham, W. V.: Inequalities in mental capacity from military data. Science, *104*:107, 1946.)

ferent countries, and another 6 to 9 per cent are so impaired intellectually that they require special education within the school system. In the United States of America, various estimates have shown that 3 per cent of the children born annually will never achieve the intellect of a 12-year-old, 0.3 per cent will fall below the level of the 7-year-old, and 0.1 per cent will be so impaired in their intellectual capacity that they will remain completely helpless throughout their lives, incapable of caring for themselves in any way.

In Great Britain, where registers of the mentally retarded have been kept by local health authorities commencing with the Mental Deficiency Act of 1913, the rate of subnormality may be drawn well for specific population groups. Susser reports that in the industrial town of Salford this rate was 44 per 1000. A similar rate was discovered in rural Anglesey.

When the age and sex of the mentally subnormal are examined as to distribution from such local register reports, it becomes clear that the rates for both young and old are very low when compared with the figures for the adolescents and young adults. Susser states that permanent biological attributes present at birth could produce such a distribution. His conclusion is that *recognized* mental retardation must be a social attribute. Furthermore, recognition is determined by the social roles demanded of individuals at each stage of life. Although the capacity to fulfill such roles rests upon the biological inherited structure of each individual, the complexity of the social roles determines the stress of those roles for each individual. In modern societies, education and training are necessary to undertake many of the new roles, and, in consequence, the standardized school system makes it impossible for many to achieve the skills and aptitudes necessary to succeed. A new type of retardation has come into being.

The more physically impaired an individual is at birth, the earlier his social limitations will be recognized. The profoundly retarded individual, or idiot, scores less than 20 on intelligence tests; the severely retarded people will have I.Q.s from 24 to 39; the moderately retarded from 40 to 54; and the mildly retarded from 55 to 69. The percentages of those with I.Q.s in these classificatory terms are shown in Table 29–2.

It is the mildly retarded who are discovered in adolescence and early adulthood when confronted by the complex social roles of modern society. Those severely retarded owing to obvious biological deficiencies are discovered early in life as they fail to keep pace with other infants and children in their growth and development. The medium grade retarded become conspicuous as their weaknesses are exposed during schooling. In the Susser analysis, only 1 in 20 of the middle grade had been detected by age 5, 7 of 10 by age 15. Thirty per cent of this group were not recognized until after leaving school.

The vast majority of the retarded live in their communities, and many make satisfactory social adaptations. Others require special training to perform simple tasks and care for their own needs. The remainder require institutional care. In the past it was estimated that one bed per 1000 population should be provided in institutions for the mentally defective; however, the nature of those admitted has been changing in recent years. In the U.S.A., there has been an increased admission of those with lower grades of defect, associated with brain damage.

Today some point out that civilization tends to preserve the unfit and that therefore a general decline in human physique and intelligence is to be feared. Penrose, an outstanding English investigator of mental deficiency, is of the opinion that the number of defective and subnormal individuals is not steadily increasing. He concludes that propagation of the unfit is not a danger to the community because such persons tend to propagate less efficiently. In his opinion, decisions about segregation or other disposition of high-grade retardates should be based solely on medical, psychological, and social grounds; he maintains that the equilibrium with respect to biological fitness and intelligence level will be retained. Probably the only areas where the average intelligence is falling are certain small rural communities in which there has been inbreeding of poor mental stock and a rapid emigration of better stock. The incidence of mental retardation, particularly at the high-grade level, is distinctly higher in rural than in urban areas.

TABLE 29–2   I.Q. Range, Percentage, and Number Per Population of One Million

LEVEL	IQ RANGE	PERCENTAGE	NUMBER
Mild Retardation	55 to 69	2.16	21,600
Moderate Retardation	40 to 54	.14	1,400
Severe Retardation	24 to 39	.06	600
Profound Retardation	Less than 25	.05	500

(From Friedman, E.: The recent changes in the American Association on Mental Deficiency Definition of Mental Retardation and the public policy ramifications [unpublished].)

DETERMINATION OF INTELLECTUAL RETARDATION

To determine whether a child who is suspected of being mentally retarded really is, and in order to outline constructive treatment, one should study the many factors which led not only to his intellectual defect but also to his unique personality pattern. If one or both of the child's parents are known to be defective, it may be found that heredity has been an important factor. It should be kept in mind, however, that intellectually retarded parents contribute not only defective genes but also, usually, a home atmosphere deficient in intellectual, social, and personality-forming influences, thus restricting the potentiality of mental growth.

In many of the severely subnormal, there is some evidence either of a general biological inferiority or of the sequelae of former traumatic or inflammatory processes in the central nervous system. Other evidences of a biological inferiority are anomalies of the skull, such as microcephaly, oxycephaly or tower-shaped skull, hydrocephalus, the spherical skull of the mongoloid, and asymmetry of the skull. Low frontotemporal hairline, asymmetries of the face, malformations of the external ear, anomalies of the eye and its appendages, uncomeliness of the nose, thickness of the lips, receding or protruding mandibles, imperfectly formed or irregularly erupted teeth, and malformation of the palate are much more frequent in mentally defective individuals than among persons of average intelligence. For those who wish to consult an atlas demonstrating extraordinarily well through color photographs the many varieties of physical deformity encountered among those with severe mental retardation, the one prepared by Gillis and Feingold, published by the United States Government Printing Office, is recommended. In addition to the physical deformities often seen in the severely retarded, electroencephalogra-phy frequently reveals abnormality in both standard and sleep recordings.

In most severely retarded children, there will be a history of delay in the development of physiological, psychological, or social functions. In the newborn, early indications of deficit are shown in weakness or absence of the sucking, Moro, and grasping reflexes, and of crying in response to painful stimuli, closure of the eyelids, and contraction of the pupils. The infant shows apathy, difficulties in sucking, and, later, delay in commencing to use his motor apparatus at the customary stage of maturation.

The healthy child smiles by the second month, and crying is now accompanied by tears. The head and eyes turn toward sounds. At the fourth month, the child usually begins to hold up his head; two months later he should be able to sit for several minutes. At this time, he should begin to crawl, may grasp for objects, holds up his arms to be taken, and distinguishes people. At the tenth month, he should stand, and at one year he should take a few steps, say "Mama" and one or two other words and recognize toys. At 18 months, he should be walking well. Delay in the acquisition of these motor skills suggests impaired cerebral development.

There exists an important relation between intelligence and the capacity for development of correct and distinct speech. The degree of intelligence is closely indicated by the age of acquisition of speech; by the character of articulation, i.e., whether the articulation is clear, slovenly, slurring, or jerking; by lalling, or the substitution of one consonant for another; and finally, by the extent of vocabulary, since this measures rather well the stock of ideas. Usually the normal child should be speaking a few words at one year and should articulate clearly between the ages of three and four.

A more valuable indication of the presence or absence of defect than either the history of school progress or an examination in school work is the practical knowledge and general information possessed by the individual. Here we find that the ability for breadth and accuracy of observation, and the capacity for comparison, planning, and discrimination essential for the successful solution of the practical problems connected with occupation and the business life, are inadequate in the mental retardate. His range of knowledge, too, concerning common objects and events in his environment is limited. The retarded often vary in their ability to apply their intelligence to concrete life situations.

In considering the field of social history and behavior, it should be kept in mind that social incompetency does not necessarily mean social delinquency. Such chronic social problems as poverty and recidivism are associated not so much with mental defect as with a population of borderline intelligence. The extent to which criminality is a result of mental defect is usually overestimated. Studies by English psychiatrists show that the percentage of criminals who are retarded mentally is about 3.5. The percentage of criminals of borderline intelligence is doubtless higher. Although acquisitive crimes occur most frequently both among the retarded and those of normal intelligence, it is estimated that serious sexual offenses are nearly ten times as common among the former as among ordinary criminals. The mentally retarded contribute more than others to traffic offenses.

Individual psychological as well as social factors contribute to delinquency among the retarded. In the borderline defective, especially, it will be found that the precipitating factors of his delinquencies are emotional ones. Some behavior disorders may represent a rebellion against, or a flight from, a difficult environment. If the retarded child is rejected by his home, feelings of hatred and resentment may be stimulated in him, as in others, and trans-ferred to all parental surrogates. Again, aggressive and destructive behavior may represent a compensation for an underlying sense of inadequacy. Some defective individuals, through their wish to gain recognition, are easily led into delinquency by stronger, dominant personalities. Because the defective person obtains thrills and satisfactions so quickly, he is apt to follow those who show evidence of bold and vicious behavior.

Degree of Retardation

In Chapter 28, Disorders Usually First Evident in Infancy, Childhood, and Adolescence, the methods of examination of the child were described, including the various psychological tests now used to determine mental functioning. From such tests as the Wechsler-Bellevue may be derived an Intelligence Quotient, which, as stated there, must be recognized as representing only the current functioning of the individual at the time the test was administered. The term *borderline intelligence* is often used for those with I.Q. scores consistently in the 70 to 90 range.

Since general intelligence tests are valid only if they measure overall capacity to solve mental problems, in recognition of the limitations of all presently available tests, the American Association on Mental Deficiency has proposed a *behavioral classification* of deficit, which consists of the two dimensions of *measured intelligence* and *adaptive behavior*. Thus the measured intelligence dimension is scaled into five levels in terms of Standard Deviation units* that describe the distribution of test scores in the general population. The adaptive behavior dimension classifies four levels of behavior in the two areas of degree: to function and maintain oneself independently and to meet

---

*A statistical unit which expresses the dispersion from the mean of a range of measurements in a sample.

satisfactorily the culturally imposed demands of personal and social responsibility. This scale is given in Table 29–3.

Additional scales should be used to supplement the clinical judgments. For example, the Vineland Social Maturity Scale is useful at the preschool level and may be supplemented by items from the Gesell and Amatruda's Developmental Schedules, Cattell Infant Intelligence Scale, and the Kuhlmann Tests of Mental Development.

TERMINOLOGY. Today the use of the descriptive terms idiot, imbecile, and moron is uncommon. Since, however, they are still occasionally used, their definition, as adopted in 1934 by the American Association on Mental Deficiency, may be quoted: "An idiot is a mentally defective person usually having a mental age of less than three years, or if a child, an intelligence quotient less than 25. An imbecile is a mentally defective person usually having a mental age of three years to seven years, inclusive. A moron is a mentally defective person usually having a mental age of eight years or upwards, or if a child, an I.Q. of 50 or more." As for the I.Q., the Association stated: "As a rule, the upper limit for a diagnosis of mental deficiency should be an I.Q. of 69, but this limit should not be adhered to in cases where medical, social, and other factors clearly indicate that the patient is mentally defective."

TABLE 29–3   Adaptive Behavior Classification*

	PRE-SCHOOL AGE 0–5 MATURATION AND DEVELOPMENT	SCHOOL-AGE 6–21 TRAINING AND EDUCATION	ADULT 21 SOCIAL AND VOCATIONAL ADEQUACY
Level I	Gross retardation; minimal capacity for functioning in sensorimotor areas; needs nursing care.	Some motor development present; cannot profit from training in self-help; needs total care.	Some motor and speech development; totally incapable of self-maintenance; needs complete care and supervision.
Level II	Poor motor development; speech is minimal; generally unable to profit from training in self-help; little or no communication skills.	Can talk or learn to communicate; can be trained in elemental health habits; cannot learn functional academic skills; profits from systematic habit training. ("Trainable")	Can contribute partially to self-support under complete supervision; can develop self-protection skills to a minimal useful level in controlled environment.
Level III	Can talk or learn to communicate; poor social awareness; fair motor development; may profit from self-help; can be managed with moderate supervision.	Can learn functional academic skills to approximately 4th grade level by late teens if given special education. ("Educable")	Capable of self-maintenance in unskilled or semi-skilled occupations; needs supervision and guidance when under mild social or economic stress.
Level IV	Can develop social and communication skills; minimal retardation in sensorimotor areas; rarely distinguished from normal until later age.	Can learn academic skills to approximately 6th grade level by late teens. Cannot learn general high school subjects. Needs special education, particularly at secondary school age levels. ("Educable")	Capable of social and vocational adequacy with proper education and training. Frequently needs supervision and guidance under serious social or economic stress.

*Reprinted from Sloan, W., and Birch, J. W.: A rationale for degrees of retardation. Am. J. Ment. Defic., *60*:258–264, 1955–1956.

Among these severely retarded, the expectations for life are less than for the general population. Losses from this population are less than in the past; as medical care has improved, their survival time has been prolonged. Thus in the group with Down's syndrome (mongolism) alone, prevalence rose from 1 per 4000 in 1929 to 1 per 1000 in 1958.

As for those with mild retardation, it is of interest that in the Salford studies, reported by Susser, in adulthood two thirds of these persons were no longer carried in the local register as impaired. In terms of their social functioning they had improved! Such findings have been reported from other countries, as well, where many later are found well employed, married, and with families.

The groups who fail socially in adult life are those who have been detained for antisocial behavior, because of either delinquency or transgressions of the sexual codes. The majority come from broken homes or severely disrupted families known to social agencies. Their failure to adapt derives essentially from the deficiencies in the family structure, which establishes the capacity for affective ties and inculcates the necessary superego standards and ego ideals upon which depend much of successful adult adaptation.

APPARENT DEFECT. Several writers have called attention to a group of children who have often been neglected. This is composed of those who may be described as apparently retarded or pseudo-feeble-minded. In many cases persons have been declared retarded solely upon the basis of their intelligence quotients. Although usually the I.Q. correctly measures a person's intellectual capacity, at times conditions may mask a child's intellectual potentialities. Among such conditions are blindness, deafness, spasticity, specific reading or numerical disability, or emotional blocking, with consequent inhibition of intelligent behavior or of responses in psychometric tests.

The child with sensory defects often leads an isolated existence, full of frustrations and confusion and deprived of certain necessary types of stimulation and information, with the result that he may not demonstrate his real intellectual potential. Sometimes a learning difficulty actually caused by emotional retardation may be mistaken for an organic deficiency. Occasionally the awkwardness of the examiner stimulates a negativism that prevents an accurate assessment of intelligence. There are on record cases of children whose admission to the public school system was refused because of alleged low-grade mental retardation, as demonstrated by psychometric tests. Some demonstrate superior intelligence and even go on to a college education.

The "idiot savants" are an uncommon subgroup among those of subnormal intelligence, who often amaze by their highly developed intellectual capacity in some isolated area of functioning. One such patient known to the authors accurately and rapidly added six-digit numbers presented quickly to him. He could stand at a railroad crossing and add the numbers painted on the sides of successive cars in trains of over seventy units. In the pair of "idiot savant" twins studied by Horwitz et al., these brothers demonstrated a phenomenal capacity as calendar calculators. Given a remote date, they were capable of instantly replying with the weekday of the date requested.

Some brain-damaged children develop exceptional reading ability (hyperlexia), prematurely. They read indiscriminately and compulsively, often shutting out interest in other matters about them. If interrupted, they return to the same reading at the same point. The material they read is usually verbalized in a repetitious, rhythmic fashion.

To explain this unusual incongruity in intellectual behavior, suggestions range from the existence of an unusual eidetic imagery, of mechanisms utilizing memory and repetition as substitutes for usual learning, to the existence of computer-like mechanisms in the brain. In the twins studied by Horwitz et al., the conclusion was reached that the subjects memorized a conventional calendar—one mastering a range of 400 years—an effort to which they devoted 15 years and in which they were assisted by a photographic memory. They were observed from the age of six spending hours looking at an almanac that contained a perpetual calendar, and later their father gave one a "perpetual" calendar with which they played for hours and hours.

ETIOLOGY

Mental deficiency, then, is a symptom associated with a large number of disease entities that affect the organism in its earliest stages of growth and development. It is not a clinical entity itself. The group of mentally retarded is by no means homogeneous; it is marked by wide dissimilarities in etiology, clinical phenomenology, and pathology, linked only by the common criterion of subnormal intellect. To be excluded from the group are those instances of impairment of intellect that occur as the result of brain damage after adolescence, to which is applied the term dementia.

In the past, it has been the custom often to classify the mental deficiencies in terms of the temporal relationship of the impairment factor to birth. From a clinical standpoint, it is convenient to divide them into those operating prior to birth, those resulting from injuries at birth, and those resulting from injuries or disease occurring after birth but before mental development has been fully attained.

The American Association on Mental Deficiency has recommended an etiological classification of mental retardation with supplementary qualifications to indicate the existence of a genetic component, secondary cranial anomalies, impairment of special senses, and motor dysfunction. Since both classificatory systems are in use, a brief statement

is provided of the etiological factors recognized to function in the *prenatal, neonatal,* and *postnatal* periods. Later, specifically defined entities are described under the suggested etiological headings of the American Association on Mental Deficiency.

CAUSES ACTING BEFORE BIRTH. It is often difficult to determine whether a mental defect was caused by factors inherent in the genes or whether toxic, infectious, endocrine, traumatic, nutritional, and other prenatal pathogenic factors operating on the germ cell or within the pregnant mother tended to weaken or distort developmental capacity of the brain. Among prenatal factors may be pertussis, mumps, and other viral infections, particularly the virus of rubella, which late in the first trimester of pregnancy may pass through the placenta and damage the brain. Anomalies of various organs often coexist with the defect.

Other causes may be toxoplasmosis, Rh incompatibility (usually if the fetus is Rh-positive and the mother Rh-negative), the influences responsible for the chromosomal nondisjunction causing mongolism, and also damage to the fetus by therapeutic doses of roentgen rays. Fetal oxygen deficiency as a cause of brain damage and subsequent mental defect usually occurs during labor but may happen earlier also. The mental deficiency of cretinism may be caused by thyroid deficiency at a very early prenatal age or may be coincidental with the hormonal defect rather than caused by it. Toxic, anoxic, and infectious states which, in the adult nervous system, may be reversible or completely recoverable can produce permanent changes in the fetal neural structures, leading to impairment of developmental potentiality.

Premature births, particularly those with birth weight less than 2500 gm., and maternal malnutrition are associated as well with the birth of a greater number of children with mental defect than average.

Probably from 50 to 65 per cent of

the cases of retardation arise from poorly understood causes existing prior to birth. It is now agreed that hereditary transmission of mental defect plays a much less important role than was previously believed.

CAUSES ACTING AT BIRTH. Birth trauma resulting in either mechanical injury to the brain or asphyxia with resulting anoxia may be a cause of mental defect. In recent years, the surgical removal of subdural hematomas has prevented some degree of mental defect which would otherwise have followed birth injury. The most frequent immediate causes of cerebral hemorrhage at birth are prematurity and difficult labor. Asphyxia at birth is a common cause of mental defect. If the resulting anoxemia lasts sufficiently long, it will produce permanent degeneration of the ganglion cells of the cerebral cortex, with resulting impairment of mental capacity. It is estimated that about 8 per cent of the mental defects result from causes acting at birth. Probably, however, 50 per cent of the children showing clinical evidence of brain injury are not mentally defective.

CAUSES ACTING AFTER BIRTH. The various forms of viral and bacterial encephalitis and of meningitis are the most frequent factors acting after birth in the production of retardation. Although head trauma with brain damage in infancy or early childhood occasionally results in retardation, this is much overemphasized by the laity. In institutionalized mental defectives, it will be found that the defect in about 1.5 per cent of the patients is the result of postnatal cerebral trauma. Toxemia and vitamin deficiency in infancy and early childhood may, if long continued, produce irreversible changes in the cortex with varying degrees of mental retardation. Convulsive disorders often accompany mental defects resulting from organic disease of the brain.

In the congenitally blind and deaf, the reduced number of stimuli received from exteroceptors results in a certain degree of mental defect unless compensatory training is provided. It is generally agreed, too, that retardation in intellectual development may be caused by emotional factors without organic defect. Probably from 25 to 30 per cent of the cases of retardation result from causes acting after birth.

ETIOLOGIC CLASSIFICATION

DUE TO INFECTION

Although there remains controversy over whether maternal infections cause congenital brain damage without direct infections of the growing fetus, there is much evidence to show that, in many conditions, a direct fetal brain infection does take place. At times this infection may occur without clinical evidence of illness of the mother.

Cytomegalic inclusion body disease is the most common viral cause of mental retardation. About 1 per cent of infants are born infected with this virus. A mild or subclinical virus infection in the mother causes fetal brain damage, impairment of hearing, hepatosplenomegaly, erythroblastosis, and jaundice. It is recognized by inclusion bodies in the urine, cerebrospinal fluid, and other tissues of the infant. A vaccine for cytomegalovirus is now available.

Congenital rubella, associated with illness of the mother in the first trimester of pregnancy, causes mental deficit and other congenital anomalies, such as deafness, cataract, and cardiac malformations. It has been found that there is a direct relationship between the period of the maternal infection and the frequency of occurrence of abnormality in the infant. Approximately 50 per cent of live-born children are abnormal if the mother is infected in the first month of pregnancy, 15 per cent in the second month, and 10 per cent in the third month.

Influenza contracted by the mother during pregnancy has been associated with mental deficiency consequent to malformation of the infantile brain.

Congenital syphilis is diagnosed on the basis of maternal infection with positive serologic tests for syphilis and the various signs of congenital syphilis in the child, including Hutchinson's teeth, interstitial keratitis, choroidoretinitis, and pupillary abnormalities. Juvenile paresis, another form, is discussed in Chapter 12.

Toxoplasmosis is due to infection *in utero* from the mother with the protozoan-like organism, *Toxoplasma.* At birth, or shortly thereafter, the infant may show wasting, convulsions, spasticity, choroidoretinitis, hydrocephalus, or microcephaly.

Finally, other infectious processes incurred by the fetus, such as meningococcal meningitis and equine encephalitis, can cause mental deficiency.

DUE TO INTOXICATION

Bilirubin encephalopathy (kernicterus) may follow any condition that produces jaundice with a high level of serum bilirubin in the newborn. Since kernicterus may now be prevented by exchange transfusions, recognition of the potential danger of high levels of bilirubin in the first few days of birth is highly important. It is now widely accepted that a value of 20 mg. of bilirubin per 100 ml. of plasma is indication for such transfusion, even though there is wide variability in the occurrence of this encephalopathy when correlated directly with plasma levels of bilirubin.

Stern and colleagues have found that phenobarbital administered to expectant mothers during the last weeks of pregnancy will lower the newborn infant's serum bilirubin. They recommend that such treatment be started in Rh-immunized mothers in the 32nd week of pregnancy. Infants with diabetic mothers, infants with prenatal distress, or those badly bruised with excessive red cell breakdown have been given the drug for the first five days of life in doses of 8 mg. per kg. per day.

Such infants cleared bilirubin from the blood by the drug enhancing the liver's glucuronide-forming capacity. Exposure of infants with neonatal jaundice to sunlight also lowers the serum bilirubin level, by converting bilirubin to its water-soluble derivatives, which do not cross the blood-brain barrier and are readily excreted. Infants so exposed seem to be protected from kernicterus. In many patients this exposure appeared to eliminate the need for exchange transfusion.

The cause of the increased bilirubin levels in the blood is related to insufficient glucuronide formation in the newborn period, due to a reduced amount of liver glucuronyl transferase, the enzyme responsible for conjugating bilirubin, as well as a deficiency in the donor substrate, uridine diphosphate. Often it is due to Rh incompatibility between the fetus and the mother, but it also may result from other blood incompatibilities, including those between A, B, and O types.

In the absence of blood incompatibility, kernicterus is associated often with prematurity and neonatal sepsis. The early stages of kernicterus are difficult to determine, but the condition may be assumed in the presence of drowsiness, poor feeding, unstable body temperature, a high-pitched cry, and alterations in the Moro reflex. Opisthotonus, loss of the Moro reflex, and ocular signs are indicative of marked damage. Mental defect, choreoathetosis, and deafness are the common late sequelae.

Pathologic studies of the brain show yellow staining with bilirubin in the basal ganglia, cerebellar nuclei, hippocampus, and medulla. When severe, loss of cells, glioses, and demyelination are noticed.

Encephalopathies, caused by lead or carbon monoxide or following the postserum and postvaccinal encephalitides, are other more frequent causes of retardation due to intoxication. Lead poisoning has been discussed in Chapter 16.

DUE TO TRAUMA OR PHYSICAL AGENT

Difficulties of labor, such as those occurring with malposition or malpresentation of the child or disproportion between the head of the child and the pelvis of the mother, can cause damage to the infant's brain at birth. Common lesions with birth injury are meningeal tears and rupture of blood vessels and brain substance, often with intracerebral bleeding. Considerable hemorrhage leads later to brain softening and cyst formation, particularly after difficult forceps delivery. The falx cerebri or tentorium may be torn, resulting in subarachnoid or subdural hemorrhage. With time, the structural evidence of acute injury at birth is supplanted in the process of repair with such nonspecific tissue changes as glioses, cavitation, and areas of defective myelination.

The *diagnosis* of severe injury at birth may be immediately inferred with pallor of the infant, inability to make sucking movements, respiratory distress, high-pitched feeble cry, tense or depressed fontanel, nystagmus, and retinal hemorrhage. At later stages of growth, the brain-injured child may be overactive or underactive and show fluctuations of muscle tone, impaired associated movements, primitive reflex activity, difficulties in convergence, and trouble with posture.

Mental deficiency of this type is caused as well by asphyxia at birth due to interference with the placental circulation, overdosage with anesthetic agents or drugs depressing respiration, or, much more rarely, by prenatal irradiation of the uterus.

DUE TO DISORDERS OF METABOLISM, GROWTH, OR NUTRITION

Perhaps in no other area has so much new understanding accrued from research related to the inborn enzymatic defect. Nearly 150 different metabolic disorders are now recognized as associated with abnormalities of brain development. This group of conditions may be separated into those due to abnormalities in lipid, carbohydrate, and protein metabolism. Early recognition of many of these defects is highly important, since institution of proper dietary measures may prevent or appreciably reduce the amount of brain damage and subsequent impairment of mental function.

Lipoidoses (Sphingolipoidoses)

For the clinician, the lipid storage diseases of the brain may be grouped as those without marked visceromegaly, those with visceromegaly, and those associated with and recognized by degeneration of the brain white matter. They may also be grouped according to the age of onset. Today, perhaps they are best categorized by the enzymatic defect discovered to occur in the condition, or the characteristic accumulating glycosphingolipids, as summarized in Table 29–4.

Of the forms of rare lipoidoses, the following were first differentiated and are best known: in amaurotic familial idiocy (Tay-Sachs disease), GM_2 ganglioside accumulates in the central nervous system; in Niemann-Pick disease, deposits of sphingomyelin exist in the nervous system as well as in the reticuloendothelial system and in parenchymal cells; in Gaucher's disease, the cerebroside glucosyl ceramide collects in the nervous system only in the infantile form of the disease, but regularly is found in excess in phagocytic cells in the spleen, liver, lymph nodes, and bone marrow; while in metachromatic leukodystrophy, sulfatides accumulate in the white matter of the nervous system as well as in the liver, spleen, and kidney. These substances are normally present in all tissues, but are present in greater amounts in the nervous system. The metabolic dysfunction which leads

TABLE 29–4   Lipid Storage Diseases

CONDITION	STORAGE MATERIAL (BRAIN)	ENZYMATIC DEFECT	CLINICAL CHARACTERISTICS
Without marked visceromegaly			
Infantile amaurotic idiocy (Tay-Sachs disease)	GM$_2$ ganglioside	Hexosaminidase A Hexosaminidase A and B Unknown	Cherry-red spot, onset first year of life.
Late infantile amaurotic idiocy (Batten-Bielschowsky)			Onset between second and sixth year of life. Intellectual deterioration, ataxia, myoclonic seizures. Retinal degeneration usually late.
LIAI with CL bodies	Unknown – EM: CL bodies	Unknown	
LIAI with LF bodies	Unknown – EM: CL bodies	Unknown	
Generalized gangliosidosis GM$_1$	GM$_1$ ganglioside	Galactosidase B and C	
"Juvenile" GM$_2$ gangliosidosis	GM$_2$ ganglioside	Hexosaminidase A (partial)	
Niemann-Pick (group C)	Unknown – Sphingomyelin stored in viscera	Unknown	Similar course as other forms of LIAI. Retinal cherry-red spot is common.
Juvenile amaurotic idiocy (Spielmeyer-Vogt)	Unknown – EM: LF bodies	Unknown	Onset between sixth year and puberty.
	Unknown – EM: pleomorphic bodies	Unknown	Intellectual deterioration, generalized seizures.
Juvenile GM$_2$ gangliosidosis	GM$_2$ ganglioside	Hexosaminidase A (partial)	
Dystonic juvenile lipidosis	Unknown – EM: variety of cytoplasmic inclusions	Unknown	Dystonia a prominent part of symptoms.
Late onset lipidosis (Kufs)	Unknown – EM: LF material	Unknown	Mental deterioration of adult life, psychotic symptoms predominant in early stages.
With marked visceromegaly			
Infantile onset			
Generalized gangliosidosis	GM$_1$ ganglioside	Galactosidase A, B, and C	Hurler's appearance, bony abnormalities, retinal cherry-red spots common.

Disease	Accumulated substance	Enzyme defect	Clinical features
Infantile Gaucher's disease	Unknown; ceramide glucose in spleen	Absent glucocerebrosidase in spleen	Bulbar signs common early in disease, occasional cherry-red spot.
Niemann-Pick (group A) disease	Sphingomyelin	Sphingomyelinase	Intellectual deterioration, anemia, hepatosplenomegaly.
Juvenile onset Juvenile Gaucher's disease	GM_3 ganglioside	β Galactosidase	Slow intellectual deterioration, hepatosplenomegaly.
Niemann-Pick (group D)	Unknown; sphingomyelin in viscera	Unknown	
White matter degenerations Infantile onset Globoid cell leukodystrophy		Cerebroside galactosidase and sulfotransferase	Progressive spasticity. Loss or reduction of deep tendon reflexes, elevated cerebrospinal fluid protein. Seizures rare.
Spongy degeneration of white matter Alexander's disease		Unknown Unknown	Spasticity, enlarging head, early optic atrophy. Enlarging head.
Pelizaeus-Merzbacher's disease		Unknown	Usually sex-linked, unusual eye movements. CSF normal.
Late infantile onset Metachromatic leukodystrophy		Sulfatidase	Spasticity, loss or reduction of deep tendon reflexes, nonfunctioning gallbladder, elevated cerebrospinal fluid protein.
Juvenile onset Metachromatic leukodystrophy		Sulfatidase	Genu recurvatum, spasticity with loss or reduction of deep tendon reflexes, elevated cerebrospinal fluid protein.
Sudanophilic leukodystrophy		Unknown	Sex-linked, Addison's disease may precede or follow neurologic symptoms.
Adult onset Metachromatic leukodystrophy		Sulfatidase	Organic dementia, corticobulbar involvement.

Abbreviations: LIAI = Late infantile amaurotic idiocy, EM = Electron microscopy, LF = Lipofuscin, CL = Curvilinear.
(From Menkes, J. H., Andrews, J. M., and Cancilla, P. A.: J. Pediatr. 79:183–196, 1971.)

to their abnormal accumulation and their relationship to the impairment of brain function is thought to be due to deficiencies of hydrolytic catabolic enzymes. Recently, however, Brady reported the instance of deficiency of synthetic enzyme, which impaired catalytic formation of the ganglioside—a defect the opposite of that occurring in Tay-Sachs disease.

Of the lipoidoses, the infantile form of Tay-Sachs disease is the most common. The condition is transmitted by a single recessive gene. Thus, although both parents may appear healthy, if both are carriers, the probability exists of one out of four children suffering the disease. Marriages producing affected children represent an increased occurrence of consanguinity.

At birth the infant seems normal, but within the first year the child's development is impeded. He becomes apathetic, appears to have muscular weakness, cannot hold his head steadily, and regresses in his ability to grasp objects. There is advancing visual deterioration, and ophthalmoscopic study of the retina shows a typical "cherry-red spot" in the macula. The course is progressive, with death ensuing in one to three years. In a late infantile form of the disease (Bielschowsky's disease) the onset is in the second or third year.

Prenatal diagnosis of Tay-Sachs disease is now possible through culture of the cells of amniotic fluid obtained by transabdominal amniocentesis as early as the 16th week of pregnancy. In high risk pregnancies, marked reduction is found in the enzyme hexosaminidase A in the amniotic fluid, in both cultured and uncultured cells from that fluid. Such diagnosis has allowed termination of pregnancy before the birth of the affected child. After birth, assay of hexosaminidase in tears alone will identify homozygotes and heterozygotes for the Tay-Sachs gene.

Within the nervous system, pathologic changes are found in the brain, cord, and sympathetic system. Swelling and distortion are seen in the ganglion

cells; their cytoplasm is often vacuolated and some are necrotic.

Niemann-Pick disease, transmitted as an autosomal recessive, manifests itself symptomatically by the time the infant is six months old. There is usually a regular progression to a fatal termination by the third year. Abdominal enlargement due to splenomegaly and hepatomegaly precedes the indications of intellectual retrogression which end in amentia, and is associated with such neurological signs as spasticity, abnormal movements, tremor, and convulsions.

Vacuolated leukocytes may be found in the blood of some patients with Niemann-Pick disease. Similar leukocytic vacuolation has been found in some unaffected parents and siblings of the patients, perhaps indicating that they are heterozygous carriers.

In the infantile form of *Gaucher's disease*, consisting of about one-third of the cases, the clinical picture is very similar to that of Niemann-Pick disease. The course is rapidly downhill. Diagnosis may be made by bone marrow aspiration. Plasma acid phosphatase is often elevated.

Metachromatic leukodystrophy is a familial condition, found in many countries, in which the affected child develops well during the first year or two but then becomes incoordinated and shows muscular weakness. Progressive impairment of brain function takes place, with both neurological and intellectual deficits leading eventually to death between the third and sixth years.

Chemical analysis of urinary sediments from a 24-hour collection for individual glycosphingolipids from affected patients with the illnesses will allow the differentiation of the specific glycosphingolipid through its abnormal accumulation. In the case of many of these conditions, the diagnosis has been made by discovering that the level of activity of the respective enzymes is markedly reduced in preparations of the patient's leukocytes.

The only existing treatment for lipoidoses consists of nursing and maintenance of general health.

Aminoacidurias

Within the past decade, a sizable number of specific defects in amino acid metabolism that cause mental deficiency have been discovered. All are transmitted through a recessive autosomal gene. While these conditions are rare, their early diagnosis becomes increasingly important as some dietary regimens have been devised that prevent the evolution of brain damage and subsequent mental deficiency.

PHENYLKETONURIA. This is the most frequently encountered and most thoroughly understood of the specific metabolic disorders of protein. The condition was recognized in 1934 by Fölling, a Norwegian biochemist. Since the associated mental defect in this condition, as with other disturbances of protein metabolism, may be prevented by diagnosis shortly after birth and treatment with proper diet, early recognition is highly important.

This form of familial mental deficiency is inherited as a rare autosomal recessive. Since each parent is a heterozygous carrier, a quarter of the children will have the illness, one-half will be carriers, and a quarter will be healthy noncarriers. For each pregnancy, the chances are one in four of having a phenylketonuric child and three in four of bearing a normal child. Approximately one case of phenylketonuria occurs in 25,000 births; in institutions, 1 per cent are estimated to have this condition.

As Yu and O'Halloran report, there is a high rate of retardation among the children of mothers with phenylketonuria. In their series, all of 12 children born of such mothers were retarded; ten were heterozygotic for the disease and two had a typical phenylketonuria. As serum phenylalanine levels are high in pregnant heterozygous women and this and other amino acids are readily transported across the placenta, Yu and O'Halloran recommend that measures be taken to reduce the occurrence of mental retardation in the nonphenylketonuric children of affected mothers. Such mothers should not nurse their children. Also, pregnancies should be planned and the diets of such women should be low in phenylalanine some weeks before conception. When pregnancy ensues and the mother has high serum levels of phenylalanine, consideration should be given to therapeutic abortion.

Phenylketonuria is rarely suspected in adults of apparent normal intelligence. It does occur, and is sometimes associated with acute psychotic reactions. Perry et al., studying such cases, recommend that the ferric chloride test, described later, be performed on every woman during her *first* pregnancy, even if she is apparently not mentally disabled. Furthermore, they recommend that if positive, abortion should be prescribed if the level of phenylpyruvic acid is above 10 mg. per ml. They believe the possible existence of this condition should be checked in all schoolchildren with unexplained learning disorders or mental retardation.

Heterozygous carriers may be detected through the use of the phenylalanine tolerance test. Four hours following the oral ingestion of L-phenylalanine in a dose of 0.1 gm. per kilogram of body weight, the blood level of such carriers will be in the neighborhood of 20 mg. of phenylalanine per 100 ml. A considerable proportion (5 to 15 per cent) of parents of these patients represent cousin marriages.

Diagnosis. Clinically, retardation in motor and mental development is observed before the end of the first year, and it is thought that all damage to the nervous system takes place within the first two years of life. Although most untreated patients learn to walk, few speak; a quarter have grand mal convulsions, and electroencephalographic abnormalities are even more common.

The mental defect is severe, with the intelligence quotients usually below 50. Less than 10 per cent develop normal intelligence or only mild mental defect. The children usually have fair hair and blue eyes, and there is frequently an associated dermatitis. The stature is somewhat dwarfed, head measurements are less than normal, and the incisors are widely spaced. Accompanying the marked mental deficiency and the metabolic error are neurological manifestations generally regarded as an extrapyramidal syndrome. The posture of the patient is usually that of general flexion, with bent head and body; both flexor and extensor muscles are rigid, the deep reflexes are active, and many patients show hyperkinetic or dyskinetic manifestations, such as tremor and athetosis. Encephalograms suggest that the extrapyramidal signs may be referred to cortical atrophy of the frontal lobe.

The urine has a penetrating, musty odor and contains abnormal amounts of phenylalanine and its derivatives, phenylpyruvate and phenylacetate. Phenylpyruvic acid can be easily detected in the urine by adding a few drops of ferric chloride to an acidified specimen. An intense green color develops in the presence of phenylpyruvic acid. Other conditions and substances may lead to a false-positive test. For this reason the serum level should be examined, as the amino acid phenylalanine is found in increased amounts in the blood, spinal fluid, and perspiration. The blood levels reach 30 to 50 mg. per 100 ml. While the blood phenylalanine level is elevated within a day after birth, the urinary excretion of the amino acid and its derivatives does not occur for at least the first week of life. It is now recognized that a significant number of infants with elevated blood phenylalanine levels do not have the disease. Thus, to establish a firm diagnosis in the early weeks of life, both a positive blood test and a positive urine test should be obtained. This confirmation is needed because the early treatment by dietary restrictions, which carries with it the potential for inducing serious nutritional handicaps, should not be undertaken lightly.

All infants should have their urine tested for this condition between the third and ninth weeks. For siblings of a phenylketonuric, tests should be repeated every two weeks until the tenth week if serum phenylalanine levels cannot be obtained. A few normal children show elevations of serum phenylalanine during the first six weeks of life.

According to present knowledge, the defect is caused by a blockage in the conversion of phenylalanine into tyrosine due to a deficiency of the enzyme phenylalanine hydroxylase. Thus the unmetabolized amino acid accumulates in the body fluid and large amounts of its deaminated products — phenylpyruvic, phenyllactic, and phenylacetic acids — are excreted with it in the urine. The metabolism of the amino acids tyrosine and tryptophan is affected secondarily. The mechanism by which the defect in metabolism leads to failure in cerebral development remains unknown.

Pathologic findings consist of a diminution in brain size, glioses of the white matter, and retardation of myelinization. In brains of those dying later in life, degenerative changes have been reported in the cortex and basal ganglia. There is a marked failure of myelinization of the nervous system.

Treatment. Treatment with a diet restricted in phenylalanine appears both to prevent and greatly limit cerebral damage, particularly when commenced before the child is 15 months of age. There is now available commercially an acid hydrolysate of casein with phenylalanine removed, but supplemented with additional amino acids, minerals, and choline. It may be given at the level of 2.0 to 2.5 gm. per kilogram of body weight, with additional fats and carbohydrates to meet caloric requirements. The casein hydrolysate is supplied as Lofenalac, and the manufacturer provides full instructions for the diet. The phenylalanine levels of the blood serum should be maintained below 10 mg. per 100 ml. during the first year of life. How long the dietary restriction must be maintained in order to insure full cerebral maturation remains undetermined.

Brambilla and his colleagues recently have treated a few phenylketonuric children with anabolic steroids. They report that not only do these agents induce a significant improvement in the blood levels of phenylalanine and tyrosine, but also the patients' growth curves approximate the normal more closely than those on diets restricted in phenylalanine. The work remains unconfirmed.

MAPLE SYRUP URINE DISEASE. This specific inherited defect in amino acid metabolism was described in 1954 by Menkes; it received its name from the characteristic maple syrup-like odor of the urine. Within the first week of life, the infant appears spastic, loses the Moro reflex, and then undergoes progressive cerebral deterioration, with death in a few months. Studies of the urine show marked increase in excretion of the branched-chain amino acids leucine, isoleucine, and valine, as well as methionine, but cystine and other amino acids are abnormally low. In this disease, transamination of methionine and the branched amino acids occurs normally, with formation of ketoacids, but further degradation is blocked, with accumulation of these four ketoacids and amino acids in the blood owing to absence of the enzyme that catalyzes decarboxylation. There also appears to be a secondary disturbance of tryptophan metabolism. Therapeutic studies with diets low in these acids are encouraging, but require further evaluation.

Cystothioninuria, argininosuccinuria, citrullinuria, aspartylglycosaminuria, and histidinuria are other aminoacidurias discovered in a few mentally defective patients. All these conditions are inherited, probably as autosomal recessives. They are diagnosed by chromatography. There are several conditions in which the body metabolism is normal, but a defective renal reabsorption leads to overflow and loss of amino acids. The familial *Hartnup* disease is a generalized aminoaciduria associated with a pellagra-like rash, cerebellar ataxia, and often mental deficit. Other patients have been reported to have little mental deficit, but personality disturbances and dermatitis occur later in life.

Hereditary hyperammonemia, caused by an enzymatic defect in the liver at the ornithine transcarbamylase step of the urea cycle which impedes conversion of ammonia to urea, is of interest in that the brain astrocytic structure is transformed to Alzheimer II type. This cell type is found in the brain of adult patients with chronic liver disease.

Hyperuricemia in infants is associated with mental retardation in boys only. This condition, known as Lesch-Nyhan syndrome, is sex linked and is characterized by deficiency of hypoxanthine-guanine phosphoribosyltransferase, leading to increased purine synthesis.

The child born with this condition demonstrates an extraordinary aggressiveness toward his own body and toward others. The symptoms become apparent about the age of four months. The affected children develop spasticity, choreoathetotic movements and compulsive self-biting of the mouth area and fingers. Later on this aggressivity may be directed toward others through hitting, punching, and biting. The condition is associated with elevation of the serum and cerebrospinal fluid uric acid. Those with a less severe deficiency of the significant enzyme present a clinical syndrome of childhood gout, excessive production of uric acid, and uricemia, but no behavioral drives for self-mutilation. Rockson and his associates have found that there exist in this syndrome an elevated plasma dopamine beta-hydroxylase activity and an absence of pressor response to acute sympathetic stimulation, but only in those presenting self-mutilating behavior. Treatment with probenecid or allopurinol diminishes the uricosemia.

A prenatal diagnosis may be made by study of cells obtained through transabdominal amniocentesis. Amniotic cells from affected infants fail to take up hypoxanthine in the absence of the enzyme. Termination of pregnancy may be undertaken if such prenatal diagnosis can be made.

It is of interest that hyperuricemia, diagnostic with gout in adults, has also been found by Anumonye and his associates to be associated with the capacity for drive and a wide range of activities in business executives.

In Menkes' *kinky hair syndrome*, of X-linked recessive inheritance, children show progressive mental retardation, deficient growth, pili torti, hypothermia, and generalized degeneration of the blood vessel walls. Both serum ceruplasmin and copper content of various organs are low. It appears that this condition may be due to malabsorption of copper, in contrast to the situation in hepatolenticular degeneration in adults.

Defects in Carbohydrate Metabolism

GALACTOSEMIA. Galactose diabetes, a specific metabolic defect of carbohydrate metabolism inherited as an autosomal recessive trait, is productive of profound disturbance in growth and development and leads to mental retardation unless recognized early and properly treated. It appears that galactosemia represents a single block in the formation of the enzyme galactose-1-P-uridyltransferase, which leads to collection of galactose-1-phosphate in cells. The eventual effects of galactosemia relate to the amount and duration of galactose consumption and are reversible by removal of this substance from the diet.

The infant born with galactosemia seems to be normal for several days but shortly commences to show difficulty with feedings, vomits, and may develop diarrhea. If milk feeding is continued, there may occur jaundice, enlargement of the abdomen because of ascites and hepatomegaly, nuclear cataracts, and the indications of mental defect in delay in standing, walking, and talking. Sugar is present in the urine, which is nonfermentable with heat.

The condition may be diagnosed just after birth by incubating erythrocytes of cord blood with galactose; in the galactosemic blood, galactose-1-phosphate accumulates in the cells. Galactose tolerance tests are abnormal, and the cephalin flocculation is elevated. If milk is eliminated from the diet and soybean or casein hydrolysate substitutes are utilized in its place, the symptoms subside. Early diagnosis, with proper treatment, may prevent permanent cerebral damage.

Mental deficiency may also accompany *glycogenosis* (von Gierke's disease), which is associated with deposition of glycogen in various organs and sometimes involves the brain. Transient hypoglycemia with later retardation has occurred in the children of hypoglycemic mothers.

Gargoylism

This condition, also known as a lipochondrodystrophy, is characterized by deposits of mucopolysaccharides in the organs and connective tissues of the body. In the brain are extensive deposits of gangliosides in neurons, giving rise to intracellular structures known as zebra bodies because of their appearance under electron microscopy. It is now recognized that there exist several variants of this condition. The most widely studied are the Hurler, the Hunter, and the Sanfilippo syndromes, but others exist as well (Scheie, Maroteaux-Lamy, and Morquio types). A major difference between the Hurler and Hunter syndromes is the mode of transmission; the former is carried as an autosomal recessive, and the latter is sex linked. Thus in the Hunter syndrome women, the carriers, transmit to their sons but not to their daughters. The Sanfilippo variant is also an autosomal recessive, characterized by severe mental retardation, but few general physical defects.

At birth, the infant's head may be enlarged, joint movements are limited, and later the cornea appears clouded. At three months, the upper lumbar vertebrae and long bones show deformities by x-ray, and kyphosis is evident. The characteristic features are protrusion of the forehead out of proportion with the stunted body, saddle nose, bushy eyebrows, coarse features, and a deep crease between the thick lips and chin. Abnormal bodies are found in the leukocytes, and there exist both hypermucopolysacchariduria and hyperaminoaciduria. Later in life, wedging of the vertebrae, shortened and flexed deformity of the hands, flexion deformities at the hips and knees, and enlargement of the liver and spleen develop. Most children die in their teens. No treatment is known.

These conditions are diagnosed by finding a secretion of mucopolysaccharides—chondroitin sulfate B (CSB) and heparitin S (HS)—in the urine in amounts in excess of 15 mg. daily. In the Hurler syndrome, CSB exceeds HS in excretions by 2 to 1; the ratio is equal in the Hunter syndrome. Mainly HS is excreted in the Sanfilippo syndrome. Fibroblasts cultured from the skin of these patients show signs of accumulation of mucopolysaccharides. Toluidine blue staining of lymphocytes discloses mucopolysaccharide inclusions in high proportions of these cells. It is now possible to diagnose these conditions by withdrawing amniotic fluid before birth and examining the cells contained therein for such accumulations. This prenatal test has been used successfully for prenatal diagnoses in mothers who have previously given birth to afflicted children and thus allowed the termination of pregancy by abortion.

The evidence suggests that the mucopolysaccharide accumulations are the result of failure in the degradation process. The absent enzymes for the Hurler syndrome exist in the Hunter cells and vice versa.

Hypothyroidism

Either congenital or acquired, this condition may lead to retardation in mental growth. Sometimes recognizable at birth, it usually is not manifest until later months when it may be noticed that the infant is dwarfed, particularly with failure in growth of length. The subcutaneous tissues are thick so that the features are coarse, the skin dry and cold. The child appears dull and puffy. The tongue protrudes and the lips are thick. The forehead may be wrinkled, the hair is thin, and the anterior fontanel is widely open. There is often abdominal distention with associated umbilical hernia, slow pulse, and such neurological signs as ataxia, rigidity, and hyporeflexia. The basal metabolic rate varies from -20 to -50, the protein-bound iodine value of 4 to 8 μg. per 100 ml. is much below values found in healthy subjects, and the uptake of radioactive iodine is reduced. Usually, after the age of two the blood cholesterol is elevated, and x-ray studies show recurrent development of ossification centers and epiphyseal union.

In areas where goiter is common, the congenital type may be the consequence of maternal iodine deficiency. The congenital type also includes those cases with absence or hypoplasia of the gland and those with a genetically determined enzyme defect causing inadequate synthesis of thyroxin (biochemical hypothyroidism). In the latter cases, the thyroid appears to be morphologically normal, although a goiter may develop later. However, the degree of mental retardation found in each individual is related as well to the familial occurrence of low, average, or high intelligence and opportunities for education.

Treatment consists in establishing a euthyroid state as early and rapidly as possible without the induction of cardiac decompensation. Desiccated thyroid is as effective as thyroxin and triiodothyronine. The dosage of these agents must be carefully regulated to protect the heart from damage. In young infants, a daily dose of 15 to 30 mg. of desiccated thyroid is indicated initially. Every two or three weeks this dose may be elevated by 15 mg. Daily doses of 45 to 60 mg. are adequate to maintain the euthyroid state at ages below one year. Between 1 and 3 years of age, 75 to 120 mg. is needed daily, and at later ages, 150 to 180 mg.

Studies have shown that approximately half of those with the most severe types of cretinism, commencing before birth and apparent in the first months of life, attain nearly average intelligence quotients if treated before the age of six months. Less than one fifth of the group have persisting moderate retardation. Delay in beginning treatment is less disastrous for those with an insidious onset commencing from birth and not clinically recognized until they are over 1 year of age. It has been suggested that there exists a critical period of brain development in the prenatal or early postnatal life, when irreparable failure may occur as the result of thyroid deficiency.

The neuropathological findings are reduction in the number of cells in the cortex; failure in myelinization, and delays in maturation of fiber tracts and neurons. The electroencephalogram shows low amplitude and slow alpha rhythm; these are reversible with thyroid medication.

DUE TO NEW GROWTHS

Tuberous Sclerosis

This clinical form of retardation, sometimes known as epiloia, is characterized by epilepsy, mental defect, and a butterfly-shaped rash of cutaneous nodules resembling sebaceous adenomas, but really consisting of hyperblastic connective and vascular tissue. The disease results from a congenital blastomatous malformation involving the neuroectodermal system. The brain shows diffuse disturbances in cytoarchitecture and localized neoplastic glial formations.

It is transmitted by a dominant gene with reduced penetrance. Neurofibromatosis, inherited in a similar way, and trigeminal cerebral angiomatosis (Sturge-Weber-Dimitri disease), which is characterized by the "port-wine stain" or cutaneous angioma of the face, may both be associated with cerebral defect and mental retardation.

DUE TO CHROMOSOMAL ABERRATIONS

Down's Syndrome

This frequent variety of mental deficiency is perhaps most widely known as mongolism, because the physiognomic features are suggestive of those normally exhibited by the Mongolian race. It is estimated that three to four infants of each thousand births will be mongoloid and that 5 to 10 per cent of all defectives fall into this category.

Clinically, the patient is characterized by short stature and a small, round skull, with a flattening of both the occiput and the face. The hair is scanty and coarse. The palpebral fissure is narrow and oblique, with the inner end lower than the outer; a fold of skin continued from the upper eyelid over the inner angle adds to the resemblance to the Asiatic countenance. The tongue is large and fissured, with its papillae hypertrophied, and it is often constantly protruded and withdrawn through the open mouth. The nose is short and broad, with a depressed bridge; the hands are large and stubby, the fifth finger being particularly short and often incurved. The joint ligaments are lax, and the muscles are hypotonic, giving the joints an unusual mobility. The palate is often deformed, the abdomen is large, and the genitalia are underdeveloped. The palm and fingerprints are characteristic, as the two main creases across the palm are replaced often by a single crease (simian line). In a tenth of the patients, a congenital heart defect is found. The mongoloid's good disposition and tendency to imitativeness often conceal at first the seriousness of his mental defect. Most mongoloids have an I.Q. between 15 and 40, with an upper limit in the 50s.

Many Down's sufferers display signs of presenile dementia during the fourth decade of life. Slowly progressive mental and emotional changes emerge as shown in lessening of vocabulary, continued to loss of speech; apathy; increasing inability for self-care of bodily functions; irritability; and temper tantrums.

There are no distinctive pathologic changes in the bodily organs. The brain tends to maintain the embryonic convolutional patterns and to have a disproportionately small cerebellum and brain stem. The ganglion cells of the third cortical layer are sparse and irregularly dispersed. The brains of those living long enough to expose the early signs of presenile dementia characteristically show senile plaques and neurofibrillary tangles similar to those found in Alzheimer's disease. These pathologic findings suggest a genetic-biochemical interrelation between the two conditions. Abnormal changes are reported in the pituitary, thyroid, and adrenal glands, and the heart and arterial systems are poorly developed.

Hyperuricemia is the rule in this condition, and many develop diabetes. Blood serotonin is abnormally low in those with Down's syndrome. There exists a lack of response to tryptophan loading, as well as a fall in blood serotonin level after administration of *dl*-penicillamine. The latter may be corrected by administration of pyridoxine. These findings suggest a depression of decarboxylation of 5-hydroxytryptophan in Down's syndrome. The fact that low blood platelet serotonin exists in 60 per cent of those with Down's trisomy 21 syndrome and remains unassociated with changes in the catabolites of this monoamine in the cerebrospinal fluid suggests that the peripheral abnormality may not be associated with central nervous system disturbance of serotonin or dopamine.

Cytogenetic studies by Lejeune in 1959 showed that the somatic cells of patients with mongolism have 47 chromosomes instead of the normal 46, owing to a trisomy of chromosome 21. (See Fig. 29–1.) It is suggested that, during meiosis, nondisjunction persists, with the mongoloid receiving the undetached segment. Since then there have been reported a number of cases with a normal chromosome count of 46, but an excess of genic material attached to chromosome 21 because of a translocation. In this latter form of mongolism, now recognized as constituting approximately one fourth of the cases, one of the parents, usually the mother, carries the translocation. She has only 45 chromosomes, but one holds excess genic material, usually found in two chromosomes in the healthy. Mosaicism, in which there exist differing chromosomal aberrations between the skin and blood cell, occurs in some with the syndrome. It is of interest that a chromosomal trisomy resembling the Down condition has been found in a chimpanzee.

Late maternal age long has been related to the birth of children with this syndrome. It now appears that the form due to nondisjunction, in which there are 47 chromosomes, is more typically related to births occurring in older women. The form due to translocation, on the other hand, characterizes births in younger mothers. The cause of both chromosomal nondisjunction and translocation remains a mystery. Radiation exposure, autoimmune reactions, and vascular deficiencies in the ovary all have been suggested as etiologic for these chromosomal aberrations.

Treatment. By tissue culture of leu-

Figure 29–1 Cytogenetic analysis of chromosomes in Down's trisomy, in a male. Note chromosome 21. Courtesy of John Rainer, M.D., Professor of Medical Genetics and Chief, Department of Medical Genetics, Columbia University and New York State Psychiatric Institute.

kocytes and subsequent chromosome counts, it has been possible to establish the diagnosis within a few days of birth. However, specific therapy is unknown. Mothers may be advised that the risk of bearing a child with this condition increases with age. Over age 40, the risk is 1 in 50. For mothers with a translocation defect and only 45 chromosomes, the risk is one in ten.

Prevention. Prenatal diagnosis through amniocentesis and study of fetal chromosomes now allows the opportunity for termination of pregnancy before birth. A New York State court has determined that a physician may be held negligent for not advising an older patient of the risk of Down's syndrome and of the means of prenatal diagnosis and prevention.

Klinefelter's Syndrome

This condition, found in males only, with a mental defect in approximately one fourth of those affected, is associated with an anomaly of the sex chromosomes. Those affected are tall, lean individuals with breast enlargement (gynecomastia) and small or underdeveloped testes. There exist aspermia and increased secretion of follicle-stimulating hormone; cytologic examination shows chromatin-positive nuclei. Men and adolescent boys with this condition have limited sexual drives. They often feel inferior, owing to the delay in achieving physical maturity, and react to the body image conflict with resulting personality disturbances. Thus, in addition to mental retardation, there have been observed schizophrenic, passive-dependent, and antisocial personality disorders with this genetic abnormality.

It is now known that clinically undistinguishable cases may have different cell karyotypes. A little over a half have 47 chromosomes, with the count due to an XXY arrangement rather than the normal XY sex chromosomes. In some, there have been observed XXXY or XXXXY sex chromosomes. In all such cases, cytogenetic studies show one or several extra chromatin-positive bodies, depending upon the number of X chromosomes. In less than half the cases, various mosaic patterns are found in the somatic cells, a condition in which two types of cells are found due to a nondisjunction considered to take place in mitotic division after fertilization.

Turner's Syndrome

This condition, also due to nondisjunction, occurs in females and is associated with the presence of one X chromosome and the absence of Y. It is called the XO variant. Such females lack secondary sex characteristics and show, in addition to mental defect, other congenital abnormalities, including short stature, "webbed" neck, deafness, and aorta malformation.

DUE TO UNKNOWN PRENATAL INFLUENCE

Conditions for which no definite etiology has been established are those associated with various cranial and cerebral anomalies. *Craniostenosis* of various types, hydrocephalus, and hypertelorism fit into the first group. Among the relatively small number of retarded persons who exhibit distinctive charac-

teristics of the skull or general bodily conformation, or of brain structure, that entitle them to recognition as clinical varieties are the *microcephalics*. Arbitrarily, those defectives, mostly imbeciles or idiots, whose skulls on completion of development do not exceed 17 inches in circumference, are designated as microcephalic. Those of this clinical variety show a peculiarity not only in the size of the head but also in its shape, which is characterized by a receding forehead and a flattening of the occiput. The hair, which is wiry in texture, extends low on the forehead. The scalp is greater in amount than is necessary to cover the cranium, with the result that the excess becomes arranged in corrugations. The chin is usually receding and the stature is short. As might be expected from the limited cranial capacity, the brain of the microcephalic is markedly underdeveloped. Histological defects are the rule, and gross anomalies in addition to those of size are common.

PSYCHOSOCIAL DEPRIVATION

Among the group of mild retardates are those in whom it is caused essentially from deprivation of the necessary experiences in the local culture or subculture to develop their potential for social adaptation. This condition usually is recognized in school children with I.Q.s in the range of 50 to 80. The inadequacy of intelligence tests and computation of the I.Q. is demonstrated well by Mercer's study, which disclosed that, in a North American community, 91 per cent of the diagnosed black children and 60 per cent of the diagnosed Mexican Americans with a standard deviation one point below 70 on the I.Q. passed adaptive behavior tests. These results indicate the unreliability of the use of the standard intelligence tests in defining retardation in those reared outside the dominant culture. No pathologic findings are discoverable on extensive physical, neurological, and laboratory studies, nor is there history of brain or metabolic disturbance. Generally, the father will be found to be a manual or blue collar worker, and any older siblings will be discovered in the higher levels of secondary education, including the advanced technical schools.

In other instances, the child from a minority group that ignores or denigrates the advantages of academic or technical education, or that speaks a language other than that used in the public schools, will have lacked the motivation to perform in school. The condition is most common in boys and also in children from large families. Often more than one child in the family is so classified.

When the family is intact and stable, the outlook for effective social adaptation is favorable. When parents have been lost or the parental relations are broken or pathological, the later social history often reveals erratic work records and frequent transgressions of the law. Children from such families are at high risk for long-term confinement in institutions for the retarded.

Treatment requires special schooling for acquisition of reading and simple numerical skills, redefinition of attitudes to others, and development and use of technical abilities that allow acceptance socially. Schooling should be more prolonged than for other children, to make allowances for the existing slowness in learning. To allow such schooling, the family's attitudes must often be persuaded and influenced by their involvement with the teaching services.

Early screening of the school populations detects such backward children. It is this high risk group for whom the special programs should be made available early, to prevent the social consequences of late adolescent or early adult failure and the consequent deleterious effects in damaging mental health further.

Psychoses with Mental Retardation

It is generally agreed that most of the mental disorders that afflict persons of normal intelligence may also afflict the mentally defective. Sometimes, also, defectives suffer from psychoses of an acute transitory nature, presenting episodes of excitement with depression, paranoid trends, or hallucinatory experiences. The psychoses are often situational in origin.

PREVENTION

Mental retardation, as the reader realizes, is the consequence of a variety of factors operating from the time of conception, throughout fetal maturation, and during the early childhood and developmental phases. Prevention, then, must be applied through a variety of strategies, many of which are now well known but remain employed haphazardly.

Of the causes of mental retardation, the cultural-familial syndrome is certainly the most common. For this, the strategy is modification of the children's learning environments. At high risk for retardation due to deprivation of stimulation and intellectual experiences are those children born of retarded mothers, living under deprived socioeconomic conditions, such as occurs both in ghetto-ized urban areas and isolated rural districts. On a small scale, children at such risk have been provided structured nursery and preschool experiences during their first five years. In these experiments, the ratio of adults to children has been as high as 1:2. The adults provided a program of daily activities that focused upon teaching self-help and verbal, numerical, and problem-solving skills. High-risk children in this group proved far superior in social, verbal, and numerical skills to similar children at high risk for retardation who remained in their own homes and communities.

Many more such children in Western industrial societies today have the opportunity for such stimulation through regular television viewing of preschool educational programs. But many remain deprived of this large-scale opportunity, for the retarded or low-grade parent often is unaware of or disinterested in guiding the child to such viewing or may even actively discourage it. Parents at high risk for rearing children with sociocultural retardation may also be introduced into educational programs—and learn by the process of *modeling*.

The causes of profound and severe retardation are most frequently genetic or embryogenetic forces. Here the practical preventive strategies involve detection of that mother at high risk for bearing a defective child; the opportunity for her of prenatal diagnosis through amniocentesis and analysis of amniotic fluid for chromosomal or biochemical aberration; and, in the event of discovery of abnormality, elective abortion. These procedures are applicable now for mothers at high risk for bearing children with the chromosomal aberrations, particularly the common Down's syndrome, as well as for those at risk for Tay-Sach's disease and other lipoidoses, and defects of the neural tube, including anencephaly. The latter may be detected through finding high levels of alpha fetoprotein in the amniotic fluid.

In Down's syndrome, women over age 40 face a risk of 1 in 50 of bearing a child with this condition; the risk for those between ages 35 and 40 is 1 in 200. While the number of women over 40 bearing children is small (1.5 per cent of pregnancies in New York City), they give birth to 16 per cent of the children with Down's syndrome. Women who have one child with this condition also have a higher risk. Social policy should establish for all such women the opportunity of prenatal diagnosis by amniocentesis. The diag-

nosis may be established after the fourth month of pregnancy.

The same principles and practices should pertain to those at risk for bearing children with Tay-Sach's disease and other lipoidoses in which the carrier may now be identified by blood tests and prenatal diagnosis. Here, too, the diagnosis may be made by amniocentesis after the fourth month of pregnancy.

The third strategy involves biochemical screening of the newborn, now widely practiced in some states to prevent phenylpyruvic oligophrenia, in particular. It is also available for other conditions, such as galactosemia.

The massive social experiments of postnatal screening of infants for phenylketonuria through urine tests appear to have reduced the incidence of retardation through early detection and remedial dieting. One drawback has been false diagnoses with unnecessary dietary restriction of phenylalanine which, in some, has led to malnutrition and secondary retardation. As noted, the screening of mothers for PKU by the ferric chloride urinary test early in pregnancy offers the opportunity of detecting carriers.

Other methods for preventing the biologically determined brain pathology causing retardation are the programs of immunization for pregnant women. A rubella immunization and a vaccine for cytomegalovirus are available now.

Stein is of the opinion that if all the preventive efforts now known to protect against the birth of children with chromosomal or inheritable metabolic defects were widely applied, the prevalence of severe mental retardation might be reduced by 30 per cent.

Emotional Problems

The emotional problem created for the parents by the retarded or defective child may be a difficult one, and the manner in which it is met has much influence upon the child's future development. The knowledge that one's child is not developing normally often comes slowly; the mother may refuse to face the situation and develop a sense of personal shame, failure, and even guilt. Her tearfulness and the father's angered disappointment may leave the child confused, frustrated, and isolated. If rejected, emotionally deprived, coerced, and perhaps beaten, the child is restless, insecure, aggressive, and hostile, and perhaps becomes delinquent.

Feelings of frustration and futility are more common among parents of the mentally retarded child than among parents of the physically handicapped child. The latter can often experience a feeling of compensation in the child's intellectual and emotional growth. Since such satisfactions are lacking in the case of the mentally retarded child, the underlying problems of the parents are intensified and often expressed in their attitude toward him, with the result that he develops hostility and behavior problems. Many, perhaps most, retarded, like normal individuals, have conflicts regarding their hopes, fears, anxieties, and frustrations. The manner in which these are met by parents and teachers will have much influence on their behavior and social adjustment. Many mentally defective persons are more incapacitated by their emotional difficulties than by their intellectual deficit. As with children of normal intellectual endowment, frustrations, humiliations, ridicule, anxieties, emotional deprivations, and insecurities may be expressed in delinquent behavior.

The extent to which the parents are capable of providing healthy nurturance of the retarded child, as well as their stamina in sustaining a constant supportive interpersonal climate, should be assayed by the psychiatrist. Evident inability to provide this support may be a deciding factor in suggesting residential care outside the family. Recommendations for respite care in times of transitory parental inability should certainly be made.

TREATMENT

Early involvement of the retarded child in stimulating transactional experiences with others is now recommended and widely practiced as the knowledge and significance of the child-mother or mother surrogate bond for development have achieved solid support from numerous researches and ethological observations. For the infant and young child either at home or placed in residential care, sensitivity training through manipulation and play involving body contact and rocking may be scheduled to stimulate the audiovisual sensory apparatus, as well as the surface and deep receptors of the tactile, aversive, kinesthetic, and gustatory systems. Commencing in the preschool age, it is important to teach both parents and nursery school educators how to relate to, observe, and work with the child. This may be done by *modeling*, in which the parent or child is taught to imitate the techniques of action of the teacher. To what extent such early therapeutic efforts are successful in producing sustained and progressive development, particularly in the severely and profoundly retarded, remains unknown. Some parents have responded to such efforts as modeling with increased guilt.

While excessive early stimulation is thought by some to lay the groundwork for spoiling and later overly dependent or aberrant behavior, the general impression is that most retarded children who are provided early stimulation display social and cognitive skills that otherwise would not have evolved. Perhaps even more important, they appear to be motivated later to become involved in more advanced social, educational, avocational, and vocational activities.

In the field of education, teachers should concentrate from the start on those abilities and aptitudes with which the child is most fully endowed. Perhaps nothing is so devastating to the mental health of a defective child than to be offered lessons that are beyond his powers of comprehension. For this reason, careful assessment of his strengths and weaknesses is desirable. Many schools for the retarded employ special educators or educational consultants for such assessments and to provide advice about the programs to be emphasized or avoided for the individual child. A variety of new test devices is available now to evaluate the child's assets and liabilities in sensorimotor integration and social, adaptive, behavioral, and prevocational skills.

Training in recreational and avocational skills takes on major significance as a means of relating to others, providing the stimulus to develop body awareness, and enhancing the potential for assertiveness and pleasure.

Behavior modification, described in more detail in the next chapter, has been used with success in training the severely and profoundly retarded in such skills as toileting, dressing, feeding, and grooming, and in aiding them to shed socially undesirable traits or habits.

The social training of retarded children is of immense importance and of far greater significance to them than mere educational attainments. The extent to which they are accepted as agreeable individuals by and in a community is directly proportionate to their social adjustment. This attitude of the community has a direct relation to the mental health of the growing child. If he is accepted, he will feel that he has fulfilled his main ambition of being somebody in the eyes of others. If he is not accepted, he has a feeling of failure and frustration, or grievance and ill will against society, all of which breed discontent and unhappiness, leading to emotional difficulties and maladjustment and perhaps even to delinquency and crime.

Lack of intelligence is not by any means a bar to gainful employment. In many unskilled occupations, what counts in obtaining and retaining a job is not so much skill, literacy, or information as steadiness, reliability, honesty, and the ability to get along well with workmates and supervisors. With happiness will come mental health, and a child who has good mental health, even if he is intellectually defective, is an asset to the community.

It should be considered an obligation of the state to discover, classify, and provide suitable education for all retarded children as early in their lives as possible. In some states, an attempt is now made to meet this obligation by requiring an examination of all public school children who are retarded three years or more in their classes, and by directing that special classes be provided for such children. Probably with most of these defectives it would be better if they were discovered and assigned to special classes earlier. By assignment to a special class, the child is removed from too difficult a curriculum in which he has no interest, from critical classmates, perhaps from an antagonistic teacher and other humiliating conditions that create feelings of inferiority, destroy a sense of security, and lay the foundations for the easiest method of defense, that of overt unsocialized behavior and socially maladaptive compensations.

Since the child in the special class can compete with his fellows, undesirable reactions are not stimulated and there is created a feeling of security, self-reliance, satisfaction, and success that has great constructive value in personality formation. Approbation, attention, and praise afford great satisfaction and, within reasonable limits, may produce a desirable, stimulating effect on the individual's effort to fit into a world that is always going to be beyond him. Retarded children should be encouraged to take part with normal children in all those games in which the defective child can compete on equal terms with the normal one.

Today, the indications for recommendation of placement of a retarded child outside his own home have become increasingly complex as appreciation has sharpened about the human and environmental forces conducive to or inhibiting development of the individual's full potential. Those with the most severe degrees of retardation—multiple handicaps and major physical deformities—are most likely to be recommended for such care because of the burden their living demands and social acceptance imposes upon families. The less severely retarded, who are rejected or abandoned by families, also often require care in residential facilities other than the primary home.

There still persists in the minds of many medical practitioners the belief that placement in institutions is preferable, particularly when the child comes from a large family. The psychiatrist is often confronted with parents who have received such a recommendation; his convictions of the potential for better development of the child in the family home, and his attempts to counsel the parents to persist in such care, frequently are severely compromised by such advice. When, indeed, it is apparent that care in the home will not be beneficial to the child, the psychiatrist will recommend their acceptance of the separation and care by others—a situation that generally accentuates their guilt. Parents need to have a full explanation of the child's condition and prognosis. The psychiatrist is often psychotherapeutically useful to bring relief of parents' pathological anxiety and guilt relating to the child's retardation.

Some elderly parents request residential placement for their older retarded child as they become anxious for the child's care in the face of their own increasing weakness and potential death.

Today, in many countries, there exists a wide variety of facilities for residential care. Placement in a community residence offers the potential of continuing contacts with society in general, as well as the advantages of educational, recreational, and vocational opportunities similar to those offered to others. Community residences are varied: foster care in another home, group homes, halfway houses, and apartment clusters offer in differing ways a variety of living circumstances with differing degrees of support. Information about the availability of such living arrangements and advice about the appropriate placement should be given by the physician or consultant, assisted by the local knowledgeable voluntary or social agencies.

The attempt is made now to avoid institutional care for all those who have sufficient social skills to reside elsewhere. There remain many, nevertheless, so impaired and dependent that the only available resource is the private or state-supported facilities. In the state facilities, many of the less severely retarded are now, through the efforts of the staff, trained and placed in alternative residences in the community to achieve what is termed *normalization*.

Sterilization

Opinions about the value and wisdom of sterilization of the intellectually retarded are varied. Suggested as a means of preventing retardation, its eugenic value is much more limited than was at first appreciated. The legal provision for sterilization applies in most states to those committed to public institutions, but experience shows that a large proportion of high-grade defectives, who of all defectives are most frequently afflicted with a familial disease, are not so placed. Experience has thus far shown that, even when the law provides for their sterilization, only a few of the retarded who are supported by their families are subjected to this operation. Those in the upper levels of the subnormal group are the most highly reproductive.

Contrary to the opinion of many, most high-grade retardates are not prolific. Statistics show that only a very small percentage of male defectives who are committed and subsequently discharged ever marry or have children. Experience indicates that a majority of the detrimental behavior on the part of mental retardates is not their sexual irregularity and reproduction but vagrancy, dependency, and delinquency. The mortality rate among the retarded is so high that danger from their unrestrained propagation is limited. It is now recognized, too, that society does not need protection from the retarded girl as much as the retarded girl needs protection from society.

Many retarded couples will live a successful, happy life if not burdened with the financial, physiological, and other strains incident to rearing a family, yet many suffer social and economic collapse if obliged to assume these burdens. Much neglect and ill-treatment of children would be forestalled if persons intellectually or emotionally unfit to rear children could be sterilized, but such a measure can scarcely be determined solely on the basis of I.Q. Its usefulness is more individual than social.

It must be concluded now that, as a general social policy to prevent retardation, sterilization provides only a superficial approach to its control.

BIBLIOGRAPHY

General

Birch, H. G., and Gussow, J. D.: Disadvantaged Children. Health, Nutrition and School Failure. New York, Grune & Stratton, 1970.

Boyce, L., and Dax, E. C.: The police and the less intelligent driver. Aust. N.Z. J. Criminol., 110:5–16, 1977.

Feinberg, I., Braun, M., and Shulman, E.: EEG sleep patterns in mental retardation. Electroencephalogr. Clin. Neurophysiol., 27:128–141, 1969.

Gillis, S. S., and Feingold, M.: Atlas of Mental Retardation Syndromes: Visual Diagnosis of Facies and Physical Findings. U.S. Department of Health, Education and Welfare, Division of Mental Retardation. Washington, D.C., U.S. Government Printing Office, 1968.

Heber, R.: Epidemiology of Mental Retardation. Springfield, Ill., Charles C Thomas, 1970.

Horwitz, W. A., Deming, W. F., and Winter, R. F.: A further account of the idiot savants, experts with the calendar. Am. J. Psychiatry, 126:412–415, 1969.

Knobloch, H., and Pasamanick, B. (eds.): Gesell and Amatruda's Developmental Diagnosis. 3rd ed., Hagerstown, Md., Harper & Row, 1974.

Mehegan, C. C., and Dreifuss, M. B.: Hyperlexia: Exceptional reading ability in brain-damaged children. Neurology, 22:1105–1111, 1972.

Mercer, J. R.: I.Q., the lethal label. Psychol. Today, 6:46, 1972.

Penrose, L. S.: The Biology of Mental Deficiency. 3rd ed. New York, Grune & Stratton, 1963.

Susser, M.: Community Psychiatry. Epidemiologic and Social Themes. New York, Random House, 1968.

Tarjan, G., Wright, S. W., Eyman, R. K., et al.: Natural history of mental retardation: Some aspects of epidemiology. Am. J. Ment. Defic., 77:369–379, 1973.

Due to Infection

Marx, J. L.: Cytomegalovirus: A major cause of birth defects. Science, 190:1184–1186, 1975.

Wortis, J. (ed.): Mental Retardation and Developmental Disabilities: An Annual Review. Vol. VII. New York, Brunner/Mazel, 1975.

Due to Intoxication

Bruton, J. L., Corsellis, J. A. N., and Russell, A.: Hereditary hyperammonaemia. Brain, 93:424–434, 1970.

Diamond, I., Lucey, J., and Schmid, R.: Prevention of hyperbilirubinemia and kernicterus by exposure to light. Studies in newborn guinea pigs and premature infants. Trans. Am. Neurol. Assoc., 93:70–71, 1968.

Stern, L., Khanna, N. N., Levy, G., et al.: Effect of phenobarbital on hyperbilirubinemia and glucuronide formations in newborn. Am. J. Dis. Child., 120:26–31, 1970.

Due to Disorders of Metabolism, Growth and Nutrition

Brady, R. O.: Inherited metabolic diseases of the nervous system. The pathogenesis and strategies for the control of heritable neurological disorders are examined. Science, 193:733–739, 1976.

Lipoidosis

Desnick, R. J., et al.: Diagnosis of glycosphingolipoidosis by urinary sediment analysis. N. Engl. J. Med., 284:739–743, 1971.

Menkes, J. H., Andrews, J. M., and Cancilla, P. H.: The cerebroretinal degenerations. J. Pediatr., 79:183–196, 1971.

Singer, J. D., Cotlier, E., and Krimmer, R.: Hexosaminidase A in tears and saliva for rapid identification of Tay-Sachs disease and its carriers. Lancet, 2:116–119, 1973.

AMINOACIDURIAS

Boyle, J. A., Raivio, K. O., Astrin, K. H., et al.: Lesch-Nyhan syndrome. Preventive control by prenatal diagnosis. Science, 169:688–789, 1970.

Brambilla, F., Giardini, M., and Russo, R.: Prospects for a pharmacological treatment of phenylketonuria. Dis. Nerv. Syst., 36:257–260, 1975.

Cunningham, G. C., et al.: Phenylalanine tolerance tests. Am. J. Dis. Child., 117:626–635, 1969.

Danks, D. M., Campbell, P. E., Walker-Smith, J., et al.: Menkes' kinky hair syndrome. Lancet, 1:1100–1102, 1972.

Dunn, H. G., Perry, T. L., and Dolman, C. L.: Homocystinuria. Neurology, 16:407–420, 1966.

Perry, T. L., Hansen, S., Tischler, B., et al.: Unrecognized adult phenylketonuria. Implications for obstetrics and psychiatry. N. Engl. J. Med., 289:395–398, 1973.

Rockson, S. G., Stone, R. A., Vander Weyden, M., and Kelley, W. N.: Lesch-Nyhan syndrome: Evidence for abnormal adrenergic function. Science, 106:934–935, 1974.

Yu, J. S., and O'Halloran, M. T.: Children of mothers with phenylketonuria. Lancet, 1:210–212, 1970.

CARBOHYDRATE METABOLISM

Neufeld, E. F., and Fratantoni, J. C.: Inborn errors of mucopolysaccharide metabolism. Science, 169:141–146, 1970.

Zelson, J., and Dekaban, A. S.: Biological behaviour of lymphocytes in Hunter-Hurler's disease. Arch. Neurol., 20:358–361, 1970.

Due to Chromosomal Aberration

DOWN'S SYNDROME

Benda, C. E.: Down's Syndrome. Mongolism and Its Management. New York, Grune & Stratton, 1969.

Ellis, W. G., McCulloch, J. R., and Corley, C. L.: Presenile dementia in Down's syndrome. Neurology, 24:101–106, 1974.

Kaufman, J. M., and O'Brien, W. M.: Hyperuricemia in mongolism. N. Engl. J. Med., 276:953–956, 1967.

Lilienfeld, A. M.: Epidemiology of Mongolism. Baltimore, Johns Hopkins Press, 1969.

Lott, I. T., Murphy, D. L., and Chase, T. N.: Down's syndrome: Central monoamine turnover in patients with diminished platelet serotonin. Neurology, 22:967–972, 1972.

McClure, H. M., et al.: Autosomal trisomy in a chimpanzee. Resemblance to Down's syndrome. Science, 165:1010–1011, 1969.

Penrose, L. S., and Smith, G. F.: Down's Anomaly. Boston, Little, Brown & Company, 1966.

KLINEFELTER AND RELATED SYNDROMES

Beeker, K. L., et al.: Klinefelter's syndrome. Clinical and laboratory findings in 54 patients. Arch. Int. Med., 118:314–321, 1966.

Swanson, D., and Stepes, A. H.: Psychiatric aspects of Klinefelter syndrome. Am. J. Psychiatry, 126:814–822, 1966.

Prevention and Treatment

National Institute of Child Health and Development Task Force Report: Predictors of Hereditary Congenital Defects. Washington, D.C., U.S. Department of Health, Education, and Welfare, 1979.

Stein, Z. A.: Strategies for the prevention of mental retardation. Bull. N.Y. Acad. Med., 51:130–142, 1975.

Taft, L. T., and Cohen, H. J.: Mental retardation. In Barnett, H. L. (ed.): Pediatrics. 15th ed. New York, Appleton-Century-Crofts, 1972.

30

PSYCHOTHERAPY

"Philoperio. . . . I never saw yet two hypochondriacal Cases exactly alike. Misomedion. Then what is your Secret in the Cure of this difficult Distemper?
Philoperio. I have several: I allow myself time to hear and weigh the Complaints of my Patients . . . I take pains to be well acquainted with the manner of living of my Patients, and am more curious in examining them than there is occasion for a Man to be in any other Distemper; not only to penetrate into the Procatartick Causes, but likewise the better to consult the Circumstances as well as (a) Idiosincrasy of every particular Person . . ."

Mandeville, *A Treatise of the Hypochondriack and Hysterick Passions*

Franz Anton Mesmer
He believed his hands could produce cures through "animal magnetism." (From Roback, A. A., and Kiernan, T.: Pictorial History of Psychology and Psychiatry. New York, Philosophical Library, 1969, p. 60.)

Psychotherapy, as practiced today in this country, is confusing to students, who must sift through the claims of a multitude of practitioners, each asserting that their technique is the one that has the greatest potential for expansion of personality or relief of troublesome symptoms. Medical practitioners must recognize that simply seeking their help and their prescription of any form of treatment embodies a powerful psychotherapeutic element for patients. This element, the nonspecific factor in medical treatment, originates in the biologically determined attachment bond that is reflected in human behavior beyond the infantile period. From this bond derive all placebo effects as well. Preserving the bond during the course of doctor-patient or client-therapist transactions enhances the effectiveness of any procedures and also diminishes much of the anxiety that arises upon recognition of the existence of illness.

Psychotherapy is the treatment of emotional and personality problems and disorders by psychological means. The most important therapeutic factor common to all types of psychotherapy is the therapist-patient relationship. Through this relationship, the patient comes to know that he or she can share feelings, attitudes, and experiences with the therapist. In most psychotherapy, the therapist will not depreciate, censure, or judge, no matter what may be revealed, but will respect the patient's dignity and worth, with warmth, understanding empathy, acceptance, and support.

The intensity of this relationship varies, depending on the type and duration of the therapeutic method employed, as well as through the intermesh of the personalities of the patient and the treating person.

Since the patient goes to the physician for help and the latter offers this, the patient usually brings a positive attitude to the therapeutic situation. This positive transference attitude is found in the vast majority of patient-physician relations that exist in medicine. It underlies the expectations for recovery and explains many magical cases of cure. Its psychogenesis derives from the human being's long period of dependent development, in which early pains and fears were frequently and repeatedly alleviated and relieved by the attention, interest, and strength of the parents and those they took the child to for aid. This learned expectancy of help from the early support of parents is transferred to the physician as a professional person and forms the fulcrum for all successful psychotherapeutic ventures.

It must be recognized that not every patient brings to the therapeutic situation the hopeful expectancy that characterizes the positive transference. Pervasive attitudes of distrust, suspicion, and hatefulness may make it impossible for the patient either to initiate or to accept under pressure contact with the physician, whether in need of medical or psychological treatment. Patient attitudes of this kind, which prevent the early establishment of an effective psychotherapeutic relationship, usually are found in those deprived of parents in early life, frequently shifted from one institution or foster home to another, or brought up in a home situation limited in loving support and encouragement by too demanding or rejecting parents. For individuals whose development has taken place under these circumstances, the opportunity has been limited to learn and ingrain the important ego attitudes of hopefulness and trust. In such patients, the effort to overcome the initial distrust — the initial resistance — may resist change in spite of many months of visits. There is theoretical reason to believe that some individuals have undergone such serious deprivations in mothering at critical periods during early infancy and childhood that an effective therapeutic relationship may never be established.

In this text, we described only the cardinal treatment principles of these major psychotherapeutic processes from which derive the multitude of modern variations. For our purposes, we have subdivided these into the *psychotherapies*, in which the treatment is conducted between two persons, and the *sociotherapies*, in which groups of people are brought together to effect behavioral change.

Two quite separate techniques are recognized today within the psychotherapeutic arena. We have classified these as the *expressive-suppressive therapies*, which depend upon either facilitation of or suppression of affect or emotion between persons as a means of alleviation of symptoms, with cognitive processing used variably to bring insight. The classic model for these therapies is the psychoanalytic. The *behavior therapies* are based upon learning theory and reflect a primary dependence upon cognitive processes, with emotive learning considered secondary. As Karasu has pointed out, others have classified the psychotherapies differently: philosophical, motivational, scholarly, ethical, or curative-scientific schemes. His tridimensional schema of dynamic, behavioral, and experiential therapies and their features is presented in Table 30–1. We discuss his experiential category under expressive-suppressive therapies.

Marmor posits that the rash of therapies that focus mainly on emotional release and differ largely in technical vari-

ations have sprung up as a reaction to the presumed mechanistic views of human behavior contained in the psychoanalytic and behavioral models.

Non-Specific Features

To elaborate upon the non-specific features common to the majority of psychotherapeutic modalities, the patient develops new information, trans-

TABLE 30–1 Summary of Thematic Dimensions of Three Kinds of Psychotherapy

THEME	DYNAMIC	BEHAVIORAL	EXPERIENTIAL
Prime concern	Sexual repression	Anxiety	Alienation
Concept of pathology	Instructual conflicts; early libidinal drives and wishes that remain out of awareness, i.e., unconscious	Learned habits: excess or deficit behaviors that have been environmentally reinforced	Existential despair: human loss of possibilities, fragmentation of self, lack of congruence with one's experiences
Concept of health	Resolution of underlying conflicts: victory of ego over id, i.e., ego strength	Symptom removal: absence of specific symptom and/or reduction of anxiety	Actualization of potential: self-growth, authenticity, and spontaneity
Mode of change	Depth insight: understanding of the early past, i.e., intellectual-emotional knowledge	Direct learning: behaving in the present, i.e., action or performance	Immediate experiencing: sensing or feeling in the immediate moment, i.e., spontaneous expression of experience
Time approach and focus	Historical: subjective past	Non-historical: objective present	Ahistorical: phenomenological moment
Type of treatment	Long-term and intense	Short-term and not intense	Short-term and intense
Therapist's task	To comprehend unconscious mental content and its historical and hidden meanings	To program, reward, inhibit, or shape specific behavioral responses to anxiety-producing stimuli	To interact in a mutually accepting atmosphere for arousal of self-expression (from somatic to spiritual)
Primary tools, techniques	Interpretation: free association, analysis of transference, resistance, slips, and dreams	Conditioning: systemic desensitization, positive and negative reinforcements, shaping	Encounter: shared dialogue, experiments, or games, dramatization or playing out of feelings
Treatment model	Medical: doctor-patient or parent-infant (authoritarian), i.e., therapeutic alliance	Educational: teacher-student or parent-child (authoritarian), i.e., learning alliance	Existential: human peer–human peer or adult-adult (egalitarian), i.e., human alliance
Nature of relationship to cure	Transferential and primary for cure: unreal relationship	Real but secondary for cure: no relationship	Real and primary for cure: real relationship
Therapist's role and stance	Interpreter-reflector: indirect, dispassionate, or frustrating	Shaper-adviser: direct, problem-solving, or practical	Interactor-acceptor: mutually permissive or gratifying

From Karasu, T. B.: Psychotherapies: An overview. Am. J. Psychiatry, *134*:852, 1977.

mitted through example (modelling or identification). There is also the percept of self-discovery, the development of a variety of new skills, and an enlargement of the patient's capacity to perceive and accept his or her emotionality. This is in addition to the rewards of the trusting attachment bond between patient and therapist, which brings confidence to the patient that help will be obtained and that he or she has the ability to cope.

Qualities of Therapists

Regardless of the type of therapy or therapies employed, it is recognized generally that therapists must have certain personal assets. They should possess an empathic capacity for projecting themselves into the situations experienced and felt by others and be capable of understanding human motivation. They should be able to accept the emotional reactions of others with equanimity and simultaneously maintain their own personality integrity without defensiveness. Their own personal motivation must be to assist but do no harm. Their ethics must stand against exploitation of their patients in any way. They will hold and respect a theoretical knowledge of their particular psychotherapeutic field of endeavor, buttressed by a wide experience.

EXPRESSIVE-SUPPRESSIVE THERAPIES

The majority of the expressive dynamic psychotherapies have in common the assumption that the patient's emotional or personality difficulty had its genesis in significant psychological experiences and developed in accordance with the dynamic processes that determine psychopathology. They assume that the patient's present attitudes and modes of reaction to life experiences are largely governed by reactions and attitudes to experiences in the past, by patterns of behavior laid down in the

brain systems through prolonged learning and through experiencing pain and pleasure, aversion and reward, in the stream of family and social life. Yet these therapies vary significantly in their theoretical assumptions and their technical application.

Since the theory and practice of psychoanalytic therapy have been most intensively studied and clearly defined, *its assumptions and methods form a convenient model* against which other treatment methods and variations in technique may be examined. For this reason, psychoanalytic treatment is described first.

PSYCHOANALYSIS

It should be borne in mind that the term psychoanalysis is used in two very different senses. Freud originally applied the word to a particular therapeutic method, but it is now employed also as the name of a system of theoretical psychology. The psychoanalytic techniques may be used both for the investigation and the treatment of mental and emotional disorder.

Value and Indications

Psychoanalysis has elucidated many aspects of human behavior that had baffled interpretation and has led to a deeper understanding of the factors that have been responsible for personality development and patterns. Through psychoanalysis it has been learned that phenomena in adult life that are seemingly unintelligible take on meaning when understood in terms of chronologically earlier experiences. It has, too, been of immense value in bringing into awareness the unconscious roots of the problems of the mentally ill.

As a system of psychotherapy, psychoanalysis aims to establish its methods on the general principles and knowledge of the dynamics of emotional life. Psychoanalysis makes possible a study of deeply repressed psychological forces and attempts to demonstrate how certain inner situations and roles persist and result in attitudes and motivating mechanisms that lie behind consciousness, but may determine the whole course of life. It emphasizes, more than other psychological theories, the role of infantile experience in determining adult behavior.

Psychoanalysis is an etiological, uncovering, or insight type of therapy, in contrast to the supportive, nonexploratory types described in a subsequent section. The goal of psychoanalytical therapy is the uncovering and modifying of unconscious psychological forces. Through the analysis, patients should discover the influences of these forces upon the patterns of their daily life, the behavioral manifestations of their condition, their character and its traits, and their relationship to other persons.

Provided the patient's personality is sufficiently mature, his motivation for change is strong, and he has the requisite time and personal resources, psychoanalysis is the choice of psychotherapy if the goal of treatment is a thoroughgoing modification of the personality. The analyst seeks to bring about changes in personality structure by undoing the unfavorable patterns established in earlier years. Psychoanalysis aims to explore the hidden forces determining the behavior that brings suffering to the patient, with the hope that thereby the patient may acquire a maximum of self-knowledge and effect an alteration in the personality structure by undoing and reorganizing the unfavorable patterns that were established in an earlier period.

PREPARATION OF THERAPIST. It is now generally agreed that an analytical psychotherapist should have a personal analysis as a basic preparation for analytical therapy. In this analysis, the prospective therapist undertakes a penetrating psychological study of himself or herself. Such an analysis helps the therapists to recognize their own impulses, wishes, anxieties, and defenses and reduces the danger that these will interfere with the therapeutic relationship with the patient. Well-analyzed therapists will avoid the anxieties that can be aroused by overtly expressed hostility or affection of their patients. Because of their comprehension of the transference implications of behavior, the apparently personally directed comments or actions of patients do not arouse hostile or exploitative impulses.

As in all patient-physician relationship types of psychotherapy, the therapist must avoid treating the patient as a projected part of himself or herself. The personal analysis enables the therapist to avoid many problems that may otherwise arise out of countertransference, discussed later. Also, the personal analysis is extremely helpful in acquainting one's self with the technique of an experienced analyst. The future therapist should also receive a long period of supervised clinical work before undertaking psychoanalytical therapy without the guidance of a trained therapist.

INDICATIONS. Psychoanalysis finds its greatest therapeutic usefulness in the psychoneuroses, character disorders, and the borderline states. The success obtained in these disorders is characterized by a greater potentiality for transference than exists in other neuroses. In the psychoses, the usefulness of psychoanalysis is limited.

Rarely can much be accomplished by the analysis of persons over 45 years of age, although more depends upon the plasticity and receptivity of one's personality pattern than upon chronological age. Psychoanalytic therapy is unlikely to be successful in highly dependent individuals, who demonstrate through their life history little evidence of self-reliance or efforts to gain a personal independence away from parents or parental substitutes. Where the life history shows that the patient has made efforts to give up infantile attachments to the parents, even unevenly and irregularly, the potential for success is enhanced.

Principles and Technique

Psychoanalytical therapy involves recognition of and usage of principles such as *unconscious content, free association, resistance, transference, countertransference, interpretation,* and *analysis of dreams.* These are discussed briefly. No attempt is made either to present them in detail or to examine the many problems that arise in the actual employment of the technique.

The analyst should have had considerable experience with both psychotic and neurotic patients, and be well acquainted with the principles of dynamic psychology. In classic treatment, interviews are held four or five times per week for periods extending from 45 minutes to one hour. Today many analysts conduct less intensive treatment at two or three sessions per week. From one to three years are usually required for an analysis. It is generally considered desirable that the therapist and the patient should not have been previously acquainted, also that their relationship continue to be a strictly professional one, free from social contact. In order that free association may be facilitated, the patient usually reclines during the interview, relaxed on a couch, while the analyst is seated a little behind and to one side. The analyst can observe the patient, but the patient cannot see the analyst, so does not constantly seek signs of the therapist's response. In some instances, the patient and therapist may conduct the analytic process seated when this posture seems more effective in facilitating free association.

Free Association

The principal technique of psychoanalysis is that of free association. To obtain such consciously unguided association, the therapist asks the patient to say whatever comes to mind and advises against changing the sequence of undirected thoughts and against withholding anything because it seems irrelevant or distressing. There should be an uncensored, uninhibited verbalization of everything and anything that comes to mind.

The permissive atmosphere of the therapeutic relationship facilitates free association. Opinions and feelings are expressed with a minimum or no guidance by inquiry. As material through the free association process emerges, often in symbolic form, from the consciously inaccessible portion of the mind, it becomes conscious. To be used therapeutically, however, it is necessary that the patient's repressed material be made conscious and that interrelations and implications of the material be recognized.

It is essential that the therapist be exceedingly guarded and discreet in pointing out connections among the material produced by free association or suggesting interpretations of it. The meaning of the material, as pointed out elsewhere, must be largely discovered by the patient himself. Through the free association process, the patient explores early memories, recreates significant experiences and the feelings contingent on them, reactivates relations with parents, siblings, or other persons, and tries to bring into consciousness feelings and ideas about himself and his attitudes as they existed in childhood. The purpose of the analysis, however, is not in any way to secure a history but rather for the patient, through free association and his interpretation of its products, to discover the tendencies, motives, desires, and other influences that have led to his personality problems and his defenses against anxiety and have constituted dynamic forces in his life.

Gradually, as associations increase in number and in their richness, what has appeared irrelevant and meaningless to the patient begins to assume significance. Because of the great degree of self-revelation that it makes possible, free association is perhaps the most valuable of all methods in disclosing psychodynamics.

Resistance

Free association does not, however, assure smooth and easy passage of all repressed memories and emotions into consciousness. Although the patient's trust in the analyst and the confidence that he is not being judged by the therapist aid him in facing emotional constellations with which he could not deal in the past, as certain repressed and forgotten experiences and emotions are about to be brought within the scope of immediate observation, an opposition to their complete awareness or an aversion to facing the unconscious basis of his motive appears. This opposition, known technically as *resistance,* may be manifested by sudden silences, denials, blockings, forgettings, evasions, embarrassments, and strong emotional reactions. It derives from the patient's transference distortions of the therapist as a punitive, critical, or punishing replica of some significant person in his own past life experiences.

The dynamic significance of the repressed material may be estimated by the degree of resistance to its emergence, and by the severity of the defensive reaction. By noting the occasion and the topics that evoke the patient's defensive resistances, the analyst secures clues about the nature of the repressed material. Usually, the patient's inflection or sudden change of subject indicates that the nucleus of a conflict is being approached or that he is unwittingly attempting to avoid recognition of an unconscious motivation.

Resistance serves as a defense mechanism against the anxiety that would be aroused by a threatening self-knowledge of repudiated feelings and impulses. Care is taken not to probe too deeply or too rapidly in the early stages of an analysis so as not to arouse too great anxiety.

Sandler and his colleagues have outlined the various forms of resistance. There is *depression-resistance* that emerges when impulses, memories, or affect arise against which the patient must defend himself in order to escape conscious distress. The common affects the patient attempts to avoid are those of anxiety, guilt, and shame. *Transference resistance,* sometimes regarded as the most difficult obstacle to analysis, occurs when the patient struggles against revealing his innermost thoughts and feelings about the therapist—many, of course, revelatory of infantile and childish desires. Another important resistance is that which would expose the gain or value of the illness, the secondary gain in the advantages derived from being cared for, gratifying aggressive, domineering, or revengeful impulses toward caretakers, or satisfying masochistic trends. *Id resistance* refers to the unwillingness to change well-established behavioral patterns derived from one's basic drive. Here the patient must "work through" his resistance. *Superego resistance* is that aroused when the patient feels threatened by unconsciously perceived guilt or shame as the analytic work tends to loosen his rigid inhibitions in expression of aggressive sexual or dependency drives, producing what is designated as the "negative therapeutic reaction."

Resistances may evolve as the changes in the patient produce difficulties in important interpersonal relations; by fear of detachment from the analyst as the treatment approaches its ending; by threat to his self-esteem through need to expose infantile behaviors that induce shame; and by the potential of having to give up well-established character traits which sometimes have taken on an autonomous gratifying existence.

Transference

What is perhaps regarded as the most significant concept in psychoanalytical therapy, and perhaps the most important discovery of Freud, is the emotional reaction of the patient toward the analyst, known as the *transference.* Transference is usually defined as a repetition in the patient's present life, and particularly in his relationship to the analyst, of unconscious emotional attitudes developed during childhood within the family group and especially toward the parents. It represents a carrying over, and attaching to the therapist, of the friendly, hostile, or ambivalent attitudes and feelings that the patient formerly entertained in relation to the parent or other meaningful person of the past who played a significant role in his life. The patient reacts toward the therapist as if the latter were this person. He projects upon the therapist the significant images of those to whom he was related in the past.

The significance of the transfer is that it throws light upon the patient's relationship with the individual whom the therapist represents. The patient comes to react as if the therapist were actually the other person and therefore interprets the behavior of the analyst in conformance with his concept of the person toward whom he originally had the reaction. Important unconscious factors are therefore revealed by transference behavior. In the resulting reaction, often referred to as the *transference neurosis*, the original pathogenic conflicts of the early family relationships are repeated with less intensity in relationship to the analyst. This may lead to extreme anxiety, illogical hostility with paranoid implications, clinging affection, or serious acting out of aggressive or sexual impulses or both in order to invite the therapist's punishment.

Three types of transference phenomena may be distinguished: transference of infantile wishes and strivings emerging toward the analyst (libidinal transference); transfer of early defensive processes to the analyst (transference of defense); and transfer of actions into the patient's life (acting in the transfer). The latter may prove disruptive and needs quick recognition and interpretation by the analyst to effect its interruption.

Therapists must remain undisturbed by hostile, critical, or overdetermined loving attitudes of the patient toward them. Instead, they study those feelings objectively with patients, pointing them out and seeking to trace their origins. Through interpretation, patients are brought to realize how their feelings arose out of earlier relationships. The sudden discovery of the transference distortions reveals to the patient, with major impact, the means by which they have frequently misperceived and misjudged their relationships during their recent life.

One aspect of the transference situation that may arise is the tendency of the patient to repeat in relation to the therapist a pattern of dependent emotional relationship such as the one that hampered his emotional adjustment and personality development in the past.

Countertransference

A phenomenon that accounts for many mistakes and failures of psychotherapy is that known as *countertransference*. This consists of such negative attitudes of physician to patient as anger, impatience, or resentment. These and similar attitudes are almost certain to interfere with the therapeutic effectiveness of the physician. For the most part, the countertransference reactions arise in the therapist as a result of the patient's influence on the physician's unconscious feelings and have their origin in the latter's irrational projections and identifications. The therapist must not permit his own unconscious feelings and attitudes, aroused during phases of treatment, to intrude in his relations with the patient.

It should be added, however, that just as countertransference can account for failure in therapy, so it can also in the hands of a skillful therapist be put to good use diagnostically and therapeutically.

Some of the modifications of classic psychoanalysis, such as *existential analysis,* use the revelation of the psychoanalyst's own inner feelings as a therapeutic tool in an encounter between two individuals. Such revelations have been used quite consciously by psychoanalysts to relieve shame or guilt in their patients and thus provide a permissive model that allows patients to disclose their own aggressiveness or sense of failure, thereby bringing about change in the inhibitions imposed by a pathological superego development (see Kolb and also Ward).

Interpretation

Another technique, especially important in its relation to therapy, is *interpretation*. The therapist helps the patient to understand the meaning of his mental phenomena and behavior. Usually, the patient is unaware of the existence of the mental phenomena. As the therapist perceives connections between the experiences revealed by the patient through his free associations and the behavior and symptoms of which he complains, he offers tentative explanations as interpretations. From these interpretations the patient is brought to insight into the dynamic motivations leading to the persistence of his impairing social behaviors.

Often when such interpretations are correct but arouse the anxiety of the patient, he will evidence that anxiety in denial, anger, or other manifestations of resistance. However, the reaction formation against the interpretation is usually followed by further verifying free associations which lead the patient to an insight.

An added task for the therapist is to assist the patient through interpreting resistance. The therapist never confronts the patient with a blunt interpretation of the meaning of his or her symptoms. The more obvious their meaning, the more cautious the therapist must be in explaining them. It has been said that whenever patients cannot see the obvious it is because they need their blindness. Therapists do not impose their own interpretations. These are best offered as tentative observations.

Patients are likely to gain more insight into their problems and behavior through making their own associations, or at least in being merely guided and helped to draw their own conclusions and fully assimilate their interpretations into their psychology.

Timing of interpretations is important. The more experienced the therapist, the more likely that his guidance through interpretation will occur at those moments when they may be most useful to the patient. Frequency of interpretation is important as well. The inexperienced therapist is likely either to remain too passive or to impede the patient's own growth by interrupting too frequently to offer his interpretive remarks. Intellectually able patients with the ego assets of courage work well at analysis with minimum need for such interpretative assistance.

REPRESSION AND ANXIETY. The efforts of the therapist and patient should lead to an undoing of repression in order that the repressed may be brought to consciousness and its critical judgments. Rational decisions can be made if all the facts are at hand instead of having only part of them available, as was previously the case when some were unconscious. One aim of analysis is to bring about such a state that the conscious ego, with its reason, logic, and critical abilities, may assume control when it is confronted with unrealistic, pleasure-seeking, infantile demands that cannot be satisfied by reality.

In every neurotic individual there is overt anxiety when the repressed material approaches consciousness. This anxiety then causes ego functioning to renew its efforts to secure repression, often through the aid of other defense mechanisms. In the analytical transference situation, the patient allows himself to experience the anxiety without renewed efforts at repression by the ego. This the patient can do, since he identifies himself with the analyst who is there to help him and will, he is confident, protect him from danger. Thus, over a period of time, derepression leads to progressive lessening of anxiety, guilt, and shame, and of the need for pathological defenses. The release of energy to use personality assets occurs and self-esteem accordingly increases.

Dream Material

Another important method employed by psychoanalysis for rendering contents of the unconscious available for conscious scrutiny is the examination of *dream material.* The dream is regarded as a phenomenon directly connected with psychic life. Since it represents a product of the patient's thinking that lacks the directing and inhibiting forces exercised by awareness, the material it presents for examination discloses more clearly than does consciously directed thinking the underlying strivings of the personality. Tendencies that may not be expressed in the presence of clear consciousness work freely in dreams. They serve as a convenient disguise for the patient's unacceptable, rejected emotions. In them the analyst finds a symbolic expression of the patient's inner tensions, and clues to his repressed thoughts, feelings, childhood memories, and experiences. When a dream persists in memory or is repeated, it has special significance because it specifically reveals something constant and basic in the forces that make the personality.

Freud divided the content of thought of dreams into two categories. One he called the *manifest content*—the content as it appears to and is recalled by the dreamer. The recollected or obvious content is not, however, the significant element, which is contained in what is known as the *latent content.* The latent content, were it to appear in its naked form, would be too disturbing and painful and is therefore distorted and disguised so that its recollection will not disturb the dreamer. The disguise of mental material is brought about by the mechanisms of displacement, condensation, symbolization, dramatization,

and elaboration. The joint activity of these mechanisms is known as the *dream work,* a process by which the latent dream content is transformed into the manifest content. By condensation, two or more ideas, wishes, or persons are fused into one, emphasis on significant mental material is displaced, and the content is dramatized and filled out by a deceptive secondary elaboration.

As a result of the dream work, the manifest content appears an irrelevant, confused product, yet it represents the symbolic expression of inner tensions and of other important material, the hidden meaning of which must be interpreted in terms of the total life situation of the individual. The mechanisms that in the dream work cause the latent content of the dream to assume the form presented in the manifest content are the same ones that operate to produce many neurotic symptoms. Such symptoms are in their dynamics identical with dream processes. In both, one notes the operation of the psychological laws of the unconscious.

In psychoanalysis, the dreamer is encouraged to report to the physician any recent or recurring dream. Starting from the manifest content of the dream, free associations are employed. The patient is requested to report all that comes into mind in regard to the various objects, actions, and affects revealed in the manifest dream content; in other words, to free associate in relation to the dream and its contents. The latent or underlying significance of the symbolic imagery in the manifest content is brought to light. The analyst must not impose an arbitrary acceptance of fixed symbols as the patient attempts to unravel the hidden meanings represented in the dream content. The object in dream interpretation is not so much the translation of certain symbols as it is the discovery of the ideas and motives that are dynamic in determining the patient's reactions in waking life.

OTHER SYMBOLIC MESSAGES. In addition to the analysis of dreams, the skilled therapist will recognize in the patient's reporting of unusual interest in particular passages of books, dramatic productions, or art forms a possible symbolic representation of some internal conflict situation. Gifts proffered by the patient also contain this potential. Therefore, the therapist seizes these spontaneous presentations to bring the patient to free associate to the objects of interest brought into the analysis. The analytic work here is similar to that with dreams; its result is as revealing as or even more revealing than dream analysis.

Personality Reorganization

To be successful, psychoanalysis should so thoroughly reveal to the patient his underlying strivings and problems that, with the assistance of the therapist, he can reorganize the forces of his personality, redirect his affective energy into constructive channels, and prevent its further dissipation in dissociation, substitution, and other evasive, neurotic ways. It aims to give the patient freedom from disabling fears, distress, and inhibitions and to enable him to achieve insight sufficient to handle ordinary conflicts and reasonable reality stress. In psychotic patients, it is usually too difficult to overcome resistance or to establish transference to a degree that will permit extensive personality reorganization, but much has been accomplished with many such patients.

Modified Psychoanalytic Theories and Techniques

Work with patients with psychoses and differing character pathologies, with neurotic individuals of cultures other than American and European, and with various socioeconomic groups led to modifications or expansions of the original Freudian psychoanalytic theory. Recognizing varying symptoms of neuroses between generations of the 19th and 20th centuries and between populations in Europe and the United States, Karen Horney concluded that more than a purely biological theory is required to explain these differences. She remained dissatisfied with the outcome of traditional psychoanalytic therapy embodying the original technique.

Horney visualized the personality as developing over time in attitudes toward the self and others, and in social values, expectations, and conflicts, as derived and learned from the family. She postulated the need to recognize within the self three parts—the actual, the real, and the idealized self. A total of the individual's experience constitutes the actual self. The central force within the individual, while commonly shared with others, and unique to each person, provides the integrating and harmonious sense of the real self.

The third concept of self, the idealized, represents the neurotic presentation.

Horney believed that, if exposed to early parental rejecting attitudes, the growing child develops basic anxiety and thereby evolves fixed attitudes of submission, aggressiveness, or attachment toward the parents; she identified these as neurotic trends. These attitudes lead to intrapsychic conflict which, in turn, is productive of further anxiety. Horney considered that excessive preoccupations with genital or other organ functions were reactions to parental attitudes, rather than being based upon the biological phases of development that were emphasized by Freud. She emphasized the significant role of hostility in the development of personality function.

To solve the neurotic conflict, Horney thought, the individual evolved self-effacing, expansive, or resigned characterological attitudes. In self-effacement, the neurotic individual's pressing need is to be loved rather than to assert himself through initiative, competitiveness, and striving toward success. Those with expansive characterological development strive toward mastery over individuals and obstacles in their lives and seek to lessen anxiety through power, prestige, or both. The neurosis leads to avoidance of expressions of affection and sympathy and rejection of trustfulness, as these are seen as weaknesses. This neurotic type is sensitive to admissions of imperfections of any kind. The resigned individual has a wish to be independent and self-sufficient. He therefore avoids others and feels anxious when exposed to them because of their possible demands upon him or their efforts to place him in a position of obligation, to influence him, or to coerce him. Horney emphasized that treatment is directed toward self-realization in the present and not to concepts of cure, for the consequences of the warped developmental processes may never be rectified.

Harry Stack Sullivan derived his interpersonal theory of personality from his work with the schizophrenic and obsessive-compulsive, the influence of Adolf Meyer, and the knowledge he absorbed from association with the principal American thinkers of his time pertaining to the influence of social forces upon the personality. Sullivan emphasized the potentially human mode of functioning, as against the animal or biological. To him, anxiety was a consequence of the expectation of unfavorable estimation by another significant individual. Such expectation might arise from real experiences, from fantasy, or from unconsciously held tensions derived from early experiences with significant others, particularly parents. Sullivan recognized as the first goal of all humans the satisfaction of biological needs; the second goal is to achieve good relationships and status with others. He designated the first as the need for satisfactions and the second as the need for security.

Sullivan's concept of dynamism, as a characteristic way in which an individual relieves his inner tensions, whether to satisfy biological needs or needs for security, resembles in many ways Freud's ideas of defenses. Sullivan pointed out that in modern societies tensions are largely derived from a person's need for security, which is sustained only through development of meaningful interpersonal relations. From his accomplishments in feeding his needs, anxiety is subdued and, with increasing confidence about security, there arises self-esteem. Self-esteem is seen as necessary to cope with the realistic aloneness and powerlessness that occur throughout the lifetime of an individual. Like Horney, Sullivan emphasized the role of learning in personality development, although he indicated that empathy, the willingness to move forward through trial and error, the suffering or pleasure in punishment and reward, learning through imitation, and, finally, deduction and conceptualization were critical in human development. He believed that learning occured when anxiety existed at an optimal level to provide motivation and drive.

Anxiety in the interpersonal field is communicated and perceived either realistically or incorrectly. Incorrectly perceived, it may be experienced in the *prototaxic mode* through the suffering of diffuse and undifferentiated emotional states derived from infancy and childhood, and re-represented in the psychoses, particularly schizophrenia. Anxiety may also be experienced in the *parataxic mode* expressed through temporal and serial connections, but without logical representations. Paranoia develops from this type of distorted thinking.

The characteristic of psychoanalytic treatment using interpersonal theory is the focus on the detailed study of the patient's interpersonal relationships through examining the realistic feelings experienced in his relationship with the psychoanalyst. The psychoanalyst is defined and functions as a participant observer in the patient's life, though this is often distorted through the patient's prototaxic or parataxic modes of experience. Intrinsic to treatment, therefore, is detailed exposure of the events and related emotional states of interpersonal contacts with others, present, past, or future, through use of the analytic principles of free association. The intent is to provide a more realistic appraisal of the social perceptiveness of the individual, so as to increase social competence, self-assurance, and self-esteem, and to sharpen the individual's perception of here and now in social relations for himself and others.

As participant observer, the interpersonal psychoanalyst holds himself highly alert to the countertransference as well as the transferences of his patient. Thus he is anxious to know what transpires between himself and the patient, and vice versa. He attempts to get the patient to verbalize misperceptions of himself, as a means of clarifying the interpersonal relationship. The emphasis is on the communicative process and its revelations, as it pertains to the patient's response to anxiety. Although genetic reconstruction provides the open explanation of his experience, free association and dream analysis are also used. These latter processes are held secondary. Perhaps for this reason the interpersonal psychoanalytic process, which derived largely from work with the schizophrenic and obsessive-compulsive neurotic, is particularly useful in resolving the fixed usage of fantasy, intellectualization, denial, symbolization, and other defenses felt characteristic of these states.

Others who have contributed to emphasizing the process of socialization significant to personality development and expressions in psychopathology are Erich Fromm and Erik Erikson. The reader is referred to their works for further elaboration.

Existential psychoanalysis had its origins in phenomenological philosophy based upon a concept of *being in the world*. This concept emphasizes the polarity from man and the world in the here and now situation. Anxiety is defined as stemming from the fear of not being—the fear of death. The goal is recognized as achieving "the courage to be" rather than preoccupation with the desire for conformity to the opinions of others, the playing of expected roles, or involvement in extensive distractions. Existentialist psychoanalysis has been less well elaborated theoretically and practically than the other forms discussed. Leston L. Havens has discussed the method in action as he uses it, providing examples from clinical experience. He describes the states of *being, staying,* and *leaving behind* as the early, middle, and late stages of existential work. The emphasis is on expression of feelings by the patient and also the therapist. Through such progressive expression there evolves comprehension of the other's ideas and a sense of understanding and closeness that deepens as the individuals' revelations to each other expand. The act of being in the therapeutic situation is empathic; objections about the personality of one by the other emerge openly to be understood. The therapeutic process is, therefore, highly subjective. Havens indicates that the existential therapist is little interested in defining unconscious material while listening to the patient's free associations. He takes at face value all the patient's statements. Conversely, existential psychiatry suggests a greater degree of frankness in exposure of the therapist's feelings toward the patient.

Among the existential psychoanalysts is Victor Frankl, who designates his method as logotherapy. He emphasizes that the therapeutic relationship that develops between the therapist and the patient is necessarily conflictful, as the therapist brings to the treatment situation the extremes of human closeness versus scientific detachment. The therapist must strive for a posture in which neither his desire to assist his patient nor his insistence on technique becomes omnipotent. Frankl teaches the importance of anticipatory anxiety in

relation to the compulsion of self-ob-
servation. To him, excessive attention is
a significant factor in the etiology of
neuroses, as well as excessive intention.
The forced intention of attaining a goal
leads to excessive striving, which often
inhibits that very attainment. Recognizing these aspects of personality functioning, he has devised a particular
technical variation for treatment of
phobias, also sometimes used in sleep
disturbances, called "paradoxical intention." Logotherapists encourage the patient to intend or wish exactly that
which the patient fears, even if only for
a moment or two. Frankl observes that
patients can couple this paradoxical intention with a change in attitudes toward the symptom. Thus, the patient is
directed not only to confront his symptoms but even to exaggerate them. The
humorously toned, exaggerated attitude provides a self-detachment from
the symptoms. Frankl suggests that the
technique is particularly applicable to
short therapy and argues that it is not a
method of persuasion (to be described
later in this chapter), but its opposite,
for the patient is required to exaggerate
his fears rather than to suppress them.
Logotherapists also employ a technique called "de-reflection" to counteract the compulsive inclination for self-
observations. The patient is brought to
de-reflect from his anticipatory anxiety.
to something else. Strategies such as
these have been described by Haley
and are included by certain behavior
therapists under the category of negative intention.
Comparative evaluations of the
various modifications from the traditional psychoanalytic therapy, as well as
comparative analysis of the actual differences in technique, remain to be
done. We are convinced that this may be
done with great benefit using the modern technology of television. Unfortunately, most psychoanalysts rationalize
their unwillingness to expose their
technical maneuvers audiovisually on
the ground that recording for public

analysis will distort the therapeutic
process.

Outcome

Although there exist reports of numerous studies of the effectiveness of
psychoanalysis and other psychotherapies, there is now a widespread
recognition that for the most part the
research, design, and conduct of these
studies leave much to be desired. There
is, in fact, little in the literature to
suggest that we have scientifically validated outcome studies of effectiveness
of any of the therapies reported in this
chapter. Comparisons between forms
of therapy are, at best, tenuous, because most reporters have failed to
specify the goals of the treatment before its application. Obviously a treatment directed to personality reorganization and prevention of further
disturbance attempts an achievement
much more complex than one directed
to symptom alleviation.
Effective designs for evaluating treatment should state the theoretical basis
for the treatment to be examined and
the goals in behavioral changes. Also,
such reports should state the details of
the treatment, including the setting.
The patient population should be defined by age, sex, sociocultural, diagnostic, and symptomatic classification.
The measuring devices need descrip-
ton, standardization in various populations, and evaluation, and should be
performed by others than those providing treatment. Such studies should include a design which compares the psychotherapeutic effectiveness of two or
more treatments. Decisions must be
stated as to whether the controls will be
sought within the behavior of the patient over time or by comparison
groups, both methods presenting considerable weaknesses. For a thorough
discussion of the design of research on
effectiveness of psychotherapy and a
body of information useful in assessing

reports on outcome now in the literature, the article by Fiske et al. is recommended.

Weber, Elinson, and Moss have presented a highly sophisticated study that meets many of the requirements outlined for evaluative study and compares changes in behavior over time in 1329 patients treated by the psychoanalytic method and a briefer psychodynamic psychotherapy. Using as indicator of change an ego balance scale in which the coders quantitated modification of behavior in nine areas of functioning (dependency, pleasure, sex, affects, defense, emergency emotions, guilt, pathology, social), they report that the length of time patients are in treatment bears a direct relationship to the improvement recorded. With both forms of treatment there occurred a rising rate of improvement over time.

With the less intensive psychodynamic psychotherapy, this improvement reaches its maximum in six months to a year and then levels off. Patients in analysis did less well during the initial year than those in psychotherapy, but a greater number improved over the succeeding years and achieved higher levels of functioning than those in psychotherapy. Analytic patients showed significantly greater net improvement on the sex, defense, and pathology balances than the other group over one to two years. The changes for the better on the dependency balance were equal for both groups. (See Figure 30–1.)

For patients in the different diagnostic groupings, psychoanalysis proved most effective for those with neurotic character disturbances. The psychoneurotic and psychotic did about equally well in both forms of treatment.

PATHOLOGY BALANCE —ALL PATIENTS
CHANGE IN SEVERITY

TIME IN TREATMENT

Figure 30–1   Change in severity rating on the Pathology Balance from the beginning to the end of treatment is shown for groups with varying times in treatment. Patients in psychoanalysis and psychotherapy are compared.

(Modified from Weber, J. J., Elinson, J., and Moss, L. M.: Application of ego strength scales to psychoanalytic clinic records. *In*: Goldman, G. S., and Shapiro, D. (eds.): Developments in Psychoanalysis at Columbia University. New York, Hafner Publishing Company, 1966.)

BRIEF PSYCHODYNAMIC PSYCHOTHERAPY

Because of the time required for an analysis, and therefore the relatively few persons who can be treated thereby, various brief and modified psychotherapeutic techniques that utilize psychoanalytic understanding are now employed. Many psychiatrists combine selected features from psychobiological, supportive, and psychoanalytical therapies. Franz Alexander, while making use of psychoanalytical principles and techniques, emphasized certain shortcomings in that procedure. He believed that prolonged, uninterrupted daily interviews may favor the development of a too dependent relationship and consequently postpone recovery. He therefore reduced contact with the patient as much as possible, gave the patient more independence, and discouraged regressive tendencies.

Even in modified psychoanalytic therapies, the therapist seeks to bring the patient to recognize the significance of patterns of behavior and their relationship to early environmental and cultural influences or to interpersonal relationships and experiences. In some instances, the therapist sets a time limit for the treatment. Frank emphasizes that the results in these treatments bear a strong relationship to the expectations of both the patient and the therapist. When both are expectant of improvement and change, the outcome is usually gratifying. Clearly, outcomes that rest upon the expectations of the patient derive from the infantile experiencing of constancy of dependency and trust.

Mann, Sifneos, and Malan are among those who have described most clearly their technical approaches and the indications they seek for selecting patients for their particular forms of short intervention. Mann focuses upon the issues stemming from separation—that is, dependency and passitivity. In a treatment transaction, he maintains a constant and empathic relation to his patient's feelings, much like an existential therapist, commenting upon and supporting the feelings in the context of a treatment contract fixed at no more than 12 sessions. The contract in itself clearly faces the issue of separation anxiety with the ambivalent emotional conflicts. Mann believes those most likely to benefit are younger adults confronting the conflicts that arise in relation to personal autonomy and establishment of their personal identities, for which separation from others upon whom they have been dependent is important.

Following the initial diagnostic assessment, the effective therapist generally formulates for the patient the nature of the problem and the goal or goals toward which the psychotherapeutic work will be directed. Also, the patient is advised clearly what to attempt to do in the treatment sessions. Patients are sometimes given the termination date and requested to state their willingness to accept the treatment arrangements. As Mann describes the course of time-limited brief psychotherapy, the initial sessions are characterized by magical expectations that all will go well. During the middle phase, the patients express in their behavior their desire to avoid that which they have disliked confronting in the past. In general, this relates to separation without resolution from a significant but "ambivalently experienced person." In the end phase, the therapist actively interprets the conflict situations. Transference interpretations are limited to the last session.

Such psychotherapy seems indicated for patients who have had no prior treatment, and who have a disturbance of recent origin, no physical complaints, and a referral by a physician. The selection of patients who do well in time-limited treatment correlates with the high responders for termination of time-unlimited treatment as found in the terminator-remainer tests devised some years ago, as well as with their high scoring on the Bass Social Acquiescence Scale.

Sifneos and Malan use dynamic interpretative techniques, including those related to transference. Sifneos seldom continues patients beyond 20 sessions, while Malan remains less definitive in his timing. Neither sees patients at the frequency of psychoanalysis. For these two therapists there is also a focus for therapy—unconscious conflicts, generally oedipal in nature, which impair a person's capacity to establish and maintain satisfying intimacy with another. In their therapeutic efforts, both are much more active with interpretation than is traditional in long-term psychoanalysis. The attempt is made to bring quickly to the patient's awareness the unconscious fixations that intrude upon daily life. Sifneos is more confronting and deliberately attempts to arouse anxiety; Malan is more patient—he offers the patient insight into the "triangle of conflict," as he puts it, which consists of defense, anxiety, and hidden feeling, and the "triangle of person," which includes others, transference, and parents. Malan insists that defense always should be interpreted before impulse (affect).

In general, Sifneos and Malan select for their brief dynamic therapies those young people confronted by challenges in the establishment of intimacy and adult relations in family life, occupation, or other social relations. Malan advises against this therapy for those with a history of suicidal attempts, alcoholism or drug dependency, long-term hospitalization, more than a single course of electroshock treatment, long-term incapacitating phobic or obsessional symptoms, destructive acting out, or homosexuality.

A comparison of these brief dynamic psychotherapies is given in Table 30–2. A careful reading of the respective texts of Sifneos, Malan, and Mann will delineate more fully their styles. All illustrate their work with case reports.

Beck includes cognitive and behavioral models in his brief psychotherapy with depressed patients. He attempts to enable his patients to comprehend that their dysphoria is secondary to their "automatic thought" in which they denigrate and criticize themselves. Like a behavior therapist, Beck teaches his patients the responses and behaviors that may be useful.

Such short-term psychotherapy has been modified specifically for use in those with particular neuroses. Suess, for instance, describes a technique of treating people who have compulsive personalities and obsessive-compulsive symptoms. Using the Sullivanian model, he focuses on the current feeling of the patient in the interview and in daily living experiences. This relieves guilt, self-doubt, and anxiety. The therapist actively intervenes to cut off repetitive and tangential communications, intellectual discussions (including those of psychogenetic account), and descriptions of symptoms, and in so doing interprets directly the defensive character of such verbalization. He openly interprets the hidden hostilities he sees in the daily transactions of the patient, which are present in everybody in similar situations. Ward and also the senior author have commented on these and other variations in psychotherapeutic technique in treating persons with differing psychopathology.

Psychobiological Therapy

With this technique, problems are approached largely at a conscious level and discussed directly in the form of an ordinary conversation, with attention directed toward definite situations and the patient's reactions to them. Psychobiological therapy does not recognize nor does it systematically use the patient-physician relationship, the transference, to explore the genetic dynamics of the patient's behavior. The therapist seeks to modify the unhealthy attitudes that have prevented the patient from carrying on his daily tasks without disturbing his relations with others or creating anxiety within himself. The therapist aims to assist the patient in establishing a more rational, more con-

TABLE 30–2 Comparison of the Modern Short-Term Dynamic Psychotherapies

	SIFNEOS	MALAN	MANN
Patient selection	Rigid standards; no borderlines, psychotics, or character disorders	Rigid standards; like Sifneos	Character disorders OK; no severe depression, or acute psychotics; usually no borderlines
Focus	Neurotic conflict (preconscious or unconscious) especially oedipal; well circumscribed	Like Sifneos, especially oedipal	Affective state (presently and chronically endured pain); preconscious or conscious
Technique			
Style	Unemotional teacher	Nondirective teacher	Empathic helper
Method	Provoke anxiety by interpretation and confrontation	Provide insight by interpretation	Impose rigid structure and explore affect
Alliance	Rational	Rational	Irrational
Contract			
Fixed termination?	No	Yes	Yes
Patient agreement on focus?	Yes	No	Yes
Transference			
Quality	Positive, then ambivalent	Same	Same
Management	Actively considered	Same	Same
Emphasis	Middle of treatment	Same, but variable	Termination
Termination	Downplayed; focus on loss of therapist, not loss of past objects	Flexible	Crucial to therapy; related to central issue
Curative factor	Insight into conflict	Insight into conflict	Mastery of separation
School	Analytic	Analytic	Existential-analytic

Modified from Burke, J. D., White, H. S., and Havens, L. L.: Which Short-Term Therapy? Arch. Gen. Psychiatry, 36:184, 1979.

structive, and therefore healthier pattern of living.

Because of the principles involved, Adolf Meyer characterized as distributive analysis and synthesis this technique of psychotherapy. Attention is directed more to actual situations and circumstances than to the discovery of unconscious attitudes and mechanisms. The therapist does not, as in psychoanalysis, attempt to have the patient relive early experiences but to understand the present meaning of them and his present attitude toward them. The therapist's interested and receptive attitude and his noncritical acceptance of the patient's problems, feelings, and fears help the patient to recognize his own emotions and to understand himself better. As in psychoanalysis, one must be careful not to overwhelm the patient with interpretations and thereby cause him to build up his defenses and resistances.

The discussions aim to help the patient trace genetically the origin of his complaint in past experience, both in that of which he is aware and in that which has been excluded from memory. Such a biographical analysis includes a study of somatic factors, drives, and activities and a survey of the patient's psychosexual development. It emphasizes human relationships in general, including difficulties with others and social successes and failures.

The therapist asks questions frequently, not so much for the purpose of securing an answer as for promoting a study by the patient himself of his modes of reaction to life experiences. After various experiences, situations, and symptoms have been discussed and analyzed, the patient may be asked to reformulate them into a dynamic life story with its motivations, to as nearly as possible reproduce the origin and development of his problem and understand the means taken to meet it. Great care must be exercised lest any interpretations to which an effort is made to guide the patient be made too early, without fact, or in unacceptable terms. Usually, the therapist also makes use of other measures, such as reassurance, guidance, persuasion, desensitization, and ventilation.

Confrontation Technique

From what has been stated earlier about the need for caution in interpretation, confrontation would seem largely undesirable as a psychotherapeutic technique. Yet it has been employed in brief therapies and as an aid to interpretation in the longer dynamic expressive treatments.

Garner has most clearly defined a confrontation technique, which he employs in his psychotherapeutic approach. His goal is problem solving, in contrast to the permissive dynamic psychotherapeusis of the coercive suppressive approaches. Recognizing a crucial problem within the patient that the patient vaguely perceives, the therapist clearly states the issue. Moreover, he suggests a realistic solution. Garner does this in an exaggerated manner, to illustrate the needed action. Finally, he provides a statement of the repetitive conflicts deriving from the status quo, to emphasize the lack of gratification through its continuance. The patient's thoughts and feelings in regard to the confrontation are then sought.

OTHER EXPRESSIVE THERAPIES

In the discussion of psychoanalysis, it was noted that free association and an observation of its sequence of ideas, dreams, and the associations to them (transference phenomena and defensive reactions, such as resistances) served as the means both of exploration and of expression of unconscious material. In the following description of special expressive therapies, various techniques, sometimes with associated adjunctive devices (such as drugs that alter the level of consciousness), are employed for the purpose of exploring and securing expression of the preconscious and other relatively superficial mental content. Among the superficial expressive therapies are narcosynthesis, hyponosis, ventilation, and abreaction.

Narcosynthesis

In this form of therapy, the patient is given an intravenous injection of pentothal sodium or sodium amytal to the point of thorough relaxation, but not of sleep. In general, 300 to 500 mg. of the barbiturates injected slowly over a period of three to five minutes achieve the appropriate level of consciousness. This is known when the patient gives evidence of impairment of cerebral functioning through slight slurring of speech on counting backwards. In this state, censorship is less active, and suppressed or repressed material emerges. Conscious control is obliterated and inhibitions removed. The patient's subconscious is revealed relatively rapidly and with the minimum of psychic trauma. Positive or negative feelings may be overtly expressed and trends disclosed. The patient forgets any expressed material and acting out. Recently, some therapists have filmed the procedure and then later reviewed the recorded actions with the patient.

The technique is of considerable value when the patient has recently been subjected to severe traumatic experiences that stirred impulses and anxiety to a degree that they could not be handled without repression and symptom formation. Under these circumstances, abreaction often contributes to the therapeutic process. The greatest usefulness of narcosynthesis is in acute anxiety states, early traumatic neuroses, conversion hysterias, and the dissociative amnesias and fugues. It is not satisfactory in obsessive-compulsive states or in chronic neuroses. The technique not only breaks down inhibitions but favors the establishment of rapport, puts the patient in a suggestible frame of mind, and is appealing because it uses a physical approach, which is usually accepted readily. Resistance, or an unconscious effort to evade memories and insight, is reduced by the narcosis, and interpretation is thereby facilitated.

Although Dysken and his colleagues report that under the influence of such drugs no more information may be elicited than through ordinary interviews, the technique's principal objective is the emotional abreaction. Narcosynthesis may be used for such responses in the 70 per cent of persons incapable of induction of trance through hypnosis.

Hypnosis

Hypnosis has been defined as an induced state of dissociation produced through suggestion. Some have considered the trance state as a condition of hypnosis, a special state of consciousness in which the subjects are more responsive than others to suggestions for anesthesias, amnesias, age regression, and hallucinations. In recent years this view has come under question through the work of a number of experimenters. In an exhaustive review of the trance state, Barber has proposed that a better explanation for hypnosis and the hypnotic state is that certain individuals, more responsive than others to suggestions, respond appropriately when their attitudes, motivations, and expectancies to the situation are positively inclined.

Without using the trance induction technique customarily applied by hypnotists, Barber and others have been able to induce all the characteristics of the hypnotic trance in groups of unselected men and women exposed merely to brief "task motivational instructions." He found among these unselected groups of individuals as much response to the task motivational instructions in bringing about body immobility, aggression, hallucination, analgesia, and amnesia as among another unselected group exposed to the usual trance induction techniques.

As an analogy to the hypnotic trance state, Barber suggests the state of a member of an audience viewing a staged dramatic presentation, who projects himself to identify with the affects, actions, and communication of the actors. In so doing, his attention is diverted from the initial awareness that the performance is contrived and that he is a passive viewer. He enjoys the emotional experiencing into which he has projected himself. The hypnotic state may be considered a behavioral change based upon the patient's hopeful preconceptions of that state and of the therapeutic interpersonal relationship. The therapist is perceived as an authority.

Clearly, the selection of patients—those responsive individuals amenable to rapid behavioral change through induction of hypnotic trance—is an important precondition of the decision to use hypnotic technique. Hilgard and Hilgard and others have devised various methods to identify the trance-responsive or highly suggestible individual. Approximately 5 to 10 per cent of the general population are susceptible to trance induction and 25 per cent are minimally so.

Hilgard and Hilgard offer a full description of the method of testing an individual's potential for hypnosis, as well as the following protocol of trance induction:*

(Patient may be seated in any kind of chair with arms, or may be in bed, sitting or lying.)

Introductory Remarks

In a moment I shall hypnotize you and suggest to you a number of experiences that you may or may not have, and a number of effects that you may or may not produce. Not everyone can have the same experiences or produce the same effects when hypnotized. People vary greatly. We need to know which experiences you can have so we can build on them and know how to make hypnosis best serve you. Please remember always to respond to what you are *feeling*, so we can use hypnosis in ways that are natural for you.

Induction

Please close your eyes and listen carefully to what I say. As we go on, you will find yourself becoming more and more relaxed. . . . Begin to let your whole body relax. . . . Let all the muscles go limp. . . . Now you will be able to feel special muscle groups relaxing even more. If you pay attention to your right foot, you can feel the muscles in it relax . . . feel the muscles in the right lower leg relaxing . . . in the right upper leg relaxing. . . . Now on the left side, concentrate on the way that the left foot is relaxing . . . and the left leg, how the lower part and the upper part are both relaxing more.... Next, you'll be able to feel the muscles of the right hand relaxing, the right lower arm and the right upper arm relaxing. . . . Now direct your attention to your left hand. Let it relax, let the lower arm and the upper arm relax. . . . As you have become relaxed, your body begins to feel rather heavy. Just think of the chair (bed) as being strong, sink into it, and let it hold you. . . . Your shoulders . . . neck . . . and head, more and more relaxed. . . . The muscles of your scalp and forehead, just let them relax even more. . . . All of this time you have been settling more deeply and more comfortably into the chair (bed).

Your mind has relaxed, too, along with your body. It is possible to set all worries aside. Your mind is calm and peaceful. You are getting more and more comfortable. . . . You will continue to feel pleasantly relaxed as you continue to listen to my voice. . . . Just keep your thoughts on what I am saying . . . more and more deeply relaxed and perhaps drowsy but at no time will you have any trouble hearing me. You will continue in this state of great relaxation until I suggest that it is time for you to become more alert. . . . Soon I will begin to count from 1 to 20. As I count, you will feel yourself going down further and further into this deeply relaxed hypnotic state. You will be able to do all sorts of things that I suggest, things that will be interesting and acceptable to you. You will be able to do them without breaking the pattern of complete relaxation that is gradually coming over you. . . . One — you are becoming more deeply relaxed . . . two — down, down into a deeper, tranquil state of mind . . . three — four — more and more relaxed . . . five — six — seven — you are sinking deeper and deeper. Nothing will disturb you. You are finding it easy just to listen to things that I say . . . eight — nine — ten — halfway there . . . eleven — twelve — thirteen — fourteen — fifteen — although deeply relaxed, you can hear me clearly. You will always hear me distinctly no matter how hypnotized you are . . . sixteen — seventeen — eighteen — deeply relaxed. Nothing will disturb you . . . nineteen — twenty — *completely relaxed.*

You can change your position any time you wish. Just be sure you remain comfortable and relaxed.

You are very relaxed and pleasantly hypnotized. While you remain comfortably listening to my words, I am going to help you learn more about how thinking about something affects what you do. Just experience whatever you can. Pay close attention to what I tell you, and think about the things I suggest. Then let happen whatever you find is happening, even if it surprises you a little. Just *let it happen by itself.*

The remainder of the induction, needed to complete the various sections of the Stanford Hypnotic Susceptibility Test, is given in the Hilgards' book.

Some therapists believe that those identified as highly suggestible among patient populations, who will be found in large numbers among those with hysterical, anxiety, and depressive neuroses, are the least likely to profit

---

from long-term intensive psychotherapies. If this is corroborated, identifying
easy responsivity to suggestions becomes of major clinical import in choosing the appropriate treatment method.
Spiegel's method of eye-roll levitation
rapidly identifies subjects likely to respond. Spiegel and Spiegel suggest that
those resistant to trance induction are
most often the least flexible and most
likely to suffer serious psychopathology.

INDICATIONS AND VALUE. Hypnosis
occupies an important and valuable
place in the therapeutic armamentarium of the psychiatrist. Its greatest
value is to modify conversion symptoms, recover amnesic defects, and examine childhood behavior through
suggestion of age regression, and as an
anesthetic means in dentistry, obstetrics, and certain surgical conditions.

Marks et al. compared the hypnotic
techniques to the desensitization variant of the behavior therapies in the
treatment of phobias, with each patient
exposed to 12 successive weekly treatments by the two methods. Both treatments brought about equally significant
improvement, but not complete relief
of disability. The hypnotic techniques
appeared to be superior with the most
anxious patients, and desensitization
with the opposing groups in whom
habituation was more rapid and coun-
terconditioning occurred readily.

As with other suppressive therapies,
although a symptom may often be made
to disappear dramatically through
hypnosis, the factors that produced
it are merely repressed and the fundamental personality problem is unchanged. Another reason why hypnosis
is not a measure that is permanently
successful when used alone is that
suggestions lose their effect after a
time. It also has the disadvantage that,
when the patient's symptoms are
suggested away, he may become dependent on the hypnotist instead of developing an ability to solve his problems
independently. For these reasons hypnosis should be supplemented by an in-
sight-producing and constructive form
of psychotherapy. Any real change in
personality functioning requires a
knowledge of the underlying factors
that produced the symptoms.

Hypnosis may be of value when painful experiences have been repressed
and have given rise to symptoms. The
memory of the traumatic experience
may be revived by hypnosis and the
symptom made to disappear with an accompanying abreaction, in which the
patient goes over and over the traumatic situation, crying and sobbing or
showing other expression of pent-up
emotions.

Under hypnosis, forgotten experiences may be revived, and the patient
can discuss material about which he
cannot or does not want to talk in the
waking state. The use of intravenous
barbiturates as a means of recovering
repressed memories is more certain
and requires less time than does hypnosis. It does not, moreover, involve the
emotional dependence often prerequisite to successful hypnosis and provides
the patient a "face-saving" device, particularly if he lives in a technologically
inclined culture.

The relationship of hypnosis to acupuncture in providing relief of complaints of pain has attracted much attention. It is said that those responsive
to acupuncture are similar in personality to those responding to hypnosis. Yet
the mechanisms of the actions of the
two techniques may differ. Li and his
colleagues reported that under hypnosis, the average intensity of an electrical stimulation needed to produce
sensation was greater than before the
trance. Acupuncture and placebo-
acupuncture produced no significant
changes in the subjects' reaction to
painful stimulation.

Ventilation

Ventilation is an expressive type of
therapy in which the patient's anxiety is
relieved to some degree by the oppor-

tunity in a tolerant, empathic setting frankly to "talk out" and discuss with the therapist personal problems and "worries" that he ordinarily would not discuss with others. The physician, with an attitude of understanding and encouragement, interrupts the patient as little as possible, although occasional questions may be necessary to keep the thread of the story in meaningful channels.

Among topics that may require ventilation may be doubts, impulses, conscious anxieties, family problems, and feelings of guilt. Some phases of the material expressed often represent confession of thoughts or actions considered intolerable and for which relief from guilt or shame is needed to alleviate anxiety. Others may consist largely of "blowing off steam" regarding resentments. Frequently a joint discussion of present conflicts and past life situations as they seem to relate to emotional or psychosomatic symptoms may bring relief to troublesome aspects of the patient's life. Perhaps in this way the patient may discover a linkage of events and feelings with present reactions and symptoms.

An occasional question may help the patient to find the meaning of his symptoms himself. A correction of misinformation regarding personal problems may result in some diminution of the patient's anxiety. The patient-physician relationship adds to the therapeutic effect of ventilation. Ventilation may at times be supplemented by a superficial psychotherapy based on a knowledge of psychodynamics.

Abreaction

There is a superficial expressive type of psychotherapy in which anxiety is lessened by an emotional reliving of the stress situation that produced the neurosis. A therapeutically beneficial discharge of dammed-up emotions associated with the recall of a repressed memory occurs. The existence of a high degree of emotional tension is the basic indication for abreaction. It often tends to produce a desensitization, i.e., a reduction of emotional tension related to a repressed psychological conflict. The emotional reactions discharged are usually those of grief, rage, or fear. Sometimes the abreaction may include an expression of hostility toward the therapist.

Abreaction, with its beneficial effect in bringing about a reliving and possible working out of the emotional aspects of a stressful experience, may be spontaneous, suggested under hypnosis, or facilitated with barbiturates.

SUPPRESSIVE THERAPY

Suppressive psychotherapy aims to strengthen repression and other usual defenses or to lessen the intensity of a disabling symptom using such means as dogmatic assurance, persuasion, suggestion, and hypnosis. It makes no search for, or any effort to solve, the actual dynamic problem. If, therefore, it produces any relief, the problem still remains and may readily return under any stress or strain.

Persuasion

Persuasion as a form of psychotherapy is particularly associated with the name of Paul Dubois of Berne. This therapy is based upon the principle of intellectual explanations and moralizing discussions. It is explained to the patient how faulty intellectual and emotional attitudes on his part were reactions to certain difficulties; also how such tendencies led to undesirable habits and unhealthy emotional and mental conditions. According to Dubois, an important method of therapeutic approach is through self-criticism and through reasoning about the nature of the symptoms and the false ideas and bad mental habits that led to the symptoms.

In persuasion, the emphasis is on rationalism and on moral suasion, on an appeal to "reason" and to will. By means of persuasion, the therapist seeks to create, convert, or strengthen certain impulses and to remove or diminish others, to create or strengthen some inhibitions and to free the patient from enslaving ones. It is the aim of the physician, through reasoned argument, to implant in the patient's mind the conviction that his symptoms will disappear. Persuasion probably overestimates the potency of rational processes in any attack upon the products of emotional factors.

Suggestion

In suggestion, the therapist seeks to aid the patient by subtly, often indirectly, implanting or inducing the idea or belief that unpleasant or disabling symptoms are being relieved. The successful use of suggestion requires that the physician manifest an attitude of assurance, professional authority, and sympathy. The patient, because of his respect for and confidence in the physician, tends to accept the idea presented. His critical ability is lessened and his mood is influenced. His attention becomes narrowed. In his state of expectancy, he comes to believe that the results predicted will actually take place.

The best results in suggestion therapy are secured when there is no deep-seated disturbance of the personality, as in hysterical conversion symptoms of recent and superficial origin, or in anxiety states following accidents. The employment of electricity, massage, or manipulation in conjunction with suggestion is not advisable, since the patient may attribute the recovery to external agencies. In such cases, the recovery is frequently not permanent and at best is only the disappearance of a symptom and not a cure. In the event of a probable recurrence, the same agencies must be employed in exactly the same manner and frequently by the same person.

Suggestion does not, of course, give the patient any understanding of the cause or dynamics of his disability, and in hysteria, it tends to fix even more firmly the usual propensity to receptivity so characteristic of that disorder. It tends to restrict rather than increase insight. Even though a symptom is relieved by suggestion, the problems and psychological needs that produced it remain unchanged and their evasion may soon be sought by some other symptom. For this reason, the use of suggestion should be accompanied by some kind of re-education.

INDICATIONS AND APPLICATION. In spite of the limitations of suggestion, its use may be considered permissible in children, in persons of limited intelligence, and in immature, hysterical personalities.

Assuming, for example, that the symptom to be removed is a conversion symptom, such as a recent paralysis, the physician deals with it by direct suggestion accompanied by some explanation about the nature of the paralysis. The attitude must be one of conviction and certainty, inspiring confidence in the patient. The physician demonstrates that the capacity for passive movement still exists and informs the patient that no organic disability that can interfere with function is present. In referring to the patient's disability, the physician comments about what a nuisance the disability must be. At the same time, the patient is instructed to attempt to move the extremity naturally and without forced effort. The patient is apt to make the mistake of attempting the movement by a strenuous effort that leads also to an innervation of the antagonist group of muscles, resulting in a rigid immobility. The initial movement usually is very small. By persistent encouragement, its range is increased slowly.

The interview, with its atmosphere of conviction, must continue until voluntary exercise of the function is restored, even though an hour or two is required. Additional persuasive sessions may be necessary to bring about full function. The physician, through the very full life story he has obtained from the patient and through a knowledge of the circumstances under which the disability occurred, must be able to convince the patient of the meaning and purpose of the symptom.

The physician must be careful both in word and manner not to create the impression that he considers the patient to be either feigning or exaggerating his inability. Anything that will tend to offend the patient's self-respect must be avoided. Ross emphasizes that the atmosphere of the interview during which the physician attempts removal of the symptom must be one of reasoned logic and of scrupulous avoidance of dramatic demonstration or of artful deception. The patient would prefer to believe that manipulation or some agency outside of himself removed the disability, but he must be made to see that no external interference was instrumental. The patient must be convinced that the disability disappeared because he recognized its purpose and unreality.

The loss of the symptom is at first accompanied by a feeling of relief and pleasure, but unless he fully recognizes the sequence and relation of events and feelings, the patient may suffer a relapse when again confronted with the same problem or unpleasant situation from which the symptom had unconsciously provided an escape. In that case, the sense of relief is followed by anxiety, sleeplessness, mild depression, physical distress, and perhaps by disability. A frank discussion of the situation with the patient may enable him to make an emotional adjustment to it; again, if the problem springs from the environment, a removal from the source of the difficulty may be wise.

Suggestion often is done with narcosynthetic uncovering and is repeated later with the patient fully conscious.

Supportive Therapy

Supportive psychotherapy is anxiety suppressive. It seeks to diminish anxiety through reassurance, modifying the social environment through changing living quarters, hospitalization, or by prescription of anxiolytic medication. It may be either prolonged or brief, depending on the nature of the patient's problems. No attempt is made to produce insight, although the therapist recognizes resistant defenses or removes the patient from the anxiety-provoking environment. This permits respite and time for the restoration of personality organization. Sifneos believes that anxiety-suppressive psychotherapy of the brief type is the method of choice for those who are able to maintain a job yet feel strongly the need for assistance, recognize that their symptoms are psychological in origin, and are willing to cooperate with the therapeutic effort.

The patient is seen one or two times a week; medication is prescribed when indicated to relieve symptoms while the therapist ascertains the social pressures to which the patient is exposed. The therapist may assume the decision-making functions of the patient for a short time, as well as encourage specific actions that may resolve the conflict situation. He gives concrete and detailed advice on how to achieve the patient's desires. The therapist will predict the patient's future behavior on the basis of his past performance and rehearse his reactions to an anxiety-provoking task to cope with the affects which will be aroused when he takes action. In many respects, anxiety-suppressive techniques are similar to those used by many in crisis intervention.

BEHAVIOR THERAPY

Behavior therapies have evolved from the methods devised by Pavlov, Watson, and others to produce conditioned reflexes in animals, as well as from the various studies on reinforcement theory by American psychologists, commencing with the studies by Thorndike and elaborated by Hull, Skinner, and their colleagues. The behavior therapies are founded on the premise that all social behavioral expressions, healthy or maladaptive, are learned or represent distortions or deficits in the learning processes of the growing human being. Therefore, they are considered to be subject to modification through processes that extinguish those original learning experiences that led to the establishment of a repetitive pathological response. Where deficits in behaviors are considered the cause of the abnormality, more effective behavioral responses will be engendered by exposure to new learning experiences. Such experiences must be associated with arousal of emotion in the form of gratification (pleasure) or aversion (pain). Mowrer provides a historical review, a critical commentary, and a significant bibliography on the subject. Eysenck's recent revision of theory is described in Chapter 22, The Neuroses.

Perhaps the major difference between behavior therapy and the psychodynamic therapies is the emphasis that the former places on the control of behavior through its "consequences," rather than identifying its origin in antecedent experiences so change can be effected. The emphasis in behavioral analysis on identifying ongoing and current factors that maintain pathological behavior has greatly clarified treatment concepts because it demands more extended and careful scrutiny of the constant rewarding or aversive social controls to which the patient is exposed. Following the recent controversies between those espousing one or another approach, a desire is emerging to examine the operations of the several methods of treatment to determine their similarities and differences.

As Hunt has stated, in practice behavioral theories are so general that they often fail the behavioral therapists in formulating treatment plans to assure the desired behavioral change. Some of the difficulty rests in the obscurity of the subtle rewards offered in the social environment, and in the lack of importance attached to the internal rewarding or aversive systems of the individual, as contained in his or her ego ideals and superego. Hunt believes that those behavior techniques that rely upon extinction are confronted with serious difficulties. Eventually, he believes, the more successful procedures in behavioral therapy will be those that directly strengthen or substitute desirable or constructive behaviors for the undesirable.

Behavior therapy demands both a careful analysis of the stimulating situation inducing or perpetuating psychopathology and also individualization of the learning situations to bring about change in the individual patient. As practiced today it often consumes as much time as more traditional psychotherapies. Its rudiments will be found in the treatment of phobias by Freud and persuasion techniques for conversion symptoms described by Ross.

Indications

Precise recommendations for the prescription of behavior therapy remain obscure. At present it may be said that the method of desensitization is successful in treating phobic states. In a study reported by Gelder and his colleagues, patients with phobic symptoms who were treated with nine months of weekly desensitization sessions showed more improvements than a comparable series treated by individual psychotherapy once a week for one year. There were, however, more dropouts from the behavioral therapy group. Symptom substitution did not occur over a two-year period, and patients who showed improvement in symptoms also reported similar changes in their adaptation with others, both at work and during leisure. Wolpe and Lazarus, particularly, report the successful use of the method in a variety of neurotic conditions, including compulsive states and sexual aberrations, and include in their series patients treated without success by other psychotherapies.

Operant conditioning methods have been tried with some success in improving the verbal performance of mute, autistic, and mentally defective children, stutterers, and enuretic children. They have been used to mold constructively the socially deficient behaviors of regressed and nonproductive schizophrenics as well as the senile demented. *Reality orientation programs* for the elderly fit into these categories of treatment. Goals are clearly specified and reinforced with "*token economies,*" in which patients are rewarded with a token by exhibiting the desired behaviors. They exchange the tokens for food, bed, hospital privileges, and small luxuries. Under such treatment programs, many long-term hospital patients increase their self-care and group activities. Sustained behaviors in extra-hospital adaptation will be produced only when reinforcement techniques are planned for and sustained in outpatient settings.

It is possible that excessive bureaucratization of token economy programs may lead to such antitherapeutic effects as rewarding or aggravating pathology and diminishing socialization and interpersonal growth.

Treatment Techniques

Major characteristics of behavior therapy, as practiced now, are as follows:

(1) The focus is on maladaptive behavior rather than on any assumed disease process in a personality disorder or conflict. The therapist attempts to find observable and measurable aspects of behavior; compulsive handwashing, phobic avoidance, or a cardiac irregularity are examples. The therapist will pay attention as well to cognitive processes, imagery, and subject affect when they are related to the analysis for modification of symptoms. Use is made of the patient's verbal reports, self-rating scales, and any autonomic indicators that might be studied.

(2) The treatment of an individual's problem with behavior therapy is essentially experimental manipulation of variables to lead to a modification of the unwanted behavior—the dependent variable. The approach is direct, based on a hypothesis about the genesis and maintenance of the symptoms.

(3) Goals are specifically declared, after discussion with the patient and the family. This requires very detailed clarifications of the patient's objectives in seeking treatment and the possible consequences for the patient, his family, and those in his social environment if change takes place.

(4) The therapist will establish suitable measuring techniques so that the change consequent upon the behavioral interventions that provide either rewarding or aversive control may be monitored.

In treatment, the therapist directs his attention particularly to the patient's overt behavior, ignoring the subjective aspects of the patient's life. He attempts to define the identifiable life conditions which control and perpetuate the undesirable behavior. No effort is made to identify the underlying precursors in experience, the associated subjective symptoms, or the presumed motivating forces. In contrast to other psychotherapeutic procedures, little attention is paid to the patient-therapist relationship and transference phenomena. The aim of treatment is modification of symptoms rather than personality characteristics.

Through a careful history, the therapist notes the patient's complaints, their expression in overt behavior, the situations in which they are expressed, and particularly the preceding associated situations and the succeeding behavior of the patient. The therapist analyzes this information to decide whether the symptom represents a conditioned response to an isolated fear-arousing situation, a response aroused through generalization of the initial emotionally charged situation, or a response that is perpetuated through its social consequences. It is then necessary for the therapist to devise a series of experiences capable of easy manipulation by him that may be applied to modify the antecedent, emotionally arousing stimuli. Such experiences or techniques now are commonly referred to as (1) desensitization, (2) reciprocal inhibition, or (3) combinations of the two. If the analysis of the behavioral response indicates that the behavior is maintained as the consequence of the social relationships after the act or as a deficit in experience, methods are arranged of *positive* and *negative reinforcement, aversive control,* or *extinction.*

In the *desensitization technique* the patient is repeatedly exposed to stimuli similar to those inducing the abnormal response (phobias) but at such low intensity that arousal does not occur. Over time, the intensity of the exposure is increased by slight degrees until the patient is able to expose himself to the original stimulating situation without responding inappropriately. The *reciprocal inhibition* technique exposes the patient to a situation in which the original, emotion-inducing response is elicited but in competition with another emotion of greater intensity. For example, stimuli directed toward muscular relaxation may be provided simultaneously with the original anxiety-inducing stimuli. Wolpe and Lazarus have been the major proponents of techniques combining the two methods just described. The reader is referred to their writings. For the treatment of antisocial behavior, such as abuse of alcohol or drugs, *conditioned avoidance* methods have been tried. These methods have been used with varying success for a number of decades. Here the therapist pairs the pleasure-giving situation with an unpleasant response, such as the induction of vomiting with

apomorphine or creation of a neurovascular response with Antabuse.

Reinforcement methods are those in which desirable behavior is rewarded on its appearance by the immediate provision of a pleasurable substance or response. In the case of nonspeaking children, as soon as a patient utters a sound, the therapist gives a candy. With successive trials and appropriate shaping of the sounds to words and later sentences, the reward is provided, though not necessarily on a regular repetitive schedule. In animal experiments, schedules of intermittent reward have proved more effective in inducing learning than regular schedules.

Negative reinforcement schedules also have been tried. Here an unpleasant or painful situation is established and the production of a wanted behavioral response is the signal for relief. *Social conditioning* used in psychiatric hospitals, such as isolation through detention, or deprivations later mitigated upon good behavior probably represents long-tried shaping techniques of this type. Extinction technique has been successful in some instances when the undesirable behavior was reinforced by the obvious attention of family members or of hospital or clinic staff. Here, instructions that the patient's behavior be ignored have in some instances led to improvement. Another technique of value in the treatment of some patients has been that of *negative practice.* The patient is requested to practice the undesired behavior particularly at those times when he experiences the usual emotion inducing the behavior. The explanation for the value of this method is not clear in the theories of behavior therapy. Very likely it rests upon the personality trait of negativism, and the use of this technique is indicated when such a factor is clearly present. Here the reader is referred to Haley's *Strategies of Psychotherapy.*

In *implosion technique,* the therapist directs the patient to close his eyes and imagine situations from his history known to induce anxiety—thus important areas of conflict in a patient's life are discovered. The patient is instructed to imagine these key scenes and attempt to experience as much as possible the related anxiety, tension, or other affect. Observing the reactions of the patient, such as crying, muscle tension, or anguish, the therapist then suggests more imaginations likely to elicit the most anxiety. He will progressively bring the patient to imagine his most fearful conflict situations, which are generally related to aggression, past rejections, sexual matters, and guilt. The clinician symbolically reproduces the original stimulus cues that elicited the symptoms. Since there is no recurrence of the feared event, primary reinforcement does not occur and extinction takes place.

Biofeedback

Biofeedback training is a form of behavioral therapy. Through bioelectric instrumentation, the subject is provided immediate visual or tonal feedback indication of change in action potential information, i.e., his conscious efforts to modify physical status. As an example, verbal instructions are given to individuals with anxiety-related muscular disorders, such as tension headaches or backaches, about programmed relaxation. In the training sessions, the patient is connected to an electromyogram, which provides a recording of the degree of muscular tension. The impulse is modified and amplified in the form of an auditory tone, which becomes lower in pitch as the muscles relax. In visual training, a light diminishes as muscles relax. Instrumentation or programming for biofeedback training has become increasingly sophisticated, to allow the individual to modify various physiological states, including muscle tone, to visualize changes in blood flow in fingers, and to monitor

alpha rhythms in electroencephalograms or electrocardiograms. Biofeedback has been used in an attempt to modify a variety of psychophysiological disorders. In reviewing the literature, Blanchard and Young find that critical assessment today supports its value only in the elimination of tension headaches and of subvocal speech while reading. At the present time, there is little evidence that biofeedback eliminates cardiac arrhythmias, lowers blood pressure, or reduces epileptic seizure frequency.

Alpha biofeedback—the visual feeding back of brainwave patterns to the subject who is instructed to attempt to produce alpha (7.5 to 13.5 cycles per second) brain wave activity—has been tested to produce the "alpha" state of relaxation and peaceful awakefulness. Acoustic tone is commonly used as the feedback mechanism when the alpha waves are not being produced.

Interestingly, the *transcendental meditation techniques* of Eastern religious groups are associated with prominent alpha wave activity, as well as other physiological changes, including decreases in heart rate, cardiac output, and respiratory rate, with increase in skin resistance. The metabolic rate of the body is also reduced during meditation. Whether the biofeedback technique, which requires extensive instrumentation, or the meditative technique will be preferred as a means of providing relaxation and associative physiological change is under assessment now. Some believe that meditation is preferable to biofeedback in providing states of general and muscular relaxation whereas biofeedback is preferable for patients with specific psychosomatic symptoms. Very probably the personality organization and values of the individuals will decide their choice to learn personal control of bodily functions and to bring relief from anxiety, tension, and associated abnormal, psychophysiologically induced states.

SOCIOTHERAPIES

Contrasting with those therapeutic processes in which the patient is treated by an individual therapist—the dyadic transactions described earlier in the chapter—in which the goals are directed to changes within the individual personality, there are various sociotherapies or group transactions directed to the alleviation of stresses and conflicts between the personality and the social system.

There are many existing variants of group treatments concerned with aiding the individual to cope more effectively with the social milieu. He may be in need of a clearer perception of the interrelations, modes of communications, emotional conflicts, and related defenses existing within his family. He may have been deprived of socializing experiences beyond the family, or may have projected his perceptions of the idiosyncratic social relations of his own family onto those relations beyond the family group.

The effective diagnostician will assess not only the individual pathology of the patient but also that reflected in his transactions within the social system of which he is a member. Through the use of one or several of the group processes available, he has at his command methods of effecting the social perceptivity and transactional capacity of his patient that in many instances seem more suitable and more effective in inducing social adaptation than the individual psychotherapies alone.

Perhaps the concept of the sociotherapies and their contribution is best realized in the context of contributions of the various psychotherapeutic disciplines to the ego development of the hospitalized patient. All of those working within a well-run and organized hospital, a therapeutic milieu, must be imbued with the concepts of acting as agents in treatment of the admitted patient. In their contacts, they constitute the members of a therapeutic community.

Today the term *therapeutic community* is most often used for the functions of small face-to-face units employing group processes, organized toward democratic decision making and permissiveness, yet linked to reality confrontation of unacceptable behaviors. A small group of patients and staff live and work together and struggle toward improved communication and understanding of each other's behaviors. Behaviors that disturb individuals or the group are subject to direct confrontation.

Thus Edelson describes the *work group* in a therapeutic community as functioning to give to the individual participant and his ego system an input, generating, maintaining, or restoring reality testing and mastery through improvement of his skills. Its organization contributes to goal orientation to directly validated measures of accomplishment. On the other hand, the group in the *activities program* stimulates the individual's commitment to seek and enjoy, to accept gratification in esthetics, and social transactions, and their attending excitement, thus reducing the affective sense of despair in deprivation. Such groups contribute to the expansion or restoration of the positive affective response within the personality. *Patient governments* or community councils motivate the participants to identify or achieve common and shared ends, thus establishing the value systems of acceptable or nonacceptable between members of the group. The contribution to the personality system here is to the superego. Finally, the small *family group* motivates to respect of institutional values and assists the inclusion of daily experiences with values and meaning, thus confirming the value system. In turn, these groups influence the individual personality through development and support of the ego ideal.

One may view the sociotherapeutic subsystem of the hospitals in the various group experiences directed by occupational and recreational therapists, nurses, social workers, and mental health aides as assisting the patient's ego and superego development. He is helped to master the social system through development of the skills and methods needed for adaptation.

GROUP PSYCHOTHERAPY

Group psychotherapy had its beginnings in the work of J. Pratt, who, in 1905, initiated the use of didactic discussion and inspirational group meetings to bring about a favorable change in the morale of physically ill patients whose activities were restricted. The first patients to be treated in such groups were the tubercular; later, others with various psychosomatic conditions were treated. As experience has broadened through successive testing of this treatment technique for the psychoses, the psychoneuroses, and the various behavior disorders of adults, adolescents, and children, there have evolved both theory and technique that are significant in understanding, recommending, and pursuing treatment. Since the number of patients that may be treated simultaneously by a single therapist is considerable as compared with individual treatment, those concerned with management of massive programs of patient care have actively encouraged the widespread dissemination of the various group psychotherapeutic techniques. However, presumed expediency is the least powerful argument for recommending group psychotherapy.

Indications

Group psychotherapy neither supplants individual psychotherapy nor necessarily offers itself as a substitutive treatment for those to whom other psychotherapeutic doors are closed. On the contrary, there are specific indications for its use. Slavson notes that certain patients manifest aversion to the individual therapies because of fear,

competitiveness, distrust, or antagonism toward all authority figures. Individual psychotherapy is too threatening and the patient finds in the group the acceptance and support necessary for the examination of his problems. For such persons, group psychotherapy alone may be successful, or it may serve as a preparation for individual treatment. Patients lacking sibling experiences, having antagonistic sibling attitudes, living in situations without opportunities for participation, experiencing destructive family relations, showing character disorders, presenting evidence of generalized social maladjustment, or fearing homosexual involvement with an individual therapist are often selected for group treatment. Patients with dull intelligence may benefit more from group therapy in peer groups than from individual therapy. Generally, all children gain from group association, and it is believed that many children who need therapy are suitable candidates for the activity form of group treatment. Exclusive group treatment is frequently considered successful when feelings of inadequacy, sibling rivalry, and social maladjustments are the presenting problems in children. Analytical group psychotherapy is considered the treatment of choice for adolescent girls with confused sexual identifications.

Group psychotherapy provides an opportunity to relive and correct in capsular form many distorting experiences of earlier life which have arisen in the context of situations creating destructive sibling rivalry, anxiety-provoking separations, loneliness, excessive spoiling, or exploitation.

The Psychodynamics of Group Process

Perhaps the most significant consideration giving rise to the concept of group interaction as a method of psychotherapy is the sociodynamic pattern of human maturation. The development of the infant from helplessness and dependency to tempered autonomy and acculturation takes place through a continuing series of transactions within a family and a series of extrafamilial social relations. If maladjustments are caused to develop by inadequate or unwholesome group situations during the formative periods of life, it should be possible to undo and modify them by exposing the maladaptations to continuous, structured group action in a more adequate and more wholesome setting.

Within all groups, the emotional processes that take place over time are centered upon the leader. In psychotherapeutic groups, the therapist occupies this role initially. The patient members of the group are tied to each other through their common bond with the leader. The group functions unconsciously as a family, with the leader representing the parental role, usually initially that of a parent, as an authority figure. Each member of the group then assumes the role of a sibling in relation to the other group members. Toward the therapist the various members project their transference expectations and fantasies, while toward their fellows in the group they find similar expectations derived from their family experiences or they live through processes of sibling interchange lacking in early life.

In the newly constituted group, the patient members are individually dependent and submissive to the therapist. The formation of the group around the leader in an authoritarian position is enhanced when the members are anxious and unsure; thus patient groups more rapidly assume the regressive position in relation to the therapist than do other nontherapeutic groups concentrating on some task orientation. Authoritarian leadership is considered to enhance the submissive dependent relationship and therefore is eschewed in the therapeutic group, where the leader allows a free interchange. In this interchange the group members are encouraged to respond to

each other and the leader freely. Thus disagreement and criticism are possible, as is a new type of identification in which the critic may identify with the criticized. This opens to the individual patient in the group a new opportunity for personal evaluation and opinion.

In this treatment process, the therapist may become a model for admiration and thereby a focus for a new ego ideal, a model for superego change or growth, or a source for identification through either love or fear. Similarly, the relation to other group members later provides opportunities for alternative identification.

In the therapeutic group, the individual member may act out his ambivalent affects toward authority and his peers. In his revelations through both verbal and nonverbal communications within the group, the individual has the permissive support of the leader and his peers in assisting him to reveal himself. Also he is exposed to awareness of his verbal distortions and the unconscious meanings of his mannerisms through the interpretative comments of his peers, a process which creates much reality checking and re-evaluation of personal motivations. Some group members live through new emotional experiences within and through the group transactions and thereby achieve greater understanding of both personal and interpersonal reactions.

Experience with therapy groups has revealed that the principles of treatment employed in individual psychotherapy are applicable to groups. The relationship between each member and the therapist possesses the qualities of individual therapy, and in addition all the patient-members become, in a sense, auxiliary therapists, thus increasing the emotional interplay. The group setting is a continuous reality factor, which presents an ever-fresh stimulus and provocation to behavior that may be therapeutically directed. Although the group support diminishes individual anxiety, many group therapists feel that the amount and character of affective interactions may be increased and accelerated.

The group situation is such that mechanisms are mobilized for self-defense against real or imagined threats occasioned by the presence of others. In large part, this is a result of *transference*, the avenue through which projections, displacements, and other mechanisms operate. While the entrance of this attitudinal force into the group work presents a barrier, it becomes the very focal point toward which therapeutic interpretations and insight formations are directed.

Systems of Group Therapy

From the early group techniques of inspirational lectures, there evolved group and individual discussions with the leader following his didactic presentations. Simultaneously Trigant Burrow applied to the evolving group therapy theoretical principles derived from psychoanalysis while Kurt Lewin in Germany was working out his field theories and explanations of group dynamics.

From these early experiments in group treatment many variants have been developed. Thus S. R. Slavson, who pioneered analytic group psychotherapy in the United States, derived his conceptual schemes from his experiences in the study of group psychodynamics of children with behavior disorders, a form of treatment organized around manual activities which he designated *activity group therapy*. J. L. Moreno developed the procedures of *psychodrama* and *sociodrama*. In the former, two or more patients interact with each other but are instructed to act out differing roles; in the latter the patients are the audience.

In England, during the 1930s, Joshua Bierer initiated experiments in which, through group discussions, a passive therapist attempted with a circle of approximately ten patients to bring about attitude change through impersonal discussion of interpersonal issues. S. H. Foulkes, the founder of the Group Analytic Society and the first to utilize psychoanalytic principles in group psychotherapy in England, initiated this treatment procedure at the Maudsley Hospital.

Other groups have been established with problem-centered approaches directed toward guidance. Among these may be included Alcoholics Anonymous, as well as those groups established for narcotic addicts and homosexuals and for parents of children with cerebral palsy or mental deficiency. In such groups, ego strength is enhanced through identification and sharing with others and the growing awareness of and increasing ability to cope with common problems shared by the group members. Later, if such groups remain cohesive, they, too, bring into the open the conflicts and associated emotions, as well as the early contributing parental transactions, upon which the individual psychopathologies rest.

There now exist group therapies which are essentially nondirective and which have a psychoanalytic orientation, as well as others which rely on more directive procedures based upon didactic or educational principles.

To be separated from the above are the nonclinical groups that aim to improve understanding of the group process to assist in development of assets for leadership, management, counseling, or other roles.

Such "sensitivity," "encounter," training or "T" groups are widely sponsored now by industries, universities, social agencies, and other organizations. In contrast to the group psychotherapies, the conduct of the group process differs in that the leader or trainer initially and generally assumes a nonresponding role—the group is structured to appear leaderless. The members of the group struggle to effect group structure, including leadership, procedures, and task orientation, and in so doing, reveal to themselves and others their customary patterns of behavior in relating to others. The conduct of such groups often has been given to leaders or trainers whose psychological knowledge and training remain undefined. Nor, until recently, have there been efforts to screen those enrolled in the group, many of whom have been participants on the basis of pressure from the organization in which they are employed. It has become apparent that a number of participants develop acute emotional disturbances during such encounters, and a few have become overtly psychotic. The incidence of such psychopathological reaction is currently unknown. Stone and Tieger surveyed 105 applicants for a church-sponsored "T" group experience and screened out 15 whom they considered to have evidence of psychopathology, while 8 failed to attend. Even following screening, two had disruptive emotional reactions. In another study of a wide variety of encounter group experiences Yalom et al. report 16 casualties among 209 individuals participating in encounter group experience—a high rate of disturbance. Lack of structure, the lowering of psychological defenses, and in some, the encouragement of extra-group contacts, including the physical, seemed to have precipitated ego disorganization through emergence of unacceptable aggressive, sexual, or dependent striving.

To prevent such reactions, it has been recommended that participation be voluntary and informal, that participants be screened, that leaders define the limits of permissible behavior and that those in need of psychiatric assistance be excluded.

In some instances, group processes are used to modify attitudes for political purposes, as in "brainwashing" methods employed by certain political organizations. Religious revival meetings also rest upon principles of group interactions that influence individual behavior and attitudes.

Among the group psychotherapists and those concerned with the use of group processes for other purposes, there are controversies today about whether the principles upon which both rest are similar and convergent. There are those who believe that the group process, with its aim of bringing awareness of the interactions for the benefit of the group as a whole, tends to diminish psychotherapeutic processes for the group members. Others, such as Durkin, stress that all groups are comparable as they have a dynamic basis in ego interaction.

Technique

When possible, it is considered desirable to convene interview groups in round table formation in esthetically pleasant surroundings with an informal atmosphere predominating. Activity therapies may require work tables and a meeting room constructed of especially durable materials. Because of extratherapeutic acting-out, which may limit group work or fragment the group, it is usually desirable to separate the sexes. Groups may meet at any time of day or evening on a rigidly scheduled basis. Except for the intensive therapies, the group convenes once a week for periods of 60 to 90 minutes. More frequent meetings are necessary for groups having deep insight goals.

The proponents of the analytical psychotherapies urge that the *group leaders* have had personal intensive psychotherapy and further training in psychopathology. It is believed that group psychotherapists should have special training in the therapies, including a broad didactic educational background as well as a penchant for this form of treatment. The personality and motivations of the group leader are of importance; it is felt that therapists who normally experience discomfort in groups should not undertake group therapeutic leadership. A competent therapist of either sex may be a group leader.

When both group and individual therapy are required for a patient, the therapist must be the same person.

When leaders provide a preparatory session in which the group participants are advised as to the nature of group therapy in dynamic terms, it has been observed that there evolves the development of those transactions conducive to the goals of treatment. The therapists advise that the aim of the group work is toward fostering group and personal maturation. To effect change, the members are to immediately express their feelings and thoughts in relation to the group interactions.

Many groups maintain "open" *membership*, allowing participants to terminate therapy when they wish to do so and permitting others to join at any time. As a rule, the deeper the insight goal, the less variable the group membership. Some groups set date limits, while others go on indefinitely for several years. Goals, number of participants, and systems of therapy vary according to whether the groups are composed of hospital or clinic patients. Group psychotherapy is used in mental hospitals, outpatient clinics, private practice, affiliate therapeutic agencies of educational institutions, family agencies, with relatives of hospitalized patients, and with children. Certain groups employ a totally permissive atmosphere without rules. Some groups employ agreed-upon taboos relative to group work. Many leaders, for example, regard it as desirable to inculcate ethical principles in the group relative to privileged communication and to forbid physical acting-out during meetings.

Group homogeneity and the number of participants are still debated subjects. Too much unification of interest may present the therapist with a symptom wall used as a rallying point for group resistance in the form of monothematic ruminations. On the other hand, too little homogeneity causes scattered interest. Extreme heterogeneity, e.g., alcoholic patients mingled with symptom-neurotic patients, or psychotic persons with transference-neurotic patients, may engender name-calling and mutual distrust. The groups should be large enough for an adequate amount of interaction, yet not so large that members are neglected. In formation of groups for psychotherapy, experienced group therapists suggest that the patients selected be of the same sex, reasonably close to one another in intelligence, reasonably close in age, and fairly well balanced as to traits. Homogeneity of sex helps prevent acting-out. Similarity in intelligence is found to be important because misplaced retarded patients may delay group development. Closeness in age is significant because of the need for some uniformity in social values, outlook, and philosophical points of view. Group balance is needed in order to avoid overloading with a particular group of symptoms that may, as mentioned, serve as a wall of resistance against the therapeutic effort. Generally, groups fare well when they are made up of multiples of a basic triad of patients: the activator, the mollifier, and the passive recipient.

The criteria for denying patients admission to therapeutic groups depend largely upon the orientation of the therapy involved. Most groups suffer from the inclusion of acute psychotic, aggressive paranoid, regressed schizophrenic, and manic patients. Patients with psychoses tending toward depression or those with potential or overt perversion, suicidal behavior, psychopathic personality, involutional states with compulsive and obsessional drives, or hallucinated thought-life are generally excluded from analytical groups. Such patients tend to disrupt, dominate, and exploit the group. They may also stimulate pathological processes in a deleterious way in other patients. In general, it is the feeling among group therapists that patients must have some capacity to participate in groups and at least a minimal amount of social hunger to gain from a therapy group.

The most significant factors which

lead to early *dropout* from group psychotherapy appear to rest upon such personality disturbances as inability to tolerate intimacy; shame resulting from maladroit self-disclosures; marked deviancy from the group norms (in terms of age, ethnic difference, or degree of pathology), or need to compete with the leader by setting up a competing subgroup or acting as the group provocateur. Other factors which lead patients to separate from therapeutic groups have to do with personal incapacity to share the leader, inadequate orientation to the group treatment procedure, conflicts engendered when the patient is simultaneously in individual psychotherapy, and various external reasons related to undue stress and anxiety in the life of the patient. Failure to continue in group psychotherapy bears no relationship to the individual's ability to profit from some other form of psychotherapy or treatment.

Group Dynamics

In contrast to individual therapy, group psychotherapy more closely resembles actual life situations and ordinary social intercourse, thus endowing the process with continuous reality meanings. In individual psychotherapy, all attitudes, conditionings, and transferences are isolated in the patient and channeled into the one participant-observer, while in group interaction there exist a multiplicity of targets and a dilution of transference. These have both positive and negative values. On the one hand, these factors reduce anxiety and fear activated by hostile and aggressive feelings toward figures of authority, and they allow for redirection or deflection of the hostilities and resentments toward fellow members. On the other hand, these factors may add an almost insuperable complexity to the production of insights. This is due to the multiplicity of possible emotional interrelationships.

MECHANISMS. Probably all groups traverse phases of development roughly approximating three periods: (1) a stage of *group unification* with the emergence of group identity; (2) a stage of *group interaction* with the observation of dynamisms; and (3) a final stage of understanding and *resolution of dynamisms* with the production of insights.

Therapy takes place at different levels according to group goals. The factors of mutual support and reliance engendered by group sanction parallel the formation of group esprit and contribute toward the establishment of morale, which may be all that is desired for some groups. Simple ventilation through the phenomenon of emotional release may relieve tensions in given situations. Popular superstitions and ignorance may respond to educative group reorientation, with the consequent lessening of fears and anxieties.

Analytically oriented group psychotherapies make use of the classical factors of catharsis, resistance, analysis of transference, interpretation, and insight formation. The leader plays an important role in interpretation when resistance must be overcome, also in the resolution of transference. The group setting offers opportunities for the manifestation of social mechanisms and dynamisms not ordinarily found in individual psychotherapy. In addition to those mentioned above, the following are a few commonly encountered.

Displacement. A variety of feelings toward the therapist, which the patient may be afraid to express, are displaced on less threatening group members or on persons not present.

Escape. This is achieved by selective silence or by a change of subject.

Deflection. This may be used for escape by redirecting attention to another group member.

Catalysis. This dynamism represents the manner in which each member activates all the others. Frequently it is valuable, especially in institutional group psychotherapy, to transplant a particularly alert or well-indoctrinated member as a nuclear cadreman, around whom new groups may be built. Such a catalyst accelerates early group work.

Identification. This primary mechanism in personality development is the insigne of civilization and enters importantly into the therapeutic process.

Universalization. This is the term given the dynamism occurring in patients when they discover that other people have problems similar to their own, that others entertain the same forbidden thoughts or experience similar unacceptable impulses. This mechanism alone is considered by some to be therapeutic. It reduces guilt, heightens self-esteem, and diminishes emotional burdens.

ADVANTAGES. Frequently small groups not only have supportive value but permit the expression of hidden anxieties and conflicts. Also members, by seeing their unconscious motives in action in the ways the members feel toward each other and the therapist, may gradually gain insight into their difficulties.

Anxiety, shame and guilt may be reduced and transference modified in group psychotherapy. Some therapists claim that a depth of insight comparable with that of individual psychoanalysis may be attained.

An important consideration of group therapy is the realization that in chronically aggressive children the very antagonisms and violent hostilities that constitute their antisocial tendencies are factors common to such groups and tend to promote unit formation, while the non-neurotic elements of the ego respond to the persevering interest and patient of the group leader.

The mobilization of certain defenses may be all that is desired in the treatment of many psychotic patients. The group process often encourages re-repression of unconscious fantasies that present themselves clinically as delusions. As the psychotic mechanisms are removed from consciousness, more normal ego elements resume their supremacy and the patient may become eligible for noninstitutional life or individual psychotherapy.

Mention should be made of the ever-increasing senile segment of the population, with whom considerable group therapeutic work is now being done in some institutions. A significantly greater number of senile patients so treated are enabled to return to better levels of adjustment than without group therapy. The group process appears to increase alertness, dispel confusion, bring affects toward normal, and improve memory and orientation. Often, incontinence is found to diminish in many patients on this program.

Results of Group Therapy

The statistical evaluation of therapeutic results of group work, as in all the therapies, remains largely impressionistic. A recent study of 22 juvenile delinquents treated with interview and activity group therapy and of the same number of controls revealed statistically significant improvement in the experimental group as measured by psychometric tests, school achievement, and maturity tests, as well as by Rorschach personality assessment technique. Also, neurotic depressions are said to respond well to group psychotherapy. Most therapists of well-constituted groups report results that compare favorably with those of individual psychotherapy.

FAMILY THERAPY

With the expanding awareness of the importance of the interactions between family members in shaping and maintaining behavioral patterns of the individual (the psychic defenses and adaptative processes), family therapy has emerged within recent decades as an important new therapeutic technique. Experience with individual psychotherapies in the correction of psycho-pathology revealed the difficulty of bringing about changes in symptoms or maintaining gains achieved when individual patients were treated separately from the family group and then returned to the still-existing pathogenic milieu in the home. Too, when individual psychotherapy succeeded in bringing about substantial changes in symptom expression and more effective social adaptation, sometimes there were observed shifts in family homeostasis that led to frank appearance of psychopathology in other family members and, at times, dissolution of the nuclear family. Several decades ago a number of psychoanalysts and child psychiatrists commenced experimentation with various forms of family therapy. In some instances, members of the family were treated individually, with the therapists meeting regularly to consult each other; in others, married partners were treated simultaneously, either on a regular basis or through spaced conjoint meetings with a single psychotherapist. Family therapy as it is practiced today is best represented in the efforts of Ackerman, Jackson, and their associates. In their practice, the therapist meets regularly with the members of the nuclear family, significant relatives, or members of the extended generational family—that is, parents and grandparents.

Indications and Contraindications

Family psychotherapy has found its greatest application in the treatment of those neurotic, psychotic, and personality disorders in which individuals "act out." Thus indications for its use are aggressive behaviors leading to maladaptation of children or adolescents at school or in the community, the various addictive states in adolescents and adults, and marital disharmonies with their roots in the complicated transactional processes of an extended family. Where psychotic defenses in an individual are perpetuated or clearly aggra-

vated by re-exposure to a conflict-ridden family situation, family psychotherapy may prove the necessary adjunctive method to assist in establishing social rehabilitation.

Family psychotherapy is not advised for children or adolescents when one or both parents are known to have an established paranoid psychosis or a history of a personality disorder with traits of dishonesty, deceitfulness, untruthfulness, or recurrent antisocial behavior. The existence of a threatening family secret or of fixed cultural or religious prejudices against such treatment also contraindicates its trial. Treatment is inadvisable if there is a physical disease that precludes participation by one or more family members, or if a family nember has fixed rigid psychological defenses which, if stressed by the anxieties of the treatment, might induce ego disruption and a psychosomatic crisis or a psychosis. Further, family therapy should not be initiated if breakup or dissolution of the family by an irreversible conflict is imminent.

Family Theory

The family is the indispensable social unit necessary for the growth and maturation of its various members. Without the maturing protection from excessive emotional arousal and the learning processes so important to later social adaptations that take place in the family, the growing members suffer personality warp or even failure. The transactions within the healthy family determine the stability of the later social adaptations of its various members. Within the family, its members express both similarities and differences in their modes of interaction. Their individual character traits and talents supplement and complement each other or may be the source for frustration of needs and desires and thereby induce family conflict and fragmentation.

The complementary aspects of family

transactions enhance the self-esteem of the individual members, satisfy their needs, support their defenses in the face of anxiety induced within or without the family, assist in their efforts at solution of conflict situations, and support the development and fulfillment of each member's personal abilities and drives.

As the capacities of the maturing individual change and his personality emerges, it is inevitable that conflicts should wax and wane within the family. Family conflict has potential for both assistance and restriction of growth of each individual within the group. As Ackerman points out, "Competition and cooperation in family relations are not necessarily opposites. The true opposite of cooperation is not competition but apathy and indifference."

When the differences within the family become threats to the individuals, instead of being perceived as valuable, then family conflict leads to splits, with family members aligning against each other or selecting one or several members as scapegoats. The family conflict organizes around the selected member, who may be ill or who may be the family troublemaker, pet, clown, or presumed most talented.

Family conflicts center over differences and their presumed perquisites, passivity versus activity, controlling domination versus pleasure seeking, obedient versus defiant behaviors, drives for positions of power and wealth versus their relinquishment or destruction. Various members of the family group may alternately or regularly play the domineering role, that of persecutor, scapegoat, or mediator.

Family conflicts may be resolved rationally through their clear perception by the involved members or through their containment by various compensations while solutions are sought. When the family members misperceive or distort their relations with each other, then the conflict situation leads to such accretions of emotion that one

or several members act out or become isolated in the special roles mentioned beforehand. The theories of Bateson and Jackson and of Johnson and Szurek, mentioned in earlier chapters, are most pertinent in the comprehension of family conflict as it relates to pathological behavior and defective communication. It is under these circumstances that family psychotherapy may assist in a solution of the family crises and of the pathology engendered in the family members.

Technique

The primary aim of the family therapist is the mobilization of a rational and effective communications system between the family members—one which brings to awareness the hidden and distorted expressions of emotion that pervade the disturbed family and adversely affect the sick member or members.

The family therapist must take the position of a participant observer within the family group. He initially invites the family to meet with him as a group to discuss the problem of the referred member. In the initial discussion, he may see husband and wife, parents and children, or the extended group. It is considered preferable to meet with the group without prior effort at gaining a formal history of the family. The therapist notes how the family members enter the room and the seating arrangement they establish spontaneously. On successive treatment sessions he ascertains whether repetitive patterns of association and communication exist between particular family members. He notes those who dominate the commentary, those who interrupt, coerce, deny, or express their reaction through such nonverbal communications as frowns, smiles, or other bodily movements, or by withdrawal.

It is then his function, through clarifying questions and interpretations of behavior, to assist the family to become more open in their communications, to reassay and reorganize their patterns of coercion and malalliance, and resolve conflicts by exposing their emotional responses to the real and unreal differences they perceive among themselves. The therapist uses his own personality and requires that the family members express their transference perceptions of him. He must be active, questioning, and at the same time supportive of those family members who bear the brunt of family attack in the course of the treatment sessions.

Family psychotherapy differs from group psychotherapy; the members of the family bring to the psychotherapeutic process various roles and patterns of interaction long since established. The therapist's role as a leader is less sharply perceived in the initial phases of family psychotherapy, whereas in group treatment that position is evident from the initial meeting. Furthermore, the aim of the therapist differs. His hope is to bring about a change in the family as an ongoing social institution. The group psychotherapist uses processes that emerge in an artificially constructed group to assist the individual members in achievement of useful personality change, but is not committed to shaping that process for any permanent function.

BIBLIOGRAPHY

Psychoanalysis

Abraham, K.: Selected Papers on Psychoanalysis. London, Hogarth Press, 1927.
Adler, A.: The Practice and Theory of Individual Psychology. New York, Harcourt, Brace & Company, 1956.
Freud, S.: The Interpretation of Dreams. New York, The Macmillan Company, 1933.
Fromm-Reichmann, F.: Notes on the personal and professional requirements of a psychotherapist. Psychiatry, 12:361–378, 1949.
Fromm-Reichmann, F.: Principles of Intensive Psychotherapy. Chicago, University of Chicago Press, 1950.
Glover, E.: The indications for psychoanalysis. J. Ment. Sci., 100:393–401, 1954.
Greenson, R. R.: The Technique and Practice of Psychoanalysis. New York, International Universities Press, 1967.
Havens, L. L.: The existential use of the self. Am. J. Psychiatry, 131:3–10, 1974.
Kubie, L. S.: Practical and Theoretical Aspects of Psychoanalysis. New York, International Universities Press, 1950.
Langs, R.: The Technique of Psychoanalytic Psychotherapy. 2 vols. New York, Jason Aaronson, 1974.
Sandler, J., Holder, A., and Dare, C.: Basic psychoanalytic concepts: IV. Counter transference. Br. J. Psychiatry, 117:83–88; V. Resistance. 215–221, 1970.
Shapiro, A. K.: Placebo effects in medicine, psychotherapy and psychoanalysis. In Bergen, A. E., and Ganfield, S. L. (eds.): Handbook of Psychotherapy and Behavior Change: Empirical Analysis. New York, John Wiley & Sons, 1971, pp. 439–473.
Silber, A.: A patient's gift: Its meaning and function. Int. J. Psychoanal., 50:335–341, 1969.
Ward, H. P.: Shame—a necessity for growth in therapy. Am. J. Psychother., 26:232–243, 1972.
Weber, J. J., Elinson, J., and Moss, L. M.: Psychoanalysis and change. Arch. Gen. Psychiatry, 17:687–709, 1967.
Weber, J. J., Elinson, J., and Moss, L. M.: The application of ego strength scales to psychoanalytic clinic records. In Goldman, G. S., and Shapiro, D. (eds.): Developments in Psychoanalysis at Columbia University. New York, Hafner, 1967, pp. 215–273.

Psychotherapy

Bure, J. D., White, H. S., and Havens, L. L.: Which short-term therapy? Matching patient and method. Arch. Gen. Psychiatry, 36:177–189, 1979.
Fiske, D. W., et al.: Planning of research on effectiveness of psychotherapy. Arch. Gen. Psychiatry, 22:22–32, 1970.
Frank, J. D.: The influence of patient's and therapist's expectations on the outcome of psychotherapy. Br. J. Med. Psychol., 41:349–356, 1968.
Garner, H. H.: Interventions in psychotherapy and confrontation technique. Am. J. Psychother., 20:391–404, 1966.
Haley, J.: Strategies of Psychotherapy. New York, Grune & Stratton, 1963.
Karasu, T.: Psychotherapies: An overview. Am. J. Psychiatry, 134:851–863, 1977.
Karush, A., and Ovesey, L.: Unconscious mechanisms of magical repair. Arch. Gen. Psychiatry, 5:55–69, 1961.
Kolb, L. C.: A new look at psychotherapeutic evaluation. In Talkington, P. C., and Bloss, C. L.: Evolving Concepts in Psychiatry. New York, Grune & Stratton, 1969.
Malan, D. H.: Individual Psychotherapy and the

Science of Psychodynamics. Boston, Butterworths, 1979.

Mann, J.: Time-Limited Psychotherapy. Cambridge, Mass., Harvard University Press, 1973.

Marmor, J.: Recent trends in psychotherapy. Am. J. Psychiatry, 134:409–416, 1980.

Miller, W. B.: The telephone in outpatient psychotherapy. Am. J. Psychother., 27:15–26, 1973.

Ross, T. A.: The Common Neuroses. Baltimore, William Wood & Company, 1937.

Sifneos, P. E.: Short-Term Dynamic Psychotherapy. New York, Plenum Press, 1979.

Suess, J. F.: Short-term psychotherapy with the compulsive personality and the obsessive compulsive neurotic. Am. J. Psychiatry, 129:270–275, 1972.

Narcosynthesis

Dysken, M. W., Kooser, J. A., Haraszti, J. S., and Davis, J. M.: Clinical usefulness of sodium amobarbital interviewing. Arch. Gen. Psychiatry, 36:789–794, 1979.

Marcos, L. R., and Trujillo, M.: The sodium amytal interview as a therapeutic modality. Curr. Psychiatry, 18:129–136, 1978.

Naples, M., and Hackett, T. D.: The amytal interview: History and current uses. Psychosomatics, 19:98–105, 1978.

Hypnosis

Barber, T. X.: Suggested (Hypnotic) Behavior. The Trance Paradigms Versus an Alternative Paradigm. Medford, Massachusetts, The Harding Foundation, 1970.

Clark, W. C., and Young, J. C.: Acupunctural analgesia? Evaluation by signal detection theory. Science, 184:1096–1098, 1974.

Frankel, F. H.: Hypnosis and related chemical behavior. Am. J. Psychiatry, 135:664–668, 1978.

Hilgard, E. R., and Hilgard, J. R.: Hypnosis in the Relief of Pain. Los Altos, Cal., William Kaufmann, Inc., 1975.

Kroger, W. S.: Acupunctural analgesia: Its explanation by conditioning theory, autogenic training and hypnosis. Am. J. Psychiatry, 130:855–860, 1973.

Li, C. L., Ahlberg, D., Lansdell, H., et al.: Acupuncture and hypnosis: Effects on induced pain. Exp. Neurol., 49:272–279, 1975.

Marks, I. M., Gilder, M. G., and Edwards, G.: Hyponosis and desensitization: A controlled prospective study. Br. J. Psychiatry, 114:1263–1274, 1968.

Spiegel, H., and Spiegel, D.: Trance and Treatment. Clinical Uses of Hypnosis. New York, Basic Books, 1978.

Behavior Therapy

Behavior Therapy in Psychiatry. Task Force Report No. 5. Washington, D.C., American Psychiatric Association, 1973.

Chesser, E. S.: Behavior therapy: Recent trends and current therapy. Br. J. Psych., 129:289–307, 1976.

Gelder, M. G., Marks, I. M., and Woolff, H. H.: Desensitization and psychotherapy in the treatment of phobic states: A controlled inquiry. Br. J. Psychiatry, 113:53–73, 1967.

Hewett, F. M.: Teaching speech to an autistic child through operant conditioning. Am. J. Orthopsychiatry, 35:927–936, 1965.

Hunt, H. F.: Behavior therapy for adults. In Arieti, S. (ed.): American Handbook of Psychiatry. Vol. 5. New York, Basic Books, 1974, pp. 290–318.

Liberman, R. O., McCann, M. J., and Wallace, C. D.: Generalization of behavior therapy with psychotics. Br. J. Psychiatry, 129:490–496, 1976.

Miller, E.: The management of dementia. A review of some possibilities. Br. J. Soc. Clin. Psychol., 16:77–83, 1977.

Mowrer, O. W.: The behavior therapies, with special reference to modeling and imitation. Am. J. Psychother., 20:439–461, 1966.

Wolpe, J., and Lazarus, A. H.: Behavior Therapy Techniques: A Guide to the Treatment of Neuroses. New York, Pergamon Press, 1966.

Zeldow, P. B.: Some antitherapeutic effects of the token economy. A case in point. Psychiatry, 39:318–321, 1976.

Biofeedback

Blanchard, E. B., and Young, L. D.: Clinical applications of biofeedback training. Arch. Gen. Psychiatry, 30:573–589, 1974.

Gaarder, K. R., and Montgomery, P. S.: Clinical Biofeedback; A Procedural Manual. Baltimore, Williams and Wilkins, 1977.

Glueck, B. S., and Stroebel, C. F.: Biofeedback and meditation in the treatment of psychiatric illness. Compr. Psychiatry, 16:303–321, 1975.

Miller, N. E.: Applications of learning and biofeedback to psychiatry and medicine. In Freedman, A. M., Kaplan, H. I., and Sadock, B. J. (eds.): Comprehensive Textbook of Psychiatry. Vol. 11. Baltimore, Williams & Wilkins, 1973.

Raskin, M., Bali, L. R., and Peeke, H. V.: Muscle biofeedback and transcendental meditation. Arch. Gen. Psychiatry, 37:93–97, 1980.

Robbins, J., and Fisher, D.: Tranquility without Pills. All about Transcendental Meditation. New York, Bantam Books, Peter H. Coyden, Inc., 1972.

Shapiro, D. H.: Meditation and psychotherapeutic effects. Arch. Gen. Psychiatry, *35*:294–302, 1978.

Sociotherapies

Ackerman, N. W.: Treating the Troubled Family. New York, Basic Books, 1966.

Ackerman, N. W. (ed.): Family Psychotherapy in Transition. Boston, Little, Brown & Company, 1970.

Clark, D. H.: The therapeutic community. Br. J. Psychiatry, *131*:553–564, 1977.

DeWitt, K. N.: The effectiveness of family therapy. Arch. Gen. Psychiatry, *35*:549–561, 1978.

Durkin, H. E.: The Group in Depth. New York, International Universities Press, 1964.

Edelson, M.: Sociotherapy and psychotherapy in social psychiatry. Res. Publ. Assoc. Res. Nerv. Ment. Dis., *47*:196–211, 1969.

Jaffe, S. J., and Scherl, D. J.: Acute psychosis precipitated by T group experiences. Arch. Gen. Psychiatry, *21*:443–448, 1969.

Jones, M.: The Therapeutic Community. London, Tavistock Publications, Ltd., 1952.

Kadis, A. L., Krasner, J. D., Winick, G., and Foulkes, S. H.: A Practicum of Group Psychotherapy. New York, Harper & Row, 1963.

Kaplan, H. I., and Sadock, B. J. (eds.): Comprehensive Group Psychotherapy. Baltimore, Williams & Wilkins Company, 1971.

Minuchen, S.: Families and Family Therapy. Cambridge, Mass., Harvard University Press, 1974.

Semrad, E. V., and Arsenian, J.: The use of group processes in teaching group dynamics. Am. J. Psychiatry, *108*:358–363, 1951.

Slavson, S. R.: Analytic Group Psychotherapy with Children, Adolescents and Adults. New York, Columbia University Press, 1950.

Stone, W. N., and Tieger, M. E.: Screening for T groups: The myth of healthy candidates. Am. J. Psychiatry, *127*:1485–1490, 1971.

Whitaker, D. S., and Lieberman, M. A.: Psychotherapy Through the Group Process. New York, Atherton Press, 1964.

Yalom, I. D.: A study of group therapy dropouts. Arch. Gen. Psychiatry, *14*:393–414, 1966.

Yalom, I. D., Houts, P. S., Newell, G., and Rand, K. H.: Preparation of patients for group therapy. Arch. Gen. Psychiatry, *17*:416–427, 1967.

Yalom, I. D., and Lieberman, M. A.: Encounter group casualties. Arch. Gen. Psychiatry, *25*:16–30, 1971.

31

SOCIAL AND COMMUNITY PSYCHIATRY

"The characteristic traits of a clinic for mental diseases according to my conception should be, first, service to the patient rather than to an administrative system; second, elaboration of the study of the diseases rather than of means of wholesale handling of patients; third, possibilities of following up the studies of nature's experiments beyond the hospital period, and preventive work through extramural efforts outside of the hospital.... I consider it of the greatest importance that the clinic may itself be responsible for the mental health work of a fairly well circumscribed unit of population so as to make possible studies of the social situation and of the dynamic factors which lead to the occurrence of mental derangement that must be attacked for purposes of prevention."

Adolf Meyer

ADOLF MEYER
(From National Library of Medicine, Bethesda, Maryland.)

The elements of the field of social and community psychiatry were formed from pressures dislodged by the humanitarian movements of the nineteenth century. In that great ferment arose a multitude of observations upon the extent of psychiatric disability, its attendant emotional stress upon others, its social and economic consequences, and its more frequent occurrence in certain forms among the most deprived.

From its earlier impressions of the wide extent of impaired personality functioning, the scientific community has progressively extended studies of prevalence and incidence in differing cultures, under varying circumstances of social stress. New instruments detect the existence of impairment and provide quantitative measurements of degrees of social stress and also impairment. Sociologists, cultural anthropologists, social psychologists, and psychiatrists have contributed to these investigations. Those whose principal interests are therapeutic and preventive have examined both the individual and the institutional framework surrounding their efforts, pieced out the weaker or deleterious treatment methods, and proposed new hypotheses for treatment intervention or prevention of disability. This chapter incorporates many of the social influences determining occurrence and expression of mental illness that were mentioned in Chapter 6, and elaborated in the description of the clinical syndromes—most notably in those chapters discussing the psychoneuroses and psychiatry in medicine. This chapter also describes the newer hypotheses and methods now applied in attempts to expand the benefits of mental health intervention to those who in the past have been relatively neglected or even deprived of the opportunity for assistance.

The terms community psychiatry, social psychiatry and preventive psychiatry are often used interchangeably. Here, *social psychiatry* is defined as the research effort to discover newer methods to delineate and suggest information required in the practice of psychiatry. Changes are sought in the social settings, either in small or in large groups, that would sustain mental health, prevent mental disability, or expand therapeutic or social rehabilitative intervention.

Community psychiatry defines the practice of psychiatrists who are interested in applying all measures that are directed to the promotion of mental health and the prevention of all mental disabilities to large population groups in all their diversity. The commitment is to continuity of care and the provision of treatment for the patient as close to home as possible and within the catchment area. Community psychiatric practice employs professionals in all mental health disciplines as well as indigenous nonprofessionals. Local citizen participation is encouraged in planning, advising, and evaluating. Prevention is emphasized, and the programs are perceived as a part of both the general health care system and the public human network system.

Community psychiatrists, therefore, will acquire information from the social sciences, particularly the disciplines of sociology, anthropology, and political and economic science. They are required to comprehend to the fullest all the social stresses that impinge upon the groups to whom their professional talents are to be devoted.

The concept of *preventive psychiatry* has been extended by psychiatric epidemiologists beyond that of *primary prevention* to include interruption or modification of the environment in such a way as to avoid entirely the occurrence of a psychiatric disability. The development and widespread application of vaccination to prevent smallpox is an example of a primary preventive measure. Primary prevention has sharply reduced the occurrence of the psychiatric disabilities caused by organic brain disease consequent to infectious and toxic processes. Identifying metabolic disorders in infancy to prevent the development of mental retardation in such conditions as phenylketonuria is another highly successful primary prevention. *Secondary prevention* is taking therapeutic measures to restore an individual suffering from a mental or emotional disability to improved health or to the pre-existing status. *Tertiary prevention* includes all those measures and interventions taken to establish a maximum degree of personality functioning in those who are suffering disabilities that are persistent, progressively deteriorating, or both.

History

It is worth noting that, from the very beginning, the movement to improve and expand services for the mentally disabled has been characterized by the energy and driving force of members of the lay public. They, along with interested physicians, psychiatrists, and other health professionals, urged and participated in persuading political leaders to support the evolving mental health services and organizations that have proved highly successful in modifying public attitudes toward the mentally disabled. They also pointed out the need for public and private support for these services, the training of mental health workers, and research.

In the U.S.A., in 1908, Clifford Beers (1876–1943) published *A Mind That Found Itself,* in which he described the treatment he had received in a mental hospital. He initiated the mental hygiene movement; in that same year, there was founded in Connecticut a society for mental health, with membership drawn from the educational, religious, and legal fields, as well as from workers in general medicine and psychiatry. A national society was established the following year. Beers allied with Dr. Adolf Meyer and the distinguished psychiatrist Dr. Thomas Salmon, who was in charge of the psychiatric services of the U.S. Army during World War II and was later the first professor of psychiatry at Columbia University, to establish the National Committee for Mental Hygiene. The goal of this society held to the public health principles of prevention and early detection and treatment, as well as calling for research into the etiology of all mental disabilities.

During the 1920s and supported by a grant from the Commonwealth Foundation, the child guidance movement in the United States of America was initiated. This movement was influenced strongly by psychoanalytic concepts, particularly by those hypotheses that emphasized the evolution of personality disorders in the adult as a result of conflictful situations occurring in the course of childhood development. At that time, prevention was sought through the establishment of child guidance clinics. Such clinics were characterized by the development of the team concept, in which a psychiatrist worked with psychologists and social workers. Both these clinics and the psychiatrists of the general hospitals provided services on site. The clinics functioned largely as receiving units for the acutely mentally ill and offered some clinic services to outpatients. The circumscription of practice then was due to the small number of professionals interested in the field of psychiatry, few of whom practiced outside the confines of city, county, or state mental hospitals, plus a few private ones.

The general burden of mental illness became increasingly apparent to state governmental agencies in the United States as more and more people were hospitalized for psychiatric disorders. This burden was particularly evident in the states exposed to the mass emigration from other countries. The continuing pressure from the high prevalence of mental illness and retardation was brought to the attention of the federal health agencies, and led to the development of screening techniques to prevent immigration of the mentally disabled to the U.S.A. The United States Public Health Service initiated training in psychiatry among a few of its personnel as early as 1915.

The enormity of personality malfunction in the American armed forces was discovered before the United States entered World War I in studies conducted among troops along the Mexican border. Similar findings were found in British soldiers engaged in trench warfare in France. For these reasons, the Surgeon General of the United States Army approved a selection process in the recruitment of troops to avoid induction of psychotic and mentally retarded men. Psychiatrists were assigned to the various services and a psychiatric organization was established to provide treatment as extensively as possible in therapeutic stations at major hospitals in both Europe and the United States. Because of then existing manpower shortages, the plan had a limited effectiveness. Nevertheless, it brought widespread public recognition of the existence of mental illness and the potentialities of effective treatment. Following the return of the many mentally disabled from the military services after World War I, the U.S. Veterans Administration was established and opened hospitals for the care of the psychiatrically ill. Simultaneous concern over the extent of narcotic addiction in the U.S.A. led to the initiation of research related to narcotic abuse by the United States Public Health Service. Within a few years, two large federal narcotic treatment centers were established, in which the medical-psychiatric administration and treatment were provided by the U.S.P.H.S. The expanding role of this federal service in screening of immigrants, research, and treatment of narcotic addiction brought about the development of its Division of Mental Hygiene.

Prior to World War II, the Division of Mental Hygiene of the U.S.P.H.S. initiated planning for the development of a National Institute of Mental Health. The goals of this institute were conceived of as providing federal government support of research and education related to the etiology, prevention, and treatment of mental disabilities in the U.S. Army. With the advent of World War II, the experiences of World War I were remembered and the Selective Service Commission was established to screen civilians for both physical and mental disabilities before entering the armed services of this country. Accepting volunteers, the U.S. Navy and Air Force developed their own neuropsychiatric screening groups and assigned psychiatrists to provide diagnostic and therapeutic direction to their various units.

Both during induction and after entry, large numbers of men were eventually discharged as unfit for military duty because of mental and emotional disturbances. Of these, relatively few suffered from the acute stress disorders of warfare. The need for large numbers of psychiatrically trained personnel led the armed forces to establish short training courses for physicians, to provide the needed psychiatric diagnostic and therapeutic services in all the combat areas, as well as in the areas to which the disabled were evacuated within the continental United States. From this wartime experience emerged a recognition of the importance of morale and leadership in preventing widespread emotional disability. The military initiated studies of organizational arrangements and administration as they affected military group interactions, both in Great Britain and the United States. Later, the new insights were applied in some business organizations.

Many physicians were influenced positively by the psychodynamic knowledge gained through their experience with psychiatry in the armed forces. On their return to civilian life, they formed an influential nucleus in development of psychiatric services in the community and in general hospitals, as well as in support of the development of a strong national program in mental health. The prewar plans of the U.S.P.H.S. for a National Institute of Mental Health were revived, and were supported by public pressure generated from the evident necessities of managing wartime manpower. Their pressure resulted in the federal legislation known as the National Mental Health Act of 1946.

The National Institute of Mental Health, as patterned under this legislation, made available grant monies for research, as well as for education in the four major mental health professions (psychiatry, psychology, social work, and nursing) and initiated community mental health services throughout the states. Grants from the N.I.M.H. made possible the expansion of psychiatric training in medical schools throughout the country, so the number of mental health specialists rose rapidly during the next 25 years. This cardinal federal legislation was followed in 1963 by the Community Mental Health Centers Act, which authorized financing of the cost of constructing and staffing comprehensive community mental health centers throughout the country. Such centers offer five major services and are directed to serve specific catchment areas—that is, to provide total mental health services for a delineated population living in a particular geographic area. But various states also legislated the development of community services. New York's Community Mental Health Act was passed in 1956 and California followed with similar legislation in 1957 and 1969. California's revolutionary legislation brought about decentralization of services to the county level.

The American legislation had been preceded in Europe, however, by a series of developments that demonstrated the potentials of delivering more effective psychiatric services through alternative facilities to those offered in the then existing institutions operated by the State. In England, as the result of the legislation that established national health services, and under the organizational structure established thereby, the *catchment area* principle was established throughout the country. Each service facility was responsible for all individuals who became mentally disabled within the assigned geographic catchment. Furthermore, such outstanding mental hospital superintendents as T. P. Rees (Warlington Park Hospital, Croydon, England), Duncan McMillan (Mapperley Hospital, Nottingham, England), and G. Bell (Dingleton Hospital, Melrose, Scotland) initiated the *open door policy* by allowing increasing numbers of patients full privileges to move about in the surrounding community. Their practical experience demonstrated the capacity of many of those who had been institu-

tionalized over long periods of time to function acceptably in a social setting outside the institutions. They and others observed that the stimulating experiences of life in the open society led to a lessening of the abnormal behavior and extreme withdrawal of large numbers of patients who had previously been considered hopeless. That social experiment for the institutionalized lessened the use of locked doors and physical and chemical restraints. As their experiment became widely known, it was adopted by the mental health authorities of many countries and shorter voluntary hospitalizations were attempted successfully.

In the meantime, owing to a housing shortage, the U.S.S.R. was forced to experiment with holding many seriously disabled patients in their homes, but provided *partial hospitalization* through *day care programs*, with respite for the families. The development was pushed by the psychoneurological clinics, to which were attached extensive workshops. These clinics also related their work to designated population groups and provided an outstanding demonstration of alternative methods of treatment of the mentally ill, organized countrywide as with the British system. Under the leadership of Querido in Holland evolved crisis intervention teams that made home visits to people reported as being disturbed and manifesting signs of mental illness. Through such visits, the teams were able to demonstrate that immediate intervention into the family or small living group was able often to relieve the conflict-inducing situation and prevent the necessity for psychiatric hospitalization.

Public support for the transition from institutional care of those with mental and emotional disabilities and the retarded to diagnosis and treatment in the community grew with the development of well organized and politically strong voluntary groups. In the U.S.A., the National Association of Mental Health, with its subsidiary state groups, and the Association for Retarded Children have been particularly important in educating the public and influencing legislative bodies about the needs for those so disabled. Other organizations that have advocated support for particular constituencies and are of importance to community mental health programs are the United Cerebral Palsy Association and the American Epilepsy Association. Some groups have come into being to provide therapeutic support of individuals with special symptomatic problems. We mentioned Alcoholics Anonymous. Others concern themselves with the prevention of drug abuse, with suicide, gambling, and autistic children. They, too, have now evolved roles of public education and advocacy. Finally, a variety of community agencies, including schools, churches, the Young Men's and Women's Christian Associations, and clubs in various countries, have offered support toward the social rehabilitation of the mentally disabled and retarded, as well as assistance in establishing facilities on a widespread and continuing voluntary basis.

CONCEPTS SIGNIFICANT FOR COMMUNITY MENTAL HEALTH PRACTICE

Those whose interests are directed to the goals of social and community mental health services must recognize that the level of operation is the *societal system*. This subsystem of the living system in general has properties particular to itself which are more than the sum of the individual components. Leighton points out that societal systems (the community) live on beyond the birth and death of the individual members of the society. Societies maintain or modify the value systems that define the acceptable goals, and the codes of conduct that establish conventional transactions between individuals and groups. Within each society, a variety of institutions evolve that enforce, protect, and maintain those values. One finds as examples governmental structures, legal structures, working or industrial structures, and educational, religious, and health structures. Such institutions insure protection, the necessary energic substances, and communications between the members of the individual communities within the different societies. Social systems across the world vary in many ways: the languages that they use to communicate, their capacity to provide this communication in symbolic (written) terms, the values and concepts they hold of the world, time, and space, appropriate relations between kind, and so on. The diverse sociocultural variants become of major significance to the community mental health practitioner. He or she must comprehend the various segments of the society to be able to influence change to foster support or modification of values.

In societies composed of individuals of diverse ethnic background, perception of differences in the origins of those he seeks to assist will alert and prepare him to develop procedures that will be acceptable to the individual or group who seeks or is found in need of care.

To put it another way, the values and orientations of differing ethnic groups, the impoverished, those with religious affiliations other than his own, or those who speak in another language, must be seen as a challenge to the community mental health worker to foresee the obstacles to making contact, planning, organizing, and effecting actions necessary to prevent or modify the course of any of the disturbances.

Leighton has hypothesized that societal systems may be adjudged to function well or poorly; he conceives a sociocultural disintegration of a societal system, or ineffective functioning of one or another of its subsystems. Such ineffectiveness is manifested in deficiencies in communication, weakness of leadership or followership, the inability of successful parenting in families, and the breakdown of shared values, expressed in increasing intergroup hostility and violence. Cultural disintegration has been manifested, particularly in the last several centuries, as different cultures have come into contact with each other. Predominant Western technological values have tended to erode and supersede those of the social systems with less technological advance. Increasing migrations of vast numbers of people from differing social systems into urban areas have produced almost worldwide breakdown of the cultural values of the immigrant groups, who often gather together in ghetto areas of today's vast metropolitan complexes. It is in these areas that the various studies conducted by psychiatric epidemiologists and other social scientists have disclosed the largest concentrations of those suffering from mental illnesses, drug abuse of various kinds, as well as other indicators of poor health, and from high rates of antisocial behavior demonstrated in delinquency and criminal activity.

In disintegrating communities, the breakdown of the family leads to deficiencies in child-nurturing and child-rearing patterns, with dissolution of values regarding acceptable social conduct. This leads to an increase in delinquency, later criminal activity, and the lessening of the influence of education. The assessment of the impairment in the child-nurturing effort is evident in higher frequencies of maternal deprivation, the absence of father figures, and difficulties in peer relations.

Furthermore, with psychosocial disintegration, the social stress is magnified as the individual becomes exposed to excessive frustration, fear, and disappointments in his aspirations. As mentioned in an earlier chapter, new techniques assessing the social stresses to which the individual is exposed have been devised. Perhaps the best known are those of Holmes and Rahe and those evolving from the Sterling County studies by Langner. The attempts to assess the degree of social disintegration in relation to psychological-psychiatric disability that have achieved the most recognition are the Sterling County studies, and the Midtown Manhattan studies undertaken by Srole, Langner, Michael and others. In addition to these studies, made largely in North America, there are many investigations of psychiatric disability frequency in a variety of other isolated communities, and in selected ethnic groups such as the Eskimos and differing African cultures.

In the next section, some of these findings will be described.

SOCIOCULTURAL SYSTEMS AND PSYCHOSOCIAL DISORDERS

Reliable evaluations of the extent of mental disabilities in various populations permit planning and development of the necessary manpower and facilities to assist those in need. Beyond that, examination of the relationship of social stress to the etiology or manifestations of such disability becomes useful in understanding what maintains or modifies it and what policies of government agencies might reduce its incidence and prevalence.

For over a century, researchers have reported a relationship between social status and psychological disorders. The paper of Jarvis in 1856 concluded that the "pauper class" in Massachusetts contributed disproportionately to the number of cases of "insanity." From the studies of Ferris and Dunham in 1939, which disclosed that the highest rate of disability occurred in slum sections in the central areas of cities, the hypothesis evolved that social disorganization might cause psychological disabilities. Others have suggested that the accumulation of people with mental disabilities in urban areas is due to their downward drift in the socioeconomic scale and the cheaper rents for the run-down housing there. Some argue that as genetic factors lead to the reproduction of disability, the consequence will be a higher retention of it in pools of people in certain areas. However, this argument is weak, since individuals living under adverse social and environmental conditions of urban ghettos may be situated there as the result of other biological and environmental deficits, such as poor nutrition and deficient family developmental processes, education, and socialization.

The relationship of age, sex, and social status to psychiatric disability has been discussed in the chapter on precipitating and predisposing causes. The relationship of ethnic and class status is less clear. *Ethnicity* is defined as distinction among individuals relating to skin color, religion, language, and national origin. *Social status* relates to the opportunities for obtaining acceptance from others, job successes, and the material resources available from the individual's own family and lineage. Sociologists have differentiated a series of status groups and have pointed out the many significant interclass differences, not only in styles of living, but also in the presumed degrees of stress to which those in differing styles are exposed.

Within the field of psychiatry, most epidemiologists have been concerned with individuals who have been admitted to the system for treatment, but it has become increasingly apparent that such studies provide inaccurate estimates of the incidence and prevalence of disability, since the availability of services varies so widely in different areas of the world, and even within different sections of countries. Also, it is clear from numerous studies that attitudes toward entrance into the mental health system—that is, the willingness to accept treatment, vary between different cultural groups and social classes. These attitudes are influenced by possible shame or anxiety arising from perceptions of the social significance of

such treatment and the changes it might occasion in the social network in which they live. We may state, then, that rates of prevalence measured by individuals who come to treatment are inadequate as evidence of the extent of psychological disorder in general populations.

As the Dohrenwends concluded from their critical analyses of some 44 studies performed to date, it is not possible to come to any firm conclusion about the etiological significance of the social status of the individual and his psychological disorder. The range of those presumed to have psychological disorder extends from 1 to over 60 per cent of the population. The explanations of these differences are many and varied: the designs of the studies were different; the lengths over which the rates were computed are in no way comparable; age ranges vary as well as sex, race, and social class.

In certain of the studies questionnaires alone were used, from which the evidence for psychiatric disability or psychological disorder was extracted solely from the responses. In others, questionnaires were followed by interpretations made with information provided by the responders. In some, records of individuals were reviewed, as well as some direct contact with those who were regarded as disabled; in still others, all subjects considered to be mentally or emotionally disturbed were interviewed. In the latter studies, only a few had an associated physical examination. An analysis of the questionnaire methods disclosed that when the responses obtained from the index used (Cornell) were analyzed by physicians, many questions were found that would allow the interpretation of the existence of a physical disorder. It is known, too, that response bias to interviewers as well as to questions varies, depending upon the interpretation of the nature of the question when given to individuals of certain social classes or when wide variations exist between the social class of the interviewee and interviewer. This is particularly so when the response would be shame-inducing or when the interviewee tends to be passively acquiescent or to have been culturally trained to give positive answers about physical disabilities while repressing answers that might indicate emotional-psychological problems.

Another reason for the wide variation in the reported prevalence of psychological disorders in the general population is the failure to discriminate between acute and transient stress-induced symptomatology and the more enduring forms of mental disorder. It is well known, for instance, that when individuals diagnosed in the emergency rooms of general hospitals as suffering from chronic or transient emotional disturbance and receiving no treatment are examined after a short interval, one third will report themselves free of symptoms, another third will report some continuing manifestations, and another third will indicate the persistence of symptoms.

Within recent decades a number of psychiatric-sociological studies of populations within the United States of America have generated much discussion about the nature and interpretation of the findings, the strengths and weaknesses of the methodologies, and their usefulness as a basis for planning and construction of services to prevent mental disability. The well-known Midtown Manhattan Study carried out in New York City by Leo Srole and his colleagues demonstrates the differences in the findings when one compares the data derived from patients in the existing mental health systems to those derived from patients who are defined as suffering a psychological disorder on the basis of questionnaire survey methodology. For every 1000 people living in the Midtown section, according to the criterion used, 5 were confined to psychiatric hospitals at the time of the 1953 survey. In contrast, Table 31–1 shows the symptom expression classi-

TABLE 31–1 Home Survey Sample (Age 20–59), Respondents' Distribution on Symptom-Formation Classification of Mental Health		
Well	18.5%	
Mild symptom formation	36.3	
Moderate symptom formation	21.8	
Marked symptom formation	13.2	
Severe symptom formation	7.5	
Incapacitated	2.7	
Impaired*		23.4
N = 100%	(1,660)	

*Marked, Severe, and Incapacitated combined. (From Srole, L., Langner, T. S., Michael, S. T., Kirkpatrick, P., Opler, M. K., and Rennie, T. A. C.: Mental Health in the Metropolis; The Midtown Manhattan Study. (Revised and enlarged.) New York, Harper Torchbooks, 1975.)

fication of 1660 Midtown adults. It is evident that roughly one in five — 18.5 per cent of the respondents — was viewed by the team psychiatrists who examined the responses of questionnaires as free of other than inconsequential symptoms and regarded as "essentially well."

However, as stated, such surveys do not determine the numbers suffering from time-limited acute stress reactions, transient symptoms of anxiety and depression, or from the long-continuing and seriously impairing disorders as classified by the International Classifications of Disease or the American Psychiatric Association. Percentages in Table 31–1 indicating those incapacitated and with severe symptom formation closely parallel the figures in studies of those who are actually brought into the existing mental health systems in industrialized countries for treatment.

It is evident that the computed rates for those who use mental health systems in urban areas vary tremendously according to the districts compared. Table 31–2 shows the variations of the usage rates in the Washington Heights section of northern Manhattan. Hospitalization rates of the more disadvantaged areas, populated by blacks and Puerto Ricans, are from two and a half

TABLE 31-2 Psychiatric Admissions from Washington Heights Health District to Receiving Mental Hospital by Health Area in 1964 (Both Sexes)

HEALTH AREA		POPULATION CENSUS 1960	NUMBER OF ADMISSIONS	RATE PER 1000 POPULATION
North	1.10	25,313	54	2.13
	1.20	23,731	72	3.03
	2.10	25,246	78	3.09
	2.21	22,607	51	2.26
	2.22	18,000	25	1.39
Central	3	21,490	57	2.65
	4	26,366	107	4.06
	5	26,061	115	4.41
South	6.10	15,780	101	6.40
	6.20	18,299	107	5.85
	7.10	9,382	59	6.29
	7.20	14,617	95	6.50
	9	22,385	101	4.51
Total		269,277	1,022	3.80*

*Rate for total admissions in 1964.
(From Gruenberg, E. M., Kiev, A., Stein, Z., and Wiehl, D.: Who are the Washington Heights psychiatric patients? In Kolb, L. C., Bernard, V. W., and Dohrenwend, B. P. (eds.): Urban Challenges to Psychiatry. Boston, Little, Brown & Company, 1969, p. 157.)

to three times greater than those from an immediately adjacent area where first, second, and third generation Irish-American and German-Jewish Americans reside. But even here interpretations must be made with care, since services other than hospitals were lacking for the high usage groups, whereas there were a number of community hospitals with psychiatric services and also a large medical center geographically available to the white groups, who came from a slightly higher socioeconomic class. What one may derive from the information presently available is the necessity for a more even distribution of mental health services for the mentally ill, the mentally retarded, and the drug abusers. Provision of local preventive, rehabilitative, and educational supports is also necessary.

A stronger central administration of the mental health services appears required. The fact that all the other indicators of social disintegration—impaired physical health, increased delinquency, and criminality—are high in those urban areas with high rates of psychiatric hospitalization suggests that much more must be done by government in general to improve the quality of life there.

Similar suggestions of the correlation of mental disorder with evidence of social disintegration have come from the studies of Leighton and his colleagues of a number of rural communities in Nova Scotia. The Hollingshead-Redlich study of services given to various socioeconomic classes revealed the differential care given. It has proved invaluable in directing the attention of those practicing community psychiatry and responsible for the allocation of resources to the necessity for a more equitable distribution of services to the populations that appear at greatest risk—those in the lower socioeconomic groups.

Role of the Psychiatrist

From the foregoing, it is evident that the social role of the psychiatrist practicing in the community may vary considerably from that generally held in the private office, mental health clinic, or general or psychiatric hospital. This is particularly so when he or she relates to those in need from ethnic and socioeconomic groups other than his own and when to provide care he must extend his professional knowledge by training and working with other nonprofessionals.

The terms "role" and "transaction" require definition. *Transaction* defines those reciprocal and reverberating processes ongoing in any system, including behavioral systems, whether between two individuals or the members of a group, phasic or cyclical. The transaction interchanges in a behavioral system tend to be self-regulating and self-correcting to maintain the overall function of the system.

Social role is defined as the description of behavior from the vantage point of a social situation. The term does not describe the artificial role-taking of an actor. Rather, it relates to the cultural standards that define the part in which the individual functions in the social system. Thus the recognized roles in the mental health system are those of physician, psychologist, nurse, technician, rehabilitation worker, social worker, dietitian, and so on. Role descriptions are used constantly as a means of signifying actions of others and comprehending their talents, skills, or the potential stresses to which they are exposed. For example, physicians in their history-taking define patients in such roles as housewives, students, lead miners, ceramic workers, sailors, and others.

Such roles evolve from what motivates the individual, from social opportunities, and from cultural value orientations. For example, the role of a patient in pain will be expressed in the transaction with the physician in different ways depending upon the patient's cultural background. Zborowski described some variations well in a study of pain-complaining in a Veterans Hospital in the Bronx, New York City, where the patients came from old American (second generation U.S.A.), Jewish, and Italian families. In their transactions with the medical staff, the Italian and Jewish first-generation Americans were intense, voluble, and demanding in their requests for help. The "old" Americans tended to be quiet and stoical. The physicians in attendance, mostly old American, perceived the "new" Americans as highly emotional and tended to feel uncomfortable with or dislike them as too insistent. This attitude was reflected in their care-giving to those whose cultural backgrounds trained them to express pain and emotion in a manner other than that to which the physicians were personally accustomed. All the patients were equally motivated in their patient role to gain relief from the pain or distress they suffered, but the manner in which they behaved in the patient role was based on their cultural values.

Social roles are complementary—in the sense that the communication system between individuals in differing roles generally has certain expectable interchanges or transactions. The physician is allowed—indeed, is expected—by most societies to ask questions about various behaviors (sexual, excretory) that are denied to others except family or intimates. In addition, the allowable expectation or transaction is that the patient will respond. In this respect, one must recognize the difference between the concept of transference as used in psychoanalysis, in which the individual projects onto another the expectations and emotional sets derived from interaction over time with significant parental or other persons in his past, as against the role-learned transactions that arise from later experiencing in learning. In all transactions, both implicit (transference-like) and explicit, roles may be intertwined.

In community mental health, the role of the psychiatrist is unlikely to be that learned as a physician or a psychiatrist in a hospital or clinic setting. There the model of the physician is established as the medical expert in charge of a team of technical assistants, in transaction with a patient who is lacking in knowledge, and who, if given too much, is likely to respond emotionally, thereby interfering with necessary diagnostic and therapeutic procedures. A patient's expectable role attitudes are usually those of respect and gratitude. Such a model of physician-psychiatrist must be recognized as often inappropriate in the other roles the psychiatrists may be called upon to assume in the community mental health networks, where the roles may vary from administrator—to team leader—to team member—to consultant. Furthermore, the hospital-based expectable transactions with patients or clients will also differ, since the community psychiatrist must circumvent his own culture-bound values (often middle-class) in meeting and undertaking treatment with ethnic and deviant groups with which he may have little previous acquaintance or knowledge, and whose attitudes toward him may also be highly divergent from the role expectations of hospital practice.

The possibility of failure of the match between professionals in the mental health field (psychiatrists, psychologists, social workers, and rehabilitation workers) and their patients and clients has fostered the development of *nonprofessional indigenous mental health workers.* Because of their potential of making contact with the often doubtful, suspicious, or already denigrated individuals in various subcultures or deviant social groups, such workers have come to plan an increasing role in many community mental health centers.

Many of the difficulties in the community mental health operations stem from the failure of the psychiatrist and other mental health workers to recognize their particular roles in the system network of their commitment. Interprofessional conflicts have resulted over issues of authority, leadership, and specific forms of caretaking (who is the primary therapist?). Failures in the therapeutic bind and in its maintenance have frequently ensued owing to ignorance of differences in cultural values. Those in the community mental health centers need the information now available from the multitude of cultural anthropological works and reports in the field of *transcultural psychiatry.* The professional must define the subcultures to which he is related and know their values and social customs if he is to be successful in his social role of healer to the community.

Crisis Theory

Central to crisis theory is the homeostatic principle of the personality's tendency to maintain a stable level of functioning. In the face of a personality crisis, various psychological and physiological forces act to achieve balance and rectify the dysequilibrium — the latter is associated always with affective disturbance. Crisis theory embodies the notion of "coping" with stress. The theory also holds that in working through a crisis situation the potential exists both for further personality development and growth and for personality disruption.

Social role theory, just discussed, is significant in crisis theory as the individual is recognized as pursuing roles in relation to one or more social groups. Loss, threat of loss, or significant disruption of these roles constitutes the crisis situation. The individual threatened by or exposed to crisis is exposed to the affective discharge (sadness, anxiety, and so on) as a consequence, as well as to the need to learn a new role. Thus, the successful worker at retirement generally suffers loss of satisfaction in exercise of his skills, sadness because of that and because of the disrupted relationships with his fellow workers, as well as the necessity to "learn" the "retirement role" or some other role.

Crisis theory has its roots in psychoanalysis, social work, and sociology. To guide practice, three postulates may be derived from the theory:

(1) Major attention in any attempt at intervention will focus on the details of the crisis event and its subsequent course and outcome. In contrast to other psychotherapeutic methods, less attention is given to historical events or psychological processes.

(2) The potential is maintained throughout the crisis for growth of the individual through effective coping.

(3) People are perceived in an ecological perspective in their human and natural environments, with consideration of their view both of the psychosocial and physical world around them and their inner psychobiological world; interactions between the two can create crisis effects upon the individual.

Caplan, the leading exponent of crisis theory, outlines four stages of crisis. There first takes place an initial rise in tension that initiates the individual's automatic problem-solving responses. Second, with a further rise in tension, a state of partial or complete ineffectiveness follows. Third, with further tension, external and internal resources are mobilized to cope. Fourth, if these fail, a breaking point is reached with consequent personality disorganization. In the later stages, mounting anxiety, depression, and feelings of helplessness and hopelessness are accompanied by progressive degrees of regressive behavior.

At any stage, the personality crisis may end with removal of or solution of the problem in such a way that compensatory satisfactions are gained for the threatened loss or after recognition and acceptance of the loss. Generally, the duration of the acute stage of a personality crisis runs from four to six weeks.

It is clear that for centuries personal crises have been supported by many, other than psychiatrists. Family members, friends, clergymen, and physicians have constituted the most common group of caretakers. The active role of the psychiatrist in crisis intervention relates to care of those at high risk for psychotic or neurotic personality breakdown; his function for the majority in crisis is as consultant.

Crisis Intervention

The general principles of crisis intervention were stated as: focus on the immediate event; recognition of the event as both a threat and an opportunity; and direction of the intervention to resolve the crisis problem within the individual's ecosphere. Crisis intervention arose from and is similar in many respects to the short-term dynamic psychotherapy described in the previous chapter.

At initial contact, avoid the assumption that the contacting individual is necessarily the person in need of help, but he or she should be involved in the process of discovery of the crisis event. His eventual role will be determined as the crisis intervenor proceeds with the first step in the therapeutic process—identification of the event that has precipitated the crisis. That analytic process is not unlike good general psychiatric history-taking, with the exception that concentration is focused upon discovery of some occurrence in the immediate past which has disturbed the equilibrium of an individual, a family, or group. In that analysis, any individual may or may not be recognized as clearly suffering psychopathology, as the person presenting in crises in some instances is responding to the psychotic or neurotic behavior of another. The intervention then may be directed to assisting an individual, a family, or a group.

In individual crisis intervention, the intervenor will keep in mind the more common crises for the age and development of the person. Deaths of family members, divorce, separation, loss of lovers, sudden disillusionment over behavior of an idolized person, serious physical illness of self or loved ones, arrests and sentencing for antisocial behavior, failures at school or work, and sudden unemployment or retirement are the most common crisis events. At different age periods, the likelihood varies. In adolescence and young adulthood, the common crises are the vicissitudes of dating, engagement, marriage, or childbirth. School or college activities or various jobs that test capacity of the individual to relate both to peers and to those in positions of authority, as well as aspirational strivings and failures can cause crises. These events also affect the parents of children and adolescents. In adulthood, vocational and social threats are more likely. At later ages, the most likely threats are the menopause for women, illnesses, bereavements, and retirement.

Once the intervenor, through his analytic probing, has identified the crisis event, he will attempt to formulate its emotional and psychodynamic effect upon the sufferer and decide the most effective intervention. Generally, interpretations are made of the intervenor's assessment of the event, its probable affective arousal on the individual, and the influence of that arousal on his and others' immediate behavior, and the related interactions. Subsequent discussions may touch on the changes common in working through the affective state, the alternative solutions to the social quandary, and the processes which may alleviate the affective state. The therapist will prescribe medication if this is indicated by the intensity of the emotional arousal and is appropriate to the personality disruption he sees. He will aid in the expression of affect when this has been suppressed or repressed. When rage and anger are to be uncovered, the therapist will make sure that the guilt and sometimes the shame associated with this affect are exposed and relieved beforehand.

The therapeutic approach emphasizes the reality situation. For this reason, the expression of infantile or childish affect and desires will be ignored and their expression discouraged. However, this does not mean that the therapist will force suppression of the appropriate affect—quite the contrary.

Adaptation is then aided by reviewing the possible solutions to the crisis. Those coping mechanisms which are foreclosed will generally be defined by the sufferer, who must be helped to see the inevitable loss, his affective reaction, and the solutions that will prove ineffective.

In closing the crisis intervention, the therapist reviews with the patient those matters that have been recognized and worked through, the positive changes that have followed, and the patient's plans for future coping. If there is evidence of ongoing psychopathology, the patient should then be referred to the appropriate source for continued treatment.

Family crisis intervention follows the same principles. The therapist here works with all family members along the lines described in the previous chapter. Often the therapeutic process is conducted in the home, resulting in a more rapid assessment of other significant persons and factors that might go unreported or be easily missed at the crisis center. Generally, in crisis centers the participation of other family members is suggested only to those who present themselves with the complaint.

Crisis group intervention involves the referral of the complainant to a crisis group who work through his problem with him, utilizing the principles and techniques described above for individual intervention. Here, too, attendance is limited to five or six sessions. Crisis group intervention is said to be particularly useful for the deprived and disadvantaged. It offers the members the unique opportunities of sharing experiences and thereby of providing ego and superego support, particularly for those of similar ethnic and cultural backgrounds.

Consultation

As a means of clarification of individual or group problems that have gone unresolved, and as an educational process to expand mental health manpower, consultation has played an increasing role in the mental health field.

The consultant should be an experienced individual with training in psychiatry or a related mental health profession. His consultation capacities are utilized in the areas of his singular competence. The client may be a colleague or peer, a student, or a group desirous of improving its functioning through transactions with the consultant. Consultation may be patient-centered, colleague-centered, or agency-centered. Psychiatrists are sought as consultants by their colleagues not only for individual patient problems, but also to guide their efforts in individual and group therapy, for administrative matters of all varieties of mental health, mental retardation, and drug abuse centers, and for research projects. The clients may comprise the range of mental health workers.

In his function as a consultant, the psychiatrist must ascertain initially the desired goals of his client; that is, the questions on which the client wishes to have an opinion, or the aims or emergent problems of the colleague or group to which he is to address himself. Often, the explicit reasons given for the consultation cover other less easily articulated or hidden requests, which emerge only as the consultant pursues his exploration.

As a consultant, the psychiatrist must attempt to identify all the significant groups in the network concerned as they affect the care of the patient or the achievement of the group's goal. Through judicious questioning and exploration, he will clarify the use or avoidance of alternative therapeutic processes in patient-centered consultation, or present positive and negative potentials of differing arrangements for administration, organization, decision-making, and acquisition of support to colleagues or agencies. In his role of clarification and facilitation, the able consultant avoids authoritative positions, and fosters open discussion and eventual decision-making through a transactional process. This process, if pursued with tact, patience, and avoidance of critical appraisals, has proved effective in setting or resetting therapeutic processes, alleviating group tensions and conflicts, and effecting needed change to aid facility and agency operations. In a sense, the keen consultant sets in motion and fosters the process of self-evaluation.

Consultants in the mental health field offer much through their knowledge and experience of personality, psychodynamics, and group process to others within and without the field. Beyond that, their special expertise in the areas of psychopathology and the various therapeutic modalities are of major value during patient- or colleague-centered consultation.

NETWORK THEORY AND PRACTICE

Approximately two decades ago, the concept of social networks was first used in the study of a small community. It use in the clinical field is recent. A social network may be defined as a set of linkages among an identified set of persons that is capable of interpreting the social behavior of the individual involved within the network. In practice, network concept is more loosely defined as the set of kinship or friendship links existing between an individual patient and close others. In general, it is valuable as (1) a recognition of a potentially curative grouping of individuals; (2) a location of resources; (3) a means of understanding the utilization of services; and (4) a means of analysis and eventual organization of an effective therapeutic concept of families involved with community-supporting agencies.

In use of the network concept as a potential for therapeutic grouping, the attempt is made to identify all significant friends, neighbors, and relatives of the family. In treatment, as many as possible of the total network will be mobilized into a social force with the aim of moving against the depersonalizing trend that is considered to have contributed to the pathology. The application of network theory in this way represents an expansion of family therapy. The reader will recognize that, although derived from another source, the network theorist works within the interpersonal definition of anxiety as given by Sullivan and referred to in earlier chapters on psychodynamics and psychotherapy.

As a resource group, the network is considered to provide for its members emotional, welfare, educational, and economic supports to complement those provided by other social institutions. By extension, employers, possessors of specific skills, and those capable of involving the patient in a belief system may be recognized as members of the network.

Some have pointed out the potential of network overload upon the individual patient who is incapable of sustaining the complexity of the context within which he lives. This potential exists particularly in families of schizophrenics. Others have emphasized that professionals may attempt to extract more resources for support than exist within the capacity of small networks related to an individual.

Network concept has been applied to research on the utilization of health and social services. The characteristics of those under-utilizing such services differ in terms of their network patterns of communication of standard behavior from those who do use formal health and social services. Also, network concepts have been helpful in studies of patient or client dropouts following one or two health-seeking visits to health, mental health, and mental retardation agencies.

Acceptance of the fact that social networks have characters of their own makes the concept useful in the attempts to unravel and make cohesive the health and social welfare contacts of those families who seek care from many organizations. "Interassistance conferences" become essential. It is known that the contacts of several agencies with a family may combine inadvertently, often to defeat each other's activities. To recognize the family and all of its caregivers as members of a network establishes criteria for intervention, as distinct from the traditional case conference.

Network therapists arrange to bring in as many as possible of the identified persons in the personal scheme for five or six sessions. The network generally meets with several therapists. Indications for network therapy are evidence that the network itself is moving from a closely integrative to a loose-knit form, or contrarywise to the distress of the concerned individual or individuals. Network intervention, too, is useful in the service sector in providing care to the kinship and friendship sectors at large when they are poorly connected and the caregivers lack knowledge of or acquaintance with each other. Another indication for such intervention is the interruption of the flow of communication from the personal to the kinship sector so that the distressed person is the recipient of behavioral advice from the others without reciprocal opportunity for himself. By such communication, the individual feels stigmatized. In such situations, the distressed person may be the continuing focus of "prescriptions for action." In treatment, it is possible for the therapist to clarify and compare the prescriptions given by the many in the network, to evaluate their effective quality and their ambiguity, de-emphasizing or modifying their conflicting messages, thus assisting the distressed person in his own determination of the course of action to follow.

Again, network therapy is helpful when it appears the patient has a problem maintaining contact with his family, his friends, and his caretakers. In this instance, the network's therapist will take the responsibility for bringing all together to define maintenance of needed supports.

Garrison gives in some detail a description of the therapeutic process. He refers to that process as a Screening, Linking, Planning Conference. As a form of crisis therapy, the initial conference should occur in time as closely as possible to the crisis itself. It can be conducted within the usual living space of the person in crisis or in his community. The participants convened should include the primary members of the ordinary social network of the distressed person. Usually, the most difficult to convene will be the most alienated and most significant network members. The therapist should, from the beginning, make clear the expectation of the distressed person's rapid resumption of social functioning, as well as the limits of therapeutic contact.

At the time of the initial contact with the patient, the therapist will identify the significant members in the social network and the current and past relation of these persons to the individual. He will assume the responsibility of convening a network gathering. At the meeting, the therapist will determine whether any significant persons are absent, and decide whether to proceed without those persons or attempt to make contact. From the members of the network, the therapist can start to define the complaints about the behavior of the individual in distress. It is the responsibility of the therapist to present this complaint list in terms of positive expectations for behavioral change, which will involve not only the patient but other members of the network. The therapist must be open to identifying the network resources available for providing satisfaction of the patient's needs, including biological drives, personal identity, intercession with one or more persons to assure the opportunity for a dignified relationship, provision for financial support if required, and assistance in the definition of the value system that will provide the resources for the patient to relate to his social world.

To support a positive identity for the distressed individual, the therapist will encourage reminiscing by the members of the network. Here will usually be discovered recollections demonstrating the ability of the person to cope in previous crises. If it is determined that the sick person requires hospital care

or other change in environment, the therapist will arrange for visits by the network members on the basis of the information obtained in the conference. He will hold himself responsible for establishing links to other agencies and helping groups. Each conference should end with explicit statements of the efforts to be made by the members before the next meeting, and a statement by the therapist that he is available for consultation.

PRACTICE OF COMMUNITY PSYCHIATRY

It is seldom that a single facility or institution in any community has the capacities to provide total care because of the diverse individuals who are suffering from mental disorder, the wide range of disabilities, and the differing degrees and stages of disability extant at one time. The goal of community psychiatry and the mental health center functioning as an organizer is to discover and fill the needs of those within its geographic or functional area. The population may be defined in terms of a "catchment area," as is most often the case when a community mental health center is established under the aegis of government. Sometimes, however, the responsibility of those working in the mental health center may be centered upon particular groups of individuals employed within an industry, the students of universities or colleges, clients of a social welfare agency, a prison population, the aged, or unmarried mothers.

In addition to providing care for those who are judged mentally disordered, the psychiatrist working in areas undergoing social disintegration finds himself involved with many problems that extend beyond delivery of psychiatric service. He or she will be confronted with families who make simultaneous demands upon social welfare systems, educational systems, and many areas of the health system (so-called "multiproblem families"). His particular knowledge and skills may be called upon in diagnostic, therapeutic, or consultant capacity, in the management of drug addicts, alcoholics, prostitutes, delinquents, probationers, people expressing degrees of social incompetence, or the individual who becomes a focal point of social unrest. Frequent and ready identification of the immediate emotional crisis will be his task. He may work with the crisis therapy team to bring about transactional changes to alleviate social distress.

Recognition of the extent of emotional problems within the members of all communities means taking the leadership in organizing much more than the resources of the primary mental health system. A cohesive therapeutic unit must be brought to bear, utilizing the public and private social organizations, the educational system, vocational training, and, at times, the correctional system. The attempts to assist multiproblem families living in areas of social disintegration amply demonstrate this need, as well as the need to integrate the efforts of these human support subsystems, as they often have intervened unbeknown to each other, resulting in fragmented, discontinuous, uneconomic, and ineffective service to distressed individuals or families.

Psychiatry has recognized in the past the necessity for the support of a variety of social agencies in attempting the rehabilitation of those who come to mental health systems with a distinguishable disorder appropriate for help. In some facilities, it has called upon and organized aid from social and vocational agencies, the religious community, and the legal societies, as well as voluntary organizations of one type or another.

The community mental health movement emphasizes the organization and administration of collaborative efforts of human resource networks for individual or family care from the point of ingress to the appropriate treatment,

residential support, reintegration into the community through resocialization plans, and vocational and avocational rehabilitation. Use of the network principles requires the community mental health center to build linkages between organizations that facilitate provision of appropriate services to the patient or client. At the point of entry into the mental health system through the community mental health center, the center either assumes the follow-up responsibility or sees to it that the admitted are provided the proper information, referral service and follow-up to assure that needed care is given.

With a central organization assuming responsibility there are variations in the functioning of the network. Where services are generally complete, the centers' primary focus is information and referral. Where gaps exist in the variety of facilities (general hospitals, psychiatric services, general hospital clinics or freestanding clinics, halfway houses, partial hospitalization, hostels, residential care facilities, county or state hospitals), the organization must assume the leadership in devising service network arrangements. For example, a university service might become the nucleus for aggregating all of the related subsystems to collaborate in providing the full range of services for the patients or clients in the area. This has been done in some cities. In communities where mental health services are seriously deficient, the opportunity exists to establish a comprehensive center maintaining representatives of all of the health, education, and welfare subsystems that provide assistance. Thus, the direct services that are necessary to provide psychiatric treatment in the community will extend beyond the direct clinical contact with patients to that sector of the population at high risk. Many of these find their way initially into other segments of the social system, such as caregiving agencies and the professions and organizations mentioned earlier.

In community mental health practice, patients and clients are encouraged to use all of the basic community services available to other citizens, to provide what is commonly called "normalization." In addition, every attempt is made to educate those in leadership positions in these services for understanding and full assistance of all who come with mental disabilities. Community mental health practice, therefore, involves both the psychiatric and nonpsychiatric resources of the community—a comprehensive network of caregiving agencies and professions which in Western societies includes both publicly and privately supported facilities.

ADMINISTRATION

Current goals in the practice of public psychiatry, particularly within the frame of the community mental health movement, determine the role practiced by the psychiatrist. He or she may function as the executive of a large federal, state, county, or city organization, or as a middle-level administrative person. He may be a team leader in the community clinic, a day care facility, a hostel, a department of psychiatry, an outpatient unit, or a community network of care, or serve only as a consultant or a team member.

According to Greenblatt, one may view administration as a technological system, as a system for policy formulation and decision-making, as a system of responsibility and accountability, or as a clinical social system. All such elements of system operation of administration will be discovered in any major administrative post, although weighted variously from organization to organization.

In a *technological system*, the administrator will concern himself principally with the efficiency of the operation. This model derives largely from the business world. Levels of authority and lines of communication are well defined, like those in the military organization. This organizational structure is seldom found suitable for health agencies, particularly those working with the social networks so characteristic of community mental health efforts. Nevertheless, today it is apparent that the health system is increasingly held accountable and greater demand exists for organization similar to the technological system. There is exposure from without to peers or groups set up to determine its responsible actions—in other words, assessing accountability. Today, various accrediting bodies regularly inspect hospitals to certify, recommend changes, and establish accountability. Their power rests upon public announcement of full certification, limited or probationary certification, or removal of certification. Such bodies provide a strong incentive to develop and maintain quality work and operation of health-related facilities; and confer respectability on facilities in the eyes of those who provide voluntary contributions. The administrators of the institution and its various subsections thereby are held openly responsible through the process of recurrent review.

Large organizational structures generally have within them today a program evaluation unit. In state organizations, such a unit may function through the process of providing certification before new units are established and reaccrediting the operating units at specified intervals thereafter. The administrator himself will recognize his responsibility for continuous analysis of the efficiency of the system he operates, and for monitoring those responsible for the variety of tasks that are required to assure human and safe care for the patients.

Evaluations of the influence of community mental health centers on utilization of various services, such as that made by Babigian, have shown that utilization rates increase in areas with such centers while hospitalization rates at large public institutions diminish. Furthermore, the generally underserved poor, children, and young adults are reached. Other evaluation studies have demonstrated the effectiveness of brief hospitalization programs versus standard hospital procedure for the majority of patients and have disclosed the strengths and weaknesses of such alternatives to long-term hospitalization of the chronically ill in relation to foster home care.

Administrative offices of the organization are concerned with general support, relationships with the business world outside, as well as with personnel throughout the total system. The executive or administrator must have knowledge of all units to assure himself of the effective and ongoing maintenance of all operations.

Another major responsibility of the administration of a large organization is the ongoing concern with the development of general policies, and planning for the future. The organizational administration must develop or rely upon an information system and devote time to the analytic processes that allow monitoring of the efforts and support processes of the operation, appropriate budgeting, and the decision-making necessary for both short- and long-term goals.

Final decision-making rests with the duly appointed executive, who may or may not be a psychiatrist. The alternatives and choices to be decided by the executive should be presented to the deputies in charge of the various subunits for analysis, criticism, and development of other options. The final decision rests with the executive, but is best obtained from within the group of deputies who must evaluate a unit's capacity for achieving the goals in mind.

The administrator may view his organization as a *clinical system*. This assists him in recognizing the necessity to maintain a continuing high level of morale, which fosters the best performance of each individual and, therefore, stimulates the most likely milieu for providing attentive and compassionate care to those who come for treatment.

Finally, the administrator may view the organization as a *social system* relating to other social systems. The organization, per se, will be recognized as a group of human beings with unique skills, values, and personalities, who relate to the administrator as well as to each other in various peer or hierarchical ways. In addition, relations will be identified with many extraorganizational groups—other departments or operating units, political and advocacy groups, and the senior authorities, whether governmental, voluntary or proprietary.

Greenblatt is of the opinion that the psychiatrist functions best as executive and administrator, perceiving the organization in which he works as a social process. In this way, he utilizes his professional knowledge best. Psychiatric practice relies on good communication. Seeking open expression of opinion from patients and staff encourages the opportunity for innovations to arise at any level of the organization and provides the potential for maximizing self-esteem and certainty of support, and lessening anxiety.

As the senior executive or administrator, the psychiatrist will be confronted with the necessity of working with those in the political system, in which the goals and tactics may vary often from his own. While the goals of the political system are to assure benefits to the public at large, the tactics are adversarial, for incumbents in office and aspirants for office must seek public attention. The mental health administration must be sensitive to the fact that the political aspirant seeks power by obtaining public notice. This is often done through focusing attention upon the need to improve institutional management and disclosing its presumed or existing deficiencies. An administrator in the large state, city, and public organizations must expect and be prepared for political scrutiny and attack—whether deserved or not. The administrator must learn to relate to the executive branch of government and its various departments and also to the legislative bodies at many points. Furthermore, as a means of arousing public concern, consumer and provider advocates for the mental health movement may employ adversarial strategies and tactics focusing on the administrator and the organization through public criticism or, nowadays, forcing legal suits to obtain the rights of patients.

Knowledge of political and group strategies and tactics for confrontation, coupled with the understanding of group dynamics and transference phenomena, may prove to be extraordinarily important in the administrator's capacity to withstand such attacks and to maintain the functioning of the organizational unit that he leads.

The significance of the emotional stability of staff in health care organizations and psychiatric facilities is evidenced by the studies of Stanton and Schwartz and others. They found a temporal association between rivalries, disagreements, and misunderstandings among staff members, and episodes of abnormal behavior and outbursts of aggressive disturbance among schizophrenic patients in the same institution.

Far more significant are the role difficulties that confront those working in the various treatment units of the network of community mental health services. Physicians and mental health workers trained in the hospital system often find it difficult to adapt to the consultative or subordinate roles they may play on the community mental health team. In such teams, other professionals or nonprofessionals may be appointed team leaders because their skills are more suitable for effecting the appropriate contacts with the community leaders and those needing help among disadvantaged minority population groups. In contrast to the respectful hospital environment, the psychiatric or mental health worker new to community care may have to defer to others the position of leadership so customarily given to the physician in the clinic service or hospital.

BIBLIOGRAPHY

General

Beers, C. W.: A Mind That Found Itself. New York, Doubleday, 1939.

Caplan, G.: Principles of Preventive Psychiatry. New York, Basic Books, 1964.

Jahoda, M.: Current Concepts of Positive Mental Health. New York, Basic Books, 1958.

Joint Commission on Mental Illness and Health: Action for Mental Health. New York, Basic Books, 1961.

Kennedy, J. F.: Message from the President of the United States Relative to Mental Illness and Mental Retardation, February 5, 1963, 88th Congress, First Session, House of Representatives, Document 58. Washington, D.C., U.S. Government Printing Office, 1963.

Meyer, A.: The Aims of a Psychiatric Clinic. Trans. Int. Congr. Med., Sec. 12, 1–9, 1913.

Sociocultural Factors and Psychosocial Disorder

Brody, E. B. (ed.): Behavior in New Environments: Adaptation of Migrant Populations. Beverly Hills, Cal., Sage Publications, 1970.

Caudill, W.: The Psychiatric Hospital as a Small Society. Cambridge, Mass., Harvard University Press, 1958.

Dohrenwend, B. P., and Dohrenwend, B. S.: Social Status and Psychological Disorder. New York, Wiley-Interscience, 1969.

Hollingshead, A. B., and Redlich, F. C.: Social Class and Mental Illness. New York. John Wiley & Sons, 1958.

Kardiner, A.: The Individual and His Society. New York, Columbia University Press, 1939.

Kolb, L. C., Bernard, V. W., and Dohrenwend, B. P. (eds.): Urban Challenges to Psychiatry. Boston, Little, Brown & Company, 1969.

Leighton, A. H.: Social Disintegration and Mental Disorder. In Arieti, S. (ed.): American Handbook of Psychiatry. 2nd ed. Vol. II. New York, Basic Books, 1974, pp. 411–423.

Linton, R.: Culture and Mental Disorders. Springfield, Ill., Charles C Thomas, 1956.

Opler, M.: Culture, Psychiatry, and Human Values. Springfield, Ill., Charles C Thomas, 1956.

Reissman, F., Cohen, J., and Pearl, A. (eds.): Mental Health of the Poor. New York, Free Press of Glencoe (Macmillan), 1964.

Scheflen, A.: Living space in an urban ghetto. Family Process, 10:429, 1971.

Sherl, D. J., and English, J. T.: Community mental health and comprehensive health service programs for the poor. Am. J. Psychiatry, 125:1666, 1969.

Srole, L., Langner, T. S., Michael, S. T., Kirkpatrick, P., Opler, M. K., and Rennie, T. A. C.:

Mental Health in the Metropolis; The Midtown Manhattan Study. (Revised and enlarged.) New York, Harper Torchbooks,
1975.

Social Role

Spiegel, J. P.: The social roles of doctor and pa-
tient in psychoanalysis and psychotherapy.
Psychiatry, *17*:369–376, 1954.
Spiegel, J. P.: Transactions: The Interplay Be-
tween Individual, Family and Society. New
York, Science House, 1971.
Zborowski, M.: Cultural components in responses
to pain. J. Sci. Issues, *8*:16–30, 1952.

Crisis Theory and Practice

Bartolucci, G., and Drayer, C. S.: An overview of
crisis intervention in the emergency rooms
of general hospitals. Am. J. Psychiatry,
130:953–960, 1973.
Caplan, G.: Theory and Practice of Mental
Health Consultation. New York, Basic
Books, 1970.
Jacobson, G. F.: Programs and techniques of
crisis intervention. *In* Arieti, S. (ed.): American Handbook of Psychiatry. 2nd ed. Vol. II.
New York, Basic Books, 1974, pp. 811–825.

Network Theory and Social Systems Intervention

Bott, E.: Family and Social Network. 2nd ed.
London, Tavistock, 1972.
Erickson, G. D.: The concept of personal net-

work in clinical practice. Family Process,
14:487–498, 1975.
Garrison, J.: Network techniques: Case studies in
the screening-linking-planning conference
method. Family Process, *13*:337–353, 1974.
Pattison, E. M.: Social systems psychotherapy.
Am. J. Psychother., *47*:396–409, 1973.
Polak, P.: Social systems intervention. Arch. Gen.
Psychiatry, *25*:110–117, 1971.
Polak, P., and Jones, M.: The psychiatric nonhos-
pital: A model for change. Community Ment.
Health J. *9*:123–132, 1973.

Administration

Babigian, H. M.: The impact of community men-
tal health centers on the utilization of serv-
ices. Arch. Gen. Psychiatry, *34*:385–394,
1977.
Barton, W. E.: Administration in Psychiatry.
Springfield, Ill., Charles C Thomas, 1962.
Feldman, S. (ed.): The Administration of Mental
Health Services. 2nd ed. Springfield, Ill.,
Charles C Thomas, 1980.
Greenblatt, M.: Administrative psychiatry. Am.
J. Psychiatry, *129*:373–386, 1972.
Greenblatt, M.: Psychopolitics. New York, Grune
and Stratton, 1978.
Kolb, L. C.: Group dynamics and resolution of
conflict in community psychiatric practice.
Group Psychother., *22*:155–172, 1969.
Murphy, H. B. M., Engelsmann, F., and Tcheng-
Laroche, F.: The influence of foster home
care on psychiatric patients. Arch. Gen.
Psychiatry, *33*:179–183, 1976.
Reibel, S., and Herz, M. I.: Limitations of brief
hospital treatment. Am. J. Psychiatry, *133*:
518–521, 1976.

32

PHARMACOLOGICAL THERAPY

"We must recollect that all our provisional ideas in psychology will some day be based on an organic substructure. This makes it probable that special substances and special chemical processes control the operation..."

Sigmund Freud

J. P. L. DELAY
Codiscoverer (with P. Deniker) of tranquilizing effects of chlorpromazine.

(From Kline, N. S.: Psychopharmacology Frontiers. Boston, Little, Brown & Company, 1959. And: International Congress of Psychiatry, 2nd, 1957. Proc. of the Psychopharmacology Symposium, p. XIII.)

For the treatment of the most severe mental disorders, psychotropic drugs are the primary therapeutic agents. Certain of these drugs are useful in providing symptomatic relief in the psychoneuroses and physiological disturbances, while others act specifically in relation to certain symptoms, or are useful as enhancers for the effects of other drugs.

The agents now well recognized as modifying pathological behavior may be classified into the neuroleptics, the antidepressants, the anxiolytic sedatives, the psychostimulants, and the somnifacients. The classification in Table 32–1 is based on the recommendation of the Special Committee of the World Health Organization.

The neuroleptics modify psychotic behavior in general and have become the major therapeutic agents, particularly in the treatment of the schiz-

TABLE 32–1   Classification of Psychotropic Drugs Used Therapeutically

CATEGORY	REPRESENTATIVE MEMBERS
Neuroleptics	Phenothiazines Butyrophenones Thioxanthenes Dihydroindolines Dibenzoxazepines Rauwolfia alkaloids
Antidepressants and affective modulators	Monoamine oxidase (MAO) inhibitors Tricyclic compounds Lithium compounds
Anxiolytic sedatives	Glycerols Diphenylmethanes Benzodiazepines
Psychostimulants	Amphetamine, methylphenidate, dibenzoxepin Caffeine
Somnifacients	Barbiturates Chloral Hydrate Ethchlorvynol Flurazepam Glutethimide Methyprylon Methaqualone Paraldehyde

(Modified, updated, and expanded from the classification recommended by the Special Committee of the World Health Organization, 1967.)

ophrenias. The neuroleptics have the capacity to modify affective states without seriously impairing cognitive functions. In this respect, they differ from the somnifacient drugs. In addition to their reaction upon the central nervous system in modifying behavior, they affect the functioning of the extrapyramidal nervous system and the autonomic system. Generally, they act by blocking dopamine receptors in the brain. Included in the group are the phenothiazines, the butyrophenones, the dihydroindolines, the dibenzoxazepines, and the rauwolfia alkaloids.

The antidepressants are complex agents, with pharmacological effects in particular on the biogenic amines norepinephrine and serotonin. They include the tricyclic compounds and the hydroxide and nonhydroxide monoamine oxidase inhibitors.

The cerebral stimulants include the dextroamphetamines and methylphenidate. These agents tend to produce a transient increase in psychomotor activity. They must be considered as stimulants and are not effectively antidepressant. However, they enhance the activity of certain of the antidepressants.

The anxiolytic agents are sedative hypnotics that generally depress brain function. Pharmacologically, they do not affect the extrapyramidal or the autonomic nervous systems, as do the neuroleptics. Benzodiazepines are the most frequently prescribed drugs in this class. These drugs are more frequently prescribed than any other in America. Although they were thought to exert their psychotropic effects through action on the GABA or glycine neurotransmitter systems, it has recently been shown that human brain contains receptors for benzodiazepines. Thus, the possibilities exist that these drugs act by direct stimulation of receptors, and that the brain may synthesize compounds quite similar to the benzodiazepines.

Individuals receiving these agents develop a tolerance and may become habituated or addicted or both. Because of the possibility of addiction, they have been classified in many countries as controlled substances.

The somnifacients include the well-known barbiturates, chlorohydrate, ethchlorvynol, glutethimide, methyprylon, methaqualone, and flurazepam. Pharmacological effects are generally of shorter duration and are more intense than those of the anxiolytic drugs.

The anticholinergic agents are significant as they are effective in the treatment of drug-induced parkinsonism, so common in administration of the neuroleptics.

Since it is expected that the able psychiatrist comes to practice fully knowledgeable from previous medical studies of the well-known properties of and clinical indications for using central nervous system depressants such as the narcotics, anesthetics, hypnotics, and intoxicants, as well as the stimulants, consideration is not given to these drugs in this text. Their skillful prescription, often in conjunction with that of the neuroleptics, is demanded in practice.

PHARMACOLOGICAL ACTION AND BRAIN FUNCTION

The active psychotropic drugs exert complex actions upon various neural systems and the neuron itself. These actions have been demonstrated through changes brought about in animal behavior (particularly through analysis of responses obtained by classical and instrumental conditioning), through depth electroencephalography, through electrophysiological and biochemical studies of synaptic transmission, and through studies of drug metabolism within bodily tissues and changes in endocrine functions.

It is well known now that the psychotropic drugs have a long half-life in bodily fluids. The drugs and their metabolites accumulate in bodily tissues as administration is continued over time. This accumulation ceases when the saturation level is achieved. With cessation of administration, the tissues slowly release the accumulated drugs. Thus, traces may be found in the urine for two or three months after discontinuance. The psychopharmacological properties are generally manifest days to weeks later than the early effects on the other segments of the central nervous system. Thus, the side effects frequently precede the therapeutic response. These well-recognized pharmacodynamic properties are most important, particularly in relation to the modes of administration, prescription, and assessment of therapeutic response, as will be described.

Much of the variation in effect produced by the differing agents is thought to depend upon their differing actions at the synaptic junctions within the brain. It is considered that the passage of a nerve impulse from activated neurons takes place across the synaptic junction by discharge into the synaptic cleft of the neurotransmitters. These substances then activate the receptors of the postsynaptic neuron.

In Chapter 3 (The Brain and Behavior) and Chapter 18 (Schizophrenic Disorders), respectively, the synaptic action of the various biogenic amines and the "dopamine hypothesis" as it relates to schizophrenia were described. Norepinephrine, dopamine, the indoleamine serotonin, gamma-aminobutyric acid or acetylcholine are differentially disposed through the brain stem. Certain pathways have been identified as principally containing and thereby activated by dopamine and noradrenaline (Fig. 32–1).

As the storage, release, action, and

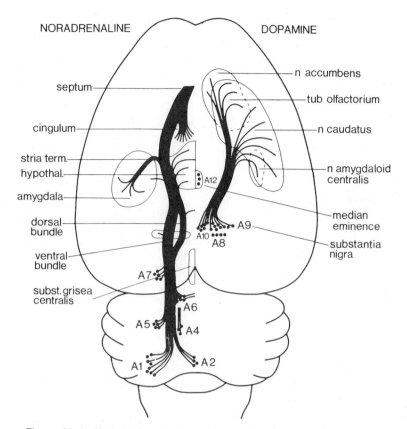

NORADRENALINE   DOPAMINE

Figure 32–1 Horizontal projection of the ascending NA and DA pathways. A1 and A2, cells in medulla oblongata; A4, cells sending axons to locus ceruleus; A5 and A7, cells in pons; A6, cells in locus ceruleus; A8, cell bodies caudal to substantia nigra; A9 and A10, cells in substantia nigra; A12, cells in N. arcuatus. (From Ungerstedt, U.: Stereotaxic mapping of the monoamine pathways in the rat brain. Acta Physiol. Scand. (Suppl.)367:1–48, 1971.)

later re-uptake of the biogenic amines, believed significant particularly in the affective disorders, are now well worked out, certain of the psychotropic drugs have been shown to affect these processes. For example, the catecholamines exist in the neuron in two forms: the labile form, capable of release by stimulation or by sympathomimetic drugs such as amphetamine, and that form contained in storage granules and released by reserpine. When released from the interneuronal structure, catecholamines flow into the synaptic cleft and then are returned to the cell, where they are stored or oxidized by the enzyme monoamine oxidase. The monoamine oxidase inhibitors, such as iproniazid, increase the amount of intraneuronal biogenic amines, making more available. Reserpine depletes the intraneuronal amines, thus diminishing the amount available for activation.

The tricyclic antidepressants decrease the re-uptake of serotonin and norepinephrine. For this reason, these neurotransmitters are partially prevented from returning to the neuron and their concentration in the synaptic cleft is prolonged over time.

The principal action of the phenothiazines is to render the receptor sites for dopamine less available so that the effect of the neurotransmitter is diminished. Thus those drugs that deplete or inactivate biogenic amines in the brain usually produce sedative or depressive actions, while those that increase or potentiate it commonly bring about excitatory behavior and have antidepressant effects. Norepinephrine and serotonin are found in highest concentration in the hypothalamus. Dopamine exists in greatest concentration in the caudate and lenticular nucleus.

Most psychotropic drugs exert their major effects upon the brain stem and limbic systems, the structures of which, as has been noted in Chapter 3, are principally concerned with systems modulating and shaping emotional behavior.

The explanations given for the effects of the various neuroleptic agents on synaptic transmission and on functions of limbic or reticular activating systems and other organ systems do not entirely explain their impressive actions in modifying affect in the major psychoses. What emerges from the pharmacological physiology is an appreciation of the differences of action of the various series of agents, and a recognition that their functions vary. The underlying neurohumoral constitution of the class of patients in which each is effective may well be idiosyncratic for that disorder. Constitutional differences may have origins in genetic differences, expressed in subtle variations in production, transport, storage, and metabolism of neurotransmitters within the brain. Both the effectiveness and the toxicity of drugs may be based as much on such variables as on dosage levels, routes of administration, and absorption.

Administration

There now exists a wide range of drugs in the various categories of the classification described in Table 32–1. Table 32–2 lists those presently available in the U.S.A., and gives the generic name, the brand name, and the recommended range of daily dosage.

The selection of the appropriate drug depends upon the nature of the psychopathology observed in the individual patient. In general, neuroleptics will be used in the treatment of schizophrenia and psychotic conditions other than the affective. The antidepressant agents will be used for the affective psychoses, while the anxiolytics are indicated for symptomatic relief in the neuroses, psychophysiological reactions, certain personality disorders, and some special symptoms.

It is recommended that the psychiatrist become experienced in the use of a single agent or two in each class and generally prescribe such agents in practice. The administration of more than one agent in a class to a patient (polypharmacy) is to be avoided. There are both synergic and anergic antagonistic effects when prescribing across categories. These must be fully understood and will be described later in this chapter. The value of having available the large number of analogues in the various classes is the potential of varying the medication as the patient is found unresponsive to one or another in a series. In other words, the treatment may be varied to fit the peculiar metabolic constitution of the individual.

As with other pharmacological treatment, the physician will consider in determining the dosage the individual's body weight, age, sex, and type and severity of illness. The dosage and type of drug will be varied, depending upon the individual's tolerance or resistance. As with other agents, the dosage should be prescribed within the ranges recommended in the provider's descriptive package insert, except where there are clear clinical indications otherwise. In keeping with the known pharmacological properties of these drugs—their long half-life in serum and their tendency to accumulate in tissues—administration is unnecessary more than once or twice a day. Generally, since in most of the psychopathological conditions sleep is affected, and also as a means of

TABLE 32–2   Classification of Psychotherapeutic Agents and Daily Dosage Range

GENERIC NAME	BRAND NAME	DAILY DOSE	CHLORPROMAZINE MG. EQUIVALENT
	NEUROLEPTICS		
	PHENOTHIAZINES		
	Aliphatic		
Chlorpromazine	Thorazine, Sonazine	30–1000 mg.	100 (Standard)
Promazine	Sparine	40–1000	200
Triflupromazine	Vesprin	20–200	25
Levomepromazine	Levoprome	150–300	–
	Piperidine		
Piperacetazine	Quide	20–160	10
Mesoridazine	Serentil	25–400	50
Thioridazine	Mellaril	50–800	100
	Piperazine		
Acetophenazine	Tindal	80–120	20
Butaperazine	Repoise	15–100	10
Carphenazine	Proketazine	25–400	25
Fluphenazine	Prolixin,		
	Permitil	1–20	2
Perphenazine	Trilafon	4–64	10
Prochlorperazine	Compazine	15–150	15
Thiopropazate	Dartal	10–150	10
Trifluoperazine	Stelazine	2–40	5
	MISCELLANEOUS		
	Thioxanthenes		
Chlorprothixine	Taractan	30–600	100
Thiothixene	Navane	6–60	2
Flupenthixol	–	0.5–1	–
	Butyrophenone		
Haloperidol	Haldol	1–100	2
	Dihydroindoline		
Molindone	Moban	20–225	10
	Dibenzoxazepine		
Loxapine	Loxitane	20–250 mg.	10
	ANTIDEPRESSANTS (PSYCHOANALEPTIC DRUGS)		
	Tricyclic Derivatives		
Amitriptyline	Elavil	20–300	
Desipramine	Norpramin,		
	Pertofrane	25–200	
Doxepin	Sinequan	25–300	
Imipramine	Tofranil	30–300	
Nortriptyline	Aventyl	30–100	
Protriptyline	Vivactil	15–60	
	Monoamine Oxidase Inhibitors		
	Hydrazines		
Isocarboxazid	Marplan	10–30 mg.	
Phenelzine Sulfate	Nardil	15–75 mg.	
	Nonhydrazines		
Tranylcypromine Sulfate	Parnate	10–30 mg.	
	CEREBRAL STIMULANTS		
Acetamidobenzoate	Deaner	50–300 mg.	
Amphetamine	Benzedrine	5–60 mg.	
Dextroamphetamine	Dexedrine	5–60 mg.	
Methamphetamine	Desoxyn	2.5–25 mg.	
Methylphenidate	Ritalin	10–60 mg.	
Pemoline	Cylert	37.5–112.5 mg.	
Pentylenetetrazol	Metrazol	300–600 mg.	

TABLE 32–2   Classification of Psychotherapeutic Agents and
Daily Dosage Range (*Continued*)

GENERIC NAME	BRAND NAME	DAILY DOSE	CHLORPROMAZINE MG. EQUIVALENT
	ANXIOLYTIC AGENTS		
	Glycerol Derivatives		
Meprobamate	Equanil, Miltown	1200–2400	
Tybamate	Tybatran	750–3000	
	Diphenylmethane Derivatives		
Hydroxyline	Atarax, Vistaril	50–400 mg.	
	Benzodiazepine Derivatives		
Chlordiazepoxide	Librium	10–200	
Clorazepate	Tranxene	15–60	
Diazepam	Valium	2–40	
Oxazepam	Serax	30–120	
	SOMNIFACIENTS		
	Barbiturates		
Amobarbital	Amytal and others	65–500 mg.	
Aprobarbital	Alurate	40–160 mg.	
Butabarbital	Butisol and others	50–120 mg.	
Mephobarbital	Mebaral and others	100–400 mg.	
Pentobarbital	Nembutal and others	30–200 mg.	
Phenobarbital	Luminal and others	100–600 mg.	
Secobarbital	Seconal and others	50–300 mg.	
Vinbarbital	Delvinal	100–400 mg.	
	Nonbarbiturates		
Chloral Hydrate	Noctec and others	500 mg.–2 g.	
Ethchlorvynol	Placidyl	200 mg.–1 g.	
Ethinamate	Valmid	500 mg.–2 g.	
Glutethimide	Doriden	250 mg.–1 g.	
Methaqualone	Quaalude, Sopor	150 mg.–400 mg.	
Methyprylon	Noludar	150 mg.–300 mg.	
Flurazepam Hydrochloride	Dalmane	15 mg.–30 mg.	
	ANTICHOLINERGIC DRUGS		
Benztropine Mesylate	Cogentin	1–8 mg.	
Biperiden	Akineton	2–8 mg.	
Cycrimine HCL	Pagitane	3.75–20 mg.	
Trihexyphenidyl HCL	Artane	1–15 mg.	
Procyclidine HCL	Kemadrin	6–20 mg.	

The list contains commercially available psychotherapeutic and anticholinergic agents. Doses listed are those suggested in the manufacturer's package insert. (Modified from the Manual for the Use of Psychotherapeutic Drugs in the New York State Department of Mental Hygiene Facilities. Prepared by the N.Y.S.D.M.H. Committee on Therapeutics: S. Malitz, Chairman, H. Glassman, B. Kobrynski, E. E. Scerebim, and G. Simpson, 1977.)

avoiding the minor side effects, it is sometimes advisable to prescribe the total daily dosage at bedtime. If there is a need to continue a tranquilizing effect early in the day, one third of the dose may be given in the morning and two thirds before bedtime. Such an administrative regimen not only has been found to increase the likelihood of the patient regularly taking medication, but also is less costly since it allows the utilization of larger tablet strength, and, in hospitals, saves staff time in administration of the compound.

For the elderly, the initial dose recommended is one third to one half that for younger adults. The customary formula relating to children should be applied to each child, with particular attention to bodily weight.

When the most effective maintenance level of the appropriate agent has been achieved, it is both possible and advisable to reduce the dosage to a lower level, in view of the accumulating potential of the agents as described. Furthermore, it is then possible to allow the patient drug-free days. Many physicians discontinue administration one day a week following establishment of the maintenance level. It has been found that this does not modify the therapeutic effect.

It is particularly important for the psychiatrist to recognize that many who are presumed resistant to pharmacological therapy are simply failing to take the prescribed medication. This resistance arises often as a direct expression of the psychopathology, of their personality make-up and consequent attitudes toward physicians, or of certain ingrained cultural attitudes toward the taking of medicine. For example, many psychotic patients deny the existence of illness. Particularly in the paranoid, sometimes the ingestion or acceptance of medication is perceived delusionally as a means of poisoning. Others reject medication as a result of family attitudes equating illness as weakness or from fear derived from early childhood experiences of illness. Still others will refuse to accept medications prescribed by routes other than the ones customarily used within their culture. Thus, in the U.S.A. and Great Britain, sedative medications are customarily taken by mouth, in Italy by injection, and in France by anal suppository.

The prescribing and giving of medication should be recognized in the context of the patient-physician relationship. All medications, as with placebos, hold the potential for meeting the magical expectations of the sick individuals, who often eagerly anticipate relief or cure of their distress. It is important that the attending medical staff support these expectations by indicating the potential efficacy of the prescribed medications, while at the same time providing an outlet for the later use of analogues by describing the individual differences in metabolizing specific agents.

The attitude of the attending physicians is particularly significant, as shown by studies examining the differences in approach of those physicians successful in treating patients in low socioeconomic groups, where dropouts in treatment programs are common. The successful physicians tend to be more active in their relations with these patients, to be more positive in dealing with and responding to them, and to practice more personalized interviews. The inference made from these investigations is that the successful physicians seemed to be more empathic with their patients, yet did not give them direct reassurance. These physicians rate their patients as sicker and at the same time tend to have a more positive prognostic outlook. They more frequently call their patients by name, are vocal and facially animated, and expend more time with the individual.

In contrast, "high dropout" therapists are passive, wait for the patient to speak, are less enthusiastic and more certain that the drugs will act. The same traits then are necessary to maintain patients in pharmacological treatment programs as in psychotherapeutic programs. The experienced psychiatrists, nurses, and mental health personnel will understand the transactional meaning between themselves and the patient and recognize their roles as parental surrogates and authorities.

Before prescribing, the physician will inquire into the patient's family's attitude and responses to drug-taking in the past. The prescription then will be tailored to suit the individual attitudes of the patient. Those likely to reject prescriptions may often be identified. If this is not the case, the sensitive therapist noting nonresponse will inquire from both the patient and members of his family or others, particularly if the individual is in outpatient treatment, whether the individual has filled the prescription, delayed its usage, forgotten to take medications, taken less than indicated, or discontinued before recommendation.

In the instances of those individuals who discontinue medication, and who frequently have exacerbations of symptoms, it is wise to place them on the long-acting injectable depot products.

NEUROLEPTIC AGENTS

Phenothiazines

The phenothiazine nucleus from which the various analogues have been synthesized consists of two benzine rings joined by a sulfur and a nitrogen atom. By the addition of side-chains to the formula, numerous derivatives have been developed. From the attachment of a dimethylamopropyl side-chain are derived chlorpromazine, promazine, and triflupromazine. Substitution of the piperazine side-chain in this position leads to the development of perphenazine, prochlorperazine, and trifluoperazine. The piperidine side-chain results in thioridazine, piperacetazine, and mesoridazine. Compounds in the piperazine-substituted group are the most potent, but also have the greatest tendency to produce symptoms of extrapyramidal dysfunction.

The general indications for the prescription of the phenothiazine derivations are the same as those for chlorpromazine. These drugs differ more in their toxic properties than in their abilities to modify selectively various "target symptoms."

Pharmacological experiments in animals show that the phenothiazines reduce conditioned avoidance responses. They do not inhibit escape, nor do they affect the response to conditional stimuli, as do the barbiturates. They impair vigilance but not cognitive actions. Seizure threshold to both electroshock and convulsive drugs is unchanged. With large doses only, there appear slow (5 to 6 per second), low-voltage waves in the electroencephalogram. Hypothalamically regulated activities are disrupted. Thus thermoregulation is impaired, adrenocorticotropic hormone (ACTH) secretion is diminished, and growth is diminished. Another endocrine effect is reduction in urinary gonadotropins. In animals, the estrous cycle and ovulation are suppressed by the phenothiazines. The decidual reaction is prolonged by them and lactation is induced. Infertility occurs. In women patients receiving phenothiazines who develop inappropriate lactation and amenorrhea, prolactin levels become elevated, basal luteinizing hormone levels vary, and absence of midcycle peaks occurs, while estrogen and progesterone levels have been reported as similar to those during the follicular phase of a normal cycle. In men receiving such drugs, plasma testosterone is either low or normal and rises on withdrawal of the drug.

These agents are well absorbed from the intestine (60 to 80 per cent) and widely distributed in the body tissues, where they remain bound for prolonged periods (6 to 12 months) after administration has ceased. They are metabolized in the liver through hydrolysis and glucuronidization.

Of the classes of phenothiazines in general, the aliphatic and piperidine series provide more sedative effect than the piperazine. The latter series, by weight, contain the more potent compounds, but these also are more likely to produce the parkinsonism and other basal ganglia side effects. The therapist has available many analogues in these various groups, and some, notably fluphenazine, may be prescribed in long-acting injectable forms.

There follows a description of the

therapeutic action of the first introduced, still the most widely used, and the least expensive of the series—chlorpromazine. The description serves as a model for the actions of all the neuroleptics. The variable indications and complications will be reviewed later.

ADMINISTRATION. Chlorpromazine is available in 10-, 25-, 50-, 100-, and 200-mg. tablets, and also in 25-mg. (1-ml.) and 50-mg. (2-ml.) ampules. There is no standard dose of the drug; this must be individualized. Chlorpromazine may be administered by oral or by intramuscular routes; however, it is so irritant that it should not be administered subcutaneously. Intramuscular injections should be given deeply in the upper and outer quadrant of the buttock; the solution supplied by the manufacturer should be diluted with physiological salt solution or a 2 per cent procaine solution and administered very slowly. Some physicians add hyaluronidase to facilitate absorption and prevent abscess formation. If quick action is desired, the patient may receive 25 mg. by deep intramuscular injection, and if this amount is not effective, an additional 25-mg. injection may be given within an hour unless contraindicated by marked hypotension. Subsequent intramuscular dosages may be increased gradually, even up to 400 mg. every six hours. The higher doses should be reached over a period of several days.

If, as frequently occurs, the acutely disturbed patient becomes quiet within 48 hours, oral doses (milligram for milligram or higher) may gradually replace intramuscular doses. Injections should not be continued for more than three or four days. It will not usually be necessary to increase oral administration to more than 800 mg. a day, but if sedation is not secured, the dosage may gradually be increased up to as much as 1200 mg. a day. Usually, this amount is sufficient for a maximum dose, although some psychiatrists give a maximum of 2000 mg. in 24 hours.

SPECIAL THERAPEUTIC REGIMENS.

Rapid Tranquilization. The immediate treatment of the acutely psychotic with the maximally tolerated dosages of phenothiazines is advocated by some to facilitate ego reorganization and social adaptation. Such treatment seems to be particularly valuable when the patient is seriously confused and incapable of engaging in meaningful verbal communication with others.

This method of treatment requires the quick establishment of a maximal daily dosage for each individual. Polak and Laycomb recommend that the patient be given an initial dose of 25 to 50 mg. of chlorpromazine orally and be observed closely for side effects for one hour. If none are noticed, the drug is prescribed in 50 to 200 mg. doses orally every hour for six to eight hours, depending upon the behavioral state. When the initial disturbed psychotic behavior has diminished within the first six hours—including as end points strong sedation or sleep—the dosage is arranged in successive days at two thirds the total required initially. Each day thereafter the dosage is reviewed and modified, depending upon the observed behavior. In the first several days, well-tranquilized patients sleep a good part of the day. After the third day, there generally takes place a considerable reduction of drowsiness. Often, side effects, too, diminish at this time. Only after this day is the total level of medication reduced.

If oral medication is refused, intramuscular dosages of one third the oral may be substituted.

High Dosage Regimens. On the effectiveness of high dosage regimens of chlorpromazine (over 2000 mg. per day) against low dosage treatment among groups of chronic schizophrenics, Prien et al., reporting from the Psychopharmacology Research Branch Collaborative Group Study on 120 such patients, found that high dosages were significantly more effective when given to patients under 40, hospitalized less than 15 years, who had been receiving a nonpiperazine phenothiazine beforehand. There was little difference in high dosage and low dosage regimens in other patient subgroups. Those who had been on higher dosages beforehand were more likely to fail. For older patients, high dosage caused a great increase in side effects. Dyskinesias occur in as high as 25 per cent of patients treated with high dosage regimens, particularly among the aged.

Long-Acting Agents. Fluphenazine hydrochloride has been found to retain its physiological activity longer than any other phenothiazine. This is probably due to its higher fat solubility than that of the other analogues. When combined with various acid esters (enanthic, decanoic, and lauric), its release from fatty tissue is further slowed. Thus the hydrochloride will demonstrate action for from two to six days in animals, whereas the ethanate acts for up to three to seven times that period and the decanoate ten times as long. In humans, their therapeutic action commences to recede after two weeks.

Experience has demonstrated that the intramuscular injection of these agents is effective in the acute psychotic states when oral medication is either difficult to administer or the patient refuses it. In the chronic stages, where the rate of failure of schizophrenic outpatients to take prescribed oral medications amounts to 50 per cent, the use of these intramuscular depot phenothiazines reduces that figure to 20 per cent.

The decanoate preparation appears to be slightly more long-lasting and less likely to produce the side effects. These agents, in particular, produce extrapyramidal symptoms, which may be controlled in most, but not all, with antiparkinson agents.

THERAPEUTIC RESPONSE. In the use of all neuroleptics, the physiological side effects caused by their actions on the central and autonomic nervous systems generally precede the therapeutic effects on pathological behavior. One of the early effects of the administration of chlorpromazine is a fall in blood pressure, according to dose and individual reaction. Other effects are slowing of the pulse and of respiration, lowering of temperature and of basal metabolic rate, and transient leukopenia. Frequently the drug causes dryness of the mucous membranes and nasal congestion. It has an antiemetic effect as well. In large doses, chlorpromazine produces motor retardation, muscular hypotonia, and an unsteady gait. During the first two or three days of treatment, patients show varying degrees of somnolence, but can be awakened without difficulty and are able to take food. However, as a rule, the increased need for sleep is reduced after a few days. Patients may complain of feeling faint, weak, cold, and drowsy, but the sensorium remains clear. The action of the drug is maximal at one hour after administration and appreciable effects continue for six hours. It potentiates the effects of barbiturates and of narcotics.

As the patient begins to grow quiet, the dose may gradually be reduced over a period of weeks or months. If symptoms return, the amount should be increased immediately and additional parenteral doses should be given if necessary. When the patient is no longer disturbed, the dose may usually be reduced gradually and then continued for an indefinite period, the amount being the smallest that will control symptoms. Usually, in the chronically disturbed patient this will be approximately 600 to 800 mg. daily. If there has been no improvement in symptoms after the patient has received these amounts daily for two months, the drug should be gradually discontinued.

In the less acutely agitated patient, treatment may be begun with 50 mg. given orally three times a day. This may be increased gradually until an effective and tolerable level is reached. Frequently, doses of 100 to 400 mg. daily, if continued over a long period, will maintain sedation.

The most obvious response to chlorpromazine is somnolence, varying from slight drowsiness to deep sleep. The somnolence is most marked within 15 to 20 minutes after an injection; however, even when the somnolence is deepest, it is possible to rouse the patient easily. He shows little or none of the residual clouding of consciousness that follows comparable barbiturate sedation. Acutely agitated, restless, or excited patients show a greater response than do less disturbed patients. The tranquilizing effect does not seem in any way related to the underlying nature of the excitement: whether it is schizophrenic, manic, or confusional. If the patient responds well to the drug, he develops an attitude of indifference both to his surroundings and to his symptoms. He shows decreased interest in and response to his hallucinatory experiences and a less assertive expression of his delusional ideas.

INDICATIONS FOR USE OF PHENOTHIAZINES. These and other neuroleptics exert a tranquilizing effect in a wide variety of disturbed psychiatric states — tension, psychomotor overactivity, agitation, impulsiveness, aggressive outbursts, destructiveness, and overtly anxious, antagonistic, paranoid reactions.

They are the drugs of choice in *schizophrenia,* both in acute reactions and in overactive chronic reactions. The more destructive and aggressive the patient, the more likely is he to respond. In the acutely ill, schizophrenic hallucinations and delusional ideas frequently disappear within the first two weeks of treatment. The longer the schizophrenic patient has been ill, the less are his chances of attaining a moderate or marked improvement. Of schizophrenics who receive these agents relatively early in their illness, more are able to leave the hospital and make adequate social adjustment than has been the case with any previous method of treatment. Among them will be many who, despite other forms of treatment, have shown no improvement. Chronic psychotic patients should be treated for extended periods

(six to eight months) before the results are assessed. Best results are secured with patients who have not been ill for more than two years. Among these the results will depend largely on the clinical manifestations of the disorder, the degree of improvement being much greater in the overactive, disturbed patients.

Many patients, previously so ill and preoccupied with the symptoms of their illness that they remained indifferent or hostile to attempts to alter their behavior, thinking, or emotional set, become more amenable to therapy when taking chlorpromazine. Although many schizophrenics who have been hospitalized for years show some improvement, few develop social competence to the extent of independent living outside the facility.

The care of the approximately 60 per cent who do improve but are not able to leave the hospital is greatly eased. Delusions and hallucinations may persist but are usually no longer disturbing to the patient. The sullen, sarcastic, and antagonistic patient is less irritable and frequently becomes quiet, cooperative, and accessible, and there is a remarkable improvement in disturbed patients. Although the withdrawn, inactive, unresponsive, regressed schizophrenic may not usually improve sufficiently to leave the hospital, he frequently is able to modify his behavior, discontinue soiling, and no longer discard his clothing. The relief from the anguish, bitterness, hostility, and despair from which many patients suffer is of incalculable value. The chronic schizophrenic who improves should continue on a carefully determined maintenance dose for an extended period. When stabilization of behavior has occurred and been maintained, the dosage should be lowered to that level capable of continuing the behavioral evidences of therapeutic improvement. Changing or discontinuing neuroleptics, once one has been proved effective, carries a sizeable risk of deterioration or relapse. Many of those stabilized on chlorpromazine and remaining in hospital over long periods of time are maintained well on dosage levels of 250 mg. or less daily.

In *manic-depressive psychosis,* chlorpromazine is a useful adjunct if the patient is manic, overactive, and unmanageable.

The usually difficult handling of the restless or agitated patient suffering from *senile dementia* is often rendered much easier by the use of a neuroleptic, which is far superior to prescription of a somnifacient. The dosage ranges must be much less than for the middle-aged adult. With chlorpromazine, in amounts of 25 to 50 mg. three times a day, the patient often becomes calm and manageable and can be cared for at home. Memory loss and disorientation are, of course, unaffected.

Various neuroleptics have proved of value in treatment of patients with the psychophysiological disorders, including the pruritic dermatitides, acne, rheumatoid arthritis, and asthma.

Occasionally, institutionalized *epileptic patients* are subject to episodic or chronic disturbed states, in which they may be hyperactive, noisy, hostile, aggressive, resistive, assaultive, destructive, and given to temper outbursts or furor states. A parenteral injection of 100 mg. of chlorpromazine is highly effective in quieting the acute, excited states. Most epileptic patients who exhibit chronic disturbed states are also quieted and relaxed by the drug. This may at first be given as 300 mg. daily and later reduced to 150 mg. Since chlorpromazine tends to potentiate the activity of barbiturates, it is well to reduce the dose of the latter drug during the administration of the former.

In relatively large doses, the phenothiazines are extremely helpful in the management of *acute alcoholic states.* They produce prompt control of motor excitement and of nausea and vomiting, permit restful, relaxed sleep, and contribute to the relief of tension and anxiety. Their sedative effect hastens recovery in delirium tremens. They are definitely beneficial in nearly all short-lived mental disturbances of a delirious type. They should supplement and not replace the administration of glucose solution, insulin, and vitamin B complex. They are not, of course, of value in the treatment of Korsakoff's syndrome or in the alleviation of chronic alcoholism.

SELECTION OF ANALOGUES. Mention has already been made of certain general properties of the three subclasses of the phenothiazines. Not only are there variations in hypnotic, antiemetic, and potential for side effects, but also wide variation in price. The least expensive of the neuroleptics in the U.S.A. is fluphenazine, followed by chlorpromazine, loxapine, thioridazine, trifluoperazine, haloperidol, thiothixene, molindone, and perphenazine, in that order.

An aliphatic phenothiazine not shown on the general list, but important as a highly potent analgesic useful for patients with chronic and intractable pain symptoms is levomepromazine (Levoprome or Noninan). It is also reported to have antidepressive activity. It has been used successfully in the treatment of numerous chronic painful states, including posthepatic neuralgia, phantom limb pain, tabes dorsalis, and thalamic syndrome, and when given by injection it has been shown to be as effective as morphine in equivalent doses in acute postoperative and postpartum states. No addiction has been reported.

The effective dosage of levomepromazine for the chronic painful reactions ranges from 150 to 300 mg. daily. The drug is usually prescribed in 50-mg. doses three to five times each day. When relief of pain is obtained, the daily maintenance dosage often may be reduced. Levoprome is available only for parenteral injection.

URINE DETECTION TEST. A simple test for detection of chlorpromazine and other phenothiazines in urine has

been described. To a small amount of
urine (1 ml.) is added an equal volume
of a solution containing equal parts of
10 per cent H_2SO_4 and 5 per cent
$FeCl_3$. The mixture is gently shaken.
The presence of phenothiazines is indicated by the development of a violet
color.

Thioxanthenes

Of this group of neuroleptics, thiothixene (Navane) is one of the most potent. Its actions are similar in many
respects to the piperazine phenothiazines. Flupenthixol, now in trial, has
been found to have effective antidepressant effects at dosages lower than
those used in treatment of the chronic
schizophrenic.

Butyrophenones

The butyrophenones are long-acting
nonhypnotic antipsychotic drugs that
also have antiemetic and analgesic
properties.

Haloperidol was the first drug of this
series to be introduced, and continues
to be the most extensively prescribed. It
has a more rapid therapeutic effect
than chlorpromazine in the treatment
of the acute schizophrenic. It is effective in many instances where the phenothiazines fail in this condition. Today
it is generally regarded as the preferred drug in acute manic attacks and
is reported as useful in paranoid excite-
ments. Some have found it superior to
the anxiolytics in anxiety tension states
and it has been prescribed with some
success for obsessive-compulsive neuroses.

Of particular interest is its effective
action in the Gilles de la Tourette syndrome, and other multiple tic syndromes. Haloperidol has also been
used effectively in some cases of Huntington's chorea.

Recently, Cavenar and Maltbie have
described it as an effective agent in the
control of chronic pain.

Dihydroindolines

The single agent in this subseries of
neuroleptics now in clinical use is molindone (Moban), indicated for the schizophrenic.

Dibenzoxazepines

Loxapine (Loxitane) is now in use for
the treatment of schizophrenia. As
noted, it is relatively inexpensive.

Rauwolfia Alkaloids

Extensively prescribed in the 1950s
and early 1960s, these agents have been
largely superseded by the other neuroleptics. Their therapeutic effectiveness
tends to be delayed following initial administration, and Serpasil has been
found to produce depressive reactions
in some.

TOXICOLOGICAL REACTIONS. Today,
the major toxicological reactions to the
neuroleptic agents are the extrapyramidal syndromes—parkinsonism, akathisia, and, in those administered the
agents for long periods, tardive dyskinesias.

While in general the therapeutic potency of the neuroleptics appears to
bear a direct relationship to the specific
drug's capacity to induce parkinsonism
or other extrapyramidal symptoms, this
is not entirely true. The simple explanation has been that these agents block
dopaminergic synapses concurrent with
their effects on alleviating the behavioral expressions of schizophrenia and
other acute psychoses, thus bringing
about the inactivation of the pathways
known deficient in the parkinsonian
state. It is clear from both the clinical
anomalies alluded to before (effective
antipsychotic action without extrapyramidal toxicity) and from laboratory studies that the explanation is
more complex. Snyder and his colleagues have found, for example, that
different phenothiazines and butyrophenone analogues differentially affect

the muscarinic (cholinergic) brain receptors as well as blocking the dopamine receptors. They propose that the extrapyramidal effects are inversely proportional to the individual drug's anticholinergic potency and capacity to blockade the muscarinic receptors.

Parkinsonism appears in about 10 per cent of the patients receiving full doses of chlorpromazine. The clinical picture is the usual one of muscular rigidity, slowing of movement, festinating gait, sialorrhea, and at times a pill-rolling tremor. The condition is always reversible through prescription of antiparkinson agents, of which benztropine mesylate (Cogentin) is perhaps the most frequently employed. Others are listed in Table 32–2. Cogentin is usually prescribed in a dose of 1 mg. daily. Amantadine hydrochloride (Symmetrel), given in 100 mg. doses daily, is as effective as Cogentin, but does not produce the same range of anticholinergic side effects.

Much over-prescription of antiparkinson drugs has occurred in conjunction with neuroleptic treatment. As DiMascio points out, long-term continuance of these agents is unnecessary. He has shown that following abrupt withdrawal of these agents after three months of antiparkinson treatment, only about 10 per cent require its continuance (Fig. 32–2).

Akathisia is overlooked frequently as a concomitant of early neuroleptic therapy. In this condition, the patient complains of restlessness, and particularly of the inability to remain seated for more than a few minutes. The patient will be noted to frequently rise, pace, and turn around to resume his seat, and go through this cycle of movement repeatedly. This condition, too, can be immediately relieved by an intravenous injection of benztropine mesylate or other antiparkinson drug, or it will disappear in several hours after oral medication.

Tardive dyskinesia. This condition, in which oral dyskinesias are the most common and conspicuous clinical phenomena, may appear as early as three to six months after neuroleptic therapy has been initiated, but is more frequently encountered after a year or more of administration. This condition occurs in 10 to 20 per cent of those at risk. Elderly patients on high dosage regimens are at high risk, yet the fact that its incidence is so low suggests

Figure 32–2 Return of extrapyramidal symptoms and length of time on antiparkinson medication prior to discontinuation. (From DiMascio, A.: Toward a more rational use of antiparkinson drugs in psychiatry. Drug Therapy, Sept., 1971.)

that individual predisposition, probably genetic in origin, plays a major role in its development. The clinical phenomena consist of chewing movements, licking and smacking of the lips, sucking, repetitive protrusion of the tongue or tongue movements within the oral cavity, tongue tremor or wormlike myokymic movements on the tongue surface, grotesque grimaces, and facial spasms. Sometimes the oral lingual dyskinesias are associated also with spasmodic torticollis, retrocollis, torsion movements of the lip, and lip rocking. The condition may become irreversible even after withdrawal of the neuroleptic. There have been a few cases where tardive dyskinesia has been associated with parkinsonism in the same patient.

Early signs of onset after initiating neuroleptic therapy consist of facial tics, ill-defined oral or ocular movements, chewing, rocking, or swaying. The clinician should discontinue the prescribed drug on first observation of such movements, when the condition is generally reversible.

The explanation for tardive dyskinesia is uncertain. It has been suggested that it is due to dopaminergic overactivity through hypersensitivity of neurons activated by this substance. By some it is considered to be etiologically similar to Huntington's chorea. Both conditions are improved by dopamine-blocking agents and worsened by anticholinergic drugs, such as those used for Parkinson's disease. The relationship to abnormality of gamma-aminobutyric acid, the inhibitor neurotransmitter, also linked to nigrostriatal dopaminergic functions, seems likely in view of the recent reversal of the condition by administration of sodium valproate, an antiepileptic agent which increases GABA levels in the central nervous system.

At present there is no satisfactory treatment for tardive dyskinesia. The psychiatrist must weigh the risk of discontinuing the neuroleptic against continuing the dyskinesia. Tardive dyskinesia has been controlled in some sufferers by administration of thiopropazate hydrochloride, 30 to 60 mg. daily; haloperidol, 2 to 10 mg. daily; acetophenazine, 80 to 120 mg. daily; Serpasil in high doses; and, most recently, sodium valproate, 900 mg. given in three divided doses daily. Where dyskinesia exists with parkinsonism, the neuroleptics are ineffective; they even worsen it.

CARDIOVASCULAR DISTURBANCES. Most reported difficulties are from the use of aliphatic and piperidine phenothiazines. Hypotension of the orthostatic type may occur and lead to sensations of faintness or to actual fainting, especially on changing from a recumbent to a standing position. Drugs should be given with great caution to patients suffering from atherosclerosis, cardiovascular disease, or other conditions in which a sudden drop in blood pressure may be undesirable.

The cholinergic effects and dopaminergic blocking effects may lead to tachycardia, postural hypotension, electrocardiographic abnormalities (Q-T prolongation and minor S-T changes), and ventricular tachyarrhythmias.

Hypotension, if severe, is treated by volume expansion through intravenous fluids. If pressor agents are indicated, only norepinephrine or metaraminol (alpha adrenergic stimulator) should be administered. Other catecholamines may cause a further drop in blood pressure. The neuroleptic should be withdrawn and later either another agent substituted or a lower dose tested.

Skin reactions occur in some patients administered phenothiazines. The urticarial, maculopapular, edematous, or petechial response takes place within one to five weeks after initiation of treatment. When drug administration is stopped, the skin clears and may remain clear even if the same treatment is resumed later. This is regarded as a hypersensitivity response. *Photosensitivity* confined to areas exposed to sunlight may be produced by chlorpromazine and some other phenothiazines. Usually, this will result merely in redness and itching, but sometimes it will lead to edema and vesicle formation. Ordinarily, interruption of the drug, the application of bland lotions, and the administration of antihistamines are sufficient treatment of the dermatological reactions.

Abnormal skin pigmentation, appearing as a gray-blue discoloration in areas exposed to the sun, has developed in some patients after prolonged high-dosage administration. Similar deposits of pseudomelanin have occurred in the cornea and lens, but only in rare instances have such deposits impaired vision. D-Penicillamine given in doses of 0.3 gm. three times daily for six days with mineral supplement substitution on the last day has been reported successful in reducing the pigmentation.

Jaundice, usually appearing from the second to the eighth week after the drug was started, may develop, largely as a complication in those given chlorpromazine. It is today less frequently encountered than when this drug first became available. Its duration is variable. The jaundice is cholestatic in origin. The total bilirubin content of the blood is greatly elevated, and the alkaline cholesterol is much increased, as is the percentage of eosinophils. However, there is little or no disturbance of the cephalin flocculation and thymol turbidity. The obstruction is within the intralobular canaliculi and a result of pericanalicular lymphocytic infiltration.

If jaundice appears, the drug should be discontinued and glucose administered intravenously, if indicated. Vitamins should be given, and also a high-carbohydrate, high-protein, and low-fat diet.

The neuroleptics may depress the production of leukocytes. *Agranulocytosis* is fortunately of low incidence, probably less than 0.3 per cent, and it occurs within three to six weeks after the beginning of treatment. It is more frequent in women, particularly in those between 40 and 60 years of age, and its onset is sudden. Patients should be asked to report at once the sudden appearance of sore throat or of lesions in the mouth. Any rise in temperature should also suggest an immediate blood count. These cannot be relied upon as the sole criteria for agranulocytosis. In case blood dyscrasia develops, chlorpromazine should be stopped at once and penicillin and the broad-spectrum antibiotics should be given immediately. Corticotropin (ACTH) is also usually employed, and transfusion is often advisable.

A few cases of sudden death in the course of high-dosage phenothiazine treatment have been reported. It has been proposed that death was caused by ventricular fibrillation or asphyxia during a drug-induced seizure or by food aspiration.

Suicide attempts have been made with the various phenothiazines and antidepressants. These agents are much less toxic than the barbiturates or minor tranquilizers, and few such attempts have been successful. As much as 30,000 mg. of chlorpromazine has been ingested with recovery. Following these attempts, the vasopressor levarterenol is indicated. When convulsions occur, great care must be taken in attempting their control with barbiturates, as these drugs are potentiated by the phenothiazines.

Phenothiazines may lead to elevation of the cerebrospinal fluid proteins. Furthermore, immunological diagnostic pregnancy tests appear unreliable in women receiving chlorpromazine and other phenothiazines, as they yield a high incidence of false-positive results.

Miosis or blurring of vision is noted at times.

Occasionally, nurses who administer chlorpromazine develop a troublesome contact dermatitis that clears when further exposure is avoided. The irritant qualities of the drug were dramatically illustrated in the case of one patient who rubbed an eye with a tablet of chlorpromazine. An extensive and violent inflammatory process resulted in loss of vision.

ANTIDEPRESSANTS

Iminodibenzyls

Closely related to the phenothiazines, the first of these drugs, imipramine (Tofranil), was introduced for clinical use by Kuhn in 1957. It is similar to promazine, but a two-carbon chain replaces the sulfur in the latter. Imipramine is the prototype of the iminodibenzyl group and for that reason its actions are described in some detail.

PHYSIOLOGICAL EFFECTS. Imipramine reduces susceptibility to convulsions induced by either electroshock or Metrazol. It depresses the action of the reticular formation and evokes on the electroencephalogram a brain-wave pattern typical of sleep. Its action at the synaptic junction is described earlier in this chapter, in the section entitled Pharmacological Action and Brain Function. It has anticholinergic effects and thus atropine-like side effects. Unlike chlorpromazine, it does not modify the conditioned escape-avoidance response in animals.

The oral route is preferred in the administration of the drug, although it may be given by intramuscular injection. The usual initial dosage range is 75 to 100 mg. daily, the amount being increased to a total of 200 to 300 mg. within several days.

INDICATIONS. Imipramine has been more effective in the depressive phase of the bipolar affective psychoses and in certain of those with unipolar depression. As described in Chapter 21, it now seems likely to discriminate those responding particularly with retarded depression than with other conditions. With the agitated depressions, it is not effective, even when combined with the phenothiazines. Depressive reactions with organic brain syndromes have responded well, but its usefulness is limited with the neurotic depressive reactions and hypochondriacal states. In some patients with chronic pain, recurrent psychosomatic complaints, and neurotic states (and, as noted earlier, some phobic states), it has also been reported useful. Some apathetic patients with schizophrenia and catatonia have been mobilized with the drug, but, in general, it has not proved of value in the treatment of these reactions. Some believe it is contraindicated. Imipramine is also effective in the treatment of enuresis in children.

The change in mood and behavior seldom becomes noticeable within the first week of administration, and maximum benefit accrues usually after two or three weeks of medication. In the depressions, evidence of favorable response is shown with the patient first becoming less self-deprecatory and self-accusing and with reduction in his hypochondriacal complaints. Later there follow increased activity and socialization and improvement in general somatic functioning, including sleep.

Imipramine must be continued on a maintenance level after clinical improvement has taken place, as symptoms recur with its withdrawal. Many recommend that the drug administration be continued three to six months following satisfactory change in affect. The drug should be withdrawn gradually.

TOXIC EFFECTS. The majority of the side effects are minor, although they may impede acceptance of the drug by the patient. Dryness of the mouth is experienced by almost all who receive the drug and difficulties in accommodation in many. Perspiration is common, particularly about the head and neck, and by some it is thought to occur particularly in those who respond favorably. With it may occur flushing of the face. Dizziness, tachycardia, and postural hypotension are seen in the elderly and hypersensitive; thus the drug must be used with caution in patients with cardiovascular illness. With large doses, tremors may be induced. Impairment of urination has been observed. Photosensitivity occurs less frequently as a complication than it does with the use of the phenothiazines.

Insomnia is often noticed when the drug is first given. Later on, sleep tends to improve. The tricyclic antidepressants as a class tend to increase non-REM sleep while decreasing the percentage of REM sleep and the duration of each REM cycle. Thus the total number of REM interruptions during the night is increased. In the bipolar manic-depressive, hypomanic states have frequently followed its administration and require both its withdrawal and the use of a phenothiazine. Some patients suffer burning paresthesias in the forearms and hands and substernally. Rarely, incoordination and convulsive attacks have been reported.

Although eosinophilia is common, leukopenia occurs much less frequently, and only a few instances of agranulocytosis have been seen. In the presence of glaucoma or urinary retention this drug and its analogues should be avoided.

Serious poisoning has occurred from overusage with these compounds, and the frequency is rising in children, for whom the prescriptions for enuresis have increased notably. Both central nervous system and other evidences of anticholinergic blockade emerge. In the former, coma, agitation, delirium, choreoathetosis and myoclonus have occurred. These symptoms are reversed readily with physostigmine salicylate given in appropriate doses between 0.5 to 4.0 mgm. intravenously in repeated doses at intervals. Tachycardia, urinary retention, paralytic ileus, hyperpyrexia, and mydriasis may occur. Gastric lavage and continuous cardiac monitoring are usually indicated.

Amitriptyline. Marketed as Elavil, this drug has actions, indications, and side effects similar to imipramine. The dosage range is 75 to 300 mg. daily, given by mouth. There is some evidence that its untoward actions are less than those of imipramine. Elavil has hypnotic actions that make it useful when sleep disturbance is a prominent expression of depression.

Nortriptyline. Sold as Aventyl, this agent is supplied in pulvules of 10 to 25 mg. The indications, contraindications, and side effects are similar to those for the previously described analogues.

Desipramine. This agent (Pertofrane or Norpramin), stated to be produced in the body as an active metabolite of imipramine, was initially considered to be therapeutically effective more quickly than its precursors. This claim has not been borne out by double-blind studies. It is supplied in 25-mg. tablets and is usually effective in a daily dosage range of 150 mg.

Enhanced and Diminished Action of Tricyclic Antidepressants

Among the depressed group are patients who fail to respond to the tricyclic antidepressants even on high dosage regimens. It is known now that the metabolism of these agents is highly variable between individuals. Thus, the same dosage given to various persons results in radically different blood levels because of the actions of the liver microsomal enzymes, in combination with the cytochrome reductase system in this organ. Different drugs given in combination with the tricyclic compounds may either stimulate or inhibit the liver metabolic processes, thus enhancing or diminishing the therapeutic effectiveness of the prescribed agent. Genetic differences between individuals now are recognized in these complex drug-drug interactions.

Using radioimmunoassay and gas liquid chromatographic techniques, it has become possible to measure plasma levels of the tricyclic antidepressants. For some (imipramine, amitriptyline, and nortriptyline) a minimum plasma concentration is required to achieve a therapeutic response. For some tricyclics—e.g., nortriptyline—a therapeutic window of plasma concentration exists such that plasma levels between a minimum and a maximum are associated with therapeutic response. The utilization of plasma determination also allows the psychiatrist to determine patient compliance in taking tricyclic medication.

Methylphenidate (Ritalin), an inhibitor of liver metabolism, has been shown to enhance the effect of the tricyclics in patients previously resistant to these compounds alone. In this treatment, the methylphenidate may be given in 10 mg. doses three times daily for several weeks, in combination with the tricyclic antidepressant given in average or lesser dosage regimens.

The thyroid-stimulating hormone and L-triiodothyronine (T_3) enhance the therapeutic activity of imipramine in women and produce both a more rapid recovery and effective action in patients initially resistant to imipramine alone. The former appears the most potent. The explanation for the enhancing action of thyroid hormones seems to be similar to that of Ritalin. The neuroleptics, too, inhibit the metabolism of the tricyclics, but it is not clear whether the antidepressant action is increased.

On the other hand, the benzodiazepines and barbiturates increase the antidepressant's metabolic breakdown and thereby diminish its therapeutic potential. For this reason, if a hypnotic is indicated, flurazepam should be prescribed.

Monoamine Oxidase Inhibitors

The capacity of iproniazid to produce euphoria in some persons was observed during its early use in the treatment of pulmonary tuberculosis. It was found that the hydrazine iproniazid had the property of preventing the breakdown of serotonin and epinephrine in the brain on administration of reserpine, through its capacity to inhibit the enzyme monoamine oxidase. Thus the cerebral levels of these amines rise.

The monoamine oxidase inhibitors potentiate the effects of many other drugs. Thus the amphetamines may prove excessively stimulating when given to patients who are taking iproniazid. They also potentiate the sedative-hypnotic actions of alcohol and barbiturates. Of most importance are their potentiating actions when given with the tricyclic iminodibenzyls. When they are administered simultaneously, the likelihood of serious hypotension, convulsions, and circulatory collapse is increased greatly. However, if they are cautiously administered by the oral route, with careful observations of blood pressure, their usage with imipramine and its analogues may enhance the therapeutic response in some patients.

Patients receiving the monoamine oxidase inhibitors should be warned to avoid the many foods containing tyramine, like cheese, wines, and chicken livers. The pressor effect of tyramine is markedly enhanced by the monoamine oxidase inhibitors.

The therapeutic response to all monoamine oxidase inhibitors is characterized by latent periods extending from days to weeks before relief of depression is discernible. They share in common the side effects of hypotension, expressed in dizziness, vertigo, and fainting. In the elderly, vascular collapse may occur when the patient is on high dosage. Constipation, vesical atony, peripheral edema, and such anticholinergic effects as dry mouth and blurred vision are seen. With central nervous activation, hyperreflexia, tremors, insomnia, and restlessness may occur. All may induce hypomanic episodes in the depressed individual when administered over time in high doses.

The MAO inhibitors described here are those now in general clinical usage and with limited toxicity in the prescribed effective dosage range.

Isocarboxazid. Sold as Marplan, this drug is given by mouth in a dosage range of 10 to 30 mg. daily. It may induce hepatitis, blood dyscrasias, and skin disorders. It is as effective as iproniazid (Marsilid) but is regarded as less toxic than the latter, which has now been withdrawn owing to the large number of cases of toxic hepatitis apparently induced by its usage.

Phenelzine. Known commercially as Nardil, this drug is usually administered in the dosage range of 40 to 60 mg. daily. It is considered by many clinicians to be as effective as iproniazid and more so than nialamide and is said to cause fewer hypotensive symptoms than other monoamine inhibitors. Cases of liver toxicity have not been reported.

Tranylcypromine. This monoamine oxidase inhibitor differs chemically from those previously described, as it is not a phenylhydrazine. Marketed in the United States as Parnate, it is regarded as the most rapidly acting antidepressant in the MAO series, and is considered by many the most effective for the majority of patients.

The drug is available in 10 mg. tablets. The usual initial dosage is 20 mg. given in two doses, morning and evening. If little response is obtained within two weeks, an additional 10 mg. may be prescribed daily.

Paradoxical Hypertension. In some patients, severe occipital headaches develop on administration of Parnate. These may be accompanied by nausea and vomiting, pallor and sweating, pain and rigidity in the neck, or collapse—significant signs of paradoxical hypertension. Some develop photophobia. Ingestion of amphetamines or substances high in tyramine potentiates the likelihood of this reaction. Onset of headache indicates the necessity for immediate withdrawal of the drug.

It is recommended that the monoamine oxidase inhibitors not be administered with the tricyclic antidepressants. However, in depressed patients resis-

tant to both series of drugs, some have cautiously and effectively prescribed combinations, carefully monitoring the blood pressure, pulse, and other physiological indicators.

With a hypertensive reaction, phentolamine (Regitine), 5 mg., or pentolinium (Ansolysen), 3 mg., should be given slowly by the intravenous route.

Lithium

The salts of lithium are now recognized worldwide as effective agents in the treatment of mania and hypomania. John F. J. Cade of Australia first tested the use of lithium in the treatment of such patients in 1949, extrapolating broadly from his experiments in animals in which he noticed that guinea pigs injected with the carbonate salt became temporarily lethargic.

PHYSIOLOGICAL ACTIVITY. Although lithium produces numerous changes in neuronal, biochemical, electrolyte, and endocrine functions, its exact mode of action in the manic-depressive psychoses remains unclear. It increases norepinephrine turnover rates in the brain, perhaps leading to a greater intraneuronal inactivation of norepinephrine. Synaptosomes treated with lithium increase their rate of uptake of norepinephrine, which makes less available at receptor sites. Lithium increases the rate of synthesis of serotonin in the brain. Lithium may alter membrane excitability, as it can replace sodium in the isolated nerve; its active transport out of the cell is much less than that of sodium.

Lithium administration in human beings leads to a generalized slowing of the electroencephalogram, but does not necessarily increase the frequency of seizures. When given to depressed patients, it tends to "normalize" sleep, increasing the low baseline levels of delta sleep and elevated levels of REM. These changes may occur within 24 hours of initiating treatment. It increases cortisol excretion, suggesting a direct effect on the adrenal or a nonspecific effect on the pituitary adrenal axis. It modifies aldosterone excretion. Lithium administration is associated with lowering of protein-bound iodine.

On electrolyte metabolism, lithium leads to diuresis, saluresis, and kaluresis immediately following its administration. Three days of administration reverses this picture and sodium retention commences. Manic patients retain significantly more orally administered lithium than do healthy controls. Like potassium, but unlike sodium, it enhances metabolism in brain slices, suggesting that it may modify energy metabolism in that organ.

INDICATIONS. Those who respond most effectively to the therapeutic use of lithium are patients with bipolar disorders (manic-depressive psychosis, mania, or hypomania). Those with frequent alteration of manic or depressive attacks do less well. When there is impairment of thought processes with delusional or hallucinatory experiences, or the clinical picture is regarded as schizo-affective, the clinical response to the agent is generally less favorable than in the former categories of illness. Nevertheless, some 70 to 80 per cent of patients with manic or hypomanic behavior are effectively relieved of their aberrant behavior when treatment with lithium is properly carried out. Maintenance therapy with lithium prevents or alleviates both phases of bipolar affective disorders and recurrent unipolar states.

In comparison with the neuroleptics, a number of reports indicate that lithium is the more effective agent in treating bipolar disorders. The neuroleptics bring about a more rapid reduction in the abnormal behavior; yet lithium administration, which at times requires five to ten days to effect change, is often effective when the former agents fail. Treatment of the manic patients is often started with haloperidol. If control is inadequate or ineffective, lithium becomes the agent of choice. Lithium may also be used to maintain a behavioral steady state by continued administration, thus preventing recurrence of mania. Some patients have taken the agent for over 15 years. During treatment, leukocytosis and slowing of the electroencephalogram occur frequently.

In the United States of America, lithium carbonate is now available commercially in 300 mg. tablets. The effective drug dosage by mouth will generally vary from 900 to 1800 mg. daily. It is necessary to maintain a serum lithium level between 0.8 and 1.2 mEq. per liter. In Chapter 19, reference is made to the means by which the psychiatrist may estimate the appropriate daily dosage of lithium for the individual by noting the 24-hour level of serum lithium following a single test dosage.

Lithium treatment does not impair intellectual activity, consciousness, or range or quality of emotional life. Patients taking the drug fully experience joy, grief, tenderness, sexual desire, and other affects. In this respect it also contrasts with the neuroleptics. Patients frequently speak of the drug as "putting a brake" on them. Those who have obtained a secondary gain from the sense of exhilaration and power in the license of hypomanic or manic attacks sometimes dislike the drug for this reason. Polatin and Fieve point out that in those with milder forms of manic-depressive illness, this factor, as well as the denial of illness and its chronicity, leads some to discontinue or refuse lithium carbonate, both as continuing treatment and as a preventive of recurrences.

TOXIC SYMPTOMS. In the years since its introduction into psychiatry as a therapeutic agent, there have been very few serious complications. Toxic symptoms may occur above serum lithium levels of 2.0 mEq. per liter. Nausea, abdominal cramps, vomiting, diarrhea, thirst, and polyuria are symptoms associated with blood levels over 1.0 mEq/

liter. These become severe at 2.0 mEq/ liter. Central nervous system symptoms of marked lethargy, coarse tremors and muscular twitchings, ataxia, slurred speech, and convulsions occur as the blood level is increased over 2.0 mEq/ liter. The patient may lapse into coma, and death may result from severe changes in electrolyte balance with consequent cardiac and pulmonary complications when blood levels exceed 4.0 mEq/liter. The drug is contraindicated in those with impaired renal, cardiac, or central nervous system functioning.

The toxic symptoms may be reversed by prompt discontinuance of the drug and correction of the abnormalities in the fluid and electrolyte balance. When serious imbalance has occurred, correction has been brought about by sodium replacement intravenously, ingestion or infusion of urea and alkalinization of the urine by infusion of sodium lactate, or administration of acetazolamide or aminophylline, which increase lithium excretion. Dialysis may be required to exchange lithium for sodium in severely toxic patients.

Both goiter and hypothyroidism have been noticed in those receiving lithium, but findings of an increased goiter incidence in patients with bipolar disorders untreated with lithium suggest that the agent at best plays a secondary role in goiter production, probably only in those predisposed to dysfunction of this organ.

Lithium has been implicated as a teratogenic agent. During pregnancy, renal lithium clearance tends to rise and children nursed by lithium-treated women show a level of serum lithium approximately one third to one half that of the nursing person. Polyuric side effects can occur in some on lithium therapy. The diabetes insipidus–like syndrome is considered activated by vasopressor-sensitive adenylcyclase.

Folliculitis and papular pruritic dermatitides have occasionally been observed, but are rare. Excessive weight gain, sometimes noted, may be rapidly reversed on a low-calorie diet containing 100 mEq. sodium daily. T-wave depression in the electrocardiogram during treatment with lithium is benign.

ANXIOLYTICS

Of the therapeutic agents classified as anxiolytics, it is probable that the benzodiazepine derivatives have become the most widely used and today are among the most frequently prescribed of all drugs. As a group, the major indications for their use are in the anxiety disorders and particularly in those in whom overt anxiety and neuromuscular tension are evident. They are not effective in the psychoses and, if given over periods of time, tolerance develops in individual patients, with the potential for withdrawal reactions similar to those that occur with addiction to the somnifacients (the sedative-hypnotics). In contrast to the latter group of drugs, their action is longer, although less intense, and they have muscle relaxant properties not evident with the somnifacients, as well as anticonvulsant potentials. These agents do not affect activity of organs activated by the autonomic nervous system.

Glycerols

Meprobamate, a member of this series, was first introduced and sold commercially as Miltown or Equanil in the U.S.A. It is known to synchronize selectively interneuronal electrical activity in the thalamic nuclei and to act as an anticonvulsant and muscle relaxant. In contrast to the previously described drugs, it is said not to affect activity of the autonomic nervous system.

It is of value in anxiety and tension states, phobias, tension headaches, psychosomatic disorders, insomnia, premenstrual tension, and neurodermatitis. It often produces relief of headaches that are the result of constant, almost unremitting contraction of the posterior muscles of the neck.

Continued ingestion of large doses of meprobamate can create physical dependence, manifested on abrupt withdrawal of the drug by hyperirritability of the central nervous system and convulsions. The type of addiction caused by meprobamate resembles that caused by chronic intoxication with excessive amounts of barbiturates or alcohol. Especial care should be exercised in prescribing meprobamate for alcoholics or narcotic drug addicts.

A wide variety of side effects and untoward reactions has been reported with meprobamate use. Among them have been dermal hypersensitivity reactions and acute nonthrombocytopenic purpura. Large doses taken with suicidal intent may produce respiratory and vasomotor collapse. In a few persons, allergic reactions have been noted, with urticaria, erythematous rashes, and, rarely, fainting spells and bronchial spasm.

Benzodiazepines

Of these agents, diazepam (Valium) and chlordiazepoxide (Librium) have been the most widely prescribed therapeutically.

The benzodiazepines generally are rated by clinicians as more effective than other anxiolytics and the somnifacients (barbiturates, et al.) in provision of symptomatic relief. They are effective in the anxiety disorders, tension headaches and backaches, treatment of the nocturnal "restless limb" syndrome and the stiff-man syndrome, termination of status epilepticus, and in psychomotor agitation in alcoholic withdrawal, following brain or other injuries, or tonic muscle spasm, including tetanus.

These drugs are unusually safe to prescribe to the psychiatric patient, as massive overdoses seldom lead to death, and the management of the toxic effects is less difficult. They are

therefore preferred to the somnifacients when suicidal intent is suspected.

While tolerance may occur and withdrawal psychoses have been encountered occasionally, these potentials also seem less frequent than with meprobamate or the sedative-hypnotics. Furthermore, as they are bound and metabolize more slowly, withdrawal effects are less intense than with the latter agents.

Diazepam is effective in inducing and maintaining sleep over short periods. As a hypnotic, flurazepam is effective in doses of 15 to 30 mg. before bed. This agent is classified in Table 32–2 as a somnifacient and is the preferred drug when prescribing the antidepressants, as the potential for drug-drug inhibition is less than with others in that series. Common side effects are drowsiness and limitation of spontaneity, with impaired concentration. Ataxia, dysarthria, hyperactivity, and headache have been observed, and also occasional acute overactive behavioral disturbances. For major toxic responses in which respiratory depression, hypotension, hypothermia, or coma occur, it is seldom necessary to provide other than supportive care.

Forced diuresis is useless for the benzodiazepines, but is indicated in poisoning with meprobamate, for which peritoneal dialysis and hemodialysis may be employed.

BIBLIOGRAPHY

General

DiMascio, A.: Psychotropic drug overuse: An examination of prescription practices. Psychiatr. Digest, 23:39–43, 1972.

Klein, D. F., and Davis, J. M.: Diagnosis and Drug Treatment of Psychiatric Disorders. Baltimore, Williams & Wilkins Company, 1969.

Malitz, S., Glassman, A., Kobrynski, B., Scerebini, E. E., and Simpson, G.: Psychotherapeutic Drug Manual. State of New York, Department of Mental Hygiene, Albany, New York, 1977.

Porter, I. H.: The genetics of drug susceptibility. Dis. Nerv. Syst., 27:25–36, 1966.

Schader, R. I. (ed.): Manual of Psychiatric Therapeutics. Boston, Little Brown & Company, 1975.

World Health Organization: Research in Psychopharmacology. Techn. Rep. Serv., 371. Geneva, World Health Organization, 1967.

Neuroleptics

Ayd, F. J.: Haloperidol: Fifteen years of clinical experience. Dis. Nerv. Syst., 33:459–469, 1972.

Beaumont, P. J. V., Gilder, M. G., Friesen, H. G., et al.: The effects of phenothiazines on endocrine function. Br. J. Psychiatry, 124:413–430, 1974.

Carney, M. W. P., and Sheffield, P. F.: Comparison of antipsychotic depot injections in the maintenance treatment of schizophrenia. Br. J. Psychiatry, 129:476–481, 1976.

Cavenar, J. O., and Maltbie, A. A.: Another indication for haloperidol. Psychosomatics, 17:128–130, 1974.

Creese, I., Burt, D. R., and Snyder, S. H.: Dopamine receptor binding predicts clinical and pharmacological potencies of antischizophrenic drugs. Science, 192:481–483, 1976.

DiMascio, A.: Toward a more rational use of antiparkinson drugs in psychiatry. Drug Therapy, Sept., 1971.

DiMascio, A., Bernardo, D. L., Greenblatt, D. J., and Marder, J. E.: A controlled study of amantadine in drug-induced extrapyramidal disorders. Arch. Gen. Psychiatry, 33:599–602, 1976.

Donlon, P. T., Axelrad, A. D., Tupin, J. P., and Chien, C.: Comparison of depot fluphenazines: duration of action and incidence of side effects. Compr. Psychiatry, 17:369–376, 1976.

Fann, W. E., and Lake R.: On the coexistence of parkinsonism and tardive dyskinesia. Dis. Nerv. Syst., 35:324–326, 1974.

Gardos, G.: Are antipsychotic drugs interchangeable? J. Nerv. Ment. Dis., 159:343–348, 1974.

Groves, J. E., and Mandel, M. R.: The long-acting phenothiazines. Arch. Gen. Psychiatry, 33:893–902, 1975.

Jus, H., Pineau, R., Lachance, R., et al.: Epidemiology of tardive dyskinesia. Dis. Nerv. Syst., 37:257–261, 1976.

Linnoila, M., Vinkari, M., and Hietala, O.: Effect of sodium valproate on tardive dyskinesia. Br. J. Psychiatry, 129:114–119, 1976.

Marano, V., and Seapagnini, U.: Flupenthixol in depression. Acta Neurol., 30:102–108, 1975.

Polak, P., and Laycomb, L.: Rapid tranquilization. Am. J. Psychiatry, 128:640–643, 1971.

Prien, R. F., Levin, J., and Cole, J. O.: Indications for high dose chlorpromazine therapy in chronic schizophrenia. Dis. Nerv. Syst., 31:739–745, 1970.

Snyder, S., Greenberg, D., and Yamamura, H. I.: Antischizophrenic drugs and brain cholinergic receptors. Arch. Gen. Psychiatry, 31:58–61, 1974.

Task Force of the A.P.A. on Late Neurological Effects of Antipsychotic Drugs: Tardive Dyskinesia: Summary of a Task Force Report of the American Psychiatric Association. Am. J. Psychiatry, 137:1163–1172, 1980.

Lithium

Almy, G. L., and Taylor, M. A.: Lithium retention in mania. Arch. Gen. Psychiatry, 29:232–234, 1973.

Chernik, D. A., Cochrane, C., and Mendels, J.: Effects of lithium carbonate on sleep. J. Psychiatr. Res., 10:133–146, 1974.

Cooper, T. B., Bergner, P. E. E., and Simpson, G. M.: The 24-hour serum lithium level as a prognosticator of dosage requirements. Am. J. Psychiatry, 130:601–603, 1973.

Davis, J. W.: Overview: Maintenance therapy in psychiatry: II. Affective disorders. Am. J. Psychiatry, 133:1–13, 1976.

Dawson, E. B., Moore, T. D., and McGanity, W. J.: Relationship of lithium metabolism to mental hospital admission and homicide. Dis. Nerv. Syst., 33:546–556, 1972.

Dempsey, G. M., et al.: Treatment of excessive weight gain in patients taking lithium. Am. J. Psychiatry, 133:1082–1084, 1976.

Erwin, C. W., Gerber, C. J., Morrison, S. D., et al.: Lithium carbonate and convulsive disorders. Arch. Gen. Psychiatry, 28:646–648, 1973.

Murphy, D. L., Goodwin, F. K., and Bunney, W. E.: Leukocytosis during lithium treatment. Am. J. Psychiatry, 127:1559–1561, 1971.

Perez-Cruet, J., Tagliamonte, A., Tagliamonte, P., et al.: Stimulation of serotonin synthesis by lithium. J. Pharmacol. Exp. Ther., 178:325–330, 1971.

Polatin, P., and Fieve, R. R.: Patient rejection of lithium carbonate prophylaxis. J.A.M.A., 218:864–866, 1971.

Schou, M., Goldfield, M. D., Weinstein, M. R., et al.: Lithium and pregnancy. Br. Med. J., 2:135–139, 1973.

Sheard, M. H., Marini, J. L., Bridges, C. I., et al.: The effect of lithium on impulsive aggressive behavior in man. Am. J. Psychiatry, 133:1409–1413, 1976.

Antidepressants

Amsterdam, J., Brunswick, D., and Mendels, J.: The clinical application of tricyclic antidepressant pharmacokinetics and plasma levels. Am. J. Psychiatry, *137*:653–662, 1980.

Dalessio, D. J.: Chronic pain syndromes and disordered cortical inhibition: Effects of tricyclic compounds. Dis. Nerv. Syst., *28*:325–328, 1967.

Glassman, A. H.: The clinical pharmacology of imipramine: Implications for therapeutics. Arch. Gen. Psychiatry, *28*:649–653, 1973.

Gram, L. F., Overd, K. F., and Kirk, L.: Influence of neuroleptics and benzodiazepines on metabolism of tricyclic antidepressants in man. Am. J. Psychiatry, *131*:863–866, 1974.

Munoz, R. H.: Treatment of tricyclic intoxication. Am. J. Psychiatry, *133*:1085–1087, 1976.

Schildkraut, J. J.: The catecholamine hypothesis of affective disorders: A review of supporting evidence. Am. J. Psychiatry, *122*:509–522, 1965.

Spiker, D. G.: Combining tricyclic and monoamine oxidase inhibitor antidepressants. Arch. Gen. Psychiatry, *33*:828–830, 1976.

Wheatley, D.: Potentiation of amitriptyline by thyroid hormone. Arch. Gen. Psychiatry, *26*:229–236, 1972.

Anxiolytics

Garattini, S., Mussini, E., and Randall, L. O.: The Benzodiazepines. New York, Raven Press, 1973.

Presskorn, S. H., and Deuner, L. J.: Benzodiazepines and withdrawal psychosis. J.A.M.A., *237*:36–38, 1977.

Tallman, J. F., Paul, S. M., Skolnick, P., and Gallager, D. W.: Receptors for the Age of Anxiety: Pharmacology of the benzodiazepines. Science *207*:274–281, 1980.

33

SHOCK AND OTHER PHYSICAL THERAPIES

"...Pluck from the memory a rooted sorrow,
Raze out the written troubles of the brain,
And with some sweet oblivious antidote
Cleanse the stuff'd bosom of that perilous stuff
Which weighs upon the heart..."

Macbeth

The tranquilizing chair, a nineteenth century invention for treatment of the insane.
Photograph courtesy of the New York Academy of Medicine.

With the increasingly widespread usage of the pharmacotherapies and psychotherapies in psychiatric practice, the need for shock and physical therapies has proceeded toward obsolescence. The former have proved more effective and more economical to administer for the majority of patients. To a larger extent, their administration avoids temporary or permanent damage to brain tissue and function. Nevertheless, the physical therapies remain important techniques in the therapeutic armamentarium. For the most part today, their prescription occurs when a patient problem remains resistant over time to the psychotherapeutic and/or pharmacotherapeutic approach or, as in the case of the serious depressive psychosis, a prompt behavioral change is indicated to prevent either suicide or prolonged suffering.

ELECTROCONVULSIVE THERAPY

In 1938, Cerletti and Bini described a method of producing convulsions by electricity and began its use in the treatment of schizophrenia.

The generally used apparatus operates on 100-volt, 60-cycle, alternating current and contains mainly a variable transformer, ohm, volt, and ampere meters, and an automatic timer. The combined voltage and time settings constitute the "dose." Applications may range from 70 to 130 volts continuing from 0.1 to 0.5 second. Usually one starts with 80 volts for 0.2 second. If this fails to produce a convulsion, the voltage may be increased to 90 or 100 volts and the period of application increased. If this does not result in a seizure, no further application should be made until the following day. Only generalized seizures are productive of desired results.

The patient becomes unconscious immediately after the current is applied, even if no seizure follows. He will have no memory of a "shock." The convulsion conforms closely to those of spontaneous origin, with a tonic phase continuing for approximately 10 seconds followed by a clonic phase of somewhat longer duration. The convulsion is accompanied by apnea.

Techniques and Responses

In addition to the usual physical examination, including blood pressure, before the patient receives electroconvulsive therapy, a roentgenogram should be made of the chest and of the lateral aspect of the spine; there should also be an electrocardiogram. An electroencephalogram is recommended. If the patient is to be treated in the morning, he receives either no breakfast or a glass of fruit juice and one slice of toast two hours before treatment. The patient should void, and dentures should be removed before treatment. Ordinary sedation need not be withheld, but drugs producing hypotensive effects should not be prescribed beforehand.

The patient is placed in a comfortable dorsal position, or the spine may be slightly flexed. The shoulders and arms are held lightly by a nurse to prevent extreme movements of the arms. Usually a restraint sheet is sufficient for the thighs, but if they are held, the control should not be too rigid lest fractures of an acetabulum or of a femur result.

Premedication with succinylcholine (Anectine) is used regularly now to prevent fractures. Generally, the patient receives sodium pentothal or methohexital intravenously slowly until sleep has ensued. At this time, 20 to 30 mg. of succinylcholine is injected. The barbiturate relieves the usual preshock anxiety. Most therapists have the patient inhale oxygen. A padded tongue depressor or other resilient mouth gag is placed between the teeth to prevent biting the tongue or other injury. The assistant who holds the mouth gag in place holds the patient's chin firmly upon the gag so that the jaw cannot open too far and become dislocated. Electrode paste is rubbed into the skin on both sides of the forehead, and the electrodes, previously soaked in saturated salt solution, are applied to the prepared areas. The apparatus button is pressed and the patient instantly becomes unconscious. Following the clonic phase, there is a phase of muscular relaxation with stertorous respiration. It is well to roll the patient on his side to prevent inhalation of saliva. The patient remains unconscious for about five minutes, then slowly rouses during the next five to ten minutes.

After the treatment there is a period of confusion, during which the patient should be closely observed to prevent harm through falling or other actions taken in the acute confusional state. He should usually be permitted to lie for one half to one hour after treatment. If left undisturbed, he may sleep an hour or more.

Unilateral application of electrodes, in order to induce a focal seizure spreading from the nondominant hemisphere, has been recommended as a means of decreasing postshock confusion, amnesia, and memory loss. Its therapeutic effect, however, has been found by some to be less than with bilateral electroconvulsive therapy. In study of the effects of this technique, it was found that verbal learning was impaired selectively by electroconvulsive therapy when applied to the nondominant hemisphere and nonverbal learning by application to the dominant hemisphere.

In this technique of stimulation, one electrode is placed midway across and 3 cm. above a line projected between the lateral angle of the orbit and the external auditory meatus. The other, or upper, electrode is placed 6 cm. higher than the lower and at an angle of 70° to the line. The placement is made over the nondominant hemisphere, dominance being determined on the basis of preferred skeletal muscular usage. The convulsive state induced by this method is similar to that brought about by bilateral electrode placement, although occasionally contralateral (focal) convulsions take place.

Frequency

Treatments are usually given three times a week. The period for which treatment should be continued depends largely upon the results obtained and upon the nature of the disorder treated. In depressive reactions, the patient may have received the maximum benefit after five to ten treatments. In disorders in which the patient is slowly but definitely improving, treatment may continue to 25 or 30 applications, followed, if desirable, by maintenance treatments. Two treatments per day may be given for two or three successive days in the case of acutely disturbed patients who are threatened by psychotic exhaustion.

Indications

The greatest usefulness of electroconvulsive therapy is in depression. Its most frequent use, therefore, is in the treatment of involutional melancholia and of the depressive phase of manic-depressive psychosis. When depression is an associated symptom in other disorders, this form of therapy may be followed by beneficial results. Its use as a "maintenance" treatment in chronically disturbed schizophrenics and in the manic phase of manic-depressive psychosis is discussed in another section.

Clinical features which distinguish the therapeutically responsive group are a good premorbid personality; lack of evidence of psychogenic precipitants to depression; weight loss; pyknic body build; previous depressive episodes; early morning awakening; nihilistic, somatic, and paranoid delusions; and ideas of guilt. Evidence of anxiety, hysterical features, and the blaming of others correlate with poor response to electroconvulsive treatment.

Induction of the convulsive state by unilateral parietal placement of the electrodes over the nondominant hemisphere, described previously in the section on Technique, is preferred by some for patients with associated organic brain disease such as senile or arteriosclerotic syndromes, those who depend heavily on memory functions in their vocations, and paranoid and phobic individuals who manifest increasing anxiety as memory impairment increases.

Contraindications

The only contraindication to the use of electroconvulsive therapy (ECT) is increased intracranial pressure. Thus patients with brain tumors should not be given ECT. For those patients with subdural hematoma, subarachnoid hemorrhage, congestive heart failure, or aortic aneurysm, the increased risk of morbidity and mortality associated with ECT treatment must be weighed against the benefits of this treatment. The premorbid state may be severe enough to preclude the use of ECT except when the risk of death from depression, either through suicide or self-starvation, is high and the risk of ECT is less than that associated with chemotherapy utilizing monoamine oxidase inhibitors or tricyclic antidepressants.

Complications

IMPAIRMENT OF MEMORY. Impairment of memory constantly accompanies electroconvulsive therapy. It may vary from a mild tendency to forget names to a severe confusion of the Korsakoff type. At first it tends to cover a long period prior to treatment, then gradually to diminish to events immediately before treatment. It is often distressing to the patient and may continue to some degree for several weeks or a few months following the termination of treatment. Full return of memory finally occurs. Psychological investigators indicate that electroconvulsive therapy is not followed by any intellectual impairment.

It has been shown that with the impairment of retention in memory function, there simultaneously takes place improved capacity for learning. The fact that clinically improved patients complain infrequently of memory disturbance may be explained by the fact that they judge their response subjectively in terms of the greater capacity to learn and this experience dominates the impairment of retention due to the electroshock. One cannot accept then the subjective report of the patient relative to the effects of electroshock on his memory.

FRACTURES AND DISLOCATIONS. The most frequent complications in electroconvulsive therapy are fractures and dislocations caused by muscular contraction. The fracture occurring most often is a *compression fracture of vertebrae*, in the dorsal area between the second and eighth, usually the third, fourth, or fifth vertebra. A majority of the fractures occur early in the course of treatment. They are not of major clinical importance and do not require special treatment. Many are found only on roentgenologic examination. Back pain may persist for a few days or weeks. Fractures of the femur, of the acetabulum, and of the neck of the humerus have occurred. Dislocation of the jaw is frequent unless pressure is applied to prevent the opening of the mouth at the onset of the tonic phase. With the use of succinylcholine to induce paralysis, the incidence of ECT-induced fractures is extremely low.

APNEA. Apnea occurs physiologically in any general convulsive seizure, but in electroconvulsive therapy the respiratory arrest may be disturbingly prolonged. Some therapists use oxygen inhalation immediately after the convulsion as a safety measure. If apnea persists, artificial respiration should be applied. A metal airway should be available to prevent the tongue from falling back and to lead air through accumulations of saliva and mucus. Deaths as a result of electroconvulsive therapy are exceedingly uncommon.

In approximately one in a thousand patients, prolonged apnea may occur after the use of succinylcholine. It has been suggested that those sensitive to this drug and its diethyl derivative, suxethonium, have inherited a less active variant of the enzyme pseudocholinesterase, which metabolizes the drug so that the drug action persists an undue length of time. It is now possible, through a rapid screening test, to disclose those whose serum contains the atypical cholinesterase incapable of breaking down the muscle relaxants. From Motulsky and Morrow's study, the gene frequently determining the existence of the abnormal enzyme is very rare among blacks, suggesting that they are at very low risk for this complication in administration of electroshock therapy with succinylcholine.

Usually, a period of controlled respiration will terminate the apnea. Coramine (1 to 2.5 gm. in 4 to 10 ml.) may be given intravenously to counteract excessive barbiturate. Artificial ventilation should be maintained until spontaneous respiration occurs.

Any patient responding with prolonged apnea after use of Anectine should be so informed. Neither he nor other family members should be administered this agent again unless careful quantitation is made of serum esterase activity.

Results of Treatment

In patients with major depression, the improvement following electroconvulsive shock therapy is striking. In 80 per cent or more of these disorders, five to ten treatments are followed by full or social recovery. Prior to the treatment of involutional melancholia by electric shock therapy, protracted depression, sometimes lasting for years, was the rule. Early treatment of this disorder and of the depressions of depressive psychosis by shock therapy will save many patients who would otherwise commit suicide.

Electroconvulsive shock therapy has no influence on the recurrence of manic-depressive episodes. Guilt and self-punishing, self-accusatory trends are usually rapidly alleviated. Treatment is followed by improvement in less than half of the cases of the paranoid type of involutional psychosis, even though the maximum number of convulsions is induced. Senile depressions are usually relieved unless arteriosclerotic or senile brain changes have been important determinants.

The results of treatment of the manic phase of bipolar disorders are less favorable than of the depressive phase, but have been greatly improved by the practice of giving treatments more frequently. Best results are secured by giving two treatments a day for the first two or three days. These are usually followed by much confusion, but as this clears, the patient is found to be definitely improved.

Mode of Action

The use of electroconvulsive shock is entirely empirical. Many theories, both psychogenic and physiogenic, have been suggested as explanations for its therapeutic action, but no one has offered a satisfactory explanation for the results obtained either by electroconvulsive or by insulin therapy. Some investigators suggest that cerebral anoxia, a result common to all the shock therapies, may somehow be the basis for the mental improvement. In both hypoglycemic and convulsive shock therapies, the brain is deprived of energy and oxidative metabolism to a degree that renders it inadequate to support cerebral function. The mechanisms producing these conditions are different, however. With hypoglycemia the brain is deprived of glucose and the cerebral metabolic rate is depressed. With electroshock, brain activity is raised to such a high pitch that cerebral function cannot be sustained by the oxygen and glucose coming to the brain in the blood.

Electroconvulsive therapy modifies the sleep pattern profoundly, in that it leads to increase in total sleep time, with diminution of rapid eye movement (REM) sleep. In animal experiments, no drive later to make up REM time in sleep is seen. Electroconvulsive therapy apparently produces a sustained increase in synthesis and utilization of norepinephrine in the brain. It appears, as well, to produce a short-lasting inhibition of brain protein synthesis.

In animals it has been shown that electroshock convulsions selectively obliterate conditioned fear reactions and other aversively controlled and learned behaviors. Hunt has shown, too, that this effect depends upon the occurrence of convulsion and is not the result of the impairment of memory functions. Some drugs enhance or attenuate the effect of electroshock on the *conditioned emotional response* (CER) in rats; whether these drug actions found in rats may be correlated with their clinical effects in man has not been established. Chlorpromazine given after electroshock to rats increases the CER. Meprobamate, on the other hand, decreases the conditioned emotional state even more. Curiously, Dilantin given simultaneously with shock enhances the effect of the shock, while phenyrone blocks out the convulsion and prevents the attenuating action of the convulsion.

Electrosleep, which is not to be confused with electroshock, has been used extensively in the U.S.S.R. and is now under trial elsewhere. It is induced from a battery device passing a standard 100 pulses per second of pulse duration of 1 millisecond at levels of 1 milliampere for 30 minutes between electrodes placed over one eye and the related mastoid. The designation is a misnomer; many patients never fall asleep. No convulsions occur. Treatments are usually given five days per week for one or two weeks. The indications and therapeutic effectiveness of this technique are dubious.

INHALANT CONVULSIVE TREATMENT

Clinical trials have demonstrated that hexafluorodiethyl ether (Indoklon) given by a simple inhalation technique in doses of 4 to 6 ml. containing 0.05 of the agent per milliliter of solution is capable of inducing immediate convulsive responses. Indoklon has been administered intravenously as a convulsant agent in association with succinylcholine and a short-acting anesthetic.

This convulsant may be used as effectively as electroshock therapy for the same therapeutic purposes and is accepted more readily by some patients. Thus it may serve as an alternative procedure to electroshock treatment.

INSULIN SHOCK TREATMENT

In 1928, Sakel, believing that the nervous hyperactivity occurring in morphine addicts during withdrawal of that drug was caused by an excess of epinephrine, expressed the opinion that the excitement might be relieved by large doses of insulin. Later the similarity of the abstinence symptoms to other excited stages suggested to Sakel that the latter also might be influenced by the same drug. He accordingly administered insulin to excited schizophrenic patients. After a period of experimental clinical work, he published his results in 1933. The basic features in the method developed by Sakel are still regarded as most effective. At first Sakel tried to avoid the development of deep hypoglycemic states, but he soon observed that better results occurred if coma was induced. He then increased the dose with the avowed intention of producing insulin shock.

NEUROPHYSIOLOGY. Unlike other organs, which can utilize carbohydrates, proteins, and fats for energy requirements, the brain is able to oxidize carbohydrates only. Since the rate of oxidation of carbohydrates is determined by the amount of insulin in the blood stream, the injection of a large amount of insulin into the body greatly reduces the sugar content of the blood. With a decrease in the amount of sugar available, the oxidative processes of the brain are so reduced that the effects are similar to anoxia of that organ, a condition known to lead to coma. The loss of consciousness in hypoglycemia is presumably caused by the fact that the brain cells are deprived of glucose, their principal fuel, without which the metabolic processes in the brain are progressively depressed.

According to the segmental-suprasegmental concept of evolutionary development of the central nervous system, there are ascending levels of integration both of structure and function. We may therefore think of successively higher levels, beginning with the lower medulla and culminating with the cerebral hemispheres. It has been shown that the rate of metabolism in each of the higher levels is greater than in that of the level immediately lower or older. The greatest susceptibility to low blood sugar exists, therefore, in the more complex and phylogenetically more recent areas of the forebrain. With the injection of large amounts of insulin, there is a steplike depression of function and there appear progressive neurological signs and symptoms corresponding to a phyletic regression or functional disturbance in the successively lower anatomical levels of cerebral cortex, diencephalon, midbrain, upper medulla, and lower medulla.

As the blood sugar falls following the injection of a "coma dose" of insulin, various deficiency and release phenomena linked with functional patterns of different levels of the neuraxis become manifest in the signs and symptoms that characterize the successive stages of insulin coma.

PREPARATION FOR TREATMENT. Although insulin shock therapy is a relatively safe procedure in the hands of a skilled therapist, most serious complications may occur with patients in whom an organic pathologic condition has been overlooked. In addition to careful and complete psychiatric, physical, and neurological examinations, such laboratory examinations should be made to exclude the possibility of undertaking the treatment of a bad risk. It is generally agreed that there should be roentgenologic studies of the chest and of the lateral thoracic spine, a serological examination, urinalysis, blood count, and a determination of the fasting blood sugar. An electrocardiogram, especially in older patients, is highly desirable, even though the clinical examination is negative. It is advisable to discuss results and dangers with a responsible relative, and also to secure written permission for treatment.

CONTRAINDICATIONS TO TREATMENT.

The presence of any organic disease must be individually evaluated and its seriousness weighed against the urgency for treatment. The following disorders, however, are usually considered as contraindications: (1) any active infection, or any chronic or subacute infection that may be "lighted up" by treatment; (2) serious heart, liver, or kidney disease; (3) diabetes or other endocrine disorder; (4) skeletal pathology; (5) lack of adequate superficial veins; or (6) age under 16 or over 45 years. Some therapists, however, have successfully treated patients who were pregnant or had epilepsy, myxedema, or allergy.

TECHNIQUE OF TREATMENT. The patient usually receives his dose of insulin at about 7 a.m. while still fasting. He remains under vigilant nursing observation from the time the drug is given until after coma is terminated and consciousness fully regained. Because of the danger of "after-shock" or other complications, the patient should be under competent nursing supervision during the succeeding 24 hours. A physician trained and experienced in insulin therapy should watch him constantly from the time he becomes unconscious until consciousness is fully restored.

The original method of Sakel, still very widely followed, begins with the intramuscular injection of 15 to 25 units of insulin, which is increased by 10 to 15 units daily until the desired depth of coma is reached. This is usually not reached until the dosage is between 80 and 275 units and from 7 to 15 treatments have been given. After coma dose has been reached, the dosage may usually be reduced somewhat in the hope that excessively deep reactions may be avoided, but it is adjusted daily for the remainder of the course of treatment. The dose of insulin required to produce coma is not related to the degree of hypoglycemia produced.

A technique in which rapidly increasing doses are administered was developed by Shurley and is often used. With this technique, the procedure begins with the administration to the fasting patient for five successive days of small doses of insulin increasingly graduated from 5 to 25 units. The purpose of this series of injections is to ascertain whether the patient has a predisposition to allergic or hypoglycemic reactions. If there is no evidence of undue sensitivity, the course of treatment is begun.

The therapist seeks to produce the maximum physiological effect for the longest period of time permissible by the largest doses of insulin consistent with the patient's safety. Patients possess varying degrees of resistance to insulin. For that reason, the initial treatment dose does not exceed 50 units of U 100 ordinary insulin given by deep intramuscular injection. This dose is doubled each day until a clinical response is secured or a maximum dose of 1600 to 2200 units is reached. Some patients are extremely resistive to insulin. If in such cases coma does not occur within the dosage range stated, the maximum dose may be repeated for five or six days or the dose may be "zig-zagged."

This procedure may be conducted in one of several ways. The most common method is first to give double the dose with which treatment was begun, the next day to give half the maximum dose, and on the third day to repeat the maximum dose. If a patient does not respond to this routine, larger doses may be given or the route of administration may be changed to intravenous. When a clinical response is obtained, the rate of dose increase is reduced from a doubling of the amount to one of 10 to 20 per cent. When sensitization occurs as manifested by a deeper coma on the same or a smaller dose, by an earlier onset of coma, or by a somatic crisis or other complication, the dose is reduced rapidly (by halves) until one just sufficient to produce the desired depth of coma is reached. Thereafter

the maintenance dose must be determined daily as indicated by the patient's response. The depth and duration of each coma will vary in accordance with the opinion and experience of the individual therapist.

TERMINATION OF COMA. Hypoglycemic coma is terminated by giving an adequate amount of carbohydrates by one of three methods: orally, by gavage, or by intravenous administration. In emerging from the coma, the patient ordinarily retraverses the phyletic stages through which he passed in developing coma. If he is able to drink, the patient is given eight ounces of a 50 per cent sugar solution. If he is unable to drink, the coma is terminated by tube feeding or by glucose given intravenously. Each method has its proponents. Probably, however, a gavage of 500 ml. of a warm 50 per cent glucose solution is preferable, especially if the patient has had a convulsion, has been uncooperative upon waking, has inaccessible veins, or needs a reservoir of glucose during a prolonged coma. The intravenous method is always used in an emergency and routinely by many therapists.

When glucose is given intravenously, the patient receives from 20 to 50 ml. (sometimes more) of a $33\frac{1}{3}$ per cent solution. This method should be used also if the patient is not alert within 20 minutes after having received glucose by mouth. If he is suffering from simple hypoglycemia, he should respond to intravenous glucose within five minutes. If the coma is terminated intravenously, it is wise to give additional glucose by mouth lest there be a return of the hypoglycemic state. Following the termination of the coma, the patient should receive a substantial meal. It is important that he receive sodium chloride to replace that lost through perspiration.

ADJUNCTS TO TREATMENT. Atropine sulfate ($\frac{1}{150}$ to $\frac{1}{75}$ grain) is given routinely with the insulin dose and again before electroshock if that is used in conjunction with insulin therapy, to decrease vagotonia. Vitamins B_1 and C are given to supplement the deficiencies resulting from the intake of large quantities of vitamin-poor carbohydrates. Diphenylhydantoin sodium (Dilantin), $4\frac{1}{2}$ grains daily, may be given orally at the same time the patient receives insulin in order to prevent hypoglycemic convulsions. It should be gradually discontinued upon completion of the course of insulin therapy and should not be used if combined electroconvulsive therapy is employed. Postural drainage and the insertion of gauze wicks should be used to prevent aspiration of the excessive amount of saliva. Care must also be exercised to prevent aspiration of vomited material. Airways, oxygen, and artificial respiration may aid in preventing serious complications.

Some therapists use potassium chloride prophylactically to correct electrolytic balance and to prevent prolonged comas. Its value is still undetermined. Hyaluronidase, in doses of 75 to 150 turbidity reducing units (T.R.U.) added to the insulin, has been found to be of value in reducing the amount of insulin required to produce coma, to increase the effective length of treatment levels, and to increase the number of therapeutically valuable reactions (comas). It is also said to diminish the frequency of aftershocks, as well as convulsions, restlessness, and exhaustion.

DURATION OF TREATMENT. Treatment is given five or six times a week for an average total course of 50 hours of coma. Although the number of treatment days may be somewhat smaller in acute cases and in those patients who have shown no benefit from treatment, the total number of hours should be not less than 30. More than 50 coma days are given by some therapists to patients who are continuing to show beneficial results. If a relapse takes place, it usually occurs within a month after discontinuance of treatment. The patient should therefore continue under observation for nearly that period of time.

COMPLICATIONS OF TREATMENT. Since dangerous, and even fatal, complications may readily occur, it is essential that both physician and nurse possess sufficient experience and skill to enable them to recognize and deal immediately with emergency situations. Even though both possess these qualities, the mortality rate will be from 0.5 to 1 per cent. Complications include prolonged coma, respiratory and cardiovascular reactions, convulsions, and allergic reactions.

RESULTS OF TREATMENT. As already implied, the use of insulin shock therapy is limited today to the treatment of schizophrenia. There is complete agreement among therapists that there is an inverse ratio between the duration of illness and the recovery rate. The best results are obtained with patients who have not been ill for more than one year. The highest recovery or remission rate is among patients in their twenties who previously had well-integrated personalities, who have had a stormy onset of the illness, and have come to treatment within six months after its onset. Conversely, the results of treatment are poorer in the case of patients who have had limited personality resources.

There is a high rate of recurrence among schizophrenic patients treated with insulin therapy, but the remission or recovery rate for those who have been adequately treated with insulin is significantly higher than for a similar group of untreated patients. It has been said that, over long periods of time, recoveries are more stable in non-shock-treated patients than in those so treated. The use of insulin coma therapy is rapidly declining.

PSYCHOSURGERY

The operation of lobotomy, a surgical procedure consisting of a severance of the connection between the thalamus and frontal lobe, was developed by a Portuguese neurologist, Egas Moniz, and first performed by the neurosurgeon, Almeida Lima, in 1935. Moniz published his monograph in 1936, immediately following which the operation was introduced into the U.S.A. by Dr. Walter Freeman and Dr. James Watts. In 1949, Moniz received the Nobel Prize in Medicine for his work in prefrontal lobotomy.

Techniques

A variety of neurosurgical techniques were devised as a means of transecting the thalamofrontal fibers expanding from the dorsomedial nucleus of the thalamus to the frontal poles. As these procedures were tested, it became apparent that only limited transections of cortical white matter were necessary to bring about the desired therapeutic result. Progressively more limited neurosurgical procedures have been developed. The thalamotomy procedure, in which the dorsomedial thalamic nuclei are destroyed by electrolysis, and cingulectomies are more often done currently. Blocking the frontal lobe by initial procaine and later alcohol injections has been tried.

Today, the few lobotomies performed usually are carried out through open craniotomies by neurosurgeons. Transorbital lobotomy, the closed procedure initiated by Freeman and conducted by some psychiatrists, has been abandoned.

Indications

Prefrontal lobotomy is a radical procedure that will be undertaken only after other forms of treatment, including tranquilizing drugs and some form of shock therapy, have failed. Its use since the introduction of the tranquilizing drugs has almost ceased. Patients are selected for operation on the basis of symptoms rather than of diagnosis. The best results are secured in patients who show tension, agitation and distress, depression, worry, intractable pain syndromes, compulsions, hostility, and excited, impulsive behavior. Such symptoms as phobias, obsessions, hallucinations, and delusional experiences are relieved if they have not existed for extended periods, although the basic pathology of the thought process is not affected. Cruelty, avoidance of responsibility, and excessive use of alcohol before the development of the psychosis are contraindications.

In *schizophrenia*, prefrontal lobotomy has no effect on the fundamental disease process, but in well-selected cases it may be followed by a great improvement in adjustment. The better organized the prepsychotic personality, the better the results, provided deteriorated, psychotic habits have not existed for several years. If the patient is a chronically deteriorated, inactive *hebephrenic* whose affect has been "burned out," little benefit is to be expected from operation. On the other hand, the behavior of the overactive, resistive, excitable, destructive, restless, unmanageable schizophrenic may be greatly improved.

In severe obsessive-compulsive, obsessive-ruminative, and hypochondriacal types of *psychoneuroses* that have not been benefited by psychotherapy, the disabling tension and anxiety states may be relieved by lobotomy. Obsessive ideas may continue, but the relief from tension may permit the patient to pursue his normal activities.

Unpleasant Sequels

A change in personality with an accentuation of previous unpleasant traits is not uncommon but does not occur in all cases. The patient's sense of responsibility and his feeling for others may be impaired. Affect is more shallow than before the illness, and the patient usually lacks former sympathies and altruistic motives. There is an increase in self-esteem, tactlessness, and lack of self-criticism and of restraint. Imaginative foresight is usually less than normal. "He doesn't care whether school keeps or not." With less desirable results, the patient may be lazy, tactless, suggestible, and childish, and manifest a silly euphoria. He may be unrestrained in word and action, careless in eating habits and personal appearance, and perhaps vulgar and profane. In the usual case, the outstanding change is in affect and not in intellect.

The careful long-term follow-up of Smith on patients subject to topectomy has shown significant losses in their performance on various psychological tests. Some patients, particularly those schizophrenics who have led a purely vegetative existence without active mental conflict, may show no improvement and even exhibit an organic dementia also. Patients whose prepsychotic tendencies were characterized by active aggressiveness may, after operation, manifest an undesirable lack of restraint of these impulses.

Outcome

There have been published a number of reports of assessment of long-term outcome of patients treated by one of the varieties of lobotomy. Those reports vary because some represent the study of patients operated upon a decade or so past when lobotomies were frequently prescribed, whereas others, such as that by Post, Rees, and Schurr, present outcome on patients so treated more recently, after all other methods of treatment had proved ineffective in establishing a social adaptation. This later report is most pertinent to the needs of the modern psychiatric practitioner. They

found that a high proportion of the 52 patients with longstanding, continuous, and disabling illness other than schizophrenia, attained beneficial results. Thus 14 became socially well or symptom free, 14 benefited moderately, 15 benefited. marginally, and nine were unimproved. These changes were maintained or enhanced over a three-year period of observation. The conditions so treated were psychotic depression, depressions with pain, depressions with obsessions, neurotic depressions, and obsessional and other neurotic states. Yet undesirable effects occurred in two thirds, in terms of postoperative personality changes described earlier in this chapter. Those with chronic depressive symptoms were most likely to benefit, either as an isolated expression of illness or associated with other neurotic symptoms or the complaint of pain.

BIBLIOGRAPHY

General

Kalinowsky, L. B., and Hippius, H.: Pharmacologic, Convulsive and Other Somatic Treatments in Psychiatry. New York, Grune & Stratton, 1969.

Electroconvulsive Therapy

Abrams, R., Dornbush, R. L., Feldstein, S., et al.: Unilateral and bilateral electroconvulsive therapy. Arch. Gen. Psychiatry, 27:88–91, 1972.

Cohen, B. D., Penick, S. B., and Tarter, R. E.: Antidepressant effects of unilateral electric convulsive shock therapy. Arch. Gen. Psychiatry, 31:673–675, 1974.

Cotman, C. W., Banker, G., Zarnetzer, S. F., and McGaugh, J. L.: Electroshock effects on brain protein synthesis. Science, 173:454–456, 1971.

Hunt, H. F.: Electroconvulsive shock and learning. Trans. N.Y. Acad. Sci., 27:923–945, 1965.

Kety, S. S., et al.: A sustained effect of electroconvulsive shock on the turnover of norepinephrine in the central nervous system of the rat. Proc. Nat. Acad. Sci., *58*:1249–1254, 1967.

Motulsky, A. G., and Morrow, A.: A typical cholinesterase Gene Ela: Rarity in Negroes and most Orientals. Science, *159*:202–203, 1968.

Squire, L. R.: ECT and memory loss. Am. J. Psychiatry, *134*:997–1001, 1979.

Psychosurgery

Ballantine, H. T., Cassidy, W. L., Flanagan, N. B., and Mauno, R.: Stereotaxic anterior cingulotomy for neuropsychiatric illness and intractable pain. J. Neurosurg., *26*:488–495, 1967.

Culliton, B. J.: Psychosurgery: National commission issues surprisingly favorable report. Science, *194*:299–301, 1976.

Donnelly, J.: The incidence of psychosurgery in the United States, 1971–1973. Am. J. Psychiatry, *135*:1476–1480, 1979.

Miller, A.: The lobotomy patient—a decade later. Can. Med. Ass. J., *96*:1095–1103, 1967.

Post, F., Rees, L. W., and Schurr, P. H.: An evaluation of bimedial leucotomy. Br. J. Psychiatry, *114*:1223–1246, 1968.

Shobe, F. C., and Gildea, C. L.: Long-term follow-up of selected lobotomized private patients. J.A.M.A., *206*:327–332, 1968.

Smith, A.: Changing effects of frontal lesions in man. J. Neurol. Neurosurg. Psychiatry, *27*:511–515, 1967.

34

PSYCHIATRY AND THE LAW

"A society that sets out to guarantee full freedom for all will find itself enslaved by savages."

Learned Hand

"I will hide amongst the thickets of the law."

Sir Thomas More
in A Man for All Seasons
by Robert Bolt

DANIEL M'NAGHTEN
About 1855, in Bethlem.
(From Walker, M., and McCabe, S.: Crime and Insanity in England. Vol. 11. Edinburgh, Edinburgh University Press, 1973.)

Greco-Roman laws and earlier writings in other cultures recognized clearly that illness might lead to both antisocial behavior and serious impairment of judgment that would be detrimental to the sufferer or those around him. As psychiatry evolved into the special body of knowledge about abnormal behavior and its origins, it was inevitable that courts and lawyers turned to psychiatrists for advice and testimony in the decision-making processes of the judicial system. A specialized branch dealing with legal proceedings within the practice of psychiatry became *forensic psychiatry*. The psychiatrist must be aware of fundamental differences between his or her practice and its foundation in medicine and science, and the practice of law. The differences account for the tensions that have existed for decades between the professions, and contribute to the public's frequent lack of understanding of the role of psychiatrists placed in the adversarial position demanded by law's due process procedures.

Events of recent years have vastly increased the interface between the practitioners of psychiatry and the practitioners of law. Challenges of the legitimacy of the concept of mental illness have been made. Advocacy of the civil rights and the rights to treatment for those involuntarily committed to hospitals is heard. There is a growing recognition of the importance and function of psychiatric testimony as a means of protecting minor children when their future development depends upon the courts, either because of their alleged antisocial behavior, or because of court decisions in divorces or adoptions.

The psychiatrist may be called upon to testify in court about the propriety of civil commitment to mental hospitals as a means of protecting the public and the individual from potentially dangerous behavior as the consequence of mental illness. Often, he testifies as an expert witness on the mental competence of individuals to stand trial or make judgments about the custody of property and children in civil actions such as marriage, separation, or divorce. He assists the court to evaluate potential adoptive parents, or competency in the making of wills and contracts. In many jurisdictions, psychiatrists may testify in court regarding criminal responsibility.

Psychiatrists and other physicians increasingly find themselves defendants in malpractice suits. Psychiatric administrators and staff psychiatrists employed in state systems or institutions also have been named as defendants individually in the course of suits to establish the rights of patients, or have been cited in contempt proceedings for failure to comply following a state consent action to improve treatment.

Principles of Justice

It has been stated that the concept of conscience (the superego), which evolved in early Egyptian society over 4500 years ago, is man's outstanding cultural achievement. Early measures to control aggression in primitive societies led to those peculiarly human affects of guilt and shame. Actions taken against an individual offending the social mores reside in the administration of justice, throughout the world, based on the Mosaic *lex talionis,* the principle of retributive justice. The threat of retribution continues to be regarded widely as a deterrent to antisocial acts. Through the ages evolved the concepts of *mens rea* (the guilty mind) and the lack of capacity to exercise civil rights, a lack of mental competence known in Roman law as *non compos mentis* (not of sound mind). Modern jurisprudence incorporates in the criminal law, in addition, the concepts of incapacitance, deterrence, and rehabilitation.

Extant law today, in most English-speaking countries, had its origins in feudal ideals, elaborated in part in the Magna Carta and accreting over time through precedents set as one court decision followed another. A major premise in the Anglo-American law is that the civil rights of citizens as decreed by the power of the state shall not be limited except through the due process of law. This goal continues to be sought, but the necessity to control antisocial and deranged behavior of individual citizens led the various nation-states to establish correctional and, later, mental institutions, for the presumed containment and correction of such behavior. That neither the punitive, deterrent, therapeutic, nor habilitative goals charged to the administration of such institutions have been fully achieved at any time is a matter exposed repeatedly in the last several centuries. From these insights, many legislative, judicial, and executive actions have been and continue to be taken to improve the care of those confined.

The weakness of the state institutions reflects the persistence within society to isolate and avoid those who have given distress or caused anxiety because of odd and deviant behaviors. "Out of sight, out of mind." Most societies tend to denigrate the caretakers of those confined and to withhold sufficient support to allow a quality of human and physical resources that might very possibly effect habilitation and well-being.

These weaknesses and recognition of the curtailment of the rights of individuals confined to institutional care have spurred widespread civil rights legislation and court action in the United States of America in recent decades. The judicial system of the U.S.A. recognizes that all persons retain their legal rights unless these are removed by due process of law. Each individual has the right to a jury trial, representation by counsel, freedom of speech and religious beliefs, and privacy for his person and his domain. These rights may not be abridged except through an open legal process, adversary in nature. The statutes protecting the rights of individuals, as well as the legal procedures, undergo continual revisions, both at national and state levels; this makes exceedingly complex the practice of the psychiatrist who testifies in court on the variety of legal issues which may arise.

THE PSYCHIATRIST IN COURT

The Expert Witness

Generally, the psychiatrist in court appears as an expert witness, a legal role he or she must comprehend well to effectively present knowledge. As the legal procedure is adversary, it may be expected that the opposing viewpoints will be argued vigorously. The adversary process will be regulated by procedural rules and the rules of evidence enforced by the judge. The facts of each case are established either by the weighing of the evidence presented to the jury, or by the judge when a jury trial is not held. The majority of witnesses who appear must testify solely on directly perceived information relevant to the charges. "Hearsay" information usually is not allowed from such witnesses; the testimony of each witness may be clarified and challenged by the opposing lawyers.

The expert witness, differing from the ordinary witness through his command of a special body of knowledge or technical information, may give "opinions." He may inform the court of direct information he gathered in regard to the subject in question—including, in the case of a psychiatrist, an account of the illness, history obtained from the patient and relatives, as well as inferences pertaining to the psychopathology and personality organization of the subject, his motivations, matters deduced regarding the patient's relations with others (transference-countertransference influences)—provided the material derives from theoretical bases in the area of his expertise.

The psychiatrist who is asked by a lawyer to examine a client must be certain to ascertain the essential issues in question and to have them clearly defined. He must have sufficient time to conduct a thorough examination of the client, whether plaintiff or defendant. Following the examination, the psychiatrist will discuss his findings and opinions with the lawyers and from that discussion decisions will be made about relevant information. Psychiatrist and lawyer together generally plan the way to most effectively present the expert testimony in court. In the course of these discussions preliminary to the trial, the psychiatrist should be instructed by the lawyer of the law relating to the issues to be raised and the language best used to present his findings as related to the law. The psychiatrist may in turn have to instruct the lawyer about the theories and hypotheses he used to derive his construction of the psychological events relevant to the case. He will point out the pertinent data supporting his contentions in the literature. The psychiatrist may be of assistance in assessing the background and personality of jurors that would be most congenial to the lawyer's case and may recommend other witnesses who might support his testimony.

In court, the psychiatrist should present the theory or theories on which his opinions are based, state his findings and, finally, give the diagnostic formulation and legal inferences as they relate to the questions in controversy. It is the best procedure to quote directly from the patient and other sources and refer precisely to documents he has reviewed.

Often, in court the lawyer will present the issue in the form of a "hypothetical case," in which there will be detailed circumstances similar to those presumably existing in the case under consideration. The expert will be asked to provide his opinion or opinions in terms of questions related to this hypothetical case.

To be effective as an expert witness and to be responsive both to the lawyer to whom he is related as well as to the adversary, the psychiatrist might regard the court hearing as a "game," in which telling and dramatic forces are often used to "win" the case. This has been interestingly described by Slovenko. He may expect to be vigorously questioned and cross-examined. His own testimony will be most effective if he avoids overdetermined emotional responsivity in the course of the attack made upon his findings, theories, and deductions during the "game."

Privilege and Confidentiality

In all those jurisdictions where there is a statute establishing medical privilege to communication, the psychiatrist may decline to testify if served a sub-poena. There are jurisdictions where statutes defining privileged communication do not exist. There, failure to testify may result in the psychiatrist's being held in contempt of court. It is important, then, that the psychiatrist know the statutes pertaining to privileged communication in the jurisdiction where he practices.

These statutes developed from the generally held belief that the confidentiality of a patient's relations with his psychiatrist is peculiarly strong, even more so than in ordinary medicine, and is not subject to violation even on a court summons. Some courts have held that relations between a patient committed to a mental institution and a staff doctor are likewise of a privileged professional nature and are therefore protected from disclosure on a witness stand. The privilege has, in fact, been extended so far beyond the premise of protecting confidential communication that courts assume without argument that all statements of inmates to hospital doctors come within the rule.

Customarily, all information obtained by a physician or psychiatrist during his diagnostic or therapeutic examination and contacts with the patient is held privileged. Only the patient may waive the privilege. In certain cases, the patient may do so when in his opinion and that of his lawyer the testimony of the physician will be helpful to his case. But even in such instances, the psychiatrist presented with this option should discuss with the patient thoroughly both the personal and public implications of the revelations he may be brought to make.

The patient's privilege is waived automatically in relation to previous psychiatric illness if he files suit with the claim of emotional damage.

PSYCHIATRIC TREATMENT IN A RESTRICTIVE SETTING

Regarding attitudes toward admission of the mentally ill person to a hospital, the psychiatrist urges that the dignity of the patient be respected and that the obstacles to admission be no greater than those experienced by the physically sick person. Since in many instances the mental patient does not recognize that he is ill, he does not seek treatment and may even resist measures designed to provide it; since the Constitution of the United States provides that a person may not be deprived of his liberty without adequate notice and a chance to be heard, the law insists on a punctilious observance of what it regards as human rights.

A period of care in a restrictive hospital environment to effect therapeutic contact is still required for many, in spite of the major therapeutic advances of the past two decades, the growing recognition of the secondary social deterioration consequent to prolonged institutional care, and more humane and accepting attitudes toward the mentally ill. The period of care in the state institutions has been reduced from an average of eight months to a little over one month in some states. In general hospital psychiatric services, the duration of stay for the acutely distressed now averages between 10 and 14 days.

Admission of Patients to Mental Hospitals

Both voluntary and involuntary hospitalization have been increasingly challenged in the past two decades, in spite of the obviously diminishing reliance upon treatment in restrictive custody that has reduced the populations of state institutions in the U.S.A. from over a half million to less than a quarter million while the population of the country almost doubled.

From the ranks of psychiatrists, Szasz wrote in 1961 on the *Myth of Mental Illness*, strongly arguing that deviant behavior is learned socially, that psychiatric diagnoses are irrelevant and unreliable, and that psychiatrists delegate responsibility to themselves which more properly belongs to functionaries within the legal system. Careful reading of his work makes it clear that he applies his arguments only in the case of those without clearly evident biological or physiological abnormality. Yet, since he wrote, and as the many chapters preceding this one attest, the evidence mounts for genetic predisposition and biochemical and physiological abnormality as the significant etiologic factors, particularly in the psychoses – the group of disorders which have provided the large populations considered by societies to require protective treatment in restricted environments. Szasz admits the need for immediate psychiatric intervention without involving the legal processes prior to confinement, in the instances of certain psychiatric emergencies. If his argument were carried to its full length, all deviant behavior would once again be adjudged solely through legal processes. For most experienced clinicians, this course would once again lead to the detention in prisons of many, as was the custom over two centuries ago. The prison systems have demonstrated little capacity to provide surcease for those with the well known psychoses – let alone the habilitation of the criminal populations they now harbor.

The *concept of dangerousness* as a reason for hospital commitment has also been sharply challenged. Here the ability of a psychiatrist to predict future violent behavior has been examined among groups of criminal offenders with psychiatric disorders, former psychiatric inpatients and those with known organic brain dysfunction, and in populations of psychiatric patients at large. The article by Mesnikoff and Lauterbach provides a thorough review of the research literature on the subject.

As Cocozza and Steadman found in their careful studies of almost 1000 criminally insane patients who were transferred to the mental hospital system from prisons in accordance with the judicial decision in the case of Baxtrom v. Herold, of 98 patients subsequently released to the community from those hospitals, only 14 displayed dangerous behavior. Dangerous behavior was defined by them as violent assaultive behavior directed against others. The number represents only 15 per cent of the group released. They found predictive of this behavior only age and high scores on the Legal Dangerousness Scale (LDS), which is composed of such aspects of previous criminal activity as existence of juvenile record, number of previous arrests, convictions for violent crimes, and severity of the crime leading to the last conviction.

They examined as well the capability of psychiatrists to predict dangerousness in terms of later violent behavior against persons when examining individuals to determine if they were competent to stand trial. If competence was ascertained, the sentenced individual was sent to prison. For those found not competent, treatment was provided in a detention hospital. Psychiatrists apparently rely heavily on the seriousness of the current alleged offense in defining dangerousness. In a study of 'the actual number of individuals in these two groups arrested later for violent crimes, the prediction of dangerousness did not hold up, for approximately the same number in the dangerous and nondangerous groups were rearrested. There is substantial agreement now, on the basis of existing evidence, that psychiatric ability to predict future dangerousness is not accurate and, if accepted as the sole reason for commitment, would lead to confinement of many more than would ever commit a violent act. It is not now known whether psychiatrists are more capable than others to make such a prediction.

From the standpoint of social policy, the occurrence of antisocial behavior in individuals discharged from mental hospitals is a matter of some moment. Old studies (made prior to modern treatment of the psychoses with neuroleptics and early discharge into the community) tend to show different results than new studies (made after introduction of the newer methods). The earlier studies showed that ex-patients exhibited no greater and some even smaller rates of violent criminal behavior than the general population. The new studies suggest that the rates are similar or, in certain instances, higher for the ex-patients than for the general population.

The following paragraphs describe the varieties of admission to state and other facilities where care is provided in a restrictive environment.

Hospitalization and the Law

States hold the authority, vested in their police power, to commit for treatment to protect society those considered dangerous to others and to protect the individual from himself. The doctrine of *parens patriae* allows the state to intervene and act as a surrogate parent for those unable to care for or likely to harm themselves.

The Council of State Governments of the United States of America, reporting from a 1974 survey of state legislation, found commitment to a mental hospital possible: if a person was judged mentally ill and dangerous to himself or others in 29 states; if a person was unable to care for his physical needs in 15 states; if in need of care and treatment or unable to make a responsible treatment decision in 29 states; and if a person required commitment for his own or others' welfare in 7 states.

The vast majority of states have laws that permit a mentally ill person to apply for treatment in a public mental hospital. Such laws frequently state that the applicant must be mentally competent to make application and must give a certain number of days' notice in writing if he desires to leave. The extent to which persons apply for admission under the provisions of such a statute varies greatly among the states.

In addition to any laws providing for the voluntary admission of patients, every state has various laws governing the commitment of mentally ill persons. Frequently, the patient with mental disorder caused by, or associated with, impairment of brain tissue function is not mentally competent to make application for his admission to a hospital. Among such persons may be those suffering from acute brain disorders associated with intoxication or infection, or from chronic brain disorders associated with cerebral arteriosclerosis or senile brain disease. The laws of a number of states wisely permit the legal guardian or close relative of such an incompetent person to arrange for his admission. "A person who is a fit subject for mental treatment should not be denied the easy method for admission merely because he may be too indecisive, weakminded, or incompetent to sign his own papers."*

Many states provide for the emergency commitment of a patient. These commitments are temporary, and commitment for an indeterminate period must be completed before the expiration of the period for which the emergency commitment is permitted. The procedure to be followed in an emergency commitment varies greatly. In some states, the law merely requires that a petition be filed with the hospital to which commitment is desired, together with a certification of one physician that the patient is in need of immediate hospital care.

In most states, the law provides in general that when an involuntary commitment for an indeterminate period is contemplated, a petition for the patient's commitment must be filled with a judicial agency, that the patient be notified of the proposed judicial hearing on his mental state, and that he be examined by two physicians who will certify that he is suffering from mental disease. The judge presiding at the hearing is the committing agent, although in 21 states the hearing may be held before a jury if requested by the patient.

In a few states, the law permits, without a judicial hearing or order, the superintendent of a mental hospital to receive a mentally sick person and detain him for an indeterminate period. Usually in such a case, a relative or other responsible person submits to the superintendent a petition for the patient's admission. This petition contains a sworn statement setting forth reasons why the petitioner believes the patient is mentally ill. Accompanying the petition is a certification by two physicians that they have, within a prescribed period, examined the patient and that in their opinion he is mentally ill and in need of care and treatment in a hospital for the mentally sick.

The laws governing commitment, however, have gradually become more liberal and reflect the need to preserve the psychiatrically ill from humiliating publicity and deprivation of their rights, as well as to open more easily to them treatment on the same grounds as those with predominantly physical illnesses. Perhaps nowhere is this trend more advanced than in England, where under the Mental Health Act of 1959, nonstatutory admissions are allowed to the mental hospitals; patients may enter informally if they so desire, without signing papers or having them signed by others, and thereby they receive treatment under the same circumstances as those with medical or surgical problems.

In cases in which compulsory admission is required to safeguard the patient or the community, this is recognized solely as a medical decision and not a civil or judicial one. The authorization for admission consists of the recommendation of two physicians, one of whom must be experienced in the treatment of mental disorders. In cases of emergency, the patient may be admitted and detained three days on the application of a mental welfare officer or any relative on the recommendation of one physician.

*Addendum, Law of Maryland, March, 1944, page 63, 34A.

Discharge from the hospital also may be carried out informally on the decision of a physician, or at the request of the patient or relative on three days' written notice. When the patient is considered too disturbed to be discharged, he may be detained on medical recommendation, but he has recourse to appeal to the Mental Health Review Tribunals. Such tribunals are composed of legal and medical members, as well as persons qualified in administration of social service. The tribunals are independent local bodies of skilled persons, which evaluate the patient's mental condition and his need for continuing hospital care. If he is found to be without illness or unlikely to endanger himself and others, his discharge must be ordered. Each adult patient may apply to the tribunal once in the six months following his initial admission and once in each succeeding year of detention. Special provisions are established for such groups as the psychopaths.

This act guarantees certain rights to the hospitalized patient. It establishes, as well, systems for the management of criminal cases. Thus the courts may order hospitalization instead of imprisonment for the convicted mentally ill persons who are suitable for treatment when facilities exist for such care.

To many, the British Mental Health Act of 1959 represented the penetration of a new frontier in the treatment of those with serious behavior disturbances. It reflected as well a profound concern with the development of community resources for their care. Its social pioneering established the model for humanitarian health legislation in other countries. New York State law, recodified in 1972, to some extent followed the pattern of the British Mental Health Act. The law established a Mental Health Information Service, composed of lawyers and social workers, with the requirement that this service insure that each admitted individual be informed of his rights, of the availability of a judicial hearing if desired, and of a periodic review of the maintenance of his retention.

The management of psychiatrically ill criminal offenders under the British Mental Health Act has taken a course unsuspected by the progenitors of this most liberal legislation. According to Rollin, it would seem that in the courts British psychiatrists are unusually optimistic as regards the effects of treatment in mental hospitals, even for the psychopathic, as against confinement in prisons. Accordingly, more persons with criminal records, and many repeated recidivists, are entered into the British open hospital and community care system. As Rollin shows, under this method of management a greater proportion of those formerly entering the prison system now enter the open mental hospital system, which appears to be ineffective in providing the necessary management to modify the criminal tendencies and sustain public security. Here and there, when large numbers of those criminal mentally ill are entered in hospital, their easy escapes into the local community and their subsequent implication in further antisocial ills have produced adverse public reactions toward the modern mental health system in Britain and the forward-looking Act.

In the U.S.A., as indicated, each state has its own laws governing the commitment of the mentally ill. Because of this, there is great disparity among the states as to legal procedure in commitment. In many states, too, these procedures subject the patient to indignities and humiliations. For this reason, the National Advisory Mental Health Council in 1949 requested the United States Public Health Service to develop what might be considered a model act.* Very few states enacted a law patterned

---

*A Draft Act Governing Hospitalization of the Mentally Ill, U.S. Federal Security Agency, Public Health Service, Publication No. 51, U.S. Government Printing Office, 1951.

on this "Model Act," but presumably, as states gradually modified their commitment laws, there was a tendency to incorporate into concrete legal procedure the principles of this model. Attention is called to some of its most important features:

The model act facilitates *voluntary admissions*, but provides that upon the patient's written request he shall be forthwith discharged. If, however, in the opinion of the head of the hospital the release of the patient would be dangerous to himself or others, this official may notify the court and the patient's discharge may be postponed for as long as the court deems necessary for the commencement of proceedings for judicial hospitalization, but in no event for more than five days.

The model act distinguishes between *involuntary hospitalization* and compulsory hospitalization. Commitment proceedings may be involuntary in the sense that they are initiated by someone other than the patient himself, but the patient accepts the judgment of the physician and his family. In that case, there is no judicial hearing, and the commitment procedure consists merely of the filing of a request for the patient's admission and the certification of two qualified physicians that they have examined the individual and that in their opinion he should be hospitalized. It is presumed that most patients would be admitted on this medical certification, were statutes based on the model act adopted.

If the patient refuses hospitalization, a judicial hearing is necessary before a *compulsory commitment* may be made. In such a case, a petition for the patient's commitment may be filed with the court. This petition must be accompanied by a certificate of a physician stating that he has examined the patient and is of the opinion that he is mentally ill and should be hospitalized. Upon receipt of the application, the court gives notice thereof to the patient and appoints two physicians to examine him. If the examiners report that the patient is mentally ill, the court sets a date for a hearing at which the patient is afforded an opportunity to appear. If, upon completion of the hearing, the court finds that the patient is in need of custody and treatment, it orders his hospitalization for an indeterminate period or for a temporary observational period not to exceed six months.

The model act also has humane provisions for the emergency commitment of a patient, pending opportunity to initiate proceedings for an indeterminate commitment.

The draft contains various provisions designed to promote the welfare and protect the rights of the patient requiring hospitalization. Among these is one that, pending his removal to a hospital, a committed patient shall not, except because of and during an extreme emergency, be detained in a nonmedical facility used for the detention of individuals charged with or convicted of penal offenses. As is already provided in many states, the model act would, except under unusual circumstances, permit the patient to communicate with official agencies inside or outside the hospital; to receive visitors and confer with counsel; to exercise all civil rights, including the right to dispose of property, execute instruments, make purchases, enter contractual relationships, and vote, unless he has been adjudicated incompetent. The act also greatly restricts the information that may be divulged concerning a patient except with the permission of either himself or his guardian.

For evidence pertaining to the judgment to commit civilly, the U.S. Supreme Court recently established "clear and convincing evidence" as the standard of proof, contrasted with the criminal standard of "beyond a reasonable doubt," thus placing the mentally ill person in the role of patient.

Several states have legal provision whereby a person charged with, or under indictment for, a criminal offense, or if having been found guilty is awaiting sentence, may be committed to a public mental hospital for a limited period of observation. This constitutes an *observation commitment*. Following the examination of the prisoner, the hospital submits a report to the court. The hospital does not, of course, express any opinion about the guilt or innocence of the prisoner. If he is found to be psychotic, commitment will usually be recommended. Frequently, the report may include a statement on whether or not the prisoner's mental condition is such that he is capable of conferring with counsel and preparing his defense.

COMMITMENT, COMPETENCY, AND CIVIL RIGHTS

In most states, mentally ill patients are not adjudged incompetent or deprived of their "civil rights" by their commitment. If, at the time of commitment, patients are formally adjudged "insane" by judicial action, they are thereby rendered incompetent and deprived of certain civil rights. They may not buy or sell property or sign legal papers or vote or hold office. Their drivers' licenses are suspended. The judgment usually vacates licenses to practice medicine, law, or other learned profession; takes away the right to consent to or refuse to consent to the adoption of a child; casts doubt on their right to make a will; and impairs their right to marry, although usually, if they do marry while psychotic, the marriage will be valid unless specifically set aside. In most states, they cannot start a divorce action.

The methods of erasing the adjudication and of restoring legal competency vary from state to state. Generally speaking, if commitability and incompetency are determined by separate procedures, then discharge (not leave-of-absence or parole) will vacate the commitment order, but have no effect on the finding of incompetency. Another court action will be necessary to declare the patient competent and to discharge a guardian.

Habeas Corpus

A right that the psychotic person preserves, even though he has been legally adjudicated insane, is that of applying for a writ of habeas corpus. This writ has for its object an inquiry by the judiciary concerning the legality of detention. Under American and English law, this writ may be proclaimed on behalf of anyone who claims he is being deprived of his liberty illegally. Since a commitment may continue only so long as the patient needs care and custody, he may at any time petition for the issuance of such a writ on the ground that he is now sane and so entitled to release. At the hearing on the petition, the sanity of the patient is inquired into and, if the court finds him sane, he may be discharged. In some jurisdictions, the court impanels a jury to determine the issue of sanity. In only a few jurisdictions are there any restrictions imposed on the frequency with which application for a writ may be made.

Right to Treatment

All patients in a hospital, whether received voluntarily or committed involuntarily, are there under either the explicit or the tacit assumption that they will receive the most appropriate treatment available for the disorder leading to their admission. Yet in many states throughout the country, and in the world, the staffing and the physical accommodations of the facilities to which the mentally disabled have been committed are such that the provision of active, effective, and appropriate treatment for the individual is deficient. Birnbaum posed the question in 1960 whether, if the state deprives an individual of freedom and places him in a hospital, he is entitled to treatment. By raising this question he sought to attack the propensity of society, in its apportionment of support for mental disability and retardation, to neglect and ignore those involuntarily committed. In 1966, this issue was raised in the District of Columbia, first in the case of Rouse v. Cameron and settled by the court with Judge David Bazelon defining the state's obligation, as stated above. Neither the court nor organized psychiatry rose to the occasion to define treatment.

The case that attracted national recognition (Wyatt v. Stickney, 1971) was a class action in Alabama on behalf of the patients of a number of state mental hospitals. The court not only declared the necessity for the state to provide adequate treatment to those deprived of their liberty upon confinement, but went much further in elaborating in detail minimal standards for supporting the adequate treatment of the mentally ill. In so doing, it defined the basic hospital staffing ratios and qualifications, the prescription of individualized treatment plans, and the necessary quality of the physical plant in which the individual was confined. In its Appendix A (1972) to the original opinion, the court defined the contents to be included in the treatment plans. These include, as does the earlier description of a case formulation in this text, a statement of the specific problems and needs of the individual and, beyond that usual formulation, a statement of the *least restrictive environment* necessary to achieve the purposes of the commitment, as well as other details regarding future goals and necessary therapy, specifications of individual staff responsibility, and criteria by which to judge release to less restrictive treatment conditions, as well as discharge.

Heard before the U. S. Supreme Court, the case of O'Connor v. Donaldson, while not explicitly laying down a federal constitutional right to treatment, has marked the first recognition at the highest judicial level of the legitimacy of judicial consideration in decision making previously considered largely the domain of psychiatry. In a narrow decision, the Court set forth the impropriety of nontherapeutic confinement of those mentally ill not considered dangerous.

Juvenile Courts and Delinquency

Juvenile courts have their origin in the ancient legal concept of *parens patriae* that defined the state's role and interest in assuring the development of all children, and provided support of state intervention in the areas of child rearing and child disciplining. Juvenile courts function more as administrative than judicial tribunals. They may legally intervene and take jurisdiction of a child on the grounds of delinquency, neglect, or a decision that the child is "in need of supervision or is incorrigible." The latter determinations are made generally about runaway children or children whose parents have stated their inability to control their children. A delinquent act by a child or adolescent is one that would be adjudged criminal if committed by an adult. Children are not declared delinquent until the court has so adjudicated.

The services of psychiatrists, psychol-ogists, and social workers have been used extensively by juvenile courts. The testimony in establishing the finding of delinquency has been criticized in recent years. This criticism led to a number of U. S. Supreme Court decisions in the 1960s that children have the same procedural rights as adults when charged with criminal activity.

The court attempts to make decisions about future care to insure the child's developnent and welfare. To be effective, psychiatrists providing evaluations to these courts must present their findings and recommendations clearly and practically. In general, those observing the operations of the juvenile justice system find that the courts tend to accept psychiatric testimony with caution, owing to the continuing doubts regarding its predictive ability. A frequent decision is to supervise the parent's care of the child temporarily while maintaining jurisdiction of the case.

Persons in need of supervision (P.I.N.S.) are those children brought to court with disturbed behavior that is often induced by intrafamilial conflicts. If the psychiatrist overlooks the parental role in causing the child's disturbed behavior, and if he or she fails to recommend involvement of the parents or parent surrogates in the corrective process, the court may make a placement decision that will be detrimental to the child. The psychiatrist must also assist the court by assessing the parental capacity for corrective involvement.

COMPETENCY AND CIVIL ACTIONS

Marriage

In most states, the criterion of legal capacity to marry is the ability to understand the nature of the marriage contract and the duties and obligations such a contract entails. The statutes are of little help in defining the degree of mental unsoundness that will suffice to void a marriage. If it is clear that if one party was so psychotic, drunk, or defective at the time of marriage that he or she did not understand the obligations entailed in the marriage contract, an annulment will usually be decreed. In general, however, courts are reluctant to declare a marriage void. Some states have laws forbidding mentally ill persons to marry. The objective of such laws was presumably to prevent the procreation of defective children. Some courts will not annul a marriage on the grounds of fraud if a concealment of previous mental disease is the basis of the charge. Concealment of previous commitment to a mental hospital is not a ground for annulment on the basis of fraud unless the party concerned had affirmed that he never was in a mental hospital.

Divorce

In most states, insanity is not a ground for divorce; however, in some states divorce will be granted if the insane spouse has been committed to a hospital for mental diseases for a period of years. The statutes in some states specify that the spouse must be "incurably insane." Today, most psychiatrists are reluctant to testify that any mental illness is absolutely incurable. Perhaps the most that may be said is that, in the light of present-day medical knowledge, it is one's opinion that the patient's disorder is incurable.

Child Custody in Divorce

A most important aspect of each divorce decree is the assumption by the court of the supervision of all children of the terminated marriage until each reaches his or her majority. Formerly, in divorce proceedings, one parent was required to be found at fault and the other blameless. Under such proceedings, the recriminations, bargaining, and legal sparring led frequently to later ongoing difficulties as they affected one or the other or both parents' relationship to the children of the mar-

riage. With "no fault" divorce, a new approach, there is hope that the best of the parental relations with the children, no matter who is awarded custody, will be preserved. Because of the unfortunate aspects of the adversary process in divorce, a proposal has been made that counsel should be appointed for the children. Such a procedure remains to be tested.

When the psychiatrist is involved in the divorce proceeding, he and counsel for one or the other party should strive to determine the best interests of the child or children. Certain criteria for these interests have been stated in the model child custody act presented by the National Conference of Commissioners for Uniform State Laws, such as: the affectional ties between the children and the competing parties; the capacities of the individual parents to provide the needed affection, guidance, and education necessary to foster growth and development; provision of the physical nurturance, care, and medical aid that may be needed; the likely permanence of the existing or proposed custodial home; the moral fitness and physical and mental health of the two parents; the children's records at home, school, and in the community; and the preference of the child for placement with one or other parent.

With these guidelines, the psychiatrist may advise counsel or the court of his opinions.

Adoption

Occasionally, psychiatrists are requested by the court to assess potential adoptive parents, or the child being placed for adoption. Psychiatrists should recognize that adoption is best when accomplished as early as possible after birth, is deemed final upon placement, and excludes supervision as an intrusion in the development of a successful attachment to the adopting parents.

Wills

A person's competency to make a will is known as testamentary capacity. This capacity must meet three criteria. The testator, or person making a will, must (1) know that he is making a will, (2) know the nature and extent of his property, and (3) know the natural objects of his bounty. Expressed a little more simply, the person signing a will must know clearly what he is doing when he signs it. Although it is not necessary that he know the minutest details concerning his property, he must have a substantially accurate knowledge of what he owns. By "natural objects of his bounty" is meant the members of the testator's family, his warm friends, others to whom he feels especially grateful, or institutions or organizations in which he has felt an interest. Although he must know who are his living near relatives, the law does not require that he bequeath them anything. The failure of a testator to include a member of his family because of paranoid delusions of a psychotic intensity concerning the relative would probably render the will invalid, since the delusion would affect his understanding of the natural objects of his bounty. Statutes sometimes state that the testator must be of "sound mind and memory." This phrase means, in effect, that the testator must possess the testamentary capacity just described. The fact that the testator was psychotic or was committed to a hospital for mental disorders when he made the will does not necessarily mean that he lacked mental capacity to make a will, nor does it necessarily render it invalid. The psychiatrist must at all times bear in mind the three basic criteria of testamentary capacity.

Since it is often difficult to draw a line between simple senility and senile dementia, the question of testamentary capacity of the elderly person may arise. Even though the testator's mental processes are slow, the courts will consider him competent if he can call to mind his property and the natural objects of his bounty. Senile persons may suffer not only impairment of mind and memory but also increased suggestibility and therefore may be subject to undue influence. Many aged individuals are easy prey to the flattery of younger persons. The courts will hold invalid a will obtained by deception, threat, or the persistent suggestion of a domineering relative or of a flattering confidant.

Occasionally, the psychiatrist will be requested to testify in court concerning the testamentary capacity of a testator, now deceased, at the time he made his will. The attorney will ascertain from witnesses every possible fact concerning the testator's behavior that will be helpful to the psychiatrist in forming an honest opinion about the testator's capacity on the day he made his will. These facts will be assembled in the hypothetical question describing the testator's behavior.

A lawyer may request that his client be examined as to his competency at the time the client prepares his will. The psychiatrist's examination will then be directed with special reference to the three basic criteria of testamentary capacity. He will secure from the testator a description of his property and its estimated value. He will ask the patient to name the members of his family and indicate their relationships. As he secures a description of each relative, the psychiatrist will note the nature of the emotional response evoked by the discussion concerning each. The psychiatrist's report to the lawyer should contain the verbatim statements made by the patient that will later suggest his testamentary capacity.

Guardianship

Every person of legal age is presumed to be mentally competent, i.e., to have the mental capacity to carry on his or her everyday affairs. The burden of proof is, therefore, on one who would declare the adult incompetent. To determine that a person is incompetent, it must be shown that he has a mental disorder, that his mental disorder causes a defect in judgment, and that this defect in judgment renders him incapable of managing his property, of the prudent making of contracts, or of taking some other specific action.

The establishment of a mental disorder is not sufficient to warrant a finding of incompetency. It must also be shown that the mental disorder causes an impairment of judgment. No valid generalization can be made on the relationship of the various mental disorders to competency. The diagnostic label attached to the disorder is not as important as the degree to which judgment is impaired. Consideration must also be given on whether the condition is static, progressive, or improving. A progressive organic disease of the brain is typically a disorder that renders a patient incompetent, but many patients suffering from psychogenic disorders, such as manic-depressive psychosis, schizophrenia, or paranoid disorders, suffer from such seriously impaired judgment that they are rendered incompetent.

If a person is considered incompetent and he has business affairs that require attention, a petition for the appointment of a guardian will be filed with the appropriate court. The issue of incompetency is usually tried before either a probate or a county court, without a jury. In several states, a jury is still used. Usually, a member of the patient's family is the petitioner, but anyone who has an interest in preserving the patient's estate may petition the court for the appointment of a guardian. Notice of a hearing on the petition must be given to the person, and in many states to certain others, such as his next of kin. A few states provide that his presence is required. It must be shown, usually by medical evidence, that there is danger that, in the absence of a guardian for the person's estate, he will dissipate his property or become the victim of designing persons. Some courts require personal testimony by a physician, while others will accept a certificate of incompetency in lieu of personal testimony. If the person is declared incompetent, the court will decide whether his interests are best served by the appointment of a friend, relative, stranger, or corporation as the guardian.

In some states, the fact of commitment automatically adjudges the patient as incompetent. In such a case, the appointment of a guardian is merely an administrative matter and requires no judicial hearing. Usually a guardianship pertains only to the patient's estate and does not, unless so specified, include guardianship of his person.

Contracts

Courts will usually rule that a contract or other legal transaction will not be set aside on the grounds of mental incompetency if the person had sufficient mental capacity to understand the nature and effect of the particular transaction. A higher degree of mental capacity may be required to understand a complex instrument or transaction than a simple one. The degree of judgment needed may vary greatly. It is sometimes claimed that a contract was executed during a lucid interval of a person admittedly disordered. Psychiatrists are inclined to question whether in most cases the patient's lucidity during such intervals was not more apparent than real. It is the prevailing theory that where the incompetency of one party was not known to the other party, where no advantage was taken of the incompetent, and where the contract has been executed and the parties cannot be put back *in status quo*, the contract is binding and cannot be voided on the grounds of incompetency.

Informed Consent

Increasingly in recent years, following revelations of harm done to patients during clinical experimentation, general physicians and now more frequently psychiatrists have become sensitized to the necessity to obtain "informed consent" from their patients before undertaking treatment or clinical researches. The legal antecedents of the current doctrine are found in the 18th century case of Slater v. Baker and Stapleton, which put on record the then professional custom to treat patients only with consent, and the necessity to adhere to that practice if liability were to be avoided. Roth quotes Justice Cardozo in the Schloendorff case as establishing the modern dictum underlying the necessity to obtain approval for treatment: "Every human being of adult years and sound mind has a right to determine what shall be done with his body." The patient thus has the *right to refuse treatment* unless adjudged incompetent.

Informed consent requires that the patient receive from the responsible physician information about the nature of the treatment he is to receive, the best knowledge available about benefits and potential risks of the proposed treatment, as well as its discomforts, side effects, long-term consequences, and the results if the procedure fails. Being of "sound mind," the patient then should make a valid decision. This decision must be taken voluntarily, that is, without coercion. Exceptions to obtaining informed consent and proceeding with limited or no disclosure are recognized legally, in the regulations of many governmental bodies, in cases such as emergencies, when the patient is unable to comprehend (as in unconsciousness), or when it is judged that disclosure of the risks may be so emotionally stressing to the patient that capacity to provide consent would be impaired. In such circumstances, the physician has a "therapeutic privilege" to withhold information. However, the physician will always attempt to obtain informed consent from a responsible relative.

As indicated, it is presumed that the patient is capable of comprehension as a "reasonable man." If the patient is not competent, his decision will legally be held invalid. The definitions of competency are unclear and are particularly murky when the psychiatrist attempts to provide treatment to the psychotic individual, whose civil rights generally are held inviolate, but whose motivations to be "reasonable" may be seriously askew as the result of his psychopathology. The situation is equally obscure and complex when attempting to obtain consent from the mentally retarded adult or the child with an emotional disorder whose parents too are found suffering personality aberrations. The legal rulings that have been made do not clarify any of these conflicts between the concept of man as "reasonable" versus the motivational deterrents, conscious and unconscious, to a valid decision—even after the psychiatrist has shared with his patient the available knowledge of the potential benefits and harm that might ensue in the proposed treatment.

Perhaps the most illustrative example is the suicidally motivated, depressed individual who has proved unresponsive to treatment with psychopharmaceuticals. Given information about electroshock therapy and its usual benefits and side effects, his suicidal drive and obsessive thinking often lead to a denial of consent. The able psychiatrist, in these instances, will attempt to work with both the patient and responsible relatives. It is wise to have witnesses present when the patient is given the needed therapeutic information. If the necessary therapeutic measures continue to be denied, legal action questioning competence may be required.

The therapeutic procedures most in question today in psychiatry are the shock therapies and psychosurgical procedures.

In some instances, psychiatrists have been requested by lawyers to evaluate whether informed consent for medical, surgical, or psychiatric treatment has occurred under coercion. Following a careful examination of the patient concerning the human transactions and the circumstances that occurred when his consent was allegedly secured, the psychiatrist will have available for testimony in court a description of the process of the consent, his professional evaluation of the individual's capacity to give the consent, as well as the possibility of actual or implied threats or coerciveness perceived in the situation.

Emotional Damage

There has been a rapidly rising trend to sue for emotional damage in recent years, both secondary to physical injury or as a consequence of witnessing a stressing act, and from the suffering endured under the stress of such circumstances as concentration camp experience. The West German government has heard many of these claims from persons detained in Nazi camps during World War II. In the United States, the courts have moved from a conservative to a more liberal position in awarding damages for such claims. Psychiatric examination and testimony are sought in this type of case often by both plaintiffs and defendants.

MALPRACTICE

Suits against all physicians, including psychiatrists, are on the increase. The charge in malpractice suits is essentially a charge of negligence in practice, through failure to provide "reasonable care." The quality of care considered appropriate in the courts is that provided by the professional peer group. Courts now tend to measure the quality of practice issue beyond that provided in a local community. It is the responsibility of the plaintiff to prove the physi-

cian's negligence by producing a preponderance of evidence. Usually, he calls in experts from the medical profession as witnesses to support his claims. As lawyers complained over the years of the trouble in proving medical malpractice owing to the difficulty of obtaining medical testimony against the defendants, they more frequently now bring suits on the issue of informed consent. The aftereffects of electroconvulsive treatment are most likely to involve psychiatrists in such suits. There have been a few suits brought for sexual abuses alleged to have occurred during psychotherapy. Psychiatrists are unlikely to have difficulty if they follow in their practices the ethical codes of the specialty, obtain informed consent, maintain good clinical records and, in prescribing the somatic therapies, obtain beforehand complete physical and laboratory examinations, electrocardiograms, and radiographs of the spine.

Psychiatrists employed in state and county institutions and caring for the involuntarily committed should know that they may be charged with liability in the release of patients, particularly if an individual has demonstrated recent violent and aggressive behavior or has threatened third parties while in hospital and then, following release, has assaulted, harmed, or killed others. Courts will impose liability under certain circumstances following the release of a patient who then acts dangerously, as is evident in the Sember v. Psychiatric Institute of Washington case and the Hicks v. United States case. In the first, the decision to impose liability was based on the court's judgment that the release decision violated prior orders of the court and overlooked the necessary participation of the court in changing the treatment plans about the degree of supervision. In the second case, the court imposed the penalty for failure to produce a complete case history. The information submitted to the court about the individual did not include the full hospital report, which contained statements that his family should not be regarded as a community resource and described his conflictful relation with his wife, whom he killed following release. The court found for the plaintiff's survivors.

Nevertheless, the courts in the United States of America continue to follow the premise of release of patients to the least restriction available; they recognize the risk in the decision to effect release; and they do not find against the institution or psychiatrists on "error in judgment" alone.

CRIMINAL RESPONSIBILITY

Unquestionably, in no area of social action where the functions of the law and psychiatry meet is the disparity between the concepts and practices of the two professions so evident as in determination of criminal responsibility. The adversary process, which pits one party against the other in deciding right or wrong, reaches its peak publicly today as courts attempt to make decisions in criminal cases amid highly emotionally charged dissemination by the mass media for its ultimate material advantage. The adversary process and the attempts to make decisions on the basis of cognitive processes relying on precedents often overlook modern psychobiological knowledge. This system reveals the dissonance between the several professions, as well as the continuing inability to decide the proper role of the psychiatrist in the courts. In the criminal trial, the attempt to determine responsibility utilizing psychiatrists by opposing litigants as adversaries hardly assists that decision.

What a modern system of law, cognizant of the special knowledge that psychiatrists have, should request of this specialty is a definition of the appropriate corrective management of an offender after his act has been judged and found guilty by a jury. On the basis

of a clinical evaluation, the psychiatrist, as expert, might recommend: psychiatric treatment with attempts to modify pathological affect through treatment by pharmacotherapy or other somatic therapies under professional care; a prescription to attempt development of superego controls through emotional attachment and relearning in group and individual psychotherapies in a permissive, but closed, institution; for some, a restrictive prison experience punishing of his act when it is apparent that the offender's development excluded such exposure.

Unfortunately, neither the practice of law nor that of psychiatry has achieved sufficient understanding of the other, or of the potentials of the behavioral sciences, to the point that this appropriate use of psychiatric testimony is made in the courts today.

In the legal system, the defendant may enter the plea that he be found not guilty as he lacks the appropriate capacity of *mens rea* — the guilty mind — to have committed the act with deliberation and "malice aforethought." Consequently, there has arisen, in law, the concept of diminished responsibility in the judgments made regarding actions generally considered criminal.

The differences between the practices of law and psychiatry result from the gradual development of psychological knowledge. In ancient times lunatics were not regarded as suffering from disease, but were believed to be possessed by demons and were beaten, kept in chains, or sentenced to death by burning or hanging. Even if the alleged lunatic had committed some crime, there was no consideration of the offender's responsibility. Gradually, however, rules to determine criminal responsibility were formulated. Since American law is based largely on English law, it is of interest to note the early application of responsibility tests in the laws of England. In 1723, an English court declared that for an accused to escape punishment he must "not know what he is doing, no more than...a wild beast." This requirement, that to qualify for immunity the accused shall know no more than a wild beast, was altered and moderated somewhat about 1760 when the terms "right and wrong" were substituted for "good and evil." Slightly earlier, however, an accused person was executed after it had been determined that he had not shown a "*total* want of reason."

The American law prevalent for many years stems directly from the famous British M'Naghten case. In 1843, Daniel M'Naghten was tried for the willful murder of Edward Drummond, the private secretary of Sir Robert Peel. For several years, M'Naghten had suffered from delusions of persecution. He had attempted to escape from his persecutors by leaving Scotland and going to England or to France. On many occasions he had complained to his father and to various public authorities. He became increasingly embittered and finally determined to right his imaginary wrongs by killing Sir Robert Peel. With this objective in mind, he watched Peel's house. Seeing Drummond come out, he followed and shot him under the belief that he was shooting Peel. At M'Naghten's trial, his counsel entered a plea of "partial insanity." He was declared of unsound mind and committed to an institution for the criminally insane.

This case caused a great sensation in England, with the result that a few days after the trial a discussion took place in the House of Lords that proposed five questions to the 15 Judges of England regarding the law of insanity. The answers of the Judges can be reduced to two rules to determine the responsibility of a person who pleads insanity as a defense to a crime:

(1) "To establish a defense on the ground of insanity, it must be clearly proved that, at the time of committing the act, the party accused was laboring under such a defect of reason, from disease of the mind, as not to know the nature and quality of the act he was doing, or if he did know it, he did not know he was doing what was wrong."

As a rule, the defendant "knows" the facts concerning the particular criminal act that he has committed, knows its harmfulness ("quality"), and its unlawfulness and consequences, but does not know the unconscious basis for it.

(2) "Where a person labors under partial delusions only and is not in other respects insane" and commits an offense in consequence thereof, "he must be considered in the same situation as to responsibility as if the facts with respect to which the delusion exists were real."

It should be borne in mind that the M'Naghten Rules are a test of responsibility in law for acts done. They do not relate to the matter or existence of "insanity" or any defined mental disorder. In many states, the M'Naghten formula is the sole test of responsibility, and in American Military Law it is still the main test, supplemented by "the irresistible impulse test."

Although many courts have clung tenaciously to the M'Naghten "right and wrong test," it has been severely criticized, not only by psychiatrists but also by many eminent lawyers. In 1953, Justice Felix Frankfurter stated, in testifying before the British Royal Commission on Capital Punishment: "The M'Naghten Rules were rules which the Judges, in response to questions by the House of Lords, formulated in the light of the then existing psychological knowledge.... I do not see why the rules of law should be arrested at the state of psychological knowledge at the time when they were formulated."

This opinion of one of the most eminent American jurists reflects the view of many lawyers.

In 1869, influenced by Dr. Issac Ray, who was doubtless the most enlightened American psychiatrist in the medical jurisprudence of insanity, the Supreme Court of New Hamshire handed down an opinion sweeping aside the M'Naghten Rules. The court recognized simply that an accused person is not criminally responsible if his unlawful act was the result of mental defect. Under this decision, insanity is no longer defined as a matter of law; instead, it is made a question of fact to be determined by the jury like any other fact. This determination rests upon testimony of the psychiatric expert based on the latest knowledge of human behavior and his interpretation of such knowledge in terms of his observations of the accused. If the accused has a mental disease and if the criminal act is the product of it, he is found not guilty by reason of insanity.

In Massachusetts, the law (the so-called Briggs law) provides that a person who commits a capital offense or commits more than one felony, or who commits the same crime more than once, must be referred for examination by experts appointed by the State Department of Mental Health. The examinations are usually made at the jail where the defendant is being held. The psychiatrist's report is filed with the clerk of the court and is accessible to the court, to the district attorney, and to the counsel for the accused. If the examiner reports that the prisoner is suffering from mental disease, he is not directly asked to say whether the patient is able to distinguish between right and wrong, or whether he is able to refrain from doing wrong because of an irresistible impulse, but he is asked whether the patient suffers from a mental illness sufficiently severe to affect his responsibility and to require treatment in a mental hospital. It is apparently assumed that the examiner bases his opinion on the right-wrong test and the irresistible impulse test, but the reports submitted to the courts neither ask nor answer the question in these terms.

Under this law, juries have shown a commendable tendency to take the word of the impartial examiner as against that of psychiatrists hired by either side. The "battle of experts" has become almost unknown in Massachusetts.

In 1954, in the case of Durham v. United States, the Court of Appeals for the District of Columbia Circuit handed down a decision adopting in substance the same rule as the New Hampshire one. This case involved a defendant, Durham, who had been convicted of housebreaking. He had previously been committed to a hospital for mental disease. At Durham's trial, the issue of responsibility was raised. A psychiatrist testified that he thought Durham was of unsound mind, but that he might give the correct answer if a question of right or wrong were put to him. The appeal court ruled that the trial court was in error in declaring Durham sane on an obsolete test of responsibility. The essence of the decision is contained in the following passage:

"We find that as an exclusive criterion the right-wrong test is inadequate in that (a) it does not take sufficient account of psychic realities and scientific knowledge, and (b) it is based upon one symptom and so cannot validly be applied to all circumstances. We find that the 'irresistible impulse' test is also inadequate in that it gives no recognition to mental illness characterized by brooding and reflection and so relegates acts caused by such illness to the application of the inadequate right-wrong test. We conclude that a broader test should be adopted. . . .

"The rule we now hold must be applied on the retrial of this case and in future cases is not unlike that followed by the New Hamsphire court since 1870. It is simply that an accused is not criminally responsible if his unlawful act was the product of mental disease or mental defect."

Unfortunately, while the Durham decision of Judge Bazelon provided the opportunity for psychiatrists to testify more completely about their understanding of the motivational forces underlying the criminal act, they continue in the main to conduct themselves in court as in the past. They fail to go beyond presenting diagnostic labels to describe and explain the origins and development of the manifestations of the disordered psychological processes which underlie an act—that is, psychiatrists fail to give the dynamic formulation for the disordered behavior.

Because of this failure on the part of

psychiatric witnesses, and because of the concern of the legal profession, which believed that juries would be unlikely to function easily under the Durham rule, the American Law Institute wrote an alternative proposal:

"(1) A person is not responsible for criminal conduct if at the time of such conduct he lacks substantial capacity to appreciate the criminality of his conduct or to conform his conduct to the requirements of the law. (2) As used in this article the terms "mental disease" or "defect" do not include an abnormality manifested only by criminal or otherwise antisocial conduct."

This standard has become part of the criminal codes of several states. Meanwhile, in 1971, the Durham decision was set aside and the A.I.L. recommendation was adopted in the District of Columbia as a consequence of the decision Brawner v. United States.

In the states of California and Colorado, the defendant has the opportunity of a "bifurcated trial." In the first trial, psychiatric testimony may be entered in an attempt to reduce the level of criminal responsibility; for example, the defendant might stand for second rather than first degree murder. If the defendant elects the second trial, it may utilize the same testimony as a defense of insanity.

The senior author is of the opinion that all of this fails to support the sole purpose of the law in judging the act *per se* criminal, by allowing the plea of diminished responsibility. A judgment of the act as criminal reinforces the social codes of behavior. Only after the act of the individual has been judged does he consider psychiatric testimony as socially desirable, provided he is found guilty. Then the psychiatrist's knowledge might assist the court in deciding degree of punishment and disposition, whether to prison or to a hospital for treatment. The period of detention should be stated by the court in either case.

When testifying at a trial, the psychiatrist should remember that the determination of responsibility is a legal issue. The psychiatrist's function is to present the data; the application of the law to the facts is for the court and the jury. He will therefore not express any opinion about whether or not the defendant can distinguish between right and wrong. Any testimony beyond professionally recognized medical data descriptive of the defendant's mental status, and informative to the court and jury, is therefore beyond the province of the psychiatric experts. All expert testimony should be free of moral and value statements. The psychiatrist will be wise not to attempt to scale degrees of responsibility in terms of symptoms.

If a person charged with crime is found not guilty by reason of insanity, in some states he may be committed to a state hospital for mental diseases at the discretion of the court. In other states, it is mandatory that he be committed. In some states, the patient may, upon recovery, be discharged by the court that ordered his commitment; in other states, if regarded as no longer dangerous if allowed at large, he may be discharged by the governor. In one state the patient may be discharged only by act of legislature.

Competence to Stand Trial

Throughout the United States today, a defendant with mental illness who is unable to understand the charges against him and to work with counsel to prepare his defense is deemed incompetent to stand trial. While all defendants are considered as competent to stand trial when presented before the court, the court itself, the defending counsel, or the prosecutor may question the presumptions. The court then will order a psychiatric examination to make the determination. If found incompetent, the individual is hospitalized under commitment until such time as he is recovered sufficiently to have his competency status restored. By this means, some individuals have remained throughout life in state mental institutions. This improper outcome is no longer legally sanctioned as a consequence of the Jackson v. Indiana decision of the U. S. Supreme Court. Both psychiatrists and lawyers have worked to protect those individuals lost and held in hospitals improperly by reason of this decision.

BIBLIOGRAPHY

Allen, R. C., Ferster, E. Z., Rubin, J. G.: Readings in Law and Psychiatry. (Revised and expanded.) Baltimore, Johns Hopkins University Press, 1975.

Brooks, A. D.: Law, Psychiatry and the Mental Health System. Boston, Little, Brown & Company, 1974.

Cocozza, J. A., and Steadman, J. H.: Some refinements in the measurement and prediction of dangerous behavior. Am. J. Psychiatry, 131:1012–1014, 1974.

Cocozza, J. A., and Steadman, J. H.: The failure of psychiatric predictions of dangerousness: Clear and convincing evidence. Rutgers Law Review, 29:1084–1101, 1976.

Diamond, B. L.: Isaac Ray and the trial of Daniel M'Naghten. Am. J. Psychiatry, 112:651.–656, 1956.

Gurevitz, H.: Tarasoff: Protective privilege versus public peril. Am. J. Psychiatry, 134:289–292, 1977.

Guttmacher, M. S.: The Role of Psychiatry in Law. Springfield, Ill., Charles C Thomas, 1968.

MacDonald, J. M.: Psychiatry and the Criminal Courts. (3rd ed.) Springfield, Ill., Charles C Thomas, 1976.

Mesnikoff, A. M., and Lauterbach, C. G.: The association of violent dangerous behavior with psychiatric disorders: A review of the research literature. J. Psych. Law, Winter, 1975, pp. 415–446.

Morris, G. H.: The Insanity Defense: A Blueprint for Legislative Reform. Lexington, Mass., Lexington Books, 1975.

Ray, I.: A Treatise on the Medical Jurisprudence of Insanity. Boston, Charles C. Little & James Brown, 1838.

Roby, J., Getting caught in the "open door": Psychiatrists, patients, and third parties. Mental Disability Law Reporter, Nov.-Dec., 1976, pp. 220–228.

Rollin, H. R.: The Mentally Abnormal Offender and the Law. New York, Pergamon Press, 1969.

Roth, L. H., and Meisel, A.: Dangerousness, confidentiality and the duty to warn. Am. J. Psychiatry, 134:508–511, 1977.

Roth, L. H., Meisel, A., and Lidz, C.: Tests of competency to consent to treatment. Am. J. Psychiatry, 134:279–284, 1977.

Slovenko, R.: Psychiatry and Law. Boston, Little, Brown & Company, 1973.

State Responsibilities to the Mentally Disabled. Lexington, Ky., Council of State Governments, 1976.

Szasz, T. S.: The Myth of Mental Illness; Foundations of a Theory of Personal Conduct. New York, Hoeber Medical Division, Harper & Row, 1961.

Szasz, T. S.: Law, Liberty, and Psychiatry. New York, MacMillan Company, 1963.

Walker, N. and McCabe, S.: Crime and Insanity in England. Vol. II. Edinburgh, University of Edinburgh Press, 1973.

Watson, H. S.: Forensic Psychiatry. In Freedman, A. M., Kaplan, H. I., and Sadock, B. J. (eds.): Comprehensive Textbook of Psychiatry. Vol. 2, 2nd ed. Baltimore, Williams & Wilkins Company, 1975, pp. 2421–2436.

Williams, D. W.: New developments in civil commitment of the mentally ill. J.A.M.A., 242: 2307–2309, 1979.

INDEX

Note: Page numbers in *italics* indicate illustrations; those followed by (t) indicate tables.